1001 BUILDINGS
YOU MUST SEE BEFORE YOU DIE

1001 BUILDINGS
YOU MUST SEE BEFORE YOU DIE

GENERAL EDITOR MARK IRVING

PREFACE BY PETER ST. JOHN

← Phæno Science Center rendering,
Zaha Hadid Architects (*page 894*)

UNIVERSE

A Quint**essence** Book

First published in the United States of America in 2007 by
Universe Publishing
A division of Rizzoli International Publications, Inc.
300 Park Avenue South
New York, NY 10010
www.rizzoliusa.com

ISBN-13: 978-0-7893-1564-9
QUIN.KBLD

Library of Congress Control Number: 2007924705

2007 2008 2009 2010 / 10 9 8 7 6 5 4 3 2 1

This book was designed and produced by
Quint**essence** Publishing Limited
226 City Road
London EC1V 2TT

Senior Editor	Jodie Gaudet
Editors	Mary Cooch, Lucinda Hawksley, Carol King, Fiona Plowman, Frank Ritter, Jane Simmonds
Editorial Assistants	Helena Baser, Andrew Smith
Picture Researcher	Jo Walton
Designer	Nick Jones
Editorial Director	Jane Laing
Publisher	Tristan de Lancey

Manufactured in Singapore by Pica Digital Pte Ltd.
Printed in China by SNP Leefung Printers Ltd.

Endpaper, front (from top left)
Royal Alcázar, Spain (*page 97*)
British Council Nairobi, Kenya (*page 870*)
Villa Eila, Guinea (*page 714*)
Architects' Housing, Hvittrask, Finland (*page 336*)
Casa Planells, Spain (*page 389*)
Terminal 1, Charles-de-Gaulle Airport, France (*page 591*)
Jerónimos Monastery, Portugal (*page 133*)
Kimbell Art Museum, USA (*page 576*)
Gran Teatro de la Habana, Cuba (*page 370*)
Great Mosque, al-Ukba, Tunisia (*page 56*)
Leça Swimming Pools, Portugal (*page 556*)
Church of St. Mary Magdalene, France (*page 268*)

Endpaper, back (from top left)
Merchants' Houses, Netherlands (*page 177*)
Monadnock Building, USA (*page 319*)
Renaissance Theater, Germany (*page 396*)
Roof Roof House, Malaysia (*page 628*)
Monticello, USA (*page 239*)
Palacio de Correos, Mexico (*page 343*)
Church of San Apollinare, Italy (*page 41*)
Monreale Cathedral, Sicily (*page 74*)
Palais des Congrès, Canada (*page 845*)
Baptistery at Pisa, Italy (*page 87*)
Monastery of Santa Maria da Vitória, Portugal (*page 104*)
Sheldonian Theatre, England (*page 184*)

Contents

Preface

An Interview with Peter St. John

Caruso St. John, led by Adam Caruso and Peter St. John, is a small London-based architectural practice with a big international reputation. The practice is known for its intelligent approach to architecture and a sensitive, tailored response to individual sites. Established in 1990, it received worldwide acclaim for the New Art Gallery in Walsall, West Midlands, UK. Since then, Caruso St. John has produced a range of carefully conceived projects, from the addition to the Bethnal Green Museum of Childhood in East London to the redesigned artists' studios at Spike Island, Bristol, and a planned renewal of Tate Britain, London.

Mark Irving (MI): **What would be your criteria for including buildings in this book?**

Peter St. John (PSJ): Good architecture is affecting. We have all had the experience of walking through a building, of it catching our attention, making us suddenly more aware of what is around us. It is a complex impression, never the same, but there is a connection between the way people walk and sit around, and the scale of the details of the building. My best memories of buildings are bound up with sensual pleasure in their sounds, the weather, a special view out of a window, or perhaps the reflection of light off a shiny floor. Ancient buildings, with their mineral presence, naturally have the capacity to provoke an emotional response—the interior of Hagia Sophia comes to mind—but there also can be poetry in the simplest of situations. A social housing project by Aldo Rossi on the outskirts of Milan did that for me once—the repeated sharp shadow of the concrete columns of the arcade seemed so dramatic, like standing in a painting.

MI: **How should one look at buildings?**

PSJ: Buildings are a backdrop to everyday life and usually only architects raise their eyes when they are walking down the street. That is how it should be. I assume everyone has their own way of looking. For me, a visit to a building might be quite short and leave an impression, but if it is a good building I will think about it later. I will find it in a book, read about it, and trace my remembered route on the plan drawing as a way of understanding its organization. But this all sounds rather methodical. What do you think?

MI: **I think the way one looks at buildings is always influenced by mood. I do not think there is an objective way of looking at them. Architecture is affected by what you project onto it. It is about a set of choices made by the architect and how you react to these. Architecture is about emotion. Does this relate to the issue of style?**

PSJ: I try to ignore the question of style. It can be useful in terms of placing people and understanding the connections between architects who might see themselves as independent, but who are strongly connected. But I am interested in other things than style. I feel too sensitive about it.

MI: **But what if people ascribe your work to a certain style?**
PSJ: You always bridle, because the label can be prescriptive. "Minimalist," for example, has become a put-down, a way of excluding content, as it were.

MI: **Labeling architecture was made all the more "important" after the advent of Postmodernism, of course.**
PSJ: There was a period in the late 1970s and 1980s when it became very important to give names to different kinds of architecture that were proliferating at the outset of Postmodernism. A lack of consensus meant things were becoming more diverse and confusing. Now people have got used to this diversity. I suppose to me the more evenhanded organization of buildings you have suggested for this book seems much more relevant. It is more appropriate than structuring the buildings according to labels. Inevitably, all architects would feel this to be unsatisfactory.

MI: **Have you been inspired by specific architects or buildings? You have described in the press your respect for architects such as Denys Lasdun, Alvaro Siza, and Peter Zumthor.**
PSJ: When I was a student, there were certain architects whose work I thought was enormously affecting. I used to spend a lot of time studying their projects. I am a great admirer of James Stirling, for example. Now, as I get older, I am becoming interested in a much wider range of buildings. There are not good or bad buildings, just different ones. I am just as interested in Lord Burlington's Chiswick House as I am in Stirling's Engineering Building. It is crucial to avoid the issue of style by choosing a starting point—it could be at any point in architectural history—from which to work out your ideas. That is what is different about working in architecture now.

MI: **So good architecture is about what you do with your starting point?**
PSJ: Yes. There is context and situation. That can be the starting point. At this practice we are interested in working with familiar things that provoke a memory. Then we will alter them to give them a fresh identity. It is as much about how you change them as it is about how you use them.

MI: **Is there a risk that architecture becomes a bit of an "in-house" discussion to which most people have no access?**

PSJ: The process may not be grasped by most people, but there is a kind of trigger that comes from working with "found" things. In the end, architecture is about making places, and I agree when you say that this is influenced by mood. Good buildings have an atmosphere, and old buildings with their material density have this naturally. A ruin can be extraordinarily physical, and this is part of its atmospheric potential. Contemporary buildings have this effect more rarely, because they are not built to last.

MI: **How does the opportunity for good architecture happen? Is there not always pressure to conform to economic pressures?**

PSJ: Good architecture happens because clients find architects they want to work with. They like your work. As a client, if you want to make a piece of architecture happen, you have to be trusting. You have to clear a path for your architect without knowing where that architect is going to take you.

MI: **There seems to be frenzy of building happening around the world now. What condition does this create for thoughtful architecture?**

PSJ: Architects are now working on projects where they may never visit the site or see the building completed. The design may be modified out of their control during construction. We try to resist that by working more slowly and concentrating on aspects of construction. Thinking about construction rather than image is one way of getting the time needed to do things well.

MI: **The building frenzy is aided by technological innovation.**

PSJ: Yes, but it is also globalization. People come from the other side of the world looking for architects who will give them a picture of a building without worrying about how to build it. This happens quite a lot now. Projects are given credibility by the publication of a famous architect's drawing, even though it may have little to do with the final result.

MI: **The effect of this is that the local becomes subsumed into the global, the "you-can-find-it-anywhere" architectural gesture.**

PSJ: Absolutely. You get the "brand." Computer renderings of buildings can be a problem because you get the impression that they are actually built, when for certain architects they do no more than extend a reputation for built projects, even though some of these may never have been constructed.

MI: But what about the view that such technologies, for example Computer Aided Design (CAD), liberate the architect, by changing the forms that are realized and articulating the hitherto impossible?

PSJ: That is a naive thing to believe. We are all making choices about what is possible. We use computers all the time, but it does not follow that we want them to influence our choice of form or construction. The possibility of the curve, which is what we are talking about, is not a new threshold of architecture. It is one way of making complex space and is in danger of becoming a restrictive style. Architects have to build spaces for different functions and rhetorical forms of this kind are only purposeful for certain kinds of things. They are not very useful for housing, for example.

MI: Was there ever a specific book on architecture you found useful?

PSJ: There have been many, but perhaps not a single one. But *1001 Buildings* would be one I would dip into and enjoy. I guess it would inspire me to travel to see that amazing Indonesian longhouse, for example.

MI: One thing I have gained from doing this book is a respect for vernacular forms of building that still continue, using materials and techniques that have worked for generations.

PSJ: It is a strength of this book to show examples of the vernacular alongside works of architecture, so that people can see their true value. In the vernacular there is a language of building that has been built up as part of a culture, such that these buildings appear natural, like plants and rocks. I first understood the beauty of this after looking at Bernard Rudosky's famous book *Architecture without Architects*, in which those amazing Trulli houses in Apulia are shown, the same ones you include in *1001 Buildings*.

MI: The temptation to clear away buildings and start afresh must be so great for architects. Does the desire to erase ever tempt you?

PSJ: The opposite, in fact. That is why I love London for its extraordinary diverse collection of buildings. It is a kind of background city that, because of its organic realization as a growing together of villages, has always escaped the overarching vision of planning. For me there is something beautiful about that constantly changing ordinariness, that makes for a city that is tolerant of diversity and a pleasant place to live.

London, March 2007

Introduction

By Mark Irving, General Editor

Why 1001? The extra "1" is important. It signifies that, even after the landmark figure of 1000, the possibilities are potentially endless and the choices available to the editor of this compilation truly legion. In choosing buildings for this book, I have relied on both my instinct and knowledge and, where the latter has been lacking, on the advice of others with more specialist expertise. The resulting selection is a mixture of rational consensus, personal whim, and, in some cases, individual obsession. This is a collection of opinions that may confirm your existing thoughts, pique your curiosity, or perhaps incur your wrath, but which I hope will inspire you to read further about or even visit the buildings.

The format of the book has been regulated by that of the wider *1001* series, one that has carved out its own space in publishing, being neither a coffee-table book, a pocket travel guide, nor an academic compendium, but rather a set of accessibly written and informed perspectives. The main text for each entry totals around 300 words, requiring that the writers exercise their minds clearly and succinctly about the significance of the building in question. Such brevity has its advantages and disadvantages. Suffice to say that many of these buildings merit having hundreds of pages written about them, but there is no great building to which 300 carefully chosen words cannot do justice.

My first decision was to consider what constitutes a building. Ruins were initially excluded, as were buildings that are no longer extant, since the series subtitle requires that there is something for readers to "see." I have stuck to this rule in general, excepting some very early examples of buildings from the ancient world that, while no longer inhabited, are substantive enough today and of such particular architectural or historical merit (presenting early prototypes or solutions) to deserve inclusion. Some buildings are included for the quality or notability of their interiors or their exteriors, or both, with the caveat that inclusion itself does not guarantee public access inside or even close to them. Occasionally, dedicated trackers of the buildings on this list may have to content themselves with a semi-distant view or the detail found in other literature.

Some structures, such as bridges, tidal barriers, giant satellite dishes, pylons, masts, or certain towers (the Eiffel Tower in Paris, for example) are feats of engineering rather than buildings and could not be included, although Raul Mesnier de Ponsard's Santa Justa Lift in Lisbon slips in under the net because of its expressed architectural camouflage and its integral role in and intelligent response to its immediate, densely urban context.

Deciding which buildings should be included was a stimulating, occasionally fraught process. The variety in this book is dazzling. Our list draws from the following: palaces, castles, châteaux, churches, mosques, synagogues, temples, shrines, villas, country retreats, government and corporate offices, schools, hospitals, tombs, restaurants, memorials, university faculties, railway and bus stations, airports, libraries, hotels, apartment blocks, museums, galleries, concert halls, theaters, cinemas, treasuries, markets, retail outlets, factories, gymnasiums, abattoirs, courts of justice, artists' studios, sports and swimming-pool complexes, cafés, park pavilions and hideaways, tree-houses, tea-houses, follies, fire stations, casinos, prisons, warehouses, monasteries, banks, custom houses, barns, prayer rooms, playrooms, showrooms, guild houses, ski jumps, sanatoriums, signal boxes, and ventilation buildings. I believe that all kinds of buildings offer lessons about human nature and the great spectrum of materials—found in nature, adapted from it, or produced entirely artificially—with which we construct buildings. Some of the buildings in this book are made from marble, stone, steel, and concrete; others, from wood, bark, and bamboo. Some, like the Portuguese royal palace at Mafra, cover many acres, have consumed vast quantities of materials and resources, including manpower, only to become soulless crypts for disintegrating dynasties; others, like the Batak Toba houses of Samosir Island, Indonesia, rely on cooperative sharing of resources and space and are produced for communal use, although they are made of materials that a wrecking ball could demolish in seconds. Others still, such as the public lavatory in Groningen, the Netherlands, by Dutch architects OMA, or the quayside shelter at An Turas on the Scottish island of Tiree by Sutherland Hussey Architects, perform incidental roles at the edges of urban or rural experience respectively. But they are buildings nonetheless and their significance to those using them, however few in number, cannot be underestimated.

The materiality of these buildings—whether they be made of stone or grass—as well as their location or the supposed education of their builders may have determined whether in the past they were considered as "architecture," but as this book has developed, that term has become less and less useful. "Architecture" is a politically volatile term; building is not, although of course its effects can be and increasingly are in a world of decreasing space and resources and growing human needs. Just as our list of buildings reflects the whole panoply of human life, from its inception to its aftermath, so it cannot escape the moral judgments that shadow our lives. Some of these buildings, such as Francesco Borromini's San Carlo alle Quattro Fontane, Rome, reveal human ingenuity, compassion, admiration for different cultures, emotional understanding, and elegant control, just as others, such as the Ryugyong Hotel, Pyongyang, North Korea, evidence human brutishness, vain excess, and dictatorial contempt for common man. I was determined to include some buildings notable for their odious qualities because the act of building in itself is no guarantor of public benefit or historic significance, although this is a book primarily about buildings with much to offer in ideas and inspiration.

When compiling the list I quickly became aware of a bias in the existing literature toward the "great civilizations" of the West, Islam, China, and India, with Western architects and their buildings featuring more highly than any other. Architecture in Africa has been ignored by most writers, while in India, China, and Southeast Asia architecture has long been synonymous with traditional heritage; coverage of postcolonial and contemporary building is scant in the extreme. Some of the responsibility for this lies with the countries themselves, saddled as they often are with the paradoxical burden of representing themselves as zoos of "traditional" (that is, not modern) culture. Much more lies with Western education, and publishers who have tended to evaluate buildings in the rest of the world by a rather limited set of criteria.

Finding writers who can write with personal knowledge of contemporary building practice in Africa, for example, proved nearly impossible, given the tight schedule of this book, while many people wanted to write about buildings, both modern and old, in Italy and the United Kingdom. All too often, "contemporary" or "modern" was taken to mean Western or Japanese architecture, whereas I consider it significant that much vernacular architecture in the developing world continues to be built (or rebuilt) according to principles established centuries if not millennia ago. This imbalance was one factor in deciding to run the list chronologically rather than by region, although the argument that chronology threw up more interesting neighbors on a list drawn from across cultures was persuasive regardless. I am pleased to have a list of buildings from around 100 countries, albeit some countries are much more amply represented than others. We have also tried to surprise those readers familiar with certain architects by including some of their less well-known buildings.

The task of ascribing the names of architects and designers to each building reflected the way that buildings in certain cultures (especially those in the West) serve as important vehicles for conveying changes in fashion and the power structures of the elite. "Newness," or the idea of the novel and innovative, has been synonymous with architectural practice in the West for centuries. Even when making perfect replicas from the past or interpretations of the past, Western architects seem to produce buildings with inverted commas around them, and most have wanted their names identified with their projects.

In the non-Western world, for centuries pride has been taken in building buildings as they always were (or should have been) and the idea of a "signature style" is almost meaningless. The habit of "copying the copy of the copy of the original" has made the task of ascribing a particular completion date to some buildings especially difficult. In general, we have settled on dates that reflect the period when the idea or manifestation of a particular building at that site was first apparent, even if today's structure is a modern reconstruction, full or partial. A similar problem has occurred with buildings—such as Hampton Court Palace in England—that have been changed and added to continuously over the centuries: which version of Hampton Court Palace is our building? And what about great cathedrals such as Notre Dame, Paris, or St. Peter's, Rome: when were these truly completed? In such instances, our writers have chosen to focus on a moment or period in the building's history when a significant and sustained architectural gesture was made, or when, as in the case of Antonio Gaudí's still-unfinished Sagrada Familia, the genius of the project was substantially achieved. Dating buildings is a dangerous game, and despite our careful considerations, some of the dates we have used may need revising in the future.

Choosing the team of writers was also important, and here I have striven to find wherever possible writers equipped with either specialist knowledge of the building or architect in question, or firsthand experience of seeing it. The writers include university professors, postgraduate researchers, architects, historians, experienced travelers, museum curators, architectural journalists, structural engineers, and more. I am particularly delighted to include Phyllis Lambert, who has written on the Canadian Centre for Architecture. She has played a pivotal role as patron and creative collaborator in the evolution of twentieth-century architecture itself. Many of the writers live in Europe or the United States, but others are based in regions as diverse as South America, China, Singapore, and Canada. Most took on their writing assignments despite mountains of work and tight delivery deadlines and their evident enthusiasm for both their buildings and the project overall has been terrific. I have benefited a great deal from their independent views while I was constructing the list. Some writers recognized this book as a chance to highlight neglected buildings deserving of attention as much as an opportunity to reassess, however briefly, celebrated masterpieces.

There is now, as Peter St. John suggests in his preface, a frenzy of building across the world, just as the past century saw an explosion of architectural ideas, technical building capabilities, and human demand for infrastructure. That is why our chapters on the twentieth century are so rich and full of variety. The implications of such a rush of building are many, not least the necessity to continue to look at buildings with questioning minds, so that the lessons, good and bad, of the past and the present can inform our future actions.

Buildings
Index

Buildings from the ancient world were held in high esteem by subsequent generations. Their exotic forms and decorative vocabulary provided new generations with inspirational, authoritative prototypes that led numerous patrons and architects to copy, adapt, and subvert the architectural ideals of the ancient world. In the West, these ideals were fervently analyzed and reformulated during the Renaissance, while in the Islamic world, ancient forms were blended with innovative architectural paradigms to suit new needs and doctrines. In India, China, and much of the rest of the world, the authority of ancient prototypes reigned supreme.

ANCIENT WORLD *to the* RENAISSANCE

PRE-**1600**

Newgrange Burial Chamber (3200 BCE)

Architect Unknown **Location** Brú na Bóinne, Donore, County Meath, Ireland **Style** Neolithic **Materials** Stone slabs, turf, quartz pebbles

Newgrange, a UNESCO World Heritage Site, is one of the finest examples in Western Europe of a passage grave. It consists of a 36-foot-high (11 m) stone and turf mound, through which a narrow, slab-lined passage leads to a burial chamber. At the winter solstice on December 21, a shaft of light shines through a roofbox at the entrance and along the passage to the tomb's furthest recesses. The complexity of carvings on the stone walls suggests a religious significance; the design may be evidence of sun worship. The cremated remains of four or five people, laid on large stone basins and found when the tomb was excavated, suggest that only priests and rulers were buried there. The passage tomb is surrounded by ninety-seven curbstones; the most impressive is the large entrance stone, which is covered in swirls and designs. Inside the large mound, there is a long passage leading into a chamber that branches off three ways. The corbeled roof inside the burial chamber is still watertight and supports an estimated 200,000 tons. Newgrange predates the pyramids of Egypt by 400 years. Excavation has revealed evidence of human occupation in the area as early as the fourth millennium BCE. The immediate area is known as Brú na Bóinne—the Bend of the Boyne. The mounds at Newgrange, Knowth, and Dowth dominate the area, which is to be designated a National Archaeological Park. **BMC**

"This is Europe's largest and most important concentration of prehistoric megalithic art."

UNESCO

Step Pyramid of Zoser (2611 BCE)

Architect Imhotep   **Location** Sakkara, Egypt   **Style** Ancient Egyptian   **Material** Stone

Sakkara is an ancient Egyptian necropolis that lies 18.6 miles (30 km) south of Cairo. The vast site covers an area of approximately 4.3 miles (7 km) by 0.9 miles (1.5 km), and served as a royal burial ground when Memphis was the capital of ancient Egypt, before it was superseded by Gaza. There are various *mastabas* on the site, which are flat-roofed, mud-brick, rectangular buildings used as burial tombs, as well as seventeen pyramids. The most notable pyramid is the Step Pyramid of the Third Dynasty pharaoh Zoser, which is the oldest complete, hewn-stone building known. The Step Pyramid of Zoser was designed by Imhotep (*c.* 2667–48 BCE)—the first architect and physician known by name in written history. He is thought to have been responsible for the first known use of columns in architecture, and is recognized as the founder of Egyptian medicine. When constructing the Step Pyramid of Zoser, Imhotep enlarged the basic *mastaba* structure to make it square. He then built similar *mastaba*-like square blocks of stone on top of the first course in ever-decreasing size to arrive at the final, impressive, stepped shape. The casing blocks are set at an angle to take up the thrust of the successive layers. The pyramid has six terraces and measures around 203 feet (62 m) high. Most of its outer casing and part of its masonry have disappeared over the centuries. The pyramid's eastern side is the most intact. It is thought that the original surface was encased in smooth white limestone, or polished white marble, which would have meant the structure caught the rays of the sun and reflected its rays to dramatic effect. At the heart of the pyramid, 92 feet (28 m) underground, lies the royal burial chamber. A vertical shaft leads to the tomb, the entrance of which was originally sealed with a 3-ton slab of granite. **CMK**

Great Pyramid of Khufu (2560 BCE)

Architect Hemon, vizier to Pharaoh Khufu   **Location** Giza, near Cairo, Egypt   **Style** Ancient Egyptian   **Materials** Limestone, granite

The Great Pyramid of Khufu is the largest and most northerly of the three famous pyramids at Giza, and the only one of the Seven Wonders of the World left standing today. As the largest pyramid ever built, it is a wonder mainly because of its sheer scale, and the incredible precision with which the building work was executed. It is assumed to be the burial place of Egyptian pharaoh Khufu, who ruled from 2589–66 BCE, but only an empty sarcophagus has been found. Designed by Khufu's cousin Hemon, the pyramid originally stood 482 feet (147 m) high with four equal sides each measuring 755 feet (230 m). The giant, stepped sides were originally covered with highly polished limestone casing stones. When in place, these stones, weighing some 15 tons apiece and slotted together with unerring accuracy, would have lent sheen to the structure in the sun. Some Egyptologists believe that the pinnacle of the structure may have been gilded. Inside the pyramid, there are three burial chambers. The King's Chamber contained a huge granite sarcophagus; the smaller Queen's Chamber, a large angular doorway or niche. There are two narrow shafts, about 8 inches (20 cm) wide, extending from the chamber toward the outer surface of the pyramid. The other main features of the Great Pyramid are the Grand Gallery, ascending and descending passages, and the lowest part of the structure dubbed the "unfinished chamber." **DT**

"From the heights of these pyramids, forty centuries look down on us."

Napoleon Bonaparte, Battle of Giza (1798)

Ziggurat at Ur (2096 BCE)

Architect Unknown **Location** Ur, near Nasiriyah, Iraq **Style** Sumerian **Materials** Mud brick, fired brick

The Ziggurat at Ur sits on a vast plain in southern Iraq, near the modern city of Nasiriyah. Ziggurats are pyramidal structures built by the Sumerians, Babylonians, and Assyrians of ancient Mesopotamia—the region between the Tigris and Euphrates rivers. There are thirty-two surviving ziggurats, and the Ziggurat at Ur is one of the best preserved. It once sat within a walled precinct. Its core was constructed with bricks made from mud and reed pressed into molds and dried in the sun. Seven million bricks were used for the core, which was strengthened with reed matting and sandy soil sandwiched between every six layers of brick. The core was clad with glazed bricks mortared with bitumen to create a waterproof surface, punctuated by "weeper holes" to allow water to evaporate from the center. Many of these facing bricks were stamped with the name of King Ur-Nammu (2112–2095 BCE). In Ur-Nammu's time, the ziggurat had three tiers and three buttressed staircases probably leading to a temple on the flat surface at the top. Each tier formed a terrace that may have been planted with vegetation. Evidence of continuous repair and maintenance indicates that this was an important building for at least 2,000 years. In the sixth century BCE, four more tiers were added to make it a seven-story structure. Only the first two tiers now survive. The discovery of the Ziggurat at Ur in 1922 sparked a brief craze for tiered buildings. **MC**

"I fell in love with Ur, with its beauty in the evening, the ziggurat standing up, faintly shadowed ..."

Agatha Christie, *An Autobiography* (1977)

Temple of Hatshepsut (1458 BCE)

Architect Senenmut   **Location** Deir el-Bahri, Egypt   **Style** Ancient Egyptian   **Material** Stone

Queen Hatshepsut was the fifth pharaoh of the Eighteenth Dynasty of ancient Egypt. She founded a vast number of buildings during her reign, the most spectacular of which is her own funerary temple at Deir el-Bahri, a site on the west bank of the Nile opposite Luxor. It is positioned in a straight line from the tomb she commissioned for herself in the Valley of the Kings that lies on the other side of the mountain. Archaeologists estimate that it took fifteen years to build the temple—between the seventh and the twenty-second years of her reign. They have also suggested that originally the approach to the temple was along a 121-foot-wide (37 m) causeway lined with sphinxes. The focal point of the temple is the Djeser-Djeseru or "The Sublime of Sublimes," which consists of three elegant colonnaded terraces standing 97 feet (29.5 m) high, and dramatically built into a high mountain face that rises above it. It is notable for its perfect symmetry, which predates Greece's Parthenon by 1,000 years. Djeser-Djeseru is reached by two ascending ramps that were once planted as gardens. The second ramp leads to the upper terrace, and the Punt Portico that is supported by two rows of square columns. It is decorated with statues of Queen Hatshepsut sculpted to appear as the god Osiris, and its walls bear reliefs depicting a trading expedition to Punt, which is thought to be a region in what is now known as Ethiopia or northern Somalia. **CMK**

> *"Senenmut built one of the most beautiful monuments of ancient Egypt, the style . . . never repeated."*
>
> John Julius Norwich, historian

Temple at Luxor (1408 BCE)

Patron Amenhotep III **Location** Luxor, Egypt **Style** Ancient Egyptian **Material** Stone

The Temple at Luxor is an ancient Egyptian temple complex that lies on the east bank of the Nile, at what is now called Luxor, and what was the ancient city of Thebes. It was dedicated to the Theban triad of gods—Amun, his wife Mut, and their son Chons—and was built on the site of a smaller Middle Kingdom structure for the god Amun. The earliest parts of the temple existing today date from 1408 BCE and were built during the reign of Amenhotep III of the Eighteenth Dynasty of the New Kingdom. Access to the temple is via the Avenue of Sphinxes, built by Nectanebo I, which replaced the ram-headed sphinxes built by Amenophis III. The avenue once stretched the 1.86 miles (3 km) from the Temple at Luxor to the Temple of Karnak in the north. A 78-foot-high (24 m) obelisk built by Ramesses II of the Nineteenth Dynasty in 1300 BCE lies at the end of the avenue at the entrance to the temple. Originally there were two obelisks, but the second obelisk was given to France's King Louis-Philippe in 1829 and now stands in the Place de la Concorde in Paris. The gateway leads into a peristyle courtyard, also built by Ramesses II. Both it and the obelisk were built at an oblique angle to the rest of the temple. The courtyard leads into a processional colonnade, 328 feet (100 m) long, built by Amenhotep III, and lined by fourteen papyrus-capital columns. A second peristyle courtyard lies beyond the colonnade. The inner part of the temple is accessed via a hypostyle court with thirty-two columns. This inner sanctum comprises an antechamber that contains a mix of both Egyptian carvings and Roman stuccoes, reflecting the fact that at one time the Romans also used the site as a place of worship. The temple also has a shrine dedicated to Amun, and the Birth Room of Amenhotep III, which contains reliefs depicting the pharoah's birth. **CMK**

Parthenon (432 BCE)

Architects Iktinos, Kallikrates, Pheidias   **Location** Athens, Greece   **Style** Ancient Greek   **Material** Marble

"The sumptuous temple of Athena stands out and is well worth a look."

Heracleides of Crete, geographer

⬆ A view of the Doric frieze above the columns showing alternating metopes and triglyphs.

➡ The Parthenon on top of the Acropolis, showing its splendid position and the damage done over the ages.

The silhouette of the ruined Parthenon has become a symbol of Western culture. Originally built as a pagan temple to the goddess Athena and funded by the profits of Athens's empire, it was not the largest temple of antiquity, but certainly the most richly adorned. The surviving sculpture (controversially divided between Athens and London since the nineteenth century) came from the building's exterior and celebrated the religious tradition, myth, and history of Athens. The most important piece, however, has long been destroyed: a 40-foot-high (12 m) gold-and-ivory "cult statue" of the goddess that stood inside. In fact, the function of the Parthenon was not congregational. The purpose of the building (which comprised just two simple chambers) was to house this statue and other Athenian treasures.

Historians do not know exactly who was responsible for the design. The sculptor Pheidias is associated with the statue of Athena and he may have had some control over the architecture too. The names of Kallikrates and Iktinos are also mentioned. But whoever played the leading part, the architectural details have been praised and minutely examined since the nineteenth century—especially the so-called "optical refinements," those tiny adjustments in its dimensions to make the building appear perfectly regular to the naked eye. Calculations show that the columns at either end, if continued upward, would actually meet 31 miles (50 km) above ground.

The Parthenon was used long after the end of antiquity—converted first into a church and in the fifteenth century into a splendid mosque. It became a ruin only after a Venetian cannonball hit it in 1687. Since then it has inspired imitations worldwide, from Ludwig I's Walhalla in Bavaria to an exact replica in Nashville, Tennessee, and the unfinished "Parthenon" on Calton Hill, Edinburgh. **MB**

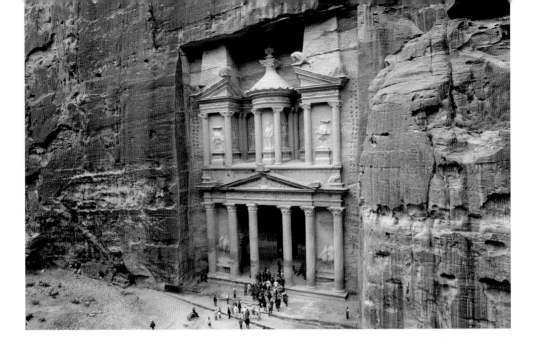

Treasury at Petra (100 BCE)

Architect Unknown   **Location** Petra, Wadi Mousa, Jordan   **Style** Classical Roman / Hellenistic   **Material** Sandstone

Petra is the stuff of true archaeological fantasy. Its location in Jordan remained a mystery to Europeans until its discovery by Swiss explorer Johann Burckhardt in 1812. The Nabeteans, or "monument carvers," are not famous for anything else apart from Petra. They built their city to be an important stop on a trade route that linked China and Rome. Petra covers 3.8 square miles (10 sq km) and boasts a 3,000-seat amphitheater as well as temples and a monastery. The origins of the so-called Treasury are shrouded in mystery. It is known to be one of the later buildings constructed at Petra. The Greco-Roman facade shows the influence of first-century Roman architecture, in contrast to earlier monuments at Petra, which do not have Classical antecedents. The Treasury was probably carved from the top, working downward. It has two levels. Corinthian columns divide the top level, which has a central circular *tholos* topped with a figure—possibly the goddess El-Uzza. The lower level is a pedimented portico with six columns and two sculptures believed to be the Roman deities Castor and Pollux. The facade has a Classical look, but it is a completely original rendering of a Classical facade. The inner chamber is a huge space with three smaller antechambers. At the back of the main chamber is an ablution basin. The grandeur of the facade, the empty space, and the presence of the basin suggest that the building actually may have been a temple. **WB**

> *"Match me such marvel save in Eastern clime / A rose-red city half as old as time . . ."*

John William Burgon, "Petra" (1845)

Maison Carrée (16 BCE)

Patron Marcus Vipsanius Agrippa **Location** Nîmes, France **Style** Classical Roman **Material** Limestone

The Maison Carrée, or Square House, represents a perfect definition of the Vitruvian principles of proportion and beauty in architecture in their most classical guise. As an austere moral symbol of Republican values expressed through its simplicity of form, the building has inspired the Church of the Madeleine in Paris and Thomas Jefferson's Virginia State Capitol in the United States. It was commissioned by Marcus Vipsanius Agrippa, politician and friend of Emperor Augustus, the original patron of the Pantheon in Rome, and later dedicated to his sons, Gaius Julius Caesar Vipsanianus and Lucius Caesar. Constructed of locally quarried limestone, the temple remains in its preserved state and original proportion thanks to its dedication as a Christian church in the fourth century. The rectangular building is in a symmetrical proportion of 2:1—86 feet (26.42 m) long by 44 feet (13.54 m) wide—and stands on the south side of the forum, resting on a podium 9 feet (2.8 m) high. It is approached by fifteen entrance steps on the west entrance facade with six Corinthian columns under the pediment. Behind is a portico, three columns deep, extending to nearly one third of the total length of the building. Along the length of the temple walls are eight half-embedded columns. The architrave and frieze are decorated with exquisite ornamental relief carvings including egg-and-dart motifs, rosettes, and acanthus leaves. The windowless inner chamber is entered through a large door, 22.5 feet (7 m) high by 11 feet (3.27 m) wide, made in 1824. The original shrine has at various times been a house, stable, and storage for archives. It became a museum after 1823 and now exhibits mosaic, sculpture, and archeological information. Its modern counterpoint, the Carré d'Art, an art gallery designed by Norman Foster, stands on the far side of the square. **JEH**

Pyramid of Cestius (12 BCE)

Architect Unknown **Location** Rome, Italy **Style** Classical Roman, Egyptian influence **Materials** Concrete, white marble, travertine marble, brick

This white mausoleum, built in the first century BCE during the last years of the Roman Republic, looks incongruous at first glance. The tomb's pyramidal form is a reflection of the "Cleopatra fad" that swept through the empire's capital after the conquest of Egypt just a few years earlier, in 30 BCE. That victory had made the monuments and funerary practices of the powerful province very fashionable indeed. The fact that a single citizen was able to build a personal tomb worthy of a pharaoh says much about the wealth of ancient Rome. Already considered one of antiquity's most significant monuments back in the 1400s, this Roman pyramid has a burial chamber inside once adorned with vibrant frescoed panels of female figures. Discovered during excavations in 1660, it was found to contain the ashes of Caius Cestius, magistrate, tribune, and *epulonum* (member of the *septemvirate*, one of Rome's four great religious organizations). The strength of the materials—brick-faced concrete overlaid with white marble slabs on a travertine foundation—made possible a truly firm construction, built at a much sharper angle than any of its Egyptian counterparts. Inscriptions on its eastern and western faces record the names and titles of the deceased as well as the circumstances relating to the construction. Built in less than a year and intact to this day, Caius Cestius's funerary monument has proved far more enduring than anything he achieved while alive. **AA**

> "Well-designed buildings [such as the Pyramid of Cestius] exhibit outstanding firmness."
>
> Vitruvius, Roman architect

Colosseum (80)

Architect Unknown **Location** Rome, Italy **Style** Classical Roman **Materials** Travertine cladding, brick and concrete skeleton

One of the most impressive monuments surviving from the Roman empire, the Colosseum is the largest of all the Roman amphitheaters. Its elliptical form covers a surface of 617 feet (188 m) by 512 feet (156 m) on its major axes. It was built for the Flavian emperors on a site previously occupied by a private lake adjoining the luxurious palace-villa of Nero. Entirely clad in travertine blocks, it filled a nodal position at the intersection of the Imperial Forum and the Sacred Way. The Colosseum was the prime venue for gladiatorial contests and venations—wild beast hunts—and it could accommodate around 70,000 people. Entry and exit to the building influenced its design: the seventy-six arcaded and numbered openings—*vomitoria*—on the ground-floor exterior corresponded to stair ramps that brought spectators directly to their seats on the different levels of the 157-foot-high (48 m) building. The outer facade is arranged on four levels, and presents the canonical arrangement of the Classical orders; the first three levels are formed by arcades framed by half-columns from the Doric ground floor, through the Ionic and Corinthian, and terminate with the flat surface of the attic story with its Composite pilasters. This crowning attic story contains the bracketing elements that originally supported masts from which a great awning was stretched like a sail to provide shade. The amphitheater was a central component of the imperial policy of "bread and circuses," as the poet Juvenal described it, which aimed to control the citizens of Rome. But the building has long outlasted the empire that built it and the reasons for its construction. Having served as a castle in the Middle Ages for the Frangipani family, the travertine monument functioned almost as the city quarry and many Renaissance buildings were constructed using its materials. **FN**

The Pantheon (126)

Patron Marcus Vipsanio Agrippa   **Location** Rome, Italy   **Style** Classical Roman
Materials Basalt, *pozzolana* cement, concrete, marble

Conceived as a temple to all the gods by Agrippa, the Pantheon suffered damage by fire in 80 and was restored by the emperors Domitian and Trajan. In 118–25 Emperor Hadrian turned it into a classical study of space, order, composition, and light—it is no coincidence that the height of the dome and the diameter of the rotunda fit within a perfect sphere.

The Pantheon's circular composition, designed to reflect the heavens and the sun, deviates from earlier Greek and Roman architecture where rectangular enclosures served as temples. Raising a circular vault over a square base was made possible by inserting hidden wall niches and brick arches as supports. Ever-smaller coffers and walls become progressively thinner and reduce the downward thrust of the dome's weight while redirecting the mechanical stress placed on the foundations. This remnant of Roman glory has survived with its concrete dome intact, making it the best-preserved building of its kind. It inspired Michelangelo's design for the cupola of St. Peter's Basilica, and over the centuries it has proved multifunctional, serving as an imperial reception area, a court of law, and a mausoleum for Italy's royals and artists. It has been used as a church since 609.

The building's only source of light is the oculus or "great eye" in the domed ceiling, and around noon sunlight enters and sets aglow this extraordinary space with its polished marble interior and coffered geometry. The interior has a sloping floor to drain away rainwater entering through the opening. **AA**

↖ The Pantheon with its portico of Corinthian columns dominates the area with its historical resonance.

↩ The dome's technical skill and grace has inspired writers, artists, and architects for nearly 2,000 years.

Castel Sant'Angelo (139)

Patron Emperor Hadrian　**Location** Rome, Italy　**Style** Classical Roman　**Materials** Tufa, stone, travertine overlaid with marble

The Hadrianeum—the circular construction designed and commissioned by Emperor Hadrian in 130 as his personal mausoleum—was completed by Antoninus Pius a year after Hadrian's death. The adjoining bridge, Pons Aelius, another of the emperor's projects, was begun in 136. In 270–75, Emperor Aurelian incorporated the tomb within the inner city by means of the fortified walls bearing his name. In the sixth century, Castel Sant'Angelo (see page 20) ceased to function as a tomb at all and became a papal fortress. During the thirteenth century, Pope Nicholas III linked the current structure to the Vatican City by means of a *passetto,* or corridor, along the top of the encircling wall. This "secret" emergency escape route saved the lives of several besieged pontiffs.

Overlooking the encircling panorama from the building's roof terrace is a massive eighteenth-century statue of the Archangel Michael. It replaced an earlier statue that commemorated Pope Gregory the Great's vision of a hovering angel unsheathing his sword over the ramparts to mark the end of the plague epidemic in the sixth century. A spiral ramp leads to the imperial mortuary chamber at the heart of the monument, while a broad staircase opens out into the large, open-air courtyard and apartments on the upper floors. Nothing can prepare visitors for the stark contrast between the dark, dank cells of the lower levels and the well-ventilated and refined upper rooms and galleries. Do not miss the Hall of Justice, Hall of Apollo, loggia of Julius II, Treasury, Clement VII's apartments, and the Sala Paolina with its *trompe l'oeil* frescoes. Castel Sant'Angelo has been pivotal to the growth and development of Rome as a focal point for Western civilization, dutifully guarding both its living and dead in times of war and peace. **AA**

Hunting Baths at Leptis Magna (200)

Architect Unknown　**Location** Leptis Magna, Libya　**Style** Roman vernacular　**Materials** Limestone, concrete

The distinguished archaeologist Mortimer Wheeler (1890–1976) argued that the Roman passion for cleanliness—and the construction of public bathhouses throughout the Roman empire—stimulated the development of spacious interiors. The Hunting Baths are plain, squat, domed, and vaulted buildings resembling modern industrial units—the name comes from frescoes depicting men baiting leopards and other wild animals in the vaulted main hall. The baths were built at the end of the first century at a time when Emperor Septimius Severus was

> *"It is the astonishing reach of the Roman mind that compels the imagination."*
>
> Mortimer Wheeler, archaeologist

lavishing money on rebuilding his birthplace. The Severan expansion of the city created suburbs that needed their own baths. The Hunting Baths were originally surrounded by seaside villas.

The almost complete survival of these baths is extraordinary and is partly to be explained by the resilience of Roman concrete. The Hunting Baths's long, barrel-vaulted roofs and dome were fashioned in concrete that was laid, not poured as is usual with modern concrete. The contemporaneous dome of the Pantheon in Rome was made in the same way. The Hunting Baths demonstrate that concrete roofing was quite commonplace in the late Roman era. Domes and barrel-vaulted roofs were widely adopted after the fall of the Roman empire, but concrete was not reinvented until the twentieth century. **MC**

Arch of Constantine (316)

Patron Constantine **Location** Rome, Italy **Style** Classical Roman **Materials** Stone, porphyry, marble including Numidean yellow marble

Rome's Arch of Constantine commemorates the triumph of Constantine I (272–337), the last pagan emperor of Rome, after his victory over Maxentius in the Battle of the Milvian Bridge in 312. It is located between the Palatine Hill and the Colosseum, along the Via Triumphalis taken by victorious armies of the time. Triumphal arches were erected as permanent commemorative monuments and seen as physical manifestations of political power, a practice followed by others through the ages, such as France's Emperor Napoléon I with Paris's Arc de Triomphe du Carrousel.

The arch is particularly notable for its attention to geometric proportion. The lower part is built of marble blocks, and the top is brickwork riveted with marble. The 65-foot-high (20 m) arch is 82 feet (25 m) wide and 23 feet (7 m) deep. It houses three archways; the central archway is 39 feet (12 m) high, and the two side archways are 23 feet (7 m) high. Each facade had four columns of yellow Numidean marble in Corinthian order; one has been replaced since the Roman era. Spandrels above the main archway depict figures of victory, and those above the smaller arches show river gods. Above each side of the archway lie two medallions measuring 8 feet (2.4 m) in diameter and depicting hunting scenes, and on the top level are oblong bas-reliefs and statues.

Many of the sculptures were taken from earlier monuments. For example, the bas-reliefs on the north and south faces of the arch at one time showed episodes in the life of Emperor Marcus Aurelius but were remodeled so that Aurelius's features were made to resemble those of Constantine I. **CMK**

↖ The Arch has been a source of ideas for architects, artists, and urban planners for centuries.

← The pictorial space created by the reliefs would have been animated by people passing under the Arch.

Church of Santa Costanza (361)

Architect Unknown   **Location** Rome, Italy   **Style** Early Christian   **Materials** Brick, marble and granite columns, mosaic

Santa Costanza was built as the mausoleum or *martyria* of the daughter of the emperor Constantine, Constantia (Costanza), who died in 354. As was commonly the case for Roman mausolea, although on a grander scale than is usual, this was a centrally planned circular building that originally had at its center, beneath the dome, the porphyry tombs of Constantia and her sister, Helena (now removed to the Vatican museums).

The building adjoins the nave of the Basilica of Sant'Agnese, to whom Constantia had a particular devotion. The circular design of the building is especially striking on the interior, where two concentric rings of twenty-four paired, freestanding, granite columns with an architrave on composite capitals separate the central space from a barrel-vaulted ambulatory. Rising above the central volume is a large ribbed dome 74 feet (22.5 m) in diameter, built using a technique similar to that of the Pantheon. It is likely that the design inspired the *martyria* of the Holy Sepulchre in Jerusalem, commissioned by Constantine and his mother, Helena.

Santa Costanza is richly decorated with mosaics, some of the earliest from the Christian era to survive, although many of these have been lost over the centuries, and only a few of the New Testament scenes survive. However, it is the exquisite decorative panels and frames in the ambulatory, showing interwoven crosses, foliage, and geometrical patterns, as well as vines with *putti* that are most striking. The mausoleum was consecrated as a church in 1254 by Pope Alexander IV and is still in use today. **FN**

↗ The beautiful church of Santa Costanza takes the circular form of traditional Roman mausoleums.

⊡ Light from the clerestory windows fills the chamber, which contains twelve pairs of radiating columns.

Shaolin Temple (495)

Patron Emperor Xiaowen **Location** Shaoshi Mountain, Henan, China **Style** Buddhist **Materials** Stone, timber

In 464 an Indian monk named Bada, the twenty-eighth successor in a line of religious leaders that could be traced back to Buddha, arrived in China to spread Buddhist teachings. The Shaolin Temple, the construction of which began in 495 under the orders of Emperor Xiaowen, bears testimony to his success. It was from here that Indian scriptures were translated into Chinese and the precepts of Zen Buddhism formed. Bada is also reputed to have introduced martial arts as a complementary practice to meditation—a practice that developed into the notorious, highly skilled Shaolin Gongfu.

The original temple structure was simple but with each succeeding dynasty the Shaolin Temple became increasingly extensive—many of the current structures date from the Ming and Qing dynasties. Great care was taken to preserve symmetry in the temple's design with all crucial buildings being constructed along the site's central axis. These include the Gate of the Temple, the Bell and the Drum towers, the Heavenly King Hall, the Main Hall, the Abbot's Room, the Mahavira Hall, and the Sutra-Keeping Pavilion. The largest and most impressive building of the complex is the Thousand Buddhas Hall, the interior of which is decorated with exquisite, well-preserved murals.

Close to the temple is one of China's greatest architectural records, the Pagoda Forest. Here 246 burial sites are marked by an astounding variety of pagodas. This structural diversity, along with the temple's significance as the birthplace of Zen Buddhism, makes the Shaolin Temple one of China's most important Buddhist sites. **JF**

↖ The building has been destroyed and rebuilt many times over the centuries, and today is partially restored.

↩ The red-colored temple with its green deviations and splendid roof is a fine example of Chinese architecture.

Hagia Sophia (537)

Architects Anthemius of Tralles, Isidore of Miletus   **Location** Istanbul, Turkey   **Style** Byzantine   **Materials** Brick, marble, stone

Hagia Sophia (or the Church of Holy Wisdom) is a former church that was converted into a mosque in 1435, and then into a museum in 1935. It was originally built as part of the newly founded Constantinople for the Emperor Constantine in 326. It was rebuilt by Emperor Justinian in 537. Its plan was drawn up by two men who were better known as scientists than architects—Anthemius of Tralles, an expert in projective geometry, and his colleague Isidore of Miletus, a teacher of stereometry and physics.

It is perhaps the designers' theoretical approach that resulted in the rather foolhardy project, which challenged structural norms. The vast central dome spans 107 feet (32.6 m) and is raised more than 164 feet (50 m) above the nave, which is in turn compressed by a series of interlocking domes, semidomes, and apsidal spaces. Beneath it, forty clerestory windows allow shafts of suffused light to cut into the structure so that the dome appears to float. The dome was the first to be built using the pendentive—an architectural device that resolves the meeting of the curve of the dome and the right angle of the wall below; this redistributed the weight of the dome, though there have been collapses over the years.

From the exterior, the building is striking above all for the evident complexity of massed geometric forms, although there is no clear facade to the design. Sixteenth-century minarets, added when the church was converted to a mosque, give the building an intelligible frame. Once the largest cathedral in the world, Hagia Sophia is still regarded as a sacred space by many Christians and Muslims. **FN**

↗ An exterior view showing Hagia Sophia with the waters of the Bosphorus beyond.

➡ The billowing forms of the church are enhanced by the sloping marble walls and shimmering gold mosaics.

Basilica of San Vitale (548)

Patron Bishop Ecclesius **Location** Ravenna, Italy
Style Byzantine **Materials** Greek marble, stone

Ravenna's cultural heritage derives from its position at a crossroads between East and West. This church was consecrated by Bishop Maximian in 548. Its double octagonal plan contains an inner and outer shell with the aisles and galleries creating a series of uniform trapezoidal spaces. There is a cloister-vaulted domed center and an apse for the altar and presbytery. Between the eight columns around the church's core are eight two-story niches framed by wedge-shaped capitals. The architecture of San Vitale signals the shift from strong Roman influence—visible in the shape of the doorways, steeped towers, and dome—to Byzantine ascendancy as seen in the polygonal apse, column capitals, and use of narrow bricks.

The floor, choir, ceiling vault, galleries, and apse contain the best-preserved secular and religious mosaics outside of Constantinople. The double procession panels of Justinian and Theodora, the greatest of early Byzantine mosaics, showcase the power of art being used as political propaganda. At the foot of the apse, Emperor Justinian and his retinue solemnly gaze across at the bejeweled Empress Theodora and her ladies-in-waiting on the other side. Golden bands of birds, flowers, and cornucopia abound plus representations of Jesus Christ, the Lamb of God, and Old and New Testament figures.

San Vitale's layout was a model for the Church of Saints Sergius and Bacchus in Constantinople, the Palatine Chapel of Charlemagne at Aachen, and Brunelleschi's dome for the Duomo in Florence. **AA**

↖ Beneath the church's central dome are eight two-story niches; the upper gallery was set aside for women.

← The Church of San Vitale was established on the site where St. Vitale reputedly was buried.

Church of San Apollinare (548)

Architect Unknown **Location** Classe, near Ravenna, Italy
Style Byzantine **Materials** Julian bricks, *cipollino* marble

Skellig Michael (550)

Patron St. Fionán **Location** Ballinskelligs, County Kerry, Ireland
Style Celtic **Material** Slate rock

Only Rome has churches older than this sixth-century rectangular basilica with its cylindrical bell-tower, the most beautiful of Ravenna's *campaniles*. This building commemorates a shrine dedicated to Apollinare, the first bishop of Ravenna, who was martyred in the third century. The semicircular crypt houses a Greek marble urn containing St. Apollinare's bones. The basilica was originally built in the late fifth century for the Ostrogoth Theodoric—a follower of Arian Christianity. In the mid-sixth century, it was reconsecrated to Neonian or Catholic Christianity, Arian beliefs having been declared heretical.

The solemnly suggestive, well-proportioned interior was designed as a tangible evocation of the celestial order. The uppermost sections of the nave walls showcase scenes from the life of Christ and his apostles in mosaic and date from 493 to 526. The lower sections feature bishops, martyrs, and saints in mosaic dating from 527 to 565. The nave and two aisles are divided by two rows of twelve columns in veined marble with ornate acanthus-leaf capitals. The vibrantly colored mosaics of the apse mark the transition from Classical naturalism to a more stylized symbolism. A new theophany uniting the glory of God with that of St. Apollinare and the church of Ravenna is presented here through an allegory of the Transfiguration of Christ—a jeweled cross against a blue sky. Around it are shimmering mosaics depicting holy figures in stylized poses—among them St. Apollinare preaching, Abraham and Moses, and the Three Magi visiting the Christ child. The basilica is a Classical space dressed in Byzantine style. Its glittering mosaics contrast with the luster of marble columns deemed so resplendent that they are reputed to shine even at night. **AA**

The island of Skellig Michael, a pyramidal rock 714 feet (217 m) high, 8 miles (13 km) off the coast of County Kerry, is an outstandingly well-preserved early Christian settlement. It was declared a UNESCO World Heritage Site in 1996. St. Fionán is thought to have founded the settlement in the sixth century, but the earliest written records date from the end of the eighth century.

The Skellig settlement is the most dramatic expression of the early Christian monastic belief that intimacy with God was best achieved in harsh and

> *"An incredible, impossible, mad place ... [Skellig Michael] is part of our dream world."*
>
> George Bernard Shaw, writer and critic

isolated settings. There are six slated, beehive-shaped cells, their drystone walls curving gradually inward, covered with corbeled-stone roofs. Along with two oratories and the monks' garden, they stand on a terraced shelf at the island's northeast pinnacle, 600 feet (183 m) above sea level, reached by winding steps from the landing stage below. At its largest, the community is thought to have comprised twelve monks and an abbot, but climate change in the twelfth century forced the monks' departure.

Recently, archaeologists found evidence of the remains of a hermitage near the Skellig's South Peak, built on the ledges of a rock rising vertically from the sea below to a height of almost 700 feet (213 m); this was, in their words, "a place as near to God as the physical environment would permit." **BMC**

Hanging Monastery of Xuan Kong Si (600)

Architect Unknown   **Location** Datong, Shan Xi Province, China
Style Vernacular Chinese   **Material** Wood

Church of St. Hripsime (618)

Patron Komitas I, Catholicos of Armenia   **Location** Vagharshapat
(Echmiadzin), Armenia   **Style** Eastern Christian   **Material** Tufa

Some 40 miles (65 km) from the forbidding industrial city of Datong, which boasts one of the world's largest coal mines, is an architectural marvel that figuratively and physically transcends the relationship between man and nature. Perched on the side of Heng Shan Mountain, on the west face of Jinxia Gorge, is the Hanging Monastery of Xuan Kong Si. Construction began in 491, though various additions and renovations have occurred since, including a major restoration in 1900. Sheltered from the elements, the inspiration for this ethereal monastery derives from the Taoist notion of tranquility, where concentration is undisturbed by commonplace sounds, such as the crowing of roosters and barking of dogs.

The monastery is a must-see for its sheer uniqueness, not only of its beauty and precipitous setting, but also for being the only surviving example of a temple built on the basis of China's three main philosophies: Taoism, Buddhism, and Confucianism. Evidence of this is to be seen inside the temple in the sculptures of Sakyamuni, Confucius, and Laotzu.

The method of construction used to suspend this monastery from the face of the gorge was a series of chiseled openings in the rock into which wooden beams were inserted. The protruding beams served as the building's foundation onto which wooden boards and pillars were attached to create the walls and roofs. As a safety measure, a wooden balustrade skirts each building and vertical wooden poles further support the walkways and buildings from underneath.

The monastery complex comprises forty rooms with a combined space of 1,635 square feet (152 sq m), interconnected by exterior walkways. The highest of these, formerly 295 feet (90 m) above the riverbed, is now 190 feet (58 m) above, due to river silting. **ED**

The Church of St. Hripsime stands over the tomb of St. Hripsime, one of the thirty-three virgin martyrs who helped bring about the creation of Armenia as the first Christian kingdom at the start of the fourth century. One of a group of almost identical buildings in both Armenia and Georgia, the church represents religious architecture simultaneously at its most complex and playful. The church was designed around its ground plan, a geometric exercise in interlocking circles, semicircles, and rectangles. At its heart is a square nave, over which hangs the huge masonry dome. To

> ## "Lord Christ, remember Komitas, Catholicos of the Armenians, builder of St. Hripsime."
>
> Inscription on the facade of the church

each side of the square is a semicircular apse; and at each corner, between the apses, is a tall, narrow, almost circular niche that leads through to a rectangular chamber in each corner of the building.

From the outside, it is almost impossible to discern this geometric game; only the pairs of deep triangular niches on each facade hint at the interior divisions of space. Instead the church stands as a solid, austere mass of stone, rigidly contained within its rectangular footprint. The severity is offset, however, by the profusion of apses (most are ecclesiastically unnecessary) and the variegated colors of the local building material: the black blocks of tufa, which might have appeared oppressively plain and massive, are interspersed with orange, enlivening the walls with a sense of movement and lightness. **AE**

Great Mosque at Mecca (632)

Patron Caliph Omar Ibn al-Khattab   **Location** Mecca, Saudi Arabia
Style Early Islamic   **Materials** Gray stone, marble

The Great Mosque (Al-Masjid al-Hāram Mosque) began as a small, unassuming, unroofed building with low walls made of rough stone. Over the centuries it has evolved to become a superstructure with six minarets, a dome, and a courtyard capable of holding 800,000 people during the most important Muslim pilgrimage—the annual *hajj* to Mecca.

Practicing Muslims pray in the direction of the Great Mosque's shrine five times a day wherever they are. The shrine—or Kaaba—is the focal point of prayer and the center of the faith. The structure has been destroyed and rebuilt several times since the Prophet Mohammed removed pagan idols and rededicated it to Allah in 632. It is now a tall oblong of around 50 feet (15 m) in length covered in black silk brocade with a gold frieze. The most important symbol in Islam, the Black Stone—thought to be a meteorite—is embedded in the shrine. The nearby Zamzam well holds the sacred waters of Islam, into which pilgrims dip their white pilgrimage clothing, ready for burial.

The mosque has been added to extensively over the centuries. Most importantly, early porticoes surrounding the courtyard, which were erected during the Ottoman empire in the sixteenth century, were only narrowly saved when the Saudi King, Abdul Aziz, sponsored the extension of the structure in the 1950s. Further modernization, in the latter half of the twentieth century, saw the courtyard emptied of obstacles that blocked the circumambulating movement of the pilgrims visiting the mosque. **ADB**

↗ The mosque is almost more a delineation of sacred space than a mere building.

→ The great mystery of the Kaaba remains tantalizing, its secrets shrouded forever beneath ritual vestments.

Great Kyz Kala (651)

Architect Unknown **Location** Merv, Bairam Ali, Turkmenistan **Style** Sassanid **Material** Mud-brick

The Great Kyz Kala is an awe-inspiring and dramatic mud-brick structure. It comprises a rectangular earth platform with sloping sides containing the lower-story rooms. The massive corrugated external walls rise dramatically from the mound and enclose the rooms of the upper story and parapet. Enough of the interior survives to suggest at least sixteen rooms built around a central space. Each corrugation is half-octagonal with a diameter of 4.3 feet (1.3 m), rising from a pointed base to form a pointed top. The walls are 6.5 feet (1.98 m) thick, gently tapering toward the top, and survive to a height of 39 feet (11.8 m). The Great Kyz Kala stands adjacent to a smaller monument—the Little Kyz Kala—also constructed from mud-brick, sharing a similar corrugated construction. This is the best surviving example of a *köhsk*, a type of structure found in Central Asia. These buildings perhaps served as residences for the wealthy and powerful. This is an architecture ideally suited to a hot, arid climate, with life based around a shady central space, protected from the extremes of weather by thick enclosing mud-brick walls. The Great Kyz Kala has survived relatively unscathed from a period in which the majority of buildings have been lost. The fact that this is an abandoned mud-brick structure, retained without its protecting roof and without any regular maintenance, is astounding. The whole of Merv has been designated a UNESCO World Heritage Site. **LC**

"... it is difficult ... even to suggest what might have been the purpose of these unusual ... piles."

V.A. Zhukovsky, archaeologist

Ise Shrine (690)

Architect Unknown **Location** City of Ise, Mie Prefecture, Japan **Style** Ancient Shinto **Material** Wood

Ise Shrine is one of the most sacred examples of *Yuiitsu-shinmei-zukuri*, the purest and simplest form of Shinto architecture. Ise Shrine actually refers to the two main shrines, the Naiku and the Geku, as well as many smaller subsidiary shrines nearby. The Naiku is dedicated to Amaterasu Omikami, the sun goddess and the ancestral deity of Japan's imperial family. At the Geku is enshrined Toyouke Omikami, the goddess of grains and cereals. The main sanctuary buildings of both the Naiku and Geku resemble images of grain warehouses etched on bronze mirrors from the fifth century. What is remarkable about Ise Shrine is that these sanctuary buildings are all rebuilt in the exact same manner every twenty years. At both the Naiku and Geku, there are two main sanctuaries next to each other, and these alternate as sites to be rebuilt each time. Thus, the current shrine buildings, which were all newly constructed in 1993 on the occasion of the sixty-first *shikinen sengu* "transfer ceremony," should be identical to the first ones built, in 690. Ise Shrine is considered to represent the most purely Japanese tradition (Buddhist architecture and official court buildings, first introduced to Japan in the late sixth and seventh centuries, all have their roots in China and Korea). Thus, modernist architects such as Bruno Taut, Walter Gropius, and Kenzo Tange all visited Ise Shrine in their own search for the roots of Japanese architecture and its "modernity." **YZ**

> *"I have roamed through tradition until, at its furthest limits, I was confronted by Ise ..."*
>
> Kenzo Tange, architect

Dome of the Rock (691)

Architect Caliph Abd al-Malik **Location** Jerusalem, Israel **Style** Islamic **Materials** Stone, marble, porcelain, gold

Built by the Umayyad Caliph Abd al-Malik, this holy shrine surrounds the rock from where the prophet Muhammad ascended to heaven on a horselike creature, Buraq, accompanied by the angel Gabriel. It is one of Islam's most holy buildings, and within the Jewish faith the rock is revered as the site where Abraham fulfilled God's test and offered his son Isaac as a sacrifice. Further, it is thought that Solomon's Temple once stood on this site, and that during its period of tenure the Ark of the Covenant was placed upon this sacred rock. The octagonal building is perhaps best known for its stunning gold dome, which stretches 66 feet (20 m) across the rock, rising to an apex of almost 115 feet (35 m) above it. The dome was originally made of gold; however this was replaced by copper and finally, aluminum. The aluminum is now covered with gold leaf, a donation from the late King Hussein of Jordan. Right at the top of the dome sits a full-moon decoration, referring to the more familiar crescent-moon motif of Islam; the moon is positioned so that its aperture faces toward Mecca, the most holy site in the Islamic world. Beautiful polychromic tiles from the Turkish town of Iznik are layered over the shrine's exterior. These are accurate copies, made in the 1960s, of the original tiles, commissioned by Suleiman the Magnificent and made in Persia in the sixteenth century. Some of the tiles assemble into Arabic inscriptions that narrate the story of Muhammad's night journey to heaven, as described in the Koran. The mosaics within the interior feature both realistic and stylized representations of vegetation. (Islamic custom prohibits the images or representations of people or animals in art in religious buildings.) Together, these poetic decorations evoke an exotic garden, perhaps even the long-awaited gardens of Paradise. **AT**

Cathedral of St. Domnius (699)

Architect Filotas   **Location** Split, Croatia   **Style** Classical Roman, Gothic   **Materials** Limestone, brick, marble

In 305 Emperor Diocletian retired to his fortified palace, situated on a small peninsula on the eastern shores of the Adriatic Sea. In 316 he was laid to rest in his mausoleum, an octagonal building within the palace complex. (Centuries later, in 639, the palace was used as a refuge for the people of nearby Salona who, safe within its fortified walls, constructed the town now known as Split.) In the seventh century, Diocletian's mausoleum was converted into a Christian cathedral dedicated to St. Domnius, an ironic turn because Diocletian is largely remembered for his persecution of the early Christians, and St. Domnius was one of many Christians killed during the persecution. The cathedral is a fascinating fusion of Christian church architecture and Classical Roman building. The octagonal floorplan has been retained, and Roman columns and arches are still in place along with reliefs of Diocletian and his wife around the

dome. Later additions to the cathedral include a thirteenth-century, hexagonal stone pulpit and belltower, inspired by a Classical triumphal arch. The fifteenth-century Altar of Domnius, in Lombardic Gothic style, is attributed to Bonino of Milan. George the Dalmatian, who built Sibenik Cathedral, designed the sixteenth-century Gothic canopy above the Altar of Anastasius. St. Domnius is the oldest Roman Catholic cathedral in the world, but its bones are those of a Roman mausoleum. **MC**

"No province . . . could have afforded Diocletian a more elegant place of retirement."

Robert Adam, *The Ruins of the Palace of Diocletian* (1764)

Big Wild Goose Pagoda (704)

Patron Emperor Gaozong   **Location** Da Ci'en Temple, Suzhou, China   **Style** Buddhist temple design, Tang Dynasty   **Material** Brick

The Big Wild Goose Pagoda is situated in the Da Ci'en Temple, a grand complex in Chang'an, near today's Xian City. Construction of the temple began in 648, during the reign of Emperor Gaozong. The pagoda's construction began four years later, an example of how the Chinese Buddhist pagoda tradition had taken root. Many Tang Dynasty constructions were, like the Big Wild Goose Pagoda, simple in design, although they became more elaborate with subsequent centuries. The original mud-and-brick construction reached five stories high but was reconstructed between 701 and 704 in gray brick and elevated to seven stories, attaining a height of 210 feet (64 m). The pagoda was constructed expressly for the purpose of holding the Buddhist Sanskrit scriptures acquired by the monk Xuanzhuang on his travels to India. As seen today, the seven stories of the Big Wild Goose Pagoda are strongly delineated by small roofs projecting from each level; above these, arched entry portals puncture each wall. On the lintels of the four ground-level gates are delicately carved Buddhist images and architectural designs, along with two stone tablets engraved by the eminent Tang Dynasty calligrapher Chu Suiliang. Simple but impressive, the Big Wild Goose Pagoda that we see today still towers over its surroundings and tells us much of the manner in which both Buddhist teaching and architectural principles traveled from India through to China. **JF**

"Its high pinnacle pierces the boundless blue. A violent wind is blowing without a pause."

Tu Fu, poet

Umayyad Mosque (715)

Architect Caliph al-Walid bin Abd al-Malik   **Location** Damascus, Syria   **Style** Umayyad   **Materials** Limestone, white marble

From the time of the Assyrians, this site in the heart of old Damascus has housed sacred buildings. During the Roman era it was occupied by a temple to Jupiter and, after Emperor Constantine's conversion to Christianity, it became a Byzantine basilica. Following the Islamic conquest of 636, it was converted into a mosque shared by Muslims and Christians, before being demolished as the rise in power of the Umayyad caliphate demanded a new monument. The plan for al-Walid's mosque consists of a rectangular courtyard with external walls from the days when the building functioned as a temple, and three minarets—the eastern, thirteenth-century Minaret of Jesus; the western, fifteenth-century Minaret of Qat Bey; and the Minaret of the Bride, a square tower-shaped minaret near the northern gate. In the middle of the courtyard are the Dome of the Hours, the ablutions fountain, and the ancient treasury called Beit al Mal. The tomb of

Saladin (1138–93) stands in a small garden adjoining the north wall. The mosque building occupies the southern length of the rectangle and opens out into a magnificent, white, marble-paved courtyard flanked by a two-story, mosaic-covered arcade on three sides. The rectangular basilica plan of the prayer hall has three aisles separated by a gilded mosaic transept, topped by the octagonal Dome of the Eagle on four great pillars. The interior walls, embellished by colored and gilded glass mosaics, are thought to depict paradise and house the marble-clad, green-domed shrine of St. John the Baptist, venerated by Christians and Muslims alike. The Umayyad Mosque became the model for hundreds of mosques in newly established territories throughout the Islamic world. Ranked in sanctity alongside Jerusalem's Dome of the Rock, it comes second only to the pilgrimage destinations of Mecca and Medina. **AA**

Pyramid of the Great Jaguar (743)

Patron Hasaw Chan K'awil   **Location** Tikal National Park, Guatemala   **Style** Mayan   **Material** Local stone

The imposing pyramids at Tikal are the evocative remains of one of the most important civilizations of the Mayan Classical Period. Now a UNESCO World Heritage Site, surrounded by rainforest, Tikal was once home to some 100,000 people. The Jaguar Temple, also known as Temple One, is the most famous pyramid on the site. Standing 144 feet (44 m) high, it was built as a tomb for the body of the Mayan leader Hasaw Chan K'awil, and as a symbol of his defeat of a rival Mayan tribe. The temple was groundbreaking in its construction, a deliberate change from all previous Mayan buildings, emphasizing Hasaw Chan K'awil's supremacy over other Mayan leaders. It was built under the direction of his son, Yik'in Chan K'awil, who became ruler of Tikal in c. 743. Construction work began on the temple in c. 741. The north-facing tomb was constructed first and the great pyramid built on top of it; the building material was all local stone, including flint. The pyramid is square-sided with dangerously steep steps ascending via a series of smaller platforms to a dominating platform near the top. On this platform, inside what appears from the ground to be a forbiddingly cavernous doorway, are three rooms. Above this section is an arched and carved roof-comb. The temple takes its name from the original wooden carving of a jaguar—now in a museum in Switzerland—that was once an important feature. Other carvings and reliefs in wood were also once attached to the structure, but archaeologists are divided in opinion as to their content and scale. The Jaguar Temple commands impressive views—emphasizing the strategic might of Tikal at the time. As the primary city of the Peten region, Tikal was in a coveted position and the building of the Jaguar Temple demonstrated the ruler's intention to keep his city safe from further invasion. **LH**

Jotab-dong Pagoda (750)

Architect Unknown **Location** Gyeongsangbuk-do, South Korea **Style** Buddhist **Materials** Granite, brick

Jotab-dong Pagoda has its origins in the Indian funerary monument known as a *stupa*. In the course of its migration east, the *stupa* took on, in China, the form of a tower. The building of such towers accompanied the spread of Buddhism beyond into the Korean peninsula. There, in the Silla Kingdom, they were often built in stone rather than in wood, and sometimes in brick in imitation of wooden constructions. The five-story Jotab-dong Pagoda is all that remains of an unknown Buddhist monastery. It is exceptional because it combines two construction materials normally used separately: the tower is in two parts, with stone at the bottom supporting an upper section of brick. Erected on an earth terrace, the structure, a little less than 30 feet (9 m) high, lacks the additional elements—often made of bronze—that usually crown a pagoda top. The square base, about 75 square feet (7 sq m), is raised by a few steps and consists of

five or six courses of granite blocks cut in various shapes. On the south side, the stone frame of a doorway gives access to a rectangular room that was probably used to hold sacred relics; to the sides, two sculptures represent two protecting deities, called *Inwang* in Korean. Surmounting the pagoda's stone base, bricks form an additional five stories. The brick stories reproduce, by a succession of courses that increase in circumference and then decrease, the tiered-roof arrangement of wooden pagodas. **FM**

"By that time in Gyeongju . . . pagodas stood in unending lines like flights of wild geese."

Legend in *Samguk Yusa* (1284)

Temple of Kailashnath (773)

Patron Krishna I, Rahstrakoota Dynasty **Location** Ellora caves, Maharashtra, India **Style** South Indian (Dravidian) **Material** Carved local stone

There are thirty-three shrines dug from the volcanic rock at Ellora. Twelve are Buddhist from the Gupta Period, four are Jain, and seventeen are Hindu. Undoubtedly the most striking, and one of the best stone temples in all of India, is the Kailashnath temple. It is dedicated to Lord Shiva and symbolizes Mount Kailash, the Himalayan peak attributed to be the abode of the deity. This building's architectural grandeur makes it stand from the myriad of religious halls of worship carved into the Charanandri Hills of Aurangabad. The monolithic structure is built in the architectural style of the south Indian temples, and contains a shrine, inner sanctum, and open porches. But it is all the more brilliant because it was not constructed by laying stone upon stone, but was carved out of the rock by excavating nearly 40,000 tons of sandstone, thus making it an achievement of sublime sculptural splendor. It was conceived and executed from the topmost point—the *shikhar*—of the temple with stonemasons working all the way through to the pedestal, creating a multistoried temple 64 feet (50 m) deep, 109 feet (33 m) wide, and 98 feet (30 m) high. Its crowning glory is the largest cantilevered rock ceiling in the world. The entire external and internal surface of the temple is intricately carved with symbols and figures from Hindu scriptures, helping to explain why the temple is said to have taken more than a century to complete. **BS**

"… one of those rare occasions when men's minds, hearts, and hands work in unison."

Percy Brown, architectural historian

Church of St. Donat (800)

Architect Unknown **Location** Zadar, Croatia **Style** Romanesque **Materials** Brick, limestone, wood

Zadar, founded in the first century during the reign of Emperor Augustus, was a typical Roman town with a forum, basilica, temple, theater, and marketplace. As the Roman empire declined, Christianity became the dominant religion, and a fourth-century bishop's palace was built on the site of the forum. By the ninth century, it had become part of "Byzantine Dalmatia," along with other cities and islands on the Adriatic coast that belonged to the Eastern empire. But, to complicate matters, Zadar and other coastal towns, including Split and Dubrovnik, remained under the ecclesiastical jurisdiction of the Church of Rome. The entire region became an ideological faultline between East and West, Rome and Constantinople, Orthodox and Roman Catholic Christianity. The response of local builders was to innovate. Many ninth-century churches survive along the Croatian coast, and they differ considerably in ground plan and

form. But one common feature is the use of vaulting, apses, and domes merging with walls in a continuous surface without any articulation of the supports and joins. St. Donat's Church is the largest of its type. The rotunda is 75.5 feet (23 m) in diameter and 65.5 feet (20 m) high, interrupted by three rounded apses with arched entrances supported by Roman columns. The columns form part of an arcaded ambulatory that encircles the ground floor. The upper story is supported by brick piers and topped by a wooden roof that replaces the original dome. St. Donat's is similar to the sixth-century church of San Vitale at Ravenna, Italy, although San Vitale is hexagonal. The arches are reminiscent of the Palatine chapel at Aachen Cathedral, which was also constructed in the ninth century. However, St. Donat's primarily expresses Zadar's adaptability to the political and religious pressures of the early Middle Ages. **MC**

Aachen Cathedral (800)

Architect Odo von Metz **Location** Aachen, Germany **Style** Byzantine, Franconian **Materials** Italian marble, granite, limestone, sandstone

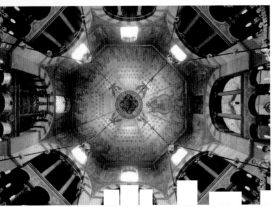

Nowadays we are so accustomed to the idea of churches having spires that we almost consider both inseparable in Western architecture. But the evolution of spires marks a particular characteristic of European architecture and can be considered a novelty to architectural history. Towers in traditional architecture used to be relegated to defensive structures and were not typical of church buildings.

When Charlemagne commissioned his palace and palatine chapel in Aachen, there was no local tradition in masonry buildings. He therefore drafted builders from Italy and other southern countries to construct a church that would become one of the first examples of this new building typology.

The cathedral's main central space is based on an octagonal ring of arches, which are flanked by a circular gallery about 100 feet (32 m) in diameter. The east side held the altar and was later enlarged by a Gothic choir. The real innovation was the introduction of the west end, the gated access to the church, where the emperor would have resided. It forms a distinct opposition to the clerical east end and establishes the ruler firmly as a second power in the edifice.

At Aachen the west end was built in a more defensive style, which leads to a "hybrid" building merging elements of a castle and a church. This discrepancy would later be resolved by Gothic architects in their use of more ornamental additions. But the template had been laid down: from then on nearly all church designs boasted one, two, sometimes even four spires, dominating the skylines of so many European cities to this day. **LT**

↖ Aachen cathedral's main central space was the first vaulted structure north of the Alps since antiquity.

↩ The view up to the splendidly decorated ceiling of the dome in the center—and heart—of the cathedral.

Borobudur Temple (835)

Architect Unknown   **Location** Near Magalang, Java   **Style** Sailendra with Gupta influence   **Materials** Black, volcanic, andesite rock

By the seventh century, Indianized kingdoms were dominant in Java and Sumatra. They were unified by the Sailendra Dynasty, which built Borobudur after converting to Mahayana Buddhism. Once the heart of Buddhist worship in southeast Asia, Borobudur was mysteriously abandoned in the twelfth century until Java's Lieutenant-Governor, Sir Stamford Raffles, rediscovered it in 1814, hidden under volcanic ash.

Situated on a hill, the stepped, four-sided pyramid is made up of ten levels: six square stories, three circular terraces, and a central *stupa* (dome-shaped shrine) at the summit. Its plan combines five symbols in one: a *mandala* (a mystical map of the cosmos combining a square for the earth with a circle for the heavens), the blossoming lotus (Buddha's secret symbol), the *stupa* shrine, the temple-mountain (Mount Meru), and a three-dimensional path to enlightenment. The 160 relief panels on the base illustrate the realm of worldly desires. Starting with those on the eastern staircase, a pilgrim traverses around the monument in a clockwise direction, before ascending to the next level. The panel carvings comprise a pictorial biography of the Buddha's life and teachings, each familiar story a step in the pilgrim's progress toward attaining higher consciousness. This shift is conveyed architecturally as the square platforms of the lower terraces give way to circular ones in the upper levels. The latter display seventy-two life-size Buddha statues within wall niches. The crowning *stupa*, representing enlightenment, is empty. Borobudur set a precedent for future Buddhist sites, influencing structures like Cambodia's Angkor Wat. **AA**

↗ Borobudur is the largest non-monastic Buddhist temple on the planet.

➡ The greatest treasure of this massive monument are its relief panels depicting scenes from Buddhism.

Great Mosque, al-Ukba (836)

Patron Ziyadat Allah   **Location** Kairouan, Tunisia
Style Islamic, Aghlabid   **Materials** Stone, marble, wood, porphyry

Legend has it that the famous Muslim conqueror, Akbar, of the Umayyad Dynasty founded a city and mosque at Kairouan when one of his soldiers kicked a golden goblet out of the sand and recognized it as one that had been lost from Mecca, the holiest city of Islam. A spring, thought to have its source in the sacred Zamzam well in Mecca, flowed from the spot and established this as a holy site that is still referred to as the Mecca of the Maghreb. The mosque that was built here in 670 was completely destroyed by an Aghlabid sovereign and was rebuilt in 836. But, even today, the mosque is often referred to as al-Ukba, in memory of the revered original and its founder, Akbar. Kairouan is now the holiest Islamic city in North Africa.

The Great Mosque, once an important site of pilgrimage for Muslims, is the model for all mosques in North Africa and is thought to have the earliest and most beautiful prayer niche in Islam as well as a very early towering, square minaret. Its main structure and features remain in place from the ninth century and it is considered to be the most important monument of the Aghlabids left standing today. Its sanctuary, or prayer hall, is made up of seventeen arcades of 414 pillars in marble and porphyry, which were taken from various ancient buildings and as a result are all of different heights. They are connected by pointed horseshoe-shaped arches. Restoration took place in 862 when the *mihrab*, the prayer niche indicating the direction of Mecca, was added and decorated using rare, luster tiles imported from Baghdad. The *minbar* (carved wooden pulpit) is thought to be the oldest preserved example today. In the thirteenth century, the Hafsids added arcades around the courtyard and porches at the gates. This mosque's design set the style for later North African Islamic architecture. **ADB**

Mosque of Ibn Tulun (879)

Patron Ahmad Ibn Tulun   **Location** Cairo, Egypt
Style Abbasid, Tulunid   **Materials** Mud brick, brick, stucco, stone

The monumental Mosque of Ibn Tulun is one of the few remnants from the classical Islamic period when Abbasid caliphs ruled the Islamic world from their capital Samarra in Iraq. The governor who built this mosque declared his independence from his masters in 868 and founded the short-lived Tulunid Dynasty. When the Abbasids reconquered Egypt in 905, they left nothing standing save for Ibn Tulun. Over the centuries Cairo's oldest mosque and the world's third largest has served as a *caravanserai*, or travelers' inn, as well as a hideout for body snatchers.

> "... this blessed and happy mosque [uses] the revenues from a pure and legitimate source ..."

Ancient calligraphy in ninth-century Kufic script

The complex consists of a mosque surrounded by an enclosure. Around it on all but its *qibla* side (the one facing Mecca) are narrow enclosed wings or *ziyadas*. The *ziyadas* protect the sanctified inner space and lead into the immense courtyard where thirteen pointed arches distinguish every side of the mosque. The northern *ziyada* contains a helical-shaped minaret with a Babylonian ziggurat-influenced spiraling external staircase. Inside the mosque the *mihrab* (prayer niche) of the prayer hall is flanked by two columns with perforated capitals. Behind the *qibla* wall was the Dar al-Imara giving access to the *maqsura*, a private area used by the caliph and his close circle during Friday prayers. A sycamore-wood frieze runs around the inner arches and the Kufic calligraphy running above it retells one-fifth of the Koran. **AA**

Saminid Mausoleum
(Tomb of Ismail Samani) (c. 943)

Architect Unknown   **Location** Bukhara, Uzbekistan
Style Saminid   **Material** Brick

The Saminid Mausoleum is a masterpiece of tenth-century Islamic architecture and marks a significant period of development in Central Asian architecture.

The mausoleum is a slightly tapered cube, 35 feet by 35 feet (10.6 by 10.6 m), topped with an inset hemispherical dome. Each facade is identical, comprising an arcaded gallery, portals, and engaged corner columns. The building finds its inspiration from the earlier Sogdian and Sassanian structures—the domed square, arched opening on each side, upper gallery, and circular bricks in particular—while the Islamic geometry, squinch (small arch allowing a drum or dome to meet an angled base) and *chortak* (domed hall) design were to influence future buildings.

Elaborate brick decoration is on every surface but the dome. Tripled or quadrupled stretchers alternate with smaller bricks in vertical bonds, while curved shapes increase the range of decoration, bordered by thick borders of plain bricks. The interplay of brickwork and shadow creates the spectacular effect of lightness, the whole seeming like a delicately woven basket. The brick decoration marks a significant shift from earlier uses of stucco and is possibly a preliminary to the eventual use of molded terra cotta.

The mausoleum is popularly known as Ismail Samani's tomb, and was erected before 943 in the emir's cemetery. It was excavated in 1934 by the Russian painter Ivan Shishkin and underwent sympathetic conservation work in the 1990s. The mausoleum now stands alone in a public park. **LC**

↗ The building's stark symmetry suggests its scale is more monumental than its actual size.

→ Its richly textured exterior surfaces are cast into relief by the crawling shadows of the day.

Tiger Hill Pagoda (961)

Architect Unknown   **Location** Yuyan Temple, Suzhou, China   **Style** Buddhist temple design, Song Dynasty   **Materials** Brick

Constructed in the Song Dynasty, the brick Tiger Hill Pagoda—also known as Cloud Rock Pagoda—was constructed to replace and imitate in its design, a previous wooden Tang Dynasty structure. It is, for this reason, a valuable resource for information regarding Chinese wooden pagoda design.

Built 1.8 miles (3 km) northwest of Suzhou, as part of the Yunyan Temple established at the summit of Tiger Hill, the Tiger Hill Pagoda is the oldest of such structures in the area. It is octagonal in plan and consists of seven stories that reach to a height of 258 feet (48 m). What is of particular interest, however, is the fact that the 600-ton pagoda has been tilting for more than 400 years and today leans to the northwest, 8 feet (2.5 m) off-center.

Despite this tilt, the gentle tapering and subsequent graceful curving of the pagoda's exterior walls make it particularly elegant. Upon the structure's surface, constructed in fine brickwork are distinctive brackets that appear to support the projecting ledges, which wind around each story. These, in fact, have no structural purpose and, like the lintels above the many doorways, have been added for purely decorative reasons. Remnants of red paint that would have originally decorated the lintels can still be seen surrounding the numerous pointed doorways, the scalloped edges of which are relatively unusual in Chinese pagoda design.

The extent of the decoration demonstrates the increasing ornamentation of Chinese Buddhist pagodas, but the plainer structure of today has lost none of its charm. Indeed, the entire pagoda, in its aged state, has become an intrinsic part of the hill upon which it stands and serves as an icon for the ancient city of Suzhou. As declared by Su Shi, the Song Dynasty poet, "It is a lifelong pity if having visited Suzhou you did not visit Tiger Hill." **JF**

Great Mosque (998)

Patron Abd Ar Rahman I | **Location** Córdoba, Spain | **Style** Moorish | **Materials** Stone, jasper, onyx, marble, granite

After defeating the Spanish Visigoth empire in 711, the Moors founded an independent caliphate in Spain. In 756 Córdoba was chosen as residence and became one of the most prosperous cities and important Islamic centers in medieval Europe. To assert his independence, the caliph Abd Ar Rahman I (731–788) founded a mosque to compete with the greatest ones in the East.

Construction of the Great Mosque (Mezquita) began in 785 and subsequent rulers consistently extended the building. In 998 the structure reached its current length of 587 feet (179 m) and width of 423 feet (129 m). The architects stipulated giant double-story horseshoe arches, modeled on the archetype of Latin aqueducts, to provide a greater ceiling height. These imposing arches, made out of alternating red and white stone, stand on 856 columns made of jasper, onyx, marble, and granite to form the nineteen naves of the mosque. The use of double arches is unique in Islamic architecture. A crenelated wall surrounds the complex, also enclosing the splendid *Patio de los Naranjos* (Orange Tree Courtyard). In 1236 Ferdinand III, Christian king of Castile, recaptured Córdoba. In 1523 the mosque was converted into a cathedral, with the first of many Christian features being added, including a nave and several shrines.

Despite the implementations of the Christian church, the interior of the Great Mosque still has great visual impact: in half-light, its forest of stone columns gives the impression of an infinite labyrinth and the mosaics in the *mihrabs* (prayer niches or rooms) are among the most beautiful in the world. **CWH**

↗ The double arches, a new architectural feature at the time, provide height as well as striking visual interest.

➡ The Great Mosque is unique among other mosques in that its main *mihrab* is not orientated toward Mecca.

Observatory at Chichén Iztá (1000)

Architect Unknown **Location** Yucatán Peninsula, Mexico **Style** Mayan **Material** Stone

Chichén Iztá is one of the best-preserved Mayan sites in Mexico's Yucatán Peninsula. The area was first settled in 550, and then later abandoned, perhaps because of a Toltec invasion. It was resettled *c.* 1000, but by the thirteenth century it had been abandoned once more. The observatory is thought to have been built during this later period of settlement. The site is believed to have been a religious, military, political, and commercial center that would have been inhabited by 35,000 people in its heyday.

The 74-foot-high (22.5 m) observatory was known as *El Caracol* or "The Snail" by the Spaniards when they first arrived because of the circular design of its central domed tower and its spiral staircase. It is believed that the structure was used as an astronomic observatory, since the Mayans used the stars to predict when to sow crops and when to time religious rituals. For example, shadows inside the observatory cast from the angle of the sun hitting a doorway would have been used to predict solstices. Around the edge of the building lie large rock receptacles that are likely to have been filled with water in order to see the reflection of the stars and enable Mayan priests to decide dates in their calendar system. Four entrances face in the direction of the cardinal points of the compass and carved masks of the rain-god Chac sit above each doorway. The 42-foot-high (13 m) tower rests on two rectangular platforms. Inside are some small windows that align with the appearance of certain stars on certain dates and were probably used to study the stars. A staircase leads to the top of the structure for closer observation of the skies. **CMK**

◹ Mayan ingenuity in using architecture to serve science is superbly demonstrated by this building.

◿ The stylized deities on the building's exterior reveal the Mayan's overall religious world-view.

Brihadishvara Temple (1010)

Patron Rajaraja I **Location** Thanjavur, Tamil Nadu, India **Style** South Indian (Dravidian) **Material** Granite

The Brihadishvara Temple is just as much a symbol of power and wealth as it is a shrine to the Hindu god Shiva. Inscriptions—made on the walls detailing the ruler Rajaraja I's (985–1012) lavish gifts to the temple—are evidence enough of the wealth of the Chola empire. They list jewels, gold, silver, attendants, and 400 female dancers who were brides of Shiva. When Brihadishvara was constructed, it was the biggest temple in India. Moving away from the small-scale design of earlier temples, it set the standard for a new age of grandiose design. The temple's design also starts a shift toward favoring larger and more ornate gateways or *gopuras* until they eventually overshadow even the main shrine in stature.

At a height of more than 200 feet (60 m), the main shrine of the temple is the highest pyramidal shrine tower in south India. Legend says its domed cupola—which weighs over eighty tons—was transported to the structure's apex via a gently sloping 4-mile-long (6.5 km) ramp. Inside the main shrine sits a 13-foot-high (4 m) *lingam,* or sacred object, which represents the Hindu deity Shiva. Murals depicting Rajaraja I decorate the walls and are thought to be the most extant important examples of Chola painting, even though much of these have been partially obscured by a later Nayakas mural. A shrine and a pavilion to house a huge stone Nandi—Shiva's bull—were also added during the Nayakas period in the seventeenth century. With its soaring pyramidal shrine, heavy doorways, and early paintings, the Brihadishvara Temple is a must-see and the unrivaled masterpiece of Chola art and architecture. **ADB**

↗ Carvings of an army of gods adorn every outer surface of the building, creating a highly textured facade.

➡ A fine example of Dravidian-style temple architecture, the structure is now a UNESCO World Heritage Site.

Cathedral of St. Sophia (1052)

Patron Prince Vladimir **Location** Kremlin, Novgorod, Russia **Style** Russian Orthodox **Materials** Stone, pink lime mortar, dressed brick

The Cathedral of St. Sophia, built under Bishop Luke for Prince Vladimir, son of Yaroslavl the Wise, Prince of Novgorod, was the seat of an archbishop from 1165. The nucleus of the church is domed and cruciform, with five aisles, the whole supported by twelve pillars. There are only three apses, although these have the traditional complement of five domes. Originally, single-story galleries supported by flying buttresses surrounded the church, but these were raised by another story and the buttresses were enveloped. At the end of the fifteenth century, the Chapel of the Nativity of the Virgin was added and subsequent additions were matters of detail rather than substance. The church was inexpertly restored in the late nineteenth century, and again after World War II following bomb damage in 1941. The interior—despite many alterations made over 900 years—still conjures up an impression of severity and sublimity.

The architecture has a muscular Classical severity reminiscent of Nicholas Hawksmoor or Sir John Soane. Original mural paintings of c. 1144 by artists from Constantinople survive only in fragments, as does a picture of the Emperor Constantine and his mother Helena painted *al secco* (painted on dry plaster) on a pillar c. 1108. Otherwise the decorations date from the late nineteenth century or post-1945. In the west portal is a famous pair of bronze doors made at Magdeburg from 1152 to 1154, one of the finest surviving products of the German High Romanesque. Brought to Novgorod c. 1187 from the captured Swedish fortress of Sigtuna, these doors bear portraits of the masters who originally cast them, as well as a later one of the man who reconstructed the panels of the doors in Novgorod. Other panels are embellished with images of saints and bishops and a centaur shooting a bow and arrow. **CWH**

San Miniato al Monte (1059)

Architect Unknown   **Location** Florence, Italy   **Style** Romanesque   **Materials** Marble, green serpentine and other colored stone

San Miniato al Monte was founded in 1018, to serve a Benedictine abbey sponsored by Countess Matilda of Canossa, a great advocate of papal power during the late eleventh century. It is dedicated to the first martyr of Christian Florence, who was beheaded and then allegedly staggered, head under his arm, to his final resting place on the hillside location of the church. It is a fine example of Tuscan Romanesque architecture, and both its interior and exterior were to exert a great influence on the Renaissance architects of the fifteenth century. The facade is rationally ordered with a design using green serpentine stone, which is set off to great effect by the pristine white of the Carrara marble. The design combines a five-bay arcade on the ground floor, surmounted by an element resembling a Classical temple front. At the top of the elegant aedicular window (framed to resemble a little building) is a thirteenth-century mosaic showing Christ enthroned with the titular saint of the church. Crowning the facade, a bronze eagle symbolizes the wool merchants' guild that was the church's chief benefactor. The interior is ordered around a nave with two side aisles, separated by arcades that alternate columns with compound piers. The apse, rising high above the crypt and raised high altar, shimmers with thirteenth-century mosaics. Framed by the stairs up to the high altar, Michelozzo's Cappella del Crocifisso (1448) is an elegant Renaissance addition. **FN**

> *"No spot is more propitious to lingering repose than the broad terrace in front of the church ..."*

Henry James, *The Madonna of the Future* (1879)

Glendalough Round Tower (1066)

Architects Irish monks   **Location** Laragh, County Wicklow, Ireland   **Style** Vernacular   **Materials** Mica-schist, granite

In 1825 the Scottish novelist and poet Sir Walter Scott described Glendalough as "the inestimably singular scene of Irish antiquities." One of the great monastic centers of Early Christian Ireland, its 103-feet-high (31 m) Round Tower is among the finest examples of its kind. Glendalough—in the original Irish, *Gleann Dá Locha*, "the valley of two lakes"—is situated in a remote corner of the Wicklow Mountains, 30 miles (48 km) from Dublin. St. Kevin settled in the valley as a hermit in the sixth century and later established the first monastery. The settlement grew rapidly; Irish monasteries were not merely religious buildings, but also functioned as centers of economic activity. Eventually, as many as 1,000 people may have lived in Glendalough, some in the monastery, others in the lay community nearby.

The Round Tower dates from the early eleventh century, an era when marauding Vikings frequently launched raids on Ireland. It functioned as a bell tower, but was also a place of safekeeping for manuscripts, relics, and sacred utensils. While Irish monks used round towers as places of safety when under sudden predatory attack, they were not ideal for this purpose. Some round towers were burned, along with their books and treasures. Glendalough's tower originally had six timber floors connected by ladders, and it tapers inward toward a conical roof. Its top story has four windows, which face the cardinal points of the compass. Glendalough is the most perfect example of a ratio often found in Irish towers: its height is twice its circumference. Its door is some ten feet (3 m) off the ground and was reached by a ladder. Such height was necessary to add strength to the base of the tower, as foundations were often shallow. The tower's conical cap was restored in 1876, supposedly from its original stone. Today, the Round Tower has come to symbolize County Wicklow and its rural charms. **BMC**

Basilica of San Marco (1071)

Patron Doge Domenico Contarini   **Location** Venice, Italy   **Style** Venetian Byzantine, Gothic   **Materials** Gold, precious stones, marble, metal, stone

The original ninth-century Romanesque church conceived as a shrine for the stolen remains of St. Mark the Evangelist from Alexandria was destroyed by fire in 967. Doge Domenico Contarini (1043–71) commissioned builders to begin work, with the help of Byzantine architects, on expanding and restoring the structure that was to become the Basilica di San Marco. The church was finally consecrated in 1094.

Inspired by the Church of the Holy Apostles in then Constantinople, now Istanbul, the floorplan forms the shape of a Greek cross with three naves and intersecting transepts, and domes over the center and each arm. The five-domed composition is a rich blend of Byzantine and Gothic style. Across its western frontage extends a vestibule with five portals leading out to the Piazza San Marco and the glittering facade is encrusted with marble slabs and gilded mosaics.

Inside the cathedral ceiling vaults and domes shimmer with mosaics as light filters in through the cupolas to illuminate the combined polychromy of precious stones and metals. As the seat of a trading empire, Venice could have its pick of artifacts from the exotic East. Its columns, statues, jeweled icons, friezes, carvings, and mosaics were treasures removed from ancient buildings, and brought back on ships before, during, and after the Crusades. The central altarpiece, the Pala d'Oro (Golden Pall), is framed by an imposing *baldacchino* or altar canopy.

The collection of loot inside the Treasury—most of it acquired on countless raids abroad—serves as an enduring reminder of Venice's maritime prestige and supremacy over the eastern Mediterranean. **AA**

↗ The interior of San Marco, with its rich, shadowy mystery, suggests the influence of Eastern Orthodoxy.

→ The basilica's silhouette, with Asiatic finials and cupolas, betrays the building's Eastern character.

Qui Nhon Ban It Towers (1080)

Architect Unknown   **Location** Binh Dinh Province, Vietnam   **Style** Binh Dinh (Cham) style   **Materials** Brick, resin, sandstone

The Qui Nhon Ban It Towers, a group of four towers better known as the Silver Towers, are one of the best surviving examples of late Cham architecture. The Cham kingdom of Champa flourished in south and central Vietnam from the second century onward and reached the height of its power during the ninth century. Adopting Hinduism as their state religion, the Chams adapted architectural models from their Indian counterparts to create something unique to Vietnam. This is best illustrated by the Kalan complex, of which the Silver Towers are a great example. The term *kalan* refers to a main sanctuary tower centered on a single shrine, housing the main object of worship—in this case a statue of the Hindu god Shiva. But, due to the gradual decline of the Cham kingdom from the tenth century onward, the Silver Towers could not compete artistically with the beautiful pilasters and architraves of early Cham art and instead restricted itself to simpler motifs. What it lacked in refinement, however, it made up for in monumentality. To do this the *kalan* and an adjacent repository were situated at the summit of a hill, while the two smaller towers were located at a lower level to the south and east of the *kalan*. The hill was then landscaped with steps, achieving an overall pyramidal effect and creating a temple-mountain. Constant warring took its toll on the Champa, and by the early thirteenth century they had been quashed by the Khmers of Cambodia. **SAM**

"... all we have today are temple ruins, original but enigmatic works of sculpture..."

C. Noppe and J.-F. Hubert, *Art from Vietnam* (2003)

Great Mosque of Masjid-i-Jami (1088)

Architect Nizam al-Mulk **Location** Isfahan, Iran **Style** Seljuk **Material** Brick, ceramic tiles

The Masjid-i-Jami (Friday Mosque) in Isfahan was begun during the last years of the Sassanid era. When Isfahan became part of the Islamic caliphate in the ninth century, the Abbasid rulers rebuilt the mosque using a hypostyle plan with square, brick columns supporting the building throughout. The mosque was rebuilt in the eleventh century under the Seljuk caliph Malik Shah. The rebuilding was overseen by Malik Shah's vizier Nizam al-Mulk. Al-Mulk introduced a large brick dome in front of the *mihrab*, the niche indicating the direction of Mecca. An *iwan*, a vaulted arched entrance, led to the *mihrab* dome. This combination was a new development in mosque design but one that harked back to ancient Sassanid architecture. Another dome on the other side of the *mihrab* was later built by a rival of al-Mulk. Construction of the dome used the innovation of the squinch—a corner-shaped filler that supported the transition from right-angled brick walls to the curve of the dome above. When the mosque burned down in 1120, the rival dome survived and was incorporated into a new, four-*iwan* building arranged around a large courtyard. The *iwans* were arranged in an axial plan with the southern *iwan* enlarged to indicate the presence of the *mihrab*. Each *iwan* has an overhanging frontispiece known as a *pishtaq*. The four-*iwan* style also prompted the introduction of adjoining, separate buildings on each side of the mosque. This was the origin of the *madrassa*, a religious school attached to a mosque. Another innovation was the use of *muqarnas*—geometric decoration on the domes and *iwans*. The Friday Mosque became a template for mosques across the Islamic world and its innovations were borrowed by other cultures. For example, the brick ribs of the domes are thought to have inspired Gothic rib vaulting in Christian churches. **MC**

Ananda Temple (1105)

Patron King Kyanzittha **Location** Pagan, Myanmar **Style** Buddhist, Mon period style **Materials** Brick, sandstone, stucco, teak

Commissioned by the Burmese king, Kyanzittha, in c. 1105, the Ananda Temple is one of the finest examples of Buddhist temple architecture in southeast Asia. Located in the ancient Burmese capital of Pagan, it reflects the culmination of centuries of architectural tradition and design. This is best reflected in the temple's exterior elevation, which represents a perfect balance between horizontal width and vertical thrust. The structure was built primarily of brick, interspaced with sandstone. The ground plan takes the form of a Greek cross with a double ambulatory corridor surrounding the center. Access to the four central shrines, located at each of the cardinal points, is through four porches located on the same alignment. The vertical aspect of the temple is achieved by the high central *sikhara* (the tapered and decorated tower), terminating in a finial and represents one of the most innovative features of this temple. If the worshipper was awed by the temple's exterior, the experience upon entering it would have been equally memorable. The interiors of Mon-style structures were renowned for their cave temple-like atmosphere. Purposely dark to create a sense of mystery and piety, natural light was restricted via latticed windows, and with the Ananda this technique reached its peak. As worshippers entered any of the shrines, they would observe the light from the openings above falling directly on the face of the Buddha image. **SAM**

> "No building in the world is more perfectly symmetrical than Nanda [Ananda Temple]."
>
> Gordon H. Luce, *Old Burma–Early Pagan* (1970)

Basilica of St. Sernin (1120)

Architect Unknown **Location** Toulouse, France **Style** Romanesque **Materials** Stone, brick

The Romanesque Basilica of St. Sernin in Toulouse is a pilgrimage church and the largest of the churches built along the route to Santiago de Compostela in northwest Spain. The interior is a celebration of medieval culture reflecting the expansion of the boundaries of Western Christianity. The exterior, constructed mostly of local peachy-orange colored brick with structural elements in stone, has a cruciform layout, with an octagonal 213 feet (65 m) pagodalike bell tower at the crossing of the two axes of the structure. The extreme length of the basilica—377 feet (115 m) long, 210 feet (64 m) high, and 69 feet (21 m) wide—is a reminder of spiritual grace and the impression on the visitor is of a vast, calm, and humbling interior space. Charlemagne donated relics to the church which are held in the sanctuary at the eastern end of the church called the *chevet*—"pillow" in French—referring to the cruciform shape of the church and the altar that represents Christ's head. This is the oldest part of the building and consists of nine chapels, five from the apse and four in the transepts. These radiating chapels display the religious relics and are approached by an ambulatory (walkway) lined with seven large relief slabs of Christ, angels, and apostles. The walkway around the nave allowed pilgrims to approach the relics as closely as possible to benefit from their power to protect against demons, plagues, and natural disasters. The interior is renowned for its murals and 260 Romanesque decorations on the capitals, carved between the end of the thirteenth century and the sixteenth century. Above the exterior doorways on the south side of the church are Romanesque relief sculptures—the *Porte des Comtes* depicts Lazarus and Dives while the draped figures of the apostles and Christ in resurrection on the *Porte Miégeville* resemble ancient sarcophagi. **JEH**

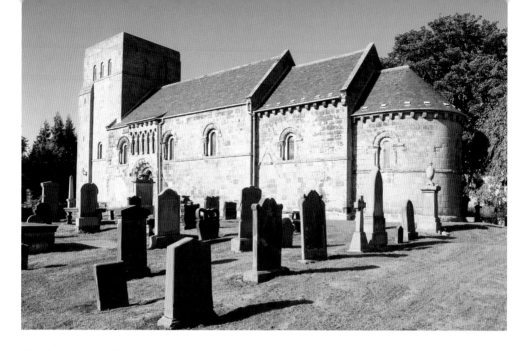

Dalmeny Church (1140)

Patron Earl Gospatric **Location** Dalmeny, Edinburgh, Scotland **Style** Romanesque **Materials** Sandstone, slate roofing

As a truly international style, Romanesque architecture spread across Europe with a fascinating multitude of local variations. Dalmeny Church is the best-preserved Romanesque parish church in Scotland. It has the round-apse plan typical of many parish churches dating from the early-to-mid twelfth century, yet its detailed sculpture shows it to be part of a distinct local group including the abbey at nearby Dunfermline. It was built for the local landowner, Earl Gospatric, from blocks of sandstone, which have helped ensure its longevity. Although its western tower was restored under the architect P. MacGregor Chalmers from 1922 to 1927 and rebuilt to the designs of Alfred Greig in 1937, the rest of the building is very much as Gospatric would have known it—its hefty construction and vaulted chancel and apse giving its interior a highly memorable sense of enclosure. The great glory of Dalmeny is its elaborate south doorway. A beguiling range of motifs fills the stones around the arch, many derived from the medieval bestiary. There are centaurs, lusty couples, and the tree of life, all figures charged with symbolism, which exercised great power over the medieval mind. Building churches was a means of trying to ensure God's approval and with a keen eye to the afterlife, Gospatric commissioned a decorated sarcophagus, which was moved from the church to the graveyard during the Reformation and now stands as a timely reminder of mortality. **NMC**

> *"Dalmeny is famous as the best-preserved Norman church in the country."*
>
> Colin McWilliam, architectural historian

Cathedral of St. Lazarus (1146)

Architect Unknown   **Location** Autun, Burgundy, France   **Style** Romanesque, Gothic   **Material** Stone

From the walled heart of the city once known as the "Rome of the Gauls" rises the slender spire of Saint-Lazare. Formerly the chapel of the Dukes of Burgundy, the cathedral's significance rests not only with its exemplary Romanesque pointed barrel vaulting, but in the quality of its sculpture, most notably its tympanum and cloister capitals. Originally a pilgrimage church for visitors to the tomb of St. Lazarus, the site was elevated to the status of a cathedral during the twelfth century. Its design draws significantly on the model of the Abbey of Cluny, which was rebuilt shortly before work began on Saint-Lazare. The cathedral is laid out in the form of a Latin cross, with an aisled nave and three-stage choir with semicircular apse. Its pilasters and arcading are clearly influenced by the Classical detailing of the city's Roman gates. The Gothic spire, tower, and side chapels were added in the fifteenth century, while the twin western towers are nineteenth-century additions. Unusually for the medieval period, the sculptor of the great tympanum is identified by the words "Gislebertus hoc fecit," carved below the feet of Jesus, the central figure in a richly animated frieze depicting the Last Judgment. The French culture minister in the 1960s, Andre Malraux, described Gislebertus as "a Romanesque Cézanne." The tympanum's remarkable state of preservation is due in part to the fact that it was plastered over during the eighteenth century and remained protected during the destructive years of the French Revolution. Inside, the sculptor's artistry is best seen in the figurative capitals of the nave, twenty of which were replaced during the nineteenth century. The originals are displayed in the chapterhouse, together with a frieze taken from the now demolished north door, illustrating the temptation of Eve and incorporating a rare female nude. **AMR**

Jaisalmer
Fort (1156)

Patron Rawal Jaisal   **Location** Jaisalmer, Rajasthan, India
Style Rajput, Islamic   **Materials** Sandstone, marble

The chieftain Rawal Jaisal, leader of the Bhatti Rajput clan, sought to establish a secure desert base for his people. This became the foundation for the Jaisalmer Fort, destined to be an alternative capital to his more vulnerable one at Lodurva. The second oldest fortress town in Rajasthan, Jaisalmer lies in the middle of the expansive Thar Desert. Its ramparts rise out of the desert, standing tall at more than 250 feet (76 m) high. The external boundary with its numerous bastions encloses the self-sufficient habitat of more than 10,000 people. The town comprises the palace grounds, merchants' *havelis* (villas), residential complexes, military quarters, and temples, each competing as a symbol of the medieval prosperity of Jaisalmer.

The fort, known locally as the *sonar quila* (golden fort), now forms the heart of the city of Jaisalmer. Its buildings are a subtle blend of Rajput and Islamic architectural styles, the most elaborate and elegant of these being the *Patwon ki Haveli*, a group of five residences commissioned by Guman Chand Patwa, an affluent local merchant. Every inch of the houses were intricately carved in stone, reportedly over a span of fifty years, a fitting tribute to the local craftsmanship. Sadly, modern times are taking their toll on this once glorious settlement. The local population is expanding and demanding an increased infrastructure, but a failure to address this change is threatening Jaisalmer. This large desert fort continues to stand tall, however; glowing in the first light of dawn, only just retaining its dignity and sense of indestructibility. **BS**

↖ Buildings are not only made by the people who build them; here, the Indian sun completes the apparition.

← Until now, the Fort's power was undiminished by rival structures; India's economic might is a new challenge.

Le Thoronet Abbey (1176)

Architect Unknown **Location** Provence, France
Style Romanesque **Materials** Limestone, terra cotta

The first view of the Cistercian abbey of Le Thoronet is typically from one of the surrounding hills. Snatched glimpses of pale limestone, terra cotta roofs, and a belfry finally give way to a clear prospect of the monastic city rising from densely wooded slopes of pine and olive trees. From this distance, the tiled wings of accommodation arranged around a courtyard are reminiscent of a Roman villa, the volumes appearing modest, even agricultural in character. Walk down to the site and step from the sunlight into the relative darkness of the church, however, and you are

---

"Light and shade are the loudspeakers of this architecture of truth, tranquility, and strength."

Le Corbusier, architect and writer

---

presented with one of the purest architectural forms to have survived from medieval Europe, fully expressive of the simplicity and lack of adornment that St. Bernard of Clairvaux had advocated as key elements for the ideal Cistercian church. One of the "Three Sisters of Provence," alongside Silvacane and Sénanque, Le Thoronet was completed toward the end of the Romanesque period. The church is resolutely simplistic in style, with a nave arcade of pointed arches surmounted by a barrel vault, transepts giving onto cavernlike chapels, and a round apse punctured by three round-headed windows. Le Thoronet was one of the first buildings in France to receive listed status, and Le Corbusier spent time here in the 1950s when preparing his design for the Dominican monastery of La Tourette. **AMR**

Abbasid Castle (1180)

Patron Caliph An-Nasir li-Din Allah **Location** Baghdad, Iraq
Style Abbasid **Material** Brick

The Abbasid Dynasty (750–1258) descended from an uncle of the prophet Muhammad. In 762, the first Abbasid ruler chose Baghdad as the new capital. Over the next 500 years, Baghdad became a large, prosperous city and the center of a Golden Age of Islamic culture and education.

Abbasid Castle (Qasr Al-Abbasi) was constructed in the late Abbasid period. It is believed to have been built for Caliph An-Nasir li-Din Allah (r. 1179–1225), although modern excavation suggests it may have been built as a *madrassa* (religious school) rather than a caliph's palace. It is a two-storied, rectangular, brick building situated on the west bank of the Tigris River in the al-Maiden area of Baghdad. In the courtyard, a west-facing facade features a large, brick, barrel-vaulted hall or *iwan* with carved brick decoration of intricately flowing lines or arabesques in the Seljuk style. Two small archways on either side lead to an arcade that borders the courtyard. The arcade is supported by square, brick pillars topped by elaborately carved corbels in tiered geometric patterns, known as *muqarnas*, that vault the arcade's arches. From within the arcade, doorways lead off to small chambers that originally may have been study rooms. The west side of the courtyard is believed to have once led to a large prayer room. A modern *iwan* has been built here to face the original one. Some scholars believe that Abbasid Castle was the Sharabiya School, a renowned university in the Islamic world in the twelfth century. This is because of its resemblance in plan and structure to the Mustansirya School, which is located in the same area as the castle. In 1258 Baghdad was devastated by a Mongol invasion. The castle is a rare survivor of a time when Baghdad was the richest and most cultured city on earth. **MC**

Monreale
Cathedral (1182)

Patron King William II of Sicily   **Location** Palermo, Sicily
Style Romanesque   **Materials** Stone, mosaics

Durham
Cathedral (1189)

Architect Unknown   **Location** Durham, England
Style Romanesque, Gothic   **Materials** Stone, timber

Monreale Cathedral of Santa Maria la Nuova is one of the greatest medieval buildings in the world. It overlooks Palermo and the Conca d'Oro from Mount Caputo. The name Monreale comes from *Mons Regalis,* meaning royal mountain. The Norman King William II of Sicily began its construction between 1172 and 1176, a century after the Arab emirate in Sicily ended in 1072. The cathedral's exterior is rather stern but the Neo-Arabic decorated triple apse, with its interlaced arches of limestone and lava, is very fine. The bronze west doors by Bonanno da Pisa (1185) are well worth an examination, but it is the splendidly decorated golden interior that is overwhelming in its beauty and spiritual energy. It is a glorious hymn of praise, synthesizing Byzantine, Romanesque, Lombard, and Provençal art with Arab craftwork.

The plan of the cathedral is simple—a Latin cross, 334 feet by 131 feet (101 m x 39 m)—but it is decorated with 70,000 square feet (21,000 sq m) of glorious Byzantine mosaics completed in 1182. The apse is dominated by a mighty image of Christ the Pantocrator surrounded by golden mosaics illustrating the story of the creation and the life of Jesus.

Stepping into the majestic interior is like walking into an illustrated manuscript. An arched arcade is supported by twenty-six paired columns on four sides; there are 216 pairs in all. Each column has a different design and richly decorated capitals. An elegant marble Arabic fountain, resembling a stylized palm tree, gently cools a corner. Adjacent to the cathedral are the elaborately decorated Benedictine cloisters of the monastery. Monreale Cathedral shows that the great Mediterranean cultures, Christian and Islamic, can come together to produce art and architecture of unique beauty and passion. **ATB**

The mighty cathedral (see page 20) and castle of Durham offer the most spectacular architectural grouping in England. Their location reflects the city's vulnerable location, not far from the Scottish border, as a result of which the Bishop of Durham was granted exceptional temporal powers comparable to those of the prince-bishops of Germany. The cathedral was raised above the grave of St. Cuthbert of Lindisfarne, a seventh-century saint. The current building replaced a Saxon cathedral and was begun in 1093, with the main vault completed in 1133. The western chapel known as

"… this unexpected combination of primeval power with a consummate mastery of scale …"

Nikolaus Pevsner, *The Buildings of England* (1951–74)

the Galilee Chapel, with its five aisles of serrated arches calling to mind a Moorish mosque, was finished in 1189, while the lovely eastern Chapel of the Nine Altars and adjoining choir vault were begun in 1242. Externally the cathedral is dominated by the Gothic central tower, completed in 1488, but internally the overwhelming impression is Romanesque, with great pillars incised with bold geometric patterns in spirals, flutes, chevrons, and diamonds. The view east is majestic without being oppressive. The building's real significance lies in the nave's rib-vaulted roof and its concealed flying buttresses. Durham is the earliest surviving example of this type of rib vaulting, which later became a feature of Gothic cathedrals. In this sense, Durham became the template for cathedral building throughout medieval Europe. **RW**

Angkor
Wat (1190)

Patron King Suryavarman II **Location** Siem Reap, Cambodia
Style Khmer **Materials** Sandstone, laterite

The Angkor Wat temple complex, with its exquisite mural carvings, multitiered domes, and kabbalistic conception, is an architectural wonder. Built by King Suryavarman II (*r.* 1113–45) in the twelfth century, it combines a main temple to the Hindu god Vishnu and a royal mausoleum. As a state temple within the ancient capital of the Khmer empire, Angkor Wat combines two classic layouts from a golden era of religious architecture: the temple mountain with its quincunx of towers and the surrounding galleried temples. Initially a Hindu, then a Buddhist religious center, the entire structure is steeped in mystical significance. Visitors can access the inner sanctuary of this temple-mountain via the main causeway with its balustrades shaped like *naga* (mystical serpents).

Inside, the main temple rises up on three ever-diminishing terraces, one for each of the universal elements (earth, water, and wind), while its great central tower and smaller surrounding ones symbolize the peaks of Mount Meru, the epicenter of the Hindu universe. The plethora of bas-relief carvings represent the world's most complete iconographic record of Hindu mythology. The eastern gallery wall is famous for its depiction of "The Churning of the Ocean of Milk," which powerfully conveys a universe in flux.

Angkor Wat was imitated across the Khmer empire, but no other temple was created on such a grand scale. It has been in more or less continuous use, from its origins as a Hindu temple through centuries of Buddhist worship, and now as a tourist attraction. **AA**

↗ The beatific smile of one of Angkor's remarkable carved faces still beams over the site.

⊡ The use of varied heights and tapering towers produces a disorienting sense of immense scale.

Minaret of Jam (1195)

Architect Ali ibn Ibrahim of Nishapur   **Location** Firuz Koh, Afghanistan   **Style** Ghurid   **Materials** Mud brick, ceramic tiles

The Minaret of Jam is a mysterious structure. Located halfway between Kabul and Herat, it is so isolated that it was completely forgotten until the nineteenth century. It stands in a deep river valley between soaring mountains in the remote Ghur province. It is possibly the last standing building of the summer capital of the Ghurid Dynasty (*c.* 1150–1212). The minaret is circular, built on an octagonal base and is made up of two shafts that rise to 213 feet (65 m). The two shafts differ structurally. The lower shaft has thick brick walls rising to a height of 124 feet (38 m). Its diameter narrows from 32 feet (9.7 m) at the base to 19.5 feet (6 m) at its top. The 98 feet (27 m) narrower upper shaft is spanned by six wooden cross-vaults resting on four internal buttresses. From a single doorway, the interior can be accessed via two flights of spiral staircases. They lead to the remains of two wooden balconies—one at the top of the lower shaft and one in the middle of the upper shaft. The upper shaft is topped with a cupola with an open space beneath, which probably held a lantern.

The minaret is richly decorated with tiles and terra cotta in relief. On the lower shaft, eight vertical tile panels in geometric shapes frame a continuous inscription in turquoise-glazed tiles of the Surat Maryam from the Koran, which tells the story of Mary, the mother of Jesus. The use of this inscription is unique in an Islamic building, which also complicates scholarly interpretations of the minaret's origin. The upper shaft is inscribed with religious texts, the names of the Ghurid ruler, and the architect. It is thought to have been the inspiration for another minaret, the Qutub Minar in Delhi, also built by the Ghurids. After the Qutub Minar, the Minaret of Jam is the second-tallest brick minaret in the world. It has been added to UNESCO's World Heritage Sites in Danger List because it is at risk from flooding and earthquakes. **MC**

Koutoubia Mosque (1199)

Architect Yacoub-el-Mansour **Location** Marrakech, Morocco **Style** Almohad, Moorish **Materials** Brick, stone

The Koutoubia Mosque was built under the auspices of the twelfth-century Muslim Berber Almohad dynasty that ruled over most of North Africa, Spain, and parts of sub-Saharan West Africa. While traveling in the country, writer Edith Wharton observed that "no later buildings in northwest Africa equal the monuments of the great Almohad sultans" (*In Morocco*, 1920). The Koutoubia was named after the sellers of manuscripts (*kutubiyin*) who gather in front of the mosque. Although hidden from view within the old town, its skyscraping minaret is unmissable as you enter the *souks* (markets) from Place Djemaa-el-Fna.

Although closed to non-Muslims, the mosque's T-shaped, hypostyle plan can accommodate 25,000 faithful. The interior combines austere forms and materials with geometric, floral, and epigraphic ornamentation in restrained luxury. The eleven cupolas are decorated with *muqarnas* (corbels carved in tiered geometric patterns) and the prayer hall consists of sixteen parallel aisles, a wider central nave, and 112 columns. A wall prayer niche indicates the direction of Mecca. The ornate *minbar* (pulpit) at the far end of the prayer hall was a gift from Córdoba, Spain, by the Almoravid sultan Ali ben Youssef and belonged to a previous mosque that was later destroyed. The Almohads introduced to the new mosque the square-shaped minaret in monumental style. Topped by four copper globes, it contains an inner shaft with six vaulted rooms, one on each story, and a ramp to the top. The tower's four facades display cusped arches, floral motifs, and carved stonework tracery, and its pink masonry bears traces of the blue, turquoise, and white frieze tiles that once adorned the top. The Koutoubia minaret set an architectural precedent across the ancient Islamic world and later masterpieces—the Giralda of Seville and the Hassan Tower of Rabat—were directly modeled on it. **AA**

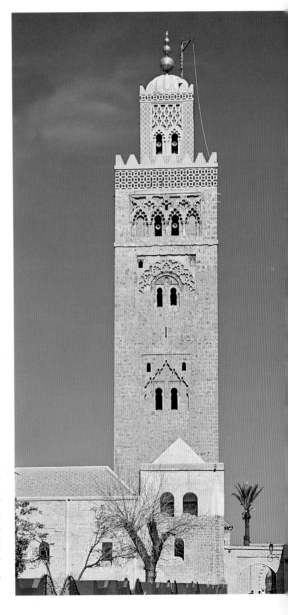

Church of St. George (1200)

Architect Unknown **Location** Lalibela, Ethiopia **Style** Medieval Ethiopian **Materials** Monoliths carved from red volcanic rock

"Edifices, the like of which— and so many—cannot be found anywhere else in the world."

Francisco Álvares, Portugese explorer

⬆ Visitors to Lalibela are shown around by robed priests who guard the gold crosses and ancient manuscripts.

➡ The Church of St. George's architectural form is an extruded Greek cross standing on a stepped plinth.

The Church of St. George, or Bet Giorgis, is the finest of eleven extraordinary, rock-hewn churches in the town of Lalibela in northern Ethiopia. These churches are sculpted out of solid rock, standing free from the surrounding land with their roofs at ground level, like ships in dry docks. They are unique both for the technical expertise of their construction and their architectural refinement. A visitor cannot help being impressed by the sheer amount of labor involved in their creation. Scholars have estimated that a workforce of 40,000 would have been required, and legend has it that angels took over the work at night.

King Lalibela (1118–1221) was inspired to create a new Jerusalem here in this dusty town. Ever since, it has been a center of pilgrimage, and the churches have been in continuous use for 800 years. St. George's stands slightly apart from the other churches, where the others are connected by passages and bridges, it sits on its own. The roof, the most visible part of the building at ground level, is carved with concentric Greek crosses, while the sheer walls are decorated with simple carved bands. The few small windows are surprisingly decorated with pointed arches topped with flowing, leaf motifs. Unlike the other churches in the complex, which are colorfully painted, the interior is undecorated, and it houses artifacts including a wooden chest said to contain King Lalibela's tools. The historical independence and geographical isolation of Ethiopia, as well as the fact that it is a Christian country surrounded by Muslim ones, has meant that the country's architecture and visual arts have always had their own strong identity. The wide variety of style and decorations of the churches, including the cruciform plan and pointed arch windows of St. George's, suggest a variety of cultural influences and an awareness of Christian forms of the time found elsewhere in the world. **SJM**

Cathedral of Santiago de Compostela (1211)

Architects Various   **Location** Santiago de Compostela, Galicia, Spain   **Style** Romanesque, Baroque   **Material** Granite

The Cathedral of Santiago de Compostela is the last of the pilgrim churches that stretch along the Christian pilgrimage route across the Pyrenees to Galicia in Spain. It is said to house the remains of the apostle St. James. Work began on the church in 1075 during the reign of King Alphonse VI, under the direction of Bishop Diego de Peláez, and the church was consecrated in 1211. It has been added to over the years, with a Baroque facade that forms part of the Plaza del Obradoiro, a large square surrounded by public buildings. The main entrance is via a quadruple flight of steps, flanked by statues of David and Solomon. The Baroque Torre de Reloj, or clocktower, was completed in 1680 by Domingo de Andrade. The interior chapel is similar in style to that of other Romanesque churches along the pilgrim route. It is arranged so that pilgrims can enter and use the church without disturbing any services that are being held at the high altar. It is built in granite and laid out in a Latin cross, measuring 320 feet (98 m) long and 220 feet (67 m) wide, with a three-aisled, barrel-vaulted nave. The ambulatory links the aisles behind the high altar. The architectural jewel of the cathedral is the twelfth-century Pórtico de la Gloria, behind the Baroque facade. Mounted on the tympana and archivolts of the three arches of the doorway, which opens onto the nave, are more than 200 sculpted figures in scenes from the Last Judgment. **CMK**

"In this church there is no fault . . . large, spacious, light, with harmonious dimensions."

Aymeric Picaud, *Pilgrim Guide* (1140)

Chartres Cathedral (1220)

Architect Unknown   **Location** Chartres, France   **Style** Gothic   **Materials** Limestone, copper

The Cathedral of Notre Dame at Chartres is one of the foremost examples of High Gothic architecture. It houses a relic of the veil of the Virgin Mary and is also known for its prestigious medieval school for humanistic studies, where the seven liberal arts were taught. The new cathedral displayed innovations in building techniques, sculpture, and stained glass that set the standard for thirteenth-century architecture. Construction on the Romanesque foundations was begun in 1145, and the body of the cathedral was rebuilt between 1194 and 1220. Built of limestone, the cathedral is a prominent landmark due to its green copper roof and two contrasting spires. The first of these is a 345-foot (105 m) plain pyramid dating from the 1140s; the second is the 370-foot (113 m) northwest spire, the Clocher Neuf, completed in 1513. The cathedral plan is cruciform, with a spacious nave, 118 feet high (36 m) and 420 feet long (128 m), with a floor labyrinth where pilgrims can walk. The cathedral used external flying buttresses in its original plan to provide structural support for the weight of the extremely high vaults. The architectural sculptures at Chartres, carved between 1145 and 1170, are among the first since Roman times to reflect more naturalistic, individualized characteristics. The cathedral is justly celebrated for its 150 stained-glass windows from the early thirteenth century and especially for the color used, known as "Chartres blue." **JEH**

> "... such a degree of beauty that on entering one would think oneself transported to heaven."
>
> Jean de Jandun, philosopher and theologian

Castel del Monte (1240)

Patron Emperor Frederick II   **Location** Near Bari, Puglia, Italy   **Style** Gothic   **Material** Limestone

The Castel del Monte is a remarkable octagonal structure erected for the Holy Roman Emperor Frederick II (1194–1250) in the southernmost reaches of the empire, in Puglia, southern Italy. During his reign, Frederick Caesar engaged in an extensive fortification campaign that included many castles in Sicily as well as the imperial fortress at Prato in Tuscany. It is thought that the building's distinctive design may be the result of the emperor's direct involvement. The design is rigorously geometrical; the eight corners of the exterior are marked by bastions, which are also octagonal in form, as is the internal courtyard. Consequently the rooms are all the same size; there are eight trapezoidal rooms on each of the two floors of the building, many of them finely vaulted with delicately carved bosses. Although its name and outer appearance suggests that this was a castle—it has massive walls, towers, and a portcullis gate—it seems that its purpose had little to do with defense. The grand entrance, framed by fluted pilasters, flanked by lions, and topped by a classicizing pediment, suggests a ceremonial function. The castle's unusual form and location—it appears like a massive crown on a hill—as well as its luxurious materials seem designed to evoke the splendor of the emperor in his dominions. The building, originally decorated with colored marble as well as mosaic floors, was a grand residence for the ruler and may well have served as a hunting lodge. **FN**

> *"Frederick Caesar and his son Manfredi, followed after elegance and scorned what was mean."*
>
> Dante Alighieri, poet

La Sainte-Chapelle (1248)

Architect Unknown   **Location** Boulevard du Palais, Paris, France   **Style** Gothic   **Materials** Stone, stained glass

This magnificent chapel, which resembles a richly ornamented jewelry box or metalwork reliquary, was designed to house religious relics that King Louis IX acquired from Constantinople, including the relic of the Crown of Thorns and part of the True Cross. The chapel is surrounded by the Palais de Justice on the Île-de-la-Cité near to the Cathedral of Notre Dame; until the second half of the fourteenth century the Palais de Justice was used as the royal palace by the kings of France. As a palace chapel, the main entrance was originally on the first floor, connected directly with the royal apartments. The chapel has been altered a little during its long life, and in the mid-nineteenth century extensive restoration works took place. The building combines structural technology with, on the exterior, richly ornamented decoration, including pinnacles and gables. The buttresses are relatively plain and sheer, and carry much of the weight of the vaulting and roof. The building has a simple plan, with two floors to separate the king from the rest of the court. But it is the structural elements and decoration of the interior of the chapel that is awe-inspiring. The colored decoration, sculpture, stained glass, and the lightness of the structure combine to create a breathtaking interior. The lower chapel's main features are the slender but short painted columns and ribbed vaulting, giving the impression of a crypt. The upper chapel is a complete contrast in its height and the amount of daylight that pours in through its long windows. The holy relics were displayed here, and this part of the building is the most richly decorated. The ornament includes carved spandrels of the wall arches, carved capitals, wall paintings, and decorative metalwork. The stained glass is spectacular and colorful, with sequences from the Old and New Testament. **EG**

Djenné Mosque (1250)

Patron Koi Konboro   **Location** Djenné, Mali   **Style** Sudano-Sahelian   **Materials** Mud brick, timber

The Grand Mosque is the largest mud brick building in the world. It is also utterly distinctive in form with its profile of three stepped minarets each topped by an ostrich egg. The mosque faces onto the main market square of the ancient trading city of Djenné. The present structure dates from 1906, but there has been a mosque on the site since the thirteenth century. The original mosque was built c. 1240 by Koi Konboro, a local ruler who converted to Islam. It was a significant act of devotion on the part of this new convert, because he replaced his own palace on the site to make way for the mosque's construction. During the next 600 years, Djenné developed into a major religious center. Travelers' and traders' tales of the building and its extraordinary scale—further exaggerated in the mind perhaps by the deep shadows formed by the gridwork of exposed wooden beam-ends being misread as windows—ensured it gained legendary status as far away as Europe. The original mosque was demolished in 1834 and was rebuilt in the same style. At that time its layout was simplified. The primary division is between a prayer hall with ninety pillars and an arcaded courtyard that is also used for prayer. The building is made of sunbaked mud bricks coated in mud plaster. Horizontal bundles of deleb palm timber act as expansion points, to prevent the building from shifting in the extreme temperature. The timbers also act as convenient scaffolding for the annual repair of the fabric after the rainy season, which badly erodes the fabric of the mosque. The annual replastering has become an event known as La Fête de Créppisage, and plays an important part in the social life of the city. This building is an embodiment of the geographical and cultural factors that formed it and of the local community that continually rebuilds it. **RGW**

Salisbury Cathedral (1258)

Architect Unknown **Location** Salisbury, England **Style** Early English Gothic **Materials** Portland stone, marble

Known as the Cathedral of St. Mary, this building was raised to help found a new city, then called New Sarum. Boasting the tallest surviving pre-fifteenth-century spire in the world, it is unique among medieval English cathedrals because it was mostly completed within a century—the main part being constructed in only thirty-eight years—with no substantial later additions. Surrounded by cloisters, it is built in the shape of a double cross. The main entrance at the west end is decorated with some impressive religious statues, ten of which date from the medieval period. Inside, rib-vaulted ceilings are supported by typically Gothic arches, with a second tier of smaller arches supporting the ceiling over the main aisle. Outside the south transept is an elegant octagonal chapter house complete with a vaulted, ribbed ceiling of breathtaking beauty, supported by a single, decorated, central column of Purbeck marble.

The cathedral's Portland stone-clad tower and spire were added fifty years after the main building. This was due to the advent of revolutionary new building techniques whereby flying buttresses helped to carry the load, enabling medieval architects to create much taller buildings. However, the unplanned addition of the daring 404-foot (123 m), 6,500 ton, cross-tipped spire has caused noticeable deflections in the four stone columns that provide its support, mainly because the cathedral was built on marshy ground. **JM**

> "[Salisbury is] a rare example of an English Gothic church built entirely to one basic design."
>
> Sir Banister Fletcher, *A History of Architecture* (1896)

Cliff
Palace (1260)

Architects Unknown **Location** Mesa Verde National Park, Colorado, USA
Style Pre-Columbian vernacular **Materials** Sandstone, wood

The largest cliff dwelling in North America was created by geology and exploited by man's ingenuity. Skilled farmers, architects, and engineers, the Puebloans worked the level land on the cliff top and the canyon bottom, and lived "vertically" inside the cliff face. When they scouted locations for a new community more than 800 years ago, they saw a large alcove in the cliff face high above the canyon floor. Protected from the elements and virtually safe from attack, the Puebloans created a multistory, diverse community.

They lived here only seventy years, possibly forced out by a prolonged drought. Approximately one-quarter of the 150 rooms have hearths, suggesting that there were probably about 110 residents. Above these rooms are nine food stores, reached by steep ladders with handholds carved into the sandstone. Multistory towers dot the complex, as do *kivas*—circular walled excavations for ceremonial use or council chambers. The central *kiva* is located at a demarcation of walls with no doors or access between each side. It is thought that the central *kiva* was an attempt to integrate two separate communities.

The Puebloans carved sandstone blocks and joined them with mortar made of soil, water, and ash. Tiny pieces of stone called "chinking" dot the mortar and provide structural integrity. Thin plaster with pictographs covers some surfaces. Surviving wood roofs provide evidence that trees were cultivated to grow in a way that provided purpose-made beams without killing the tree. **DJ**

⬉ Unlike much architecture that works against Nature, this complex works hand-in-hand with it.

⬅ The huge, protective embrace of the tabletop cliff mesa creates a world of its own.

Baptistery at Pisa (1265)

Architect Dioti Salvi **Location** Pisa, Italy
Style Romanesque, with Gothic additions **Materials** Stone, marble

Pisa was a center for the arts in the eleventh and twelfth centuries and attracted artisans and craftsmen from all over Italy. One result is the circular Baptistery at Pisa, one of four impressive buildings that make up the Pisa Cathedral complex. This, known as the Piazza dei Miracoli—the square of miracles—also includes the cathedral, the bell tower (also known as the Leaning Tower of Pisa), and the cemetery. Although the buildings were built over three centuries, from 1063 to 1350, they form an impressive stylistic unit. Excavations have shown that the current baptistery

> *"There is music that can exist only in this place. . . . The resonance, the vibrations, are incredible."*
>
> **Professor Leonello Tarabella, academic**

replaced an earlier brick one, presumably because it would sit more harmoniously with the cathedral.

The current baptistery was designed by Dioti Salvi (1152–*c*. 1180) in the Italian Romanesque style. He used decorated, columned, surface arcading made of white marble inlaid with gray bands. It is thought that Dioti Salvi designed the baptistery to resemble the Church of the Holy Sepulchre in Jerusalem. It has an outer hemispherical roof, which was added later, along with the Gothic finishing to the upper levels and the beautiful marble pulpit. The dome skirts the original roof—a truncated cone—which can be seen protruding through the outer roof and is itself capped by a small dome. Recent analysis of the resonance inside the baptistery suggests it was designed to mimic the pipes of a church organ. **JM**

Hospital of Santa Maria della Scala (1270)

Architect Unknown **Location** Siena, Italy
Style Gothic, Renaissance **Materials** Brick, stone detailing

Until it was recently emptied of its last patients, the Hospital of Santa Maria della Scala was the oldest functioning hospital in Europe, tracing its origins back to the ninth century. The building as it stands today largely results from accretions initiated in the thirteenth century. It owes a great deal to the layering of successive buildings that has raised it up to as many as seven stories in places, fusing medieval Gothic style with the later Renaissance forms of the hospital church. The bowels of the building are literally that—*pozzi di butto* or cesspits—where refuse from the medieval hospital was thrown. Recent archaeological digs have revealed medieval crockery as well as, far deeper, burial sites from Etruscan times.

On the surface, facing Siena Cathedral, are the huge rooms of the medieval hospital, which were mostly designated for the care of pilgrims on their way to Rome. Vast halls, such as the *Pellegrinaio* or Pilgrims' Hall, were lined with beds, and are decorated with frescoes that explain the functions of the hospital, from the feeding and clothing of the poor and needy to the raising of orphans and the caring for the sick.

But the hospital is also a holy place, a destination for pilgrims, who visited it to experience its renowned collection of relics, on show in the sacristy of the Holy Nail and the vast church of the Annunciate Virgin Mary. Far more private devotion was also reserved to the confraternity meeting rooms, a number of which can be viewed in the underground portion of the hospital. A visit to Santa Maria della Scala is perhaps the closest you can get to the medieval period, while the recently restored Palazzo Squarcialupi, which forms part of the building, is a refreshing step into contemporary museum design and a successful fusion of ancient and modern. **FN**

Lincoln Cathedral (1280)

Architect Unknown **Location** Lincoln, England **Style** Gothic **Materials** Stone, timber

No English cathedral apart from Durham has a more striking position, set on a steep-sided hill with its soaring trio of towers visible for many miles across the flat Lincolnshire countryside. The character of the cathedral, begun in the 1070s, was formed by successive rebuildings in the twelfth and thirteenth centuries. The view down the nave, completed in the 1230s, is one of the most majestic in English cathedral architecture—a stately procession of arches that manages to combine nobility, elegance, and serenity. The style is the phase of Gothic known as "Early English." Compared to French cathedrals of the same date, the proportions characteristically avoid extreme verticality. The great length of the building, also typically English, is emphasized by the prominent ridge rib to the vault, leading the eye ever eastward.

The choir, rebuilt under St. Hugh of Lincoln in the 1190s and named after him, is the work of an unknown but willfully original architect who gave it its so-called "crazy vault"—a landmark in European architecture for its purely decorative use of ribs. The eastern section, rebuilt and extended to contain St. Hugh's shrine, was completed in 1280. Architecturally, it is the richest section of the cathedral, much embellished with sculpture and dubbed the "Angel Choir" after the exquisitely carved angels that appear above the gallery arches. Richer still, is the sumptuous choir screen that was created in the 1330s. The ensemble was completed by the three towers, which once sported spires. The spire of the central tower made it one of the tallest of the Middle Ages, but it was blown down in 1548. **RW**

◹ The "Bishop's Eye" window, completed between 1325 and 1350, is in the west transept of the cathedral.

◁ The cathedral's accretion of different period styles is especially evident on its west elevation, shown here.

Raabjerg Church (c. 1320)

Architect Unknown **Location** Raabjergvej, Raabjerg, Ålbæk, Denmark **Style** Late Romanesque **Materials** Brick, granite

Raabjerg Church rests in the middle of the North Jutland wilderness, an area of sandy soil, heath, pine trees, and glorious, ever-changing light. Only a few houses and farms populate the flat landscape, and it is clear that untamable nature, not human presence, governs this part of Denmark. Not far from the church is Raabjerg Mile (Raabjerg Dune), the only migrating dune in Denmark. It is the largest dune of its kind in Northern Europe, approximately 1.25 miles (2 km) long, and it migrates approximately 49 feet (15 m) a year toward the northeast, away from the church.

It is estimated that Raabjerg Church was built some time between 1290 and 1320. The building is characterized as Late Romanesque, yet the choir arch is pointed, indicating that the church was built at the transition from the Roman to the Gothic style. The building rests on granite boulders and is constructed of so-called *munkesten*—a type of large brick—predominantly used in the Middle Ages. In 1620 the church was extended toward the west, and in 1720 the east gable and the nave were rebuilt. In 1931 the church went through a major restoration— a new roof was fitted, and the south and east gables were faced with new brickwork. Significant is the church's bell frame, one of the oldest in Denmark, which is placed somewhat independently of, yet close to, the church.

Raabjerg Church is sparsely decorated, and the white walls—both externally and internally—are prevailing characteristics. On its own, this small, low-ceilinged church is not making a big architectural statement; rather, it stands out as a symbol of purity, of a space filled with tranquility that allows room for thought. Raabjerg Church is a building that epitomizes the aspiration to unite nature with the manmade. It represents a symbiosis of religious thought and natural humility. **SML**

Great Enclosure and Chief's House (c. 1330)

Architect Unknown   **Location** Great Zimbabwe, Zimbabwe   **Style** Bantu   **Material** Granite

When Portuguese traders first saw the stone ruins of Great Zimbabwe, or "houses of stone," in the sixteenth century, they thought they had discovered Ophir, the capital of the Queen of Sheba. Archaeologists now concur that the complex of ruins was a city created by the Munhumutapa empire, the ancestors of one of Zimbabwe's Shona-speaking ethnic groups—the Lemba—and that it was inhabited by as many as 40,000 people in its heyday.

Built between the eleventh and fifteenth centuries, the 1,800-acre (728 ha) site is the largest ancient stone construction in sub-Saharan Africa. Set on a high plateau in wooded savanna, it is divided into three areas: the hill complex, the valley complex, and Imba Huru, or the Great Enclosure. The latter is thought to been built in the early fourteenth century, and is where the chief or king lived, remote from the surrounding land in order to escape disease carried by the tsetse fly. More than 300 stone structures lie within the Great Enclosure, which is surrounded by a wall that snakes sinuously over the hilly terrain. Both the structures and the walls were built using a dry-stone technique. The wall is built from 15,000 tons of granite blocks, and is 800 feet (244 m) long, 16 feet (5 m) thick at the base, and 32 feet (10 m) high. It is covered with intricate zigzag fretwork patterns in brick. Originally, the buildings of the complex were decorated with stone carvings and gold and copper ornaments.

The site was abandoned c. 1450 for unknown reasons. It has been suggested that it may have been because of drought, overfarming that depleted the land's resources, or a decline in the gold trade. **CMK**

↖ No mortar binds the stone blocks of the impressive walls surrounding the enclosure.

← The walls of the ruins consist of many thousands of shaped stones fitted together without mortar.

Notre Dame de Paris (1330)

Architect Maurice de Sully   **Location** Paris, France   **Style** Early Gothic   **Material** Stone

Notre Dame de Paris has been the cathedral of the city of Paris since the tenth century. It is a Gothic exemplar of a radical change in the Romanesque tradition of construction, both in terms of naturalistic decoration and revolutionary engineering techniques. In particular, via a framework of flying buttresses, external arched struts receive the lateral thrust of high vaults and provide sufficient strength and rigidity to allow the use of relatively slender supports in the main arcade. The cathedral stands on the Île de la Cité, an island in the middle of the River Seine, on a site previously occupied by Paris's first Christian church, the Basilica of Saint-Étienne, as well as an earlier Gallo-Roman temple to Jupiter, and the original Notre Dame, built by Childebert I, the king of the Franks, in 528. Maurice de Sully (d. 1196), Bishop of Paris, began construction in 1163 during the reign of Louis VII and building continued until 1330. The spire was erected in the 1800s during a renovation by Viollet-le-Duc.

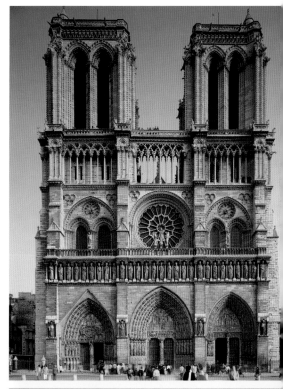

The western facade is the distinguishing feature of the cathedral. It comprises the Gallery of Kings, a horizontal row of stone sculptures; a rose window glorifying the Virgin, who also appears in statue form below; the Gallery of Chimeras; two unfinished square towers; and three portals, those of the Virgin, the Last Judgment, and St. Anne, with richly carved sculptures around the ornate doorways. The circular rose window in the west front and two more in the north and south transept crossings, created between 1250 and 1270, are masterpieces of Gothic engineering. The stained glass is supported by delicate radiating webs of carved stone tracery. **JEH**

↗ The west facade shows carefully managed symmetry, blending sturdiness and delicacy in equal measure.

→ Notre Dame Cathedral's vault, at 112 feet (34 m) high, was the first to be built on a truly monumental scale.

Ightham Mote (1340)

Architect Unknown   **Location** Near Sevenoaks, England   **Style** Vernacular   **Materials** Timber with wattle and daub infill, brick, Kentish ragstone

Ightham Mote is almost the ideal English manor house—a cluster of stone and timber-framed buildings around a courtyard, surrounded by a moat, and entered by a gate beneath a tower. It is typically picturesque and also typical in that it is a building that has grown and changed over hundreds of years.

Ightham Mote was begun around 1330, when the great hall, crypt, original chapel, and a pair of upper rooms were constructed. No one knows who the original builder was, although a knight called Sir Thomas Cawne lived there soon afterward, in 1340. Additions in the late fifteenth century turned the building into an inward-looking house centered on its courtyard; an owner called Sir Richard Clement enriched the interiors in the 1520s and 1530s, adding stained glass, paneling, and a finer ceiling in the New Chapel. The seventeenth-century owners built the drawing room and nearby buildings. In 1889 Sir Thomas Colyer-Fergusson bought the house and began a program of repair and restoration.

The house's vernacular charm found many admirers, not least the U.S. businessman Charles Henry Robinson, who bought it in the 1950s and left it to the National Trust. By 1989 the Trust had launched the most in-depth restoration project in its history, virtually taking the house apart and putting it back together again and in the process revealing much about its growth and development. So painstaking was this conservation project that even hidden parts of the house—hidden roof supports, nineteenth-century wallpaper concealed under later paneling, attic plasterwork—were conserved. **PW**

↖ The half-timbered upper story of the fifteenth-century south front projects over the stone lower story.

↩ Ightham Mote's charm lies as much in its agglomeration of historic character as in its romantic setting.

Tower at Pisa (1350)

Architect Bonanno Pisano **Location** Pisa, Italy **Style** Romanesque **Materials** Stone, marble, lime

The cross-shaped duomo at Pisa, with its cylindrical *campanile* (bell tower) and circular baptistery, make up one of the world's most distinct architectural groupings. The *campanile*, bizarrely positioned toward the rear of the cathedral instead of at the front as would be expected, is visible from all sides of the aptly named Field of Miracles. Its marble masonry, encircled by eight tiers of colonnaded arches and topped by a belfry, provides a thematic link to the church's apse.

The tower was designed to be vertical, but it appears to have been jinxed from the start. The first stones were laid down on a slippery substrate of clay, fine sand, and shells. With subsidence in evidence, work ceased in 1178 after only three stories had been constructed. As the angle of the tilt deepened, the structure began to rotate on its axis, causing its south side to begin moving up toward the surface. In 1272 heavier materials were introduced to counterbalance the pull of the lean. In 1360 gravity was fought yet again when different numbers of steps, six and four respectively, were added to the south and north sides, from the seventh cornice up to the bell chamber—all to no avail. Another error was made in 1838 when a walkway was dug around the base, triggering a flood that added to the existing inclination.

The bell tower's inclination has been the object of very special attention ever since 1173. From 1991 to 2001, the foundations were subjected to serious rehabilitation in one of the all-time great feats of engineering, which involved experts successfully experimenting with soil extraction methods in order to preserve the tower for future generations. **AA**

↗ The Tower's infamous lean has deflected attention from the superb quality of its architecture.

➔ The tiered galleries of columns serve as outer supports to the inner core, creating a deeply textured exterior.

Alhambra (1354)

Architects Nasrid dynasty **Location** Granada, Spain **Style** Moorish Islamic, Renaissance **Materials** Stone, timber

The Alhambra—from the Arabic, *Al Hamra*, meaning The Red—is an ancient mosque, palace, and fortress complex built by the Moorish monarchs of Granada. The name is perhaps derived from the color of the sun-dried bricks that make up the buildings. Much of the Alhambra resembled typical medieval Christian strongholds in its three-fold arrangement of castle, palace, and residential quarters. After the Christian reconquest of the city in 1492, Charles V rebuilt portions of the complex in the Renaissance style. Some buildings were given a new role, such as the Palace of Mexuar, which was turned into a Christian chapel. Others were demolished to make way for the new Palace of Charles V, which was designed by Renaissance architect Pedro Machuca. Moorish features survived elsewhere: at the Palace of Comares, the Ambassador's Room has its original cedar-wood ceiling representing the seven heavens of Islam. The Hall of the Mozárabes was named for the Christian architects who adapted its Moorish style. At the Palace of Muhammad V, the celebrated Court of the Lions is dominated by the Fountain of Lions—a magnificent alabaster basin surrounded by twelve lions in white marble. The lions once functioned as a clock, with water flowing from a different lion each hour. The Christians were fascinated with this device and took it apart to see how it worked. Inevitably, the contraption never functioned correctly again. **AT**

> *"... the song of nightingales mingles with the fresh orchestral sounds of running water ..."*

C. J. Lim, architect

Castelvecchio (1356)

Architect Unknown **Location** Verona, Italy **Style** Gothic **Material** Brick

The Castelvecchio in Verona was constructed as the fortified residence of the prince of the city, Cangrande II della Scala. Positioned on the west side of the city, adjacent to a bend in the Adige River, it was designed both to dominate Verona and to provide an easy, protected escape for the ruler from urban uprisings, by means of a private bridge—the Ponte Scaligero. Cangrande amassed considerable wealth from overtaxing the population, depositing much of the money in banks in Florence and Venice, so that he was reviled by his subjects and was eventually murdered by his brother. The large castle has a trapezoidal plan that follows the curvature of the river, while a severe crenellated facade, seven towers, two rings of walls, and gates with portcullis separate it from the city. The interior is ordered around two courtyards with ample space provided for the mercenary guard that protected the ruler. The prince's residence is distributed around the more heavily protected second court, which is protected by the Torre del Mastio and has direct access to the private bridge. The latter was an integral part of the castle project and is also fortified. The castle was converted to a museum by the architect Carlo Scarpa, who deftly inserted modern materials. Inside, cast concrete walkways crisscross the medieval brick fabric and the objects are displayed against contrasting material surfaces, so that the installation is an artwork in its own right. **FN**

"With its fast-rushing river, great castle, and prospect so delightful and so cheerful! Pleasant Verona!"

Charles Dickens, novelist

Alfriston
Clergy House (1360)

Architect Unknown **Location** Alfriston, England
Style English vernacular **Materials** Timber with wattle and daub infill, thatched roof

The typical medieval English "Wealden" house, named for the Weald of Kent where it was once common, was a structure with a central double-height hall, flanked on either side by smaller rooms—private rooms for the family off one end of the hall, service rooms such as kitchen and pantry off the opposite end. Few of these buildings, which were usually of timber-framed construction, have survived in anything like their original form. With changing fashions, double-height halls were divided horizontally to make rooms of normal height; extensions were added; timber structures were replaced with brick.

Alfriston Clergy House was probably first built in the fourteenth century as the house of the local parish priest or vicar. As a priest's house, the use of the rooms may have been slightly different from those in the standard Wealden house, with service rooms and a private chamber for the priest at one end and accommodation for a servant at the other.

In 1896, the house was sold to the National Trust for £10; it was the very first building that the Trust acquired. The Clergy House retains its black-and-white timber-framed walls and its steeply pitched roof, which was probably originally tiled although it has been thatched since at least the nineteenth century. Inside, the chalk-floored hall rises to ancient, blackened roof timbers. Two-story wings are preserved on either side. This modest but beautiful building offers a glimpse of the kind of life lived by members of the clergy in the late Middle Ages. **PW**

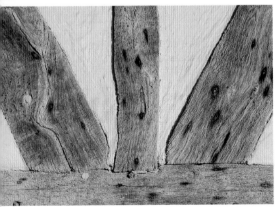

◩ The thatched roof, brick chimney, and timber-frame painted walls are quintessentially English.

◪ Much of the building's appeal derives from the craftsmanship that has gone into its construction.

Royal Alcázar (c. 1364)

Patron Pedro of Castile   **Location** Seville, Spain
Style Mudéjar, Gothic, Renaissance   **Material** Stone

Qutub Minar (1368)

Patron Qutub-ud-din Aibak   **Location** Delhi, India   **Style** Islamic,
Mu'izzi   **Materials** Brick masonry, red sandstone, white marble

The Royal Alcázar of Seville (see page 21) is not a single castle but an arrangement of palaces built in several reigns, in different periods and styles. While the Alcázar's origins go back to a Roman fortification, greater parts of a twelfth-century Almohad palace, called Al-Muwarak (the Blessed), are integrated into the Alcázar's current setting. However, most of the building on view today was constructed after Ferdinand III reconquered Seville in 1246. In 1364 Pedro of Castile (1334–69), also known as Peter the Cruel, commissioned the royal residence, core of the

> "... the world beyond was softly, but inexorably, shut out from this garden of Eden ..."

Elizabeth Robins Pennell, writer

Alcázar, to impress his beloved Lady Maria Padilla. He gathered craftsmen from Seville, Toledo, and Granada, who created one of the best remaining examples of Mudéjar architecture, a style that under Christian rule in Spain remained under Islamic architectural influence. Following monarchs contributed their own additions to the Alcázar, sometimes mixing the Islamic style with Gothic and Renaissance elements. The palace comprises a mazelike arrangement of rooms and patios where each provides its own special treasures. The design of the Alcázar's lovely garden, a relaxing, green oasis, is inspired by Arabic and Renaissance styles. Listed as a UNESCO World Heritage Site since 1979, Reales Alcázares de Sevilla is still home to the Spanish royal family in that city. The Alcázar and its gardens are a unique architectural jewel. **CH**

One of the first structures of the Islamic architectural legacy, the Qutub Minar stands tall in the midst of the sprawling Qutub complex. The best-preserved building of the complex, it may have been inspired by the Minaret of Jam in Afghanistan.

The tower was probably commissioned by the first Muslim ruler of Delhi, Qutub-ud-din Aibak, although only the first tier was completed during his rule. His successor, Iltumish, and thereafter Firoz Shah Tughlaq, commissioned the subsequent tiers, raising its height to an astounding 238 feet (72.5 m), making it the tallest brick masonry tower in the world. The diameter of the tower is 47 feet (14.3 m) at the base, gradually tapering to less than 11.5 feet (3.5 m) at the top. The tiers are multifaceted cylindrical shafts, with intricate carvings and verses, illustrative of the refinement and evolving craftsmanship of Islamic styles over the different ruling dynasties. Each of the five tiers is marked by a balcony supported by corbels.

There continues to be speculation about the purpose of the tower. Traditionally, all mosques had minarets to call people to prayer. Though the Qutub Minar seems modeled on a similar style, and flanks the Quwwat ul Islam mosque, its scale supports the idea that it was envisaged as a victory tower, marking the overthrow of the Chauhans, the last Hindu rulers of Delhi by the Afghan Sultan Muhammad of Ghur. The surrounding complex is thought to have been constructed out of the material salvaged from the demolition of over twenty Brahman temples.

The name *Qutub* means axis, and is believed to denote a new axis for Islamic dominion. However controversial the historical pedigree of the tower, it has stood the test of time and continues to be synonymous with the south Delhi skyline. **BS**

Swayambunath Stupa (c. 1372)

Architect Unknown   **Location** Kathmandu Valley, Nepal
Style Buddhist, Newari   **Material** Stone

While the earliest record of the sanctuary at Swayambunath dates from a fifth-century stone inscription, its history begins in mythology. Legend has it that the Kathmandu Valley was once a huge lake. The god Swayambunath, which means "self-created," appeared on this lake in the form of a blazing lotus flower. Bodhisattva Manjushri split the mountains with a giant sword to provide access to the miracle, and the water of the Kathmandu Valley disappeared, leaving the lotus on the top of a hill. Later, to protect Swayambunath from invaders, the monk Shantikar Acharya covered the lotus flower with a *stupa*, a massive dome typical of Buddhist architecture.

Swayambunath sanctuary's present appearance dates from the fourteenth century, when it was reconstructed after Bengal troops destroyed it, and the sixteenth century, when King Pratapa Malla expanded and embellished the complex. Its central building, the *stupa*, is structured as thirteen rings, representing the steps of enlightenment. Painted on the *stupa*'s hemispherical top, Buddha's all-seeing eyes stare out in every direction. Shrines and temples from different periods and two Tibetan monasteries complete the UNESCO World Heritage Site.

To reach the *stupa*, pilgrims and visitors climb a staircase of more than 300 steps that represents the final part of the path of enlightenment. At the end of the exhausting climb is an unforgettable view of the *stupa* and all its shrines and temples, combined with a breathtaking panorama of the Kathmandu Valley. **CH**

↖ The Stupa is a synthesis of architecture and religion, its form and spiritual narrative working in unison.

← The painted eyes of the Buddha on all four sides of the tower command the attention of all around them.

Temple of the Floating Stone (1377)

Patrons Uisang, King Munmu of Silla **Location** Yeongpung-gun, Gyeongsangbuk-do, South Korea **Style** Jusimpo **Material** Wood

The Buseoksa Monastery was established by a monk, Uisang (625–702), on the orders of King Munmu of Silla (*d.* 681) in 676, but little remains of the original structure. According to legend, the monastery became known as the Temple of the Floating Stone because a daughter of a Tang Chinese official fell in love with Uisang while studying in China. She warned Uisang of a possible attack on his homeland, and he returned home to warn his countrymen. The girl wanted to join him and rushed to the shore, only to see his ship had set sail. She flung herself into the sea and drowned, and her sacrificial act caused her to be turned into a dragon. Once Uisang had averted the possible attack, he set to building a temple.

The series of buildings that now make up the monastery are located on a mountainside terrace and dominate the valley. One building, the Jodasang, is dedicated to the memory of the now Venerable Seon Master, Uisang. Built in 1377, and then rebuilt in 1490, it is one of the rare remaining wooden buildings from the Goryeo kingdom (918–1392). However, the monastery is most famous for its main shrine, the Muryangsujeon, meaning "room of infinite longevity." According to records, the present elegant wooden shrine also dates from 1377, but it reflects an older construction style in the harmony of its proportions and finish of its framework. The rectangular hypostyle shrine is built on a granite foundation, and has a gabled roof covered by large gray tiles. Wooden columns with slightly curved sides are capped by joints in the shape of an inverted pyramid that support the roof eaves. Latticed windows adorn the south side of the building. The Muryangsujeon is one of the oldest wooden buildings in Korea and a beautiful example of Korean carpentry skills. **FM**

Jongmyo Shrine of the Yi Dynasty (1394)

Architect Unknown **Location** Seoul, South Korea **Style** Ikkong **Materials** Stone, tiles, wood

The founders of the Choseon Kingdom adopted Confucianism. According to Chinese customs propagated by that philosophy, a king must honor with offerings the four past generations of his paternal ancestors, as well as the ancestor who had obtained for him the heavenly mandate to govern. Therefore, after the foundation in 1394 of their new capital city (today's Seoul), the kings of the Yi Dynasty built a sanctuary to the east of their royal palace.

The first sanctuary was designed to hold seven tablets invested with spirits of the deceased. The

> *"The Mandate of Heaven is not easy, but [the state] flourishes when there is virtue."*
>
> Beginning of "Botaepyeong," Korean ritual music

sanctuary disappeared during the Japanese invasion of 1592, although the tablets had been taken to safety. This sanctuary was reconstructed in 1608 and, over time, it was enlarged several times with additional cells, built in a row toward the east. The Jongmyo Shrine now consists of a long house, 330 feet (100 m) in length, with short wings at either end defining a large paved terrace. This is the main building of the funerary sanctuary of the Yi kings and is impressively solemn and severe with its limited color range of white stone, gray tiles, and dark red columns. Each deceased king had his tomb placed in an auspicious site within the building. The shrine's walled park encloses, in addition to the main sanctuary, a secondary sanctuary (the Yeongnyeongjeon) and several buildings used to prepare for ceremonies. **FM**

Temple of the Golden Pavilion (1397)

Architect Shogun Ashikaga Yoshimitsu   **Location** Kyoto, Japan   **Style** Muromachi, Heian, and Zen influences   **Materials** Wood, lacquer, gold leaf

The Temple of the Golden Pavilion (*Kinkaku-ji*) in Kyoto's northern hills was originally built by Shogun Ashikaga Yoshimitsu (1358–1408) as a *shariden* (hall) for relics of the Buddha. In 1408 he asked that it be posthumously converted into a temple for Zen Buddhism's Rinzai sect. Following the decline in power of the shogunate, Zen temples struggled financially and many perished during the Onin War (1467–77). This temple escaped destruction until it was set alight by a deranged monk in 1950. What exists today is an exact replica from 1955 that was last relacquered and gilded in 1987. The temple's rooftop is crowned by a gilded finial in the shape of a Chinese phoenix, and the second and third stories are coated in Japanese lacquer covered in gold leaf. Each level of the three-story pagoda is characterized by a distinctive style. Inspired by the eleventh-century residences of Heian nobility, the first-story Temple of Dharma Water

(*Hôsui-in*) is built in the palace style (*shinden-zukuri*) and consists of a large room with sliding panels that allow light and air to enter the veranda-surrounded interior. A Chinese-style Buddha hall on the second story, called the Grotto of Wave Sounds (*Chôon-dô*), reflects the style of samurai houses (*buke-zukuri*). The third-story Buddha hall is called the Superb Apex (*Kukkyôchô*) and is in the Chinese Chan or Zen temple style (*karayo*), and boasts gilded ornamentation, cusped windows, and sacred relics. **AA**

"Each piece must . . . look as if it was designed for that particular building."

Minoru Yamasaki, architect

Trullo Stone Houses (1400)

Architect Unknown **Location** Alberobello, Apulia, Italy **Style** Vernacular **Materials** Whitewashed limestone, stone

An ingenious response to the local landscape and readily available materials, the *trullo* is a dry-wall or mortarless construction made from local stone called *chiancarelle*. A *trullo* is erected on a square or round base with thick stone walls to keep the rooms warm in winter and cool in the summer. The conical, watertight roof is raised in concentric circles of piled-up, hand-cut, limestone boulders covered by weathered slabs. Decorative rooftop finials of different shapes, sizes, or combinations of geometric forms—orbs, triangles, columns, and stars—personalize each limestone dwelling and evoke the sun-worshipping cult of the region's earliest inhabitants. The history of the *trulli* of Alberobello began when local landed gentry, the counts of Conversano, came up with a scheme for evading the taxes associated with obtaining royal approval for building a new settlement. Local farmers were thrown off their lands and were forced to relocate to the Selva—an oak forest—and live in temporary shelters that could be rapidly dismantled and reconstructed elsewhere. Ironically, these dwellings proved sturdier than their mortar-built equivalents. Finally, in 1797, after nearly four centuries of itinerant subsistence, the community successfully appealed to Ferdinand IV, king of Naples, to legitimize their way of life. Today, the local people are proud of their heritage and happily rent out *trulli* to tourists for a unique accommodation experience. **AA**

> *"... [these] timeless ghostly cones raise the specter of a forgotten age for a fairytale setting."*
>
> Émile Berteaux, architect and academic

Gur-i Emir (1405)

Patron Timur **Location** Samarkand, Uzbekistan
Style Timurid **Materials** Brick, ceramic tile cladding

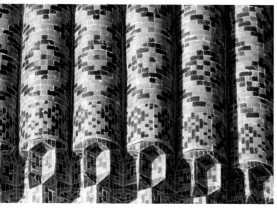

The Gur-i Emir is the mausoleum of Timur (1330–1405), known in the West as Tamurlane and by his contemporaries as "the scourge of God" and "conqueror of all the Earth." The greatest of the Turco-Mongol rulers of Central Asia, Timur actually built this vast mausoleum for his favorite grandson, but it became the dynastic tomb of the Timurids. Beneath the dome lies Timur's black jade sarcophagus—the largest block of jade in the world—although his remains reside in the crypt below.

The building is a partial ruin, but this preserves its authenticity, unlike many of the Timurid buildings in Uzbekistan that the Soviets restored to a theme-park sheen. As mausoleums go, this is grandiose, but then it is characteristic of the colossal scale of Timurid architecture and certainly befitting of Timur's ego.

The fluted, melon-shaped dome with its aquamarine ceramic tiles is specific to Central Asia. Around its drum the glazed brickwork spells "God is immortal," along with the names of Allah and the prophet Muhammad in giant Kufic script. But whatever the flourishes of the exterior, the real glory is inside. It takes a while for the eyes to adjust to the slight gloom, but it soon becomes apparent just how elaborate the surfaces are. A kaleidoscope of onyx marble, alabaster tiles, and gilded, filigreed stucco shifts in geometric shape from the square room through a series of pendentives up to the circular dome. This chamber is to be admired not just for its craftsmanship, but also as a powerful vision of paradise. **JMc**

↖ This form of Islamic architecture achieves a balance between abstracted form and ornamental detail.

← The startling blue and green tiles on the outside of this mausoleum are reminders of paradisal gardens.

Hall of Prayer for Good Harvests (1420)

Architect Commissioned by Emperor Yongle (Zhu Di) **Location** Temple of Heaven Park, Beijing, China **Style** Taoist **Material** Wood

Hospital of the Innocents (1429)

Architect Filippo Brunelleschi **Location** Florence, Italy **Style** Renaissance **Materials** *Pietra serena*, plaster

The Temple of Heaven (*Tiantán*) Park is about 3 miles (4.8 km) south of Beijing's Forbidden City. The park is a dignified complex of Taoist temples set in gardens, where the Ming and Qing emperors would conduct seasonal ceremonies, praying for good weather and harvests. The temple's layout, and that of individual buildings, symbolizes the relationship between Earth and Heaven—the everyday and spiritual dimensions of life—at the heart of Chinese traditional cosmogony. The emperors had a special role of mediating between the natural and the spiritual worlds; their prayers were considered essential to the empire's well-being.

The largest building in the Temple of Heaven is the Hall of Prayer for Good Harvests. The hall is a circular wooden structure, 125 feet (38 m) high and 98 feet (30 m) in diameter. It has a triple conical roof, covered in deep-blue glazed tiles representing heaven, and topped by a bulbous golden finial. The construction of the hall is entirely in wood, with no iron nails or cement. The whole structure is supported by twenty-eight large pillars. These are in red-lacquered *nanmi* (a fine hardwood) and symbolize the twenty-eight constellations. The four central pillars are arranged according to a traditional symbolic calendar. The coffered ceiling is carved with dragons and phoenixes. In the center of the flagstone floor is a marble slab with veining also representing a dragon and phoenix. The whole interior is splendidly decorated in gold and traditional Chinese colors.

The hall stands on a *Qigutan*, a three-level circular terrace from which a causeway, planned according to Taoist geomancy, leads to the Earthly Mount altar. The hall was destroyed by lightning in 1889 but underwent restoration a year later. It was designated a World Heritage Site in 1998. **ATB**

Some consider the Hospital of the Innocents to be the building that first defined a new style of architecture during what is now known as the Renaissance—a style that was based upon a rejection of Gothic forms and a return to the language of the Classical Roman past. It is a foundling hospital established and funded by a wealthy merchants' guild to provide for the city's orphans. Brunelleschi (1337–1446) used freestanding columns supporting round-arched arcades. By boldly contrasting the gray stone of the *pietra serena* architectural elements against the white stucco of the

"He also designed the loggia and residence of the Innocents … it can still be seen by all today."

Giorgio Vasari, biographer and critic

smooth surfaces, the building's design was made easily comparable to Roman models.

In an original reworking of Classical Roman elements, Brunelleschi used plain, not fluted columns without a balustrade above them. Above each column is a ceramic *tondo* depicting a baby in swaddling clothes lying on a blue wheel. The blue wheel referred to a rotating horizontal wheel on which mothers could leave their babies at the hospital anonymously. The hospital accepted unwanted children until 1875.

The hospital's striking design is also innovative for its clear and eloquent addressing of the adjacent public space. The open arcade expands into the public space. Raised on a plinth of steps, the *loggia* offers an open and protective facade, in a symbolic language expressive of the building's function. **FN**

Monastery of Santa Maria da Vitória (1434)

Architect Master Huguet   **Location** Batalha, Portugal
Style Portuguese Gothic   **Materials** Stone, stained glass

Florence Cathedral (1436)

Architects Di Cambio, Giotto, Pisano, Brunelleschi   **Location** Florence, Italy   **Style** Gothic, Renaissance   **Materials** Marble, brick, wood, glass

The monastery at Batalha (Portuguese for "battle") was built to commemorate the victory of the Portuguese over the Spanish in 1385, and was commissioned by King John I (1357–1433). Of the master builders involved it was the English architect Master Huguet (d. 1438) who made the biggest impact, being instrumental in turning the monastery into the most impressive example of Gothic architecture in the entire Iberian region. He raised the nave and altered the proportions of the church in a style reminiscent of the English Early Perpendicular. The Founders' Chapel

> "Master builders were just waiting for the chance to demonstrate their skill, and Batalha was that chance."

Pedro Dias, *Portuguese Gothic Architecture* (1994)

in particular is a monument to his genius. The star vault of the cupola, which spans 62 feet (19 m), was a daring achievement and a highly innovative structure for its time.

Under Manuel I (1495–1521), construction of seven chapels began. They were intended to house the remains of all the members of the Aviz dynasty, but they were never finished—the massive, carved-stone pillars that would have supported the vaulted ceiling are in place, but the chapels are open to the sky. Batalha, with its stone pillars, sculptures, and gargoyles, was highly influential in architectural terms. It kickstarted the style now known as Portuguese Gothic, which began at Batalha and matured in the later Manueline style as exemplified at Jerónimos Monastery in Lisbon, built a century later. **MDC**

The Cathedral of Santa Maria del Fiore (see page 21), or Duomo, forms part of an architectural complex that includes the baptistery—Battistero di San Giovanni—and Giotto's bell tower. All three buildings are linked visually by the distinctive vertical and horizontal bands of colored marble decorating their external walls.

By the end of the thirteenth century, the Cathedral of Santa Reparata was crumbling, so Florence decided to build a church over it that would surpass those of Pisa and Siena. Work began on the floorplan by Arnolfo Di Cambio (1245–1302)—a nave and two aisles divided by Gothic arches, culminating in an octagonal dome at the rear of the building. Giotto di Bondone (1267–1337) worked on the *campanile* before his death, and Andrea Pisano (1270–1348) continued the construction until he died of the plague. A series of architects quickly succeeded one another to complete the bell tower, expand the apse and side chapels, and finish off the naves. Six lateral stained-glass windows were also added with only the four closest to the transept allowing in light. There is a marked contrast between the elaborately decorated exterior and its spartan interior—a reversal of what was typical for cathedrals of the period.

In response to the challenge of erecting a cupola over the chancel, Filippo Brunelleschi (1377–1446) presented plans for a wooden and brick model inspired by the Pantheon's double-walled circular dome. His revolutionary engineering design solution—an octagonal double-walled cupola with horizontal reinforcements resting on a drum instead of the roof—bypassed any need for scaffolding and produced history's first octagonal dome. When the Duomo was finally completed, it was the largest Christian church in the world. **AA**

Ca' d'Oro (1436)

Architects Giovanni Bon, Bartolomeo Bon **Location** Venice, Italy
Style Venetian Gothic **Materials** Stone, polychrome marble

Best seen from a gondola on the Grand Canal, this aristocratic waterside mansion gets its name from the exquisite gilt and polychrome embellishments that once graced its facade but which have long since faded. Built for the public prosecutor Marino Contarini, the palazzo bears the unmistakable signature of the pair of sculptor-architects behind the Doge's Palace and the Porta della Carta.

The Ca'd'Oro is a uniquely Venetian design, blending Gothic elements with Byzantine and Arabic influences derived from the city's trade links with Constantinople, Moorish Spain, and the Islamic east. Its famous facade—a harmonious contrast between the empty spaces of the portico and *loggias* on the left-hand side and the solid planar wall studded with nine inset windows on the right-hand side—gives the visual impression of two houses in one. The recessed ground-floor colonnaded loggia leading directly from the pier into the entrance hall of the palazzo, the enclosed Moorish-style balconies supporting rows of quatrefoil stonework tracery on interlinking arcades and open arches, and the lacy parapet with exotic crestings all lend the palace an air of wistful romance. With the collapse of the Venetian Republic in 1797, ownership of the mansion changed hands several times. In 1895 Baron Franchetti began an extensive restoration program that included building a museum in his name—the Galleria Giorgio Franchetti—and restoring the Gothic stairway that had originally stood in the tiled inner courtyard. **AA**

↗ Venice turns the seemingly impossible into stone, with buildings striving to be as insubstantial as water.

→ The influence of the Orient on the Ca' D'Oro can be seen in the lacy window architecture.

Kumbum Chorten (1440)

Patron Prince Rabten Kunzang Phag   **Location** Gyantse, Tibet   **Style** Fifteenth-century Tibetan   **Materials** Stone, wood, clay

The Kumbum, commonly known to Tibetans as the Pango Chorten, has probably been Tibet's most famous *chorten*, or *stupa*, since its construction in the early fifteenth century by the then prince of Gyantse, Rabten Kunzang Phag. The *chorten* is a Tibetan development of the Indian Buddhist *stupa*, a solid reliquary monument enshrining the remains and belongings of the Buddha. One of the unique features of the Kumbum is that it contains a number of floors and rooms. Although there are several Tibetan *chorten*s containing a chapel that can be entered, it is rare for them to have more than one or two rooms.

The symbolism and design of the Kumbum and most other Tibetan *chorten*s is far more complex than that of the original Indian *stupa*. The term *"kumbum"* literally means "100,000," and in this context refers to the fact that the building houses a vast number of images of enlightened beings. Within its walls, the Kumbum contains a large and complex pantheon of Tibetan Buddhist lineage masters, Buddhas, Bodhisattvas, and tantric deities. These are sequentially enshrined in seventy-five chapels, from exoteric figures such as those of the Buddha Shakyamuni on the ground floor up to the secret meditational deities enshrined in the *chorten*'s spire.

The complex building is eight stories high and has a whitewashed exterior. Pilgrims and visitors are guided by the layout from the ground floor to the top. At first they encounter images of public figures, after which they slowly make their way through a realm of ever more profound and esoteric imagery that aids them on their path to enlightenment. **JR**

↖ Friezes of painted auspicious motifs such as wheels, lotuses, and flaming jewels decorate the exterior.

← The form of the *chorten* and its chapels allows pilgrims to journey upward through the structure.

Palazzo Medici (1450)

Architect Michelozzo di Bartolomeo **Location** Florence, Italy **Style** Renaissance **Materials** *Pietra forte* sandstone

The first major residential palace of the Renaissance in Italy was built for Cosimo de' Medici, *pater patriae* or godfather of the Florentine state during the second quarter of the fifteenth century. Cosimo turned to the local sculptor-architect Michelozzo di Bartolomeo (1396–1472) whom he had already employed for the construction of the stripped-down monastic complex of San Marco, in the north of Florence. Michelozzo, a master at combining innovative features with local building traditions, fashioned an entirely new residential type for his Medici patron.

Centered on a grand, columnated courtyard, the tripartite facade with its rusticated lower level, large round-arched windows on the second story, and massive cornice set the template for Florentine *palazzi* for years to come. Reminiscent of a Roman villa, the proud exterior gave way to an softer interior, the courtyard opening onto an intimate enclosed garden.

Beyond the courtyard, on the first floor— the so-called *piano nobile*—an impressive sequencing of rooms led to the domestic quarters. At the heart of the home was the private chapel, the Capella dei Magi, designed by Michelozzo and decorated by the painter Benozzo Gozzoli with frescoes showing the journey of the Magi. The immense luxury of this room was rivaled only by Cosimo's private study, which was lined with precious objects whose collective value far outstripped the construction cost of the entire palace.

In 1659, Gabbriello Riccardi bought the palazzo and adjacent buildings. He set about merging the buildings, but maintained the Renaissance exterior as far as possible while giving it a Baroque interior. **FN**

↗ The inner courtyard combines graceful open colonnades with defensively rusticated upper stories.

➡ The principal rooms on the main floor provide an essay in Baroque sensibility.

Hôtel-Dieu Hospital (1451)

Architect Jacques Wiscrère **Location** Beaune, Burgundy, France
Style Flemish Gothic **Materials** Brick, wood

The Hôtel-Dieu at Beaune is an elegant hospital for the poor, founded by Nicolas Rolin, chancellor to Philippe le Bon, Duke of Burgundy, and his wife Guigone de Salins. The design, by Flemish artist Jacques Wiscrère, followed the style of the Hôpital Saint-Jacques in Valenciennes and is the best-preserved example of Flemish Gothic, transported by its architect to become a symbol of Burgundy. The construction was conceived and completed in a little more than eight years and dedicated on December 31, 1451.

The long, half-timbered building has a picturesque galleried courtyard with towers and gables in the roofscape. The architectural jewel of the building is the iridescent roofs decorated with red, yellow, and black glazed tiles arranged in geometric patterns. The current roof design dates from between 1902 and 1907, and is an interpretation of a mid-eighteenth-century model of the hospice and some existing colored tiles. The courtyard contains a wrought-iron well-head in front of the main ward.

The Hôtel-Dieu functioned in its traditional role until a modern hospital was built in 1971. From the beginning of the hospital's foundation, Nicolas Rolin had planned to supply the institution with paintings, sculpture, furniture, and tapestries. The building now houses a museum holding around 5,000 items, including a large polyptych, *The Last Judgment* by Rogier van der Weyden. Visitors can also see the old hospital ward, the chapel, the kitchen, and the pharmacy, all with their original furnishings. **JEH**

↖ The colored roof tiles are among the most celebrated examples of what became the Burgundian style.

← The lavish roof decoration, pillared galleries, and costly glass emphasizes the building's expense.

San Francesco and Tempio Malatestiano (1455)

Architect Leon Battista Alberti   **Location** Rimini, Italy

Style Renaissance   **Materials** Istrian marble dressing

San Francesco in Rimini is a double monument, where the medieval church of San Francesco is encased by the Tempio Malatestiano, or Temple of the Malatesta family. The warlord prince Sigismondo Malatesta decided in the 1440s to create a mausoleum for himself, his forebears, and his mistress—later wife—Isotta degli Atti. He turned to Alberti (1404–72), charging him with the transformation of the church into a funerary monument.

Alberti's design preserved the original building, encasing its entirety within a new skin of a marble. On

---

"No aspect requires more care and diligence than the establishment and ornament of the temple."

Leon Battista Alberti, architect

---

the interior, this gave rise to an extraordinary program of sculptural architecture that entirely renewed the interior in luxurious colored stone. The exterior is monochromatic and uses exclusively white Istrian marble from across the Adriatic. Alberti adopted a design for the facade that was based on the idea of superimposing a Classical temple front upon a three-bay Roman triumphal arch, connecting the two with lateral scroll-like elements.

This simple yet revolutionary solution was never fully completed, and it seems that initial plans had ambitiously proposed the addition of an enormous apse, modeled on the domed Pantheon in Rome. The sides of the building were also encased in stone arcades, containing sarcophagi with the mortal remains of Sigismondo's ancestors and courtiers. **FN**

Brussels Town Hall (1455)

Architects Jacob van Thienen, Herman de Voghele, Jan van Ruysbroek

Location Brussels, Belgium   **Style** Brabantine Gothic   **Material** Stone

The focus of the city's Grand Place, Brussels Town Hall is perhaps the most significant secular building constructed in the Brabantine Gothic style. The principal facade of the building is arranged to face the square and is centered on a massive, 315-foot-high (96 m) bell tower, at the base of which is the building's main entrance. The overall design, which included a lower bell tower, is attributed to Jacob van Thienen, and dates to the early 1400s. Expansion of the town hall was begun from 1444, when the ten-year-old Duke Charles the Bold officiated at a foundation ceremony for the enlargement, which was designed and supervised by the city architect Herman de Voghele. A final phase, completed in 1455, was overseen by Jan van Ruysbroek, the court architect of Philip the Good, and included the extension of the bell tower and the addition of a rich crowning portion to the octagonal tower in the Flamboyant style. A 16-foot-high (5 m) gilt bronze sculpture of St. Michael tops the tower.

In spite of this complex building history, and the vicissitudes that saw the building gutted in various military events (it was sacked during the French Revolution), the town hall offers a unified and impressive facade to the city. Serried ranks of Gothic arcading articulate an open ground-floor gallery, which is imitated on two successive stories of cross-mullioned windows, topped by crenellations, and a steeply pitched roof with dormer windows. The entire facade is encrusted with lively figural sculpture representing nobles (some of whose houses were demolished to make way for the palace), saints, and allegorical figures. It is the continuous nature of this decorative scheme that helps bind together the facade into an ordered whole. **FN**

Malbork
Castle (1457)

Patron Siegfried von Feuchtwangen   **Location** Malbork, Poland
Style Gothic   **Material** Brick

The Teutonic Knights were descended from the Brotherhood of the Hospitaliers and were originally a spiritual order before being transformed into a military organization. It soon began to play an important role in European politics with the intention of founding its own state. In 1309, the Grand Master Sigfried von Feuchtwangen (d. 1311) moved the capital of the Teutonic Order from Venice to a monastery at Malbork. The fortified monastery, constructed in the preceding three decades, was due for redevelopment.

The subsequent periods of construction only truly finished with the purchase of the castle by the Polish king in 1457, by which time the fortress had become the most powerful in Europe. It is divided into three main sections, the High, Middle, and Low Castles. The High Castle is an extraordinary fortress defended by multiple circuits of moats and curtain walling dotted with numerous towers. The Middle Castle consists of the former bailey converted into residential quarters, the Infirmary, the fan-vaulted Great Refectory, and the Great Masters' Residence. The castle underwent a further program of improvements that took another century to complete, involving enlargement of the Low Castle area, which included St. Lawrence's Church, workshops, an armory, stables, and other buildings.

The complex is beautifully executed in brick with figurative friezes, fine window traceries, and sculpted portals, all built on an imposing scale. Malbork Castle is one of the largest brick structures ever built, and was made a UNESCO World Heritage Site in 1997. **BK**

⬉ The imposing sight of Malbork would have instilled fear and respect in all those approaching its gates.

⬅ The extensive layout of the complex makes this site an extreme example of defensive urban planning.

Palazzo Piccolomini (1462)

Architect Bernardo Rossellini **Location** Pienza, Tuscany, Italy
Style Renaissance **Materials** Sandstone, travertine

Palazzo Piccolomini is the centerpiece of perhaps the most perfect piece of urban design of the fifteenth century—the diminutive urban core of Pienza—the birthplace of Pope Pius II Piccolomini (1458–64). When he was appointed pope in 1458, Pius set about rebuilding his former village, elevating it to a bishopric, and thus making it a city. Piccolomini's personal response to the buildings of ancient Rome is at the heart of Pienza's design, which was seen to completion by the executant architect, Bernardo Rossellino. Around the central square he arranged a cathedral,

> "The beauty and nobleness of the building helped me forget the irritation at its expense."

Pope Pius II Piccolomini

residential palace, episcopal palace, and a city hall. The cathedral fused a grand facade modeled on Roman triumphal arches, with an interior that evoked the high, luminous interiors of German hall-church design.

The papal palace is directly evocative of Rome. Its exterior is dressed in coursed stonework, and is marked by a grid design of pilasters and cornices that imitates the use of the Classical orders on the exterior of the Colosseum. Behind this magnificent facade lay a large, regular courtyard, closely modeled on that of the Medici Palace in Florence. Perhaps the most remarkable feature of the palace, however, is its open loggia, articulated over all three stories on the garden front of the building. Here, Classical columns frame access to the imposing hanging garden and the marvelous views over the Val d'Orcia. **FN**

Palazzo Schifanoia (1470)

Patron Alberto V d'Este **Location** Ferrara, Italy
Style Renaissance **Materials** Brick, marble

Palazzo Schifanoia is a Renaissance palace that lies outside of the medieval walls of Ferrara in northeast Italy. Begun by Alberto V d'Este (1347–93), who ruled Ferrara from 1370, the building was originally designed as a country retreat. The name Schifanoia is a contraction of the phrase *schivar la noia*, meaning escape from boredom, and the palace was certainly a place of leisure for members of the court. Building began in 1385 with the construction of a single-story structure. The palazzo's initial style was that of a Roman villa with a plain brick facade, small windows, and a large wooden door leading to an atrium. The facade was originally crenellated.

In 1465 Alberto's nephew Borso d'Este (1413–71) commissioned Pietro Benvenuto degli Ordini to extend the palazzo. A second story was added, and the facade was lengthened to 315 feet (96 m). Fake marble murals and an elaborate marble portal, carved with the Este coat of arms, were added to the facade. The portal survives, still bearing traces of colored paint. In the 1470s, the sculptor Domenico di Paris painted stuccoes in a frieze of *putti* and symbols of virtues in the Sala delle Virtù (Hall of Virtues). Painters, including Francesco del Cossa and Ercole de' Roberti, were commissioned to paint allegorical frescoes in the main hall. The stunning *Ciclo dei Mesi* (Cycle of the Months) frescoes depict the life of Borso d'Este, the months of the year, and related astrological signs.

Later, the court architect Biagio Rossetti (c. 1447–1516) worked on the palazzo, removing the unsafe crenellation from the facade and adding a brickwork cornice. He also added new rooms. The architecture of the d'Este buildings influenced future pleasure villas such as the Cortile del Belvedere, the papal palace in Rome that was begun in 1506. **MC**

Milan Cathedral (1480)

Architects Various **Location** Piazza del Duomo, Milan, Italy **Style** Gothic Lombard **Materials** Brick, white marble

The original plan for a Gothic cathedral with a cruciform nave and transept was commissioned by Archbishop Antonio da Saluzzo in 1386 on an ancient Roman site—a location so central that all of the Milan's main streets radiate from this spot. Its construction paved the way for the introduction of High Gothic into mainland Italy from across the Alps and northern Europe. Progress stalled on and off for the next five hundred years because of a lack of funds and ideas. Unsurprisingly, the church's appearance is a contradiction in visual terms, being massive yet delicate, both confused and inspired. It has an eastern apse that is French Gothic in flavor with a profusion of pinnacles, flying buttresses, and intricate tracery window panels; an octagonal Renaissance cupola; seventeenth-century doorways; an eighteen-century spire; and a Neo-Classical facade. The amazing roof bursting with spires, gargoyles, and marble statues offers fabulous views of the city. The building's enormous dimensions—one-and-a-half football fields or 126,000 square feet (11,706 sq m)—make it the world's third-largest Roman Catholic cathedral after St. Peter's in Rome and Seville Cathedral in Spain. Inside the vast interior capable of containing 40,000 visitors, five great aisles stretch from the entrance to the altar, and enormous stone pillars dominate the nave. The walls and niches house more statuary than any other building in the world—a staggering 3,159 images—2,245 of which can be found on the exterior alone. The most famous effigy, that of the *Madonnina* (Little Madonna), rests on top of the tallest spire covered in 3,900 pieces of gold leaf. Love it or loathe it, Milan Cathedral (Duomo di Milano) is a towering achievement that exalts the lofty pretensions of all the madmen who wished to press on with such an arduous project. **AA**

Knole (1486)

Patron Thomas Bourchier **Location** Sevenoaks, Kent, England **Style** Tudor, Jacobean **Material** Kentish ragstone

Set in a deer park near the town of Sevenoaks in Kent, Knole is one of the largest houses in Britain, and there is a tradition that it contains 365 rooms. It is arranged around half a dozen large courtyards and looks more like a small town than a house. Knole began as the palace of the Archbishop of Canterbury, Thomas Bourchier (c. 1411–86), who built much of it after he bought the estate in 1456. During the next century, King Henry VIII appropriated the house and then enlarged it. His daughter, Queen Elizabeth I, passed it to her cousin Thomas Sackville, who carried out the last major remodeling from 1603 to 1608. Members of his family have lived at Knole ever since, although the house is now in the care of the National Trust. Much of Bourchier's building survives, but its rather austere stone walls and rows of mullioned windows are enlivened by curvaceous gables in the Dutch style that were added during Sackville's time. Beyond the imposing front are gables, turrets, and clusters of tall chimneys signaling suite upon suite of rooms that can accommodate a large family, a small army of servants, and many guests. Inside, many rooms survive from King Henry VIII's time, with ceilings by the royal master-plasterer Richard Dungan and woodwork thought to be that of the king's carpenter, William Portinton. There are also many interiors from Sackville's remodeling, including the richly painted staircase and cartoon gallery. **PW**

> "I … must be a very great admirer of Knole. I think it is the most interesting thing in England."
>
> Edmund Burke, philosopher

Santa Maria dei Miracoli (1489)

Architect Pietro Lombardo   **Location** Venice, Italy   **Style** Renaissance   **Materials** Pink, gray, and white Istrian marble; wood; stone

So many rumors began to circulate about a miracle-working image of the Madonna and Child in fifteenth-century Venice that the icon soon became the object of pilgrimages. Veneration ran so deep that the Venetians raised funds to build first a shrine—and subsequently a church and convent—in her name.

Located at a canal crossing in a corner of the residential section northeast of the Rialto Bridge, the church has two entrances: one on the canal side with white stone steps, and the other on the street side. Crowned by a distinctive semicircular pediment, the polychromatic facade shimmers with colored sheets of marble and the red and green porphyry encrustations of its flat surfaces. A series of blind arches and a false colonnade create a sense of perspective around the external walls of the building to give the illusion of greater size.

The interior is composed of a raised balcony above the portal, so the nuns could remain hidden from view, and a single nave dominated by a raised chancel with a stairway between two pulpits at the opposite end. An ornately pierced marble parapet borders the altar of the raised presbytery on which the Marian icon is enshrined, and floral and figurative carvings ornament the chancel.

Windows and dark borders frame light-colored marble in the upper wall registers, and the lower sections are sheathed in soft-hued panels encased by pink and dark-gray borders. The painted barrel-vaulted, wooden ceiling is made up of fifty panels depicting faces of saints, prophets, and Old Testament figures, all framed by gilded coffer moldings. **AA**

↖ Santa Maria dei Miracoli is one of the best examples of Venetian Renaissance architecture.

← The church is lavishly decorated with exquisite polychrome marbles that shimmer in the sun.

Palazzo Ducale (1490)

Architects Luciano Laurana, Francesco di Giorgio Martini **Location** Urbino, Italy **Style** Renaissance **Materials** Brick, marble

The Palazzo Ducale at Urbino is among the grandest princely residences of the early Renaissance. Built for the mercenary general, Duke Federico of Montefeltro by the Dalmatian architect Luciano Laurana (c. 1420–79), and completed by the Sienese Francesco di Giorgio Martini (c. 1439–1502), it commands an impressive site on the highest point of the hilltop city of Urbino in the Marches, on the Adriatic side of central Italy. The palace has two monumental facades, one facing into the city, the other grandly projecting a sequence of superimposed triumphal arches framed by turrets toward the Duke's dominions.

On the city front, the palace is ordered by beautifully sculpted marble-framed windows, incised with the coat of arms and name of the duke. Beyond the entrance, an elegant courtyard opens up; the marble columns of the arcade contrasting with pale pink brickwork of the surfaces. Switchback staircases rise to the upper floor where there is a sequence of grand ceremonial rooms. At the heart of the palace, adjoining one of the three-tier arched balconies facing the countryside, is the patron's study furnished with intricate wooden marquetry, showing fictive landscapes, and the Montefeltro heraldic symbols. Immediately below, a suite of chapels, exquisitely carved in stone, are dedicated to Christian devotion on one side and the pagan Muses on the other. Farther below lie massive buttressing cellars that accommodate diverse facilities, including a cold storeroom where ice was preserved through the summer months, as well as a bath complex modeled on the ancient Roman thermal designs. **FN**

↗ The palace expresses the status and wealth of its patron through its enormous scale.

➡ The fine attention to detail and nod to Classical architecture reflect the owner's sophistication.

Mosque of Masjid-i-Jami (1498)

Patrons Ghiyath al-Din Muhammad, Shah Rukh, Ali Shar
Location Herat, Afghanistan **Style** Timurid **Materials** Brick, tile

The Masjid-i-Jami (Friday Mosque) in Herat is a stunning building with a long and checkered history. Its foundations were laid in the tenth century at a four-way intersection close to the city center. It was rebuilt in 1200 at the decree of the Ghurid ruler Ghiyath al-Din Muhammad (1162–1202). Within a century, Herat was invaded by the Mongols, and the mosque was devastated by fire and an earthquake. The exterior was refurbished by the Timurid ruler Shah Rukh who governed Herat from 1397 to 1447. When Shah Rukh became the supreme ruler of the Timurid empire in 1405, he made Herat his capital, and for fifty years it flourished as the leading intellectual and artistic center of the eastern Islamic world.

In 1500, the mosque was rebuilt under the supervision of the author and philanthropist Ali Shar (1441–1501). He refashioned the building in its present form following the traditional, four-*iwan* (vaulted hall) Iranian style. The 59-feet-span (18 m) *iwan*s face north, south, east, and west, and lead to domed hypostyle halls around a large courtyard. The western *iwan* is a *maqsura*, or screened *iwan*. A *madrassa* (religious school), which is still in use today, and the thirteenth-century mausoleum of Ghiyath al-Din Muhammad lie outside the northern *iwan*. In the twentieth century, the mosque was reconstructed and extended. There are now five entrances along the north and east walls, including a portal from the original mosque. Richly decorated tilework in geometric and floral designs in the Timurid style cover the entire building. **MC**

◥ The vivid blue, green, and saffron-colored tiles still shimmer with their original glory.

◿ Although substantially rebuilt over the centuries, the mosque remains a fine example of the Timurid style.

Temple of Confucius (1499)

Patron Duke Ai of the State of Lu   **Location** Qufu, Shandong Province, China   **Style** Confucian   **Materials** Wood, stone, marble

The Temple of Confucius (Kong Miao) originated shortly after the death of the sage and philosopher, Confucius in 479 BCE. The sage is buried under a tumulus at the temple. The complex expanded over more than 2,000 years, although it was badly damaged by Red Guards during the Maoist Cultural Revolution. A fire in 1499 damaged much of the temple, and most of the current complex dates from that time. The temple has nine courtyards, entered through a series of gates. It is laid out around a central axis, similar to the Forbidden City in Beijing. The Star of Literature

> *"I am not bothered … that I am unknown. I am bothered when I do not know others."*
>
> Confucius, *Analects of Confucius* (c. 479–221 BCE)

Pavilion was built in 1098, rebuilt in 1191, and houses a library on the upper story. Farther into the temple is the Hall of Great Achievement (Dachengdian), which has four towers at the courtyard corners. In front of the Dachengdian is the Apricot Pavilion (Xingtan). All the pavilions and halls are constructed in the traditional Chinese manner, with elegant use of red walls, yellow roofs, and carved white marble stonework. Confucian temples do not usually display images; their purpose is to honor the sage's teachings. However, at Qufu, which is still managed by Confucius's descendants, there are statues of him. As Confucian philosophy spread across East Asia, temples were progressively built in Korea, Vietnam, Indonesia, and Japan. The design of such temples was influenced by the original temple in Qufu. **ATB**

Basilica of St. Mary (1502)

Architect Henryk Ungeradin   **Location** Gdansk, Poland   **Style** Gothic   **Material** Brick

In 1343, having received permission from the Grand Master of the Teutonic Order Ludolf Konig of Wattzau, a foundation stone was laid to commence the 159-year construction of a new parish church in Gdansk. The first phase, completed in 1361, produced a modest structure subsequently incorporated into the west part of the basilica proper. Between 1379 and 1447 a major extension was constructed, including the transept, presbytery, and raised bell tower. Erection of external walls and internal vaulting completed the third phase of the project in 1502.

The Basilica of St. Mary is built on a Latin cross plan with a 346-feet-long (105 m) triple-aisled nave and 217-feet-wide (66 m) transept. The verticality is emphasized by a 269-feet-tall (82 m) bell tower, seven steeply pointed pinnacles, and pointed arch windows. It provides a good balance to the heavy, horizontal mass of the nave, capable of accommodating a 20,000-strong congregation. The internal location of buttresses breaks up the basilica's long elevations into a row of flanking chapels leaving smooth wall surfaces on the external facades, punctuated by the regular pattern of the thirty-seven stained-glass windows. The most conspicuous window is positioned on the east elevation and covers an area of 1,367 square feet (416 sq m). The refined quality of the architecture is matched by intricate net-and-crystal ceiling vaults, elevated to 98 feet (30 m) above the stone flooring by twenty-seven columns. The basilica is a prime example of brick architecture and the largest church in the world expressed in this material. It is also one of the largest brick Gothic buildings in Europe. The brilliance of French Gothic cathedrals is clearly evoked here, not with stone, however, but with simple modular blocks. **BK**

Tempietto di San Pietro in Montorio (1504)

Architect Donato Bramante   **Location** Rome, Italy
Style High Renaissance   **Materials** Travertine marble, stone

This martyrium, or sanctuary dedicated to a martyr, lies hidden within the cloister of San Pietro in Montorio, on the supposed site of St. Peter's martyrdom on the cross on the Gianicolo—one of the seven hills of Rome. King Ferdinand II and Queen Isabella I of Spain owned the land and ordered the construction of the complex in 1480 as fulfillment of a vow taken after the birth of their firstborn child.

Modeled on the Temple of Vesta at Tivoli, the proportions of the double-cylinder, two-story memorial are designed to Doric-order specifications with an encircling sixteen-pillar colonnade, an entablature modeled on the Theater of Marcellus, a balustrade, and a hemispherical dome with niches carved into its walls.

Donato Bramante's (1444–1514) first construction in Rome is one of sculptural grandeur. His emphasis on volumes and his command of form, proportions, lighting, spatial arrangements, and composition are evident in the sanctuary's design. His original plans for a centralized chapel inside a circular colonnaded cloister were never realized but he understood the principles of ancient architecture and chose to reshape its Classical forms. He conceived space not merely as a vacuum but as a positive, almost tangible presence. Bramante is credited with introducing the High Renaissance to Rome, a style of architecture that fused the ideals of Classical antiquity with those of Christian inspiration. His approach proved instrumental in ushering in Mannerism. **AA**

↖ The pleasing proportions of this High Renaissance building come from its emphatic symmetry.

← Bramante's design for a centralized chapel was never realized.

Hostal de Los Reyes Católicos (1509)

Architect Enrique de Egas **Location** Santiago de Compostela, Galicia, Spain **Style** Plateresque **Material** Stone

Santiago de Compostela is the last stop on the Christian pilgrimage route that stretches along across the Pyrenees to Galicia in Spain. Its cathedral is said to house the remains of the apostle St. James. The Hostal de Los Reyes Católicos lies adjacent to the Baroque facade of the cathedral on a large square called the Plaza del Obradoiro. It was founded *c.* 1492 after the Spanish reconquest of Granada by Queen Isabella I of Castile and King Ferdinand II of Aragon, who stipulated that part of the income from the war should be used to build a hostel and hospital for Santiago's visiting pilgrims. Since 1958, the building has been used as a *parador* (state-run hotel).

The Spanish-Flemish architect and sculptor Enrique de Egas (active 1490–1534) was commissioned to design the building. He was also the chief architect of the Santa Cruz Hospital at Toledo. Pilgrims and patients first used the building as a hospital in 1509, when it was one of the most well-equipped hospitals of its time. It is an elegant example of the ornate Spanish Plateresque style. Its stone facade has large areas of bare wall relieved by narrow windows, with touches of decoration in the form of sculpture and coats of arms around the windows and main entrance. The richness of the decoration is typical of the period, reflecting the wealth that Spain accumulated as it colonized Latin America. A narrow pathway in front of the Hostal de Los Reyes Católicos is delineated by a rope chain—at one time any criminal could seek refuge in this area and be free from arrest.

Inside the sumptuous building lie four colonnaded and interconnected courtyards; two were created in the sixteenth century complete with fountains; the other two courtyards, laid out in a Baroque style, were added in the eighteenth century. **CMK**

Villa Farnesina (1511)

Architect Baldassare Peruzzi **Location** Rome, Italy **Style** Renaissance **Materials** Brick, marble, stone

This two-story villa on the banks of the Tiber was built for Agostino Chigi, papal banker, arts patron, and richest man in Europe. The mansion underwent a period of decline before being snapped up by Cardinal Alessandro Farnese—hence its present name—in 1577, who connected it to the Palazzo Farnese opposite by means of a bridge.

Typical of early sixteenth-century Classical architecture, the villa's balanced and harmonious U-shaped plan consists of a garden facade with two lateral wings projecting from a central recessed block

> *"[Villa Farnesina's] perfection appears [to be] born rather than built ..."*
>
> Giorgio Vasari, biographer and critic

with loggia arcades. The frescoes on the front have long since vanished but there are terra cotta friezes crowning the second story, and slender pilasters interrupting the flat surfaces of the external facades.

The entrance hall on the ground floor leads visitors to the richly frescoed Galleria di Psiche (Loggia of Psyche), which looks out onto formal gardens. The Sala delle Prospettive (Hall of Perspectives) on the upper floor uses *trompe l'oeil* techniques that create the illusion of looking out onto views of sixteenth-century Rome through a marble colonnade. In keeping with Renaissance ideals, all of these astonishing frescoes provide a commentary on Chigi's hedonistic lifestyle, his interests in the pagan and Classical worlds, and his desire to be associated with the patricians of ancient Rome. **AA**

King's College Chapel (1515)

Architects Robert Ely, John Wastell **Location** Cambridge, England **Style** Perpendicular Gothic **Materials** Limestone, stained glass

"Where light and shade repose, where music dwells / Lingering— and wandering as loth to die . . ."

William Wordsworth, *Ecclesiastical Sonnets* (1821–22)

↑ Three different kings were involved in building King's College Chapel, which took more than seventy years.

→ The chapel features the world's largest fan vault, with enormous stained-glass windows.

King's College was founded by King Henry VI in 1441. Work on the chapel started in 1446, but was rudely interrupted in 1461 when the king's fortunes took a nosedive in the Wars of the Roses. Work began again in earnest in 1506, under the politically more stable regime of the first Tudor king, Henry VII. The building was completed under his son, King Henry VIII, in 1515.

For a structure with such a long building history, the chapel at King's College is remarkably simple and unified. It is essentially a single rectangular space lined with enormous stained-glass windows and topped by a fan vault of amazing delicacy. It is this very simplicity that makes the building so breathtaking—inside, the visitor or worshipper can take in at a single glance a glorious space in which the vertical lines of the window tracery lead the eye upward to the intricate vault, which seems to float with little visible support above the vast areas of glazing.

The overall design was the brainchild of King Henry VI's master mason, Robert Ely (active 1440s), although the vault was the work of his Tudor successor, John Wastell (c. 1460–c. 1518). Together, these two men created an outstanding example of a style of architecture called Perpendicular, a way of building in which all the elements—pilasters, columns, window mullions, paneling—have a vertical emphasis, leading the eye upward. This is a uniquely English style of later medieval architecture, as English as the heraldic symbols—portcullises, Tudor roses, and crowns— with which the chapel is decorated. And King's College Chapel is the finest example of the style.

Most of the stained glass is the work of Netherlandish craftsmen working under Henry VIII's master glaziers. The screen and stalls are outstanding pieces of Tudor carpentry and carving. In no other building of the period do these elements combine together so complementarily. **PW**

Imcheonggak Estate Buildings (1515)

Patron Yi Jeung **Location** Beopheungdong, Andong, Gyeongsangbukdo, South Korea **Style** Joseon **Material** Wood

Imcheonggak is one of the largest and most ancient examples of wooden housing used by Korea's Confucian nobility during the sixteenth century. Korean society at this time was deeply influenced by Confucian ideology. The upper classes in particular adopted the philosophy and were classified according to gender, age, and social status. The hierarchical division of society was reflected in the design of their homes, particularly in the case of the large homes of the nobility. Imcheonggak in Andong is representative of these imposing houses that were built in the provinces among the thatched cottages of the peasants. Such houses indicated a family's power and illustrated the simplicity and austerity of Confucian teachings. For example, in an effort to curtail extravagance, a law prohibited civilians from building houses with more than one hundred rooms; Imcheonggak originally had ninety-nine rooms, the largest number permitted for a civilian's home. Part of the estate was demolished to build a railway, and approximately fifty rooms remain today. Imcheonggak was built by the mayor of Yeongsan-hyeon, Yi Jeung, who fell in love with the area's scenic beauty. It consists of three elements: the main house and dwelling place; the Prince Pavilion (Gumjajeong); and a small building holding memorials of the ancestors, erected in the most private part of the residence. The house has a succession of rooms that are typified by their use, stretching from the semipublic to the most private. The outhouses form a barrier to the outside world. The so-called "inside outbuildings" lie around courtyards, and are for domestic use. They comprise the men's living quarters, the women's living quarters, and an area for close relatives. The Prince Pavilion was used by the male elders as a reception or a study. Outside is a veranda surrounded by a balcony. **FM**

Seville Cathedral (1520)

Architects Bartolomé Morel, Diego de Riaño **Location** Seville, Spain **Style** Gothic **Materials** Masonry, cut stone

Seville Cathedral is the third largest church in the world and one of the finest examples of Gothic architecture. After the Spanish reconquest of Seville in 1248, the existing Almohad mosque was consecrated as a Christian church. The mosque was demolished as Spain sought to build a cathedral on a massive scale that would symbolize the country's wealth and power. All that remains of the mosque is the entrance court, the *Patio de los Naranjos* complete with a fountain, and part of the Giralda bell tower that was originally a minaret. The latter was altered over the centuries to transform it into a bell tower, culminating in the addition of a weathervane of a woman, representing Christian faith, between 1566 to 1568 by Bartolomé Morel. Building began *c.* 1401 on the rectangular foundations of the original mosque and took just over a century to complete. The church has five aisles housed under a vaulted ceiling and Gothic central nave, flanked by small, decorative chapels. The main aisle opens onto the Capilla Mayor that houses a Gothic wooden retablo of scenes from the life of Christ. Behind it is the domed Renaissance burial chapel, and at the end of the first aisle is a series of rooms in Plateresque style designed in 1530 by Diego de Riaño (active 1526–34). An antechamber leads to the Renaissance-style chapter house with a domed ceiling. Beside it lies the main sacristy, again in the Plateresque style. **CMK**

> *"There are fully forty towers, which are lofty and well built, the largest of which has fifty steps ..."*
>
> Hernán Cortés, Spanish conquistador

Château de Chenonceau (1521)

Architects Philibert de l'Orme, Jean Bullant   **Location** Chenonceaux, Indre-et-Loire, France   **Style** French Renaissance   **Material** Stone

Chenonceau is a picturesque château and former royal residence built on and over the River Cher, in the city of Chenonceaux in the Loire Valley, set in formal gardens and a 173-acre (70 ha) park. Château de Chenonceau was begun in 1515 for Thomas Bohier, who built the simple, rectangular, four-towered keep standing on piles in the River Cher on the site of an old fortified mill of the Marques family.

A medieval keep, the Marques tower was transformed in the Renaissance style. The forecourt reproduces the layout of the former medieval castle, which was demarcated by moats. Externally, the building is elaborate, with ascending architectural masses, decorative windows, chimneys, and slate turrets. The château is surrounded by water and is connected to the left bank by an elegant three-story gallery built upon a five-arched bridge. The bridge was built by Philibert de l'Orme (c. 1510–70) for Diane de Poitiers between 1556 and 1559. The magnificent long gallery above it was built for Catherine de Medici by Jean Bullant (1515–78) in 1576. The gallery has a black-and-white checkered floor, exposed ceiling joists, and eighteen Mannerist windows.

The building is known as the Château de Femmes because it owes its development to two women: Diane de Poitiers, mistress of King Henry II, who was given the château by the king; and the king's wife, Catherine de Medici, who appropriated it when he died in 1559. The château changed its name from Chenonceaux to Chenonceau during the French Revolution to differentiate what was a symbol of royalty from the new republic. **JEH**

⬈ A former royal residence, Château de Chenonceau is completely surrounded by water.

⬅ The château is connected to the river's left bank by an elegant three-story gallery built on top of a bridge.

Villa Madama <small>(1525)</small>

Architect Raphael **Location** Rome, Italy **Style** Renaissance **Materials** Brick, marble

The Villa Madama was built for Cardinal Giulio de Medici, the nephew of Pope Leo X, and himself later Pope Clement VII. The villa stands outside the northern walls of Rome, on the slopes of the Monte Mario, and has marvelous views over the city and Vatican precinct. Its position made it an ideal summer retreat from the heat of the city, and sufficiently close for it to be used as luxurious lodgings for guests.

Raphael (1483–1520) was chosen to design the villa; at this time he was the leading figure of the artistic life of Rome and a connoisseur of Roman ruins. He built a villa replete with Classical references. Stretched out along the hillside, the villa has an amphitheater carved out from the hillside, and water garden or *nymphaeum* fed by water from springs channeled from the hillside. Only partially completed, the circular courtyard formed the centerpiece of the design, and a hippodrome and a theater were planned on either extremity of the building. These grandiose forms imitated the examples decribed in the writings of Pliny and seen at newly excavated sites such as the villa of Hadrian at Tivoli.

The external ornament was articulated by accurately reproduced rustic columns in the Doric and Ionic orders and was innovative for its balance between literary and archaeological references. The interior introduced techniques learned from the ruins of the Golden House of Nero. Its pristine white stucco low relief, vivid decorative *fresco grottesque* coffering, and mythological designs, combined to recreate the Roman palace villa as a setting suited to the ecclesiastical elite of the day. **FN**

↗ Raphael's sophisticated design draws on the technique and style of Classical Roman architecture.

→ The interior exemplifies the paradox of humanist teaching, blending pagan and Christian imagery.

Chapel of King Sigismund I (1533)

Architect Bartolomeo Berecci   **Location** Krakow, Poland   **Style** Renaissance   **Material** Stone

The year 1500 marks the beginning of the Golden Age in Poland, a period of unrivaled cultural, social, and scientific development in the country's history. The marriage of the Polish King Sigismund I to Bona from the Milanese Sforza dynasty brought about an explosion of Renaissance art and initiated an influx of renowned Italian artists to Poland. A significant number of notable designs were conceived during this era—the Chapel of King Sigismund I, contained within the royal castle complex on the Wawel Hill, being the most outstanding of these magnificent buildings constructed in the sixteenth century. Designed as one of eighteen tomb chapels flanking the Wawel Cathedral, its floorplan is based on a shallow Greek cross and houses the tombs of King Sigismund I, his children, and Poland's monarchs, Sigismund II Augustus and Anne the Jagiellon. Its upper section, a stone octagonal drum punctuated by

circular windows, supports a gold-finished dome topped with a glazed lantern, and a cross. The identical design of three internal walls, reminiscent of a Classical triumphal arch, includes ornamental scenes from Roman mythology. Numerous sculptures, medallions, stuccoes, and paintings executed by eminent Renaissance artists complete this architectural gem. Inside and out, this finely proportioned chapel constitutes one of the best-preserved examples of the essence of Renaissance style in architecture. **BK**

"[The Chapel is] the pearl of Renaissance architecture built north of the Alps."

August Essenwein, architectural historian

Palazzo del Te (1534)

Architect Giulio Romano **Location** Mantua, Italy **Style** Mannerist **Materials** Marble, stone

This moat-surrounded residence was originally a farm with stables. Duke Federico II, philanderer and scion of the local Gonzaga dynasty, invited Giulio Romano (c. 1499–1546), a former pupil of Raphael, to carry out major architectural and pictorial renovations for what was to become his mistress's summer villa, and his own personal pleasure-palace complete with guest rooms around a grotto and cascade—the *Playboy* mansion of its day. Mannerist architecture places greater emphasis on decorative qualities than on structural relationships, and the Palazzo del Te is no exception. A square block organized around a cloistered courtyard with formal gardens enclosed by colonnaded outbuildings framing contrived vistas through their arches and doors, its four facades flirt with Classical elements such as columns, pediments, archivolts, and triglyphs, as well as Palladian motifs and grotesques. Visually, there is much to divert the

visitor. The frescoes inside feature steamy erotica, and larger-than-life murals of gods and nymphs. The Fall of the Titans, a grand-scale, illusionistic sequence of the destruction of the Titans at the hands of the Olympian gods, is furiously unleashed across the walls, windows, and ceiling of the Sala dei Giganti (Hall of the Giants) like a three-dimensional film projection. Even the chamber's formidable acoustics operate like a stereophonic sound system where paper can be heard being torn several rooms away. **AA**

"One cannot hope to see a more terrifying or naturalistic work than [Palazzo del Te]."

Giorgio Vasari, biographer and critic

Cotehele House (1539)

Patron Sir Richard Edgecumbe   **Location** St. Dominick, Saltash, Cornwall, England   **Style** Medieval, Tudor   **Materials** Granite, slatestone, slate

Little has changed at Cotehele since the mid-seventeenth century. Set in formal gardens near the River Tamar in Cornwall, the architecture of Cotehele today flaunts its history. Cotehele consists of a huge stone triple-court-plan house with castellated tower, chapel, and dovecote. Many of the windows are small, and look out onto enclosed courts. The house has grandly named rooms, such as King Charles's Room, so called because the king purportedly slept there in 1644. Initially built on land owned by the De Cotehele family from the mid-fourteenth century, when Hilaria de Cotehele married William Edgecumbe it stayed with the Edgecumbes for the next six centuries. Sir Richard Edgecumbe (c. 1433–89) began to remodel the medieval remains of Cotehele in the last four years of his life, followed by his son Piers. Maintaining much of the medieval stonework, Richard rebuilt the chapel and the north range, using granite and a Gothic style.

The medieval-style grand hall, with its decorative and strong arch-braced trusses, is an exquisite example of sixteenth-century carving. Small changes were made in subsequent centuries, such as the spiral staircase being replaced by straight stairs in the 1650s, and the ceiling of the White Room in the tower decorated with geometrically arranged wooden ribs, believed to date from the 1750s when antiquarianism was at full height. It is a building subtly altered, whose renovations tell the story of a grand house through the ages. **SL**

> "Mansion after mansion posssessing even the interest of Cotehele . . . was taken down."
>
> Reverend F. V. J. Arundell, author and archaeologist

Palazzo Vecchio (1540)

Architects Arnolfo di Cambio, Michelozzo di Bartolomeo **Location** Florence, Italy **Style** Gothic **Material** Sandstone

The fortified medieval city hall of Florence is attributed to the sculptor and architect Arnolfo di Cambio (c. 1245–1310), and was originally named Palazzo dei Priori after the priors who governed the city. Reflecting the internal conflict and factionalism that characterized the era, the Palazzo Vecchio was built on land confiscated from the opposition Uberti family, thus creating an architectural expression of the force of the commune to overpower internal rivalries. Fierce rusticated stonework in local *pietra forte* (strong stone) gives the building a militaristic feel that is reinforced by the high windows, prominent heraldry, and projecting balcony topped with crenelations. The bell tower, topped by a belfry resembling the palace's forms in miniature, creates a pivot around which the public space and government palace interact. Running along the front of the building is a high stone podium from which the government announced decisions to the city community. Behind the defensive exterior is a sophisticated Renaissance palace, focused around an arcaded courtyard resembling that of the Medici Palace. This is the result of reordering of the building around 1450, promoted by the Medici family who increasingly came to control Florentine affairs and were able to ensure that their favored architect, Michelozzo di Bartolomeo (1396–1472), supervised the improvements. Beyond the courtyard a mazelike sequence of rooms originally housed diverse political offices, but was transformed in the mid-1500s to serve as a palace for the Medici family, who had become rulers of the city. The most impressive architectural space of the interior is the Sala dei Cinquecento (Room of the 500), so called for the number of citizens it could accommodate for government assemblies held during the last gasps of the Florentine Republic prior to the rule of the Medici family. **FN**

Falkland Palace (1541)

Patron King James V of Scotland **Location** Cupar, Falkland, Fife, Scotland **Style** Renaissance **Materials** Stone, slate roofing

Not only did King James V of Scotland (1512–42) like dressing up as a peasant and wandering around incognito, he was an obsessive Francophile. When he decided to rebuild his hunting-lodge at Falkland he went scouting around the Loire Valley with a French master-mason, Moses Martin, to get ideas to ensure his latest edifice would pass muster with the French court. He had his reasons: he was married in 1537 to Madeleine de Valois, daughter of King Francis I of France. When she died a few months later, he then married Marie de Guise, daughter of Claude, Duke of Guise. Significantly, the treaties setting up both marriages detailed that Falkland Palace was to be given to his brides in the event of his predeceasing them. Built largely by French masons, and resplendent with Renaissance detailing up to date with the latest architectural styles of the French court, Falkland was laid out on a square plan around a central courtyard.

The south courtyard front has some of the most engaging stone carvings of its period in Britain, an array of character types from young woman to venerable soldiers, set within luxuriant wreaths. Yet the main street frontage adopts a veneer of subterfuge. It is in Late Gothic style, misleading historians into thinking it was earlier than the Renaissance courtyard on the other side when it was in fact contemporaneous but represents a serious, churchlike foil to the more frivolous splendors within. **NC**

"The facade is purely French, of the Loire school [and is] earlier of its kind than anything in England."

John Summerson, architectural historian

Palazzo Pitti (1549)

Architects Filippo Brunelleschi, Luca Fancelli, Bartolomeo Ammannati   **Location** Florence, Italy   **Style** Renaissance   **Materials** Stone, marble

Luca Pitti, Florentine merchant, politician, friend, and sometime rival of Cosimo de' Medici the Elder, commissioned Filippo Brunelleschi (1377–1446) to design a residence that would surpass Palazzo Vecchio in size and content. The original design was a central block, equal in both height and depth, over three floors with three entrances at ground level, and seven windows on each side of the two upper floors. The project lay unfinished until the property was sold to Eleonora of Toledo, wife of Cosimo I de' Medici, in 1549. Numerous additions followed. The heavily rusticated stonework facade, later incorporated into the vast extensions made at either side of the palace, was originally characterized by three rows of seven-arched bays reminiscent of a Roman aqueduct. Six hundred years later, the result is a massive building complex: twenty-three bays long on the first floor, and thirteen on the top floor. Sixteenth-century floorplans indicate there were major divisions between the ceremonial and residential functions of the palace. Bartolomeo Ammannati's (1511–92) clustered family apartments may be seen as a characteristic feature of Medicean residences, and records of official visits suggest the vastness of the residence was due to diplomatic protocol and the constant entertaining of visitors at the Medicean court. The setting of Palazzo Pitti extends to the Boboli Gardens, one of the earliest examples of Italian gardens with fountains and grottoes, created by the Medicis in 1550. The architectural merit of Palazzo Pitti is in its outer severity. Stuffed with treasure, it houses the Royal Apartments of the Medicis, the Palatine Gallery, paintings, sculptures, porcelain, silverware, and a costume gallery. The official residence of one ruling family, it has also played host to other dynasties such as the Bourbons, Bonapartes, and Savoys. **AA**

Tomb
of Askia (c. 1550)

Patron Askia Muhammad Touré **Location** Gao, Mali, West Africa
Style Sudanese **Materials** Earth, acacia wood

At the end of the fifteenth century, Gao was the capital of the Songhai empire, stretching from the Atlantic coast to Saharan and central Africa. With city populations to rival those in Europe, this massive empire was ruled by Askia Muhammad Touré (c. 1442–1538). Credited with the establishment of Tombouctou as a seat of religious learning, he is best known for his work to consolidate the progress of Islam across the region. In 1528 he ceded power to his warring sons and is said to be buried in the mausoleum in Gao.

The complex is built entirely of earth and timber, and at its center stands a burial pyramid. It is ascended by a set of narrow spiraling steps, punctuated by a hazardous, vertical drop, and terminating in a small opening which permits a *muezzin* (the person who leads the call to prayer) to access the loudspeakers mounted on the summit. The pyramid stands in the assembly courtyard between two low mosques, which are supported by elephantine columns. There is no shortage of remarkable earth buildings in the Sahel region. Mosques and grand dwellings alike are cited as examples of the Sudanese style later popularized by colonial-era postcards. However, where others tend to a regular geometry, the Tomb of Askia, with its more sculptural form and free arrangement of the scaffold timbers, is unique. In a city where the trade of gold, salt, and slaves has ebbed but not died, and where tourists are still a novelty the Tomb of Askia is a fusion of Sahel urbanism, African Islamic architecture, living heritage, and audacious form-making. **HF**

↖ The pyramid is covered with gnarled stakes of wood that provide scaffolding for replastering the mud.

← A view through the prayer room that forms part of the long rectangular building adjacent to the tomb.

Jerónimos Monastery (1552)

Architects Boitac, De Castilho, De Torralva **Location** Belém, Portugal
Style Manueline **Materials** Stone, wood

Originally called the Hieronymites Monastery, Jerónimos was commissioned in the sixteenth century by King Manuel I, on the site of the Santa Maria chapel, a popular place of worship among the seafaring community that was originally built at the behest of Manuel's ancestor Prince Henry the Navigator. It was intended to be a burial monument for the Portuguese royal lineage. However, its purpose was changed to honor the return of explorer Vasco de Gama from India, who prayed at the chapel on the eve of his epic journey and whose tomb is one of the monastery's historical monuments.

Diogo Boitac (c. 1460–1528) designed the monastery, and was later succeeded in 1517 by João de Castilho (c. 1475–1552). At that time Belém was the main port of Lisbon, and Portugal was arguably the richest country in the world. The workmanship on its highly detailed facades and interiors is masterful. The architect Diogo de Torralva (1500–66) resumed construction in 1550, adding the main chapel, the choir, and completing two stories of monastery. Jérôme de Rouen (1530–1601) continued his work from 1571. Its style is a synthesis of Late Gothic with Spanish Plateresque, shot through with nautical references, and can be described as Manueline. Eminent sculptors such as Costa Mota and Nicolau Chanterene also made contributions to the project. The vast ornate building has chapels, cloisters, a church, and the tombs of many Portuguese monarchs. The monastery also houses the remains of the poets Luis de Camões—the Portuguese Shakespeare—and Fernando Pessoa. Jerónimos features designs, such as the two-story cloister, that were seen as daring at the time. It is considered to be the best example of Manueline period architecture in the world. **MDC**

Süleymaniye Mosque (1557)

Architect Mimar Sinan **Location** Istanbul, Turkey
Style Ottoman **Materials** Stone, Iznik tiles, stained-glass windows

Crowning the Third Hill in Istanbul is the vast complex of domes and minarets that is the Süleymaniye (see page 20), the finest of the city's mosques. It dominates the skyline, just as its founder, Süleyman the Magnificent, dominates Ottoman history. It stands as a monument not only to the greatest of the sultans but also to Mimar Sinan (1489–1588), his chief architect. Born a Christian, Sinan was drafted into the elite Corps of Janissaries and forcibly converted to Islam. He was the chief architect of the Ottoman empire, responsible for no fewer than eighty mosques, thirty-four palaces,

> *"Architecture is the most difficult of professions, and he who would practice it must … be pious."*
>
> **Mimar Sinan, architect**

and countless schools, hospitals, tombs, and public baths. When Süleyman decided to raise his own mosque in 1550, he inevitably turned to Sinan.

The basic plan, with a huge, 90-foot-wide (27 m) central dome flanked by two semidomes, follows that of Hagia Sophia, built one thousand years earlier. However, in Hagia Sophia the central area beneath the dome is separated from the aisles by colonnades on each side. In the Süleymaniye, Sinan made his supporting piers so tall and spaced them so far apart that he created the impression of a single vast continuum. Decoration is restrained: only the stained-glass windows and the Iznik tiles—turquoise, coral red, and deep blue—provide color. With four minarets that are the highest in Turkey, the Süleymaniye mosque is the crowning glory of Islamic Istanbul. **JJN**

Cathedral of Our Lady, Antwerp (1559)

Architects Jan Appelmans, Pieter Appelmans **Location** Antwerp, Belgium **Style** Gothic, Renaissance **Material** Stone

This Gothic building—built between 1353 and 1533—replaced an earlier Romanesque church on the site. Its north tower of 405-feet-high (123 m) north tower was completed in 1518 and was intended to be accompanied by a second, which was never built further than the main roof level. Consecrated as a cathedral in 1559, it is a dominant landmark in the city, while its interior, with its triple aisles, is typical of northern Gothic "hall church." Although it is unusually large, the Holy Roman Emperor Charles V laid the foundation stone for an extension that would have

> *"The luminosity of the upper stories . . . contrasts with the dim ground story aisles and chapels."*
>
> Jacques Thiébaut, architectural historian

made it three times its existing size. In 1533, the still unfinished building was partly destroyed by fire. The reconstruction coincided with the Flemish Renaissance, resulting in an elision of Gothic and Classical forms that blend harmoniously beneath a coat of whitewash inside the cathedral. The bulbous lantern over the crossing creates a light-filled heaven.

Much of the cathedral's original decoration was destroyed by iconoclastic Protestants in the mid-sixteenth century. Among the main attractions is the series of paintings by Peter Paul Rubens. The pulpit is dated 1713 and was brought to the cathedral in 1814. With the carved organ case, it is the perfect accompaniment to Rubens. Changes to the building include the carving of the main portal in a Neo-Gothic style in the early twentieth century. **AP**

Villa Farnese (1559)

Architects Antonio da Sangallo, Giacomo Barozzi da Vignola **Location** Caprarola, Viterbo, Italy **Style** Mannerist **Material** Stone

Temperatures in Rome rise to unbearable levels in the summer months, and led to the affluent members of Renaissance society to leave for cooler and more pleasant areas around the city, the so-called *villeggiatura*. A rich and powerful family, such as the Farnese, demonstrated their wealth and social position by creating splendid, dominant, buildings. Their *palazzo* (town house) in Rome—now the Italian president's official residence—is a powerful building in itself. However, it does not have the dramatic impact of their country residence, sited as it is on a slight hill dominating the little town of Caprarola, in the province of Viterbo.

The building looks like a fortress, with massive, stone walls looming high over the small houses of the town. In the manner beloved of the Renaissance rediscovery of antiquity, the architecture of the building is harmoniously united with the gardens. Indeed the whole of the little town beneath the villa was reordered around a wide new main street, the better to frame the approach to the building.

The builder was Cardinal Alessandro Farnese, the grandson of Pope Paul III. The project was begun by Antonio da Sangallo (1484–1546) who probably devised the pentagonal plan and the innovative circular courtyard—a Renaissance invention that deviated from the usual layout of ancient Roman villas. When Sangallo died in 1546, Giacomo Barozzi da Vignola (1507–73) took over. He worked on the villa until his death and turned the project into a Mannerism masterwork.

Vignola was the author of two architectural treatises, one on the Classical orders and another on the art of perspective. Villa Farnese at Caprarola is his chief surviving building. **EG**

Villa
Barbaro (1560)

Architect Andrea Palladio **Location** Maser, Veneto, Italy
Style Renaissance, Palladian **Materials** Brick, plaster

Andrea Palladio (1508–80) remodeled an existing house to create a villa that is one of his most famous works, although it is also the least typical of his authenticated works. The reason can be found in his clients—the brothers Daniele and Marc'Antonio Barbaro—and the villa's appearance owes as much to them as to Palladio. Daniele was a scholar, diplomat, and, in due course, a churchman who published a translation of Vitruvius, illustrated by Palladio. Marc'Antonio was a statesman, diplomat, and amateur sculptor, to whom some of the sculpture around the Nymphaeum in the garden is attributed.

Construction of the villa began after a visit to Rome by Palladio and Daniele Barbaro. More eclectic in its sources than any other villa by Palladio, it shows evidence of his studies of modern buildings as well as antique ones, particularly Raphael's Villa Madama and Pirro Ligorio's designs for the Villa d'Este, which inspired the Nymphaeum. It is alone among the villas of his middle period in not having a portico, but is still templelike in projecting boldly forward from its wings and having Ionic pilasters and a pediment. Unusually, the wings always contained living accommodation rather than forming part of the farm buildings, and the fronts of the pavilions at each end bear sundials. The T-shaped plan is probably in part a response to its setting, against a hill with views down over the Barbaro estates. The frescoes in the villa by Paolo Veronese, executed 1559–62, mostly depict divine dalliances or celebrate the Barbaro family. **CWH**

↗ The facade of the villa, with its pilasters and pediment, gently integrates Classical references.

→ The villa revels in the act of sight itself: as viewed subject and as the provider of splendid views.

Cathedral of St. Basil the Blessed (1561)

Architect Postnik Yakovlev   **Location** Red Square, Moscow, Russia   **Style** Russian Orthodox   **Materials** Brick, limestone

The Cathedral of the Virgin of the Intercession on the Moat—or as it is popularly known the Cathedral of St. Basil the Blessed—is both a monument and a symbol. It was built on the chief marketplace of Moscow by order of Ivan IV (1530–84), known as Ivan the Terrible, to commemorate the capture of Kazan in 1554, thus finally freeing Russia from the threat of the Golden Horde. Its location in the busiest part of the city also reminded the people of the strength and might of the czarist state. The popular name commemorates St. Basil the Blessed, who became famous for his denunciation of the atrocities of Ivan IV.

Like the capital city itself, the church was to represent on earth the Heavenly Zion. The architect, Postnik "Barma" Yakovlev, planned a symmetrical group of eight chapels around a central pillar structure. The plan is extremely complex and resembles an eight-pointed star. The interior spaces are small, gloomy cells, apart from the central church, which is 210 feet (64 m) high. There are no paintings, which allows the wall surface to be articulated with pilasters, arches, niches, and cornices. According to a traditional story, the czar had Yakovlev blinded to prevent him from ever building anything so beautiful again.

The basic structure of the building has remained unchanged, apart from minor modifications. The key changes were made in the 1670s, when the building was painted in bright colors reminiscent of folk embroidery. As a result, the building typifies for non-Russians what a Russian Orthodox church should look like and formed the model for numerous Russian Revival churches of the nineteenth century. **CWH**

◥ The distinctive appearance of the Cathedral of St. Basil the Blessed has come to typify a Russian church.

◁ The onion-shaped domes with their swirling colors dominate Moscow's Red Square.

Ali Ben Youssef Madrassa (1565)

Patron Abdallah Ghâlib **Location** Marrakech, Morocco **Style** Saadian **Materials** Stone, mud brick, tile, cedar wood, marble

This is one of the largest *madrassas* (Koranic schools) in the Maghreb, the area of Islamic North Africa that lies west of Egypt and north of the Atlas Mountains. Until it closed down in 1960, up to 900 students lived here, studying religion, rhetoric, and Koranic law.

Founded by the Merinid Sultan Aban el-Hassan in the mid-fourteenth century, it was named after the twelfth-century Almoravid Sultan Ali Ben Youssef (*d.* 1142). It was subsequently almost completely rebuilt during the Saadian dynasty in 1564 to 1565 by Abdallah Ghâlib and laid out on a quadrilateral plan around a central courtyard.

The *madrassa* is accessed from the street down a richly ornamented corridor, with marble basins at either end. It leads directly into a main courtyard with a large white marble pool at its center. Every surface is covered in intricate decoration, with marble and tiles below stuccowork, crowned by carved cedar wood coving, all decorated with patterns, and calligraphic passages from the Koran. The ornament bears striking similarities to that of the Alhambra Palace in Granada, Spain, pointing at the possibility that the same craftsmen worked on both buildings.

Along either side of the courtyard run two parallel arcades; above lie rooms for students that are basic and plain in their appointment, in contrast with the decorative courtyard. Seven subsidiary courtyards are tucked away from view. The main focus of the *madrassa* is an elaborate prayer hall at the back of the courtyard. It has a pyramidal cedar wood dome and elaborate carving, with an exquisitely carved horseshoe-shaped arch framing a prayer niche. **RGW**

↗ Every surface of the Ali Ben Youssef Madrassa is intricately decorated with patterned tiles and marble.

↱ The elaborate horseshoe-shaped arch in the prayer hall is exquisitely carved from cedar wood.

Virupaksha Temple (1565)

Architect Unknown   **Location** Karnataka, India   **Style** South Indian (Dravidian)   **Materials** Granite (chloritic schist and soapstone)

Toward the south of the Indian Peninsula, in a bowl of rocky granite terrain reined in by the intemperate Tungabhadra River lies the spectacular ruins of Hampi. This fourteenth-century city was the capital of the great Vijayanagar empire and reached its zenith under Krishnadevaraya (r. 1509–29). The city spreads over an area of about 16 square miles (41 sq km), and at the core is the Virupaksha, or Pampapati Temple, which predates the Vijayanagar empire. It was extended between the thirteenth and sixteenth centuries while Hampi was built around it. The temple's stones carry masonry marks referring to orientation and location, which suggests that they were dressed and shaped at source before being brought to the current location. The temple has three towers, the largest of which has nine tiers and rises to 160 feet (48 m). The tower, a *gopuram*, is typical of Hindu temple entrances in southern India. It leads to an inner precinct full of shrines and pillars that date back to the thirteenth century. From here the complex extends like a colonnaded street for more than half a mile through two smaller, tiered towers leading to a huge statue of the bull deity, Nandi. While the rest of Hampi lies in ruins since its destruction in the sixteenth century, this Dravidian temple, dedicated to Shiva and his consort Pampa, continues to be used for pilgrimage. It is a living remnant of an extraordinary city that was once the center of a dynamic and sophisticated empire. **BS**

"As you enter the site great mountains of granite rock burst out of the earth ..."

Shobita Punja, Indian National Trust executive

Château de Chambord (1566)

Architect Domenico da Cortona **Location** Chambord, Loire et Cher, France **Style** Renaissance **Material** Stone

The Château de Chambord was constructed for King François I soon after his return from the French campaign in Italy, and its style can be directly linked to the monarch's wish to adopt new Italian models. Leonardo da Vinci, who is known to have accompanied the king on his return from Italy, has been tentatively connected to the château, although he died at Amboise soon after the building's inception in 1519. Domenico da Cortona, a Tuscan artist involved in other royal castle projects, supervised construction of the château and provided wooden design models. The castle is built on an unprecedented scale, a rectangular plan of 511 feet (156 m) on its major facades, marked at each corner by enormous round towers, the fantastic outline of the upper parts bristle with 300 chimneys, dormer windows, and turrets. The core of the building is its keep, or *donjon*, a centralized structure 144 feet square (44 m sq), with a main hall built to a Greek cross plan that may derive from Donato Bramante's original plans for St. Peter's Basilica in Rome. Beyond its massive scale, fairytale skyline, and Italianate use of classical ornament, the château's most remarkable feature is the unusual interlocked, double-helix, open-work staircase that people can ascend and descend simultaneously without meeting. It is this feature in particular that has been linked to Leonardo. The actual function of the castle is not entirely clear, and in spite of the fact that François I paid special attention to the project, it is known that he visited it rarely and died before its completion. While it may therefore be considered an architectural testament to the monarch's Italian ambitions, its setting within a massive park of 13,425 acres (5,433 ha) demonstrates that it also served as a very grand hunting lodge. The park was landscaped in 1682 by Jules Hardouin-Mansart. **FN**

Lahore Fort (1566)

Patrons Mughal and Sikh rulers   **Location** Lahore, Pakistan   **Style** Mughal   **Materials** Marble, brick masonry, red sandstone, tiles, mosaic

The history of Lahore Fort reaches back into the recesses of Indian history, with excavations at the site suggesting it was inhabited before the conquest of Lahore by Mahmood of Ghazni in 1021. The substantial and imposing structure seen today is one that has been added to over the centuries, starting most significantly in 1566 when the Mughal emperor Akbar replaced and extended the existing mud-built fort with one of brick masonry. Lahore was an important city in the Mughal empire, strategically located between the other great Mughal strongholds of Kashmir, Kabul, and Multan. It was also the site of the first Mughal conquests in India, so it was both fitting and necessary for the city to boast a grand and functional fort. Following Akbar's initial rebuilding, the successive emperors—Jahangir, the Shah Jahan, Aurangzeb, and Maharaja Ranjit Singh—greatly enhanced the fortification by adding new and highly decorative buildings. The layout is strictly organized and not dissimilar to that of the Agra Fort, with areas divided into private and public (administrative) sections. The palatial private quarters occupy the northern side and are accessed through the Elephant Gate, while the more public areas used by the emperors for state occasions are accessed via the impressive Alamgiri Gateway built by Aurangzeb. The monumental gates, which substantiate the power and prestige of the different emperors, also needed to allow for an elephant to pass through them. Shah Jahan is remembered for his love of ornate and opulent architecture—he also built the Taj Mahal. The Hall of Mirrors (Shish Mahal) and white marble Naulakha Pavilion are other examples of his elaborate style. He was also the first to build a Mughal mosque inside the fort, again crafted from white marble, which is now a distinctive feature of the fort complex. **TP**

Villa Emo (1567)

Architect Andrea Palladio **Location** Fanzolo di Vedelago, Italy **Style** Renaissance Classicism **Materials** Brick, plaster

Until 2005, the Villa Emo was the only villa by Palladio to have passed by direct male descent from the original client. It was designed for the Venetian nobleman Leonardo Emo to celebrate his impending marriage to Cornelia Grimani in 1565. The villa faces a public road, and all its decoration is concentrated on that side. The rear is totally plain and lacks any architectural elaboration. The villa is one of the very few to correspond almost exactly to the woodcuts of it in Palladio's *I Quattro Libri dell'Architettura* (1570). It has a grand simplicity that appealed particularly to English Palladian architects in the early eighteenth century. Unusually, the *piano nobile* is approached by a sloping ramp rather than a formal flight of steps, which has led to the unlikely suggestion that it was used as a threshing floor. Inside, the plan is strictly symmetrical, with three rooms on each side flanking a central square salon, the three rooms all being in proportion to each other—1:1, 1:2, and 1:3. The unusually well-preserved frescoes are by Giambattista Zelotti, a frequent collaborator of Palladio. They depict episodes from mythology, Roman history, and allegorical subjects, the general theme being that the subjugation of passion and the practice of virtue can only be achieved in the countryside. The painted architecture in each room is more than usually well proportioned. Outside, the formal garden was laid out in the late nineteenth century. **CWH**

> *"In its simplicity, the Villa Emo observes the basic principles of Palladio's architecture . . ."*
>
> Bruce Boucher, art historian

Palazzo dei Conservatori del Campidoglio (1568)

Architect Michelangelo Buonarrotti, Giacomo della Porta   **Location** Rome, Italy   **Style** Renaissance   **Materials** Travertine marble, stone

Embarrassed by the state of the Capitoline Hill (*Campidoglio*) following a visit to Rome by Emperor Charles V in 1536, Pope Paul III ordered Michelangelo (1475–1564) to draw up plans for a dramatic makeover. The scheme involved a trapezoid-shaped piazza and remodeling of the existing buildings—Palazzo dei Conservatori and Palazzo Senatorio. Michelangelo's space-saving design included a paving pattern with an interlaced twelve-pointed star to mark the epicenter of Roman might, and a new building—the Palazzo Nuovo—that would thematically link the other two structures. Work began on this building one year before Michelangelo's death. The flatness of the facade is broken up by giant Corinthian pilasters that link the upper and lower stories, and by smaller Ionic pillars framing the sides of the loggias and second-story windows. A balustrade with statues adorns the straight entablature and flat roof to accentuate the upward pull of the columns. Palazzo dei Conservatori and Palazzo Nuovo constitute the Capitoline Museums, the oldest existing public collection in the world, begun by Pope Sixtus IV in 1471. Michelangelo effectively shifted the orientation of Rome's civic center to the west: away from the Roman Forum toward the Vatican. The square's layout with its flanking palazzi is the first urban instance of "the cult of the axis"—*Caput mundi*—that so influenced later Italian and French garden design. **AA**

> *"The Capitoline Hill remains a magnificent setting overlooking the heart of this ancient city."*
>
> J. Carter Brown, Pritzker Prize jury for architecture

Town Hall (c. 1570)

Architect Hans Hendrik van Paesschen   **Location** Lübeck, Germany   **Style** Romanesque, Gothic, Renaissance   **Materials** Brick, limestone

Lübeck was the most important city among the 100 cities forming the Hanseatic League, a trading organization established by merchant communities across the Baltic Sea and northern Europe. The League commanded the region's seaborne economies from the thirteenth to the fifteenth centuries, bringing huge wealth to its cities. The Town Hall (Rathaus) was begun in 1226 in a late Romanesque style, still evident in its great pillared and vaulted cellars. Arranged over three houses, it functioned as a cloth hall and interior market. The tall house gables, constructed in dark glazed brick, conjoin into an astonishing top story featuring pointed spires and pierced roundels open to the wind. When Lübeck was granted the status of free imperial city by Holy Roman Emperor Frederick II in 1226, the result was a statute of laws known as the "laws of Lübeck" adopted by the League. Large parts of the Rathaus were subsequently rebuilt, with a Long

Hall added in 1298 and a further reception hall or *Audienzsaal* built in the Gothic style in 1442. This in turn was redecorated as a Rococo setting in the eighteenth century. The last major architectural addition to the Rathaus was the elegant Dutch Renaissance style limestone building added to the wing looking onto Breitenstrasse in c. 1570. Authorship of this new addition is possibly owed to Hans Hendrik van Paesschen (1510–1582), an architect of great feeling working across Northern Europe some consider should be accorded the praise given to his contemporaries Andrea Palladio in Italy and Philibert Delorme in France. The great Renaissance doorway (1573) leading into the Audienzsaal from the Market Square is credited to Tonnies Evers the Elder (c. 1540– c. 1580). The League dissolved in 1630 due to competition from the Dutch, but the Lübeck Senate still convenes in the Rathaus. **MI**

Florence Baptistery (1571)

Architects Andrea Pisano, Lorenzo Ghiberti, others | **Location** Florence, Italy | **Style** Tuscan Romanesque | **Materials** Marble, stone, gilded bronze

"A masterpiece of ... construction, intriguing modifications, and priceless embellishments."

Giorgio Saviane, architect

⬆ Visitors enter by the baptistery's south gate, with gilded bronze doors by Andrea Pisano.

➡ Christ surrounded by hierarchies of angels, apostles, patriarchs, and saints on the baptistery ceiling.

The imposing Baptistery of San Giovanni situated across from the Duomo has sixth-century foundations that hark back to a time of cultural rebirth in Florence following centuries of barbarian invasions. The building's octagonal geometry—which includes the lantern-topped pyramidal-shaped roof—is defined by classical proportions and ancient heraldic symbols, such as the Florentine lion. Complex white and dark-green marble patterning distinguishes all eight sides, with each face characterized by horizontal bands, rectangles, blind arches, and deep-set windows that allow light into the interior. The upper fascia contains windows set within a series of three-panel designs.

The figurative art of the celebrated doors marks the dawn of the Renaissance. Pisano (c. 1290–1349) cast the south entrance in gilded bronze with figures in relief taken from the life of John the Baptist. Ghiberti (1368–1445) crafted those of the north entrance to show scenes from the New Testament. Using a workmanship similar to Pisano's, but showing greater perspective, depth, and naturalism, he went on to create ten masterpiece panels for the east entrance. Michelangelo dubbed these "the Gates of Paradise" for their astonishing beauty.

The interior is fairly somber, but the walls are faced with colored marbles and gilded capitals. Granite columns separate wall niches, and arches resting on pilasters open on the ambulatory or gallery. The architrave, semicircular apse, and domed ceiling are encrusted with gold Byzantine mosaics. Red, green, black, and white Moorish-style inlays adorn the floor.

San Giovanni's breathtaking compositional equilibrium fuses architectural perfection, exquisite craftsmanship, and precious materials to convey the salvation of the spirit inherent in the Christian baptismal rite. Traditionally, all infants born in Florence of Catholic parents are baptized here. **AA**

Casa de Pilatos (1571)

Architects Tortello, De Bisono, De Aprile, Pulido brothers **Location** Seville, Spain **Style** Mudéjar, Renaissance, Gothic **Materials** Brick, marble

The Casa de Pilatos is one of Seville's finest palaces, and is currently a museum and the residence of the Duke of Medinaceli. The house is a mix of Mudéjar, Renaissance, and Gothic styles, and its dimensions are supposedly the same as that of the building inhabited by the biblical figure, Pontius Pilate, hence its name. The house was bought by Don Pedro Enríquez, the former governor of Andalucia, and his wife Catalina de Ribera. But it was his son, Fadrique, who initiated its redesign. Fadrique returned from a pilgrimage to Jerusalem and tour of Europe in 1519. He was so impressed by the architecture he had seen—in Italy in particular—that he resolved to make the family home a showcase of innovative style. The house was completed by Per Afán de Ribera, first Duke of Alcalá. The main entrance is a Renaissance marble arch, built in 1529 by the Italian artist Antonio de Aprile. It leads into a porticoed courtyard, typical of Andalucian mansions, used for the entry of horses and carriages. This, in turn, leads to the 270-square-foot (25 sq m) main courtyard, which is surrounded by a series of irregular arches consisting of Mudéjar plasterwork, Classical columns, and Gothic balustrades. A stunning staircase decorated with elaborate tilework and covered by a coffered ceiling leads to apartments on the upper floor of the building. The courtyard opens onto two gardens—the larger one contains loggias created by the Italian architect Benvenuto Tortello in the 1560s, and the smaller one has a pool with a bronze of Bacchus, the Roman god of wine. Apartments surround the main courtyard, including a rib-vaulted chapel with Gothic moldings. **CMK**

◱ The crisp Mudéjar plasterwork contrasts with the smooth gray-blue marble columns.

◲ The building is a brilliant mix of styles, being at once a Renaissance gem and a Moorish palace.

Laurentian Library (1571)

Architect Michelangelo Buonarroti **Location** Florence, Italy **Style** Early Mannerist **Materials** *Pietra serena* (gray stone) and stucco

The Laurentian Library was commissioned by Pope Clement VII de' Medici to house the valuable manuscripts and early printed books that his family had been collecting for about a century. Michelangelo was awarded the project, and although he left the site in 1534 to work mostly in Rome, his precise drawings and instructions enabled Tribolo, Vasari, and Ammannati to complete it in his absence.

Site constraints were a major factor in the design, because the library is positioned above the pre-existing second floor of the cloister adjoining the Basilica of San Lorenzo and squeezed on one side by the transept and Old Sacristy of the church, built the previous century by Brunelleschi. Michelangelo overcame these problems with virtuoso prowess, creating first of all a vestibule—the so-called *ricetto*—that creates the transition from the old structure to the new. Top-lit by clerestory windows, the massive, almost oppressive use of *pietra serena* paired columns and blind windows are set into the wall, an expedient that allowed space to be saved in this enclosed area.

Beyond the *ricetto*, the architect created an open-plan reading room, a rectangular space nearly 164 feet (50 m) long, amply lit by windows on both sides, with a flat, wooden, coffered ceiling, the elaborate design of which is mirrored in the floor paving. The room is articulated by pilasters that clearly evoke fifteenth-century precedents in the rest of the religious complex, thus melding the new library with its context. Michelangelo also provided drawings for the unusual benches that serve as desks behind, as well as a clay model for the *ricetto* stairs. **FN**

⬈ Michelangelo has managed to produce a feeling of intense atmosphere within tight spatial constraints.

⇥ The Laurentian Library is located near the transept of Brunelleschi's domed Basilica of San Lorenzo .

Selimiye Mosque (1575)

Architect Mimar Sinan **Location** Edirne, Turkey **Style** Ottoman **Materials** Brick, polychrome glazed tiles

Mimar Sinan (1489–1588), chief architect for successive Ottoman sultans, considered this mosque his masterpiece, and history has not disagreed. Born a Christian to either Greek or Armenian parents, Sinan was converted to Islam when he entered the elite Janissaries corps, as was customary. The mosque, commissioned by Sultan Selim II and begun in 1568, is the highpoint of a *kulliya* or complex of buildings that originally included a school, hospital, library, shops, time-keeper's room, and bathhouse, all arranged axially. This expressed density of functions reflects the central place the mosque has in Islamic life.

The mosque is an essay in structural inventiveness. Its spherical dome is supported by eight giant piers detached from the outer walls, themselves forming a giant square. Four semi-domes rise from the corners of the square, taking the huge load of the massive dome, measuring more than 102 feet (31.25 m) in diameter. Outside, this weight is also offset by the slim rocketlike minarets that rise dramatically from each corner. Inside, a graceful sequence of arches springs off from the eight piers, producing an ambulatory space inside the walls. It is possible to view the *mihrab* (prayer niche) from any point within the mosque. Instead of merely pressing the niche into the wall, Sinan has innovatively pushed it further back and punctuated the walls on three sides around it with glazed windows, thus throwing light upon the gleaming wall tiles. Color and decoration have been used judiciously inside the mosque, with its tectonic structure picked out in red offset with sections of dark-gray wall and intricately patterned tiling. **MI**

↖ Sinan's dome was designed to rival that of the Hagia Sophia, the great church-turned-mosque in Istanbul.

← The soaring dome is the culmination of an upward thrust suggested by the ring of supporting arches.

El Badi Palace (1578)

Architect Ahmed el-Mansour **Location** Marrakech, Morocco **Style** Saadian **Materials** Stone, mudbrick, timber

The name of this palace can be translated as "The Incomparable"—one of the ninety-nine names given to Allah—and reflects the fact that when built it was almost legendarily sumptuous, with imported Italian marble, Indian onyx, Irish granite, and Sudanese gold leaf covering the surfaces of its 360 rooms. Based on the original Moorish design of the Alhambra in Spain's Granada, El Badi Palace was built by Sultan Ahmed el-Mansour—his name means The Victorious—and was constructed immediately after his victory over the Portuguese in the Battle of the Three Kings at Ksar el-Kebir in 1578. Indeed, it was in part paid for by ransoms extracted for the return of Portuguese nobles after that battle.

The palace is laid out around a huge, 426-foot-long (130 m) central court, which—with its series of pools and canals—was built on a substructure of vaults so that water flow could be controlled. A central, 295-foot-long (90 m) reflecting pool was divided by an island that was originally graced with a fountain, and around which were four smaller pools. Originally there were also four adjacent summer pavilions of which only the floor of one remains intact—the Koubba El Hamsiniya, or Pavilion of the Fifty Pillars.

In 1683, Moulay Ismaïl, a scion of a new ruling dynasty, stripped the palace of anything of value and transported it to his new capital at Meknès, where he adorned his own palaces with the loot. El Badi Palace is still a vast and impressive structure today, but sadly it is just the carcass of one of the most spectacular buildings ever constructed. **RGW**

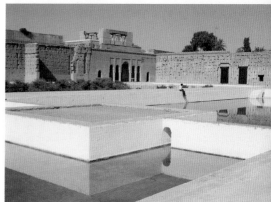

↗ The palace's grandeur is still evident in these somber walls, wrecked by eager despoilers.

➔ The sequence of pools with their trickling fountains underscores the importance of sound in architecture.

Uffizi (1580)

Architect Giorgio Vasari   **Location** Florence, Italy   **Style** Mannerist   **Materials** Stone, stucco

The massive Uffizi project of Giorgio Vasari (1511–74) is an early example of the architecture of absolute monarchy, built for the newly established Florentine Duchy of Cosimo I de' Medici. Cosimo ordered the relocation of city-guild and other administrative offices to a location immediately adjacent to his residential palace—the former city hall, the Palazzo Vecchio. United in one location, these *uffizi* or offices were ordered along the course of a newly cut straight street that linked the Piazza della Signoria to the Arno river, a distance of more than 492 feet (150 m). Each office had an opening onto the grand Doric portico, and upper rooms on a mezzanine level, which was lit by high windows cut into the coffering of the barrel vaults. The sense of order created by the serried ranks of Doric colonnades that enclose the new piazza are characteristic of authoritarian architecture. The Uffizi were not simply an administrative hub, however. The two upper levels of Vasari's design were reserved for the Duke's court and residence and were soon filled with the works of art that form the core of the present-day museum collection. Lighting of these spaces was one of Vasari's major concerns, and he ordered the facade into units of three bays punctured by large aedicular windows. At the Arno end of the U-shaped structure, a vast triumphal arch-like Serliana window affords vistas back to the Palazzo Vecchio, and south to the Arno and the Boboli gardens beyond. **FN**

> *"The loggia . . . had to be constructed over the river, as it were, in the air."*
>
> Giorgio Vasari, biographer and critic

White Heron Castle (1581)

Architects Hideyoshi Toyotomi, Ikeda Terumasa   **Location** Himeji, Japan   **Style** Medieval Japanese   **Materials** Wood, white plaster

Few original Japanese landmarks survive because their wooden structures were so vulnerable to fire. White Heron Castle is perfectly preserved because its walls were covered and reinforced with white, fireproof plaster. The building's name derives from this peculiarity as well as from its gracefully upturned eaves, which give the impression of a heron taking flight. Built on Mount Himeyama, the castle was originally a fortification for the Akamatsu clan against attacks from local shoguns. When Shogun Hideyoshi Toyotomi (1536–98), one of the three great unifiers of Japan, took control during the turbulent Warring States period, he added a turreted three-storied castle. The world-famous five-storied central tower and keep were erected by Ikeda Terumasa (1564–1613), who received it as a gift from his father-in-law, Shogun Ieyasu Tokugawa, in 1601 after their victory at the battle of Sekigahara (1600). Although the castle

proved crucial for asserting Tokugawa rule over the local districts, it has never been damaged by warfare and miraculously escaped the bombings of 1945. The effective organization of its key buildings, the high stone foundations, watch-towers, fortified passageways, and ramparts confirm that White Heron Castle was built as an impenetrable defense stronghold but also devised to wield subtle psychological warfare. The theory has never been tested, but the gates, baileys, and outer walls of the complex are apparently laid out so that the enemy would be to forced to circle around the castle on their way to the keep, facing many dead-ends along the way and becoming disorientated, as if in a maze. Exposed in such a way, intruders could be observed and fired upon during their entire approach. Today, the seemingly endless stairs and passages continue to unsettle and confuse people trying to get in—or out—and visitors easily lose their way. **AA**

Royal Monastery of
San Lorenzo de El Escorial (1584)

Architects Juan Bautista de Toledo, Juan de Herrera
Location Madrid, Spain **Style** Herrerian **Material** Granite

Lying northwest of Madrid, the Royal Monastery of San Lorenzo de El Escorial is an enormous complex that is part basilica, part palace, part monastery, part museum, part library, and part mausoleum.

The building complex was ordered by King Philip II of Spain to commemorate the victory at the Battle of Saint Quentin in 1557 over the French. Construction was started in 1563 by the architect-in-chief of the royal works, Juan Bautista de Toledo (1530–67), and after his death it was completed in 1584 by his assistant, Juan de Herrera (1530–93). The austere appearance of the structure, with its absence of decoration, and carefully proportioned geometric lines, is attributed to de Herrera.

Built of granite and laid out in a rectangular shape, the El Escorial complex has 180-foot-high (55 m) towers at its four corners. The basilica's two *campaniles* are 236 feet (72 m) high, and the cupola is 301 feet (92 m) high. The main entrance, which faces west, leads into the Kings' Courtyard. To the north is a school and to the south a monastery, both of which are still in use. Straight ahead lies the flat vault of the *coro*, or choir, which leads into the dark interior of the basilica. Next to it, to the north, is the Bourbon Palace, while to its south is the Cloister of the Evangelists, complete with white marble statues of the apostles and one of the world's largest garden courts. A staircase at the back of the church leads down to the Kings' Pantheon and the final resting place of the Spanish monarchs housed in marble tombs. **CMK**

↖ The library at El Escorial contains a treasury of the most valuable collection of books in Spain.

↙ At the center of the complex lies the Basilica El Escorial, with its dome and two bell towers.

Church of Il Gesù (1585)

Architects Giacomo Barozzi da Vignola, Giacomo della Porta
Location Rome, Italy **Style** Baroque **Materials** Marble, brick, stone

Dedicated to the sanctity of Jesus's name, this church was conceived by Ignatius Loyola, founder of the Jesuits, in 1551. The Society of Jesus had acquired Santa Maria della Strada, Rome's first Jesuit church, to house a fifteenth-century Madonna image, but then decided to build a larger mother church.

The sober scrolled marble facade, a reworking of Classical elements, is the earliest example of Counter Reformation architecture, while the church's features provided a model for subsequent Jesuit churches the world over, especially in the Americas. The floorplan is

"The significance of Jesuit architecture was not its novelty but its functionalism."

Father Tom Lucas, University of San Francisco

a Latin cross with the intersecting transepts barely discernible. The extended nave celebrates the glory of the high altar, visible from all directions. Lining the sides are twelve chapels, six on each side. Walking through these now interconnecting shrines becomes a spiritual experience that culminates in the glory of the tomb of St. Ignatius, a Baroque explosion of lapis lazuli, alabaster, semiprecious stones, colored marbles, gilded bronze, and silver plate.

The Church of Il Gesù represents the architectural and artistic pinnacle of Jesuitic hopes for the Counter Reformation. The painted apse, cupola, and ceiling by Il Baciccia glorify God, the sacraments, and the Jesuit order itself. In favoring liturgical needs over artistic vanity, the Church of Il Gesù was a building specifically devised for preaching the word of God. **AA**

Fatehpur Sikri (1585)

Patron Mughal Emperor Akbar **Location** Near Agra, Uttar Pradesh, India **Style** Mughal **Materials** Red sandstone, marble

A UNESCO World Heritage Site, Fatehpur Sikri was commissioned by the Mughal emperor Akbar the Great. This fort city is one of the best-enduring examples of the Mughal architectural legacy, even though it was only occupied for about fifteen years.

Situated on the top of a rocky outcrop, it has been realized entirely in red sandstone quarried from the same rock. The city is dotted with numerous architectural points of interest, each one evidence of Akbar's attitude of tolerance for different cultures and religious beliefs. Primarily in the Persian style, there are also rich influences of Gujarati and Rajasthani vernacular schools, attributed to the use of masons and craftsmen of those regions. One of the most elegant of the architectural jewels is the Jodha Bai palace—the house of Akbar's Hindu wife and mother of the crown prince—which, although simple in layout, has ornamentation inspired by Hindu architectural motifs combining two diverse cultures in one edifice.

The highlight of the fort city, however, is the tomb of Salim Chisti—a Sufi saint who was consulted by Akbar about the birth of his son. A destination of pilgrimage for his devotees, this tomb lies in the center of the Jami Masjid, or Friday Mosque. Being the only structure there to be constructed in pristine white marble, it is framed by the magnificent 147-foot-high (45 m) Buland Darwaza—a colossal triumphal arch— in stunning contrast to the backdrop of red sandstone.

Fatehpur translates as the city of victory. This explains why, although only for a short period, the fort city was meant to share the duties of the imperial court. The magnitude and calm of the place is best experienced in the first hours of the day, when the golden glow of the sandstone is truly revealed. **BS**

Burghley House (1589)

Patron Sir William Cecil **Location** Stamford, Lincolnshire
Style Elizabethan **Material** Stone

Sir William Cecil (1520–98), later Lord Burghley, was Lord Treasurer to Queen Elizabeth I and one of her key advisers. He became one of the most powerful men in England, and in the 1560s he began to build his principal house near Stamford, on the borders of Lincolnshire and Cambridgeshire. It was a structure that increased in grandeur and elaboration as Cecil's power increased over a period of more than two decades. The building became one of the most amazing houses in a period of sensational houses—structures so lavish that they became known as the prodigy houses of the Elizabethan age.

All four of Burghley's facades are different, and each is enlivened with the whole Elizabethan vocabulary of towers, bays, and mullioned windows. The entrance has a tall gatehouse, but there is nothing defensive or castlelike about this feature—it is grand, ornate, and filled with large windows. Striking as the gatehouse is, the glory of the building is the roofline, a riot of turrets, cupolas, tall chimneys, obelisks, and pinnacles, all leading the eye up to the climactic feature, a spire.

If the gatehouse and spire are reminders of the Gothic architecture of the previous century, most of the details, from pilasters to cupolas, owe more to the Renaissance. Some are drawn from French buildings or pattern books, some from Italian sources. There is the same mix of influences inside, although only a few interiors survive intact from Cecil's time, notably the Gothic-looking Great Kitchen, the French-Renaissance staircase, and the hall, with its Italianate fireplace. Many other rooms were remodeled in the seventeenth century by the Fifth Earl of Leicester who employed masters of decoration such as painter Antonio Verrio and carver Grinling Gibbons. **PW**

Villa Rotonda (1591)

Architect Andrea Palladio **Location** Vicenza, Italy
Style Classical **Materials** Brick, plaster

Palladio's client was a retired clergyman, Paolo Almerico, who had spent most of his life in service at the Vatican. The house (see page 20) is a suburban rather than a country villa and provided the limited accommodation that its bachelor owner required. Its exterior has become one of the most widely recognized domestic works of the Renaissance.

This is the first of the villas that Palladio intended to be seen from all four sides (each portico faces a cardinal point); he designed the others for viewing from only one or two viewpoints. Here, Palladio

> *"Far more space has been lavished on the stairs and porticoes than on the house itself…"*
>
> Johann Wolfgang von Goethe, poet

brought together in one building a number of references to his studies of ancient Roman structures, while pursuing the Renaissance ideal of man as the measure of all things and the hub of the universe. The very name of the villa is a memory of Santa Maria Rotonda (the Pantheon), while the porticoes are modeled on the Portico of Octavia, also in Rome.

As is usual with Palladio, the plan is strictly symmetrical. Almerico lived in the eight rooms of the *piano nobile*. The basement provided service accommodation and storage, and the ground floor was a granary (as was the custom with villas in the Veneto). Controversy has always raged over the dome, which is low and tiled, but which Palladio illustrated in his *I Quattro Libri dell'Architettura* (1570) as having a much higher and more architectural outline. **CWH**

Library of San Marco (1591)

Architects Jacopo Sansovino, Vincenzo Scamozzi **Location** Venice, Italy
Style High Renaissance **Material** Istrian stone

The Library of San Marco was begun in 1537 to house the famous manuscript collection of Cardinal Bessarion of Trebizond. A public project funded by the Venetian state, it was erected on a central site in front of the ducal palace and facing the Grand Canal, after the demolition of various taverns and other untidy buildings. Jacopo Sansovino (1486–1570) was a Florentine sculptor and architect who had worked extensively in Rome, before settling in Venice after 1527, where he was instrumental in introducing a new style of Classical architecture based on ancient Rome.

The library facade is ordered as a twenty-one-bay arcade, which is lined with shops, while the central bay leads to a grand barrel-vaulted staircase that grants access to the library rooms on the *piano nobile* (upper floor). Passing through a generously proportioned vestibule, which was used as a school for young nobles, the main reading room is set along the front of the building, so as to benefit from the full illumination of the seven windows. The sumptuous decoration of the walls and ceiling with paintings and stucco was carried out by a team of the most renowned Venetian artists of the day. The ground floor is ordered with a Doric arcade and frieze, above which rise Ionic columns topped by a weighty entablature that compresses the building and reinforces its horizontality. Sansovino's intuition was to "sculpt" the facade, thus enlivening the Colosseum-inspired design with reclining figures, lions' heads, and obelisks, which create a sense of massiveness and grandeur. **FN**

↗ The ceiling of the main chamber is filled with *tondo*s (circular paintings) by Veronese, Salviati, and others.

→ The library contrasts with the larger but more delicately articulated mass of the Doge's Palace.

Church of the Redeemer (1592)

Architect Andrea Palladio **Location** Venice, Italy **Style** Classical **Materials** Istrian stone, brick

The Church of the Redeemer (Il Redentore) was built after the Venetian senate vowed that a new church be built to abate the terrible plague that afflicted Venice from 1575 to 1577; in the event, about thirty percent of the population died. The site was selected and the foundation stone was laid in May 1577. The liberation of the city from the plague was celebrated on July 20 by a procession across a bridge of boats, an event now commemorated annually. The pontoon bridge is aligned to the west facade. Building progressed quickly and was completed in 1592, eight times over budget. Palladio's design provided for all the functions of the Franciscan church—ceremonial, votive, and monastic. Although influenced by contemporary Franciscan church projects, Palladio's solution owed most to his studies of Roman baths. The friars required a large nave for sermons and side chapels for private prayer. The crossing combines the ceremonial and

votive functions, for this is where the doge and senate would worship on their annual visit. The tri-conch shape gives the impression of a church wider than it actually is. There is a satisfying and stately rhythm set up between nave, crossing, and choir, solids contrasted against voids, and views created through the screen of columns behind the altar. Although the interior is not elaborate, Palladio deliberately provided a lighter element by copying the intricate profile of the column bases of the Temple of Diana at Nîmes. **CWH**

> *"[The Church of the Redeemer] is small and contemptible, on a suburban island ..."*

John Ruskin, art historian

Basilica of St. Peter (1593)

Architects Michelangelo, della Porta, Bernini, Bramante, Maderno   **Location** Vatican City, Italy   **Style** Baroque Classical   **Materials** Stone, marble

Some buildings radiate power: St. Peter's is one such, as the world center of Roman Catholicism. The basilica is not the cathedral of Rome or the Catholic Church—that is St. John Lateran—but it is the religion's focus, in its own city-state. Michelangelo's dome is elegant and impressive. He worked on it until his death in 1563, and it was completed by Giacomo della Porta and Domenico Fontana in 1593. Visitors ascend to an external gallery surrounding the lantern at a height of 394 feet (132.5 m). The view over St. Peter's and Rome is magnificent. The basilica—mainly the work of Donato Bramante and Gianlorenzo Bernini—is huge. The nave is 692 feet (211 m) long—one of the longest in the world. Bernini's Baroque interior contains many sacred masterpieces and his sumptuous *baldachin*, or canopy (1633), above the high altar, is splendid. St. Peter's Chair (1666) is a very fine example of Bernini's work at the height of his powers: the epitome of High

Baroque art. The east front by Carlo Maderno is rather sober and formal, but it works well as a background to papal blessings and homilies from the central balcony. Bernini's Piazza San Pietro is a work of genius because its extended "keyhole" plan both excludes Rome—creating a formal, sacred space—and includes by surrounding the faithful pilgrims with the encircling colonnade, which was built between 1656 and 1667. The colonnade comprises rows of columns, 4 feet (1.2 m) deep, surmounted by Baroque statues. At the piazza's center is an Egyptian granite monolith, carved in 1 BCE, re-erected here in 1585. A tour of the Vatican gardens is recommended since this allows visitors to see the more humble but still important minor buildings of the city-state. St. Peter's enormous size, solemn composition, and powerful authority have influenced the design of many large churches and state buildings across the world. **ATB**

House of Tiles (1596)

Architect Unknown **Location** Mexico City, Mexico **Style** Mexican Colonial, Baroque, Art Nouveau **Materials** Stone, tiles

The House of Tiles is a two-story building that was constructed as a residence for the second count of the Valley of Orizaba and his wife, Graciana Suárez Peredo. It is distinctive for the Spanish and Moorish blue-and-white tiles that cover its outside walls and that gave it its name. The tiles were added in 1737 by the fifth count of Orizaba. There is a story that the count's father said that his young son would never build a house of tiles, because a tiled house was seen as a sign of success, and the count had little faith in his son's future. When the son became wealthy, he renovated his home in a Baroque style and covered it with tiles.

The Orizaba family sold the building in 1871 to a lawyer, Martínez de la Torre. After his death the building passed into the hands of the Yturbe Idaroff family, who were the last to use it as a private residence. From 1881 the building functioned as a private men's club, and the ground floor became a women's clothing store. The revolutionary leaders Pancho Villa (1878–1923) and Emiliano Zapata (1879–1919) are said to have breakfasted upstairs when they entered Mexico City in 1914. From 1917 to 1919 the building was remodeled in an Art Nouveau style as the Sanborn Brothers drugstore and soda fountain. In 1978 it was remodeled once again as a restaurant and department store; which essentially it remains today. The main restaurant is set in a glass-covered courtyard that houses a Mudéjar fountain. Surrounding the stone-columned courtyard are tiled murals, and there is a staircase decorated with waist-high tiling. The building was renovated from 1993 to 1995, with the aim of preserving its mix of original styles. **CMK**

◥ The house is an early example of a Mexican colonial palace built for the emerging Creole-Spanish nobility.

◁ The tiles, or *talavera*, covering the building's exterior were made in Puebla, to the east of Mexico City.

Ali Qapu Palace (1597)

Patron Shah Abbas I | **Location** Isfahan, Iran | **Style** Safavid | **Material** Brick

"That brick boot-box" is how the travel writer Robert Byron described the Ali Qapu Palace in the 1930s. It is not high praise, but then Byron was an unforgiving critic. Even if one is immune to the pleasures of the building itself, the Ali Qapu can be enjoyed for its chief function, which is as a balcony from which to observe perhaps the grandest formal vista in the Islamic world.

Imam Square, in Isfahan, is the second-largest square in the world. The Ali Qapu sits on the west side, opposite the Sheikh Loft Allah mosque. Originally built as a gateway to the complex of royal gardens and pavilions behind it, the Ali Qapu—meaning high or sublime gate—was later converted by Shah Abbas (1587–1629) into a covered veranda from which he and his courtiers could watch the parades, executions, and polo matches taking place in the great square.

Sitting above the brick portico, this broad balcony is covered by an elaborately carved wooden ceiling supported by elegant wooden columns, creating a delicate counterbalance to its heavy base. Inside is a series of chambers used for listening to music or housing the shah's collection of Chinese porcelain. Here, the walls are covered with rich, though faded, murals depicting courtiers at play in the gardens.

Although broadly continuous with the arched arcades around the edge of the square, the Ali Qapu adds to the diversity of architectural gestures on each side of it, from the Sheikh Loft Allah mosque to the majestic Shah Mosque to the south, and the entrance to the bazaar to the north. With these buildings reflected in the long pool at its center, Imam Square is one of Iran's most dramatic spectacles. **JMc**

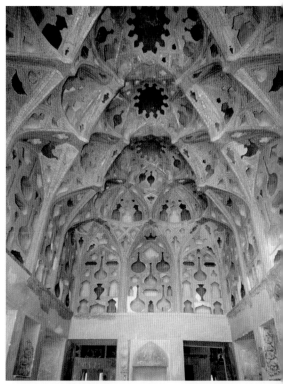

↗ This grotto-like interior consists of walls of niches that originally housed rare porcelain and glass.

→ The covered balcony looks over old Isfahan, allowing its residents to be displayed to the people below.

Triangular Lodge (1597)

Architect Sir Thomas Tresham   **Location** Rushton, Northamptonshire, England   **Style** Elizabethan   **Material** Sandstone

The Triangular Lodge at Rushton is a sensationally strange little building with a sharpness that seems to slice into the senses. Smothered with symbols on its striped sandstone body, it is a sermon in stone—a proclamation of faith—by Sir Thomas Tresham. Having been hounded for his Catholicism, he created this covert declaration of his beliefs between July 28, 1594 and September 29, 1597. A pious and exquisite Elizabethan conceit, the building embodies its principal inscription, "There are three that bear witness," a reference to the Holy Trinity, as well as being a pun on Tresham's name and his emblem of a trefoil. Everything about the tiny building revolves around the number three. Each side of the triangle is 33 feet and 4 inches—an exact third of 100 feet—or 10 meters long, tapering up to 33 feet exactly. All three sides of the three stories have a trio of fanciful trefoil windows. The three main rooms are hexagonal, each with triangular corner chambers. Nine gables soar up to the sky, ablaze with stone flames, and carved with symbols and creatures, then crowned with three-sided pinnacles, topped with trefoils. The triangular chimney is carved with symbols of the Mass. Nine stone angels bulge forth, bearing on their chests some of the many other inscriptions that abound on this building, including Tresham's declaration, "Behold not for myself alone have I laboured." Carvings encrust every aspect of the Triangular Lodge: on the southeast wall is a seven-branched candlestick and seven eyes of God, representing God the Father; and on the north wall is a hen and her chicks and "the pelican of piety", symbolizing God the Son. To the southwest, a dove on a serpent, as well as the hand of God, represent God the Holy Ghost. Thomas Tresham spent fifteen years either in prison or in confinement for his beliefs. Thank God for this little building. **LL**

Hardwick Hall (1597)

Architect Robert Smythson **Location** Doe Lea, Chesterfield, Derbyshire, England **Style** Elizabethan **Materials** Stone, timber, glass

"Hardwick Hall, more glass than wall," goes the jingle learned by children in their history lessons. Glass was an expensive commodity in the late sixteenth century and, like almost everything else about Hardwick, the intention was to impress. Work began on the house for the Countess of Shrewsbury, better known as Bess of Hardwick, in 1590, following the death of her fourth husband, the Earl of Shrewsbury. Bess wanted a new house that would reflect her huge wealth and status. Hardwick combined Renaissance ideas imported from Europe with the latest English building technology. Robert Smythson (1535–1614), the designer of Longleat, was almost certainly the architect—a drawing by him associated with the house is now in the RIBA collection—and the building is symmetrical on every side, in accordance with the modern style. The house is built using local stone, with fireplace flues running through internal walls, thus allowing space for the broad window openings. In section and plan, Hardwick also contains some innovations: the great hall, used as a servants' dining room, runs from the front to the back, while the state rooms are at the top of the house on the second floor. The high great chamber, built on a magnificent scale, still comes as a surprise after the more compact rooms on the lower floors. Now owned by the National Trust, Hardwick Hall is one of the finest examples of the Elizabethan country house in England. **MF**

> *"The house is not Gothic, but of that betweenity that intervened when Gothic declined ..."*
>
> Horace Walpole, writer and politician

The expansion of Western empires and their colonies allowed Renaissance ideals to encounter those of other cultures, producing hybrid forms that led fashionable taste. Elsewhere, empires encompassed vast new territories and a wealth of building traditions. Advances in building technologies, greater access to material and human resources, and faster communications influenced the international spread of architectural ideas. Political radicalism and the Industrial Revolution in the West provided patrons and architects alike with opportunities to co-opt the language of the past and explore new forms to articulate these ideals.

EMPIRE *to* REVOLUTION

1600–1900

Montacute House (1601)

Architect William Arnold **Location** Montacute, Somerset, England **Style** Late Gothic, Renaissance **Material** Limestone

One of England's best-preserved Elizabethan mansions, Montacute House was built by Sir Edward Phelips, Master of the Rolls to Queen Elizabeth I, who made his fortune as a lawyer, entered parliament in 1584, and commissioned a house befitting his elevated station four years later. Most likely the work of local master mason William Arnold (active 1595–1637), everything about the house is designed to communicate the status and taste of its owner. Of the original gatehouse, only the flanking ogee-roofed pavilions survive. Ahead stands an imposing three-story facade of ocher-colored limestone, rising from a symmetrical, E-shaped floorplan and enriched with a wealth of carving, including the monkeys and other beasts that clamber over flamboyant Dutch gables and parapets, and the Classically-inspired "Nine Worthies," set in niches along the upper story. Arnold's scheme combines Late Gothic motifs with Renaissance forms and detailing fashionable in Europe at the time. Unusually for English architecture of this period, the design incorporates expansive mullioned windows. Montacute's interior is equally impressive, most noteworthy being the Long Gallery that extends the 172-foot (52 m) length of the house. It contains a collection of Elizabethan and Jacobean portraits. Most of the original furniture was sold after the English Civil War to settle debts. In 1780, Montacute's only significant remodeling added a porch and screen to the central portion of the west elevation, using ornamental stonework acquired secondhand, following the demolition of a local house. Montacute remained in the Phelips family until financial difficulties forced its sale in the early twentieth century. The house was bought in 1931 for the Society for Protection of Ancient Buildings, from whence it passed to the National Trust. **AMR**

Golden Temple (1601)

Patron Guru Arjan Dev **Location** Amritsar, India **Style** Indian (Sikh) **Materials** Stone, marble, gold

The evolution of architectural legacy within the Indian subcontinent is indebted largely to the conception of religious places of congregation. The Harimandir Sahib, or Golden Temple, is one such iconic place, establishing what many believe to be the Sikh style of architecture. A shrine of worship of immense sublimity and elegance, it is said to have found its origins in the fourteenth century when the founder of the Sikh religion, Guru Nanak Dev, came to live and meditate at the lake called Amritsar, meaning "pool of ambrosial nectar." The foundation of the formal temple structure was laid by the Islamic saint Hazrat Mian Mirji of Lahore in December 1588, under guidance of the fifth Guru Arjan Dev (1563–1606). The shrine was a coevolution of Hindu and Islamic architectural motifs. Uniquely, unlike established precedents of raising iconic buildings on a pedestal, the Golden Temple was built at the same level as its surroundings. However, the uncertain political milieu of the fifteenth century turned this sanctuary into a victim and witness of nearly a hundred years of conflict, with the Sikhs defending against invasion from the Turks and Mughals. Rebuilt numerous times, the temple rose up each time, reflecting the strength and prosperity of its followers. In the relatively stable period of the 1700 to 1800s, the shrine was richly embellished in marble and precious stones, including the golden gilding of the upper stories, giving rise to its popular name. **BS**

" . . . the Golden Temple sparkling in the evening sunlight, casting a golden reflection on the water . . ."

Mark Tully, BBC reporter

Temple of the Sacred Tooth Relic (1603)

Patron King Kirthi Sri Rajasinghe **Location** Kandy, Sri Lanka **Style** Buddhist **Material** Stone

Kandy's Temple of the Sacred Tooth Relic, or Sri Dalada Maligawa, is Sri Lanka's most sacred Buddhist shrine, and a pilgrimage site for Buddhists worldwide. According to legend, when the Buddha died, his body was cremated in India, and his left canine tooth was retrieved from the ashes of the funeral pyre. The tooth had various homes before it finally arrived at Kandy.

The temple was first built in two stories *c.* 1600 during the reign of King Vimaladharmasuriya I (1592–1603) but nothing now remains of the original building. It was reconstructed during the reign of King Kirthi Sri Rajasinghe (1747–81). In 1998 Hindu Tamil separatists bombed the temple, but the damage has since been repaired. The red-roofed, white temple buildings sit on the edge of a lake and are surrounded by a moat and stonewall fortifications. The walls are intricately decorated with openwork, adding a touch of decoration to the otherwise plain design.

Although the buildings have simple exteriors, inside they are lavishly adorned with inlaid woods, ivory carvings, and lacquered paintings. Crossing a small bridge over the moat leads to a stone gatehouse. In the courtyard at the center of the complex lies a two-story rectangular shrine, known as the Vadahitina Maligawa. Its main entrance is decorated with paintings, flanked by stone statues of lions, leading to a museum. The tooth itself is kept in a series of gold and jeweled caskets housed on the top floor of the shrine. A stairway connects the temple to the Pattiripuwa tower built in 1803 by King Sri Wickrama Rajasinghe (*r.* 1798–1815), and is used as a library to house important palm-leaf manuscripts. **CMK**

↖ The walls of the red-roofed temple are decorated with openwork.

← The golden door to the temple declares the precious sanctity of the space inside.

Church of Santa Maria della Consolazione (1606)

Architects Cola da Caprarola, Antonio da Sangallo the Younger **Location** Todi, Umbria, Italy **Style** Renaissance **Material** Travertine stone

Construction of the Church of Santa Maria della Consolazione began only two years after architect Donato Bramante's audacious plan for Pope Julius II to replace St. Peter's in Rome had started. It is considered to be a simplified and scaled-down version of that project: a centrally planned church, with interior and exterior designs that closely correspond, and crowned with a dome raised up on a drum. The centralized plan, with the circle of the dome inscribed in the square of the crossing, and to which semicircular apses are added on each plane, was not new. The central-plan church was an idea pursued by the architect Leon Battista Alberti and could be seen in Giuliano da Sangallo's Church of Santa Maria delle Carceri, near Florence, during the 1480s.

The typology is closely associated with pilgrimage devotion, especially the three entranceways allowing for easy access to the relic site. In the case of Santa Maria della Consolazione, it is a miraculous image of the Virgin Mary that adorns the high altar. Such was the case in many churches built in central Italy *c.* 1500.

Here, the articulation of interior and exterior surfaces on two orders of applied pilasters, and the use of travertine stone lends the structure a measured poise. The colossal piers that support the dome are derivative of Bramante's experiments with sculpted forms, and the structural mass of the piers projects even to the exterior, where the corners appear to mark the square around which the design is ordered. This clear geometric order, coupled with the massive forms inspired by the ruins of antiquity, characterize the monumental designs of the High Renaissance. **FN**

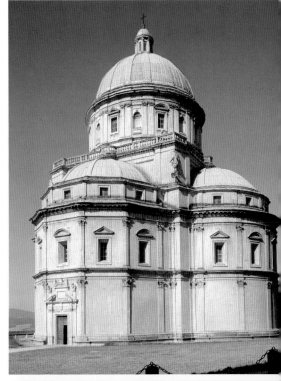

↗ Although the church is relatively small, the massing of its volumes and its detailing is monumental.

→ The interior dome is derived from Bramante's architectural experiments.

Sheikh Lotf Allah Mosque (1619)

Architect Muhammad Reza ibn Ustad Hosein Banna Isfahani   **Location** Isfahan, Iran   **Style** Safavid   **Materials** Brick, mosaic tiles

> *"Other interiors came to mind . . . to compare it with: Versailles . . . Schönbrunn . . . or St. Peter's."*

Robert Byron, *The Road to Oxiana* (1937)

⬆ The entrance to the mosque is approached across the vast Imam Square.

➡ The interior is a sublime essay in mosaic tiling, with soaring arches and complex spiral patterns.

Sheikh Lotf Allah Mosque is one of the great treasures of Iranian architecture. Built by Shah Abbas I in honor of his father-in-law, a revered cleric, it sits on the eastern side of the vast Imam Square, in Isfahan. The mosque is named after the scholar Sheikh Lotf Allah Maisi Al-Amili who came to Isfahan at Shah Abbas I's request, and lived on the site. Shah Abbas I had moved the capital to Isfahan in 1592, and his building program made the city a triumph of Safavid architecture.

The first thing that strikes the viewer is that the dome, although flecked with turquoise blossoms on its pattern of spiraling tendrils, is a sandy color. This is unusual, because mosques of the Safavid period favored a brilliant blue.

The dark entrance leads into a hypnotically exquisite room. Made up of a single square chamber topped with a dome, the mosque's simplicity in plan is complicated by the bewildering complexity of the tilework. Every surface is a haze of flowers and calligraphy. The detailing is so intricate that it is sometimes difficult to know where to look because the focal point is directly overhead.

The dome sits on an octagonal story of arches trimmed with blue cable tiles. At its center is a floral sunburst radiating blue, tear-shaped medallions, growing larger as they descend, against a golden ocher background. The way the sunlight enters the faience-work windows creates a fan-shaped reflection emanating from the apex of the dome that resembles a peacock's tail.

Like the Imam Mosque at the south end of the square, the portal hides the fact that the mosque sits at forty-five degrees to the square, and is oriented toward Mecca. However, while this jewellike object is not as imposing in scale or grandeur as the Imam Mosque, it still has a power over the senses that is difficult to forget. **JMc**

Banqueting House (1622)

Architect Inigo Jones **Location** Whitehall, London, England **Style** Palladian **Materials** Portland stone, timber, glass

Inigo Jones (1573–1652) plays a key role in the history of British architecture because he traveled to Italy to study, and afterward built the first significant Classical buildings in England. He was influenced by the designs of Andrea Palladio, whose buildings he visited on the continent. In line with Palladio's rules, the Banqueting House has a rusticated base, a first story with Ionic columns and pedimented windows, and a second story in the Corinthian order with garlanded swags linking the capitals. It is Jones's first building in Portland stone, a material he is credited with having introduced to London and that Sir Christopher Wren later used for St. Paul's Cathedral. The facade was refaced by Sir John Soane in 1829. The Banqueting House was designed as a party venue for King James I and is famous for its sumptuous double-cube hall—55 feet (180 m) wide, 110 feet (360 m) long, and 55 feet (180 m) high, complete with a gallery—that occupies the entire upper floors. The ceiling panels were painted by Peter Paul Rubens. In January 1649, King Charles I stepped out onto the scaffold of this building to be beheaded. Jones, who had already designed the Queen's House at Greenwich, went on to complete a number of other important projects, including Covent Garden Piazza, London's first real residential square. His work was highly influential on Neo-Classical British architects of the eighteenth century, including William Kent and Lord Burlington. **MF**

> *"When first built, it stood among an Elizabethan jumble ... its startling newness unimaginable."*
>
> Edward Jones and Christopher Woodward, authors

Craigievar Castle (1626)

Patron William Forbes **Location** Alford, Aberdeenshire, Scotland **Style** Renaissance **Materials** Harled stone; slate and lead roofings

If there is one castle that typifies the jaggedly romantic outline of the traditional Scottish tower house, it is early-seventeeth-century Craigievar Castle. With its jumble of oversailing gables and turrets emphasizing an uncompromising verticality, it wears the ceremonial dress of warlike display rather than the armor of battle. Bristling with features such as corbelling and fictive cannons, it was built to look fortified at a time when the need for serious defensive protection had largely passed but when the prestige associated with military endeavor was still deeply embedded in the psyche of the Scottish landowning class. Built for William Forbes (1566–1627) by local masons from almost unworkable local granite hidden beneath a layer of pinkish ocher harling (a lime-based screed), it is far more resolved than first appears. An irregular L-shape on plan, its cleverly worked congregation of spaces provides a fully integrated range of functions from kitchen to great hall—a last triumph of vertical living at a time when grand houses in England and Europe were expanding along a rather more horizontal axis. Internally, Craigievar has a match for its busy outline in its elaborate plasterwork decoration, a fashionable element inspired by royal precedent. The vaulted ceiling of the great hall is enlivened with busts of Roman emperors and there are caryatids above the main fireplace. Since the 1960s, the property has been in the care of the National Trust for Scotland. **NC**

> *"Craigievar is outstanding for no later alterations mar the perfect balance of the elevations ..."*
>
> John Dunbar, architectural historian

Rosenborg Castle (1634)

Architects Bertel Lange, Hans van Steenwinckel, King Christian IV   **Location** Øster Voldgade, Denmark   **Style** Renaissance   **Materials** Brick, sandstone

King Christian IV (1577–1648) of Denmark and Norway was celebrated for his great interest in culture, in particular architecture, and music. Many of his architectural projects can be seen in Copenhagen, such as the Old Stock Exchange, the Round Tower, and Rosenborg Castle. The castle was originally erected as the king's summer residence and it lies within the King's Garden, which he also designed. Although the castle was built and extended over almost thirty years, it stands today as a fine and whole example of the Dutch Renaissance style. Between 1606 and 1607 the king built a two-story, red-brick summerhouse with a spire-crowned turret and two bays facing east. Today, this first section of the building marks the central part of the castle's southern structure. From 1613 onward, the house was extended, and in 1624 the majority of the building was completed, so that by then it included a third story, the Long Hall, the Great Tower,

and several spires. In 1634 the king requested a more notable entrance to the main official chambers, replacing the existing stair turret with the current one, and adding an outer double staircase linking the entrance to the first floor. The castle blends together three natural colors with its use of red brick, gray sandstone, and verdigris copper roof, making for a prominent and eye-catching building. Today Rosenborg Castle is a museum that houses the Crown Jewels, the Danish Crown Regalia, and collections of parade arms, porcelain, and glass, displayed in sumptuous, Baroque settings in styles chosen by the king's successors at the end of the seventeenth century. King Christian IV was aided on structural elements of the building project by the architects Bertel Lange (active 1620–30) and Hans van Steenwinckel (1587–1639). To this day it remains uncertain how much the king participated. **SML**

Mauritshuis (1635)

Architect Jacob van Campen   **Location** The Hague, Netherlands   **Style** Dutch Classical   **Material** Brick

The Mauritshuis was designed by Jacob van Campen (1596–1657), a painter turned architect who had studied in Italy. He was one of the chief exponents of Dutch Classicism—a regional variation on the Baroque—and was inspired by the work of the sixteenth-century Northern Italian architects Vincenzo Scamozzi and Andrea Palladio. They followed the principles of Classical Greek and Roman architecture and provided rules for the design of contemporary, Classical buildings. In keeping with these rules, the Mauritshuis is strictly symmetrical. The building stands alone; the rear elevation overlooks a large pond. Each side sports two-story-high pilasters in colossal order—reaching from foundation to roof. Both stories have the same layout: an antechamber at the front with two rooms on either side and a great hall at the rear. The second story is accessed by two symmetrical flights of stairs. The great hall on the upper floor was topped with a cupola with a walkway around it. After a fire in 1704, the building was restored, following Van Campen's layout, although the cupola was not reinstated. The hall on the ground floor was refurbished in an extravagantly gilded Louis XIV style with allegorical paintings by Giovanni Antonio Pellegrini, a Venetian artist painting in the Rococo style. In 1822 the Mauritshuis became a museum of art. Van Campen's style is reputed to have influenced Sir Christopher Wren's London churches. **MC**

"He vanquished Gothic folly with Roman stateliness and drove heresy forth before an older truth."

Constantijn Huygens, poet and composer

Shir Dor Madrassa (1636)

Patron Alchin Yalantush Bahadur   **Location** Samarkand, Uzbekistan   **Style** Shaybanid   **Materials** Brick, tile

The Shir Dor Madrassa (1619–36) alongside the Ulugh Beg Madrassa (1417–21) and Tilla Kari Madrassa (1646–60) form three sides of Registan Square in Samarkand. The dramatic external facade facing into Registan Square comprises the *iwan* (vaulted hall), twin ribbed domes, and two slender minarets. The exterior is decorated with geometric and floral polychromatic tile patterns. At 167 feet (51 m) from minaret to minaret, the facade mirrors the Ulugh Beg Madrassa (religious school) opposite. The minarets are replaced on the rear elevation with turrets. The two-story *madrassa* conforms to a set design. A central courtyard made up of student cells, with central *iwans* on the northern, eastern, and southern facades, which operated as open classrooms. The surface of the interior is richly decorated with multicolored tiles. Although awe inspiring, the tile decoration is not as refined as that from the Golden Age of Samarkand in the fifteenth century. What is revolutionary is the *iwan* that depicts tigerlike lions pursuing gazelles watched by human-faced suns. The figurative representation is unusual on an Islamic building, possibly borrowing from earlier Zoroastrian or Mongol motifs. The lions depicted on the tile mosaic give the building its name: Shir Dor means "lion bearing." The structure was restored in the 1920s following the Soviet occupation of Central Asia. Repairs and extensive reconstruction work continued through the twentieth century. **LC**

> *"The Registan of Samarkand was originally, and is . . . the noblest public square in the world."*
>
> George Curzon, *Russia in Central Asia* (1889)

Tomb of Jahangir (1637)

Patron Shah Jahan   **Location** Shahdara, Lahore, Pakistan   **Style** Mughal   **Materials** Red sandstone, marble

Nuruddin Salim Jahangir (1569–1627) was ruler of the Mughal empire from 1605 to 1627, and was the son of Emperor Akbar the Great (1556–1605). The Tomb of Jahangir was built on the site of a garden designed by his twelfth wife, the Empress Nur Jehan. The mausoleum was commissioned by Jahangir's son Shah Jahan (1592–1666), and completed in 1637. It is a single-story, flat-roofed building measuring 279 square feet (85 sq m). The exterior is fashioned in red sandstone with floral marble inlay. The octagonal crypt at the center of the building is accessed through long corridors and vaulted arches. Its walls and niches are decorated with frescoes, *pietra dura* (durable stone) inlay, and colored marble. A flight of stairs leads to an open flat roof that originally had a marble balustrade. Within the crypt, the white marble sarcophagus is decorated with mosaic floral designs and the Ninety-Nine Attributes of God in the Koran inlaid in black on

two sides. Four 100-feet-high (30 m) minarets round out each corner of the building. They rise in five stages and are topped with white marble cupolas. Each is zigzagged with white and yellow marble. The mausoleum's style can be described as Late Mughal. Under Akbar, Mughal architecture was a marvelous combination of Persian, Islamic, Hindu, and other styles, as seen at the now deserted city of Fatehpur Sikri. During the reign of Shah Jahan, Hindu features disappeared. The Tomb of Jahangir, with its square, arcaded layout and minarets, is fully Islamic. However, the *pietra dura* mosaics and floral-tiled cladding are of Persian origin, and their use was perfected under Shah Jahan. In 1648 he completed the Taj Mahal that used white marble and *pietra dura* inlay to full effect. A few architectural curiosities from Akbar's day survive at this building, including baluster columns with a European feel at each corner of the tomb. **MC**

Baghdad Kiosk at Topkapi Palace (1639)

Architect Mimar Kasim   **Location** Istanbul, Turkey   **Style** Ottoman
Materials Stone, tile, wood, ivory, mother-of-pearl, tortoiseshell

The Topkapi Sarayi (Topkapi Palace) is a vast rambling complex built after the Ottoman Sultan Mehmed II (1432–81) conquered Constantinople (now Istanbul) in 1453. It differs from many royal palaces in its seeming lack of symmetrical order. This holds particularly true for some of the smaller structures within the palace, where among gardens and wooded landscape lie tentlike pavilions and "kiosks." The kiosks are domed structures on columns with open sides, and were places to eat, drink, read poetry, listen to music, and enjoy the remarkable views of the Bosphorus.

Many were built to commemorate military victories. For example, Sultan Murad IV (1612–40) was responsible for building the Revan Kiosk and Baghdad Kiosk on the belvedere platform adjacent to the tulip gardens. They were built to commemorate the conquests of Revan and Baghdad respectively.

The octagonal Baghdad Kiosk lies in the Fourth Court of the palace, and was designed by a master of Ottoman architecture, Mimar Kasim (1570–1659), who was responsible for rebuilding various parts of the palace. Behind the slender marble columns of the entrance hall is a low building with windows reaching almost to the ground ensuring comprehensive views. The walls of the kiosk are richly decorated with Iznik tiles reaching to the base of the dome. The woodwork on the doors and window frames is sumptuously decorated with inlaid mother-of-pearl, ivory, and tortoiseshell. Inside, velvet-covered divans line the walls to provide comfortable and lavish seating. **FN**

↖ The intricate tracery of the balcony is repeated in the blue tiles that cover the walls of the kiosk.

← The building is encircled by an open-pillared verandah that serves as a foil to the kiosk itself.

Merchants' Houses (c. 1640)

Architects Various   **Location** Amsterdam, Netherlands
Style Dutch Classical   **Materials** Brick, sandstone

San Carlo alle Quattro Fontane (1641)

Architect Francesco Borromini   **Location** Rome, Italy
Style Baroque   **Materials** Travertine marble, stone

Seventeenth-century Amsterdam was one of the wealthiest cities in the world. During its Golden Age, the city was laid out in a crescent shape with concentric streets and canals in ever larger rings from the port to the city boundary. The rings were bisected by straight canals and narrow streets that fanned out from the port. Within the confined spaces of the islands created by the canals, the prosperous merchants of Amsterdam built their houses.

To distinguish Protestant Amsterdam from the Gothic style of Catholic France and Spain, the Amsterdam style drew on the Classical. Sometimes referred to as Plain Amsterdam Renaissance, its main features were red-brick facades with strips of white sandstone, known as "rashers of bacon," and stepped gables. Pilasters in colossal order were crammed onto elongated facades, but high-pitched roofs could not be hidden by a Classical cornice because the zigzag shape of a stepped gable was not Classical, and architects had to be innovative.

Oudezijds Voorburgwal 239 (1634) is ascribed to Philips Vingboons (1607–78). He was influenced by Jacob van Campen whose mansion at Keizersgracht 177 (1625) is described as Amsterdam's first Classical building. Keizersgracht 319 (1639) and Rokin 145 (1642–43) are mature examples of Vingboons's style, which was widely adopted. In time, the gable became more decorative as at Oudezijds Voorburgwal 187 (1663), where figures of slaves with rolled tobacco leaves reflected the owner's business. Here the pilaster facade is topped with Ionic capitals in the central section, and Corinthian capitals on the neck gable. An imitation of Vingboons's style in humbler houses was jokingly referred to as "contractors' Classicism" as seen at Herengracht 70–72 (1643). **MC**

The design for the corner church of San Carlo alle Quattro Fontane, also known as San Carlino, was architect Francesco Borromini's (1599–1677) first solo commission; the challenge was to fit a gem of gigantic proportions into a narrow building site.

Located at the Quattro Fontane intersection with a fountain on each corner, the church has a reclining Neptune (a personification of the Arno river) incorporated into its side wall. Approaching the church, the concave and convex rhythms of the bays on its facade, its sinuous entablature, and tall

---

"[Borromini's] architectural vocabulary invested architecture with new meaning."

Paolo Portoghesi, architectural historian and critic

Corinthian columns add movement. The upper story, with its sectioned entablature and oval medallion held up by asymmetrically placed angels, looks heavier, and was done by the architect's nephew.

Borromini's pinched longitudinal oval design defied Baroque norms by using intersecting and interlocking ovals and circles to accommodate a high dome. Gradually decreasing in size, the geometric coffers of the dome trick the eye into seeing the illusion of additional height, and hidden windows make it appear as if suspended in mid-air.

The flowing design of the church blurs the boundaries between architecture and art as the walls weave in and out in a heady combination of shapes, also reflected in the dome's complex coffered pattern of crosses, ovals, and hexagons. **AA**

Fortress of
St. Peter of the Rock (1643)

Architect Juan Bautista Antonelli **Location** Santiago de Cuba, Cuba
Style Renaissance **Materials** Stone, wood

Situated at the entry to the channel leading to the port of Santiago de Cuba, San Pedro de la Roca, or Fortress of St. Peter of the Rock, dates back to the late sixteenth century when piracy was rife throughout the Caribbean. In 1638 the governor of Santiago, Pedro de la Roca y Borja, commissioned the Italian military engineer Juan Bautista Antonelli (1550–1616) to expand the fort; it was completed in 1643. The Antonelli family acted as consultants to the Spanish Crown, and their influence may be seen in the elegant fortifications of all the principal ports around the Gulf of Mexico, particularly those of Havana and Veracruz.

The fortress was built in quadrilateral form with bastions equipped with artillery manned by a garrison of thirty men. In 1662 it was damaged during attacks by pirates, and its reconstruction was hampered by a series of earthquakes. During the eighteenth century when the European powers were at one another's throats over their Caribbean possessions, the fortress repelled attacks from the English.

During the Cuban Wars of Independence in the late 1890s, it was used as a prison. The form of the castle follows the promontory upon which it is built, in the shape of an arrow pointing out to sea. The foremost section of the building, where a triangular bastion rears up from a dry moat, is particularly impressive. Entrance to the building is via two drawbridges. The parade ground is arranged over several levels linked by steps and ramps, below which are two platforms reached by stone steps. **JB**

↖ In certain inner courtyards, the fortress could almost be mistaken for a domestic building.

← The fortress commands spectacular views—and a powerful defensive position—across a vital channel.

Red Fort (1648)

Patron Shah Jahan   **Location** Netaji Subhash Marg, Delhi, India
Style Mughal   **Material** Red sandstone, marble

House of Charitable Works (c. 1648)

Patron Martín Calvo de la Puerto y Arrieta   **Location** Havana, Cuba
Style Baroque   **Materials** Brick, stone

Mughal emperor Shah Jahan (1592–1666) transferred his capital from Agra to Delhi in 1638. The foundation of the new citadel Lal Qila, or Red Fort (see page 163), was laid in April 1639, and so-called because it is built of red sandstone. It took nine years to complete. The fort is close to the Yamuna River, and the crowded Chandni Chowk bazaar runs west of its Lahore Gate.

The fort is octagonal in plan: about 3,250 feet (900 m) by 1,800 feet (550 m). It accommodates palaces along the eastern side. The Diwan-i-Khas, or Private Audience Hall, was the innermost court, where the glorious Peacock Throne once stood; fragments are now in Tehran. The hall was elaborately decorated. The Diwan-i-Am, or Public Audience Hall, has fine arches and columns. The hall was restored by Lord Curzon, the British Viceroy, who also paid for the replacement of two large stone elephants near the Delhi Gate. The Hammam, or Royal Baths, are built of marble, and the floors are inlaid with colored *pietra dura* (durable stone). The Red Fort was not just a fort; it was the home of the Mughal court. A complex of palaces arranged around classical Mughal gardens, it is an oasis of peaceful calm, contrasting with the bustling city beyond the gates. Important visitors to the emperor progressed through a series of ever more impressive spaces until reaching the imperial presence in the finest rooms. The Mughal emperors lived there until 1857, when the British took over the fort.

Under the British Raj, the military occupation of the fort was a symbol of domination. When Indian independence was declared in 1947, the Prime Minister of India addressed the nation from the fort. The replacement of the Union Jack at the Red Fort by the green, white, and saffron Indian flag symbolized the end of the British empire in India. **ATB**

One of the most distinguished of Havana's domestic buildings, La Casa de la Obra Pía, or House of Charitable Works, began as a fusion of two neighboring properties by Martín Calvo de la Puerto y Arrieta. It is one of the city's largest colonial houses. Its 1,937 square feet (180 sq m) courtyard is surrounded by galleries on three sides with stone columns and arches; it also has a grand stone staircase that leads to the upper floor. The grand entrance was sculpted in Cádiz in Spain, and brought in sections to Havana to be assembled on site. The eccentricity of its design,

---

"The elaborate and whimsical forms of this entrance ... are without equal ..."

Joaquín E. Weiss, architectural historian

---

with its imaginative interpretation of the rules of perspective and polychromed Castellón coat of arms, for Nicolás de Castellón who inherited the house, contrasts well with the building's austere exterior.

The dining room has open sides and is located between the courtyard and the rear courtyard in an arrangement typical of the time. The principal courtyard was designed as a tranquil relief from the noise and dust of the streets, and would have been decorated with plants. The rear courtyard was a service area around which would have been grouped kitchens, storerooms, and stabling. An unusual feature is a long, low construction on the roof that may have housed slaves. It is the only one of its kind in Havana; in all the other grand mansions the slaves lived in mezzanines between the lower and upper floors. **JB**

Drax Hall (c. 1650)

Patron James Drax   **Location** Saint George Parish, Barbados   **Style** Colonial Jacobean   **Materials** Coral, limestone, plaster

Drax Hall was out of style the minute its builders downed tools. Whether the owner knew this is unknown. Anglo-Dutch militia captain James Drax landed in Barbados with the first wave of English immigrants in the 1620s. Allied to cane, know-how, and slaves provided by Brazilian-based Dutch growers, he had the basis for his rise to plantation sugar boss. When Drax Hall was built some thirty years after his arrival, its Jacobean style had been out of fashion in England just as long. Did an out-of-date house model provide the blueprint? Or was a copybook by sixteenth-century Dutch architect Jan Vredeman de Vries used as inspiration? De Vries's Flemish interpretation of the five Classical architectural orders was one of the style guides available to seventeenth-century colonials, and explains many of the Northern Renaissance features of Drax Hall. The main building material, coral, reflects the locality, but the form makes few climate concessions. Rather than verandas and French doors to beat the heat, the house has formalism and fireplaces. The pitched saddleback roof of the three-story, square hall is capped with finials at the four corners. Symmetrical double-gable ends balance a full-height symmetrical triple-gable facade paired opposite with a one-story-gable porch. Coral limestone block walls are mortared with egg white and ground coral, and skinned with a plaster finish. Shutters provide sun shields for the windows. **DJ**

> *"To confess truly all the lands that I have passed by and seen unto this day, not any pleaseth me so well."*
>
> Sir Henry Colt, *The Voyage of Sir Henry Colt* (1631)

Taj Mahal (1653)

Patron Shah Jahan   **Location** Agra, India   **Style** Mughal   **Materials** Red sandstone, makrana white marble inlaid with semiprecious stones

As a monument to enduring love, this mausoleum was commissioned by the Mughal emperor Shah Jahan (1592–1666) in memory of his principal wife, Mumtaz Mahal, in the year of her death. The Taj Mahal is not solely his work, but the amalgamation of a powerhouse of master builders and craftsmen from Persia and India who saw it evolve over twenty-two years. It represents the opulence and power of the Mughal empire, and bears the scars of a violent history of pilfering and restoration thereafter. Much has been written about the Taj Mahal: its refined elegance, architectural rendition, and balanced composition. However, its sublime beauty is best appreciated from the gateway to the Charbagh—a garden with four quarters, resplendent with flower beds, tree-lined avenues, and water courses—inspired by the Persian concept of paradise. To the extreme end of this abundance sits the mausoleum erected on a base of red sandstone. Every inch of its pure white marble is detailed with bas-relief calligraphy and abstract geometric or floral patterns inlaid with sapphires, lapis lazuli, turquoise, and semiprecious stones. The internal chamber containing the cenotaphs of the empress and her husband are screened with intricate marble filigree screens. The ancillary buildings around the main mausoleum complement its sublimity, including the four minarets at the corners of the plinth. The minarets are smaller to accentuate the height of the Taj Mahal, and are erected out of plumb so that in the event of a collapse they would fall away from the main building. Set against the backdrop of the Yamuna River and the Charbagh, the Taj Mahal is transformed at different times of the day and different seasons. The reflection of dawn light on the marble renders it pinkish, while moonlight causes the semiprecious stones to sparkle giving it the appearance of a jewel. **BS**

Masjid-i-Jahan Numa (1656)

Patron Shah Jahan **Location** Delhi, India **Style** Mughal
Materials Red sandstone; black and white marble

Considered to be one of the last of the Mughal emperor Shah Jahan's (1592–1666) vast architectural legacies, the Masjid-i-Jahan Numa—meaning "mosque commanding view of the world" and popularly known as the Jama Masjid—is one of India's largest and most revered mosques.

It was constructed in the Mughal capital of Shahjahanaba (now known as Old Delhi) opposite the emperor's home, the Lal Quila (Red Fort). The royal residence had no private place of prayer, and the construction of the mosque beyond its vestiges was a

> *"… it is one of the main ingredients of the city, built to the monarch's directives …"*
>
> Veena Garella, professor of architecture

symbol that the city outside the fort was not deprived of royal patronage. The emperor came to the mosque for his Friday prayers, entering through the East Gate that frames a stunning vista of the old city.

As one ascends the red sandstone steps to one of the three imposing entrances to the complex, the frenzy of the city is left behind, and one steps into the peaceful grand courtyard.

Capable of accommodating more than 20,000 devotees, this majestic house of worship is designed in alternating strips of red sandstone and white marble in the well-established Mughal tradition. Its stunning main prayer hall, arches, pillars, and three grand domes all evoke awe, drawing devotees into the house of worship. The marble entrances are inlaid with inscriptions from the Koran. **BS**

Church of San Ivo alla Sapienza (1660)

Architect Francesco Borromini **Location** Rome, Italy
Style Baroque **Materials** Marble, stone

Formerly the chapel of the Palazzo della Sapienza (House of Knowledge), this compact gem is not visible from the street. Entry is through the courtyard of the former seat of the University of Rome. Shaped like a star of David and surmounted by a whimsical steeple, nothing about the church of San Ivo alla Sapienza (see page 163) can be appreciated merely at face value.

Gian Lorenzo Bernini, Francesco Borromini's (1599–1667) chief rival architect, recommended his colleague for the job in 1632. Because of a lack of room and an aversion to using flat surfaces, Borromini ingeniously incorporated the convex facade of the church within the palazzo's concave courtyard in a bid to challenge perspective by visually expanding and contracting space where necessary. The building's circular dome terminates in an architectural novelty for the time: a dramatic corkscrew lantern spire modeled on the Tower of Babel.

The church's walls are a complex rhythm of dazzling rationalistic geometry combined with Baroque excesses in a profusion of illusionistic shapes. The nave's centralized plan alternates concave and convex surfaces for a dizzying effect.

Borromini's architectural revolution was ahead of its time and resisted the anthropomorphic obsessions of the sixteenth century, favoring designs based on geometric configurations. Nowhere is his vision more evident than in the ground design, where a circle superimposed on two intersecting triangles forms a six-pointed Star of David creating a hexagonal array of chapels and the altar, and the calculated position of the church's innermost columns as points on a circle. San Ivo alla Sapienza represents a dramatic deviation from the rational compositions of the ancient world and those of the Renaissance. **AA**

Church of
Sant' Andrea al Quirinale (1661)

Architect Gian Lorenzo Bernini   **Location** Rome, Italy
Style Baroque   **Materials** Stone, brick, Carrara marble

Pope Alexander VII (r. 1655–67) left an indelible mark on the planning and architecture of Rome, severely impoverishing the papal coffers in the process. He was fortunate in having a remarkable team of architects, sculptors, and painters available, the most outstanding of whom was Gian Lorenzo Bernini (1598–1680). Bernini was first and foremost a sculptor, and Sant' Andrea al Quirinale was his first complete church.

Perhaps surprisingly for an architect so associated with the Baroque style, Bernini's facades are remarkably orthodox. Despite their occasional curves, they rarely break the rules laid down by the Classical architect Vitruvius. Outside, the church is no exception to this rule, but inside, in part because of the wide but shallow site, the church is highly original. The plan is oval, with the short axis leading to the altar. The domed, central space is flanked by eight chapels: four oval-shaped and four square. The chapels are in shadow while the high altar is lit from concealed windows, and its preeminence is accentuated by the plaster, painting, and sculptural decorations.

The masterpiece of the church is the oval dome that covers the nave. Tapering ribs and diminishing hexagonal coffering in white and gold lead the eye upward, while over the large windows, reclining youths in Carrara marble talk to each other in lively attitudes. Over the smaller windows, *putti* (figures of male infants) swing from heavy garlands of fruit that hang from the windows around the dome, an effect that is charming, profane, and highly theatrical. **CWH**

↗ The church's sumptuous interior reflects Bernini's skill as a sculptor as much as his ability as an architect.

➡ The oval dome covers the nave and the eye is pulled upward to the golden *oculus* at its center.

Amsterdam Town Hall (1664)

Architect Jacob van Campen **Location** Amsterdam, Netherlands
Style Dutch Classical **Materials** Brick, yellow stone

Amsterdam Town Hall (see page 162), now the Royal Palace, is one of the most confident expressions of Northern Renaissance culture of the mid-seventeenth century. It was projected in 1639 as a replacement for a Gothic town hall, and construction began in 1648, following the Treaty of Münster, an event that gave strength to Dutch political and religious independence, and boosted trade.

Jacob van Campen (1596–1657) was the architect of the Mauritshuis in The Hague, a smaller building of great sophistication, and was the leading Classicist in the Netherlands, having visited Italy around 1615. His five-story facade is organized in the traditional form of a palace, with a projecting center section and wings. A double tier of pilasters—an idea probably taken from the book *L'Idea dell'Architettura Universale* (1615) by Andrea Palladio's principal disciple, Vincenzo Scamozzi—locks the repetitive windows into a grid formation, and a fine cupola, completed in 1664, marks it on the skyline. The yellow stone was brought from Germany to replace the usual brick of the Low Countries, although it has darkened over time.

The interior was decorated with symbolic painting and sculpture—the debtor's court has a scheme based on the fall of Icarus—culminating in the double-height central hall. The lack of a grand entrance is typical of the democratic Dutch spirit, and the seven arches represent the seven provinces of the Netherlands. At ground level on the central axis is the Tribuna, arranged for trying legal cases in public view.

The Town Hall was in civic use until 1808, when it was converted into a palace for Napoleon Bonaparte's brother, Louis Napoleon Bonaparte, with furniture in the Empire style that remains in place in its current use as the official residence of the Dutch royal family. **AP**

Sheldonian Theatre (1667)

Architect Sir Christopher Wren **Location** Oxford, England
Style Baroque **Materials** Limestone, timber

Sir Christopher Wren's (1632–1723) architectural genius was still in its budding form when he was approached by Gilbert Sheldon, Archbishop of Canterbury and future chancellor of Oxford University to design a structure that would provide a secular venue for "the enactment of university business."

Inspired by reading Vitruvius, and his recent visit to Rome, where he was particularly impressed with the Marcellus Theater, Wren conceived a building that borrowed heavily from its Roman predecessor.

A 70 by 80 feet (21 by 24 m) D-shaped floorplan

> *"In one building . . . Wren [is] a neat decorative draftsman and an experimental philosopher."*
>
> Sir John Summerson, architectural historian

with tiered seating could accommodate an audience of 2,000. The column-free interior was made possible by Wren's mathematical talent that enabled him to contrive a revolutionary timber truss spanning the load-bearing external walls. The main elevation resembles Roman structures of similar type: a two-story facade topped with a broken pediment featuring the Corinthian and Composite orders respectively. The building drum is clad in limestone and punctured with rectangular windows.

The interior features a flat, painted ceiling, including large areas of blue skies that maintain an illusion of an outdoor ancient theater.

Wren's real achievement, albeit concealed behind the ceiling, lies in the ingenious roof structure that crowns the largest column-free hall of its time. **BK**

Colonnade
of St. Peter (1667)

Architect Gian Lorenzo Bernini   **Location** Rome, Italy
Style Baroque   **Material** Travertine stone

Gian Lorenzo Bernini's (1598–1680) design for the piazza facing the newly built Basilica of St. Peter in Rome was unrivaled in scale, and an expression of the Roman Catholic Church triumphant in the Baroque age. Commissioned by Pope Alexander VII, the piazza established order on the medieval fabric of the Vatican precinct, completing a ceremonial access to the vast church begun by Pope Julius II in 1506.

Bernini's project set out to create a Classical enclosure, axially aligned to the basilica. The architect's drawings suggest that the oval colonnade stands for the outstretched arms of the church, gathering the faithful together. Bernini had to incorporate an ancient Egyptian obelisk, dating back to 1200 BCE, that had been brought to Rome in 37 by Emperor Caligula. It was moved to its position in front of St. Peter's in 1586. Bernini made the obelisk the center of a massive oval. From the obelisk, radiating lines are inscribed on the pavement, marking the axial plan of the piazza.

The colonnade is three columns deep, but at the geometric source all columns align to allow a view out of the piazza, which is otherwise enclosed by a curtain of columns. A third "arm" was originally planned to screen the front of the piazza, in order to create a more dramatic impact on arrival at the piazza from the city. The enormous scale and breadth of the design accentuates the size of the basilica that is framed as the focus of the design. Above the giant travertine columns stand statues of saints reinforcing the sense of pomp and display at the center of Christendom. **FN**

↗ The colonnade embraces visitors, commanding their attention while controlling their onward path.

⊡ The colonnade is a piece of Baroque theater, its encircling saints witnesses to heaven's splendor.

Synagogue of the Holy Community Talmud Torah (1675)

Architect Elias Bouman **Location** Amsterdam, Netherlands **Style** Dutch Classical **Materials** Brick, Bremen sandstone, wood

In 1671 the leaders of the Sephardi, or Spanish-Portuguese Jewish community, of Amsterdam chose the work of local architect Elias Bouman (1636–86) from a number of designs for the new synagogue of the Holy Community Talmud Torah in Amsterdam. The synagogue replaced an older synagogue on Houtgracht that had functioned since 1639, but had become too small for the growing, prosperous Sephardi population of Amsterdam. The building was consecrated in 1675 with an impressive ceremony, followed by eight days of festivities. Some scholars believe that certain elements of the design, especially the prominent buttresses, were inspired by Rabbi Jacob Judah Leon's famous model of the Temple in Jerusalem (c. 1640). The building is one of Amsterdam's outstanding architectural monuments and is still used by the local Sephardi community.

The synagogue's majestic interior has remained intact since the inauguration. The rectangular design is dominated by a huge Holy Ark of Brazilian jacaranda wood. On top of the Holy Ark is the Decalogue, apparently influenced by a similar practice in Reformed churches. At the other end, the Tebah, the platform from which services are led, is situated opposite the usual location in many other synagogues, where this element appears right in front of the Ark. A total of 3,000 wooden piles support six brick barrel vaults, five of which can only be reached by boat. Four huge Bremen-sandstone columns support the three wooden barrel-vaulted ceilings. The vertical arrangement of the benches is typically Sephardi and provides space for 1,227 men and 440 women. **EGS**

↖ The interior is no less impressive than the exterior, monumental in both its starkness and rigorous order.

← The building's exterior presages Wren's Hampton Court facades, but seems more modern still.

Church of San Lorenzo (1679)

Architect Guarino Guarini **Location** Turin, Italy **Style** Baroque **Material** Stone

The seventeenth-century Church of San Lorenzo with its magnificent dome and ornate interior is a near perfect expression of the Baroque style.

The church owes its existence to a vow made by Duke Emanuele Filiberto in 1557. On the eve of the battle of San Quintino (held on August 10, a day traditionally dedicated to San Lorenzo) the duke made a pledge that if he was victorious he would build a church in the saint's honor. He won the battle, but it was a hundred years before work began on his chosen site of the existing church of Santa Maria del Presepio.

The church was designed by Italian architect and mathematician Guarino Guarini (1624–83), a member of a religious order of Theatine monks that owned the site. Working in a long, narrow, confined space, Guarini created an octagonal building modeled on the Greek cross, and topped it with a magnificent cupola. Its eight walls curve into the center of the domed space, and each bay has a large oval window. The dome is remarkable for its fine intersecting rib structure responsible for holding up a lantern that provides a mesmerizing interplay of light and shade.

Unfortunately, although Guarini drew up plans for a facade it was never built. However, its plain exterior hides a wealth of architectural treasure. With Gothic and Arabic elements, the interior is an ecclesiastical delight, consisting of towering altars, frescoes, statues, stuccowork, gilding, colored marble pillars, and a beautifully carved pulpit. This was Guarini's first work in Turin, and is hailed as a turning point for the evolution of European Baroque architecture between the seventeenth and eighteenth centuries. **JM**

↗ Guarini's cupola telescopes the eye upward, changing architecture into a series of sublime geometries.

→ Given the site's spatial restrictions, the cupola strongly announces the church's presence.

Santa Maria della Salute (1682)

Architect Baldassare Longhena   **Location** Venice, Italy   **Style** Baroque   **Materials** Istrian stone, marble

By 1630, one-third of Venice's population had been decimated by the plague, so the Senate decreed that if the city was delivered from such an epidemic, a new church would be built and dedicated to the Virgin. The pledge was honored one year on with a competition to find the most inspiring design for such a building. The drawings of an unknown were selected from eleven other plans, and the church of Santa Maria della Salute was completed in 1682, one year before the death of Baldassare Longhena (1598–1682). The massive two-domed basilica stands at the intersection between the Grand Canal and the inner basin of St. Mark. Approached by gondola, its balloonlike domes appear as if pinned down by the great Baroque scrolls on the facade and huge doorway. Giving the structure even greater grandeur are the white stone steps raised over wooden pilings that lead up to the entrance modeled on the Roman triumphal arch. A

platform made of more than 100,000 wooden piles prevents the octagonal brick and stone base from sinking into the Grand Canal. Divided by arches with a corresponding number of columns, the majestic octagonal interior also recalls Byzantine elements with its demarcation of architectural elements using color. There are references to the Virgin everywhere: the great dome represents her crown, the cavernous interior her womb, and the octagonal plan her eight-pointed star, yet the circle of saints crowning the balustrade in the central nave is a novel detail. This building remains inextricably woven into the character of the Venetians and their city. On November 21, during the Festa della Madonna della Salute (Feast of the Presentation of the Virgin), the city's officials cross the Grand Canal on a specially built pontoon bridge from St. Mark's to Santa Maria della Salute for a thanksgiving and remembrance service. **AA**

Wren Library (1684)

Architect Sir Christopher Wren **Location** Cambridge, England **Style** Baroque **Materials** Ketton stone, timber, iron

The Wren Library is one of Sir Christopher Wren's (1632–1723) finest buildings. The library as built closes the west side of Nevile's Court, completed in 1612, that was until then open toward the River Cam. It is a simple structure: a stone shoe-box with one room to house the books, raised up on an open, colonnaded ground floor as a precaution against damp. The two main elevations are two seemingly equal stories, designed to mask the fact that internally the upper floor is considerably taller in order to accommodate the bookcases below the windows. The side facing the court is more elaborate. The tall arched windows of the upper floor are separated by attached Ionic columns, while the ground floor has Doric columns framing an apparent arcade. The river front is simpler and even finer. The ground floor is a solid wall punctuated by unglazed window apertures and three Doric portals. On the upper floor the columns are stripped away so that the arched library windows are set within elemental stone frames. The rationalism of the facade is carried into the library interior, where the vertical rhythms of the facade are prolonged to form a grid of ceiling beams. The austerity is offset by the procession of projecting oak bookcases, ornamented with limewood carvings, and by a profusion of marble busts. Although Wren drew on the form of previous college libraries, here he set an example that was emulated for more than a century. **RW**

> *"... simplicity and ease combined with a mastery of the Renaissance idiom."*
>
> Sir Nikolaus Pevsner, *The Buildings of England* (1951–74)

Het Loo (1686)

Architect Jacob Roman, Daniël Marot **Location** Apeldoorn, Netherlands **Style** Baroque **Materials** Brick, stone

Originally a hunting lodge, Het Loo dates from 1684 when Prince William III of Orange, later William III of England (1650–1702), bought it to use as a country house. In 1685, a principal block was built linked by colonnades to wings on either side in Palladian style. The four-story main building followed the Palladian model of having a basement lying two-thirds below ground level, and an elevated main entrance accessed by steps. After William's accession to the English throne in 1689, the building was enlarged, and the colonnades were replaced by four forward-projecting wings containing new apartments more suitable for royalty. The architects, Jacob Roman (1640–1716) and Daniël Marot (1661–1752), also designed the interiors, furnishings, and the garden. Het Loo, while still presenting itself as a country retreat, became more palatial. Its grand scale and situation *entre cour et jardin* (between forecourt and garden) mimicked the Palace of Versailles, albeit on a smaller scale. The new wings created another Baroque feature, the *cour d'Honneur* (a three-sided courtyard) that served as a grand approach to the pedimented main entrance. Marot is credited with introducing French Baroque to the Netherlands; Dutch Baroque was always more restrained and austere. For example, the entrance at Het Loo is modestly pedimented, and the *cour d'Honneur* has wrought-iron gates on its fourth side, adding an air of domesticity. **MC**

" . . . the design of Het Loo . . . is relatively modest compared with other Baroque palaces."

Dr. Anthony Geraghty, architectural historian

Palace of the Archbishop at Hradcany (1694)

Architects Jean-Baptiste Mathey, Johann Joseph Wirch **Location** Hradcany, Prague, Czech Republic **Style** Baroque **Material** Stone

The mighty Vltava river cuts the city of Prague in two. A hill rising steeply from its left bank culminates in an impressive manmade geology of spires, towers, tiled roofscapes, and vast, rhythmically fenestrated elevations. Hradcany's juxtaposition of Romanesque, Gothic, Renaissance, Baroque, and Rococo forms is evidence of the cycles of construction, reconstruction, and remodeling that began with the erection of the first castle on the site in the ninth century. Next to the castle, and overlooking the cobbled main square stands the Palace of the Archbishop, itself a testimony to the shifting sands of architectural fashion. The original sixteenth-century Renaissance palace was based on plans drawn up by the German architect Bonific Wohlmut, whose surviving achievements in the district include work on the Gothic cathedral of St. Vitus's later south tower, with its "Golden Gate." While the chapel, with frescoes added in 1599 to 1600,

remained essentially unchanged, the palace itself was rebuilt in the Baroque style in the second half of the seventeenth century. The design was by Jean-Baptiste Mathey (1630–96), who had moved from France to Prague to begin working as architect to the archbishop in 1675, and immediately began working in the Classicizing French manner. Less than a hundred years later, the palace's Late Baroque facade was added by Johann Joseph Wirch (1732–83). Wirch's elegant design fuses a pleasingly symmetrical arrangement of a pediment, columns, pilasters, and glazed openings with exuberant Rococo embellishments. A decorative portal with Latin inscription from the older scheme is retained as an element of the new composition. The interior of the palace is closed to the public, but it includes an excellent collection of ecclesiastical portraits, tapestries, and a wealth of decorative eighteenth-century furnishings. **AMR**

Hampton Court Palace, East and South Facades (1694)

Architect Sir Christopher Wren   **Location** Hampton Wick, Middlesex, England
Style Baroque   **Materials** Brick, Portland stone

Hampton Court was begun for Cardinal Wolsey in 1514. At his downfall in 1529, his house was confiscated by King Henry VIII and enlarged to become a royal palace. Thereafter, little building work was done until King William III and Queen Mary II made it their Versailles. Work on the interior continued after William III's death in 1701 but only minor additions were made under King George I and King George II, and the Royal Family ceased to occupy the palace after 1760.

Sir Christopher Wren, as Surveyor to the King's Works, was the obvious choice to modernize the palace. He hoped to replace the entire building, but the royal finances were insufficient, and a reduced scheme was carried out. The result is cosy and cheerful rather than grand, but its style was enormously influential two centuries later, when what Edwin Lutyens described as the "Wrenaissance" became virtually the house style of the British empire. The use of circular windows above rectangular ones was particularly popular.

Two show fronts to the park were completed to the east and the south in contrasting Portland stone and red brick, with the Fountain Court behind. The east front is twenty-three bays wide. The centerpieces of both fronts lack sufficient emphasis to dominate, and the whole is less than the sum of the parts. A particular problem is the way that the pediment on the east front is squashed below an attic. The interiors are more successful, and the workmanship throughout is of the highest quality. **CWH**

↘ The majestic scale of Wren's architecture relies on the juxtaposition of simple geometrical shapes.

← The recently restored gardens at Hampton Court Palace extend the formal repetition of Wren's facades.

Tiger's Nest Monastery (1694)

Architects Tenzin Rabgye, Penlop Dragpa Gyatso
Location Paro, Bhutan   **Style** Bhutanese   **Materials** Stone, wood

According to legend, in the eighth century the Buddhist master Padmasambhava made a journey to western Bhutan on the back of the lady Tashi Kyidren, who had transformed into a flying tigress. The tigress landed in Paro, on the side of a sheer cliff, 2,600 feet (792 m) above the floor of the Paro Valley. Here the tantric master meditated in a cave, today known as the Taktsang, or Tiger's Nest.

In 1692 Bhutan's ruler, the Fourth Druk Desi Tenzin Rabgye (1638–96) visited the Taktsang cave, and announced that a temple would be built on the site.

> *"Paro Taktsang in Bhutan,*
> *[is] one of the most sacred places*
> *blessed by Padmasambhava."*

Matthieu Ricard, academic and Buddhist monk

After deciding on the basic design, an artist monk, Penlop Dragpa Gyatso (1646–1719), organized its construction. The first temple, Guru Tsengyed Lhakhang, was completed in 1694.

The Tiger's Nest Monastery has twelve temples that were restored following a fire in 1998. The temple complex is highly compact and only accessible via a bridge and steep winding track. The cluster of white-washed temples, with their gilded roofs, can be seen from miles away, clinging to the cliff, below an overhanging mass of rock. The main building materials used are stone and wood, which is often carved in exquisite detail and painted. The temples house a number of statues, paintings, and relics. The most sacred spot of the complex is the cave in which Padmasambhava meditated. **JR**

Hall of Supreme Harmony (1695)

Patron Emperor Kang Xi   **Location** The Forbidden City, Beijing, China
Style Imperial Chinese   **Material** Wood

The Forbidden City is a complex of buildings built between 1406 and 1420 by the Ming Emperor Yong Le (1360–1424) when he moved the capital from Nanjing to Beijing. The vast palace complex is surrounded by a 33-foot-high (10 m) wall and a 170-foot-wide (52 m) moat. Within the walls, the complex is divided into the Inner Court and the Outer Court that are aligned along a central north-south axis.

Tai He Dian is popularly called Jin Luan Dian (Hall of Supreme Harmony), and was used by the emperor to receive officials. It is located on the central axis within the Outer Court. Various vicissitudes, including three fires, have ensured various incarnations since 1420. The existing structure was built in the reign of Emperor Kang Xi (1654–1722) in 1695. Standing more than 114 feet (35 m) high with an area of 25,575 square feet (2,377 sq m), the Hall of Supreme Harmony is the largest of the Forbidden City's halls and, as the largest surviving wooden structure in China, is an excellent example of traditional Chinese architecture.

From the outside, the building is conspicuous for its dominant position above a white marble terrace, and its double-eaved roof of yellow tiles supported by seventy-two wooden columns, twelve of which form a colonnade at the front of the building at ground level. Inside the sumptuous gold interior, the extraordinarily complex structure of the roof beams and eaves and the intricate paintwork are simply breathtaking. Symbolism is used throughout the building, and dragons—the sign of the emperor—are ubiquitous: in the center of the ceiling is a sculpted dragon holding a pearl between its teeth. Dragons are carved into six wooden columns that surround the emperor's throne, which itself is decorated with dragons, as is every roof beam and crossbeam. **ED**

Potala Palace (1697)

Patron Lozang Gyatso, Fifth Dalai Lama **Location** Lhasa, Tibet
Style Tibetan Buddhist **Materials** Concrete, wood, stone

As King Songtsen Gampo's seventh-century structure was almost completely destroyed, the oldest sections of the Potala Palace date mostly from the time of Lozang Gyatso (1617–82), the Fifth Dalai Lama with additions by the Thirteenth Dalai Lama. Perched on Marpo Ri Hill, this former seat of government was also the residence of Tibet's spiritual leader.

The immense, thirteen-story, highrise quadrangle of bearing masonry with gilded roofs and inward-sloping walls consists of two separate areas accessed via stairways. The lower and outer portions of the

"Imposing ... with skyscraperlike sloping walls, gilded roofs, and bells crowning the chortens ..."

Sir Banister Fletcher, *A History of Architecture* (1896)

White Palace encase the Red Palace that rises above the center. Both constructions house chapels, private apartments, and state rooms.

A wooden staircase on the western side of the painted inner courtyard separates the secular quarters and administration offices of the White Palace from the prayer and study rooms of the Red Palace. Within the White Palace are the Great East Hall on the fourth floor of the western wing and two small chapels, the Phakpa Lhakhang and the Chogyal Drubphuk. The Red Palace contains galleries, halls, chapels, shrines, and libraries on different levels. Its richly decorated central chamber, the Great West Hall, consists of four chapels dedicated to deities, saints, and past Lamas. The Saints' Chapel on the north side of this room is the Potala's holiest shrine. **AA**

Fortress of San Juan de Ulúa (1701)

Patron Holy Roman Emperor Charles V **Location** Veracruz, Mexico
Style Spanish Colonial **Material** Stone

Raised on an island just off the coast of Veracruz, the Fortaleza de San Juan de Ulúa (Fortress of San Juan de Ulúa) castle fortress was built to protect the shallow waters and exposed position of the galleons at these maritime doors of sixteenth-century New Spain, now Mexico. The target of pirate attacks seeking the fabled gold and silver bound for the motherland, the fortress also resisted invasions from the French, British, and Dutch. A support base for Spain until the Royalist forces were finally driven out in 1825, the fort was captured during the Mexican-American War of 1846 to 1848 that resulted in the ceding of all lands north of the Rio Grande, and was turned into a prison during Porfirio Díaz's presidency.

The island bastion is connected to the mainland by a walk bridge that leads to a rear gate of the fort. Shortly after the Spanish Conquest, Holy Roman Emperor Charles V (1500–58) ordered a Franciscan chapel, the first building on the site, and proceeded to build a formidable floating fortress. The vast majority of the fortress was completed in 1701, and it is one of seven such forts constructed over the course of sixteenth and seventeenth centuries, claiming the lives of thousands of indigenous slaves. The island bastion is equipped with five powerful bulwarks, battlements, bridges, arched breezeways, passageways, stairways, plazas, cannons, a moat, a watchtower, a hospital, and dungeons.

Fortress San Juan de Ulúa is one of the few representations of colonial military architecture still standing today. It evokes the spirit of a bygone era of swashbuckling adventure, slave traders, and New World buccaneers. More silver and gold have been collected, stored, and shipped from Veracruz and its fortress than any other place on earth. **AA**

Hôtel de Soubise (1709)

Architects Pierre-Alexis Delamair, Germain Boffrand
Location Paris, France **Style** Rococo **Material** Masonry

The Hôtel de Soubise is a city mansion built for the Prince and Princess de Soubise. In 1700 François de Rohan bought the Hôtel de Clisson, and in 1704 the architect Pierre-Alexis Delamair (1675–1745) was hired to renovate and remodel the building. Delamair designed the huge courtyard on the Rue des Francs-Bourgeois. On the far side of the courtyard is a facade with twin colonnades topped by a series of statues by Robert Le Lorrain representing the four seasons.

In 1708 Delamair was replaced by Germain Boffrand (1667–1754), who carried out all the interior decoration for the apartments for the Prince's son, Prince Hercule-Mériadec de Rohan-Soubise, on the ground floor, and for the Princess on the *piano nobile*, (principal floor) both of which featured oval salons looking into the garden.

The interiors are considered among the finest Rococo decorative interiors in France. In the Prince's salon, the wood paneling is painted a pale green and surmounted by plaster reliefs. The Princess's salon is painted white with delicate gilded moldings, and features arched niches containing mirrors, windows, and panels. Above the panels are shallow arches containing cherubs and eight paintings by Charles Natoire depicting the history of Psyche. Plaster *rocailles* (shellwork) and a decorative band of medallions and shields complete the sweetly disordered effect. At the time of the French Revolution, the building was given to the National Archives. A Napoleonic decree of 1808 granted the residence to the state. **JEH**

↗ The twinned columns supporting the pediment bring texture to the otherwise restrained front elevation.

→ The magnificent courtyard carves out a space within the crowded city, declaring wealth and status.

St. Paul's Cathedral (1710)

Architect Sir Christopher Wren   **Location** London, England   **Style** Baroque   **Materials** Portland stone, Oxfordshire stone

The medieval Old St. Paul's was destroyed during the Great Fire of London in September 1666. A week before the Fire, Wren had delivered proposals for repairs and alterations to the old building, but he now had the freedom to design a completely new church. The present cathedral is a brilliant compromise that grafts a domed Classical structure onto a cruciform, Gothic plan, designed to meet the needs of the clergy. Although Wren first proposed a centralized domed church in the form of a Greek cross, the clergy demanded a traditional Latin cross plan. They also wanted a choir that could be closed off to contain the smaller daily services and, lastly, a cathedral that could be built in stages, for it was evident that money might be short. The sources of many of Wren's ideas in designing the building were French, particularly François Mansart's church of Val-de-Grace in Paris. His only foreign trip was to Paris in 1665, but he built up an extensive library, including a collection of engravings, so Italy and particularly Rome also furnished ideas. For example, Wren clearly studied Michelangelo's proposals for the dome of the Basilica of St. Peter. His building's interior is enhanced by the woodwork of Grinling Gibbons and the frescoes in the dome by Sir James Thornhill, although Wren did not approve of the latter. The purity of the original design has been further blurred by the addition of large sculptures and nineteenth-century mosaics in the choir. **CWH**

> "... inside the cathedral shows a balance between carved detail and massive scale that is perfect."
>
> Colin Amery, journalist and architectural historian

LaBrang Tashikyil Monastery (1710)

Architect Unknown   **Location** Southwest of Lanzhou, Gansu Province, China   **Style** Tibetan   **Materials** Wood, mud, stone

Located on a mountainside, facing Da Xia river, and at an altitude of more than 9,842 feet (3,000 m), LaBrang Monastery is considered among the six most significant monasteries of the Gelug Tradition and is the biggest outside Lhasa. LaBrang conforms to a traditional Tibetan plan, though its buildings evidence Han Chinese and curious fusions of Han and Tibetan styles. The many buildings that make up the extensive monastery complex are concentrated around the great hall of Mayjung Tosamling, established by the First Jamyang-zhaypa in 1710. This impressive wooden structure is supported by 140 wooden columns and can seat 3,000 monks. The interior is very elaborately decorated with a strong Nepalese influence and dominated by a 32-foot-high (10 m) golden Buddha, fashioned by Nepalese craftsmen. The entire monastery contains more than 10,000 religious statues made from a wide range of materials including jade, gold, ivory, clay, bronze, and wood. It also houses more than 65,000 Tibetan Buddhist manuscripts covering a wide range of subjects, such as philosophy, medicine, history, and literature. The walls of the buildings are constructed from wood and mud or stone and mud, with their exteriors faced with black stones. The style is intended to be simple and elegant. Around the cornice line of the taller buildings are typical Tibetan elements of low walls made of grass, which add height, sometimes by as much as two stories. **ED**

> *"No sight of wood from outside and no sight of stone from inside."*
>
> Local proverb

Golden-Domed Monastery of St. Michael (1720)

Patron Svyatopolk II Iziaslavych **Location** Kiev, Ukraine **Style** Ukrainian Baroque **Materials** Limestone, brick

The eleventh-century Monastery of St. Demetrius was a complex of buildings that included three churches. The main church, later cathedral, was dedicated to Michael the Archangel by Svyatopolk II Iziaslavych (1050–1113). Its dome is believed to be the first of the Kievan Rus's region to be gilded, hence the description "golden-domed." The monastery complex was damaged by the Mongols in 1240 and fell into disrepair, but it underwent many restorations and enlargements during the sixteenth century.

St. Michael's Cathedral became a place of pilgrimage because relics of St. Barbara were kept there. The original cathedral followed the plan of a Greek cross with six pillars, three apses, and only one dome. In the eighteenth century, the cathedral was given a Baroque exterior with additional domes. The Byzantine interior was remodeled in a more Baroque style to include a five-tier iconostasis—a wall of religious paintings separating the nave from the sanctuary. Medieval mosaics and frescoes were plastered over. The monastery bell tower with its pear-shaped dome was built from 1716 to 1720. The style, known as Ukrainian Baroque, is a less elaborate and less ornamented form of Western Baroque. In the 1930s, the cathedral and monastery were demolished by the Soviet government. The shell of the cathedral was dynamited. Of the monastery, only the eighteenth-century refectory survived. In the late 1990s, excavation of the site uncovered parts of the eleventh-century cathedral and several ancient artefacts. The cathedral was rebuilt in its eighteenth-century form and reopened on May 30, 1999. **MC**

↖ The startling color scheme and abstraction of Western architecture creates an air of fantasy.

← The monastery, as it currently stands, is a recent reconstruction of a still older series of buildings.

Church of St. John of Nepomuk (1722)

Architect Jan Blazej Santini-Aichel   **Location** Zdár nad Sázavou, Czech Republic   **Style** Baroque Gothic   **Material** Stone

This curious white church is situated on top of Zelená Hora (Green Hill) in a forested area near the Cistercian monastery at Zdár nad Sázavou, a town in the Bohemian-Moravian highlands. It was formerly a Gothic construction erected in honor of the national saint, John of Nepomuk (1340–93). During the Czech Counter-Reformation, orders were given by the local abbot, Vaclav Vejmluva, to begin reconstruction of the monastery, its church, and the surrounding buildings. Santini-Aichel, a Prague-born architect of Italian origin, was chosen to renovate the Gothic church. John of Nepomuk's canonization one year before the church's completion made it the region's most popular pilgrimage destination.

Santini-Aichel transposed the existing elements of the church into Baroque form. Surrounded by cloisters laid out in the pattern of a ten-point star and crowned by a star-shaped roof, its pentagram plan and five entrances have mystical significance. Local legend relates how a five-star halo miraculously appeared above the body of St. John, who drowned in the Vltava River after being thrown off Prague's Charles Bridge. The interior consists of twenty-five chapels with pointed windows and culminates in a dramatic altarpiece set into arcades that reach into the upper gallery on the eastern side. The sculpture shows the martyr being carried up to heaven by five angels. Santini-Aichel's masterpiece, with its complex, interconnecting spatial forms, use of light, and dynamic proportions, bypasses the conventions of eighteenth-century architecture to foreshadow the Gothic Revival of the nineteenth century. **AA**

↗ The seemingly haphazard ordering of windows is governed by the twenty-five chapels inside.

⇥ The delicate tracery around the chapels' windows anticipate the nineteenth century's Gothic Revival.

Schloss Belvedere (1723)

Architect Johann Lukas von Hildebrandt **Location** Near Vienna, Austria **Style** Baroque, Rococo **Materials** Brick, stucco

The two parts of Schloss Belvedere, southeast of Vienna, were built for Prince Eugen of Savoy. The Lower Belvedere, built first, is a single-story pavilion with a mansard roof and a raised centerpiece containing the Marble Hall, with frescoes by Martino Altamonte. The Upper Belvedere, built about ten years later, stands on higher ground to the south, and is a more complex structure with three stories and an attic in the center, winged by octagonal pavilions. The two palaces face each other on the main axis of formal gardens. Lukas von Hildebrandt, who trained in Rome with Carlo Fontana, was the chief successor in Austria to Fischer von Erlach, and introduced the High Baroque style with French influence. He was at first a military engineer, working for Prince Eugen on his campaigns in Northern Italy, from whence many of his architectural mannerisms derived. Hildebrandt was, however, an accomplished master of space and form in his own right, and the Upper Belvedere is probably his finest work, with an especially fine entry sequence leading from the entrance up the stairs to the Sala Terrena, overlooking the gardens. The stuccowork of both buildings was completed by Giovanni Stanetti, of Venice, with a team of assistants. Both also feature allegorical or illusionistic ceiling paintings by Italian artists. The Upper Belvedere was severely damaged during World War II, but after restoration both it and the gardens are due to reopen in 2008. **AP**

"Hildebrandt's feeling for space, so superbly revealed in the exterior, appears equally ... in the interior."

Eberhard Hempel, historian

Church of St. Charles Borromeo (1725)

Architects Johann Bernard Fischer von Erlach **Location** Vienna, Austria **Style** Baroque **Material** Stone

Also known as the Karlskirche, this church is set in open space originally beyond the city walls, and is one of the landmarks of Vienna. It was built to fulfil a vow made in 1713 by the Emperor Charles VI, in recognition of the intercession of St. Charles Borromeo in saving the city from plague. The commission came to Johann Bernard Fischer von Erlach (1656–1723), the favored architect of the Habsburg court in Vienna, and was completed by his son Joseph (1693–1742). The church has a grand, symmetrical facade, made especially wide to fulfill its scenic purpose as viewed from the Hofburg, the Royal Palace. The main portico is in a scholarly Corinthian order, its freestanding columns more Neo-Classical in style than the Baroque forms of the rest of the building. There are open pavilions at each end of the facade, recalling the termination of Bernini's colonnade in front of the Basilica of St. Peter. Two freestanding columns in the manner of Trajan's column in Rome are a unique feature, carrying bas-relief narratives of St. Charles Borromeo's life, based on reconstructions of the Temple of Solomon in Jerusalem. A complex iconography for the whole church was devised by Karl Gustav Heraeus. The main oval body of the church supports a tall dome, with its long axis toward the high altar. On the skyline of the west front are three figures, with Charity represented by the saint in the center (he was also the Emperor's name saint), and Faith and Hope on either side. **AP**

> *"In its spiritual conception it has no predecessor, and in … its realization it has no successor."*
>
> Hans Aurenhammer, historian

Peterhof (1725)

Architects Various   **Location** Near St. Petersburg, Russia   **Style** Russian Baroque   **Materials** Brick, plaster

"If Petersburg is Lapland in stucco, Peterhoff [sic] is the palace of Armida under glass."

Marquis de Custine, diplomat

⬆ In front of the Grand Palace, the Grand Cascade flows from beneath the palace into the Marine Canal.

➡ Peterhof's recently restored interiors feature a riot of freshly gilded carvings, moldings, and statuary.

The palace complex at Peterhof—called Petrodvorets since 1944—is extensive and varied. More than twenty palaces and pavilions are set out in huge interconnecting parks along the Gulf of Finland. The royal palaces were formerly bordered by an outer fringe of aristocratic palaces and country houses, but these were largely destroyed in World War II and not rebuilt. While many of the constituent elements are not outstanding, the whole is far greater than the sum of the parts. The feat of restoration, begun in 1945 and still continuing, is quite extraordinary.

Peter the Great first noticed the site's potential in 1709 and built a two-story palace there between 1715 and 1724, designed by Jean-Baptiste Alexandre Le Blond and Niccolo Micchetti. This remains at the heart of the present Great Palace, which, in its present form, has a third story and long wings designed for the Empress Elizabeth by Bartolommeo Francesco Rastrelli. The palace interiors are a mixture of Rastrelli's Baroque and cooler Neo-Classical rooms redecorated for Catherine the Great by Yuri Felten and others. Between the Great Palace and the Gulf of Finland stretches the Grand Cascade and the Marine Canal. Begun by Peter the Great with additions by each of his successors into the nineteenth century, the cascade and the dozens of fountains in the Lower Park form the most remarkable assemblage in the world of devices using water to entertain, amuse, and delight.

Scattered through the formal park are various Baroque pavilions by Le Blond and others, built between 1714 and 1726. Outside the park, a number of former imperial palaces have reopened to the public. The most notable are the Konstantin Palace at Strelna in the east (1797–1807, by Andrei Voronikhin), the Cottage Palace (1826–29, by Adam Menelaws), and to the west the Chinese Palace at Lomonosov (1762–68, by Antonio Rinaldi). **CWH**

Chiswick House (1725)

Architects Richard Boyle, Earl of Burlington, William Kent   **Location** London, England   **Style** Neo-Classical Palladian   **Material** Stone

Inspired by the villas of ancient Rome, Chiswick House was built largely to the design of Richard Boyle, Earl of Burlington (1694–1753), assisted by William Kent (1685–1748). Built on three different elevations and surrounded by carefully designed gardens, the house owes much to the buildings visited by Burlington on his Grand Tour. Burlington's greatest inspiration came from the works of the Italian architect Andrea Palladio, while Kent was inspired by Inigo Jones; both Palladio and Jones are commemorated in statues at either side of the sweeping external stairs.

Burlington based much of Chiswick House on Palladio's Villa Rotonda near Vicenza, although he chose to use Corinthian forms while Palladio had used Ionic. While in Italy, Burlington purchased some of the building materials to give his villa authenticity; in the Lower Tribune, eight columns of Tuscan marble support the stone floor of the room above.

One of the most unusual features of the design of Chiswick House is its consistent use of geometry, including the octagonal hall at the heart of the villa. The hall, in common with the slender spiral staircases leading from it, pays homage to Palladio's Rotonda. The remarkable ceiling of the Blue Velvet Room is supported by eight pairs of curving brackets.

The villa's lavish interiors are a deliberate contrast to the all-white exterior, with the upper floor the most elaborate of all. In recent decades it has become common to interpret carvings, details of paintings, and certain room decorations as Masonic symbols, leading to speculation that the upper floor was also a regular Masonic meeting place. **LH**

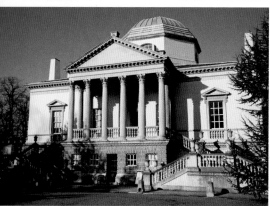

↖ The elegant exterior staircases lead directly to the *piano nobile*, where entertainments were staged.

← Rusticated (rough-surfaced) stone was used for the ground-floor walls, below the elegant portico.

Church of St. Martin-in-the-Fields (1726)

Architect James Gibbs **Location** London, England **Style** Palladian **Material** Portland stone

St. Martin-in-the-Fields today is the hinge on which swings the whole of the nineteenth-century layout of London's Trafalgar Square. Originally, the site was squeezed into the bottom of a narrow old street, and only the portico and steeple were visible from afar. A new church became necessary because the old medieval structure had become unsafe, and the parish authorities turned to Scottish architect James Gibbs (1682–1754). A Roman Catholic architect, Gibbs was unique among his British contemporaries for having undergone training in Italy in the office of Rome's leading architect, Carlo Fontana.

Gibbs produced several proposals, including a design with a circular nave, all of which he subsequently published in his *Book of Architecture* (1728). These designs proved extraordinarily influential in Britain and North America, and derivatives are still being built today. Gibbs's achievement was to combine in one structure the Gothic concept of a steeple with the Classical concept of a temple.

The temple front is monumental and unusually deep; originally it was intended to be one bay shallower. The forms of the tower and gilt-crowned steeple are influenced by architect Sir Christopher Wren's steeples in the city center of London, and Gibbs took the building committee on an educational tour of these when submitting his proposals. The interior also looks back at Wren but with a more eighteenth-century sensibility. The ceiling has an elliptical barrel vault and there are saucer domes over the aisles. The plasterwork is by Italian Giovanni Battista Bagutti and Chrysostom Wilkins. **CWH**

↗ Gibbs's combination of a Classical temple and a Gothic steeple is now often seen in the United States.

➡ The royal coat of arms within the pediment testifies to close links between the royal family and the church.

Zwinger Palace (1728)

Architects Pöppelmann, Permoser, Semper **Location** Dresden, Germany **Style** Baroque, Neo-Classical **Material** Sandstone

If ever there was a building that embodied the essence of its epoch, it is surely the Zwinger Palace in Dresden. The Zwinger is a perfect display of splendor that mirrors the abundance of art and culture in Dresden during the rule of August II the Strong. Built by Matthäus Daniel Pöppelmann (1662–1736) and the sculptor Balthasar Permoser, it was designed for lavish festivals, performances, and other amusements, framed by picture galleries, fountains, and arcades. Intended to form a U-shaped courtyard, one side was originally left open to the terraces along the River Elbe. However, in 1847, Gottfried Semper (1803–79), who had erected the Semper opera on a neighboring site, completed the Zwinger with the less ornate, Neo-Classical, northeast-wing picture gallery in 1854. The Kronentor, or Crown Gate, and the French pavilion are undoubtedly the most striking parts of this building. However, the true heart of the Zwinger lies in the carved stone and sparkling waters of Permoser's Nymphenbad, the fountain of nymphs. The Zwinger, damaged repeatedly during wars over the centuries, was almost totally destroyed at the end of World War II—a fate it shared with nearly all of the historical buildings of Dresden. This devastated city was one of the few that were rebuilt in almost exactly the same way. Pristinely restored between 1945 and 1963, the Zwinger Palace now sits immaculately in the remains of a city once dubbed "Florence on the River Elbe." **LT**

> *". . . sparkling, playful baroque ornaments with the . . . geometric lines of the Neo-Renaissance . . ."*
>
> Thomas Kantschew, art historian

Marble Hill House (1729)

Architect Roger Morris **Location** London, England **Style** Palladian **Material** Stone

Marble Hill House was intended as a retreat, not a residence, hence its comparatively small size. It was built for Henrietta Howard, Countess of Suffolk, the mistress of the Prince of Wales, later King George II, for her use as a rural escape from London. Architect Roger Morris's plans were overseen and contributed to by Lord Herbert, later the Earl of Pembroke. The gardens were landscaped by Charles Bridgeman with the poet Alexander Pope. The plans for Marble Hill House were influenced by the currently fashionable idea of a pastoral idyll, encapsulated in artistic images of Arcadia, such as the paintings of Nicolas Poussin. The house is one of London's finest examples of Palladian architecture, and its clean lines and superb use of symmetry adhere closely to Palladio's own sixteenth-century designs, as opposed to the more common Anglo-Palladian style of the eighteenth century. Inside the villa, the symmetry is maintained by use of

subterfuge when necessary, with false doors providing the illusion of a perfectly balanced room. Henrietta Howard was a prominent intellectual with a wide range of acquaintances, and for her the most important requirement of the building was as a venue where everyone could meet. Accordingly, the most striking part of the interior is the large salon, or Great Room, intended for the staging of literary and artistic gatherings. On the ground floor, the Great Room is echoed in the size of the imposing entrance hall, complete with Ionic columns. All the other rooms were intentionally made small, since the salon and entrance hall were the focal points about which the rest of the interior was constructed. The Great Room, with its exquisite moldings and grand gilt work, would not be out of place in a much larger building, emphasizing the importance of its role as the heart of this specialized and lovely villa. **LH**

Royal Palace at Mafra (1730)

Architect Johann Friedrich Ludwig (Ludovice)   **Location** Mafra, Portugal   **Style** Portuguese Baroque   **Materials** Limestone, marble

Originally intended as a Capuchin monastery, the Royal Palace at Mafra evolved into a grand building project under King John V (1689–1750). It was intended to be John V's Versailles, and a rival to Spain's Royal Monastery of San Lorenzo de El Escorial. The chief architect was Johann Friedrich Ludwig (1670–1752), known as Ludovice. He had worked in Italy designing church altars, and was influenced by the sculptor Giovanni Lorenzo Bernini (1598–1680) and the architect Francesco Borromini (1599–1667). The limestone facade is 722 feet (220 m) long, with square towers at each end sporting squat, Byzantine-style domes. The front of the basilica occupies the center of the facade, pilastered in marble with niches for fifty-eight marble statues. Two immense, white marble bell towers reach 223 feet (68 m), each containing forty-eight bells. These soaring towers and facade are reminiscent of Rome's Sant' Agnese in Agone, by

Borromini. The basilica's lavish interior is wrought in rose and white marble. Its barrel-vaulted roof rests on fluted Corinthian columns. Carved jasper altarpieces grace the side chapels, and marble statues fill the side aisles. Behind the church is a massive courtyard around which there are more buildings, including a huge library with rose, gray, and white marble-tiled floors and barrel-vaulted white marble ceilings. This is the largest palace in Europe and the most sumptuous Baroque building in the world. **MC**

"Mafra [is] at once rich and simple. Its design was grand and its execution uniformly successful."

Joaquim Antonio de Macedo, author

St. George's, Bloomsbury (1731)

Architect Nicholas Hawksmoor **Location** London, England **Style** Baroque **Material** Portland stone

St. George's, Bloomsbury was one of the so-called Fifty New Churches (actually only a dozen were built) begun after 1710 for new areas of London. Hawksmoor (1661–1736) was called upon to build six, and the plans of all of them are designed around intersecting axes. St. George's is the most complex, although the effect has been diminished by later alterations. Hawksmoor was given a deep but narrow site running north to south, but he was required to provide an east-facing altar and access through the west tower. His solution is exceptionally clever. He provided cross-axes so that the building works both north–south and east–west with an apparent central square space and a clerestory. The north and south galleries disguise the internal asymmetries required by the site. A recent restoration makes sense of the interior for the first time since the nineteenth century. The tower is based on the Tomb of Mausolus at Halicarnassus in Turkey, one of the lost Seven Wonders of the World. Square in plan, the steeple is a tall, stepped pyramid. What aroused controversy and abuse even before the building was competed were the secular elements provided by a statue of King George I (wearing a toga) on the steeple top, and pairs of lions and unicorns gamboling around the base. Removed in 1871, the latter were recently restored. The church is built on a high basement, so the handsome portico (inspired by the Pantheon, Rome) is approached up a great flight of steps. **CWH**

> *"Hawksmoor was . . . a master of architectural form [with a] powerful personal style . . ."*
>
> Sir Howard Colvin, architectural historian

Blenheim Palace (1733)

Architect Sir John Vanbrugh   **Location** Woodstock, Oxfordshire, England   **Style** Baroque   **Material** Stone

Blenheim Palace and the Woodstock estate were presented by Queen Anne and a grateful nation to John Churchill, First Duke of Marlborough, for his role in thwarting the ambitions of Louis XIV of France to dominate Europe. The building was intended as a national monument celebrating military achievements rather than the small, comfortable house desired by Churchill's wife. The result is one of the greatest Baroque buildings in England. The Duchess's virulent dislike of the architect imposed by Queen Anne, John Vanbrugh (1664–1726), led ultimately to Vanbrugh's dismissal in 1716. The building's silhouette resembles a medieval fortress, and the whole structure reflects Vanbrugh's intense Romanticism. The fantastic skyline is made up of sculptures such as the Lion of England savaging the Cock of France, while what appear to be pinnacles are revealed, on closer inspection, to be piles of cannonballs, reversed fleur-de-lys, and ducal coronets. Outlying courts also have a rugged military character. Vanbrugh was assisted by Nicholas Hawksmoor who took over once Vanbrugh fell out with the Duchess. The respective roles of Hawksmoor and Vanbrugh are difficult to distinguish before 1716, but Hawksmoor was certainly responsible for the Chapel and the sumptuous Great Library. Inside, the state rooms were altered from 1766 to 1775 by Sir William Chambers. Only the Great Hall was completed by Vanbrugh on a majestic Roman scale. **CWH**

> *"[I pay] the tribute which a painter owes to an architect who composed like a painter . . ."*
>
> Sir Joshua Reynolds, artist

Melk Abbey (1736)

Architect Jakob Prandtauer   **Location** Melk, Austria   **Style** Baroque   **Material** Rendered blockwork

For more than 900 years, Melk Abbey has been a stronghold of Catholicism and at times a bastion against reformation. This impressive edifice on a cliff above the village of Melk is the work of architect Jakob Prandtauer (1660–1726), who was commissioned by the young abbot Berthold Dietmayr to replace structurally unsound parts of the old abbey buildings. After thorough investigation, it was decided to build a new church in their place together with a monastery. Originally trained as a sculptor, Prandtauer's mastery undoubtedly lay in the composition and proportions of his designs. Unlike other Baroque monasteries, the church at Melk dominates the other buildings, but it also clearly serves as a backdrop for the impressive, palacelike outbuildings. Organized around a central axis 1,050 feet (320 m) in length, the south wing and its glorious marble hall alone are stretched 790 feet (240 m). Melk is the biggest Baroque abbey in Austria

and Germany, but it is the quality of detail that makes this building truly outstanding. The decoration can be credited to Prandtauer's nephew, Joseph Munggenast (1680–1741), who continued the work after his uncle's death. Some of the decoration was entrusted to Antonio Beduzzi (1675–1735), a theater designer from Vienna, with frescoes and gilding by Paul Troger (1698–1762) in the Austrian Baroque style. Building work was practically completed in 1736, but in 1738 a fire destroyed all roofs, the towers, and several representative rooms. Repair work went on until 1746 when the abbey church was finally consecrated. Today, Melk Abbey remains a center of pilgrimage, and is very much a living monastery where new religious life flows in its old veins. But it is without a doubt Jakob Prandtauer's magnificent creation that draws thousands of visitors to Melk, providing a financial lifeline to the town in the twenty-first century. **LT**

Lesser Basilica of St. Francis of Assisi (1738)

Architect Unknown **Location** Havana, Cuba **Style** Early tropical Baroque **Material** Local stone

Construction of Havana's great Franciscan church and monastery began in 1591. It was so close to the edge of the harbor that piles had to be driven into the seabed to support its foundations. However, by 1719 the Great Chapel was on its way to collapse. It was demolished, and the new church was completed in 1738. The original plan of the church included a nave and two side aisles with a dome at the crossing, but the latter was destroyed in the great hurricane of 1846, which also toppled the statue of St. Francis from the tower. The church was for many years the most fashionable in Havana and is still used today for important cultural events. The nave is supported by arcades resting on pillars of cruciform section, and the lateral vaults, which contain skylights, intersect perpendicularly into the principal barrel vault. The tower of the church is 138 feet (42 m) high, and an excellent view of the old city may be seen from the top. The church's principal entrance is set into a deep, shell-like arch that receives scant appreciation due to lack of space from which to view it, for the street in which it stands is narrow. Attached to the church are two three-story cloisters with perimeter galleries connected by an original staircase enhanced at ground-floor level by an arch with surprising and beautiful perspective. The external entrance to the south cloister consists of three superimposed levels of Tuscan columns, finished with Baroque detailing. **JB**

"We believe that it constitutes a primitive Baroque, before Cano, Donoso, and Churriguera . . ."

Joaquín E. Weiss, architectural historian

Drayton Hall (1742)

Architect Unknown **Location** Charleston, South Carolina, USA **Style** Palladian **Material** Brick

Drayton Hall has endured many bullets in its lifetime, plus fires, hurricanes, and an earthquake. When Charleston surrendered to the North during the Civil War, Drayton Hall escaped Union arsonists who were torching plantations on the Ashley River—they were tricked by hastily improvised smallpox quarantine flags posted along the riverbank. Or was the hall spared for use as a headquarters? Either way, it survives as the finest eighteenth-century Palladian plantation house in the United States. Few historic houses are so authentic—multiple owners and restorations make that impossible. Drayton Hall is completely original. The family who for more than 200 years owned and lived in the hall made no improvements—no electricity, no plumbing, no ducted heat, no do-it-yourself destruction. The architect is unknown, but the design suggests he used a "pattern book" imported from England. Such architectural design catalogs contain plans, elevations, and sections. One such, *Vitruvius Britannicus*, published from 1715 to 1725, popularized the Palladian style used for Drayton Hall. The symmetrical plan follows Enlightenment thinking—order through reason. The hall is a nearly square, seven-bay box with a central entry and symmetrically divided staircase; its main rooms are accessed from a large hall. The upper floors are raised above the brick half-basement service floor. A deep, double-height portico on the inland side is a major adaptation and concession to the sultry southern climate, shading the house and circulating air. Its outdoor veranda provides the ideal place to scan for marauders. Furniture rarely makes a building, and Drayton Hall's trump card is its emptiness. Nothing detracts from the architecture. The result is superbly atmospheric, and for this reason alone Drayton Hall demands a visit. **DJ**

Taj Lake Palace (1746)

Patron Maharana Jagat Singh II   **Location** Lake Pichola, Udaipur, Rajasthan, India   **Style** Indian Classical   **Material** Marble

This elegant marble palace, with its intricate mosaics and intimate courtyard gardens, seems to float tranquilly in the center of Lake Pichola. Covering about 4 acres (1.6 ha), Taj Lake Palace (*Jag Niwas*) has been a royal summer retreat for hundreds of years. It was built for Maharana Jagat Singh II, successor to the royal dynasty of Mewar. When he was young, he was given free reign over a small island in the lake by his father and he decided to create his own palace here, laying its foundation stone on April 17, 1743. The first stage of its construction was completed and royally inaugurated three years later in a lavish three-day ceremony. It was built facing east, so at dawn its inhabitants could pray to the sun god from whom the royal family was believed to be descended. The palace was built almost entirely from marble in a classic combination of columns, fountains, and baths, being beautifully decorated with inlaid mosaics, colored glass, and watercolors of historic Indian scenes. With a focus on fun, the inhabitants would have enjoyed its water-filled courtyard gardens, not to mention its peepholes and secret passages. For more than 400 years the building has been slowly extended to suit the needs of successive rulers. However, in 1955, the palace was sold by the royal family and converted into India's first luxury hotel. Now, after renovations, it has become the opulent Taj Lake Palace Hotel, which famously featured in the Bond movie *Octopussy*. **JM**

" . . . the uniformity pleasingly diversified by the light passing through glass of every hue."

Colonel James Tod, British officer and scholar

Sanssouci (1748)

Architect Hans Georg Wenzeslaus von Knobelsdorff   **Location** Potsdam, Germany   **Style** Rococo   **Material** Stone

In 1744, Frederick the Great ordered that a low, south-facing hill outside Potsdam be carved into a six-tiered terrace and planted with grapevines. He made some sketches for a proposed royal retreat on the summit of the hill and sent them to Hans Georg Wenzeslaus von Knobelsdorff. What Frederick wanted was a small, quiet retreat from the cares of state. Construction based on the king's ideas began the following year, and an inaugural concert was held in 1747; the interiors were completed in 1748. The entrance front opens onto a semicircular colonnade surrounding a forecourt. The paired Corinthian pilasters here are repeated in the vestibule and marble hall inside. The latter is the heart of the palace. It is an oval room, lit from above as well as from three windows opening onto a terrace facing south. Here Frederick entertained dinner guests, including brilliant politicians, artists, musicians, and writers. The audience chamber and music room are decorated in a particularly delicate Rococo style in white and gold. Other rooms include Frederick's circular library, to which no one was admitted without special permission, and an art gallery for paintings and sculpture. In the park, Frederick commissioned various buildings, including an art gallery (1747), the Chinese teahouse (1754–57) by Johann Gottfried Büring, and a friendship temple (1768–70) by Carl von Gontard. The royal bedchamber (1786–87) was redecorated in Neo-Classical style for Frederick William II. **CWH**

"[The marble hall is] on a par with the very best of the genre—Amalienburg, Brühl, or Benrath."

Giles MacDonogh, Frederick II's biographer

Radcliffe Camera (1749)

Architect James Gibbs   **Location** Oxford, England   **Style** Baroque   **Materials** Burford and Headington stone, timber, lead

The dome of the Radcliffe Library—known as "the Camera" from quite early on—is the most distinctive element of the Oxford skyline, otherwise celebrated for its spires. The building was funded by Dr. John Radcliffe, an enormously wealthy physician. By the time of his death, it had been decided to create a new square to provide a suitable setting. In 1733 Nicholas Hawksmoor (1661–1736) produced a scheme for a great domed rotunda, freestanding in the square. James Gibbs (1682–1754), who had previously suggested a more practical shoe-box shape, was asked to adopt and adapt the rotunda concept—the university authorities evidently felt that a rotunda better reflected Radcliffe's wishes. Gibbs transformed Hawksmoor's noble but straightforward design into something more complex, sophisticated, and Baroque. The paired columns of the main drum are placed in a syncopated rhythm between the accents of the rusticated plinth below and the ribs of the dome above. An imposing oval staircase leads to the library room on the upper floor, a magnificent domed space with the bookcases in two levels beyond the inner ring of eight stone arches. The vault was decorated by three leading artists in plaster of the day, the Italian Giuseppe Artari, the Anglo-Dane Charles Stanley, and local man Thomas Roberts. The result is Oxford's finest individual building, even if it has never functioned ideally as a library. **RW**

"The grandest feature in the grandest of all English architectural landscapes."

Alan Cunningham, biographer

Cuvilliés Theater (1753)

Architect François de Cuvilliés the Elder **Location** Munich, Germany **Style** Rococo **Material** Carved and painted wood

After a fire destroyed a wing of Munich's Residenz in 1750, Max III Joseph, Elector of Bavaria, commissioned François de Cuvilliés (1695–1768) to construct a sumptuous opera house in its place. Cuvilliés had originally served as a court dwarf in the prince's residence, but his other talents were soon discovered. He was sent to Paris to receive his artistic training from François Blondel. His opera house, which witnessed the premiere of Mozart's *Idomeneo*, ranks among the finest theater designs in the French Rococo style. The theater is no less remarkable for its beauty than the vicissitudes of its twentieth-century history. While the richly ornamented interior we see today is that of Cuvilliés, the theater no longer stands in its original place. In 1944 Allied bombing was beginning to take its toll on Munich's historical center. Seeing the danger, Swiss architect Tino Walz convinced the authorities to dismantle and store away the theater's splendid interior, made entirely of wood. After the war, the original site made way for a new public theater while the carefully numbered Rococo pieces were relocated and assembled in the fountain court in the northern part of the Residenz. After its reopening in 1958, the building became known as the Cuvilliés Theater. Nearly fifty years after its unlikely rebirth, Cuvilliés's design impresses with the harmonious unity of its décor and spatial composition. An overabundance of figurative and vegetative ornament in golds and reds glides seamlessly into an architectural order. The four-story structure reflects the hierarchy of the *ancien régime*, differentiating clearly between the princely loge at the center and the other parts of the auditorium reserved for the high aristocracy, the civil service, and the lesser urban nobility. The characteristic playfulness of the theater's Rococo style reinterprets the region's rich Baroque traditions. **MJG**

Church of the Immaculate Conception (1753)

Architect Father Martin Schmid   **Location** Concepción, Chiquitos, Chiquitanía, Bolivia   **Style** Baroque   **Materials** Adobe, wood

The first Jesuit missionaries arrived in Upper Peru, now known as Bolivia, in 1572. They founded eleven mission towns in the province of Chiquitos in Chiquitanía, ten of which have survived complete with their Baroque-style churches, built by the missionaries aided by native craftsmen. The church—now the cathedral—of La Inmaculada Concepción lies at the center of the mission town of Concepción.

The church was built between 1752 and 1753, and restored in 1982. Like many Jesuit mission churches it was designed by the Swiss priest Father Martin Schmid (1694–1774). An accomplished musician, Schmid went to Latin America in 1729, and during his stay in the region he founded choirs, made musical instruments ranging from harps to violins, wrote and copied masses and operas, and helped to build the churches, even carving some of their statues. He, like all the Jesuits, sought to train local carpenters and craftsmen, the results of which became a unique synthesis of local and European cultures and skills.

La Inmaculada Concepción is a low, wide, barnlike structure surrounded by rows of wooden columns with twisted fluting, carved from single trees. The facade is painted white with golden Baroque scrolls, shells, and balustrades around its corners, windows, and entrance. Nearby stands a tall, wooden structure, open on all four sides, with a tiled roof; this is the bell tower, which has clock faces on every side. The church has a three-section nave, as do all the mission churches, in homage to the basilicas of the early Roman Catholic church. Inside, its richly carved and gilded altars, *retablos* (painted wooden panels), statues, confessionals, and paintings were made by indigenous craftsmen of the time using a local hardwood known as *ajunau*. **CMK**

Pilgrimage Church of the Scourged Savior (1754)

Architect Dominikus Zimmermann   **Location** Steingaden, Bavaria, Germany   **Style** Rococo   **Materials** Stone, stucco

Wies, located at the foothills of the German Alps, was in 1738 the setting for a miracle. A wooden image of Jesus Christ as the scourged savior appeared to some faithful peasants to be weeping tears. The miracle resulted in a rush of pilgrims. A small chapel was built, but soon the pilgrims—arriving from Germany, Austria, Bohemia, and Italy—became so numerous that it was deemed necessary to construct a great sanctuary to house the miraculous statue.

Dominikus Zimmermann (1685–1766), one of the most talented and famous Rococo artists of his time,

> *"Everything was done throughout the church to make the supernatural visible."*
>
> James F. White, critic

was commissioned to design the church, also known as the Wieskirche. His brother, Johann Baptist Zimmermann, a painter at the royal Bavarian court, attended to the ceiling frescoes. The nave is built to an oval plan and its ceiling is supported by eight pairs of columns. An upper and a lower gallery surround a long, deep choir. The entire building displays an extraordinary fusion of paintings, woodcarving, and stuccowork. The interplay of motifs and figures, the movement of lines, and the skillful opening of surfaces create a unique impression of elegance and lightness.

Since 1983 the Wieskirche, also known as "the Lord God's Ballroom," has been listed as a UNESCO World Heritage Site. Miraculously preserved in its beautiful subalpine scenery, the Pilgrimage Church is a perfect masterpiece of Bavarian Rococo. **CH**

Independence Hall (1756)

Architects Andrew Hamilton, Edmund Woolley   **Location** Philadelphia,
Pennsylvania, USA   **Style** Georgian   **Material** Red brick

An attractive municipal building typical of the restrained yet elegant Georgian style of the mid-eighteenth century, the State House of the Province of Pennsylvania, better known as Independence Hall, is famed for its association with some of the most significant events of the American Revolution. It also functions as a nexus for the nation's relationship with its founding values. Designed and built by Andrew Hamilton (1676–1741) and Edmund Woolley (1695–1771), the two-story, red-brick building was originally surmounted by a wooden steeple with a domed cupola. Two decades after its completion, Philadelphia was a hub of insurrection, and the hall was the site of pivotal events such as the appointment of George Washington as Commander in Chief of the Colonial Army, the agreement on the design of the Stars and Stripes, the signing of the Declaration of Independence, and the drafting of the Constitution.

When Philadelphia became interim capital between 1790 and 1800, the hall was not used as the seat of government. Already in some disrepair, it was scheduled for demolition when, in 1811, it was saved for the nation. By the 1820s it had become a shrine to the Revolution, complete with a steeple reconstructed in brick housing the Liberty Bell. In 1950 the hall was acquired by the government and restored, both inside and out, to an approximation of its appearance c. 1780. With its visitors' center and new Liberty Bell pavilion, the hall now forms the centerpiece of Philadelphia's Independence National Park. **RDB**

↗ The steeple now contains a replica of the Liberty Bell; the original is displayed on the pavilion out front.

➡ A wall plaque proclaims the extraordinary significance of Independence Hall in U.S. history.

Castletown House (1758)

Architects Alessandro Galilei, Edward Lovett Pearce **Location** Celbridge, County Kildare, Ireland **Style** Palladian **Material** Stone

Built for William Conolly, a man who had come from a humble background to become speaker of the Irish House of Commons and the wealthiest man in Ireland, Castletown House is the most impressive Palladian country house in the country. With its perfect proportion, it is even said to have influenced the design of the White House in Washington, D.C.

Plans for the building were initiated by Alessandro Galilei (1691–1737), who was in Ireland working for Lord Molesworth, but it was left to Irishman Edward Lovett Pearce (1699–1733) to complete the designs. Pearce had met Galilei while on his Grand Tour, and was also a great admirer of Andrea Palladio (1508–80). The main body of the house is Galilei's, but the particularly Palladian colonnades and pavilions at either end of each wing are those of Pearce.

Conolly was offered a title, but refused it, saying he was happy to be the wealthiest commoner in the country. His heir, Tom Conolly, did marry nobility when he wed Lady Louisa Lennox. Just fifteen years old, Lady Louisa was great-granddaughter to Charles II of England, and it was she who oversaw the completion and decoration of the house, beginning in 1758. She took many of her ideas from English architect Sir William Chambers (1723–96), who never visited Ireland, but who did publish his designs.

As with all great country houses, stories and legends abound, which make a visit to Castletown more than just a trip around a piece of architectural history. There is the beautiful but flawed Long Gallery, whose blue chandeliers were ordered from Venice. The room was decorated while they were made and shipped. Colors were hard to describe in a pre-photography era, however, and the blue of the walls never matched that of the Murano glass. **GT**

Casino at Marino (1762)

Architect Sir William Chambers **Location** Dublin, Ireland **Style** Neo-Classical **Material** Portland stone

The Casino, 3 miles (5 km) northeast of Dublin city center, is an architectural gem. Ireland's first and most important Neo-Classical building was designed by Sir William Chambers (1723–96) as a garden pavilion for the Earl of Charlemont's Marino estate, of which it is now the only surviving part. It is deceptively small—only 50 square feet (15 sq m) to the outer columns. From the outside it appears to be a single-roomed, single-story Greek temple. Inside, however, there are sixteen exquisitely proportioned rooms on three floors. Chambers, who originally intended his design

> *"Never on a building so small can more care have been expended."*
>
> Maurice Craig, Irish architectural historian

as an end pavilion for Harewood House in Yorkshire, England, never visited Ireland.

Lord Charlemont, an Irish patriot, was a connoisseur of the arts, and the Casino is emblematic both of his aesthetic and political aspirations. In plan it is a Greek cross with each projecting elevation framed by a pair of columns. The main facades are north and south—with the entrance on the north—and are dominated by the solid attic story, statues, and urns. The urns were once functional chimneys, while the freestanding columns were hollowed out to conduct rainwater from the roof. Inside, the saloon is a more attractive space than the extravagant stateroom. Its ceiling's centerpiece is a head of Apollo emerging from a sunburst. Also charming are two smaller rooms, the China Closet and the Zodiac Room. **BMC**

Winter Palace (1762)

Architect Francesco Bartolommeo Rastrelli **Location** St. Petersburg, Russia **Style** Russian Baroque **Materials** Brick, plaster

The Winter Palace is one of the most famous buildings in St. Petersburg, as much for its role in Russian history as for its artistic importance. It was built for the Empress Elisabeth by her favorite court architect, and with 1,000 rooms is one of the largest palaces in Europe. Only the Russian Baroque exterior remains as built, with rich and varied ornament over three stories.

The palace was gutted by fire in December 1837 and rebuilt over the next two years, regardless of expense and with much loss of life among the workforce. The only Rastrelli interior to be restored as before was the Jordan Staircase. The rest of the palace interiors are an eclectic mix of Baroque Revival, Neo-Classical, and Gothic Revival by several architects, including Vasily Stasov, Alexander Briullov, and August Montferrand. The public rooms are large and impressive while the private rooms were relatively simple, although epitomizing bourgeois comfort.

Catherine the Great added further buildings to the north of the Palace to house her growing art collection. These included the Small Hermitage (1764–75) by Yuri Felten and Jean-Baptiste Vallin de la Mothe; the Old Hermitage (1771–87) by Felten; and the Hermitage Theater (1783–87) by Giacomo Quarenghi. To these Nicholas I added the New Hermitage (1839–51) by Leo von Klenze. By 1945 the Winter Palace had been handed over in installments to the State Hermitage Museum, with galleries replacing most of the service accommodation and rooms of both the imperial family and members of the court. **CWH**

↗ The Winter Palace exterior is lavishly ornamented with columns, arches, pediments, bays, and statuary.

⇥ Originally painted yellow with white details, the palace's green-and-white scheme dates from 1946.

Holkham Hall (1764)

Architects William Kent, Lord Burlington, Earl of Leicester **Location** Wells-next-the-Sea, Norfolk, England **Style** Palladian **Material** Yellow brick

Among the grandest of all English country houses, Holkham is a masterpiece of the Palladian style. From the outside the house is imposing, elegant, but rather forbidding. A massive central block, with a classical pediment and a pair of end towers, is flanked by four smaller corner pavilions. The whole enormous building, 344 feet (105 m) in length, is in a somewhat austere local yellow brick, designed to imitate Roman Renaissance brickwork. The main rooms are on the upper floor, and from the outside this is expressed by the row of large windows sitting on top of the rusticated masonry of the lower floor. All these features have their origins in the buildings of Renaissance Italy. None of the exterior grandeur, though, can compare with the interior, much of which survives largely as its creators left it. Whereas outside everything is restrained and austere, inside there is richness, color, and pattern aplenty. In the central

block there is a series of staterooms housing the Earl of Leicester's outstanding collection of furniture and works of art. There is a vast, triple-height entrance hall with a Derbyshire alabaster colonnade that was modeled on the Temple of Fortuna Virilis in Rome. The saloon has a gilded ceiling and walls covered in deep red Genoa velvet, and the Statue Gallery contains the most complete collection of classical statuary in an English private house. The libraries house books and paintings collected by the Earl on his Grand Tour. **PW**

> *"I look around, not a house to be seen but my own. I . . . have ate up all my neighbors."*
>
> Thomas Coke, Earl of Leicester

Ottobeuren Abbey (1766)

Architect Johann Michael Fischer **Location** Ottobeuren, Bavaria, Germany **Style** Rococo **Materials** Stone, plaster

Many dislike the Rococo style, but like it or not, the superb Ottobeuren Abbey, designed by architect Johann Michael Fischer (1692–1766), should not be missed. Originally an eighth-century foundation, it was rebuilt during the period of its greatest wealth and success by the powerful Abbot Rupert Ness and his successor Anselm Erb. The abbey is impressive and highly ornamented; the library in particular with its beautiful, dainty plasterwork feels more suitable for dancing than study. The highlight, however, is the abbey church. Its exterior has the dignity of size and restraint of Classical architecture, and is crowned by elegant onion-domed towers typical of central Europe. On entering, the same Classical language governs the architecture of the interior, but here it is overgrown with spectacular ornament. The massive excess of the decoration bursts from panels and drips over structural elements, like a vigorous plant growth.

Where the lively frescoes cannot reach, stucco curls and frills can, and generally do. Every piece of church furnishing becomes part of the uproar, with the pulpit, monuments, and above all the altar attracting major outbursts of ornament. Where the columns are unornamented, bright, pinkish marble maintains the feeling of luxury. For all its prettiness and spectacle, this is not frivolous architecture. The church is an attempt to show the people a fragment of the sensory delights awaiting the faithful in heaven. **BWC**

> *"The subsidiaries [were made] so energetic that the framework became redundant."*
>
> Sir John Summerson, historian, on Rococo

Petit Trianon (1768)

Architect Ange-Jacques Gabriel   **Location** Palace of Versailles, near Paris, France   **Style** Neo-Classical   **Material** Stone

The château of Le Petit Trianon on the grounds of the Palace of Versailles reflects the taste for the simple elegance of the Neo-Classical style prevalent from the 1760s onward. Influenced by the order and measured forms of classical Greek architecture, the exterior of the château appears sober and austere, suggestive of the idea of moral virtue. It was designed by Ange-Jacques Gabriel by the order of Louis XV for his mistress, Madame de Pompadour, and was constructed between 1762 and 1768. Its proportions are of an architecturally correct three-story cube set in a formal garden. The sides are 112 feet (34 m) in length and feature five floor-to-ceiling "French" windows along each side and a peristyle of four corinthian columns on the garden and courtyard facades. In 1774 Louis XVI gave the château and its surrounding park to Queen Marie Antoinette, who would escape here from the formality and responsibilities of court life. The queen's

private apartments are notable for their elegant woodwork, with furniture by Georges Jacob and Jean Henri Riesener that decoratively evokes flowers and harvests. The interior includes a bedroom suite, music room, reception rooms, and thirteen bedrooms. In the grounds, Marie Antoinette replaced, at great expense, the most scholarly greenhouse in Europe and, between 1776 and 1783, initiated the construction, by architect Richard Mique, of *fabriques* or follies inspired by a variety of architectural styles. **JEH**

"How delightful were these groves scented with lilacs, peopled by nightingales …"

Baroness of Oberkirch, on visiting the château

Syon House (1769)

Architect Robert Adam **Location** London, England **Style** Tudor, Neo-Classical **Material** Stone

In 1761 Robert Adam (1728–92) published his designs for the remodeling of the interior of Syon House. Commissioned by the Earl (later the Duke) of Northumberland, Adam's plans were submitted shortly after his return from an inspirational tour of Italy. His original plans were to recreate five rooms inside the house and to build an Italianate rotunda out in the courtyard—the latter was not implemented. Working within the limitations of the existing structure of a Tudor hall, Adam was often frustrated by a lack of space or awkwardly shaped rooms. For an architect inspired by the great Classical traditions and hidebound by the need to use exact Classical proportions, the remodeling of Syon House was a challenge. He overcame the obstacle of the irregularly shaped Great Hall at the entrance to the old house by dividing it into three sections. This allowed him to create two apses and one correctly proportioned hall.

The division was not merely an aesthetic requirement: the original hall had been built on uneven foundations, and creating three separate spaces enabled Adam to solve the problem of an uneven floor. Similarly, in the Anteroom, Adam used a screen to turn what had been a rectangular room into a square one. This gave him full scope to create interiors in true, lavish, Neo-Classical style, making full use of symmetry and uninhibited by awkward angles. Today, Syon House is regarded as an fine example of his revolutionary use of color. However, the house cannot be evaluated as a full work of art without taking into account its park, remodeled at the same time as the house by Lancelot "Capability" Brown (1716–83). Like Adam, Brown strove to create an idyll of an earlier age, but he did not look to Classical antiquity for inspiration, finding it instead closer to home in the deer parks made so popular by King Henry VIII. **LH**

Cromford Mill (1771)

Architect Richard Arkwright **Location** Cromford, Derbyshire, England **Style** Early Industrial **Materials** Local stone, timber

It was at Cromford Mill that the eighteenth-century industrialist Richard Arkwright (1732–92) refined his system of mechanized cotton spinning. The building was revolutionary, harnessing a workforce, machinery, and water power in a factory format. Arkwright chose the small Derbyshire village of Cromford because he was guaranteed a steady supply of water from the Cromford sough, a mine drain into which ran a warm thermal spring. To make progress as quickly and affordably as possible, Arkwright bought a house in a nearby village, demolished it, and used the stone to build his first mill. The five-story building was 98 feet (30 m) long, by 30 feet (9 m) deep. It was a plain, undecorated structure, with large windows to give the cotton spinners as much light as possible. All the interior supports, beams, and floorboards were timber. The mill was complete within four months, and producing cotton by the end of 1772. By 1776,

Arkwright began construction of his second mill a short distance downstream. It was similar in style and layout to the first, although larger—118 feet (36 m) wide and seven stories high. One notable difference was the insertion of clerestory windows in the top story. The second mill was also powered by water. In order to generate sufficient power, Arkwright placed the waterwheel in a deep pit underneath the building. Only the wheel pit and foundations have survived; fire destroyed the rest of the building in 1890. **AM**

> *"... a system of industry, order and cleanliness till then unknown in any [great] manufactory ..."*
>
> David Peter Davies, *History of Derbyshire* (1811)

Church of the Fourteen Holy Helpers (1772)

Architect Balthasar Neumann **Location** Bad Staffelstein, near Bamberg, Germany **Style** Rococo **Materials** Sandstone, stucco

This church is named for the Fourteen Holy Helpers, or *Vierzehnheiligen*, a group of saints venerated by the Roman Catholic Church, particularly in Germany. The original Gothic church, established in 1448, was replaced by the new Rococo church just as Baroque and Rococo were going out of fashion. The Vierzehnheiligen was one of the last designs by Balthasar Neumann (1687–1753), one of the leading architects of German Baroque. His design for the new Vierzehnheiligen was a fluid, organic plan in typical Rococo style based on seven interlocking or adjacent ellipses. This clever juxtaposition of shapes is responsible for the often described "spatial miracle" within the church, which boasts a nearly round central space within the stretched rectangular outer shape. Unlike his contemporary master builders, Neumann did not usually design the decoration and stuccowork himself, but worked closely with *stucateurs* and artists

to finish his compositions. At Vierzehnheiligen their biggest achievement is that the stucco appears not merely as decoration for structural walls—here, space and enclosure becomes architecture in its own right. The inner and outer buildings detach from each other with a vaulted ceiling invisibly suspended from the roof structure above. Outside, the well-proportioned, undulating facade is flanked by bell towers surprisingly topped by onion domes and steeples, giving the church a curiously Byzantine feel. **LT**

> *"[Balthasar Neumann] was truly gifted to create an aspiration for the divine in one's soul . . ."*
>
> M. H. von Freeden, historian

Château de Versailles (1774)

Architects Le Nôtre, Le Vau, Hardouin-Mansart, Le Brun, De Cotte, Gabriel **Location** Versailles, France **Style** Baroque **Material** Stone

> *"... an immense palace whose defects are more than compensated by beauties."*
>
> Voltaire, philosopher and writer

⬆ French Baroque gardens with parterres, topiary, fountains, and sculptures complement the palace.

➡ The Royal Chapel superseded four earlier chapels, which had either been destroyed or converted for other uses.

The immense Château de Versailles is a key example of Baroque palace architecture. It reflects the new taste and lighter style of King Louis XIV (r. 1643–1715), who had wearied of allegories and wanted "youthfulness strewn everywhere." It was the royal château of the king of France and home for thousands of the nobility, courtiers, and attendant government officials and functionaries from 1682 until 1789. At the center of the château are the state apartments, notable for their majestic scale—they contain 2,143 windows, 1,252 fireplaces, and 67 staircases. In the gardens there are 1,400 fountains. The original château was begun in 1624 as a modest manor house for Louis XIII, who reigned from 1610. It was used as a hunting lodge and remains at the building's heart. The palace grew through a series of expansions and was dramatically enlarged under the "Sun King," Louis XIV. Between 1661 and 1669 he added a huge garden facade, 2,200 feet (670 m) long, by Louis Le Vau, with interiors by Charles Le Brun.

In 1667 André Le Nôtre began to design one of the largest formal gardens ever created, with extensive *parterres* (ornamental gardens), terraces, fountains, and canals. Jules Hardouin-Mansart became project architect in 1678 and added the Hall of Mirrors, the north and south wings, the stables, the Orangerie, and the Grand Trianon. The Royal Chapel, begun in 1698, was completed by Robert de Cotte in 1710. Ange-Jacques Gabriel contributed the Royal Opera in the north wing in 1768. Many of the finest craftsmen in Europe worked on this vast palace, which became a symbol of Louis XIV's vision of absolute monarchy, for many years. After the French Revolution, the palace collections of paintings and sculpture were consigned to the Musée du Louvre, books and medals went to the Bibliothèque Nationale, and clocks and scientific instruments to the École des Arts et Métiers. **JEH**

San Pedro Church (1774)

Architect Unknown **Location** San Pedro de Atacama, Chile **Style** Spanish Colonial **Materials** Stone, adobe, cactus wood

San Pedro de Atacama is a pre-Inca town situated around an oasis in northern Chile's Atacama Desert, which is the driest desert in the world. Visitors generally stop there in order to visit the surrounding natural wonders, including the desert's salt flats. The Spanish conquistadors settled in the area in 1540 and evangelized the locals. The town's population today consists of descendants of the Lican Antai or Atacamanean Indians. The majority of the population is Roman Catholic and the San Pedro Church, named after the town's patron saint, is where they worship. The church is located on the west side of the central square and is surrounded by ancient pepper trees. It was built in 1774, replacing an existing one built in the seventeenth century and is one of the oldest churches in Chile. Built of stone and adobe, the church has a cross-shaped ground plan, with a nave measuring 134 feet (41 m) long by 25 feet (7.5 m) wide. What is most remarkable is the use of cardón cactus wood in its construction. These 33-feet high (10 m) cacti are used by the locals to build houses. Cactus is used for the door at the main entrance, and leather straps are used instead of nails. The roof framework is made of local woods, and the ceiling is constructed from small cactus boards, mud, and straw. An adobe bell tower was added in 1964, to replace a previous one built of wood. Inside, there is a richly decorated, carved stone *reredos* screen behind the high altar. **CMK**

> *"The hostile stones . . . took shape and form / and one by one took on / the sharp clarity of buildings."*

Pablo Neruda, "El Pueblo, Plenos Poderes" (1962)

Royal Crescent (1774)

Architect John Wood the Younger   **Location** Bath, England   **Style** Georgian Palladian   **Materials** Bearing masonry, Bath stone

Bath's Royal Crescent is one of Europe's finest crescents and lays claim to be the first to be built as a terrace. Built in the Palladian style from pale gold Bath stone, it consists of thirty houses that follow a full semi-ellipse so that the end houses face each other, all fronted by a great open lawn. Its unique continuous facade above the ground floor, consisting of a colonnade of 114 20-foot-high (6 m) Ionic columns, is only broken by double columns to mark out its center and end houses. This gives its grand sweep a noble symmetry, making it hard to distinguish the individual houses, so that it appears less a terrace and more a large country mansion in a parkland setting. Designed by John Wood the Younger (1728–82), it took eight years to complete. The uniformity of the exterior was no accident: while Wood employed different contractors to build the separate houses and the interiors were built to match the prospective tenants' wishes, the

exterior of each had to follow a very strict plan. Wood is also famous for finishing his father's celebrated Circus in Bath, as well as building Brock Street, the connecting road between the Circus and the Crescent. This unassuming terrace deliberately hides the Royal Crescent until the very last moment, helping to maximize the surprise and wonder felt by visitors as they turn the corner to be presented with Wood's novel and elegant arc. Even today, it is a view that can stop onlookers dead in their tracks. **JM**

"[The Royal Crescent] provides one of the happiest moments of European sightseeing."

Jan Morris, historian and travel writer

Chinese Palace (1774)

Architect Antonio Rinaldi   **Location** Oranienbaum, St. Petersburg, Russia   **Style** Rococo   **Materials** Plaster, brick

Oranienbaum, 24 miles (39 km) south of St. Petersburg, was the countryside estate where Catherine the Great endured many unhappy years with her husband Peter III. Months after seizing power in 1762, she commissioned Rinaldi to construct her first palace as empress there. Her desire for a summer palace that was "hers and hers alone" resulted in the Chinese Palace. She used it as a daytime retreat for meeting with diplomats and probably her lover of the time and co-conspirator, Grigory Orlov. The palace incorporated elements of *chinoiserie*, which had been taken the long way round from China to Russia via England and the rest of Europe. Secluded in a woodland setting beside an ornamental lake, it is an elegant, naturalistic contrast to Bartolomeo Rastrelli's rigid baroque style at Tsarskoye Selo, the other rural imperial estate. In true Rococo style, the palace is dominated by symbols of animals, plants, trees, and cornucopias, and in some of the rooms the effect between outside and inside is deliberately blurred. The highlight of the palace is undeniably the Glass Bead Salon where more than two million shimmering glass beads perform as a backdrop to exotic scenes of birds and flowers. The decoration throughout the palace is exceptionally rich and lavish, yet intimate and informal. Today the palace is threatened by rising damp and water ingress due to its position beside the ornamental lake, although restoration is now underway. **WB**

"There is nothing in Russia to match the richness and freshness of Oranienbaum rococo . . . "

Dmitry Schvidkovsky, architectural historian

Palacio de la Inquisición (1776)

Architect Unknown   **Location** Cartagena, Colombia   **Style** Spanish Colonial   **Materials** Stone, limestone, wood

On the west side of Plaza de Bolívar in Cartagena, an ornate portal and massive oak door studded with iron bolts topped by a stone Spanish coat of arms announces a building of far-reaching historic importance for this perfectly preserved colonial town founded in 1533. Spanish Inquisition officials claimed the original block-long row of *casas altas* belonging to wealthy Cartagenans as their headquarters in 1610, but the present yellow-and-ocher-walled mansion dates from 1776. On the side wall, just around the corner from the entrance is the small, barred window with a cross on top from which the tribunal sentences were read out in public. Over two centuries, the Inquisition tribunal in Cartagena condemned about 800 people. Under suspicion of heresy and witchcraft, countless people were tortured, had their wealth confiscated, suffered exile, or were burned at the stake until Cartagena gained independence from Spain in 1811. In the Andalusian tradition, entrance to this three-storied mansion is through a gate leading into a vestibule, a circulation area with access to rooms via a corridor or balcony to interiors that contain hidden courtyards and patios. The somber, high-ceilinged rooms include the Grand Inquisitor's chamber and the torture chamber, which display original torture instruments. A relic from a dark chapter in history, the palace is rather at odds with the charmingly picturesque image that the old city presents. **AA**

"As in the past, this citadel of the Conquistadors continues to live a colorful existence."

Matt Moffett, *The Wall Street Journal Online*

Strawberry Hill (1776)

Architects Horace Walpole, John Chute, Richard Bentley **Location** Twickenham, London, England **Style** Gothic Revival **Material** Brick

In 1747 the connoisseur Horace Walpole (1717–97), son of Sir Robert Walpole, Britain's first prime minister, moved to a small house in Twickenham, west London. He named the house Strawberry Hill and immediately set about remodeling it. Instead of using the prevailing Georgian classical style, Walpole took a radical route— he had his house rebuilt in an eighteenth-century version of the Gothic style used by the cathedral builders of the Middle Ages. Over nearly thirty years, Walpole transformed his house into a Gothic fantasy, with a round tower, battlements, and pointed windows outside, and fan vaults, arches, and Gothic paneling within. Some of the details were copied from Salisbury Cathedral or Westminster Abbey and some came from Walpole's imagination. Highlights include a library with bookcases topped with pinnacles, a vaulted gallery with details drawn from Canterbury Cathedral, and a bedchamber with a delicate Gothic canopy over the fireplace. Instead of employing an architect, Walpole gathered around him a group of friends known as his "Committee of Taste." These men were mostly connoisseurs like Walpole himself. This combination of influences made Strawberry Hill unique and it was soon much imitated. It was the first eighteenth-century house to be completely in the Gothic style, and its filigree decoration is among the best of its kind. Strawberry Hill was a trendsetting house that changed the course of British design. **PW**

> *"I do not mean to defend . . . a small capricious house. It was built to please my own taste . . ."*
>
> Horace Walpole, writer and politician

The Royal Salt Works (1779)

Architect Claude-Nicolas Ledoux **Location** Arc-et-Senans, near Besançon, France **Style** Neo-Classical **Material** Stone

The unique industrial complex of the Royal Saltworks at Arc-et-Senans is considered Ledoux's masterpiece and the major achievement of the socioaesthetic Enlightenment movement of the pre-Revolutionary era. Ledoux believed that rational architecture, urban design, and industrial organization could contribute to the development of an ideal society according to a philosophical order. His abstract plan emphasized the image of the circle to evoke the harmony of the ideal city for common activity. The site is entered through a massive Doric portico, inspired by the temples at Paestum, which opens into a vast semicircular space. Ten Neo-Classical stone buildings housing workshops and dwellings for artisans and laborers are arranged in the curve of a closed semicircle, with the director's villa at the center of the main axis. Administration buildings and workshops for the extraction of salt are connected on the straight diameter. Although conceived as the first phase of a large and grandiose scheme for the new ideal city of Chaux, this plan was abandoned during the French Revolution. The building was funded by the *gabelle*, a state monopoly and mandatory tax on the sale of salt, whereby all people over the age of eight years had to buy an amount of salt at a price fixed by the government. The complex was seen as representing the controlling intention of the state and was effectively a pseudo-egalitarian forced labor settlement, with the movements of the workers constantly observed and severely restricted. This monumental epitaph to Ledoux's unconsummated vision was never financially successful and was abandoned in 1895. Since restoration, the complex has been the headquarters of the Claude-Nicolas Ledoux Institute, which includes a Salt Museum and the Ledoux Museum. It is a UNESCO World Heritage Site. **JEH**

Grand Théâtre de Bordeaux (1780)

Architect Victor Louis **Location** Bordeaux, France **Style** Neo-Classical **Material** Stone

Conceived as a temple of the arts and light, the Grand Théâtre de Bordeaux is a masterpiece of Neo-Classical architecture and one of the most beautiful eighteenth-century buildings in Europe. Commissioned by the maréchal de Richelieu for the elegant Grands Hommes quarter of the city, the construction of the theater began in 1773 and took seven years to complete. It opened on April 17, 1780, subsequently becoming a model for many other French and European theaters.

The designer was Victor Louis (1731–1800), who was also responsible for the Comédie Française and the arcades for the Palais Royal in Paris. Situated on the place de la Comédie, this imposing structure features a Neo-Classical facade endowed with a portico of twelve colossal Corinthian columns, which support an entablature with twelve statues representing the nine muses—Clio, Euterpe, Thalia, Melpomene, Terpsichore, Erato, Urania, Calliope, and Polyhymnia— and three goddesses, Juno, Venus, and Minerva.

The Classical facade fronts an opulent interior and Louis devoted a third of the length of the building to a dramatic entry vestibule, an atrium containing the grand staircase to the auditorium, and reception and intermission spaces. The stairwell is grandiose, featuring a monumental doorway with statues of Melpomene, muse of tragedy, and Thalia, muse of comedy. The theater interiors were restored in 1991 to the original colors of blue and gold. The auditorium, in the Italian style, is admired as one of the finest in the world, seating 1,114 people. The original stage curtain, whose design extended the architecture of the auditorium, has also been reconstructed. **JEH**

⬉ The Grand Théâtre is valued as much for its distractingly opulent interior as for its productions.

⬅ For the sake of symmetry, three goddesses join the nine muses above the twelve columns of the portico.

Brimstone Hill Fortress (1782)

Architects Military engineers **Location** St. Kitts, Leeward Islands, Caribbean **Style** British Colonial **Material** Stone

Slavery was the stone and sugar the mortar that built Brimstone Hill Fortress. Human capital and cash crops created vast colonial wealth that needed to be defended. The purpose and design of the fortress is that of a panic room—a refuge for plantation bosses, merchants, and their families.

Small enough to be surveyed with a sweep of a spyglass, yet large enough to support sugar plantations, St. Kitts was settled in the seventeenth century by English and French entrepreneurs. Their *entente cordiale* was brief, and the British-built fortress became the flashpoint for these competing colonial powers until the treaty that ended the American Revolution in 1783 gave the island to Britain.

Brimstone Hill Fortress's vantage, design, and materials contributed to its success. It crowns a hill 700 feet (213 m) above sea level, and the topography allows successive defensive levels. Building materials were on site: blocks hewn from the volcanic core and mortar mixed from powdered limestone crust were used to build 7-foot-thick (2 m) defensive walls on a 40-acre (16.2 ha) site with fifty-plus structures, including a hospital, infantry quarters, a defensive redoubt, and a bastion with cannons pointing out over the Caribbean Sea. Huge cisterns allowed the fort to store 400,000 liters of water. By the nineteenth century, absentee plantation owners, a shift of colonial interests to Africa and India, slave emancipation, and hurricanes finished the fortress without a shot fired or a wall breached. The abandoned buildings inevitably decayed over time, but restoration got underway in the 1900s. **DJ**

↗ Inclined, well-constructed fortress walls were designed to deflect bombardment from the sea.

⇥ The British fort commanded its part of the Caribbean and was known as "the Gibraltar of the West Indies."

Lak Muang
City Pillar Shrine (1782)

Patron King Rama I **Location** Bangkok, Thailand
Style Traditional Thai **Material** Chaiyaphruek wood

The city of Bangkok is known to its inhabitants as "Krungthep," meaning City of Angels, and was established as the capital of Siam (now Thailand) by King Rama I, in 1782. Today in this modern metropolis, rickshaws rattle past contemporary tower blocks and the city successfully juggles rapid modernization with its traditional charm. This charm is highly evident in the graceful temple structure that houses the Lak Muang Pillar. In Thailand such pillars are traditionally erected to commemorate the establishment of cities. This lacquered and gilded pillar was created on the orders of King Rama I (r. 1782–1809)—founder of the Chakri Dynasty—when he chose to move the capital of Thailand from Thon Buri to Bangkok. Measuring 9 feet (3 m) in height, it occupies a prominent position opposite the Grand Palace and represents the official city center. It also has a practical function, as from this point distances to all other city shrines in the country are measured. The pillar encases the city horoscope, which was originally intended to provide prosperity for Bangkok and help ward off invasions from the Burmese. It is commonly believed that the shrine houses the guardian deity, Phra Lak Muang, as well as other protective deities, and locals frequently worship at the site. In exchange for answered prayers, offerings of incense, flowers, and food are left. In 1982 Bangkok celebrated the 200th anniversary of its establishment. As part of the festivities, the old dilapidated pillar was joined by a new one and the two of them are visited by hundreds of people every day. **KGB**

◥ The multi-tiered roof and abundant carved wooden details are typical of traditional Thai architecture.

◲ In 1982, the shrine housing the city pillars was demolished and replaced by a new building.

Jefferson's Monticello (1782)

Architect Thomas Jefferson   **Location** Charlottesville, Virginia, USA
Style Colonial Georgian   **Materials** Brick masonry

Jefferson's Monticello is one of the great presidential homes, and yet it was largely finished before Thomas Jefferson (1743–1826) was elected as the third president of the United States. The man primarily responsible for writing the American Declaration of Independence lived in this small corner of Virginia virtually all his life; he built and remodeled Monticello over fifty-eight years from 1768 to his death. Monticello, "little mountain" in Italian, is an iconic image of power. It sits on a small grassy peak in the Southwest Mountains, near to Charlottesville, where

> "... Palladio, [Jefferson] said 'was the bible' ... you should get it and stick close to it."

Colonel Isaac A. Coles, statesman

the natural elevation adds to the building's stately grandeur. Jefferson was a self-taught architect who had gathered a comprehensive library of architecture books, including copies of Palladio's *Quattro Libri*. He absorbed the principles of Palladio and the didactic qualities of Roman architecture, and applied these to his own designs. Although Monticello was built over a number of years there is a great sense of continuity through the design, which is based on a cross-axial plan with emphasized horizontal wings. Jefferson was a consummate designer and he continually remodeled the building. He incorporated many innovative technical details such as hidden closets, automatically swinging and sliding doors, and all manner of gadgets, including a mechanical clock in the portico that tells the time and day of the week. **TP**

Vilnius Cathedral (1783)

Architect Laurynas Gucevicius   **Location** Vilnius, Lithuania
Style Neo-Classical   **Material** Stone

The Lithuania that emerged from the collapse of the USSR is a relatively young country but the area's history goes back long before the Soviet era. Lithuania was one of the last countries in Europe to adopt Christianity in the mid- to late-thirteenth century, replacing the pagan worship of Perkunas, the god of thunder, rain, mountains and the sky; part of Vilnius Cathedral can be dated to this transitional period. Today, a leaning Italianate bell tower standing next to a Neo-Classical Greek temple is the central meeting point in Vilnius. The fairytale, white tower and the solid, colonnaded cathedral form part of Gedimino Prospect and are the center of this optimistic capital city.

Vilnius Cathedral is an incarnation of three previous buildings, the first of which was built in the late thirteenth century. A storm felled the south tower in 1769, which prompted a complete rebuilding of the church. The colonnaded rectangle seen today was built by Laurynas Gucevicius (1753–98), considered to be Lithuania's first professional architect. He studied in Paris under Jacques-Germain Soufflot and Claude-Nicolas Ledoux. Gucevicius's reconstruction is in strict Classical style. The church is a quadrangular Roman temple complete with a pedimented, open-air portico with Doric order columns topped by statues of St. Helena, St. Casimir, and St. Stanislaus. St. Casimir is the patron saint of Lithuania, and the return of his remains to the cathedral after the collapse of the Soviet Union in 1989 was highly symbolic. In contrast to the Neo-Classical church around it, the Casimir Chapel is early Baroque with black-and-brown Italian marble. Gucevicius's Roman temple-turned-cathedral may seem strangely out of place, but it has become a key symbol of a rejuvenated national identity. **WB**

Hameau
de la Reine (1784)

Architect Richard Mique **Location** Versailles, France
Style French Vernacular **Materials** Masonry, stone, wood, plaster

In the eighteenth century, picturesque landscape gardens became fashionable among Europe's aristocracy. In 1783 Marie Antoinette commissioned her architect, Richard Mique, to build an ornamental lakeside hamlet, the Hameau de la Reine (Queen's Hamlet), in the grounds of the Châteâu de Versailles. Inspired by the architecture of rural Normandy, the aesthetic style of the ornamental farm was rustic half-timbering, painted to simulate age, with thatched and tiled roofs. However, the interiors were luxurious, endowed with the latest technical and decorative refinements. The Hameau consisted of twelve buildings, six of which were reserved for the use of the queen: the Queen's House, Billiard Saloon, Boudoir, Mill, Laiterie de Propreté (Dairy), and the Marlborough Tower. The tower was the most imposing structure in the Hameau, dominating the small buildings around it. Four buildings made up the farm: a barn, later converted into a ballroom after 1787 when a second barn was built closer to the farm proper; a pigeon loft; and the *laiterie de préparation* (working dairy). The *rechauffoir* was used for housekeeping and preparing dinners for the Queen's House. The last building was the residence of the guardian of the Hameau. Each building had its own garden planted with cabbages, cauliflowers, and artichokes, enclosed by a low hedge. The staircases, galleries, and balconies were decorated with pots of flowers. Plants, vines, and espaliers climbed the walls of the buildings and the trelliswork that shaded some of the pathways. **JEH**

↖ The semblance of a poor but self-sufficient community is reinforced by the beds of vegetables.

← Centered on a landscaped pond, the hamlet has the feeling of being deep in the French countryside.

Agate Pavilion and Cameron Gallery (1785)

Architect Charles Cameron **Location** Pushkin, St. Petersburg, Russia
Style Neo-Classical **Materials** Brick, plaster, stone dressings

When Catherine II seized power in Russia in 1762, she rejected the baroque tastes of her predecessors in favor of Neo-Classicism. The finest buildings and interiors of her reign were by the Scottish architect, Charles Cameron (1743–1812). Cameron was invited to Russia by Catherine II on the strength of his book on Roman baths and the Agate Pavilion was his first commission for the empress. Catherine wanted "an ancient house with all its decor" and she thought Cameron would be the ideal architect to "craft baths with a hanging garden and a gallery for walks." So

---

"We are fashioning here ... a terraced garden with pools beneath ... this will be beautiful."

Catherine II, Empress of Russia

---

successful was he in this that the Cameron Gallery is the only eighteenth-century building in Russia to be known by the name of its architect. In its basement, the Agate Pavilion contained a near reconstruction, on a small scale, of the baths of ancient Rome. Upstairs on the *piano nobile* (principal floor) are three rooms of the most exquisite Neo-Classical design, the Agate and Jasper Studies, which flank a central hall. The studies are lined with semiprecious stones and adorned with bronze mounts and inlaid floors. Adjacent to the pavilion is the Cameron Gallery, overlooking a flower garden on one side and a sweeping view over a picturesque landscape park and lake on the other. A tremendous substructure bears a delicate Ionic arcade with an internal glazed corridor to allow walking in all weathers. **CWH**

Chinese Pavilion at L'Isle-Adam (1785)

Architect Jean-Honore Fragonard **Location** L'Isle-Adam, France
Style Baroque **Materials** Stone, iron, wood

The Chinese Pavilion at L'Isle-Adam is a rare surviving example of an eighteenth-century oriental folly in France. It reflects its period's taste for landscaped parks with *fabriques* or architectural follies, in which a Romantic vision of the landscape was created with arcadian gardens composed like paintings. Other examples include the garden of Marie Antoinette at Le Petit Trianon, Versailles. At L'Isle-Adam, a building program of nineteen fabriques was initiated. The follies, some of them "ruined" in character, were built to suggest antiquity or recall historical and exotic influences and might include a Persian pavilion, Greek temple, Chinese pagoda, or Egyptian obelisk.

The creator of the park and pavilion, Pierre-Jacques Bergeret, was a painter and architect drawn to the vogue for the *jardin à l'anglaise* as opposed to the formal French *parterre* (ornamental) garden. In 1778 he purchased the Cassan Domain and developed ostentatious plans that were only partially realized between 1781 and 1785. Bergeret tried to emphasize the undulating contours and water sources of the landscape by creating a number of picturesque structures around the meandering ponds and islands. The design of the Chinese Pavilion has been attributed to the artist Jean-Honore Fragonard, a frequent visitor to Cassan. The pavilion is a composite Italian–Chinese octagonal structure with a base of stone arches over a shallow water overflow, a peristyle with eight wooden columns, and a double-pagoda roof crowned by a bronze mast with small bells that chime when activated by the wind. It stands in a serene, idyllic, tree-lined setting on the edge of a lake. The French Revolution prevented the completion of Bergeret's project, but the pavilion was restored in 1975 and re-created within a public park. **JEH**

Somerset House (1786)

Architect Sir William Chambers **Location** London, England **Style** Neo-Classical **Material** Stone

Somerset House, one of Britain's greatest public buildings, is the masterpiece of Sir William Chambers (1723–96). It was designed as an office building to house various civil service departments together with the Royal Academy and the Society of Antiquaries. Chambers seized the opportunity to design a grand public building by the River Thames, no doubt seeing the chance to trump his rivals, the Adam brothers, who had recently built a successful development at the Adelphi not far upstream. Chambers's exercise in the grand style was a success. On the Thames front, he used the fashionable classical vocabulary of pilasters and columned porticoes, set on a row of arches. The structure was an instant London landmark. On the Strand side, visitors enter through a trio of tall arches into an elegant vestibule adorned with sculpture, then into a vast courtyard surrounded by beautifully detailed facades. The public only saw small parts of the interior, such as the glass-lanterned Great Room, where the Royal Academy displayed its paintings. In the nineteenth century the building was extended with eastern and western wings designed by Robert Smirke and James Pennethorne. For decades Somerset House was little visited by the public, but it is now a vibrant center for the visual arts. Architects Inskip and Jenkins have upgraded the building and enhanced the courtyard with fountains that cascade from the pavement and offset Chambers's great building. **PW**

> *" . . . A polished academic jewel intended as an appropriate casket for the academic bodies inside."*
>
> John Harris, architectural historian

Pavlovsk Palace (1787)

Architect Charles Cameron **Location** Pavlovsk, St. Petersburg, Russia **Style** Neo-Classical **Materials** Brick, plaster

Although it was built for the heir to the Imperial Russian throne, Grand Duke Paul Petrovich and his second wife Maria Fedorovna, the choice of architect for Pavlovsk Palace was dictated by the Grand Duke's mother, Catherine II. Charles Cameron (1743–1812) was her favorite designer. Although Cameron's concept for Pavlovsk was never fully realized, it represented a complete and ideal world that remained dear to him long after he had fallen out with its owners. When Catherine gave the estate to Petrovich in 1777, it consisted of dense, virgin forest and only a few small garden pavilions were built in the next few years, none of which Cameron liked. In 1781 he was assigned to design a new palace and lay out the park. The palace is loosely Palladian, with a central block and curved wings that lead to square pavilions. Combining monumentality with an air of lightness, the building is crowned by a remarkable, flat dome based on the

Pantheon in Rome, its drum surrounded by sixty-four columns. The park layout is romantic, taking full advantage of the natural landscape, and Cameron's buildings are brilliantly placed for picturesque effect. Cameron was dismissed in 1787 before he had completed the interiors, and Vincenzo Brenna took over. When Brenna's interiors were destroyed by fire in 1803, the palace was rebuilt by Andrei Voronikhin, and it was this version that was superbly reconstructed after damage during World War II. **CWH**

"… Pavlovsk in its entirety constitutes an enormous and integrated poetic world …"

Mikhail Alpatov, art historian

Column House, Désert de Retz (1789)

Architects François Racine de Monville, François Barbier
Location L'Isle-Adam, France **Style** Rococo **Material** Stone

The Désert de Retz is a witty and playful conceit in the form of an eighteenth-century French *jardin Anglo-chinois*, designed between 1774 and 1789 as a philosophical and poetic entertainment. The ornamental park originally extended over 99 acres (40 ha) of botanical and horticultural gardens around the ruined village and church of St. Jacques de Retz. It was the creation of François Racine de Monville, a wealthy aristocrat, assisted by a young architect, François Barbier, who designed and built seventeen follies, or *fabriques*, to create an arcadian and idyllic environment for reflection and contemplation.

The collection of fake antique buildings arranged as theatrical backdrops included an Egyptian obelisk, a temple of Pan, and a Tartar tent on the l'île du bonheur or Island of Happiness. Of the original structures there exist an ice-house in the shape of a pyramid, a Chinese pavilion, and a truncated Tuscan column. The sixteen-sided column is an extraordinary, 50-foot-high (15 m) false ruin that contained a four-story summer house for Monville, accessed by a central spiral staircase and illuminated by a glass skylight hidden below the parapet. The facade contains manmade fissures and irregular window holes intended to replicate architectural antiquity.

The term "désert" referred to an isolated and unpopulated place; "Retz" is a variant spelling of "roi," or king. The Désert was designed to create noble emotions of splendor, pleasure, reverie, surprise, and awe. It sought to pictorialize nature, to create intimate historical and mythological scenes related to the *vanitas* and *memento mori* paintings of Nicolas Poussin and Claude Lorrain. The ruin was praised by Denis Diderot as a stimulant to meditation on vanity with the effect of inducing nostalgia and melancholy. **JEH**

Groot Constantia (1790)

Architects Various **Location** Constantia, Cape Town, South Africa
Style Cape Dutch **Materials** Whitewashed masonry, thatched roof

Perhaps the most majestic of all Cape Dutch homesteads, Groot Constantia's sober form and elegant gables sum up the charm of a farming tradition that has become known throughout the world alongside the growing popularity of South African wine. Although considered "New World" by connoisseurs, local vineyards and the viticulture on which they depend boast a history almost five hundred years old. Simon van der Stel, who arrived from Holland as Commander of the Cape in 1679, was Groot Constantia's first occupant. He acquired the

> *"In its full stylistic splendor Cape Dutch has come to typify the winelands . . ."*
>
> Roger Fisher, architectural academic

farm in 1685, naming it Constantia after his wife, Constance, and erected a two-story building. Vegetables and wine were produced, not only to feed the household but also to supply passing ships on the spice route between Europe and India. Today's building dates back to the eighteenth century and to the industrious efforts of Hendrik Cloete, who rebuilt the house. In 1791 Cloete added sash windows to the old house and a wine cellar on the same axis as the farm entrance; structural changes included raising the roof. New gables were designed by French architect Louis Michel Thibault, incorporating a sculpture depicting fertility by artist Anton Anreith. At Groot Constantia today, winemaking and tourism coexist bringing local history to life by preserving the *raison d'être* of the homestead as a working vineyard. **MJB**

Court Theater, Drottningholm Palace (1791)

Architects Carl Fredrik Adelcrantz, Louis Jean Desprez **Location** Stockholm, Sweden **Style** Neo-Classical exterior **Materials** Timber frame, brick, papier-mâché

The 1766 exterior of the Court Theater at Drottningholm Palace, Sweden's lakeside Versailles, is in an austere Neo-Classical style. Built for Queen Louisa Ulrika, the theater replaced an earlier one burned down in 1762. A number of the rooms were altered in 1791 in the French style, with delicate colors, white, and gold, relief ornament, and a *trompe l'oeil* painted ceiling. The work was carried out for Queen Louisa's son, King Gustav III, by his French court architect, Louis Jean Desprez, who also designed some new furniture. Despite its relatively large auditorium, Drottningholm has more the air of a drawing room than a public space. The deep stage allows for the use of painted scenery in the Italian Renaissance tradition, of which Drottningholm has a unique collection from the eighteenth century. The stage machinery has also survived, including a special mechanism based on a ship's capstan to remove one set of side wings and bring on another.

When Gustav III was assassinated in 1792, the theater fell out of use. In 1922 historian Agne Beijer rediscovered it and, recognizing its value, devoted the rest of his life to conserving the fabric of the building, also promoting the performances that continue to this day. Few eighteenth-century theaters survive in Europe, and among these, only Drottningholm has such a rich hoard of original scenery. The park contains other decorative buildings, including a fine Chinese pavilion. In 1991 the Royal Domain of Drottningholm was inscribed as a UNESCO World Heritage site. **AP**

↗ The lamps and the doors' simple moldings provide some of the only exterior ornamentation.

↘ The Neo-Classical rear elevation of the theater is plain and even less ornamented than the front.

Custom House (1791)

Architect James Gandon   **Location** Dublin, Ireland

Style Neo-Classical   **Materials** Portland stone, Ardbraccan limestone

The Custom House, built at a cost of $390,000 (£200,000), encapsulates a brief moment of political confidence in eighteenth-century Dublin, when it acquired the architectural qualities of a capital city. Designed by architect James Gandon (1743–1823), it is probably the city's most important public building. It stands on the banks of the River Liffey on Custom House Quay, to the west of the present-day port. Elegantly proportioned, with a long classical facade of graceful pavilions, arcades, and columns, its central dome is topped by a 16-foot-high (4.8 m) statue representing Commerce; fourteen keystones over the doors and windows represent the Atlantic Ocean and thirteen Irish rivers. The Custom House's four facades are richly decorated with sculptures and coats of arms by Agostino Carlini, Thomas Banks, and Edward Smith. Gandon himself was the most influential Irish protagonist of Neo-Classical style.

Dublin's merchant class opposed the building of the Custom House, foreseeing that the chosen location, on reclaimed land, would move the city's focus to the east, away from its medieval nucleus. Initially the Custom House was the headquarters of the Commissioners of Customs and Excise. Today it houses Ireland's Department of the Environment. The original interiors were destroyed during the Anglo-Irish War in 1921, when the IRA set fire to the building in an attempt to disrupt British rule in Ireland. The dome of the Custom House was reconstructed by the Irish government after independence, using Ardbraccan limestone, which is noticeably darker than the Portland stone used in the original. The building underwent further restoration in the 1980s, when a new Portland stone cornice was put in place to replace the substandard one fitted after the fire. **BMC**

Palace of the Captains General (1791)

Architects Antonio Fernandez Trevejos, Pedro de Medina

Location Havana, Cuba   **Style** Baroque   **Material** Local stone

The Palace of the Captains General (Palacio de los Capitanes Generales) is Cuba's most celebrated eighteenth-century building. Built to house the council office, prison, and residence of the captains general, work on the structure began in 1776, and in 1791 Captain General Luis de las Casas moved into the impressive apartments on the upper floor. All the Cuban captains general lived there until the end of Spanish rule and the establishment of the Cuban Republic in 1902, after which the building functioned as the Presidential Palace until 1920. Occupying an

> *"I tried to lock [Havana] up in the stony confines of a museum and she … imprisoned me … for ever."*
>
> Eusebio Leal Spengler, city historian

entire block in Old Havana, it is monumental but not forbidding; its stately, sober Neo-Classical composition is softened by its linear Baroque detailing. The facade is relatively austere, its decorative emphasis being concentrated upon the window surrounds. The first floor is arcaded, and the upper facade is divided by pilasters into five sections. The main entrance hall opens through an *arco trilobulado* (triple-lobed arch) into an elegant courtyard planted with palms, yagruma trees, lilies, and jasmine. Between the first and upper floors is an *entresol*, the galleried balconies of which overlook the courtyard.

Thanks to the energy and commitment of Dr. Eusebio Leal Spengler, the City Historian of Havana, the building was restored in the early 1960s and now houses the Museum of the City of Havana. **JB**

Culzean Castle (1792)

Architect Robert Adam   **Location** Maybole, Ayrshire, Scotland
Style Neo-Classical   **Materials** Stone; slate and lead roofing

Born in Scotland, Robert Adam (1728–92) is widely regarded as the greatest British architect of the eighteenth century. The celebrated "Adam style"— which integrated Neo-Classical architectural form and elaborate interior decoration—was derived from the architect's research into the Classical art and architecture of ancient Rome.

At Culzean, on the dramatic west coast of Scotland, Adam created his most romantic house in the castellated style that became the hallmark of his later commissions. Viewed from the sea, the heftlike shape of the castle appears to have grown from the rugged rocks on which it stands. Yet seen from the landward side, it presents a more refined and balanced composition, using the idiom of fortification as no more than a playful veneer. Set within grounds that include woodland, formal gardens, and romantic follies, Culzean represents an exceptional example of aristocratic eighteenth-century taste.

Built for David Kennedy, the tenth Earl of Cassillis, incorporating elements from earlier ancestral buildings on the site, the house almost bankrupted him. Nevertheless, it remained within the Kennedy family until the National Trust for Scotland assumed stewardship in 1945. Although it has the full panoply of grand apartments and a circular drawing room, the highlight of the interior is the colonnaded oval staircase. Lit dramatically from above, this element was a late addition to the Adam plan but acts as the compositional core of the building. **NMC**

↗ The massive castellated bulk of Culzean Castle looms dramatically over lush, landscaped gardens.

→ The castle completely dominates its promontory on the southwestern coast of Scotland.

Panthéon (1793)

Architect Jacques-Germain Soufflot **Location** Paris, France **Style** Neo-Classical **Material** Stone

The Panthéon is the quintessential Neo-Classical monument in Paris and an outstanding example of Enlightenment architecture. Commissioned as the church of St. Geneviève by Louis XV (r. 1715–74), the project has become known as a secular building and a prestigious tomb dedicated to great French political and artistic figures including Mirabeau, Voltaire, Rousseau, Hugo, Zola, Curie, and Malraux, who have been honored and interred in the vaults following the ceremony of Panthéonization.

Soufflot (1713–80) was a self-taught architect and tutor to the Marquis de Marigny, general director of the king's buildings, who had been influenced by the Pantheon in Rome. Soufflot claimed that his principal aim was to unite "the structural lightness of Gothic churches with the purity and magnificence of Greek architecture." His Panthéon was revolutionary: built on the Greek cross plan of a central dome and four equal transepts, his innovation in construction was to use rational scientific and mathematical principles to determine structural formulas for the engineering of the building. This eliminated many of the supporting piers and walls with the result that the vaulting and interiors are slender and elegant. The Neo-Classical interior contrasts with the solidity and austere geometry of the exterior. The initial scheme was considered too gracious and lacking in gravity, and was replaced with a more funereal scheme, which involved blocking forty windows and destroying the original sculptural decorations. The Panthéon was the location for Foucault's pendulum experiment to demonstrate the rotation of the earth in 1851. **JEH**

↗ Although it has served as a church, the Panthéon today is a mausoleum for great French intellectuals.

← Above the Panthéon's decorative inner dome are two additional, superimposed dome structures.

Pump Room (1795)

Architects Thomas Baldwin, John Palmer   **Location** Bath, England   **Style** Neo-Classical   **Materials** Bearing masonry, Bath stone

Located in the Georgian city of Bath, England, the Pump Room and Roman Baths have formed its social heart since 1795. They also provide one of the reasons why Bath is the only English city to be granted World Heritage status. Built above a natural thermal spring, the Pump Room's set of elegantly decorated chambers were designed by Thomas Baldwin (1750–1820) and John Palmer (1738–1817) in the 1790s to replace a smaller building. Their brief was to provide comfortable surroundings in which to drink the "health-giving" waters.

The Pump Room is an imposing structure of Bath stone, with one entrance marked by an elegant colonnade of Ionic columns matching a similar colonnade that already existed next to it. The North facade of the building bears a large pediment carrying a Greek inscription meaning "Water is Best," supported by four Corinthian columns. Located inside the striking Neo-Classical salon of the Pump Room are a beautiful mineral water fountain and more giant Corinthian half-columns.

At the same site are the monumental remains of a great Roman temple and magnificent bathhouse. It was not until 1755 that the original Roman Baths of Aquae Sulis were discovered underneath the Georgian-built baths. The ancient ruins have since been excavated out of the river silt, which had protected them for so long. Although the open-air terrace and the statues that surround the baths are a Victorian folly, the bath itself is of Roman design. Taken together, the Pump Room and Roman Baths receive more than one million visitors per year. **JM**

↗ Visitors may draw salty-tasting spa water from the faucets of this fountain in the Pump Room.

⇥ The eighteenth-century King's and Queen's entrance to the Roman Baths is in Romanesque style.

Pfaueninsel (1796)

Patron Frederick William II **Location** Berlin, Germany **Style** Gothic Revival **Materials** Whitewashed timber and hardwood

In 1793 Frederick William II bought Pfaueninsel, an island in the River Havel outside Berlin, to create a park. Based upon his ideas, two buildings were erected from 1794 to 1796 at each end of the island, the little Schloss and the Dairy. Construction was supervised by Johann Gotlieb Brendel, the Court Carpenter. A cattle stall and a farmhouse were added in 1802. The farmhouse was remodeled by Karl Friedrich Schinkel, incorporating the facade of a late-Gothic house from Danzig, and renamed the Kavalierhaus. The eye-catching little Schloss turns toward Potsdam. Externally it is unassuming; two towers of unequal height are joined by an obviously painted timber wall and a pretty Gothic iron bridge above it. The interior is quite remarkable and includes intimate rooms retaining their original furnishings, wallpapers, and textiles. Of particular note, the Tahiti Room is painted to look like the interior of a native hut with views out over South Sea islands. The architectural elements of this large Neo-Classical room are entirely made of polished woods—elm, nut, black poplar, plum, apple, and walnut—and the walls are veneered. Outside, the original landscaping was simple with paths cut through the island's woodland. But, in the 1820s a new park was laid out by Peter Joseph Lenné, Germany's leading garden designer. English in character, it had ornamental trees and animal shelters housing exotic animals, such as kangaroos, llamas, and bears. **CWH**

> *"If outside this building seems little more than a conceit, the interior is mesmerizing."*
>
> Marcus Binney, journalist

Castle Coole (1798)

Architect James Wyatt **Location** Enniskillen, County Fermanagh, Northern Ireland **Style** Neo-Classical, Georgian **Material** Portland stone

Castle Coole, set in 700 acres (283 ha) of parkland, is an outstanding example of the uniquely Irish response to the Palladian ideal. Coolly classical, this mansion house is a model of symmetry. The quality of its Portland stone masonry is consummate, with all four frontages equally perfect. The house was designed by James Wyatt (1746–1813) for Armar Lowry-Corry, the first Earl of Belmore, a member of the Irish Parliament. Early designs were by Richard Johnson, but he was replaced once the foundations had been laid. The interior is the finest of its period in Ireland, created as it was by some of the leading craftsmen of the late eighteenth century with chimney pieces carved by Westmacott, plasterwork created by Rose, and scagliola columns and pilasters fashioned by Bartoli. (Scagliola is a technique to make architectural elements resemble marble.) Much of the furniture was designed by Wyatt and made on the premises. Lord Belmore intended that Castle Coole be a showpiece to proclaim his standing in Irish society and influence in the Irish House of Commons, where his family held five seats. However, the 1800 Act of Union between Britain and Ireland left both the house and builder high and dry. Belmore, because he opposed the Union, was not offered a British peerage in the new parliament. The eventual building costs were twice those originally estimated, and Lord Belmore died in 1801, leaving massive debts, the majority of which were attributable to the building of Castle Coole. The second Earl furnished the house in Regency style, and in 1821 a magnificent bedroom was prepared in anticipation of a visit by King George IV. In the event, the king never came, preferring to dally at Slane Castle with his mistress, Lady Cunningham. The National Trust, which has taken care of Castle Coole since 1951, has restored the estate and redecorated the interior. **BMC**

Hawa Mahal (1799)

Architect Lal Chand Ustad   **Location** Jaipur, Rajasthan, India   **Style** Rajput   **Materials** Red sandstone, white quick lime

Regarded as one of the iconic symbols of the state of Rajasthan, the Hawa Mahal (Palace of Winds) sits peacefully in the center of the busy city of Jaipur. Built as an extension to the women's chambers of the city palace, it was intended as a viewing screen. Through this screen—a kind of architectural veil—women of the royal family and harem could freely view the bazaar and its vibrant proceedings unseen. The term *mahal* in this context is almost misleading, as the building was never meant to serve as a residence. The five-story building is actually quite shallow, with the top three stories being barely a room deep and containing quaint chambers in which the women sat. In keeping with the visual language of the "Pink City" of Jaipur, the structure is built entirely in red sandstone, which in the sunlight glows with a pink hue. Although it is credited to the Rajput style of architecture, it also has very strong Mughal influences manifested in the symmetry of the facade. This 50-foot-high (15 m) facade has more than 950 windows, each painted with motifs in white limewash. The main entrance is at the rear of the building, where a series of ramps lead to the upper stories. These were designed to facilitate *palanquins* (chairs carried on men's shoulders). The Hawa Mahal, as its name suggests, continues to be a fitting vernacular response to the harsh climate—its numerous windows allowing the breeze to keep the internal spaces cool in the desert heat. **BS**

> "... Alladin's magician could have called into existence no more marvelous abode."

Sir Edwin Arnold, poet and journalist

Batak Toba Houses (1800)

Architect Unknown   **Location** Lake Toba, Sumatra, Indonesia   **Style** Vernacular   **Materials** Timber, bamboo, rattan, sugar palm tree fiber

The Batak Toba houses of Sumatra can be divided into two categories: the *ruma* (dwelling house) and the *sopo* (granary). The *rumas* stand facing the *sopos* across a *halaman* (square). Today the majority of the *sopos* that survive have been converted into dwellings, although they retain the name *sopo*. The houses are constructed without the use of nails, with a traditional notch-technique involving pegging and wedging to reinforce the structure. The pillars are not buried in the earth, but rest on large individual stones that prevent damage to the wood from termites and rot. This also allows the building a degree of movement during earthquakes. By being suspended on pillars, the houses protect their inhabitants from the monsoon mud and preserve stored food from rats. The most striking elements of both the *ruma* and the *sopo* are their exterior decorative carvings and paintings. The Bataks, an ethnic group of Sumatra, at Lake Toba tend to use red, white, and black to accentuate their decorations and this makes for an intricate, colorful design. Both the *ruma* and the *sopo* can be divided into three levels. The lower level, where the supporting pillars are situated, is used to stable animals. The second level of the *ruma* is where the Batak live and sleep, although there are no inner walls to divide up the space. In the *sopo* this level does not have outer walls and is used as a work area or as accommodation for guests. The largest *sopo* belonged to the village chief, and this second level was then used for village meetings. The third level is covered with a saddle-backed roof and, in both the *ruma* and the *sopo*, is used for storage. One of the most distinctive features of a Batak Toba house is its roof, which curves upward at each end. Sadly, this unusual 2,000-year-old tradition of building is fast disappearing in favor of more modern structures. **IS**

Tower Houses (1800)

Architect Unknown   **Location** Sana'a, Yemen   **Style** Vernacular   **Materials** Mud brick, gypsum, lime plaster

"The tall buildings ... offer a paradigm for green architecture in unpromising circumstances..."

Peter Popham, journalist

⬆ A rocky outcrop provides a good defensive position as well as raising the building into cooling winds.

➡ The patterns of the white gypsum decorations vary according to local and family traditions

For centuries the need for security has driven the fiercely tribal inhabitants of Yemen to live together in towns that can be easily defended. Although there are distinct regional differences, the vernacular house is a tower, built to a height of up to 100 feet (30 m). Sana'a, the capital of the Yemen, has about 14,000 of these tower houses. Typically they are six stories high, made of mud bricks decorated with thick layers of whitewashed gypsum. Openings, doors, and windows in the houses are usually emphasized in white. Mud bricks are often still handmade in the traditional way out of earth and straw mixed with water and then dried in the sun. Gypsum is obtained locally and is also used for shelves and decorative effects inside. Each tower has to accommodate a family, its goods, and guests, with animals, such as sheep, goats, and cattle, on the first floor. The foundations are of stone to protect the walls from damp. Walls get progressively thinner as the tower extends upward, and a broad staircase paved with stone links the different levels.

Above the animals is usually a floor for storage, and thereafter floors for residential use. The fifth floor, for instance, might house the kitchen, being high enough to benefit from the ventilation that comes with height above the ground. On the top floor is the traditional *mafraj*, a large room with a view where guests are welcomed and the men of the family gather to drink coffee, smoke, and talk. Often there will be a bathroom on each floor, with a lavatory that opens into a chute that ends in a sealed room at ground level. Solid matter soon dries out and is then used for fuel. Urine goes down a channel outside the tower and into a communal drain. Frequent scrubbing tries to keep odors at bay. A well on the first floor can be accessed by all levels. The introduction of modern amenities is, unfortunately, proving a threat to this delicately balanced ecology of house building. **CWH**

Peasant Housing (1800)

Architect Unknown   **Location** Corripo, Ticino, Switzerland   **Style** Vernacular   **Materials** Granite, chestnut wood

It is often assumed that true architecture can only be achieved by the involvement of an architect or master builder. It is therefore even more surprising to find an entire village and even an entire valley of extreme architectural value. Corripo, a tiny settlement perched steeply against a remote mountainside, boasts an urban quality in uniformity yet diversity that even the most respectable contemporary architects seem to fail to achieve. The use of material, the proportions—restricted by local natural stone and wood—and the positioning of the different buildings seem to respect the harshness of their location. Every house provides only the bare minimum to ensure its farming inhabitants survival in the alpine environment. In a construction method that has stayed the same over several centuries, each "Rustico," as the houses are known, is built from simple stacked granite blocks; even the roof tiles are sourced from the same natural stone slabs. All wooden parts from structure to joinery were "farmed" by using local chestnut trees. Although mostly built around the 1800s, the village of Corippo was only connected to the Swiss road network in 1838. Luckily Corippo was never completely abandoned, and after being rediscovered in the 1980s by Swiss urbanites as potential weekend retreats, a careful and extensive restoration project followed, which enabled this small but vibrant community to sustain a lifeline well into the twenty-first century. **LT**

"The inhabitants were obliged by a not always benign nature to seek sustenance in places."

Chiara Cereda, writer

Basilica of Our Lady of Copacabana (1805)

Architect Unknown **Location** Copacabana, Bolivia **Style** Spanish Colonial **Material** Brick

Copacabana lies close to Lake Titicaca near the sacred sites of the Incas, the islands of the Sun and Moon. Our Lady of Copacabana is the patron saint of Bolivia and the basilica is a pilgrimage site for Roman Catholics, housing a statue of the Virgin. The basilica is situated at the foot of a small hill that was sacred to the Incas. The 4-foot-high (1.21 m) statue of the Virgin Mary is made of plaster and maguey fiber, and was created by a local craftsman and descendant of Incan nobility, Francisco Tito Yupanqui. It is a concrete synthesis of the indigenous religious practices and Roman Catholicism, and is said to have miraculous properties. The Virgin took the name of the pre-Hispanic idol—Copacabana—she replaced. The statue is covered in gold leaf and decorated with jewels, and is dressed like an Inca princess. It was first housed in an adobe church in 1583 that was built over Incan temples, before being housed in 1805 in the Hispanic Colonial-style church it

is in today. The statue was crowned by Pope Pius XI, and its sanctuary was promoted to a basilica in 1949. The church itself is Colonial in style, with a mixture of Spanish and Indian detail. Its *trompe l'oeil* facade appears to be made out of large stone blocks rather than the small bricks that have actually been used. The walls are whitewashed with earth-colored stonework around the top of the building and around its arched entrances. A large bell tower, two stories high, stands at its main entrance. **CMK**

"[The Virgin image] manifested its miraculous nature by emitting glorious light at night ..."

María Rostworowski, academic

Sir John Soane's Museum (1812)

Architect Sir John Soane   **Location** London, England   **Style** Neo-Classical   **Material** Portland stone

Sir John Soane's House is a magical, labyrinthine space and a must-visit for anyone with an interest in design, architecture, arcane history, and the illusions that can be played with light, shade, and mirrors. The building is situated in Lincoln's Inn Fields, the largest public square in London. Neo-Classical architect Soane (1753–1837) designed the building as his house, but also as a public museum from which "amateurs and students" could learn. The building grew out of Soane's demolition and subsequent rebuild of three buildings on the north side of Lincoln's Inn Fields. He began with the rather plain brick No. 12, between 1792 and 1794, then bought No. 13—the home of the museum today—when he was made professor of architecture at the Royal College of Art in 1806, then No. 14, which he rebuilt in 1823–24.

The exterior features a projecting facade of Portland stone rising from the basement to first and second floors and finishing in the center bay of the third floor. But the building's most interesting points are almost entirely to do with its rich, bewilderingly complex, and playful interiors. Some of the most famous spaces in the house are the top-lit ones in the museum at the rear, which echo spaces Soane designed for the Bank of England's banking halls. The ingeniously designed picture gallery has a clever space-saving device with large, folding panels of paintings. Other subtle tricks and elements include the mirrored, domed ceiling of the breakfast room, a study featuring a collection of Roman architectural statues and fragments, a "Gothic" library in a deep red, and two external courtyards. **DT**

↖ Removal of London soot from the facade of No. 13 Lincoln's Inn Fields has revealed the Portland stone.

↤ The library contains Soane's collection of more than 6,000 titles; nothing has been added since 1837.

Dulwich Picture Gallery (1817)

Architect Sir John Soane **Location** Dulwich, London, England **Style** Neo-Classical **Material** Stone

Britain's first public art gallery was created thanks to the will of Sir Francis Bourgeois, who bequeathed his private collection to the public in 1811, together with a bequest for building a gallery to house them and the request that his friend Sir John Soane (1753–1837) design it. The picture gallery opened in 1817. Soane's design has since become the inspiration for a number of museums and galleries worldwide.

Soane's work was idiosyncratic, fed by his private collection of Greek, Roman, and Egyptian antiquities and the many varied properties of light. His inspiration for Dulwich Picture Gallery came from his memories of monumental architecture from the classical world, and the play and illusion of light effects created by them. Evocative of a Grecian temple, the plan for the gallery was basic: a collection of interlinking rooms all lit directly from above by large skylights to display the works of art to their greatest advantage, making full use of natural light. The skylights are curved and graded, with the location of each pane of glass designed as carefully as the facets of a cut diamond. The panes allow the light to fall naturally over the paintings, but also allow diffusion of the light before it makes contact with the pictures, minimizing the risk of damage.

Twentieth-century additions to the structure of the picture gallery by Rick Mather Architects are in sharp but pleasing contrast to the eighteenth-century building. The new areas have been built as a cloistered entrance—fully enclosed yet making use of huge glass panes that are suggestive of walking through an outside space. **LH**

↗ Sir John Soane's innovatory gallery lighting showed a modern concern for safeguarding art from sunlight.

⇥ Simple piers and arches characterize the east facade; the design originally called for an arcaded walkway.

Dinh Cam Pho Communal House (1818)

Architect Unknown **Location** Hoi An, Vietnam **Style** Nguyen Dynasty **Materials** Brick, wood, convex terra-cotta tiles

Located in the historic port town of Hoi An on the coast of central Vietnam, the Dinh Cam Pho Communal House is an excellent illustration of the specific architecture and function of the Vietnamese *dinh*. A *dinh*, or community hall, represents the most important building within any Vietnamese village or town. In a uniquely Vietnamese architectural innovation, the *dinh*'s roof features convex tiles and upturned edges. It is thought that this style of roof stretches as far back as the Dong Son era of the first millennium BCE, and the complex framework of the *dinh*'s roof further suggests a long and venerable architectural tradition. Unlike the *dinhs* of earlier periods however, the Cam Pho Communal House is a fusion of Vietnamese and Chinese architecture and design. The Cam Pho Communal House went through several phases of construction. A storeroom was added in 1875, while the antechamber was added in

1903. The building would have served as a courtroom, a banquet hall, and a theater for entertainments such as plays and puppet shows. It also incorporated a temple in honor of the local patron divinity, as well as a shrine to commemorate the deceased. To enter the Cam Pho Communal House is to enter the heart of traditional Vietnamese society. The *dinh* represents a lasting link with Vietnam's past while simultaneously reminding us of the vibrancy of the culture in Vietnam that continues to exist to this day. **SAM**

"When I pass the dinh, I tip my hat to it. I love you as much as its roof tiles are numerous."

Ancient Vietnamese saying

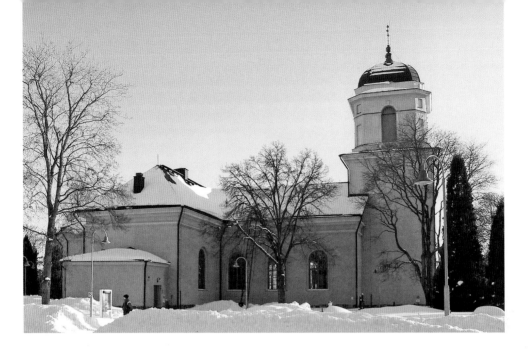

Vihti Church (1822)

Architect Carlo Bassi **Location** Vihdintie, Vihti, Finland **Style** Neo-Classical **Materials** Concrete; copper roof

Vihti Church in southern Finland is an elegant example of Nordic Neo-Classicism, known as the Gustavian style. It is named after the Swedish king Gustav III who reigned in the late eighteenth century. He had spent some time in France and returned influenced by the style favored there during the reign of Louis XVI. Gustavian style is defined by Classical simplicity, with some surface decoration and muted colors. Vihti Church is built in the shape of a crucifix, and the cruciform church is a tradition that runs through Finnish ecclesiastical architecture. Lutheran churches like this one are customarily less decorated than, for example, Roman Catholic churches. The religious message is communicated by more minimal and subtle means, reflecting the Lutheran belief that salvation can be found through faith alone. The Italian architect Carlo Bassi (1772–1840) moved to Finland around 1800, having grown up in Sweden and studied in Stockholm. He established himself as an architect of churches, designing in the Gustavian style, and was mainly based in Turku. After the old Vihti Church was severely damaged by lightning in 1818, it was rebuilt according to Bassi's design. It is a delicate, almost pretty building with a tower and tall windows. After the church was again damaged by lightning in 1848, it was rebuilt with some Neo-Gothic touches, such as windows that narrow at the top. During the renovation in 1929, these features were removed, returning the church to its original, Gustavian look with arching windows. Inside, the church is almost homely in its friendly proportions. The color scheme is typical of its style, with pastels combined with darker accent colors. The large windows allow light to flood the church. In rural Finland, churches were important communal spaces. This approachable and graceful church fulfills this purpose perfectly. **RK**

Royal Pavilion (1823)

Architect John Nash **Location** Brighton, England **Style** Neo-Classical, Indo-Islamic **Materials** Stone, cast iron, copper

"The turban domes and lofty pinnacles might ... attract and fix the attention of the spectator ..."

John Nash, architect

⬆ The Music Room, decorated in Chinese style, is lit by nine extraordinary, lotus-shaped chandeliers.

➡ John Nash's Indian-styled extravagance led to one of England's most distinctive and best-loved buildings.

This impressive palatial building, with its mosquelike domes, minarets, and Chinese-styled interior, looks as though it would be more at home in the Middle East or India than in East Sussex. Home to three British monarchs, the Pavilion originated as a farmhouse that was rented as a seaside retreat by the Prince of Wales, later George IV, in 1786.

In 1787 the Prince commissioned Henry Holland to convert the farmhouse into something more befitting his status. Holland designed and built the "Marine Pavilion," a small Neo-Classical structure, around the original building. It consisted of a central rotunda surrounded by Ionic columns and two wings with bow windows. It was extended by P. F. Robinson in 1801, and a few years later William Porden added in its grounds an enormous, Indian-styled, domed stable large enough to house sixty horses.

The Prince was so impressed with the novel nature of the stables—now the Dome concert hall—that he commissioned the famed architect John Nash (1752–1835) to transform the Pavilion into the exotic fantasy that exists today. Nash completely concealed Holland's original form under a cast-iron framework to support his new exterior. Once finished, the resplendent creation boasted a giant lantern ceiling kitchen, an entrance hall with a Chinese-motif wall design, a spectacular music room, and—the *pièce de résistance*—the shallow-domed Banqueting Room with a one-ton crystal chandelier hanging from the claws of a silver dragon positioned at the apex of its 45-foot-high (13 m) painted ceiling.

Recently restored to its original theatrical grandeur by Brighton city council, which bought the stripped building from Queen Victoria in 1850, and now standing in replanted Regency gardens, this glorious, full-scale folly cannot help but delight with its display of master craftsmanship. **JM**

Shaker Barn (1826)

Architect Unknown **Location** Hancock Shaker Village, Pittsfield, Massachusetts, USA **Style** Regional Vernacular **Materials** Stone, wood

The United Society of Believers was a religious sect founded in the eighteenth century; it was given the pejorative name of "the Shakers" by observers affronted by their visible trembling during devotion. Work was worship, so it seems reasonable to assume that the Hancock community of Shakers spent a large percentage of their shared equity on this cow barn. Based on regional barns but with significant innovations, the design adheres to the belief that it is better to be beautiful on the inside than outside. The exterior is economical and spare, while the interior marries the practical with the spiritual. The circular, three-story structure comprises a stone base, a twelve-sided wood clerestory, and a cupola crown; the barn's latter two elements replace the original conical roof and cupola, destroyed by fire in 1864. The circular shapes and small windows give the barn the air of a giant dovecote, and form a metaphor for the Father, Son, and Holy Ghost. At ground or wagon level is an internal perimeter "roadway," entered through one large door. Cows enter and exit at manger level through a wood-covered bridge on granite pillars. Walls up to 3.5 feet (1 m) thick ensure heat retention but also exacerbate steam accumulation, which makes the superb ventilation design essential. Cows face inward to the central haymow from manger-level perimeter stalls. Split-wood posts in the center create a tight base bundle that fans upward to the apex to aid air circulation; from beneath, it resembles the underside of a mushroom cap. The floor has holes through which the manger-level animals receive feed. The top of the haystack is accessed via a third-level earthen ramp. The later addition of a manure pit with trapdoors beneath the stable and manger allows waste to drop by gravity directly into wagons stationed below. **DJ**

Altes Museum (1828)

Architect Karl Friedrich Schinkel **Location** Berlin, Germany **Style** Neo-Classical **Materials** Stone, render

In the nineteenth century, the German bourgeoisie increasingly believed that every citizen should have the chance of a comprehensive cultural education. Accordingly, Frederick William III of Prussia (1770–1840) commissioned architect Karl Friedrich Schinkel (1781–1841) to design an art gallery to house his collection in a museum complex on an island in the Spree River in Berlin. The museum was built on a plinth to raise it up from the island, which was prone to flooding, and Schinkel also changed the course of the river to protect the island. The subsequent construction of the Neues Museum, the Alte Nationalgalerie, and the Bode Museum gave the island its name of Museuminsel. Schinkel's concepts for the Altes (Old) Museum were based on drawings and sketches by Frederick William himself, which showed a Classical, templelike building with a row of columns facing the square in front. The interiors are organized around two courtyards connected by a central rotunda—loosely based on the Pantheon in Rome—all architectural elements that previously would have been used solely in palatial or ecclesiastical buildings. Work began in 1825, and the museum opened to the public in 1830. With its articulate, well-proportioned appearance and simple internal layout, it is widely considered to be one of the most important buildings of the Neo-Classical period in Germany, and it is certainly the most distinguished of Schinkel's creations. **LT**

> *"Schinkel's Altes Museum with its grand facade shaped the triad of museum, cathedral, and palace."*
>
> Christina Weiss, ex-German Minister for Culture

Schloss
Charlottenhof (1829)

Architects Karl Friedrich Schinkel, Ludwig Persius   **Location** Potsdam,
Germany   **Style** Neo-Classical   **Materials** Stone, brick, plaster

In 1825 Frederick William III of Prussia purchased an estate south of Sanssouci Park as a gift for the Crown Prince Frederick William. The estate already had an eighteenth-century manor house, which was remodeled jointly by Karl Friedrich Schinkel (1781–1841) and the Crown Prince to create the Charlottenhof Palace. Schinkel was abroad while much of the reconstruction work was underway, so his assistant, Ludwig Persius (1803–45), supervised the project.

The fabric of the old house was transformed, although as much as possible was retained to reduce costs. On one side, the ground was raised to conceal the basement, and a pedimented Doric portico was added to the original centerpiece. The interiors were simply but elegantly redecorated, and Schinkel designed much of the furniture.

The house was extended out into the landscape by means of pergolas, terraces, steps, paths, and formal architectural seats. The prince envisaged the idealized landscape around Charlottenhof Palace as a utopian domain. Thus the Court Gardener's House—built from 1829 to 1845 and now known as the Roman Baths—formed an important feature in the views from the palace. This house was conceived in the style of an Italian country villa, with tiled roofs and towers. The strongest influences on Schinkel and the prince were the then recent discoveries made at Pompeii and Herculaneum. Charlottenhof Palace and the Court Gardener's House are the epitome of nineteenth-century picturesque Classicism. **CWH**

↖ This palace, built for German royals, is now named after a former owner, Maria Charlotte von Gentzkow.

↩ Some of the living rooms at Charlottenhof have been restored to how they looked in the Crown Prince's time.

Royal High School (1829)

Architect Thomas Hamilton   **Location** Edinburgh, Scotland
Style Greek Revival   **Materials** Stone, lead, slate roofing

With the building of the Royal High School on a rocky outcrop overlooking the center of the city, Edinburgh cemented its reputation as the "Athens of the North." Its complex massing of Greek Revival elements was entirely appropriate for the main public school in a city famous for the "democratic intellect" heralded by the cultural ferment of the Scottish Enlightenment.

The Royal High School was the building that really made the reputation of Thomas Hamilton (1784–1858) as a master of the Classical language of architecture. The son of a local mason, Hamilton never visited

---

"[It shows] how well the lessons of the Anthenian Propylaea were learned by Scottish architects."

Henry-Russell Hitchcock, architectural historian

Greece, yet the way in which he integrated the central "temple" core of the building with Doric colonnades and pavilions is masterly. The setting on Calton Hill, just below the Parthenon-inspired National Monument, is so sensitively integrated with its site, it almost appears to be hewn out of the living rock.

Symmetrical in plan, the principal focus of the building is the galleried central hall with gilded columns, its details an array of Grecian motifs such as anthemions, palmettes, and rosettes. Cleverly lit from above by windows at gallery level, the heavily coffered ceiling seems to float rather than weigh heavily, and the overall result pays elegant homage to Classical sources without being slavish or pedantic. The Royal High School is a key element in making Edinburgh the greatest Neo-Classical city in the world. **NMC**

Nat Taung Kyaung Monastery (1830)

Architect Unknown   **Location** Taung-bi, Myanmar
Style Buddhist, Late Konbaung Period   **Material** Teakwood)

To fully appreciate the all-pervasive nature of Buddhism in Burmese society, one needs to look no further than to its religious architecture. This is perfectly illustrated by the Nat Taung Kyaung Monastery, which is one of the oldest and finest surviving wooden monasteries in Myanmar. Designed according to well-established architectural traditions and constructed almost entirely of teak, it is built on wooden piles that raise the floor from ground level. A covered veranda is located at the northern end of the main structure; the central room functioned as a reception area, with the main shrine room being located off to the east.

Two multi-tiered spires tower over the main shrine room and living area respectively. This architectural feature is known as a *pyatthat*, and is a unique Burmese innovation. The *pyatthats* here each consist of five roofs, separated by paneling, that decrease in size with their ascent, terminating in a bulbous finial. According to the Burmese, this architectural feature represents the three palaces that served as the seasonal abodes of Prince Siddhattha, the Buddha-to-be.

The most outstanding feature of this monastery however, is its exceptional wood carving, which dates to the late Kon-Baung Period (1850–80). The veranda doors are some of the finest to be seen in all of Myanmar, with low-relief leaf designs decorating the jambs, which are in turn flanked by pairs of dancing *kinnari*—a mythical Burmese creature. The roof decoration of the *pyatthats* is also exceptional and exhibits some exquisite wood carvings.

The Nat Taung-Kyaung Monastery represents not only one of the finest surviving examples of Burmese wood carving but also encapsulates the beauty of Myanmar's Buddhist architectural tradition. **SAM**

Arc de Triomphe (1836)

Architect Jean François Thérèse Chalgrin **Location** Paris, France
Style Neo-Classical **Material** Ashlar stone

The Arc de Triomphe is the world's largest triumphal arch, standing 167 feet (51 m) high by 148 feet (45 m) wide. Inspired by the Arch of Titus in Rome, it was commissioned by Emperor Napoleon I in 1806 after the victory at Austerlitz, to commemorate all the victories of the French army; it has since engendered a worldwide military taste for triumphal and nationalistic monuments. The astylar design consists of a simple arch with a vaulted passageway topped by an attic. The monument's iconography includes four main allegorical sculptural reliefs on the four pillars of the Arc. *The Triumph of Napoleon, 1810*, by Jean-Pierre Cortot shows an imperial Napoleon, wearing a laurel wreath and toga, accepting the surrender of a city while fame blows a trumpet. There are two reliefs by Antoine Etex: *Resistance*, depicting an equestrian figure and a naked soldier defending his family, protected by the spirit of the future and *Peace*, in which a warrior protected by Minerva, the Roman goddess of wisdom, is sheathing his sword surrounded by scenes of agricultural laborers. The *Departure of the Volunteers of '92*, commonly called *La Marseillaise*, by François Rude, presents naked and patriotic figures, led by Bellona, goddess of war, against the enemies of France. In the vault of the Arc are engraved the names of 128 battles of the Republican and Napoleonic regimes. The attic is decorated with thirty shields, each inscribed with a military victory, and the inner walls list the names of 558 French generals, with those who died in battle underlined. The Arc has subsequently become a symbol of national unity and reconciliation as the site of the Tomb of the Unknown Soldier from World War I. He was interred here on Armistice Day, 1920; today there is an eternal flame commemorating the dead of two world wars. **JEH**

Church of St. Mary Magdalene (1842)

Architect Pierre-Alexandre Vignon **Location** Paris, France
Style Neo-Classical **Material** Stone

In 1806 Napoleon commissioned Pierre-Alexandre Vignon, Inspector–General of Buildings of the Republic, to build a Temple to the Glory of the Great Army and provide a monumental view to the north of Place de la Concorde. Known as "The Madeleine," this church was designed as a Neo-Classical temple surrounded by a Corinthian colonnade, reflecting the predominant taste for Classical art and architecture. The proposal of the Arc de Triomphe, however, reduced the original commemorative intention for the temple and, after the fall of Napoleon, Louis XVIII

> *"With a temple destined to last … one must look for the maximum grandeur and solidity possible."*
>
> Pierre-Alexandre Vignon, architect

ordered that the church be consecrated to St. Mary Magdalene in Paris in 1842.

The Madeleine has no steps at the sides but a grand entrance of twenty-eight steps at each end. The church's exterior is surrounded by fifty-two Corinthian columns, 66 feet (20 m) high. The pediment sculpture of Mary Magdalene at the Last Judgement is by Philippe-Henri Lemaire; bronze relief designs in the church doors represent the Ten Commandments.

The nineteenth-century interior is lavishly gilded and overdecorated. Above the altar, is a statue of the ascension of St. Mary Magdalene by Charles Marochetti and a fresco by Jules-Claude Ziegler, *The History of Christianity*, with Napoleon as the central figure surrounded by such luminaries as Michelangelo, Emperor Constantine and Joan of Arc. **JEH**

Pentonville Prison (1842)

Architect Colonel Joshua Jebb   **Location** London, England
Style Italianate   **Material** Brick

Pentonville Prison combined what were seen as the best qualities of a number of previous prisons in Britain and the United States, incorporating the ideas of several prison reformers. Its designer was a military engineer who was seconded to the Home Office in 1837 to advise on the development of model prisons; by 1842, he was the first Surveyor-General of Prisons.

The style was Italianate rather than the castellated style that was currently a popular option, which meant that the building was a little less forbidding and fortresslike. Staff could observe the whole prison from the central hall, from which four wings of cells radiated. Bay windows allowed the governor and visitors to see into the hall. Balconies and stairs were all of cast iron so as not to obstruct the view. Food was lifted from the basement on trays for distribution to the cells on trolleys that ran along the wing gallery handrails. The prison originally held 520 prisoners; a further 220 places were added when the wings were heightened and lengthened from 1865 to 1872.

The regime was harsh. The prisoners were held in solitary confinement, working, eating, and sleeping in their cells, which were provided with handbasins and water closets. Masks were used to prevent recognition when taking exercise or worshipping in the chapel. There were individual, high-sided pews in the chapel to prevent sideways contact between prisoners, who could see only the chaplain. In the cells, they could not see out of the windows, which were set high up in the wall. Pentonville is still in use as a jail today. **CWH**

↗ Open staircases and slim metal corridor handrails improve observation of prisoners in the cell blocks.

➡ The gate's pediment and the stylized columns of the central block behind show the Italianate influence.

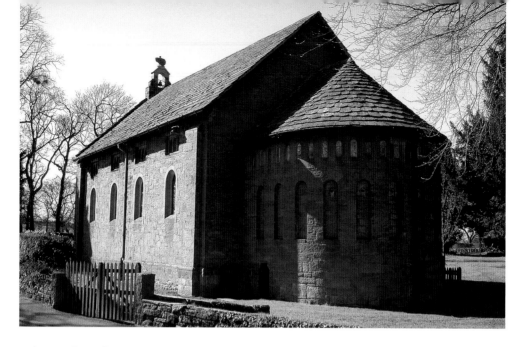

Church of St. Mary (1842)

Architect Sara Losh   **Location** Wreay, Cumbria, England   **Style** Romanesque Revival   **Materials** Sandstone, marble, stained-glass

The word "Romanesque" was coined by William Gunn in 1819. The idea of a European basis for this round-arched precursor of Gothic was taken up by scholars and architects such as William Whewell and Edmund Sharpe. The finest example of the style is St. Mary's Church at Wreay, which owes its origins to the independent travels and learning of Sara Losh (1786–1853). Independently wealthy, Losh used her inheritance to travel in France, Italy, and Germany, sightseeing and mixing with a European intellectual circle. On her return she began building at Wreay; early examples of her antiquarian interests were a schoolmaster's house based on a Pompeian villa and a copy of the Bewcastle Cross. In 1835 she embarked on a new parish church in what she herself described as "early Saxon or modified Lombardic." The church has the simple plan of a single nave and a semicircular colonnaded apse, intended to reproduce an early Christian basilica. What marks out the church is its scholarly and consistent use of a style for which there was virtually no English precedent, and its breathtaking use of carved decoration and materials. The alabaster font was carved by Sara and her cousin; the stonework was carved by the local builder's son, Willian Hindson; and the woodwork—some with its bark still on—was crafted by Sara's gardener. There were more exotic imports; the altar is of Italian marble, and some of the stained glass is French in origin. **FK**

> "Very original and beautiful . . . much more so than the things done by the young architects now."
>
> Dante Gabriel Rosetti, poet and artist

Walhalla Hall of Fame and Honor (1842)

Architect Leo von Klenze **Location** Donaustauf, near Regensburg, Germany **Style** Neo-Classical **Material** Marble

The young crown prince Ludwig I of Bavaria was highly educated and a lover of arts and literature. He built the Walhalla Hall of Fame and Honor as a monument to "glorious and honorable Germans." At this time, Germany as a united country did not exist—the German states united in 1871—so it was German speakers whose achievements he intended to recognize. In 1816 Ludwig approached the architect Leo von Klenze (1784–1864); after lengthy disputes over the location and the style, work began in 1830 on a structure that drew inspiration from the great Greek temples such as the Parthenon in Athens. Similar to the Parthenon, the Walhalla Hall has only one row of Doric columns on the outside, while on the inside there is a large, column-free space. Here, the busts of the famous and honored could be displayed on lightly decorated walls lit by large rooflights. The interior is a rather free interpretation of Greek architecture, but

that does not detract from this imposing building, which embodies the best intentions of Classicist architecture. Today the Walhalla Hall houses 191 busts and plaques of scientists, writers, composers, clerics, and artists spanning almost two millennia of European history. Leo von Klenze's work became highly regarded across Europe, and beside his work for the Bavarian king he also took on other commissions, most notably the formidable New Hermitage in St. Petersburg, completed to his designs in 1852. **LT**

"Everything else is just styles, only the Greeks mastered the art of architecture."

Leo von Klenze, architect

The Grange (1844)

Architect Augustus Pugin **Location** Ramsgate, England **Style** Gothic Revival **Materials** Brick, Caen stone

The great Gothic Revivalist Augustus Pugin (1812–52) is best known for his decorative design work at the Houses of Parliament in London, but this small house with its adjacent church has in its own way been just as remarkable and influential. Pugin was becoming widely recognized as an architect and polemical writer on design when he drew up plans for his own family residence atop a cliff at the western edge of the Channel port of Ramsgate. At this time, a few years into Queen Victoria's reign, almost every middle-class detached house shared the same plan: a corridor leading from the entrance door would run centrally between two principal rooms. The front elevation was imposing; stairs were squeezed into the central corridor, or ran from one side of it. Pugin's house was completely different. A bold, double-height, central stair hall sits at the middle of the plan, and the rooms are arranged around it to create a dynamic, rotating layout. Each room is part of a block that is expressed distinctly on the exterior yet held together visually by a common ridgeline and a consistent architectural language. The main entrance is located alongside the back wall of a kitchen that projects into the front yard—a startling deviation from Georgian convention, which typically hid the functional parts of a house at the rear. Within a short time, features like these appeared in new houses all over Britain. Pugin had transformed the design of residential architecture. **TBC**

"There should be no features . . . not necessary for convenience, construction, or propriety."

Augustus Pugin, architect

Albert Dock (1846)

Architect Jesse Hartley   **Location** Liverpool, England   **Style** Classical, industrial   **Materials** Brick, sandstone, granite, cast iron

Albert Dock is the finest of the nineteenth-century dock buildings in Britain. It comprises a single dock basin surrounded by a massive granite wall for security, and five linked stacks of five-story warehouses around the quays, all of fireproof construction. Along the waterfront, massive iron columns support the wall on a combination of straight lintels and elliptical arches. These arches, which allowed valuable bonded cargo to be swung from ship to shore, add a graceful note to the austere brick elevations. Inside, the structure is carried by cast iron with vaulted brick ceilings, which undulate to give greater strength. The roof design was original, being made of wrought-iron plates riveted together as a form of skin, stressed by iron trusses. Jesse Hartley (1780–1860), dock engineer to the Port of Liverpool, brought practical bridge-building experience with an eye for architectural effect. Albert Dock survived decades of redundancy and threats of demolition, partly because it was such a tough building from the start, and partly because it provided such a compelling image of Classicism blended with utility. One can read the rationale of every stone and brick, granite replacing sandstone where friction was expected, and corners curved to prevent ships' rigging from snagging in narrow places. Although the docks were built well into the Victorian period, they retain the attractive simplicity of fifty years before—the spirit of Soane or Ledoux. **AP**

> "… its sublime grandeur [is] unquestionably the architectural climax of the Liverpool docks."
>
> Joseph Sharples, historian

Church of St. Giles (1846)

Architect Augustus Pugin   **Location** Cheadle, Staffordshire, England   **Style** Gothic Revival   **Material** Hollington sandstone

Until the religious revival of the late-Georgian and early-Victorian period, most of England's Gothic churches were in a state of advanced neglect or decay. The will to revive their past glories was there, and yet architects lacked the skills to do it—until Augustus Pugin (1812–52) showed them how. Because Pugin built for the newly enfranchised but still poor Roman Catholic community, most of his churches were modest affairs. The Church of St. Giles, at Cheadle in Staffordshire, built under the patronage of the wealthy Earl of Shrewsbury, was the exception. With its soaring 200-foot-high (61 m) spire, this spectacular building was intended to advertise both the revival of the English Catholic Church and the splendor of medieval architecture. Externally, the building resembles a fine early-fourteenth-century Gothic church; the interior, however, is one of the most spectacular in Britain. Every inch of the walls is decorated in bold colors, the

spaces glowing and sparkling in red and gold. Pugin designed everything in the church: the stained glass, the wall and floor tiles, the metalwork, and the furnishings. Above his own rood screen Pugin placed a painting of the Last Judgment by an obscure Swiss artist known only by his surname, Hauser. At Cheadle, Pugin showed architects the potential of the Gothic Revival. Too often compromised by unsympathetic clients, this extraordinary architect saw St. Giles's Church as his greatest achievement. **TBC**

" . . . Cheadle. Perfect Cheadle. Cheadle, my consolation in all afflictions."

Augustus Pugin, architect

Thorvaldsen's Museum (1848)

Architect Michael Gottlieb Bindersbøll **Location** Copenhagen, Denmark **Style** Neo-Classical **Materials** Brick, plaster

Bertel Thorvaldsen (1770–1844) was one of the finest Neo-Classical sculptors in Europe. Born in Copenhagen, he studied in Rome from 1796 and spent most of the rest of his life there, accepting commissions from all over Europe. In 1838 he decided to return home for good, founding a museum to house his collections of plaster models of his entire output, as well as contemporary paintings and antique artifacts. Thorvaldsen's Museum is a key building in the history of Danish Classicism, built just as the old Neo-Classicism was passing out of fashion but before historicism had taken root. The museum was the first and most important work of its architect, Michael Gottlieb Bindersbøll. It was built on the site of the old Royal Carriage House, not far from the Christiansborg Palace. The reuse of that building's foundations largely dictated the museum's dimensions. Bindersbøll's study of polychromy in the decoration of antique buildings materially affected his design. The basic color of the simple and massive exterior is a rich ocher, with architectural elements picked out in white, green, and blue. The portal motifs of the entrance front are carried around the sides, where they contain windows and frame a remarkable s'graffito ("scratched" plaster) frieze by Jørgen Sonne depicting the transport of Thorvaldsen's collections from Rome to Copenhagen, in a modern-dress equivalent of an ancient Roman triumph. The museum's interior is decorated with plain dark colors to set off the sculpture, and the ceilings are decorated in paint and stucco in the Pompeian style. The entrance vestibule is large and barrel-vaulted. Beyond, a glazed peristyle surrounds the courtyard while the side wings contain a series of small rooms or alcoves to house individual major works of art. At the far end is a hall for the display of Thorvaldsen's figure of Christ. **CWH**

Palm
House (1848)

Architects Decimus Burton, Richard Turner   **Location** London, England
Style Victorian   **Materials** Glass, iron

At the Palm House at Kew Gardens, 16,000 panes of glass combine with a delicately curving structure of iron supports to make a greenhouse some 362 feet (110 m) in length and 63 feet (19 m) tall. This was the first really large-scale glasshouse in Britain, a perfect building to house Kew's world-class collection of palm trees, and a structure of simple beauty in its own right. It was also highly influential, being one of the inspirations of Joseph Paxton's famous Crystal Palace exhibition building, and of many other large glasshouses since.

The Palm House is a building of elegant simplicity, but its construction was far from simple. Architect Decimus Burton (1800–81) produced plans that were criticized for their large number of internal columns. Engineer Richard Turner (c. 1798–1881) produced new plans, which Burton disliked, resulting in further revisions from Burton. Historians have since struggled to work out who was responsible for which part of the design. The overall design and structure were probably Turner's, while Burton was responsible for the proportions of the building's central part, much of the detailing, and the boiler tower to the east.

The original glass was tinted green to minimize the scorching effect of the sun, but this produced a gloomy interior and was replaced with clear glazing. As the interior floods with sunlight, the combination of the tracery of the steel glazing bars and the overlapping green leaves of the trees makes the Palm House a memorable architectural experience. **PW**

↖ The design took advantage of sheet glass recently invented by Chance Brothers and Co. of Birmingham.

← The Palm House, built using shipbuilding technology, has been likened to an upturned ship's hull.

Church of St. Savior (1853)

Architect Sophia Gray **Location** Claremont, Cape Town, South Africa **Style** Ecclesiastical Vernacular **Material** Stone

All but hidden beneath years of additions and alterations, St. Savior's is a gem of South African architectural history. This small Anglican church, where "Sophy" (as she was known) Gray (1814–71) was buried in 1871, was the best-loved of her large legacy of ecclesiastical works, which included churches and clergy buildings in parishes up and down the country, often in remote settings.

Gray's personal story is more interesting than much of her design output. Originally from England, she is usually cited as South Africa's first woman architect—true in a strictly professional sense, although it should be noted that women masterminded home-building in most traditional African cultures long before Gray made her mark on the nineteenth-century colony. Sailing for Cape Town in 1847 with her husband, Bishop Robert Gray, Sophy brought their children, servants, clergymen—and plans culled from the best of British church architecture. Their new home became base camp for numerous "visitations" around the episcopal territory, often made in unforgiving conditions and usually on horseback. Always carrying her portfolio, she would leave plans at each small town they passed, and by 1861 she was managing twenty-one building projects, corresponding with far-flung parish councils.

But her favorite project was closer to home. St. Savior's was built on donated land. Records show that Sophy had workers on site only two weeks after the property transfer, with the first stone laid in September 1850. Doting on the scheme, she personally brought encaustic tiles from London, which she laid around the altar. Today her contribution to South African architecture is honored in the annual Sophia Gray Memorial lecture series. **MJB**

Salt's Mill (1853)

Architects Fairbairn, Lockwood, Mawson **Location** Saltaire, West Yorkshire, England **Style** Industrial Italianate **Material** Sandstone

In 1850 Titus Salt, a prominent Yorkshire mill owner who had made a successful business out of making alpaca and mohair cloth, decided to move his factory to a new site outside Shipley. The mill he built is a gargantuan structure—at 557 feet (170 m) in length it was said to be longer than St. Paul's Cathedral, and its chimney, 208 feet (76 m) high, was slightly taller than another celebrated London structure, the Monument. Salt was making a point by putting up a building in Yorkshire that was bigger than anything in the capital. The size and scale of his building showed what

> ## "[Its] walls look more like those of a fortified town than a building destined to . . . peaceful pursuits."
>
> *The Builder*, 1852

Yorkshire was capable of, and above all Salt produced a practical building, with space for 4,500 workers and two very powerful steam engines.

Salt and his engineer, Sir William Fairbairn (1789–1874), chose the Italianate style. They brought in their favorite architects, Henry F. Lockwood (1811–78) and William Mawson (1828–89), to add Italian detail to the facades—*campanile*-like pavilions and the occasional Classical window surround. Inside, fireproof construction, with stone vaults and iron roof trusses, was the order of the day. This robust building, surviving many years as a hardworking textile mill, has been restored as a combination of art gallery, museum, and shopping center. Now visitors can enter the vast interiors of this monumental mill and appreciate Salt's grand conception first hand. **PW**

Customs House (1854)

Architect Edward Salmons   **Location** Paita, Peru
Style Early Victorian Colonial   **Materials** Cast iron, wrought iron

The manufacturer E. T. Bellhouse of Manchester was one of the world's most successful suppliers of prefabricated buildings sheathed in galvanized, corrugated iron. In 1853 the Peruvian Treasury Department commissioned Bellhouse to design an iron customs house for the Pacific port of Paita. It was to replace the existing and partially derelict structure at the end of the pier. The need was urgent: Paita was a busy port near large deposits of guano, Peru's most lucrative export. Working with architect Edward Salmons, Bellhouse designed a 70-square-foot (21 sq m)

"[The Customs House] is one of the most important works in iron ever executed."

Practical Mechanics Journal 1854

---

two-story structure, with a cantilevered veranda at the upper floor, topped by an ornamental belvedere and a two-stage circular tower crowning a pyramidal roof. The structure was supported on a cast-iron frame, and clad in sheets of corrugated iron arranged vertically between cast-iron pilasters. The simple, balanced design achieved a substantial volume with minimal materials, elegantly demonstrating the structural efficiencies possible with iron building components.

Prior to export, the Customs House and a corrugated-iron warehouse were erected temporarily at Bellhouse's Manchester works; it was an opportunity to check for defects and to number the components. The building attracted more than 25,000 visitors. The Customs House still stands in Peru, albeit hidden behind a skin of crumbling stucco. **AM**

Paddington Station Trainshed (1855)

Architects Brunel, Wyatt   **Location** London, England
Style Victorian industrial   **Materials** Wrought iron, cast iron, glass

Nineteenth-century Britain's greatest gift to the world was the railway, and Paddington Station was the first terminus to express the dynamism and the adventure of this revolutionary form of travel. The Great Western Railway Company was established in 1833, and its chief engineer, Isambard Kingdom Brunel (1806–59), personally directed the layout and design of the route from London to Bristol; this was operational by 1841. At the very end of 1850, Brunel sketched out ideas for a permanent London terminus; a month later he had already completed his detailed plans.

Sadly, we can no longer enjoy Joseph Paxton's Crystal Palace, site of the Great Exhibition at Hyde Park in 1851. But Paddington Station is its closest surviving progeny. Brunel planned it as the palace was going up, and it was the palace's contractors, Fox, Henderson & Company, that built Paddington. The original three great vaults of the station, the widest of which spans more than 100 feet (30 m), proudly demonstrate Victorian Britain's spirit of adventure. Like the Crystal Palace, Paddington was built with "transepts"; here they allowed Brunel's locomotives to make three-point turns before the invention of the turntable. Matthew Digby Wyatt (1805–55) assisted Brunel by designing decorative detailing, including the Venetian-looking doors and windows along the western side of the concourse and the unusual organic patterns of ironwork at either end of the trainsheds.

Today, people may travel from Paddington to Penzance, at almost the southwesternmost point of England, but in Brunel's day the station was the London terminus for the New York service. Passengers would travel to Bristol, and thence by steamship—another Brunel invention that cut the journey time across the Atlantic by more than half. **TBC**

Dolmabahçe Palace (1855)

Architect Garabet Amira Balyan   **Location** Istanbul, Turkey
Style Ottoman Baroque   **Material** Stone

On the European shore of the Bosphorus in Istanbul stands one of the most lavish palaces in the world. It was built for the Ottoman sultan Abdülmecid I, who wanted a building to accommodate his harem (the imperial family quarters), the court administration, and enormous state rooms, where visiting rulers and ambassadors could be entertained. The imperial architect, Garabet Amira Balyan (1800–66), delivered a building that performed all of these functions with a grandeur and a scale that is almost overwhelming.

The style Balyan chose was an ornate Neo-Baroque. Double-height porticoes and rich carving produce an effect that combines grandeur with ornate and expensive decoration. But the long facades and the array of accommodation wings are nothing compared to the interiors. Here again, vast scale is combined with rich and intricate ornament. Grandest of all the many rooms is the ballroom, with its 118-foot-high (36 m) dome and its rows of columns and arches. On a similar scale is the staircase hall, its double-horseshoe-shaped stairs famous for their crystal balusters. The palace also boasts seemingly endless series of reception halls, richly gilded private rooms, and alabaster-lined bathrooms.

When Turkey became a republic in the twentieth century, the palace became the Istanbul residence of the country's leader, Mustafa Kemal Atatürk. In 1938, he died in the palace and lay in state there. In Turkey the building is now seen as a monument to him as much as to the extravagant sultan who created it. **PW**

↗ Neo-Baroque pillars and ornate window tracery hint at the extraordinary splendor within the palace.

⇥ Ottoman palaces on the Bosphorus benefited from the deep water's cooling effect, and boat transport.

St. George's Hall (1856)

Architects Harvey Lonsdale Elmes, Charles Robert Cockerell   **Location** Liverpool, England   **Style** Neo-Classical   **Materials** Stone, brick

One of Europe's finest Classical buildings, St. George's Hall is a monument to the wealth and civic aspirations of a great commercial city in the early nineteenth century. Liverpool continued to thrive and expand in this period, despite the abolition of the slave trade in 1807, yet its citizens were increasingly aware that it was lagging behind in cultural matters. A competition was held in 1839 for a public hall for meetings, concerts, and dinners, and won by the twenty-five-year-old Harvey Lonsdale Elmes (1814–47), who shortly afterward won a separate competition for the new courts of law. He subsequently revised his designs to produce a multifunctional building, and work began in 1841. Ill health forced Elmes to withdraw before work had begun on the interior, and he died in Jamaica. Charles Robert Cockerell (1788–1863) took over the supervision and was largely responsible for designing the interiors. Although Elmes's competition designs were in the Greek Revival idiom, Roman elements—notably the giant Corinthian order that marches around and unifies the exterior—were introduced as he revised them, and the result is a highly original and complex synthesis of the two styles. The scale is vast, and deliberately so, since the citizens of Liverpool wanted to trump rivals such as the recently completed Birmingham Town Hall. Elmes's relatively chaste shell contains Cockerell's sumptuous sequence of halls and courtrooms, including a circular and lavishly decorated Small Concert Hall. The central space is the enormous Main Concert Hall, reminiscent of a Roman basilica, with an elaborate tiled floor, fabulous bronze doors and gasoliers, and a crowning barrel vault. St. George's Hall shows Elmes to have been an exceptional architect, despite his tragically short career, and he was fortunate to have had such a brilliant, sympathetic successor. **RW**

Brevard-Mmahat House (1857)

Architect James Calrow   **Location** New Orleans, Louisiana, USA   **Style** Greek Revival   **Material** Timber

After the 1803 Louisiana Purchase, which transferred New Orleans to the United States, U.S. business descended on the city to exploit the newly booming economies of the Mississippi Delta. Fortunes built on cotton and the slave trade were soon made and, disinclined to rub shoulders with Creoles in the cramped French Quarter, wealthy entrepreneurs headed upriver to Lafayette. Developed between 1840 and 1900, Lafayette's residential Garden District was built across the site of several former plantations to a grid plan originally devised by Barthelemy Lafon, an architect and planner who turned to piracy and smuggling in later life. In an area renowned for its elegant mansions and lush gardens, the Brevard-Mmahat House is one of the most beautiful and representative. Designed and built by James Calrow, whose hand is seen in several local buildings, the antebellum house was erected shortly after Lafayette

was annexed to the city of New Orleans. A two-story, gray, timber mansion in the domestic Greek Revival style, it has the later addition of an Italianate double bay boasting porches lined with intricate cast-iron railings, fluted Classical columns, and an unusual Egyptian keyhole doorway. The interior is no less splendid, with decorative murals, 14-foot-high (4.2 m) ceilings, and a 27-step grand staircase. The house inspired horror author Anne Rice, who has used it as the setting for several of her novels. **RDB**

" . . . a deep secretive house, full of graceful designs yet somehow ominous."

Anne Rice, *The Witching Hour* (1990)

British Museum (1857)

Architects Sir Robert Smirke, Norman Foster and Partners   **Location** London, England   **Style** Greek Revival   **Materials** Stone, iron, concrete

A number of British collectors left their antiquities and works of art to the nation in the mid-eighteenth century, and these items were displayed in a building called Montague House in Bloomsbury. At the beginning of the nineteenth century, a purpose-built museum was planned to house these collections together with the library of George IV, which the king had sold to the museum. The architect, Sir Robert Smirke (1780–1867), conceived a grand Classical Revival building arranged around a courtyard, a fitting home for the world-class collections displayed within.

The British Museum contains several outstanding interiors, including the west wing, which houses the Egyptian collection, and the King's Library, purpose-built for the royal books and roofed with a forward-looking structure made of iron and concrete. Both of these spaces preserve some of the atmosphere and decoration of the museum as it would have been in its early days. Another remarkable interior is the circular Reading Room, designed by Smirke's brother, Sidney.

After the Reading Room was completed in 1857, the building was extended and altered on several occasions, with extensions to the north carried out between 1900 and 1914 and to the west in the 1930s. But the museum's greatest transformation came about at the end of the twentieth century, when the national library was moved to St. Pancras. The Great Court—the area around the Reading Room—was cleared, remodeled, and given a stunning glass roof by Norman Foster and Partners. This development gives the visitor yet another reason to linger in one of the world's greatest museums. **PW**

◿ The circular Reading Room houses the Paul Hamlyn Library and a multimedia database of the collections.

◺ The Greek Revival exterior, with its imposing rows of Ionic columns, reflected architectural trends in Europe.

Leeds Town Hall (1858)

Architect Cuthbert Brodrick **Location** Leeds, England **Style** Neo-Classical, Renaissance influence **Material** Stone

In 1852 Cuthbert Brodrick (1821–1905) was awarded first prize in a competition to design Leeds Town Hall; he was also awarded £200 ($393) in prize money. At the time Brodrick was an unknown architect, but his monumental classical design caught the eye of Sir Charles Barry, the competition's judge. Brodrick's vision was intended to rival the architecture of southern English municipal buildings.

The building's design is created around a square, enclosed by an imposing colonnade of Corinthian columns. These are unbroken even for the entrance—visitors pass through the colonnade to gain entry. Atop the columns rests a balustraded cornice and in the center of it all is an imposing tower. The tower was not part of the original design; it was an addition suggested by Barry. The building's main entrance is flanked by a pair of lions created in Portland stone and added in 1867 to increase the building's regal aspect.

The internal design's centerpiece was the tunnel-vaulted Great Hall, now known as the Victoria Hall, which was restored in the 1970s after problems with the plasterwork. The hall's fittings include an organ, which when installed was one of the largest organs in the world, standing almost 50 feet (15.25 m) in height.

The Town Hall was designed as a multifunctional building, constructed with both lavish entertainments and civic meetings in mind. A number of rooms are designed as administration and council offices. There are also the old cells, sited under the front steps and constructed for the housing of prisoners before their appearance in court. These contained ankle- and wrist-shackles to secure the prisoners to the wall. **LH**

↗ Work on the bell tower continued after the Town Hall was officially opened. The bell was hung in 1860.

→ The Town Hall's uninterrupted succession of columns is echoed above in the twenty columns of the tower.

Church of All Saints (1859)

Architect William Butterfield **Location** London, England **Style** Gothic Revival **Material** Brick

All Saints, Margaret Street, is a building of exceptional originality and significance. It was built as a model of what churches in England should be to exemplify the observation of ritual needs and English architectural precedent. One of the prime movers in its construction and the provider of most of the funds was Alexander Beresford-Hope, a wealthy and influential promoter of the Gothic Revival. It was Hope who commissioned William Butterfield to design the new church.

The initial plans were modified after the publication of John Ruskin's *The Seven Lamps of Architecture* (1849) and it was decided to make All Saints a gorgeous display of colored stones and tiles. Inside and out, the church is an example of constructional polychromy. The influences of the decoration are both Italian and German, although the architectural structure of the interior is clearly derived from English thirteenth-century Gothic. German Gothic is the main influence on the exterior, where the use of brick and the spire in particular can be compared with the great brick churches of northern Germany. Butterfield succeeded brilliantly in providing a spacious building on a very restricted site.

Butterfield and Hope fell out over the style and type of decoration of the interior and little work was carried out in the roofed shell of 1853–56. Much that was done by way of frescoes and glazing Butterfield replaced or removed in the 1870s or in 1895, when he was recalled to do some restoration work. Twentieth-century restorations and decorative additions have probably left it closer to Butterfield's original intentions than it was during his lifetime. **CWH**

◳ The soaring brick spire is 227 feet (69 m) high—taller than the towers of Westminster Abbey.

◰ Polychromatic brickwork frames one of the church's few windows—the restricted site limited their number.

Dohány Street Synagogue (1859)

Architect Ludwig Förster **Location** Budapest, Hungary **Style** Moorish, Byzantine **Materials** Brick, steel, glass

In 1844 the Neolog Jewish community of Pest acquired a site at Dohány Street to build a new synagogue for its community of then 30,000 members. The architect chosen was German-born Ludwig Förster, whose Moorish synagogue in Leopoldstadt, Vienna, was being built at the time.

The Dohány Synagogue (Dohány utcai Zsinagóga), also known as the Tabak-Shul, is considered the second largest synagogue in the world, with no fewer than 2,964 seats—1,492 for men and 1,472 in the women's galleries. The building measures approximately 173 by 87 feet (53 x 26.5 m) and was designed as a genuine basilica with two balconies. The western facade has arched windows with decorations of carved stone and brickwork in Budapest's heraldic colors blue, yellow, and red. A stained-glass rose window rises above the entrance, and the gateway is flanked on both sides by two copper-domed towers with long arched windows.

Inside, the Holy Ark is situated on the eastern wall, facing the *bimah* (a platform used to perform services). The choir appears above the Holy Ark, and the galleries for the women are located on the upper levels. The 5,000-tube organ was built in 1859 and played by, among others, Franz Liszt and Camille Saint-Saëns.

During World War II, the synagogue served as an internment camp for the city's Jews. More than 2,000 Jews who died in the ghetto of Budapest are now buried in the synagogue's courtyard. After the war the Jewish community used the damaged synagogue, but renovations of the temple did not begin until 1991, following the return of democracy to Hungary. **EGS**

↗ Byzantine-Moorish elements mixed with Romanticism give this Hungarian synagogue an Eastern aspect.

→ The towers of the western front are decorated with geometric stone carvings and large clocks.

Main Cell Block, Fremantle Prison (1859)

Architects Royal Engineers (using convict labor)   **Location** Fremantle, Australia   **Style** Neo-Classical   **Material** Limestone

Australia was initially founded as a British penal colony, so it is not surprising to find that a number of its early buildings were built using convict labor. Numerous public works, including roads, were realized in this way from the late 1780s until the middle of the nineteenth century. In fact, one of Australia's most notable early architects, Francis Greenway, had arrived in New South Wales a convict in 1814.

Unfortunately, many of the buildings that once formed Australia's main penal settlements either no longer exist or are in ruin. Fremantle Prison in Western Australia, however, is the largest and best-preserved example of this type of architecture in the country.

Founded in 1850, the Convict Establishment—as the prison was originally known—was constructed in large part from limestone quarried on site. One of the earliest and most substantial buildings in the precinct is the Main Cell Block, designed in a severe and unadorned Neo-Classical style. Constructed between 1852 and 1855, it initially had running water in every cell. At either end of the four-story main block were two large dormitories known as Association Rooms. These housed up to eighty men sleeping in hammocks and were designed for prisoners with an upcoming "Ticket of Leave" or as a reward for good behavior.

The single cells of the rest of the prison were less salubrious, being a mere 7 by 4 feet (2.1 x 1.2 m). The front of the Main Cell Block is dominated by the Anglican chapel, which is among the finest and most intact of early prison chapels in Australia. **GAB**

↖ The Neo-Classical Main Cell Block, completed in 1855, was based on Pentonville Prison in London, England.

← In 2005, restorers of the prison gatehouse began to remove concrete rendering to reveal the stonework.

St. Vincent Street Church (1859)

Architect Alexander Thomson   **Location** Glasgow, Scotland
Style Greek Revival   **Materials** Stone, slate and lead roofing

Although Glasgow is rightly famous for the work of Charles Rennie Mackintosh, at an earlier period it produced another world-class architect in Alexander "Greek" Thomson (1817–75). Although his designs have traditionally been perceived as a difficult and demanding, opinion has recently warmed to his unique brand of architectural eclecticism.

Thomson never left Britain and, although he was nicknamed "Greek," he utilized published sources showing Egyptian and Indian architecture as well as those illustrating classical buildings. Unlike most of his British contemporaries, he was prepared to experiment boldly with traditional forms, introducing adventurous features and compositions that find their closest kinship in the work of Karl Friedrich Schinkel (1781–1841) in Berlin.

Although built on a difficult, sloping site, St. Vincent Street Church represents Thomson at the height of his powers. A masterpiece of architectural massing, it raises the traditional classical porticoed form onto a colossal two-story plinth. Positioned in bold asymmetry is an extraordinary tower that mixes Assyrian with Egyptian details and culminates in a fluted egg-shaped dome of Indian derivation.

While the building seems almost unnervingly massive on the exterior, the use of top-lit spaces gives the interior a beguiling lightness. With a range of highly resolved details such as attenuated cast-iron columns terminating in capitals, which subvert the traditional acanthus form, this is a building where every last detail has been considered from a unique perspective. Sadly, many of Thomson's other works have been damaged or demolished, adding an extra level of importance to this most idiosyncratic of Victorian churches. **NMC**

Sheerness Boat Store (1860)

Architect Godfrey Thomas Greene   **Location** HM Dockyard, Sheerness, England   **Style** Early Industrial   **Materials** Iron, concrete, wood (oak)

The Boat Store at Sheerness, completed in 1860, is one of the world's earliest examples of a multistory, iron-framed building. In style, structure, and quality, it bears comparison with the work of the twentieth-century Modern masters—it is a frame and panel construction with ribbon windows running from end to end. However, it is unlikely that Modernists such as Gropius and Mies van der Rohe would have been familiar with the Boat Store. The architectural significance of the structure lay unrecognized until 1957 when it was photographed and documented as part of a research

> ## "[Built] eight years later than the Crystal Palace, [the Store] seems to belong to a different age…"
>
> A. W. Skempton, professor

study into early industrial architecture in England.

The Boat Store was designed by Godfrey Thomas Greene, a military engineer. It consists of two identical buildings (or "aisles") either side of a full-height void ("nave"). The whole is 210 feet (64 m) long and 135 feet (41 m) wide, with a skylight running the length of the void; across the width of the building are three pitched roofs each spanning 45 feet (13.7 m).

There are four rows of columns in each of the two aisles. The cast-iron H-section members are 40 feet (12 m) high. The ground level is a concrete slab; the three upper levels consist of oak planks supported on transverse I-section beams. The nave is spanned by three traveling girders; one on each level. Boats were maneuvered into position on the ground, then lifted onto a trolley and hoisted to the required level. **AM**

Long Room Library (1860)

Architects Thomas Burgh, Thomas Deane, Benjamin Woodward   **Location** Dublin, Ireland   **Style** Victorian   **Material** Stone

The 400-year-old campus at Trinity College is full of architectural gems, with the grandest buildings clustered around Front Square, and stretching back past the Campanile to Library Square beyond. Behind these, contemporary architecture finds its place, with an impressive mix of styles and periods sitting alongside the gardens and cricket greens. Built in the early eighteenth century, the massive Long Room—also known as The Old Library—once dominated views of both college campus and city. The main construction is the work of Thomas Burgh (1670–1730), son of a bishop, and also responsible for the Royal Barracks in Dublin. Originally designed with open colonnades at ground level, these were enclosed in the nineteenth century to create more space for scholars and books. The defining addition, however, came in 1858–60 when Irish duo Thomas Deane (1792–1871) and Benjamin Woodward (1816–61)

removed the original flat roof, giving the building its beautiful, wooden, barrel-vaulted ceiling. Known for both drama and Neo-Gothic whimsy, Deane and Woodward's work can also be seen next door in the wonderful Museum Building and in the Museum of Natural History in Oxford, England. At 210 feet (12 m) in length, the Long Room at Trinity is the largest single chamber library in the world, and houses 200,000 of Trinity's oldest books in its oak cases. The library is still used by students and academics at the college. **GT**

> "The arched nave stretches in seeming infinity, cathedral-like in its majesty and dignity."
>
> P. D. James, *New York Times* (1981)

Red House (1860)

Architect Philip Webb **Location** Bexleyheath, Kent, England **Style** Arts and Crafts **Materials** Brick, timber

One of the most outstanding buildings of the Arts and Crafts era, Red House was built for William Morris by Philip Webb (1831–1915). One of Webb's overriding principles was the use of vernacular, which he put into practice in his designs for Red House. He followed Morris's own maxim that one should have nothing in one's home not known to be useful or believed to be beautiful. Every feature and fixture of the house serves an identifiable purpose, such as the well in the garden, which is often erroneously believed to be ornamental, but was actually the house's water source. Webb was inspired by Augustus Pugin and by the works of architects William Butterfield and George Edmund Street. The steep red-tiled roof, the leaded windows and the arched doorway all pay homage to the Gothic Revival, yet the interior is entirely of its time, with every attention paid to the practicalities of everyday domestic family life. The sense of internal space and

the embracing of natural light were a deliberate move away from conventional Victorian homes. Several Pre-Raphaelites and Arts and Crafts artists took a hand in the decoration of Red House. Edward Burne-Jones and Dante Gabriel Rossetti provided stained glass for the windows and painted decorations on the walls and furniture, William de Morgan created ceramics and Morris's own company created the wallpapers. The garden was intended by Morris to "clothe" the house, deliberately linking it to the surrounding fields. **LH**

> *"It is a most noble work ... and more a poem than a house ... but an admirable place to live in, too."*
>
> Dante Gabriel Rossetti, poet and artist

Adare Manor (1862)

Architects James Pain, Windham Henry Quin   **Location** Adare, County Limerick, Ireland   **Style** Gothic Revival   **Materials** Limestone, slate

Adare Manor, now a five-star hotel, was the family seat of the earls of Dunraven and is set within 840 acres (340 ha) of formal gardens and parkland beside the River Maigue. The nearby village, also built by the Dunraven family, is one of the prettiest in Ireland. Building work on the manor began in 1832 and was completed thirty years later. It is likely that James Pain (c. 1779–1877) was the architect, despite the insistence of Windham Henry Quin, second earl of Dunraven and Mount-Earl (1782–1850), that he had carried on the work "entirely from my own designs and without any assistance whatsoever."

The Great Gallery, inspired by the Hall of Mirrors at Versailles, is at 132 feet (40 m), one of the longest in Ireland. Lined with Flemish choir stalls, the gallery also has a timbered roof and stained-glass windows, and the effect is almost monastic. The structure is a series of visual allusions to famous Irish and English homes that the Dunravens admired: a turreted entrance tower stands at one corner; there are 52 chimneys to commemorate each week of the year, 75 fireplaces, and 365 leaded-glass windows. During the Irish potato famine in the 1840s, building work provided vital employment for many villagers. In 1850 the third earl commissioned Augustus Pugin (1812–52), architect of the Houses of Parliament, to design a dining room, library, and terrace. But Pugin was very ill by then, and his work was never fully executed. P. W. C. Hardwick completed the building.

Adare Manor is a fascinating evocation of early Victorianism, reflecting the personalities of the two generations of the family that built it. **BMC**

◩ The manor references other stately homes, persuading the visitor the building is older than it is.

◪ A feature of medieval architecture, these crowned heads convey an impression of both age and nobility.

Oranienburgerstrasse Synagogue (1866)

Architect Eduard Knoblauch **Location** Berlin, Germany **Style** Moorish **Materials** Brick, steel, iron, zinc, gold leaf

Rising 164 feet (50 m) above the Oranienburgerstrasse street facades, the restored golden dome of the Neue Synagogue is an exotic presence above the dour apartment blocks. The synagogue was designed by Eduard Knoblauch (1801–65), and opened in 1866. It could seat 3,000 worshippers, and was a strong cultural statement in the Moorish style by the established German-Jewish middle classes.

The building was advanced for its time, with central heating and gas lighting placed next to the stained-glass windows, causing them to glow at night, and the extensive use of iron as both a structural and expressive material. The spectacular dome was constructed with a light armature of wrought iron, clad with timber boarding before being finished with zinc sheeting, and gilded fretwork. The street elevation is built of richly ornamented polychromatic brickwork, flanked by two domed towers heralding the entrance, also gilded.

The synagogue survived 1938's Kristallnacht (Night of Broken Glass) thanks to the courage and determination of the local police chief, who defended it against the Nazi mob. At the onset of World War II, the golden dome was daubed with pitch to make it less conspicuous, but in 1943 Allied bombs damaged the main hall, and it was demolished in 1958. Restoration of the entrance halls and dome began in 1988; when workers found the remains of the synagogue lamp under the rubble, it was restored and sent on a tour across the United States to raise funds for the restoration. The synagogue was opened as the Centrum Judaicum in 1995. **CB**

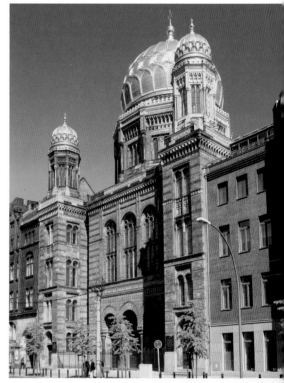

↗ The synagogue is a testament to the integration of liberal Jews within nineteenth-century Berlin.

→ Damaged during World War II, the restored dome continues to convey an almost Eastern opulence.

Tyntesfield (1866)

Architect John Norton **Location** Wraxall, North Somerset, England **Style** Gothic Revival **Material** Stone

William Gibbs (1790–1875) inherited a trading company that made most of its money from importing guano from Pacific islands, and selling it as fertilizer. Gibbs used part of the fortune he made from the business to buy an estate near Bristol, and in the 1860s he employed the architect John Norton (1823–1904) to remodel the house. Norton incorporated the original house into the new Tyntesfield, but the resulting extravaganza of turrets, bay windows, pointed arches, and pinnacles was his own: a lavish country house in the mid-nineteenth-century Gothic Revival style. Tyntesfield is striking from outside, but its unique quality comes from the interiors that have changed little since the Victorian period. Timber roofs, Victorian decorations, and Gibbs's original furniture have created a Victorian time capsule. In many of the rooms, such as the library with its oak shelving and oak-lined walls, and the billiard room with its Gothic

table, the atmosphere of the Victorian country house is preserved intact. When Tyntesfield was put up for sale in 2001 the National Trust recognized its value and bought the house. Since then, the National Trust has embarked on a conservation program. Given the interest in the house, the National Trust took the unusual step of opening part of the building to the public while the conservation project was proceeding, so that as many people as possible could appreciate the building's special qualities. **PW**

> *"A masterpiece: one that fully reflects the serious architectural aspirations of the period . . ."*
>
> James Miller, historian

Galleria Vittorio Emanuele II (1867)

Architect Giuseppe Mengoni   **Location** Milan, Italy   **Style** Classical Revival   **Materials** Iron, glass, stone

On the northern side of Milan's Piazza del Duomo, presenting a magnificent facade in the form of a triumphal arch, a five-story arcade of shops and cafés opens enticingly, with its iron-and-glass roof leading to a central glass-domed octagon, ringed with fresco paintings in lunettes, a secular counterpart to the historic churches of the city. Four arms of the Galleria Vittorio Emanuele II converge at this point, which is marked by the decoratively tiled walkway. The internal elevations with their arcades, pilasters, and continuous row of balconies surmounted by caryatids represent everything about nineteenth-century architecture that is excessive, theatrical, and incomparable in its ability to create a sense of occasion in a public space. The Galleria Vittorio Emanuele II celebrates the liberation of Milan from Austrian rule under the House of Savoy, capturing the confidence of the newly independent secular nation in its leading commercial and industrial city. Architect Giuseppe Mengoni (1829–77) studied the Passages de Paris shopping complex, but no shopping emporium before this date had been conceived on such a large scale. At the time, many opposed the construction of the Galleria Vittorio Emanuele II because it destroyed the historic urban fabric, but posterity has proved that it gives something of substance in return. It was financed with English money when attempts to raise funds by lottery locally failed, and attracted international attention. The gas lighting was itself a spectacle, with an automatic ignition system by which a small instrument traveled on rails, and sparked the flints of each gaslight. Known as *il salotto di Milano* (Milan's drawing room), this vast shopping mall is one of the earliest glass-and-iron structures of its kind. It also proves that even a humble shopping arcade from the nineteenth century can powerfully evoke the period. **AP**

Houses of Parliament (1870)

Architects Sir Charles Barry, Augustus Pugin   **Location** London, England   **Style** Gothic Revival   **Materials** Limestone, metal, stained glass

The medieval royal Palace of Westminster burned down in 1834, leaving only the great Norman Hall with its timber roof, an undercroft, cloisters, and a few walls. At the time of the fire, proposals for rebuilding were under consideration, although on past precedent, so the disaster ended prevarication by committee. The competition rules for the new Houses of Parliament stipulated that the style was to be either Gothic or Elizabethan. The winners were Sir Charles Barry (1795–1860) and Augustus Pugin (1812–52). Temperamentally and often intellectually opposed, the pair worked in harmony, and the building is a joint creation. Barry produced a plan that combined clarity with good sense and all the work on the building's execution was his. Pugin did the drawings for the competition, and designed all the details in metal, stained glass, and tiles, down to the inkstands and coat hangers. The plan is formal and symmetrical, with the Victoria Tower and the clocktower (known as Big Ben) the major asymmetrical elements. The building established Gothic as the dominant national style for many years to come. During the twentieth century, much of the palace's Gothic decoration was toned down and the original furnishings removed, but from the late 1970s onward they have been restored or replaced. The Commons Chamber was destroyed by bombing in 1941 and Sir Giles Gilbert Scott (1880–1960) designed its successor, in a neutered Gothic style. **CWH**

> *"The Houses of Parliament are a monument to public stupidity and official mismanagement."*
>
> *The Architect* (1870)

Royal Albert Hall (1871)

Architects Francis Fowke, Henry Scott **Location** London, England **Style** Classical Revival **Materials** Red brick, wrought iron, glass, terra cotta

It was Queen Victoria's consort, Prince Albert, who conceived the complex of museums in South Kensington, and when he died in 1861 plans were quickly put in train to build not only the famous Albert Memorial in Kensington Gardens, but also a public concert hall nearby. The original designer was not an architect, but an engineer, Captain Francis Fowke (1823–65), who was also working on the nearby building that became the Victoria & Albert Museum. Fowke produced plans for a vast elliptical building, rather like a roofed version of a great Roman amphitheater. But he died in 1865 and the project was taken over by Lieutenant Colonel Henry Scott (1822–83), another military engineer who also took over Fowke's work at the museum. The Royal Albert Hall opened in 1871, and holds an audience of around 8,000 beneath a dome 135 feet (41 m) high. Fashioned from glass and wrought iron, the dome covers the building's 219-foot (67 m) width. But it is not just the size that is impressive. The designers were at pains to emphasize the building's importance as a cultural center. So the red-brick exterior is adorned with a terra-cotta frieze, depicting the great and good in the fields of the arts and literature. The terra cotta decorations around the outer walls complement and offset the huge areas of red brick. Inside, the audience sit in a swath of seats around the central arena or in the tiers of boxes that rise above. **PW**

"*The mind becomes filled with an impression of endless space and sublimity.*"

Illustrated London News (April 8, 1871)

Mark
Twain House (1874)

Architect Edward Tuckerman Potter **Location** Hartford, Connecticut, USA
Style Victorian Stick **Materials** Brick, timber

The house built for the writer Samuel Clemens (known as Mark Twain) mixes influences to create a building full of character and atmosphere. The Victorian Stick Style, popular in North America during the second half of the nineteenth century, referred to central European alpine chalets and English Tudor. Edward Tuckerman Potter (1831–1904) was commissioned to design the house in Hartford so that Twain could be near his publishers. Tuckerman Potter was best known for his ecclesiastical buildings on the U.S. East Coast.

The nineteen-bedroom mansion's eclectic, richly colored interiors were designed by Louis Comfort Tiffany. The house utilized the latest technologies available at the time, including a telephone system that was one of the first to be installed in a private home. Twain and his family moved out of the house in the 1890s. Since then, it has had many uses including a period as a school building. It is now a National Historic Landmark that has seen various stages of restoration. A separate building housing the Mark Twain Museum opened in 2003.

The house has a warm atmosphere, and it is unsurprising that Twain created his well-loved characters Tom Sawyer and Huckleberry Finn while living there. Moving through the building, the visitor can sense a story: unexpected turns, cozy corners, and views over the central winding staircase. Not only is the house an example of architectural styles fashionable in the United States at the time, it also nurtured the work of a great American writer. **RK**

↖ The hand-carved mantle in the library was bought by the Twains in Scotland. The iron fireplace is Indian.

← The irregularity of the house's external appearance was echoed by quirky internal arrangements.

Palais Garnier (1875)

Architect Charles Garnier **Location** Paris, France
Style Neo-Baroque **Materials** Iron, cut stone, copper, marble, onyx

The Palais Garnier (see page 162), or Opéra National de Paris, is a sumptuous and flamboyant nineteenth-century Neo-Baroque opera house, designed by Charles Garnier (1825–98). Conceived as a grandiose centerpiece for the boulevards being constructed by civic planner Baron Haussmann, it was representative of the official art of the Second French Empire.

Garnier created an opera house in the traditional Italian style on a grand scale with seats for an audience of 2,200, and a stage for 450 performers. The venue was intended for promenading by the emperor's entourage and the wealthy Belle Epoque audience, and the loggias, foyers, staircases, and rotundas occupy a larger area than the theater itself.

Garnier personally supervised the opulent decorative schemes, commissioning figurative academic statuary and paintings from seventy-three painters and fourteen sculptors. The building has an iron-frame structure covered with ornate interiors, rich with marble friezes, Venetian mosaic, gilt mirrors, chandeliers, columns, and caryatids. The luxurious Foyer de la Danse is lined with chandeliers, and thirty paintings of allegories of dance and music by Paul Baudry. The magnificent central staircase, the Grand Escalier, is decorated in marble and onyx. In the auditorium the great central chandelier illuminates the ceiling painted by Marc Chagall in 1964.

The facade has a Classical structure but is draped with statues and eclectic Baroque decoration. The green copper roof is crowned by a gilded sculpture, *Apollo, Poetry and Music*, by Aimé Millet. Gold-leafed sculptural assemblages of Harmony and Liberty by Charles Gumery sit on either side of the pediment. The vestibule has seven arcades decorated with four monumental sculptural groups. **JEH**

Midland Grand Hotel at St. Pancras Station (1876)

Architect Sir George Gilbert Scott **Location** London, England
Style Gothic Revival **Materials** Red brick, limestone, marble

There is no more evocative symbol of Victorian pride and industriousness than the Midland Grand Hotel at St. Pancras (see page 162). Built by a passionate Gothic Revivalist, this great sanctuary of steam is one of the most exciting examples of this rip-roaringly English style and a masterpiece. The Midland Railway wanted a building to add luster to its station; the winning design by Sir George Gilbert Scott (1811–78) was the largest and most expensive, offering 300 rooms.

The exterior is a feast of gables and pinnacles, with dormers, towers, and turrets spiking into the sky from

> *"Railway termini and hotels are to the nineteenth century what cathedrals were to the thirteenth."*
>
> The Builder (1875)

a richly decorated polychrome body of 60 million Nottingham red bricks and a variety of English stone. Ironwork abounds, with spires, crests, balustrades, and decorative detailing. Friezes are carved with writhing sea horses, shells, flowers, and stars.

The interior of the Midland Grand Hotel is breathtaking. In the dining and coffee room are pillars of pink and green polished limestone. The Ladies Smoking Room—the first in the world—boasts granite pillars, carved stonework, and two marble fireplaces. With elaborate stenciling and gold leaf on the walls and ceilings, plus flamboyant wallpapers, no inch of the hotel was undecorated. Arched stairwells give the appearance of an Italian palazzo. Designed to allow two ladies in crinolines to pass, its wide corridors run to 500 feet (152 m) long. **LL**

Old Government Buildings (1876)

Architect William Henry Clayton **Location** Wellington, New Zealand
Style Renaissance Revival **Material** Timber

New Zealand in the late nineteenth century was a flourishing British dominion. In 1876, with the decision to eliminate the old state governments, the national government commissioned a new administration block large enough to be able to hold the entire public service, and parliamentarians, too.

Tenders were called for a building in Renaissance Revival style, in concrete or timber. It is unsurprising that the estimates in timber came in lower, given the country's plentiful forests, which then made timber the most common building material.

> *"One of New Zealand's most important historic buildings and an icon of Wellington City."*

New Zealand Historic Places Trust

The 143-room structure became the largest timber building of its type in the world. It is conservative in style, yet lively in expression. The H-shaped plan is broken down by projecting side wings, and a central projecting entry bay. Detailing usually seen in stone is executed in timber, such as string courses, the projecting window hoods on the upper floors, quoining, eaves brackets, and even the urns. Much of the interior is also finished in timber.

Its architect William Henry Clayton (1823–77) was born in Tasmania, trained in England, returned to Tasmania to practice, moved to New Zealand, and then became the country's first government architect in 1869. His government connections were close; in 1867 his daughter married Julius Vogel, who served as premier twice in the 1870s. **RS**

Manchester Town Hall (1877)

Architect Alfred Waterhouse **Location** Manchester, England
Style Gothic Revival **Materials** Spinkwell stone, brick

Alfred Waterhouse's (1830–1905) Manchester Town Hall is one of the great public buildings of the nineteenth century. Its plan occupies an almost triangular site. The Great Hall is placed within the hollow triangle, perpendicular to the west side. The main entrance, below the 286-foot (87 m) clocktower, faces Albert Square. Other entrances lead to grand staircases and corridors. Although Waterhouse used a Gothic idiom—normally thirteenth century—his pragmatic and eclectic approach informs the design. He selected durable Spinkwell stone, which

> *"It is widely known as a classic of its age, but now after that age, it justly transcends that limit."*

John Archer, architectural historian

weathered well in Manchester's sooty atmosphere (the interior courtyard walls are still dirty and black).

The exterior has four stories and steeply pitched slated roofs. Its picturesque, robust, and varied skyline of towers, spires, and carvings is both vigorous and impressive.

Internally, the landings, stairwells, and corridors are richly and majestically decorated. The Great Hall is 100 feet (30 m) long by 50 feet (15 m) wide, and has seven bays beneath a paneled wagon-roof ceiling. Ford Madox Brown's murals, six on each side, allude to incidents in Manchester's history. The council chamber is richly decorated. The sculpture hall and reception rooms have fine collections of Victorian sculpture and art. The bee, symbol of Manchester, and the red rose of Lancashire are frequent motifs set in mosaics. **ATB**

Semper
Opera House (1878)

Architect Gottfried Semper   **Location** Dresden, Germany
Style Neo-Baroque   **Materials** Stone, marble

The Semperoper, or Semper Opera House, is in the heart of Dresden. Its plan is visible on the exterior, with the curve of the auditorium joining the higher roof of the stage house, rather than the whole being enclosed in a rectangle. Three entrances project into the surrounding square, with carriage porches to the sides and a royal entrance on the main axis, surmounted by a niche and a *quadriga* (four-horse chariot) of Dionysus and Ariadne. Inside, the foyers are restrained in style, but rich with colored marbles and paintings.

The opera house is a rebuild of one of the first major works by Gottfried Semper (1803–79), a major architectural theorist of his time whose buildings do not always illustrate his ideas directly. The theater aimed to turn the audience's attention toward the drama with a new seriousness. The early operas of Richard Wagner were performed here, and he enjoyed a turbulent friendship with Semper. They shared a desire to restore the Dionysian qualities of drama as exemplified by ancient Greece, and Semper's rich decoration was a contribution in that direction.

In 1869, the first theater burned down, and Semper was distraught. He beat off competition for the rebuilding, and accomplished the task to great acclaim. Changes were made to improve the plan, but many sculptures were salvaged for reuse. In this building one comes closest to Semper's remarkable personality as a thinker, with ideas that are the architectural equivalent not only of Wagner's operas but of Friedrich Nietzsche's interpretation of art. **AP**

↗ Destroyed by Allied bombing in 1945, Semper Opera House was rebuilt and reopened in 1985.

→ The interior features rich stucco craftmanship and Neo-Renaissance wall and ceiling paintings.

Schloss Neuschwanstein (1880)

Architects Christian Jank, Eduard Riedel   **Location** Hohenschwangau, Germany   **Style** Gothic Revival   **Materials** Stone, steel

This building is instantly recognizable from countless postcards, jigsaw puzzles, and advertisements—and from its famous imitator, the Sleeping Beauty Castle at Disneyland. It is one of the most dramatic castles ever built, and the story of its creation is as memorable as the building itself. Ludwig II, King of Bavaria (r. 1864–86) was on the throne for only two years before military defeat by the Prussians removed his autonomy and made him a client king. A fragile personality, the strain of this change led him to withdraw into a Wagnerian dreamworld of noble kings and muscular Germanic gods. He retreated to a hilltop near his childhood home, where he spent most of his reign—and most of his money—building a number of superb, fantastical medieval castles, including Schloss Neuschwanstein. Although incomplete at his death in 1886, the rooms he built are magnificent. Although the castle appears medieval, it enjoyed modern facilities with central heating, running water, flushing lavatories, and even telephones. Christian Jank (1833–88), who architecturally realized Ludwig's dreams, was a stage designer, and this is reflected in the building. Rather than a faithful reconstruction of a medieval castle, it is a vigorous mix of Romanesque, Byzantine, and Gothic styles. In every room, carvings and frescoes depict the legend of Tristan and Isolde and other Wagnerian themes, and throughout are references to medieval Grail legends. **BWC**

" . . . The desecrated gods [will] come to live with us on the lofty heights, breathing the air of heaven."

Ludwig II of Bavaria

Museum of Natural History (1880)

Architect Alfred Waterhouse   **Location** London, England   **Style** Neo-Romanesque   **Materials** Brick, iron, terra cotta

The Natural History Museum in South Kensington, London, was the first building to be completed on the site bought out of the profits of the 1851 Great Exhibition, and was intended to provide a cultural campus. First considered in 1866, the commission was confirmed only in 1870, with construction beginning in 1872. The building was a complete redesign of a project of 1859 by engineer and architect Captain Francis Fowke, who won the contest for its design but died before he saw it built. For reasons of economy the museum was to be built in two stages, the second of which, the side wings and rear, were never built. Architect Alfred Waterhouse (1830–1905) had continually to contend with arguments about the budget, and the building is an extraordinary tour de force brought off in the face of government parsimony. The main facade, Great Hall, and study galleries were essential, and the planning demonstrates Waterhouse's usual clarity of thought—not least because most spaces had to have natural lighting. Gas lighting was regarded as a fire risk because so many specimens were preserved in spirit. The proportions are cathedrallike, and climbing the flying staircase in the Dinosaur Hall is an exhilarating experience. The style is Waterhouse's own version of German Romanesque, but what strikes the visitor most is the decoration. The museum immediately established Waterhouse as the leading figure in the use of terra-cotta, and his use of the material is both witty and inventive. The modeled figures, all designed by the architect and executed by Farmer & Brindley, reflect the museum's contents; creatures both living and extinct climb, swim, and fly across every surface. The museum has a particularly exotic skyline, the excuse for which (when the Treasury quibbled) was the need to hide the extensive water tanks. **CWH**

Cologne
Cathedral (1880)

Patron Konrad von Hochstaden   **Location** Cologne, Germany
Style Gothic   **Material** Carved stone

Of all the breathtaking Gothic churches with their gravity-defying arches and light-flooded aisles, the Cathedral of St. Peter and St. Mary is one of the most impressive. Situated on the banks of the Rhine in the heart of Cologne, this is a monument to faith and spirit. Its sheer size with the 470-foot-long (144 m) nave and choir, and its 515-foot-tall (157 m) spires pushed the boundaries of structural design.

The cathedral was commissioned by the Archbishop of Cologne, Konrad von Hochstaden (1205–61) after the previous church burned down. The master builder Gerhard von Rile knew the architect of Notre Dame in Paris, Jean de Chelles, and was familiar with works at Amiens Cathedral from where he took inspiration for the shape of the arches, and the structural order that he tried to elaborate. Progress on the main choir was initially rapid, but it would take 600 years and eleven more architects to complete the cathedral in 1880, although work stopped between 1560 and 1842.

The cathedral is among the finest examples of Gothic architecture in a period that reached and sometimes went beyond the limits of traditional stone construction. Only the invention of cast iron and steel, which was used to finish the roof, would eventually enable architects to push designs further.

Luckily, damage inflicted on the cathedral during World War II proved insubstantial, and the building continues to tower above the city of Cologne as an awe-inspiring achievement of the human spirit. **LT**

↖ For four years after its completion in 1880, Cologne Cathedral was the tallest building in the world.

← Soaring columns and distant ceilings make Cologne Cathedral a classic of Gothic architecture.

Royal Exhibition Building (1880)

Architect Joseph Reed **Location** Melbourne, Australia
Style Italianate **Materials** Brick, bluestone, timber, cast iron

The Royal Exhibition Building in Melbourne is a monument to Victorian optimism and enterprise. Built for the 1880 Melbourne International Exhibition, it was intended to signify the colony of Victoria's significance on the world stage as part of Britain's ever-expanding global empire. It was conceived in the tradition of large, open-plan exhibition buildings typical of the international exhibition movement of the late nineteenth and early twentieth centuries, and remains one of the few intact examples of its kind in the world. Stylistically it is a mixture of Classical motifs combined in a free Italianate manner. When completed it was the largest building in Australia, and the tallest in Melbourne. The Great Hall alone consists of more than 39,000 square feet (3,623 sq m) of display space.

The building's architect, Joseph Reed (c. 1823–90), of the Melbourne-based firm Reed and Barnes, was born in Cornwall, and immigrated to Australia in 1853. For a time he was Melbourne's most important architect, dominating the profession from the 1860s through the 1880s. In 1863 Reed made a trip to Europe, which inspired an enthusiasm for the architecture of Italy. This enthusiasm later returned in his design for the Royal Exhibition Building, the dome of which is based on that of Filippo Brunelleschi's great exemplar at Florence Cathedral. Reed also played a role in laying out the ceremonial gardens in which the Royal Exhibition Building is situated.

The Royal Exhibition Building in Melbourne has been the site of numerous events of local and national significance. It was the location for the 1888 Melbourne Centennial Exhibition, celebrating a century of European settlement in Australia, and the venue for the inauguration of the sovereign Commonwealth of Australia in 1901. **GAB**

Church of the Savior Not Made By Hand (1882)

Architect Viktor Vasnetsov **Location** Abramtsevo, Moscow, Russia
Style Russian Vernacular **Materials** Stone, tile

This is one of the most exquisite works of art created under the patronage of railway millionaire Savva Mamontov (1841–1918). It is part of the Abramtsevo Estate on the outskirts of Moscow. There is an ensemble of buildings from the restrained Classical lines of the main house to the wooden House on Chicken Legs illustrating a Russian fairy tale.

The estate was purchased in 1870 by Mamontov, and intended as a retreat from Moscow. He invited artists, sculptors, architects, wood carvers, and musicians to live and work in residence. It became a

> "... distinctions between the arts were consciously elided to create an organic whole."
>
> Rosalind Blakesley, *The Arts and Crafts Movement* (2006)

key center of the Russian Revival, the renewed interest in medieval and folk motifs in the Russian arts.

Mamontov embellished the estate with other buildings, created by the artists, including a wooden guesthouse in the style of a peasant *izba* (cottage), and a workshop organized by Savva's wife Elizaveta, where Elena Polenova taught locals carving and joinery to ensure that these crafts did not disappear.

In 1881 artist and set designer Viktor Vasnetsov (1848–1926) created designs for a church. Its form and plain, whitewashed walls were inspired by medieval church architecture. Its austerity is countered by stone carving and glazed tilework. The artists executed all the work themselves, including painting icons for the iconostasis, laying the mosaic floor, and sewing shrouds and banners. **CC**

Gravers Lane Station (1883)

Architect Frank Furness   **Location** Philadelphia, Pennsylvania, USA
Style Victorian   **Materials** Brick, wood, tile

The quirky buildings of Frank Furness (1839–1912) fell heavily from popularity during the twentieth century. Of the many suburban railway stations he built for the expanding commuter network in his native Philadelphia, Gravers Lane is the only survivor. Thanks to a restoration in 1982, it is in good condition.

Sitting in the middle of a sloping lawn, the station is too small for the quantity and type of architectural features that Furness has given it. The building contains only modest accommodation for the caretaker, a small waiting room, and a ticket counter.

"The whole sweep of the structure there, relatively unimportant as it is, is masterful."

Albert Kelsey, architect and planner

They are decked out in porches, gables, a turret, ornamental woodwork, and ample pitched roofs with dormer windows. Each part looks as if it ought to be much larger, producing a curiously toylike whole. The effect is endearing, and the distinctive little building must have contributed considerably to the sense of domestic paradise that the nineteenth-century speculators building Philadelphia's suburbs sought to give to prospective residents.

At the same time, there is function in some of its quirks, especially the extended sweep of the roof to each side of the main building. These attractive wooden structures provide on one side shelter for those arriving at the station by vehicle, on the other a good area of platform that is protected from the rain. It is a lovely little building. **BWC**

Palace of Justice (1883)

Architect Joseph Poelaert   **Location** Brussels, Belgium
Style Baroque Revival   **Material** Stone

This edifice was the largest building constructed in the world during the nineteenth century. It is 344 feet (105 m) high, has a footprint of 525 by 492 feet (160 by 150 m), covers 853,000 square feet (79,246 sq m), and contains eight courtyards, twenty-seven large courtrooms, and 245 smaller rooms. The building looms even larger by virtue of the fact that it was built on the hill above an area previously known as the Gallows Field—where criminals were executed.

The design of the building was the subject of a competition in 1860, but when there were no declared winners, King Leopold II awarded the relatively unknown architect Joseph Poelaert (1817–79), the project in 1861. The style of the building, eclectic and grandiose, is typical of the pompous overscaled mishmash of influences of much late-nineteenth-century official architecture in Europe. The building has variously, and confusingly, been described as Assyrian, Byzantine, Roman, and Neo-Gothic.

The project seemed somewhat cursed from the beginning, suffering such delays that Poelaert did not live to see it finished, allegedly having been sent mad by the project. Once completed, the building work had overrun the original budget six times. Further controversy was provoked when, in order to clear the site for construction, a section of the poor neighborhood of Marolles was demolished, causing much ill feeling. A café that later opened in the neighborhood was called De Scheve Architect, meaning "the crooked architect."

The Palace of Justice was one of Adolf Hitler's favorite buildings, and in September 1944 German soldiers retreating from the city were ordered to burn it down, but only managed to collapse the dome, which was rebuilt even higher after the war. **RWN**

Academy
of Athens (1885)

Architects Theophil Freiherr von Hansen, Ernst Ziller
Location Athens, Greece **Style** Neo-Classical **Material** Marble

When the new kingdom of Greece was established in 1834, Athens was an unplanned and untidy small town huddled amid the decayed glories of Classical antiquity. It needed to be equipped with the amenities of a nineteenth-century capital city: a parliament building, university, national library, museum, and palaces for the royal family.

A number of the buildings were funded by rich expatriates. The Academy of Athens was paid for by Simon Sinas of Vienna, founder of the National Bank of Austria, who gave three million drachmas for the purpose. Its architect was the Dane Theophil Freiherr von Hansen (1813–91), and the supervising architect was Ernst Ziller (1837–1923).

The building is in the form of an amphiprostyle temple (one with a portico both at the front and the rear). In the center is a projecting temple front, its Ionic portico based on the east porch of the Erectheion, on the Acropolis. The coffering and architectural members were given a fully polychromatic treatment, in line with contemporary views on the use of color in architecture by the Ancient Greeks. Flanking the portico are gigantic Ionic columns, bearing statues of Athena, goddess of wisdom, and Apollo, god of light and music, carved by Leonidas Drosis, who also made the pediment sculpture.

Inside, the Assembly Hall contains eight murals depicting the myth of Prometheus, painted by Christian Griepenkerl. The other decorations of the interior echo the purity of the exterior. **CWH**

↗ The Athens Academy is acknowledged to be one of the finest Neo-Classical buildings in the world.

→ The pediment sculpture by Leonidas Drosis represents the birth of Athena, sculpted in the round.

Palacio da Pena (1885)

Architect Baron von Eschwege   **Location** Sintra, Portugal
Style Victorian   **Materials** Stone, wood, brick

"There can be no surprise that Lord Byron and William Beckford fell in love with its beauty."

C. T. North, *Guia dos Castelos Antigos de Portugal* (2002)

⬆ Of the original sixteenth-century monastery, the chapel and a Manueline cloister were preserved.

➡ The Palacio da Pena is remarkable for its eclectic mixture of styles, from Neo-Gothic to Neo-Islamic.

In 1838 the German Prince Ferdinand Saxe-Coburg Gotha acquired the ruins of the Pena Monastery at auction. At the time he had the intention of restoring the building to its original glory. However, perhaps influenced by an illicit affair, he changed his plans and in 1840 the prince commissioned the German engineer Baron von Eschwege (1777–1855) to build a country residence and grounds. The architect proposed radical designs for an awe-inspiring new palace and gardens at Pena that were happily accepted by the prince.

The turreted building sits unevenly across giant rocks on a mountaintop 18 miles (30 km) from Lisbon. It possesses an awkward yet charming style. The colorful palace is influenced by a dizzying array of architectural styles: Bavarian, Romantic, Gothic, and Moorish are the principal influences, but there are Renaissance details, too, in the form of the original sixteenth-century chapel by master builder Diogo Boitoc and sculptor Nicolau Chanterene, both of whom worked on the Jerónimos Monastery in Lisbon. When finished, the building was mainly used as the summer residence of the royal family. The palace is full of precious objects, collections, and works of art.

The landscaped palace gardens are spectacular, and there are excellent views of the Sintra mountains. The original ornamental ponds, bird fountains, groves of exotic trees, and expanses of wild flowers all remain intact. Later, Prince Ferdinand was to build a more modest chalet in the grounds of the palace for his second wife, the Countess of Edla, who also contributed ideas for the gardens. She inherited the estate in 1885 when the prince died just as the palace was completed. She later sold it to the state. In 1910 Palacio da Pena (Palace of Pena) was listed as a Portuguese National Monument, and in 1995 the town of Sintra was listed as a World Heritage Site. **MDC**

Cragside (1885)

Architect Richard Norman Shaw   **Location** Rothbury, Morpeth, Northumberland, England   **Style** Tudorbethan   **Materials** Stone, timber

Cragside was originally foreseen as a country retreat for Lord William Armstrong, the Northumbrian inventor and hydraulics engineer. Dramatically located on top of a large rock overlooking a deep gorge and set within 1,000 acres of land, the house was developed over a period of fifteen years by the architect Richard Norman Shaw (1831–1913). The original building started life as a small hunting lodge but Lord Armstrong wanted this to be enlarged for his retirement. Additions were made to the existing Jesmond Dene Banqueting Hall that was previously too small and badly lit. A square gallery was added, built into the steep hillside, lit from above and linking the old and new sections, Shaw created an organ loft for the entertainment of guests. He also improved the steep access from the road above, and behind the main house he built an attractive small lodge. As well as structural changes, Shaw redesigned the interiors and some furniture of several existing rooms, namely the library, dining room, and drawing room. The dining room has an inglenook fireplace in carved stone, and the drawing room contains a large fireplace, decorated in highly ornate plasterwork. Cragside was also the first house in the world to be lit by hydroelectricity, and the first to use the incandescent light bulb. Lord Armstrong successfully dammed the local rivers and diverted the water to new lakes, providing the source for hydroelectricity. **FO**

"I had a tremendous talk with … William about his gallery … and think I am to have my own way."

Richard Norman Shaw, architect

Summer Palace (1888)

Patrons Emperor Qianlong, Dowager Empress Cixi   **Location** Beijing, China   **Style** Imperial Chinese   **Materials** Stone, brick, wood

Beijing's Yi He Yuan, or the Summer Palace, is a complex of halls, towers, kiosks, and pavilions in a 720-acre (290 ha) park around Kunminghu lake, about 12 miles (19 km) northwest of Tiananmen. It was commissioned by Emperor Qianlong (1711–99) in 1750 as the Qingyi Yuan (Garden of Clear Ripples), which developed into the imperial summer residence. It was attacked by foreign armies in 1860 and 1900, and rebuilt on each occasion. The Dowager Empress Cixi (1835–1908) lived here from 1889 until her death, and she is said to have funded the restoration and expansion of the Summer Palace with money diverted from funds for the Chinese navy. In 1924 the palace was declared a public park. Notable structures in the park include the Yiledian (Hall of Nurtured Joy) with a three-story theater; the Leshontang (Hall of Joyful Longevity), the Dowager Empress Cixi's residence; and the Shiqi Kong Qiao (Seventeen-Arch Bridge). The

Chang Lang (Long Gallery) is a 2,388-foot-long (728 m) covered walkway elaborately decorated with more than 14,000 paintings depicting scenes from Chinese classical literature. The Shi Fang (Marble Boat) is a lakeside pavilion built of wood and painted to look like marble. Imitation wheels on either side make it resemble a Mississippi paddle steamer. Although the individual buildings are pleasantly decorative and historically curious, it is the traditional Chinese landscape with, for example, views across the lake that are most attractive. The natural landscape of hills and the ornamental lake combines with artificial features such as the pavilions, halls, palaces, temples, and bridges to create a harmonious atmosphere of great charm. The design epitomizes the philosophy and practice of Chinese garden design, reflecting the profound aesthetic of this internationally influential Chinese cultural form. **ATB**

Chhatrapati Shivaji Terminus (1888)

Architect Frederick William Stevens   **Location** Mumbai, India   **Style** Victorian   **Materials** Brick, stone, wood, iron

The Chhatrapati Shivaji Terminus (formerly known as Victoria Terminus) in Mumbai is one of the most prominent vestiges of British colonialism in India. Designed as a railway station and administrative hub, it took ten years to complete and is the only functional building to be listed as a World Heritage Site by UNESCO. The station was designed by English architectural engineer Frederick William Stevens (1847–1900), who worked for the India Public Works Department from 1867, until his services were loaned to the Great Indian Peninsula Railway in 1877 to consult on the railway station. Stevens visited Europe to look at railway stations before creating his design, and the Chhatrapati Shivaji Terminus is said to be modeled on St. Pancras railway station in London. It is a marvelous example of two schools of architecture, Venetian Gothic Revival and traditional Indian school, with flying buttresses and traditional wood carvings

existing in harmony. Externally the building has a spectacular edifice of carved friezes and stained-glass windows, while the interiors are detailed in decorated tiles, ornamental railings, and grills that tie together the grand staircases and ticket offices into one stunning volume. The terminus is capped with a central dome on which stands a statue of the figure of Progress. Originally called the Victoria Terminus after Queen Victoria, it was officially renamed the Chhatrapati Shivaji Terminus in 1996 after a seventeenth-century Maratha king. The station also holds importance because India's first steam engine was flagged from here. Today, the station houses the headquarters of the central railway and supports a network of local trains transporting more than 2.5 million commuters every day. "VT," as it continues to be referred to by the locals, ably sustains the metropolis of Mumbai as one of its gateways. **BS**

Hotel del Coronado (1888)

Architect James Reid **Location** Coronado, San Diego, California, USA **Style** Victorian **Material** Timber

The Hotel del Coronado is one of the oldest and largest all-wooden buildings in California, and has been part of San Diego's history since the 1880s. It was designated a National Historic Landmark in 1977 for being a fine example of a Victorian seaside resort where architectural style has been allowed to roam free to become a cityscape itself. Built as a luxury hotel, the Hotel del Coronado is located on the island of Coronado, close to San Diego; it is the largest beach resort on the North American Pacific coast ever to be built. The Hotel del Coronado was the creation of three men. In 1885 retired railroad executive Elisha Babcock, Hampton Story of Story & Clark Piano Company, and Jacob Gruendike, president of the First National Bank of San Diego jointly bought Coronado and North Island for $110,000. Along with Indiana businessmen Josephus Collett, Herber Ingle, and John Inglehart, they formed The Coronado Beach Company.

They appointed Canadian architect James Reid (b. 1851) to design the beach resort complete with its profusion of turrets and tiered verandas. Construction began in 1887, and it took just eleven months to complete, costing $1 million. Reid later set up an architectural practice in San Francisco with his brother Merritt. The pair were responsible for many buildings erected after the destruction caused by the 1906 San Francisco earthquake, including the Fairmont Hotel (1906), and Call Office Building (1914). **FO**

"It would be built around a court ... a garden of tropical trees, shrubs, and flowers ..."

Elisha Babcock and Hampton Story, owners

Allegheny County Courthouse (1888)

Architect Henry Hobson Richardson **Location** Pittsburgh, Pennsylvania, USA **Style** Romanesque Revival **Material** Granite blocks

Henry Hobson Richardson (1838–86) has been called "the father of U.S. architecture." Allegheny County Courthouse in Pittsburgh was one of the last commissions Richardson accepted before his untimely death at the age of forty-eight. Although he did not live to see its completion, he regarded it as his best building design.

Built to replace an earlier structure destroyed by fire in 1882, Allegheny Courthouse is imposingly constructed from massive, rusticated granite blocks rising to four stories around a central courtyard. A tower soars up 280 feet (85 m) on the courtyard's open side while a covered bridge—a facsimile of the Bridge of Sighs at the Doge's Palace in Venice—stretches over an intervening road to connect the main building to its neighboring jail.

The courthouse's steep roofs, projecting bays, dormer windows, round arches, and Byzantine capitals achieve a synthesis that is quite distinct from contemporary Gothic or Baronial Revival. French Renaissance organizing principles are augmented with an English Arts and Crafts attention to structural polychromy, but Richardson's main inspiration originated from the medieval architecture of southern France. These influences merged together in a wholly original fashion to create a language that has been called Richardsonian Romanesque. It was a style that was to prove extremely influential in the years after his death. Its characteristic "heavy massing" and celebration of the sculptural qualities of stonework has echoes in the work of Louis Sullivan and Frank Lloyd Wright. **RDB**

↖ The windows clearly show medieval influence, with their arches and pillars recalling the Romanesque.

← The bridge reinterprets the Venetian Bridge of Sighs in a monumental, powerful register.

Burgtheater (1888)

Architects Gottfried Semper, Karl Freiherr von Hasenauer   **Location** Vienna, Austria   **Style** Neo-Baroque   **Material** Limestone

The Burgtheater, or Imperial Court Theater, is one of a group of colossal buildings that define the Viennese Imperial style. Its architects Karl von Hasenauer (1833–94) and Gottfried Semper (1803–79) were responsible for a number of landmark buildings constructed during the brief Austro-Hungarian empire, including the Kunsthistorisches Museum (Museum of Art History) and the Naturhistorisches Museum (Natural History Museum), which show a strong Baroque influence. The Baroque style had blossomed in the seventeenth and eighteenth centuries, defined by curves, statues, and elaborate columns.

Von Hasenauer earned the title "Freiherr" for his work, which included being the chief architect for the 1873 Vienna World Fair. Semper had written texts such as *Four Elements of Architecture* (1851). Although his buildings refer to past styles and use an abundance of motifs, his written work has modern insights and influenced future generations of architects.

The Burgtheater took years to complete and saw extensive rebuilding works after damage during World War II. The theater's round facade is built to impress. Above the name of the building is a relief of Bacchus, the god of wine, in procession. The building's use as a space for performing arts is visually signposted by busts of writers and statues depicting allegorical figures such as Love, and the muses of Tragedy and Comedy. The interiors are lavishly decorated with stucco ornament and frescoes by Gustav Klimt, one of the best-known Austrian artists of this period. The Burgtheater is a testament to its time, reflecting the opulence of nineteenth-century Imperial Vienna. **RK**

↗ The grand staircase, together with the towering windows, leads the eye up to the stunning ceiling.

→ The facade is topped with a statue of the god Bacchus, flanked by further statues of the Muses.

Palau Güell (1890)

Architect Antonio Gaudí **Location** Barcelona, Spain **Style** Art Nouveau, Sculptural **Materials** Stone, iron, wood, ceramic

A visit to Barcelona is incomplete without paying homage to one of its greatest sons, the highly individual architect Antonio Gaudí (1852–1926). And Palau Güell (Güell Palace), the town house Gaudí lovingly created with the help of a team of artisans and craftsmen for Catalan textile industrialist and friend Count Eusebi Güell, is a fine place to start. The house is situated on a back street in an unfashionable area that the Güell family had traditionally lived in, and was the first large-scale work to clearly show the architect's search for new ideas and forms in construction

Externally, two large parabolic arches serve as entry gates, dominating the lower facade. The gates are made of intricate wrought iron and feature the owner's initials, with a Catalan coat of arms between them. The gates allowed horse-drawn carriages into the complex that is a grand vertical space that is topped by a large, beautiful, parabolic dome with star-shaped windows. Around this, Gaudí arranged the other luxurious main spaces: salons, living rooms, and corridors featuring marble columns, precious-wood-paneled ceilings, ironwork, stained-glass windows, paintings, and stylish furniture. Visitors to the rooftop have more treats in store, with twenty sensuously shaped, almost Gothic, chimneys and ventilator shafts decorated with broken pieces of ceramic.

The house was one of a number of buildings and features that Count Güell commissioned from Gaudí in an attempt to bolster his profile on the architectural scene. It was a scene Gaudí conquered at the head of a new wave of Catalan patriotism, and continued to give expression to at La Sagrada Família. **DT**

↖ Organically shaped windows partly glazed with stained glass contribute to the hallucinatory effect.

← Chimneys and ventilator shaft openings received Gaudí's trademark decoration with broken ceramics.

Castell Coch (1891)

Architect William Burges **Location** Tongwynlais, South Glamorgan, Wales **Style** Gothic Revival **Materials** Red limestone, white limestone

Nestled in the hills to the north of Cardiff like a remnant from a bygone era, Castell Coch is a Victorian vision of a fairytale castle. In the late nineteenth century, William Burges (1827–81) was commissioned to build Cardiff Castle, a new mock medieval residence for the Third Marquis of Bute. At the same time, he managed to persuade his patron to finance a summer home for the Butes in the Welsh countryside. Burges proposed to redevelop an existing eleventh-century motte castle, known as the "Red Castle," and this appealed to Bute's enthusiasm for archaeology. The ruined motte was all that remained of a stronghold built to defend the River Taff, and was later developed into a masonry fortress by the De Clare lords of Glamorgan and used in their battle against the Welsh in the late thirteenth century. By the mid-nineteenth century when Burges discovered it, only one tower remained. Burges rebuilt using the De Clare plan but radically altered the silhouette of the castle.

Three towers of varying heights, joined by a curtain wall, were constructed, with smooth, sloping roofs inspired by the Château de Chillon on Lake Geneva. Sadly, Burges died after the shell was completed, leaving only sketch designs for the decoration of the interior. Another architect, William Frame, completed Burges's work, creating a highly decorative interior, full of vivid imaginings. The Drawing Room glitters with colorful animals, birds, and butterflies. To visit Castell Coch is to be immersed in the Victorian obsession with recreating the medieval. Here, one of the most brilliant architects of the time realized his romantic fantasy of a castle. **JS**

↗ Carvings of the Fates, goddesses who control destiny, dominate one of the lavishly decorated interiors.

→ William Burges admitted that the picturesque conical roofs of Castell Coch were "utterly conjectural."

Silver Pagoda (1892)

Patron King Norodom   **Location** Phnom Penh, Cambodia
Style Khmer   **Materials** Concrete, marble, silver

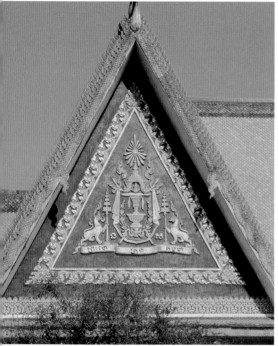

Phnom Penh's Silver Pagoda is situated in the compound of the Royal Palace that serves as home to King Sihanouk and his family.

It was originally constructed in 1892 by King Norodom (1834–1904), but the wooden structure suffered much damage and was rebuilt in the twentieth century by King Sihanouk. No expense was spared to create the Silver Pagoda in the native Khmer style, and it was elaborately decorated inside and out.

With its bright clean lines and colors, the building makes a spectacular impact. Its architecture clearly shows the influence of Wat Phra Kaeo in Bangkok, a revered Thai shrine. Similarities include the ornate gold detail, and successive, recessing decorative pediments. Although some say that the complex in Phnom Penh feels slightly artificial and lacking in atmosphere, the magnificent treasures inside more than make up for any lack of originality in the exterior.

The Silver Pagoda owes its name to the 5,329 handcrafted silver tiles that adorn its floor. Its official name is Preah Vihear Preah Keo Morakot but is commonly referred to as Wat Preah Keo (Temple of the Emerald Buddha). The Emerald Buddha is an attraction of the temple, but is believed to be made of baccarat crystal. Another feature is the Buddha Maitreya (Buddha of the Future), a solid gold Buddha encrusted with more than 2,000 diamonds. The walls of the building are lined with cabinets housing gifts presented to the king by visiting dignitaries. It remains a treasure trove in the heart of this bustling city. **KGB**

↖ The royal crest of the King of Cambodia signifies this is a palace as well as an architectural treasure.

↤ Looted by the Khmer Rouge during the late 1970s, the Silver Pagoda has been restored to its former glory.

Georgetown Cathedral (1892)

Architect Sir Arthur Blomfield **Location** Georgetown, Guyana
Style Neo-Gothic **Material** Timber

The British colonists in Georgetown were devout Christians, and built a brick church on the silt of the nearby Demerara River in 1842. Unfortunately the church required better foundations, and by 1877 it had to be abandoned as unsafe. With a temporary cathedral bursting at the seams, a renowned British architect, Sir Arthur Blomfield (1829–99), was asked to design a new cathedral. The commissioning committee, concerned about both the expense and the possibility of another masonry cathedral disappearing into the alluvial silt, insisted on the use of local timber. Blomfield never visited Guyana, but the cathedral opened its doors in 1892. It was the tallest timber structure in the world until 2003.

The builders of the cathedral chose their timbers well, using tropical woods distasteful to termites for the structure, and pitch pine for the ceiling. The local greenheart hardwood possesses exceptional strength, allowing large spans and slender columns to make a spacious interior with good sightlines. The cathedral sits on an oval close, chosen for its conspicuous location, and is clad in white clapboarding. But its complex roof form is unsuited to tropical downpours, and keeping water out is an ongoing battle.

The building is eccentrically marvelous, but not a masterpiece. The use of dark, varnished structural timbers with whitewashed infill boarding creates an almost mock-Tudor effect of black-and-white patterning to the interior, but this does not lessen the drama of the soaring space, punctuated by colored light streaming through stained-glass windows. A chancel screen of white-painted wrought iron adds a jaunty touch. Externally, timber flying buttresses prop the main frames, an intriguing example of wooden construction mimicking stone. **CB**

Tenement House (1892)

Architect Clarke & Bell **Location** Glasgow, Scotland
Style Late Victorian **Materials** Stone, slate

While most buildings considered interesting are unique, some are fascinating because they are typical. Glasgow's Tenement House (145 Buccleuch Street) falls into this latter category. It is a time capsule that represents an extraordinary vignette of life at the turn of the nineteenth century and the beginning of the twentieth century. Its very ordinariness is what makes it so important.

Lived in from 1911 until 1965 by Miss Agnes Toward, a shorthand typist, it preserves the traditional features of the tenement—an apartment in a small

> *"It is ... part of the nation's heritage because it is typical of the flats so many Scots used to live in."*
>
> The National Trust for Scotland

block of similar properties. The four-story block housing is built of the red sandstone that is distinctive of much of Glasgow's architecture of this period. Plain but solidly built, with a centrally placed "close" or common entry providing access to all apartments via a stone stair, the house is typical of tenement blocks built across the city in the boom years before the start of World War I.

Owned by the National Trust for Scotland since 1982, it preserves features such as gas lighting, the coal-fired cooking range, and a bed-recess off the kitchen. It is also decorated with many of Toward's possessions, including a rosewood upright piano and a grandfather clock. It allows the visitor an understanding of how life was lived by ordinary people in one of Europe's great industrial cities. **NMC**

Hôtel Tassel (1893)

Architect Victor Horta **Location** Brussels, Belgium
Style Art Nouveau **Materials** Iron, wood, stone

Hôtel Tassel is the elegant work of Belgian Art Nouveau architect and artist, Victor Horta (1861–1947). Ghent-born Horta's work represents a landmark in world architectural history, introducing the decorative style, and developing the use of free forms in architecture. Hôtel Tassel is his first mature Art Nouveau structure, incorporating hints of the French Gothic Revival influence, and setting the pace for the style.

The two-story structure is located in the center of the Belgian capital, and was designed and built for geometry professor Émile Tassel on a narrow and deep site. A finely detailed urban house, Hôtel Tassel has an articulated facade defined around centered, stacked, bay windows with a top balcony. The architect used regularly curved forms, strongly believing in their practicality rather than seeing them as merely ornamental. He also experimented with glass and steel, both in the free-flowing interiors, and in the house's purpose-designed furniture. The facade is almost Neo-Classical in appearance, but the balcony section's oblique form suggests its decorative influences. Expressive, nature-inspired designs are found in the warm-colored patterns on the walls and floors, and in the exuberant staircase metalwork.

The architect fitted out the house in sumptuous style, although the revolutionary aspect of the structure lies elsewhere: in the free use of the interior space and the different-level access to the various rooms, breaking the traditional separated-room approach to residential planning. **ES**

↖ Curving steps, metalwork, tile patterning, and wall decoration flow in the ground-floor stair hall.

← For Horta, stained glass was as important for the way it affected interior light as for its decorative potential.

Monadnock Building (1893)

Architects Burnham & Root, Holabird & Roche   **Location** Chicago, Illinois, USA
Style Romanesque Revival   **Material** Brick

Named after Mount Monadnock in New Hampshire, the monumental Monadnock Building prompted awe almost immediately after its construction. Built for Boston developer Peter Brooks by Burnham & Root, at sixteen stories it was considered a skyscraper. It stands on a narrow half block, with two tall, slender profiles flanking a long sheer face. It is thought to be the last monolithic masonry building of its scale; soon after construction techniques transitioned to load-bearing steel frames. The Monadnock was briefly the tallest building in the world, and remains one of the tallest load-bearing masonry buildings, necessitating walls more than 6 feet (1.8 m) thick at its base.

The Monadnock Building is not only considered a significant structure for its grand scale, but for its refinement and simplicity at a time when buildings were heavily ornamented and detailed. The client demanded simple lines, and was obsessed with its practicality, asking for "no projecting surfaces or indentations" that would collect dirt or bird droppings. The resulting building was admired for its sleek profile and undulating bays that impressed architects and real-estate investors—the unusual bays offered additional rental square footage.

The corners of the building illustrate its architectural subtlety. They begin as sharp angles at the base and increasingly flare, eventually becoming rounded and flattened at the top where the walls also gently flare out forming an abstracted cornice.

Holabird & Roche designed the seventeen-story southern addition in 1893 using a steel-frame construction. The north and south buildings mark a turning point in architectural history: the transition from load-bearing masonry to steel frames that made possible the construction of tall skyscrapers. **JC**

Winslow House (1894)

Architect Frank Lloyd Wright   **Location** River Forest, Illinois, USA
Style Prairie House   **Materials** Brick, stone, plaster

The distinctive style of the Winslow House developed from Frank Lloyd Wright's (1867–1959) early house designs. The Winslow House demonstrates his synthesis of the Prairie House style, and laid the foundation for a revolutionary approach to domestic U.S. architecture, particularly in the development of open-plan living.

In contrast to the more traditional approach to domestic buildings, the Prairie House style offered a modern, light, and airy living space. Wright used his interior walls to define space rather than enclose it,

> "Without an architecture of our own we have no soul of our own civilization."

Frank Lloyd Wright, architect

creating a fluid transition and pathway through the dwelling, and used furniture such as high-backed chairs to further create space within space.

The Prairie House style was so called because the long, low horizontal lines of the houses reflect the Midwestern prairies of Wright's youth. They create a sensation of the building both evolving from nature, and being separate from it in its function as a shelter. The Classical lines of the front facade of the house create a sense of stillness associated with the prairie, while the horizontal feel is evoked through a series of different layers. The street facade of the Winslow House is formal, strongly horizontal, and symmetrical. In contrast, the rear facade is irregular and consists of grouped segments of living space that interrelate with an undulating harmony. **TP**

Reichstag (1894)

Architects Paul Wallot, Foster & Partners **Location** Berlin, Germany **Style** Neo-Renaissance, High Tech **Materials** Stone, aluminum, glass

The Reichstag's colorful and checkered history stands as a testament to the symbolic power of certain buildings. As a symbol, it has experienced both the depredation of political fanatics and the attention of one of the world's leading contemporary architects.

The Reichstag was built in an imposing Neo-Renaissance style in 1894 by Frankfurt architect Paul Wallot (1841–1912) to house the assembly of the Second Reich. Conceived as a powerful statement of German national pride in which regional representatives would have their voices heard, it was burned down in 1933 by Nazi Party activists bent on undermining national democracy and casting blame on the Communists. Only just escaping demolition, it was then damaged in Allied bombing raids in World War II. A ruin, it was patched up between 1958 and 1972 to serve as government offices. After the fall of the Berlin Wall in 1989, the Reichstag became the home of the legislative assembly of the reunited Germany, the Bundestag. The building's uneasy resonance was expressed when it was wrapped in sheeting by artists Christo and Jeanne-Claude in 1995.

In 1999 British architect Lord Foster (b. 1935) stripped the building to its bare walls and inserted a lightweight glass and aluminum dome over the internal courtyard. This is flanked by two suspended interior spiral ramps, enabling the public to witness their parliament at work. Foster's mastery lies in his use of light: a mirrored funnel plunges down from the dome, providing daylight and ventilation to the lower debating chamber. Illuminated at night, the dome acts as a beacon for German democracy. **JM**

↖ The Reichstag mixes old and new, with the new glass dome capping the nineteenth-century building.

← Foster's dome replaces the original Neo-Renaissance Revival structure, which was destroyed in World War II.

Guaranty Building (1896)

Architects Dankmar Adler, Louis Sullivan **Location** Buffalo, New York, USA **Style** Beaux Arts **Materials** Steel, terra cotta

The Guaranty Building rises sheer from the downtown grid of Buffalo, no longer the tallest, but infinitely more expressive in its upward thrust than its neighbors. Nearly identical elevations, one two bays wider than the other, emphasize this verticality. Consistent with the principles declared by Louis Sullivan (1856–1924) for a new building type, the skyscraper, the base is expressed separately from the main body of the building, while the continuous verticals are gently brought to a halt with arches and circular openings at the top where the cornice swells like a breaking wave. The surfaces are lightly encrusted from top to bottom with Sullivan's distinctive ornament of oval milkweed pods, molded in warm brown terra cotta. The flat panels are in low relief, but the column capitals close to the ground are as curly as endive, and deeply recessed for the effect of shadow. The upper parts of the lobby survive, with a skylight of shallow stained-glass domes and a stenciled frieze. Critics have objected to the lack of connection between the ground section and the main shaft of the building above, but the discrepancy could be explained in terms of the different views obtained when walking along the street close to the building, and when viewing it from further away.

Sullivan primarily designed commercial buildings, but posterity has not been kind to the legacy of this architect in his home city of Chicago. The Guaranty Building is perhaps best understood as one of a series, including such Chicago buildings as the Jewelers' Building and the Kaufmann Store and Apartments, and the Wainwright Building in St. Louis. **AP**

↗ Following Louis Sullivan's principles, the building's base is expressed separately from the main body.

→ The arched window above the entrance betrays a debt to Romanesque architecture.

Chapel of St. Kinga (1896)

Architects Józef Markowski, Tomasz Markowski, Antoni Wyrodek   **Location** Wieliczka, Poland   **Style** Neo-Gothic   **Material** Salt rock

Salt manufacturing in Wieliczka began *c.* 3500 BCE, and rock salt was first mined there in the thirteenth century. The Wieliczka mine has been extended continuously ever since. Spread over nine levels, it reaches to a depth of 210 feet (327 m), housing 186 miles (300 km) of galleries with works of art, chapels, and statues sculpted in the salt, in addition to the mine workings.

St. Kinga's Chapel—St. Kinga is the patron saint of the local miners—is the largest of the chapels in the mine, located 331 feet (101 m) below the surface. It is literally carved out of the salt rock and decorated with sculptures, bas-reliefs, and chandeliers made from salt crystals. Even the floor is made from salt, but it has been carved so that it appears to be a tiled surface.

Work began on the chapel in 1896. It is 39 feet (12 m) in height, 178 feet (54 m) long, and 59 feet (18 m) wide. The chapel is the work of miner-sculptors, most notably Józef Markowski. Together with fellow miners, Markowski created an altar in the presbytery that contains sculptures of St. Joseph and St. Clement. Sculptures of the crucified Christ, kneeling monks, and the Virgin Mary were placed on the right and left sides of the chapel. He later created a vestry, pulpit, and side altar. In 1918, the chapel's salt chandeliers were adapted for electric current. Józef Markowski's younger brother Tomasz continued the work from 1920 to 1927, with additional bas-reliefs, and more were added by Antoni Wyrodek, who worked in the chapel from 1927 to 1963. .

The chapel is in use as a sacred space every Sunday morning, and during certain religious festivals. It is a truly breathtaking and unique structure. **CMK**

◥ The statues, pillars, and main altar of St. Kinga's were all carved in situ from the salt rock of the chapel wall.

◩ Deep underground, the chapel requires electrical lighting to reveal the details of ornamental carvings.

Great Market Hall (1897)

Architect Samu Petz **Location** Budapest, Hungary **Style** Neo-Gothic **Materials** Iron, brick, glass

Close by the River Danube in Budapest is one of Europe's liveliest nineteenth-century market halls. After the 1867 Act of Compromise, when Hungary achieved self-government within the Austro-Hungarian Empire, Budapest grew rapidly. The old infrastructure for food distribution was inadequate and the city required a new wholesale market.

Designed by a group of architects led by Samu Petz (1854–1922), the Great Market Hall has a symmetrical facade featuring patterned brickwork around a large main window and four smaller ones. At each end of the facade is a small tower. The entrance is stone and Neo-Gothic, but it is the interior that impresses—one can climb up three floors and look down on a bustling, colorful scene of over 180 stalls selling flowers, fresh vegetables, cheeses, meats, and fish. Most distinctive are stalls of red Hungarian paprika and peppers, reputed to restore fertility and good health, and, near Christmas, tanks of live carp.

The barrel-vaulted roof is six stories high, constructed in a lattice of iron. The overall impression is of an iron and glass cathedral devoted to fresh produce and good food. Hungarian author Mihály Gera first visited the hall when he was six: "My dazzled eyes gazed with wonder at the mightiness of the building, the ornamented iron pillars firmly supporting the roof, and the hurly-burly." Since the renovations of 1991–94, the market has served the retail trade. Elsewhere, markets like this have been demolished—Les Halles in Paris is one example—or redeveloped into sterile shopping malls. Luckily, Budapest decided to keep and repair its foodie heaven. **ATB**

↗ The Great Market Hall's Neo-Gothic facade features decorative brickwork in a variety of patterns.

➡ Small walkways branch off from the main aisle of the iron and glass hall, increasing the retail space.

Castel Béranger (1898)

Architect Hector Guimard **Location** Paris, France **Style** Art Nouveau **Materials** Brick, enamel tiles, stone, cast iron

Hector Guimard (1867–1942) was the initiator of French Art Nouveau, his ornamental entrances to the Paris Métro being his most visible legacy. At Castel Béranger, in the fashionable area of Auteuil, he designed an impressive building of thirty-six apartments as an Art Nouveau showpiece.

The building is a rectangle pierced with irregular windows and a varied facade of red brick, enamel tiles, white stone, and red sandstone. Metalwork was a feature with a spectacular red copper entrance gate and ironwork in the balconies. The elaborate interior

---

"Each apartment has its individual character: the bourgeois, the worker, the artist . . ."

Paul Signac, painter

---

stairwell is of red sandstone decorated with bespoke rich wallpapers and fabrics, and a mosaic inventively decorated with steel and copper. Guimard applied the principles of French Art Nouveau where the decoration was integral to the building. Like many of his contemporaries, he was influenced by the theories of Viollet-le-Duc (1814–79) in rejecting flatness and symmetry. Guimard's unique stylistic vocabulary is derived from plants and organic forms in abstract two-dimensional patterns.

Castel Béranger was described on its inauguration as the Maison des Diables (House of Devils) after its profusion of swirling, chimeraic figures. Although critics called it "subversive" and "deranged," it won first prize as the most beautiful facade in Paris in 1898. The painter Paul Signac lived in the building. **JEH**

Crown Liquor Saloon (1898)

Architects E. Byrne, J. Byrne **Location** Belfast, Northern Ireland **Style** Victorian **Materials** Brick, marble, tile

The Crown Liquor Saloon (see page 162) gloriously epitomizes its era. The closing years of the nineteenth century saw Belfast boom. All the vitality of a wealthy industrial town in the Late Victorian age was embodied in great buildings, such as Belfast City Hall, and smaller ones, such as the Crown Liquor Saloon. Located opposite the terminus of the Great Northern Railway, the Railway Tavern public house opened as a relatively plain building in 1846.

In 1885, it was renamed The Crown by its new owner, Michael Flanagan, and it was his son, an architecture student, who brought it to its present state. Local architects E. and J. Byrne oversaw the remodeling of both interior and exterior with a riot of ornate *faience* (tin-glazed earthenware), carved wood, ceramic tiles, brass, glass, and mirrors. A row of snugs opposite the ceramic bar, including a heated foot rest, lent additional charm to the interior. Local legend has it that Italian craftsmen, who had come to Ireland to decorate the churches that sprang up following Catholic Emancipation, moonlighted for extra cash by working on The Crown. Nobody knows if this is true, but what is documented is that the decorative tiling firm Craven Dunhill—also responsible for the woodwork on the ill-fated *Titanic*—supplied the tiling and created the magnificent curved bar.

The wonder of The Crown is that it has been so well preserved. Despite damage from bombs during the Troubles in the twentieth century, The Crown was never directly targeted. When the National Trust purchased the bar in 1978, all they needed to do was restore the original gas lighting and install a Ladies toilet. While great architecture can undoubtedly refresh the soul, a visit to The Crown for a well-pulled pint will also refresh the spirits. **GT**

Secession Building (1898)

Architect Josef Maria Olbrich **Location** Vienna, Austria
Style Viennese Secession, Jugendstil **Materials** Stone, metal

Even from today's viewpoint, the Secession Building (Secessionhaus) is a bold, ambitious edifice with its open-fretwork cupola of golden laurel leaves and its pared down, regimented facade. This fin de siècle building is seen as an icon of the Viennese Secession— an anti-traditionalist group of artists—of which Josef Maria Olbrich (1867–1908) was one of the founding members. With his fellow Secessionists Gustav Klimt, Otto Wagner, and Josef Hoffman, Olbrich looked to contemporary British architects such as Charles Rennie Mackintosh for inspiration. Determined to explore the possibilities of art outside the restrictions of academic tradition, Secessionists hoped to create a new style owing nothing to historical influence.

The ground plan and section of the Secessionhaus reveal the use of simple geometric forms, creating a unified, meditative space that was intended to serve as an "exhibition temple dedicated to the new art." The motto of the Viennese Secession is carved in gold above the main entrance: "To Every Age, Its Art. To Every Art, Its Freedom." The tendril-like motif of the Secession is a core part of the facade's ornamental detailing, and creates moments of delicacy and poise in the large swaths of white space that dominate the front elevation. In 1902, Klimt painted the Beethoven Frieze at the Secessionhaus, which predates the work he did at another Secession-inspired building, the Palais Stoclet in Brussels, designed by Josef Hoffman. Fittingly, the Secessionhaus functions today as an exhibition space for contemporary fine art. **AT**

↗ The facade declares the credo of the Secessionists: "To every age, its Art. To every Art, its freedom."

⊡ The dazzling cupola, with its golden laurel leaf design, sits atop a contrasting framework.

Karlplatz Metro Station (1899)

Architect Otto Wagner   **Location** Vienna, Austria   **Style** Jugendstil   **Materials** Steel framework, marble slabs

A professor at the Vienna Academy of Fine Arts, architect Otto Wagner (1841–1918) was highly influential for a whole generation of architects. He became famous for a lecture he gave in 1894 in which he advocated that Vienna's architectural style should be radically renewed and spurn any imitation of classical architectural styles. In 1883 he was one of the two prizewinners of a competition to reconstruct parts of Vienna's urban district. He went on to become an adviser for the Vienna Transport Commission and the Commission for the Regulation of the Danube Canal, and was appointed to design the urban-rail network, the Stadtbahn. He designed the bridges and tunnels for the network, as well as the platforms, staircases, and ticket offices of the stations. Karlplatz Metro Station is one such station entrance and was opened in 1899. When the rail network changed from the Stadtbahn to the U-Bahn in 1981, the station entrance became defunct. However, the two facing buildings above the ground are still in use. One is used by the Wien Museum Karlsplatz as a temporary exhibition space, the other is a café. The structures are built using a steel framework with marble slabs mounted on the exterior. Each building has a central curved entrance, flanked by symmetrical walls. Inside each entrance is a glass doorway and the sides of the buildings contain large windows. The green and gold painted metalwork that supports each building is exposed in the functional style that Wagner promoted. But what is most striking is the use of simple, flowing curved lines, gilded metal, and inset panels of decorative floral imagery to create an impressive facade. The buildings are an example of Viennese Jugendstil, a style of Art Nouveau developed from 1897 by members of the Vienna Secession art movement who influenced Wagner. **CMK**

Majolica House (1899)

Architect Otto Wagner   **Location** Vienna, Austria   **Style** Jugendstil   **Materials** Stone, majolica tiles, wood, iron

Derided as "hideous beyond measure" when it was first built, Otto Wagner's Majolica House marks a pivotal point in the architect's career. Turn-of-the-century Vienna was a crucible of artistic experiment, as architects such as Wagner, and his students Josef Maria Olbrich and Josef Hoffmann, turned away from the eclectic historicism that had marked Viennese architecture. It was in reaction to this that Art Nouveau—which developed as Jugendstil in the German-speaking regions of Europe—came to prominence in Vienna, and the Majolica House is Wagner's best example of this style. Highly decorated, the house takes its name from the majolica tiles that face the building. The wrought ironwork of the first two stories gives way to a facade that is creepered with curving abstract flowers, spreading as if from a stem as they go up to meet lions' heads, molded in relief beneath the overhanging eaves. The exuberance of the decorative tiles masks the clean modernist lines of the building. This was a radical architectural development at the time, and would find its own high point in Vienna with the Loos House at Michaelerplatz, built in 1911 by Adolf Loos, and denounced as the "house without eyebrows" due to its lack of ornamental stuccowork. Majolica House is one of the earliest examples of the *Gesamtkunstwerk*, or total work of art, in which art, architecture, and interior design all conspire to create the perfect whole. **GT**

"... our artistic sense must tell us that today only modern things can be considered beautiful..."

Otto Wagner, architect

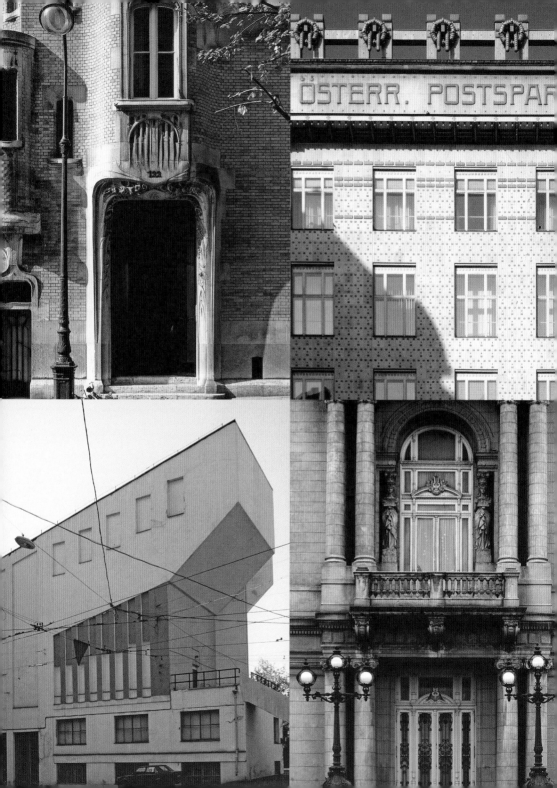

The Machine Age promised new utopias—few of which were delivered. The horrors of World War I ended the hitherto unquestioned authority of the past, with city-dwellers urging greater social mobility, speed of transport, and ease of living, along with increased political and social emancipation. Architecture was a vital symbol of radical reform, with patrons and governments keen to end the restrictions of the Victorian era. Clashes between the economic and military might of the West and traditional cultures in China, India, and other regions of the world produced stark contrasts between Modernist principles and traditional, vernacular architecture.

BIRTH *of* the MODERN

1901–1935

Blackwell (1900)

Architect M. H. Baillie Scott **Location** Bowness, Cumbria, England **Style** Arts and Crafts **Materials** Roughcast rendered masonry, green slate roof

Blackwell is the greatest and most accessible house by the architect M. H. Baillie Scott (1865–1945). Baillie Scott was a follower of the Arts and Crafts movement. He deplored modern "mass-produced" housing built without regard to location, craftsmanship, or the needs of its occupants. He advocated an "artistic" approach to house building that did not spurn the use of old materials, such as eighteenth-century oak paneling and firebacks, that would blend in with purpose-built plasterwork and metalwork. He built Blackwell for Sir Edward Holt, a rich Manchester brewer, on a superb site beside Lake Windermere. From the outside of the house, its plain rendered walls, casement windows in sandstone surrounds, and local Westmorland slate roof fit harmoniously into the scenery and local style of architecture. Inside, big windows look out onto views of the lake from rooms with timber-framed walls or decorated with low-relief

plasterwork depicting fruit and leaves in the tradition of William Morris. The blend of plain walls, wooden floors, and bay windows creates the kind of living spaces that Morris loved. The use of alcoves and inglenook fireplaces is also typical of this idiom. In the twentieth century, Blackwell suffered from use as a school and as offices, but at the end of the century it was lovingly restored. At a time when most of the Arts and Crafts houses are still private homes, Blackwell offers the unique chance to visit one of the best. **PW**

" . . . Not shallow, showy, and pretentious as most modern mansions are . . . "

M. H. Baillie Scott, architect

La Ruche Studios (1900)

Architect Gustave Eiffel   **Location** Paris, France   **Style** Early Modernist   **Material** Brick

La Ruche (The Beehive) is a circular structure with a steel frame and was originally designed by Gustave Eiffel (1832–1923) as a temporary wine pavilion for the Great Exposition of 1900. Sculptor Alfred Boucher (1850–1934) dismantled and transferred it from the Champ de Mars to its present location in a secluded garden off the Passage de Dantzig in Montparnasse. Here it was transformed into a complex of low-cost artists' studios and lodgings, exhibition space, and a theater, which was active until 1934. The twelve-sided wooden rotunda is on three levels and made up of wedge-shaped segments, subdivided into cells around a central stairwell. At its inauguration in 1902, it housed forty-six artists and eighty studios. It currently provides eighty-four private working artists' studios. Boucher was a successful, monumental, figurative sculptor and contemporary of Rodin and Claudel who was "in the situation of the hen who sits on the eggs of

the duck." At La Ruche he sought to help artists with low-rent space: "Here everyone has a share of the cake, each artist is judged by his own. He has a space at his disposal that is the same size as his neighbor." La Ruche housed an astounding array of artistic talent. Artists from all over the world went there to become part of L'Ecole de Paris, including Léger, Soutine, Modigliani, Chagall, Zadkine, Cendrars, and Max Jacob. Chagall once said, "You either died there or left famous." La Ruche declined during World War II and by 1968 was threatened with demolition, but, thanks to support from leading cultural figures, such as Jean-Paul Sartre, Jean Renoir, and Réné Char, it was preserved and restored in 1971. Paintings, sculptures, films, and photographs from its heyday can be seen at the Musée du Montparnasse. The interior is not open to the public, however, the exterior of La Ruche alone is well worth a visit. **JEH**

Mole Antonelliana (1900)

Architect Alessandro Antonelli **Location** Turin, Italy **Style** Neo-Baroque **Materials** Brick, iron

The Mole Antonelliana is an unusual structure that rises 132 feet (167.5 m) high and dominates the Turin skyline. In 1861, just before construction of it began, Turin became the capital of unified Italy. The building has become a landmark for the city. It was designed by Alessandro Antonelli, an architect and urban designer with a particular taste for vertical limits, as is also demonstrated by his dome for the Baroque church of San Gaudenzio in Novara, which soars to a height of 400 feet (122 m). The construction of the Mole Antonelliana, started in 1863, owes much to the San Gaudenzio design, relying largely on the structural capabilities of brickwork.

Originally designed as a synagogue for the Jewish community of Turin, it was bought in 1877 by the city council of Turin and converted into a monument dedicated to King Victor Emanuel II. Rising up from the massive base of extensive vaults and lower stories, the heart of the building is filled by a great hall, almost a covered courtyard, which is crowned by a domelike structure. Four bulging planes converge toward a lantern, which is arranged like a Classical portico from the exterior, and is topped in turn by a spire. This ambitious project occupied Antonelli until his death in 1888, at which time his son Costanzo oversaw completion of the building. Today, the structure houses a museum of cinema, and visitors can rise up through the massive hall in a memorable elevator ride, which is timed to coincide with dramatic lighting changes as the shutters of the dome automatically close and become screens for the projection of historic film footage. **FN**

↖ This building, originally a synagogue, has become a beacon, rising from the surrounding city.

← For all its command over the landscape, this strange building offers few views from inside.

Subotica Synagogue (1902)

Architects Marcell Komor, Dezö Jakab   **Location** Subotica, Serbia   **Style** Art Nouveau   **Materials** Concrete, steel, brick, glass, wood

The Jewish community of Subotica in northern Serbia was founded in 1775 and, toward the end of the eighteenth century, consisted of at least thirteen families. Under the leadership of the novelist Isidor Milko, the community ordered a synagogue to be built in 1901–02 by the Hungarian architects Marcell Komor and Dezö Jakab. In spite of its critical state of conservation, it is generally considered to be one of the most beautiful synagogues in central Europe, and it is used occasionally for religious services.

The Secessionist style of the building was highly innovative for a Jewish house of prayer. Between 1923 and 1926, the synagogue underwent renovation and was altered slightly. The central part of the synagogue is dominated by a huge dome, surrounded by smaller ones on the four corners. The original design provided 850 seats for men on the ground floor and 850 seats for women in the galleries on the three sides. The exterior is richly decorated and includes plastered and plain brick surfaces. The glazed terra-cotta elements were produced by the Zsolnay Factory in Pécs, Hungary. The interior design is dominated by gilded gypsum stuccoes and colorful wall paintings. Since the majority of the community embraced the enlightened Neologic movement, there is no *bimah* (altar) in the center and an organ was situated above the Torah shrine. In 1940 there were 6,000 Jews living in Subotica—six percent of the city's total population of 100,000—but only 1,200 of them survived the Holocaust. In 1996 the synagogue was included in the One Hundred Most Endangered Sites by the World Monument Watch program. **EGS**

↗ The interior of the dome is a remarkably florid affair, with cerulean blues, roses, and pale yellows.

→ The grand exterior belies the synagogue's fragility and its status as an endangered site.

Maison and Atelier Horta (1902)

Architect Victor Horta **Location** Brussels, Belgium **Style** Art Nouveau **Materials** Iron, wood, cut stone facade

Revolutionary Belgian architect Victor Horta (1861–1947) designed this graceful Art Nouveau complex to serve as his house and atelier (studio). Maison Horta was constructed between 1898 and 1902, followed by a long period of renovations and alterations that brought the house to its final form; it was sold in 1919, when Horta moved to nearby Avenue Louise. This narrow town house and atelier are representative of the height of his career, showcasing his maturely perfected Art Nouveau skills.

A sublimely detailed organic staircase dominates the entrance, leading to the more private areas of the bow-windowed house, and is the main circulation-well connecting most of the major spaces within. Above the top of the main staircase there are a number of curvaceous skylights crafted in glass and metalwork that perfectly demonstrate the Art Nouveau decorative tendency. Horta's nature-inspired patterns appear throughout most of the house's fittings and furniture, ranging from balconies to doorknobs and from drainpipes to the master bed, all designed in pure Hortian style. Even though the two parts of the complex—house and studio—were conceived together and communicate from the inside, they each have their own individual character, distinguishing residential from professional space.

In 1969, the house and atelier became the Horta Museum; a few years later the buildings were restored and interconnected. In 2000, the Maison and Atelier Horta and Horta's town houses—Hôtel Tassel, Hôtel Solvay, and Hôtel van Eetvelde—were designated as UNESCO World Heritage Sites. **ES**

↖ This exuberant facade, combining Horta's house and studio, is a mature example of Art Nouveau.

← Horta's design sensibility extended to almost every object in the house, from furniture to fittings.

Santa Justa Lift (1902)

Architect Raul Mesnier de Ponsard   **Location** Lisbon, Portugal   **Style** Hispano-Moorish   **Material** Iron

This striking structure located in Lisbon was created by Portuguese-French structural engineer Raul Mesnier de Ponsard. Its iron form is rather like a scaled-down version of the Eiffel Tower but with more emphasis on function than form. The Santa Justa Lift (Elevador de Santa Justa), also known as the Carmo, was built to transport people and commerce between upper and lower downtown Lisbon. The original steam-powered traction engine was replaced by an electrical one five years after its inauguration.

The structure is 147 feet (45 m) high and features two lifts, each with a twenty-five passenger capacity, that counterbalance one another. A complicated excavation project was required in order to build a tunnel for the elevator. To save costs the decorative top of the Santa Justa was never constructed. Instead, it was replaced by a simple observation deck with superb views of the south Pombal district of Lisbon.

The use of iron as the primary structural material liberated the need for solid walls, allowing elegant windowed elevations to soar upward on delicate supports, giving views out over the surrounding area. Iron also proclaimed a desire for the modern and an escape from the supposed restriction of labor-intensive stone or marble. The delight of this building is that it accommodates motion as its core purpose, a paradox that would not have gone unnoticed by its creator. The slim silhouette of the structure is also an ingenious response to its immediate context, a heavily built-up area of the city. That historical references could still be articulated so finely using this dazzling new technology at the time would have seemed miraculous to De Ponsard's contemporaries.

The lift was made an official national Portuguese monument in 2002 and attracts tourists from all over the world. Officially, it is also part of CARRIS, the Lisbon suburban public transport service. **MDC**

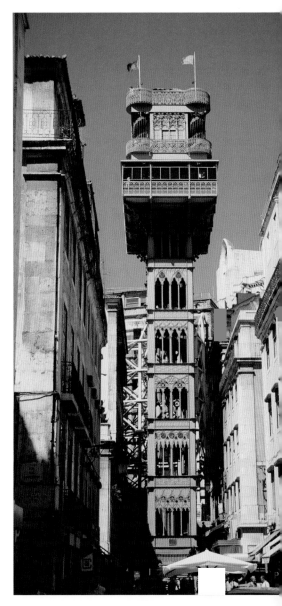

Architects' Housing at Hvittrask (1902)

Architect Eliel Saarinen   **Location** Kirkkonummi, Finland   **Style** Arts and Crafts, Vernacular   **Materials** Stone, timber, glass

With its magical sylvan setting on the edge of a lake, this exquisite home of stone and wood has come to epitomize the European Arts and Crafts ideal of a *Gesamtkunstwerk*, or total work of art. It was designed by the Finnish architect Eliel Saarinen (1873–1950), initially as a small studio and workshop with living quarters above it. Subsequently, it was expanded to form an office and three dwellings around a courtyard for the communal living of Saarinen and his architect partners, Herman Gesellius and Armas Lindgren. The three architects, who trained together at the Polytechnic of Helsinki, had collaborated in 1900 on the Finnish Pavilion at the Paris Exposition.

This building complex represented a kind of manifesto for Finnish National Romanticism, a movement that sought to revive the country's vernacular building forms and to reinterpret them in a modern way. Therefore, Hvittrask—named after the nearby lake—resembles a cluster of homely cottages, with granite walls, picturesque windows, and hunkering, gabled roofs.

Inside, the handcrafted timber furnishings and fittings are influenced by the Viennese Secession and British Arts and Crafts movements. The interconnecting nature of the spaces suggests the looser, more communal way of living proposed by these movements, as well as by the early houses of U.S. architect Frank Lloyd Wright. (At Hvittrask, these ideas were interpreted literally when one of the architects' wives swapped partners.)

In 1923 Saarinen emigrated to the United States, where he continued to practice as an architect, also becoming an influential teacher. However, his body is buried at Hvittrask. The complex is now open as a public museum. **MF**

Eliseev Brothers Food Shop (1903)

Architect Gavriil Vasilievich Baranovsky   **Location** St. Petersburg, Russia   **Style** Art Nouveau   **Material** Granite

The Eliseev family fortune had humble beginnings: from selling pies on trays at Nevsky Prospekt to the late nineteenth century, when they were one of the richest merchant families in Russia.

The St. Petersburg branch of their shop reflected their various interests and is one of the finest buildings of its date surviving in the city. At ground level is a shop, on the second floor a theater (now the Comedy Theater), and on the third floor was a restaurant. The basement storage stretched beyond the building and included a bakery and laundry. Externally, the building

> *"To eat in public in St. Petersburg is beyond the means of all but the most opulent traveler . . ."*
>
> Charles Piazzi Smyth, Astronomer Royal for Scotland

is granite faced and mostly in the classical version of the Style Moderne. Huge bronze statues by Amandus Heinrich Adamson represent Art, Commerce, Industry, and Science. The shop front and first-floor interior are full-blown Art Nouveau with stained-glass panels depicting flowers, lacy metalwork, and gilded plaster. Lighting comes from elaborate cornucopias of metal lilies as well as crystal chandeliers. The counters are mahogany with gilded panels and glass vitrines.

After the Russian Revolution, the shop was nationalized and renamed Gastronom No. 1. During the siege of the city, from 1941 to 1944, the basement remained open for business. Despite considerable damage, the interior survived and was restored in 2000. The shop has recovered its historic name and is once more part of a commercial chain of shops. **CWH**

Hill House (1902)

Architect Charles Rennie Mackintosh   **Location** Helensburgh, Scotland
Style Art Nouveau   **Material** Rendered brick masonry

Far outside the city of Glasgow, at the top of a hill in Helensburgh, stands Charles Rennie Mackintosh's (1868–1928) finest domestic project: Hill House is a lesson in the manipulation of light, construction, and the art of interior design. It is the epitome of Mackintosh's holistic approach to architecture both within and without. While he was widely venerated in turn-of-the-century Vienna, where enthusiasm for Art Nouveau was at its peak, Mackintosh's stark white walls with delicate flower stenciled designs were not fully appreciated in Victorian Britain. However, he had the perfect patron in wealthy publisher Walter Blackie. On receiving the commission for Blackie's family home, Mackintosh spent many months with the Blackies, gaining an insight into the needs of their way of life. He then worked on the interior layout before starting on the exterior elevations.

The articulation is in the form—every space imagined fully and complete in his mind. With its distinctive cylindrical stair tower, large asymmetric gable-end, steeply sloping roofs, and many small, stone-framed windows set into thick, gray rendered walls, the underlying theme is of a Scottish baronial keep or castle. It even has a tower in one corner, some narrow arrow-slit windows, a parapet, and a gardener's hut that looks like a dovecote. Internally, the home is an orchestrated balance of light and shadow. Furniture and light-fittings, designed with his wife Margaret, line the walls. Hill House is one of the highlights of Mackintosh's, sadly small, Scottish portfolio. **BG**

↗ Mackintosh's design appeals to the Art Nouveau sensibility, eschewing needless ornamentation.

→ This facade displays the unusual combination of Scottish baronial castle and sleek Continental design.

Rue Franklin Apartments (1904)

Architect Auguste Perret **Location** Paris, France **Style** Early Modernist **Materials** Reinforced concrete frame, tile surface

Auguste Perret (1874–1954) came from a family of building contractors and trained as an architect in order to bring the profitable work of design within the capabilities of the family business. This background gave Perret an understanding of how buildings are actually made, far outstripping that of most architects of his time. His buildings have all the classical rigor of his architectural training, combined with the structural logic and technical mastery learned within his family firm—a mastery in particular of the then-new building material, reinforced concrete.

The Rue Franklin apartment block was one of the first fruits of this fertile coupling, although, unusually for Perret, the concrete frame was in this case subcontracted to another builder as being too complicated for the Perret firm at that date. The building uses a concrete frame structure rather than treating the entire wall area as support, and this frame is visible on the outside. To profit from good views, Perret moved the legally obligatory light-well to the street front, producing a C-shaped facade, and enlarged the windows as far as building regulations then permitted. The clear structural framework is enlivened by a symmetrical pattern of bay windows, balconies, tiled panels, and windows flush with the walls. A shop at the bottom and receding balconies at the top increase the visual interest. This attractive building is most famous as the first residential building to use a reinforced concrete structural framework. Modernist critics have often attacked it for the rather flowery ornament on the tile-covered facade; however, it remains a fine piece of architecture. **BWC**

↖ The block shows a firm grasp of construction principles—unusual for an architect of the time.

← Perret has been criticized by Modernists for the building's ornamental tiled facade.

Antwerp Central Station (1905)

Architect Louis de la Censerie **Location** Antwerp, Belgium **Style** Neo-Renaissance **Materials** Stone, brick, marble, iron, glass

Visitors arriving in Antwerp, Belgium's principal port, are invariably astonished by the grandeur of the city's Central Station. It is a cathedral of the railways and one of Europe's most impressive stations. Belgium was an early adopter of railways: the first line, from Antwerp to Mechelen (Malines), opened in 1836. The present building is the third on this site since then.

The ornate station building, by Louis de la Censerie (1838–1909), uses marble and decoration extravagantly in an overblown Neo-Renaissance style, known locally as Léopold II. De la Censerie is said to have been inspired by Lucerne train station in Switzerland and the Pantheon in Rome. An impressive staircase and the giant glass roof dome, centered on an elaborate clock, add to the splendor. Clement Van Bogaert's immense iron and glass roof is 140 feet (43 m) high, 610 feet (186 m) long, and 216 feet (66 m) wide. The building was officially opened in 1905, when Antwerp was a wealthy, thriving port city. Although Belgium is a small country, part of its empire was the Congo basin in Africa, and Antwerp Central Station acted as the European gateway to the Congo's immense wealth. The station has survived two world wars and German occupations. It was designed as a dead-end terminal out of which trains had to reverse. Since 1998, ambitious rebuilding has allowed high-speed train services between Paris, Brussels, and Amsterdam, to travel via tunnels across the city. The station building was restored between 1993 and 2005; it now has three levels and fourteen platforms. One of the world's great railway stations, it must enliven even the dullest daily commute to this European city. **ATB**

↗ Visitors to the station are always astonished by its unexpected cathedral-like grandeur.

→ The architecture is extravagantly overblown and speaks much of the wealth taken from the Congo.

Casa Lleó Morera (1905)

Architect Lluís Domènechi Montaner **Location** Barcelona, Spain **Style** Catalan Modernisme **Materials** Stucco, ceramics, glass

Due to a wave of immigration to Barcelona in the middle of the nineteenth century and to increasingly difficult living conditions, the city's government decided to construct a new district called Eixample ("extension"). This area became a playground for the architects of the Catalan Modernisme (Catalan Art Nouveau), such as Josep Puigi Cadafalch, Antoni Gaudí, and Lluis Domenèchi Montaner. At Passeig de Gracia, Eixample's splendid boulevard, these three masters of Modernisme competed with one another to build the most beautiful house. Domènechi Montaner (1849–1923) was commissioned by industrialist Albert Lleó Morera to transform technically and aesthetically his house. Through his work as an architect, professor, and critic of architecture, Montaner had already played a key role in defining the style of Modernisme. His buildings displayed a mixture of rationalism and fabulous

ornamentation. For Casa Lleó Morera he designed a facade dominated by floral decoration and fluid forms. A round pavilion sits like a throne on the roof, and its shape is echoed in the curved balconies and windows beneath. Inspired by the technology of the era, Montaner incorporated sculptures into the building's facade of women holding a camera, a telephone, a gramophone, and an electric light bulb. The floral designs used in the colorful windows are reminiscent of the work of Louis Comfort Tiffany. Casa Lleó Morera impresses with its serene play of extraordinary decor, ornament, glasswork, and sculpture merging into a fairytale world. This house, along with Gaudí's Casa Batlló and Puigi Cadafalch's Casa Amatiller are each masterpieces of architecture, and although the Barcelona Municipality chose Casa Lleó Morera as building of the year in 1905, the real winner of the competition is in the eye of the beholder. **CH**

Kinloch Castle (1906)

Architects Leeming & Leeming   **Location** Rhum, Small Isles, Scotland   **Style** Edwardian   **Materials** Sandstone with slate roofing

It is always a special thrill to find sheer opulence in the middle of wild countryside. Kinloch Castle is an extraordinary example of Edwardian excess situated on a beautiful but remote island off the west coast of Scotland. Fitted out with the finest furniture and fittings of the period, it survives as one of the richest and most evocative interiors of the Edwardian age. Built for the wealthy industrialist Sir George Bullough, who inherited a massive fortune based on textile production in Lancashire, England, it was a sporting retreat used principally as a base for stalking red deer. Although there had been a previous house nearby, Sir George had it replaced with the present building, a castle in mock Tudor style with Scottish Baronial inflections, laid out around a central courtyard and filled to overflowing with eye-catching furnishings and the latest modern conveniences. Designed by the London firm Leeming & Leeming, building began in

1897, and the red sandstone used for its construction was brought by ship from the south of Scotland. With no expense spared, the house had its own hydro-electric plant, air conditioning, and telephone system, almost unheard-of luxuries at the time. With the finest paneling and furniture, much of it supplied by James Shoolbred & Co. of London, Kinloch Castle was also filled with mementos of Sir George's travels to exotic places. Altogether, it represents supreme Edwardian frivolity in the years before World War I. **NMC**

> *"I can scarcely describe the effect of the crowded Edwardian interior of Kinloch Castle..."*
>
> John Betjeman, writer

Albert Street
Apartments (1906)

Architect Mikhail Eisenstein   **Location** Riga, Latvia
Style Art Nouveau   **Materials** Stone, brick, plasterwork

Albert Street, or Alberta ieia, in Riga is lined with an extraordinarily rich gallery of Art Nouveau apartment blocks designed by Mikhail Eisenstein. Although the five-story blocks are each distinct, they form a continuous streetline of the most astonishing Art Nouveau architecture in Europe. Eisenstein designed the blocks in Albert Street, each one displaying an abundance of ornamental decoration including Jugendstil female figures, plaster sphinxes in pharaonic headdresses, grotesque masks, swirling plasterwork, sternly gazing caryatids, and *passant* (walking) lions. The blocks are decorated with a subtle palette of colors used in Baroque-era buildings in the region. No. 2 Albert Street (1906), with its sphinxes, has a false sixth-story attic, pierced by five balconied apertures. The British philosopher, Sir Isaiah Berlin, was born in the fourth-floor apartment there in 1909. No. 4 (1904) is more exuberant, with its almost Neo-Egyptian entrance. Nos. 6 (1904) and 8 (1903) are also very ornate, with the latter boasting an unexpected lion's head adorning the roofline.

In the early twentieth century, Riga was the third most important city of the Russian empire and was wealthy due to a booming timber export trade. In 1901 it held an Exhibition of Industry and Crafts where the Art Nouveau style gripped the local middle classes. Local architects adapted the style for the growing city and Riga thus has one of the most exciting concentrations of Art Nouveau architecture in the world. **ATB**

⬉ Eisenstein's buildings are dizzying fantasies, with extravagant, theatrical ornamentation.

⬅ Despite the formal symmetry, the buildings' facades delight in multicolored, patterned ostentation.

Palacio de Correos (1907)

Architect Adamo Boari   **Location** Mexico City, Mexico
Style Neo-Classical, Art Nouveau   **Materials** White limestone, marble

The Palacio de Correos (Postal Palace) in Mexico City was built between 1902 and 1907 by Italian architect Adamo Boari (1863–1928). It still serves as the city's central post office today.

At the time of its construction, Mexican president Porfirio Díaz (1830–1915) was keen to emphasize Mexico's modernity, and he commissioned a number of public buildings that tended to imitate grandiose European architectural style. The Palacio de Correos was one such building, along with the Palacio de Bellas Artes opera house, also designed by Boari; both of which are situated in the historic center of Mexico City. Boari favored Neo-Classical and Art Nouveau styles, and the Palacio de Correos is an eclectic and heady mix of these as he sought to give it the look of a European palace.

In 1985 an earthquake caused serious damage to the building, and during the 1990s the Mexican government restored the building according to Boari's original design. The outside of the building consists of a white limestone facade carved with Renaissance motifs. Inside, the elegant main hall has Carrara marble floors and is peppered with stuccoed columns in the form of imitation marble. The central staircase is constructed from wrought iron, as are the counter, tables, and post boxes.

The gold-colored bronzework on the banisters, doors, and windows was made by the Italian Pignone Foundry in Florence. The elaborately decorated plasterwork walls of the lower floor and the two upper floors are visible through the main hall and staircase. The top floor of the Palacio de Correos is separated from the rest of the building by a window covering the staircase, and it houses a museum dedicated to the history of the postal service. **CMK**

Tampere Fire Station (1907)

Architect Olivia Mathilda "Wivi" Lönn   **Location** Tampere, Finland
Style Jugendstil   **Materials** Granite, steel, copper

Although the Tampere Fire Station has something of the fairy castle about it, its pragmatic design still serves its original purpose.

Having qualified as an architect in 1896, Wivi Lönn (1872–1966) won the competition to design it in 1905. She was a Tampere native and the first Finnish female architect to open her own practice. Her reputation paved the way for other Finnish women to take up architecture as a profession. Lönn is perhaps best known for her school buildings around Finland. She was concerned with the functionality of buildings and

> *"It ... incorporated rustification, archaism, Naturalism, Symbolism, and story-telling in its details."*
>
> Jennifer Opie, *Art Nouveau: 1890–1914* (2000)

this is apparent in the Tampere Fire Station, which is designed in the Jugendstil style. The main body of the building is a semicircle, creating more space at the forecourt and allowing more room for practicalities. The tower, in which the fire hoses were dried, is a traditional feature in such buildings. Inside, the structure is built so that there are fewer columns to disrupt the inner space. The use of natural stone has allowed the building to age well, and although it was constructed during the horse-drawn era, it has proved to be adaptable for modern fire engines.

Lönn was one of the most prominent practitioners of Jugendstil, which came to define Finland's civic architecture. Tampere Fire Station combines the best aspects of Jugendstil: a robust, practical design with an attractive, approachable appearance. **RK**

Unity Temple (1908)

Architect Frank Lloyd Wright   **Location** Oak Park, Illinois, USA   **Style** Prairie, Early Modern   **Materials** Concrete, glass

> *"[He was drawn] to what he called 'the elemental law and order inherent in all great architecture.'"*

William Curtis, architectural historian

⬆ The closed, minimalist exterior reveals little of the open, airy design of the Temple's interior.

➡ Inside, clerestory windows, amber-colored skylights, and pendant lamps balance the weighty architecture.

Frank Lloyd Wright (1867–1959), perhaps the most important U.S. architect of the last century, is widely regarded as the one of the founders of Modernism. His innovative ideas about buildings became as significant as the buildings themselves. The Unity Temple is one such example where Wright synthesized theories on space and human needs. The idea of wholeness and unity is fully expressed in its form, leading one to experience the space both physically and spiritually.

Originally the Unitarian Church in Oak Park wanted a traditional, churchlike space for their congregation, but Wright insisted on redefining the idea of a place for worship and assembly. He wrote, "[It must be] a noble room, for worship in mind, and let that great room shape the whole edifice. Let the room inside be the architecture outside." Thus the Unity Temple, with its massive, monolithic, concrete exterior form reveals itself to be a light-filled, airy room on the interior. It is bound to the earth, but open to the heavens. This contrast between its exterior and interior, and the process of eroding away the solid mass to create a voided space, underline the building's complexity.

The design of the Unity Temple echoes the personal path of spiritual discovery in its procession from street to inner temple. With its multiple pathways leading to the main temple, the journey is a celebration of discovery and arrival, typical of Wright's buildings. This democratic treatment is further reflected in the main temple, where no seat is more than 45 feet (13 m) from the pulpit. The square volume emphasizes symmetry, harmony, and unity, as the congregation surrounds the pulpit within full view of one another. Clerestory windows create the impression of a floating roof and amber-colored skylights emulate "a happy cloudless day," according to Wright, allowing for a truly powerful spiritual experience that is both personal and communal. **AC**

Teatro Colón (1908)

Architects Tamburini, Meano, Dormal **Location** Buenos Aires, Argentina **Style** Renaissance **Materials** Various

Buenos Aires's first opera house, the Teatro Colón (see page 328), opened in 1857. By 1888, the theater was closed, and the building had been sold to a bank because the local government realized the city needed a larger and more modern facility. Construction began in 1889, and it took almost twenty years to complete. The lavish result is a testament to opulence. The initial architect on the project was an Italian, Francesco Tamburini (1846–90), but due to his untimely death, his assistant, another Italian, Vittorio Meano (1860–1904), took over the project until he was assassinated. The building was then completed by Belgian architect Jules Dormal (1846–1924).

The majestic building is typical in style of those built in the city after independence in 1816, drawing on classical European style and in particular that of the French and Italian Renaissance. The building is vast, measuring 26,250 square feet (2,439 sq m). Its imposing facade is harmoniously divided into three distinct sections adorned by windows, columns, arches, and architraves, and is capped by a gable roof. Several entrances allow access for both performers and opera-goers. The main entrance hall has a white marble floor that leads to a wide staircase providing access to the stalls, which then divide to lead up to seating spread across seven levels. The building also houses two other ornately decorated halls. The horseshoe-shaped auditorium is richly decorated in red and gold, and seats 2,478, with room for 500 people standing. It measures 95 feet (29.2 m) in diameter at its narrowest point, 107 feet (32.6 m) at its widest diameter, and rises 92 feet (28 m) high. Suspended from its frescoed 1,043 feet square (96 m sq) dome is a 23-foot (7 m), burnished bronze chandelier lit by 700 electric light bulbs. **CMK**

House Hohe Pappeln (1908)

Architect Henry van de Velde **Location** Weimar, Germany **Style** Art Nouveau **Materials** Stone, timber

The House Hohe Pappeln (Lofty Poplars) is the second home that Belgian architect Henry van de Velde (1853–1957) built for his large family. Located on the outskirts of the old German capital Weimar, it is set within a large garden, surrounded by tall poplar trees, hence its name. Van de Velde is known for his Art Nouveau furniture, but he was also an early pioneer of Modernist design. In 1902, he was invited by the Grand Duchy of Saxony to become the adviser for industrial design and crafts; in the following year he started an arts and crafts seminar, which in turn led to the

> *"Ugliness corrupts not only the eyes, but also the heart and mind."*
>
> Henry van de Velde, architect

foundation of the School of Arts and Crafts in Weimar. This later became the predecessor of the Bauhaus.

It was during this time that Van de Velde built the Hohe Pappeln, primarily to provide large and open spaces for his children to enjoy. Its rather strange exterior is a result of the unusual, asymmetric planning of the spaces inside. All the living spaces seem to flow effortlessly between each other, allowing a freedom of movement unconstrained by the more traditional home layout. A twisting staircase that winds its way up through the floors to the attic forms the heart of the house. Much is made of the generous outside space with a second-floor balcony, raised walkway, and steps down into the gardens both at the front and rear of the house. Hohe Pappeln is a hybrid of old and new house design, unlike any other. **FO**

AEG
Turbine Factory (1909)

Architect Peter Behrens **Location** Berlin, Germany
Style Early Modern **Materials** Steel, glass, brick

The Turbine Factory for the Allgemeine Electricitäts Gesellschaft (AEG) was completed in 1909 by Peter Behrens (1868–1940). AEG was the foremost electrical company in Germany, a pioneer in the development of electrical consumer devices and one of the first companies to develop a coherent brand identity. Behrens was not just an architect; AEG also employed him as an artistic consultant from 1907 onward, aware of the work he had done at the Darmstadt Artists Colony, where his synthesis of art and lifestyle embodied the *Gesamtkunstwerk* ("total work of art") approach. For AEG, he created posters, lamps, and furniture, as well as the company's logo.

The turbine assembly hall is a seminal early modern work, a paean to the triumph of the machine age. Designed in collaboration with the structural engineer Karl Bernhard, the building is monumental. It is also perhaps the first example of a building intended as a corporate symbol. Situated at the edge of the factory complex, it signified AEG's aspirations, paring them down to a simple, Neo-Classical form. Oft referred to as a "temple of power," its form was defined by the function within—the progression of huge industrial turbines along an assembly line. The rhythm of the structural columns mimics the orders of classical architecture, pre-dating the modern movement's often shadowy and unacknowledged relationship with formal arrangements. In an age that favors outsourcing and cost-cutting, the factory has fallen from favor as an architectural archetype **JBL**

⬈ Behrens went further than a traditional architect, his designs extending to the company's hexagonal logo.

➡ For all its status as a Modernist icon, the underlying form is borrowed from the Classical temple.

Ashton Memorial (1909)

Architect John Belcher **Location** Lancaster, England **Style** Edwardian **Materials** Portland stone, Cornish granite, copper

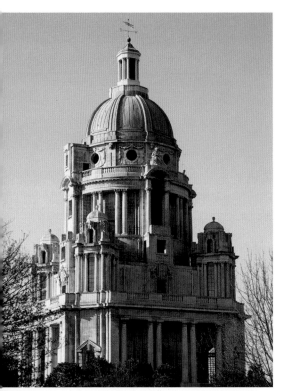

In the latter half of the nineteenth century, Lancaster was the center of British linoleum production, with two firms, Storeys and Williamsons, dominating the industry. The Williamson family became great civic benefactors and paid for Lancaster Town Hall. By the turn of the twentieth century, James Williamson, now Lord Ashton, decided to build a family memorial.

There is nothing modest about the Ashton Memorial; it is Lancaster's most notable landmark from the passing motorway. Its hillside site dominates the city and provides views for miles across Morecambe Bay to the Lake District fells. Its white Portland stone and green copper dome stand in stark contrast to the materials with which nearly every other building in Lancaster was built. The memorial was designed by John Belcher (1841–1913), the author of *Later Renaissance Architecture in England*, which became a textbook for the sort of monumental architecture of which this building is an outstanding example. It stands some 150 feet (45 m) high, built on a platform approached by grand staircases sweeping up from the park. The first floor is square in plan with beveled corners, and the east and west entrance facades have Tuscan screens. Above a rich entablature is a copper dome with a lantern. The whole is richly decorated with sculpture, both within and without. Although described in the *Dictionary of National Biography* as "a gargantuan folly," the memorial was conceived by Lord Ashton as a monument to the second of his three wives who died in 1904. And despite the essentially English classicism of its architecture, Ashton Memorial has a touch of India's Taj Mahal about it. **FK**

⬉ Ashton Memorial is a living symbol of Lancaster's historic importance as a commercial center.

⬅ The Memorial is approached by staircases that would be equally at home in a theater or opera house.

Flatiron Building (1909)

Architect Daniel Burnham   **Location** New York, New York, USA   **Style** Beaux Arts   **Materials** Steel, limestone, terra cotta

One of the oldest surviving skyscrapers in New York, the Flatiron Building (Fuller Building) on Fifth Avenue is significant not only in its unusual appearance but also as one of the key buildings in the Beaux-Arts Classicist movement. Its architect, New York–born Daniel Burnham (1846–1912), is better known for his work and plans in Chicago—the home of the skyscraper—than for that in his city of birth. In 1873 he formed a partnership with John Wellborn Root that was significant in creating the Chicago School.

The commercial office tower scheme, named initially after the building's promoter George Fuller, is situated on a tight triangular site, which gave it its distinctive form, in the Madison Square Park area of Manhattan. Also famed as one of the first buildings to use a steel skeleton, it is constructed in three sections horizontally, like a Greek column, and, unusually for the time, uses extensive lifts. Horizontals are laid out as strongly, as the verticals and the prowlike exterior features a regular, repeated exterior. The nickname, flatiron, comes from its resemblance to the clothing irons used at the turn of the twentieth century. At the very top of its 22-story, 285-foot (87 m) structure, the building is incredibly narrow—just 6.5 feet (2 m) wide.

The Flatiron Building is a popular landmark in the New York landscape for camera-wielding tourists and for the publishers who now inhabit it—so much so that the district it sits in is now named after it. It is a must-see building for its individualism and as one of the early precursors in the development of what would become a dramatic, although aesthetically very different urban building form, the skyscraper. **DT**

↗ The Flatiron Building brings a touch of Chicago to New York, albeit in a particularly idiosyncratic way.

→ The building resembles an old-fashioned clothes iron, although it could also double for the prow of a ship.

Glasgow School of Art (1909)

Architect Charles Rennie Mackintosh **Location** Glasgow, Scotland **Style** Arts and Crafts, Art Nouveau **Materials** Sandstone, glass

The brief for the Glasgow School of Art was a specific one, and a competition was held for an architect to design a "plain building." The winning architect also had to take into account that the site available was a difficult one to accommodate. It was long, narrow, and on a steep incline of 30 feet (9 m). Charles Rennie Mackintosh (1868–1928) beat eleven other architects with his groundbreaking, practical, and fittingly simple design. One of the building's most striking features is the clever use of windows. Tall and slender, they echo the size of the rooms within the building, individual rooms having differently sized windows. Inside the school, maximum use is made of natural and artificial light. As an artist himself, Mackintosh understood the importance of being able to work by natural light. The school's east wing was built between 1897 and 1899; the west wing between 1907 and 1909. The new building included attic studios, a design so popular

that similar studios were added to the east wing. The western doorway is more elaborate than the rest of the building, with its gradation of stone carvings suggestive of an entrance to an Egyptian pyramid. It is a fascinating anticipation of Art Deco design. Externally the building owes a debt to the grandeur of the Scottish Baronial tradition, with its forbidding outer walls, yet the internal spaces are refreshingly modern. It is a building of sharp contrasts: the exterior appearing austere, the interior welcoming. **LH**

"The only art school in the world where the building is worthy of the subject."

Sir Christopher Frayling, rector, Royal College of Art

Gamble House (1909)

Architect Charles Greene, Henry Greene **Location** Pasadena, California, USA **Style** Arts and Crafts **Materials** Wood with platform framing

The Gamble House, built as a winter residence for David and Mary Gamble of the Proctor & Gamble company, is widely considered to be one of the best surviving examples of the Arts and Crafts style in the United States. Charles (1868–1957) and Henry Greene (1870–1954) designed the house holistically, and were responsible for every detail, fixture, and fitting, internally and externally. This approach gave the building great continuity in feel and spirit, and contributes toward it being a domestic architectural masterpiece. The brothers turned to nature for their inspiration and incorporated the Arts and Crafts style along with Oriental details and knowledge of Swiss design, to create a house in contrast to popular U.S. building styles of the time. Although it is a three-story building, the Greenes used the term "bungalow" to describe it because of its low roofs with broad eaves. Inside, the floorplan is fairly traditional with low

horizontal and regularly shaped rooms radiating from a central hall, but the detail and ideals of the house were different. The entire interior is conceived around different types of lustrous wood including teak, maple, oak, redwood, and Port Orford cedar, buffed to glow with a natural and warming radiance that creates a restful and harmonious effect. This was further evoked through the use of stained-glass windows designed to filter soft, colored light into the house. The Greene brothers also developed the concept of indoor-outdoor living, by including partially enclosed porches leading from three of the bedrooms, which could be used for sleeping or entertaining. These spaces, along with the extensive use of wood inside, blurred the boundaries between the interior and the exterior of domestic dwellings. The notion of indoor-outdoor living spaces was one that suited the Californian lifestyle and location of the house very well. **TP**

Masía Freixa, Terrassa (1910)

Architect Lluís Muncunill i Parellada **Location** Terrassa, Spain
Style Modernist **Materials** Masonry, glass

It is hard to believe that this outlandish Modernist creation used to be a factory. Its elegant, open parabolic arches, undulating domed roofs, and minaretlike tower are a joy to behold while its aesthetically pleasing smooth curves seem to ache to be touched. Located in the city of Terrassa, which is known for its fabric manufacturing, Masía Freixa was originally a textile mill. In 1910 it was converted into this Gaudí-inspired, organic yet austere sea of arches as a private residence for the industrialist José Freixa. It was designed by the Modernist Lluís Muncunill i

"Modernism in Terrassa … can be summed up in two simple words … industrial and Muncunill."

Neus Peregrina, curator, Museum de Terrassa

Parellada (1868–1931) who, as the municipal architect for Terrassa, happily applied his knowledge of Modernist principles, especially the Catalan vault, to every type of building from the town hall to industrial warehouses. With a style based on elliptical shapes, he created more than forty buildings in the area, each one more daring than the last, with one of the most celebrated being Masía Freixa.

This white stucco building, with its glimmering glass roof, is situated in the suburbs of Terrassa, within extensive and sumptuous gardens that date from 1917. The town council bought the site in 1958 to create the city's first public park, the Sant Jordi. Masía Freixa remains a lasting testament to a creative architect who helped reinvent a principally industrial town into the unique jewel of Modernist architecture it is today. **JM**

First Church of Christ Scientist (1910)

Architect Bernard Maybeck **Location** Berkeley, California, USA
Style Arts and Crafts **Materials** Reinforced concrete, local wood

Bernard Maybeck viewed the architectural canon as a style smorgasbord. Gothic, Romanesque, Asian, Arts and Crafts, Classicism—all were there to be sampled, interpreted, and reintroduced as California Craftsman. His belief in pure materials—untreated redwood shingles, exposed reinforced concrete, raw timber trellises—was balanced by unbridled curiosity for new materials, colors, and patterns combined in untested ways. But whereas his contemporary Frank Lloyd Wright knew where to stop before exuberance skids into excess, Maybeck's church teeters on the brink between cohesive whole and bricolage assemblage.

Maybeck was influenced by Arthur Page Brown while working on his Swedenborg Church of New Jerusalem (1895) in San Francisco. Brown introduced a key feature found later in Maybeck's work—the incorporation of church and home. Both churches have fireplaces and homespun-style chairs. While central to Brown's design, Maybeck relegates these to an important, but secondary feature with this church.

The wood and concrete exterior is sober in color but no less exuberant in rhythm. A visual mix of Japanese temple and Gothic cathedral, its multilevel, low-pitch gable roof has wide eaves, bargeboards, and trellises. Harlequin-patterned panels and colored diamonds brighten the reinforced concrete between columns and walls. The modular windows are topped with Gothic glazed traceries on the east and west windows. Concrete columns have "nonce" figurative capitals. This mix of classical order with imaginative elements is used to express the soul of the structure and enrich its meaning. This system of "speaking architecture" was taught at the Ecole des Beaux Arts, Paris, where Maybeck studied. It personifies his interplay of the classical with the non-conformist. **DJ**

Robie
House (1910)

Architect Frank Lloyd Wright **Location** Chicago, Illinois, USA
Style Prairie style **Materials** Roman brick, gray stone, steel

The ideal of peaceful, natural, architectural beauty developed in the United States toward the end of the nineteenth century, leading to the birth of the Prairie-style house, an architectural idiom headed by the idiosyncratic architect Frank Lloyd Wright (1867–1959). According to Wright, prairies have "a beauty of their own, and we should recognize and accentuate this natural beauty." A significant landmark in architectural history, Robie House was commissioned by Frederick C. Robie and is one of the last and more mature works in Wright's "Prairie House" series, a supreme example of its revolutionary, for the time, form.

Dominated by horizontal lines and accentuated by the equally horizontal raked brick joints, dramatic overhangs, and big glass windows—especially in the southern front—the elegantly functional open floorplan and low-pitched roof qualify the building for the accolade of the ultimate Prairie-style residence. The house features masonry and Roman brick, and is renowned for its beautiful art glass windows, which bathe the interior spaces with light and color. Incorporating all the elements of the Prairie style, it is also one of the very first houses to include a car parking space in the original design.

Robie House is a Prairie gem, which perfectly demonstrates Wright's well-honed skills and experience. The house has served in the past as a film set and as a gathering place for University of Chicago alumni, and today the Frank Lloyd Wright Preservation Trust operates tours of this extraordinary building. **ES**

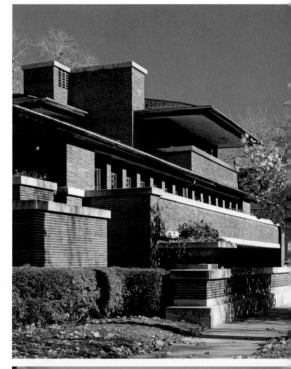

↗ Frank Lloyd Wright famously designed Robie House in 1908 in his iconic studio in Oak Park, Illinois.

→ Robie House values natural beauty, exemplified by the importance of natural light in the building.

Kuala Lumpur Railway Station (1910)

Architect Arthur Benison Hubbock **Location** Kuala Lumpur, Malaysia **Style** British Colonial **Materials** Concrete, iron, glass

All visitors arriving at Malaysia's capital city were once greeted by the astounding spectacle of spires, domes, minarets, and arches that constitute the Kuala Lumpur Railway Station. Sadly this is no longer the case. Falling victim to the inevitable march of modernization, the station now only sees the arrival and departure of commuter trains. Nonetheless the architectural magnificence of the building remains undiminished. Designed by architect Arthur Benison Hubbock, who had previously worked with the British administration in India, the Kuala Lumpur Railway Station makes distinct references to Mughal architecture, a style that prospered in northern India during the Mughal empire (1526–1857). Hubbock designed many other structures on the Malaysian peninsula in a similar style, including the Jamek Mosque, Old High Court, and the Selangor Railway Office Building. However, the Kuala Lumpur Railway Station is a particularly fine example of his

work, self-assuredly demonstrating the grandeur of colonial architecture in old Malaya. Every surface of the station's exterior is painted a pale pink color while the main columns, arches, and domes are painted bright white. This results in the building having a brilliant luminosity, which contributes to its fantastical appearance. The domed minarets at each corner of the four-story building, together with the structure's colonnades, conceal the station's heavy glass and cast-iron train sheds. Although the functional interior of the building conforms to Victorian standards of the age, its confinement within the majestic, Mughal-inspired exterior exemplifies the merger of Eastern and Western influences so prevalent in colonial architecture. Kuala Lumpur Railway Station may no longer be the hive of activity that it once was, but its lavish extravagance remains a sight to behold amid today's skyscrapers and busy highways. **JF**

Steiner House (1910)

Architect Adolf Loos   **Location** Vienna, Austria   **Style** Modernist   **Materials** Reinforced concrete, metal

Adolf Loos (1870–1933) was as much a cultural critic as an architect. His 1908 essay, entitled "Ornament and Crime," became a theoretical manifesto on the Modernist ideal. In it Loos argued that ornament should be eliminated from useful objects; he believed that beauty was in function and structure. Lack of ornament was, to him, a sign of spiritual strength, and excessive embellishment wasted materials and labor in an industrial age. His call for an unadorned style of building was a reaction to the decorative Secessionist movement at the turn of the century. The Steiner House is one of the most emblematic buildings of European Modernism. Built for the painter Lilly Steiner, it was constructed in a Viennese suburb where strict planning regulations stipulated that the street front must be only a single story with a dormer window in the roof. The house extends to three stories at the rear, and Loos cleverly used a semicircular, metal, mansard

roof to slope smoothly down to meet the second floor on the street facade. Loos's belief that the exterior of a house is for public consumption is reflected in the sparse, white walls. One of the first private homes to be constructed from reinforced concrete, the Steiner House established Loos as the pre-eminent Modernist architect outside of Vienna. It became a compulsory reference point for other architects for its radical austerity and extreme functionalism, and is regarded as the first completely modern dwelling. **JS**

"[We should] concentrate . . . upon the production of buildings well formed and comely in the nude."

Adolf Loos, architect

Casa Milá (La Pedrera) (1910)

Architect Antonio Gaudí **Location** Barcelona, Spain **Style** Catalan Modernisme, Art Nouveau **Materials** Stone, brick, iron, mosaic

Casa Milá, or La Pedrera (The Quarry), was designed by the famous Catalan architect Antonio Gaudí (1852–1926). It is his largest residential project and one of the most imaginative and magnificent buildings ever created, considered more a piece of sculpture than a building. Gaudí was commissioned to produce La Pedrera by the Barcelona businessman Roger Segimon de Milá and his wife Roser. At the time, Gaudí was the most expensive and famous architect in Spain, renowned for his sculptural and unconventional architecture, influenced by forms taken from nature, and for his use of colored mosaic and tiles.

Located on a large corner site, the structure of the house is open plan with supporting columns, allowing the facade to be load-free. The exterior consists of a series of undulating wave formations in which windows and balconies emerge like caves from the mass of sculptural stone. Among the balconies are abstract iron railings that twist and turn randomly. However, La Pedrera's crowning glory is its roof, which begins by rising up like a giant sand dune, pierced by tiny attic windows and behind this, bizarre, abstract chimney stacks, covered with pieces of colored mosaic. The interiors are just as remarkable; two courtyards act as a central axis rising up through the building with the apartments fitting around the voids and the attic space is made up of a series of brick arches, similar in shape to the keel of a boat, supporting the weight of the terrace roof above.

La Pedrera, like many of Gaudí's buildings, is a total one-off. And although it is loosely described as Art Nouveau, it is unlike any other existing building. **FO**

↖ The central courtyard bears a relatively conventional exterior, compared to the facade that fronts the street.

← La Pedrera has been described as a surreal, lunar landscape, like a Dalí painting come to life.

Casa Comalat (1911)

Architect Salvador Valeri i Pupurull **Location** Barcelona, Spain **Style** Catalan Modernisme **Materials** Stone, glass, wood

This lavishly decorated apartment building is a tale of two facades. While its organic curves and intricate mezzanine balconies are a miracle of stonework at the front, the more imposing undulating curves, bulging protuberances, and colorful tiling at the rear provide a rather different but equally impressive sight.

Designed by Salvador Valeri i Pupurull (1873–1954), a second-generation Modernist architect who trained in Barcelona's School of Architecture, parts of the structure are clearly Gaudí-inspired. Its organic forms and the ornate, balustraded front balconies in particular are very reminiscent of Gaudí's Casa Batlló. The balconies frame a decorated front door that interconnects with the base of a double-story oriel window above. As the eye is drawn upward, it takes in the intricate wrought-iron balconies on the upper levels until it reaches the strikingly decorated crest.

The back facade, covered with arabesque mosaics, flows around an irregular-shaped corner, and above the first level it juts out over the pavement. Elongated bone-shaped stone arches that appear to be melting, hold up the higher stories. Crowning this side of the building is a decorated curving cornice with a large oval perforation at its center. Inside, it is beautifully decorated with carved wooden furniture, bespoke lighting, and stained glass. Now that the exterior facades, glasswork, and wooden blinds have been restored, Casa Comalat once more stands out on this busy street like something from a fairy tale. With this late Modernist creation Valeri undoubtedly helped ensure that the architectural style continued to be celebrated as Barcelona's aesthetic trademark. **JM**

↗ Although this entrance is Gaudí-inspired, the ribbed arches are also reminiscent of cathedral porches.

⬈ A decorated curving cornice with large oval windows crowns one facade of the building.

Flinders Street Station (1911)

Architects James W. Fawcett, Henry P. C. Ashworth   **Location** Melbourne, Australia   **Style** Edwardian   **Materials** Brick, stone

Flinders Street Station is Melbourne's main hub of commuter activity, housing overland and underground metropolitan train lines. A competition was held in 1899 for a new station building to accommodate growing public transport needs. James W. Fawcett (1863–1934) and Henry P. C. Ashworth (c. 1871–1903), both railway workers, won with an opulent design which would provide a grand gateway to the wealthy Victorian city. Placed at a busy city intersection, adjacent to the Yarra River and Princes Bridge, the building itself is unmissable: its bright colors and architectural lines contrast with the surrounding city buildings and developments. The rusticated arch of the main entranceway, aligned diagonally with the southwest corner of Flinders and Swanston Streets, heralds passenger arrival and departure. It encloses a stained glass *lunette* (half-moon window), beneath which are a series of clock faces displaying train

departure times. Above, a grand dome punctuates the skyline, while down at the Elizabeth Street intersection a clocktower draws further attention to the building. Designed to house offices, amenities, the Victorian Railways Institute club, and even a ballroom, the four-story building dominates Flinders Street. Since the building's completion in 1911, the concourse, platforms, and subways have been refurbished, yet old subway tiles bearing the quaintly stenciled words "Do not spit," still provide a source of amusement to today's passengers. Throughout the day people use the steps beneath the main entrance's clocks as a meeting place. Many sit on the steps to watch the pedestrian traffic pass by, themselves watched by people using the opposite street corner who are taking in the view of the station. As night falls, strategic illumination ensures that the building continues to catch the eye. **KW**

Palais Stoclet (1911)

Architect Josef Hoffmann   **Location** Brussels, Belgium   **Style** Vienna Secession   **Materials** Marble veneer over brick

Although located on a Brussels boulevard 570 miles (900 km) from Vienna, Palais Stoclet is perhaps the most iconic of all the Secession movement's creations—not least because as a millionaire's private house its lavish interior has been hidden from the public gaze since its completion. The Secession movement began when German and Austrian artists broke from academic art institutions to start their own movement. The Vienna Secession became a more restrained version of Art Nouveau style. Josef Hoffman (1870–1956) designed the house for Adolphe Stoclet, who allowed Hoffmann and the artist-craftsmen of his newly established Wiener Werkstätte to create complete interiors in which the design of every object was part of the whole. With its marble cladding, bronze edgings, and cascading composition of towers, the exterior of the house is geometrically complex but comparatively restrained; although, in a

dramatic statement, four huge figures by sculptor Franz Metzner stand atop the soaring tower. This is Arts and Crafts with a distinctly Modernist twist. The interior is awash with precious stones and metals, opulent veneers and enamels. The dining room is decorated with one of the most astonishing of all the works of Gustav Klimt. His glittering 46-feet-wide (14 m) frieze, *Fulfilment*, runs in two sections around the room. The Palais Stoclet provides a field day for enthusiasts of fin-de-siècle Vienna. **TBC**

"[Palais Stoclet's] exquisitely spaced openings and light walls are a joy to the eye."

Nikolaus Pevsner, architectural historian

Palais Idéal (1912)

Architect Ferdinand Cheval   **Location** Hauterives, Drôme, France   **Style** Folkloric   **Materials** Stone, concrete, lime, wire

Ferdinand Cheval (1836–1934) was a mailman who spent thirty-four years building the Palais Idéal, a naive and whimsical "fairylike palace beyond imagination." Cheval collected images of the outside world from the pages and pictures in *Le Magazin Pittoresque*, and he included in the facade of his four-sided castle a mix of different architectural styles, periods, and countries. The mix includes diverse visual, religious, and mythological influences from biblical, Islamic, Chinese, Gothic, and Hindu sources. Cheval recorded that his structure was inspired by a dream of 1864 in which he built a fantastical rock palace of grottos. More prosaically, he also claimed inspiration from tripping over a stone while he made his rounds through the eroded landscape of Hauterives. In April 1879, he began his work by collecting stones, eventually taking twenty years to construct the outer walls. Cheval intended to be buried in his unique edifice but, denied by the authorities, he spent eight years building a mausoleum, the Tomb of Silence and Eternal Rest, for himself and his wife in the local cemetery. The fantastic style of this structure was praised by the Surrealists as an example of dream-life entering the real world. Recognition from artistic luminaries such as André Breton and Pablo Picasso made the Palais Idéal a tourist attraction, and the site is now visited by more than 120,000 people annually. In 1969, André Malraux declared the Palais Idéal as a cultural landmark. **JEH**

> *"I thought of Napoleon, who said the word 'impossible' does not or should not exist ... I agree with him."*
>
> Ferdinand Cheval, mailman and architect

Church at Kiruna (1912)

Architect Gustaf Wickman **Location** Kiruna, Sweden **Style** Arts and Crafts **Material** Wood

In 2001 the church at Kiruna was voted Sweden's most beautiful building. It is situated in Lapland, in the northeastern part of Sweden. The church was built for the people of Kiruna by the LKAB mining company, headed by the geologist Hjalmar Lundbohm, as part of the town's foundation in 1900. Lundbohm wanted Kiruna to be an ideal town, and the church to be its centerpiece. He therefore gathered the finest artists, architects, and town planners of the time, including Prince Eugen, who painted the altarpiece, Christian Eriksson, who designed the cross and the gilt bronze statues standing by the edge of the roof, and the architect Gustaf Wickman (1858–1916). "You must build a church which is like a Lapp hut," Lundbohm told Wickman. Based on a slim, stone foundation, the exterior slanted walls ascend and merge into the low, steeply pitched roofs. The exterior is constructed of red-painted wood; inside, beams and rafters of dark timber interweave, creating an exciting setting in which rays of light split and meet in the great room below. The architect has placed large windows in the upper section of the main room to bring light into the dark, lower part of the building. In front of the church stands the detached bell tower, which is also constructed from timber posts and red-painted wood. Covered with winter snow, the contrasting dark red and white presents a wonderful, fairy tale-like scene. However, in reality, the iron ore that led to Kiruna's creation is now proving to be its undoing—the ground on which the town stands is affected by mining-related subsidence. Over the next decade, the center of the town will be relocated, building by building, a few miles northwest of its current site. In its new location, Kiruna Church will continue to enhance the grandeur of the northern lights and the solemnity of the raw Nordic landscape. **SML**

Hôtel Guimard (1912)

Architect Hector Guimard **Location** Paris, France
Style Art Nouveau **Materials** Stone, brick

The Hôtel Guimard (see page 328) was built by the architect as a wedding present to his rich American wife, the painter Adeline Oppenheim. More polemical than his earlier turn-of-the-century houses, such as the Castel Beranger, the Hôtel Guimard is the culmination of his mature Art Nouveau style, and a unified masterpiece of harmonious integration between architecture and decoration. It is arranged over six stories, with a narrow footprint of 968 square feet (90 sq m) per floor, featuring oval room interiors and unique pieces of furniture, as well as an elevator

> *"… the terrifying and edible beauty of Art Nouveau architecture."*
>
> Salvador Dalí, artist

and central staircase. Guimard lit his wife's painting studio with north-facing windows on the top floor, and installed his own office on the ground floor.

The building suggests some of the influences of other Art Nouveau architects, including Victor Horta and Charles Rennie Mackintosh. In particular, the elegant, buff-colored, brick facade displays a fluid and sinuous use of masonry, featuring melting Flemish windows with decorative floral and organic motifs. The building has an irregular arrangement of balconies and windows of different sizes, reflecting the internal structure of the building. Guimard detailed the exterior and interior decoration himself, working with craftsmen in the fabrication of furniture, stained glass, iron gates and balconies, furniture, and even the door locks. **JEH**

Post Office Savings Bank (1912)

Architect Otto Wagner **Location** Vienna, Austria **Style** Early Modern, Secessionist **Materials** Concrete, glass, marble tiles

When, in 1897, a group of architects and artists, including Otto Wagner, Josef Maria Olbrich, and Gustav Klimt, founded the Vienna Secession, their aim was to break away from both architectural historicism and from the excessive over-ornamentation that had characterized Art Nouveau's illogical extremes. This intention did not stop Olbrich from running a frieze of topless dancing girls in relief around the exterior walls of his Secession building of 1897, but nonetheless it was the ideals of the Secession, and Otto Wagner's own handbook, *Modern Architecture* (1895), that paved the way for the clean lines and practical nature of Modernist architecture.

Occupying an entire city block, the massive Post Office Savings Bank (*Postparkasse*; see page 328) in Vienna is one of the cornerstone buildings in the transition from Classical and Historicist architecture to Modernism. It has ornamentation, including, for example, the cast-aluminum, winged female figures atop the cornices, and there are definite Classical elements to the design (evident from the grand symmetry of the facade), but it was the clean functionality of the architecture that proved highly influential. "Nowhere," wrote Wagner in his design proposal, "has the slightest sacrifice been made for the benefit of any traditional form."

Reached via a flight of stairs, the *Kassenhalle* (main public hall) is an atrium, lit by an enormous, arched, glass skylight above. The floor is made up of glass tiles, dispersing light into the sorting rooms below. Compared with the exuberance of some Secessionist decoration, this building is restrained. There is now an Otto Wagner museum in the Post Office Savings Bank, which should inspire visits to other Wagner buildings in Vienna, such as the Kirche am Steinhof of 1907. **GT**

Fagus
Factory (1913)

Architects Walter Gropius, Adolf Meyer **Location** Alfeld-an-der-Leine, Germany
Style Early Modern **Materials** Steel, reinforced concrete, brick masonry, glass

The early twentieth century saw architects beginning to embrace the Machine Age and all the possibilities in construction and design that it encompassed. There was a boom in factory building, with radical evolution in industrial architecture. Walter Gropius (1883–1969), who would later become the founder of the Bauhaus school of design, believed that it was an architect's duty to provide well-conceived working environments for people. He was a utilitarian architect, rejecting ornament in favor of functionalism. He worked with a partner, Adolf Meyer (1881–1929), who translated Gropius's ideas onto paper.

Gropius and Meyer had begun their careers in the office of Peter Behrens when he was designing the AEG Factory in Berlin. After three years, the pair left to form their own practice and their first significant project was the Fagus shoelace factory. While the building refers to Behrens's AEG, they rejected his Classical influences and the heavy stone with which he had built. Instead, their building was the first to have a completely glass facade, the three floors supported by a steel and concrete framework. Its stark linearity places an emphasis on the horizontal and the cubic, the feeling of light and openness enhanced by the apparent lack of structural support at the corners.

This building is essential viewing for anyone wishing to experience what Frank Lloyd Wright called the "etherealization" of a previously solid form of architecture—factory design. It paved the way for a generation of architects to come. **JS**

↗ Fagus is one of the earliest examples of a building containing all the features of International Modernism.

⇥ For the first time in history, a large expanse of clear glass unified a building's interior and exterior.

Théâtre des Champs Elysées (1913)

Architect Auguste Perret **Location** Paris, France
Style Art Nouveau **Material** Reinforced concrete

Auguste Perret (1874–1954), the architect who brought together serious concrete engineering with serious architecture in the early years of the twentieth century, was not initially appointed architect for this avant-garde theater. The Belgian Art Nouveau master Henry van de Velde was to be the architect, but Perret edged him out after his family firm of building contractors was called in to help with the structural design.

The theater is renowned as the first public building using a frame of reinforced concrete for its structure. For the visitor, however, the great elegance of this frame, especially the paired shallow arches spanning the auditorium, is mostly concealed behind understated decorative moldings. Only in the foyer did Perret permit himself a full expression of the frame. Simple cylindrical columns rise through two tall stories, supporting a balcony on their way up, and the beams of the floor level above form a sort of Classical coffering. The Modernist overtones of this expressive concrete structure go remarkably well with the unequivocally Art Nouveau staircase, which appears almost to drip down from the upper floor like candle wax. Outside, a few sculpted panels enliven a characteristically restrained Perret facade. The underlying frame is implied here by the emphasized verticals and horizontals.

One of the first performances in the theater was the 1913 premiere of Stravinsky's *Rite of Spring*, much of it infamously drowned out by fistfights between opponents and supporters of the new sound. **BWC**

↖ This restrained facade gives way to the expressive foyer, which emphasizes the concrete frame.

← The severity of the front facade is broken by the inclusion of lively sculpted bas-relief panels.

Villa San Michele (1913)

Architect Dr. Axel Munthe   **Location** Anacapri, Capri, Italy
Style Architectural fantasy   **Materials** Stone, render

In 1929, this small but exquisite house on the island of Capri became world famous when its owner, the Swedish doctor Axel Munthe (1857–1949), published his memoir of how he built his remarkable home. *The Story of San Michele* details how Munthe, who made his fortune treating patients in Rome, found a series of crumbling, traditional stone buildings on a narrow street in Anacapri, and set about extending and embellishing them to make his fantasy villa, complete with an atrium, studio, dining room, salon, and a large bedroom. Rather than use new materials, Munthe

> *"I built it on my knees ... where I would seek knowledge and light from the radiant God ..."*
>
> Axel Munthe, *The Story of San Michele* (1929)

gathered a wildly eclectic collection of architectural fragments, including Roman columns and mosaics, Norman windows, and Moorish tiles, and incorporated them into the building, which was constructed using local labor. The villa is spread out over several levels, built as it is on a rock overhanging the Gulf of Naples.

Over several decades, Munthe decorated and furnished the house with original pieces that included a fifteenth-century iron bed, English pewter, and an antique head of Medusa that Munthe claimed he discovered on the seabed. The garden features an avenue of cypress trees, a little chapel, a 3,000-year-old sphinx, and the remains of an imperial villa. Shortly before his death in 1949, Munthe bequeathed his house to the Swedish nation. Sweden runs the villa as a museum, and it is now open to visitors. **MF**

Apartments, 26, rue Vavin (1913)

Architects Henri Sauvage, Charles Sarazin   **Location** Paris, France
Style Art Nouveau   **Materials** Reinforced concrete, ceramic tiles

Henri Sauvage (1873–1932) collaborated with Charles Sarazin (1873–1950) between 1898 and 1912 to build apartment blocks for the Society for Hygienic Low-cost Housing. Sauvage had already built one such apartment block in Paris for the society—the unusual building at No. 7, rue Trétaigne, built in 1904, which demonstrated his concern with providing space and light in multiple-occupancy buildings.

Visually and functionally a benchmark building, the six-story apartment block, called the Maison à Gradins Sportive or La Sportive, draws inspiration from Art Nouveau, but presages the International Style in its concern with providing light, airy living spaces. Sauvage and Sarazin designed the block with two dwellings on each floor, and shops at street level. The building is tiered, with each upper floor receding to allow for the implementation of a balcony or *gradin*. This innovation ensured that each apartment had adequate light, and gave the building an almost sculptural aspect. The building facade is in reinforced concrete completely overlaid with rectangular white ceramic tiles, with occasional geometric patterns in navy blue tiles. The blue-and-white tiles are the same as those used throughout the Paris Metro system, supplied by the manufacturers Boulenger. This lends the apartment block a distinctly nautical appearance, reminiscent of a public bath or sports club.

Sauvage's signature buildings include the Paris department store, La Samaritaine (1930), designed with Frantz Jourdain, and the artists' studios on rue la Fontaine. He is probably best known for his simple but ingenious design for the social housing apartment block at rue des Amiraux, Paris, which was completed between 1922 and 1927, and restored in the 1980s by the architects Daniel and Patrick Rubin. **JEH**

Abattoirs de la Mouche (1913)

Architect Tony Garnier **Location** Lyon, France **Style** Industrial **Materials** Concrete, steel, glass

The building now known as La Halle Tony Garnier was built as the city abattoirs of Lyon. Construction began in 1909 but, following completion in 1913, the building was used as a munitions factory during World War I. It reopened as Les Abattoirs de la Mouche in 1928. The abattoir was closed in 1978, and now the vast space of the hall is used for concerts and exhibitions.

Tony Garnier (1869–1948) was one of the greatest French architects and urban theorists of the twentieth century. His plans for *la cité industrielle*, published in 1917, were revolutionary. He proposed—foresaw, as it turned out—urban zone planning and the use of reinforced concrete. His designs anticipated the undecorated, streamlined shapes of the 1920s and 1930s. His sketches, reminiscent of science fiction, were astonishingly progressive for the time.

The abattoir, located in a new industrial zone, reflects his ideas. Processing large numbers of different species of animals required logical workflows, meticulous planning, and space. The main hall is 721 feet (220 m) long, 260 feet (80 m) wide, and 72 feet (22 m) high. The interior is uninterrupted by pillars and the great roof is supported on strong *rotules*—ball-and-socket joints—along the building's sides. It is a triumph of daring engineering, developing from Dutert and Contamin's 1889 designs for the Galerie des Machines in Paris. The external walls have nine large, clear glass windows in descending sizes, which saves on lighting costs. With so many live animals, ventilation and waste clearance were carefully engineered. The vastness and lightness of the space, and the technical innovation are impressive. **ATB**

◹ The majestic facade of the abattoir bears witness to Garnier's work both as an architect and city planner.

◿ The interior is a vast space, uninterrupted by pillars, and a triumph of daring engineering.

Hodek Apartments (1913)

Architect Josef Chochol   **Location** Prague, Czech Republic   **Style** Czech Cubist   **Materials** Brick, render

This corner apartment building in the Prague suburb of Vysehrad, with faceted forms, most visible under the deep projecting eaves, is a startlingly unusual edifice. The placing of the balconies at the apex of the block adds to the dynamism of the form and the sense that the corner column is like a tree.

The Hodek Apartments are among the best representatives of the short-lived style of Cubist architecture in Czechoslovakia, and are loosely based on the contemporary art movement in Paris. The Czechs (who were politically within the Austro-Hungarian empire) viewed Cubism as an opportunity to engage with the European cultural mainstream and "open the windows onto Europe." The small group of architects involved in the movement broke away from the dominant influence of Otto Wagner in Vienna. Josef Chochol (1880–1956) wrote an article in 1913 calling for architecture to capture the effect of speed in the modern world. The architecture also drew on the memory of the "diamond vaults" of late Bohemian Gothic, which were very similar in effect. Old-fashioned ornament, which was still normal for buildings in 1913, was an impediment to this effect, and to the desire to create a sense of space in architecture.

World War I cut the movement short, and Chochol himself moved on to become a strong advocate of a fully developed modern style. For a time, Czech Cubism, which also extended to decorative arts and graphics, was heavily criticized, but it was rediscovered around the time of the "Velvet Revolution" in 1989 and celebrated afresh as a distinctive national style with international connections. **AP**

↗ The plain exterior and angular ground floor windows of the apartments are typical of late Cubist style.

→ The placing of the balconies at the apex of the block adds to the sense that the corner column is like a tree.

Union Buildings (1913)

Architect Sir Herbert Baker   **Location** Pretoria, South Africa   **Style** Imperial Classical   **Material** Sandstone

It is ironic, or perhaps appropriate, that the Union Buildings—rooted as they are in the colonial age—formed the backdrop to the inauguration of Nelson Mandela as South Africa's first democratically elected president in 1994. The architect, Sir Herbert Baker (1826–1946), would have argued that permanent place-making is a more powerful force than passing political opinion. Although he belonged to an imperial culture, his fondness for the South African landscape was born out in his work, particularly in the use of local stone. Cape Town's Rhodes Memorial and a series of homes in Johannesburg demonstrate his belief that an important building should be anchored to its site. Baker's fascination with the interplay of stone, nature, and symbolism of place is exemplified by the Union Buildings. From an elevated base, a semicircular colonnaded main building overlooks an amphitheater set in terraced gardens. The huge wings on either side

are said to represent the English and Boer sides of the political union for which the buildings are named. At 902 feet (275 m) from end to end, this is, in effect, three buildings joined into one. In what is called English monumental style, the Union Buildings are Classical, with Renaissance details such as the two 180-foot-high (55 m) *campanile*-like towers and low-slung tiled roofs. Sir Herbert also designed South Africa House in London's Trafalgar Square, and is famous for his substantial remodeling of the Bank of England. **MJB**

> *"[He extended his clients' power] into the South African wilderness through the idiom of stone ..."*
>
> David Bunn, academic

Hala Ludowa (1913)

Architect Max Berg **Location** Wroclaw, Poland **Style** Expressionist **Material** Reinforced concrete

On June 28, 1911, the final decision was made to build a multipurpose hall—or *Jahrhunderthalle*—for the city of Breslau, which could house exhibitions, sports events, and public rallies. The building, designed by architect Max Berg (1870–1974), is set on a quatrefoil plan, with a centrally positioned, circular, 426-foot-wide (130 m) hall connected by a double-ring foyer to fifty-six auxiliary exhibition spaces offset outward. Each side of the floorplan's main axis is marked by an entrance hall with the main west access point, facing the city center, emphasized by double-story height, and an oval floor. The stepped form of the dome enabled the insertion of a virtually uninterrupted area of exotic hardwood-framed windows, which let in natural light. To provide appropriate acoustic conditions, the walls are partially constructed of concrete mixed with wood or cork. The elevations' concrete finish, textured with the imprints of wooden

shuttering, adds to the brutal charm of the building. It has a well-deserved place in the annals of architecture because of its unprecedented and inventive use of reinforced concrete in the design process of a dome spanning 213 feet (65 m)—at the time of construction, it was the largest of its kind in the world. This pioneering structure marks a turning point in the exploitation of new steel construction methods. UNESCO recognized the building's character by listing it on July 13, 2006 as a World Heritage Site. **BK**

"He created a . . . monumentality without concealing the boldness of his structure."

Nikolaus Pevsner, architectural critic

Lisbon Metro Headquarters Building (1914)

Architect Manuel Norte Jr. **Location** Lisbon, Portugal
Style Art Nouveau **Materials** Teak, mahogany, glass, brick

Gran Teatro de La Habana (1915)

Architects Gerónimo de León, Paul Belau **Location** Havana, Cuba
Style Baroque Revival **Material** Coral limestone

Around 1900, it was not uncommon for those Portuguese who had made fortunes in the colonies to return to Portugal with the ambition of flaunting their new wealth by commissioning extravagant "arriviste" constructions. This structure is a fine example of this trend, which was strongly supported by the teaching of architecture as one of the fine arts in the schools of Lisbon and Porto. It was originally commissioned by businessman José Maria Moreira Marques in 1910 as a luxurious cosmopolitan family house with spacious gardens. The house was among the first in Lisbon to have an elevator, and his children even had a specially designed gymnasium. Upon its completion in 1914 ,the project was immediately awarded the prestigious Valmor architecture prize. In 1950 the house was sold to Lisbon City Council, and in 1954 it became the headquarters building of the Lisbon Metro.

Due to the pristine condition of its original interiors, visiting the building is like stepping back in time. The entire building is in working order, a testament indeed to the high quality of its decorative Art Nouveau apparel and its turn-of-the-century workmanship. Every room boasts ornately decorated cornices and other plaster objects. Some have been adorned with gold leaf. The rooms originally for the entertainment of guests still retain their eclectic character and details, such as purpose-made glass vitrines and dumbwaiters, although these days the rooms are used as offices.

Some of the collection of nineteenth-century works owned by the Lisbon Metro are housed in the building. In fact, a connection with art and culture seems to be an important factor for the Lisbon Metro—numerous public art commissions may be viewed in many of the Lisbon metro stations. **MDC**

Havana's Gran Teatro is the result of a sizeable theater having been enveloped by an even larger and more lavish building. The Gran Teatro de Tacón was constructed between 1836 and 1838. It was designed by Gerónimo de León with master mason Antonio Mayo and carpenter Miguel Nin y Pons, and built by slaves, local laborers, and ex-prisoners.

The current building was erected between 1910 and 1915 by Purdy and Henderson at a cost of over two million *pesos de oro*, after the theater and surrounding land had been purchased by the Galician

> *"… a permanent, vital evocation of cultural and artistic continuity, with universal resonance."*
>
> Alfredo Acosta-Pérez, vice director of the theater

Center of Havana for their club building. Designed by Belgian architect Paul Belau, it represents one of the most important architectural expressions of the Cuban Republican period. The structure's exterior has whimsical visual variations on the Baroque detailing of the city's earlier buildings. The facade, which overlooks Parque Central, is lavishly embellished with curved balconies, windows, cornices, and sculptural groups in Carrara marble by Moretti. The building is crowned with three towers, each bearing a bronze Nike. Notable interior features of the building include the Sala Garcia Lorca (the original Teatro Tacón); an impressive marble staircase curving elegantly up three floors; murals by Fernando Tarazona; ceilings decorated with exuberant Classical frescoes; and a plethora of decorative plasterwork. **JB**

Retiro Station (1915)

Architects Eustace Conder, Sydney Follett **Location** Buenos Aires, Argentina **Style** Edwardian **Materials** Steel, glass, stone, brick

By the start of the twentieth century, the Argentine railway system was one of the largest in the world. The northern-line network terminates in the Estación Retiro Ferrocarril Central Argentino, or Retiro Station, one of the three large terminals in Buenos Aires.

The Retiro Station project crystallized the debates around the changes in British architecture in the period between the Victorian era and World War I. Edwardian architecture combined the possibilities of industry with the Baroque. This particular case reflects the Classical education of Sydney Follett (1883–1935), who studied at the Edinburgh School of Art. Sir Edwin Lutyens, with whom Follett had worked after winning the Pugin Studentship Medal, recommended him to Eustace Conder (1863–1935) for this project in 1911.

The facade is rich in references to buildings such as the National Museum in Cardiff, the Westminster Central Hall, and Cardiff City Hall. A refined sequence of spaces starts at the carriageway. Defined by the colonnade, there is first the access hall, where English Baroque religious architecture is combined with the late Victorian ticket counter. This space, covered by ceramic pieces matching the original floor, provides the transition to the waiting room, a basilicalike hall modulated by a complex decoration of giant ordered columns. Finally, the two 820-foot-long (250 m) steel-and-glass sheds that cover the platforms create an outstanding space. A third train shed and a wing on Avenida del Libertador were part of the original project plan, but neither was ever built. **JPV**

↗ Follett's vaulted waiting room with its coffered dome brought Edwardian dignity to Argentine rail travel.

→ The facade emulates the National Museum, Cardiff, with its Edwardian and Neo-Classical elements.

Torre de los Ingleses (1916)

Architect Sir Ambrose Macdonald Poynter **Location** Buenos Aires, Argentina **Style** Palladian **Materials** Portland stone, brick

Situated in the Retiro area of Buenos Aires, the Torre de los Ingleses, or Tower of the English, was a monument erected by the city's Anglo-Argentine community for the 1910 centenary celebrations of the country's May Revolution. A design competition for the tower was won by the British architect Sir Ambrose Macdonald Poynter, grandson of the founder of the Royal Institute of British Architects. Almost all of the materials used to construct the tower—cement, Portland stone, and red Leicestershire brick—were imported from England. The foundation stone was laid in 1910, and the tower was completed in 1916, its construction having been delayed by the outbreak of World War I.

The 248-foot-high (75.5 m) tower is constructed in an ostentatious Palladian style that was undergoing a revival at the time, and has eight stories. It measures 918 square feet (85 sq m) at its base, and its four corners are laid according to the cardinal points of the compass. The main entrance faces west, and is adorned with stone emblems representing the British Isles: the Tudor rose, the Scottish thistle, the Welsh dragon, and the Irish shamrock. More stonework can be seen one floor up: the British emblems of the lion and the unicorn, the motto of the British monarch, *Dieu et mon droit*—God and my right—and the motto of the English Order of the Garter, *Honi soit qui mal y pense*—shamed be he who thinks evil of it—with shields representing Argentina and Britain. At the top of the tower are four clocks on the four sides, each being 15 feet (4.5 m) in diameter. Five bronze bells weighing three tons each are rung every fifteen minutes in imitation of the bells of London's Westminster Abbey. After the 1982 Falklands War between Argentina and the United Kingdom, the tower was renamed the Torre Monumental, or Monumental Tower, although locals still refer to it as the Torre de los Ingleses. **CMK**

78, Derngate (1917)

Architect Charles Rennie Mackintosh **Location** Northampton, England **Style** Art Nouveau, Modernist **Materials** Brick, timber, glass

Surprisingly, one of the most important examples of early Modern architecture in Britain consists of a remodeled Georgian terraced house in Northampton. What is more, its architect is a Scottish designer best known for his work in the Art Nouveau style.

Charles Rennie Mackintosh (1868–1928) was commissioned to refurbish the house in 1916 by W. J. Bassett-Lowke, a manufacturer of model railways who had a strong interest in continental design. The architect, by now down on his luck and living in London, added two small extensions to the house and provided all the furniture and decorations for the interior. The front door leads directly to the lounge-hall, one of the two most notable rooms in the house. Here Mackintosh moved the staircase to create more space and designed an exotic decorative scheme. The walls were painted a velvety black and then stenciled with a white checked pattern topped by a frieze of blue, green, purple, and red triangles. The triangle motif appears again in the leaded glass of the black staircase screen. Together with the zigzag lines of the fireplace and black-stained furniture, the effect evokes an Expressionist movie set. The guest room at the top of the house is also decorated dramatically, with striped wallpaper and a suite of oak furniture.

Most important of all, however, is the remodeled rear elevation. Here Mackintosh added a new square bay that provided larger rooms downstairs, together with a veranda and balcony for the bedrooms above. The simple, rationalist lines of the extension anticipate the Paris houses of Le Corbusier, that were to be built several years later. **MF**

↗ For the rear extension, Mackintosh designed windows to suit the rooms within, rather than impose uniformity.

➡ The hall-lounge, with its black wallpaper and stenciled yellow inverted triangles, is a decorative tour de force.

Gellért Hotel and Baths (1918)

Architects Artúr Sebestyén, Ármin Hegedus, Izidor Sterk   **Location** Budapest, Hungary   **Style** Art Nouveau, Neo-Baroque   **Materials** Stone, brick, tiles, glass

The Gellért Hotel and Baths face Szabad ság híd (Liberty Bridge) at the foot of Gellérthegy Hill in Buda. Saint Gellért, or Gerard, was pushed from the hill and martyred by heathen Magyars. The hill has long been known for its thermal springs, which are used in the local tradition of spa baths, dating from Ottoman Turkish times. Budapest is a city of spas and the Gellért Hotel and Baths is by far the grandest. Thirteen springs feed thermal pools inside elaborately decorated spa baths built in the Magyaros National Romantic style of Ödön Lechner (1845–1914), who influenced a generation of Hungarian architects.

Lechner used modern materials and technology, decorated with traditional Hungarian motifs. His use of ceramics and color in architecture was innovative. Edwin Heathcote, the architectural historian, considers Lechner to have been "an eccentric genius and prophet of modernism." At the Gellért Hotel, three of his students—Artúr Sebestyén, Ármin Hegedus, and Izidor Sterk—interpreted his ideas with enthusiasm. The interior has glazed, marbled tiles and fine mosaics that shimmer in the warm, steamy atmosphere. The main indoor pool is surrounded by tiled galleries. A semicircular thermal bath lies at one end, and a glass roof slides open in fine weather. The opulent splendor, exotic decoration, and dark recesses combine into a fabulous feast of bath architecture. The main entrance, the corners, and the entrance to the baths are covered with Baroque cupolas. There are sun terraces and an open-air pool outside, carved from the hillside. The whole Gellért complex evokes an era of exquisite luxury and sensual opulence. **ATB**

⬈ The full magnificence of the architects' design is best experienced by bathing in the main pool.

⬅ The imposing 243-foot-long (74 m) entrance hall is covered by an elegant, arched stained-glass roof.

Helsinki Railway Station (1919)

Architect Eliel Saarinen   **Location** Helsinki, Finland   **Style** Jugendstil   **Materials** Granite, copper

Helsinki Railway Station is one of the best-known Finnish landmarks, not only because it is a major travel thoroughfare, but because of its breathtaking design. Eliel Saarinen (1873–1950) won the competition at a relatively early stage of his career, having only graduated as an architect in the late 1890s. The design echoes the then-popular Jugendstil style—a Nordic version of European Art Nouveau—which acted as an early influence on Saarinen, alongside the Arts and Crafts movement and Classicism. After creating an impressive portfolio of buildings in Finland—such as the Finnish National Museum—he relocated to the United States. Later in his career, Saarinen moved on to a more unadorned style, a good example of which is his design for Crow Island School in Illinois.

Helsinki Railway Station is defined by its vertical lines, its rows of windows, and the clock tower. The red Finnish granite makes the building appear weighty, solid, and dynamic—an impression that is reinforced by the stern-faced, gigantic male statues holding lamps at either side of the entrance. These statues have become so much part of the Finnish visual vernacular that they appear as animated characters in advertisements for Finland's national railway. Inside, the ceilings arch high with floods of light, a sight that greatly impresses arriving travelers.

Helsinki Railway Station belongs to a group of fine buildings in the capital that combine international influences with a certain Finnish simplicity. Saarinen's National Romantic style was a strong influence on architects in the fledgling country, working toward a visual style that defined a nation. **RK**

↗ The huge granite statues towering either side of the station contribute to its distinction as a local landmark.

➡ Helsinki Railway Station demonstrates the Jugendstil style that was an early influence on Saarinen.

Basilica of the Sacred Heart of Christ (1919)

Architects Paul Abadie Jr., Louis-Jean Hulot   **Location** Paris, France   **Style** Byzantine Revival   **Material** Travertine stone

The Roman Catholic Basilique du Sacré Coeur is a popular landmark in Paris. The harmonious edifice, built of white travertine stone, is located at the summit of Montmartre, the highest point in the city. From the 272-foot-high (83 m) dome there is a south-facing panoramic view of 18 miles (30 km). At its consecration in 1919, the building was declared not a parish church but a basilica, an independent sanctuary and place of pilgrimage where the Sacred Heart of Christ is venerated. Architect Paul Abadie Jr. (1812–84) designed the basilica, but he died in 1884, and five successive architects continued the work. The last of these, Louis-Jean Hulot, built the 275-foot-high (84 m) bell tower with a garden and fountain for meditation; he also commissioned the monumental sculpture. Abadie had restored several medieval churches, and the style of the structure shows a strong Romano-Byzantine influence. The original idea of constructing the church developed in France after the Franco-Prussian War. It was intended to expiate the spiritual and moral collapse held to be responsible for the defeat of 1870. Many design elements of the basilica are based on nationalistic themes. The portico, with its three arches, is flanked by bronze equestrian statues of French national saints—Joan of Arc and King-Saint Louis IX—by Hippolyte Lefebvre. In the apse is a 5,113-square-foot (475 sq m) mosaic of Christ in Majesty, the world's largest, by Luc-Olivier Merson. **JEH**

" … raise a temple calling for divine protection … in a place that can be seen from all parts of the city."

Joseph-Hippolyte Guibert, Archbishop of Paris

Spaarndammerbuurt Housing Blocks (1921)

Architect Michel de Klerk **Location** Amsterdam, Netherlands **Style** Amsterdam School **Material** Brick

Of the three housing blocks designed by Michel de Klerk (1884–1923) for Amsterdam's growing industrial working class, the third, Het Schip—The Ship—is the best known. While that design loosely resembles a ship, the group of buildings are more significant as an example of the humanitarian and benevolent approaches to social housing that were developed in the Netherlands following the passing of the Housing Act in 1901. Het Schip is in Spaarndammerbuurt, an area of Amsterdam defined by the railway and maritime industries. De Klerk added his own architectural spirit to the letter of the new housing laws and, borrowing from the traditions of craftsmanship associated with the shipbuilding industry, he designed an apartment block that broke with existing utilitarian notions of working-class housing. The city council was outraged that De Klerk's plans included such luxuries as cast-iron window

casements, winged horses, patterned brickwork, and a functionless, yet emblematic tower. However, De Klerk got his way and Het Schip still stands complete with its mastlike tower. It was described as a "worker's paradise," and, given that De Klerk incorporated eighteen different types of apartment into the 102 units, each with its own bath, at that time it probably was. His belief in the expressive capacity of architecture contributed in these buildings to material improvement for thousands of Dutch workers. **GT**

"[De Klerk's] host of imitators ... copy his mannerisms without comprehending his ideals."

Howard Robertson, *The Architectural Review* (1922)

Einstein Tower (1921)

Architect Erich Mendelsohn   **Location** Near Potsdam, Germany   **Style** Expressionist, Early Modern   **Materials** Brick, poured concrete, render

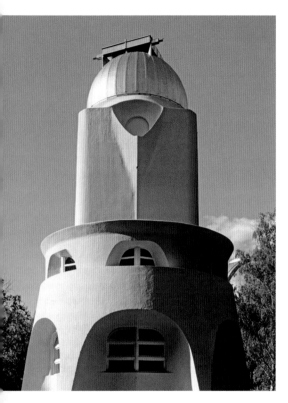

The Einstein Tower by Erich Mendelsohn (1887–1953) is a one-off—a tour de force that defies categorization but which encapsulates a dynamism and a vision of the future for post–World War I Germany. The odd-looking building is an observatory and laboratory, built for the famous physicist Albert Einstein and his research team. Originally it included dormitories for the men who were expected to toil around the clock there, all in the name of science. Einstein's theories of relativity were intended to be put to the test here by German astronomer Erwin Finlay Freundlich.

Constructed from a mixture of brick, concrete, and block render (sadly, the latter has required much maintenance over the years), the scheme unites an underground laboratory with a stationary vertical telescope within a domed observatory. On either side of the building, outcroppings perform as drain spouts, while other unusual features include angled windows placed in streamlined niches, which are themselves molded into rounded corners.

This Expressionist wonder hints at Mendelsohn's military past (he served with the German Imperial Army in World War I), the tower looming up like some lookout post, armored vehicle, or submarine conning tower. But the plan of the building actually owes more to the limitations imposed by its staircases, together with the delicate optical equipment that had to be accommodated. Today, the small, curvaceous, streamlined tower is a national monument, and it is still in use as a working solar laboratory for the Potsdam Astrophysical Institute. It sits as one of a group of beautiful nineteenth- and twentieth-century observatories and scientific institutions at Science Park Albert Einstein, near Potsdam. It is an example of a period of history when a new freedom could be glimpsed and then distilled in an eccentric, individual, and highly innovative building form. **DT**

"A man of genius must constantly renew himself, otherwise he is ossified."

Erich Mendelsohn, architect

↑ Light is directed through the telescope in the tower to the underground solar laboratory.

→ The overall effect of this highly original building's exterior is one of smooth, molded edges.

Schindler-Chase House (1922)

Architect Rudolph Schindler **Location** West Hollywood, California, USA **Style** Modernist **Materials** Concrete, wood, canvas, glass

The reputation of Rudolph Schindler (1887–1953) languished after his death. He was damned by the faint praise of his mentor, Frank Lloyd Wright, who downplayed Schindler's contribution to his own projects, and overshadowed by a contemporary, Richard Neutra. Designed as a shared studio and home, the Schindler-Chase House, also known as Kings Road House, is radical yet understated, complex but not complicated. It became a prototype for a recognizably Californian style of building. Built of four main materials—concrete, wood, canvas, and glass—the concrete foundation/floor and wood frame give 2,500 square feet (762 sq m) of living space. Three interlocking L-shapes pivot from a central fireplace and provide a system of three studios with bathrooms. Each studio is enclosed on three sides by concrete walls; the fourth is open and faces a communal patio and outdoor fireplace. The sunken lawn beyond

repeats patterns from the house. Schindler created shelter and space through variance of the flat roofline. Ground-floor rooms rise to a clerestory window ventilation system, and open through sliding canvas doors into the enclosed garden. Japanese elements complete the house's grammar. Redwood-and-glass corner window-walls flip and repeat in the adjacent space. Concrete walls are panelized with vertical glass slits between. The house unites the outside world with a shared yet individual interior life. **DJ**

"One of the most original . . . designs of the present century— and one of the most . . . habitable."

Reyner Banham, architectural historian

Imperial Hotel (1922)

Architect Frank Lloyd Wright   **Location** Tokyo, Japan   **Style** Early Modernist   **Materials** Poured concrete and concrete block

If a building, so admired that its parts are reassembled after being pulled down and removed from its site, is not iconic, then what is? Demolished in 1968, the Imperial Hotel in Tokyo by Frank Lloyd Wright (1867–1959) is one of the few works located in Japan of the talented and controversially eccentric U.S. architect. Wright worked for this project beyond his usual style to produce a rich, playful, yet disciplined space that had many references to the architecture of Japan. Wright's design was a redevelopment of the pre-existing and original wooden, Victorian, ultra-luxurious Imperial Hotel, founded in 1890, only a stone's throw away from the emperor's palace. The new hotel was a constellation of small but perfectly formed spaces. Different levels hosted little rooms and unexpected terraces formed an ornate composition around two parallel wings of guest rooms. Cubic forms dominate most of the building's sections. Although these cubic forms utilize the space in a standardized way, amazingly almost every room appears different from the rest—one of Wright's greatest design achievements as far as this building is concerned. The Great Kanto Earthquake of September 1, 1923 struck Japan on the very day of the hotel's grand opening ceremony, strangely defining the hotel's fate. After miraculously surviving that earthquake, the building suffered intermittent irreparable damage in later years from floods, other earthquakes, bombs, and pollution, until the management was finally forced to dismantle it in 1968. However, the building was partially reconstructed in 1970 at the Meiji Mura architecture museum in Nagoya, where it is constantly visited by students of Frank Lloyd Wright's style. The Japanese, in particular, appreciate how the masterpiece of the great architect manages to capture so perfectly the essence and spirit of Japan. **ES**

Hermann and Steinberg Hat Factory (1923)

Architect Erich Mendelsohn **Location** Luckenwalde, Germany **Style** Industrial **Materials** Reinforced concrete, brick, wood, glass

When, in 1921, the Hermann and Steinberg families set up in the hat-manufacturing town of Luckenwalde, Gustav Hermann asked his friend Erich Mendelsohn (1887–1953) to build their ambitious new factory. Mendelsohn was comparatively unknown, but the quality and elegance of his design amply vindicated his appointment. The owners fled Germany in 1939, and the plant became an armaments factory, first for the Nazis and then the Soviets, before being abandoned; it is currently being restored. The bulk of the large site is occupied by top-lit production sheds, roofed with concrete arches on columns. On the central axis of the sheds, both entrances are marked by blocklike Modernist buildings, one housing administrative offices. On the same axis are the remains of the building that gained most attention at the time, although it has long been mutilated. Designing for specialist chemical processes requiring

good ventilation, Mendelsohn gave the roof of this shed a memorable pointed profile that simultaneously assisted with ventilation and produced the definitive image of the factory. Perhaps the aspect to enjoy most, however, is the use of materials. Internally, witness the dignified march of its columns and arches and the easy relationship between their concrete and the timber elements above. The simplicity in the details raises this industrial structure from a plain shed to an expressive architectural statement. **BWC**

"The primary element is function. But function without a sensual component is construction."

Erich Mendelsohn, architect

Stockholm City Hall (1923)

Architect Ragnar Östberg   **Location** Stockholm, Sweden   **Style** National Romantic, Renaissance Revival   **Materials** Brick, stone, copper

Stockholm City Hall stands beautifully on the bank of the Riddarfjärden. Östberg's graceful architecture complements the site perfectly. Two courtyards link offices and ceremonial public spaces beneath the elegant, gently tapering, 348-foot-tall (106 m) tower. The exterior uses dark red, handmade bricks. The picturesque National Romantic southern facade, with its delicate windows, open colonnade, and golden crescent above a minor onion-dome tower, relate handsomely to the shimmering waters. The interior is an architectural hymn to Swedish arts and crafts. The Prince's Gallery, with its colonnade of fifteen pairs of dark marble pillars, is so-called because it has fresco paintings by Prince Eugen of Sweden. The Blue Hall— its excellent brickwork was to be blue-plastered originally—is a covered courtyard, often used as a banqueting hall. The Golden Hall is a magnificent space. Sixteenth-century French Tureholm tapestries adorn the Ovale, which is used for civil weddings. The Council Chamber boasts an imitation open ceiling, reminiscent perhaps of Viking ships' timbers. Östberg also commissioned Sweden's finest craftsworkers to decorate and furnish the City Hall, which took twelve years to construct. Östberg's design, using a low, massive, brick-built box with a dominant tower at the corner, was greatly influential outside Sweden; it can be seen reflected even in Art Deco and Modern factories, civic buildings, and metro stations. **ATB**

> *"[There has been no comparable work] since the Italian cities felt the excitement of the Renaissance."*
>
> W. B. Yeats, Irish poet and statesman

HSBC Building (1923)

Architects Palmer & Turner Architects **Location** Shanghai, China **Style** Neo-Classical **Materials** Concrete, granite

As the last building to be designed by the Hong Kong–based firm Palmer & Turner in the full Classical style, the HSBC Building stands as a proud monument to Shanghai's decadent past. Chief architect George Wilson's simple brief was to "spare no expense, but dominate the Bund," a goal he triumphantly achieved. Even today, despite the towering skyscrapers that face the HSBC Building across the frenetic Huangpu River, it retains its prominence.

The monumental facade is divided vertically into three main parts, with the central section consisting of a gateway topped by imposing Ionic columns. These rise to the fourth story, effectively breaking up the facade and giving support to a heavy cornice, above which rises the spectacular concrete dome, reaching 180 feet (55 m) above street level. Two bronze lions, positioned in accordance with the rules of the Chinese geomantic art of *feng shui*, flank the entrance and guide visitors into the opulent interior. Here, for the first time in Shanghai, Chinese decorative techniques were adopted within a Western-styled building.

HSBC's evident confidence in its own longlasting prosperity was misplaced, however. The bank was occupied by the Japanese in World War II and later seized by the new communist government. The building today serves as the headquarters of the Shanghai Pudong Development Bank. Despite its turbulent history, the HSBC Building continues to bear testimony to the diverse mix of international influences that existed in Shanghai in its trading heyday. It remains as one of the finest examples of Neo-Classicism in Asia. **JF**

↖ Towering above the triple-arched gateway, six Ionic columns dominate the front elevation of the building.

← The monumental bank's crowning dome proclaims Shanghai's success to all who enter the city by river.

Lingotto Fiat Factory (1923)

Architects Giacomo Mattè-Trucco, Renzo Piano **Location** Turin, Italy **Style** Industrial **Materials** Concrete, steel, glass

Traffic, fuel prices, and global warming compromise our appreciation of cars. It has not always been so. The Italian Futurists celebrated speed. Le Corbusier's *Vers une architecture* identified mass production, manufacturing, and transportation as symbols of our time. His manifesto featured Fiat's factory at Lingotto in Turin as the personification of technology.

In the design by Giacomo Mattè-Trucco (1869–1934), raw materials went in at ground level, circulated the ramped five floors, and emerged as cars on the rooftop test track. The track runs the perimeter of the plant's 800,000 square feet (74,320 sq m). After the factory closed in 1982, it was converted by Renzo Piano (*b*. 1937) to a multi-use complex with two hotels, a polytechnic, museum, and shopping area. It was Piano's first chance to display his talent at managing technology and human needs. The internal shopping streetscape is open plan. The steel-beam ceiling supports a glass roof. An alternate system of solid and open web beams creates a contemporary yet industrial pattern repeated throughout the complex.

Piano complements the roof track with a museum and conference center. The boxlike museum is raised on thin footings on top of an original roof structure. Its projecting flat roof looks like a sheet of condenser coils tethered to the main box structure by thin tensile leads at each corner. Piano's transparent *bolla* (onion dome) conference center is located on a projecting slab that abuts a heliport. Although it references traditional trackside media booths and airport control towers, its look is decidedly space age and echoes Piano's biosphere in Genoa. **DJ**

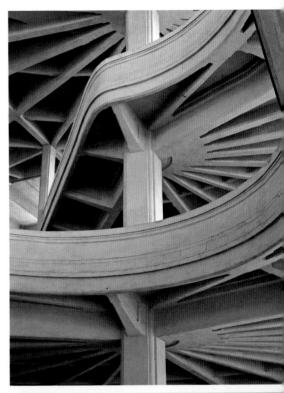

↗ Partly built cars were moved on shallow ramps to assembly areas on higher floors of the building.

➡ Completed cars were tested on this rooftop track before being released from the factory.

Schröder House (1924)

Architects Gerrit Rietveld, Truus Schröder-Schräder   **Location** Utrecht, Netherlands   **Style** De Stijl   **Materials** Brick, steel, glass

Located at the end of a dull strip of houses, the Schröder House is a surprise: small, colorful, and utterly radical. The contrast between solid, middle-class, nineteenth-century taste and a lighter, more open, twentieth-century clarity is starkly obvious. The client, Truus Schröder-Schräder (1889–1985), a young widow, had strong views about her commission for herself and her three children. All rooms had to have a bed, washbasin, and gas-point for a cooking ring.

The ground floor had to conform to local planning rules. By calling the living space an attic, architect Gerrit Rietveld (1888–1964) and Mrs. Schröder were able to create a flexible living area using sliding and movable panels. Colors were radical too: white and gray surfaces with black window and door frames, and including a few features in De Stijl primary colors. Rietveld thought that too much color would compete with the architecture. He was also a furniture maker, and the house illustrates his delightful ingenuity. Space-saving, built-in furniture and fittings were economical and often witty. To reduce costs the house was built with plastered brick, not concrete. The house was light and fun; the children recall jumping over painted lines on the floors.

Truus Schröder lived in the house until her death in 1985. Rietveld and Schröder together created an astonishing spatial work of art—humane, light, and flexible—that changed the way we think about domestic space. In its radical approach to design and the use of space, the Schröder House occupies a seminal position in the development of architecture in the modern world. **ATB**

↖ Rietveld's design was playful and radical. Inside, the distinctive color schemes and lines are repeated.

← With its abstract planes and strips of primary color, the house has been described as "a cardboard Mondrian."

Chilehaus (1924)

Architect Fritz Höger **Location** Hamburg, Germany **Style** Expressionist, Amsterdam School **Materials** Dark red clinker

Henry Brarens Sloman, already originating from a wealthy family, had made a fortune dealing with saltpeter from Chile. When he held an architectural competition for his new office building in Hamburg, he wanted it to be a true status symbol. The architect Fritz Höger (1877–1949) had already built some rather conventional office buildings in the city, clad in Hamburg's most conventional material, clinker.

With the Chilehaus, Höger designed a paradigm for Expressionist clinker architecture in Europe. On an area of nearly 65,000 square feet (6,000 sq m), a massive building block arose with a facade of dark red clinker. The bad subsoil of the site made it necessary to ram 50-foot-long (16 m) poles of iron and concrete into the earth. Being close to the River Elbe, the cellars were especially protected against floods, constructed in the form of a floatable caisson.

Working on the detailed facade, Höger developed a unique style, mixing elements of Expressionism, Gothic, and Art Deco, akin to the Amsterdam School of Hendrik Berlage and Michel de Klerk. He arranged ornamental elements of clinker and ceramics in a playful and lighthearted way, almost completely dissolving the massive bulk of the building's body. Additionally, the uppermost stories are set back, lined by metal railings painted white.

The strong vertical structuring of the facade, the explicit surface structures, the nuances in color of the clinker, and the gently curved flank give the building an additional lightness. All this culminates in the building's sharp prow, which has earned the Chilehaus its popular association with a powerful ship. **FH**

↗ The building is a characteristic example of the urban style of Hamburg's Kontorhaus office district.

→ The clean design lines of the Chilehaus have often been compared to those of a ship.

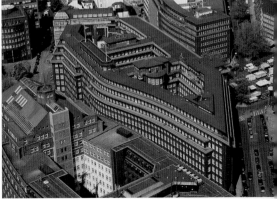

Cathedral Church of Christ in Liverpool (1924)

Architect Sir Giles Gilbert Scott, Son & Partners **Location** Liverpool, England
Style Gothic Revival **Material** Sandstone

High on St. James's Mount, the Cathedral Church of Christ in Liverpool dominates the city and the Mersey estuary. Construction began in 1903 when Liverpool was at the peak of its prosperity as Britain's principal transatlantic port. Despite two world wars, the end of the British empire, and the city's economic decline, work continued—using stone quarried at Woolton—until it was formally completed.

Sir Giles Gilbert Scott (1880–1960) was twenty-two years old when he won the 1903 architectural competition. At first he worked with George Frederick Bodley, architect of the cathedral's Lady Chapel. After Bodley's death in 1907, Scott was sole architect.

The building is the largest Anglican cathedral in the world. The 331-foot-high (101 m) tower impresses by its height and subtle bulk. The lower part is square, punctuated by the maw of the Rankin Porch. The tower tapers to an eight-sided upper stage, topped with a crown of lanterns. The interior spaces awe and impress: the immensely high central tower space; the 457-foot-long (139 m) nave; and the round-arched bridge at the eastern end. Reflecting the wealth of local merchants, the interior is richly furnished with monuments, glass, and furniture.

The painstaking masonry work supported a team of craftspeople for many years. They were involved in training stonemasons working on New York's Gothic cathedral of St. John the Divine, symbolizing the links between the two transatlantic port cities and the international Anglican community. **ATB**

↖ The tower houses the thirteen bells of the cathedral, which have the highest ringing peal in the world.

← The cathedral is made primarily out of sandstone quarried from the nearby suburb of Woolton.

Gut Garkau Farm Complex (1924)

Architect Hugo Häring   **Location** Lübeck, Germany
Style Modernist   **Materials** Concrete, brick, wood

This group of farm buildings is key in the genesis of modern architecture. Hugo Häring (1882–1958) worked closely with Hans Scharoun, a proponent of an organic Modernism whose portfolio includes public buildings such as the Berlin Philharmonic. Häring's oeuvre is more considered, but he had few occasions to demonstrate his principles.

The Gut Garkau complex is perhaps the most demonstrative of his works. A barn and cowshed, grouped picturesquely around a courtyard, the buildings illustrate Häring's belief that architecture

---

"This ... complex has been called one of the masterpieces of modern architecture."

Dennis Sharp, architectural historian

---

should appear to arrive naturally and spontaneously from its surroundings. Eschewing the overstyled organic approach that characterized Art Nouveau and its associated movements, Häring preferred that the structure evolve around its function and environment. The cowshed and barn demonstrate an avoidance of traditional vernacular forms, while remaining recognizably agricultural in their profile and materials.

Häring used concrete, brick, and wood to build the horseshoe-shaped cowshed. Its curving facade is a complex composition of all three components, with bands of structural concrete expressed on the brick lower stories, and the upper levels clad in painted wood. The floorplans were shaped by considerations such as animal welfare, with the concrete construction allowing for a tall, light-filled interior. **JBL**

Casa Planells (1924)

Architect Josep Maria Jujol   **Location** Barcelona, Spain
Style Catalan Modernisme   **Materials** Masonry, stucco, ironwork

Carlos Flores's 1965 assertion that this small residential building is "possibly the most important of [Jujol's] works" is intriguing considering it is the architect's least well-known project. Casa Planells is untypical of Jujol's oeuvre. Compare it with the earthy tectonics of Vistabella Church, the "hallucinated geometries" at Torre de la Creu, or his exuberant collaborations with Antonio Gaudí on icons such as Casa Batlló, Casa Milá, and Park Güell. From the end of Jujol's most creative decade, 1913 to 1923, the building is both pivotal in his own career and a mirror of Catalan architecture's stylistic transformation at the time. Under political and social influences, the "art nouveau" vitality of Catalan Modernisme succumbed to the rationalist stringencies of the International Style championed by Le Corbusier.

Casa Planells stands sentinel at the convergence of Carrer Sicilia and Diagonal, the grand downtown boulevard of the Eixample district. Vigorously modeled and detailed, yet almost abstract in form, it is both cave and a machine for living. The building's appearance results from the third design Jujol executed for the site and his contractor patron Planells. Stylistically an oxymoron—a pure hybrid of Modernisme's undulating vertical surface and almost edible play of light, shadow, and rich texture—it nevertheless expounds Modernisme's lack of ornament, smooth stucco, and uncompromising lines.

Originally it was intended as the pedestal for a monument to the Immaculate Conception. Enigma lies in the spiritual, psychological, and economic voyage the friends must have endured to arrive at this final uncanny artifact; its importance in that its architectural expression so clearly reflects the wider unresolved political contradictions that led to the Spanish Civil War. **MP**

St. La Salle Hall, De La Salle University (1924)

Architect Tomás Mapúa **Location** Manila, Philippines
Style Beaux Arts **Material** Concrete

Capitol Theatre (1924)

Architects Walter Burley Griffin, Marion Mahony **Location** Melbourne, Australia **Style** Art Deco **Materials** Concrete, steel, glass, plaster

Filipino resistance to colonial rule after Spain ceded the archipelago to the United States in 1898 was ended with rifles and superior numbers. But what shaped the Philippines into the most U.S.-like of southeast Asian countries was a typical imperial-style architecture allied to reinforced concrete.

Architecture was part of the U.S. pacification strategy. The imposition of Beaux-Arts monumental buildings as part of the "City Beautiful" movement meant Washington, D.C., Chicago, and Manila would reflect harmony and social order. As part of the new order, the 1903 Pensionado Law awarded U.S. university scholarships to Filipinos. In exchange, they agreed to work on reconstruction projects. Tomás Mapúa (c. 1890–1965) graduated from Cornell University in 1911, and later won the commission to design De La Salle College, now University.

Mapúa's H-shaped, three-story, reinforced-concrete building is pure Classical expression. A triangular pediment crowns an entablature of cornice, frieze, and architrave supported by Corinthian columns to create a three-bay portico main entrance. Wide, open-air portico wings extend from either side; the square openings on the third floor balanced over the rectangular openings of the upper floors' balustrade level. Corinthian pilasters and a dentiled cornice unite the floors between each arch. The interior quadrangle is similarly ordered but stripped to basic flat elements without benefit of pediment and entablature. A later addition of an exterior green metal slope-roof walkway wraps the ground-level quadrangle side. The ground-floor interior offsets Corinthian grandeur with the geometric simplicity of Tuscan columns, and a square-coffered ceiling. Mapúa added a barrel-vaulted Art Deco chapel in 1939. **DJ**

Walter Burley Griffin (1876–1937) and Marion Mahony met in the office of Frank Lloyd Wright, married, and moved to Australia in 1915 on winning a competition to design Canberra, the new capital of Australia. Parliament was then situated in Melbourne, and they set up practice in that city. Their most notable design in the city is Newman College (1918–36).

Further down Swanston Street—Melbourne's so-called "civic spine"—opposite the City Hall, stands another building by Griffin, Capitol House, which includes the Capitol Theatre. The building Walter

> *"A great gift to the city are the discoveries of Marion Mahony Griffin and Walter Burley Griffin . . ."*
> Leon van Schaik, author and academic

Burley Griffin designed was a combination of offices, shops, and the theater—a novel concept in Australia at that time. For the ten-story office block, Griffin's style is Chicagoesque with large horizontal stretches of glazing between flat vertical pilasters.

Only the upper levels of the Capitol Theatre survive today, the ground level's foyer and stalls having been removed to make way for a shopping arcade in the 1960s. The theater's upper level is an Aladdin's cave of V-shaped plaster elements backed with rows of red, blue, and green light bulbs controlled by four dimmers. The theater in a full kaleidoscope of color variations is still an experience today. Saved from destruction by RMIT University, it is used as a lecture theater during the day, and hosts the Melbourne Film Festival, and other events in the evenings. **LVS**

Café de Unie (1925)

Architect Jacobus Johannes Pieter (J. J. P.) Oud **Location** Rotterdam, Netherlands
Style De Stijl **Materials** Concrete, glass

Café de Unie has sometimes been dismissed as "facade architecture" for its eye-catching design that more closely resembles a Piet Mondrian painting than a building. Red, blue, and yellow dominate a three-dimensional geometric graphic design meant to attract passersby into the café. It is typical of the De Stijl movement of which Mondrian, J. J. P. Oud, and Gerrit Rietveld were the main proponents. A utopian movement, it advocated pure abstraction and a reduction to essential form and color. The movement was holistic and spanned art, architecture, and furniture design. The facade of Café de Unie, with its graphic lettering, is quite close in format to the cover of the seminal *De Stijl* journal, the publication created by painter Theo van Doesburg to propagate the movement's theories.

The café was designed by Oud (1890–1963), who was influenced by the esteemed architect Hendrik Petrus Berlage as well as his friendship with Van Doesburg, but developed a formal vocabulary of his own. The commission for Café de Unie came from the Rotterdam Housing Authority, for which Oud was Municipal Housing Architect between 1918 and 1933.

Café de Unie is now located on Mauritsweg, near Rotterdam Central Station. It was built to fill a site on the Calandplein between two nineteenth-century buildings, and was only meant to be temporary. It survived fifteen years until it was bombed during World War II. In 1985 the café was reconstructed 1,640 feet (500 m) from its original site. **KAB**

↗ Café de Unie has provided a popular meeting place for Rotterdam's students and intellectuals.

→ The graphics on the café's facade, shown in this sketch, echo the design of the *De Stijl* journal.

La Sagrada Família (1926)

Architect Antonio Gaudí   **Location** Barcelona, Spain   **Style** Catalan Modernisme   **Materials** Granite, tile

> *"Like a giant, decayed tooth,
> [La Sagrada Família] is full
> of possibilities."*

Salvador Dalí, artist

⬆ The tactile, organic form of the Sagrada Família
is Barcelona's most famous landmark.

➡ The fantastical carved facades of this astonishing
building are laden with Christian symbolism.

Begun in 1882 and still to be completed, the tactile,
organic form of the Roman Catholic basilica of La
Sagrada Família (The Holy Family) is the city of
Barcelona's most famous landmark. In an industrial
setting, it is an unexpected sight, with its bold, flying
buttresses, and twisted towers looming over the city.

Commissioned in 1882, the cathedral was funded
by donations to encourage Christianity in Barcelona,
which was in decline at the time. In 1883 Antonio
Gaudí (1852–1926) took over as chief architect, and
changed the original Neo-Gothic design to one based
on the strange and outlandish geometric forms found
in nature. It was to be Gaudí's Expressionist vision of a
twentieth-century cathedral, where he would use
visual symbolism to express the many mysteries of the
Christian faith.

Gaudí's design and models, most of which were
tragically destroyed during the Spanish Civil War, show
a monstrous form capable of accommodating 13,000
people. Built on a basic basilica plan, the Latin cross is
surrounded on three sides by porticoes. To the east
stands the Nativity facade with scenes celebrating
Jesus's birth, on the west is the Passion facade
depicting the crucifixion, and the main entrance
boasts the Glory facade showing how humans can
celebrate the Divine Glory. Overhead, several huge,
spindle-shaped bell towers rise to the heavens, each
symbolizing different biblical figures: the apostles, the
evangelists, the Virgin Mary and, tallest of all, a central
tower representing Jesus.

When Gaudí died in 1926, only the Nativity facade,
one tower, the apse, and the crypt were finished.
Gaudí knew he would not live to see the completion
of his vision, believing it would take 200 years, but as
he said, "The patron of this project is not in a hurry."
Unfinished it may be, but it is a marvel, and should
Gaudí's vision be realized, it will be a masterpiece. **JM**

Bauhaus (1926)

Architect Walter Gropius   **Location** Dessau, Germany   **Style** International Style   **Materials** Steel, brick, glass

In 1919, German architect Walter Gropius (1883–1969) took over as the master of the Grand-Ducal Saxon School of Arts and Crafts, transforming it into the Bauhaus. In moving the school from its home in Weimar to Dessau in 1925, Gropius had the chance to design a headquarters that expressed the principles of Modernist architecture, while creating the perfect working environment for his pupils.

The building was to serve as a training center, workshop, and residence. True to the principles of Modernism Gropius believed that the structures should differ in style according to their various functions. He separated these areas into three wings—the school and workshop connected via the studio, which is effectively a two-story bridge that spans the road. The studio consists of unbroken glass curtain walls for greater light, and to expose the activity within to external scrutiny. The color scheme also differentiates between the different constructive elements of the building. Much of the tubular-steel furniture was designed by Marcel Breuer. Gropius was keen to point out that the building had experimentally, and successfully, combined diverse aspects of design. In 1933 the Bauhaus was closed by the Nazis, and the building suffered heavy bomb damage during World War II. Today, it is fully restored, and once again open as an institution for research and investigative design.

There are other buildings designed by Gropius in Dessau, such as the Arbeitsamt (1928–29) and the Törten Housing Estate (1926–28), but the Bauhaus remains one of the largest and most innovative Modernist buildings ever conceived. **JS**

◸ Cantilevered balconies create a sense of depth on the facade of the Bauhaus's studio.

◂ The Bauhaus movement went beyond architecture— even the typography of the name proved influential.

Paris Great Mosque (1926)

Architects Robert Fournez, Maurice Mantout, Charles Heubès **Location** Paris, France **Style** Hispano-Moorish **Materials** Marble, concrete

The magnificent Grande Mosqué de Paris (Paris Great Mosque) was built between 1922 and 1926, following the Mudéjar style in a composite Hispano-Moorish design. The architects, Robert Fournez, Maurice Mantout, and Charles Heubès, based their design on plans drawn up by Maurice Tranchant de Lunel, chief of the Beaux-Arts service in Morocco. Partially financed by the French state and constructed on land donated by the city of Paris, the mosque is a memorial to the 100,000 Muslim soldiers who died in World War I fighting with the French Army. The mosque is an active place of worship, and serves as the main religious center for the Islamic community in Paris. The white-walled, green-roofed building surrounds a 108-feet-high (33 m) square minaret, and includes a prayer room noteworthy for its decoration and magnificent carpets, Islamic school and library, and a marble *hammam* (Turkish bath). At the heart of the building is a courtyard surrounded by finely carved colonnades, featuring eucalyptus and cedar wood and modeled on the Alhambra in Granada. The structure is of reinforced concrete, and is decorated with mosaics, floor tiles, green roof tiles, faience ceramics, wrought iron, plaster molding, and carvings illustrating Islamic calligraphy. These materials were imported from Morocco for the interior decoration that was created in situ by North African artists and craftsmen. The mosque's fine gardens, tiled entrance patio, Arabic tearoom, and restaurant cluster around the axis of the central courtyard. Open to the elements, shaded by fig trees, and cooled by fountains, it provides an oasis of calm and seclusion. **JEH**

↗ Although a modern design, the mosque appears much older through its use of the medieval Mudéjar style.

→ The courtyard links the mosque with the architectural home of the Mudéjar style—the Alhambra.

Renaissance Theater (1927)

Architect Oskar Kaufmann   **Location** Berlin, Germany
Style Art Deco   **Materials** Brick, rosewood, wrought iron

Originally built in 1902 by architects Reimer & Körte, the Motiv-Haus experienced a fast history of refurbishments, turning into a double-storey cinema in 1919, and into a theater in 1922. Theater director, Theodor Tagger commissioned architect Oskar Kaufmann (1873–1956) with a complete refurbishment to turn his theater into something special.

The Renaissance Theater was Kaufmann's seventh theater in Berlin, and it was to be his masterpiece before he emigrated to Palestine in 1933. With his previous theaters, he was mostly obliged to the Art Nouveau and Jugendstil movements, continuously developing his idea of the "intimate theater," where stage and auditorium form an architectural unit, pure in form yet rich in materials and detail.

While leaving the exterior of the theater untouched except for a half-round entrance building, he transformed the rooms inside into a fluent play of colors, décor, and materials. Kaufmann uncaged the rooms from their rectangular shells determined by the acute-angled building, through an organic floorplan with curved walls and ceilings. The inside is lavishly decorated with floral ornamentation in stucco and drapery. Corridors and foyers are resplendently colored in shades of blue and green. The walls of the auditorium are clad with French rosewood in dark red, and the back of the curved balcony is covered by a mural of geometrical wooden inlays.

It seems like all of Kaufmann's previous theaters were samples for this one: the architectural strictness of the auditorium and the opulent ornamentation of the foyers are not contradictions, but harmonious parts of a cohesive interior, making the Renaissance Theater a masterpiece of a theater; it is also the best preserved Art Deco theater in Europe. **FH**

Custom House (1927)

Architects Palmer & Turner   **Location** Shanghai, China
Style Neo-Classical Revival   **Material** Concrete

Designed by Palmer & Turner Architects and Surveyors, the most prominent architectural firm in Shanghai in the first half of the twentieth century, the Custom House retains its function upon the historic Bund district to this day.

Situated next to the dominating HSBC Building built four years earlier, also a Palmer & Turner design, the Custom House, like the bank, is Neo-Classical but is simpler and more linear in form, showing the Modernist influences that Palmer & Turner were beginning to adopt. Constructed using reinforced

> *"The Custom House . . . is like a one-hundred-year-old person who can endure anything."*
>
> Zhang Xiaochun, *Walking Shanghai* (2002)

concrete, the Custom House was initially the tallest building in the city having been designed to dwarf the HSBC Building. The extra height came from the addition of a clock tower that rose to 295 feet (90 m). The clock was hailed for its accuracy, having been based upon the design of London's Big Ben; earning the tower the affectionate nickname "Big Ching."

The ten-story, eastern elevation of the building overlooks the Bund, and is faced with largely unornamented granite. At the base of this facade are four massive Doric columns that form the entrance. The columns support a simple shallow cornice, above which begin the vertical strip windows that climb the height of the five floors. They serve to amplify the Custom House's height, and lead the eye up toward the pinnacle of the clock tower. **JF**

Weissenhof
Housing Estate (1927)

Architects Ludwig Mies van der Rohe, others **Location** Stuttgart, Germany
Style Bauhaus **Materials** Concrete, steel, glass, render, brick

The *Siedlung*, or housing estate, fascinated pioneering modern architects: it was a chance to create a grouping of idealized housing that conformed to both aesthetic and social requirements, and was affordable and functional. The Weissenhofsiedlung (Weissenhof Housing Estate) in Stuttgart was built in 1927 to accompany an exhibition by the Deutscher Werkbund (German Work Federation), a trade association that united architects and designers. Ludwig Mies van der Rohe (1886–1969) was its curator, and the resulting roll call of architects presents a snapshot of the first wave of Modernist innovators, including Le Corbusier, Walter Gropius, Bruno Taut, Hans Scharoun, J. J. P. Oud, Mart Stam, and Victor Bourgeois.

The estate's white walls and geometric precision had the unfortunate effect of unifying many disparate architectural approaches, and the Expressionist end of the movement, notably the work of Scharoun, was subsumed by the dazzling render, metal windows and flat-roofed uniformity that ran through the site. The estate was modern, and was seized on with misguided enthusiasm by the burgeoning Far Right, who saw modern architecture as alien and communist. The International Style had arrived into an uncertain world. The estate survived willful neglect by the Nazis, and the apartments have been protected structures in Germany for more than half a century. All are still inhabited, although some were damaged in World War II and rebuilt in the 1980s. One of the Le Corbusier houses is now the Weissenhofmuseum. **JBL**

↗ The Weissenhof estate remains one of the most important Modernist constructions in Germany.

⇥ The boldness and unrepentant starkness of the design was considered degenerate by the Nazis.

Fox Theatre (1928)

Architect Charles Howard Crane   **Location** Detroit, Michigan, USA   **Style** Oriental, Art Deco   **Materials** Steel, concrete

The Fox Theatre is referred to as the "jewel of Detroit," and was built in 1928 for William Fox, founder of 20th Century Fox. It was designed for maximum visual effect: it is a towering ten-story structure, with an Art Deco facade, and opulent entrance. It was the first of the Fox Theatres to be built, and it is the largest, with a seating capacity of 5,045 spread over three levels. It is also the second largest theater in the United States, behind Radio City Music Hall, New York. Revolutionary for its time, it was the first movie theater to be built with sophisticated sound-engineering equipment that catered for talking movies. The extent of the building's innovations and lavish decor was reflected in its estimated $12 million cost. The interior of the theater is as sumptuous and unusual as the exterior, and is full of rich Oriental decor, blood-red marble columns, and silk wall hangings. The vast lobby area is covered with the largest wool rug ever made by a U.S.

manufacturer. The building was planned down to the last detail, including 3-foot (0.9 m) aisles between the rows of seats to allow a clear passage without disturbing people. The architect responsible for this landmark theater was Charles Howard Crane (1885–1952) who designed 250 theaters across the United States with more than fifty of them in the Detroit area. The scale of his theater projects propelled him to be a leader in his field, and his influence subsequently extended across the country. **TP**

"Detroit's Fox Theatre has the largest clear span balcony in the world."

Detroit Free Press (1928)

Second Goetheanum (1928)

Architect Rudolf Steiner   **Location** Dornach, Switzerland   **Style** Expressionist   **Material** Concrete

Rudolf Steiner (1861–1925), a scholar of the works of the poet, dramatist, novelist, and scientist Johann Wolfgang von Goethe, founded the Anthroposophical Society in 1912, as a breakaway from the Theosophical Society. Goethe's ideas remained central for Steiner, and in 1913 he designed a meeting hall for his followers at a rural site near Basel. The large timber building on a concrete base was completed during World War I, but was destroyed by fire on New Year's Eve, 1922. Steiner adapted the first design for construction in concrete, a project completed in 1928, three years after his death. It is a striking and original building, on a hilltop with fine views amid Alpine meadows, representing his belief that architecture should represent in abstract form the growth principles of nature, with sculptured forms similar to those of the contemporary Expressionist movement in German architecture, although suggestive today of

Frank Gehry's designs with their faceted and concave forms. The interior contains an auditorium with a deep stage, with foyer spaces around it, although without the ornamental detail and stained glass of the First Goetheanum. The fascination of this building lies perhaps as much in the ideas that it represents as in its intrinsic architectural qualities. A visit can be both inspiring and disturbing, for it represents a challenge to mainstream beliefs. There have been a number of architects in different countries since the 1920s practicing according to Steiner's beliefs. Le Corbusier saw it incomplete in 1926 and 1927, and his companion on the visit, Norwegian engineer Ole Falk-Ebell, was convinced that it influenced the design of his chapel of Notre Dame du Haut at Ronchamp. There is a cluster of other Steiner buildings on the site, dating from the period of the First Goetheanum and owing more to Steiner's personal involvement. **AP**

Stockholm
Public Library (1928)

Architect Gunnar Asplund **Location** Stockholm, Sweden
Style Neo-Classical, Modernist **Material** Brick

Gunnar Asplund's (1885–1940) architecture has its origins in Classical architecture, in particular the titanic scale of the stripped-back schemes created by the Frenchmen Etienne-Louise Boullée and Claude Nicolas Ledoux. These nineteenth-century architects forged a Neo-Classicism that is best remembered for colossal speculation, and schemes that swamped their simple detailing with oversized Classical orders.

Public libraries were a new concept in 1920s Sweden, and Asplund went to the United States to research the topic. He noted that libraries were "the meeting place between people and books."

Constructed as part of a designated cultural and administrative quarter around Observatoriekullen (Observatory Hill) Asplund's Stockholm Library is, at its core, a cylinder contained within a box. The "box" is a three-story, U-shaped building, its facade divided horizontally with a monumental entrance, and an ordered run of windows on the upper stories. Above it rises the cylindrical form of the reading room, reached from an internal staircase that ascends toward the rotunda; the approach is articulated so that visitors to the library feel they are ascending into a repository of intellectualism refined into pure geometry. The rings of bookshelves above culminate in a circular roof light. Detailing is minimal, as much a consequence of economic necessity as of Neo-Classical purity. Asplund's architecture is functional, but it presented a confrontational challenge to the functionalist orthodoxy of the Modern movement. **JBL**

↖ The cylindrical shape of the reading room creates a calming, cocoonlike atmosphere to read in.

← Gunnar Asplund's impressive building is the largest public library in Sweden.

Villa Stein (1928)

Architect Charles-Edouard Jeanneret (Le Corbusier) **Location** Garches, France **Style** Modernist **Material** Reinforced concrete

Kameleon Department Store (1928)

Architect Erich Mendelsohn **Location** Wroclaw, Poland **Style** Expressionist **Materials** Glass, travertine, bronze

The Villa Stein is one of a series of white Cubist villas designed for rich, architecturally enlightened clients by Le Corbusier (1887–1965) early in his architectural career. Architects ever since have been haunted by the images of these remarkable houses: stark in their plain materials and lack of ornament, but complex in their arrangement of rooms, staircases, ramps, and windows. The villas proposed a new architectural language derived from industrial and engineering structures, and from planes, boats, and cars.

The Villa Stein is substantially larger than it looks in photographs, and is approached via an entrance lodge. The front is mostly simple; strip windows run the entire width that is otherwise white stucco. The arrangement of doors, balconies, and garage is at once formal and asymmetrical, in a manner that is unmistakably deliberate and uncomfortable. The rear is more complex, with a wide terrace cutting right into the building, and a strong diagonal introduced by the stairs down to the garden. Inside, the straight lines give way in a few carefully chosen spots to S-shaped and parabolic partition walls, and a spiral staircase. There is also a characteristically Corbusian ramp running up through the center of the house.

The Villa Stein has a slightly sad air of being less perfectly made than it ought to be, and not living up to the purity of its early photographs. The sermons it preaches on rebuilding cities went stale long ago. Nevertheless, this is a superb building. The haughtily self-confident oddity of its proportions and eccentricity of its planning seem to defy one to dislike it. So loudly does the building proclaim a superior way of life that one feels guilty to admit that one would be uncomfortable to live there. Its beautiful inhumanity almost seems to mock the lesser mortal. **BWC**

The German Jewish architect Erich Mendelsohn (1887–1953) belonged to the most eminent group of pioneers of Modernism along with Le Corbusier, Ludwig Mies van der Rohe, and Walter Gropius. His talent propelled the realization of some ingenious buildings that defied contemporary trends and technical obstacles, often fusing simplicity with sophistication. His motto—"The primary element is function. But function without a sensual component remains construction"—resonates in his design for a former Petersdorff department store.

> *"Erich Mendelsohn took up the motif of the curved facade . . . and made [it a tool] of Expressionism."*
>
> Sir Nikolaus Pevsner, architectural historian

The building's volume delights with its elegant boldness and uncompromising modern appearance. The facade is made up of horizontal bands of travertine cladding, broken up by bronze cornices, and enormous areas of glazing covering the best part of the elevation. The horizontality of the mass culminates with a gracefully curved-glass corner overhanging the street intersection. The building was designed to turn into a gleaming beacon at night using a sophisticated lighting system of slot fittings placed under windows, combined with bright-colored curtains made of highly reflective fabric and illuminated from inside. The interior complements the external form with a variety of high-quality materials ranging from white Japanese lacquer to mahogany, and benefits from a functional layout maximizing the natural light inside. **BK**

German Pavilion (1929)

Architect Ludwig Mies van der Rohe **Location** Barcelona, Spain **Style** Modernist **Materials** Steel, reinforced concrete, travertine, onyx, marble

An enormous amount has been said about the importance of this small building designed by Ludwig Mies van der Rohe (1886–1969) and a surprising amount of it is true. The original was demolished in 1930 after the closure of the Barcelona International Exhibition, and the present pavilion is a faithful reconstruction from the 1980s. Despite the brief life of the original, it has since stuck firmly in the imaginations of almost all Modernist architects. The basic idea is simple: a flat concrete roof slab supported on a regular grid of cross-shaped steel columns. Partitions divide the space without fully cutting off any area from another. In execution it was slightly less pure than it appeared, with structural supports concealed in some of the partitions to assist the main columns. However, this trivial compromise was outweighed by the beauty of the materials and execution. Mies van der Rohe was the son of a master mason, and truly understood

stone. The travertine base and the onyx and marble partitions were treated with absolute simplicity; nothing distracted from their beauty. The columns were chrome, as were the legs of the special chairs he designed for the pavilion, and which have been in continuous production ever since. The most widely praised aspect of the pavilion has always been its use of space. Undoubtedly the vision the architect offered here has proved of real value: a vision of a future architecture in which minimal structure could be reconfigured flexibly by partitions. In addition, the notion of dividing without fully segregating has inspired many. In the end, the most impressive thing about the German Pavilion is its sheer quality. At a time when most serious Modernist architecture had surfaces of white-painted plaster with slightly wobbly edges, Mies van der Rohe offered a beautifully made and luxurious specimen. **BWC**

Lovell House (1929)

Architect Richard Neutra **Location** Los Angeles, California, USA **Style** Modernist **Materials** Steel, concrete, glass

Six years after immigrating to the United States from Vienna, Richard Neutra (1892–1970) built Lovell House, which was to forge his reputation. It is also known as the Health House because its owner, Philip Lovell, advocated preventative medicine in the form of good diet and exercise. The *Lebensreform* movement that swept from Europe to California in the early twentieth century influenced both Lovell and Neutra. It promoted the lifestyle Lovell sought and Neutra delivered. This was the first U.S.-built, steel frame house. Neutra chose steel for its strength and superior structural capacity but also for the fact that it was seen as "healthier." The steep grade prevented a traditional on-site build so all the components were prefabricated off site. The frame was made in sections and took forty hours to erect. Neutra's biographer says work was held to a "decimal tolerance" to avoid costly changes. This suggests that Neutra anticipated the critical need for dimensional variation control. Low variation means a tight fit, fewer defects, and better appearance. Innovations abound in the house: ribbon concrete walls; expanded metal backed with insulation panels; and balconies suspended from the roof frame. The third-level entry terrace has outside sleeping porches. The lower-level gym extends to an outdoor pool, hung in a U-shaped concrete sling. Vast expanses of glass were introduced to deliver sun and vitamin D, and to ensure oneness with the landscape. **DJ**

"Design me a house that will enhance by its design the health of its inhabitants."

Philip Lovell, owner

Victoria Ocampo House (1929)

Architect Alejandro Bustillo   **Location** Buenos Aires, Argentina
Style Modernist   **Material** Stucco-covered brick

The construction of the Victoria Ocampo House in the late 1920s in Buenos Aires's Palermo Chico district caused a scandal. Like most Latin American cities of the period, Buenos Aires was populated by structures that aped those of European classical architecture. The arrival, therefore, of a building that revealed the influence of the Modernist architect Le Corbusier was shocking to its citizens. Many locals thought that its austerity was more akin to a stable or a factory.

In 1929 Le Corbusier was invited to give a series of lectures in Buenos Aires. Prior to his visit, the

> *". . . she has taken a decisive step in architecture, by constructing a house that causes a scandal."*

Le Corbusier, architect

local writer, critic, and socialite Victoria Ocampo commissioned what would be the first Modernist house in the city. She invited Le Corbusier and a local architect, Alejandro Bustillo (1886–1982), to submit plans for her house, although she had already created her own design. She picked Bustillo.

The resulting white, cuboid three-story structure is built of stucco-covered brick with rectangular windows, large, plain, white rooms, and terraces overlooking the sea. In keeping with the Modernist aesthetic, Bustillo adopted a no-frills approach using clean symmetrical lines and smooth surfaces. Bustillo at this time, however, was more interested in conventional Neo-Classical architecture, and it is said that he disliked the house so much that he refused to have his name on it. **CMK**

Narkomfin Communal House (1929)

Architect Moisei Ginzburg   **Location** Moscow, Russia
Style Constructivist   **Material** Reinforced concrete

The Narkomfin Communal House (Narkomfin Dom Kommuna) was designed by a team of architects and engineers headed by Moisei Ginzburg (1892–1946). Located on Ulitsa Chaikovskogo, just behind the Garden Ring Road in Moscow, this Revolutionary Rationalist masterpiece was a key influence on Le Corbusier's Unité d'Habitation (Housing Unit) design.

A blueprint for communal living, the Narkomfin building housed employees of the Ministry of Finance. It featured Ginzburg's famous, minimal F-units with their innovative, Frankfurt-style kitchens. As well as private living spaces with built-in furniture, the six-story building boasted communal facilities such as a solarium and garden on the flat roof. An adjoining two-story annex held a public restaurant, communal kitchen, fitness center, library, and daycare nursery.

The site and surrounding park itself was an attempt to realize a utopian vision, which came to underpin the aims of the Constructivist movement of the 1920s. It strove to overcome the divisions between city and country by the creation of new "disurbanist" landscapes across the Soviet Union: as Ginzburg put it himself, communes "where the peasant can listen to the songs of larks." The park remains with its complex of housing, communal dining, and freestanding laundry facilities all surgically inserted, preserving as much as possible of the forested, earlier Neo-Classical landscape in which it was built.

The structure of the Narkomfin Communal Hall itself has deteriorated terribly, with some of the units rendered uninhabitable by decomposing walls due to leaks. This uniquely built landscape—dismembered and severely dilapidated with only a few remaining inhabitants—is currently scheduled for demolition by the Russian government. **VB**

Melnikov
House (1929)

Architect Konstantin Stepanovich Melnikov **Location** Moscow, Russia
Style Constructivist **Materials** Brick, glass

A blossoming of avant-garde architecture, art, and design took place in 1920s, post-revolutionary Russia. Konstantin Melnikov (1890–1974) was one of the most original Constructivist architects. He designed the exciting Soviet Pavilion for the 1925 Paris Exposition, as well as six workers' clubs, including the Rusakov. Unusually for a private citizen in the Soviet Union, he designed his own house, just off the Arbat in Moscow.

The geometry of the house's design is complex and ingenious. Two interlocking white cylinders, with walls pierced by dozens of hexagonal windows, meet at the point of a spiral staircase. This means that some rooms are wedge-shaped. The second-floor, double-height study has large, plate-glass windows. The studio above it is filled with diamond-shaped windows. There are 200 windows and apertures in the house, filling it with light. The door at the top of the stairs can open to allow access to both the living room and the sleeping area. A spiral staircase links the studio to the living area. The external walls of the cylinders are built of brick in diagonal frames, creating a honeycomb pattern. Modernist architecture was suppressed during the Stalinist era, but the house survived. Melnikov lived there until his death, and his son Viktor began restoring it in the 1980s, determined to respect the original integrity of his father's creation. Standing in a prime real estate area of Moscow, it is miraculous that the house has survived war, political upheavals, and predatory property developers, thanks to the tenacity and vision of the Melnikovs. **ATB**

↗ The Melnikov House is the best surviving example of the architect's Constructivist work.

→ The hexagonal windows of this unorthodox house add to the exterior's honeycomblike appearance.

E-1027 (1929)

Architect Eileen Gray **Location** Roquebrune-Cap Martin, France **Style** Modernist **Materials** Concrete, steel

The E-1027 house represents a highlight in the career of Ireland's only Modernist architect. Eileen Gray (1878–1976) is now regarded as the most significant woman of early twentieth-century architecture and furniture design. The name "E-1027" is a cipher of Gray's initials, entwined with those of her long-term collaborator Jean Badovici, the Romanian architect. The numbers represent the alphabetical positions of J, B, and G respectively. Occupying an enviable position above Monte Carlo, the house's elegant, white profile emerges from the clifftop it inhabits. The living area's floor-to-ceiling windows overlook the harbor, and the bedrooms face the rising sun—a spatial predilection that Gray displayed throughout her career. The L-shaped floorplan allowed her to keep the social areas of the house segregated from the private spaces. Surplus space contains cleverly concealed compartments that were designed to house specific objects. The rooms were populated with custom-made furniture, including Gray's tubular steel E-1027 table and Bibendum armchair. The house was much admired by the architectural community, and was coveted by Modernist pioneer Le Corbusier, who incurred Gray's wrath by painting eight murals onto its walls. Corbusier's link with the house led to his mistaken identity as its designer, and it is only in recent years that Eileen Gray has received due credit for this compact Modern masterpiece. **JS**

"[Gray] knows that our time, with its new possibilities of living, necessitates new ways of feeling."

Jean Badovici, editor of *L'Architecture Vivante*

Villa Savoye (1929)

Architect Charles-Edouard Jeanneret (Le Corbusier)　**Location** Poissy, Paris, France　**Style** International Style　**Materials** Concrete, steel, glass

Le Corbusier's (1887–1965) most celebrated domestic work encapsulates his Five Points of Architecture—an iconoclastic manifesto for domestic design. Raised up above its site on slender columns, Villa Savoye has a striking presence. The absence of load-bearing walls allows for a free facade and floorplan, with a row of horizontal windows bringing in maximum natural light. A ramped circulation system culminates in the flat roof, where Le Corbusier imagined the enlightened inhabitants of his new architecture breathing in gulps of fresh air, even in the densest suburb. Villa Savoye has retained its iconic status partly because it was never subsumed beneath advancing rows of identical houses. Still alone and, since its restoration, pristine, Villa Savoye represents the tenets of the International Style on a macro scale, with a compact footprint that preserves the landscaping of the site—one of the original rationales for the high-density tower block.

For many years the house was a near-ruin, and even today in its restored state, it is uninhabited, with just a few pieces of original furniture scattered around the space. The villa's concrete construction uses a basic layout grid, with supporting pillars that run through the space allowing the thin concrete walls to be independent of the structure. Villa Savoye has come to represent the domestic ideal for many architects, both in terms of its stark, theoretically guided exterior and in the skilled manipulation of interior space. **JBL**

" . . . a work of consummate artistry in which freedom and order exist in subtle and ever-shifting tension."

R. Weston, *The House in the Twentieth Century* (2002)

Club Náutico (1929)

Architects José Manuel Aizpúrua, Joaquín Labayen   **Location** San Sebastian, Spain
Style Modernist   **Materials** Masonry, metal, wood

The seaside promenade of La Concha overlooks Concha Bay in San Sebastian. Approaching the end, promenaders are presented with what appears to be a beached boat: portholes, mast, and all. This is the ship-shaped Club Náutico, home of the town's royal yachting club, designed to blend in with its harbor surroundings. In 1905 the Royal Club Náutico society managed to get hold of the site of a fish factory that was strategically located at the entrance to the port and bay. There they erected a simple, temporary structure known as "the chocolate box." This served as the clubhouse for more than two decades before the current building was built in its place.

Clearly inspired by its nautical setting, the new building was designed by two twenty-seven-year-old architects: José Manuel Aizpúrua (1904–36) and Joaquín Labayen (1904–74). Both of them were keen proponents of the Rationalist movement, and as a result the design was deliberately linear and symmetric, with a form appropriate to its function. Club Náutico was soon acknowledged around the world as an original Modernist masterpiece, and this enabled the Royal Club Náutico society to attract not only international regattas, but also exhibitions by artists such as Pablo Picasso and Max Ernst.

The building has been recognized as a site of cultural interest, and its classic design has inspired other yachting clubs around the world to build clubhouses according to its groundbreaking, boat-shaped, Rationalist blueprint. **JM**

↖ The clean lines and white hue of the club bring to mind the work of Modernist master Le Corbusier.

← From a distance, the clubhouse has the appearance of a beached boat, waiting to return to the water.

Rusakov House of Culture (1929)

Architect Konstantin Stepanovich Melnikov   **Location** Moscow, Russia
Style Constructivist   **Materials** Concrete frame, glass

As part of the new typologies emerging from post-revolutionary Russia, workers' clubs were certainly one of the most successful. Most young architects of the period proposed buildings that tried to translate the new ideology into innovative architecture. Konstantin Melnikov (1890–1974) was one of the few who actually built workers' clubs, and he took the opportunity to turn this one into his most important building—a masterpiece of the Constructivist movement.

The Rusakov House of Culture (see page 328) visually separates itself from the rest of the city: its plan is introverted as it organizes three main auditoriums around a central space. Particularly forward-thinking for the time was the layout of the halls that could be used as a single space with room for 1,200 seats or subdivided into six distinct room through the use of mechanized, soundproofed panels. The internal layout provides a number of relatively small spaces, but from the outside the building is monumental in scale. Inspired by the dynamism of a tensed muscle, Melnikov deployed a formal vocabulary composed of radical and distinct forms evoking an uncompromising relationship between the club and the surrounding context. This is largely achieved by irrepressibly exhibiting the programmatic elements as part of the aesthetic of the composition. The three bulky masses of the auditoriums stick out to create a perfect synthesis between form and function.

The building triggered much criticism. Stalinists labeled it "a left-wing deviation," while Constructivists condemned Melnikov's symbolism of the human body as too formal. Nonetheless, the Rusakov House represents one of the Modernist movement's greatest peaks in its coupling of form and function, and in the resolution of aesthetic and social issues. **RB**

Medical-Dental Office (450 Sutter Street) (1929)

Architect Miller & Pflueger   **Location** San Francisco, California, USA
Style Art Deco   **Materials** Steel, concrete, terra cotta, marble

To call it "Maya mania" may seem excessive, but the frenzy for all things Mayan that gripped the United States during the 1920s was, quite simply, manic. Universities sent expeditions to the Yucatan peninsula, where the archeological equivalent of a gold rush took place. The media romanticized the Mayans as a mysterious civilization that had suddenly vanished. The effect on U.S. popular culture was electric. The First Lady broke a Mayan vase over a bow to christen a ship, Mayan balls were held, and Mayan architecture was encouraged as the new architectural style.

"There is no reason [why the Mayans] should not be the means of enriching our architecture ..."

Alfred C. Blossom, *New York Times* (1925)

Architect Timothy Pflueger (1892–1946) saw the potential. The "original" city dwellers, the Mayans had anticipated the development of the skyscraper.

At 450 Sutter Street, Pflueger's steel frame skeleton with concrete infill rises twenty-six stories without setbacks. Rounded at the corners, it is clad in monochrome terra cotta tiles. The pattern extends from tile to tile and alternates with solid block areas. Triangular window supports create an upward, zigzag rhythm, and a shadowplay on the facade that references Chichén Itzá's Kululk pyramid. A bronze entrance canopy leads to a lavish lobby. Imported French marble lines the walls to three-quarter height where they meet the step-vaulted, gilded and silvered ceiling decorated with Mayan glyphs. And bronze chandeliers echo the step-vault style. **DJ**

Chrysler Building (1930)

Architect William van Alen   **Location** New York, New York, USA   **Style** Art Deco   **Materials** Stone, stainless steel, chrome

"Art Deco in France found its American equivalent in the design of the New York skyscrapers ..."

John Julius Norwich, architectural historian

⬆ With its supremely Art Deco outline, the Chrysler Building is one of the world's best-known edifices.

➡ The stainless-steel design was intended to catch the sunlight, drawing up the eye from the street.

Following the Paris Exhibition of 1925, Art Deco was in full flight. So too, was the desire of wealthy building patrons—such as car magnate Walter P. Chrysler—to have the tallest possible landmarks shout out their names. The convergence of both of these drives gave birth to New York's Chrysler Building, briefly the tallest building in the world.

Designed by William van Alen (1883–1954), the tip of this most elegant of New York's skyscrapers stands some 1,046 feet (319 m) above the Manhattan sidewalk, but the seventy-seven-floor tower was eclipsed in height terms at least by the Empire State Building, which opened a year later. Entered via a lavish marble and chrome-steel lobby, the building's most notable stylistic treatment is the way it is clad in silver-colored stone. Its Art Deco upper part is decorated with semicircular, stylized Chrysler forms that recall the design of hub cabs, along with radiator-cap and eagle-headed gargoyles at the sixty-first floor level. A seven-story spire of stainless steel pierces the sky, above a sensuous, layered, sculptural form. As a sensational construction celebration akin to a waiter whipping off a plate cover in a restaurant, the entire seven-story pinnacle was first assembled inside the building, then hoisted into place through the roof opening and secured, all in just one and a half hours. This also served to steal a march on competitors and secure the "world's tallest" tag.

Brooklyn-born Van Alen was known for his very tall commercial buildings, but Chrysler is the most celebrated, especially as an elegant, glinting, unique homage to the world of corporate advertising and mercantile wealth. The building is a deft and beautiful counterpoise to the more rectilinear skyscrapers that followed it—an instantly recognizable monument, proclaiming the age of the automobile, New York City, and American capitalism alike. **DT**

High and Over (1930)

Architect Amyas Douglas Connell   **Location** Amersham, England   **Style** International Style   **Materials** Concrete, glass

Set among suburban, Neo-Tudor, semidetached houses and Arts and Crafts–style homes, High and Over was, and still is, uncompromisingly Modernist in its style, design, and materials. The house was designed by New Zealand architect Amyas Connell (1901–80) who greatly admired the work of Le Corbusier. On arriving in Britain, he set up practice with fellow New Zealander Basil Ward, and they quickly became leading exponents of the International Style. Connell was commissioned by Professor Bernard Ashmole, the director of the British School in Rome, who later became director of the British Museum. The house had a Y-shaped ground plan to maximize exposure to sunlight, to protect against wind, and to give the best possible view of the beautiful Misbourne valley from all the rooms. Connell also designed a glazed inner courtyard with a central stairwell that included a fountain projecting water as high as the middle floor. The windows form long bands that wrap around the corners, and on the roof is a series of large, covered roof terraces to encourage outdoor living. At the highest point of the property, a water tower with a lookout platform and covered playground was built. In 1962 the building was narrowly saved from demolition by being successfully split into two separate houses. High and Over is regarded as Britain's first Modernist house, and an important example of the International Style in the United Kingdom. **FO**

> *"... one of the first [houses] in this country to accept the style of Le Corbusier's early villas."*
>
> Nikolaus Pevsner, architectural historian

Castle Drogo (1930)

Architect Edwin Lutyens   **Location** Drewsteignton, Devon, England   **Style** Edwardian   **Material** Granite

By the time, in 1910, that Julius Drewe commissioned Sir Edwin Lutyens (1869–1944) to design his Devon retreat, the architect had become a society favorite, working with the garden designer Gertrude Jekyll to create idyllic, sprawling houses for the new moneyed classes. Drewe wanted a modern interpretation of the traditional family seat. Looming above Dartmoor, the finished building is stark and brooding, topped with battlements and defensive turrets that are pure fantasy. Inside, there is little of the richness of decoration one might have expected from a genuine Tudor castle, and granite walls and floors, wood-paneled rooms, and bare finishes are occasionally lightened by original tapestries and furniture. The floorplan follows the country house ideal, with servants' quarters tucked beneath a series of grand function and reception rooms. It took two decades to construct Drogo, with its austere, finely modeled

elevations, thick-mullioned windows, fluted towers, and overlapping levels of fenestration. The house is, in one sense, an abstract composition equal to any of the great Modernist projects. The extensive use of arched forms in the interior, particularly in the central staircase, brings to mind the later work of Louis Kahn, although admittedly Lutyens's detailing occasionally descended into pure quasi-medieval kitsch. Drogo was donated to the National Trust in 1974, becoming the Trust's first twentieth-century acquisition. **JBL**

" . . . Dramatic effects [are] produced by changing floor levels and a web of masonry staircases."

David Watkin, *English Architecture* (2001)

Church of St. Antoninus (1930)

Architect Karl Moser **Location** Basel, Switzerland
Style Modernist **Material** Reinforced concrete

This late masterpiece of Karl Moser (1860–1936) is a concrete basilica on a busy suburban street. It has six tall windows and a 203-foot-high (62 m) bell tower. The west end is marked by projecting bays formed by the choir galleries. Inside, the gray walls, bathed in color from the stained glass, rise nobly to a coffered barrel vault—the only major curved form in the whole building—supported on square piers.

Moser's reworking of a traditional Romanesque church design in a Modernist material represented a shift in the architect's thinking. He had previously put forward a Neo-Romanesque design, but then he transformed the basic shape in response to Auguste Perret's recently completed Notre-Dame de Raincy. The influence of Perret's simplified medieval form, reinterpreted in concrete and acting as a display case for stained glass, is unmistakable at St. Antoninus, although there are many differences in the balance between window and wall, and the more unified internal space of Moser's design.

A competition was held for the stained glass, and two artists, Otto Staiger and Hans Stocker, both from Basel, were selected. Each window contains a narrative central panel, with a broad surround of abstract color, responding to the grid of concrete mullions. Moser's scheme for the east end was not completed. The furnishings are mostly plain, although the altars are enriched with relief sculpture and Modernist textiles. The whole commission was an act of bravery on the part of the church, which was only beginning to respond to Modernism. Visitors to Basel can enjoy many fine buildings from the early Modernist period, including Moser's central railway station and art gallery, but St. Antoninus is the most impressive in its restrained drama. **AP**

Tugendhat House (1930)

Architect Ludwig Mies van der Rohe **Location** Brno, Czech Republic
Style Modernist **Materials** Steel, reinforced concrete, marble

Mies van der Rohe (1886–1969) built this luxurious private house for Greta and Fritz Tugendhat, a young couple each born to wealthy textile families. The sloping site of the villa allows an unusual organization of the rooms, with the street entrance and service rooms on the top floor, and living areas below.

Shortly after the architect had started early studies for the Tugendhat House (see page 329), he was commissioned to design the German Pavilion in Barcelona, Spain. Some elements—most obviously the travertine floor and the chrome, cruciform steel

---

"Mies's very narrowness permitted his passionate integrity and purifying artistry to come to focus."

William H. Jordy, architectural historian

---

columns—are used in both. Less immediately obvious is the way he applies the ideas of the simple pavilion to the more complex needs of a house. There is a similar system of a roof slab on columns, with partitions providing room divisions within. Here, unlike the pavilion, there are extra rooms on top, staircases, and private areas, but the skeleton is the same.

The domestication of Barcelona ideas is apparent in the design of the windows. An exciting development in the pavilion had been the equivocality between outside and inside resulting from the avoidance of continuous walls. Here, Mies van der Rohe provided windows that, on the main floor, can be entirely lowered into the basement, restoring the openness of the German Pavilion. This house is one of the great buildings of early Modernism. **BWC**

IG Farben Building (1930)

Architect Hans Poelzig   **Location** Frankfurt am Main, Germany
Style Modernist   **Materials** Steel, travertine

The administration building for IG Farben, the German drug and chemical cartel (at its time the fourth largest in the world), was the last major work of one of the pioneers of Modernism. It was also the largest office complex in the world until the 1950s.

On the large site, then at the edge of the city, Poelzig (1869–1936) laid out the longitudinal axis on a curve. The convex side of the arc is oriented toward the city and forms a monumental but daunting gesture. The fenestration is completely regular, in the style often called "stripped Classical," and involves the use of smooth stone facings on a steel and concrete frame. The design is not quite Classical, however, for it retains some of the horizontal emphasis of Modernism.

The office areas are housed in six projecting wings. They are connected in perfect symmetry by the long and slender arc, which is gently curved, containing corridors and more offices. The entrance is positioned in the center of the convex side, with a semicircular gallery above it. Inside, the entrance hall is impressive with flights of stairs rising on either side of a wide, low-ceilinged space. The concave side of the building creates a courtyard with a glass pavilion.

The company was prosecuted and disbanded at the end of World War II because of its connection with Hitler's regime. The building served as the U.S. headquarters for reconstruction in Europe, and was occupied by the U.S. administration until 1995. It reopened in 2001 as part of Frankfurt University, and is now known as Poelzig Bau. **FH**

↗ A plaque at the entrance commemorates those who died as a result of Farben's work with the Nazis.

➡ The grounds were landscaped by Max Bromme, and the building still seems to be standing in parkland.

Hotel Nacional de Cuba (1930)

Architects McKim, Mead & White **Location** Havana, Cuba **Style** Art Deco **Material** Stone

Constructed on a rocky outcrop above the Malecón ocean drive, on the site of an old defensive battery, the Hotel Nacional was the first luxury hotel to be built in Republican Havana. Its construction was initiated by President Gerardo Machado. A deal was struck: the Cuban government would retain a permanent right to use the Presidential Suite, and after sixty years of commercial exploitation by the U.S. developer the hotel would pass to the Cuban state without cost. The Nacional was built in two years and opened on December 30, 1930. It was an immediate hit with important visitors to Havana, including Frank Sinatra, Marlene Dietrich, and Winston Churchill. The main entrance stands at the end of an imposing driveway lined with royal palms—the Cuban national tree. The building is surrounded by broad terraces overlooking the Bay of Havana and encloses an elegant garden with long galleries on three sides; there are several

formal restaurants and a high-ceilinged bar. The famous Cabaret Parisién also stands within the hotel at the northern end of the long, ground-floor lobby. The interior is lavishly decorated with hardwoods, bronzes, tiles, and marquetry in a flamboyant combination of styles from Art Deco through Mediterranean Revival, Neo-Baroque, and Neo-Classicism to Hollywood Hacienda, with such flair that a remarkable visual coherence is achieved. The hotel remains popular; the Presidential Suite is seldom empty. **JB**

" . . . the 'glamour' of film and its 'stars' is an important ingredient in [the Nacional's] atmosphere . . ."

Alejandro G. Alonso, architectural critic

Bacardi Building (1930)

Architect Esteban Rodríguez Castells   **Location** Havana, Cuba   **Style** Art Deco   **Materials** Bavarian granite, brick, marble, brass

The Bacardi Building is one of Havana's principal landmarks, standing on the western edge of the city's historical center. Its architect originally won the international competition for its construction with a Neo-Renaissance proposal, but after visiting the 1925 Exposition Internationale des Arts Décoratifs et Industriels Modernes in Paris he completely reworked his design into an extravaganza of Art Deco style. The facade of the twelve-story building is lavishly decorated with red Bavarian granite inlaid with brass embellishments, including a stylized Art Deco version of Havana's coat of arms. The upper part of the building is faced with glazed terra-cotta reliefs of geometric patterns, flowers, and female nudes by Maxfield Parrish. Its sumptuous interior details include blue mirrors, stucco reliefs, brushed and polished brass, murals, mahogany and cedar paneling, stained and acid-etched glass, marquetry, gold leaf, and pink,

pale green, and black marble from Germany, Sweden, Norway, Italy, France, Belgium, and Hungary—the supplier of marble for the building claimed it contained stone from all the nations of Europe. The lamps and other fittings throughout are superb examples of the Art Deco style, and the atmospheric mezzanine bar has retained all its original furniture and decorative details. The restoration of the Edificio Bacardí by the Office of the City Historian of Havana was completed in 2003. **JB**

> *"... a sort of brilliant* horror vacui *... characterizes all areas, within strict design control."*

Alejandro G. Alonso, architectural critic

Villa Noailles (1930)

Architect Robert Mallet-Stevens **Location** Hyères, Côte d'Azur, France
Style Modernist **Materials** Stone, reinforced concrete, plaster

Van Doesburg House (1930)

Architect Theo van Doesburg **Location** Meudon (Paris), France
Style Modernist (De Stijl) **Materials** Concrete, stucco, glass

One of the Modernist masterpieces of Robert Mallet-Stevens (1886–1945), the Villa Noailles was built for Charles and Marie-Laure de Noailles at Hyères, in the south of France. As he had previously demonstrated at Villa Poiret in Mézy, outside Paris, Mallet-Stevens was a thorough Modernist—embracing the stylish cult of Mediterranean living, sea views, and terraces—but also a Neo-Classicist and functionalist in his industrial design and ornamental features and decoration.

Villa Noailles was extended and modified over ten years and became a place of experimentation in new ideas for interior and furniture design. It was decorated in collaboration with a team of artists: sculptors, glaziers, lighting specialists, ironsmiths, locksmiths, and interior designers, including Louis Barillet, Eileen Gray, Pierre Chareau, Francis Jourdan, Sybold van Ravensteyn, Theo van Doesburg, and Jacques Lipchitz. The French Riviera was a fashionable meeting place for artists and socialites, and guests attracted to the Villa Noailles included Buñuel, Cocteau, Giacometti, Stravinsky, and Poulenc. Man Ray's Surrealist film *Les Mystères du Château de Dé* was partly made here.

The building was constructed using traditional masonry and reinforced concrete with a facade of roughcast plaster. The original design envisaged *une petite maison dans le Midi*—a little house in the south of France—but this evolved into a 19,375-square-foot (1,800 sq m) complex of forty-two rooms, gymnasium, squash court, and swimming pool serviced by twenty servants. The Cubism-inspired garden, by Gabriel Guévrékian, is triangular in plan and is conceived as a descent and ascent along olive terraces, punctuated by pools and channels of water, garden rooms, and small pavilions. The house now hosts exhibitions of photography, design, and architecture. **JEH**

This small house and studio near Paris is the only independent structure realized by Theo van Doesburg (1883–1931), the Dutch artist, writer, critic, theoretician, and founder of the avant-garde magazine *De Stijl*. It is less well known than Van Doesburg's earlier involvements with architecture and urbanism, such as his color concepts for buildings by J. J. P. Oud, among others. Van Doesburg built the house for himself and his wife, Nelly, a concert pianist, but never actually lived there because he died from tuberculosis in Davos in 1931, shortly before the house was ready.

"It seems to be a manifesto against intuitive composition, or rather construction…"

Evert van Straaten, architectural critic

After Nelly's death in 1975 it went to the Dutch state, which uses it as a residence for Dutch artists working in one of Theo and Nelly van Doesburg's artistic fields.

The design concept is based on two cubes. One cube, with a large glass wall facing the north, contains the studio and is raised slightly to allow for a covered terrace underneath. A balcony gives access to a roof terrace on top of the other cube. This second cube, which faces the street, contains a kitchen, garage, and maid's room on the ground floor; on the upper floor are the main entrance, a tiny library, a music room, a small bedroom, and the bathroom. Van Doesburg designed several mosaics and a monumental concrete table for the house. The abstraction of the concept in relation to the actual experience of the spaces evokes Piet Mondrian's robotlike dancing to jazz music. **BL**

Villa
Müller (1930)

Architect Adolf Loos   **Location** Prague, Czech Republic
Style Modernist   **Material** Concrete

In 1908, Adolf Loos (1870–1933) wrote *Ornament and Crime*, a polemic against prevailing fashions for ostentatious ornamentation in fin de siècle Austria. Loos was not calling for the total abrogation of decoration. Instead, he believed that unnecessary ornaments and superficial design were symptoms of a dying society; he wanted craft to be directed toward making perfect utilitarian objects, regardless of cost.

Loos's own architecture is eclectic and often confusing, especially coming from a man widely assumed to have a hatred of the applied arts. The Villa Müller epitomizes this contradiction. From the exterior, the structure is plain and simple; Loos reserves his surprises for inside. To the color-deprived minimalist, Loos's approach is a revelation. The house is a riot of contrasting colors, richly veined marble, bold red radiators, wood paneling, and lacquered ceilings, plus all the trappings of a wealthy bourgeois lifestyle, including a boudoir, dressing rooms, photo studio, and staff quarters. Kitchens and bathrooms were of the highest quality with the very latest technology.

Internal planning was done according to Loos's concept of the "Raumplan," a series of interlocking "contiguous, continual spaces, rooms, anterooms, terraces," that were not unified by a floorplan or grid, but rather allowed to adjoin one another in a freeform arrangement, complete with differences in ceiling height and many floor levels. Loos was adamant that for all its complexity, the house was as straightforward a statement as he was able to make. **JBL**

↗ The plain, unrevealing street facades bear only small, yellow, metal-framed windows in various sizes.

➡ The arrangement of windows at the Villa Müller barely hints at the complex use of space within.

Central Market Halls (1930)

Architects P. Dreimanis, Riga Market Construction Office   **Location** Riga, Latvia   **Style** Functionalist   **Materials** Brick, steel, glass

Crowds of Riga shoppers pass under the main railway line to enter one of Europe's most remarkable markets. Five large, high-roofed halls are lined alongside the former city moat, close to the bank of the Daugava River. They were originally hangars for German Zeppelin airships, built by the German Naval Airship Division at Vainode, in western Latvia. The halls were 787 feet (240 m) long, 137 feet (42 m) wide, and 114 feet (35 m) high. The Germans planned to use the airships to attack St. Petersburg, only 400 miles (643 km) away. In 1917, more airships arrived; new hangars were built to house them, as well as military aircraft. After the war, in 1926, the new Latvian state dismantled the hangars and moved them to Riga. Construction was interrupted in 1928 for reasons of cost, but on November 2, 1930 the market was officially opened. Only the upper parts of the hangars were rebuilt, with concrete and brick facades and lower exterior walls in a mildly Art Deco style. The market was the largest building in pre–World War II Riga. The pavilions provide 615,000 square feet (57,000 sq m) of space for up to 1,250 traders. Each hall specializes in different products—meat, fish, dairy, vegetables, and fruit. The halls have, despite their huge size, a cozy, bustling atmosphere. During the Soviet annexation of Latvia, they declined briefly but since independence, and Latvia's entry into the European Union, they have prospered anew. **ATB**

"Rigans can be proud of having Europe's largest and most updated market in their city."

Aleksandrs Neilands, architectural historian

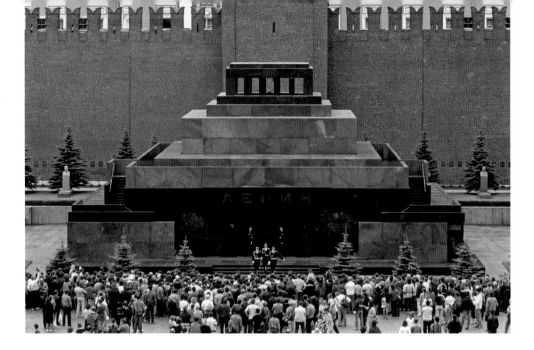

Lenin Mausoleum (1930)

Architect Alexey Shchusev **Location** Moscow, Russia **Style** Constructivist **Materials** Reinforced concrete, brick, marble, labradorite, porphyry, granite

This small but monumental tomb holds the embalmed body of Vladimir Ilyich Lenin, the Russian revolutionary leader and thinker, and occupies an ambiguous position among great architectural structures. To some, the highly polished, ziggurat-like mausoleum is an eternal reminder of a past better forgotten; to others, it is an immortal monument to a cherished history and national leader. Alexey Shchusev (1873–1949) was commissioned to design and build the mausoleum in a short space of time, and initially he erected a temporary wooden structure near the Kremlin Wall, where the stone tomb is now located. His plan was based on a cube, representative of eternity. A primary consideration was the need for a space that allowed a steady progression, from one side to the other, of the many people wishing to pay their respects to their dead leader. The initial wooden structure was replaced by a larger mausoleum, still wooden, with a stepped pyramidal form; there was a platform at its pinnacle from which party officials could make speeches. Eventually the mausoleum was rebuilt in stone. Shchusev was experimenting with Constructivism, while adhering to the example of ancient monuments. The tomb's skeleton consists of reinforced concrete, and the walls are brick faced with highly polished marble, labradorite, porphyry, and granite, creating a somber pattern of red and black throughout. The original floorplan was largely unchanged, with visitors entering through the main entrance and descending down a stairway into the memorial hall. They are guided around three sides of the sarcophagus before ascending stairs to the right of the hall and exiting through a door in the wall of the mausoleum. Shchusev's design was considered a great success, and he was subsequently awarded the Stalin Prize and the Order of Lenin. **TP**

Church of St. Martin (1930)

Architect Arthur Gordon Shoosmith **Location** New Delhi, India
Style Modernist **Materials** Brick, concrete, stone

Plaza de Toros Monumental de Las Ventas (1931)

Architects José Espeliús y Anduaga, Manuel Muñóz Monasterio
Location Madrid, Spain **Style** Neo-Mudéjar **Material** Brick

The construction of New Delhi, as capital of British India, meant the creation of a new military district or cantonment, close to the city, in 1928. A new garrison church was needed. Sir Edwin Lutyens's assistant, A. G. Shoosmith (1888–1974), was delegated the commission. Lutyens encouraged him to use simple brickwork: "My dear Shoo, Bricks! . . . The Romans did it. Why should not Britons? You will get a fine wall, and their mass, proportion, with precious fenestration, will do the rest." Shoosmith ultimately used 3.5 million bricks, partly because the material was cheap and easy to use by a mainly unskilled labor force.

The great tower and its massive brick walls step back to create an austere, monumental building. The use of handcrafted Indian bricks, with very little decoration, evokes a spartan, masculine, military style, reminiscent of adobe frontier forts. Soldiers thought that the church was a fine place to defend in an emergency. Its plan echoes that of English parish churches, hinting at a colonial nostalgia for the familiar forms of Anglicanism. Lutyens's advocacy of massive Roman brickwork forms suggests the often self-conscious identification of British imperial authorities with the grandeur of the Roman empire.

The church was built in the 1920s when Modernist architectural forms in Europe and North America were increasingly in vogue. The architectural historian and critic, Christopher Hussey, felt that, "Had this church been the work of a French or German architect, Europe would be flabbergasted by the magnificently simple and direct design. But since it is the work of an Englishman, it will probably never be heard of abroad." The British military have left, and the church now serves the Church of North India, which runs a school inside the high, cool interior. **ATB**

Situated in the east of Madrid, the Monumental Bullring is one of the most important buildings of its kind in the world—built to enhance Spain's favorite art form. One of Spain's most famous bullfighters, José Gómez Ortega (1895–1920), known as "Joselito," spearheaded the project, and it was his friend, architect José Espeliús y Anduaga (1874–1929), who began work on it. Espeliús had designed various hotels and theaters, including Madrid's Reina Victoria Theater. But Espeliús died before he could see his project realized, and it was completed by Manuel

---

"Bullfighting is the only art in which . . . brilliance in the performance is left to the fighter's honor."

Ernest Hemingway, *Death in the Afternoon* (1932)

Muñóz Monasterio, who later designed the Santiago Bernabéu football stadium.

Designed in Neo-Mudéjar, or Neo-Moorish, style, the outside of the circular building with its horseshoe-shaped arches is adorned with ceramic tilework decoration representing the shields of Spanish provinces. In the center lies the sand bullring arena, 196 feet (60 m) in diameter. The seats around the ring are divided into ten groups of twenty-seven rows each, called *tendidos*. The bullring seats almost 25,000 spectators. The arena has eight gates that allow access for the bulls and horses. A triumphant bullfighter is taken out of the bullring through the largest gate, the Puerta Grande, also called the Door of Madrid. The building now also contains a museum of bullfighting memorabilia, a small hospital, and a chapel. **CMK**

Majorelle House and Studio (1931)

Architects Jacques Majorelle, Paul Sinoir **Location** Marrakech, Morocco
Style Art Deco, Islamic **Materials** Stone, concrete, timber

This house and its blue studio—painted *à l'ouvrier blue*, a color inspired by that of French workers' overalls—is set in lush gardens. It is named after its original owner, the French painter Jacques Majorelle (1886–1962). Majorelle, born in Nancy, originally traveled to Morocco to convalesce from tuberculosis in 1917 and fell in love with the intense light there. In 1923 he bought the 12 acres (4.8 ha) on the edge of Marrakech that would form the basis for this complex of gardens and buildings, turning a former palm plantation into his personal vision of paradise.

The gardens are laid out around four walkways with a profusion of planting. Abundant green foliage contrasts with vivid flowers: orange nasturtiums, pink geraniums, bougainvillea, and hibiscus, all reflected in pools covered by enormous water lilies. The whole is further animated by the plash of water and a hubbub of birdcalls. The gardens' backdrop is the intensely colored architecture, in particular the blue of the Art Deco studio, designed by the French architect Paul Sinoir in 1931. Attached to this are pergolas, decorated with distinctive Art Deco interpretations of traditional Moroccan decorative patterned tilework or *zellij*. Other richly hued objects, such as giant gourds and pots, also punctuate the gardens.

Open to the public since 1947, the gardens were sold by Majorelle in 1962 after he suffered a bad auto accident. Their condition then deteriorated until 1980, when Pierre Bergé and his partner, the couturier Yves St. Laurent, lavishly restored them. **RGW**

↗ The clever use of light and shade make this a tranquil place to visit and escape the midday sun.

→ The house and its studio are set in luxurious grounds, filled with stunning plants and pools.

Rashtrapati Bhavan (1931)

Architect Sir Edwin Lutyens **Location** New Delhi, India **Style** Lutyens Baroque ("Wrenaissance") **Material** Stone

Rashtrapati Bhavan is the official residence of the President of India. When it was built, it was known as The Viceroy's House after the British viceroys who ruled India in the setting years of the Raj. Its construction followed the decision to move the capital of India from Calcutta to Delhi. The principal architects of the new city were Sir Herbert Baker and Sir Edwin Lutyens (1869–1944). Rashtrapati Bhavan is located at the Raisina Hill end of the long, formal Raj Path, which runs from India Gate. Lutyens wanted the processional approach to be gradually inclined, focusing on the house's dome, but Baker was allowed to retain the level space between his two Secretariat Buildings, which frame the Raj Path. Lutyens was upset by this decision; he called it his "Bakerloo." Today, though, the approach to the house reveals itself dramatically as you crest the hill, so perhaps Baker's decision was the right one. This palatial house consists of a central block capped by a copper dome 177 feet (54 m) high, and four wings. Thirty-two broad steps lead to the portico and the main entrance of the Durbar Hall. The hall is a circular marble court, 75 feet (23 m) across. Off this are wings containing private apartments, fifty-four bedrooms, accommodation for more than twenty guests, offices, kitchens, a post office, and courtyards and loggias. The house is 600 feet (183 m) long. It covers 4.5 acres (1.8 ha) and used 9.8 million cubic feet (279,000 cu m) of stone. The colors of the stone are subtle and carefully considered: the lower parts are in deep red sandstone, the upper parts cream. A thin red stone line is inserted at the parapets, contrasting with the blue sky most effectively. The Moghul Gardens—designed by Lutyens, working with William Robertson Mustoe—are patterned geometrically with red and buff sandstone. Everything is beautifully maintained. **ATB**

Hilversum Town Hall (1931)

Architect Willem Marinus Dudok **Location** Hilversum, Netherlands **Style** Art Deco **Materials** Brick, reinforced concrete

This lovely building, built for the council of a relatively small Dutch town, was one of the most influential buildings of the 1930s. Willem Dudok (1884–1974), who was made Hilversum's city architect in 1928, realized that the town hall commission was his chance to make an impression on the architectural world. He threw himself into it, giving his attention to every detail of the design, from structure to garden layout and planting. Even the furniture and fittings were predominantly designed by Dudok and his assistants. The town hall contains a mixture of fine public and municipal spaces, smaller meeting rooms and offices. It is surrounded by gardens, pools, and fountains. Good materials, simple shapes, and careful control of proportions produce a succession of attractive spaces, sensitively modernized and restored in the early 1990s. The exterior, however, is the true delight of the building. Here, Dudok formulated an architecture of

strong, simple shapes. An elegantly proportioned tower indicates that this is a public building. A few circular portholes and diagonally projecting windows apart, the building is composed of rectangular masses. The juxtaposition of plain surfaces, dark slit windows, and massive forms produces variety and interest. The town hall showed practitioners a way to create fine architecture with neither the expensive technological experimentation of the avant-garde style, nor the need for unfashionable historical ornament. **BWC**

"This is something so beautiful . . . from a better, more beautiful world, suddenly set before us."

A. H. Wegerif, Dutch architect

Empire State Building (1931)

Architects Shreve, Lamb and Harmon Associates **Location** New York, New York, USA **Style** Art Deco **Materials** Steel frame, stone cladding

"Standing in lonely dignity in the midriff of Manhattan . . . the quadri-faced Pharos of the city."

G. E. Kidder Smith, *Looking at Architecture* (1990)

⬆ The construction used 60,000 tons of steel, shipped to New York from Pennsylvania.

➡ The slender, tapering building was inspired by the simplest of design objects: a pencil.

The United States spent the 1920s in the midst of a building boom. The first skyscraper was built in Chicago in 1885, and the nation's cities had been growing taller ever since. At the close of the decade, two of New York's most affluent citizens, Walter Chrysler of Chrysler Corps and John Jakob Raskob of General Motors, competed to see who could build the tallest building, resulting in two of the world's most iconic structures—the Chrysler Building, and the Empire State Building.

Raskob selected architects Shreve, Lamb and Harmon Associates to design the Empire State Building. His inspiration was a simple pencil, which he stood on its end, asking the architects "How high can you make it so that it won't fall down?" By the time construction began, in 1930, the Wall Street crash had plunged the United States into the Great Depression. Raskob wanted his skyscraper to cost the least amount of money possible, and to take a maximum of eighteen months from drawing board to occupancy. The steel frame rose by four and a half floors every week until, after one year and forty-five days, it reached 1,252 feet (381 m) high, eclipsing the already completed Chrysler Building by 204 feet (61 m).

Despite the restrictions, architect William Lamb wanted to create a beautiful building as well as a tall one. Influenced by the simple, elegant designs of Finnish architect Eliel Saarinen, such as his second-place proposal for Chicago's Tribune Tower, Lamb produced a tapering tower that still dominates the New York skyline. The building is familiar worldwide, having appeared in more than ninety films, including *King Kong* and *An Affair to Remember*. However, to see it in person is to be truly impressed by a stunning feat of architecture that remained the tallest building in the world for forty-one years, until it was surpassed in 1972 by the World Trade Center. **JS**

Van Nelle
Factory (1931)

Architects J. A. Brinkman, L. C. van der Vlugt **Location** Rotterdam, Netherlands **Style** Modernist **Materials** Concrete, steel, glass

The Van Nelle Factory is an icon of Dutch Modernist architecture. It is well-loved within the Netherlands, but lesser known outside of the country, owing perhaps to its status as a tea and coffee factory and to the fact that a number of architects, none of whom became household names, worked on the project.

The buildings in the scheme are constructed from reinforced concrete, steel, and glass, all materials emblematic of the International Style. The main group of buildings includes a stunning curved office block; an eight-floor factory building with a circular reception room, which is a magnificent example of the curtain wall system; a shed-roofed, five-story warehouse; an L-shaped garage; and a boilerhouse with a profiled chimney. Van Nelle's signature element is a system of glazed, elevated transport bridges that cross diagonally over the street, allowing workers to move easily between the various buildings.

The factory was designed to refine and pack coffee, tea, and tobacco, and the architects made a thorough analysis of its functions. The system was designed to manage raw products that enter at the top of the buildings and move down a floor after each stage of processing. Also important in the design was improving the social aspects of working in a factory, and outdoor sporting and leisure facilities were included for the workers. These are still in existence today, although the assembly and production lines have been taken over by media and IT offices.

One of the best ways to experience the Van Nelle Factory is by train. Leaving or entering Rotterdam Central Station on the main line between Amsterdam and Rotterdam, there is a commanding, but brief, view of the factory. The distinctive "Van Nelle" lettering on top of one of the buildings is illuminated at night. **KAB**

Boots'
D10 Building (1932)

Architect Sir Owen Williams **Location** Beeston, Nottingham, England **Style** Industrial **Materials** Concrete, glass

One of the most innovative British practitioners of High Modernism or Functionalism was not actually an architect. Sir Owen Williams (1890–1969) was a trained engineer specializing in industrial buildings who innovated with reinforced concrete—then a relatively new material—for most of his working life. His favored method was to exploit the material's suitability for great internal spans and large expanses of fenestration, and then ornament the resulting structure.

Williams designed the Daily Express building in London, the Empire Pool in Wembley (now Wembley

> *"The . . . result is architecturally somewhat confused but the total effect is confidently stunning."*
>
> Dennis Sharp, *Twentieth Century Architecture* (2002)

Arena), and planned the infrastructure for the M1, Britain's first motorway. His most high–profile client was the pharmacist Boots, which commissioned him to build a new factory at the firm's site in Beeston, outside Nottingham. Williams devised an enormous concrete–framed structure that had much in common with U.S. industrial architecture.

Known as the D10 Building, the factory once housed 1,200 staff on four levels, with large atria and a part-glazed roof bringing light into production areas. Now protected by English Heritage as a Grade I- listed building of exceptional historic and architectural interest—the largest industrial structure in Britain in this category—D10 underwent a restoration in the mid-1990s and remains one of Britain's most coherent works of Functional architecture. **JBL**

Diego Rivera and Frida Kahlo Studio-House (1932)

Architect Juan O'Gorman **Location** Mexico City, Mexico
Style Modernist **Material** Concrete

The romance of Mexican artists and communist political activists Frida Kahlo and Diego Rivera was at its height when the couple commissioned their friend, painter and architect Juan O'Gorman (1905–82), to build them a house. O'Gorman had studied at the art and architecture school at National University, Mexico, and was influenced by the work of Le Corbusier. The artists' house was one of his first commissions, and one of the first built in a Functionalist style in Mexico.

The house is built of reinforced concrete, and the artist couple lived there until they parted in 1934. It consists of two separate buildings: the larger was Rivera's studio, and the smaller served as living space and Kahlo's studio. Restored in 1997, Rivera's studio is bright pink with a light blue concrete stairway, and wrought ironwork painted red. Kahlo's studio is blue. A bridge at the level of the rooftop terrace connects the two buildings. A line of cacti, replanted in keeping with the original design, fences the studios, its green contrasting with the brightly colored structures.

In keeping with his Functionalist aesthetic, O'Gorman's finishes are austere and economic. He left the electrical and plumbing installations exposed inside both buildings, the ceiling concrete slabs were not plastered, and only the walls built with structural clay tiles were stuccoed. Painted water tanks stand proudly on top of both buildings, and asbestos boards with iron frames were used as doors. The steel-framed studio windows are large, almost stretching from floor to ceiling to allow in natural light. **CMK**

↗ Towering cacti provide a strong vertical element and a carefully calculated color contrast with the studios.

→ The two independent painters' studios are connected symbolically by a bridge at rooftop level.

Le Grand Rex (1932)

Architects Auguste Bluysen, John Eberson **Location** Paris, France **Style** Art Deco **Materials** Stone, plaster

The Grand Rex is a truly impressive Art Deco example of the theater as a kitsch temple of cinema and Hollywood glamour. It opened on December 8, 1932, the work of impresario Jacques Haik and architect Auguste Bluyssen; they had been advised by John Eberson, who constructed around 400 cinemas across the United States in the 1920s. The facade is pure Art Deco, with its illuminated ziggurat crown, ocean-liner styling, and angled *pan coupé* corner entrance.

The interior continues the Art Deco style, melding Ottoman, Hispanic, and Moorish fantasia. Designer Maurice Dufrêne took inspiration from *Arabian Nights* and created an opulent auditorium, complete with antique statues, Moroccan plasterwork, palm trees, arcades, and Classical pediments. The illuminated ceiling features moving clouds and the constellations of the night sky. When the Grand Rex auditorium was renovated, its original 3,300 seats needed to be reduced to 2,750, but it is still the largest auditorium in France, arranged in three tiers: orchestra, 950 seats; mezzanine, 500 seats; and balcony, 1,300 seats. It also features the largest screen in Europe, *Le Grand Large*. Three new screens were added in the 1970s, replacing the original nursery and kennels. In the basement, there is a first aid station and a police station.

It is possible to take a tour with special effects, "*Les Etoiles du Rex;*" which allows visitors to go behind the scenes, transported in a glass elevator. Le Grand Rex also features a spectacular show, "*Féerie des Eaux,*" in which thousands of gallons of water dance on the stage. The safety curtain, installed in 1993, is by the English artist Edward Allington. **JEH**

↖ The overtly Art Deco design was initially unpopular and seen as out of character in this part of the city.

← Le Grand Rex, now considered a Parisian icon, included one of the very first escalators in France.

Maison de Verre (1932)

Architect Pierre Chareau   **Location** Paris, France   **Style** Functionalist   **Materials** Metal, concrete, glass blocks

Pierre Chareau (1883–1950) presents a dual paradox: just one work made him world famous. Furthermore, he was not an architect or an interior designer; however, he had a special aptitude for architecture and the decorative arts. His fashionable friends included Jean Lurçat, the painter; Louis Dalbet, a craftsman in wrought iron; and Marcel L'Herbier, the moviemaker. Chareau himself was a brilliant, self-taught designer.

Dr. Dalsace and his wife were Chareau's first clients, and they entrusted him with the challenge of turning an unlit *hôtel particulier*, situated on the trendy rue Saint-Guillaume, into a modern house and an office for Dr. Dalsace. Chareau reshaped the inner space entirely through unique volumes distributed within a massive void bathed in dimmed light. Abstraction, geometry, authenticity of materials: all these characteristics of 1930s avant-garde were emphasized by Chareau's boldness. The glass wall—until then a technical device used only for industrial purposes—softly filters daylight into the heart of a domestic interior. Steel structures arrange the stages of modern living. Non-simplistic Functionalism offers more than a cold response to the brief.

Chareau set up practice in the United States in 1940 and died ten years later, leaving no other significant work beyond that first and only masterstroke. Maison de Verre is currently owned by a U.S. architectural historian who also rescued Jean Prouvé's tropical house in the Congo, the Glass House remains today an iconic achievement, a place of pilgrimage for a happy few: Chareau's dandyism has outlived him. **YN**

↗ The use of glass walls in a domestic building was a revolutionary concept at the time.

→ This glass and steel structure was created amid eighteenth-century Parisian buildings.

Memorial to the
Missing of the Somme (1932)

Architect Sir Edwin Lutyens **Location** Thiepval, France
Style Modernist **Materials** Brick, Portland stone

Sir Edwin Lutyens (1869–1944) was one of the most prolific and successful British architects to undertake memorial works in the aftermath of World War I. Many of his designs were made for the Commonwealth War Graves Commission, including the Memorial to the Missing of the Somme at Thiepval. This structure was conceived as the Commission's major memorial to the more than 72,000 British soldiers who went missing in action during the fierce fighting on the Somme.

The monument's striking mass is created by a series of interlocking arches of various heights, three on each face, aligned on a cross-axis. The brick superstructure enclosing these arches is alternately stepped back in a pyramidal fashion, a pattern that increases in complexity toward the monument's apex. The multiple arched passageways piercing the structure are a pragmatic as well as aesthetic design solution, providing sufficient wall space for the display of the tens of thousands of names, while allowing natural light to flow throughout. Placed centrally at the intersection of the two largest archways is Lutyens's Great War Stone, a secular commemorative feature suggesting both altar and grave. The vast monument is a powerful architectural expression of the ultimate toll of war. The relative lack of figurative ornament allows the names to dominate the surface, while the arrangement of archways invites movement throughout the monument. Visitors are surrounded by the names of the missing at every turn—a moving experience conducted in penetrating light. **KW**

↖ While reminiscent of a Roman triumphal arch, the monument speaks most strongly of loss and absence.

← The monument serves as a gravestone for those British soldiers whose remains were never found.

Church of the Sacred Heart (1932)

Architect Jože Plečnik   **Location** Prague, Czech Republic
Style Plečnik Classical   **Materials** Klinker, stone, steel

A short metro ride from the tourist crowds in Prague's Old Town will take you to the suburb of Vinohrady, where the Church of the Sacred Heart is as astonishing today as it was in the 1930s. The architecture of Jože Plečnik (1872–1957) defies classification, but here the influence of early Christian basilicas is discernable.

Two-thirds of the walls of the main church consist of dark brown brickwork, punctuated with klinker (bricks fired twice). Brighter squares of granite and artificial stone are inserted in the walls. The upper third of the walls is finished in white plaster with an

---

"No one, from the Ancients to the moderns, has been able to build halls like these; this is real progress."

Jože Plečnik, architect

---

outward-leaning cornice. The door portals punctuate the brick skin. Above the nave is the unforgettable clock tower—also in brick, topped by a white pediment. The 138-foot-high (42 m) tower is pierced by two large, clear, glass-faced clock dials, which lighten the tower's bulk. The bell tower is hollow and has a ramp zigzagging inside as an atrium gallery.

The interior, an open nave, has brick walls decorated with gilded crosses within a grid of pilasters. Daylight enters through clerestory gallery windows beneath a polished, coffered, timber ceiling. The floor is laid in stone mosaic arranged in circular red and gray patterns. The crypt, too, is a powerful space: a brick hemispherical "tunnel" focused on a simple altar at the end. Plečnik created an ardent, spiritual space—possibly his finest work of sacred architecture. **ATB**

Paimio Sanatorium (1933)

Architect Alvar Aalto   **Location** Paimio, Finland
Style International Style   **Material** Concrete

With its whitewashed concrete walls, ribbon windows, and cantilevered balconies, the Paimio Sanatorium (see page 329) has long been lauded as one of the outstanding examples of the International Style. Yet Alvar Aalto (1898–1976) created this building about much more than a mere aesthetic—it was designed, from the ground up, to make the sick well.

After winning an architectural competition to build the sanatorium in 1928, Aalto consulted widely with doctors and health professionals so that he could design a building that would act as an integral part of the cure for tuberculosis. At this time, the only known treatment for the disease was fresh air and rest, with patients typically spending years in hospital.

Aalto's solution was to arrange the sanatorium—which is located in a large forested area—into four main wings, each with its own specific function, all linked by a central spine. The orientation of the wings was dictated by functionality—for example, the main element of the complex, the six-story patient wing, was built on a southwest axis so that patients' rooms could face southeast to catch the morning sun. The patient wing is also home to a series of spectacular cantilevered sun terraces, orientated to the south, enabling the patients to make the most of the sun.

Aalto was also responsible for the design of much of the furniture and lighting. The now-iconic Paimio chair, which is still manufactured today, was conceived specifically for the building, being designed so that its angle helped to improve patients' breathing. Patients each had their own sink, designed to lessen the noise of splashing water, although, as with the chair, the genuine health benefits of these innovations are now doubtful. Today, the building belongs to the University of Turku Central Hospital. **GB**

Hangar One (1933)

Architect U.S. Navy Bureau of Yards and Docks **Location** Moffett Federal Airfield, California, USA **Style** Industrial **Material** Steel

One of the largest unsupported structures in the United States, Moffett Field's airship Hangar One has been a landmark on the San Francisco Bay Area skyline for more than seventy years. Constructed to house the USS Macon, the largest rigid-frame dirigible ever built, the hangar's network of steel girders is anchored to concrete pilings and encloses a surface area of 8 acres (3.2 ha). More than 1,100 feet (335 m) long, 300 feet (91 m) wide, and ascending 200 feet (61 m) to a curved roof, the structure is so vast that fog occasionally forms within it. Hangar One's almost unprecedented scale necessitated numerous design innovations. The massive "clam shell" doors were so shaped to help reduce turbulence as the airship maneuvered through them, and their graceful profile seems to place the structure in the late Art Deco school of Streamline Moderne. The crash of the Macon off Monterey in 1935 signaled the end of the government's commitment to the great airship program. However, Hangar One received a new lease of life when it became the home of Navy reconnaissance balloons during World War II. In 1994 Moffett Field was turned over to NASA, but plans to convert Hangar One into an air and space center came to a halt in 2003, when it was discovered that the exterior paint was leaching toxic lead and PCBs into the surrounding soil. The structure has since become the subject of heated argument as to whether it should be demolished or preserved. **RDB**

"Simple lines are modern . . . they allow us to feel ourselves master of the machine."

Paul T. Frankel, Art Deco designer

Isokon Building (1934)

Architect Wells Coates **Location** London, England **Style** Modernist **Materials** Concrete

Isokon was a design firm established by Jack and Molly Pritchard in 1931 for the purpose of designing furniture and building apartments and houses. In 1932 the firm commissioned Wells Coates (1895–1958), a Canadian émigré architect, to build a block of apartments in Lawn Road, north London. The plan was to build each dwelling to a standard specification, fitting it out with the latest Isokon-designed furniture. The simple living spaces were strongly influenced by the many years that Coates had spent in Japan as a youth. The Lawn Road apartments showcased Coates's belief in the benefits of minimal living. Rejecting the unnecessary ornamentation of the Victorian home, he designed a small, clean, furnished, centrally heated apartment. Coates's design was so sharp and striking that the crime writer Agatha Christie, one of Lawn Road's many celebrity residents, compared the exterior to a giant ocean liner. The block also became home to many

high-profile refugees from Nazi Germany, such as Walter Gropius, Marcel Breuer (who designed many items of Isokon furniture, and went on to design the communal restaurant, the Isobar), and László Moholy-Nagy. World War II led to the demise of the Isokon company, due to difficulties in importing materials from the continent. Transferred to the local council in 1972, the block had become derelict by the 1990s, but it was refurbished in 2003 and it now has Grade I listed status as a protected building by English Heritage. **AT**

"We cannot burden ourselves with tangible possessions, in short, what we call 'life.'"

Wells Coates, architect

Tempe à Pailla (1934)

Architect Eileen Gray **Location** Castellar, near Menton, Provence, France **Style** Modernist **Materials** Stone, concrete

This house was designed by Eileen Gray (1878–1976) for her own use, and refined over the twenty years she lived here. Gray studied at the Slade School in London, before she went to Paris, becoming well known as a designer, notably for a series of elaborate lacquerwork screens. Through her friendship with Jean Badovici, editor of *L'Architecture Vivante*, she met architects such as Le Corbusier, becoming familiar with their work. Embarking on her own career as an architect, in 1926 she built a celebrated villa, E1027, on the coast at Roquebrunne, designed with advice from Badovici.

Tempe à Pailla is a more assured design than that earlier house; even its name, a local phrase for harvest, seems to reflect this maturity. Crucially, the site Gray chose, while inaccessible and awkward, was occupied by the masonry shells of three old water cisterns. She was able to reutilize these as the base for the house, and so did not require new foundations. This base contains a garage, chauffeur's accommodation, and storage, and has the effect of bedding down the house into its site, at the same time lifting up the main living floor to float over the landscape, affording prospects of both mountains and sea.

The main accommodation, approached across a terrace screened from the road, consists of a living room, dining room, and bedroom, with service rooms attached. While very much a wealthy woman's leisure retreat, the villa has a small footprint. Its interior is a masterpiece of space efficiency, with beautifully made multifunctional fitted furniture, sliding screens, and invisible storage areas. Tailored to a particular site and to individual needs, this house anticipates later developments in Modernism. It presages a more contextual architecture, one tuned to the reality, rather than the theory, of how people live. **RGW**

Shrine of Remembrance (1934)

Architects Philip Hudson, James Wardrop **Location** Melbourne, Australia **Style** Classical **Materials** Granite, freestone, marble

The Shrine of Remembrance was envisaged as an expression of a community's gratitude to those who served in World War I. Its architects, both returned servicemen, won a widely publicized competition with this design in 1923, but controversy delayed the project for several years.

Hudson (*c.* 1887–1951) used Classical architecture to reflect his belief that the war had given birth to an Australian national tradition. His main inspiration was a nineteenth-century drawn reconstruction of the Mausoleum at Halicarnassus. The building has three

> *"Here … our Memorial must be of a monumental and arresting design with a 'soul.'"*
>
> **Philip Hudson, architect**

levels—the crypt, the sanctuary, and the balconies. The crypt has a coffered blue-and-gold ceiling, twelve bronze memorial panels separated by pilasters, and is draped with military standards. The sanctuary is a centrally located inner chamber with a sepulchral atmosphere. An austere space, it is surrounded by an ambulatory, which is supported by sixteen marble Ionic columns. On its walls there are forty-two bronze caskets containing hand-written books of remembrance. At 11 AM on November 11 each year—the time and date of the 1918 Armistice—a beam of sunlight streams through an aperture in the ceiling and crosses the marble Stone of Remembrance. Excessively and unashamedly emotional, the Shrine of Remembrance is a deliberately monumental structure, and a dramatic tribute to Australia's war dead. **KW**

Park
Hotel (1934)

Architect László Hudec **Location** Shanghai, China
Style Art Deco **Materials** Steel, concrete, brick

Opened in December 1934, the Park Hotel represents arguably the zenith of architectural achievement in Shanghai before World War II, and in the career of its Shanghai-based and Hungarian-born architect, László Hudec (1893–1958). Hudec had arrived in Shanghai in 1918, where he enjoyed the most prolific years of his career, marked by a transition from traditional European styles to an espousal of Modernism. Hudec's key influences, including Expressionism and the United States' experimentation with the skyscraper, are epitomized in his design of this hotel.

The Park Hotel was originally known as the Joint Savings Society Building, and was the tallest building in Shanghai until the 1980s. The soaring structure comprises two elements: a twenty-one-story tower at the front, and a lower section to the rear. A 300-foot-high (92 m) tensile-steel frame is supported on 400 wooden piles, each 150 feet (46 m) long, and a 24-foot-deep (7.3 m) reinforced concrete raft that prevents sinking into Shanghai's infamously boggy soil.

Hudec accentuated the building's verticality by tapering the tower's outline, using slender windows separated by continuous vertical bands of brick from the fourth floor to the top of the building. He also employed heavy buttressing above the thirteenth floor, the contours of which are maintained down to the second floor, again through brick detailing. Above the third floor, the building is finished in tessellated brick and tiles of contrasting brown hues. The first three floors of the building, faced in black granite, provide a weighty base for the tower and are emphasized by their horizontal form, bound by parallel bands of granite that skirt the building. Although the building has lost some of its old-world charm, it remains an architectural highlight of old Shanghai. **ED**

Prague Castle (1934)

Architects Jože Plečnik, Otto Rothmayer   **Location** Prague, Czech Republic   **Style** Plečnik Classical   **Materials** Granite, stone, brick, timber

Prague Castle, with St. Vitus's Cathedral, dominates the city of Prague; Bohemia's rulers have always lived here. When the new republic of Czechoslovakia was created in 1918, Jože Plečnik (1872–1957) was commissioned to reconstruct and renovate the castle and its gardens. He designed the bull staircase, from the third courtyard to the southern gardens; created the Plečnik Hall in the west wing; and constructed the presidential apartment. After Plečnik's return to Ljubljana, reconstruction continued under his assistant, Otto Rothmayer (1892–1966), who designed the Rothmayer Hall and an open spiral staircase, enveloped in an elegant cage, by the Theresian Wing. Plečnik's projects included a granite monolith obelisk (1928); two pine flagpoles (1920–23); a limestone pyramid in the Ramparts Garden (1920–27); and the elegant small belvedere (1925–30) in the Na Valech Garden. The granite bowl in the Paradise Garden

(1920–27) is truly remarkable, and a fine example of Plečnik's genius and the skill of Czech masons: 13 feet (4.2 m) in diameter, it is carved from a solid block of Mrákotín granite. Plečnik was probably influenced by Schinkel's stone bowl in front of the Altes Museum in Berlin. The flagpoles, too, are exceptional: tall columns of varnished timber, they seemingly rest on blocks of granite. Plečnik had a perfect eye for garden design, public art, and urban landscaping. He could position an obelisk or a pyramid in exactly the right place. **ATB**

> *"Plečnik ... used architecture to convey his symbolic and spiritual messages ..."*
>
> Ivan Margolis, architectural historian and critic

Ufficio Postale (1934)

Architect Adalberto Libera   **Location** Rome, Italy   **Style** Italian Rationalist   **Materials** Concrete, aluminum, marble

The architectural styling of a mail office may not immediately seem obvious as an antiauthoritarian gesture. But Rome's recently restored Ufficio Postale on the Via Marmorata was designed by Italian architect Adalberto Libera (1903–63), who was one of the leading Italian Rationalist architects of the 1930s and 1940s. Libera played a vanguard role in the development of Italian Modernist architecture, and helped spearhead the Italian Rationalist movement that emerged from the shadow of Benito Mussolini. Italian Rationalism was part of a movement in architecture—and furniture and graphic design— away from antidemocratic dictatorship. It sought to shift architecture away from the predominant Facist predilection for Neo-Classical and Neo-Baroque revivalism. Italy at that time was increasingly isolated from the Modernism taking hold elsewhere, and the Rationalists sought to innovate in the International

Style, by employing simple geometric forms, refined lines, and new industrial materials such as linoleum and steel. Libera won a competition to design the building, which he constructed according to strict geometrical proportions, and using simple, cuboid shapes. When viewed from the front, the symmetrical, white, concrete, U-shaped building is divided into three sections, and access is via a low-stepped, fan-shaped stairway. Two rows of small, square windows can be seen in the central body of the building, lining its internal corridors. The structure houses three floors of offices, and a mail hall for the public is on the ground floor. The hall is made of differently colored marbles, and is supported by aluminum pillars. Rectangular windows on the lateral sides of the buildings light the offices within. At the end of each side section, the walls consist of a diagonal weft of windows contained in large concrete panels. **CMK**

ANZAC Memorial (1934)

Architect Charles Bruce Dellit **Location** Sydney, Australia **Style** Art Deco **Materials** Granite, marble

Sydney's monument to the Australian and New Zealand Army Corps—the ANZAC Memorial—was one of the last Australian World War I memorials to be designed. The winning scheme of Sydney architect Charles Bruce Dellit (1898–1942) expressed his belief that postwar society should look forward, not back, and honor the veterans in a modern idiom. The building's most striking feature is the remarkable synergy between architecture and sculpture. George Rayner Hoff (1834–1937), a Sydney-based sculptor and war veteran, built upon Dellit's original ideas to produce some of the most evocative and provocative public sculpture of the time: two external sculptural groups for the building were abandoned following an outcry against their perceived sacrilegious content. The building's clean, external lines are relieved by buttresses, which support sculpted depictions of Australian servicemen and women. Upon entering the building, visitors are drawn to a carved marble balustrade surrounding an opening in the floor. The bronze figure of a dead warrior, naked and stretched across a shield, is visible below. There is a domed ceiling, and amber glass windows in each wall bathe visitors, sculpture, and architecture in soft light. On descending to a lower hall, the visitor can identify the poignant figures supporting the bronze shield— previously viewed from above—as three women: mother, sister, and lover, the last holding a child. **KW**

" . . . traditions are the foundations from which new creative forms should be developed."

Charles Bruce Dellit, architect

Glaspaleis (1935)

Architect Frits P. J. Peutz **Location** Heerlen, Netherlands **Style** Modernist **Materials** Glass, steel, concrete

The oeuvre of Frits Peutz (1896–1974) underwent stylistic changes as he adapted his architecture to the wishes of his client. Here, the client, Peter Schunck from Heerlen, knew exactly what he wanted: a truly modern, innovative department store. After studying contemporary paradigms, such as Les Grands Magasins Decré in Nantes by Henri Sauvage, Peutz created one of the most innovative and intransigent glass buildings of European Early Modernism. He designed the store as a 323-square-foot (30 sq m) concrete rack with mushroom-shaped pillars that narrowed to the top of the seven-story building. The mushroom-shape makes the structure rigid in any direction, so additional bracings are unnecessary. The rack of concrete is encased in a facade with oversized glass panels on three sides. The big offset between facade and the first row of pillars, the extremely thin steel frames, and the absence of any inner wall make the building seem almost completely transparent. Not surprisingly, the building was dubbed Glaspaleis—the Glass Palace. Peutz's design included opening glass hatches and a 19-inch (50 cm) gap between the floor slabs and the facade—one of the first naturally de-aerated facades ever. All enclosed rooms, notably the stairs, four elevators, toilets, and the dispatch area, are located at the south side of the building. Today, after a careful renovation in 2003, the building houses a restaurant, library, gallery, and theater. **FH**

> *"... Peutz proved ... that there is an abstract modern city that can indeed be human."*
>
> Nic Tummers, architectural activist

Highpoint I
Apartments (1935)

Architect Berthold Lubetkin **Location** London, England
Style International Style **Material** Reinforced concrete

The architectural revolution—proclaimed across Europe in the 1920s by the likes of Walter Gropius and Le Corbusier—was late to influence Britain. Hoping to rehouse the poor and bring light and greenery to the slums, Modernist architects had to start by building middle-class villas and apartments in suburbs that lacked neither greenery nor light. Nevertheless, Highpoint and its best contemporaries heralded a glamorous new world of scientific planning techniques and ever-improving building technology.

The sixty apartments are disposed around two staircases in a double cross, with stylish communal spaces on the ground floor, and a large, shared garden laid out behind. The original interiors, where they survive, are highly elegant, with custom-designed fittings throughout, right down to the sanitary ware—none of the usual kind had a sufficient Modernist simplicity for Lubetkin (1901–90). The engineer, Ove Arup, employed innovative concrete techniques, avoiding traditional scaffolding by using a system of molds that climbed as the building rose. Functionality and efficiency were not enough for Lubetkin, though: the finished building had to be beautiful.

Highpoint is as thrilling today as it was on completion. It has been beautifully maintained, and retains a remarkable feeling of 1930s Modernist luxury. At the same time, despite its age, it continues to thrill with its perfect white modernity—it seems impossible that it could house anyone but the sophisticated, intellectual, and artistic. **BWC**

↖ The floating curves of the balconies provide a counterpoint to the perfectly flat walls behind.

← Molding the balconies was difficult and messy for the engineers, but they were essential to the design.

Villa Girasole (1935)

Architect Angelo Invernizzi **Location** Marcellise, Verona, Italy
Style Modernist **Materials** Concrete, aluminum

This summer villa was the brainchild of the engineer Angelo Invernizzi, who lived and worked in Genoa but brought his family here on vacation. On a gently rising slope in vine-growing country, a rectangular concrete platform supports an L-shaped house, the top level of which is cut away to form a roof terrace. At the angle of the L-shape is a spiral staircase that literally forms the pivot of the plan—the upper section is mounted on a steel track and is connected to two motors. These enable the house to rotate on small wheels through 360 degrees in the course of nine hours and twenty

---

"Invernizzi … attempts to harness the reproductive, regenerative, and transformative energy of nature …"

David Lewis, Marc Tsurumaki, Paul Lewis, architects

---

minutes, hence the house's name—*girasole*—the Italian word for a sunflower.

It is perhaps the most extreme example in the world of the Modernist cult of sunlight. While other Modernist architects adopted curved forms to allow for the path of the sun, Invernizzi went one better by making the building itself turn as well.

The limited practical benefits of his idea scarcely justified going to such lengths—it is far easier to walk from room to room in a house in pursuit of the sun, than to move the room itself. Over time, the use of the motor has begun to erode the platform, and the house is now seldom set in motion, although it may be visited by application. As a poetic and philosophical idea, however, it is a work of genius, built in defiance of tradition. **AP**

Collective House (1935)

Architect Sven Markelius **Location** Stockholm, Sweden
Style Functionalist **Materials** Concrete, stucco, steel

From the start of the 1930s, Modernist architecture flourished in Sweden. The Swedish architect Sven Markelius (1889–1972) particularly favored a Functionalist style. He became involved in social housing and wanted to create architecture that emancipated women from their household chores. Childcare and cooking would be carried out in common kitchens and childcare centers.

The Collective House in central Stockholm comprises seven floors and sits in a line with neighboring apartment blocks. The yellow-plastered house consists of fifty-seven apartments; some are single-bedroom apartments; others have two or four bedrooms. Due to the open and free planning of the interior, all appear spacious, even the smallest studio. The childcare center and communal kitchen were located on the ground floor, where there was also a public restaurant. If a working woman did not have time to cook, she could order food from the restaurant, to be delivered by means of a small food lift straight into her apartment. Each apartment has its own balcony, which recesses from the exterior walls. With vertical sections of curved balconies next to the solid walls, Markelius created a shifting and also stringent pattern between the opened and the closed. Here is room for privacy but also space to observe what goes on outside. Behind the complex and away from the street is a communal courtyard and garden area.

The Collective House was the first of its kind in Sweden. Markelius's social project and design was groundbreaking in its time, and it firmly steered Swedish Modernism and Functionalism toward an international group of Modernist colleagues within Europe. The house was thoroughly restored in 1991, and is now a protected building. **SML**

Modernism became the dominant architectural language and variants appeared across the world, from South America to colonial Africa, India, and East Asia. Totalitarian states regarded it with suspicion, producing instead a building language that reinforced the grip of central state authority. The devastation of World War II resulted in rebuilding programs that loosely interpreted Modernist principles. In postwar U.S. architecture, Modernism was bound with growing American power, as the International Style spread across the globe along with American consumer tastes and ideals. In the Communist world, politics constrained architectural innovation.

MODERNISM *goes* GLOBAL

1936–1965

Aalto House (1936)

Architect Alvar Aalto   **Location** Munkiniemi, Finland   **Style** Modernist   **Materials** Brick, steel, reinforced concrete, timber

It is the view of many, especially his fellow architects, that Alvar Aalto (1898–1976) was the greatest architect of the twentieth century. He built the modest Aalto House with his wife Aino. It might seem, at first glance, an odd object for such veneration. The house is irregular, with various balconies and irregular rooflines projecting from an overall L-shape. The structure is a mixture of vertical steelwork, horizontal reinforced concrete, and walls of brick, stone, or timber. This patchwork approach is evident both outside and in, with materials colliding in a casual, domestic fashion, sometimes painted, sometimes left bare. Aalto's charming plywood furniture is used in many rooms. The sliding walls and steel and concrete structures are Modernist, but the focal fireplace and extensive, characteristically Scandinavian use of exposed wood belong to a longer architectural tradition. Comfort is never sacrificed to technological display, but nor is

tradition allowed to hamper innovative design. Rooms are interconnected, but retain a homely identity at odds with the more radical breaking down of internal divisions typical of Modernist architecture. Aalto's house appears at ease with itself. Rather than using his buildings to further design polemics, Aalto seems to be simply trying to make the best building he can, and with tremendous imagination and thought. The lovely wooden stairs, which rise from the top of the brick fireplace, is just one such successful experiment. **BWC**

"The house an architect builds for himself ... [is] a manifestation of his aspirations, a kind of witness ..."

Ernesto Rogers, architect

Tsentrosoyuz Building (1936)

Architects Charles-Edouard Jeanneret (Le Corbusier), Nikolai Kolli **Location** Moscow, Russia **Style** Modernist **Materials** Concrete, tufa stone

Until Stalin turned against the avant-garde, the confidence of the Russian Revolution tallied well with Modernist architecture's hopes for a new world. Soviet interest in German and French Modernism was heartily reciprocated, with close links between the Bauhaus, Paris, and Moscow. It was in this context that Le Corbusier designed a characteristic project of the moment: a central office to administer Soviet grain supplies. Tsentrosoyuz is one of the largest buildings Le Corbusier built; it was faithfully carried to completion by the Russian architect Nikolai Kolli after Le Corbusier fell out with the Soviet establishment. The complex consists of three principal slabs of offices, each entirely glazed on one side, and encased with red Armenian tufa stone with small square windows on the other. Within the site stands a curved mass containing a large auditorium. There were problems from the start, notably from the failure to put in the

intended heating and cooling system in the glazed walls. In the Moscow climate this has made the offices a disagreeable place to work. Some ill-considered modifications have also done damage, although poverty and indifference have preserved more of the building's original features than employees within would perhaps have wished. The building is magnificent today in its dilapidation, like so much of Russia's wonderful 1920s architecture. Beneath its superb composition, however, is something darker: it is a vast, depersonalizing, totalitarian structure in its function, and the architects have intentionally heightened that impression by the endless repetition of identical windows and the factory-like implications of its movement of human traffic. The building displays the cold, mechanistic detachment that attracted Le Corbusier to totalitarian regimes. It also demonstrates his incomparable artistic genius. **BWC**

De La Warr Pavilion (1936)

Architects Erich Mendelsohn, Serge Chermayeff **Location** Bexhill-on-Sea, Sussex, England **Style** Modernist **Material** Concrete

The construction of the De La Warr Pavilion was part of a major investment program by seaside resorts on England's south coast to counter the growing threat posed by the middle classes vacationing abroad. It was promoted by the Earl De La Warr, a socialist and aristocrat who owned most of the land on which Bexhill was built and who was mayor of the town from 1932 to 1934. The architects were selected from a competition run by the Royal Institute of British Architects. Erich Mendelsohn (1887–1953) was a highly successful Expressionist architect whose career in Germany was cut short by the rise to power of the Nazis, and Serge Chermayeff (1900–96) was a Russian who had lived in England since 1910. Their pavilion exemplified a contemporary vision for a new society, not exactly what the retired colonels of Bexhill really wanted. The architects rejected traditional brick and stone in favor of concrete and steel, which resulted in a streamlined, industrially influenced building with metal-framed windows. Innovatively the structure used a welded steel frame. Both architects later made their careers in the United States and elsewhere, but they were among the small group who brought continental Modernism to Britain. The pavilion originally contained a repertory theater, a small auditorium, a restaurant, a reading room, and a lounge. The pavilion was restored to its original design in 2005 and is now a contemporary arts center. **CWH**

> *"Delighted to hear that Bexhill has emerged from barbarism at last ..."*
>
> George Bernard Shaw, playwright

Casa del Fascio (1936)

Architect Giuseppe Terragni **Location** Como, Italy **Style** International Style **Materials** Concrete, glass

It is a bitter irony that one of the most iconic structures of the International Style—an architectural movement with a commitment to social progression and egalitarianism—should be designed by an Italian fascist, Giuseppe Terragni (1904–43). His masterpiece is ideologically challenged, to say the least. It also unravels the received wisdom that the political right wing eschews innovation for tradition. A pristine white cube set among the terra-cotta roofs and copper domes of the city of Como, Casa del Fascio was intended to be a symbolic representation of Fascism's organizational power. The Party Secretary's room led directly to the balcony overlooking the square, allowing him to step outside and address the adoring, black-shirted throng. The building's key innovation is in the treatment of its facade. Facing the square, two-thirds of the house is broken up into modules, a concrete grid that stands proud of the main facade to provide an ordering to the structure and work within. Glass brick and steel walls provide divisions, allowing light to penetrate into the heart of the building, and strengthened glass and opaline glass were applied throughout. Terragni's intention was to make Casa del Fascio a perfect object, reflecting the glory of the political system he so admired. The building is a remarkable survivor, its sublime aesthetic transcending the wrong-headedness of its function, and ultimately existing as a blank monument to a faded world. **JBL**

"It ... was not [a] haunt or a refuge or a fortress, it was to become a House, a School, a Temple."

Giuseppe Terragni, architect

Kavanagh
Apartment Building (1936)

Architects Gregorio Sánchez, Ernesto Lagos, Luis María de la Torre   **Location** Buenos Aires, Argentina
Style Art Deco   **Materials** Reinforced concrete frame, glass

This spectacular, 393-foot-high (120 m) apartment block was for many years the tallest building in South America. When completed in 1936, it was also the largest reinforced concrete structure in the world. Its attenuated, dramatic profile, in part generated by the step-backs demanded by Buenos Aires's zoning restrictions, but also reflecting the shape of its difficult, wedge-shaped site, is one of the most distinctive in the city. The Kavanagh's narrow prow, pointing toward the River Plate, has been compared to that of an enormous gray ship.

When built, it was ahead of its time structurally, and it also offered unparalleled luxury for affluent Porteños—a nickname for the natives of this port city. The block, with 105 apartments, arranged in six wings, on thirty stories, was equipped with European oak floors and mahogany doors, central air conditioning, twelve elevators, a central telephone exchange, and even refrigerated rooms for meat.

The apartments on the upper floors have terraced gardens enjoying views over the adjacent park, river, and city. The largest of these terraces is that of the apartment on the fourteenth floor—at around 7,530 square feet (700 sq m), the only one to occupy a whole floor of the building. Not surprisingly, this was occupied by the extremely wealthy Porteño who commissioned the block in 1934, Corina Kavanagh, and its construction almost bankrupted her.

By the 1930s, Argentina was one of the richest countries in the world, and Buenos Aires had come to see itself, like New York, as a city that epitomized the confidence of a modern new world. The radical, severe, stripped design of the iconic Kavanagh Apartment Building—still a highly coveted address— is the most celebrated symbol of this aspiration. **RGW**

Newman College (1936)

Architects Walter Griffin, Marion Mahoney **Location** Melbourne, Australia **Style** Art Deco **Materials** Sandstone, concrete

Newman College is the most notable design of husband-and-wife team Walter Burley Griffin (1876–1937) and Marion Mahoney (1871–1961), although it is just one of the many buildings they designed for Melbourne's "civic spine." The college building is a compelling union between the horizontality of the Prairie style and a medieval Oxford college.

Sandstone arches fan out above windows on the street facade; an internal three-sided quadrangle is contained by a wide, low cloister with an ambulatory on its roof. Rooms are reached via stairs and open onto

> "No student who has dined here ever forgets this architecture. It marks them for life."
>
> Peter Corrigan, architectural theorist

the ambulatory with its steel-framed windows. The chief glory of the building is the domed Dining Hall surmounted by a set of spires reminiscent of Frank Lloyd Wright. The dome springs from a mezzanine, and is thus pulled low over the space.

A new Study Center, by Edmond & Corrigan, was built in 2004 as a contemporary tribute to the Dining Hall. Reticent in its external form, it contains a library, ovoid in plan, that rises through two stories and is bridged by a roughly circular mezzanine around a void that echoes a lantern above. Peter Corrigan has wrought through shifting and elusive geometries a space for study that is every bit as powerful in a minor key as Griffin's masterly space is in the major. The effect is rather like entering a time machine that warps perceptions of time and space. **LVS**

Villa Rebbio (1936)

Architect Giuseppe Terragni **Location** Rebbio, Italy **Style** Italian Rationalist **Materials** Concrete, plaster

Few architects have been as controversial or as rich in their work as Giuseppe Terragni (1904–43). Giuseppe Pagano refused to publish his designs in the 1930s because he considered them too decorative; Bruno Zevi saw in Terragni's buildings a formal dynamism that had little to do with the orthodoxy of the Fascist regime; more recently, Peter Eisenman used Terragni as a pretext to formulate his studies on form.

Terragni was a founding member of the Fascist Gruppo 7, and a leading exponent of Rationalism. Villa Rebbio—commissioned by a floriculturist—reveals Terragni's deep interest in architecture as a linguistic manifestation. It is also one of the few buildings built by Terragni outside the town of Como. The exterior has all the essential elements of modern architecture as put forward by Le Corbusier, but the Italian architect tweaked them to create a personal vocabulary.

Although the main volume of the house is cleanly suspended on slender pillars, the corners of the box are opened up to suggest movement. The long, horizontal windows do not follow any symmetry, as in many Modernist buildings. The Functionalist agenda that animated many Modernists at the time is here used as a formal vocabulary to expand the repertoire of spatial languages. The interior also treats the partition walls as "canvases" on which the architect composes abstract and dynamic forms.

Although some of the most daring elements had to be dropped from the final design, Villa Rebbio is an extraordinary example of Terragni's talent. The formal concerns of his design language and the dynamism that he brings to the most basic geometric forms had an enormous influence on several generations of architects, and today can be detected in the work of Peter Eisenman, Alvaro Siza, and others. **RB**

Magnitogorsk Metal Kombinat (1937)

Architect Ernst May   **Location** Chelyabinsk Oblast, Russia   **Style** Industrial   **Materials** Steel, concrete

"An important record of political, social, and manufacturing history."

Andrew Garn, architecture photographer and writer

⬆ During World War II, half of the steel required to manufacture Soviet tanks was made at Magnitogorsk.

➡ Today the steel town remains operational, although supplies of iron and coal must now be imported.

Magnitogorsk was "Stalin's Pittsburgh." A model industrial town for the purpose of making steel, it was part of Joseph Stalin's first Five-Year Plan. Construction of the town was extremely rapid. Work began in 1929, when the site, an isolated outpost in a corner of the southern Urals rich in iron ore, was home to a few hundred workers living in tents. By 1932, when the first steel was smelted, the population was more than 250,000. At its peak, in the middle of the twentieth century, the city had a population of 500,000.

In the late 1920s and early 1930s, the Soviet Union lacked the skills and experience required to build a major steel plant, so foreign expertise was called upon. This included a team of architects and planners led by Ernst May, a German responsible for progressive models of decentralized planning and worker housing in Frankfurt. May envisaged Magnitogorsk as a linear city, with rows of "superblocks"—system-built accommodation units with zones for production, eating, sleeping, and communal activities. These were to run parallel to the long factory buildings, which included blast furnaces, welding shops, soaking pits, combination mills, and the other facilities required for the fabrication of steel on a mass scale. The idea was for workers to live as close as possible to the industrial zone relevant to their skill, minimizing travel time and maximizing output. Residential and production zones were to be separated by a belt of green space.

However, when May arrived, construction was already underway; his vision was also compromised by geography, notably the orientation of the Ural River. At more than 13 miles (21 km) long, the city became more elongated than originally planned. During the Soviet period, thousands of cities were based on principles applied at Magnitogorsk, and the mills were a great success, although living standards and the quality of life in them were very low. **AM**

Budapest Aerodrome (1937)

Architects Virgil Bierbauer, László Králik **Location** Budapest, Hungary **Style** Modernist **Materials** Concrete, steel, glass

Budapest Aerodrome evokes the glamorous world of 1930s air travel. At that time, civil aviation was the preserve of the fashionably rich, and Budapest was an aviation crossroads for central Europe. When it was built, the aerodrome was considered to be one of the most modern in Europe, a model for airports such as those of Dublin and Liverpool. The plan, with its separated traffic system and modern departure building, was influential when engineers and architects were beginning to create an entirely new architectural form—the airport for civilian traffic. The new buildings were expected to handle demanding passengers stylishly as well as processing cargo, enforcing customs and immigration regulations, and maintaining aircraft. The plan is largely symmetrical, with two wings connected to the cylindrical central section. The streamlined, curving plan clearly resembles an aircraft. A gallery and top-lit passengers'

lobby is on the upper floor of the central drum. Originally the columns were glass-faced. An aerial photomontage stretched around the circular lobby space, to which a bar and lounges were attached. Interior fittings, such as door handles, were designed in a smart, Modernist style. On the roof of the central section, a pretty control tower projects out like the bridge of a ship, evoking the glamorous world of ocean liners. Open observation balconies and rooftop decks on the side wings add to the smart nautical effect. During World War II, fighting between the Germans and the Soviet Red Army was fierce and damaging around Budapest, so it is remarkable that the aerodrome survived the war largely intact. The aerodrome remained the principal air-traffic hub for Budapest until 1950, when Ferihegy Airport opened. It was later used as a military airfield, but now it handles small private planes and charter traffic. **ATB**

Zeppelin Field Tribune (1937)

Architect Albert Speer **Location** Nuremberg, Germany **Style** Fascist **Materials** Limestone, brick

Adolf Hitler commissioned Albert Speer (1905–81) to design a series of colossal buildings across Germany to overlook the assembled thousands at Nazi Party rallies. Speer, a student of Heinrich Tessenow, an early Modernist, had been drawn into Hitler's close circle. Before he was commissioned, the Nazis had already held several rallies on the site, just outside Nuremberg. Hitler wanted a parade ground to hold up to 320,000 participants, with a main tribune to house 70,000 spectators. Speer's Zeppelin Field Tribune was loosely based on the Pergamon Altar, an ancient Greek relic housed with great pride in the eponymous museum in Berlin. This deliberate reference to a superb example of ancient architecture therefore had a propagandist charge. Centered on Hitler's pulpit and combining theatrical elements such as artificial landscapes, banners, lighting effects, and the use of organized crowds, the tribune is effectively a giant stage. Its persuasive rhetoric is expressed in Leni Riefenstahl's infamous movie footage of the Nuremberg rallies. In one scene, featuring Speer's "Cathedral of Light," the Zeppelin Field is flanked by anti-aircraft searchlights pointed skyward, engulfing the spectators in an infinite dome of light. A monument to the darkest hours of European history, the partially demolished Zeppelin Field Tribune still oozes an unsettling feeling of mastery and intimidation, a grim reminder of architecture's power as a tool for propaganda. **LT**

> *"Hitler wanted to impress. Ideology was present in the brief, but not in the style."*
>
> Albert Speer, architect

Sant'Elia
Nursery School (1937)

Architect Giuseppe Terragni   **Location** Como, Italy
Style International Style   **Materials** Concrete, glass

In Italy, Functionalist architecture was strongly favored by the far-right administration of Benito Mussolini. However, some of the most important buildings from the Fascist era were surprisingly progressive, such as the provision of nursery care. Giuseppe Terragni (1904–43) designed the Sant'Elia nursery as a series of large classrooms arranged around a central courtyard, avoiding "long and monotonous" corridors and using the materials and palette of the International Style.

Located in one of Como's new urban districts, the facade of the classroom block adjoins the garden, facing south. A series of large canopies were rigged up on a concrete and steel frame to provide solar shading in the summer months. A fixed canopy runs from the enclosure to the central courtyard, and the simple plan allows the entire space to be easily understood by the children there. The structure, still used as a nursery today, is carefully maintained, and presents a generous environment for its present users.

Generous expanses of floor-to-ceiling glazing, 14-foot-high (4.5 m) ceilings, and windows that could open up the space in the summer were all seen as logical and healthy devices and aids to improving the quality of education. There was even a solarium on the flat roof, reached by a ramp, while areas were left free for a vegetable garden, a lawn, playpool, and pergola.

Terragni was an avowed Fascist and headed Gruppo 7, an organization of Rationalist architects determined to stop historical revivalism. His early death meant he never saw the end of his beloved Mussolini, and the major role that the new architecture would play in the reconstruction of Europe and its social structures. As his Como nursery attested, he was architecturally advanced if politically misguided, and his potential career remains a tantalizing what-if. **JBL**

Passos
Manuel Garage (1938)

Architect Arq Mario de Abreu   **Location** Porto, Portugal
Style Art Deco   **Materials** Brick, steel, wood, glass

This distinctive Art Deco building takes the car as its theme. On the facade of Passos Manuel, two strong vertical lines mark the levels of three parking lot floors like a giant harness. The lines seem to disappear into the building on the fourth floor and through the garage entrance. The impressive silhouette of the building is testimony to De Abreu's skill as a draftsman.

When it first opened, the building housed a variety of offices, workshops, studios, and a car showroom as well as the garage. There was even a famous brothel on the very top floor of the building.

"The classic and modern elements [are] united in the promotion of one thing—the motor car."

Fernandes/Cannata, *Arquitectura Moderna* (2002)

These days the auto workshops and "red lights" have disappeared but, as a result of regional political rationalism and the Portuguese love affair with the motor car, the garage has been meticulously preserved. The current BMW-Mini branding at the garage entrance somehow seems to complement the integrity and history of the building.

In 2001, a local cultural association led by photographer Daniel Pires converted the derelict top floors of the building into a contemporary culture space called Maus Habitos or Bad Habits. Culture breathed new life into the building and the surrounding area, and it soon featured exhibition spaces, studios, a café, a bar, a nightclub, and a performance space. It now enjoys international acclaim for its avant-garde programs. **MDC**

Fiat Tagliero Building (1938)

Architect Giuseppe Pettazzi **Location** Asmara, Eritrea
Style Futurist **Material** Reinforced concrete

From 1935 to 1941, Italian architects, engineers, and planners set about creating Mussolini's vision of an Italian empire in east Africa. Asmara, capital of Eritrea, was transformed into Africa's most modern city, with more traffic lights than Rome, a road network that reached out as far as Sudan, southern Ethiopia, and Somalia, and more than 50,000 motor cars.

In Eritrea, far from watchful eyes in Rome, the architects allowed their imaginations to run wild, designing and constructing a wide range of flamboyant structures. Probably the most audacious structure was the airplane form of the Fiat Tagliero service station. The two-story main body of the volant structure suggests a cockpit with its sleek wrap-around windows; on top of this soars an ornamental tower, its height accentuated by the vertical lines of its window frames. But more impressive and far braver are the building's cantilevered, 98-foot-long (30 m), reinforced-concrete wings, which hang from the structure with breathtaking weightlessness.

Pettazzi's design was a puzzle for the municipal authorities. Disbelieving the architect's calculations, they insisted that supporting columns be included in the final design. Pettazzi submitted his design with wooden pillars supporting the wings, but, according to legend, at the building's unveiling he put a gun to the contractor's head and ordered him to remove the supports. Under duress, the builder did so. When the supports were taken away, the wings stayed aloft, and they have remained that way for seven decades. **ED**

↗ Although originally looked upon with skepticism, Pettazzi's masterpiece is now a listed building.

➡ The reinforced concrete wings are remarkable, adding to the building's sense of unreality.

Church of St. Michael (1938)

Architect Jože Plečnik **Location** Ljubljana, Slovenia **Style** Plečnik Vernacular **Materials** Stone, concrete, timber

A short distance to the southwest of Ljubljana, in the *barje* or marshlands district, Jože Plečnik (1872–1957) constructed St. Michael's church at the request of his nephew, a priest. The church was intended to be temporary, and the budget was limited. Nevertheless, Plečnik's invention and genius created a beautiful wooden interior within a highly original building. Plečnik had wanted to construct the body of the church in unpolished stone. "You won't fool God with concrete," he told his nephew. However, concrete was used, with brick and stone for the upper floors. Concrete drainage pipes stood between masonry walls and the gaps infilled with wooden beams. More pipes were polished and painted for use as pillars.

It is the wood-paneled and pillared interior that impresses. The timber roof is beautifully decorated. Fine copper and metal fittings, such as the lights and door handles, combine with the woodwork to create an interior of refined folk architecture. The altar is set along the broad side of the hall, giving the church an unusual layout. Aware of the tight budget, Plečnik used polished brass for the pulpit and behind the altar. Shortage of funds encouraged other inventive details, such as a substitute bell consisting of a hanging metal ring, with a metal stick to sound it.

In the center of the church is an enclosed space where children can be watched by their parents during services. Externally, the belfry, with its long, tiered steps, is pierced for bells. The tower is structurally separate from the church because of the nature of the site. St. Michael's rests among the birch trees, an exquisite jewel box in the fields. **ATB**

↖ Plečnik took much of his inspiration from rural Slovenia; the rustic influence can be seen here.

← The warm colors of the woodwork and timber roof conjure the atmosphere of folk architecture.

All-Russia Exhibition Center (1939)

Architect Unknown **Location** Moscow, Russia **Style** Socialist Realist **Material** Reinforced concrete

Joseph Stalin ordered the All-Union Agricultural Exhibition of 1939 as a celebration of Soviet economic achievements and the success of the planned economy. The venue, then called the Exhibition of Economic Achievements (VDNKh), was a showground of monumental pavilions built in the high Socialist Realist style. The showground is still in use, although it has been extended significantly since the late 1930s.

The focal point of the development's first phase was the Central Pavilion. The original interior included a colossal illuminated map of the Soviet Union, and heroic scenes of a hydroelectric power station and Lenin's hometown. Other surviving elements of the first phase of development include an octagonal square surrounded by nine smaller pavilions, each dedicated to a different profession, theme, or sphere of economic activity. In the center of the square is a fountain featuring gilded statues of young women in the national dress of the sixteen Soviet republics.

As well as reflecting Stalin's rejection of the International Style—which was outlawed in 1931— the architecture of the showground is a legacy of Stalin's 1934 ruling that cultural expression should be, "national in form and socialist in content." Architects were encouraged to draw upon ethnic motifs; for example, in reference to architectural forms of Central Asia, the facade of the so-called Culture Pavilion features a starlike pagoda and tiled arabesques.

The 1939 event was a great success. After World War II, in 1954, the Agricultural Exhibition was revived. Following the Soviet Union's collapse in 1991, the ground became the All-Russia Exhibition Center. **AM**

↗ The Central Pavilion is a stepped, Neo-Classical structure topped by a 115-foot-high (35 m) spire.

→ The showground grew over the years; more than eighty pavilions now surround the Central Pavilion.

Museum of Modern Art (1939)

Architects Philip L. Goodwin, Edward Durell Stone   **Location** New York, New York, USA   **Style** International Style   **Materials** Concrete, steel

The Museum of Modern Art (MoMA), especially in its present incarnation, provides a transparent window into its art collections. The museum, established in 1929 exclusively to show modern art, occupied three different buildings before finally opening at its present location. New York, despite being a vital city in the early twentieth century, boasted few truly "modern" buildings until the late 1930s. Most of the steel-framed skyscrapers, which contribute so much to Manhattan's celebrated skyline, were dressed up in either Gothic or Classical disguise. Although, at first, only a small building by New York standards, MoMA made a great impact through assiduous propaganda and, of course, through its collection of contemporary art. The rich young dilettante Philip Johnson and his mentor, Henry-Russell Hitchcock, had taken a prolonged European tour in 1929, and the buildings they photographed formed the basis for their exhibition,

The International Style, in 1932. The style of the original MoMA building is a compendium of motifs of the International Style. Philip Johnson altered the museum in 1951 and 1964, adding the Abby Aldrich Rockefeller Sculpture Garden, an outdoor courtyard where visitors could contemplate sculptural art. Other architects intervened as the collections grew and the expectations of the curators changed. In late 2003, MoMA reopened after a huge refit by Yoshio Tanaguchi with Kohn Pedersen Fox Associates. **EG**

"The architects doubtlessly read all that Le Corbusier ever said about houses being 'machines to live in.'"

Henry McBride, critic

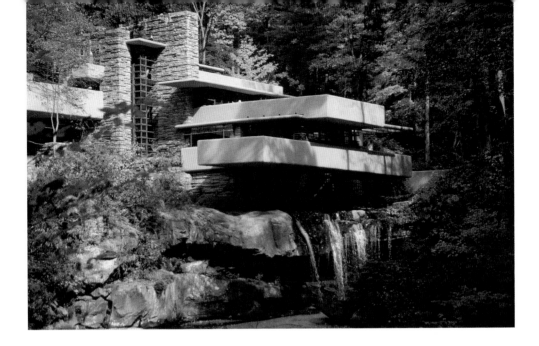

Fallingwater (1939)

Architect Frank Lloyd Wright   **Location** Bear Run, Pennsylvania, USA   **Style** Modernist   **Materials** Limestone, reinforced concrete

Frank Lloyd Wright (1867–1959), possibly the most famous U.S. architect of the twentieth century, developed the Prairie style of building—long, low structures in natural materials with roofs seeming to float unsupported above the walls. By the time he designed his most famous work, Fallingwater, his style was beginning to evolve. In 1935 Edgar J. Kaufmann, a Pittsburgh department-store owner, hired Wright to design a vacation house for his family in the western Pennsylvania mountains. The Kaufmanns loved a wooded area where a stream, known as Bear Run, turns into a waterfall, and they wanted their house to reflect the beauty of the site. They were unprepared, however, for Wright's suggestion that the house be built over the waterfall itself, allowing its inhabitants to live within the scenery rather than simply to observe it. Turning this idea into reality was a formidable feat of engineering. Anchored by limestone verticals, and a huge stone chimney at the rear, horizontal concrete planes cantilever out over the water, mirroring the shapes of the rocks 30 feet (9 m) below. Walls of glass emphasize the lack of boundaries between interior and forest. Fallingwater is a house of new ideas, with significant risks taken to achieve a unique and timeless piece of architecture. Wright created a building of elegant simplicity, ideally suited to the serenity of its setting, and one that fully embodied his client's empathy with the landscape it occupies. **JS**

> *"[Wright] created the most vivid example of manmade forms complementing nature."*
>
> Patrick Nuttgens, author and honorary professor

Prora Seaside Resort (1939)

Architect Clemens Klotz **Location** Prora, Rügen Island, Germany **Style** Fascist **Material** Concrete

This vast building by Clemens Klotz (1886–1969), gently curving along the Baltic coast, is one of the largest surviving structures built by the Nazi state in Germany. It is still, after seventy years, the longest building in Europe, measuring over 2.5 miles (4.4 km) from end to end. Built as a monolithic seaside resort for 20,000 people—it was due to open to its first vacationers for the 1940 season—it was never used due to the outbreak of war. Advertised as "a seaside resort for German workers," it was the first of five planned for the north German coast, a series of mass, state-run camps organized through the *Kraft durch Freude* (Strength through Joy), or KdF, program, led by leading Nazi Dr. Robert Ley. The KdF program was designed to synchronize the worlds of leisure and work, enabling the German workforce to be controlled and indoctrinated even when on vacation. The groundbreaking for the new building took place on May 2, 1936, the third anniversary of the breaking of the independent trade union movement, which Ley had been instrumental in implementing. For what was effectively a new small town, a railway line and station were built and a farm planned to supply fresh food. There was also to be a vast subterranean parking lot to cater for that most famous product of the KdF program, the Volkswagen (People's Car). On the seafront, there were docking facilities for KdF cruise liners to take workers around the Norwegian fjords, while cinemas, swimming pools, and a people's hall and rally ground were also planned. All the bedrooms were identical and, at 8.2 by 16 feet (2.5 by 5 m), small for two people. Linked into a loudspeaker system, they all open onto wide internal walking halls where the workers were to be encouraged to take exercise on inclement days. This is grim, monotonous architecture: an embodiment of the ideology that built it. **RGW**

Villa Mairea (1939)

Architects Alvar Aalto, Aino Aalto **Location** Noormarkku, Finland **Style** Modernist **Materials** Brick, plaster, timber (teak, fir)

In 1937, Alvar Aalto (1898–1976) was commissioned by the wealthy industrialists Harry and Maire Gullichsen to design their country retreat. Aalto's brief was to be experimental, and he created a villa not only bursting with ideas but also arguably one of the most important buildings in the Modernist style. Aalto's wife Aino (1894–1949) was also a qualified architect, and they worked as a team, with Aino taking responsibility for the interiors. Aalto was also a talented furniture designer—his bent-plywood pieces are among the most iconic examples of twentieth-century furniture. By the time Aalto worked on Villa Mairea, he had already designed one of his early masterpieces of Functionalism, the Paimio Sanatorium. Although he is undoubtedly a Modernist architect, Aalto's work has a warmth and humanity that is sometimes lacking in the designs of European contemporaries. In Villa Mairea, Aalto combined machine-made angularity with wood in warm tones. The presence of the surrounding woods was emphasized indoors by the use of wood and open-plan rooms that let in light and views. A sense of well-being permeates the house, which encloses a swimming pool and a children's play area with bars embedded into the wall for exercise. The interior detailing is impeccable. Villa Mairea encapsulates elements of Aalto's style: the practical and manmade combined with a concern for quality of life. **RK**

"The villa is undisputedly the crowning achievement of young Aalto's architectural oeuvre."

Göran Schildt, *Alvar Aalto* (1994)

2 Willow Road (1939)

Architect Ernö Goldfinger   **Location** London, England
Style International Style   **Materials** Concrete, brick

No. 2 Willow Road (see page 445) is the central house of a row of three designed by Vienna-born Modernist Ernö Goldfinger (1902–87), who created the house as his own home. This unique example of a 1930s house is now preserved together with the belongings of its architect. Included are furniture items designed by Goldfinger and works of art by twentieth-century masters such as Henry Moore and Roland Penrose.

Goldfinger saw his design as following in the tradition of the eighteenth-century row houses nearby. Completed just before World War II began,

> *"The greatest honor that can now be paid to him and his example is carefully to look after his work."*
>
> James Dunnett, architectural consultant

the elegant design has garages and entrances on the ground floor, a strip of windows signaling the main living rooms on the upper floor, and smaller square windows, slightly protruding in their concrete frames, on the bedroom floor above. The interiors are masterly, with splashes of color, brighter the higher up the house you go, complementing walls clad in oak and plywood. A mixture of concealed lighting and Goldfinger's neat, wall-mounted uplighting adds to the effect of the natural light that pours in through the generous glazing. Movable screens and folding doors make for adaptable living spaces.

Willow Road was the first important building by Goldfinger. It was fitting that it became the first Modernist building to be acquired by the National Trust, which opened it to the public in 1996. **PW**

Zale Cemetery (1940)

Architect Jože Plečnik   **Location** Ljubljana, Slovenia
Style Plečnik Classical   **Materials** Stone, concrete

After working in Vienna and Prague, Jože Plečnik (1872–1957) returned in 1921 to Ljubljana, Slovenia, as professor of architecture at the city's new university. In the late 1930s, a new cemetery for the city was needed (see page 444). Plečnik proposed his All Saints Garden, in which chapels, a mortuary, a casket workshop, and other administrative buildings would be gathered into a city of the dead. He designed and planned all the buildings and benches, tombstones, stretchers, and a fountain. Even the sextons' uniforms, with their wide brimmed hats, were to his design.

The main entrance is a formal propylaeum (monumental gateway) of three stories, consisting of a concave Classical colonnaded screen pierced by a high ceremonial portal. Here the arch symbolizes the passage from this life to the unknown world beyond. Symmetrical, two-story, administrative wings lie on either side of the colonnade. The central oratory building, with its fine *baldachin* (fixed altar canopy) is aligned to the main gate. Located about the cemetery are chapels named after Ljubljana's patron saints: John, Peter, Andrew, and Francis. A nondenominational chapel celebrates humanity as Adam and Eve. Each chapel is an exquisitely subtle composition. The weathered, green, bell-like dome of St. Peter's is supported on slender columns that enclose an octagonal drum. St. Andrew's has a robust barrel roof, while St. John's templelike facade is divided: half dark grotto, half bland wall fronted by a Classical urn.

Plečnik's work defies classification; he has even been seen as Postmodern, which would seem to trivialize his intensely serious work. At Zale, he combined his intellectual seriousness with a compassion for the grieving mourners, creating a moving assembly of ritual spaces. **ATB**

Rockefeller Center (1940)

Architects Reinhard & Hofmeister; Corbett, Harrison & MacMurray; Raymond Hood, Godley & Fouilhoux
Location New York, New York, USA **Style** Art Deco **Materials** Reinforced concrete, limestone, steel, glass

Rockefeller Center is the world's finest Art Deco civic and commercial urban ensemble, and quite probably the most successful and loved public/private space in the United States. It consists of nineteen commercial buildings of varying height, form, and content on an 11-acre (4.5 ha) private site. It was conceived as a whole, but made allowances for diversity and growth. The only major Depression-era commercial building in New York City, it was the vision of one of the country's richest men—John D. Rockefeller. He assembled a team of architects who worked collaboratively under chief architect Raymond Hood.

Hood's plan resembled that of the original thirteen colonies of the United States: a nascent federation of independent states that contribute to the strength of the whole. Thirteen satellite buildings—completed within an eight-year span—sacrificed height to consolidate air rights to the fourteenth. These air rights allowed the GE/RCA skyscraper to soar to seventy stories and create a flagship beacon. This building is a streamlined slab-shaft with a narrow profile that accentuates its verticality. The famous sunken plaza at the base feeds into a grid pattern of buildings and streets that allows a constant stream of visitors to enter and exit, aided by an undercroft of mass transit, parking, delivery, and heating and cooling systems. The entire plan has massing, hierarchy, symmetry, and logic, but the beauty resides in the care taken to create a living, accessible, and adaptable organism. **DJ**

↗ A series of setbacks heightens the visual suspense to the summit, which is crowned by the Rainbow Room.

→ The narrow profile is heightened by the tapering effect of the supporting towers.

Woodland Crematorium (1940)

Architect Erik Gunnar Asplund **Location** Stockholm, Sweden **Style** Modernist **Material** Stone

The Woodland Crematorium in Skogskyrkogarden cemetery is not only the swan song of Erik Gunnar Asplund (1885–1940), but also a mature illustration of his Modernist architectural idiom. The building is part of a burial complex that includes additional works by Asplund and architect Sigurd Lewerentz. The crematorium sits on a hilly, tree-covered part of Stockholm. A spacious entrance and a large granite cross in the courtyard dominate the site. The complex is formed by three chapels: Faith, Hope, and the larger Chapel of Holy Cross, all linked by the main facilities area—the vault containing the funeral urns and the actual crematorium space. The varied-height volumes break up the facade into separate units, allowing the crematorium subtly to follow the hill's slope. The complex's serene clarity is also reflected in its furnishings, designed to be comfortable and functional but simple. The building attracts worldwide attention from architects and historians for its elemental Modernist simplicity, in which the basic forms of the building blend harmoniously with the surrounding natural environment: a unique example of authentic monumentality and religious architecture. Asplund's creation stands peacefully, joining Neo-Classical architecture and Modernism, beauty and symbolism. Ironically, the architect himself was the first person to be cremated there. In 1994, the complex was put on the UNESCO World Heritage list. **ES**

> *"The monumental quality was deliberately reserved for the 'Biblical' landscape."*
>
> Erik Gunnar Asplund, architect

Helsinki Olympic Stadium (1940)

Architects Yrjö Lindegren, Toivo Jäntti **Location** Helsinki, Finland **Style** Functionalist **Material** Concrete

The Olympic Stadium in Helsinki is a landmark piece of Finnish Functionalist architecture. The architects, Yrjö Lindegren (1900–52) with Toivo Jäntti (1900–75), won the competition to design the stadium in the 1930s. The Helsinki Olympic Games were due to take place in 1940, but were canceled with the outbreak of World War II; Helsinki finally got its moment in the spotlight in 1952. A statue of the runner Paavo Nurmi by the sculptor Wäinö Aaltonen stands outside the stadium. He appeared in the poster for the Olympics, and carried the Olympic torch into the stadium at the opening ceremony. The design of the stadium combines two very different elements: a low, bowl-like stadium and a slim, white tower soaring to a height of 236 feet (72 m). The tower, blindingly white when lit by the summer sun, encapsulates the idealism and achievement associated with the Olympic movement. Other stadia since have been influenced by this balance between flat and upright features; one example is the stadium in Montreal designed by French architect Roger Taillibert for the 1976 Olympics. The Helsinki stadium has seen a number of additions and phases of building. It was renovated between 1990 and 1994, and more recently a new roof has been added to the east side. The stadium is regarded with great affection and nostalgia among the sports-mad Finns, and it serves as a remarkable example of mid-twentieth-century Utilitarian architecture. **RK**

"If an object is made to function well, it will by definition be beautiful."

George H. Marcus, *Functionalist Design* (1995)

Grundtvig Church (1940)

Architect Peder Vilhelm Jensen-Klint **Location** Copenhagen, Denmark **Style** Expressionist **Materials** Brick, timber, glass

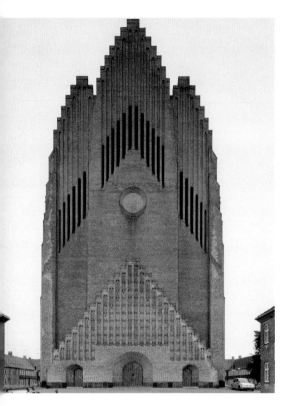

"He strove to achieve synthesis of . . . European Gothic churches and contemporary Expressionism."

Gerd Hatje, author

⬆ A forceful upward movement links Jensen-Klint's architecture with that of Gothic church builders.

➡ The visitor searches the nave in vain for a trace of the ornamentation associated with a Gothic interior.

Nothing quite prepares the visitor for the extraordinary sight of this towering brick church, a building resembling a cross between a gigantic pipe organ and a German Expressionist movie set.

In 1913, architect Peder Vilhelm Jensen-Klint (1853–1930) won the competition to design the church as a memorial to the popular hymn writer N. F. S. Grundtvig, but it was not until 1921 that the foundation stone was laid. The site is a square in the residential suburb of Bispebjerg, in the northwest of Copenhagen, where Jensen-Klint also designed the surrounding houses. The church is conceived in an Expressionist style, but the form also draws on the Gothic brick churches of northern Europe and the buildings of the Danish National Romantic movement. As an indication of the church's size, more than six million yellow bricks were used in its construction.

Among the most striking features of the church is the soaring entrance facade, with its tripartite gable, complete with lower ziggurat pattern and projecting central section. Further Expressionist stepped brick gables run down the sides of the building, interspersed with etiolated windows and topped with pointed arches. The interior is a modern interpretation of the Gothic cathedral, with a long nave and aisles, pointed arcades, and a ceiling height of some 115 feet (35 m). However, in this case the traditional carved stone decorations are replaced by exposed courses of projecting and receding brickwork. Even the two pulpits, one located at the end beneath the tower and one in the choir, are made of brick.

In 1930, before the building could be completed, Jensen-Klint died. The final works, including the organ front and many of the furnishings, were finished by his son, Kaare Jensen-Klint. The church was finally consecrated in 1940, on the one hundred and fifty-seventh anniversary of the hymn writer's birth. **MF**

Martienssen House (1940)

Architect Rex Martienssen   **Location** Johannesburg, South Africa
Style International Style   **Materials** Concrete, brick, timber, glass

Modernism did much to shape South African architecture. The idea that towns could perform like machines was appropriated by the apartheid regime, resulting in dislocated and paradoxically inefficient cities. Racial divisions were mapped out according to Modernism's principles of separate urban functions: "industry" zones became "township" slums for black workers, while the "town" was reserved for whites. Modernism and apartheid seemed inseparable.

However, the Modern movement's utopian dimension was not entirely lost in South Africa. Its most significant exponent was Rex Martienssen (1905–42). Dynamic and inspirational, his enthusiasm caught students, colleagues, and famous international Modernists in its wake: he corresponded with Le Corbusier, Terragni, and Léger. Always at the center of debate, he edited the *South African Architectural Record* as well as teaching and designing. A belief in modern design's capacity to drive social and spiritual change fueled his tireless networking. Societies such as the Alpha Club and the Transvaal Group were springboards for Martienssen's activism, and his writing—especially the journal *Zerohour* (1933)—reads as a manifesto for what his biographer, Gilbert Herbert, calls a "living architecture in South Africa."

Martienssen's own house in Greenside is canonical, a regional interpretation of Modern movement principles. Most significant is the composition of the front elevation, which draws on Léger and Helion, and the aesthetic theories of Kandinsky. Le Corbusier's influence can be seen in the character of the plan and in proportional relationships. After only two years in his new home, Martienssen died, aged thirty-seven; tribute was paid to his lasting achievement in a special issue of the *Record*. **MJB**

National and University Library (1941)

Architect Jože Plečnik   **Location** Ljubljana, Slovenia
Style Plečnik Baroque   **Materials** Stone, brick, marble

The National and University Library of Slovenia (see page 444) may be the masterwork of Jože Plečnik (1872–1957). Work began in 1936 on the site of the Auersperg Palace, destroyed in an earthquake in 1895. Plečnik limited his plans to the palace's site and volume. He viewed the library as a symbolic temple of knowledge and culture. The student passes through the entrance doors and ascends a monumental staircase lined by thirty-two pillars of black marble, to enter the grand Reading Room. It is a passage from darkness to light, in a dramatic metaphor for learning.

> *"This building is a powerhouse as well as a storehouse; a bastion of the Slovenian language."*
>
> Mel Gooding, architectural historian

The exterior reflects the Baroque influences of the Roman artist Federico Zuccari (1543–1609). The facade is of stone and brick mixed in an interplay of textures. A large statue of Moses, by Lojze Dolinar (1893–1970), and projecting windows suggest Viennese influences.

The interior of the Reading Room has a handsome Arts and Crafts dignity. Readers study in a light, beautifully crafted room, traversed by narrow gallery bridges supported by charming spindly columns of brass and metal. The light fittings are inventive and appealing. The doors to the Exhibition Room feature dark marble panels enclosed by marquetry frames. The brass door handles are stylized eagle heads.

The building was damaged by a airplane crash in 1944, but was repaired, with Plečnik taking the opportunity to redesign the ceiling. **ATB**

Århus
Town Hall (1941)

Architects Arne Jacobsen, Erik Møller **Location** Århus, Denmark
Style Modernist **Materials** Reinforced concrete, marble, white cement

In 1937 Arne Jacobsen (1902–71) and Erik Møller were chosen by Århus town council to create what turned out to be one of the most celebrated and innovative buildings of twentieth-century Danish architecture. Despite World War II and the Nazi occupation, their town hall was inaugurated in 1941; it was marked for preservation due to its unique design in 1994.

The building, situated in the center of Århus, consists of four stories. It is split into three overlapping blocks, each of which represents a different service function. The block pointing toward the main part of the city, including the main vestibule, acts as the area of representatives. The central office block, with a long corridor dividing all the offices on both sides, is intersected into the main hall, which links the vestibule with the third building, a smaller and lower section containing the citizens' service area. The town hall's monumental blocks are lifted by the 197-foot-high (180 m) tower. Like the rest of the building, the tower is covered with Norwegian Porsgrunn marble.

Århus Town Hall expresses many aspects of the Modernism of Arne Jacobsen and Erik Møller. The rigid yet open and light design works superbly well, particularly with the outdoor surroundings. The cool gray of the marble, concrete, and white cement contrasts strongly with the verdigris copper-covered roof and the detail of the clocks. With a sense of majestic dignity the town hall fuses the classic tradition of monumental architecture with a calm, open, and progressive design style. **SML**

↗ The tower, which so dominates the building, was added on the instigation of the citizens of Århus.

→ The tower is framed by a scaffoldlike concrete structure with two clock dials and five balconies.

Ministry of Education and Health (1943)

Architects Lucio Costa, Oscar Niemeyer   **Location** Rio de Janeiro, Brazil   **Style** Modernist   **Material** Reinforced concrete

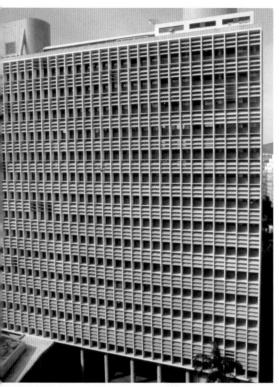

This was the first of many big Modernist buildings commissioned by a South American government, and remains one of the best. The original winners of a competition for the job were paid their prize money but then dismissed by the strong-willed minister, Gustavo Capanema, who wanted something more innovative. He appointed Lucio Costa (1902–98) to the job, and Costa called in his hero Le Corbusier to advise. An ambitious young draftsman in the office, Oscar Niemeyer (*b.* 1907), was so excited by the contact with Le Corbusier that he would privately trace the master's sketches in order to teach his hand to produce similar line drawings. Soon Niemeyer had pushed his way up to a role nearly equal to Costa's in the team.

The ministry, also known as Capanema Palace, is a tall block. High stilts lift it from the ground to open up a street-level piazza in the crowded city; although it later became a cliché of Modernist office blocks, at the time it seemed miraculous to stand such a large building on such slender legs. The other defining feature of the building is its control of sunlight. In the subtropical sun of Rio, offices easily become unbearably hot. To allow breezes in, but shade the sun-drenched north facade, the architects covered it in a grid of concrete sunshades, of which the vertical fins were fixed, the horizontal ones adjustable according to the position of the sun.

The impact of this office block was all the greater for its completion during World War II, when most of the world had put architecture entirely on hold. It promised a world of scientifically planned, Modernist, beautiful buildings once the war was over. **BWC**

↖ Le Corbusier's Ministry was a landmark building, signaling the arrival of Modernism in South America.

← The clever system of concrete sunshades controls sunlight and ventilation inside the building.

Casa Malaparte (1943)

Architects Adalberto Libera, Curzio Malaparte   **Location** Capri, Italy   **Style** Italian Rationalist   **Materials** Pompeian stone, red stucco

The gorgeous island of Capri has undeniably had its days of glamour—however, the luxury lifestyle is not its sole attraction. Conceived by Italian Rationalist architect Adalberto Libera (1903–63) for the eccentric journalist Curzio Malaparte (1898–1957), a beautiful yet bizarre house sits theatrically on the Massullo Peninsula, on the eastern part of Capri. With its geometric forms and bright color, the villa is a perfect expression of Italian Rationalism.

Situated at the top of a steep slope, the villa is a red-stuccoed masonry residence in the shape of a simple box, and possesses a wonderful rooftop patio overlooking the Gulf of Salerno. The roof area, decorated by a freestanding wall of increasing height, is reached by a monumental reverse pyramidal staircase, an element so strong that from a distance it seems that the whole building transforms into a wedge of steps. Rumor has it that Malaparte was the real force behind the design; dismissing Libera's original plans, he followed his own vision, assisted by the expertise of local stonemasons.

Casa Malaparte is notoriously hard to reach, accessed after an almost two-hour walk from the nearest town and via private property—or by sea, on a calm day. It has become—thanks to its design, location, and the owner's idiosyncrasy—a genuine architectural myth. Its dramatic shape and surrounding scenery prompted film director Jean-Luc Godard to use it for *Le Mépris* (1963), which helped raise awareness of the house, abandoned after Malaparte's death. Today, the villa retains the original furniture, but is still private property. **ES**

↗ Perched high on its exposed promontory, Casa Malaparte is as uncompromising as its once-owner.

➡ Pompeii-red walls, steps without handrails, and the white, curving wall all promote a sense of unreality.

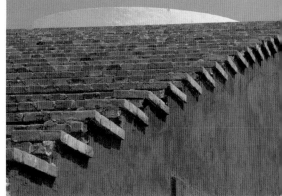

Pentagon (1943)

Architect George Bergstrom   **Location** Arlington, Virginia, USA   **Style** Neo-Classical Revival   **Materials** Reinforced concrete, wood, slate

The Pentagon is notable not just as the military nerve center of the United States, but also as the office building with the highest capacity in the world. Shaped as it sounds—the result of a former site's shape—the Pentagon is known to those who work within its walls as "the Building." Its sheer size yields some dizzying statistics. It houses around 23,000 military and civilian employees and about 3,000 nondefense support personnel. The building has five floors above ground plus two basement levels, and five ring corridors per floor, with a total of 17.5 miles (28 km) of corridors. It boasts a floor area of 34 acres (14 ha). It lists 131 stairways, 19 escalators, 13 elevators, and 7,754 windows. The building rests on 41,492 concrete piles, the combined length of which would stretch 200 miles (322 km). Its five concentric pentagonal rings are separated by interior courts that serve as light wells—a design feature of civilian

architect George Bergstrom (1876–1955)—that increase the number of windows and allow natural light. The inner- and outermost rings have sloping slate roofs, while the other three rings have flat roofs. Since these were the early years of World War II, very little steel was used in its design. Although not considered a design masterpiece, and bearing the emotional scars of being hit by an airborne terrorist attack in 2001, the building remains a massive achievement in constructional speed and scale. **DT**

" . . . a hundred architects and nearly as many engineers worked around the clock . . ."

James Carroll, *House of War* (2006)

Italian Chapel (1945)

Architect Domenico Chiocchetti   **Location** Lambholm, Orkneys, Scotland   **Style** Vernacular   **Materials** Concrete, salvaged materials

Two Nissen huts placed end to end are all that remain of Camp 60, a prisoner-of-war camp on the small island of Lambholm, in the Orkneys. From 1943 until the end of World War II, Italian prisoners converted the huts into a chapel. Italian prisoners had been sent to Lambholm in 1940, to assist with the construction of the Churchill Barrier, a concrete barricade blocking the eastern approach to Scarpa Flow. In January 1942, 550 Italians were relocated to Camp 60, which comprised thirteen Nissen huts. Almost as soon as they arrived, the Italians began to improve their surroundings. They used concrete left over from the construction of the camp to build paths, a theater, and a recreation hut, complete with a concrete snooker table. But their greatest undertaking was the chapel, on which work began toward the end of 1943. The project was managed by artist Domenico Chiocchetti (1910–99). Once the huts had been repositioned, work began on the chancel, followed by the altar, stoop, and the elaborate facade. All were constructed from concrete and scrap materials. Behind the altar, Chiocchetti created his masterpiece, a painted window portraying the Madonna and Child. The interior walls were paneled with plasterboard and painted with scenes of Italian churches. In total the work took eighteen months. The prisoners were repatriated early in 1945. The chapel was rededicated in 1960, with Chiocchetti in attendance. **AM**

"Decorated by Italian prisoners of war, it has been preserved as a reminder of Camp 60."

Simon Holloway, *Corrugated Iron* (2007)

Hamdi Seif al-Nasr Rest House (1945)

Architect Hassan Fathy   **Location** Fayyum, Egypt
Style Islamic Revival   **Materials** Clay, mud brick

Built in 1942, and expanded in 1945, the Hamdi Seif al-Nasr Rest House (see page 444) is a family home. What makes it notable is that it is the work of one of Egypt's most important architects, Hassan Fathy (1900–89). Fathy was an Islamic Revivalist who advocated the adaptation of existing Egyptian Mamluk, Cairene, and Nubian styles. He pioneered the use of elements such as the *malkaf* or wind catch, *shukshaykha* or lantern dome, and *mashrabiya* or wooden lattice screen, which he combined with mud-brick construction, believing this would lead to distinctive, economical,

> ## "Architecture is music frozen in place, and music is architecture frozen in time."
>
> Hassan Fathy, architect

and environmentally friendly structures in keeping with tradition. His promotion of this type of mud-brick architecture to house the poor, earned him the nickname the "Barefoot Architect."

The house is located on a peninsula of land that lies in Lake Fayyum. It was built to be used by a landlord as a weekend retreat on his visits to his estate. The building is raised up on a podium above the water level to protect it from floods, and is accessed by a small set of steps. A square, arcaded courtyard lies at its center, and vaulted and domed private rooms, such as the dining room, are situated around it. The main vaulted space at one end of the property is left open to serve as a loggia. Typically, it has a dome raised on squinches, and uses colored glass windows to serve as wind catches and protection against the sun. **CMK**

Dymaxion House (1946)

Architect R. Buckminster Fuller   **Location** Dearborn, Michigan, USA
Style Prefabricated   **Materials** Aluminum, steel

Dymaxion House, designed by R. Buckminster Fuller (1895–1983), is one of the great dead-ends of modern architecture; a prefabricated house for global mass production that barely made it out of the prototype stage. Now installed and fully restored at the Henry Ford Museum in Dearborn, Michigan, it nonetheless continues to inspire contemporary practice.

"Dymaxion" is a hybrid word coming from the words "dynamic," "maximum," and "tension." Early Dymaxion prototypes never made it beyond model form. Fuller envisaged using new materials and construction methods to create a hexagonal, mast-supported structure that could be "deliverable in 24 hours." It was not until the end of World War II that the concept found its most fitting sponsor. Developed in conjunction with the Beech Aircraft Corporation of Wichita, Kansas, the Dymaxion House was built using surplus aircraft production technology, drawing on the skills the company had accrued during the war.

The circular structure uses glistening, ultra-light, curved, aluminum panels clad onto a mast-supported framework. Inside, it is a masterpiece of packaging, fitting two bedrooms, two bathrooms, kitchen, and living area into 1,000 square feet (92 sq m), using clever, space-saving devices such as revolving clothing racks and an integral vacuum-cleaning system. Best of all, the house could be carried on a single truck and erected in a day with the right team at hand.

Fuller's dream of nationwide mass production looked imminent. But, for whatever reason, he wavered, conjuring up endless technical and logistical reasons why production could not commence immediately. Interest waned rapidly, and this brief flurry of futurism was swiftly subsumed beneath the Levittown-driven future of suburban sprawl. **JBL**

Kaufmann Desert House (1946)

Architect Richard Neutra   **Location** Palm Springs, California, USA
Style International Style   **Materials** Stone, glass, stucco

The desert setting is key to the Kaufmann Desert House. Twenty years after he introduced European Modernism to Los Angeles, Richard Neutra (1892–1970) imported the suburban garden—manicured lawn and plants that know their place—to the desert habitat. When he tamed the Sonoran Desert, Neutra did what countless others have tried to do before and since—control and alter what they believe to be barren and intolerant.

That the Kaufmann House is iconic is undisputed. That it is innovative is apparent. Seamless windows frame the view. The "gloriette"—a modern medieval keep—is a second-story aerie with three sides of vertical louvers to attract or repel the elements. It neatly sidesteps the one-story zoning restriction and is the main focal point. The house is a series of interconnected blocks in the shape of a serifed cross. Flat roofs create welcome overhangs. A central living area leads to long wings for the bedrooms and bathrooms. Breezeways augment internal galleries and route past patios and pool. Massive drystone walls ensure that the precinct is protected.

Compared to nearby building designs by fellow European Modernist architect Albert Frey that draw inspiration from the desert landscape and attempt to integrate with their environment, Neutra's Kaufmann House reflects a widespread U.S. belief that nature should bend to humanity's will. Neutra created a masterpiece. But whether house should master landscape is the question. **DJ**

↗ The gloriette's view takes in the landscape, but is cut off from it by the pool and surrounding walls.

→ The large windows ensure the interlocking blocks of the house remain open and inviting.

New Gourna (1948)

Architect Hassan Fathy   **Location** Luxor, Egypt   **Style** Vernacular   **Material** Mud brick

The villagers of Old Gourna near the Valley of the Kings, Queens, and Nobles in Egypt made their living by looting the local Pharaonic tombs. The Egyptian Department of Antiquities hoped to put an end to this ransacking by moving the 7,000 locals from the area. Hassan Fathy (1900–89), an architect noted for his rural housing and traditional methods was the obvious choice to design the new village on a site 50 miles (80 km) away. His plans for the village reveal the careful attention he paid to the individual at a time when Modernists were building uniform units. Each of the five tribes of Old Gourna would live in their own zone of the new village. Large public central spaces would lead to smaller courtyards and narrow alleys would wind their way back to the private area of family home. Preserving customs was central to his thinking. For example, communal wells were used in the new design because the daily parade of women to the well in Old Gourna afforded suitors the only chance to spot a marriage match. Fathy erected an agricultural marketplace, hotel, and craft market which he hoped would give the villagers new sources of income. But his vision fell apart when the Gournii refused to move. Building ground to a halt with only a fifth of the village complete. It was left largely uninhabited with only the mosque—the first part of the village to be built—still maintained. Nonetheless, the design of the village remains a great example of rural planning. **ADB**

> *"When planning a city one has to consider the man who is being planned for..."*

Hassan Fathy, "What is a City?" lecture (1967)

Breuer House II (1948)

Architect Marcel Breuer   **Location** New Canaan, Connecticut, USA   **Style** International Style   **Materials** Timber, concrete

Breuer House II is a modern version of the traditional "longhouse" plan—one room deep and connected in a straight line. It is built into a gently rising hillside and entered from the windowless northwest side. The main living spaces are in the upper part, which is built of timber, with a broad overhanging balcony on the southeast corner, from which a slender ladder stair descends into the garden. In 1938, Marcel Breuer (1902–81) arrived in the United States and became known as a younger Modernist with Bauhaus roots who was pioneering a more romantic form of architecture with natural materials and rough textures. He worked in New York and subsequently joined a colony of Modernist architects building their own houses at New Canaan, of which Philip Johnson's Glass House is now the best known. The first Breuer House in Lincoln, Massachusetts, was designed with Walter Gropius. Breuer House II is a timber box that floats on a concrete base. It attracted admiration worldwide, despite a difficult construction process, and was widely imitated. The process of hanging the balcony from a steel cable took many attempts to achieve successfully, although this feature provided the best photographs during its construction, including one of Breuer and his wife eating lunch and enjoying the view. Inside, there was a freestanding, white-painted fireplace, another typical Breuer feature. The Breuer House II survives, but in a much altered form. **AP**

> *"It gives you a feeling of liberation, a certain élan, a certain daring, while [also] a sense of security."*
>
> Marcel Breuer, architect

Casa Barragán (1948)

Architect Luis Barragán   **Location** Mexico City, Mexico   **Style** Modernist   **Materials** Stone, plaster

The combination of Modernism with the warm and uniquely vibrant Mexican character has never found a more perfect expression than in the architecture of Luis Barragán (1902–88). In what better place can architects apply their theories than in their own home? Casa Barragán is the second residence that the architect designed for himself in the Tacubaya district of Mexico City; the first was on 20–22 Ramirez Street, only a stone's throw away.

Casa Barragán, at No. 14 Ramirez Street, is a house defined by its simple, geometric spaces, colored surfaces, and wide interiors. From the outside, a completely unmemorable facade, with materials left in a near-natural state, represents the structure's intrinsic modesty. Inside, lower walls separate the high-ceilinged main space, assisting in the diffusion of sunlight throughout the house. The use of primary colors on walls and furnishings reflects Barragán's love of Mexican culture. A large window allows visual access to the wall-enclosed garden. Barragán often called himself a "landscape architect," and his outside spaces were intended to be extensions of the interior.

Throughout the house and garden, Barragán's interest in animals and his religious beliefs are evident in the form of horses and crucifix-shaped icons. The house was continuously remodeled until his death in 1988. Throughout his career, Barragán became a specialist in designing intimate private spaces, perfect for isolation from the outside world. His other favorite themes—the combinations of flat planes and light, and the use of strong, vivid colors—are all repeated in Casa Barragán. **ES**

◥ The restrained use of color, texture, and form are key to the tranquil, harmonious character of the house.

◄ The building, with its unprepossessing facade, makes no attempt to stand out on the quiet Mexican street.

Case Study House No. 8 (The Eames House) (1949)

Architects Charles Eames, Ray Eames **Location** Pacific Palisades, California, USA **Style** International Style **Materials** Concrete, glass

Chicken wire appeared on the June 1950 cover of *Arts & Architecture* magazine—John Entenza's publication about modern architecture, which launched the Case Study House movement, which called for modern alternatives to suburban housing. Chicken wire also appears as visible glass reinforcement in the house of Charles (1907–78) and Ray Eames (1912–88). Its use indicates the role industrial and off-the-shelf materials held for the husband-and-wife team. But it was more than just wire. For the Eameses, it was a collection of holes incidentally held together with wire. This highly original way of looking symbolized their simple yet revolutionary style.

Their prefabricated house sits on a hillside, which allows the upper floor to open at ground level, while a concrete retaining wall allows the lower level to do the same. Courtyards balance two live-work blocks. The corrugated flat roof is hidden outside, but its wavy raw profile is visible inside. The steel frame house featured sliding walls and windows, contributing to spacious, light, and versatile spaces.

Color blocks delineated by black perimeters suggest Mondrian. Seemingly minor details, such as the pull-cord triple-doorbell, celebrate labor and love of mechanical functions. The main door has a "finger pull" circle above, and opens onto a splay-foot open circular stair. The Eameses' love of science is evident in the mirroring of the two main living units, and in details such as panel voids versus hardscape voids. Case Study House No. 8 demonstrates how the materials and patterns of the ordinary can combine to produce an extraordinary lifestyle. **DJ**

↗ The Mondrianlike lines of the house are balanced by the organic forms in the surrounding landscape.

→ It took five men sixteen hours to raise the rectangular steel frame of the structure.

Glass House (1949)

Architect Philip Johnson   **Location** New Canaan, Connecticut, USA   **Style** International Style   **Materials** Steel, glass, brick

The Glass House is the epitome of Modernism and Modernist space—a spare glass and steel box. It is flooded with light, open visually to the natural world around, yet austerely in contrast to it. Philip Johnson (1906–2005) drew closely on the tradition of the classical villa in his design: a place of retreat and repose in the country. The house is an hour's drive north of New York, and Johnson, who built it for himself, commuted for many years to his office in Manhattan. Internally, the division of space seems provisional and fluid as there are no partition walls—yet it is highly defined. The dominant element, a brick cylinder, separates the space between bedroom and study, and living and dining areas. This cylinder contains a bathroom opening onto one area and an open hearth facing the other. The latter element completes the *mise en scène* of the main living space, centralized in the house like the salon in a classical villa, but here defined only by the edges of a large rug on the floor, and bounded by a fictive wall implied by the positioning of a Poussin painting on an easel. The house is set up on a small bluff and looks down onto a lake and pavilion. The latter is just one of many folly-type structures Johnson built, making the grounds of the house seem like a small-scale, eighteenth-century English garden. One of the most iconic buildings of the twentieth century, the house is also a sophisticated essay on architectural history. **RGW**

"Philip, should I take my hat off or leave it on? Am I indoors or am I out?"

Frank Lloyd Wright, architect

Turin Exhibition Hall (1949)

Architect Pier Luigi Nervi   **Location** Turin, Italy   **Style** International Style   **Material** Reinforced concrete

In autumn 1947, the Turin authorities commissioned Pier Luigi Nervi (1891–1979) to build an exhibition hall on the site of the former fashion institute that had been destroyed during World War II. The hall had to be completed by the spring of 1949, in order to host the first postwar International Automobile Show. The schedule was tight, and Nervi was chosen because the design he submitted took into account time and cost-effectiveness. Nervi was already one of Italy's most influential engineers. He had developed novel ideas for the use of reinforced concrete, including the invention of *ferrocement* (a strong, light material made of layers of steel mesh grouted together with concrete), and with it a new architectural language. The Turin Exhibition Hall was the first major building where Nervi used an innovative structural method of precasting he had developed in 1944, and which he was to adopt throughout his career with great results.

The dome of the hall was subdivided into small elements forming grooves into which concrete could be poured. The ribs so-formed served a dual purpose of establishing the monolithic nature of the structure and eliminating the need for columns. Movable scaffolding with a built-in lifting device was installed to raise and position the precast elements. The roof of the main hall spans more than 269 feet (82 m). The undulating ribbing structure that holds it up has a plastic richness because of the light entering through the windows, which are arranged in the corrugation of the prefabricated roof elements. The Turin Exhibition Hall is exemplary for Nervi's approach to fusing form and construction. His designs made reinforced concrete the main construction material of the time, and buildings such as the Turin Exhibition Hall are exceptional in terms of inventive construction, conceptual realization, and aesthetic perfection. **CH**

Rose Seidler House (1950)

Architect Harry Seidler   **Location** Turramurra, New South Wales, Australia   **Style** International Style   **Materials** Concrete, timber

With the uncompromisingly modern Rose Seidler House, Harry Seidler (1923–2006) introduced east coast Modern to a country more used to building and living in cottages that would not have looked out of place in late-nineteenth-century Britain. An Austrian émigré, Seidler first studied architecture in Canada, before leaving for New York to be taught by Walter Gropius and Marcel Breuer. After finishing his studies, Seidler worked in Breuer's studio before leaving for Australia, a journey he made via Brazil and Oscar Niemeyer's studio. The influence of these Modernist masters is plain to see in the house at Turramurra that Seidler designed for his parents. It is one of three houses he designed on a site overlooking a valley in Ku-ring-gai Chase public reserve. The house is open on all sides to make the most of the spectacular views, and is essentially a hollowed-out square with separate living and sleeping areas joined by a central family room. The central terrace can be reached by a ramp, which, together with stone retaining walls and a louver fence, anchors the partly suspended house to its surroundings. While the interior is characterized by cool, purist colors and textures, the central terrace is dominated by a vibrant mural painted by Seidler himself, the reds, yellows, and blues of which are picked up through accent colors in the furnishings, thus maximizing the spatial flow and heightening the sense of bringing the outside space indoors. **GB**

> *"There can be no more captive client than a mother!"*

Harry Seidler, architect

Farnsworth House (1951)

Architect Ludwig Mies van der Rohe   **Location** Plano, Illinois, USA   **Style** International Style   **Materials** Steel, glass

Usually cited as the ultimate monument to Modernist purity, but also a prime example of bull-headed, architectural arrogance, Farnsworth House is one of the icons of the Modern movement. Dr. Edith Farnsworth hired Ludwig Mies van der Rohe (1886–1969) at the height of his powers. After moving to the United States in 1937 having been expelled from the Bauhaus by the Nazis, he embraced the commercial opportunities of the New World. The pared-down Modernism evolved from the classical simplicity of his early works; the next stage was to exploit the rigid perfectionism of glass and steel construction to the full, with soaring office and apartment blocks that inspired a multitude of imitators. Farnsworth House is a glass box bracketed by thin, white floor and roof slabs. The vertical steel columns raise the entire structure above the ground—a flood plain—accentuating the sense of the house as a sculptural object placed within the landscape. Dr. Farnsworth complained bitterly about the house's failings—the lack of privacy, the impractical layout, and the baking interior. The house's free plan and minimal servicing made it awkward to inhabit. Peter Palumbo bought the house from in 1972, and spent a lot of time and money improving upon its terrible environmental performance. The house stands as a monument to purity and obstinacy, an unattainable yet fascinating state of domestic perfection. **JBL**

"The paraphernalia of traditional living ... abolished in a puritanical vision of simplified ... existence."

Maritz Vandenberg, *Farnsworth House* (2003)

860–880 Lake Shore Drive
Apartments (1951)

Architect Ludwig Mies van der Rohe   **Location** Chicago, Illinois, USA
Style International Style   **Materials** Steel, glass

The form of the steel-framed high-rise is so familiar today that it is hard to imagine the impact the twin towers of 860–880 Lake Shore Drive Apartments—the first of their kind—had when they were completed in 1951. For Ludwig Mies van der Rohe (1886–1969), however, they were not a novel concept but the realization of a thirty-year-long ambition. He first proposed a lightweight skeletal skyscraper in a 1921 competition in his native Germany. But it was not until the late 1940s, when he was living in the United States, that he was able to put his ideas into practice. The opportunity came when he was commissioned by real-estate developer Herbert Greenwald to design apartment blocks for a prime Chicago site on the edge of Lake Michigan.

The result is a pair of 26-story towers placed at right-angles to each other that has become one of the most copied schemes in the world. On first impression the buildings look simple. But, for the architect whose style has been summed up by the aphorism "less is more," this is his greatest achievement because of the scrupulous attention to design and engineering detail required to achieve such an effect. The towers utilize frames of steel beams and cantilevered floors that make possible their floor-to-ceiling wrap-around glass skins. Because the buildings appeared to achieve the Modernist ideal of form following function, the most controversial detail is the addition of nonstructural I-beams on the facades. They were added by Mies to express the nature of the real structure that remained concealed in accordance with fire-safety regulations. Mies brushed off the criticism and repeated the same detailing in one of his greatest creations, the Seagram Building in New York (1958), this time expressing the structure in bronze just for good measure. **MF**

Beverly Hills Hotel Refurbishment (1951)

Architect Paul R. Williams **Location** Beverly Hills, California, USA
Style Mission-style, Modernist **Materials** Stone, pink stucco

The hillside Hollywood sign is not the only famous symbol in Los Angeles. In 1949 Paul R. Williams (1894–1980) was commissioned to redesign large parts of the Beverly Hills Hotel. His work included a sweeping drive leading to the signature colors of the portico entry and a green entablature block resting on a narrow pink cornice supported by two round, shell-pink columns. He also spelled out the hotel's name in his own handwriting on the facade. Williams did all this as an African-American in an era when discrimination was openly practiced, proving he was unusually gifted

---

"If I allow the fact that I am a Negro to checkmate my will, I will form the habit of being defeated."

Paul R. Williams, architect

---

and tenacious. Known as the "architect to the stars," his clients included Frank Sinatra and Tyrone Power.

The signature areas of the present-day hotel were designed by Williams and married to the original Mission-style structure. To fuse Modern on Mission could be a disaster, but Williams's genius was to create a unique architectural style: a mix of Palladian and French empire made modern by materials, layout, and interplay of radical elements. Williams redesigned the lobby, added the Crescent Wing, and revamped the Polo Lounge and Fountain Coffee Shop. His elegant style can be quickly identified—round columns, circular sweeping staircases curved in tandem with the wall, and Greek temple details among other features. The hotel is a theatrical stage set on which the fantasies of architect and guest are played out. **DJ**

Aula Magna (1952)

Architect Carlos Raúl Villanueva **Location** Caracas, Venezuela
Style Modernist **Material** Concrete

In his long association with the Central University of Venezuela, Carlos Villanueva (1900–75) succeeded where most had failed. Over a period of more than twenty years he managed to collaborate with some of the most eminent artists of the time, such as Alexander Calder, Andre Block, Jean Arp, and Fernand Léger.

The core of the university campus is the cultural center that consists of the Aula Magna, the Paraninfo, and the central library. The Aula Magna auditorium is the stunning centerpiece in this composition. The uncompromising use of exposed concrete clearly turns it into the visual focus of the entire scheme. The entrance to the building is filtered by a series of open spaces connected by ramps and stairs that also link it to the rest of the campus. Villanueva here mitigates the strong presence of the concrete by using local materials such as bricks to filter natural light.

The dynamism of the entry finds its logical conclusion inside the auditorium. Villanueva invited Alexander Calder to design the ceiling acoustic panels, the large colorful shapes of which are distributed irregularly to contrast with the symmetry and monochromatic quality of the space, and float above the auditorium like clouds. A special lighting system varies the intensity of the lights to create different atmospheres. All the building's elements complement one another to create an architectural spectacle.

The combination of this building and the urban plan constitute one of the highest peaks reached by modern architecture. In a historical period in which Functionalism was running out of steam, Villanueva opened up new perspectives for architecture by breaking away from rigidity and abstraction to embrace local traditions and materiality as equally important elements of design. **RB**

Unité d'Habitation (1952)

Architect Charles-Edouard Jeanneret (Le Corbusier)   **Location** Marseille, France   **Style** Modernist   **Material** Concrete

The Unité d'Habitation (Housing Unit) crystallized many of Le Corbusier's groundbreaking, radical ideas about architecture. Building vertically, using modern construction technology, in blocks set in landscaped open spaces, meant that it was possible to increase housing densities while maintaining healthy, green spaces for play and recreation. In the 1920s and 1930s the health benefits of sunlight and fresh air were encouraged, partly to counteract diseases such as tuberculosis. The Marseille Unité is the first and most definitive of this example of Modernist residential housing. It is a 12-story slab of 337 apartments raised on 23-foot high (7 m) *pilotis* (supporting blocks on structural columns) above the ground. The "vertical city" is 450 feet long (137 m), 66 feet wide (20 m), and 200 feet tall (61 m). There is an internal street of shops on the fifth floor, where you can stay at the Hotel Le Corbusier. The roof design, which was very influential,

is a private piazza in the sky behind high parapets. Between sculptural vents and lift-housing towers, there are play areas, a roof garden, benches, and a swimming pool. By using weather-boarded and bush-hammered concrete, Le Corbusier created a robust, primitive finish that provides good sound insulation. While this textured concrete looks attractive in sunny Marseille, it is less so in wetter climes. Originally the Marseille Unité was intended as low-cost housing, but its residents now tend to be more bourgeois. **ATB**

"Any architect who does not find this building beautiful had better lay down his pencil."

Walter Gropius, architect

Säynätsalo Town Hall (1952)

Architect Alvar Aalto **Location** Säynätsalo, Finland **Style** International Style **Materials** Brick, copper, wood

Säynätsalo Town Hall showcases the remarkable talent of Alvar Aalto (1898–1976) as an all-around designer. The detailing and furniture designed specifically for the town hall contribute to a coherent, visual whole. As well as designing a variety of buildings, Aalto also painted, sculpted, and was an industrial designer. His art fed into his architecture, and this is apparent at Säynätsalo Town Hall. Red brick gives the building a solid, monumental presence. This is a civic center, housing a library, government offices, and the local council chamber. The chamber—at the top of the building—lends the layout a visual hierarchy. Its wooden ceiling is supported by fan-shaped wooden struts or *perhoset*, one of several elements of visual quirkiness that were typical of Aalto. The first floor houses the library, apartments, and offices. The third floor courtyard is a tranquil square with a water feature and a sculpture. Aalto intended the space to be used by the building's occupants, showing his interest in their comfort and enjoyment. Unlike the rest of the complex, the council chamber has a slanting roof, emphasizing its importance. The town hall is almost eccentric in its layout: the asymmetrical structure offers unexpected views, around corners, downstairs, and through windows, with zigzagging lines and vertical sweeps. The building appears in harmony with its surrounding woods, the sunburned trunks of pine trees repeating the red hues of the brick. **RK**

"Taste is so incredibly rare that you would need three or four decimal places to express its frequency."

Alvar Aalto, architect, in his student journal

Dublin Central Bus Station (1953)

Architect Michael Scott **Location** Dublin, Ireland **Style** International Style **Materials** Reinforced concrete, Portland stone, mosaics, brick

Dublin Central Bus Station, or Busáras, is one of the first postwar examples of the International Modern style in Europe. The architectural team led by Michael Scott (1905–89) was strongly influenced by Le Corbusier's Maison Suisse in Paris. The bus station faces James Gandon's Custom House—Dublin's finest eighteenth-century building—and mirrors its use of Portland stone. Busáras was controversial at the time because of its heavy cost. Standing on an island site flanked by three streets with facades of equal detailing, there are four distinct sections: two rectangular office blocks, a top floor pavilion, and the station itself, which is irregularly shaped. The bus station, a curved block capped by a wave-contoured, cast concrete canopy, emerges from beneath the two office buildings and appears to link them. This canopy, cantilevered out into the forecourt far enough to cover the passengers, was exceptional for its time. Busáras integrated art with architecture, meticulously detailed as it was with stone, mosaics, handmade bricks, and assorted woods. It incorporated a basement theater and a restaurant on the top floor. Scott's visionary project failed, however, due to a lack of funding to exploit the building's potential. The theater and restaurant closed, and the building became drab. Now a listed building, however, its iconic status is being belatedly recognized, and conservation is underway to restore this classic of Irish modern architecture. **BMC**

"A tour-de-force of glass, metal, and mosaic immediately beside Gandon's great Custom House."

Robert Furneaux Jordan, architecture critic

Yale Art Gallery (1953)

Architect Louis Kahn **Location** New Haven, Connecticut, USA **Style** Modernist **Materials** Concrete, glass, steel, red brick

Can any other art gallery boast a staircase that is a pilgrimage destination? The triangle-inside-a-circle stair by Louis Kahn (1901–74) is not, however, boastful. His modestly sized, mid-century art gallery addition to the Beaux-Arts, main space is classically inspired but modern in delivery. Kahn is a maverick materials man and statesmanlike Modernist, as is evident in details such as the concrete slab dual-purpose ceiling/floors. These are triangular shapes formed in tetrahedral pans to create depth and texture. Each floor is visible through the crisp glass and thin, vertical scrim, steel frame, and combined they create a formal yet warm space. Kahn contrasts the glass/steel side with Chapel Street—a concrete facade composed of blocks. The lobby continues this blending of different materials with a red-brick stretcher bond wall. The exhibition floors are open spaces. The gallery was recently renovated by the Polshek Partnership, which honored the form while updating selected materials. Masters of the curtain wall, the Polshek Partnership sandwiched the glass and metal with reinforced insulation. They released Kahn's sunken court from a clumsy roof addition. The famous staircase rationalizes the layout and provides a circulation feature. Stand at the top of the stairs and look down. Light filters over your head from clerestory windows that peek around a cast triangle panel. This vantage point crystallizes the reason why Kahn's quiet gem must be seen. **DJ**

> *"Somewhere up there Louis Kahn is smiling down on Yale once again."*
>
> Nathaniel Kahn, filmmaker, after the restoration

Moscow State University (1953)

Architect Lev Vladimirovich Rudnev **Location** Moscow, Russia **Style** Soviet **Material** Concrete

In 1755, Moscow State University was founded in central Moscow by the scholar Mikhail Lomonosov. In the late 1940s, Stalin decided to build a new university building, designed by Lev Rudnev (1885–1956), on Moscow's Sparrow Hill. Stalin's consolidation of power saw the demise of the Constructivist architectural period in Moscow and its replacement with a new monumental style. He wanted to rebuild large areas of the city in "Stalinist Gothic" style. Seven matching skyscrapers, known as Stalin's "seven sisters," were erected at key points in the city, the idea being that wherever you stand in Moscow you can always see one of them. Their description as "wedding cake" architecture is misleading as there is nothing inviting about these intimidating structures. Moscow State University is the tallest of the sisters. Indeed, at 79-feet (240 m) high, it was the tallest building in Europe until 1988. The style is influenced by the Kremlin towers and European Gothic cathedrals. Built by German prisoners of war, it contains 20 miles (33 km) of corridors and 5,000 rooms. The star on top of the central tower is said to weigh 12 tons, while the facades are decorated with wheat sheaves, Soviet crests, and clocks. The terrace below is ornamented with students gazing confidently into the future. Newlyweds go to Sparrow Hill, which has panoramic views over Moscow, to have their picture taken, but with the city, not the university, as the backdrop. **WB**

"[Stalin's] Gothic Imperial [style] was designed to create a sense of awe, power, history, and dread."

Simon Sebag Montefiore, *Stalin* (2003)

Smithdon School (1954)

Architects Alison and Peter Smithson **Location** Hunstanton, Norfolk, England **Style** Brutalist **Materials** Steel, brick, reinforced concrete

Smithdon School was one of many built in Britain in the 1940s and 1950s to accommodate the large generation of children conceived by couples settling down after the war. In a country hampered by war and debt, the schools were built cheaply with minimal materials, but every effort was put into ensuring the new buildings provided the best conditions for children. Alison (1928–93) and Peter (1923–2003) Smithson were both under thirty when they won the competition to build the school. The austere purity of Smithdon School struck a chord with many of their generation internationally, and, although it does not use much exposed concrete, it has long been seen as a key building in the growth of the Brutalist movement, which was to dominate architecture in the next two decades. Planned formally, like a Renaissance palace, around two courtyards, the main building avoids long, institutional corridors by positioning all

the classrooms on the second floor, accessible by staircases. Steel and brick are always visible, and the lighting and plumbing pass along walls and ceilings unconcealed. In photographs, the building looks more forbidding than it is, and you cannot appreciate the detail. The steel is arranged into a system of posts and beams as logical and satisfying as the columns in a Greek temple. It is also finely cut and welded to avoid ugly bolts, and what little there is beyond steel and brick is elegantly economical. **BWC**

"An attempt to make architecture out of brute materials, but with . . . self-denying restraint."

Reyner Banham, architecture critic and theorist

Niemeyer House (1954)

Architect Oscar Niemeyer **Location** Rio de Janeiro, Brazil **Style** Modernist **Materials** Reinforced concrete, steel

Oscar Niemeyer (b. 1907) has enjoyed a lifetime of commissions beyond the dreams of most architects, with many museums and government buildings. At the smaller scale of this private house for himself, however, he produced what may well be his greatest work. Indebted to the glass-box houses popularized by Mies van der Rohe, the basic organization of the ground floor is a roof standing on columns, with the interiors minimally separated from the outside world by glazing. But unlike Mies's houses, Niemeyer's roof is an irregular and curvy shape, beneath which the glass meanders with equal freedom. The proximity of nature is heightened by boulders from the garden, which come through the windows and into the house, as though the glazing were as insubstantial as a soap bubble. For all the striking beauty of the house, comfort is not sacrificed to architectural ideals: the remarkably open first floor is the entertaining area, but

bedrooms are given privacy and insulation from the heat by being sunk into a basement below, with windows giving glimpses up to the garden. The Canoas House, as it is sometimes known, is not only smaller than most of Niemeyer's work, it is also less formal. In most of his buildings he organizes the functions into a simple, large-scale volume with a distinctive, overall shape. Yet here we see another side to the architect—the Niemeyer of perfect details and thoughtfully relaxed planning. **BWC**

"[I respect] all architecture, from the chill . . . of Mies van der Rohe to the . . . delirium of Gaudí."

Oscar Niemeyer, architect

Maison Curutchet (1954)

Architect Charles-Edouard Jeanneret (Le Corbusier) **Location** La Plata, Argentina **Style** Modernist **Materials** Reinforced concrete, glass

The buildings in the later career of Le Corbusier (1887–1965) are often full of playful surprises, a feature you tend not to expect from one of the founding fathers of Modernism, with its rationalist language, strict tenets, and reputation for monastic simplicity. Maison Curutchet is a good example: from the street this three-story house—in the grid-patterned city of La Plata in Argentina—looks rather austere, however, inside a secret world of beauty, color, and complexity is gradually revealed. The house was constructed as an office and home for a medical doctor named Curutchet, with a clinic in the front section separated from the main house at the rear by a pleasant, open courtyard planted with a poplar tree. As with Le Corbusier's most famous house, the Villa Savoye, a sculptural ramp provides the pivotal point in the building. In accordance with the architect's principles, a concrete structure of slabs on slender pillars allows for a free plan which makes possible the curved bathrooms and large, double-height living room on the second floor. A certain hedonistic lifestyle is also suggested by the shaded roof terrace, and the way in which views over the living room are provided through louvered openings in the master bedroom. Although Le Corbusier had visited Argentina in 1929, he never saw this site or the completed building, and its construction was supervised by a local architect, Amancio Williams. Maison Curutchet—which is now open to the public—stands as a transitory example of work in the architect's career. While there is obviously a link to his earlier Parisian houses, the imaginative narrative experience created by a separation of work and living quarters, linked by the ramp in the courtyard, looks forward to the building designs of Postmodern architects such as Rem Koolhaas and Richard Meier. **MF**

Notre Dame du Haut (1955)

Architect Charles-Edouard Jeanneret (Le Corbusier)   **Location** Ronchamp, Franche-Comté, France   **Style** Modernist   **Materials** Concrete, render

The hilltop chapel of Notre Dame du Haut designed by Charles-Edouard Jeanneret (know as Le Corbusier, 1887–1965) occupies an ancient site of religious worship, having previously been the location of a pagan sun temple and a fourth-century Christian sanctuary. Canon Lucian Ledeur approached Le Corbusier to design the chapel in 1950, telling him, "We do not have much to offer, but we do have this: a wonderful setting and the possibility to go all the way." Le Corbusier did not disappoint the canon with his extraordinary chapel, more redolent of a sculptural installation than a building. The chapel is an organic composition of convex and concave surfaces, without the strong symmetry and axiality of the traditional church. The thick volume of the battered south wall, with its deep reveals and irregular windows of colored glass, sharpens to a prow at the southeast corner, while the inverted whale-back of the "breton-brut"

(raw concrete) roof oversails the rough-cast walls and lends a geological quality. The east wall is sparsely fenestrated and cradles an exterior altar and pulpit to mirror those in the interior; outdoor pilgrim gatherings are part of the chapel's remit. The vertical elements in the composition are provided by the three cylindrical light cowls that tower above the dark concrete roof. With its bold, almost naive forms, the chapel seems indelibly part of the hilltop and has echoes of vernacular building. It quite different from the urbane, intellectual architecture that preoccupied Le Corbusier before World War II. The spatial qualities are visceral in effect and daylight is used in a masterful way: a soft glow in the light cowls, aspirant shafts of light at sliced openings, a sharp line of daylight separating the south wall from the dark bulge of the roof that hovers, magically, above. Whether you are spiritually inclined or not, this is an inspiring building. **CB**

Tate & Lyle Sugar Silo (1955)

Architect Tate & Lyle Engineers Department   **Location** Liverpool, England   **Style** Functionalist   **Material** Reinforced concrete

At times the most interesting buildings that surround us are not necessarily the most beautiful. A good case in point is Liverpool's former Tate & Lyle sugar silo. Liverpool was once an internationally important port, thanks partly to the lucrative sugar trade. Henry Tate of the firm Tate & Lyle began his business in Liverpool and the immense wealth he accrued from sugar later funded the various Tate art galleries. Traders in granular products such as sugar had long found storage problematic because when poured in quantity they form a natural mound. At the turn of the twentieth century, reinforced concrete became available, and North America—the source of many granular crops such as wheat and sugar—was soon dotted with enormous silos. Unexpectedly, these stark, utilitarian structures were to inspire many Modernist architects. In Britain in the 1920s, Imperial Chemicals had built a series of parabolic arched silos to store fertilizer, which had been inspired by the airship hangars built at Orly, France. The sugar silo is a 528-foot-long (161 m), 90-foot-high (26 m) unobstructed space with a rough, ribbed exterior that contrasts with the smooth, unadorned interior. To stand in it while empty is to stand in a space unlike any other. The scale and simplicity of the building is ample compensation for its lack of traditional beauty, and it is a superb example of the Modernist credo of form following function. **ER**

"[The use of concrete] in the soaring curves of this silo shows [concrete's] possibilities . . ."

English Heritage, on the silo's historic status

Kresge Chapel (1955)

Architect Eero Saarinen   **Location** Cambridge, Massachusetts, USA   **Style** Modernist   **Materials** Brick, reinforced concrete

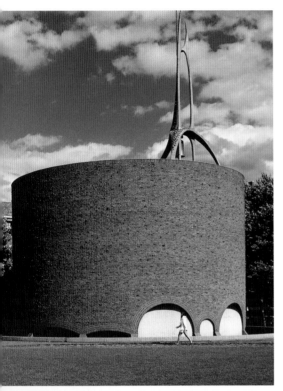

The nondenominational Kresge Chapel and the nearby Kresge Auditorium, both designed by Eero Saarinen (1910–61), were part of a conscious attempt in the 1950s to introduce a new social and community hub to the Massachusetts Institute of Technology. The original plan was to include more facilities and to landscape the open spaces. However, this plan was never completed, and the two Saarinen buildings have, as a result, a slightly unsatisfactory relationship with each other and their surroundings.

From the beginning the chapel was controversial. Unsurprisingly, traditionalists disliked it for not looking like the rest of the campus. Modernists, too, often expressed reservations. Whereas the spectacular engineering of Saarinen's other works—the TWA Terminal and the Ingalls Rink—drew many admirers, the Kresge Chapel does not seek to astonish through technical wizardry.

The building is a simple cylinder from the outside. Apart from the base, which is cut away into low arches and circled by a shallow moat, the exterior could hardly be simpler. Going in, there is a surprise: the inside is not a cylinder, but waves in and out in sinuous curves. The most striking feature is the highly theatrical lighting: a circular window above the altar lets in most of the illumination, like a giant spotlight. This effect is enhanced by a Harry Bertoia sculpture made from suspended flecks of metal which pick up and dramatize the beam of light like smoke. The chapel revels in visual effects and refuses to bow to European Modernist prejudices about the inside and outside of a building being the same shape. **BWC**

↖ The Kresge Chapel evokes a 1950s spirit of optimism and demonstrates the power of light and shape.

← Harry Bertola's floating metallic sculpture introduces a strong theatrical element to the chapel's interior.

Casa Antonio Gálvez (1955)

Architect Luis Barragán   **Location** Mexico City, Mexico   **Style** Modernist   **Material** Stone

There are few Mexican architects as important in architectural history as Luis Barragán (1902–1988). He is renowned for reinventing the International Style, offering a colorful, even sensuous, Latin American version of Modernism. Casa Antonio Gálvez, situated in Mexico City's San Angel area, is one of his most poetic masterpieces and showcases his notion of the house as a space of peace and retreat.

The house is located on a cobblestone street in a formerly suburban area of the city, on a piece of land measuring a mere 7,217 square feet (2,200 sq m). Barragán has used the space to create a family house with an enclosed garden. Modernist influences are evident in the lack of ornament and the sharp geometry of the plan's design, a play of lines and surfaces. But the Mexican master's personal style and his philosophy of "regionalism" in architecture are also clearly outlined. The colors of the house—intense pink, a warm shade of ocher, and a bright white—help to separate the shapes and screen the entrances and facades. A fountain, enclosed by the tall walls of the entrance patio, causes the patio's heat to rise and cooler air to be wafted into the house.

Tall walls with relatively few windows define the interior/exterior relationship—with the exception of the floor-to-ceiling glass opening that leads to the courtyard and brings together living space and nature in typical Barragán style. This arrangement perfectly suits the hot Mexican climate, enabling the house to breathe and stay cool during hot summer afternoons, while at the same time accentuating the sense of intimacy and privacy that the architect so valued. **ES**

↗ Barragán's use of tall, brightly colored walls was borrowed from traditional Mexican architecture.

⇥ Bright pink and white surfaces are offset by the ocher of the geometric porch and the pale gray paving.

House
Fox (1955)

Architect Revel Fox **Location** Worcester, South Africa
Style Modernist **Materials** Stone, timber, glass

Traveling inland from the Cape offers a rich variety of landscapes. The beaches and lush lawns of the coastal belt give way to wine country. Passing through a range of majestic mountains takes one to an entirely different terrain, ascetic but not arid. There you can see for miles to the craggy boundaries of this serene flat land or *platteland* as it is known.

This sublime topography sets the scene for the early work of Revel Fox (1925–2004). Responding to the spirit of the place, as well as the zeitgeist of 1950s Modernism, his designs—like Frank Lloyd Wright's

---

"... a link in the search for a South African style within the framework of modern techniques ..."

Alan Lipman, architecture critic

Prairie style but in a different idiom—keep a low profile. They hug the ground and lazily blink in the dazzling sunlight. House Fox exemplifies this aesthetic: it is an archetypal "Fox Box"—the nickname that has become synonymous with the Fox oeuvre.

Scandinavian "New Empiricism" influenced Fox as much as the local vernacular. The overall form consciously mimics South African farm buildings just as elements of the design look to European precedent. Critics have seen echoes of Eliot Noyes and Raphael Soriano in the set-back glazing and the delicate veranda columns. It is in the balance between the restrained simplicity of the design and the sophistication of its detail—of attention to proportion, materials, and environmental performance—that this modest house stakes its claim to greatness. **MJB**

Pedregulho
Residential Complex (1955)

Architect Affonso Eduardo Reidy **Location** Rio de Janeiro, Brazil
Style Modernist **Material** Reinforced concrete

Pedregulho Residential Complex represents a peak of Brazilian Modernism. Up to 1946, Paris-born Affonso Reidy (1909–64) was mainly involved in academic research. Pedregulho gave him a strong presence, not only among Brazilian architects, but also as an international designer.

The masterplan, which included housing blocks for low-income families, schools, and support services, was commissioned in 1946. Reidy, who worked with Carmen Portinho and Roberto Burle Marx, had to confront the significant size of the program and the topographical constraints of such a rugged site. Through a single, large-scale gesture, he was able to accommodate most of the housing units along the hill in a 853-foot-long (260 m) building that incorporates 272 apartments. In this way, aesthetic concerns and social issues created a spectacular solution.

In section the building is split into two main parts by a long path, which provides access to the various residential units. The open space cutting into the building also brings together all the public spaces and provides a stunning view of the bay. Below this path all the single-bedroom apartments are located, whereas the upper part is occupied by duplex apartments for families to maximize density.

The elevation that faces Rio's bay emphasizes the horizontality of the intervention with a long *brise-soleil* (sunshade) in concrete, which is only interrupted by the verticality of the supporting columns. By contrast, the rear elevation employs a simple, but quite poetic screening device built with simple bricks that produce a sense of domesticity in a development of otherwise mega-structural scale.

Reidy's design brings together social concerns and a dynamic, almost sensual, formal language. **RB**

Chandigarh High Court (1955)

Architect Charles-Edouard Jeanneret (Le Corbusier) **Location** Chandigarh, India
Style Modernist **Material** Reinforced concrete

The planning of Chandigarh as the administrative capital of the redefined state of Punjab began in 1947, immediately after the partition of India. Le Corbusier (1887–1965) designed the city according to the principles laid down by the Congrès Internationaux d'Architecture Moderne (CIAM), which the architect had co-founded. These design principles called for functional order. Le Corbusier demanded "honesty of materials"—exposed brick, boulder stone masonry, and concrete surfaces forming geometrical structures, which became the defining elements of Chandigarh.

Le Corbusier's work in Chandigarh is concentrated in Sector 1—the Capitol Park stands aloof like a modern Acropolis, dominating the city with the four huge solitaires of the Secretariat, the Assembly, the Governor's Palace, and the High Court. The latter was the first completed building in Chandigarh and consists solely of reinforced concrete, demonstrating the sculptural possibilities of this building material.

The High Court is a linear block with a gracefully arched roof, meant to shade the entire building. The main entrance has three 59-foot-high (18 m) slabs of concrete colored light green, yellow, and red. The facade toward the plaza is a playful composition of cutouts and niches, reconciling its size with the human scale while fully expressing the majesty and force of the law. It contains nine law courts with offices, each one having its own entrance. The design embraces furniture, fittings, and nine huge tapestries, which cover the back wall of each court room. **FH**

↗ Reinforced concrete provides the building's structural integrity and its sculptural ornament.

➡ Simple blocks of color contrast with the surrounding concrete, marking the entrance to the courthouse.

Palace of Culture and Science (1955)

Architect Lev Vladimirovich Rudnev   **Location** Warsaw, Poland   **Style** Soviet   **Material** Reinforced concrete

Warsaw's Palace of Culture—originally known as the Joseph Stalin Palace of Culture and Science—was a "gift" from the Soviet Union to Poland. It was built during the early 1950s, when the USSR was asserting its influence over every sphere of life in Poland, and other states in eastern and central Europe. The Soviets originally proposed a university based on Moscow State University, a monumental Stalinist edifice designed by Lev Rudnev (1885–1956). However, the Poles expressed a preference for a center of culture and science. But while the building's function changed, the architect, style, and tower form were retained. Rudnev led a team of four architects on the design of the 754-foot-high (230 m) skyscraper—the height includes the 140-foot (43 m) spire. In its "wedding cake" composition, Gothic trappings, and monumental scale, the Palace of Culture is classically Stalinist. However, much of the detail, including 550 ornamental sculptures, was inspired by Polish design convention. Construction lasted 1,175 days and was carried out by 7,000 workmen—3,500 from Poland, and 3,500 from the Soviet Union. The building contains 3,288 rooms over 42 floors, including cinemas, theaters, and museums. From the beginning, the structure was highly controversial; to the residents of Warsaw, it was inescapable evidence of Soviet domination. Today it has many uses, including as an exhibition center and office complex. **AM**

"The ornamentation ... inspired Warsawers to baptize the Palace 'an elephant in lacy underwear.'"

Emporis Buildings website

Berlage Institute (1955)

Architect J. J. P. Oud **Location** Rotterdam, Netherlands **Style** Neo-Modernist **Material** Brick

The Berlage Institute is one of the most prestigious architecture schools in the world, named after the great Dutch architect H. P. Berlage, and presided over by Alejandro Zaera-Polo, one of the co-founders of Foreign Office Architects (FOA). Some of the best-known architects practicing today have participated in the Berlage's two-year postgraduate program. With its cutting-edge character and dynamic dean, one would expect it to be housed in a temple to avant-garde architecture. It is, however, housed in a sober historic building that was designed originally as a *Spaarbank* (savings bank) by legendary Dutch architect J. J. P. Oud (1890–1963) in the late 1940s. One of Oud's later buildings, it represents a departure from his earlier forays into Neo-Plasticism. As a proponent of De Stijl, alongside Mondrian and Van Doesburg, Oud argued for simplicity of form and the use of primary colors. Here one sees a more restrained palette indicative of Oud's postwar style: the use of white brick is reminiscent of his hero Berlage and symbolizes a more subtle architecture. The facade is symmetrical and restrained with a central entrance with glass-brick curved walls. Inside, the floorplan is rational and conventional. Oud was considered one of the great Modernist architects, alongside Mies van der Rohe, Walter Gropius, and Le Corbusier although he has not received the recognition afforded to his Modernist colleagues. **KAB**

"The characteristic feature of architecture is relief ... the art of the definition of space ..."

J. J. P. Oud, architect

Rødovre Town Hall (1956)

Architect Arne Jacobsen   **Location** Rødovre, Copenhagen, Denmark   **Style** International Style   **Materials** Reinforced concrete, steel, stone, glass

Arne Jacobsen (1902–71) believed in the universality of the designer's art; whenever possible he designed not only the buildings themselves but also the fittings and furniture that went inside them. As he was to state, "the fundamental factor is proportion." The town hall at Rødovre, a suburb of Copenhagen, demonstrates him working at all scales of design. Replicas of the clock he designed for the council chamber are still manufactured, and his chair, door-handle, and cutlery designs in general are perhaps better known than his architecture. Rødovre Town Hall is almost painfully simple and regular in its design. A large rectangular block contains the offices and most other functions; a small box to the rear houses the council chamber. That is all. The open sides of each block are unvarying curtain walls of glass and steel; the closed end walls are clad in plain black stone. Only a freestanding porch relieves the entrance front. Inside is a wide central corridor, open to the public, flanked by the paired structural columns on which the building stands. The interiors are almost as sparse as the exterior. Such simplicity is difficult to execute with conviction—the architect risks being seen as unimaginative rather than restrained. Jacobsen, however, avoided large-scale gestures for a reason: by keeping the shape simple, the intimate perfection of the building's every detail is allowed to set the tone. A good place to start learning to love this wonderful, unemotional building is on its main staircase, where very slim treads run between zigzagging beams. The stair rises through all three stories of the building, but never touches the walls. Instead the whole thing is hung from three thin, steel bars. Here and throughout the building, Jacobsen seems to take to extremes the famous aphorism attributed to one of his architectural heroes, Mies van der Rohe: "less is more." **BWC**

Hiroshima Peace Center (1956)

Architect Kenzo Tange   **Location** Hiroshima, Japan   **Style** International Style   **Material** Reinforced concrete

Hiroshima's Peace Memorial Park commemorates the world's first nuclear attack. It is hard to distinguish the emotions raised by the architecture from those arising from the poignancy of the place. In the immediate aftermath of World War II, Hiroshima directed most of its effort to providing housing, schools, and other essentials. There was, however, a feeling that a proper memorial was required as a matter of urgency. A competition was held, and won by Kenzo Tange (1913–2005), a young professor of architecture in Tokyo. With a budget constrained by the cost of wider reconstruction, Tange could not make expensive gestures. The main building, the Memorial Museum, is a simple glazed box on paired columns. Seen from the Peace Memorial (Genbaku Dome), it is translucent and light—a quiet backdrop for gatherings, reminiscent both of the Japanese tradition of pavilion building and of the work of Mies van der Rohe. From an angle,

however, the museum looks more monumental and solid, with rough concrete surfaces like those being employed by Le Corbusier at the time. Tange continued to add to the complex into the 1990s, using similar architectural elements to maintain the unity of the overall group. The Hiroshima Peace Center is in a way more about what has gone than what is there now. Tange's simple, dignified buildings were intended as calm places to come together with others and think about the horror of nuclear war. **BWC**

> *"Tradition is a catalyst that furthers a chemical reaction, but is no longer detectable in the end result."*
>
> Kenzo Tange, architect

University Library (1956)

Architects Juan O'Gorman, Gustavo Saavedra, Juan Martinez de Velasco   **Location** Mexico City, Mexico   **Style** Functionalist   **Material** Stone

Although all three architects produced early examples of Mexican Functionalist architecture, each eventually tempered strict Le Corbusier–style Modernism with an idiom that was uniquely Mexican. Part organic and part progressive socialism, the style was authenticated with native materials, construction, and the unity of structure and content. The architects' careers hit an exhilarating high when they collaborated on the Central Library of the National Autonomous University of Mexico. This modern building references ancient terrace structures with a ten-story core stack that hugs a corner of the much wider three-story, flat roof base, and crests in a small roof block echoing Aztec sanctuaries atop the main temple form.

Five years before work on the site began, Xitle volcano erupted and left behind waves of volcanic stone. This *piedra volcanica* supplied not only much of the building materials, but inspired elements of the form allied to structural and spatial arrangements of Mayans and Modernism. Echoing tiered temple registers, and geologic layers of igneous rock, the first floor, double-height reading room has rectangular sequences of eleven-by-seven rows of striated, translucent amber onyx squares stacked atop sets of two-pane, three-row glass windows. The onyx shifts from opaque to glowing.

At night the whole becomes a backlit magic lantern that pulls one's vision across the vast public forecourt in preparation for the visual shift upward to the massive mosaic stack. O'Gorman selected ten native rocks to create 10-foot-square (1 m sq) panels, which when assembled across the four faces, creates a unified mosaic design depicting the history and culture of Mexico. The mosaic's exuberant use of color pays homage to the once glorious polychrome stucco surfaces of what are now bare limestone Mayan and Aztec temples. **DJ**

"I invented this technique . . . I had to, because I didn't know any other way to do it."

Juan O'Gorman, architect

⬆ The style of the mosaic adorning the University Library was inspired by indigenous Mexican art.

➡ The building brings to mind ancient Mayan temples, with a central block topped by a smaller sanctuary.

Clock Tower, Church of St. Joseph (1957)

Architect Auguste Perret   **Location** Le Havre, Normandy, France   **Style** Art Deco, Modernist   **Materials** Concrete, stained glass

In 1945, Auguste Perret and his colleagues were appointed to reconstruct Le Havre after the city center was reduced to ruins by British and Allied bombing the previous year. The new city is an outstanding example of postwar urban planning and architecture based on the unity of methodology, and the innovative use of prefabrication and of reinforced concrete. Much of the work was supervised by Jacques Tournant, but Perret reserved the design of St. Joseph's Church for himself. Work began in 1951 and was completed after Perret's death by Georges Brochard and Raymond Audigier. The church, which was formally consecrated in 1964, is central to the rebuilding of Le Havre. The 360-foot (110 m) octagonal lantern tower is both a memorial to the 5,000 air raid victims and a spiritual lighthouse that can be seen far out at sea: Le Havre was then France's principal transatlantic port. Perret intended it as a landmark for travelers on the ocean. Architectural historian Andrew Saint described the interior: "Inside, raw piers of concrete thrust up from the corners then lurch inward to carry the open lantern which, you feel, must sooner or later come crashing down." In addition to the concrete is stained glass by Marguerite Huré, which consists of 12,768 small pieces in colors carefully interpreted with spiritual meaning. Huré intended the changing daylight to alter the atmosphere using shifting colors: at midday the south side appears aflame. The effect, within Perret's concrete framework, is profound and intense. The Perret reconstruction of Le Havre, including St. Joseph, was declared a UNESCO World Heritage Site in 2005. **ATB**

⬏ The tower commemorates the victims of Allied bombing raids in the form of a beacon to the sea.

⬅ The tower acts as a lightwell, illuminating the interior with colored light from the elaborate stained glass.

Israel Goldstein Synagogue (1957)

Architects Heinz Rau, David Reznik   **Location** Jerusalem, Israel   **Style** Modernist   **Material** Reinforced concrete

From 1948 to 1957, the original campus of the Hebrew University of Jerusalem on Mount Scopus was, in practice, inaccessible, so an alternative one was founded at Givat Ram to the west of the modern city. This new site was laid out by Richard Kaufmann, Joseph Klarwein, and Heinz Rau, and was landscaped by Lawrence Halperin. It eventually housed some of the most interesting architecture in the fledgling state. The main block of the Israel Goldstein Synagogue consists of an elevated concrete shell that resembles a puff ball raised on arches. The visitor passes through these and ascends via a delicate staircase into a simple domed room; because its floor is detached from the sides of the walls, the space seems to be floating. The furnishings, simple and restrained, enhance the poignant austerity of the room; the design everywhere is crisp and original. Later in 1957, Walter Gropius sketched a university mosque for Baghdad along similar lines, albeit on a much larger scale. The synagogue is in an isolated place, its entrance approached along a path that runs between two low, orthogonal stone buildings that form part of the architects' composition. Few buildings, anywhere, can match the masterful, dreamy poise of this delightful structure. Rau's young architect partner, the Brazilian-born David Reznik, had worked for the acclaimed Modernist Oscar Niemeyer, and went on to create some of the most sensitive stone buildings in Jerusalem, a city he finds somewhat "melancholy." He remarked that the inspiration for the Israel Goldstein Synagogue came from the old synagogues found in upper rooms in Venice, Italy. **TBC**

↗ The Israel Goldstein Synagogue serves the Givat Ram Campus of the Hebrew University of Jerusalem.

→ Respite from the fierce Israeli sun is offered by the deep shadow of the arched entrance to the synagogue.

Pirelli Tower (1958)

Architects Gio Ponti, Pier Luigi Nervi   **Location** Milan, Italy   **Style** Modernist   **Materials** Glass, reinforced concrete

Opposite the central station, greeting travelers arriving at Milan, the Pirelli Tower rises thirty-two stories in a slender diamond shape quite unlike any skyscraper before, with its feeling of lift emanating from the recessed base and its floating roof plane. The narrow ends of the tower converge on a dark recessed gap, and the floors are tapered to the edge to reduce the appearance of weight.

Ponti was a multifaceted designer. His work ranged from decorative ceramics, textiles, and tiles to the classic "Superleggera" chair—a miniature Pirelli Tower in its tapering profiles—and his diverse buildings included classical styles. He understood the structural and decorative aspects of Modernism; he also became preoccupied with the structural and decorative potential of the diamond form.

For the Pirelli Tower, he worked with Italy's most famous postwar engineer and architect, Pier Luigi Nervi, to develop a novel structural system for such a slender building, relying on the twin, triangular, service zones at each end, with additional support from the lift core and the internal concrete piers, which diminish in size as they rise through the structure. The test was a model 36 feet (11 m) high, as it pushed the boundaries of existing knowledge. Not everything was quite as Ponti wished in the finished building, however, and he disliked the "striped pajama" effect of the glazing and the narrow balconies visible in what should have been the dark voids of the ends. Nonetheless, the height and location of the building made it immediately an international landmark.

The Pirelli Tower represented one of Italy's most potent global brands during the period of postwar reconstruction, rivaling the sophistication of New York with a form that was copied by Walter Gropius himself in the less successful Pan-Am Building, and by Richard Seifert at Centre Point in London. **AP**

Seagram Building (1958)

Architect Ludwig Mies van der Rohe **Location** New York, New York, USA **Style** International Style **Materials** Glass, steel, concrete

On Park Avenue, skyscrapers jostle one another for space, with one exception: the Seagram Building stands back coolly from the throng. A plain rectangle, with none of the setbacks that characterize its neighbors, the Seagram has instead an open plaza. Deriving from his experimental models of office towers built in the 1920s, the Seagram Building is a realization of Mies van der Rohe's dream of a tall glass block. Though the impact seen in early illustrations is now somewhat diminished by many hundreds of inferior copies in business districts all over world, the Seagram continues to retain something of its original spirit when actually experienced, even in the bustle of present-day New York.

In part, this quality is due to the fanatical care Mies van der Rohe expended on the details of the building; he is often quoted as saying, "God is in the details" a free adaptation of an aphorism of Thomas Aquinas. The details all contribute to the overall effect. Mies van der Rohe was able to build what he considered a "pure" version of the steel-framed skyscraper.

Some of that impact is due to the careful siting; Mies van der Rohe suggested to Samuel Bronfman, his client, that part of the site be given over to a raised public plaza fronting onto Park Avenue. In a city where land is enormously expensive, it is a bravura show of waste, conspicuous consumption on the very grandest scale. Incorporating the plaza also allowed Mies van der Rohe to avoid adhering to the setbacks that are part of the New York zoning laws, permitting him to make full and inspired use of the space.

Inside the Seagram is another unmissable sight, the Four Seasons restaurant, designed by Philip Johnson and still retaining the style of the late fifties. In this supremely civilized space the titans of industrial America ate—and continue to eat—their steak and lamb chops. **EG**

Atomium (1958)

Architects Eugène Waterkeyn, Andre & Jean Polak   **Location** Brussels, Belgium   **Style** Futuristic   **Materials** Aluminum, steel

The Atomium is a giant model of a crystal molecule of metal, magnified 165 billion times. It stands 335 feet (101 m) high on the Heysel plateau close to the site of the 1958 World's Fair, for which it was built. The structure consists of nine spheres, 59 feet (18 m) in diameter, linked by diagonal tubes 75 feet (29 m) long and 11 feet (3 m) wide. A large model was tested in a wind tunnel, which is why the "molecule" is supported by three pylons, called "bipods," needed for stability and for emergency evacuation stairways. An elevator leads to the panoramic view at the top and escalators—the longest in Europe when built—link the spheres. Rather optimistically, Waterkeyn hoped the Atomium would "encourage young people to seek careers in the technical field or in scientific research." Originally, some of the spheres contained scientific and medical displays; since restoration in 2006, exhibitions have also featured 1950s design. The

Atomium is now seen as a relic from the time when atomic symbols were used in popular domestic designs. It was imagined the beneficent science of the Atomic Age would provide limitless, clean, and cheap energy. The Atomium's construction dates from when Brussels was rebuilt after World War II and military occupation. Today it is a popular symbol of the European Union's capital city and perhaps relates to a deeper taste for the surreal. Belgium is, after all, the home of René Magritte and Hieronymus Bosch. **ATB**

"The Atomium symbolizes this age of ours in which men of science have deepened our knowledge."

Eugène Waterkeyn, architect

Palazzetto dello Sport (1958)

Architects Pier Luigi Nervi, Annibale Vitellozzi   **Location** Rome, Italy   **Style** Modernist   **Material** Reinforced concrete

Although Vitellozzi, a mid-ranking Italian Modernist, was officially the architect for this superb stadium, there is so little architecture and so much engineering in its construction that it can only really be seen as the work of its engineer and contractor, Pier Luigi Nervi. Nervi's genius for the design of large vaults had been allowed to develop unfettered, because he ran his own construction company: he would be the one to lose if his experiments failed, and as a result his courage and imagination were his only limits. By the 1950s he was one of the best engineers in the world, and one of the cheapest, quickest, and most elegant for spanning a large space. This stadium, the smaller of two built by Nervi for the 1960 Rome Olympics, seats 5,000. Nervi's belief that beauty does not come from decorative effects but from structural coherence is demonstrated perfectly in this building. The vault is 194 feet (59 m) in diameter, and was constructed

through concrete being poured over a thin wire mesh of reinforcement. The underside is covered in diagonal intersecting ribs, which not only make a beautiful pattern when seen from within, but also give rigidity to the thin roof. So light is the dome that the Y-shaped, leaning columns that support it appear to hold it down like guylines tethering a tarpaulin. Above each Y, the vault slopes up slightly, like the edge of a pie crust, allowing more natural light into the stadium, and creating a strong, repeating pattern around the perimeter. Now that clever engineers can cobble together a structure for almost any shape an architect chooses, a visit to one of Nervi's great projects is more of a pleasure than ever. The lesson that this building teaches is that for covering large spaces engineering itself can provide the beauty that architects seek. There could not be a better engineering solution, nor a more attractive stadium. **BWC**

Church of the Three Crosses (1958)

Architect Alvar Aalto **Location** Vuoksenniska, Imatra, Finland
Style Modernist **Materials** Brick, reinforced concrete, copper

The Church of the Three Crosses (Kolmen Ristin Kirkko; see page 445) was built not only as a church but also as a social center for a deprived industrial area of Finland. To fit it for this double function, the interior can be divided up by 16-inch-thick (42 cm) acoustically insulated sliding walls, as Aalto put it, "for playing ping-pong, for instance, if the sermon isn't very good."

The church's main body is a low, oddly shaped hump with a sullen, dark roof. Above it rises a large bell tower, Aalto's counter-statement to the area's many industrial chimneys. Inside, the apparent arbitrariness of the exterior becomes more explicable: the strange profile derives from the special acoustic shapes of the internal volume. On the other hand, the ground plan remains asymmetrical and irregular. Throughout its history, architecture has almost always been made subject to some clear overall order, whether it be regular columns or a standardized ceiling grid. Aalto, here and elsewhere, goes further in the direction of abandoning regulating order than any other architect, and carries it off with remarkable grace.

The Church of the Three Crosses is a lesson in architectural daring, but it is more than that. As ever with Aalto, small details are beautifully thought out, and designed as part of the whole. Also characteristic of Aalto is the fall of the distinctive Finnish light through oddly shaped windows over curving walls. The contrast between the extravagant shapes and the restrained Lutheran white of the interior here is magnificent. Descriptions of the building tend to make it sound restless, but, when experienced, the opposite is the case. Sit in the church for as long as you can spare, and rest your eyes on the calm, self-assured oddity of the altar, pulpit, and organ case around the central three crosses. **BWC**

Ingalls Hockey Rink (1959)

Architect Eero Saarinen **Location** New Haven, Connecticut, USA
Style Modernist **Material** Reinforced concrete

Eero Saarinen died prematurely in 1961, having been America's most glamorous architect of the 1950s, and one of its best. In 1956, he was commissioned to build this ice hockey rink for Yale (see page 444). Neither the beauty and daring of his design nor the reputation and charm of the architect, however, was enough to win the project easy acceptance in the university's conservative atmosphere. Without the massive efforts of Alfred Whitney Griswold, Yale's president, the project would almost certainly have been abandoned. Although widely known as the "Yale Whale," in

> *"A great university should look at architecture as a way of expressing itself."*
>
> **Alfred Whitney Griswold, former president of Yale**

affectionate mockery of its appearance from above, the rink is officially named for David S. Ingalls and David S. Ingalls Jr., both former hockey captains.

The design of the Ingalls Rink is so simple it seems almost inevitable: a single, arching concrete beam runs the length of the pitch, and a cable-hung roof hangs in a gentle curve from this ridge to the low outer wall. The great beam curves back up again at each end like a Cupid's bow, the ends providing an entrance canopy. The cooling equipment, locker rooms, and offices are under the rink; the seating rises on all sides. Materials are simple: the underside of the roof is bare planks, the concrete is rough, and the benches utilitarian, making a spectacular artistic statement as the roughness of the materials somehow makes the elegant shapes even more poignant. **BWC**

Great Hall
of the People (1959)

Architect Unknown   **Location** Beijing, China   **Style** Soviet
Material Reinforced concrete

The Great Hall on the west edge of Tiananmen Square was one of ten urban projects to commemorate the tenth anniversary of the founding of the People's Republic. Built by volunteers, it is the leading venue for Communist Party meetings, events, and conferences.

Topped by a green- and yellow-glazed tile roof, the complex consists of a central block with a series of bronze doors, a colonnaded portico at the front, and extensive wings. Above the main doors is a red shield, the emblem of the People's Republic of China. Visitors are admitted to the building, which contains more than 300 conference halls, assembly rooms, lounge areas, and offices, via the East Gate. Government speeches are given here and representatives of China's governing body hold their annual meetings in the central auditorium, capable of seating up to 10,000 officials. This vast interior boasts central heating, air conditioning, and the latest technology.

The auditorium's ceiling is decorated by a massive red star surrounded by a galaxy of lights: indicative of the centrality of China within a Communist universe. Several reception halls, each named after a Chinese province, are decorated in a style particular to each region. The state banqueting hall can house 5,000 guests. During the ascendancy of Communism and the frenetic construction program of the 1950s, the government swept away ancient aesthetics in favor of Soviet models. Beijing became a paradigm for socialist realism through grand-scale constructions advocating national form and socialist content. **AA**

↗ The red star in the center of the auditorium's ceiling represents the People's Republic of China.

→ The Great Hall of the People was built by Communist volunteers in just ten months.

Mausoleum of the Aga Khan (1959)

Architect Fareed El-Shafei **Location** Aswan, Egypt **Style** Islamic Revival **Materials** Pink granite, sandstone, marble

Aswan lies on the first cataract of the east bank of the Nile; a frequent stopping point for tourists traveling to the Ancient Egyptian monument of Abu Simbel. One of Aswan's most visited monuments is the Mausoleum of the Aga Khan, a small square building with turrets at its corners and a fanned staircase leading to the entrance. Inside, housed under a domed structure, lies a tomb carved from one piece of white Carrara marble. The building's popularity lies not only in its simple architectural beauty—the pink granite structure appears to glow at sunset—but in the love story that led to its being built, and the esteem with which the late Aga Khan III is held within the Islamic world. Three years before his death, Sir Sultan Mahommed Shah, Aga Khan III (1877–1957) chose the spot as his resting place. His third wife, French-born Princess Yvonne Aga Khan, known as the Begum, was given the task of building the mausoleum. After consulting a British

professor of Islamic architecture, a friend of her husband's, the Begum took Cairo's Fatmid Giushi mosque and its *mihrab* (a niche in the wall of a mosque) as her inspiration. She also chose a young architect, Fareed El-Shafei. The mausoleum was completed and her husband laid to rest there sixteen months after he died. After the Aga Khan's death, the Begum stayed at her nearby house for six months of each year, when she placed a rose on her husband's tomb every day until she died in 2000. **CMK**

"I am thinking of him all the time. As long as you live and are thinking of someone, he is alive."

Princess Yvonne Aga Khan

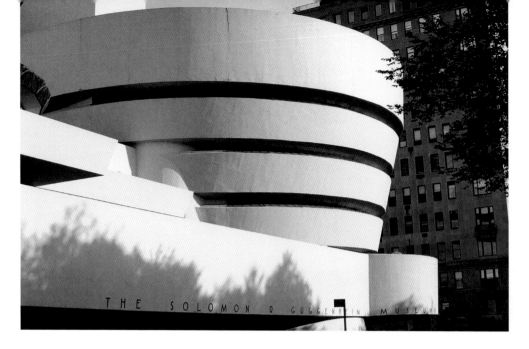

Solomon R. Guggenheim Museum (1959)

Architect Frank Lloyd Wright **Location** New York, New York, USA **Style** Modernist **Material** Concrete

Frank Lloyd Wright (*b.* 1869) was in his seventies when he received the commission in 1943 to design a museum for the modern art collection of Solomon R. Guggenheim. He worked on the project for sixteen years, until his death, at the age of ninety, just before its completion. Wright was not a fan of New York, a place he considered overcrowded and overdeveloped, so his design is something of a rebuff to the city of straight-edged buildings. In contrast to its neighbors, the main part of the museum is circular in plan, and from the outside it resembles a giant white funnel that tapers toward its base above a podium. The concrete structure was poured and sprayed on site as if the building were a massive sculpture. Inside, Wright proposed a new kind of gallery in which the art would be hung on the curved walls of a central ramp that spirals up through the building to a skylight. Visitors were whooshed to the top of the rotunda in an elevator, and then walked back down the ramp along a promenade of art. Niches were provided for separate displays, but even here the walls are not flat, and therefore not ideal for hanging art. In 1992, a large rectangular building by Gwathmey Siegel & Associates was added to the rear of the site to provide additional, and more conventional, gallery space. Although critics and artists are still divided over the Guggenheim's merits as a museum, it remains one of the world's most recognizable and best-loved buildings. **MF**

> *"Inappropriate ... for viewing works of art, but as an exercise in formal geometry [it is] remarkable."*

James Stevens Curl, architectural historian

Hooper House II (1959)

Architect Marcel Breuer   **Location** Baltimore County, Maryland, USA
Style Modernist   **Materials** Stone, steel

This house, despite being the size of a full-blown country property—with seven bedrooms, stables, and maids' accommodation—presents a supremely simple face to the world. Its main bulk—single-story, long, and low slung—is arranged between two parallel rough fieldstone walls in the Maryland woods.

This was the second house Breuer built for Arthur and Edith Hooper, a wealthy Baltimore couple with an impressive art collection. The plan is "bi-polar" with public rooms—living, dining, kitchen—at one end and private rooms—bedrooms and family room—at the other, separated by a square courtyard. The further two sides of the courtyard are formed by the fieldstone walls, one forming the facade to the long, thin entrance hall and the other pierced by a single, oblong cut-out, framing views to a lake and woods.

Breuer, born in Hungary, studied and taught at the original Bauhaus in Weimar. After living briefly in Paris, he taught at the re-established Bauhaus in Dessau. He became celebrated as a furniture designer and his designs remain influential today. Breuer left Germany in 1933 and, after settling in England for a few years, emigrated to the United States in 1939. It was for his series of east coast houses, completed in the 1940s and 1950s, of which the Hooper house is one of the most refined, that he became celebrated for a second time; this time as an architect. Hooper House II is a fine example of the Bauhaus legacy and its functional spare aesthetics transferred to and filtered through the culture of affluent postwar America. **RGW**

↖ The camouflagelike brickwork allows the house to blend into its woodland surroundings.

← The low-slung design transplants the sleek, European Bauhaus style into the American woods.

Century House (1959)

Architects John Godwin, Gillian Hopwood   **Location** Lagos, Nigeria
Style Modernist   **Material** Concrete

Century House was built to house the offices of the pharmaceutical firm Allen and Hanbury. Fronting one of old Lagos's principal squares, it nestles in the old Brazilian quarter of Lagos Island. It contrasts with adjacent buildings in its controlled rationalism that updates the European architectural tradition of the Portuguese-influenced Renaissance buildings close by, built by returning Brazilian slaves.

This was John Godwin and Gillian Hopwood's first commission. Century House sits in a narrow traditional plot, and tested the building codes by reaching six floors—local regulations decreed it should only have four. It is composed of two simple volumes: a main accommodation block slipped into an elegant thin concrete portal frame. At the top, between the main block and the portal, a terra-cotta–colored wall is set back and wraps inward to conceal the interior from the street.

The service zones of the building are coded in this terra-cotta color, dropping into the offset gap and cloaking or marking the stair shaft in the process. The main block has a double facade separating the functions of enclosure and solar protection. The outer skin comprises six modular panels housing louvers, inset in a frame that sits proud of the line of enclosure revealing a slight shadow gap. The louver modules are independently operated, and consequently animate the street facades as the occupants adjust the skin of the building to suit their requirements.

Proportionally, despite towering above its neighbors, Century House belongs, somehow mimicking the horizontal proportions of the nearby Olaiya House, built in the 1840s. Its restraint pushes both old and new to the foreground calling attention to its context and ultimately to itself. **GO**

Song Festival Complex (1960)

Architect Alar Kotli   **Location** Tallinn, Estonia
Style Modernist   **Material** Reinforced concrete

Tallinn's Song Festival Stage was built for the twentieth anniversary of the Estonian Soviet Socialist Republic. It was one of the key landmarks of "thaw era" Soviet architecture—an era initiated by Nikita Khrushchev following his denunciation of the repressive, brutal Stalin period. The sculptural form of the Song Stage, and the complex structural engineering required to erect it would have been unthinkable a decade earlier.

Alar Kotli is one of the most influential Estonian architects of the twentieth century. In this design, Kotli was inspired by Matthew Nowicky's Dorton Arena in

> ## "The re-connection … of Estonian architecture with contemporary international architecture."
>
> Mart Kalm, art historian

North Carolina (1952). Kotli chose an asymmetric design, with one of the arches unsupported and raised up allowing the internal surface of the suspended hyperbolic, parabola-shaped ceiling to operate as an acoustic screen. The 239-feet-wide (73 m) ceiling amplifies sound, and the back arch shields the sound from sea winds. The extensions are punctuated toward the north by the tower, designed for the festival flame, and toward the south by a wing for the press. The audience sits on a natural slope; the back rows have a breathtaking view of the 15,000-strong audience, the stage, and the medieval city of Tallinn.

As the Song Stage was a symbol of the officialdom of Soviet Estonia and a symbol of Estonian resistance, it was a main venue of the "singing revolution," which led to Estonian independence in 1991. **AM**

Planalto Palace (1960)

Architect Oscar Niemeyer   **Location** Brasilia, Brazil   **Style** International Style   **Material** Reinforced concrete

In the 1950s, under President Juscelino Kubitschek, the capital of Brazil was moved from Rio de Janeiro to Brasilia. The new capital was inaugurated in 1960, with the government and legislature moving to their fresh homes, including the new headquarters of the executive: the Planalto Palace. One of three major government buildings built around the Square of the Three Powers, the Planalto Palace is characteristic of Niemeyer's work in Brasilia. The vast open spaces and symbolically important buildings encouraged him to design strikingly theatrical architecture, the simplicity of shape of which only makes it all the more memorable. In the Planalto Palace he places all the functions in a rectangular, glazed box, then raises the box off the ground on a series of balletic buttress columns that reach in to touch their thin fingers on the lowest floor deck, before carrying on up to the roof. Niemeyer had a good understanding of engineering,

and elsewhere used it boldly. Here, however, much of the weight is in fact taken by columns hidden under the body of the building. This pretense of impossible engineering is beautiful, but also makes a political point: Niemeyer's columns refer to the classical architectural tradition, placing Brazil's government in a long tradition of European governments, but by using the columns to achieve inconceivable structural feats he suggests that Brazil is a modern country that will outdo its colonial founders. Brasilia has been regarded by some as a failed urban experiment—its remarkable government buildings spread over vast areas of open space are in stark contrast with the suburban slums. There can be little doubt, however, that it is a fascinating place. The city is rare in being a postwar UNESCO World Heritage Site, and attracts tourists from all over the world to admire Niemeyer's urban acropolis. **BWC**

Malin Residence ("Chemosphere") (1960)

Architect John Lautner   **Location** West Hollywood, California, USA   **Style** Modernist   **Materials** Steel, wood, concrete

This octagonal wonder is Lautner's best-known house. Leonard Malin, an aerospace engineer, commissioned the house to perch 100 feet (30.5 m) above the home of his parents-in-law. Clearly, client and architect were well-matched as the house is an engineering wonder. The fact that it is sited on a steep hillside in an earthquake zone adds kudos. Lautner's site solution was a wood-beam skeleton-cage tied to a steel compression ring mounted on a 5-foot-wide (1.5 m) cast-concrete column with eight steel supports to each vertices. The beams create the ceiling and surge toward the central skylight, like a whale's ribcage. In a nod to Exhibitionist style, a hinged beam reveals a one-way glass into the shower. Windows circle the octagon equator and separate the roof from the base. All that was left was how to get inside; this was solved by a steep-grade funicular and skybridge. In 2001, Escher GuneWardena renovated the house for new owner, publisher Bernard Taschen. Features dropped because they were too costly or technologically impossible in 1960 were reintroduced: razor-thin slate replaces tile; framed windows are now frameless glass; ash replaces the vinyl kitchen counter. Taschen has also commissioned a design for a new building on the site of the original residence: the underbelly of the masterpiece may one day be viewed from a Rem Koolhaas house. Two Plexiglas floorplates will allow Chemosphere's occupants to stare back down. **DJ**

"It is like having [the movie] Independence Day *above you."*

Bernard Taschen, owner

Capuchinas Chapel (1960)

Architect Luis Barragán **Location** Tlalpan, Mexico City, Mexico
Style Modernist **Materials** Concrete, glass, timber, stone

There are many who judge Tlalpan's Capuchin Chapel to be Pritzker Prize–winner Luis Barragán's greatest achievement. Standing in the nave, in a sculptural blaze of amber-stained sunlight, the impression is indeed one of apotheosis.

By the time he moved to Mexico City in 1935, Barragán had already made two journeys to Europe. In the chapel of the Franciscan convent in Tlalpan— once an autonomous village, now a suburb of Mexico City—one sees aspects of traditional Mexican architecture mixed with elements of European Modernism. Executed in collaboration with the artists Jesús "Chucho" Reyes and Mathias Goeritz, the chapel grew out of a modest commission to remodel the convent. In the end, Barragán's work for the nuns fell into three phases, spanning three decades. As both architect and patron, he created a work of art whose scope included furniture, altar cloths, and chasubles.

Solitary by inclination, Barragán explored ideas of an architecture of retreat. In the chapel he constructed a place of contemplative withdrawal, secluded from the turbulence of outside. Visitors pass from the street into a small courtyard framed by high white walls, and laid with black volcanic stone. Reflecting on the surface of the raised pool, a latticework screen of yellow masonry shields the route to the chapel door.

Behind the altar falls the shadow of a vast, offset crucifix. A monumental prismatic keel mediates the relationships between the choir loft, the nave, and the transept, while focusing light and attention forward. A grill separates the transept from the nave, and thus the congregation from the religious community, and also filters the light falling across rough-textured yellow stucco, successfully rendering even this simplest of surfaces richly suggestive. **AMR**

Trenchard Hall, University of Ibadan (1960)

Architects Maxwell Fry, Jane Drew **Location** Ibadan, Nigeria
Style Modernist **Materials** Concrete, stone

Trenchard Hall was designed by Maxwell Fry and Jane Drew during their extremely influential architectural involvement in the latter days of colonial British west Africa. Fry and Drew were commissioned by the University College Ibadan to draw up a masterplan for a new campus, including a series of residential halls and Trenchard Hall, primarily an auditorium complex. It was completed in 1960, the year of Nigeria's independence from Great Britain.

Located at the end of a tree-lined boulevard, Trenchard Hall marks the beginning of the campus core, with a cluster of residential halls behind and adjacent. The hall is composed of the auditorium, clock tower, office, and library block linked together with open walkways. This composition is informed by a response to the climatic conditions of Ibadan, situated in the heart of Nigeria's tropical rainforest belt and typified by heat, intense sunlight, and high humidity. It is imperative that any buildings address this by encouraging cross ventilation, reducing solar gain by introducing deep overhangs, and keeping the interiors as light and airy as possible. The architects introduced local stone-clad walls juxtaposed against white stucco walls.

The courtyard features native plant species, with trees and shrubs housed in planters and pots. The main auditorium has a fully glazed louvered clerestory with the front facade set back. A slender clock tower rises over with a hovering offset lid.

Overall, Trenchard Hall and the campus must be viewed as an extremely important example of the introduction of a revised Modernist architecture in tropical Africa. This fusion was dictated primarily by the local climate, spatial culture, and, obliquely, traditional building typologies. **GO**

Case Study
House No. 22 (1960)

Architect Pierre Koenig **Location** Los Angeles, California, USA
Style Modernist **Materials** Steel, glass

One of the most famous and influential house designs of the late twentieth century, Case Study House No. 22 is, for many, the embodiment of the Californian dream.

The Case Study program was initiated by *Arts & Architecture* magazine in 1945 with the goal of promoting the design of cheap, easily assembled residential homes—the solution to a massive postwar housing demand. Editor John Entenza said he hoped it would "lead the house out of the bondage of handcraftism into industry." In the late 1950s, Entenza approached San Francisco–born architect Pierre Koenig, who had been experimenting with exposed steel frame houses ever since building his own while still a student at USC. After the completion of his first commission for Entenza (Case Study House No. 21) he immediately began work on its successor.

Situated on an awkwardly shaped hillside lot—which had been considered "unbuildable"—Koenig fashioned an L-shaped, single-story building with open-plan rooms and flat roof decks. Combining one exposed steel framework aligned to the plot dimensions with another set over the cliff edge to the southwest, the plate glass windows of the overhang afforded spectacular views over Los Angeles.

Koenig's principles were about more than eye-catching design however. He was seeking a truthful aesthetic for simple, mass-produced materials, and he was a lifelong advocate of passive solar heating and energy conservation in the home—values that today are more relevant than ever. **RDB**

↗ Water plays an important part on the site, reflecting light back into the house through the large windows.

➡ Koenig's open-plan rooms, clean lines, and minimal ornament prefigured late-twentieth-century design.

Monastery of Sainte Marie de la Tourette (1960)

Architect Charles-Edouard Jeanneret (Le Corbusier)   **Location** Eveux-sur-Arbresle, Rhône, France   **Style** Modernist   **Materials** Concrete, glass

The rigors of monastic life inspired Le Corbusier from the earliest days of his career. So it was with great enthusiasm that he agreed to design this home for a community of Dominican monks. The challenge was to create a building to accommodate the contrasting needs of individual and collective life within an organized whole. As a result, the plan of La Tourette is derived from the daily rituals of the monks, with communal spaces on the lower floors and individual cells arranged in a U-shape around the upper levels. A rooftop garden provides a place for solitary meditation and exercise. In form, the building is one of the most extraordinary the architect ever built. Great volumes of brutal, battered concrete lie on the side of a steeply sloping hill, their scale recalling medieval monasteries such as Le Thoronet in Provence, which inspired Le Corbusier's design. Inside, the finishes are of exposed concrete and pebbledash—partly because the budget was halved during construction. The monks' simple cells have their own balconies, and are designed to provide framed views over the landscape. Most dramatic of all is the church. When entering via a ramped walkway, its moody darkness and unadorned primitiveness come as a surprise; the light can only enter through slits in the walls and the perimeter of the roof. In contrast, the side chapels are housed in an organic-shaped enclosure lit from above through brightly painted "light cannons." **MF**

"This monastery . . . is a work of love. It does not show off—it is from the interior that it lives."

Le Corbusier, architect

Park Hill (1961)

Architects Ivor Smith, Jack Lynn   **Location** Sheffield, England   **Style** Brutalist   **Materials** Concrete, brick

Park Hill was the site of the first large-scale slum clearance in Britain. The area had previously consisted of back-to-back housing, known as "Little Chicago" because of its high crime rate. It was hoped a new housing development of quality homes in a deprived area, would signal the regeneration of a fading city. Consisting of 995 units and housing more than 2,000 people, the estate occupies an entire hill overlooking Sheffield city center. The building is constructed of an exposed concrete frame with yellow, orange, and red brick curtain walling; although, today it is difficult to discern the intended polychromy. Park Hill consists of snakelike blocks containing duplex apartments and the famous "streets in the sky." In an attempt to preserve the communal aspects of street life, the front door of each dwelling opens out on to a 12-foot-wide deck, which runs continuously from one end of the scheme to the other, originally allowing milk delivery trucks to trundle from dwelling to dwelling. Park Hill's problems soon became apparent: with the reduced communal visibility normally afforded by ground-level street buildings, muggings and break-ins became common. The decks became more like quick getaway routes rather than streets in any real sense. Yet, Park Hill has earned its place in the history of postwar British housing and within Modernist architecture. It was awarded Grade II listed status (a building of special interest warranting preservation) in 1998. **AT**

> *"Park Hill housing development will draw the admiration of the world . . ."*
>
> Harold Macmillan, housing minister

Student Housing,
Sussex University (c. 1960)

Architect Basil Spence **Location** Falmer, Sussex, England
Style Brutalist **Materials** Brick, timber

The University of Sussex is one of a wave of so-called "red brick" universities founded in the 1960s. The 160-acre, campus-style university, with its student housing, study blocks, library, and administrative buildings was designed by Sir Basil Spence, although it has been added to over the decades.

The university's innovative Modernist campus, architecture, and layout includes the administrative, social, and student recreational block Falmer House, which won a Royal Institute of British Architects' medal in 1962. It stands at the main entrance to the university around a central quadrangle, in a gesture toward the layout of existing traditional universities. Sir Basil Spence intended Falmer House to appeal to the curiosity of the developing minds it housed. In contrast with the traditional perception of 1960s architecture as being made up of regular, repeating concrete patterns, the subtle irregularity of the building is striking. Arches never seem to have an exact partner on the other side of the quadrangle, for example, and each wall seems to differ slightly from those to which it abuts. Appropriately for the only UK university to be housed in a government-designated Area of Outstanding Natural Beauty, the architecture echoes the surrounding Sussex Downs, with curves taking their inspiration from the gentle roll of the hills.

Falmer House was awarded Grade I listed status (by English Heritage as a building of "exceptional interest") in 1993; there is only one other educational building in Britain to be given such status. **CMK**

◥ The courtyard at Sussex University is both a brutal and beautiful example of Modernist architecture.

◁ The red brick campus has a villagelike quality and a sense of playfulness incorporated into its design.

Teatro General San Martin (1961)

Architects Ruiz, Álvarez **Location** Buenos Aires, Argentina
Style Modernist, Functionalist **Materials** Steel, glass, concrete

In 1953 Mario Roberto Álvarez and Macedonio Oscar Ruiz presented the winning entry in a competition for the city's new theater organized by the Buenos Aires city government. By the time of its opening, the Teatro Municipal General San Martín had already become a key piece of Buenos Aires architecture due to its strict adherence to the rules of Functionalism and Modernism.

The facade's main block is made up of seven levels of offices with a cinema on the top floor. Three double-height halls reveal the building's structure. The independent volume that houses the Sala Martín Coronado is the main theater, which is dedicated to comedy. This lies above the main access hall, extending it into the building. This magnificent resolution of the ground floor could suggest a reference to earlier projects by Argentine architects Juan Kurchan and Jorge Ferrari Hardoy. The vertical relations continue in the basement, which houses the Sala Casacuberta theater, used mainly for drama.

Located one on top of the other, each theater space is an independent structure, and this makes it possible for the building to house extensive, non-theatrical, cultural programs—exhibitions, studios, storage spaces, offices, cafeteria, parking lot, and a theater school.

Considered the emblematic work of Rationalist architecture in Argentina, the theater brings together extraordinary formal resolution and a social commitment befitting its time and context. Indeed, the functioning of the institution over the course of four decades has not required any modification or expansion to the building. The importance of its contribution to Brazilian, and indeed, South American architecture is undeniable. **PAB**

Kingo Houses (1961)

Architect Jørn Utzon **Location** Helsingør, Denmark
Style Modernist **Materials** Unit masonry, tile

Jørn Utzon (b. 1918) has always aspired to create architecture that is accessible to all people. He has also concerned himself with topography, immediate environment, and how people contribute standards of living to their surroundings. These thoughts are exemplified and carried through in his residential housing scheme, the Kingo Houses. The scheme comprises sixty houses, locally referred to as the "Roman Houses" because of their Roman atrium style.

The Kingo Houses are spread across a beautiful undulating landscape next to a pond. Each house is

> *"Architecture is our room, but also our communal space . . . your own and part of the wider community."*
>
> **Jørn Utzon, architect**

L-shaped, and has its own courtyard. The tiled roofs are all evenly slanted, adding a particular dynamic to the overall structure. Seen individually the units make up private spheres, but when they are seen in their entirety the units also represent a communal environment wherein a particular sense of the collective and the communal exists. Three-quarters of the estate is laid out for communal areas.

Although each house appears sheltered and inward, their zigzag positioning allows the buildings to maintain a connection with the outer surroundings; inside each unit, this transparency is heightened by large floor-to-ceiling windows. Utzon was able to give full rein to his ideas in Helsingør, bringing an original vision to housing schemes, which at the time received little attention. **SML**

Upper Lawn Pavilion (1962)

Architects Alison and Peter Smithson **Location** Wiltshire, England
Style Brutalist **Materials** Reinforced concrete, wood, zinc

Archaeological Museum (1962)

Architect Patroklos Karantinos **Location** Thessaloniki, Greece
Style Modernist **Material** Concrete

This is a small house with a lot to say. It was designed as their own weekend house by the radical architect and theorist couple, Alison and Peter Smithson, and served as such until 1982, when noisy neighbors drove them away.

The solar pavilion, as the architects sometimes called it, is a simple, two-story, wooden box, with the upper floor resting on a pre-existing estate wall supported by a pair of concrete columns within the body of the house. The upper part of the building is clad in zinc to protect the wood from the weather. As often with the Smithsons, simple ingredients are used to make wider architectural points. The bare wood indicates a rejection of the Modernist emphasis on high technology. The preservation of old paving and a ruined wall shows their belief that architects should accept and adapt to the existing surroundings of a building—a reaction against the tendency of many architects of the 1950s and 1960s to sweep away everything and start from scratch. The Smithsons also use the house to show their admiration for the work of earlier Modernist masters. The structural idea comes from Le Corbusier, and something in the simplicity of the windows and the overall shape seems to originate with Mies van der Rohe.

The Upper Lawn Pavilion sets an example of architects building for the perfect clients: themselves. This building's complete lack of theatricality and its relaxed understatement give it an apparently superficial ordinariness, but it is an ordinariness well worth spending time seeing. The longer you allow yourself to look around, the more details you will notice, right down to the way the taps in the bathroom are made to look bright, perfect, and alien by their close juxtaposition with the rough wall behind. **BWC**

Patroklos Karantinos may not be the most famous architect outside his native Greece, yet he was a true inspiration—one of the leading exponents of Greek Modernism. Karantinos was particularly interested in the application of Modernism, the study of museum typology and, more precisely, in the relation of sculpture and natural light; a journey traced in its purest form in the Archaeological Museum of Thessaloniki, one of his most mature works.

The museum is a clearly delineated building carefully respecting the rules of Modernism, yet

> "Knowledge, sense, and sensitivity are the basic principles in the creation of a work of art."
>
> Patroklos Karantinos, architect

enriched by elements central to the Greek climate and tradition. The structure's main area is a rectangular space with a central atrium, but with a twist—there are extra smaller connected spaces that formulate a visually interesting relationship between interior and exterior, colonnades and courtyards, thus separating the gallery area from services and administration. The atria along with the facades' recesses result in an amazing diffusion of sunlight offering constant variation. The intense Greek sunlight complements perfectly the general airy feel of the museum's high-ceilinged halls, creating a geometrically austere yet warm and comfortable space.

The museum was completed in 1961 and inaugurated the following year. It was extensively restored in 1980, 2001, and 2004. **ES**

TWA
Terminal (1962)

Architect Eero Saarinen **Location** Queens, New York, USA
Style Modernist **Materials** Steel, glass, concrete

Eero Saarinen is famed for his sweeping arches, chevron angles, and curved, uplifting structures. When he was commissioned to design the TWA (Trans World Airlines) Terminal, JFK Airport in New York was breaking new ground by allowing airlines to design and maintain their own bespoke airport terminals. This new direction offered unique opportunities for courageous designers such as Saarinen to leave their mark on some of the most iconic transit spaces in the United States today.

The billowing volumes of the exterior shell of the TWA Terminal building have been sculpted as metaphors for the excitement of modern air travel—lightweight, gestural shapes that are intended to distill the featherweight notions of flight. Saarinen employed these curving vaulted domes to create spacious halls and a rare degree of exhilarating breathing space. He intended to extend the architecture to create a fully designed environment, with every object created specifically to take into account the way it related to its neighboring objects, whether small and large. All elements, right down to the formal constructions of the signs, display boards, railings, and check-in desks, were made to match.

Tragically, Saarinen met an untimely death at the age of 51 in 1961, just one year before his iconic TWA Terminal project was completed. Saarinen's other major airport building, the main terminal at Washington Dulles International Airport, was also unveiled in 1962. **AT**

↗ Successive layered platforms within the building are unified by Saarinen's typically curvaceous design.

→ The light, space, and soaring curves give passengers the impression of having already become airborne.

Olivetti Nuova ICO factory (1962)

Architects Luigi Figini, Gino Pollini **Location** Ivrea, Turin, Italy **Style** Italian Rationalist **Materials** Reinforced concrete, plaster, glass, iron

Adriano Olivetti took over a small but successful factory for typewriters from his father Camillo Olivetti in the late 1920s. Subsequently he made Olivetti the worldwide trademark it remains today, and broadened his activities to the spheres of urban planning, art, and social and political issues. From 1933 he launched numerous projects for new production facilities, offices, employee housing, canteens, and nurseries in his birthplace of Ivrea, engaging some of the most important architects in Italy, until he had transformed the entire village into a modern town that grew as fast as the company. For the extension of the old Olivetti workshop, built in 1896, the industrialist sought young and ambitious architects who would be able to interpret the buildings to complement the modernity of Olivetti's products. Luigi Figini and Gino Pollini were founding members of the Italian Rationalist Gruppo 7 that was striving to combine compositional principles

of Italian Classicism with the distinct materials and forms of early Modernism. The fast expansion of Olivetti made it necessary to extend the building four times between 1934 and 1962. All the extensions were designed by Figini and Pollini, thus creating a building complex that reveals four different stages of their architectural style over a time span of more than twenty years: from the first extension, which shows a modest two-story factory slab with white plastered walls, and long rows of iron-framed windows; to the third extension, with a beautiful formative 328-foot-long (100 m) facade along Via Jervis with a glass curtain wall, the inner facade structured by rectangular consoles of reinforced concrete and their sunblinds. In 2001, the factory complex and almost 200 of Olivetti's modern buildings in the area were transformed into the Ivrea Open-Air Museum of Modern Architecture. **FH**

Pilgrimage Church (1962)

Architect Gottfried Böhm   **Location** Neviges, Germany   **Style** Expressionist   **Material** Concrete

The Pilgrimage Church is an extraordinary example of postmodern Expressionism. It is typical of Böhm's oeuvre, concerned with the blending of traditional and contemporary elements to achieve unique internal spaces. Böhm comes from a long line of architects and took over the office of his father, Dominikus Böhm, when the latter died in 1955. Trained as an architect, Gottfried Böhm also attended the Academy of Fine Art in Munich; this training influenced his architectural practice, in particular his use of clay models that he constructs as he articulates plans for his buildings. The Pilgrimage Church is on a sloping site, which was terraced and utilized as a processional space for pilgrims. The striking concrete exterior of the church looks almost organic in form, and could be a small mountain or ragged precipice, when seen from afar. While this is imposing and original, the interior of the church is no less enthralling.

The stained-glass windows throw colored light on the concrete surfaces, creating a theatrical effect, and a dramatic open plan is flanked by sculptural concrete, reminiscent of German Expressionism as well as Bauhaus austerity. Böhm has designed a number of public buildings that have been described as post-Bauhaus. He met his architectural heroes Walter Gropius and Ludwig Mies van der Rohe when he traveled through the United States in the 1950s. Böhm was awarded the Pritzker Prize in 1986. **KAB**

> *"[Böhm] has never, in anything he has built, lost his wonderful, original humanity."*
>
> Peter Davey, architecture critic

Coventry Cathedral (1962)

Architect Sir Basil Spence **Location** Coventry, England
Style Modernist **Materials** Sandstone, concrete, stained glass, wood

On the night of November 14, 1940, the medieval cathedral of St. Michael in Coventry was almost totally destroyed in an air raid by the German Luftwaffe. Only the tower, spire, undercroft, and outer walls survived.

In 1950 a competition was held to design a new cathedral, the only stipulation being that the tower and spire of the original building should be retained. The commission was won by Sir Basil Spence, who proposed a new cathedral should be built alongside the ruin, the hollow shell of which would be turned into a garden of remembrance.

Spence trained in Edinburgh, then worked in the offices of Sir Edwin Lutyens before establishing his own practice. His design for Coventry Cathedral combined Lutyens's grandeur and monumentality with the style of textured Modernism found in Scandinavia. His soaring sandstone cathedral, with its slender columns and flat roof surmounted by a spire (flown into place by helicopter), is also famous for the art he commissioned to adorn it: Sir Jacob Epstein's bronze *St. Michael and the Devil*, a large tapestry of Christ by Graham Sutherland, and a full-height stained-glass window by John Piper, which dominates the baptistery.

Benjamin Britten's *War Requiem* was composed for the consecration ceremony, and premiered in the cathedral in May 1962. The building attracted controversy for its modern design, and remains one of the most important examples of postwar architecture in Britain. **MF**

◥ The abstract design of the baptistery window incorporates 195 panes of stained glass.

◩ The original cathedral's tower can be seen in the background, offset by Spence's reinterpretation.

House Biermann (1962)

Architect Barrie Biermann **Location** Durban, South Africa
Style Modernist **Materials** Stone, steel, monopitch

Houses designed by architects for themselves are often referred to as "autobiographical." But surely architecture is only ever a neutral container for objects and people. Can a building really communicate character? Is there more to a home than the passing life of the occupier? Barrie Biermann's House Biermann is proof that it can and there is; visitors describe it as a window onto his world—a world that formed an erudite bastion against the hostile realities of the day.

Friends and colleagues describe Biermann as something of an alchemist. He had the intellectual gift of being able to bring opposites together: the scholarly and the practical, ancient Greek and modern Zulu culture, apartheid politics and grassroots humanism. At a personal level, he lived parallel lives: privately gay, at a time when it was illegal, and publicly part of the academic establishment. Despite these apparent conflicts, his life and work impart a commonsense belief in grounded experience. For Biermann, the human character of everyday life was more important than technologies of power; accordingly, his work demonstrates a faith in place.

Rooted to its gently sloping site, its long roofline pitched parallel to the gradient, Biermann's house is like a fantasy realm at the bottom of the garden—except the garden has somehow swallowed the house. The living room blurs the boundary between inside and outside; curved internal walls reinforce the idea of space as an internal landscape, and proceeding into the depth of the home there are steps down into a lush planted courtyard. Subtle surface treatments and a sense of weightless mass contribute to the dreamlike ambience, which speaks of refinement and distinction just as it emphasizes the particulars of its African setting: the ground, the sky, and nature. **MJB**

Nedbank Centre (1962)

Architect Norman Eaton **Location** Durban, South Africa
Style Modernist **Materials** Reinforced concrete, clay block

Once described as like "going to do business in a tree," Norman Eaton's 1960s Netherlands Bank is no ordinary corporate edifice. His building furnishes the world of money with a human face. It boasts a broad, public terrace incorporating lush planting and four ceramic fountains, offering "an exchange between aesthetic and natural forms, and sense of generous abundance."

Architecture, for Eaton, was the "art of harmonious living." Yet his building designs were not idealistic or utopian but grounded in the reality of his times. The machine-age aesthetics of the Modern movement

> ## "[Eaton's] concepts and spaces and proportions and materials were derived from ... Africa."
>
> **Alexis Preller, artist**

were everywhere. Leading the field in South Africa was a smart young set known as the Transvaal Group, led by Rex Martienssen, an apostle of Modernism. He and Eaton sought an architecture both regional and universal, in which Africa made its mark on what was becoming known as the International Style.

Rhythmic pattern, spatial extensity, and an attitude to natural light color Eaton's efforts to localize the global money culture. A jacket of clay-block fretwork around the glazed banking hall shades its marble floor in dappled sunlight. Sensuous and enveloping, the creamy travertine interior seems at once like a forest glade and a fragment of ancient Rome. This rich material texture and powerful metaphoric presence— a synthesis of romanticism and restraint—signaled a mature phase in Eaton's oeuvre. **MJB**

Rosen House (1962)

Architect Craig Ellwood **Location** Los Angeles, California, USA **Style** Modernist **Materials** Steel, Norman brick, glass

Rosen House was one of the few single-story, steel houses designed by Craig Ellwood (1922–92) that was actually built, another one being Daphne House, built a year previously. The designs were among the first the architect made after absorbing the ideals of Mies van der Rohe (1886–1969). Ellwood commented, "Once I became aware of Mies's work and studied his designs, my work became more like Mies." During his mid-twenties, Ellwood worked with the building firm Lamport, Cofer and Salzman, and it was here that he developed a thorough understanding of construction materials, before turning to design. He established his own architectural firm in 1948, quickly achieving great acclaim for his innovative designs based on an acute knowledge of the technical properties of construction materials. In the Rosen House, he brought this knowledge to the fore on many levels, perhaps most visibly in his use of a single vertical steel column to support horizontal steel beams in both directions. This structural feature is part of the external skeleton of the house and appears as a rectangular design detail, marrying the effects of structure and aesthetics. The house, based upon a nine-square grid with a central open court, was entirely modern in concept but drew on the precedent of the Classical pavilion. The steel skeleton structure of the house was painted white with ceramic-faced, Norman brick panels and glass walls in between. For the interior, and along Mies van der Rohe lines, Ellwood strove for free-floating interior dividers that were unattached to any exterior walls, a feature that was complicated by the necessity for the house to function as a multiperson home. Rosen House is one of the "must sees" of U.S. domestic architecture. It is a building that satisfied the architect's artistic ideals and objectives while remaining a functional and utilitarian family home. **TP**

Temple Street Parking Garage (1963)

Architect Paul Rudolph   **Location** New Haven, Connecticut, USA   **Style** Brutalist   **Material** Reinforced concrete

The multistory parking garage is perhaps the perfect Brutalist building type: ramps, columns, and structural decks, all in hard materials. The Temple Street Parking Garage was built as part of New Haven's energetic postwar urban renewal program, providing parking for those driving in on the new expressways. Paul Rudolph (1918–97) was the head of Yale's architecture school, and a leading figure in the weighty business of urban renewal. At Temple Street, however, the serious planner is far less in evidence than the extravagant and highly accomplished artist. The program is simple enough: five decks giving a total of 1,280 parking spaces, with shops and restaurants at street level. The building does not go back far from the road, but its front to Temple Street is long, giving it a dominant, even overwhelming presence. The entire structure is in exposed, yellow-brown concrete, poured into molds of fine wooden slats, which leave their mark

once removed. This technique not only produces a rough, ribbed texture, but also offers flexibility in the construction process. The parapets curve sensuously, and the columns that support them are scooped away on four sides. The building was meticulously restored in 2004 after earlier clumsy repairs. Stroke the rough concrete, look out between the columns, and see the city from the rooftop. Note the remarkable lampposts that crown the building with a final sci-fi touch. This is concrete at its expressive, brutal, beautiful best. **BWC**

"At the top a wonderful airy world of roof-buildings and concrete lights suggesting fantastic flora."

Elizabeth Mills Brown, architectural historian

Berlin Philharmonic Concert Hall (1963)

Architect Hans Scharoun   **Location** Berlin, Germany   **Style** Modernist   **Materials** Concrete, aluminum

From the outset, Herbert von Karajan, leader of the Berlin Philharmonic Orchestra, championed the 1956 competition entry of Hans Scharoun (1893–1972) for a new concert hall. Von Karajan believed that Scharoun's revolutionary concept of performance in the round was ideally suited to the musical interpretation of the orchestra. Scharoun recognized the social dimension of this new type of concert hall layout, saying, "Is it mere chance that whenever people hear improvised music, they immediately gather round in a circle?"

In the completed concert hall, no seat is more than 115 feet (35 m) from the podium. Scharoun created an interior landscape with the seating blocks at different levels and angles, in the manner of a hillside vineyard. Working with acoustician Lothar Cremer, Scharoun tuned the folded planes, raked terraces, and canopied ceiling for acoustic advantage.

The concert hall is the centerpiece of the Kulturforum at Berlin Tiergarten, with the Chamber Music Hall attached on one side, and the State Institute for Musical Research and Museum of Instruments on the other, all by Scharoun. The concert hall was designed from the inside out, the irregular internal volume being legible on the outside, while the upper walls are boldly clad with gold-anodized aluminum. The sense of a spatial landscape is characteristic of the foyer spaces as well as the auditorium, with flowing routes from the entrance to the hall's various levels.

Scharoun was perhaps the greatest exponent of organic architecture in the postwar years, and his fluid approach to architectural space and form is now frequently copied. **CB**

↖ The organic approach to the design can be seen in the dramatically contrasting materials used in the exterior.

← The concert hall's tentlike roof sweeps dramatically upward behind the principal entrance.

Engineering Building (1963)

Architects Sir James Stirling, James Gowan **Location** Leicester, England **Style** Modernist **Materials** Glass, brick

In 1960s' Britain the vastly influential work of Sir James Stirling (1926–92) and James Gowan (*b.* 1923) was itself influenced by the later designs of Le Corbusier and the theories of Alison and Peter Smithson. The two architects instigated a trend toward using brick and exposed concrete. Their work displayed particularly Stirling's desires to create strong, muscular forms, mirroring his own character, and to construct buildings that alluded to other periods of architectural history. Most importantly, however, Stirling looked at architecture as an art form.

The Engineering Building at Leicester University represents their pinnacle. Noted for its technological and geometric character, it features a bright orange, slim, factorylike tower rising from a lower-level block, top-lit by angled rooflights and housing offices and lecture theaters. In this way, the external form reflects its internal functions. Along with Arups' Attenborough Tower and Sir Denys Lasdun's Charles Wilson Building, it signals the university campus to the outside world.

Designated as Grade II (preserved as a building of historic significance) in 1993, this "strongly individual statement," as Nikolaus Pevsner saw it, contributed to a trend away from integrated, rational masterplans toward campus environments "where every building strives to be an individual" and a "masterpiece." Stirling was awarded a knighthood in 1992, and the Pritzker Prize for Architecture in 1981, while the Royal Institute of British Architects chose to inaugurate its major award, the Stirling Prize, in his name. This building remains another fitting memorial to a still pervasive major influence on British architecture today. **DT**

↗ The clever balance of glass and brick prevents the structure from looking top-heavy.

⇥ The glass sections of the building are brilliantly lit at night to create a sense of theater.

Elder Dempster Building (1963)

Architect James Cubitt   **Location** Lagos, Nigeria
Style International Style   **Material** Concrete

Designed by the English architect James Cubitt (1914–83), the Elder Dempster Building was completed in 1963. Located on Lagos Island—in the old city—it is nine stories high, and was the first high-rise to be built on the waterfront promenade known as the Marina.

Elder Dempster, the Liverpool-based shipping company, had a long tradition of operating on the west African coast and needed a building that reflected this tradition but also was located near the hub of its Lagos operations, the waterfront. The designers took advantage of revised municipal building codes to produce the waterfront's first tall building. As with other English architects working in Nigeria at the end of the colonial period, such as John Godwin and Gillian Hopwood, James Cubitt opted for a revised Modernism that was informed by local climatic and cultural particularities. The specific response is expressed in the modulating of solar gain by continuous louvers wrapping the entire building envelope. The concrete structure of the building is protected from the demanding, tropical climate by a mosaic tile finish in a graphic pattern that reflects the Elder Dempster brand colors. The building's service plant is located on the roof, concealed behind a curve of mosaic-tiled concrete that recalls a ship's funnel—here the designer is making a reference to the client's shipping business.

Originally, the building was located close to the Marina, giving it a prominent view over the harbor. This changed in the 1970s when the harbor was filled in and an elevated roadway was built along the new water edge. Consequently, the Elder Dempster Building no longer has its commanding presence over the harbor, and dominance of the area has passed to other taller buildings built since. **GO**

Casa de Chá Restaurant (1963)

Architect Alvaro Siza   **Location** Matosinhos, Portugal
Style Oporto School   **Materials** Concrete, glass, wood

Awarded the Pritzker Prize in 1992, Alvaro Siza is a central figure of the "Oporto School"—indeed, his work embodies a theoretical, methodological, and formal synthesis of the architectural movement. Siza began his career in the shadow of his masters (including Fernando Távora) and in collaborative works. The Casa de Chá (Tea House) in the outskirts of Oporto was the project that first got him noticed.

A stone's throw north of the future site of his Leça Swimming Pools, Siza's Casa de Chá is a bold prefiguration of the architect's radical, intimate, and

> *"The shape of the building hardly seems to show on the surface from between the rocks …"*
>
> Ana Tostões, professor of architecture

restrained relationship with space. Nestled in the rocky shoreline, away from the main road and at the foot of a lighthouse, this building has an organic appearance, resembling a stretched animal. In contrast, its almost horizontal roof appears to be an extension of the sea surface, with which it seems to merge. The alternating white walls, picture windows, and wooden structures effectively transcend the surroundings with their superlative geometry.

The interior's fake-Taliesin cozy nooks and snug mezzanines provide a contrast to the sea vista beyond, as waves break in relentless bursts of foam at visitors' feet. Had the Casa de Chá been completed in 1959, Alfred Hitchcock might have been tempted to use this location for scenes such as the escape in *North By Northwest*, with Cary Grant and Eva Marie Saint. **YN**

Church
of St. Mark (1964)

Architect Sigurd Lewerentz **Location** Björkhagen, Stockholm, Sweden
Style Modernist, New Brutalist **Material** Brick

St. Mark's Church, built for a new suburban parish, includes a meeting room attached to the church and a row of single-story offices with a low belfry, where the bells are rung by hand in the English manner rather than by an automatic carillon. The little, villagelike complex of buildings is set among birch trees. The covered porch at the entrance to the church is actually a freestanding structure.

Lewerentz (1885–1975) enjoyed fame early in his career, which passed from an early Classical phase to a Modernist one. However, he spent a long period in the middle of his life making windows because he lacked building commissions. In 1956, when he was seventy years old, St. Mark's launched him in a new direction, notably in his exceptional use of brick. Visiting the site every day except Sunday, he supervised every step of the job. He required the bricklayers to use thick mortar joints and leave them in a rough state, both inside and out. Only whole, uncut bricks were used, laid in stretcher bond. The roof vaults, based on the double-curved profile of a speedboat hull, are also made of brick and were a notable achievement in their wide span. The windows are of insulated glass, fixed without frames to the exterior, with elastic sealants. The electrical wiring runs on the wall surfaces, with fittings of polished brass. The effect is at the same time rough and sophisticated, using the effects that were beginning to be categorized as New Brutalist. This is a version full of Nordic magic and charm, however, including sheepskin covers for the kneelers. **AP**

↗ The precise geometric design of the complex is in stark contrast to its birch wood surroundings.

→ The subtly undulating section of coarse brown brick wall houses the church's bells.

Marina City (1964)

Architect Bertrand Goldberg   **Location** Chicago, Illinois, USA   **Style** Modernist   **Material** Concrete

"I was revolting ... against the straight line, against ... a man made in the image of a machine."

Bertrand Goldberg, architect

⤒ The eye-catching twin towers of Marina City are organic reinterpretations of the traditional high-rise.

⤷ Goldberg acknowledged the age of the automobile by allocating nearly one-third of each tower to parking.

In the United States, the 1960s were a time of population shift from urban centers to the suburbs. The migration out of the cities had lasted nearly half a century, but in 1964 Bertrand Goldberg (1913–97) conceived a project that later would be seen as an early forerunner of the current back-to-the-city movement. Marina City is a cluster of strikingly sculptural buildings located on the Chicago River in what was a railroad district of central Chicago. The project attempted to attract small households by serving as a "city within a city," providing a full range of services and amenities within a single complex. On its completion, the project included a marina, theater, gymnasium, skating rink, bowling alley, nightclub, restaurants, commercial space, and 900 apartments. Goldberg had to overcome zoning laws of the day that forbade mixing commercial and residential uses.

A student of Mies van der Rohe during the last year of the Bauhaus, Goldberg also diverged strongly from many Modernist tenets of the day. His buildings fully engaged with the street and were designed for mixed uses, rather than standing in isolation on a plaza. The architect also had a fascination for technological innovation and organic form.

What began as an otherwise conventional cluster of rectilinear towers on Goldberg's drawing board would develop into one of Chicago's most strikingly original and photographed constructions. Goldberg designed a plinth on which he placed low commercial buildings and two round sixty-story towers of reinforced concrete. The first eighteen stories are a helical parking garage; above these stories are apartments. The scalloped edges of the towers create rounded balconies and angled views within each apartment. Favored from the start, the towers have been likened to corncobs or the grain silos that once lined the Chicago River. **AC**

Royal College of Physicians (1964)

Architect Sir Denys Lasdun   **Location** London, England   **Style** Modernist   **Materials** Reinforced concrete, brick, tiles

The Royal College of Physicians by Sir Denys Lasdun (1914–2001) is the home of one of England's oldest medical organizations. Lasdun considered resigning from the job after attending a physicians' meeting, despairing of providing a Modernist building for such an institution. In the event, though, he rose to the challenge magnificently. The college faces a corner of Regent's Park, in an area of much-loved Regency housing by John Nash. A main block clad in small white porcelain tiles presents a symmetrical entrance front to the park, with three slender columns in the middle providing a modernized reminder of a portico. The lecture theater to one side is in stark contrast—a sulky, distorted mound of black brick. Inside, the principal rooms—library, dining hall, and the Censors' Room (for grueling membership interviews)—are disposed around a large, three-story hall, with the staircase turning confidently through it. There are two major reasons not to miss the Royal College of Physicians. First, the handling of shapes is superb, with discreetly complex engineering permitting the large white volumes to hang effortlessly over the black brick lower parts. Secondly, the craftsmanship is exceptional throughout. Thirty-seven different shapes of brick were custom-designed and baked for the curves and angles of the lecture theater alone. The work in tiles, marble, and metal is similarly precise, beautifully simple, and luxurious. **BWC**

> *"Generally the scheme should not be stinted for the sake of £15,000 [$30,000] or so."*
>
> Wolfson Foundation, sponsor of the college

Vanna Venturi House (1964)

Architect Robert Venturi   **Location** Philadelphia, Pennsylvania, USA   **Style** Modernist   **Materials** Brick, plaster

In a beautiful suburb strewn with fine houses of the nineteenth and twentieth centuries, the Vanna Venturi House might initially seem an odd focus of architectural pilgrimage. It is smaller than most of its neighbors, and lacks color or obvious magnificence. However, it was in this building for his mother that Robert Venturi (*b.* 1925) first sought architectural expression for his growing dissatisfaction with the Modernist movement. It caused, and continues to cause, quite a stir. Approached from a narrow drive between high hedges and trees, the house turns its most architectural side toward the arriving visitor. Between this and another flat facade to the rear is sandwiched the house, its roof breaking with the seeming rigidity of the front and back walls. The front facade is itself idiosyncratic. It is nearly the house that every child draws, with a square, four-pane window, a pitched roof, a chimney, and a door. The break in the gable above the door, however, gives a hint of the Classical motif of a temple front that has been split in two, and a long slit window recalls European Modernist villas of the 1920s. The outrage that the building caused when it was new came from its implied questioning of Modernist ideas, especially the belief that historical references to older architecture should not be permitted in a new building. With just the front wall of a house and some wood, Venturi began a fierce debate in the architectural world. **BWC**

> *"The most significant house of the second half of the twentieth century."*
>
> David B. Brownlee, professor of art history

National Gymnasia for the Tokyo Olympics (1964)

Architect Kenzo Tange   **Location** Tokyo, Japan   **Style** Modernist   **Materials** Reinforced concrete, steel

The two gymnasia by Kenzo Tange (1913–2005) have a number of claims to attention—their ingenious cable-hung roofs are hurricane-resistant; the larger building seats 15,000 spectators and was, when built, the largest space spanned by such a roof; and the planning of supporting facilities is neat. Above all, however, they are beautiful—the smaller of the two, seating 4,000, is even more perfect than the larger. The stadia were built for the 1964 Tokyo Olympic Games—the first to be held in Asia—and Tange's buildings were perhaps a bid to outdo Pier Luigi Nervi's superbly engineered structures at the Stadio Olimpico for the 1960 Olympics in Rome. Tange's roofs curve down from majestic concrete pylons to perimeter walls that swirl like the tail of a comma. There is no distraction from this dramatic interplay of structure—no pretty details or extra rooms tacked on. The structural ties within the roof of the smaller stadium, seen from within as they spiral sharply up to a high window, are among the most memorable images of the Modernist movement. In the two buildings, Tange achieves a remarkable fusion: the engineering seems so compellingly logical that it appears universal and inevitable, but at the same time there seems to be something distinctively Japanese about the profiles—an echo of traditional roofs, perhaps. This was the perfect architectural statement for the time: advanced engineering entirely at home in an Asian context. It is hard to argue with Tange's 1987 Pritzker Prize citation, which described the gymnasia as being "among the most beautiful buildings of the twentieth century. **BWC**

◣ Tange hints at traditional Japanese design elements in his Modernist roof structures.

◀ This flying saucer stadium is an iconic Japanese building and a landmark in Tange's career.

2 Columbus Circle (1964)

Architects Edward Durell Stone; Allied Works **Location** New York, New York, USA **Style** Late Modernist **Materials** Concrete, marble, glass

The sin of 2 Columbus Circle is to be different. Called a "turkey" in a 1964 review, this exuberant, small, twelve-story building by Edward Stone (1902–78) is enrobed in white Vermont marble pierced with repeating quad sets of domino dots that allow natural light to enter at the four corners of each floor. More dots finalize the pattern at roofline beneath which runs a two-story course of lancet windows more English Perpendicular Gothic than Venetian fantasy.

This solid structure stands on a leggy Moorish-style arcade, the whole creation being one of tease and refinement. The building's diminutive stature amid a sea of high-rise developments is startling. From the vantage point of the penthouse bar of the neighboring Mandarin Oriental Hotel, 2 Columbus Circle looks small but plucky. Deplored by some for being too feminine, it was called "romantic," "airy," "pretty," and "eccentric." Le Corbusier, it was said, would have designed a more "manly" building. However, the design did attract some support. Andy Warhol warmed to the building's decorative aspects: "In some circles words like 'charming' and 'clever' and 'pretty' are all put downs; all the lighter things in life, which are the most important things, are a put down."

In 2005, the new occupant of 2 Columbus Circle—the Museum of Arts and Design—selected architect Brad Cloepfil of Allied Works to give the building a controversial facelift. Stone's confection has been stripped of its original white marble—replaced with an "S" pattern of fritted glass and skinned with 25,000 iridescent ceramic tiles. This "open" and "transparent" redesign is not gender-confused like the original. In a gilded age of wealth, raunch, and excess, it winks and flirts with its manly Trump Tower neighbor. A museum dedicated to materials, processes, and visual presence has shed its Vermont marble sheath and donned a revealing slinky number. **DJ**

Yser
Tower (1965)

Architect Robert Van Averbeke **Location** Diksmuide, Belgium
Style Dutch Moderne **Materials** Brick, concrete

The IJzertoren is a surprise in the flat landscape of Flanders. This 275-foot-high (84 m) brick and concrete tower was built to the memory of Flemish soldiers of World War I. In 1914, nearly all of Belgium was occupied by the Germans, despite the country's declaration of neutrality, except for a pocket in southwest Flanders. The IJzertoren overlooks the site of the front line where fighting was so intense that the city of Diksmuide was utterly devastated.

An earlier tower was erected in 1930 but was blown up by unknown persons in 1946. It is claimed

"My country ... endlessly flat .... Your sky-high tower proclaims that Flanders is now at peace."

Patrick Devrome, Flemish poet, author of *De IJzer*

that the tower, which is also seen as a symbol of Flemish identity, especially commemorated Flemish-speaking Belgian troops, who may have felt aggrieved by their French-speaking officers in World War I. After 1945, it has been suggested, some Walloon (French-speaking) Belgians may have felt that some Flemish Belgians were too sympathetic to the Nazi occupiers.

The present tower, begun in 1952, was built of Flemish bricks in a Dutch Moderne style. The "cube" at the top is dominated by the letters AVV (*Alles Voor Vlaanderen*—All For Flanders) and VVK (*Vlaanderen Voor Kristus*—Flanders for Christ). The twenty-two stories contain displays about war, peace, and Flemish history. The top floor overlooks the former battlefield, including the Dodengang (Trench of Death), a preserved stretch of the Belgian front line. **ATB**

National
Schools of Art (1965)

Architects Ricardo Porro, Roberto Gottardi, Vittorio Garatti **Location** Havana, Cuba **Style** Modernist **Materials** Brick, concrete, tiles

Fidel Castro and Che Guevara conceived the idea of an art-school complex for the Cuban people while playing golf at the former Country Club in Cubanacán in 1961: the grounds of Havana's most exclusive club would become the site. Three architects, Ricardo Porro (*b.* 1925), Roberto Gottardi (*b.* 1927), and Vittorio Garatti (*b.* 1927) collaborated with future students and construction workers to build the five new art schools.

The schools—Plastic Arts, Drama, Modern Dance, Music, and Ballet—were set either side of the river that bisects the park. They had sinuous organic plans that responded to the site's topography; existing ceiba trees were incorporated into the designs. Each school is distinct: the giant *stupas* of the Plastic Arts; the practice rooms and serpentine corridor of the School of Music; the broad, elevated domes of the Ballet School's performance spaces; the soaring vaults, and *brise-soleils* (sun deflectors) of the School of Modern Dance; the courtyards and irregular streets of the Dramatic Arts. The sensuous forms of the schools were an idealistic attempt to express *Cubanidad*, the potent mix of African and Spanish cultural origins that are the essence of Cuba, distinct from the European tradition.

Unfortunately, this attempt to express a uniquely Cuban cultural identity became the object of political attack when Cuba aligned itself with Soviet ideology, in which architectural expressiveness was held to be bourgeois. The funding dried up when only three of the schools were fully complete, the architects fell from grace and went in to exile, and the site became overrun by jungle. Since 2000, the schools have been reassessed as valuable cultural assets, and they are currently under restoration and completion. They have survived as the most striking built testament of Cuba's revolutionary period. **CB**

Toronto
City Hall (1965)

Architects John B. Parkin Associates, Viljo Revell   **Location** Toronto, Canada
Style International Style   **Materials** Pre-cast concrete, stainless steel, Botticino marble, glass

Described in a letter to a newspaper as "two boomerangs over half a grapefruit," the winning proposal for Toronto City Hall by Viljo Revell (1910–64) proved to be both controversial and popular. The Finnish architect's design, selected from over 500 entries from forty-two countries by a jury that included Eero Saarinen, was a new and expressively Modernist vision of what democratic government could be.

Toronto City Hall comprises a domed circular Council Chamber bracketed by two curved towers of unequal heights. Rising from a two-story horizontal podium containing public areas and a library, the towers are oriented toward each other with glass and stainless steel on the inner surfaces and textured reinforced concrete on their concave outer facades. Slightly offset, they appear at once as protective wings around the saucerlike Council Chamber and as open arms toward the city; a curvaceous counterpart to the surrounding rectangular urban forms. A generous public square with a reflecting pool, gardens, and public art serves as a forecourt to the building, its borders defined by an elevated walkway. Upper and lower plazas are joined by a ramp that swoops down from the podium roof to meet the square below.

The bold sculptural forms of Toronto City Hall embody the optimism of the postwar era. Proving wrong Frank Lloyd Wright's prediction that the new City Hall would mark "the spot where Toronto fell," Revell's design set a precedent for mindful, civic buildings and Modernist architecture in Canada. **ASM**

↗ Nestled between the crescent-shaped towers, Revell's spacepodlike Council Chamber seems poised to lift off.

⤷ Placing windows on the inner, facing walls creates a sense of community among city hall workers.

The rise of new technologies, youth culture, and various resurgent economies produced new building styles. Modernism's tired authority was questioned by architects and theorists working to find alternatives. The sureties presented by Modernism were undermined by shifts in attitudes toward traditional morality, government power, and structure. The end of the Cold War terminated most Communist architectural programs and Western building styles spread across Asia. The development of Computer-Aided Design produced building forms and strategies that challenged conventional notions of architecture.

RISE *of* POSTMODERNISM

1966–2000

Church of St. Peter (1966)

Architect Sigurd Lewerentz **Location** Klippan, Sweden **Style** Modernist **Materials** Brick, steel

Dark purple bricks, all used uncut, give character to the inside and outside of this last great building of Lewerentz (1885–1975) in southern Sweden, which he struggled against illness and depression to complete. Like St. Mark's in Björkhagen, St. Peter's includes a freestanding parish office complex that acts as an entrance space, like a village street. The church is entered through a dark, cavelike space, and inside, the ceiling is lower than at St. Mark's. In a reflection of developing views on liturgy, the congregation sits around three sides of the altar, itself made of brick. Brick vaults are held up on an arrangement of Cor-ten steel beams and a single column, suggestive of a cross; the floor is also of brick, laid not in regular lines but in shapes that echo different areas and their uses. Lewerentz, inspired by a weathered wall at the Helsingborg Steam Brickworks, decided to use misshapen reject bricks, which resulted in irregular mortar joints as a deliberate effect. The windows are even more elementary than those at Björkhagen, simply panes of glass attached to the outside of the building, although they give an effect of fragility compared to the roughness of the masonry. St Peter's Church has become a cult building among architects fascinated by its combination of modern design and timeless qualities. The details are exceptional, including the giant, natural shell that serves as a font, constantly dripping water into a gap in the brick floor. **AP**

"It seems old, as if excavated from a pre-Christian time and once again put to use ..."

Janne Ahlin, professor of architecture

Wharton Esherick House (1966)

Architect Wharton Esherick **Location** Paoli, Pennsylvania, USA **Style** Vernacular **Materials** Stone, timber

The house and studio compound built by Wharton Esherick (1887–1970) over a forty-year period places him in the august company of U.S. nonconformists. Thoreau's *Walden* (1854), kept on his nightstand, asks the reader to live deliberately and authentically, and that is what Esherick did. He quit art school and joined an Alabama utopian community. He returned to Pennsylvania in his mid-thirties and bought land and a derelict farm. Talented as a printmaker, illustrator, furniture maker, and sculptor, these skills kept him financially afloat but without the recognition he craved. He turned instead to work on his land and his retreat. He gained admirers such as Louis I. Kahn, influenced craftsmen like Wendell Castle, and inspired atypical architectural communities like Sea Ranch, California. His home defies categorization. Straight lines are eschewed. Textures, colors, forms, and materials tumble over one another yet create a

harmonious composition. A cedar deck is supported by tapered, fat columns. A "greenery-yallery" log cabin garage—the term refers to the muted color scheme— has red-stained log ends and a part-concave, part-convex roof. The circular tower is painted in camouflage; its attached wing lined in alternate width radial-sawn timber boards. Esherick learned historic joinery to build details such as butt cog drop-in square joins at building corners. The architect was awarded the AIA Gold Medal the year after his death. **DJ**

"A studio built by the craftsman's own hands out of chunks of rock and great balks of timber…"

Ford Madox Ford, writer

Liverpool Metropolitan Cathedral (1966)

Architect Frederick Gibberd   **Location** Liverpool, England   **Style** Modernist   **Materials** Concrete, metal, stained glass

Until the erection of today's popular 1960s building, the Catholics of Liverpool had no true cathedral in which to worship. Edward Welby Pugin, son of the more famous Augustus, was commissioned to design a cathedral in 1853 but only part of it was built, to serve as a parish church until it was demolished in the 1980s. After the Anglican Cathedral began to rise at one end of Hope Street in 1904, Sir Edwin Lutyens was commissioned to outdo Sir Giles Gilbert Scott's design at a new site at the other end of the same street. Lutyens conceived a monumental building, featuring a great dome, 168 feet (51 m) in diameter; the height was to be 520 feet (158 m), dwarfing the 330-foot (101 m) tower of its Anglican rival. The crypt was completed after World War II, but funds were unavailable to complete the immense superstructure.

When Cardinal John Heenan arrived in Liverpool, he opened a competition to design a new building that would relate to the existing crypt, be completed within five years, and cost no more than one million pounds for its shell. Chosen from 300 entries, the design of Sir Frederick Gibberd (1908–84) consists of a circular nave, around which are sixteen satellite chapels and anterooms. The building is flooded by natural light from a central lantern and floor-to-roof stained-glass panels. In keeping with the new spirit of the liturgy, the altar is set low in the center to facilitate greater participation of the congregation.

The Liverpool Metropolitan Cathedral of Christ the King has recently undergone a major restoration to eliminate leaks in the roof, and a new stepped approach eases access to the building. **FR**

↖ Sixteen radial buttresses support a large central lantern that represents Jesus's crown of thorns.

← The lantern features rich, multicolored glass panels designed by John Piper and Patrick Reyntiens.

Bank of London and South America (1966)

Architects S.E.P.R.A.   **Location** Buenos Aires, Argentina   **Style** Brutalist   **Materials** Reinforced concrete, steel, aluminum

At the end of 1959, the Bank of London and South America was one of the most important banking entities in the world. On the occasion of its centennial, it held a private competition for its new headquarters in Buenos Aires. The guidelines for the competition not only laid out the functions of the building, but also emphasized flexibility and image. The experienced architectural firm S.E.P.R.A.—Sanchez Elía, Peralta Ramos, Agostini—along with Clorido Testa—presented the winning project.

The original idea reflected the desired flexibility: a large virtual volume to house all the activities in a single continuous space whose parts would interact metabolically. At more than 282,900 square feet (26,280 sq m), the building becomes part of the urban landscape by making the facades of neighboring buildings into its boundaries. The lower levels, under the sidewalks, contain the vaults and the service areas. The next three levels make up a complex hall for serving the bank's customers; this hall extends into three other floors that are used as offices. The two upper levels house the management and a cafeteria.

The basement, which is partly underground, supports not only the hall's large projections but also the facade's expressive pillars and the two main circulation areas. A large, 85-foot-high (26 m) platform rests on these pillars, and from it the three upper levels of offices hang over the main space, reducing the number of inner columns. This innovative proposal entailed constructing another small branch of the bank, where the structural solutions were worked out on a full size model. **JPV**

↗ In S.E.P.R.A.'s Brutalist masterpiece, great concrete slabs are suspended above the main entrance.

→ All the interior fixtures, such as light fittings and work stations, are designed to complement concrete.

Louisiana Museum of Modern Art (1966)

Architects Jørgen Bo, Vilhelm Wohlert   **Location** Humlebaek, Denmark   **Style** International Style   **Materials** Brick, glass, wood

The Louisiana Museum of Modern Art in Denmark is an extraordinary art repository. While the collections themselves are impressive, it is the beauty of the setting within which Jørgen Bo (1919–99) and Vilhelm Wohlert (*b.* 1920) have gradually built up, over a thirty-three year period, a thoughtful, unpretentious home for these modern art collections that continues to draw many visitors each year.

In 1956, businessman Knud Jensen bought the Louisiana Estate, overlooking the Oresund Strait between Denmark and Sweden. He intended to open up his art collection to the public, and hired young architects Bo and Wohlert to build a new wing onto the existing nineteenth-century villa for this purpose. The villa was surrounded by beautiful landscape and the architects wanted to create a building that was suitable for a world-class museum without competing with the art or the natural magnificence of the estate. The result was three small pavilions, connected to the house with arching glass corridors, reminiscent of Mies van der Rohe. As the collection grew, the architects added to their design. The complex today includes a wing buried in the hillside, mirroring the slope of the land itself, and an underground building, designed to house light-sensitive photographs and prints.

This building challenges the perception of the museum as a cabinet of curiosities. The Louisiana Museum of Modern Art is an organic entity, a living part of the landscape it inhabits. The art is displayed inside and out, and the building itself is presented as an exhibit, as is the vista beyond. It is as much about the nature and scenery as it is about architecture. **JS**

↖ The glass and timber corridors linking the pavilions date from the first phase of development in the 1950s.

↙ The old villa around which the museum is based was built on the Louisiana estate in 1856.

Whitney Museum of American Art (1966)

Architect Marcel Breuer **Location** New York, New York, USA **Style** Brutalist **Materials** Concrete, stone, glass

Marcel Breuer (1902–81), the Hungarian-born baby of the Bauhaus staff when he became professor of the furniture department at the legendary German design school in 1924, aged just twenty-two, was, by the end of his life, one of the most important Modernist architects working in the United States. Among the finest of Breuer's later works in his adopted country is the Whitney Museum of American Art, an imposing and rather brutal building on New York's Madison Avenue. This is the third home of the museum that was established in 1931 by Gertrude Vanderbilt Whitney to house her collection of modern art.

When considering the form of the new Whitney, Breuer said, "It should be an independent and self-relying unit, exposed to history, and at the same time it should transform the vitality of the street into the sincerity and profundity of art." To achieve this end, he designed a highly sculptural building that steps out toward the street as it rises, like an inverted ziggurat. The elevations are finished in dark gray granite, and only one window appears on the front facade, a large projecting trapezoid that appears again in six smaller versions along the side elevation. Visitors enter the museum across a bridge, like a drawbridge to a castle, crossing the sculpture courtyard below. Inside, the building is arranged with a split-level lobby and restaurant, on the ground and basement floors, with four floors of art galleries above.

Three schemes to extend the Whitney by Michael Graves, Rem Koolhaas, and Renzo Piano have all been scrapped in favor of building a second branch of the museum on a separate, downtown site. **MF**

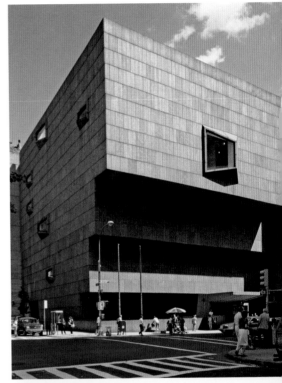

↗ The forbidding facade manifests Breuer's hope for an "independent and self-relying unit."

→ The entrance and restaurant are tucked underneath the overhanging elevations.

Leça Swimming Pools (1966)

Architect Álvaro Siza   **Location** Matosinhos, Portugal
Style De Stijl   **Materials** Concrete, copper

Only a few years after his first built work, the Casa de Chá restaurant at Matosinhos, attracted a lot of attention, Álvaro Siza (*b.* 1933) returned almost to the same spot—just a little further south along the beachfront—to create seawater swimming pools. The site was a stretch of rocky beach below the promenade, overlooked by freighters just offshore, heading for nearby Oporto. Constrained by a limited budget, Siza transcended these impediments.

A pedestrian ramp slopes gently down from street level, which is also that of the copper roof stretched

---

"I think there should always be a certain distance between the natural and what is man-made."

Álvaro Siza, architect

---

above the changing facilities and the bar, so the facilities do not obstruct the seaward view. Siza designed a canyon of concrete walls open to the sky; the visitor moves into a strange environment where the sea can be heard pounding below but at first cannot be seen. The sea is then dramatically revealed through a series of breaches carefully designed as peepholes. Exiting from this labyrinth onto the beach, the visitor finds a vista of natural rocks and low concrete walls containing a sequence of pools, allowing safe swimming in the seawater. For the bather, water, sand, stone, and concrete are an experience of the natural merged with the artificial. The experience of these pools is truly singular, with sunlight glancing off the pool surfaces and the eye-catching backdrop of Siza's concrete complex. **YN**

Church of St. Aengus (1967)

Architect Liam McCormick   **Location** Burt, County Donegal, Ireland
Style Vernacular   **Materials** Stone, concrete, steel, wood, copper

Known locally as Burt Chapel, St. Aengus's Church stands at the head of Lough Swilly, 6 miles (10 km) west of Derry. The church dramatically echoes the Grianán of Aileach, a Bronze-Age hilltop fort that dominates the surrounding countryside, and it is similarly circular in plan. A tentlike roof rising to a conical spire, both clad in copper, tops two concentric circles faced in rough-hewn stone. A split in the two circles forms the entrance; the space inside houses confessional boxes and a sacristy.

There is a historical link between St. Aengus's and the fort, which is believed to have been the palace of the northern Irish kings until the twelfth century. St. Patrick is reputed to have baptized King Eoghan there in 441. Eoghan's grandson Aengus built the first church at Burt and was later its patron saint.

Today's church accommodates a congregation of 550 people. It was built to accord with the liturgical norms of the Second Vatican Council (1962–65), which changed the way services were celebrated. Previously the priest had his back to the congregation; now he said Mass facing them. The font and altar, designed by Imogen Stuart, are of Portland stone, the latter spotlit from a lantern in the base of the spire. A sculptured wall in cast concrete depicts the site's history.

This masterpiece of Liam McCormick (1916–96) is regarded as the finest church built in Ireland since the Council. He had a natural instinct for landscape. Like his other church buildings, it provides a break with the prevailing Gothic and Italianate aesthetic, and sits naturally in Ireland's bleak west coast. Despite its avowed purpose, McCormick referred to the church as "my pagan building," because of its overt debt to the nearby fort. In 2000, it was nominated as Building of the Century in a national Irish poll. **BMC**

Shizuoka Press and Broadcasting Center (1967)

Architect Kenzo Tange **Location** Tokyo, Japan **Style** Modernist
Materials Black aluminum, concrete, steel, glass

This building forms the end of a housing and office block in Ginza, Tokyo, appearing from the highway as a terminal spike. It occupies a narrow triangular site of only 2,034 square feet (189 sq m), located directly at the Tokyo Expressway Number 1 exit. Kenzo Tange (1913–2005) designed it as a slender tower, clad in black aluminum. The stairways and elevators are accomodated in a central, cylindrical core, rising 620 feet (189 m) above the ground. The shaft extends deep into the ground in order to counteract the lateral forces on the tower. Twelve stories with 16,000 square feet (1,500 sq m) of office floor cantilever out from the tower, stretching almost randomly to different sides like the branches of a tree. The floor plan is as triangular as the site. Like Kisho Kurokawa's Nakagin Capsule Tower (1972) nearby, this is one of the seminal small towers of modern Japan.

The building marked a turning point in Tange's work. Partially emancipating his architecture from the doctrines of Le Corbusier's concrete edifices and the Metabolists' megastructures, Tange started to produce more rangy buildings that reacted strongly to their surroundings. The tower is also exceptional in Tange's portfolio: while most of his buildings convince by the skilfull structuring of their sheer mass, this one exhibits a subtle, natural, and accomplished setting of small elements.

Only two years after its completion, Tange was commissioned to build a new headquarters for the same firm a few miles to the south. The building had become too small and modular extensions of it were not feasible. The new complex, again treelike in character, consists of three buildings with office space stretching as large floors from a rectangular core, leaving here and there an open floor. **FH**

Montreal Biosphère (1967)

Architects Buckminster Fuller, Shoji Sadao **Location** Montreal, Canada **Style** High Tech **Materials** Steel, acrylic sheet

In the 1960s, student radical Abbie Hoffman famously declared, "Don't trust anyone over thirty." Yet a man in his seventies during that decade—Buckminster Fuller (1893–1983)—inspired thousands of students, and entrepreneurs. In 1965 the U.S. Information Agency commissioned Fuller to design the American Pavilion, now known as the Montreal Biosphère, at the 1967 World's Fair in Montreal. Fuller and Sadao designed a 200-by-250-foot (61 x 76 m) geodesic, three-quarter sphere. From ground to equator it is a series of parallel metal rings, above which the structure is entirely geodesic. A two-layer skin of steel rods creates an outer triangular panel system atop an inner hexagonal layer. Each panel was sealed with an acrylic sheet. Mechanically energized environments were an artistic pursuit in the 1960s, but only Fuller took the idea beyond theatrical display to living laboratory. The interior climate of the Biosphère was dynamically adjusted via internal, computer-controlled shades. Fuller's eventual plan was that the dome would evolve to include "biomimicry," by which each panel would act as a cell to shield, breathe, and photosynthesize. In 1976, a fire destroyed the acrylic panels, leaving the steel latticework intact. The dome now encloses a museum dedicated to environmental issues. A scientist who visited it in 1967 was inspired by its structure to discover the "Buckminsterfullerene" carbon molecule; he was awarded the Nobel Prize. **DJ**

"Its exterior covering was exquisitely tinted, and surprisingly it was lovely to look at."

Paper describing the architecture of Expo 67

Dr. Rogers House (1967)

Architects Richard Rogers Partnership **Location** London, England **Style** Modernist **Materials** Steel, plastic-coated aluminium, glass

The Richard Rogers Partnership is associated with the modern, technological, and social architecture of the twentieth century. Catapulted to world recognition with the Pompidou Center, which Rogers (b. 1933) designed with Renzo Piano, the Partnership is well known for its democratic, inventive, and industrial approach to architecture. This house was an early commission for Rogers, and proves his ethos that domestic projects are just as significant as larger ones. It was commissioned by Rogers's parents, Nino and Dada, as their retirement home. Rogers understood their needs well, and collaborated with them to incorporate their desire for flexible living and working spaces. It was to be a family home, with a consulting room for Dr. Rogers, who was still working part-time, and a pottery studio for Dada. The couple required an economical, expandable, easily maintained, and secluded home that merged with the landscape. In designing this house, Rogers was influenced by the Californian Case Study houses by architects such as Raphael Soriano in the 1950s, as well as by the Reliance Controls Factory project in Swindon that Rogers finished in 1967 with Norman Foster. Rogers considered the house a prototype in many ways: an exercise in using mass-produced materials to create moveable frames, achieving what in theory is itself easy to mass-produce. The house is divided into two main spaces—the house, made of five steel portals and, opposite, the studio, made of three. In the middle is a paved courtyard. Rogers calls the house a "transparent flexible tube that could be adapted and extended." The east and west elevations are glazed. This domestic building is influential in its social ideals, in pinpointing the importance of structure in design, and managing to create a seamless, economic transition from space to space. **SL**

Habitat '67 (1967)

Architect Moshe Safdie   **Location** Montreal, Canada   **Style** Modernist   **Material** Concrete

"We want to have intense urban experiences and yet we want the open space right next to us."

Moshe Safdie, architect

⬆ The construction system of stacked modular units was successful but proved prohibitively expensive.

➡ Safdie was inspired by the clustered homes of ancient hillside towns in Italy, Japan, and the Middle East.

Despite this project's Modernist credentials, Moshe Safdie (*b.* 1938) took much of his inspiration for Habitat '67 from medieval hill towns in the Mediterranean and the Middle East; this homage can be clearly seen in the formation of the apartments, as though they have grown organically via centuries of population growth. It is also suggested by the rich greenery of the trees and communal garden areas, which contrast strongly with the pale-colored brick.

Safdie was just twenty-nine when he designed Habitat '67; he hoped his vision would bring an end to what he saw as the claustrophobia and uniformity of modern urban living. Picturesquely located in the harbor of Montreal's St. Lawrence River, Habitat '67 was designed as the city of the future. Its name comes from the Montreal World Expo of 1967, the theme of which was "habitat," for which the project was created. The structures are composed of more than 350 prefab blocks, or "modules"; these make up more than 150 apartments, which range in size from between one and eight blocks. Safdie placed the apartments in a seemingly disordered manner, but when viewed from certain angles it becomes apparent that the overall shape is that of a series of pyramids.

Safdie had begun his idea for Habitat '67 when working on his university thesis, the theme of which was "A Case for City Living, a Study of Three Urban High-Density Housing Systems." Expo 1967 allowed him to bring those ideas to fruition. The complex is divided into three sections, which are connected by high walkways, as well as stairs and elevators. Aware that the project would be lived in by families as well as singles, the architect provided children's play areas and pedestrian streets. The placement of each apartment, at an opposing angle to the one beneath, means that each apartment's roof provides an outside area for its upstairs neighbor. **LH**

Church at Haparanda (1967)

Architect Bengt Larsson, ELLT Architects   **Location** Haparanda, Sweden   **Style** Modernist   **Materials** Steel, copper

The Church at Haparanda, near the Swedish border with Finland, was built to replace the previous wooden church that was built in 1825 and burned down in 1963. The Swedish architect Bengt Larsson designed this remarkable building, and called it the "clean house" because of its simple, pure features. The church is constructed of two main shapes: a base and an upper unit. The lower part appears compact and flat while the upper section rises up like an oversized, elongated church tower. It looks like a highly exaggerated version of the stacked spires of Swedish wooden churches. This barnlike structure is made up of a steel frame clad in corrugated copper plates forming a large, dark, and somewhat industrial shell. However, two window bands wrap the upper section lengthways, piercing the shell so that light streams into the bright, spacious room below. The interior stands in sharp contrast to the exterior. The room is

light and welcoming with large, unpretentious chandeliers of two concentric circles, one holding 120 lights, the other 60, creating a luminous place. Some visitors interpret the contrast between the dark facade and the bright interior as a journey through the darkness of death toward heavenly light. Purity was the architect's main theme. His design conveys a sense of aesthetic simplicity in which clear lines predominate throughout the building. Everything seems exceptionally calculated, as if arranged in geometric accordance. For example, by placing the chandeliers in the center of the room, where the open space of the tower begins, and never seems to stop, Larsson has maintained harmony and balance. Here, all the oversized lengths, heights, and widths are preserved and brought down to scale concurrently, creating a wonderfully peaceful atmosphere in a striking piece of modern architecture. **SML**

St. Catherine's College (1968)

Architect Arne Jacobsen **Location** Oxford, England **Style** Modernist **Materials** Reinforced concrete, brick

St. Catherine's College was one of a number of new colleges to be built after World War II as additions to England's oldest university, Oxford. The man who brought it into being, historian Alan Bullock, was clear that the architecture needed to be groundbreaking and resolutely modern, and for that purpose he secured Danish architect Arne Jacobsen (1902–71). Recent restoration work has brought a renewed freshness to the college, not least by replacing scrappy curtains with the louvered blinds that had proved too expensive in the initial building campaign. Two long blocks of student rooms frame a rectangular courtyard, which is divided into two smaller "quads" by the library and teaching buildings. A fine dining hall is the best internal space, its roof held free of the walls by perfect concrete columns and its floor paved with dark slate. Everywhere the detailing is impeccable. Discreetly curvaceous Jacobsen handles open plain

wood doors, and his famous furniture, including the specially designed Oxford chair, was used in many rooms. For formal dining his cutlery was provided, until pilfering made it too expensive to retain. The joy of a visit to St. Catherine's is the feeling of order and calm that it produces. From the moment the visitor crosses the bridge over a kind of moat on the entrance front, the noise of urban life is excluded, and all is surprisingly peaceful for a college complex. Simplicity, symmetry, and repetition are everything. **BWC**

"The schematic arrangement of furniture [that] an architect would prefer is rarely seen in practice ..."

Arne Jacobsen, architect and designer

New National Gallery (1968)

Architect Ludwig Mies van der Rohe   **Location** Berlin, Germany   **Style** Modernist   **Materials** Steel, glass

The swan song of one of the greatest masters of the most influential architectural style of the twentieth century, the New National Gallery in Berlin is the masterpiece of Ludwig Mies van der Rohe (1886–1969)—a mature example of his Modernist statement and the perfection of architectural cubic simplicity. An integral part of the area's *Kulturforum*, the gallery houses twentieth-century European modern painting and sculpture. Essentially, the gallery is a simple, square pavilion. Nearly all the exhibition spaces are located underground, with the lobby and ticket-sales point at ground level. The main visible space is a glass-enclosed, meticulous steel framework, a simple yet beautifully detailed structure with a flexible interior. The hall is wonderfully lit, with sunlight coming through the floor-to-ceiling glass walls and reflecting on the dark, polished flooring. Mies van der Rohe's admiration of pure geometry is ever-present, from the dark-beam grid of the ceiling construction to the sequence of slim metal roof supports in the outer walls. In structural and spatial-planning terms, the gallery resembles the master's earliest work in the United States—the architect moved there in 1937 to escape the Nazis. The gallery's minimalist elegance and structural abstraction is representative, not only of Mies van der Rohe's work, but also of the whole style he fronted. Not for nothing was it referred to as the "Classic Greek Temple" of our times. **ES**

> *"[The] detailing . . . adapts to the construction, but is admirable upon closer inspection."*
>
> **Arne Jacobsen, architect and designer**

Elrod House (1968)

Architect John Lautner **Location** Palm Springs, California, USA **Style** Modernist **Materials** Concrete, steel, glass, copper, slate

The aura of *Diamonds are Forever* lingers in the Elrod house. Stylistically related to his Chemosphere (1960), John Lautner's (1911–94) Elrod House is less flamboyant but no less spectacular. Approached by an inclined driveway, the initial view is circumspect. Curved and low, the inside is masked by darkened paneled glass. A guardrail on the protruding lip edge restrains a concrete flat roof. But wait. It intends to lull. At the end of the drive a massive, patched, copper door leads into a half-circle compound. A low, concrete entrance restrains the circular main structure. Once inside, the house pops. The vast, open living room is scaled with a reduced horizontal profile that keeps the space welcoming. The ceiling resembles a huge, 35-millimeter diaphragm shutter; its multiple blades reach to the peaked aperture and move to make an exposure of the sky. The black slate floor disappears into the night. The glass curtain wall slides open on a suspension system to reveal a half-circle pool patio area that balances the compound entrance form. The desert and mountain vista spill out beneath. A giant boulder outcrop incorporated into the living room is directional to the bedroom annex. Panoramic windows in the master bath are shielded not by curtains but by the exterior boulder landscape. A door leads to a platform hidden in the boulder outcrop, where the house can be viewed from below. What other architects dream, Lautner designed. **DJ**

"Once I get home and into my sauna, I'm so thrilled to be there that I hate to go out."

Arthur Elrod, owner

Cuadra San Cristóbal (1968)

Architect Luis Barragán **Location** Mexico City, Mexico
Style Modernist **Materials** Stone, stucco

The work of Mexican master Luis Barragán (1902–88) on residential projects is well known and widely acclaimed, including masterpieces such as Casa Barragán and Casa Antonio Gálvez, which adapt Modernist ideals to Mexico's hot climate. Of a different scale, but still according to Barragán's idiom, is the Cuadra San Cristóbal (Egerstrom House), which the architect designed in 1966.

A true Mexican hacienda, the house includes equestrian stables for the Folke Egerstrom ranch, a granary, a training track, a meadow, and a large pool for the horses, fed with water through a slot on the adjacent rusty-red wall. The architects' solution encompasses an idyllic game of light and water, the sunlight playing on the roughly stuccoed walls and then reflecting on the pool's watery surface. The complex is composed as a series of multilayered planes of varied warm colors from orange and yellow to pink and deep red, which define the spaces—the inner courts—and create areas of shade for people and animals to hide from the sun. The whole complex is conceived around the animals; the walls are designed to their scale, the horses enter and leave the main exercise space through two elegant openings on a long pink wall, and the pool has steps into the water for the horses to refresh themselves.

The theme of light and water is common in Barragán's work, but in this particular project it finds an ideal territory for experimentation owing to its scale, complexity, and need for articulation. **ES**

◹ The richly colored surfaces are also designed to provide shade for the animals.

◁ The horses' exercise yard and refreshment pool is as beautifully designed as the human accommodation.

Church of St. Mary (1968)

Architect Douglas Cardinal   **Location** Red Deer, Alberta, Canada
Style Expressionist   **Materials** Brick, concrete

St. Mary's Roman Catholic Church (see page 549) in Red Deer, Alberta, designed by Canadian-born architect Douglas Cardinal (b. 1934), is widely known as the building that established his career. When it was built in 1968, the church was on the outskirts of Red Deer, but has long since been enveloped by suburban sprawl. Notwithstanding, its forms are clearly derived from the rolling hills of central Alberta. This design language evolved not as a sculptural pretension but as a pre-design process that has come to epitomize an architect assuredly linking his buildings' users with the natural landscapes that surround them.

Cardinal reconsidered the event of the Roman Catholic Mass by promoting the feeling of a primitive church, with no separation of altar and parish. An undulating double-brick wall with a concrete cavity wraps all of the plan elements. The roof is an innovative, cable-suspended, post-tension concrete structure that is high over the entrance, creating a sense of open procession in and out of the windowed highest volumes. From the entrance the roof slopes down low to cover the altar and confessionals. The altar is a six-ton slab of Manitoba Tyndell limestone, illuminated by light piercing through the sloping roof. The spatial effect is one of somber spirituality.

In 1995, to Cardinal's dismay, St. Mary's parishioners enlisted the help of a local architectural practice to build an awkwardly conceived addition. The church entrance and one side have lost much of their visual power and elegance. The addition was designed in a pastiche of Cardinal's own distinctive style. The cloned forms visitors see today obscure the boundary of the 1960s' original and 1990s' addition. Despite all this, St. Mary's Roman Catholic Church stands proud, evoking the memory of a stoic prairie grain silo. **DMT**

Catton House (1969)

Architects Erickson Massey Architects   **Location** West Vancouver, British Columbia, Canada   **Style** Modernist   **Material** Wood

Catton House juts out of a hill high above a railway line in West Vancouver, its canted profile echoing a rocky site that slants to the sea. Arthur Erickson (b. 1924), a Vancouver native, tied the house into the slope using a tactic that appeared in his well-known and almost concurrent design for Vancouver's Museum of Anthropology. The visitor enters into private, inward-focused rooms at the top, and descends through a series of platforms and levels to public rooms with floor-to-ceiling windows.

The house is the culmination of a series of West

> *"To the horror of my colleagues, I never let structural veracity interfere with aesthetic purpose."*
>
> Arthur Erickson, architect

Coast buildings that explored an elemental, Bauhaus-inspired design approach. Erickson balances this abstract method with painterly effects derived from careful attention to site-specific phenomena: climate, vegetation, topography, light. In all his work, Erickson binds architecture and locale together, connecting both of them as much as possible to the wider physical terrain and cultural purview.

The house shows off Erickson's well-structured planning, but his higher aim is to design in the tradition of fine art: his buildings should evoke emotional responses. Catton House is covered inside and out with treated cedar cladding, which makes it appear as if the living spaces and outdoor terraces are carved from a solid wooden rhomboid. Catton House's appeal is sculptural, but above all poetic. **DMT**

Preston Bus Station (1969)

Architect Keith Ingham, Charles Wilson   **Location** Preston, England   **Style** Modernist   **Materials** Precast and reinforced concrete

The city of Preston in northwest England lies on important transport routes and draws a high volume of bus traffic, both local and long-distance. In 1959 plans were drawn up for a new bus station in Preston, but it was immediately realized that these early designs were inadequate—the increase in private car ownership called for a combined bus station and multistory parking lot.

Preston Corporation handed the scheme to Keith Ingham and Charles Wilson of Building Design Partnership. When completed, the parking lot had accommodation for 1,100 cars, and the bus station below could hold eighty double-decker buses. The structure is made of reinforced and precast concrete. The bus station is housed in a tall ground floor with mezzanine, and above, depending on the area of the bus station, four or five floors of car parking.

The side facades, clad in white tiles, have glazed ground floors with dramatic curved, concrete fronts to the upper floors. The curved form of the parking lot floor edge serves to reduce loadings; it evolved after acceptable finishes to a vertical wall proved too expensive. This curve contributes to the building's organic, sculptural character. The edges are functional, too, in that they prevent cars from hitting the vertical wall. The cover balustrade protects passengers from the weather by allowing buses to penetrate beneath the lower parking floor. Preston Bus Station is a perfect example of how a potentially utilitarian building with a mundane use can be transformed into a dramatic and bold structure in which the difficult balance of grand scale and fine detailing is achieved. **ER**

↖ The floors above Preston's Bus Station house an innovatively designed parking garage.

← In bad weather, the overhanging floors prevent bus passengers and drivers from getting wet.

Temppeliaukio Church (1969)

Architects Timo Suomalainen, Tuomo Suomalainen   **Location** Helsinki, Finland   **Style** Modernist   **Materials** Rock, glass

The Temppeliaukio Church is known affectionately as "the Rock Church." Located in the heart of Helsinki, it represents the meeting of Lutheran values and the Finnish love of the wild.

The architect brothers Timo (*b.* 1928) and Tuomo (1931–88) Suomalainen won the competition to build the church in 1961; they also designed the furniture. The church is quarried from rock, with a circular glass dome covering the space and allowing natural light to enter. The circular theme is repeated inside, with seats surrounding the altar. It was while the interior was being excavated that the decision was made to leave parts of the rock in their natural state as an integral part of the church. Traditional church decoration was omitted in favor of simple benches and the beauties of the uneven rock surface. An acoustics expert and a conductor were consulted during the design process and, as a result, the church is renowned for its acoustics. It is often used as a concert venue.

Lutheran churches are typically modest, and this church is a thorough return to basics. The natural materials and light focus the attention on the religious ceremony as well as the music. The walls, organic to the point that they are growing moss, look as though they have been there forever—encapsulating the Christian message of eternal life. Inside the church, the visitor is as close to nature as it is possible to get.

The church looks as if it has emerged from the ground, and has stood there for many centuries. Its rock walls bring to mind old Finnish fortresses, designed to survive both extreme weather and cannon fire. **RK**

↗ The interior walls were left in their original state, as a perfect illustration of God's work in nature.

→ The church appears to have grown organically from its rocky site, fitting perfectly into its surroundings.

Trinity
Car Park (1969)

Architect Owen Luder **Location** Gateshead, Tyne and Wear, England
Style Brutalist **Material** Reinforced concrete

The Trinity Car Park has achieved iconic status thanks, in part, to the central role it played in the 1971 British gangster mover *Get Carter*, starring Michael Caine. Owen Luder (*b.* 1928), a former president of the Royal Institute of British Architects, was a bold and uncompromising designer who produced several buildings during the 1960s and 1970s that were as controversial as they were dynamic. The developer of Trinity also commissioned Luder to design the equally Brutalist and equally controversial Tricorn shopping center in Portsmouth, now demolished.

The Gateshead parking garage serves the adjoining Trinity shopping complex and is raised above it in a prominent location high on the banks of the River Tyne. The decks of the parking garage have a slight "kink," breaking up the otherwise strong horizontals of the building's massive bulk. Stair and elevator access towers are at either end, giving uninterrupted views through each level when viewed from a distance. On the top level is an extra tier containing a large structure connected to the access towers; this was intended to house a restaurant.

Problems beset the parking garage almost immediately. Subsidence during construction meant extra reinforcements were needed for the foundations and within a very short time the concrete began to weather very badly. No tenant was ever found for the rooftop restaurant, and it was on this empty, unfinished floor that a key scene in *Get Carter* took place. Iconic status was assured when Michael Caine threw an adversary from the top floor. As with most Brutalist structures it is a difficult building to find beauty in, but it remains an unmistakable example of the style with the added caché of being an iconic prop of British cinema. **ER**

Torres
del Parque (1970)

Architect Rogelio Salmona **Location** Bogotá, Colombia
Style Modernist **Materials** Reinforced concrete, brick

Rogelio Salmona (*b.* 1929) worked for Le Corbusier for nearly a decade before returning to practice in his native Colombia. The Torres del Parque (Park Towers) apartments profit from European ideas on high-rise living: their curvaceous plans echo projects by Alvar Aalto, while the distorted slabs and external access galleries of the lower blocks reflect earlier English Brutalist theories on developing community spirit in apartment buildings. These foreign influences are blended with a traditionally Colombian use of high-quality red brick. This helps integrate the building with

> *"Not even in her worst moments has Colombia lost the ability to sing, dance, write, paint, and build."*
>
> Rogelio Salmona, architect

a longer history of architecture in Bogotá, and especially the fine civic bullfighting stadium nearby.

The complex consists of three towers, the tallest thirty-eight stories high. Inspired by the round stadium below, the buildings are organized around a series of interlocking circles, some expressed in the landscaping of the gardens, others only implied by the curves of the buildings. The tallest block rises sheer from pavement to roof, emphasizing its size. It is flanked, however, by two shorter buildings that, by stepping down in garden-covered balconies as they curve, help to accommodate the building to the scale of the surrounding streets. The Torres del Parque is the first example of Salmona's personal style. They show how well an uncompromisingly tall and Modernist building can be integrated into an old city. **BWC**

Metropolitan Cathedral (1970)

Architects Oscar Niemeyer, Gordon Bunshaft **Location** Brasilia, Brazil
Style Modernist **Material** Reinforced concrete, glass

One of the most important buildings of Brasilia, Brazil's then newly founded capital city, Metropolitan Cathedral is also one of the most beautiful. Here, Oscar Niemeyer (*b.* 1907), the principal architect of Brasilia's public buildings, collaborated with Gordon Bunshaft (1909–90), the leading designer of a major U.S. commercial practice, to produce a cathedral worthy of the capital of such a large, self-confident, and Catholic nation.

As with Niemeyer's other designs for Brasilia, the cathedral is remarkably simple. Its more complex functions are hidden underground. Above ground appear only the sixteen buttresses, each sweeping up to the small roof in a graceful parabolic curve. Between the buttresses is stretched a web of stained glass that, seen from outside by night, or from the inside by day, presents a vivid expanse of blues and greens.

The concrete supports are obviously modern, and the circular plan is recognizably of its period in the Catholic Church's thinking about worship spaces. There is also, though, a timeless quality to the cathedral. This comes partly from its abstract simplicity, but also from the echoes of Gothic cathedrals in the sweeping lines of the buttresses. This church looks back to the medieval tradition of daring church engineering, and forward to the advanced engineering of its own period. From outside, the strong shape is a memorable image. Inside, you are moved by the building's spacious grandeur, and by the extraordinary great window of stained glass stretched over the entire area like the canvas of a tent. **BWC**

↗ The exquisite stained glass allows in a profusion of sunlight to shine upon the cathedral's worshippers.

→ The 90-ton ribs taper as they reach the ground, giving the structure a paradoxical appearance of lightness.

Spodek Multipurpose Arena (1971)

Architect Maciej Gintowt   **Location** Katowice, Poland
Style High Tech   **Materials** Steel, reinforced concrete

The period after World War II saw a dynamic campaign instigated by the communist regime in Poland to construct superior modern structures to represent the country's new era. Katowice—the new center of Upper Silesia—needed an idiosyncratic building to mark its identity. The Association of Polish Architects organized a competition for a multipurpose hall.

The jury was so amazed by the winning entry that the proposal was eventually realized in the very center of the city, rather than on its outskirts. The clarity of the concept is striking—the floor plan is circular,

---

> *"The roof is the earliest known actual use of a cable structure based on the tensegrity principle."*

Nicolas Janberg, French-German bridge engineer

---

472 feet (144 m) in diameter. The elevated mass of the building resembles an inverted cone with its apex buried underground and the base cut off at an oblique plane. Triggered by requirements such as the rake of the seating and multipurpose usage, the design led to the remarkable tilted effect. The tensegrity method, relying on self-stressed structural components in a closed system, was employed to hold up a 300-ton steel dome by means of 120 lightweight trusses.

This building is a pioneering work of modern engineering and architecture, and it has become a key reference in the later development of the light roof structures now called "Geiger's domes." It preceded the structural methods and scale found in many later buildings, and constitutes an outstanding example of early High Tech in architecture. **BK**

Rothko Chapel (1971)

Architects Mark Rothko, Philip Johnson   **Location** Houston, Texas, USA
Style Modernist   **Materials** Concrete, brick

In 1964 John and Dominique de Menil commissioned the artist Mark Rothko (1903–70) to create a series of canvases suitable for a new chapel being built by the architect Philip Johnson (1906–2005). Rothko was to work closely with the architect, and through collaboration they were to produce a design that was both art gallery and spiritual haven, enabling the paintings and the building to develop and grow together to form a unified and devotional space.

The chapel is designed around an octagonal format, a traditional type for early Christian and Orthodox chapels, and provides an almost circular central space. Originally the chapel was to be Roman Catholic, but it was eventually conceived as a place of worship and reflection for all denominations. The interior, which is devastatingly simple, is lit from skylights above and provides an environment that is deeply moving and spiritual. After formulating the building's design, Johnson stepped down from the project, and Howard Barnstone and Eugene Aubry took on the construction.

Rothko, who was suffering from severe depression at the time, worked for three intense years on the canvases. After this period he kept returning to them, never satisfied, and tragically took his own life before the chapel was finished. Based on the Passion of Christ, the huge canvases are stark, simple, and striking. Each is a study in black with red undertones or overtones with varying paint thicknesses creating ambiguities in the colors. The symbolism of red and its associations with life, power, and spirit, and black aligned with death and deep reflection, is all the more evocative against the unadorned and dimly lit chapel interior. Consequently, this is one of the world's most intensely moving spiritual sanctuaries. **TP**

North Building, Denver Art Museum (1971)

Architect Gio Ponti **Location** Denver, Colorado, USA
Style Postmodernist **Materials** Brick, glass tiles

Dubbed "The Castle" for its apparent impenetrable solidity, the only North American building by Gio Ponti (1891–1979) is widely misunderstood. It takes its cue not from medieval fortresses but from Italian churches. The irregular, twenty-eight-sided, two-tower, seven-story structure is castellated at roofline. Slab walls are punctuated with windows shaped as squares, raised eyelids, and horizontal and vertical slits. Stretched hexagonal lozenges pair with arrow-tip windows to pattern vertical ribbon walls. Sunlight animates the glass-tiled facade to create a semiliquid glaze effect.

Divided into twin cubes linked by an elevator core, the museum appears as one from the outside. Single galleries on three floors punctuate four pairs of galleries on four floors. The design places the artwork foremost—gallery pairs eliminate the need to backtrack; moveable walls aid hanging; the double-height mezzanine ceiling moves up or down. Ponti took inspiration from his own work—the San Francesco d'Assisi al Fopponino church in Milan (1964) with its openwork lozenge facade—and from the thirteenth-century Basilica of San Francesco in Assisi. This walled compound of museums, churches, and residences includes two churches with a single shared nave decorated with Cimabue and Giotto frescoes. Ponti translated ideas from the compound to Denver—crenellated walls of monotone bricks became Ponti's glass facade; the separate but shared churches became his twin towers; the church as art patron became his museum. **DJ**

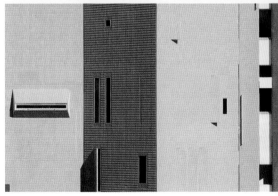

↗ The North Building enabled the museum to show all of its collections in one place for the first time.

⇥ The facade is sheathed in a million convex, rectangular, gray glass tiles designed by Ponti.

Transamerica Pyramid (1972)

Architect William L. Pereira   **Location** San Francisco, California, USA   **Style** Modernist   **Materials** Precast quartz panels, concrete, steel

Today the Transamerica Pyramid is considered a landmark building for San Francisco, yet originally it was a building of much ridicule and protest. In 1969 when architect William Pereira (1909–85) presented plans for the new headquarters of the Transamerica Corporation, his unconventional design was met with a broad mixture of enthusiasm and condemnation.

Pereira, a Los Angeles architect known for movie-set designs and futuristic buildings, had headed the team that designed the Theme Building for Los Angeles International Airport, an iconic 1960s building resembling a flying saucer. The overall form of the Transamerica Pyramid is in the shape of a slender, gently tapering pyramid with two "wings" flanking the upper levels to allow for vertical circulation. The facade is clad in white, precast, quartz-aggregate panels. It is currently the tallest building in San Francisco, and is part of the Transamerica Center.

The building's form was conceptually based on tall redwood and sequoia trees, native to the area, which with their conical form allow light to filter down to the forest floor. Similarly, the Transamerica Pyramid allows greater light to reach street level. Advocates maintained its narrow design would also allow for greater unobstructed premium views around the San Francisco Bay than a traditional tower. Critics claimed the tower was a threat to the integrity of the city and would negatively transform the urban fabric—the tower took up a full city block and required the city to sell an alley in the middle of the block to the Transamerica Corporation. A main point of contention centered on this sale of public space to a private entity. Condemning its unconventional form, one assemblyman declared it would "rape the skyline." Despite early opposition, however, the public gradually warmed, and today it is one of the city's best-known buildings. **AC**

Nakagin Capsule Tower (1972)

Architect Kisho Kurokawa **Location** Tokyo, Japan **Style** Modernist **Materials** Concrete

Nakagin Capsule Tower begins unremarkably. Square, truncated concrete pillars support a conventional first floor, which spans a ground level undercroft. The only unusual object is a model capsule display unit.

From the first floor upward, however, the tower view changes to a remarkable cluster of modular, off-site-manufactured capsules inserted in an eleven-story steel skeleton crowned with two fins. This was the very first capsule accommodation design—and looks like a giant multipin motherboard connector unit. Each tiny apartment is modular on the outside but contains a 1960s "mod" interior. The original built-in furniture is extant: a white plastic console wall begins with storage units; drop fronts create double-duty tables; and spotlights and air conditioning vents are designed to swivel and direct as needed. The console ends with a telephone, a laughably outmoded Sony reel-to-reel tape deck, radio, speakers, flip-clock, and television conveniently inserted over the bed. A 3-foot-diameter (0.9 m) porthole is the sole natural light source. A molded all-in-one plastic toilet/shower/sink unit opens with a caplet-shaped door. That is all of the 7.5-by-12-by-6.8-foot (2.3 x 3.8 x 2.1 m) unit.

Each capsule had a twenty-five-year lifespan but, eleven years past their use-by-date, the originals are still in place. The owners began to revolt when living conditions became less salubrious. Claims of defects, corrosion, and asbestos were made, and residents formed the Nakagin Capsule Tower Demolition and Reconstruction Committee.

Kisho Kurokawa (*b.* 1934) realized he had to accept criticisms of his original design and rethink the units so as to protect the overall concept. The cause is now "replacement and reconstruction," and the architect proposes identical capsules with a sixty-year lifespan. They still need one more change, however—a console sound system fit for the twenty-first century. **DJ**

Olympic Park Swimming Hall (1972)

Architects Günther Behnisch, Frei Otto   **Location** Munich, Germany
Style High Tech   **Materials** Steel cable, acrylic glass

Architect Günther Behnisch (*b.* 1922) and engineer Frei Otto (*b.* 1925) collaborated to design the remarkable complex for the 1972 Olympics in Munich. Its roofs and canopies were created using steel cables suspended from masts, and clad with panels of acrylic glass. The roof forms give a festive and organic feel to the Olympic venues, and echo the concave and convex forms of the park grounds. Clear roof panels allow natural light to filter into the enclosures, and provide a gleaming external surface. The Olympic Park Swimming Hall aquatics center is second only to the

> *"Everything man is doing in architecture is to try to go against nature."*

Frei Otto, Icon Magazine (May 2005)

Olympic Stadium for the creative marriage of high-tech engineering and a manmade landscape.

The center is built into a manmade hill so that visitors enter via a gallery overlooking the pools with spectator seating; the three-story-high glazed walls opposite give way to a grassy meadow. The changing halls, heating-plant rooms, and waiting areas are housed within the hill. One primary mast and four subsidiary masts braced by massive tension cables support the roof. A quilted fabric lines the roof to provide insulation, reduce echo, and prevent excessive glare off the water, although it unfortunately also hides the elegant overhanging structure.

The whole complex has exceptional consistency of architectural vocabulary for an Olympic site, and the park and pool are still major tourist attractions. **CB**

Kimbell Art Museum (1972)

Architect Louis I. Kahn   **Location** Fort Worth, Texas, USA
Style Modernist   **Materials** Concrete, copper, travertine blocks

The forms, shapes, and materials of the Kimbell Art Museum are familiar from Louis Kahn's (1901–74) previous buildings, but he shifted juxtapositions to echo the cylindrical shape of Hadrian's mausoleum and the arches of the Ponte Sant'Angelo in Rome.

Sixteen massive barrel vaults are grouped in parallel lines in three sections. Cast in post-tensioned concrete, the vaults are supported by pairs of square columns at either end. The roofs are skinned to eave line in lead-coated copper and infilled at each end with travertine ashlar blocks. Spatial interruptions

> *"The building feels [like] I had nothing to do with it … that some other hand did it."*

Louis I. Kahn, architect

between the vaults create Kahn's "servant and served" spaces to isolate service works as well as set up rhythmic patterns. Interior space flows uninterrupted. The servant spaces act as intimate intervals.

Kahn spoke of "wrapping ruins around buildings." Adjacent to the entrance portico a reflecting pool and sunken, walled commons reference "ruins" and temper mortality. Underneath the central entrance portico the visitor is drawn to contemplate a blank ashlar wall by directional strips of travertine marble paving intersected with solid dark blocks. The "blank" aspect is given character by manipulation of sunlight and shadows. By day the interior is lit by slit skylights that run the length of each barrel. Long light diffusers beneath reflect light upward, while a vertical version admits light to the lower-level office enfilade. **DJ**

Indiana College
Life Insurance Company Building (1972)

Architects Kevin Roche, John Dinkeloo   **Location** Indianapolis, Indiana, USA
Style Postmodernist   **Materials** Reinforced concrete, glass

The architectural firm Roche Dinkeloo is adept at rethinking contemporary urban architecture. Irish architect Kevin Roche (b. 1922) and the late John Dinkeloo (1918–81) put their names to projects of such range and diversity that they defy categorization. At College Park, Indianapolis, they created a landmark office development, turning the usual terms of dull corporate boxes on their heads.

Three pyramids rise in an offset line in a park by a lake. Each one is supported by two sides of reinforced concrete eleven stories high. This structure allows the final two faces of each pyramid to be sheer walls of glass that seem to lean, almost casually, together. The seemingly solid concrete uprights contain all the utility and service rooms, enabling the blue glass facades to house open-plan space, seemingly floating out toward the lake waters. The original designs allowed for the construction of nine pyramids in all, but only three came to fruition. They are connected by tunnels and bridges, and fulfill a corporate dream— infinitely flexible space with a kind of cutting-edge signature style.

Just as the pyramids at Giza in Egypt were testament to the wealth and power of the pharoahs who built them, Roche Dinkeloo's modern remaking of the pyramid signals where today's real wealth and power resides: in the offices of the corporate world. The simple but monumental geometry of the Life Insurance Company Building at the Indiana College park may also be seen at the UN Plaza in New York. **GT**

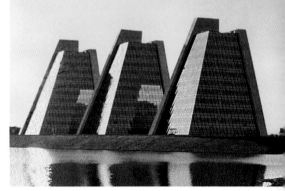

↗ The truncated tops of these pyramidal, high-rise structures give the area its unique skyline.

⇥ The massive expanses of glass mirror the reflective qualities of the nearby lake.

Trellick Tower (1972)

Architect Ernö Goldfinger   **Location** London, England
Style Brutalist   **Material** Concrete

Both loved and loathed, Trellick Tower stands tall in the heart of London's Ladbroke Grove. The work of Hungarian émigré Ernö Goldfinger (1902–87), the west London residential tower is simultaneously cherished as a pure example of Brutalist architecture and rejected as ugly and unfriendly, epitomizing the problems of Modernism. Far from taking into consideration its surroundings, the futuristic high-rise looms over the nearby buildings and was, for many years, the least popular of Goldfinger's works.

The 322-foot-high (98 m) rectangular slab with thirty-one floors has a facade of pure geometry, comparable to the facade at Le Corbusier's "vertical village" at Unité d'Habitation in Marseille, France. Goldfinger also designed Balfron Tower (1968) in Tower Hamlets, London, and actually lived in one of its apartments for two months. Trellick Tower benefited from this direct experience, for it inspired Goldfinger to design on an even larger scale. The main residential tower is composed of a mix of apartments and duplexes, while the narrow service tower contains elevators, stairs, refuse chutes, and a boiler room. As at Balfron, a staircase links together the two towers. At Trellick Tower the focus was on offering spacious apartments in nine different layouts, each detail carefully studied to add the maximum space and light.

Today, Trellick Tower is transformed, with security cameras and a concierge service. In 1998, this ugly duckling was awarded Grade II (historically significant) building status as an iconic Brutalist landmark. **ES**

↖ Goldfinger's design for Trellick Tower was greatly influenced by the work of Le Corbusier.

← Trellick Tower looms over the surrounding streets and buildings, which led to early criticism.

Bernat Klein Design Studio (1972)

Architect Peter Womersley **Location** High Sunderland, Selkirk, Scotland **Style** Modernist **Materials** Concrete, brick, glass

Set amid the rolling upland of the Scottish Borders is one of the most sculptural buildings of late twentieth-century Britain. Designed by Yorkshire-born Peter Womersley (1923–93), a talented but elusive Modernist architect, the Design Studio was built for Bernat Klein, the celebrated Yugoslavian-born textile designer. Klein's geometric house, High Sunderland, also designed by Womersley, stands nearby.

The Design Studio uses reinforced concrete and glass over a brick base-course, the floors marked by massive and daringly oversailing beams, reflecting

> *"… uncompromisingly modern … the building is as exceptional to look from as to look at …"*

Charles Strang, architectural commentator

Womersley's fascination with varied textures and structural adventurism. The balance between horizontal and vertical, and between solid and void, seems perfect. Surrounded by a gnarled battalion of wind-bent trees and founded on a step of flat ground amid hilly fields, the building has sharp lines in startling but sympathetic contrast to its surroundings. The first-floor walkway ends on an earthen mound—a fortuitous practical addition insisted upon by the planning authorities to provide an alternative fire escape—that provides a powerful symbol of the close relationship between the building and the landscape.

With a cleverly arranged suite of workspaces, the Bernat Klein Design Studio demonstrates the involvement with natural forms, changing light, and color that was key to Womersley's work. **NC**

Salto Bus Station (1972)

Architect Eladio Dieste **Location** Salto, Uruguay **Style** Modernist **Materials** Pre-stressed brick, concrete

Although Eladio Dieste (1917–2000) was mainly known as a talented engineer, his work went far beyond solving structural problems to become an original example of how local culture, technology, and form can be conflated to create an innovative spatial language. Recognizing the strong Modernist influences coming from both Brazil and Argentina, Dieste managed to embrace these neighboring tendencies and couple them with Uruguay's long tradition of building with low-tech materials. Salto Bus Station is a key example in this regard. Dieste's relatively simple brief was to provide a large, covered waiting area for people and buses, and he suggested a structural solution that used traditional materials to achieve an elegant and innovative result.

The seven self-supporting vaults are unusually executed in brick, pre-stressed to achieve the minimum thickness possible. The horizontal lines of the roof are emphasized to suggest a sense of calm. The number of columns beneath the roof is also minimal, so the effect is that of a lightweight, flying object that hovers over the activities underneath. Pairs of vaults are each supported by only one column—a technique tested in this building for the first time. The final composition is a stunning building achieved with exceptional economy. Stripping the structure down to its bare essentials does not impoverish the final composition at all. On the contrary, the building's roof, in particular, is an elegant structure that demonstrates the potential of the local construction techniques.

Dieste's work arguably represents a "third way" of understanding Modernism; it is as far from purely structural concerns as the work of Pier Luigi Nervi and Edouardo Torroya, and far from the formal language of Oscar Niemeyer's Brazilian Modernism. **RB**

Mirador del Río (1973)

Architect César Manrique   **Location** Lanzarote, Spain   **Style** Expressionist, Eco-Architecture   **Materials** Glass, rock, wood

The island of Lanzarote was regarded by the architect and artist César Manrique (1919–92) as a rugged, otherworldly canvas. One of his characteristically dramatic creations—the Mirador del Río—uses local volcanic lava deposits as the basis for a sculptural viewpoint perched 1,558 feet (475 m) up on an escarpment at the very northern tip of the island. Essentially, the building is an observation gallery, café, and souvenir shop for visitors, but it is carved into the rock and provides exceptional views out over the sea toward La Graciosa, an island of volcanic sands. The site is of historic significance: it was here that a battery of cannon was installed in the nineteenth century, during the conflict between Spain and the United States over Cuba; and before that it was a look-out for marauding pirates. The building is made up of two enormous buried domes, with sculptural arched elements supporting glazing. A narrow, winding,

white corridor leads into a large, white-walled open-plan area with a wooden floor, tables, and chairs. This space is as minimalist as possible to avoid competing with the main attraction—the view. The structure was conceived by Manrique in collaboration with Jesus Soto and Eduardo Caceres. Manrique was passionate about working in harmony with nature; his other legacies to Lanzarote include the banning of high-rise buildings and advertising billboards, and the César Manrique Foundation and gallery. **DT**

"Lanzarote is like an unframed, unmounted work of art.... I hung it and held it up for all to see."

César Manrique, artist and architect

Arango House (1973)

Architect John Lautner   **Location** Acapulco, Mexico   **Style** Modernist   **Materials** Reinforced concrete, stone, glass

Land, sea, and sky are the focal points of Arango House. Built into the hillside, the design is organic and bold. Shaped like a giant clam with exposed open edges, the roof channels downward to create the driveway entrance at the base of the roof bowl. On massive, rectangular plinth footings, the linear-combed pattern of the reinforced concrete bowl visually extends its outward reach, and gives the impression that one is standing beneath an oversize Hans Coper stoneware vessel. This inverse vantage point, exploiting the view from beneath, is a signature of John Lautner (1911–94). The dramatic overture heightens the visitor's anticipation, which is rewarded as the doorway opens into the entertainment and living room level. The floor cantilevers straight off the edge, unconstrained by windows, walls, or handrails. The stunning view across Acapulco Bay and the Pacific Ocean is unbounded. Boulders and footbridges interject into the space. Concrete furniture designed by Arthur Elrod is cast directly into the building's fabric. Offset by mobile pieces, it is a choreography of content and space. A water moat, 6 feet (1.8 m) wide, delineates the terrace edge. The perimeter water overflow creates a seamless joint between sea and sky, underlining the house's intimate relationship with the landscape. The undulation of the upper terrace forms the roof of the domestic level and counterpoints a geometric zigzag of windows. This zigzag is repeated in the stone floor's block pattern. Louvered walls protect the courtyard side of bedrooms, while the sea view is framed with windows. At swimming pool level, external Escher-like stairs ascend without visible support to a circular platform, and then move upward to terrace level; the treads look like skeletal vertebrae. Lautner's vision and genius provided the Arango family with the consummate seaside home. **DJ**

Werdmuller Centre (1973)

Architect Roelof Uytenbogaardt   **Location** Cape Town, South Africa
Style Modernist   **Materials** Concrete, glass

Faculty of Science, University of Lagos (1973)a

Architects John Godwin, Gillian Hopwood   **Location** Lagos, Nigeria
Style Brutalist   **Material** Concrete

Sculptural and bold despite the constraints of its tight, urban site, the Werdmuller Centre is an architectural paradox. Despite its heavy concrete construction, its form is light and playful. Although revered by architects, this shopping mall—built at the height of apartheid—has been notoriously unpopular with the public, and there is a campaign for its demolition as Claremont is redeveloped.

The design by Roelof Uytenbogaardt (1933–98) provides something of a mirror to his own character. Many took his reserve for aloofness, but he strongly

"[Uytenbogaardt] had the greatest contribution of an individual to South African architecture."

South African Academy for Science and Arts

believed in the humanistic duty of architecture. The Brutalism of many of his facades protects a warm sensitivity at the heart of his design approach.

Slender pillars and concrete fins raise the center's offices above the noise and flurry of street life. A ramp corkscrews up the middle of the building representing an urban design effort to extend the pavement into a spiral labyrinth of shop window displays. The idea was to make a new kind of shopping center, one that engaged customers in a spatial experience: but here the architect did not succeed; for years the center was plagued by poor commercial performance.

Despite its practical failings, the Werdmuller Centre marks an engagement with International Style trends that established Uytenbogaardt's place at the table of architectural greats. **MJB**

The Faculty of Science is located deep in the campus of the University of Lagos, at the edge of swampland bordering a lagoon. Architects Godwin (b. 1928) and Hopwood (b. 1927) were commissioned to provide a faculty block to house classrooms, laboratories, a Marine Biology block, and lecture theaters. The faculty consists of two linear blocks sitting on a finger of hard ground and auditoria lying on swampland. These ground conditions demanded different designs and, as a constraint, influenced the faculty layout.

The main block is a four-story concrete block with an aluminum sun breaker/louver system on the second and fourth floors, sitting between vertical concrete blades. Stair blocks project from the main facade, fully opened on the sides and covered in the front and top. The concrete is board finished and bush hammered recalling the finish of the main campus core. The naturally ventilated classrooms on the top floor overhang the lower three stories. A lower block is joined to the main block with walkways covered by thin planes of concrete supported by black painted steel columns. Three folded concrete shell lecture theaters project in from the middle block.

The ground-level entrance is through an open area central to the main block; this works as a gathering space where chatting students converge. The essence of the courtyard is a through space that visually connects primary arrival and gathering spaces with circulation routes at ground level.

The Brutalist Faculty of Science building marks an interesting point in British Modernism as it refers aesthetically to the attitudes to form and material expression occurring in Britain, but adapted to the particularities of site, climate, and culture presented by Lagos. **GO**

Sears Tower (1973)

Architects Skidmore, Owings & Merrell   **Location** Chicago, Illinois, USA
Style International Style   **Materials** Aluminum, glass

The Sears Tower is one of Chicago's iconic and best-loved buildings. It was commissioned by Sears, Roebuck & Co. during a boom in the U.S. economy, when a spirit of optimism resulted in a skyscraper craze in Chicago. The John Hancock Center (1969) and the Aon Building (1972) were also built at this time. The skyscrapers were emblematic of the city's ambition to rival New York as an economic and cultural destination.

The Sears Tower is clad in bronze-tinted glass and stainless aluminum. It was designed by Bruce Graham of Skidmore, Owings & Merrell (SOM). His colleague, the engineer Fazlur R. Khan, was the engineer who created the revolutionary bundled-tube configuration of the building, which results in its tiered configuration. This allowed for the very large, open office spaces and unobstructed views of the city. Another technological innovation in the scheme was a robotic window washer system to clean the impressive glass curtain facade. When the tower was being built, it competed against the former World Trade Center in New York and the Aon Building for the moniker of tallest building in the world. It remains the highest building in the United States, and it is still the largest building in terms of usable office space. Sears Tower has become a major U.S. tourist destination, with more than a million people visiting the observation deck each year.

The practice Skidmore, Owings and Merrill is one of oldest and largest architecture firms in the United States. It is best known for designing commercial buildings and for its use of the Modernist glass box. SOM is responsible for other iconic skyscrapers, including Lever House in New York and the John Hancock Center. The firm is contracted to design the new Freedom Tower, which will stand on the site of the former World Trade Center in New York. **KAB**

Sydney Opera House (1973)

Architects Jørn Utzon, Peter Hall, Lionel Todd, David Littlemore **Location** Sydney, Australia **Style** Expressionist **Materials** Concrete, tiles

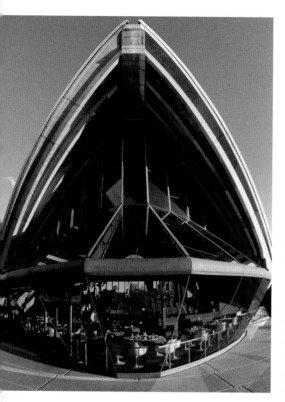

"The plan was bold, unique, brilliantly chosen—and trouble—from its inception."

John Gunther, *Inside Australia* (1972)

⬆ The beautiful curves of the Sydney Opera House have been likened to enormous oyster shells.

➡ With the harbor waters lapping around the foot of the building, the Opera House is an architectural triumph.

Sydney Opera House is an icon for an entire country. Standing in full view of where the first ships of settlers landed at Circular Quay, it epitomizes Sydney's rapid transition from a remote, inhospitable colony to a leading center of technology and culture. In the 1960s, the construction of this uniquely shaped building symbolized all that was modern, vibrant, and youthful about Australia. In 1955, the state government began a fund to finance its construction, and held an international competition for its design. Jørn Utzon (b. 1918), a little-known Danish architect, won with the striking creation seen today. Sydney Opera House's glittering, white, shell-shaped roofs are a mixture of abstract and organic forms made up of tiled, precast concrete sections held together by cables. It is often said that these were designed to mirror the sails of the boats in the harbor, but Utzon's models demonstrate that they are simply sections of a sphere.

The building's construction involved considerable innovation. It took five years just to work out how to convert the plans for the heavy, inclined roofs into reality, and involved one of the earliest uses of computers in structural analysis. In 1966, arguments about the cost and the interior design reached crisis point, and Utzon resigned from the project. This meant that the thrill of the opera house's exterior was not mirrored within, and its pink granite interior was redesigned by local architects. We will never know what Sydney Opera House would have looked like if Utzon had stayed onboard the project until its completion. He has, however, since been involved in redesigning some of the interior.

Sydney Opera House may have cost fourteen times its original building estimate, and taken nine years longer than planned to construct, but there is no doubt that it put Sydney on the world map in a way that it never had been before. **JM**

RTE Campus Headquarters (1973)

Architect Scott Tallon Walker **Location** Dublin, Ireland
Style Modernist **Materials** Steel, concrete, bronze-tinted glass

PREVI Experimental Housing (1973)

Architect Charles Correa Associates **Location** Lima, Peru
Style Modernist **Material** Concrete

The campus for Ireland's national television and radio broadcasting company, Radio Telefís Éireann (RTE), represented a new level of aspiration for Irish architecture and a visible expression of the Irish state's rhetoric of modernization. The original building, phase one of the Television Centre, was constructed as the country emerged from a recession in the 1950s with an emigration crisis that had shaken national confidence. However, the RTE campus asserted a new optimism in Irish life and echoed the admiration of its architect, Ronnie Tallon (*b.* 1927), for Miesian ideals.

PREVI, also known as the Proyecto Experimental de Viviena scheme in Lima, Peru, is one of the last, large-scale, utopian experiments in social housing ever to be built. Thirteen of the world's leading architects of the 1960s, including Charles Correa, James Stirling, and Atelier 5, together with thirteen local architects, were selected to design low-cost, low-rise, high-density housing in a scheme masterminded by British architect-planner Peter Land. The initial 1969 plan was to build a settlement for 1,500 families, with each of the twenty-six architectural firms contributing

"The RTE campus represents a model of urbanity in the setting of a suburb…"

Deyan Sudjic, architecture critic

"Architecture is not created in a vacuum. It is the … expression of belief [that is] central to our lives."

Charles Correa, architect

The architectural firm Scott Tallon Walker, which has dominated Irish architecture for most of its existence, has designed various buildings for RTE for more than forty years. Here, the campus ideal finds a more complete expression than at most universities. It has a pleasing village intimacy with Tallon's designs showing his belief in the concept of expandable buildings.

On the north campus, the Radio Centre's offices and studios are housed in a purpose-built building. Its thirteen studios are below ground level for extra soundproofing, while production staff work in open-plan offices on the upper floor. An orchestral studio with a public gallery penetrates the two levels, and the lower-level studios are grouped around a sunken garden, which is also a source of natural light. **BMC**

designs. But, by the project's end, only 502 houses were completed, using twenty-three of the designs.

Correa's (*b.* 1930) offering was designed to work with the local climate. This resulted in narrow, tubelike houses each running off a staggered party wall, locking them together in a zigzag formation. Each of the flat-roofed, concrete houses has a louvered air-scoop on top, which draws wind into the houses and can be adjusted according to the weather. An added advantage of staggering the party wall is that it gives extra earthquake protection, a necessity in this region.

Correa's houses married Modernist forms and materials—flat roofs, standardization, concrete—with the peculiarities of a particular place. Although many of the houses have since been altered, the grand husks of Correa's original design still shine through. **GB**

Casa
Bianchi (1973)

Architect Mario Botta **Location** Riva San Vitale, Lake Lugano, Switzerland
Style Modernist **Materials** Concrete, brick, steel

The small, medieval village of Riva San Vitale lies in the beautiful landscape of southern Switzerland, overlooking Lake Lugano. At the north end of the village, along a small and slowly ascending road, Leontina and Carlo Bianchi bought a 9,149-square-foot (850 sq m), steep site with a breathtaking panorama.

Casa Bianchi was the first major commission for the young Mario Botta (b. 1943), who had studied with Carlo Scarpa at the university in Venice, and worked for the renown architects Le Corbusier and Louis Kahn. The design of the house illustrates the ways in which Botta tried to gently reconcile nature and construction, developing an almost vernacular architectural language. It consists of a 43-foot-high (13 m) tower with a cubic floorplan of 33 by 33 feet (10 x 10 m). The outer frame is made of huge corner pillars built from concrete blocks. The building is carved with large geometric cuts, each aperture framing a specific view of the mountains, the woods, and the lake. The exterior gives an almost archaic impression with its basic geometrical composition. The tower is reminiscent of the bird-hunting towers, or *roccoli*, that are typical in the area.

Although the building occupies a small area of the site, it provides a surprisingly generous 2,368 square feet (220 sq m) of living area. Casa Bianchi underlines its relationship with the environment by the spectacular way in which it is entered—via a 59-foot-long (18 m) bridge made of red metal lattice girders—an unusual and dramatic entrance at the top level. **FH**

↗ The entrance bridge extends from the road to the top of the building, with living areas situated below.

⮕ The cuts made to frame the views also prevent the house from simply being a weighty concrete box.

Institute of
Public Administration (1974)

Architect Louis I. Kahn   **Location** Ahmedabad, India
Style Modernist   **Materials** Brick, concrete

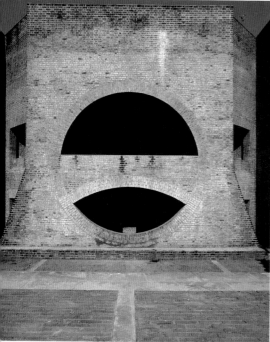

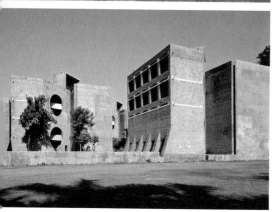

Ahmedabad is a small town in the state of Gujarat in western India, which has the unique prestige of hosting some of the country's premiere educational institutes, each one a signature design piece by some of the most influential architects of their period. One such example is the Institute of Public Administration, designed by Louis I. Kahn (1901–74).

Regarded as one of the most international architects in both his style and conception, Kahn extended his oeuvre of simple, platonic compositions and expression of material to encompass an in-depth understanding of the local culture and traditions. Set in a large, landscaped complex, the institute demonstrates the philosophy that education should be imparted in a spiritually enriching environment.

The design follows a traditional courtyard pattern, creating many open spaces that can be visually and physically accessed from different levels. This not only gives a feeling of openness, but moderates the harsh brilliance of the Indian sun, which is left outside to wash the exposed brick walls in a warmer hue. It appears as if the spaces have been conceived around the collage of openings—the sweeping full circle openings and subtle arcs spanning concrete beams—and yet they are all held together by an austere discipline of spatial scale and construction technique.

The building of the Indian Institute of Public Administration represents an example of how an elegant, modern architectural language can continue to be perceived as colossal in its legacy. **BS**

↖ Kahn worked closely with engineers and construction experts to perfect the refined curves of his design.

← The heavy brickwork fends off the sun and the layered walls capture any passing breeze.

Dick
House (1974)

Architect Jean Nouvel **Location** Troyes, France
Style Modernist **Materials** Concrete, brick

Can
Lis (1974)

Architect Jørn Utzon **Location** Mallorca, Spain
Style Modernist **Materials** Sandstone, concrete, tiles

By the time architect Jean Nouvel (*b.* 1945) designed this house, he was still very much involved in shaking up post-1968 French architecture from the torpor of both its lack of debate and the conservatism of public bodies—issues that proved critical in the case of the Dick family residence.

For the Dick House, redefining the design process involved a meaningful dialogue with the users to identify the most suitable living spaces for each individual, as well as for the family as a whole. The result was a carefully considered yet radical house

> ## "[Nouvel] is an exemplar in the very best tradition of European innovation and adventure."
>
> **Marco Goldschmied, president of RIBA**

featuring a spacious living room under an impressive white painted barrel vault, and a large functional children's play area where each child had an apse that doubled as a bedroom.

The house was initially denied a permit by the local authorities on the grounds that the design was reminiscent of Byzantine architecture, a style not in keeping with the medieval look of Troyes at the time. Nouvel reluctantly made changes to the exterior, which he presented in such a way that the authorities were duped into agreeing to the design. As a result, the house incorporates lines of red brick across its facade indicating the alterations the architect was forced into making by the local style bureaucrats. Here, and throughout his career, Nouvel was to prove that there is no such word as can't. **YN**

Jørn Utzon (*b.* 1918), recipient of the Pritzker Prize in 2003, has a magnificent sense of space combined with a great respect for the environment within which he builds. Utzon is a pioneer in shaping and interpreting architecture, and is best known for designing the Sydney Opera House. Named after his wife, Can Lis was built for the Utzons' own use. It is situated on the southeastern coast of Mallorca, perched on rocks overlooking the sea.

Can Lis is made up of four detached houses that are linked into a single whole by walls and courtyards. Resting at the edge of the sea, the houses are filled with strong sunlight and reflective warmth. Through variously sized window openings the light is reflected in many different ways; in some locations it fades via deep oblique openings, in other areas the light is sharp due to large expanses of glass. Furthermore, in one corner of the large living room area there is a small, narrow aperture that allows the sun's rays to illuminate a wall for just twenty minutes per day. Utzon used blocks of indigenous yellow sandstone and yellow tiles throughout the complex to unify his design with the surrounding Mediterranean terrain. The buildings are positioned at slightly different angles in relation to the line of the cliff that drops down 65 feet (20 m) in front of them.

The furniture inside the buildings and in the courtyards, which are also of sandstone, has been decorated with glazed terra-cotta, blue, and white tiles. In clean, geometric patterns, similar tiles are also used to adorn some of the walls. Simplicity, balance, and a great attention to the characteristics of light are prevalent features right through the house. Utzon has created a delightful environment in which he and his wife can live in constant contact with nature. **SML**

Walden 7
Apartments (1974)

Architect Ricardo Bofill **Location** Barcelona, Spain
Style Postmodernist **Materials** Concrete, glass

Ricardo Bofill (*b.* 1939) was born in Barcelona and inspired by the works of Antonío Gaudí and Le Corbusier. In the 1960s, he set up the Barcelona-based Taller de Arquitectura. His Walden 7, known as "the city in space" is a futuristic residential complex, whose otherwise plain facade is decorated with non-uniform rows of bulbous, friendly looking windows, and smoothly protruding balconies; giving an overall impression of a building in a science fiction movie.

Bofill had already spent several years working on designs for a "city in space" that he had hoped to build in Madrid. When he was commissioned to create social housing—on a very low budget—for Barcelona, he was able to put many of his ideas into use, although budget restrictions meant that the full extent of his vision could not be realized.

The site chosen for Walden 7 was an old cement factory in Sant Just Desvern, on the western rim of Barcelona. The complex contains 446 apartments, recreation areas—including two swimming pools on the roof—bars, commercial premises, meeting rooms, a parking lot, and internal courtyards complete with fountains. The apartments range from studios to four-bedroom homes. The complex is made up of a system of "towers"; rounded and thick, each pair is attached at the top and bottom, but curve outward away from each other in the middle, like a bowlegged giant. There are eighteen of these towers, and residents navigate their way through them by a system of connecting corridors, stairways, and elevators. **LH**

◥ Cantilevered balconies and cylindrical niches provide an array of vantage points for each apartment.

◿ The unique shape of the towers, attached only at the top, allows light to penetrate into interior chasms.

Terminal 1, Charles-de-Gaulle Airport (1974)

Architect Paul Andreu **Location** Roissy, France
Style Modernist **Materials** Concrete, glass, metal

Paul Andreu (b. 1938) considers the architectural legacy of the 1990s to be "the age of the air terminal," as earlier eras were the age of the great railway stations. It is rather apt that the Terminal 1 (CDG) building of Charles-de-Gaulle International Airport is of a similar scale to the Colosseum in Rome. Charles-de-Gaulle, originally called Paris Nord and renamed in 1974, was conceived as a showpiece to highlight and celebrate French knowledge in civil and aeronautical engineering. Chief architect Andreu went on to design more than forty airport projects.

"Paul Andreu ... is a god of airport terminal design. He appreciates the theater of the places."

Archiseek, online architecture resources

The futuristic 1960s design consists of a ten-story, circular, Brutalist, concrete structure, softened by an exterior decorated with figurative designs; it is surrounded by seven satellite buildings each with four gates. The design embodies the concept of the "plane-less terminal" and separates the planes from the central terminal. The central building is composed of three main levels—levels 3, 4, and 5—organized into arrivals, departures, and a connecting level that houses all services from car parking and security, to customs and luggage handling. Finger piers with undulating horizontal escalators provide access to the planes and minimize walking distance. To change levels and access the piers, passengers use one of three suspended, angled transparent tubes providing moving walkways in the open central area. **JEH**

Vacation House I at Oxylithos (1974)

Architects Atelier 66 **Location** Oxylithos, Greece
Style Modernist **Materials** Concrete, plastered masonry

Dimitris (b. 1933) and Suzana (b. 1935) Antonakakis established the architectural firm Atelier 66 with three partners and a small team of architects. The practice's work represents a landmark in Greek architectural history for developing a unique style combining European Modernism with the modern local vernacular. Vacation House I, built in 1974 in the village of Oxylithos on Euboea Island, is representative of their architectural idiom.

The house—a composition of volumes in varied heights—is situated on a steep slope and is completely exposed to the elements—in particular very strong winds. All the different spaces are laid out in zones on an east–west axis, following the slope's angle, but also coordinating with the gusty winds so as to diminish their impact.

These zones dominate the grid-based design, incorporating interiors and exteriors. The living and dining rooms, kitchen, and guest room are part of the main zone, while the master bedroom, storage areas, and bathroom belong to the second one. Each zone connects to a different outdoor space, offering a variety of views and orientations. This zoning sets the building in harmony with the natural environment, and also demonstrates Atelier 66's belief in the importance of movement.

The clear-lined, geometrical character of the building references both traditional Greek island architecture and classic Modernist villas. The firm's architectural vocabulary is clearly identified in the Vacation House I, bridging the practice's early work to more mature examples, such as the Hotel Lyttos in Crete (1976) and the Oxylithos House II (1977), and setting the pace for the Antonakakis's equally important solo work of the future. **ES**

Barbican (1975)

Architects Chamberlin, Powell & Bon **Location** London, England **Style** Brutalist **Material** Concrete

A devastating night of wartime bombing in December 1940, during which a 35-acre (14 ha) site was wrecked, became the impetus for building a new residential housing estate in the Barbican area of London. Chamberlin, Powell & Bon were selected by the London County Council (LCC) to carry out the design. Initial ideas for the estate, located in the City district of the capital, made numerous references to the definition of the word "barbican," meaning a fortified outpost, or gateway, and early plans included such features as moats, turrets, and arrow slits.

The LCC challenged the architects with two apparently conflicting requirements: they insisted on a great deal of open space, but also demanded the development of as many flats as possible, in order to maximize the commercial success of the project. For inspiration in solving this problem, the architects looked to Venice as "the best example of a city where foot and service traffic is completely segregated . . . supplies are carried to the city on canals, while pedestrians walk on pavements which cross the canals by bridges." By building much of the Barbican on platforms and podia, the architects were able to create a spacious layout despite the high density of housing.

The thirteen terrace blocks within the estate are positioned at right angles to each other in a deliberate imitation of residential squares in Kensington and Bloomsbury. They are raised on columns so that the enclosures are not oppressive, adhering to the LCC's request that wide, open space be a predominant aesthetic throughout the scheme, and highlighting the design debt to the layout of Venice. **AT**

↖ The cohesion of the Barbican's design made it a landmark example of Brutalist architecture in Britain.

← The Barbican buildings and the spaces between them create a clear sense of order without monotony.

Camino Real Hotel (1975)

Architects Legorreta Arquitectos   **Location** Mexico City, Mexico   **Style** Modernist   **Materials** Concrete, stucco, glass

Ricardo Legorreta's (*b.* 1931) low-slung "hotel museum" compound occupies 8 acres (3 ha) in the center of the Mexican megalopolis. Influenced by Mexico's first city, Teotihuacán, which flourished 1,500 years ago, Legorreta defied convention at a time when city-center hotels were built vertically, and combined a modern tectonic and minimalist build with the terraced, planar forms of the Pre-Columbian empire.

Camino Real is no pastiche, however. Legorreta created a unique design vocabulary. To three geometric shapes—circle, square, and triangle—he added textured stucco, light, sound, and surprise. Legoretta's signature blocks of bold color provide enclosure, emotional charge, definition, and direction. A shocking pink, outdoor screen greets guests in the reception driveway. It references the Mexican art of *papel picado* (cutting paper into intricate patterns), and is the first indication that this is no ordinary hotel.

Legoretta's compound adheres to a given within the canon of Mexican architecture—the link between landscape, building, and local context. He complies with surprises such as the caldera water vortex, a sunken bowl that honors both the extinct volcano in which the city sits and the Mayan rain god Chaac.

Integration carries on through to the interior public spaces where art and furniture relate harmoniously. The Blue Lounge is definitely worth a visit. It has a cube floor comprised of hundreds of stones, covered by a veneer of water over which a clear glass floorplate allows guests to float. It captures perfectly the surreal, magic realism that is part and parcel of Mexican life. **DJ**

↗ Legoretta reintroduced Mexican "wall culture" and courtyards, which denote sanctuary not fortress.

→ Illuminated by night, Legoretta's stunning use of block color is shown off to dramatic effect.

Miró Foundation (1975)

Architect Josep Lluís Sert   **Location** Barcelona, Spain   **Style** Modernist   **Materials** Concrete, timber

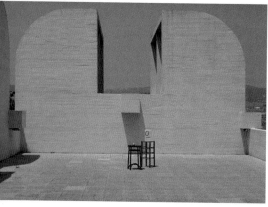

Josep Lluís Sert (1902–83) was a Barcelona-born architect whose work was heavily influenced by the nature of the Mediterranean, sunlight, and community. The Fundació Joan Miró (Joan Miró Foundation) is a museum of modern art in Barcelona in honor of Sert's friend, the Catalan-Spanish artist Joan Miró.

The building housing the museum is itself a notable example of Modernist design, which also draws on regional traditions. Completed in 1975, the white, light-filled building is arranged in sections around a square patio. Its simplicity of form, coupled with the proportions and layout of the interior, contribute to easy and effective circulation for visitors.

Catalan architectural features, such as the tiled floor, staircase treads, and shallow vaulted ceilings enhance its Mediterranean appearance. The building's distinctive exhibition spaces are informed and enriched by the exterior scoops or monitor features. These curvaceous rooftop elements allow diffused light into the gallery areas, thereby avoiding the harsh sunlight and shadow that might hinder the visitors' appreciation of the artworks. Another interesting feature is a tall, octagonal tower that houses the foundation's auditorium and library. The proportions of the different galleries complement the diverse scale and forms of the Miró artworks they display.

Sert had settled in the United States in 1939, where he worked on town-planning schemes, many of them in Latin America, using the principles of Le Corbusier, with whom he worked in his early career. The building was extended in Sert's style in 1986 by Sert-trained architect Jaume Freixa. **DT**

◥ Pilar Juncosa, Miró's widow, made a generous donation toward the costs of the museum.

◀ The unusual curves of the monitors seem to soften the outline of the concrete building.

Dominican Institute (1975)

Architect Demas Nwoko **Location** Ibadan, Nigeria **Style** Modernist **Materials** Concrete, laterite block

This building commission for the Dominican Institute was originally a request to design an altarpiece for the Dominican Community in Ibadan, Nigeria. However, architect Demas Nwoko (b. 1935) convinced the client he could do a larger commission.

The institute sits on a slight incline amid green manicured lawns with a striking tower rising up over the main building. Demas explored the theatrical relationship of worship between the clergy and congregation. He paralleled this using the concept of performance and audience to inform the plan of the building. The altar is placed within the intersection of minor and major sectors, which form the compact plan of the building. The choir separates the altar from the concentric circles of pews. A semicircle of carved columns formally denotes this transition. A concrete shell tower rises over the altar, tapering as it rises. A sacristy lies on a central axis with the altar and entrance doors on either side; two garden pools flank the entrance porch leading into the building. A circulation zone between the back of the pews and the garden pools acts as a gathering space for the congregation before and after services.

Nwoko's work as a sculptor is evident in the exterior line of columns, and the tower's design shows his sculptural expression at its most potent. The church pulls together a central theme in the synthesis of Christianity in African society, the appropriating of symbols and rituals within the context of African mystical leanings. The extreme plastic expressionism that Nwoko resorts to is disciplined and evokes the surreal qualities of his paintings. **GO**

↗ Nwoko designed the line of exterior columns to resemble tree trunks shorn of their branches.

⇥ The aluminum roof of the institute falls away from the middle of the highly distinctive concrete tower.

House VI
(Frank House) (1975)

Architect Peter Eisenman   **Location** Cornwall, Connecticut, USA
Style Deconstructivist   **Materials** Concrete, timber

Although he is now highly sought after as an architect of large, important commissions, the influential Deconstructivist Peter Eisenman (*b.* 1932) began his career with a series of rather small, yet highly elaborate, almost sculptural, private houses. The most famous and characteristic, House VI, is a family house set in the countryside of Cornwall, Connecticut. It is also known as Frank House, after its owners Richard and Suzanne Frank. The structure is a playful constellation of tricks, twists, and architectural experiments.

The house's modular base produced a flexible plan of airy, open spaces with numerous large openings. Using a post-and-beam system, large timbers hold the structure's typical residential wooden frame. The house includes some rather unconventional features, among them a column that does not reach the ground and a linear slot on the master bedroom floor that allows no room for a marital bed. This unique house may not be a model of clarity and structural honesty, but it established Eisenman's disjunction and discontinuity design theme. This was a theme he revisited at the controversial Wexner Center for the Arts (1989) on the campus of Ohio State University, which needed extensive renovations within a few years of opening.

Although the Franks initially had an enthusiastic and understanding attitude toward Eisenman's bizarre design proposals, the continual changes and updates he made to the project were expensive and threw them seriously off budget. The experience prompted Suzanne Frank to write a book describing the construction of the house—*Peter Eisenman's House VI: The Client's Response* (1994). This tale of black humor is considered to be one of the most revealing documents on contemporary architecture. **ES**

Casa
Bofill (1975)

Architect Ricardo Bofill   **Location** Montrás, Girona, Spain
Style Postmodernist   **Materials** Concrete, sandstone brick, tiles

In 1973, entrepreneur Emilio Bofill asked his son Ricardo Bofill (*b.* 1939) to design a summerhouse near the town of Montrás on the southern part of the Costa Brava. The family residence was Bofill's last project before he achieved his international breakthrough in France during the dying years of Franco's military dictatorship in Spain. In 1963, Ricardo had founded the Taller de Arquitectura (Studio of Architecture) in Barcelona, bringing together an international team of architects, engineers, sociologists, writers, and artists from theater and film.

> *"[René] Magritte is more important than Mies van der Rohe."*
>
> Manifesto of the Taller de Arquitectura

Casa Bofill is set in a landscape of woods, a few miles inland from the sea. The complex is built around the remains of a Catalan farmhouse that has been preserved as a ruin amid the new structures. Several rectangular pavilions are arranged around a central exterior space, which is occupied by a stagelike dining room and a swimming pool with striking, red ceramic tiles. The main three-story pavilion is furnished with an exterior staircase leading directly to the pool. The exterior and interior contrast greatly: the striking white inside evokes Bauhaus and Le Corbusier, while the brick cladding shares an affinity with the work of James Stirling. Casa Bofill is the most intimate work of this controversial figure of Postmodernism, whose large-scale Baroque designs were carried out under the motto of "Versailles for the people." **MJG**

Dhaka
National Assembly (1975)

Architect Louis I. Kahn **Location** Dhaka, Bangladesh
Style Brutalist **Materials** Concrete, marble

The opportunity to design the main seat of government in Dhaka, Bangladesh, was a gift for architect Louis I. Kahn (1901–74) as his final project (although he did not live to see it completed) because it proved to be the chance to fulfill his architectural vision. From his early admiration of radical visionary R. Buckminster Fuller, Kahn worked through formal geometric layouts to produce an architecture full of emotional resonance and with a hankering for ancient worlds that lifts the austerity of his work.

Construction began in 1961 under the Pakistani government as a seat for the federal administration of west and east Pakistan. However, work was halted by Bangladesh's Liberation War with Pakistan, which ended in 1975, and when it finally opened in 1982, it was as the home of the National Assembly of Bangladesh.

The building consists of nine blocks with eight blocks set around a central octagonal building. All nine blocks are interlinked horizontally and vertically via corridors, elevators, stairs, and courtyards so that the whole structure appears, from a distance, to be a single building. Light filters through the layers of concrete and marble to penetrate the chambers of government, and through a series of huge geometric shapes in the outer skin of the complex.

Louis I. Kahn believed that natural light brought architecture to life. In this way, the National Assembly building at Dhaka is part fortress, having the strength to protect democracy, and part hymn to humanity's relationship with nature. **GT**

↗ The natural light that filters through the ceiling is an aesthetically pleasing and efficient light source.

⊟ Only one of Bangladesh's eight parliaments has not used the complex to house its activities.

Ho Chi Minh Mausoleum (1975)

Patrons Communist followers of Ho Chi Minh   **Location** Hanoi, Vietnam   **Style** Constructivist   **Material** Granite

Visiting a mausoleum is always a somber experience. In Vietnam, thousands still line up daily to visit the Ho Chi Minh Mausoleum. Their chattering turns to silence as they wait in deep reverence to pay their respects to the small preserved corpse of this iconic leader, complete with wispy beard. It is highly unlikely that Ho Chi Minh (1890–1969) would have approved of this grandiose, monumental construction. Apparently, he wished to be cremated and have his ashes buried on three different hilltops in Vietnam—one in the south, one in the center, and one in the north. Following his death on September 2, 1969, his followers ignored his wishes and created a massive mausoleum for their hero, continuing the communist fashion first set after the death of Lenin. The site of the mausoleum is highly significant. It was constructed near the spot where Ho Chi Minh proclaimed the independence of Vietnam in 1945, after eighty years of French colonial rule. By tirelessly leading the fight for independence, he earned himself a place in the hearts of all Vietnamese people, and is often affectionately referred to as "Uncle Ho." The gray, austere building is raised up on steps. The severity of its design reflects the disciplined and serious manner of the revolutionary leader whose body it houses. It is simple and solemn, and decoration is minimal with the exception of the purple engraving on the facade, inscribed with the president's name. The visitor enters through a marble entrance hall and is greeted by one of Ho Chi Minh's most frequently cited phrases: "Nothing is more important than freedom and independence." Passing through a series of passages leading upstairs, is the cold, dark chamber where Ho Chi Minh's body, dressed in faded khaki clothes, is kept in a glass box. The precious, embalmed corpse is taken to Russia for three months every year for maintenance and preservation. **KGB**

Museum of Anthropology (1976)

Architect Arthur Erickson **Location** Vancouver, Canada **Style** Modernist **Material** Concrete

Once confined to a few rooms in the library basement, the Museum of Anthropology at the University of British Columbia has become a hub of coastal Northwest culture. The elegant building, located in a stunning natural location, is a distinct and powerful architectural statement that convincingly springs from a thoughtful consideration of its collection and the user's experience. Despite its urban location, visitors arrive at the museum through a lush, forested landscape. From a secluded entry, the building unfolds down a broad ramp flanked by large carvings from the coastal Northwest. At its base the ramp opens up to a light-filled Great Hall that boasts a 40-foot (12 m) wall of glass with a view of the Strait of Georgia and the North Shore Mountains. The hall also features a series of now iconic concrete posts and beams of a gigantic scale with skylights between them inspired by the log houses of coastal native peoples and the totem poles

that it now showcases. The museum's favorite method of display was inspired by Arthur Erickson's (*b.* 1924) astonishment that only ten percent of an average collection is available to the public at any given time. He suggested that the entire collection be available via an original system of storage and presentation. In the rooms to one side of the Great Hall, large display cases present a vast array of objects. Beneath these cases, a series of drawers contain still more items that the visitor can explore. **AC**

"Here the whole mess gives you the opportunity to train your eye and teach yourself..."

Arthur Erickson, architect

Heckscher House (1976)

Architect Edward Larrabee Barnes **Location** Mount Desert Island, Maine, USA **Style** Shingle style, Modernist **Material** Shingled timber

Secluded in the forests of Mount Desert Island off the Maine coast, Heckscher House is not the most well known or representative work of Edward Larrabee Barnes (1915–2004), but it is assuredly one of his most pleasing and timeless.

Barnes was a Harvard graduate who combined vernacular U.S. architecture with the principles of European Modernism learned firsthand from Walter Gropius and Marcel Breuer in the 1930s. During his long career, working primarily on large-scale projects such as cathedrals, museums, and schools, he proved especially adept at organizing complex plans into simple, bold, geometric designs.

Heckscher House was undertaken at the behest of the architect's friend, August Heckscher, a writer and the former arts consultant to President John F. Kennedy. Previously home to a few small fishing communities, Mount Desert Island had become a favorite destination for artists and writers in the mid-nineteenth century and, in their footsteps, members of some of the most powerful East Coast families built summer vacation homes here. Many of these were in Shingle Style, a New England variant of the more exuberant and decorative Queen Anne style that was fashionable at the time.

Absorbing this history, Barnes built a complex of four modestly proportioned timber buildings, shingle-cornered and grouped around a central wooden decking. Evoking Maine fishing villages, the rustic colonial revival of Shingle Style, and the ascetic ideals of Modernism, Barnes created a harmonious fusion that shows great sensitivity to materials and effortlessly connects the house with its surroundings. In 2007 Barnes was posthumously awarded the AIA Gold Medal for his achievements. **RDB**

Azuma House (Row House) (1976)

Architect Tadao Ando **Location** Osaka, Japan **Style** Modernist **Materials** Concrete, glass, steel

Azuma House is an unassuming two-story concrete block. Its blank and sheer windowless facade gives little clue that it hides an elegant solution to the problems of overcrowding in Japan, one that earned its architect, Tadao Ando (*b.* 1941), worldwide acclaim.

With a width of only 10 feet (3 m), this boxlike structure is completely closed off from the street, with only a small entrance in the front wall. On the ground floor the living room is at the front of the building, while a second space, housing the kitchen, dining room, and bathroom, is at the back, separated by a

> ## "[Architecture] should remain silent and let nature in the guise of sunlight and wind speak."
> Tadao Ando, architect

roofless courtyard. Above the living room is the master bedroom, connected by a suspended walkway, again open to the sky, to the children's bedroom at the back.

The central courtyard creates a tranquil space, open to the elements but protected from the hustle and bustle of city life. The courtyard also provides light to the rooms on either side and allows air to circulate. Ando believes that the fact that the courtyard must be traversed to get from one room to another in rain, sun, or snow rewards the occupants by making them aware of the cycle of nature around them. In the past, Japanese architecture embraced nature in the design of its buildings and Ando feels that the move toward the separation of inside and out, with the use of electric lighting and air-conditioning, is insulating people from the rhythms of the natural world. **JM**

National Theatre (1976)

Architect Denys Lasdun **Location** London, England **Style** Brutalist
Materials Reinforced concrete, brick

After nearly a century of campaigning to found a National Theatre for Britain, it finally emerged from a postwar consensus that the state should provide culture for the people. The theater took its place as the last component of the South Bank, a world-class arts complex that houses three concert halls, three theaters, an art gallery, and several cinema screens.

The theater's auditoria were shaped after years of lengthy discussions between architect Denys Lasdun (1914–2001), actor Laurence Olivier, the director Peter Brook, and others. By the time construction began in 1969, Britain was torn apart by strikes and inflation. The finish of the building is especially remarkable given this problematic context.

The National Theatre consists of a large "open" theater, with no arch framing the stage, a mid-sized "proscenium" auditorium, with the traditional arch, and a smaller experimental space in which galleries are fixed, but other seating and stage arrangements are flexible. The stage equipment and backstage facilities were the most ambitious in the world when completed, but the absolute highlight in architectural terms is the main foyer. The multiple levels and terraces are cut away to give glimpses down through the floors and out over London.

The National Theatre is an expression of concrete structural methods. The concrete was meticulously poured into specially roughened wooden molds, giving it a superb grain that appears almost furry and tactile—a talking point for every visitor. **BWC**

↗ Juxtaposed shapes and sculptural curves characterize this view of one of the National Theatre's stairwells.

⤷ Originally commissioned to design a single theater, Lasdun realized that three auditoriums were needed.

Church at Bagsværd (1976)

Architect Jørn Utzon **Location** Bagsværd, Denmark **Style** Modernist **Materials** Concrete, brick, aluminum

When Jørn Utzon (*b.* 1918) was commissioned to design the Church at Bagsværd, a few miles northwest of Copenhagen, he had just resigned from the Sydney Opera House project. This robust building, somewhat resembling an industrial unit with its use of materials, ranks as one of Utzon's most celebrated works. The church is drawn with a meticulous care for purity and simplicity, characteristics that typify the atmosphere of most Scandinavian churches. The ground plan of the building is rectangular, 262 by 72 feet (80 x 22 m); the exterior is clad tightly in prefabricated, white concrete panels, with a gray aluminum roof, which appears cold yet also calm and collected. Small inner courtyards adjoin the building, creating a sense of privacy. The interior is impressive; in particular the main church room stuns visitors. Almost everything is white: it has white concrete walls and floors, and the trellis around the altar is made of

glazed white tiles, which reflect the light coming in from both the skylights and sidelights. The heavy, organically-shaped, arched ceiling winds into the church room with great elegance and softness. The serenity of the building is further emphasized by the use of pale, whitewashed pine wood in the pews, doors, windows, and the organ. The addition of brightly colored textiles, floor runners, and vestments—designed by Utzon's daughter Lin—also works well in this peaceful and angelic space. **SML**

> *"The church . . . arches toward the heavens in a wonderful cascade of soft 'cloud formations.'"*
>
> Henrik Steen Møller and Vibe Udsen, critics

Fire Island House (1977)

Architect Arthur Erickson **Location** Fire Island, New York, USA **Style** Modernist **Materials** Concrete, wood, glass

The Canadian architect Arthur Erickson (b. 1924), whose career has spanned more than fifty years, is most commonly associated with his ultramodern designs for public buildings such as the Canadian Embassy in Washington, D.C. (1982), and the Etisalat Towers (1985) in the United Arab Emirates. However, he has also produced some of the most innovative domestic buildings of the twentieth century, of which the Fire Island House is one. The small community of Fire Island was first established in the 1600s when a whaling station was built by Isaac Stratford of Babylon; later, in 1825, a lighthouse was added to the western point. By the 1920s the island had become a popular haven for New Yorkers, and a bohemian and progressive culture started to develop. The artistic and relaxed nature of the area has persisted, and in 1977, when Erickson was commissioned to build this holiday home, he developed his design to reflect the island nature of the location while simultaneously creating a unique and modern dwelling. The house is located on the southern side of the island among constantly evolving sand dunes, which proved a major technical consideration during the design process. To counteract the instability of the ground, Erickson sank concrete pilings to secure the structure, then placed the strident wooden frame of the building on elevated wooden decks attached to the concrete base. The house is predominantly wood and glass, based around a cube form with simple lines and geometry suggesting the work of Le Corbusier. The result is a building that relates to its natural surroundings, while evoking the sense of indoor-outdoor living as experienced with a beach house. This is further enhanced by a 46-square-foot (4.3 sq m) sliding roof, which covers the two-story living space and retracts to open up the heart of the house to the elements. **TP**

Centre Pompidou (1977)

Architects Richard Rogers, Renzo Piano **Location** Paris, France **Style** High Tech **Materials** Iron, steel, glass

"Technology ... must aim at solving long-term social and ecological problems."

Richard Rogers, architect

⬆ Placing mechanical and air-conditioning systems on the exterior freed up space for the expansive interior.

➡ By stressing the functions of the building, the architects abolished the notion of an external facade.

The Centre Pompidou changed not only the face of central Paris, but also the nature of contemporary architecture, albeit being heavily influenced itself by Futurism, Constructivism, and the work of the 1960s U. K. collective Archigram.

The building sits in Paris's medieval Fourth *arrondissement* (administrative district) on the site of Les Halles market, and was designed by the team of Richard Rogers (*b.* 1933), Italian architect Renzo Piano (*b.* 1937), and structural engineer Peter Rice (1935–92). Famously, it was the result of a last minute entry to an architectural competition, and the "inside out" nature of the art complex is its chief signature, bearing its steel exoskeleton structure and long, snaking, glass tube-enclosed escalator "honestly" on its red, white, and blue exterior. In this sense, it may have also been influenced by Cedric Price's Fun Palace proposal.

Named after Georges Pompidou, who was president of France from 1969 until his death in 1974, in place of the former Centre Beaubourg, the scheme was built in an area in crisis, with the former market— which had supplied Paris with fresh food for decades—scheduled for demolition. Instead, the area has a one-million-square-foot (93,000 sq m) cultural center housing four main elements: an extensive museum of modern art, a reference library, a center for industrial design, and a center for music and acoustic research. Added to this mix are areas given over to office administration, bookshops, restaurants, cinemas, and children's activities, along with a popular external space, the Place Georges Pompidou, which is often peppered with a host of street entertainers.

The building was designed and built in six years, delivered on time and under budget in January 1977. Today, it boasts an average seven million visitors a year, who come to witness the amazing building as much as what is inside it. **DT**

Museum of Contemporary Art (1977)

Architect Kamran Diba   **Location** Tehran, Iran
Style Modernist   **Materials** Reinforced concrete, stone

The Museum of Contemporary Art in Tehran is one of the few examples of good modern architecture in the Iranian capital, which someone once described, not inappropriately, as "the bastard child of a Soviet city." Built in 1977, before the Islamic Revolution and at the height of the Shah's westernizing impulses, it was designed by the U.S.–trained architect Kamran Diba (b. 1937). What is most notable about the building is the way in which it mixes Western and Iranian idioms.

The building's recurring motif is a series of semi-arched skylights that evoke the wind towers used to

> ## "My interest in architecture has always transcended its physical dimensions."
>
> Kamran Diba, architect

cool houses in the desert town of Yazd. Four of these crown the central atrium, while below them an altogether different gesture is made by the circular ramp descending much like that in Frank Lloyd Wright's Guggenheim Museum in New York. Unlike the Guggenheim, however, the building is complex in its arrangement; in fact, it is rather like a castle in plan. From the higher citadel of the atrium block you progress through a sequence of galleries that are aligned diagonally around a terraced, sculpture court. The outer walls even use rough-cut stone, which alternates with smooth, Brutalist-style concrete.

Inside, the museum is moody and atmospheric. The almost Piranesian gloom suggests that looking at art is less a weekend entertainment than an activity of solemn contemplation. **JMc**

Quinta da Malagueira Housing Program (1977)

Architect Álvaro Siza   **Location** Évora, Portugal
Style Modernist   **Materials** Stone, brick

Portugal, after the fall of the dictator Salazar and a subsequent return to democracy, was no longer the country of Álvaro Siza's Boa Nova Tea House or of the Leça Swimming Pools. In a country where the Communist Party was now a key force, the question of housing a population still widely living in shameful conditions was a critical issue. Dwellers were to have a say in the construction of their future homes.

Évora—the outlying regional capital of an underdeveloped rural area—entrusted Siza (b. 1933)—one of the country's finest architects—with the task of

> ## "Malagueira grew through pain and struggle so as to achieve this degree of serenity."
>
> Laurent Beaudoin, Canadian businessman

designing a vast urban development scheme on the site of former estates expropriated from major landowners as a result of land reform. Under the master plan, which included integrating illegal housing, 1,200 housing units were built. To keep construction costs low, a degree of standardization was necessary, although some diversity in the one or two-story houses was achieved, and the streets became an extension of the houses themselves.

Initially intended for a low-income population, the Quinta da Malagueira is now a more middle-class neighborhood, reflecting the increased standard of living in Portugal. Architects and students from across the world still come in flocks to gaze at this atypical work. Even its creator Siza, returned to have a house built there for himself. **YN**

Venturi
House (1977)

Architect Robert Venturi **Location** Tucker's Town, Bermuda
Style Postmodernist **Materials** Concrete, white stucco

The house in Tucker's Town, Bermuda, is a product of Robert Venturi's (*b.* 1925) crusade against what he sees as the errors of the Modernist movement. Unlike many buildings that embody such a heartfelt architectural polemic, it is an exceptionally comfortable house with a domestic atmosphere. Indeed, this is the polemic: Venturi argues that style is less important than comfort and practicality.

Venturi also feels that a house should "look" like a house, and that it should fit in with the neighborhood style, which was also a planning requirement in this case. Built for the Brants, like so many other Bermudan villas, the building is painted white with pitched roofs—partly to catch precious rainwater. The outside is composed of traditional architectural features such as a scalloped Dutch gable over the entrance, a wide veranda resting on an open arcade overlooking the sea, and chimneys emerging from the tiled roof.

Inside, the house is more daring and complex. The rooms are spread across three connected pavilions, enabling them to be kept shallow to encourage any breeze to penetrate, and the connections between elements are handled to maximize the enjoyment of views and to create interesting spaces. A typical feature is the dramatic way in which, thanks to the sloping site, the visitor enters on the upper floor and descends toward the beach, with fine views out to sea from the staircase. In this house you see the implications of Venturi's belief in the importance of satisfying the client and pleasing the neighbors. **BWC**

↗ Venturi combines traditional design with a degree of stylization, seen here in the gently tapering chimney.

→ The house spreads across three pavilions, both for better ventilation and to maximize views to the sea.

Brion Tomb and Sanctuary (1978)

Architect Carlo Scarpa   **Location** San Vito d'Altivole, Treviso, Italy   **Style** Modernist   **Material** Concrete

The Brion Tomb and Sanctuary is a miniature masterpiece by an architect who spent a lifetime developing a very personal and completely modern style. Carlo Scarpa (1906–78) was acutely aware of the building traditions of the Veneto, and they informed all of his work. He received the commission from Honorina Brion, cofounder with her husband of the innovative electronics firm Brion-Vega. Giuseppe Brion had been born in San Vito d'Altivole, so Scarpa wrapped his design around two sides of the village cemetery. The L-shaped site has Giuseppe and Honorina's tombs in the outer corner, acting as a hinge between the two arms. They rest under mahogany and ebony sarcophagi beneath a curved concrete arched recess derived from early Christian catacombs.

To the west is a chapel set partly in a pond lit through translucent alabaster panels. Its door is framed in bronze. To the south is another pond with a contemplation pavilion at its center, approached across a bridge. But first one has to negotiate a passage with a door that sinks into the floor supported by a brilliantly designed and sculptural counterbalance system. The basic material of the complex is concrete but the textures are carefully modulated, and there are interventions of more precious materials such as bronze, gilding, ebony, and panels of polished plaster in the buildings. Paths, steps, and runnels for water, set on grass and beds of ivy, link the architectural incidents. From a distance, the outer walls evoke a medieval city wall, and the approach for visitors is made through a monumental gateway. Fittingly, the atmosphere is peaceful and contemplative. **CWH**

↖ The alabaster "windows" and bronze-framed doorway give the chapel a warm glow.

← The gently sloped roof evokes connections with an organic, undulating, ancient landscape.

Byker Wall (1978)

Architect Ralph Erskine **Location** Newcastle upon Tyne, England **Style** Postmodernist **Materials** Brick, steel, wood

The Byker district of Newcastle upon Tyne was traditionally an area of high-density, Victorian row housing. At the end of the 1960s, slum clearance required the housing in Byker to be replaced. The city council, mindful of mistakes made in the 1950s, kept the community together while it was rehoused.

The appointment of Ralph Erskine, a British-born, Sweden-based architect, was an inspired one, in that he believed that architecture was as much about the surrounding environment and people as it was about the building itself. Erskine had forged close links with potential residents on similar social housing schemes in his adopted Sweden. The rebuilding of Byker would be a rolling program; residents could stay in the area until their new homes were built, and they were to be consulted at various stages of the design process.

The main part of the Byker redevelopment is the so-called Byker Wall. To the north lies a busy highway and the Metro railway. Erskine minimized disturbance to the residents by placing only small windows in the northern facade and using this outward face only for nonliving areas such as the kitchen and bathroom.

On the inward-facing southerly side, the apartments and duplexes were given balconies to catch the sun, with ground floor apartments having gardens. Families with children were given priority for these, and all residents enjoyed car-free landscaping. Byker offers a refreshing break from the perception of high-density public housing as soulless. It is not without its problems, but it still stands as a testament to Ralph Erskine's vision and the positive effects that a strong sense of community can bring to an area. **ER**

↗ Erskine's work was greatly influenced by the clean lines of architecture in his adopted Sweden.

→ The small windows minimize the noise caused by nearby roads and train tracks.

Sainsbury Centre for Visual Arts (1978)

Architect Norman Foster **Location** Norwich, England **Style** High Tech **Materials** Tubular steel, aluminum

With his smooth-skinned, highly engineered, and perfectly finished buildings, Norman Foster (*b*. 1935) introduced the High-Tech Modernism of the United States to his native England (he had studied at Yale). Early projects were two buildings in the unlikely setting of East Anglia: first, the curvy, curtain-walled Willis Faber offices in Ipswich (1975), and then this, the Sainsbury Centre for Visual Arts, on the campus of the University of East Anglia. Foster received the commission to design the building in 1974, when he was just thirty-nine years old. The brief was for a gallery to house the collection of Robert and Lisa Sainsbury, and Foster's response was revolutionary in museum design. What he provided was a great shed, its clear-span interior providing flexible gallery space for permanent displays and temporary exhibitions. In form, the building comprises a rectangular hangar, a frame of prefabricated tubular steel clad in aluminum

panels. Many of the services for the building, including lavatories, are housed in the skin between the frame and the panels. Other services, such as lighting, are contained in the steel trusses of the roof. Full-height glass panels at one end of the building expose the structure and hint that the building could be extended *ad infinitum*. In fact, when Foster came to make an addition, he instead designed the Crescent Wing (1991), a separate building that is partially buried in the ground in front of his original pristine structure. **MF**

"The dominating building type in Foster's work is the great neutral space envelope . . ."

Axel Menges, author and editor

Gehry House (1978)

Architect Frank Gehry   **Location** Santa Monica, California, USA   **Style** Postmodernist   **Materials** Wood, corrugated metal, chain link

The extraordinary home of Frank Gehry (*b.* 1929) is a house turned inside out, a tumble of skewed angles, walls peeled back, and exposed beams. According to Gehry, his wife first saw a simple Cape Cod–style home on a suburban street in Santa Monica, and bought it knowing that he would "remodel" it. The remodeling turned into one of the most innovative approaches to Postmodern house design, and certainly one of the most controversial. Instead of pulling down the old house, Gehry built a new skin around it using cheap materials such as plywood, chain link, and corrugated metal, focusing on making the house appear unfinished—a work in progress. The old house peeps out in places from behind the new deconstructed shell. The apparent casual confusion of the design belies the architect's highly specified approach. Every deconstructed detail, disjointed angle, window, and roofline was designed for purpose and effect, so the

whole is an artwork viewed externally; from the inside looking out, every opening and architectural element offers visual stimulation. Gehry undertook a further renovation of the house from 1991 to 1992 when he smoothed off some of the unfinished quality of the building, streamlined it, and brought it more in line with the clarity of Mies van der Rohe's buildings. However, his first realization of the house is still the most talked about, effectively launching his career as one of the world's most original designers. **TP**

> *"Living there is very comfortable. It does leak a little and we are working on fixing that."*
>
> Frank Gehry, architect

East Building, National Gallery of Art (1978)

Architect I. M. Pei   **Location** Washington, D.C., USA   **Style** Postmodernist   **Materials** Post-tensioned concrete, pink granite, glass

The East Building of the National Gallery of Art brings together the progressive with the historic, and is an imposing, unequivocal statement of twentieth-century museum design. Built with a massive H-shaped facade, the museum punches almost defiantly through the Washington skyline; the clean, sharp lines of the building's silhouette commanding attention, while its monumentality pertains to a sense of timelessness, of immortality. This new wing was built alongside the main National Gallery of Art, a Neo-Classical building also of massive proportions, that was designed by the Beaux-Arts-trained architect John Russell Pope (1874–1937). The masterpiece of Ieoh Ming Pei (b. 1917) recalls the simplicity and Neo-Classical spirit of the earlier building, although it appears thoroughly modern in its conception. Both buildings have been faced in smooth, pink granite from the same quarry in Tennessee, a factor that further unites the two structures.

Working on a difficult trapezoidal site, Pei devised a plan using the triangle as its essential component, with two triangular exhibition and administrative spaces linked through a courtyard topped with multipeaked pyramidal skylights. The interior of the museum provides a vast, open, light-filled space suitable for housing large pieces of sculpture and other contemporary works.

Pei studied at Harvard under Walter Gropius (1883–1969); both architects rely on the same use of abstract form, clean lines, and materials such as concrete, steel, and glass, although Pei's designs tend not to conform to external influences or architectural fashions. **TP**

↖ Sharp edges and acute angles characterize the walls of the smaller of the two triangular buildings.

← The H-shaped facade gives no immediate clue that the main building's ground plan is triangular.

Tuol Sleng Genocide Museum (1979)

Architect Unknown **Location** Phnom Penh, Cambodia **Style** Modernist, Vernacular **Materials** Wood, brick, concrete

Located around a palm tree–lined courtyard, these four, three-story, whitewashed buildings with corridors running alongside the upper balconies were formerly a school. Under the Khmer Rouge, the compound became a brutal security prison and interrogation facility code-named "S-21." Between April 1975 and January 1979, it was enclosed by electric barbed wire, and the classrooms were turned into cell blocks with barred windows, interrogation rooms, and torture chambers. Prisoners were brought in and abused until they confessed to "crimes" against Pol Pot's regime. They were then executed and buried in mass graves at the killing fields of Choeung Ek.

Only seven out of Tuol Sleng's estimated 20,000 prisoners survived. The chilling exhibits on display include torture instruments, a rusty iron bedframe where several prisoners were murdered, and walls lined with mug shots taken before, and sometimes after, victims' interrogation and torture ordeals. A series of paintings by Vann Nath, a Cambodian artist who survived only because he was chosen to portray Pol Pot to the masses, depict life at Tuol Sleng and the various torture methods used on prisoners.

Opened in 1980 as a museum-cum-war-memorial to one of the twentieth century's most disturbing events, the buildings are largely as they were left when the Khmer Rouge were driven out by Vietnamese forces. Were it not for a noticeboard outside one of the blocks listing the security regulations to which prisoners had to adhere, it would seem unthinkable that a genocidal holocaust had taken place within this peaceful, sun-soaked compound. **AA**

↗ Tightly stretched barbed wire prevented the escape of prisoners being marched to cells for interrogation.

→ Peaceful now, the shabby buildings contain disturbing evidence of Pol Pot's brutal regime.

Crystal
Cathedral (1980)

Architect Philip Johnson   **Location** Garden Grove, California, USA
Style Modernist   **Materials** Steel, reflective glass

The roots of American "megachurches" go back some fifty years, but the phenomenon achieved its greatest expansion in the 1980s, in no small part because of the success of the rebuilt Garden Grove Community Church of Orange County, California—now known as the "Crystal Cathedral" although the church is not actually the seat of a bishopric. The church is so named because its architect, Phillip Johnson (1906–2005), together with his partner, John Burgee, built the main sanctuary around a colossal, star-shaped frame, rising to 128 feet (39 m) at its apex and filled with more than 10,000 panes of glass.

The mirrored panes reflect back ninety-two percent of the fierce Californian sunlight and are fitted with ventilation strips. This prevents the 3,000-strong churchgoers within from stifling in an oversize greenhouse, while immersing them in a diffuse, slightly ethereal atmosphere. Johnson had been a champion of the use of glass since designing his own Glass House in 1949, and later creating, in conjunction with his mentor Mies van der Rohe, the Seagram Building, the prototype glass skyscraper in New York.

However, much of Johnson's later work reflected an impatience with pure Modernism and a growing empathy for Pop Art and, later, Postmodernism. The Crystal Cathedral demonstrates this dichotomy—while it is Modernist in its use of industrial materials and geometric planes to exploit space, light, and volume dramatically, it is also defiantly populist and, to many, grandiosely kitsch. **RDB**

↖ The church was built for the television evangelist Dr. Robert Schuller, and hosts his religious show.

↙ The hundreds of mirrors are effective in reflecting the strong Californian sunlight away from the building.

Sangath Design Studio (1980)

Architect Balkrishna Doshi **Location** Ahmedabad, Gujarat, India
Style Modernist, Vernacular **Materials** Concrete, terra cotta, brick

Thorncrown Chapel (1980)

Architect E. Fay Jones **Location** Eureka Springs, Arkansas, USA
Style Postmodernist **Materials** Steel, glass, wood

Balkrishna Vithaldas Doshi (*b.* 1927) is a name synonymous with invigorating the contemporary Indian architectural landscape. He sees Sangath, his design studio and research center, as an expression of his design principles and observations. The unique aspect of the studio is that it also accommodates facilities for the neighborhood.

The planning of the complex is a playful juxtaposition of flat and vaulted surfaces embracing space to create habitable volumes of varying scales, allowing natural light to filter into the spaces. These

---

> *"Even local laborers and passing peasants like to come and sit next to it, enjoying the low mounds ..."*
>
> William J. R. Curtis, architecture critic

---

are further organized around an entrance court with a split-level water body, which acts as a natural cooling system in the hot climate. The differing scale creates a topography of internal and external spaces presenting architecture as an experiential art form.

The reinterpretation of the Indian vernacular is not restricted to formal aspects but also extends to the material construction. The vaults were cast *in situ* in ferrocement—elegant testimony to Doshi's studies under Le Corbusier. The finish is in mosaic tiles, executed by local craftsmen. More than sixty percent of the building is constructed using materials sourced locally. Brickwork and red-oxide floors interplay with the concrete post-and-beam structure to create an interface of contrasting textures that together work to create an inspirational design environment. **BS**

There are few buildings that combine the spirituality of the Gothic cathedral in a modern translation with inherent respect for the natural environment. Thorncrown Chapel is one, as is the Mildred B. Cooper Memorial Chapel built by the same architect, Fay Jones (1921–2004), some eight years later. The two buildings were conceived along similar lines and planned around simple, rectangular floor plans, from which rise magnificent, soaring structures; lofty, inspiring, and reflective of the trees around them.

The areas of wooded natural beauty for which both chapels were designed dictated to a great degree the construction of the buildings. Jones's reluctance to impinge on the areas, and to avoid the use of heavy construction machinery, led him to devise structures composed of easily moved elements that could be transported along the narrow paths to the construction site. These components were then assembled on the site, in the manner of a flatpack kit.

The frame of Thorncrown Chapel rises from a small supporting wall built from natural stone, and is almost entirely crafted from wood, hand-rubbed with a gray stain to fit with the color of the surrounding tree trunks. The strongly rhythmic, vertical structure rises to a canopy that appears to hover above the building. Inside the church, the awe-inspiring space is fragmented at its pinnacle through a series of diamond-shaped structural forms.

Jones was apprenticed to Frank Lloyd Wright before establishing his own architectural practice in Arkansas, and spent most of his life in relative isolation in the region of the Ozark Mountains. His unique, inspiring style was based on a synthesis of Wright's principles and Arts-and-Crafts ideals, to which he added his own approach to aesthetics. **TP**

Asian Games Village (1982)

Architect Raj Rewal **Location** Delhi, India **Style** Modernist
Materials Brick, concrete, crushed quartzite plaster

In the postcolonial milieu, it became a challenge for architects in the Indian subcontinent to delve into their past and eclectically reconstruct the fractured social fabric through the built environment. The Asian Games Village in Delhi is an example of one such intervention realized through the contemporary design of the traditional courtyard typology of residences. The scheme does not use the pastiche symbolism of architectural elements, but finds its reference in the way private and public spaces function with respect to each other.

> *"Architecture is not the habitat of the … individual: it is inevitably the expression of a community."*

Romila Thapar, professor and historian

Spread over a 35-acre (14 ha) site it accommodates 700 housing units. Whereas 200 of these are of the individual town-house type, the remaining 500 are apartment units organized over multiple floors. The individual units are based on very simple plans with living areas on the lower level and sleeping areas on the upper level. Each unit then forms a composite, which can be linked to other units on at least two other sides to create clusters or row houses. This allows for a range of open communal spaces both at higher and lower levels.

The complex has received some criticism for being essentially an adult space—not fluid enough to encourage informal play. However, it still stands as one of the more successful contemporary experiments at creating a sustainable community. **BS**

Church of Espírito Santo do Cerrado (1982)

Architect Lina Bo Bardi **Location** Uberlândia, Brazil
Style Postmodernist **Materials** Concrete, brick, wood

Often a philosopher's work cannot be understood without also considering the personal events that marked his or her life. Similarly, in the oeuvre of Lina Bo Bardi (1914–92), the relation between architectural and political ideas is so close as to make it impossible to consider one without the other. Educated in Italy, she moved to Brazil after World War II with her husband Pietro Maria Bardi. When in 1959 they moved to Salvador, Bo Bardi's work on the relation between social and aesthetic issues reached a new level.

The Church of Espírito Santo do Cerrado in Uberlândia beautifully captures this attitude. Situated in a deprived area of the city, the church was built using recycled materials from other buildings. Architects, local citizens, and clerics all donated their time to help complete the project. The church consists of four cylinders of different size and height. Starting from the north corner and moving to the opposite end of the site, the first cylinder is the *campanile*. Then the largest of the circular spaces contains the actual church, whereas the two volumes that terminate the composition respectively house the area for three nuns to live in and a small, semi-open area that is used as a gathering point for the local community. The lack of rectilinear walls and corners lends the space a sense of continuity and movement that dispenses with the traditional hierarchy of religious spaces. This is further reinforced by the use in all areas of the design of simple materials, such as masonry and wood, as well as the position of the skylights, which play down the solemnity of the typology.

Bo Bardi sketches an idea of religion detached from the solemn, transcendental concept developed in the Western tradition and reaffirms the need for a refreshing, democratic, new beginning in Brazil. **RDB**

Casa Rotunda
a Stabio (1982)

Architect Mario Botta **Location** Ticino, Switzerland
Style Postmodernist **Materials** Brick, glass

The Casa Rotunda a Stabio is the modern home built for Liliana and Ovidio Medici by the Swiss architect Mario Botta (b. 1943). The house is set within the Swiss countryside, with a few traditional houses close by.

The Casa Rotunda (Round House) is essentially cylindrical in shape, and divided into three floors with slices and segments cut through and across the cylinder to form window apertures, the staircase, and a glass atrium space so that sunlight shines down onto the floors below. The entrance is formed by a rectangular section cut out of the brickwork, which recedes to form a vestibule space leaving a solid fragment of wall that forms the remaining facade. What is unusual about the building—apart from it being circular in plan, which is challenging in itself—is that from the outside it appears to be solid in its form, but inside the spaces are broken up by intersecting dividing elements between the floors, making it difficult to see where one space begins and another ends. Single-height space changes unexpectedly to dramatic double-height space with huge expanses of glass and curved vertical walls.

Casa Rotunda, like many of Botta's buildings, is visually striking and highly original, challenging the conventional appearance and structure of the home. Since it was built, Botta—who was highly influenced by Le Corbusier, Louis Kahn, and Carlo Scarpa—has continued to produce innovative designs for houses, schools, churches, banks, and administrative and cultural institutions. **FO**

↗ Botta's stark, helmetlike brick-and-glass design is in strong contrast with nearby pantile-roofed homes.

⊡ Light pours in from a skylight, revealing interior spaces of varying heights and intervals.

Portland Public Service Building (1982)

Architect Michael Graves   **Location** Portland, Oregon, USA   **Style** Postmodernist   **Materials** Concrete, steel, glass

The Portland Public Service Building stands as a resplendent iconic monument to Postmodernism, soaring up among the prestigious company of the neighboring Beaux-Arts City Hall and County Courthouse, the streamlined Standard Plaza, and the shimmering Orbanco Bank Buildings. It was one of the first, and most adventurous buildings in the United States that shunned the machine-age industrialism of Modernist designs and embraced a new approach, drawing on historical and Classical precedents realized within a twentieth-century framework.

The building is divided into a tripartite form, along Classical lines, of base, middle, and top, or in anthropomorphic terms, of feet, body, and head. Similarly, the distinctive coloring of the exterior in teal, terra cotta, and blue recalls the ground, the earth, and the sky. The skin of the building is punctuated with regular, small, block windows that allude to the grid formation of Portland's town plan, and reflect the mass of surrounding structures.

This design propelled Michael Graves (b. 1934) to the cutting edge of contemporary architectural circles. The proposal itself was complex: as a public service building, function and simplicity had to take precedence over grandeur; the site itself was small; and the building needed to fit in with those around it, while also being aesthetically challenging. The biggest stumbling block, however, was the unreasonably low budget. The building has not been without controversy, and there have been functional and structural issues. However, in aesthetic and ideological terms it remains at the pinnacle of Postmodernist designs. **TP**

↖ The hammered-copper statue, *Portlandia* by Raymond Kaskey, was added to the building in 1985.

← The strong colors and blocklike structure of the building give it a commanding presence.

Renault Distribution Centre (1983)

Architect Norman Foster   **Location** Swindon, England   **Style** High Tech   **Materials** Steel, glass

On a sloping field outside a former railway town, the former Renault Distribution Centre startles with its yellow-painted frame and tentlike mast structure. The building marked an evolutionary stage in Norman Foster's architecture, sparked by a suggestion by Ken Anthony, one of the design team, that the smooth external envelope that had hitherto characterized the office's work could be replaced by something more expressive of the loadbearing structure. Anthony suggested the mast supports, but died in a car accident soon after. However, the project, involving Ove Arup in a crucial role as engineers, took forward his idea. By adopting a number of measures, such as setting the exterior wall cladding back from the line of the frame and molding the roof forms in three dimensions, the design team arrived at a distinctive new genre of High-Tech industrial building that borrowed the imagery of a tented roof for a building made out of rigid materials. The steelwork was handcrafted off site, and technical solutions were sought as the design went along.

As with all previous Foster projects, the social agenda for the project was to level the hierarchy between the white-collar office workers and the blue-collar manual workers on the site. The building became a symbol of the new attitude to the workplace in the early years of Prime Minister Margaret Thatcher, with a glamour entirely alien to the failing British motor industry. In 1999, Renault shifted their operation to the Midlands and sold the building. In 2004, it was bought by the Chinese government as a center for Far Eastern companies trading in Britain. **AP**

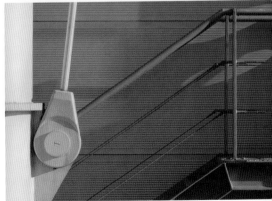

↗ The load-bearing work of the building is performed by a complex system of masts and tension cables.

→ The High-Tech aesthetic included painting significant parts of the structure in Renault's trademark yellow.

Kanchunjunga Apartments (1983)

Architect Charles Correa **Location** Mumbai, India
Style Modernist **Materials** Brick, concrete

Nordic House (1983)

Architects Ola Steen, Kollbrún Ragnarsdóttir **Location** Tórshavn, Faroe Islands **Style** Postmodernist **Materials** Steel, concrete, glass

After independence, Mumbai, the entertainment capital of India, fast developed into a commercial metropolis for the western coast of India. Located on an island in the state of Maharashtra, it had very limited land. Therefore, the rising population and concomitant housing demand forced the urban fabric to develop vertically, modeled on Western housing typologies.

Kanchunjunga Apartments, designed by Charles Correa (b. 1930), is one such high-rise solution. While modeled on Modernist lines, it integrates the essential ethos of life in a hot, tropical setting. The complex

> *"[Correa is] one of the pioneers in developing frugal, culturally rooted shelter in the developing world."*
>
> Douglas Kelbaugh, professor of architecture

contains thirty-two luxury apartments of three to six bedrooms and stands at a height of 275 feet (84 m).

In Mumbai, the preferred orientation of east-west is driven by the desire to catch the prevailing winds. Each apartment, spanning the building's width, has been designed with this orientation. As a result, each apartment also has stunning views of the Arabian Sea. A double-height recessed garden provides outdoor space, integral to traditional living patterns, and acts as a shield from the heavy monsoon rains. The building was seen as structurally groundbreaking at the time because the central core acts as the main element resisting the lateral loads.

This apartment building is a successful example of how traditional living patterns can be comfortably adapted to the modern confines of space. **BS**

Nordic House sits on a hill overlooking Tórshavn—one of the smallest capital cities in the world—as if it has been there forever. Its large windows reflect the surrounding sky, letting as much light into the building as possible—Nordic winters make daylight a very precious commodity. A steel structure, elegant yet solid, supports the sloping turf roof. The building has to be robust to withstand the sometimes extreme weather conditions.

The house was built to accommodate a center of Nordic culture. The competition to design it, held in 1977, was won by the Norwegian architect Ola Steen (b. 1942) in collaboration with the Icelandic architect Kollbrún Ragnarsdóttir. Together, they created a modern building that rises from the ground almost organically, and is perfectly incorporated into the surrounding landscape. Inside the house, the large entrance lobby and the other rooms and halls are multipurpose, with sliding walls and screens offering flexibility and variety. Different types of wood have been used throughout the building, making reference to traditional Nordic dwellings with their wood-paneled interiors.

The raw materials utilized in the construction of the Nordic House also demonstrate the collaborative nature of the building's construction. The turf roof is Icelandic; the wooden pine flooring originates from Sweden; the doors and furnishings are made from Finnish birch; slate for the floors came from Norway; and the ceilings, brass fittings, and glass facades are Danish in origin. It would be difficult to find a more fitting tribute to Nordic collaboration than this discreetly stylish cultural center, which blends in so beautifully and effortlessly with its natural mountainous surroundings. **RK**

Housing Block
"Bonjour Tristesse" (1983)

Architects Álvaro Siza, Peter Brinkert   **Location** Berlin, Germany
Style Postmodernist   **Materials** Stone, plaster

During the 1980s, West Berlin faced a paradigm change in town planning—the demolition of old buildings had allowed space for a more sensitive acquaintance with the substance of the historic city. The commission for the housing block on Schlesische Straße, known as the "Bonjour Tristesse" building, was an explicit sign of this change: to fill in an empty block corner instead of tearing down all the old houses and building something completely new.

This was the first project abroad for Álvaro Siza (*b.* 1933), already famous for his sensual, yet minimalist, buildings in Portugal. In Berlin, Siza had to learn that architecture is mostly the art of compromise. The austere design of this block arose out of the strict regulations of Berlin's social housing programs, which forced the architect to repeatedly modify his innovative housing scheme.

Siza had to add a story and simplify the facade. Initial sketches had shown a facade with curved lines in the windows, balconies, and brickwork, however, harsh economies forced him to reduce the composition to a rigid pattern of small windows in gray plaster. Instead of four big apartments on each floor, accessible via four separate staircases, the block now accommodates seven small apartments.

A graffiti artist painted the name (recalling Françoise Sagan's famous 1954 novel) on the facade shortly after completion. The name stuck and it is said that the architect himself prevented the graffiti from being removed during a refurbishment. **FH**

↗ A hole in the curved attic enabled a graffiti artist to paint the words "Bonjour Tristesse" on the facade.

→ The strict window pattern and the organic curved shape of the building make a harmonious contrast.

Cubic Houses (1984)

Architect Piet Blom **Location** Rotterdam, Netherlands **Style** Postmodernist **Materials** Concrete, wood, zinc

"The people of this region do not need more than a tree to live in."

Piet Blom, architect

⬆ The cubic houses bow down toward the streets below as though they are trees bending in the wind.

➡ The pointed triangular areas provide cozy domestic nooks and gave great scope for furniture design.

The city of Rotterdam commissioned Blom (1934–99) to design these dwellings, which are located above a pedestrian bridge across a public square from Rotterdam's Blaak station. The station's circular glass projectile roof resembles a flying saucer ready to take off and Blom's scheme of thirty-eight cubic houses and commercial shops continues this extraterrestrial theme. His houses are tilted at a forty-five degree angle and raised from ground level by hexagonal pole structures. Blom conceptualized each cubic block as a tree, creating an "abstract forest" of tree houses.

The idea for the houses originated in the 1970s when Blom built another set in Helmond. The cubes are constructed with concrete floors and a basic wood frame. Although from the outside it appears the interiors must slope, that is, of course, not the case. Yellow zinc panels cover the cubes to give them a more attractive albeit somewhat eccentric appearance. The cubes contain domestic living areas: a lower section, which is triangular in shape; a middle level with sleeping areas and a bathroom; and a top level containing either an extra bedroom or living area, which is also triangular in shape. The apex of this triangle contains a pyramid of windows that give spectacular views onto the river and across the city. The concrete poles contain staircases that lead to the apartments, as well as providing storage space.

Blom was the son of potato merchants in the Joordaan area of Amsterdam. He was trained as a carpenter and then studied architecture under Aldo van Eyck at the Academy of Architecture in Amsterdam. He became a member of the PROVO movement of the 1960s, a playful anarchist movement that advocated non-violence and absurd humor to promote social change. Blom's Cubic Houses have become such a phenomenon there is now a show house for visitors that is open daily. **KAB**

Ministry of Foreign Affairs (1984)

Architect Henning Larsen **Location** Riyadh, Saudi Arabia **Style** Postmodernist **Materials** Reinforced concrete, marble

Designing an important public project for the Saudi government frees an architect from typical cost restraints. This office building is sumptuous; the best materials—large quantities of Italian marble, for instance—were flown in from all over the world. The ministry is triangular in plan, with a substantially closed outer wall, and a central hall ringed by an internal "street." Along with office accommodation the building contains grand ceremonial rooms and assembly spaces. Air conditioning is minimized by careful design, with thick walls keeping out much of the sun's heat, and internal spaces being modeled on traditional housing and the architecture of *souk* markets. Henning Larsen (*b.* 1925) started his career in the office of another Danish architect, Arne Jacobsen. By the time he won the 1980 competition for the new Ministry of Foreign Affairs in Riyadh, he had moved a long way from Jacobsen's stripped down, ultramodern

style. Larsen's design has been attacked for its direct quotations from the Islamic tradition in architecture—some feel these quotations are closer to parody than to meaningful tribute. The Islamic influence, however, is combined comfortably with Danish Modernist style—marble aside, the interiors are simply plain white walls and well-designed lighting. The simple monumentality of the exterior echoes Louis Kahn's extraordinary capital building at Dhaka, Bangladesh, while also recalling Saudi fortresses. **BWC**

"Simplicity and complexity.... This expensive building conveys a sense of economy and clarity."

Jury of the Aga Khan Architecture Prize

Sea Ranch Chapel (1984)

Architect James T. Hubbell **Location** Sea Ranch, Sonoma County, California, USA **Style** Vernacular **Materials** Concrete, teak, stone

Sea Ranch is an architecturally significant 1960s planned community north of San Francisco. Its masterplan instituted guidelines to ensure buildings harmonized with the landscape. In contrast to U.S. suburbs, the 1,000-acre (400 ha) ranch stipulates no lawns, fences, non-native plants, or painted wood sidings. In contrast to the rectilinear houses—most designed by late Modernist architects such as Charles Moore—the nondenominational Sea Ranch Chapel, designed by the artist and architect James T. Hubbell (*b.* 1931) is more Wharton Esherick than saltbox, more diminutive exuberance than restraint. On a site near the ocean, a concrete slab foundation supports 12-inch (30 cm) walls infilled with concrete block. Teak siding was dried and molded onto the blocks to create a carapace. Boat-building skills enabled the carapace to curve. A nonequilateral drystone wall supports the offset, asymmetrical upper structure. The nave end highlights a spherical window and introduces the broad, low, weathered cedar shingle roof. From the nave the structure rises and narrows to the apex, where it flips upward like a scaled fish tail. A patinated bronze prow at the nave end pairs with a bronze finial at the roof apex, shaped to reference the Monterey pine. From the finial the roof sweeps dramatically down to the entrance. The tiny interior—360 square feet (33.5 sq m)—is fitted with curved redwood pews, Gaudí-like lights, and a white plaster, petal ceiling. **DJ**

> *"... living with nature and allowing it to manifest itself is different than ... living in a city ..."*
>
> Lawrence Halprin, Sea Ranch planner

Walter Segal Self-Build Houses (1984)

Architect Walter Segal   **Location** London, England   **Style** Vernacular   **Materials** Steel, glass, wood

"Fast track," "quick," and "cheap" are words used to describe the self-build method of Walter Segal (1907–85). But an unfair association with poor quality, high land prices, planning and zoning regulations, and reluctant mortgage lenders, all explain why Segal's approach has not taken off. It was not always so. In the 1970s, the London Borough of Lewisham responded to Segal's call for a build-it-yourself experiment. They allowed locals on the housing wait list to build their own homes the Segal way on odd-shaped parcels unsuitable for large-scale council builds. Twenty-seven detached Segal houses with gardens were built in Lewisham during the two-phase experiment. Segal prototyped the system in his native Switzerland and fine-tuned it after he emigrated to England. "Wet trades" are avoided. An engineer-free, light, easy build is achieved without bricklaying, foundation pours, or plastering. The simple, rectangular, timber balloon frame is bolted together in sections and sits on minimal footings. Standard modular dimensions avoid waste, allow for plan alterations, and use off-the-shelf materials to finish the build. A flat, thick felt roof is designed to be a green carpet. The system is affordable; structures can be added to when time and finances allow. Walter Segal wanted people to realize their potential. Two roads in the Honor Oak Park are named after Segal in honor of the man who convinced people to trust their native intelligence. **DJ**

> "It became clear to me that one can have a small path and tread it alone."

Walter Segal, architect

Neue Staatsgalerie (1984)

Architects Stirling Wilford and Associates **Location** Stuttgart, Germany **Style** Postmodernist **Materials** Stone, steel, glass

No doubt it is worth knowing your Beuys from your Picasso, but it is just as important these days to pay equal attention to the architecture hosting them. The Neue Staatsgalerie (New State Gallery) is the finest example of the work of James Stirling (1926–92) and Michael Wilford (b. 1938). The gallery is, in fact, an extension to the city's 1843 Neoclassical Altes Staatsgalerie, a series of interconnected rooms carrying a rich collection of twentieth-century art. The new gallery includes interior exhibition spaces, exterior terraces for sculpture, a theater, library, music school, and administration facilities. In its colorful, geometric, irregular shapes, Postmodernism is clearly identifiable. Bright blues and reds in the main entrance's steel pavilion, green rubber floor in the reception area, pink and purple steel handrails, green framing system, and glazed surfaces, contrast with the Classical references—warm stone and the centrally

sculpted stone-faced rotunda. The gallery's form is highly articulate, at the same time monumental and informal. Some of the original drawings can be found in the permanent MoMA collection in New York. The gallery is in the center of Stuttgart's "Cultural Mile," connected via a terrace to the History Museum and via public footpath to the city center. The complex project, though initially poorly received, developed into a great success, bringing together old and new in a very contemporary approach. **ES**

> *"I believe that the shapes of a building should indicate— perhaps display—the usage . . ."*
>
> James Stirling, architect

San Cataldo Cemetery (1984)

Architect Aldo Rossi   **Location** Modena, Italy
Style Postmodernist   **Materials** Concrete, brick, plaster

San Cataldo Cemetery is the first major building that projected Aldo Rossi (1931–97) into the international scene. Rossi had a serious automobile accident during the project, and developed his ideas while recuperating. The scheme is directly inspired by the adjacent monumental cemetery, designed by Cesare Costa in the nineteenth century.

The cemetery is a large court surrounded on three sides (the north arm is opened toward the countryside) by buildings inspired by the vernacular architecture of the local farmhouses. At the very center of the composition is the charnel house—a cube whose pure form and color is a reminder of De Chirico's metaphysical paintings. The use of blue metal panels for the roof and long concrete columns to articulate the basement level creates an abstract and poetic relation with the precedents. Despite the static and symmetrical articulation of the plan, the scheme has a certain dynamic quality, mostly because of the several parts of the project that are still unfinished—only fifty percent of the design has been implemented thus far.

By employing a language that is both poetic and pessimistic, Rossi's building marks the beginning of what Charles Jencks later defined as Postmodern architecture. In fact, all the elements of the composition are derived from historical precedents: the layout from the adjacent cemetery, the style of the buildings from the vernacular tradition.

The architect's role is no longer to invent new buildings from scratch, but rather to evolve the architectural types that have persisted over time. At San Cataldo Cemetery the result is both delicate and tragic, as architecture comes to represent the inescapable condition of humankind. **RB**

Roof Roof House (1984)

Architect Kenneth Yeang   **Location** Ampang Selangor, Malaysia
Style Eco-Architecture   **Materials** Concrete, glass

The Roof Roof House is a "life-size working prototype" of a bioclimatic design idea pursued by Kenneth Yeang, the architect and habitant of the house. Located on the outskirts of Kuala Lumpur, surrounded by rubber plantations, the house responds to the tropical climate by controlling heat without using mechanical devices. The outer curved roof works as a solar filter for the two-story structure below as does the outdoor space on top of the structure, while the swimming pool placed towards the southeast end of the site cools the prevailing wind that blows over it.

> "… an experimental design using [a] systemic approach … on the basis of climatic factors."
>
> Kenneth Yeang, architect

The internal walls and moveable glass partitions are arranged so that they effectively control the wind flow within the house—therefore the house is considered an "environmental filter."

However, Yeang's technical experiments in environmental biology, ecology, form, and design do not sacrifice the aesthetic aspects of the house. The concrete louvers on the curved roof and the slender, round columns that suspend the roof cast poetic shadows on the white surface of the building. Furthermore, a series of framed openings on the white mass create a distinctive rhythm. These formal characteristics not only express Yeang's affinity to Le Corbusier's formal vocabularies but also his unique interpretation of such vocabularies based on the regional and climatic context. **TS**

Hong Kong and Shanghai Bank (1985)

Architects Foster and Partners **Location** Hong Kong, China
Style High Tech **Materials** Steel, glass

The Hong Kong and Shanghai Bank (HSBC) by Norman Foster (*b.* 1935) dramatically displays the confidence and energy of Hong Kong in the 1980s. It bears a close stylistic connection with Richard Roger's Lloyd's Building in London, with its frank expression of services on the building's exterior, and Rogers and Piano's earlier Centre Pompidou in Paris.

Its construction on a confined site required precise off-site pre-fabrication and components were imported from across the world. The design is remarkable because there is no internal supporting structure. Eight groups of four vertical ladder masts, cross-braced with struts, hold up the floors with five levels of suspension trusses, locked into the masts. Elevators, stairs, and other services are at the east and west ends. Escalators are the main circulators, including the dramatic entrance one, which pierces the glazed atrium floor. The 170-foot-high (52 m), eleven-level atrium is an exciting and light space. It is lit by daylight scooped into the interior by computer-controlled giant mirrors.

The forty-seven story bank was one of the world's most expensive buildings when it opened (it has cost about $668 million). The plan of the bank is informed by Chinese feng shui principles: it faces water (the harbor view is not blocked) and two bronze statues, "Stephen," and "Stitt," named for former general managers, guard the building. In contrast, I. M. Pei's neighboring Bank of China is said to have bad feng shui because of its many sharp edges. Statue Square, in front of the HSBC Building, is a popular public space in Hong Kong, especially for Filipina domestic workers who flock there on Sundays. In 2004 a dramatic external lighting scheme, designed by Laservision, was installed in the building. **ATB**

Friendship Cultural Palace (1985)

Architect Garony Isakovitch   **Location** Hanoi, Vietnam
Style Modernist, Constructivist   **Material** Reinforced concrete

Spiral Building (1985)

Architect Fumihiko Maki   **Location** Tokyo, Japan
Style Modernist   **Material** Steel

Hanoi's Friendship Cultural Palace (Cung Van Hoa Huu Nghi), also known as the Trade Union Cultural Palace and the Vietnam Xo Cultural Palace, is a large reinforced-concrete structure south of the city center. It was designed and built with Soviet assistance. The white-walled building is a venue for cultural exchange. Its 120 rooms include lecture halls, meeting spaces, an observatory, library, and a 1,200-seat concert hall.

The Friendship Cultural Palace was based on a model for an exhibition and sports center developed in Moscow and replicated around the Soviet Union and its dependencies. The original prototype for this model was the Moscow Palace of Labor, the third-placed entry in a 1922 architecture competition. Legend has it that the design, developed by brothers Alexander, Leonid, and Viktor Vesnin, was the basis of the aesthetic of "form derived from function and construction" that underpinned Constructivism.

The palace, completed sixty-three years after the Palace of Labor competition, resembles a hybrid of Constructivist and Brutalist design principles, although some effort was made to accommodate local design motifs. It was built in recognition of the Socialist Republic of Vietnam's full membership of the Soviet Bloc—the Vietnamese-Soviet Treaty of Friendship and Cooperation was signed in November 1975, after the Vietnam War. Alongside Ho Chi Minh's Mausoleum, it is one of the most prominent physical legacies of the Soviet period of influence over the country.

In 1986, a year after the palace opened, the Sixth Congress of the Vietnamese Communist Party ushered in *Doi Moi*—renovation—a new era of economic and social policy, reflecting the failure of the existing system. The Soviet Union officially withdrew from Vietnam in 1990. **AM**

From the busy Tokyo street, the Spiral's facade (see page 548) hints that something worth a second look may be going on beyond. There is the logic of a grid, but none of its uniformity. The planes are slightly askew with a cone appearing in a false window. Architecture's rules are outlined, and then broken, something entirely appropriate for a center for the arts.

Behind the eclectic facade, the Spiral presents spaces for performance, movies, music, and the visual arts. A café, bar, and restaurant define it as a social space, too, and large glass areas give a sense of

"The problem of modernity is not creating forms, but rather, creating an overall image of life ..."

Fumihiko Maki, architect

openness not always achieved in arts buildings. But the real magic of the Spiral happens in its connecting staircases, and most particularly the spiral ramp that seems to glide in a floating fashion from one level to the next in the rear gallery space. The stairways running alongside windows provide quiet landings, little platforms on which to sit and gaze out at the city, proving that creativity and culture have as much to do with peaceful spaces as they do with spectacle and sensation. The spiral itself borrows, perhaps, from the archetypal ramp-in-a-gallery, the curving walkway in Frank Lloyd Wright's Guggenheim in New York. The conceit has also been repeated at the High Museum of Art in Atlanta, but here it is a more subtle intervention, a gentle upward arabesque. Fumihiko Maki (b. 1928) won the Pritzker Prize in 1993. **GT**

Museum for
Applied Arts (1985)

Architect Richard Meier **Location** Frankfurt, Germany
Style Modernist **Materials** Concrete, glass

The Museum for Applied Arts stands on the south bank of Frankfurt's River Main. It is one of the largest and most prestigious museums of decorative arts in Germany, which explains the involvement of Richard Meier (b. 1934) in the project. The museum's collections cover 6,000 years of design history, and the galleries are used for temporary and permanent exhibitions. It is located close to other museums and together they form the Museumsufer district.

Meier's scheme is organized around two factors. First, he makes use of an existing building, the Villa Metzler, a beautiful house that dates from 1803, on the site. Second, the project uses the skewed angle of the river frontage. The result is typical of Meier's oeuvre: a white geometric building with an overlapping grid structure that relates well to the existing villa. As in all of Meier's works, a sense of openness and the use of natural light are important in the design. The building conforms to Enlightenment principles—it is a place of both display and didactic purposes. Thus, the sober white architecture, while Modernist and High Tech, defer to the objects and does not overwhelm them.

Richard Meier is one of the best known American architects of the late twentieth century. His trademark purist Neo-Modernist buildings often pay homage to Le Corbusier. He has been awarded several accolades in his career: among them the Pritzker Prize in 1984 and the RIBA Gold medal in 1988. Meier was also notably the first architect to "build" for the virtual world, designing the computer game *Sim City 4*. **KAB**

↗ The all-white buildings are deliberately simple in order to serve as a backdrop to the art collections.

→ The beautifully clean lines and shimmering glass used by Meier evoke the smooth water of the Main river.

Richmond Riverside Development (1986)

Architect Quinlan Terry   **Location** Richmond, Surrey, England   **Style** Neo-Classical Revival   **Materials** Stone, plaster, brick

In the mid-1980s, the residents of Richmond, an affluent and historic suburb of London on the banks of the Thames, were given the opportunity to vote for their favorite design for the development of the riverside. The choice was between a striking, modern, concrete structure or a conservative, formal, Neo-Classical proposal by Quinlan Terry (b. 1937). The residents turned their back on contemporary designs and chose the latter. The architectural establishment was rocked; with bright red brick, white plaster, and a montage of Georgian sash windows, Palladian proportions, and all five orders of Greek architecture, it claimed the melange of past designs was pastiche rather than a model of Classicism. Terry's design includes shops, offices, pubs, and bars and encompasses the restoration of the old Town Hall. The design is notable for its distinctive disassociation between exterior and interior space. The facade is one homogenous, dignified unit; the interior functions of the building vary but individual requirements are not exhibited externally. What appears to be two separate buildings may be occupied by one office, or a bar and an office, or three offices. However, its sympathetic and varied scale, its use of solid, long-lasting materials, and the generous amount of public space—including three terraces of grass sloping down to overlook the Thames and areas for public performances—have ensured its enduring public approval. **BG**

"The first town center commercial development that added to . . . the quality of a historic town."

Architects' Journal

Lotus Temple (1986)

Architect Fariborz Sabha   **Location** Delhi, India   **Style** Expressionist   **Materials** Concrete, marble

A symbol of purity metaphorically rising out of the muddy water of life and blossoming in liberation—that is how the lotus flower has been perceived though eons of cultural and religious evolution in India. The understanding of this is what drove architect Fariborz Sabha (*b.* 1948) to conceive the house of worship for the Baha'i faith in Delhi as an iconographic abstraction of this symbol of faith. It seems paradoxically apt that the Lotus Temple, or Baha'i Mashriqu'l-Adhkar, sits in the middle of one of the densest urban, mixed-use settlements in southern Delhi. With a backdrop of random land usage and the chaos of coexisting medieval and modern transportation networks, this temple is almost a sigh of relief, evocative of less worldly concerns in its grandeur and elegant simplicity. Conceived as a nine-sided lotus with twenty-seven petals, it sits in a sprawling landscape of 26 acres (10 ha), with a nine-sided pool forming a base, which gives the illusion of the hall floating independent of any foundation. Each of the petals is constructed in concrete with white Greek marble cladding. Because of the varying curvatures of the petals, each piece of marble was individually dressed as per location and orientation and then assembled on site. Another remarkable feature of this 111-foot-high (34 m) hall of worship is that the superstructure is entirely designed to act as a light well. The core petals form a bud, which allows light to filter through, and every subsequent layer of petals reinforces the bud. The Lotus Temple, a retreat for followers of all religions to meditate in, sits peacefully within its urban bedlam, exuding an aura of divinity. It is indeed a successful icon of the translation of an ancient motif into a construct of contemporary belief. "I cannot believe it: it is God's work," exclaimed jazz musician Dizzy Gillespie on seeing it. **BS**

Snowshoe Cabin (1986)

Architect Philip Banta & Associates **Location** Soda Springs, California, USA **Style** Vernacular **Materials** Timber, concrete

A thin line exists between snow that brings pleasure and snow that accumulates and kills. Soda Springs is a ski resort in the Sierra Mountains near Lake Tahoe and Donner Summit. In a tragic episode of American westward migration in the 1840s, a group of settlers became snowbound at Donner Summit. They resorted to cannibalism to survive. Their main failure was to be ill prepared for snow. Snow in the Sierras is still unforgiving. Preparation is essential.

Snowshoe Cabin is snow smart. Beneath high peaks, the valley holds snow even in dry winters. Sited on a hill, the cabin's 1,000-square-foot (93 sq m) footprint is similar to that of a snowshoe. And just as snowshoes enable weight to be distributed evenly to prevent sinking, so the cabin rises above the snowline to achieve the snowshoe quality of "flotation."

The cabin's leading edge is a 7-foot (2.1 m) wedge. Built without removing any of the surrounding pines, the steep, enclosed, sided staircase at this north-facing end leads to the main floor. Snowfall needs to top 10 feet (3 m) before this level is affected.

The 17-foot-wide (5 m) southwest end houses the living, kitchen, and entertaining areas in a double-height open space. Two pairs of stacked, two-over-two windows at the corner overlook the valley and the deck on two sides of the cabin. The deck profile bows out like a snowshoe. A sleeping loft wraps around two sides of the living area. Thermal efficiency is assisted by a wood-stove on a tile floor. The sharply pitched roof ensures snow slides off quickly. Deep eaves vary in width and provide winter protection or summer shade. To reach the cabin from the road, the owners ski cross-country for a mile (1.6 km) with provisions. In this beautiful but treacherous environment, they know that preparation is everything. **DJ**

SESC Pompéia Factory (1986)

Architect Lina Bo Bardi **Location** Sao Paulo, Brazil **Style** Brutalist **Material** Reinforced concrete

The SESC, Social Service for Commerce, is an independent organization supported by contributions from companies with headquarters throughout Brazil. Lina Bo Bardi (1914–92) was asked to design a new social center for the SESC, which had acquired a large group of warehouses previously used as factories. These warehouses were to be demolished in order to construct the community center, but Bardi decided to use the old concrete structures; they were transformed into social areas, housing, a multipurpose restaurant, art and handicrafts workshops, a large space for

> "… it offers its ample space as a stage for a cultural citizenship practiced in its highest form."
>
> Cecília Rodrigues dos Santos, architect

meetings and exhibitions, a theater for 1,200 spectators, and video screening and reading rooms.

A smaller piece of land remained, intended for the sports center, but it was crossed by an underground rainwater drainage tunnel, over which it was impossible to build. The solution was to build two separate blocks, with pedestrian bridges in prestressed concrete connecting the two blocks at four levels. To one side is a large cylinder containing the water tower, an allusion to the factory chimney. Between the blocks there is a long wooden deck.

A walk through the SESC Pompéia is an artistic and social experience, or a "socially artistic" one, to use a Bo Bardi phrase. Enthusiastically used, the Pompéia Factory is a singular habitat that transforms a sports and cultural center into a dynamic social space. **FA**

Museum of
Roman Art (1986)

Architect José Rafael Moneo   **Location** Mérida, Spain
Style Modernist   **Materials** Cast concrete, brick

Mérida is often called the "Spanish Rome" because it was one of the most important cities on the Iberian peninsula during the late Roman Empire. The museum, built to celebrate this important period in Mérida's history, not only houses artifacts from that period, but is itself sited over part of the Roman town, the remains of which may be seen in the basement galleries.

The main body of the building is formed from a series of massive parallel walls of concrete clad in a brick facing. It has the monumental scale and ground plan—with its simple, insistent divisioning—of an archaic market, basilica, or even aqueduct, directly evoking a generic idea of "Roman-ness" without descending into pastiche Classicism. This close relationship and dialectic between the content and form of the building is what makes visiting it so powerful an experience. The museum provides a beautiful space to frame the exhibits—with a sophisticated modulation of natural light that gently picks out the white marble of the Roman artifacts—while also materially evoking through its structure the spirit of the civilization to which the artifacts belong.

In his reclaiming of the forms of historical architecture, Rafael Moneo (b. 1937) proved highly influential on other Spanish architects and on an international architectural scene mired in the stick-on period detailing of Postmodernism. Through a masterly manipulation of structure, space, and material, the Museum of Roman Art seems almost to be a synthesis of the modern and the archaic. **RGW**

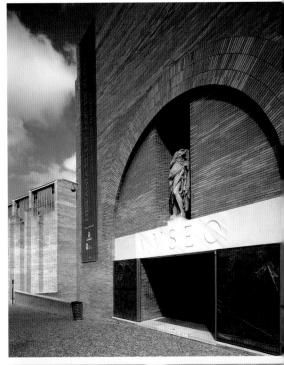

↗ The museum is in the heart of the old Roman town and stands opposite the amphitheater.

→ Moneo employed Roman building techniques, seen particularly in the sturdy brick walls.

Lloyd's Building (1986)

Architect Richard Rogers Partnership **Location** London, England **Style** High Tech **Materials** Steel, glass, stainless steel

*"Lloyd's [offers] a responsive ...
balance between permanence
and transformation."*

Richard Rogers, architect

⬆ The building rises up in the heart of one of the oldest areas of London, a proud example of High Tech style.

➡ Putting all the service areas on the outside of the building maximized the working space inside.

During the late 1970s, in new Prime Minister Margaret Thatcher's Britain, the ideals of the free market economy were beginning to gain ascendency. It was against this backdrop that the insurer Lloyd's decided it needed more space and commissioned architect Richard Rogers (*b.* 1933), to redevelop its Leadenhall Street site. Rogers responded to the brief with a highly controversial but groundbreaking design that continued a trend he had started with his Centre Pompidou project: for buildings to "wear" their insides—essentially, services—on the outside. In composition the Lloyd's Building is a futuristic blur of ducts, cranes, external glass elevators (the first of their kind in the United Kingdom), toilet pods, pipes, and braces, in a modular, repeated style and finished in silver metal. All this was to be built, surprisingly, in the hitherto conservative financial center of the City of London, with its centuries-old traditional buildings.

The building consists of three main towers and three service towers around a central, rectangular space. Its focal point is the gigantic Underwriting Room on the ground floor that houses the famous Lutine Bell. The Underwriting Room, often simply known as "The Room," is overlooked by galleries that form a 200-foot-high (60 m) atrium lit naturally through a huge, barrel-vaulted glass roof. The first four galleries open onto the atrium space.

The eleventh floor houses the Committee Room, within which is an eighteenth-century dining room originally designed for the second Earl of Shelburne by Robert Adam in 1763. The room was transferred piece by piece from the previous Lloyd's building, built in 1958, across the road. The Lloyd's Building currently standing between Leadenhall Street and Lime Street is just the latest home for the ever-expanding Lloyd's, named after Edward Lloyd, in whose coffee shop the insurance business was founded in 1688. **DT**

Archaeological Enclosure (1986)

Architect Peter Zumthor **Location** Chur, Switzerland
Style Modernist **Materials** Timber, steel, leather, cloth

Swiss architect Peter Zumthor (b. 1943) claims the status of a living legend: a recluse "architect-craftsman," a cabinet-maker by training, who places a kind of redemptive truth in natural and utilitarian beauty and resists the all-pervading arbitrariness of form-led architecture.

The archaeological enclosures were one of Zumthor's first projects. They combine the formal neutrality of primary forms with an intensely visual surface and with sculptural, oversized skylights referring to the Modernist canon. The volumes trace

> ## "I believe that the real core of all architecture lies in the act of construction."
>
> Peter Zumthor, architect

the contours of the Roman ruins they enclose and approximate their former presence while establishing an urban relationship with neighboring warehouses.

The perimeter walls, made of short, overlapping planks of timber, are interrupted only at entry and connection points and by windows, on the location of the old entrances. The timber screens are characteristic of the local barns, and their detailing seems reliant on traditional skills. The secondary elements—the steel entrance canopy, the internal raised walkway, the windows, and skylights—serve metaphorically as links to the present day. This project's poetry derives from an inherent tension between the "vibrating," three-dimensional surface and the abstract volumes it defines, from the juxtaposition of elements representing timelessness and the present. **ID**

Bank of Asia Building (1986)

Architects Sumet Jumsai Associates **Location** Bangkok, Thailand
Style Postmodernist **Materials** Reinforced concrete, brick, glass

The Bank of Asia building is one of the most distinctive buildings of its time. Sumet Jamsai's brief from the head of the Bank of Asia gave him few restrictions: he was to design a building that would "reflect upon the new generation . . . and usher in a new era involving their new computerized banking service." Jamsai conceived the robotlike form as suitably symbolic of the Bank's progressive outlook.

The 272-foot (83 m), 20-story structure is divided vertically into three main sections that taper toward the top, the apex forming the robot's "head." The large,

> ## "The robot . . . proclaims the demise of Postmodernism and of Punk Architecture . . ."
>
> Samet Jamsai, architect

apparently lidded "eyes" lend the building a curious, animated quality. Upon the east and west facades are numerous nut, bolt, and wheel shapes, which have a functional use as window casings and sun-shade canopies. The north and south facades are glazed, but the east and west elevations used masonry, to repel the sun's strongest rays. This reduces the dependency on air conditioning, making the building more energy efficient. Jamsai was ahead of his time, as such principles were not widely followed in the 1980s.

Loved by some and derided by others, it cannot be denied the Bank of Asia acquired itself a building that secured international attention. More than just an eye-catching form, the building demonstrates Jamsai's confidence and faith in the continual advancement, as opposed to the endless revivalism, of architecture. **JF**

St. Alban-Tal Apartment Houses (1986)

Architect Diener & Diener   **Location** Basel, Switzerland
Style Modernist   **Materials** Concrete, glass, render, wood

Exploring urban typologies, Diener & Diener's architecture lies at the conjunction between individual building and the city fabric in which it is embedded. The St. Alban-Tal housing project marks a shift in their early oeuvre, which combined the recognizable imagery of historical Modernism with direct references to the immediate context. With these two apartment houses, the use of such references becomes more internalized and secondary to the overall perception of the built volumes.

The project is located in an area of Basel bordering the Rhine, which has a picturesque yet ambiguous character with its medieval city walls, nineteenth-century industrial buildings, and canal. The two buildings complete this amalgam by combining traditional and Modernist elements.

The first building, parallel with the promenade, confronts its dual aspect by contrasting the industrial river facade with a more traditional, timber-boarded elevation at the back, which faces the old structures. The smaller building reveals its skeletal frame toward the canal and proposes a freer composition, determined by the internal open plan, looking toward the square. The living and quiet areas of the apartments are distributed accordingly.

The project examines the degree of literalness with which architecture may respond to its site. The Modernist canon is explored in terms of discrete images or quotations from various luminaries placed in unexpected relationships with each other. **ID**

↗ The front facade of the apartments acknowledges the nineteenth-century industrial buildings nearby.

⇥ At the rear of the building, timber boarding echoes the wooden elements of neighboring structures.

Etisalat Tower (1986)

Architect Arthur Erickson **Location** Dubai, United Arab Emirates **Style** Postmodernist **Materials** Concrete, steel, glass

Etisalat is the United Arab Emirates's state-run telecommunications company that has substantial buildings located in each of the seven emirates. Of these, Arthur Erickson's (b. 1924) Etisalat Tower in Dubai is one of the most innovative and arresting. The structure consists of two curved, concrete columns that house the elevators and utility areas of the building, joined by a glass-and-steel tower. The dark green, steel framework of the tower is broken into slim, vertical planes that are staggered outward so that the central glass and steel tower forms a prism shape. At the top of the tower, the form bends at a forty-five degree angle to the middle, and atop this sits the most distinctive feature of the building, the "golf ball" crown. From a design perspective, it is an extraordinary element, a wake-up call to the innovation of Modern and Postmodern architecture, but, and this is typical of Erickson's philosophy, it more pertinently plays a

fundamental part in the building's function. In this instance, the tower had to incorporate the needs of a telecommunications building and provide office space, as well as fit into Dubai's increasingly progressive skyline. Erickson used his design for Christ Church Cathedral in Vancouver, which was never built, and adapted it for the Etisalat Tower, with the church's glass prism evolving into the golf ball crown. The building proved popular in Dubai, and sparked a fashion for buildings with similar features. **TP**

"Architecture, as I see it, is the art of composing spaces … to answer a client's needs."

Arthur Erickson, architect

Church of Hallgrimur (1986)

Architect Gudjon Samuelsson **Location** Reykjavik, Iceland **Style** Expressionist **Material** Concrete

Recreating the characteristics and qualities of nature can be achieved by using specific materials or because the expression of nature is already embedded in the building; in the case of the Church of Hallgrimur, it is the latter. When looking at this monument by the Icelandic state architect Gudjon Samuelsson (1887–1950), towering snow-clad mountains and basaltic lava formations spring to mind. Samuelsson was commissioned to build the church in 1937; the building process continued until 1986. A small initial chapel was consecrated for worship in 1948 and several new building phases opened in ensuing years. Samuelsson died several decades before seeing the church completed, but it stands as one of his final great designs. Its site, on the top of a hill, emphasizes and extends the height of the church tower much further than its already soaring 240 feet (73 m). Vertical rows of concrete dominate throughout the building,

and when approaching the entrance, these lines are dramatically enhanced toward the center of the tower, maintaining the spectator's focus. The rows of white and gray concrete continue on the walls inside and are brought together in pointed arches. These effects allude to the Neo-Gothic style, especially with the strong emphasis on the vertical giving the nave an incredibly light, spacious appearance. The volcanolike tower can be seen from all over Reykjavik. The church is named after one of Iceland's most famous hymn poets Hallgrímur Pétursson (1614–74), and in front of the building is a statue of Leif Ericson (970–1020) who, according to Icelandic sagas, discovered North America. These two people stand as cultural symbols of Iceland, just as the church does. However, by imitating the structure of lava, and the colors of snow and ice, Samuelsson also ensured the church evoked the Icelandic natural world. **SML**

Hundertwasser House (1986)

Architects Friedensreich Hundertwasser, Josef Krawina, Peter Pelikan   **Location** Vienna, Austria   **Style** Postmodernist   **Materials** Concrete, brick

Friedensreich Hundertwasser (1928–2000), sculptor, painter, and environmentalist, turned to architecture in the 1980s with a series of designs for various buildings including incinerators, train stations, hospitals, housing, and churches. His affection for organic shapes and helices and his strong opposition to what he called the "geometrization" of humankind resulted in his highly recognizable style, a long way from the common norms of scholastic architecture.

Hundertwasser House was one of his first commissions, and remains one of the most distinguished. Sited in Vienna's Third District, this social-housing apartment building occupies a large portion of an old-town urban block. Most remarkable are the facades, which Hundertwasser broke down into small units, vastly differing in color and texture. The apartments have roof gardens with more than 250 trees, bushes, and plants.

Although the layouts of the fifty-two apartments remained fairly conventional, Hundertwasser tried to avoid flat floors and straight corridors, by introducing what he called "non-regimented irregularities," and the "right of windows," and deliberately planting "beauty obstacles." Opposed to traditional architects he initally decreed everyone should be able to build as they pleased, taking responsibility for their own space—even if this meant self-made structures would collapse—in the process of acquiring structural knowledge. He later bowed down to architects' expertise in structure and stability, but thought they should still be subordinate to the resident, who should take over in designing the external skin of a building.

Hundertwasser House is the three-dimensional application of an artist's paintings, and Hundertwasser would apply this treatment to almost all of his architectural designs making them highly personal and instantly loved or hated by the observer. **LT**

> *"Functional architecture proved to be a dead end, as much as painting with rulers would be."*
>
> Friedensreich Hundertwasser, artist

⬆ The plants and trees merge perfectly with Hundertwasser's crazily organic design.

➡ Hundertwasser softened the austerity of the apartment block with diversely decorated facades.

Stein House (1986)

Architect Günther Domenig **Location** Steindorf, Austria **Style** Deconstructivist **Materials** Concrete, steel, glass

Since the 1970s, Austrian architect Günther Domenig (b. 1934) has intensively engaged with one site on an inherited family property at Steindorf on the shores of Lake Ossiach. Stein House, situated in a lush, one-acre estate, points toward the lake, and faces undulating hills and mountain ranges. Although construction started in 1986, it remains an ongoing project and could be best described as a "built biography" that possibly will never be finished. With its beautiful shards of metamorphic rock that finger out to the lake—forming ridges, canyons, caverns—the building is inspired by the architect's sketches of Austrian landscapes. The glowing red, lava-colored finishes of the interiors contrast with the stone and metal structure on the outside. In its dramatic physicality and poetic interpretation, the house itself is a private cosmos that gives radical architectural form to human relationships and interactions. Domenig sees his project as an opposition to the Neo-Romantic Alpine style—so widely spread in this region—by providing architecture beyond the homely *Gemutlichkeit* that can be bought from do-it-yourself shops. As a manifestation of a very personal understanding of architecture, Stein House has become the underlying theme of his work. Acclaimed by architectural critics, but perhaps not to the taste of many others, Stein House is one of the most poetic, unique, and intimate buildings the twentieth century has produced. **LT**

> *"An attempt to perhaps find a way back to a native architecture that does not blur our tracks."*
>
> Günther Domenig, architect

Musée d'Orsay (1987)

Architects Victor Laloux, ACT, Gae Aulenti **Location** Paris, France **Style** Beaux-Arts Classicist, Modernist **Materials** Stone, cast iron, glass

The Tate Modern in London showed how an industrial building could be transformed into a rugged home for art, but Paris's Musée d'Orsay had done the same thing with a former railway station previously. On the eve of the 1900's World Fair, the French government planned to build a more central terminus station on the site of the ruined Palais d'Orsay, and chose architect Victor Laloux (1850–1937), who had just completed the Hôtel de Ville in Tours, to design it. The station and hotel, built within a record two years, were inaugurated for the World's Fair on July 14, 1900, its modern metallic structures masked by a hotel facade built in the academic style using finely cut stone from the regions of Charente and Poitou. However, after 1939, the station was to serve only the suburbs, as modern trains outgrew its platforms. On the initiative of President Valéry Giscard d'Estaing, the decision to build the Musée d'Orsay inside it was taken during the interministerial council of October 20, 1977, with the President of the Republic, François Mitterrand, inaugurating it on December 1, 1986. It opened eight days later. The transformation of the station into a stunning museum was accomplished by ACT architecture group, made up of Renaud Bardon, Pierre Colboc, and Jean-Paul Philippon, with leading Italian architect Gae Aulenti overseeing the transformation of the interior. The three-level scheme highlights the building's airy great hall while respecting the original cast-iron pillars and stucco decorations, with the glass awning becoming the museum's entrance. On the ground floor, galleries are distributed on either side of a central nave, these are overlooked by terraces at a median level which in turn open up into additional exhibition galleries, along with a museum restaurant—installed in the dining hall of the former hotel—bookshop, and auditorium. **DT**

Mound Stand, Lord's (1987)

Architect Hopkins Architects **Location** London, England **Style** High Tech **Materials** Tensile fabric, steel, brick

The Mound Stand at Lord's marked the start of a key chapter in the Marylebone Cricket Club's modern history of commissioning high-quality contemporary architecture. Designed by Sir Michael Hopkins (b. 1935), the stand was opened in 1987 and ushered in a series of high-quality structures at the "home of cricket." The Mound Stand essentially consists of long, curving balconies under a distinctive tent roof, and arched brickwork to the rear as it faces the street. This brickwork existed from a previous stand and forms a public concourse that stretches right around the ground. The building features a new steel superstructure supported by just six columns to avoid interfering with spectators' views. This is linked by a plate girder, from which lattice trusses cantilever out forming a skeleton for the three-story structure. Below it hang private boxes and dining rooms, featuring frameless glass doors onto raking balconies. The columns become masts, with canopies offering a lightweight, summery feel to the structure, which is held back by tension members anchored to the ground. Hopkins's work has shown a fascination with lightweight and membrane architecture and tensile fabric structures, including Hampshire cricket club stadium; the Inland Revenue building in Nottingham; and the elegant canopy for the foyer of Glyndebourne Opera House. The Mound Stand is the perfect encapsulation of the English summer. **DT**

> *"His [works] are hard to categorize. Some are ethereally delicate ... others are dark brooding affairs."*

Hugh Pearman, architecture critic

School of Electrotechnics and Electronics (1987)

Architect Dominique Perrault **Location** Champs sur Marne, Marne-la-Vallée, France **Style** Modernist, High Tech **Materials** Metal, glass, concrete

The High Tech ESIEE—École Supérieure d'Ingénieurs en Électronique et Électrotechnique—building, designed by Dominique Perrault (*b.* 1953), is the focal point of the Cité Descartes, the campus of the Polytechnicum de Marne-la-Vallée. In plan the ESIEE building resembles a large, tilted computer keyboard, 820 feet (250 m) long, with small, irregular, square and rectangular apertures to allow natural lighting. The entrance to the one-story facade is marked by a semicircular opening; this echoes the shape of the Rond Point with a sculpture by Piotr Kowalkski—*Axis of the Earth* (1989)—a symbolic spike emerging from the earth at a forty-five-degree angle. At the heart of the building is the five-story Rue Galerie, an 820-foot-long (250 m) interior street. This is the linear pedestrian spine for the building, serving 1,300 students and connecting the library, five lecture theaters, laboratories, meeting rooms, and cafeteria. From the north end of the central structure a series of six piers of five-story office buildings accommodate the research and development departments. At the south side of the building is an external semicircular vaulted gymnasium and sports area. The interior is uncompromisingly functional with exposed concrete walls, exposed supporting metal *piloti*, and glass walls. Perrault's architecture derives from a sophisticated rationale seen in several of his other projects, including the Velodrome swimming pool, Berlin (1997). **JHT**

> *"Perrault's work . . . is realized in the expression of materials to achieve tension and beauty."*
>
> *El Croquis* magazine (2001)

Institut du Monde Arabe (1987)

Architect Jean Nouvel, Architecture Studio   **Location** Paris, France   **Style** High Tech   **Materials** Concrete, stone

Nouvel's Institut du Monde Arabe (IMA or Arab World Institute) is the smallest of François Mitterrand's so-called "Grands Projets," but it cannot be called the least daring. It was crowned with the Aga Khan Award for Architecture—thus catapulting its architect to stardom. With France being a former colonial power in North Africa and the Middle East (with much debate within today's society about such issues as historical responsibility or culture mix as a legacy), IMA's purpose was to spread knowledge of Arab culture in France and throughout Europe. Housing a library, exhibition spaces, and an auditorium, it experiments with intensive cultural exchanges, mainly in the areas of science and technology. Located along the Seine, its geometrical steel and glass figure stands out like a pivotal landmark. On the north side, the curving facade becomes the mirror (in the true sense of the word) of historical Paris stretched across the river through a silk-screened, stylized reproduction of the facing skyline. On the south side, IMA opens onto a plaza bridging the gap between the building and the contemporary urban grid of the Jussieu University designed in the mid-1960s. There, a famous screen composed of thousands of light-sensitive sun-control diaphragms reinterprets the pattern of the Arab *moucharabieh*, a traditional turned-wood latticework. The theme of light was also a driving force and a common denominator when it came to dealing with IMA's inner spaces, with the blurred outlines, superimpositions, reflections, and shadows. The building may be deplored by some for the inadequate smallness of certain spaces (the entrance atrium in particular makes many a visitor feel claustrophobic), as well as for the hopeless apathy of the techno-facade, which seems never to have worked properly, yet it remains a great work of architecture, nonetheless. **YN**

Aalto Theater (1988)

Architects Alvar Aalto, Elissa Aalto   **Location** Essen, Germany   **Style** Modernist   **Materials** Concrete, granite, aluminum

Alvar Aalto (1898–1976) absorbed the teachings of southern European Modernism and adapted them to create a much-admired, and uniquely Finnish, branch of the movement. What makes his architecture so special is its rich, complex form, and the way in which it engages with nature. In 1959, when Aalto won the competition to design a new opera house for Essen, celebrated works such as the Paimio Sanatorium and the Viipuri Library were already behind him. The music theaters of this later part of his career—the Finlandia Hall in Helsinki and the Essen opera house—display many of the features for which he is famous. At Essen, the irregularly shaped building rises up like a rock face, its hard-edged southwestern elevations in contrast to the rippling curves of its northeast side. Inside, the circulation areas are shaped around the freeform bulk of the auditorium, which is designed never to feel empty. Aalto died before work could begin on the site,

so his widow, architect Elissa Aalto (1922–94), completed the building. She was able to avoid the problems encountered with certain finishes at the Finlandia Hall. White Carrara marble was found to be susceptible to pollution, so the exterior of the building is finished in granite. Inside the auditorium, the planned wood-paneled walls were ruled out as a fire risk, and are instead finished in warped aluminum. The Essen opera house, completed twelve years after Aalto's death, is now known as the Aalto Theater. **MF**

> *"… it is still the architect's duty to attempt to humanize the age of machines."*
>
> Alvar Aalto, architect

Parliament House (1988)

Architects Mitchell/Giurgola Architects   **Location** Canberra, Australia
Style Postmodernist   **Materials** Concrete, marble, steel

Parliament House is situated atop Capital Hill in Australia's capital city. It was commissioned in 1978 to supersede, not replace, the original Parliament House of 1927. It was completed for the 200th anniversary of European settlement in Australia in 1988. Its most striking feature is its low profile. The main contour of Capital Hill is carried over the top of the structure, vegetation and all, giving the impression of its being partially underground. The building is capped by a pyramid-shaped, 266-foot high (81 m), 220-tons, stainless-steel flagpole, visible throughout the city.

Principal architect, Romaldo Giurgola (*b.* 1920), had already designed several public and commercial buildings in the United States and South America. When this design was unveiled, however, it was criticized as failing to address culturally and architecturally specific issues. For instance, the Neoclassical lines, intended to echo the original Parliament House, were considered too conservative. Despite this, Parliament House is a well-conceived building, based on a simple yet effective division of space around two principal axes, highlighting the division between the upper and lower chambers of government. Visitors are surrounded by visions of Australia—a reminder that the building is owned by the people. Views take in the Brindabella Ranges to the west and the hills beyond Queanbeyan to the east. For his efforts, Giurgola received the Royal Australian Institute of Architects Gold Medal, and was made an Officer in the Order of Australia. **GAB**

◹ The grass-roofed building was constructed on top of the hill to maintain the hill's shape.

◁ Australia's most expensive building to date has an aura of otherworldliness when lit up at night.

Athan House (1988)

Architects Maggie Edmond, Peter Corrigan **Location** Monbulk,
Australia **Style** Postmodernist **Materials** Brick, timber, steel, glass

When most people think of Australian architecture,
the first image that comes to mind is Sydney Opera
House. Much lower on the list, if at all, are domestic
buildings. Yet it is there that one finds the most unique
and representative characteristics of Australian
architecture. Built in the outer-eastern, semirural
suburb of Monbulk, Athan House by Melbourne-
based firm Edmond & Corrigan is one of the newer
and most distinctive additions to this tradition.

Generally, the house is an attempt to capture the
richness and diversity of Melbourne's urban and

> ## "I've always been an unabashed fan of the suburbs. . . . I see them as a source of fabulous energy."
>
> Peter Corrigan, architect

suburban landscape. In both form and planning it is
complex and scenographic, using materials such as
brick and timber in a collagelike manner to critically
engage with and challenge one's perceptions.

The architects, Maggie Edmond and Peter
Corrigan, formed their architectural partnership in
1975. Before this, Corrigan had spent several years in
the United States studying environmental design at
Yale University. It was there that he came under the
influence of Postmodernist luminaries, including
Robert Venturi, Denise Scott Brown, and Charles
Moore. When completed, Athan House was critically
acclaimed, receiving the Royal Australian institute of
Architects Bronze Medal for Outstanding Architecture
in 1989 and is considered a landmark of late-twentieth-
century Australian architecture. **GAB**

Church on the Water (1988)

Architects Tadao Ando & Associates **Location** Tomamu, Hokkaido,
Japan **Style** Minimalist **Material** Reinforced concrete

As with many of Tadao Ando's (b. 1941) structures, the
power of the Church on the Water lies in its simple
geometric form—in this case two interlocking cubic
volumes. One of Ando's early examples of spiritual
architecture, it demonstrates his belief that religious
buildings should be at one with nature. Located in the
northernmost and coldest area of Japan, it is
surrounded by woodland and sits alongside a shallow
artificial reflecting pool created by diverting a nearby
stream. Here, the seasons are strongly differentiated: a
union of weather, water, sky, trees, and tranquility.

Embarking on a "religious journey," visitors
approach the entrance circuitously around an
L-shaped wall that runs around the back of the
building. Enhancing expectation, the lake is hidden
from view but the contemplative sound of water can
be heard. Ascending counter-clockwise, visitors reach
the smaller of the two volumes, a glass box with views
over the lake to the mountains beyond. Four
monolithic crosses, which just miss touching, are
arranged in an unusual square formulation, hinting yet
subverting an obvious Christian message. Descending
to the main chapel, worshippers are surrounded by
three exposed concrete walls their eyes drawn to the
forth, which is glazed and looks onto the pool. Based
on the idea of the Japanese shoji screen the altar wall
can be slid open uniting the interior with the exterior
and the immediate environment. When closed a
cruciform mullion echoes the large iron cross that rises
from the lake.

Unlike most contemporary architects Ando did
not receive any formal architectural training. Together
with his well-received Church of the Light, the Church
on the Water was the project that brought Ando
international fame. **JH**

Street-Porter House (1988)

Architect Piers Gough **Location** London, England **Style** Postmodernist **Materials** Brick, concrete, glazed tiles

In the 1980s, Janet Street-Porter, a TV producer famous for her radical shows, commissioned this house from Piers Gough (*b.* 1946), a friend from her student days. Gough went on to become a founding partner of CZWG, a practice that brought Pop Art sensibilities to architecture. Both the client and the architect of this house were interested in challenging conventional ideas of good taste, and in making decoration an integral part of the design.

The site of the house occupies an entire street corner in the historic Clerkenwell district of London, between the financial center of the city in the east and the fashionable West End. The choice of what was a run-down location seemed rather eccentric at the time, but the area has since become one of the most fashionable parts of the city.

The four-story house uses colored bricks to give the impression of light and shade on the facade. Inside, the concrete floors are left bare and the walls are finished with pigmented plaster. The upside-down plan has a guest bedroom on the ground floor, master bedroom and bathroom on the middle floor, and living room and kitchen on the top floor. The separate, rooftop studio, with high ceiling and huge triangular window, is accessed by an outside staircase.

The most exuberant features of the design of the house, which plays on the form of the standard London row house, are the soaring, asymmetrical, blue-tiled roof and the interlocking diamond-shaped windows. The composition of the Street-Porter house combines the joy of Art Deco with the kitschy, fun-loving hedonism that defined the Thatcher decade. **MF**

◥ Decoration is built into the house in a very literal way, through the use of contrasting bricks.

◰ In a highly decorative facade, the living space balcony stands out with a massive diamond window.

United Airlines Terminal, O'Hare Airport (1988)

Architect Helmut Jahn   **Location** Chicago, Illinois, USA   **Style** Postmodernist with Victorian references   **Materials** Steel, glass

An airport terminal is subject to perhaps more change and fluctuation than any other commercial structure; they need to be highly flexible in regard to the utilization of their space. Since the Deregulation Act was passed in the United States in 1978—and 1986 in the United Kingdom—airfares have dropped substantially and air travel has increased dramatically. In addition, airplane designs have become larger, and thus necessitate more ground space and more efficient passenger handling facilities.

These were pertinent considerations in the planning of the United Airlines Terminal Building at O'Hare Airport. The innovative design came from German-born architect Helmut Jahn (*b.* 1940). The finished design is simple in the basic layout, and incorporates two long, high-capacity buildings that run parallel, and are connected with a pedestrian corridor with a moving walkway and pulsating sound-and-light sculpture. The first building acts as a landside and airside terminal with ticketing and passenger check-in facilities on the upper story, and baggage claim on the lower story. The second building is mainly for enplaning and deplaning passengers. Both buildings have towering barrel-vaulted ceilings, and are constructed with an exposed steel framework and glass that echoes nineteenth-century railway stations.

This sense of historic respect is further emphasized inside through Jahn's use of simple geometric details and clean, classical lines. This, combined with its modern, almost futuristic elements, make the United Airlines Terminal one of the most interesting airport buildings of the twentieth century. **TP**

↗ Passengers using the long moving walkways are stimulated by sound-and-light sculpture overhead.

⇥ The steel columns and high vault ceiling mimic rail termini of the nineteenth century.

Rooftop Remodeling (1988)

Architect Coop Himmelb(l)au **Location** Vienna, Austria
Style Deconstructivist **Materials** Glass, steel

Wolf D. Prix (b. 1942) and Helmut Swiczinsky (b. 1944) founded Coop Himmelb(l)au in 1968. This is the project that put the Vienna-based architects on the architectural Deconstructivist map.

The relatively small-scale commission—an office extension brief—came from Schuppich, Sporn, and Winischhofer. Among the clients' requirements was a focus on the central meeting room and the creation of several smaller office units adjacent to this main space. With their construction site 69 feet (21 m) above busy street level, Prix and Swiczinsky decided to go for a

> *"Architecture should be … fiery, smooth, hard, angular, alluring, repelling, wet, dry, throbbing."*
>
> Coop Himmelb(l)au, architectural practice

radical solution that would make the rooftop space distinctive and unique. The glass-and-steel structure is bare of decoration or color, and resembles a wedge-filled gap, split open by an explosion on the conventional rooftop line of the otherwise Neo-Classical building. The fragmented form is visible from the street and creates an amazingly lit and spacious interior. Coop Himmelb(l)au's Rooftop Remodeling took them to the Museum of Modern Art's 1988 *Deconstructivist Architecture* exhibition in New York.

They have since won several awards creating hard-to-miss landmarks, while continuing to work on urbanism and art projects. Their strong architectural identity, expressed through this "signature" project, made them one of the most critically acclaimed design practices of the twentieth century. **ES**

Basilica of Our Lady of Peace (1989)

Architect Pierre Fakhoury **Location** Yamoussoukro, Ivory Coast
Style Renaissance pastiche **Materials** Concrete, steel, marble

The largest church in the world, the Basilica of Our Lady of Peace was intentionally modeled on St. Peter's in Rome. The work of Lebanese-Ivorian-French architect, Pierre Fakhoury, it can seat 7,000 with room for a further 11,000 standing. It is faced with Italian marble and contains an incredible 75,348 square feet (7,000 sq m) of stained-glass windows from France.

The church was commissioned by the late President of the Ivory Coast, Félix Humphoët–Boigny, who was born in Yamoussoukro, then a small village of under 500 people. In 1983 he declared it the new capital city and its population has grown to more than 200,000. Pope John Paul II laid the cornerstone in 1985 and consecrated the church after its completion. Indeed the church was built as a personal gift by Humphoët–Boigny to the Pope and the Catholic Church: a private papal villa was also built as part of the complex. The Pope made it a condition of his participating in the consecration that a hospital should be built nearby and he laid the foundation stone: this remains unbuilt.

The basilica (not a cathedral) is clearly dedicated to the memory of one man: the figure of Humphoët–Boigny is represented, like a thirteenth disciple, adjacent to the stained-glass images of Jesus and the Twelve Apostles. Its construction must be seen in the context of the Civil War, as an unequivocal demonstration of the president's personal power and authority. Its cost allegedly doubled the Ivory Coast's national debt—and that in a country where only fifteen percent of the population is Catholic. Although an excessive whim of a near-dictator, its surreal conflation of two key elements of St. Peter's in Rome—Michelangelo's dome and Bernini's colonnade—transported to an African plain, is extraordinary. **RGW**

Pyramide,
Le Grand Louvre (1989)

Architect I. M. Pei   **Location** Paris, France   **Style** High Tech, Modernist
Materials Steel, glass, reinforced concrete, stone

One of President Mitterrand's "Grands Projets," the Pyramide was part of a much-needed rationalization of France's greatest museum. Since the early nineteenth century, the sprawling Palais du Louvre has housed the extensive highlights of the state collection of antiquities and fine and decorative arts. By the 1980s, the entrance spaces were inadequate for the yearly millions of visitors, endless corridors left tourists exhausted and lost, and the curatorial facilities were appalling. Digging out the larger courtyard gave a generous foyer, the wings of the museum were united, and space was created for facilities and shops. The appointment of I. M. Pei (b. 1917), a Chinese-born American, rather than a French architect was regarded as shocking—perhaps explaining why it was the only Grand Projet not to receive an architectural award.

The great glass pyramid over the foyer solves all the problems of a subterranean entrance: it draws visitors in by its striking shape and, with the three smaller flanking pyramids, lights the space below. The pyramids, together with fountains and pools, are unequivocally modern, but also hold echoes of French garden planning, which relate them to their palatial context. The fine Egyptian collection of the museum makes the pyramid an especially resonant shape.

Initially disliked by many as inappropriately modern, the Pyramide is now widely loved. Inside, do not miss the superb interior space: the pyramid soars high above, and a great slab of perfect concrete stands on the slenderest of stone columns. **BWC**

↗ Initial controversy surrounded the merger of High Tech and Classical architectural styles at this site.

→ Illuminated by night, the Pyramide takes on an extremely delicate, latticelike appearance.

Opéra de la Bastille (1989)

Architect Carlos Ott **Location** Paris, France **Style** Postmodernist **Materials** Glass, stainless steel, limestone

The Opéra de la Bastille was developed for new creative concepts and technical innovation, as opposed to the illusionistic bourgeois theater epitomized by the layers of *trompe l'oeil* painted backcloths of the Opéra Garnier and earlier theaters. The idea of a "people's opera" is reinforced by the introduction of a subway station and commercial activities into the precincts of the building. Designed by Canadian-Uruguayan architect Carlos Ott (*b.* 1946), it is one of the *grand projets* masterminded by François Mitterrand to symbolize France's central role in art, politics, and the world economy. Conceived as a popular venue for modern classical music and opera, it replaced the Opéra Garnier, now used for ballet, as the home of the Opéra National de Paris. It offers the facilities to create three-dimensional sets, with five revolving stages, rehearsal areas, and costume and prop workshops. It has 2,716 acoustically consistent seats, each having an unrestricted view of the stage. The design was intended to present an iconic formal simplicity and to create an open and democratic invitation to enter the theater. This lack of *hauteur* is marked by the anonymous, transparent, and featureless facades, black granite floors, and the application of identical square limestone blocks for the exterior and the interior. Not everyone is convinced, however. One Parisian newspaper sniffed that it was "The Triumph of Banality." **JEH**

"This opera house is . . . sober. You don't have decoration inside the hall. The decor is on the stage."

Carlos Ott, architect

Grand Union Canal Terrace (1989)

Architect Nicholas Grimshaw   **Location** London, England   **Style** High Tech   **Materials** Reinforced concrete, aluminum, glass

Nicholas Grimshaw (b. 1939) was one of the leading exponents of the High Tech school of architecture that emerged in Britain in the 1970s and 1980s. This row of ten houses in north London was built as part of a mixed-use development with a large supermarket at its center. On the rear elevations to the south, the houses confront the store parking lot with blank, corrugated metal walls to block out the noise and pollution. On the front elevations to the north, however, they cantilever out and open up with large windows, doors, and balconies to make the most of their position overlooking the Grand Union Canal. Outside, the houses are clad in aluminum panels punched with windows like those in an Airstream trailer. The overall impression is of attempting to conform to Le Corbusier's famous diktat that a house should be "a machine for living in." Inside, however, the dwellings are more conventional, with wooden floors and plastered walls. In plan, they are arranged with a bedroom and bathroom on the ground floor, a double-height kitchen and living room on the middle floor, and a further two bedrooms and bathrooms on the top floor. The double-height window in the living room is raised by an electric motor—a reference to automobile technology—and the rooms on the top floor have skylights to let in as much light as possible. Ladders are provided to give access to boats moored alongside on the canal. **MF**

> *"A row of houses faced in what appear to be the recycled parts of airplanes."*
>
> Jones, Woodward, *The Architecture of London* (2000)

Mirage Casino (1989)

Architect Private design team   **Location** Las Vegas, Nevada, USA
Style Architectural fantasy   **Materials** Concrete, gold-tinted glass

Architecture critics are traditionally sniffy when it comes to super-casinos; yet the Mirage, owned by Steve Wynn, single-handedly revived the Las Vegas strip when it opened in 1989.

The thirty-story, 3,049-room, three-winged resort brought luxury and scale to a city that had become down at its heels. Costing $630 million, it was $500 million more expensive than any other hotel then built in Vegas. To meet its overheads, it needed to clear $1 million a day. Few thought it would succeed, yet during its first business year it reported a $200 million

> *"What [Steve Wynn] did was take another view of entertainment and how the city can grow."*
>
> Denise Scott Brown, urban planner and architect

profit. More significantly, it spawned a new Las Vegas. Its tropical theme famously included a huge, intermittently erupting volcano, with a 20,000-gallon aquarium and pseudo-equatorial glade featured within the entrance foyers. The gaming room itself was full of bronze and gold fixtures and fittings.

Las Vegas has proved an irresistible laboratory for architectural theorists. Robert Venturi and Denise Scott Brown divided architecture into categories: "ducks," buildings resembling a symbolic form; and "decorated sheds," where the design is informed purely by its use and disguised by decoration such as neon lighting. The Mirage was the strip's first "duck" and blazed a trail that other casino owners had little choice but to follow. Contemporary Vegas was kick-started by the Mirage. **GG**

Rungnado Stadium (1989)

Architect Unknown   **Location** Rungna Island, Pyongyang, North Korea
Style Modernist   **Material** Reinforced concrete

The Rungnado Stadium, built on North Korea's Taedong River is also known as the May Day Stadium. It is the world's largest stadium and the most striking thing about it is its dimensions. It stands eight stories high, contains 150,000 seats, and its total floor area covers 2,228,129 square feet (207,000 sq m).

The stadium was erected following neighboring South Korea's success in the 1988 Olympic Games. It was built to demonstrate North Korea's own sporting prowess. Since its completion, it has also become the venue for national celebrations.

The stadium's oval shape is composed of sixteen concrete arches. They resemble an open parachute and were created to be evocative of a lotus blossom floating on the Taedong. The arches also represent the waving scarves and flags used during Pyongyang's commemorative shows. Despite its oversized dimensions, the structure has an elegance unusual in North Korean official architecture, making strong reference to works of famous Western architects such as Pier Luigi Nervi and Eero Saarinen. The imposing stadium, with its 197-foot-long (60 m) canopy, is an entire sports village with a number of excellent facilities. Viewed from across the water, Rungnado looks like a UFO that has somehow landed on Rungna Island by chance.

The stadium has hosted friendly soccer games—most notably between North and South Korea—as well as the famous commemorative show for Kim Jong-Il's sixtieth anniversary. In 1999, it also achieved global status when it celebrated the visit of U.S. Secretary of State, Madeleine Albright. There are, however, queries to be addressed about how the stadium should be used—as very few true sporting events seem to take place here. **MHF**

Canadian Centre
for Architecture (1989)

Architect Peter Rose, Phyllis Lambert, Erol Argun, Melvin Charney   **Location** Montreal, Canada   **Style** Modernist
Materials Trenton limestone, anodized aluminum, reinforced concrete frame and flat slab structure, steel roof trusses

From the beginning, a building designed specifically to house the Canadian Centre for Architecture (CCA) was integral to the concept of establishing an architectural research center and museum. The most basic need was to provide a place that was large enough to store a growing collection of books, prints, drawings, and photographs, and to make them accessible. Since there was no model for such an institution there was no precedent for such a building.

Identity of place is essential for an institution whose mission is to engage the public in discourse, so the architects sought to create a contemporary building that would relate to the history and culture of the city. The new building also needed to reknit the urban tissue of an area made derelict by highway construction in the 1960s—it had to add to, and heighten, the architecture of its neighborhood.

The CCA building and gardens have become icons of Montreal. The building and wings, built around the historically listed Shaughnessy House (1874), relate to architecture past and present through their scale, siting, and the use of Montreal's traditional gray limestone juxtaposed with structural aluminum. This dialectic of old and new—rusticated old mansion and smooth ashlar new museum—is transposed to the interior, where aluminum, limestone, maple, and black granite from the Lac-Saint-Jean region of Quebec are all in evidence. The building and gardens resonate with how the past informs the present, and the present informs the future. **PL**

↗ The contemporary steel structures frame the entrance to the architecture museum.

⤷ The Shaughnessy House is one of the few nineteenth-century houses in Montréal open to the public.

Wexner Center for the Visual Arts (1989)

Architect Peter Eisenman   **Location** Columbus, Ohio, USA   **Style** Deconstructivist   **Materials** Steel, concrete, glass

The Wexner Arts Center was the first major public commission of architect and theorist Peter Eisenman (b. 1932), and his first large-scale project after a series of private residences that confirmed his radical reputation. Eisenman's design was created in collaboration with Richard Trott and landscape architect Laurie Olin, who created the amazing landscaped gardens to the building's north and west.

Interior and exterior prove to be both spacious and cramped, structured and yet confusingly disorientating. Wide passages, high-ceilinged rooms, and large openings derive from the process of superimposing two grids—the university's and the city's—a symbolic move to bring the university back into the heart of the town, incorporating elements from the site's past within the new structure. This is a technique that Eisenman was to use in numerous future projects. The east-west city grid axis dominates the building's plan, also generating both a direct entry into the center and a new pedestrian path leading to the campus. The glass-enclosed circulation spine is placed perpendicularly to the main axis, running from north to south and connecting the older buildings with the minimum of intervention.

The center's facilities include galleries, a theater, a production studio for visual arts, a bookshop, and a café. Eisenman's entry unanimously won the competition for the center's design—the jury was charmed by the boldness of his proposal. Eisenman's solution made the perfect link between the past and future of the campus location, and created a visually strong landmark. **ES**

↖ A white metal grid running along the building's east side suggests the impermanence of scaffolding.

← The towers on the south side recall a historic campus building known as the "Gymnasium" or "Armoury."

Spiral Apartment House (1989)

Architect Zvi Hecker **Location** Ramat Gan, Israel **Style** Expressionist **Materials** Stone, concrete, corrugated metal

From the early 1960s, Zvi Hecker (*b.* 1931) studied the spiral as an archetypal form, in nature and in Arabic architecture. He obsessively analyzed the staircases of minarets, which would lead inward and outward, being passages and places to sojourn at the same time. In the Spiral Apartment House each fan-shaped story of the eight-story building, thus every apartment, is stacked upon the other, while being rotated at 22.5 degrees. This created many open terraces, and a spiral staircase form enlarged to the size of a building. Hecker did not provide a supporting solid core at the center of the spiral, but an open courtyard.

Construction started with little more than the architect's sketches—Hecker wanted to incorporate spontaneous design decisions, turning the building process into a sculptor's work. One idea, that of creating inlays of stones and fragments of mirrors on the main structure of raw concrete, only emerged while working on site. The building is therefore exactly what it appears: the result of an intense process with the architect spending years on site (he lived in a building next door, the Dubiner Apartment House (1963), which he had designed with his mentors Alfred Neumann and Elder Sharon.

The two apartment blocks reveal how Hecker developed his ideas over thirty years They have the same staggered appearance, and in each case the arrangements of interior rooms, constructive elements, courtyard, and terraces are dictated by the basic geometry. But while the older building is a basic rectangular shape, the newer one has the basic shape of a spiral, with a spiral's infinite complexity. **FH**

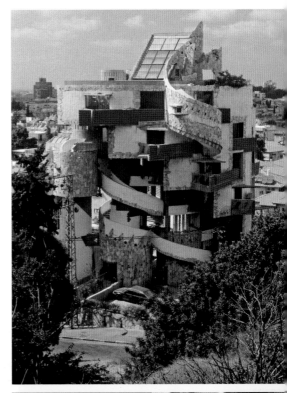

↗ Hecker's spiral-based structure offered scope for features that explored the spiral shape further.

→ Viewed from below, the apartments rotate in the manner of a stone spiral staicase.

Ice Hotel (1989)

Architects Continuously rebuilt by designers and architects   **Location** Jukkäsjarvi, Sweden   **Style** Forever changing   **Materials** Water, snow, ice

"I am drawn to explore ... refraction and reflection of light, crystalline structure, massivity, fragility ..."

Mark Szulgit, architect

⬆ The Ice Chapel, freshly built each year, provides a unique venue for weddings and christenings.

➡ The breathtaking entrance to the hotel provides an icy welcome for visitors to the subzero environment.

The culture of building with snow and ice belongs to the Sami and Inuit people. Today, in Jukkäsjarvi, 124 miles (199 km) north of the Arctic Circle, artists and architects from all over the world adapt this way of building. Inspired by the temporary conditions, permanence of architecture is challenged in an utmost way, forcing the rethinking of working with changing materials.

The Ice Hotel took its first shape in the autumn of 1989. The hotel consists of approximately sixty rooms, an ice bar, a cinema with a screen of ice, a restaurant, and a church. The main doors are clad with reindeer skin, and when entering the main lobby, the guest sees a spectacular ice chandelier—the only item from the hotel that is kept and reused every year. The atmosphere inside is calm and quiet, as if sound itself had been frozen. The hotel is built entirely from snow and sculpted blocks of ice, all sprung from the pure Torne River, which travels about 370 miles (595 km) through Lapland. Due to the fact that the ice and snow melt during the spring, the hotel is rebuilt every autumn when the temperatures once again allow for frozen building materials, creating a hotel season that lasts from December to March. Each autumn, different artists and architects are invited to design all aspects of the hotel making every season a unique experience to returning guests.

The bedrooms have an average temperature of about minus 45 Fahrenheit (-42 °C) whereas the thermometer may show minus 86 Fahrenheit (-65 °C) outside. The guests sleep in thermal sleeping bags on reindeer skins on a bed of snow and ice. This building is submitted to nature, and the architects only borrow the material that nature takes back every year. When the Ice Hotel is not standing as a solid structure, it flows with the Torne River accumulating crystal clear life for the following season. **SML**

San Nicola Stadium (1990)

Architect Renzo Piano Building Workshop **Location** Bari, Italy **Style** High Tech **Material** Concrete

San Nicola Stadium by Renzo Piano (*b.* 1937) rises majestically on an artificial plateau, surrounded by an inner ring of parking lots and an outer ring of olive groves. The stadium's gleaming, perforated form suggests a cross between a Greek temple and a marooned spacecraft. Built on the northern edge of Bari as part of a national program for urban improvement during "Italia90"—when Italy hosted the international soccer championship—it was one of the few projects to be finished on time and without scandal. Its undulating profile looks somewhat like a roller coaster, thrusting up on the short sides and dropping down toward the center. The concrete structure is lifted off the ground, leaving an unusual gap between the elevated bleachers and the lower ring of seats that steps down to the elliptical playing field. Piano and his creative engineer, Peter Rice, conceived of the upper seating sections as an opening flower with a series of twenty-six radial "petals." Each petal was made of ten hollow, banana-shaped beams that were precast and then fused together into a single piece that cantilevers over four poured-in-place pylons. The switchback stairs to the upper sections occupy the voids between the petals. In addition, the stadium is architectural policing at its most inspired: the gaps between the sections and between the lower and upper seats make it virtually impossible for warring fans to attack each other. **RI**

"Even with our most iconic works like the stadium ... we are trying to work with the immaterial."

Renzo Piano, architect

Joshua Tree Monument (1990)

Architect Josh Schweitzer   **Location** Joshua Tree, California, USA   **Style** Postmodernist   **Materials** Concrete, redwood

Josh Schweitzer's "monument" is aptly named, for although it is a domestic dwelling, in appearance it is more of a monolith, and an unequivocal statement of the architect's philosophy. After working for various architectural firms, he established Schweitzer BMI, with which he has been involved in numerous residential and commercial projects. He also designs furniture, fixtures, and fittings. The monument was built by the architect as a retreat for himself and five friends, and is located just outside the Joshua Tree National Park. It is a strange area of rugged and barren beauty, a high desert peppered with jagged rock, spiky yucca plants, cacti, and Joshua trees. The house sits amid boulders, its hard geometric form reiterating the unrelenting sharpness of the immediate environment, and its bold colors reflecting the drama of desert life. Schweitzer based the structure around a series of connecting blocks, each containing specific areas for living. In place of conventional windows, irregular holes punched through the external shell allow light to flood into the interior. The holes create geometric patterns inside and afford "snapshot" views of the land or sky. The interior is as simple in form as the exterior, with its colors diluted versions of those of the exterior. The ideology of the building—that of interior and exterior spaces being continuations of each other, and of color and spatial form obliterating the need for historical precedent—is resonant. **TP**

"I want buildings to have an overwhelming presence both inside and out ..."

Josh Schweitzer, architect

Church of the Holy Spirit (1990)

Architect Imre Makovecz **Location** Paks, Hungary
Style Vernacular **Material** Wood

The Hungarian architect Imre Makovecz (b. 1935) has created an organic architecture using timber and skilled carpentry. His style of architecture is partly rooted in central European folk timberwork but extended and manipulated into newer and more spiritually expressive shapes. Makovecz's Church of the Holy Spirit in Paks exemplifies this style.

The plan is based on the ancient S symbol, a basic symbol in Hungarian folk art. Two symmetrically placed S symbols lie along the east-west axis. They represent the dynamic opposites of light/dark, male/

"[Imre] Makovecz says that his mission is to reconcile Heaven with Earth."

Jonathan Glancey, architecture critic

---

female, sun/moon, or yin/yang. The dichotomous theme continues externally in the detached bell tower. This has three, very slender spires, capped in gold. The uppermost carries a cross; the lower spires are topped with a sun and a crescent moon. On either side of the tower are two figures: the angels of lightness and darkness.

The whole of the church is clad in dark-stained wood tiles, pierced by lighter, polished timber window frames and doors. The central porch is a tall, womblike arch, and the altar is wrapped within an open wooden cone, illuminated by almost transcendent top lighting from a stained-glass ceiling. The effect is mysterious and almost pagan. Makovecz appears to be seeking to recreate the spiritual intensity of the pagan Hungarian tribes who converted to Christianity. **ATB**

Demas Nwoko's House (1990)

Architect Demas Nwoko **Location** Idumuje Ugboko, Delta State, Nigeria
Style Modernist **Materials** Concrete, laterite block

The architect Demas Nwoko (b. 1935) trained as a painter and sculptor and was a member of the pre-independence Nigerian avant-garde art group, the Zaria Art Society, otherwise known as the Zaria Rebels.

Demas Nwoko's House is mainly single story with a two-story annex at the western end. The plan is organized as a sequence of courtyards evolved from a hierarchy of use, from service areas to the inhabited quarters. There are three entry possibilities; a formal front portico, an intermediate daily entrance, and a rear service entrance. The service courtyard holds a water cistern and electrical generator and provides a utility surface for domestic work. It is enclosed by a patterned mud wall in traditional earth construction topped with corrugated iron roofing sheets; this opens on to a corridor adjacent to a row of single rooms that wrap around another courtyard and provide accommodation for relatives. At the top of this hierarchy is a courtyard where the family lives.

The walls are built in laterite blocks, a system that utilizes the red earth of the site as a substitute for sand. These walls are left unfinished providing a durable surface that weathers naturally. The central courtyard has a bank of colored glass lights over the dining area, with bedrooms connecting to this central lobby space. Nwoko shies away from a direct inside-outside dialogue, preferring to bounce light into the bedrooms through high-level light shelves, and the entire building is ventilated naturally via low and high level louvers. The annex houses the artist's private quarters and enjoys a completely louvered timber front facade and the generous high ceiling of a peaked roof.

This building represents a careful working of the Zaria manifesto that called for the blending of new and old in an authentic new style. **GO**

Haas House (1990)

Architect Hans Hollein **Location** Vienna, Austria **Style** Postmodernist
Materials Concrete, stone, glass

Like the Museum Moderner Kunst and the Leopold Museum built in 2001 alongside the former King's Stables off Vienna's Ringstrasse, Hans Hollein's (b. 1934) Haas House is a gesture against the architectural stagnation of the city and a refusal to allow it to become a crumbling museum to the past. Built on the Stephansplatz, the great square that houses the twelfth-century Cathedral of St. Stephen, the Haas House was initially met with resistance from the local citizens. For centuries, the cathedral was the tallest church in the world, and it not only occupies Vienna's geographical heart but its emotional heart, too.

However, Hollein is also a native of Vienna, and it has been his understanding of both the city and its inhabitants that has enabled him to create a contemporary building that sits with the past, while looking toward the future. The most immediately striking features of the Haas House, an office building that also houses restaurants and shops, are the curved facade and the architect's use of glass. At street level the potentially stark lines of Postmodernity are relieved by asymmetry, and with jutting stone-clad shapes.

Hollein won his first commission in his hometown in 1965, the Retti Candle Shop. The 12-feet-wide (4 m) project won the $25,000 Reynolds Memorial Award, one of the few times that the award has gone to a work costing less than the prize itself. See the Haas House from the Stephansplatz, and from its penthouse restaurant, where it is possible to get over the price of the food by marveling at the wonderful views. **GT**

↗ Haas House reflects the cathedral and refracts it back into the square from different angles.

→ The interior of the building was designed with great attention to detail and light.

Bank of
China Tower (1990)

Architect I. M. Pei **Location** Hong Kong, China **Style** High Tech
Materials Steel, concrete, glass

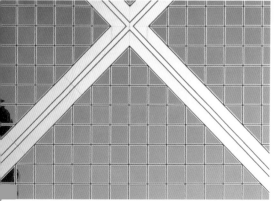

Hong Kong is famous for its tall buildings, battling each other for space on the city's crowded skyline. One of the most graceful and distinctive of these is the Bank of China Tower by I. M. Pei (*b.* 1917).

The commercial office building is immediately striking, thanks to the origami-like repeated cross-bracing and structural expression on its exterior. The form—four asymmetrical vertical elements falling away until the tallest single triangular prism remains— is said to mimic bamboo shoots, symbolizing livelihood and prosperity. The skyscraper is practical as well as aesthetically pleasing. Step-backs on the 1,210-feet-high (369 m), 72-floor tower help counteract high winds caused by typhoons. At the corners are five steel columns onto which the weight is transferred via the triangular frameworks. Inside is an imposing banking hall and 1.4 million square feet (130,000 m sq) of office space.

Ieoh Ming Pei is a Chinese-born American noted for tall buildings and a preoccupation with the triangular form, such as his extension to the National Gallery in Washington, D.C., and the pyramid at the Louvre in Paris. The buildings he designs, with his firm Pei Cobb Freed & Partners, tend to be clad in glass and loosely related to the High Tech movement.

The Bank of China was once the tallest building outside America. It should be visited not only to take advantage of its views over the city, but to see a bold, characterful expression of prosperity, writ large, with verve and drama. **DT**

↖ Pei is renowned for designing buildings on a large scale, frequently using glass and steel.

← One of the problems Pei had to contend with was to ensure his skyscraper could withstand typhoons.

La Grande Arche de la Défense (1990)

Architects Johann Otto von Spreckelsen, Paul Andreu   **Location** Paris, France   **Style** Modernist   **Materials** Concrete, granite, marble

La Grande Arche de la Défense, also known as La Grande Arche de l'Humanité, is an open cube and terminating landmark on the "Grand Ax" of Paris. The renovation of the axis was part of a series of modern cultural monuments in commemoration of the 200th anniversary of the French Revolution, in 1989.

Danish architect Johann Otto von Spreckelsen's (1929–87) scheme was chosen for its "purity and strength" and was based on simple geometrical figures. When von Spreckelsen retired from the project, it was completed by Paul Andreu (b. 1938).

"Only a grand architectural gesture can do justice to La Défense."

Jack Lang, French politician

The modern triumphal squared arch is the centerpiece of La Défense—a futuristic complex of fifty office towers. It is a prestressed concrete structure housing a 35-story office building. It rises 360 feet (110 m), faced in glass, granite, and white Carrara marble. It sits in a 328-feet-diameter (100 m) square approached by banks of steps. The building is rotated 6 degrees off center of the Grand Ax. This was not part of the original design, but had to be done so that the piles supporting the structure could avoid the network of tunnels under the site. Visitors can take a glass elevator through the sculptural "clouds" that hang within the arch's interior space, up to a three-story roof and exterior belvedere, which promises a unique perspective on the city, a new vision of the capital, and a window on infinity. **JEH**

The Wall (1990)

Architect Branson Coates   **Location** Tokyo, Japan   **Style** Postmodernist, Pop architecture   **Material** Stone

The perennially radical Nigel Coates first came to the media's attention while he was teaching in 1983. Legend has it that when two visiting professors refused to countenance the fashion-driven approach of his students, Coates simply waited until they had left, and then passed all the students regardless. Obviously feeling empowered, he went on to establish NATO—Narrative Architecture Today to its friends, or Nigel And The Others to its critics—a group of like-minded students, architects, and teachers.

Very much in touch with the contemporary city, Coates developed a style that appeared to be the architectural equivalent of music's New Romantic movement. Predictably it did not find a market in the staid architectural environment of the United Kingdom but, by the mid-1980s, he started to pick up restaurant, retail, and club commissions in Japan. And Tokyo's The Wall is a fine example of his work of that period. Located in a city where high land prices mean that commercial buildings have to start repaying their rent almost instantly, Coates's innate desire to explore pop culture found a natural home.

This bar and restaurant complex was meant to look like an ancient Roman wall that was still under construction and partially hidden behind a cast-iron gas works screen. While it was being built the building was wrapped in a huge hoarding that opined: "The concept for the building revolves around a wall of monumental proportions—a wall which could have been built by the Romans, a wall of stone and giant arches, a wall which could have encircled cities. But unlike the ruins of Rome, this wall is both ancient and still being built." In retrospect The Wall anticipated the theming fad that has gone on to become a staple of both British and U.S. shopping districts. **GG**

Seattle Art Museum (1991)

Architect Venturi, Scott Brown & Associates   **Location** Seattle, Washington, USA   **Style** Postmodernist   **Materials** Stone, glass, steel

Robert Venturi (*b.* 1925) is usually acknowledged mainly for his influential writings and teaching, yet his built work deserves equal recognition. Venturi studied under Louis Kahn in Philadelphia, absorbing Kahn's enlightened attitude to Modernism yet at the same time honing the ability to define his own reaction to the white-box aesthetic of postwar architecture. In his writings, in particular the iconoclastic *Complexity and Contradiction in Architecture*, Venturi argues for a more inclusive, contextual approach to design. His ideas, together with those of his wife Denise Scott Brown, heralded the arrival of what became known as the Postmodern era in architecture. The Seattle Art Museum, although not his most famous work, was the precursor to Venturi's Sainsbury Wing extension of the National Gallery in London and was perhaps a testing ground for his ideas. The facade is split into three horizontal bands: the roofline is formed by a thin band

of glass; the vast body by fluted sandstone; and a colorful collage of pediments and arches of granite and marble with richly colored terra-cotta tiles make up the pedestrian level. Internally, the gallery is split into what the architect describes as a "loft space system," divided into bays of varying sizes so the spaces can be as flexible as necessary to allow for changes in function from exhibitions to one-off sculptures and installations. The building takes up an entire block of the downtown area, and the silhouette of its enormous hammering man sculpture, by Jonathan Borofsky, casts a dramatic shadow over Venturi's plaza. The words "Seattle Art Museum" carved in huge serif font into the stone facade, makes sure the building will always hold its own. Venturi was awarded the Pritzker Prize in 1991, and both he and Denise Scott Brown received the National Medal of Arts in 1992. **BG**

Norwegian Glacier Museum (1991)

Architect Sverre Fehn **Location** Balestrand, Fjærland, Norway **Style** Modernist **Materials** Concrete, glass, wood

Sverre Fehn (b. 1924), the Pritzker Prize winner of 1997, is particularly known and celebrated for his exceptional and inventive use of concrete and wood. When approaching his Norwegian Glacier Museum, visitors are greeted by Fehn's remarkable vision and a memorable exercise in the flexibility of concrete. The museum is situated in a valley below the largest glacier in northern Europe, the Jostedal Glacier, and is deliberately evocative of its icy neighbor. Inside, visitors are encouraged to experiment with snow and ice, and to learn about Jostedal. Resembling its mountainous surroundings, the museum seems to have grown naturally on the site. The windows were created in various sizes and shapes, the exterior walls are slanted and leveled, and a long and narrow canopy—reminiscent of a ski slope—forms the entrance. The building is made up of geometric shapes, including a long rectangular exhibition corridor and a cylindrical lecture hall. All these variations bring a sense of dynamism to the entire structure. Fehn's angles and the steeply sloping canopy at the front echo similar traits of the mountains, and create a wonderful dialogue between concrete and nature. The museum was named the European Museum of the Year in 1994. To build in this part of the world, communicating the story of how glaciers and ice have sculpted the landscape, is a challenge the architect has taken to its utmost. **SML**

"The rocks . . . of the Scandinavian landscape . . . were the inspiration for building in concrete."

Sverre Fehn, architect

Neuendorf House (1991)

Architects John Pawson, Claudio Silvestrin **Location** Mallorca, Spain
Style Minimalist **Materials** Brick, render, crushed rock

Neuendorf House, a holiday home for a German art dealer, is set in a Spanish almond grove with sea views and a backdrop of mountains. It was designed by two arch-minimalists and has a touch of Luis Barragán.

Visitors have to climb a set of elongated steps that run along a sloping, 347-foot-long (106 m) wall, to the tiny front entrance. Clad in a render that has been reddened by crushed local rock, the house is notable for its lack of fenestration. The idea is the windows that do exist frame the space outside. The entrance, meanwhile, is a miniscule slit in the main wall that

> *"The forms themselves could be read as references to local architecture traditions."*
>
> John Welsh, architectural writer

leads into a large clear atrium, described by Pawson as "an empty cube within a cube of massed walls."

Inside, local limestone is used on the floors and to create tables, benches, and basins. In the past Pawson has been quoted as saying "furniture can ruin architecture," although the odd Hans Wegner chair is seemingly acceptable. Bedrooms are on the upper level with a dining room, living room, and office on the ground floor. An extremely photogenic swimming pool sprouts out of the house, into the olive groves and ends as a waterfall. There is also a roof terrace for those who wish to catch the sun. The project was the architects' first commission for a house and, in many respects, is a sign of what was to come for two figures who went on to become key players in the contemporary minimalist movement. **GG**

João de Deus Kindergarten (1991)

Architect Álvaro Siza **Location** Penafiel, Portugal **Style** Portuguese Modernist **Materials** Concrete, sandstone, clay, wood, glass, steel

Álvaro Siza (*b.* 1933) is a leading advocate of the "critical regionalism" movement, a philosophy developed while attending the Oporto school of architecture. Essentially, his works stress the importance of combining local and global architectural trends in a balanced way.

The Siza kindergarten in Penafiel, a quaint city northeast of Oporto, embodies this philosophy. Siza has gained most of his international renown from large-scale, award-winning public projects. This small-scale work, however, demonstrates that his approach

> *"What I appreciate and look for most in architecture is clarity and simplism."*
>
> Álvaro Siza, architect

to architecture has a global application. Materials are used to create a strong tension in the building, such as between the expanses of angular white-washed concrete and the curved traditional terra-cotta roof tiles typical of northern Portugal. Sensitivity to his local environs is a Siza leitmotif.

The kindergarten interiors have been designed as informal modern workshops, as opposed to formal teaching rooms, and somehow manage to retain a rural handicraft feel. The scale of the space was designed from the perspective of the child so that some areas possess very low ceilings, small doors, and narrow corridors. As in all Siza buildings there is ample natural light and the windows and doorways seem to frame views photographically, leading the eye through interior spaces, to the outside world. **MDC**

Nexus II
Residential Block (1991)

Architect Christian de Portzamparc **Location** Fukuoka-shi, Japan
Style Postmodernist **Materials** Concrete, glass, stone

The city of Fukouka was quickly acquiring a name as an oasis of Western architecture in Asia when distinguished Japanese architect Arata Isozaki invited six international designers to participate in a residential complex project. New buildings were to be erected along two major boulevards and around twin towers, 394 feet (120 m) high, to Isozaki's design. The client, the Fukuoka Jisho Company, was setting out to promote a more Western urban lifestyle in Japan.

French architect Christian de Portzamparc (b. 1944) belongs to the Postmodernist movement in architecture that willfully incorporates formal historic gestures. Nexus II residential proposal, consisting of four five-story residential blocks, reflects Portzamparc's interests. Two simple front buildings, facing the boulevard, are clad in white material, and are perforated by a repetitive pattern of L-shaped windows. These symmetrical volumes form a visual frame, which opens into a landscaped courtyard that contains the two remaining blocks. Irregularity and the elevation treatment of the first one resembles volcanic rock while the more distant vertical structure constitutes the composition's focal point. Its restrained mass is raised on columns, freeing up the ground-level area, and it is topped by a circular flat roof canopy.

The arrangement of the volumes of buildings, complemented by carefully designed landscaping, creates the effect of a theater set, where boundaries between reality and fiction are blurred by numerous artificial meanings and signs. **BK**

↗ Both in their structure and their cladding, the towers suggest exposed extrusions of volcanic rock.

→ The use of Classical forms makes the contrasting tower on the left reminiscent of a modern *tempietto*.

Goetz Gallery (1992)

Architects Herzog & de Meuron   **Location** Munich, Germany   **Style** Minimalist   **Materials** Steel, birchwood, glass

Compositionally and technically almost flawless, the Goetz is a little-known early masterpiece and one of the jewels in the crown of internationally acclaimed Swiss masters Jacques Herzog (b. 1950) and Pierre de Meuron (b. 1950). Surrounded by a smattering of fragile birch trees and conifers, the Sammlung Goetz collection of contemporary art is a rich and selective showcase. The gallery's art is perfectly enveloped in a long, wooden box, which is separated from the ground by a substantial milky-white glass band, and crowned by another of equal proportions. This triband division of the facade—which due to a seemingly invisible structure appears to hover above the landscape—achieves a deft lightness of touch typical in much of Herzog and de Meuron's work. The small garden appears not so much reflected into the windows, as frozen in time. Upon entering the site, one is taken aback by both the diminutive size and serene calm of the building. Restricted by height and footprint due to the neighboring residential area, the main gallery is buried in a structurally supportive concrete box in the lower basement level with even daylight falling into the room from ground-floor glazing. The second floor is a secondary exhibition space, its walls expressed by plywood and top-lit by an upper band of glass. The entrance circulation space is restricted to stairs up, stairs down, and a limited amount of administration and library space. Internally, no apparatus and no technical system of light or shading is visible, being skillfully masked behind roughly plastered walls. The building, which was constructed nine years before the architects won the Pritzker Prize, convinces the viewer of its considered design strategy. It is this element that can be so clearly seen in their major-scale works, such as Tate Modern in London. **BG**

House Aktion Poliphile (1992)

Architect Studio Granda **Location** Taunus, Wiesbaden, Germany **Style** Modernist **Materials** Brick, cedar, sandstone

When the Koening family wanted a new home, they organized an international competition entitled, "A house for an ordinary citizen." The brief requested that the thought-provoking fifteenth-century novel *Hypnerotomachia Poliphili* serve as a basis for the design. Margret Hardardottir and Steve Christer of Studio Granda submitted the winning entry. The building is the result of the successful interplay of numerous contrasting values: dark and light, introverted and extroverted, past and present. The plan consists of two volumes, one inspired by *Hypnerotomachia Poliphili*, the other by Roman mythology. The first volume—the House of Delia—is the family house. It is a stylish, rectangular, two-story block, clad in two layers of red cedar wood. It symbolizes contemporary lightness, accentuated by two rows of windows and smaller areas of glazing that puncture the building's envelope to expose its interior.

The simply treated protruding elements—stairs, decks, a roof canopy—complete the building's mass. The guest accommodation—the House of Saturn—represents the darker side of human nature. Smaller in scale, a solid block, finished with bright red render and covered with a double-pitched lead roof, it startles the visitor with its austerity. House Aktion Poliphile effectively unifies seemingly opposing principles of efficient practicality and poetic beauty. This resolution creates a highly original structure. **BK**

> *"Symbolism, beauty, and practicality . . . give meaning to the Aktion Poliphile."*
>
> Francisco Asensio Cerver, architecture writer

Metropolitan Cathedral at Managua (1992)

Architect Ricardo Legorreta   **Location** Managua, Nicaragua   **Style** Modernist   **Materials** Concrete, glass

The bible says it is easier for a camel to pass through an eye of a needle than a rich man to get into heaven. Perhaps this is why an American billionaire part-financed the replacement for Managua's Roman Catholic Cathedral, damaged irreparably in the 1972 earthquake. The donor chose Ricardo Legorreta (b. 1931) and was heavily influential in the design. Legorreta believes in "an interchange of talents" between client and architect, so the presence of a strong-willed client may explain features uncharacteristic of the architect, and why his signature elements are reduced to an understudy role. What we see is no-frills, primal Catholicism. The cathedral is a concrete mass strong-armed into urban edge greenery. It reacts against the ornate traditions of Catholicism, and disadvantages Legorreta's skill at regional and vernacular integration. The main block exterior is offset with vertical and horizontal rectangles that create both the bell tower

and the split block entrance. Spheres offset the boxes, one creating the Sangre de Christo chapel. Pierced by dozens of openings that illuminate the pink stucco interior, it provides sanctuary for a crucifix of veneration housed within a giant glass dome. The main flat roof has three ascending terraces supporting sixty-three "pods," which create ceiling ovoids through which light and air enter. Interior screens and cross-shaped apertures reveal the architect's style and channel air to cool the interior. **DJ**

"We could not just make a donation ... We had to see to it that the cathedral got built."

Joseph E. Davis, director of Mission Chapels

The Ark (1992)

Architect Ralph Erskine **Location** London, England **Style** Postmodernist **Materials** Glass, steel, brick

Traveling along the A4 highway into central London one cannot help but notice the distinctive building set hard up against the Hammersmith overpass. On a tight site, bounded by the ramped overpass on one side and railroad tracks on the other, The Ark by Ralph Erskine (1914–2005) rises up, announcing itself to be an office block unlike any other. British-born Erskine spent most of his working life in his adopted Sweden and was unafraid of challenging British ideas on architecture. Erskine was also imbued with strong ideals about how buildings should look and function, and he emphasized the importance architecture has in a social and environmental context. Erskine had built extensively in Sweden during his career and only came to prominence in Great Britain with the social housing scheme at Byker, Newcastle upon Tyne. He was a bold choice for a commercial project such as The Ark, but he won the developer over with a unique and innovative design. Externally, as its name suggests, the building resembles a large ship, with the covering of shimmering brown glass adding to this effect. Inside is bright and open, top lit with a floor-to-roof atrium. The office space is open plan, with the ship references extending to "decks" on every floor offering communal meeting places. Erskine was always aware of the environmental impact his buildings would have and The Ark is no exception. It was the first building in London to adopt the cooling method of placing radiators in the ceiling, drawing cool air upward, which negated the need for conventional ducting. Erskine built few buildings in the land of his birth, and he only gained the recognition he deserved late in his life. Stylistically it is difficult to compare The Ark to any other building and because of that it must rank as one of Britain's most unusual and interesting structures. **ER**

Fire Station at Vitra (1992)

Architect Zaha Hadid **Location** Weil-am-Rhein, Germany **Style** Deconstructivist **Materials** Concrete, glass

With its zooming, swooping forms the Fire Station at the Vitra Factory—a furniture manufacturer—is dramatically different from most of the other buildings on this site. That the building was commissioned is thanks to the chairman of the company's obsessive interest in modern architecture. The chairman, Alexander von Vegesack, sought out the most interesting young architects to build on his large industrial site, located in a corner of Germany on the border with Switzerland and France. The result is a kind of showroom of modern architecture. The Fire Station was the first freestanding building by the Iranian-born London-based architect Zaha Hadid. Other buildings on the site include a furniture factory by Nicholas Grimshaw, a conference center by Tadao Ando, and an exhibition building by Frank Gehry. Hadid's training, under Peter Cook at the Architectural Association in London, had led her to explore the architectonic qualities inherent in the work of the Russian Suprematist artists of the early twentieth century. She studied the paintings, drawings, and sculpture of Kasimir Malevich and Mikhail Chernikov, produced during the turbulent years of the Russian Revolution and she painstakingly derived her design forms from them. For many years it seemed unlikely the paintings could be translated into built forms at all, but the Fire Station proved it was possible. The building is one long mass, with sharp angled wall planes. At one end is a large, high-roofed space for the fire engines; the other end is two-stories high and includes firemen's accommodation and a roof terrace. As the town of Weil-am-Rhein grew, the municipal authorities felt the need to build a new Fire Station, so the original use of Hadid's building has withered away. It is now used as a storage and display area for part of the permanent collection of the Vitra Museum. **EG**

Kirchner Museum (1992)

Architects Gigon Guyer Architects **Location** Graubünden, Switzerland **Style** Modernist **Materials** Glass, concrete, timber, steel

The Kirchner Museum is a primary example of recent northern Swiss architecture, particularly in the way all aspects of the building collaborate into a consistent, indivisible conceptual unit. This first building from Annette Gigon and Mike Guyer is also one of their most significant. It was built to house permanent displays and temporary exhibitions of the Kirchner Foundation, whose Expressionist collection gravitates around the work of Ernst Ludwig Kirchner (1880–1938). The design responds to the collection's emotional intensity by concentrating on the painterly filtering and reflecting of Alpine light. The outside envelope is a study of the possibilities of glass: translucent for the walls; clear for entrances and windows; broken gravel-like shards on the roof; and glass components mixed into the concrete base. The factory-like outer ensemble of identical glass prisms corresponds on the inside with the four exhibition rooms. These are embedded into a lower volume—part corridor, part extension of the entrance foyer—which brings together the isolated galleries and opens to the outside through wide expanses of clear glass. The typological ambiguity of this connective space is compounded by its disorienting, overall concrete material presence. The project's mastery resides in the contrast established between two kinds of rooms: the ambient, neutral galleries and the shadowy, hard, yet sensual space between them that reaches out into the world. **ID**

"A restrained, quiet architectural language in the interior spaces ... calls for attention."

Annette Gigon, architect

National Library
of Argentina (1992)

Architects Clorindo Testa, Francisco Bullrich, Alicia Cazzaniga de Bullrich
Location Buenos Aires, Argentina **Style** Brutalist **Material** Reinforced concrete

In 1961 a competition was held to design a new building for the National Library of Argentina. The brief held that the site—a public park located on what had been the presidential residence during the Perón government—would maintain its character and the trees had to be conserved. The contract went to Clorindo Testa (*b.* 1923), Francisco Bullrich (*b.* 1932), and Alicia Cazzaniga de Bullrich (1928–68).

The library and public park are at the top of a slope on the edge of an urban development. To accommodate the large-scale program and keep the public space, the building was split in two, half underground and half raised off the ground. The rectangular volume, containing the reading rooms, is raised above a plaza. Hanging below, partially suspended by steel tensors, the administration areas and auditorium make a complex ceiling to the big open plaza and main entrance. The book repositories are underground to protect the books from sunlight and allow for future extensions.

Construction began in 1972 and continued for two decades. Among the building's outstanding elements are great views from the reading rooms, and the exterior public spaces. The heavy concrete structure was combined with smaller building units, access staircases, and ramps to the covered plaza and terraces, that generate enclaves for reading and recreation. This made it possible to provide the monumentality required for this type of project while maintaining the scale of the park. **FA**

↖ Raising the building upward meant that the site retained the atmosphere of an open space.

← Reading rooms occupy the upper floors of the building, with administration offices directly below.

La Congiunta (1992)

Architect Peter Märkli **Location** Giornico, Ticino, Switzerland
Style Modernist **Materials** Concrete, metal, translucent plastic

Peter Märkli (*b.* 1953) is an unconventional Swiss architect whose highly personal approach is grounded in a fascination with the early, exploratory stages of the established artistic periods of Western culture.

La Congiunta is Märkli's alternative to the conventional museum. An eccentric building located outside the remote village of Giornico, it was conceived as a permanent exhibition space for bronze sculptures. It dispenses methodically with the usual paraphernalia of contemporary galleries: shops, cafes, tickets, heating, water. Instead, much like a rural

"[It] reflects on the ways in which sculpture and architecture might define one another."

Marcel Meili, architect and writer

church, the building is accessible by borrowing a key from the village café. Nothing comes between the viewer and the art—except, of course, the building itself. Acutely spare, the concrete enclosure, without insulation, is lit from above through steel-and-plastic clerestories. The building grows from the inside out as a series of three rooms and four smaller cells. The rooms' carefully determined proportions respond precisely to the demands of the sculptures within.

La Congiunta's deceptive simplicity is belied by the palpable finesse of its proportions, its denial of obvious symmetries and the height variations with which each room responds to the physical presence of its collection. The play of cold, flattened light on concrete and bronze, adds to the subtlety with which one is guided through the space. **ID**

Stretto House (1992)

Architect Stephen Holl **Location** Dallas, Texas, USA
Style Postmodernist **Materials** Masonry, concrete, metal, glass

At the heart of Stretto House lies a unique location: a plot incorporating a river that feeds three ponds, each surrounded by a concrete wall that acts as a dam and allows water to flow over the top. "Stretto" is a musical term that refers to the overlapping of one musical phrase with another. The water struck American architect Stephen Holl (*b.* 1947) as fundamentally musical, and his design germinated from this. He was also inspired by a 1936 composition by Hungarian composer Béla Bartók (1881–1945), incorporating overlapping percussion with strings. Holl equated the

"The history of a physical place has meaning and influences the architectural work."

Stephen Holl, architect

heavy percussion with the solidity of the concrete walls and dam, while the lighter string instruments evoked the water. This approach was realized in the building's white expanses of wall, contrasted with the great fluidity of the light metal frame and glazed areas. The house is divided into four parts, each of which comprises two units: the static monumental walls enclosing service areas within and the smooth flowing and curvilinear metal-and-glass framework of the living areas. The interior space continues the sensation of overlapping and movement: floor surfaces transgressing into the next space, curvature of walls and ceiling leading forward. It is an extraordinarily organic house, with the sensation of movement, growth, and contrast creating both an interior and exterior that appeals to every artistic sense. **TP**

IBM Building, Menara Mesiniaga (1992)

Architect Ken Yeang **Location** Selangor, Malaysia **Style** High Tech, Modernist **Materials** Reinforced concrete, aluminum, steel

The construction of the peculiarly skeletal IBM Building, Menara Mesiniaga, signified the inception of a completely new genre of tall buildings—the so-called "bioclimatic skyscraper." Designed by Kenneth Yeang (b. 1948) and Robert Hamzah, it is a fifteen-story, 39,000-square-foot (12,000 sq m) prototype for a climate-responsive structure. Located in Selangor, Malaysia, the building is designed to utilize, as well as protect against, the tropical climate.

Although the building does have some air conditioning, most of the cooling and ventilation works on passive principles—the lifts have been placed on the hottest face of the building to act as a heat buffer, and recessed windows on the east and west provide cooling shade. The ribs circling the structure are also sun shades and much of the building has been built as a "permeable membrane," meaning that the building is never totally enclosed. To allow it to "breathe," there are many areas, such as the spiraling balconies and the sun terraces, that act as transitions between open and closed spaces.

As well as solar panels, the top of the tower has a louvered sunroof to block excess sunlight. This also acts as a wind scoop to naturally ventilate the tower's inner core. The building also features "vertical landscaping," a succession of plantings of vegetation that starts on a ramp encircling half of the base of the building and then spirals its way up and along recessed terraces across the building's face, creating a garden in the sky. These garden terraces also improve the indoor air quality by generating oxygen.

Menara Mesiniaga was the first design project to introduce low-energy sustainability to a high-density urban environment. Its low-maintenance, ecologically friendly design provides a persuasive demonstration that enclosed, boxlike, curtain-wall skyscrapers in equatorial climes may become a thing of the past. **JM**

Montjuic Telecommunications Tower (1992)

Architect Santiago Calatrava **Location** Barcelona, Spain **Style** Expressionist **Material** Steel

The 1992 Summer Olympic Games had a dramatic effect on Barcelona, not least in their architectural legacy. With its spatial dynamism and curvilinear energy, the Montjuic Telecommunications Tower—built to transmit television coverage of the Games—has since become an iconic symbol of the Catalan city.

Situated on the mountain of Montjuic, to the southeast of the city, the tower is in the heart of the Olympic park. Santiago Calatrava (*b.* 1951) produced a highly innovative design that presents a functional piece of engineering as a work of great sculptural beauty. Internationally renowned as an example of how Calatrava fuses the disciplines of architecture and engineering, the Montjuic Telecommunications Tower marks a significant point in his career and displays his later signature characteristics of daring elegance.

The soaring structure reaches 446 feet (136 m) into the sky. For some observers it represents a kneeling figure making an offering, for others, an athlete holding the Olympic torch aloft. Either way, the serene design with its smooth white curves successfully creates a sense of the human figure, and reflects Calatrava's skill as an artist. This figure is rooted in the tower base, which is covered in broken glazed tiles. This mosaic technique, known as *trencadis*, is employed in homage to the work of Antonio Gaudí. Gaudí is the most prolific architect in the history of Barcelona and his use of this technique, albeit in a more multicolored version, can be seen in many of his buildings around the city.

The smooth arc at the top of the tower hides transmitting dishes, and the positioning of the structure is such that it also functions as a giant sundial. Multifunctional and beautiful, this fluid masterpiece is a fitting legacy of the Olympic Games, and a wonderful addition to the eclectic architecture of Barcelona. **KBL**

Kunsthal Rotterdam (1992)

Architects Office for Metropolitan Architecture   **Location** Rotterdam, Netherlands   **Style** Contemporary   **Materials** Concrete, timber, glass, steel

For many years after his graduation, the Dutch architect Rem Koolhaas (*b.* 1944) was regarded as an influential theorist whose projects were likely to remain unbuilt. This scheme for a large art-exhibition space in the city of his birth proved his designs were not only exciting intellectual propositions, but also functional and buildable. As with all Koolhaas projects, the context and peculiar conditions of the site are the starting points for the design. For Koolhaas, context refers to the sociopolitical and cultural conditions, as well as the physical properties of the terrain. With the Kunsthal, the starting point was a steeply sloping site and an existing access road, now incorporated into the building. In response to these conditions, the Kunsthal steps down from the high point of the site in a series of large flexible exhibition spaces linked by concrete ramps. Outside, the building is finished in rough, cast concrete appropriate for this harsh, urban

setting, and large printed graphics of the type found on road signs. The building's interior is characterized by hard surfaces, more usually associated with outside, and bold graphics. The Kunsthal has proved to be a popular and successful environment for showing contemporary art. Meanwhile, Koolhaas and his practice, the Office for Metropolitan Architecture (OMA), have progressed from medium-scale offbeat projects such as this to number among the world's most sought-after architects. **MF**

> *"People can inhabit anything and they can be miserable in anything and ecstatic in anything."*
>
> Rem Koolhaas, architect

Ryugyong Hotel (1992)

Architects Baikdoosan Architects & Engineers **Location** Pyongyang, North Korea **Style** Soviet **Material** Reinforced concrete

The Ryugyong Hotel—with its 3,000 rooms and seven revolving restaurants—should be the largest hotel and one of the tallest buildings in the world. It has, however, been left uncompleted for more than fifteen years, due to a lack of good-quality concrete coupled with financial problems. With the hotel standing 1,082 feet (330 m) tall, Pyongyang's skyline is marked forever by this rough concrete construction, the first building over 100 floors built outside the United States. What has become a ghost tower was intended as a showpiece to demonstrate North Korea's power and grandeur to the world. Composed of three vertical triangular wings, assembled in a "Y" shape, the construction pierces the landscape like an arrow. Despite its modernity, the hotel's massive form and eerie ruination makes it look more like an ancient pyramid than a twentieth-century skyscraper. The style is neither High Tech nor Postmodern; it is somewhere between Brutalism and Constructivism, seen through the lenses of an Orwellian dimension. From a Western point of view, the hundreds of identical square windows—placed regularly along the facades—along with the pyramid form can be interpreted as a metaphor of the country's organization and ideology. It could be viewed as symbolic of North Korea's many thousands of anonymous individuals, bound together in a bid for a higher, albeit inaccessible, cause. Although the authorities have called for foreign capital in order to finish the construction, they have also completed a more modest five-star hotel, a tacit acknowledgement that the original grand project may never be completed. Today, Ryugyong Hotel, its surrounding gardens and facilities, and the $750 million it took to get it to this stage are slowly deteriorating in front of the eyes of Pyongyang's inhabitants. **MHF**

Sports Services Building (1992)

Architect Josep Lluis Mateo   **Location** Barcelona, Spain   **Style** Deconstructivist   **Materials** Concrete, steel, glass, laminated timber, brick

Josep Lluis Mateo played an integral part in the extraordinary transformation of Barcelona in the 1980s and 1990s. He also edited the seminal architectural journal *Quaderns* that monitored this change. His designs connect Montserrat, the local snaggle-toothed mountain, with contemporary global concerns about pluralism; the Sports Services Building embodies this notion. Its site is the Universitat Autonoma Barcelona campus, a humid valley in the hills north of Barcelona, where the concrete-frame main university buildings form a series of bridges spanning a watercourse and its park. Mateo's chaotic bridge building, while conforming to the existing strategy of site intervention, is nothing like the others' drab uniformity. "It's like a pipe!" exclaims Mateo of the main section of the building, a corrugated steel wall-cum-roof wrapping its changing rooms and making its sullen way across the valley. The sports building

seems to be a string of peripheral building-types, each with its own tectonic system and material language. Architecturally these represent the diverse sports activities housed within them: swimming, squash, gym, dance, even table tennis. Here, Mateo questions whether "university" is any longer possible. Once it was guided by theology, then science, now it seems a conglomerate Babel of self-referential disciplines increasingly unable to talk to one another. Water alone appears to provide life and continuity. **MP**

*"I see a conglomerate
of different worlds meeting
together in my work."*

Josep Lluis Mateo, architect

Reykjavik City Hall (1992)

Architect Studio Granda **Location** Reykjavik, Iceland **Style** Modernist **Materials** Concrete, aluminum, basalt, granite, glass

In the center of Reykjavik lies the manmade lake Tjörnin. Its immediate surroundings are characterized by a great variety of buildings that are different in terms of style, scale, materials, and color. The parliament and commercial districts are located at the north side of the lake. To the south are open views, which stretch from the city into the mountains. When Studio Granda won the competition to design a new Reykjavik City Hall and remodel its close surroundings, the practice had to take the diversity of the city into consideration. This challenge resulted in a building that bridges the buzzing capital, and the artificial lake with its surrounding rough landscape. The City Hall is split into two main buildings: one houses the city council and faces the city, the other is full of offices and fronts the lake. In comparison to the council side, the office building seems quite exposed and open. A row of concrete pillars planted into the lake, suggests

that this section has emerged directly from the water. The design communicates the linkage between the rather industrious, cool City Hall and nature beyond. The urban landscape is laid out with trees, plants, and flowers adding color and life to the concrete construction. Paving and steps of basalt stone and granite merge the urban and the rural. The architects have extended the public pathway from the city into the public hall, which invites the public into the space in which their social, cultural, and other public issues are being dealt with. The City Hall stands as an important architectural landmark in Reykjavik. It concludes and adds focus to an area in which mixed building styles used to be the main characteristic. The lake is rich in fauna, including trout, salmon, ducks, swans, and many other bird species. What at first seems to be artificial has become a feature that expresses the wildness of Iceland. **SML**

Supreme Court (1992)

Architects Ram Karmi, Ada Karmi-Melamede **Location** Jerusalem, Israel **Style** Postmodernist **Material** Jerusalem stone (limestone)

For four decades after the founding of the State of Israel in 1948 its public architecture was austere; the country had few resources for ostentatious projects. The opening of the Supreme Court in 1992, a building unparalleled locally in the richness of its references and quality of its construction, was therefore something of a sensation. It was designed by siblings Ram Karmi (b. 1931) and Ada Karmi-Melamede (b. 1936) following an international competition in 1986. The court is planned around three theoretical axes that cross Jerusalem. The first, running north to south, links major national and civil institutions including the nearby Knesset or parliament building. The second, from west to east, consists of a chain of public open spaces. The third, most significantly, places the seat of Israeli justice along a conceptual route that runs between the Old City and the modern national memorial sites to the west—and between the Judean

Desert and the Mediterranean Sea. This theme of colliding axes expresses the complex and unresolved nature of the Israeli constitution and legal system. It is illustrated at several points along the building's theatrically indirect entry route, such as in the angled juxtaposition of solid masonry with smooth white plaster walls beside the main stairs. Public spaces, including the generously proportioned, soft-edged, and light-washed principal lobby, display a remarkable variety of conscious stylistic references. **TBC**

"Unresolved conflicts between ... the fragment and the object are the conceptual design themes."

Ram Karmi and Ada Karmi-Melamede, architects

Naoshima Contemporary Art Museum (1992)

Architect Tadao Ando   **Location** Gotanji Naoshima-cho, Japan   **Style** Modernist   **Materials** Steel, reinforced concrete, glass

Some of Tadao Ando's (*b.* 1941) most accomplished buildings are those designed for areas of rural, natural beauty, such as the Naoshima Contemporary Art Museum. Publisher Soichiro Fukutake wanted to create a museum to house his art collection. This had to be expanded to include hotel accommodation, as required by Japanese planning laws, and later to include the Art House Project (1997) and the Chichu Art Museum (2004), which was also designed by Ando. Naoshima is a small and tranquil island in Japan's Inland Sea, and though it has become a thriving arts and culture center, it has lost none of its natural charm. Part of Ando's brilliance lies in his respect for the landscape, and accordingly the museum is partially buried within the rocky outcrop of the island. It is planned so that the visitor arrives by boat and ascends to the museum, which faces out over the sea with an impassive geometric facade. The primary design of

the main building is based around three overlapping cubes and a circle, with a rectangular wing set at an oblique angle. From the museum entrance the visitor descends to a two-story, open gallery bathed in light from a conical skylight above. Smaller galleries lead off the central space including one that opens up to form an exterior gallery space with concrete walls creating a frame effect and a view to the sea. Further up the hillside and above the museum is the Annex, an oval accommodation structure. Its entry corridor is entirely glass, including the floor under which flows a stream. The corridor leads to an outdoor reflection pond. This building, as with many of Ando's projects, reverberates with an innate sense of something greater, better, and more peaceful than the world around. He has brought together architectural elements, created spaces of integrity, and allowed for serene and quiet reflection in a structure appropriately devoted to the arts. **TP**

Bonnefantenmuseum (1992)

Architect Aldo Rossi   **Location** Maastricht, Netherlands   **Style** Postmodernist   **Materials** Brick, zinc, concrete, steel

The Bonnefantenmuseum is the focal point of an early 1990s redevelopment in a former industrial quarter of Maastricht. Jo Coenen (b. 1949) drew up a masterplan of a new city quarter, which had formerly been the site of the nineteenth-century Sfinx-Céramique, an earthenware pottery factory. Aldo Rossi (1931–97) was invited to design the Bonnefantenmuseum, which houses an impressive collection of Flemish painting from the sixteenth and seventeenth centuries, as well as a fine contemporary art collection. Rossi engaged the city by locating his project on the Maas River. Reminiscent of Italian Renaissance architecture, his E-shaped floorplan has its open side to the river and is crowned by a zinc dome, flanked by two steel circular stairways and a panoramic terrace. The entrance on the opposite side features double-height glass doors wedged between two towers. In addition, an old factory hall by Jan Gerko Wiebenga—a historic building and the first reinforced-concrete structure in the country—is incorporated into the museum. Aldo Rossi became one of the world's leading architects, winning the Pritzker Prize and the Thomas Jefferson Medal. His severe restraint is informed by his theories on the "analogue city," whereby unobtrusive architecture highlights the vitality of the urban context in which the building is placed. A sober floorplan and regularity of form make the museum representative of Rossi's "anti-Modernist" stance. **KAB**

" . . . Rossi's name will appear as one of those who helped to establish a wiser . . . attitude."

José Rafael Moneo, architect

Vitra Conference Pavilion (1993)

Architect Tadao Ando   **Location** Weil am Rhein, Germany   **Style** Modernist   **Materials** Concrete, glass

Rolf Fehlbaum, owner of the Vitra furniture-design company, has a remarkable eye for up-and-coming architects. After commissioning Frank Gehry's first building outside the United States and Zaha Hadid's first ever project, he went on to give the now world renowned architect Tadao Ando (b. 1941) his first commission outside of Japan: the Vitra Conference Pavilion. All three architects later went on to win the prestigious Pritzker Prize. The site chosen for Ando's design was a clearing in a forest next to Gehry's flamboyant Design Museum. With his usual sensitivity to the surrounding environment and in stark comparison to Gehry's Organic Expressionism, Ando produced an austere, low-profile building composed of unfinished concrete punctuated by large glass panels. Inside, Ando created rich interior spaces using contrasting compositions of spaces and solids formed from simple geometric shapes. Ando, true to his belief

that structures should maintain a harmony with their surroundings, buried the first floor of the building below the ground so that an existing cherry orchard could be seen blossoming over it. Vitra Conference Pavilion highlights Ando's trademark of juxtaposing powerful delineated walls against the peace provided by light and nature. Unconventionally, the whole structure is made from untreated concrete, yet Ando still manages to provide it with a smooth, almost lustrous, surface. To get this elegant finish the concrete is cast in precisely crafted wooden forms made using traditional Japanese carpentry techniques. The characteristic uniformly spaced holes found on the walls of Ando's work are a product of the bolts that hold the forms together. Although the style of Ando's work is based on traditional Japanese architecture and its connection with nature, the universality of his Minimalist Eastern designs has long been admired. **JM**

Great Mosque Hassan II (1993)

Architect Michel Pinseau **Location** Casablanca, Morocco **Style** Islamic **Materials** Concrete, granite, plaster, marble, wood, glass

In 1986 Morocco's King Hassan II commissioned a new mosque in Casablanca. His idea was to inaugurate it on his sixtieth birthday in 1989. Although several thousand laborers worked day and night, it was not completed until 1993. The mosque was inspired by a verse from the Koran that states the throne of God was built on the water. French architect Michel Pinseau (1924–99) realized the king's request by designing a building standing partly on cliffs but extending over the Atlantic Ocean. The giant complex of Hassan II mosque enfolds 22 acres (9 ha) including an Islamic school, several *hammams*, a museum of Moroccan history, a library, and a car park. The prayer room holds 20,000 worshippers, and the courtyard another 80,000. The mosque's floor is made partly from glass, so worshippers can kneel directly over the sea. Other high-tech features are heated floors, electric doors, an automatic sliding roof, and a laser integrated into the minaret pointing toward Mecca. The interior, built by more than 6,000 traditional craftsmen and artists, features gorgeous mosaics and calligraphies, marble floors and columns, plaster mouldings, and carved wood ceilings. After the mosque in Mecca, this is the second largest mosque in the world. Due to its giant minaret, reaching up to 656 feet (200 m), it is also the tallest sacral building worldwide. Yet the most spectacular characteristic of the Hassan II Mosque remains the architect's use of its stunning location. **CH**

> *"I want to build this mosque on water because God's throne is on the water."*
>
> King Hassan II

Carré d'Art (1993)

Architect Foster and Partners **Location** Nîmes, France **Style** High Tech **Materials** Glass, steel

The Carré d'Art demonstrates how a building can create a dialogue between ancient and modern architectures, and become a powerful catalyst for reinvigorating a city's social and physical fabric. The challenge was to create a building that represented its own age with integrity, while at the same time relating the new to the old. The Carré d'Art has succeeded in both. The building, which opened on May 8, 1993, is a simple box of glass, four stories tall, with five subterranean levels so as to pay due deference to the perfectly preserved Roman temple of Maison Carrée adjacent to it. The building's lower levels house archive storage and a cinema, while an elegant roofed courtyard forms the heart of the building, with upper levels connected by a cascading staircase. This links the top-lit galleries to the shaded roof-terrace café overlooking the new public square. It was this café-table-lined piazza, located in the Nîmes Roman grid, that was crucial in framing the building in its immediate context and providing a new setting for the Maison Carrée. Together, the building and the space it creates have helped to reinvigorate the social heart of Nîmes. It also helped grow the international reputation of the prolific Norman Foster (b. 1935), whose practice has now designed hundreds of high-quality buildings across the globe including Chek Lap Kok airport in Hong Kong and the remodeling of the Reichstag in Berlin. **DT**

> "[Foster's] vision forges the materials of our age into a crystalline, lyrical purity."
>
> J. Carter Brown, Pritzker Prize judge

Permanent Mission of India to the UN (1993)

Architect Charles Correa   **Location** New York, New York, USA
Style Modernist   **Materials** Steel, aluminum

Slotting into an awkward site on a narrow Manhattan block, the slender red tower of the Permanent Mission of India to the UN is a Western skyscraper with an unmistakable aura of the subcontinent. This is not surprising when one considers that Charles Correa (b. 1930) was raised in India, leaving shortly after independence to study architecture in the United States. Returning home to establish his own practice in Bombay in 1958, Correa has developed a vision that fuses the principles of Western Modernism with the styles, materials, techniques, and needs of his own

---

"In India, the sky has profoundly affected our relationship to built form and to open space."

Charles Correa, architect

---

culture. Although most of his work has been in India, Correa has undertaken a number of commissions in the Americas, of which this is perhaps the most striking example.

Rising twenty-eight stories, the red aluminium curtain wall, suggestive of Indian sandstone, that comprises the tower is surmounted by a massive open-air porch—an allusion to the rooftop *barsatis* on many Indian homes. As most of the tower is given over to the residential quarters of government employees who work on its lower floors, this reference is entirely appropriate. At the base, a darker red, granite lobby is entered through bronze double doors, and the open porch is strikingly painted in the colors of the Indian national flag. Correa has helped to forge a dynamic, postcolonial identity for Indian architecture. **RDB**

Center for Contemporary Culture (Casa del Caritas) (1993)

Architect Albert Viaplana, Helio Pinon   **Location** Barcelona, Spain
Style Contemporary   **Materials** Glass, steel, concrete, stone

Ignasi de Sola-Morales, the late professor of the Barcelona school of architecture, described the phenomenon of the transformation of the city during the late twentieth century as "a narration that is conveyed not so much by stable formal structures as by images." Many of the architects who effected this change were colleagues or former pupils of his, including Albert Viaplana and Helio Pinon. The pair have executed a number of public projects in Barcelona's periphery and center with bold wit and intellectual rigor.

The Center for Contemporary Culture is one of a series of isolated but strategically placed architectural interventions in the old town of Barcelona, aimed at the regeneration not only of individual neighborhoods, but also linking these projects together with a sequence of pedestrian routes and public spaces that focus local amenities as well as cultural identity. The former convent Casa del Caritas has been re-conceived as a conference center, the north range of its quadrangle entirely replaced with a four-story steel-and-glass facade that acts as a window onto the foyer of a museum of the city.

The plane of this facade is divided by a vertical step, which is further articulated by clear and dark glass on either side, the line of which is continued into the pink and gray halves of the courtyard paving itself. This split is taken up by the huge fourth-story glass cornice, which bows precariously over the courtyard. Only when viewed obliquely as you enter does the meaning of this—at first glance gratuitous—gesture become apparent. It is a giant mirror, reflecting the silhouette of Montjuic, Barcelona's hill of hedonistic pleasures, right into the heart of the ancient convent's chaste enclosure: an image of both identity and change. **MP**

Netherlands Architecture Institute (1993)

Architect Jo Coenen & Co Architekten **Location** Rotterdam, Netherlands
Style Deconstructivist **Materials** Glass, concrete, steel, brick

The Netherlands Architecture Institute (NAI) plays an important functional and symbolic role: it preserves and documents Dutch architectural and urban planning history, serving as a research center for local and international designers, members of the architecture community, and the general public. Situated on the northern edge of the Museum Park in Rotterdam, Jo Coenen's (b. 1949) imposing structure is an integral element of the cultural center of the city.

Coenen is an internationally renowned practitioner, who also designed the Amsterdam Public Library (2006) and currently holds the position of chief government architect for the Netherlands. His scheme for the NAI consisted of four distinct elements: a central reception hall with entrances from the north and south, a glass box suspended in an exoskeletal frame, a brick-faced exhibition hall, and a curved wing clad in corrugated steel, resting on concrete columns. These disparate elements are held together by a glass transport house containing a central staircase and lifts. The NAI also contributes to the urban fabric of the square: a public pedestrian route through the central hall connects Museum Park to a major traffic artery.

Attention has also been given to external elements, such as the concrete threshold, the pond, and the waterside terrace with café. Situated within the pond, Auke de Vrie's gigantic gravity-defying sculpture gives a vertical antithesis to the static surface of the water. In addition, Peter Struycken's light sculpture dramatically illuminates the building at night. **KAB**

↗ The NAI provides connections with and access to several surrounding areas.

→ Jo Coenen's innovative design turns a public building into a public space.

Hight Residence (1993)

Architect Bart Prince   **Location** Mendocino, California, USA   **Style** Expressionist   **Materials** Laminate wood, cedar shingles

Bart Prince (b. 1947) is perhaps the greatest contemporary exponent of the Organic or Responsive approach. His work has been compared with that of Antonio Gaudí, Louis Sullivan, and Frank Lloyd Wright. A resident of Albuquerque, New Mexico, Prince is deeply influenced by the desert landscapes of the southwest. After graduating from Arizona State University college of architecture, Prince befriended Bruce Goff, a former protégé of Wright, and a distinguished architect in the Organic school. Working intermittently with Goff in the last decade of his life, Prince developed his own practice and by the 1980s had formulated a style uniquely his own. Designed as a holiday and weekend retreat, and eventually to become a permanent home, the Hight Residence exemplifies Prince's "inside out" approach. Prince allows the building's form to evolve out of a synthesis of its environmental context, the client's personality,

needs, and budget, and his own creative responses. Inspired by the site's coastal headland, Price fashioned a low, rambling structure with an undulating roof. Acting as a wind buffer on one side, the roof also rises to afford views across the Pacific. Changes of level define different functional areas within, and beams are exposed in contrast to exterior cedar shingles. His work has drawn criticism for ignoring local vernaculars, but Prince's buildings demand to be engaged with on their own terms. **RDB**

> *"There should be as many individual designs as there are individual people."*
>
> Bart Prince, architect

Villa Anbar (1993)

Architect Peter Barber   **Location** Dammam, Saudi Arabia   **Style** Modern Vernacular   **Material** Reinforced concrete

Peter Barber (*b.* 1960) is best known as the architect who brought the Mediterranean feel to London's grim East End with the Donnybrook Quarter housing project. His Villa Anbar in Saudi Arabia's Dammam is undoubtedly an exceptional structure, the private refuge of a novelist who shares her time between London and Damman, and a skillful combination of Modernist ideals and the Arabic vernacular. Barber designed the house on a tight budget and on a rather small rectangular piece of land. The actual house is mostly hidden, a single-story building with small slit windows and high walls enclosing a roof terrace, central courtyard, and swimming pool. It is characteristic that the residence has a single west frontage and a courtyard dividing the building in two parts—the daytime section for living and receiving guests, and the more private nighttime section for resting—the whole design abiding by the rules of traditional Arabic house planning. Villa Anbar is a minimalist, cubic complex, whitewashed to perfection to reflect the sun. A Modernist simplicity and a decor-free geometric approach is effortlessly coordinated with the hot climate. The design plays with the notion of privacy and the relation of the interior and exterior, providing a welcoming house, safe from the harsh heat and also, as is traditional, from the gaze of passers-by. The project has twice been shortlisted for the International Aga Khan Award for Architecture. **ES**

> "*Minimal means are required to make a thing of beauty ... neither intricate nor expensive.*"

Peter Barber, architect

Faroe Islands Art Museum (1993)

Architect Jákup Pauli Gregoriussen **Location** Tórshavn, Faroe Islands, Denmark **Style** Postmodernist **Materials** Tarred wood, glass

Nordic architects often use traditional forms as reference points in their architecture. However, the architecture of the Faroe Islands Art Museum takes the visual reminders further, creating a kind of updated rustic architecture. The building houses the islands' art museum. The Faroe Islands, a small self-governing part of Denmark, has a population of less than 50,000, but enjoys a vibrant cultural life. The Faroe Islands Art Museum shows a program of changing exhibitions alongside the permanent collection, mainly exhibiting art by artists native to the islands.

Jákup Pauli Gregoriussen (b. 1932) designed the north wing of the museum for the Faroe Islands Art Society, opened in 1970. Gregoriussen—collaborating with N. F. Truelsen—also worked on the later addition of a run of galleries, opened in 1993. Black-tarred wood covers the facade of the run of buildings. Traditional Scandinavian architecture is dominated by the use of wood due to its plentiful availability. Vikings, who colonized the Faroe Islands at the end of the first millennium, also built their ships in tarred wood.

Three large hipped roofs, with glass tops, sit on the smaller, front-gabled buildings with a facade of large windows. The run of galleries displaying the permanent collections is here. The huge windows offer two-way views between indoor and outdoor spaces. Typically for a Nordic building, light is emphasized: during the day, the windows allow light to flood into the sparse gallery spaces, while in the evenings the warm light glows invitingly in the dark. The overall impression is one of approachability, with none of the pomposity sometimes displayed by galleries. Natural materials and friendly proportions merge harmoniously with modern building methods and the surrounding, imposing landscape. **RK**

Olympic Art Museum (1993)

Architects Snøhetta Architects **Location** Lillehammer, Norway **Style** Modernist **Materials** Wood, granite, glass

In connection with the 1994 Winter Olympics, Lillehammer decided to extend its art museum, built in 1963, and designed by Norwegian architect Erling Viksjø (1910–71). The result is a stunning experiment in the possibilities of wood and glass, adding a beautiful, pure organic structure to the existing Minimalist one.

The new extension faces a large public square, the city's main gathering space. With its voluminous, rolling, soft larch wood facade, the building appears warm and welcoming, and contrasts with the original museum, which stands out in a rather closed and cold

> *"The forms and materials are reminiscent of the surrounding mountain landscape."*
>
> Snøhetta Architects

concrete style. The ground floor, with windows facing the square, lifts up the solid timber-clad structure, which covers the entire facade of the first floor. In the new interior, some of the concrete walls have been sloped, creating an exciting space for the art. The two buildings are linked by an enclosed bridge at the first-floor level, and a garden filled with sculptures below.

Viksjø's building includes the permanent art collection, mainly of Norwegian landscape paintings. The new museum displays modern and contemporary art, and temporary exhibitions. This categorization of artworks reiterates the different styles of architecture. But when seeing the museum in its entirety, it illustrates that the styles of two different generations of architects can be combined, creating a vibrant and challenging site for the arts. **SML**

Storefront for Art and Architecture (1993)

Architects Steven Holl, Vito Acconci **Location** New York, New York, USA
Style Postmodernist **Materials** Supraboard, metal

The facade of Storefront for Art and Architecture gallery in Manhattan is ever-evolving. The nonprofit art organization commissioned the architect Steven Holl (*b.* 1947) and the artist Vito Acconci (*b.* 1940) to design the facade in 1993. The panels forming the front of the gallery and shop can be opened in a variety of combinations, or can be closed altogether.

Vito Acconci is a New York–based performance artist who has also taught in a number of art institutions and has worked with architectural concepts, looking at public and private space. Steven Holl is an American architect known for several notable buildings such as Kiasma, the Museum of Contemporary Art in Helsinki.

The facade of Storefront for Art and Architecture is flat board, with each uniquely shaped panel opening to the street like modern window shutters. The simple brilliance of the idea does not reflect the small budget with which the facade was built. The building becomes flexible, surprising, and intriguing; passers-by can catch glimpses of the gallery. The panels become a part of the street architecture and blur the line between indoors and outdoors—a familiar concept in a densely built city like New York.

Only the city that boasts the highest, glossiest skyscrapers and a street grid system could have inspired such a gallery facade. When closed, the outlines of the panels are reminiscent of the city's skyline. Storefront for Art and Architecture is quintessentially a New York–style building. **RK**

↗ The outward-opening panels offer glimpses of the gallery, intriguing and drawing in passers-by.

⇥ Some of the wall sections are hinged vertically as doors; smaller ones open horizontally to form tables.

Suzuki House (1993)

Architects Bolles+Wilson   **Location** Tokyo, Japan
Style Contemporary   **Materials** Concrete, glass, steel

Akira Suzuki, a well-known architecture critic, publisher and curator asked Bolles+Wilson to design this house for his family at the start of the 1990s, a decade of bankruptcies and recession in Japan. Suzuki House was built before the "bubble" burst, in Tokyo's classic, urban situation in which property was hugely expensive, building regulations tricky, and houses rebuilt every twenty years or so.

The brief called for an unlikely tour de force: accommodate a family of three, with a car, within a house acting both as a shelter and an urban event to

---

> *"Living in the city consists in weaving distinctive . . . bonds with an environment of quality."*
>
> Akira Suzuki, architecture critic

---

be built on a corner lot of 23 feet (7 m) by 18 feet (5.5 m). The German-based architects responded with a simple hymn to non-gravity: a narrow concrete box in equilibrium on two steel legs, clearing just enough space for the tiniest car, with just enough room within for a series of vertical stairs to a roof terrace, almost a perch, above this quiet area on the outskirts of one of the world's busiest metropolises.

Halfway between Mies van der Rohe's "Less is more," and Morris Lapidus's "Too much is never enough," this house is infused with invention and pragmatic responsibility in relation to the fulfilling of its functions. It tells us about pleasure and lightness—that of designing it, that of living in it—and about cleverness and optimism in a contemporary world in which these seem so often incongruous. **YN**

Marika-Alderton House (1994)

Architect Glenn Murcutt   **Location** Arnhem Land, Northern Territory, Australia   **Style** Modernist   **Materials** Aluminum, steel, plywood

Glenn Murcutt (*b.* 1936) is the antithesis of a starchitect. He does not command an army of juniors or seek major commissions. He is a sole practitioner. Murcutt represents the future. He should represent the present, but the West seems reluctant to live well with less, a belief evident in all Murcutt's buildings.

Arnhem Land is a wilderness where weather ranges from cyclones to floods. Yirrkala Community is Aboriginal land, and it is here that a small, ingenious, indigenous-inspired house was built for Marmburra Banduk Marika and Mark Alderton. It is a one-story, prefabricated, aluminum-finished, steel-frame structure with plywood walls and a corrugated metal, vented roof. There is no glass, but panels that lift horizontally and augment other mechanical air distribution systems that allow the house to breathe. Adjustable shutters direct sunlight, and generous eaves beat back the sun. Roofline tubes expel hot air. Large vertical fins act as spoilers to reduce wind and shield the site. The house is on short stilts that aid air circulation, protect from floods, give wildlife shelter, and reference vernacular Pacific Rim architecture.

Murcutt's respect for context and environment is reflected in his buildings. So it seems odd the house became a flash point. Some question why he built a "permanent" house for an Aborigine, as Aborigines do not build permanent structures. Others ask why the house was part-funded by a steel company negotiating mineral rights with the Aborigines. A one-word rebuttal—Chumbawumba. The anarchist, anti-globalist English band sold rights to one of their tunes to a global corporation, then gave the fee to anti-globalist campaigners. Murcutt and Chumbawumba know that to change systems you must demonstrate the accepted way is not always the right way. **DJ**

Groninger Museum (1994)

Architects Atelier Alessandro Mendini, Team 4 Architecten, Coop Himmelb(l)au   **Location** Groningen, Netherlands
Style Postmodernist   **Materials** Concrete, brick, aluminum, steel, laminate panels

Visitors leaving Groningen train station are greeted with late-twentieth-century Postmodernism's most astonishing buildings. The Groninger Museum, designed by Alessandro Mendini (*b.* 1931), may seem willfully random, but the plan is based on museum collections and functions.

The dominating, gleaming gold tower, clad in laminate panels, houses collections storage, offices, and the main entrance. It is based on a former gasometer. Beside the tower, Mendini placed two lower pavilions, green and pink, containing education rooms and a café. To the west of the tower, connected by a semi-submerged passage, is a red brick pavilion designed by Michele de Lucchi; red brick was the traditional building material of Groningen's historic quarter. Inside, designer Philippe Starck's aluminum cylindrical pavilion is a collection of 8,000 pieces of Oriental ceramics. At the eastern end of the complex is Coop Himmelb(l)au's exploded "open architecture" Modern Art Pavilion, clad in patterned laminates. The site is bisected by a blue bridge; its underside, shown when it opens for canal traffic, is covered with fifty-six panels resembling Delft tiles.

Outside the main entrance is a jokey, colorful sculpture by Mendini. Inside, the central spiral staircase covered in Italian mosaic is striking. Mendini argued that Functionalism led to impersonal, mechanical architecture: "Every person is different, so why not objects?" The Groninger Museum is a hugely expensive, ambitious way to express this point. **ATB**

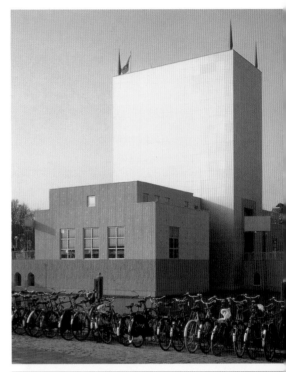

↗ The main entrance to the museum is in the side of the golden storage tower, below a triangular canopy.

➡ Coop Himmelb(l)au's Deconstructivist Modern Art Pavilion introduced a new aesthetic to Groningen.

Saint-Exupéry TGV Station (1994)

Architect Santiago Calatrava **Location** Lyon, France **Style** Expressionist **Materials** Steel, glass, concrete

The Spanish architect Santiago Calatrava (*b.* 1951) is celebrated for bridges, train stations, and public buildings designed in his sculptural, almost skeletal, style. One of his earlier stations is at Lyon Satolas airport—now called Saint-Exupéry. It is a stop for infrequent high-speed TGV *(train à grande vitesse)* trains. The station was commissioned jointly by SNCF (French Railways), the Regional Council, and the Lyon Chamber of Commerce and Industry. The clients wanted different but connected outcomes. SNCF wished to celebrate their exciting TGVs; the Regional Council wanted an iconic building for the Rhône-Alpes region; and the Chamber of Commerce wanted a new station and good transport links for the airport. The striking main hall is a 131-feet-high (40 m) curving steel, glass, and concrete structure, looking like a bird with outstretched wings, or perhaps like a human eye. From the airport, you enter the hall by a connecting pier at an elevated level. Escalators lead down into the main concourse, from which platform wings spread out on either side above the railway tracks. The central pair of arches forms a spine above the main hall. The underused, empty sculptural concrete galleries project out over the main concourse. The glazed symmetrical concourse wings project from the spine under expressive, sweeping arches. Its monumentality is impressive, but it is a shame such an exciting space is underused and relatively inaccessible. **ATB**

"Calatrava is . . . a romantic and a rationalist [with an] ability to find an equilibrium between the two."

Paul Goldberger, architecture critic

MI6 Headquarters (1994)

Architects Terry Farrell and Partners   **Location** London, England   **Style** Postmodernist   **Material** Concrete

Beloved of spy writers, the MI6 building on the south bank of the River Thames in Vauxhall has become of one London's most famous modern buildings. Its distinctive green-and-cream patterned facade, an homage to Art Deco, makes it stand out even on the grayest of London days. As one would expect of the headquarters of British espionage, the building is equipped with state-of-the-art security systems including walls and windows designed to withstand not only bullets, but bombs, too, and a "Faraday cage," which prevents electronic eavesdropping from hackers. MI6 was created in 1912 as Military Intelligence, section six. For decades, it was a shadowy legend, hinted at but not officially recognized until long after the end of the Cold War. In the mid-1990s, it was decided that MI6 should become more open and the building on Vauxhall's Albert Embankment was commissioned as a public statement of this new

attitude. This structure, known originally as the SIS Building, was designed by English architect Terry Farrell (b. 1939). It is not actually one building, but a group of three blocks interconnected by courtyards and atria, which are covered in panes of green-colored glass to coordinate with the decorated facade. Its stepped outline stretches up to a height of nine stories and extends downward deep beneath the London pavements to provide extra security. Ever since it opened, the building has excited controversy and has become both loved and loathed in equal amounts. In addition, MI6 has received criticism for its decision to stand out so blatantly; a terrorist rocket missile attack in 2000 seemed to prove the detractors' claims. Yet, despite the ferocity of the weapon used, the attack—which was attributed to a splinter group known as the Real IRA—succeeded only in damaging an eighth-floor window. **LH**

Manggha Center of Japanese Art and Technology (1994)

Architect Arata Isozaki **Location** Krakow, Poland **Style** Modernist **Material** Sandstone

In 1987 the Polish film director and long-time Japanese art enthusiast Andrzej Wajda decided to donate his Kyoto Prize, awarded by the Japanese government in recognition of a lifetime's achievement in cinematography, to help in the realization of a new project—the Manggha Center of Japanese Art and Technology, to be built in Krakow, Poland.

Clad in sandstone, the building was erected to promote cultural and technological interchange between Japan and Poland, and houses a collection of Japanese art, formerly owned and subsequently donated to the National Museum in Krakow by art collector Feliks Jasienski. The center, located on the bank of the Vistula River and overlooking the country's national symbol Wawel Castle, contains exhibition space, a multipurpose conference complex, offices, and an auditorium for concert and theater productions. The interior blends two dissimilar cultures by combining the Japanese architectural references of functional layout, carefully designed vistas, and the somber ambience of the seventeenth-century shogun castles with extensive use of typical local building materials of timber and brick.

The building's neutral typology is devoid of any obvious idiosyncrasies; however, on longer viewing, the structure appears subtly touched by both Polish and Japanese traditions. Gently undulating curves of the roof create a wave leitmotif, depicting the flow of the Vistula River in a contextual and symbolic sense, and being simultaneously reminiscent of the series of engravings *Thirty-six Views of Mount Fuji* by Japanese artist Katsushika Hokusai. **BK**

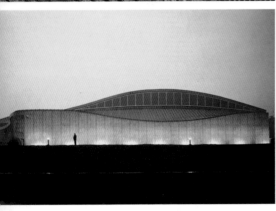

↖ The museum is a clever, harmonious mix of Japanese design and Polish building materials.

← Smooth lines and stylized lighting suggest that the structure has been superimposed into the landscape.

Channel 4 Building (1994)

Architect Richard Rogers Partnership   **Location** London, England   **Style** High Tech   **Materials** Steel, glass

Channel 4 is one of Britain's television institutions—a commercial station that considers itself on the cutting edge of consumer, political, and public life. It made perfect sense, therefore, for its central London headquarters to be designed by an architect who could stylishly and dynamically symbolize all of these assets. Richard Rogers (*b.* 1933) is one of Britain's most influential architects. He has broken new ground with his distinctive industrial aesthetic and volumes of free internal space, which he creates by siting all services, lifts, and pipes on the outside of the building.

The £35-million ($65 m) Channel 4 building is clearly designed with Rogers' Lloyd's Building in mind, as it revels in its construction and assembly: next to nothing is concealed, and the lifts and services are visible (they use innovative technology to ensure they remain warm and temperate). But it is the almost Classical form of the structure and its relationship to its urban environment that is its greatest achievement.

Set on a tight urban site in a mixed-use area near Westminster, two extraordinary concave curving glass walls—hung from a network of stainless steel rods and cables—are set back from the main street, creating a small, stepped public piazza. Flanking the central building are two four-story towers containing meeting rooms, staircases, and external circulation.

Visitors are drawn toward the striking entrance with its glass canopy. The building also includes office space for 800 staff as well as a significant amount of residential accommodation. Materials are high tech and hard-edged—perfectly suited to what is claimed to be Europe's most advanced television center. **BG**

↗ The building's High-Tech appearance and ingenious use of space belie its deceptively simple design.

→ The spectacular curved frontage and grand entrance offer visitors the prospect of an exciting new world.

Chikatsu–Asuka Historical Museum (1994)

Architect Tadao Ando **Location** Osaka, Japan **Style** Minimalist
Materials Steel, reinforced concrete

Kandalama Hotel (1994)

Architect Geoffrey Bawa **Location** Dambulla, Sri Lanka
Style Modernist **Materials** Concrete, glass

Tucked away in a verdant and beautiful area of Osaka prefecture, surrounded by hills, is the astonishing Chikatsu–Asuka Historical Museum. It rises from the landscape as a monolith of gray, faintly echoing Mayan temples, ancient pyramids, and massive monuments to the long dead. The area is home to more than 200 ancient burial mounds or *tumuli*, which date back to the Kofun Period of about the third to fifth centuries CE, and include the imperial tomb of Ono-no-Imoko, Japan's first ambassador to China. It is a place of rich historic importance for Japan—something that Tadao Ando's somber and impressive museum reflects, while also providing space for exhibitions.

The roof of the building is formed by a series of broad, shallow steps leading up to a flat, expansive platform that affords views over the surrounding burial mounds, and acts as an open-air theater for lectures and events. The entrance to the building is at first obscure. A narrow concrete path with high sides leads obliquely from the giant ritualistic staircase, seemingly going nowhere, but cleverly offering a windowlike view of the landscape ahead; it finally emerges next to the entrance. The sense of ritual is heightened as the visitor passes from the brightly lit entrance down into the dim interior whose keyhole shape reflects that of the ancient *tumuli*. Artifacts from the permanent collection are housed along the curved walls in cases, leading the visitor slowly toward a sweeping downward ramp to the lower level. Ando, who received no formal training as an architect, has produced a building of immense stature, physically and psychologically. The museum seems to grow out of the countryside, becoming a modern reinvention of the *tumuli*, and combining nature with history and pervasive spirituality. **TP**

It was the crushing of the Janatha Vimukthi Peramuna (JVP) in 1989 that brought with it a lull in uprisings in Sri Lanka and encouraged tourism to make a comeback. Hotels were needed, specifically in an area of the country known as the "Cultural Triangle" in its Dry Zone. In 1991, Aitken Spence Hotels approached Sri Lankan architect Geoffrey Bawa (1919–2003).

Bawa, whose work mixes modern techniques with vernacular themes, recommended a site around 6 miles (10 km) from the ancient rock of Sigiriya. He loved the possibility of surprise and drama for visitors

> *"Bawa exerted a defining influence on the emerging architecture of independent Sri Lanka."*
>
> **Agha Khan Award citation (2001)**

approaching through the jungle from Dambulla, a few miles to the west, toward a huge and seemingly impenetrable ridge. The cavelike hotel entrance sits near the top of this ridge, reached by a huge ramp from which the hotel's main, flat-roofed terraces lead, giving way to views beyond a stunning infinity pool toward Sigiriya. Four floors of rooms sit below the main reception level, snaking around the face of the cliff toward the east. The use of flat roofs and starkly expressed concrete frames is ideally suited to the site and climate. Walking to the rooms along open corridors alongside the overhanging cliff-face gives the impression of being at one with the landscape, a cloak of foliage lessening the building's impact. This is a luxurious eco-hotel, each room blessed with an ever-changing, natural panorama. **DT**

Signal
Box (1994)

Architects Herzog & de Meuron   **Location** Basel, Switzerland
Style Minimalist   **Materials** Concrete, copper

Swiss architects Jacques Herzog (*b*. 1950) and Pierre de Meuron (*b*. 1950) designed this distinctive Signal Box as a monument to their hometown of Basel. The sheer simplicity of the object coupled with the distinctiveness of their design speaks volumes about the architects' dedication and attention to detail. The six-story cube, entwined with bands of copper—appearing from a distance as though it is clad in shimmering pinstripes—transforms an everyday functional object into a thing of beauty. The bands of copper are not simply decorative: subtly twisted, they allow natural light to penetrate the structure, as well as being designed to deflect lightning.

The two architects, born in the same town, in the same year, studied architecture together and set up a joint practice in 1978. Since then, their work has become world famous. Herzog once compared their work to that of Pop artist Andy Warhol saying "We love to destroy the clichés of architecture." Their projects include the Tate Modern in London, the Ricola Marketing Building at Laufen in Switzerland, the Köppersmöhle Museum at Duisburg in Germany, and the Stone House in Tavole in Italy. Always looking for a challenge, their projects vary hugely in size, function, and in the materials used; for example, at the Dominus Winery in the Napa Valley, the stone walls were constructed without mortar, but held together by being encased in a mesh of wire. The pair have won major architectural prizes including the Pritzker Prize (2001) and the RIBA Stirling Prize (2003). **LH**

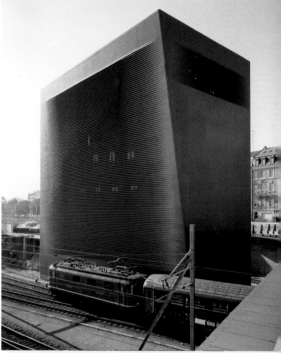

↗ At a distance an ordinary rectangular building, the signal box is actually skewed in its lower stories.

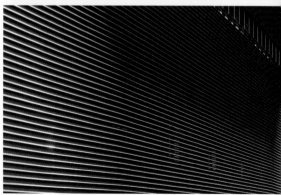

→ The cage of copper strips enclosing the building shields the sensitive electronic equipment within.

Passenger Terminal, Kansai International Airport (1994)

Architect Renzo Piano Building Workshop   **Location** Osaka, Japan   **Style** High Tech   **Materials** Steel, glass

Kansai International Airport, which sits upon an artificial island in Osaka Bay, took twenty years to plan, three years to build, and was considerably over budget. The Renzo Piano Building Workshop won an international competition to design the passenger terminal, a superlative feat of engineering and a building of extreme elegance that is difficult to compare to other structures.

International arrivals and departures are united seamlessly under one giant, curved roof, which, when seen from the air, mimics the curvature of the earth. The interior is an extraordinary exercise in spatial sequencing. Following the shape of the exterior, Piano used sinuous outlines, held up by a series of trussed supports, as an organizational tool to lead passengers to the main transitional points in the terminal. Constantly changing heights and vistas open up, allowing the user to move easily and with confidence from one area to another. The hub of the building is the "canyon," a full-height atrium that acts as a meeting point. Natural ventilation is possible as air flows without the need for closed ducts along the gracefully twisting curves.

At 1 mile (1.7 km) long, the building is one of the largest in the world. Clad in stainless-steel panels, articulated by darkened glass, its sleek, aerodynamic aesthetic was informed by the waves and wind surrounding it. The structure, services, and skin are united, resulting in a lightness that belies the building's size. Designed to withstand the seismic instability of the area, it survived the 1995 Kobe earthquake 12 miles (20 km) away without damage. **JH**

↖ This intricate structure was not only built for beauty but cleverly designed to withstand earth tremors.

← The airport was built on an island of reclaimed land, thus ensuring minimum pollution to the local area.

Glyndebourne Opera House (1994)

Architect Michael Hopkins   **Location** East Sussex, England   **Style** Vernacular   **Materials** Brick, precast concrete, steel, timber

When the owners of Glyndebourne, a country house in Sussex, England, decided to replace their famous but rather decrepit opera house they commissioned a building from Sir Michael Hopkins (b. 1935), an architect best known for his High-Tech projects that use the technology of yacht design. So the outcome, a beautifully made brick building, comes as a surprise.

The opera house is an oval drum that sits between a Neo-Elizabethan house, and the former backstage that has been converted to a bar. A trademark Hopkins tensile fabric canopy links them. Among the most striking features of the building are the two-story open arcaded sides that provide cover for picnickers during intervals in a performance, and give the opera house a Romanesque appearance.

The principal material used is handmade red Hampshire brick. Hopkins is a Modernist architect, so it was important for him that the structure of the building be clearly expressed. Thus, the concrete beams supporting the floors are exposed in the piers of the flat arches. Inside, the precast concrete floors and ceilings remain visible for the same reason. On the top floor, the structure changes dramatically, with the lead-covered roof raised up on steel columns, and timber beams. The fly tower is clad in lead.

Timber is the dominant material used in the 1,200-seat auditorium, with its three horseshoe-shaped balconies. The floor, walls, seats, and balcony fronts are made of plain, waxed wood, most of which is reclaimed pitch pine. Overall, the feeling is of a structure that is so well made and English that it could be compared to a suit from Saville Row. **MF**

↗ A classic Hopkins touch—the tensile fabric canopy—connects the old and the new Glyndebourne.

→ The seating areas are musical in their fluid shape, evoking the smooth, curved lines of a cello or violin.

Museum of Mankind (1995)

Architects Arata Isozaki, César Portela   **Location** La Coruña, Spain   **Style** Contemporary   **Materials** Galician slate, granite

The architectural genius of Arata Isozaki (*b.* 1931) lies in his ability to fuse seemingly contradictory idioms into a single coherent statement. Domus Casa del Hombre (Museum of Mankind)—a museum devoted to the mechanisms governing the human body explained using more than 200 interactive exhibits—exemplifies this synthesis. The building is on a windswept seafront cliff overlooking the Orzan Bay. The oblong floorplan includes offices, study areas, an auditorium, a restaurant, and, most importantly, cascading planes of exhibition space, linked by gentle ramps. The interior follows the rugged cliff topography with multiple floor levels and the use of different stone finishes, from rough boulders to highly polished slabs. Its external appearance emanates aloofness akin to the surrounding rough environment. A gently curving 308-by-56 feet (94 x 17 m) monolithic facade protects the interior from fierce ocean winds and traffic noise

from an adjacent motorway. Clad in greenish-gray Galician slate, from a distance it resembles a gargantuan scaly fish swept up on the shore. A strip of glazing breaks up the expanse of the facade to provide ocean views from the restaurant. The rear elevation mimics the rough context with a zigzagging solid wall treated with local varieties of granite. Domus Casa del Hombre is an ingenious building, which handles an improbable concept of lightness, expressed in one of the heaviest materials of all—stone. **BK**

"Architects such as . . . Arata Isozaki can switch from one approach to another . . . easily."

Charles Jencks, architecture critic

Takatori Kyokai Catholic Church (1995)

Architect Shigeru Ban **Location** Kobe, Japan **Style** Contemporary **Materials** Paper tubes, corrugated polycarbonate, Teflon-coated fabric

No one has forgotten the devastating earthquake that shook Kobe in 1995, killing nearly 5,500 and razing to the ground fifteen percent of the buildings, including 80,000 housing units. Providing the innumerable homeless with lasting shelters as well as with new spaces for community life (a major issue in such situations) was a primary concern. In response to these requirements, Japanese architect Shigeru Ban (b. 1957)—world famous for his innovative works with low-cost, low-tech, eco-friendly, paper-tube structures—came up with paper houses that could be built rapidly on foundations made from beer crates filled with sandbags, then dismantled and recycled. Ban was then asked to come up with a temporary paper church meant to replace the burned down original Takatori Church, a place of worship as well as a community center that was likely to provide help and solace to the population. The situation did not allow a

long design period and there was little money for the construction, which had be completed as soon as possible. Ban's response was an elliptic inner space of paper tubes encased within an exterior rectangular space under a fabric roof, accommodating eighty people. It was built in only five weeks by 160 church volunteers without heavy machinery and from materials donated by a number of companies. The result was stunning, from both an aesthetic and a spiritual point of view, a space infused with togetherness and bathed in a carefully filtered natural light. The emotive power of the building is high, not least because it addresses environmental and social issues. Ban's attitude embodies a critical approach of today's architectural production system, while claiming continuity with the Modernists. Donated to another community, the church was dismantled in 2005 and relocated to a new site in Taiwan. **YN**

Bibliothèque François-Mitterrand (1995)

Architect Dominique Perrault **Location** Paris, France **Style** Contemporary **Materials** Glass, steel, wood

Très Grande Bibliothèque (TGB, or Very Large Library): just a code name for what was an urban and bureaucratic utopia before it took shape in the form of an actual building. Certainly the most emblematic of President François Mitterrand's *"Grands projets"* (together with the Grand Louvre), it was bound to be the ultimate library, an innovative tool for culture, education, and archiving. It was meant to break new ground in a derelict industrial area and to initiate a new urbanity. Dominique Perrault (*b.* 1953), an architect who had built a mere fraction of the square feet allocated for the TGB, won the international competition. His scheme was simple: readers and researchers would use a secluded garden dug into the ground and open onto the sky, topped by a wooden deck, flanked by four book-shaped corner storage towers. The lines were pure, the surfaces seducing, and the aspiration high: replace and update the old Bibliothèque Nationale and thus shift the intellectual center of Paris toward the east of the city. The TGB was surrounded for many years by wasteland, then by construction sites. However, what long appeared as a forlorn bastion is finally becoming the heart of a multifunctional neighborhood. Some early criticisms remain (dull architecture, impractical inner spaces, unsuitable storage space, and lack thereof), yet this major facility is progressively becoming accepted as an ordinary element of the Paris cityscape. **YN**

"Designing a library in the shape of four open books may sound like a good idea ..."

Philippe Trétiack, author

Akenzua Cultural Center (1995)

Architect Demas Nwoko **Location** Benin, Nigeria **Style** Revised Modernist **Materials** Laterite block, concrete, wood

Located in the ancient city of Benin, the Akenzua Cultural Center is opposite the Oba's (King's) Palace in the old city's public square. This interesting urban juxtaposition sought to update the traditional relationship between palace and city, where the civic functions were normally incorporated within the palace complex. The subtlety emerges in the link to the public square, preserving the historical associations but asserting the independence of the center. Commissioned for the University of Benin in 1972, this building was not completed until 1995 due to intermittent government funding. It eventually became a civic building in its own right. Its core function is theater—an area interesting to architect Demas Nwoko who from 1961 studied stage design and fresco painting on a scholarship at the Academie Beaux Arts in Paris. His understanding of theater design led to a preference for thrust stages over the

proscenium stage, the former being more suited to African performance, which places the audience and performer in close proximity. The building has a strong formal composition of large intersecting volumes. A truncated cylinder is the most prominent, holding the primary spaces of performance and viewing, with a wedge-shaped block to the rear housing ancillary spaces. Entry is via a portico attached to the main block, leading into a naturally lit foyer that reveals the underside of the auditorium seating. The foyer wraps round the curve offset by the thrust stage, leading visitors into the auditorium in both directions. Actors enter the stage from an open courtyard on both wings. Local materials were used throughout—laterite blocks, colored concrete, and timber. The furniture and other details were all produced in Nwoko's workshops in Idumuje Ugboko, giving him further control over his work. **GO**

Villa Eila (1995)

Architect Heikkinen and Komonen **Location** Mali, Guinea
Style Vernacular **Materials** Local materials, stabilized earth

Eila Kivekäs (1931–99) was a Finnish anthropologist, who in 1989 founded the Indigo Association with the aim of improving the life of the local community in West Africa. She chose the Finnish architects Heikkinen and Komonen to design a series of buildings for Indigo, including her home, Villa Eila. These were an unusual commission for the architectural practice, associated as they are with High Tech structures.

To minimize the use of burned brick, which although illegal in Guinea is widely used causing massive deforestation, the architects adopted a

"Heikkinen and Komonen's architecture is one of . . . essence rather than visual image."

Juhani Pallasmaa, architect and critic

"stabilized earth" building technique. This involved adding five percent of cement into moistened earth and forming building blocks under manual pressure. The coolness of night is stored for the day and the warmth of the sun for the night. The roof tiles were made in much the same way, but with the addition of sisal-fiber for reinforcement. The flooring is laid with handmade terra cotta. Employing such materials and methods made use of the local skilled workforce, and required neither electricity nor the burning of wood.

Situated on a west-facing incline, the small home is basic and includes two circular guest rooms, an amenity block, and a living/sleeping area all arranged as independent units with porches in between. The long eastern facade is constructed of woven bamboo, which dramatically filters the light. **JH**

GIG Building (1995)

Architect Günther Domenig **Location** Völkermarkt, Austria **Style** Deconstructivist **Materials** Concrete, aluminum, glass, steel

The GIG Building (Gründer-, Innovations-, und Gewerbezentrum, or Start-up, Innovation, and Business Center) was the first to be built on a rededicated industrial park near Völkermarkt, located on a freshly flattened landscape with empty roads. Günther Domenig (b. 1934) used the commission to build a strong gesture, incorporating an expression of both innovation and welcome. As much as Domenig likes to create complex Deconstructivist compositions of forms and materials in his sculptures and stage designs, his architecture is always meant to be pragmatic and functional in the first place.

The starting point for the design was therefore a felicitous partition of the functions in a simple geometrical order: a horizontal slab containing a long workshop area, and a vertical slab with the administration. The design of the workshops with a steel structure, glass, and corrugated-iron plates is explicitly conventional. The workshops can be flexibly divided or expanded and are easily accessible from the surrounding parking lots. They are connected to the administrative wing by two small bridges, leading from the gallery of the workshops to the accentuated solid base of plain-faced concrete panels, a small ramp winding up to the main entrance.

From here loom eight rectangular concrete pillars and a tower housing the staircase and lift. Hung into this structure there are three floors of ample split-level offices and meeting rooms, accommodated in a building that sets itself apart with a filigree body of steel and glass. This explicitly light body cantilevers out of its concrete cage, dissolving and cambering around the concrete tower. It is a paradigm of an architecture that is staged as dramatically frozen movement, but at the same time cozy and handy. **FH**

Museum of Contemporary Art (1995)

Architect Richard Meier **Location** Barcelona, Spain **Style** Modernist
Materials Concrete, glass, wood, aluminum, stone

"I am still taken with the poetics of Modernism," said Richard Meier (*b.* 1934) in an interview in 1993. And his designs, more than those by any other prominent architect, continue in the heroic tradition of the bright, white, machine-age buildings created by Le Corbusier in the 1920s and 1930s. This museum is no exception.

Meier, a New York architect, was awarded the commission in 1987 as part of a scheme to rejuvenate the Catalan city of Barcelona and, in particular, the rundown quarter of El Raval to the east of Las Ramblas. His response is a monumental, sparkling white oblong—395 feet (120 m) long and 115 feet (35 m) wide—that is in dazzling contrast to the tight, narrow streets and squares that characterize the district.

Inside, the museum is planned around a long, zigzagging circulation ramp that climbs up the glazed south front of the building and provides access to suites of galleries to the north. The cylindrical entrance lobby, with its curvilinear white marble counter, is one of two "vessels" that stand apart from the main bulk of the building, the other being a double-height free-form gallery pod at the east end of the museum. The views from the front are over a new square created by Meier, now a mecca for skateboarders. Views to the north are through small slots in the rear walls of the galleries. On the outside, this northern elevation is clad in aluminum, with doors opening onto a garden.

This pristine museum is in many ways a precursor to the main event, Meier's monumental Getty Center in Los Angeles, completed just two years later. **MF**

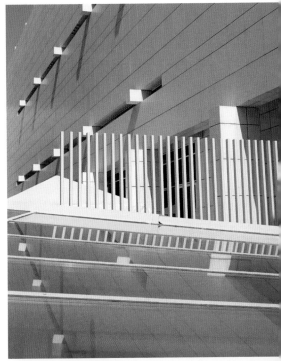

↗ Natural light from glazed roof areas is carefully regulated to ensure that exhibits are not overlit.

⊡ The glazed south front separates the main entrance lobby (at left) and a single freeform gallery pod.

Dancing Building (1996)

Architects Frank Gehry, Vlado Milunic   **Location** Nové Mesto, Prague   **Style** Postmodernist   **Materials** Concrete, glass

On a key corner site in the city center, fronting the river Vltava, an extraordinary building catches the eye. It has a glass tower, flared at the top and bottom, and a second tower beside it clad in concrete panels and surmounted by an open sphere of twisted, perforated metal sheeting, which lights up at night. The main elevation is scored with undulating lines, and the windows are unevenly distributed over its surface.

This is the Dancing Building, often referred to as "Fred and Ginger," as in Fred Astaire and Ginger Rogers. Like the Hollywood couple, it is a showstopper, and its story is extraordinary. It began as a World War II bombsite. After the Velvet Revolution of 1989, the new president, Václav Havel, who lived in the apartment building next door, wanted to fill the site with an exceptional building. Vlado Milunic (*b.* 1941), who had redesigned his apartment, was selected as architect. However, the site was acquired by a Dutch company whose rule was to employ international architects, and Milunic suggested collaborating with Frank Gehry (*b.* 1929), who had a similar approach to site-specific, irregular, and often elusive form making. This was the first project on which he used Catia software, developed for aircraft and industrial design.

The two towers were in part a practical solution, and the overhanging forms allowed the developers to reclaim some of the perimeter of the site lost to road widening under Communism. As a city, Prague stands high in the world league, and the Dancing Building would be hard to miss. It represents an optimistic, liberated country where high standards of building craftsmanship contribute to architectural design. **AP**

↖ The elegant glass tower nicknamed "Ginger" leans provocatively against the solid and upright "Fred."

← Just as Ginger's legs are represented by curved struts, "her" arm appears as a mid-height concrete platform.

Public Lavatory (1996)

Architects Office for Metropolitan Architecture **Location** Groningen, Netherlands **Style** Contemporary **Materials** Glass, steel

Dutch architect Rem Koolhaas (*b.* 1944) is globally recognized as a leading architect and theoretician of contemporary urban life. His works include Euralille in Lille, the Beijing Books Building, and the Maison at Bordeaux. But in 1996, working with colleague Gro Bonesmo (*b.* 1963) from the Office for Metropolitan Architecture (OMA), and photographer Erwin Olaf, he designed this witty public toilet as a permanent feature of Groningen's "A Star is Born" festival. The project was a conscious attempt to stimulate public debate about the nature of public space.

The toilet is located on a public square—an established meeting place for gay men—opposite an outdoor café. The structure has toilets for men and women separated by a shared wall of corrugated opaque glass. Its design, as a municipal commission, is modest. Photographer Olaf, often known for his controversial images, provided internal and external images of men and women in "the battle of the sexes." Dark-blue photographs of dancing figures appear within upper and lower border friezes of smaller dancers. The roof has a collage by OMA, themed on "the global village." Large pieces of jewellike glass are set in the roof. The interior has neat lavatory furniture in stainless steel, and also a mosaic urinal.

The Dutch critic Bart Lootsma noted that, "public and private, masculine and feminine, architecture and art, high and low culture come together" in this fun, practical work. Koolhaas and his colleagues, despite their megastar status, have distilled their inventiveness and design skills into a small but dazzling form that is normally interpreted indifferently and crudely. **ATB**

↗ Animated friezes of dancers in contrasting sizes make a lavatory visit unexpectedly entertaining.

➡ Quirkily arranged photographs by Erwin Olaf signal the presence of Groningen's popular facility.

Aronoff Center for Design and Art (1996)

Architect Peter Eisenman   **Location** Cincinnati, Ohio, USA
Style Deconstructivist   **Materials** Steel, concrete, glass

If you visit Ohio, the Aronoff Center for Design and Art, by Peter Eisenman (b. 1932), is a definitive must-see. A commission from the University of Cincinnati to unify the schools of design, art, architecture, and planning became the perfect showcase for the architect's Deconstructivist theories.

The Aronoff Center is a paradigm of Eisenman's disorientation techniques. It is a challenge to get an organizational understanding of the building. Its east, "signature" facade appears to be tiled, but this proves to be only a faux treatment of the surface. The old and

"We have, actually, to change the relationship of the body to architecture."

Peter Eisenman, architect

new parts of the building have been joined via a twisting spine that opens up to include a café and a huge staircase. Inside is spacious and well lit—despite the considerable lack of windows—and is visually stimulating, with an impressive skylit, central atrium. Apart from the rearrangement of existing spaces, the new parts include a library, theater, exhibition gallery, studios, and offices.

The seemingly ever-moving building has been one of the most talked-about architectural works of the 1990s. Even if it may seem rather complicated, there is a careful analysis of gridlines behind its design, which renders it surprisingly functional through a well-thought out geometry of joints and intersections, from its protruding wedged entrance to its delicately colored volumes. **ES**

Mooloomba House (1996)

Architects Peter O'Gorman, Brit Andresen   **Location** North Stradbroke Island, Queensland, Australia   **Style** Vernacular   **Material** Wood

Designed by husband and wife team Peter O'Gorman (1940–2001) and Brit Andresen (b. 1948), Mooloomba House seamlessly blends into its idyllic island location. Designed for the architects' own use, the two-story, timber-framed holiday home blurs the distinction between exterior and interior, with courtyards and gardens running into interior rooms, and vice versa.

Perched on a hilltop, the house is arranged in a linear fashion, with the north facade overlooking the ocean, while the living areas look east across the garden. Architecturally, the house combines two quite disparate methodologies, incorporating both local vernacular elements and a rigid prefabricated system. The western—vernacular—aspect of the house is characterized by a row of thirteen rough-hewn cypress poles with irregularly spaced rafters and slats making up a semi-enclosed, deck-style element to the building. From here, it is hard to see where the forest ends and the house begins.

The main living and working space on the ground floor, together with the four separate sleeping capsules, each large enough for a bed and little else, on the second floor, are the only fully enclosed sections of the house and are located on its prefabricated side. Because of how it merges with gardens and courtyards, the house appears much larger than its actual 645 square feet (60 sq m). To reach certain areas of the house, you must first go outside, integrating it further with its surroundings.

The house is made entirely of wood, reflecting the architects' career-long interest in using sustainable native hardwoods, in this case eucalyptus. They have created an informal, relaxed house at one with its surroundings—quite an achievement in what is one of the most beautiful locations in Queensland. **GB**

Arken Museum of Modern Art (1996)

Architect Søren Robert Lund   **Location** Ishøj, Denmark   **Style** Deconstructivist
Materials Concrete, steel, glass

In 1988, when still an architecture student and only twenty-five years old, Søren Robert Lund won a competition to design a new museum for modern art located by Køge Bay, 12 miles (19 km) south of Copenhagen. He was very conscious that the museum should correspond to its surroundings and that the lines of the landscape blended in with the building. This resulted in an imaginative design that resembles a ship berthed solidly along the coastal line. Today, Arken affords a fantastic view over the sea, taking in as well as imitating the nautical atmosphere.

White concrete walls and floors, sharp outlines of steel beams and doors, right angles, and various ceiling heights dominate the building. A 492-foot-long (150 m) axial corridor cuts through the entire structure. On one side the wall is plane, the other arched. Along the plane edge there are several exhibition areas, with large as well as smaller intimate rooms, while the curved wall borders a foyer and a multifunctional hall. The art axis not only governs the inside, it also encompasses the outdoor, seemingly wiping out any boundaries between the cultural world within and the natural settings outside. This merging with the external is also emphasized by the skylights, bringing light and spaciousness to the weighty concrete interior.

In the main foyer the visitor is greeted by a vast Norwegian granite block, which powerfully marks the entrance. The block, referring to the history of the landscape, is treated in four different ways, with a matte, rugged, smooth, and high-polished finish. **SML**

↗ Located on top of the building, simple structures suggest the mast and bridge of a tankerlike ship.

➡ Much of the interior space is shiplike, featuring metal gangways and stairs, and exposed ducting

River and Rowing Museum (1996)

Architect David Chipperfield Architects   **Location** Henley on Thames, Oxfordshire, England   **Style** Minimalist   **Materials** Concrete, glass, wood

This sleek, gray building, floating among willows and above water meadows next to the River Thames, is close to the town center of Henley, whose rowing and boating heritage it was built to display and celebrate. Its external form, while starkly and minimally detailed with bare concrete walls and large expanses of glass, is sensitive to the site and locale: its parallel sheds are reminiscent in shape of traditional Oxfordshire timber barns, the riverside boathouses at Henley, and even of upturned boat hulls. This building, distinctively modern yet echoing the past, perfectly demonstrates what its architect David Chipperfield (b. 1953), has described as the balance between "tradition and invention" in good architecture. The museum is on short supports because the site is liable to flood. The raised ground floor has special exhibition galleries, an education center, and a library, which are approached through a sequence of more open public spaces,

flooded in natural light from a full-height wrap-around glass wall. There is a café, a shop, and space for events. In contrast, the upper floor is enclosed, and houses three gallery spaces lit by skylights running their length. The lighting is designed to throw the emphasis onto the exhibits themselves, and the important boat collection the museum holds. This uncompromisingly late-twentieth-century building demonstrates a complete empathy through its form and scale with its setting and function. **RGW**

"An elegant, beautifully made pavilion in the park; a serious work."

Sir Colin Stansfield Smith, architect and academic

MAC-Niterói Contemporary Art Museum (1996)

Architect Oscar Niemeyer   **Location** Rio de Janeiro, Brazil   **Style** Modernist   **Materials** Reinforced concrete, glass

The dramatic site of this museum, a cliff overlooking the Guanabara Bay, makes the MAC-Niterói a major landmark for those approaching Rio de Janeiro by sea. Designed to house the João Sattamini Collection of Brazilian Contemporary Art, this double curving figure is an example of the search for an identity between the local and the universal, and it is realized on an exuberant Latin American scale. The MAC-Niterói is one of many seductive structures by Oscar Niemeyer (b. 1907), 1988 winner of the Pritzker Prize, and one of the principal architects of modern Brasilia. Showing the Brazilian architect's interest in volumetric monumentality and formal purity, this building refers to a previous project—the Caracas Museum of Modern Art—which was planned in 1954 but never built. The bold structure, a three-level cupola with a diameter of 164 feet (50 m), is constructed 53 feet (16 m) above the ground. The museum projects over a 817-square-foot (75 sq m) reflecting pool that surrounds the cylindrical base. The particular relation between form and landscape evokes a sense of the surreal; by night the pool's illumination lights the museum from below and emphasizes the illusion that the building is levitating. The museum is placed on a plaza open to the bay, a pre-existing viewing point. The suspended ramps lead visitors to the two points of access on the top levels. Inside, the first level is occupied by the administration, while the main exhibition hall is on the second level. Two doors lead to the spectacular viewing gallery, a promenade area offering a panoramic view of Guanabara Bay. This gallery, like the other six small exhibition rooms located on the mezzanine, is used for exhibitions. The lower level under the plaza holds an auditorium, service areas, and the restaurant; it also provides an outstanding view of the landscape. **JPV**

Bus Shelter (1996)

Architect Peter Eisenman   **Location** Aachen, Germany
Style Deconstructivist   **Material** Steel

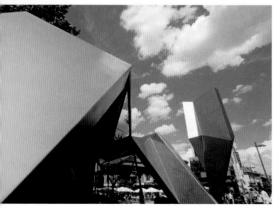

Bus shelters were rarely known for design originality, until leading figure in American Deconstruction Peter Eisenman (*b*. 1932) got involved. Eisenman, known for his unconventional theories and design style, developed his portfolio through a variety of commissions, from private houses to large cultural centers. The JC Decaux bus stop in the center of Aachen is probably his smallest-scale work—and possibly the smallest Deconstructivist creation ever—yet it remains true to his theoretical principles and unique approach.

The brief was for a simple bus shelter and street furniture prototype, to be manufactured by French company JC Decaux. Simple, though, is not a word in Eisenman's elaborate vocabulary. The design was based on the idea of "folding," using a pattern that would generate easily mass-producible, yet individual creations. The shelter essentially consists of two parts: a folded structure to serve as a point for announcements and advertising, and the actual shelter. It comprises two basic steel plates, a gray and a gold one, that form projecting benches for waiting passengers' seating, and provide the necessary functionality and comfort.

The bus shelter resembles more an oversized steel-legged insect on the pavement, than a conventional bus stop. The space created is, in true Eisenman style, deceivingly complex. Even the many "legs" are all different from each other, spawned from the playful folds in Eisenman's giant origami. **ES**

↖ Designed to be seen as high art, Eisenman's work was criticized for being insufficiently user-friendly.

← Passing motorists enjoy the shapes of the bus stop, all the more because they do not require shelter.

RMIT
Storey Hall (1996)

Architect Ashton Raggatt McDougall **Location** Melbourne, Australia
Style Contemporary **Materials** Sandstone, bronze castings, MDF

From its earliest days Melbourne has had a passion for architecture and for promulgating its own story. Storey Hall began its life as an assembly hall for the Hibernian Society, later becoming the home to the Women's Sufferance Movement. In 1954 the Royal Melbourne Institute of Technology (RMIT) acquired it as a gift from the Storey family, whose deceased son John had been studying at the institute. Modeled on the eighteenth-century type, the building had a rusticated basement, a *piano nobile*, and above that a hall with a horseshoe balcony that was supported on cast-iron columns and reached from a staircase that rose from the side of the foyer. The roof slid open to reveal the stars and release the heat and gases created within.

By the 1960s the hall had been gutted and rebuilt, with only the horseshoe balcony remaining. By the 1990s the building was unusable, as it did not meet fire egress standards. The university ran a limited competition to bring its prime public space back into use, and this was won by Ashton Raggatt McDougall (ARM), with a design that demolished two small adjacent buildings and created a new circulation system over a 300-seat lecture theater, and a new foyer at the level of the assembly hall floor, with a mezzanine gallery giving access to the balcony.

The interior of the hall itself was relined using Roger Penrose's non-periodic tiling system, in which two lozenge-shaped forms are used to cover any surface, concave or convex. This houses the air-conditioning ducts and provides an acoustic shell. The riotous, mainly green-and-white interior wins over even the most puritan of critics, and is an early, possibly the earliest, example of the use of the New Mathematics in architecture. The lozenge design also makes a striking entrance to the new section. **LVS**

District
Heating Plant (1996)

Architects Boje Lundgaard, Lene Tranberg **Location** Faaborg, Denmark
Style Postmodernist **Materials** Concrete, yellow brick blocks

When designing a heating plant, form is bound to follow function. For example, a large gas engine needs specific covering and surroundings for functional and safety reasons. Adding visual and aesthetic qualities to industrial buildings may seem challenging, but, in more recent times the challenge has been taken up, and power stations are no longer hidden.

At the southern part of Funen, the island between Jutland and Zealand, is the District Heating Plant of Faaborg, in an open area just outside the town near a lake. The plant consists of two identical mirrored

---

"One is caught, not by a special detail or a definite spectacular effect, but by the atmosphere."

Martin Keiding, architect and writer

---

buildings in which the gas engines are placed; in between the buildings is a large accumulation tank. Two smaller buildings, with control and monitoring facilities, are on the other sides of the tank, making the design of the plant symmetrical and harmonious. The concrete constructions, with facades of large yellow brick blocks, speak of geometry and stringency, which form prevalent characteristics throughout the design.

With the undulating green fields and the lake as its closest neighbors, the District Heating Plant is among natural elements, away from the public who use the energy that it produces. The architects allow the design to speak its own architectural language, not having to relate to other buildings. As a sculpture in its own right, it stands both isolated yet elegantly majestic on the green fields of Faaborg. **SML**

Solomon R. Guggenheim Museum (1997)

Architect Frank Gehry   **Location** Bilbao, Spain   **Style** Deconstructivist   **Materials** Steel, titanium, limestone, glass

"Architecture should speak of its time and place, but yearn for timelessness."

Frank Gehry, architect

⬆ Jeff Koons's 43-foot-high (13 m) topiary sculpture *Puppy* is the first exhibit likely to be seen by visitors.

➡ Thin titanium panels follow the billowing (computer-aided) contours and sharp turns of Gehry's design.

The Canadian architect Frank Gehry (*b.* 1929) was a bold choice for the design of this European outpost of the Solomon R. Guggenheim Foundation. This distinctive, titanium-clad museum opened in 1997 and was soon hailed as a leading example of the Deconstructivist style—a non-linear, fragmented thread of architecture employed by designers such as Daniel Liebskind, Bernard Tschumi, and Zaha Hadid.

The facade displays some of the common aesthetics of Gehry's work—sinuous, organically sculpted contours constructed from 0.01-inch-thick (0.5 mm) titanium panels, and an anarchic juxtapositioning of interconnected shapes and volumes to resemble a confused yet wholly unified system of architectural jigsaw puzzles. It is important to note that the structural and load-bearing complexities of Gehry's designs could not have been physically implemented without the aid of computer-modeling software. This was a key consideration emblematic of its mid-1990s context—a period when the tools with which architects dreamed up their buildings were rapidly evolving.

At sunset, the fast-disappearing sun creates a dramatic halo around the titanium shell of the Guggenheim, allowing the building for a split-second to resemble the stern of a ship, or a crane used for loading sea freight. This, together with the fishlike titanium scales that envelop the structure, is a direct reference to Bibao's role as a major port, and the fact that the museum is on the River Nervion.

The positioning of the building is problematic—surrounded on the one side by a forest of stacked-up shipping containers, and on the other by a heavily congested motorway. It is almost as if Gehry intended to integrate the building into both the cultural and the visual fabric of Bilbao—a lofty aim that appears to have been succinctly achieved. **AT**

Sheep Farm House (1997)

Architect Denton Corker Marshall   **Location** Kyneton, Victoria, Australia   **Style** Deconstructivist   **Materials** Glass, concrete

The Sheep Farm House, located in a treeless landscape northwest of Melbourne, represents a contemporary take on the classic Australian pastoral homestead. The complex, built for a high-tech sheep farm, includes the main house, a guest wing, garage, machine shed, shearing shed, and covered yards. A high concrete wall, 656 feet (200 m) long, gathers the ensemble of buildings together, helping to create an overall identity for the farmstead. The wall also helps to locate the complex in the wide, open landscape, giving substance to the buildings and a protective buffer against the elements. Access to the farmhouse and associated buildings is via a courtyard of 377 square feet (35 sq m), enclosed by austere concrete walls. The entry is denoted by a black rectangle of concrete, tilting backward and slightly higher than the rest of the courtyard. The farmhouse itself is a heavily glazed, symmetrical pavilion, two

bays wide, and open along the east side, with porches on the south and north ends that provide outdoor areas in the summer and winter. Private spaces, including the bathrooms, bedrooms, study, and storerooms, are accommodated within two "solid boxes" inside the main volume. The roof, like all the buildings in the ensemble, has a single pitch and extended eaves. Denton Corker Marshall's Sheep Farm House is widely regarded as one of the finest Australian houses of the late twentieth century. **AM**

"[The house's] heroic sculptural forms challenge all expectations of a bush homestead."

Mark Wakely, architecture journalist

Library, Delft University of Technology (1997)

Architects Mecanoo Arkchitekten   **Location** Delft, Netherlands   **Style** Contemporary   **Materials** Glass, steel, grass

Mecanoo, founded in 1984 in Delft, was a leading studio of Dutch Postmodernism. Bart Loosma, the architecture critic, wrote that "Mecanoo excels in quotations from modern and contemporary architecture, which are deployed in a variety of ways and manifest themselves in sophisticated, clear, efficient ground plans or in the atmosphere evoked by the design." Most architects, when asked to design an academic library, produce a box for books and computers. At Delft University of Technology, Mecanoo created an original design in which the ground plane folds upward at an angle, creating a sloping grassy hillock on which students can sit in fine weather. The library is accommodated in the volume below the turfed roof. A distinctive white, glass cone projects above the grass plane; at night it gleams like a beacon. The cone rests within the main hall, above the circulation desk area, on what seem like ten inward-sloping tent poles, creating an image like the underside of a resting space rocket. The hall feels very open, almost empty. Inside the cone, a spiral staircase coils all the way up, leading to the four stories of reading rooms. The library's glass walls are gently folding, contrasting with the mass of the hall. Books are stored in the central repository under the hall. Computer terminals, offices, and book stacks are layered in open galleries around the central cone atrium. Because the cone penetrates the roof, daylight suffuses the building, creating a light, open, studious environment. The lower two levels have ramps that lead to the stacks, alongside one wall. This is painted in Mecanoo's signature color blue, which contrasts with the mixed color book spines. Mecanoo rethought the idea of a library as a place of light and creativity. And how many libraries do you know where you can snowboard on the roof in wintry weather? **ATB**

Kunsthaus (1997)

Architect Peter Zumthor **Location** Bregenz, Austria **Style** Minimalist **Materials** Steel, glass, concrete

The Kunsthaus in southern Austria is an ethereally beautiful and technically masterful art gallery that offers visitors, admirers, and passersby an opportunity to indulge in the very essence of Swiss minimalist design. Winner of the Mies van der Rohe prize in 1998, the gallery also earned its creator, Peter Zumthor (*b.* 1943), the Carlsberg prize. The achievement of the Kunsthaus is not just in Zumthor's seamless and elegant design, but in his technical skill at capturing natural daylight and filtering it through the galleries, thus removing the need for complex or unsightly lighting. The Kunsthaus has three levels of galleries joined by a simple circulation system of concrete stair and lift. The external skin of brushed glass is self-supporting, hung delicately from a steel frame, and is separate from the three main galleries. A separate floor—a light plenum—is constructed above each room, and varying natural daylight is diffused through a glass ceiling and spreads evenly into the space beneath. A distinctly separate and striking black concrete building is home to the messy business of administration, shops, and café. Every detail in the Kunsthaus, from the handrails to the finely designed metal frames supporting the glass ceiling should be admired for its elegance and quality. This finesse is nothing less than could be expected from Zumthor, an architect who for his entire career has prioritized detail and construction to remarkable effect. **BG**

"Construction is the art of making a meaningful whole out of many parts."

Peter Zumthor, architect

Fuji TV Headquarters Building (1997)

Architect Kenzo Tange **Location** Tokyo, Japan **Style** Postmodernist **Materials** Steel, glass, titanium

The island of Odaiba, just in front of Tokyo harbor, was built in the 1980s as a new amusement park for the metropolis. Built on reclaimed land, this artificial landscape provides the setting for the iconic Fuji TV Headquarters Building. Architect Kenzo Tange (1913–2005), who played a key role in designing the postwar reconstruction of Japanese cities, created a Neo-Metabolist megastructure that denies any relation to human scale in its amusement park surroundings with its gigantic Ferris wheel and fun rides. The building consists essentially of two huge blocks connected by a web of enclosed corridors, over which is suspended a massive, shiny, titanium-faced sphere, that appears like a UFO that has crashed into the structure. The sphere, which is 105 feet (32 m) in diameter and weighs 1,300 tons, houses an observation platform and cafe, popular with tourists. The grid structure of the huge volume is further emphasized by recessed

banks of windows and textured columns. The escalator, encased in a tube of glass and steel, is reminiscent of the Pompidou Center in Paris, but, generally speaking, the architecture of this innovative building is unparalleled. Yet, it seems somehow to be perfectly scaled for Tokyo and, thanks to its titanium cover, it shimmers in the light like an oversized machine from the future. There is no better place to experience the work of Kenzo Tange, Japan's most visionary contemporary architect. **FH**

"Under no circumstance would I wish my buildings to appear traditional."

Kenzo Tange, architect

Tokyo International Forum (1997)

Architect Rafael Viñoly **Location** Tokyo, Japan **Style** High Tech **Materials** Steel, glass

Tokyo International Forum is Japan's largest congress center, comprising two theaters—one of the largest in the world—more than 64,583 square feet (6,000 sq m) of exhibition space, several conference rooms, a library, numerous restaurants, and shops.

The project began with an open international competition held in 1989, which was won by New York architect Rafael Viñoly (*b*. 1944). As the new project was to occupy the previous site of Tokyo's city hall, which has two of the city's busiest commuter hubs on either side of it, the designers had to work with an irregularly shaped site. Viñoly proposed a dramatic design consisting of a 196-foot-high (60 m), hull-shaped glass and steel atrium accompanied by a group of four blocklike performing arts areas that increase in size sequentially, to house the theaters, restaurants, and shops. These various buildings are linked by a granite-lined public plaza that allows for Tokyo's constant stream of pedestrian traffic. The plaza also contains the Yurakucho Canopy—the world's largest freestanding glass structure.

The atrium forms the main entrance to the complex, and from inside this immense soaring space it is said that the view is like looking through an X-ray of a whale. The atrium is crisscrossed on the inside and around the perimeter by a number of glass-encased walkways that also act as structural braces against high winds. It consists of 215,280 square feet (20,000 sq m) of laminated, heat-strengthened glass that allows natural sunlight to penetrate to the lower levels. Tokyo International Forum is a truly unique civic complex, which also has the power to astound. **JM**

↖ Viñoly's structure strikes a distinctive pose as an urban landmark of Japanese architecture.

← The interior of the great hall is bathed in natural light filtering through its curved glass roof.

National Studio for the Contemporary Arts (1997)

Architect Bernard Tschumi **Location** Tourcoing, France **Style** Postmodernist **Materials** Corrugated steel, glass

Officially known as the National Studio for the Contemporary Arts, the Le Fresnoy Art Center is located in Tourcoing, a city in northern France close to Lille and the Belgian border. The center is similar to many new museums being built around the globe, where provincial, disused sites have been transformed into ideal settings for spaces dedicated to the contemporary arts. This art center is designed for multimedia and interdisciplinary art, consisting of video, large-scale installations, and sound works.

The plan designed by Bernard Tschumi (*b.* 1944) incorporated an old structure that was due to be razed. This garish yellow building was originally designed in the 1920s as a leisure complex, which included a cinema and room for activities such as ballroom dancing, skating, and horseriding. Although in poor condition, it had extraordinary spaces that could be utilized in the new scheme. Tschumi built an umbrella, shedlike roof over the existing building to keep out the elements. The upper horizontal surface of this steel box features large letters that spell out "Le Fresnoy," punctuated by large openings for heating, ventilation, and air conditioning for the spaces below. Conceptually, Tschumi designed the structure as a box within a box, rather like a Russian doll effect.

For years Tschumi was internationally known as a theoretician and respected teacher, without having ever built a structure. His growing body of practical work, however, includes the Parc de la Villette in Paris and the New Acropolis Museum in Athens. A visit to Le Fresnoy is a must because there are simply too few of Tschumi's brilliant ideas in fruition. **KAB**

↗ The protective roof allowed the magic of the original site to be preserved, restored, and enhanced.

→ The striking spiral staircase coils down the outside of the building like a vivid blue ribbon.

Educatorium (1997)

Architects Office for Metropolitan Architecture (OMA) **Location** Utrecht, Netherlands **Style** Contemporary **Material** Concrete

The Educatorium is the centerpiece of a masterplan that OMA undertook for the Uithof, the campus of Utrecht University. "Educatorium" is an invented term meaning factory for learning. It consists of lecture and examination rooms, large public areas, and a restaurant. The main architectural distinction of this building is the remarkable use of concrete. Its ground floor morphs and wraps around the building, into the roof of the level above. A ramp bifurcates the foyer, leading down to a canteen and up to two auditoria on the first floor. Next to the entrance a covered area features bubblelike sculptural elements that serve as places for students to hang out, as well as an area for bicycle parking. The design shrewdly appropriates precedents from both architectural history and contemporary art. The reflective surfaces of the building seem to expand the space infinitely, evoking the aesthetic sensibility of U.S. artist Dan Graham.

Meanwhile, the open-plan arrangement of the lecture halls and offices bring to mind the work of Mies van der Rohe. Such eclectic references are synonymous with Rem Koolhaas and OMA. The practice, which prides itself on having no style, can be categorized as compact urbanism. Rem Koolhaas and OMA have been responsible for some of the most groundbreaking buildings in recent years including Casa de Musica in Porto, the Prada shops in New York and Los Angeles, and Seattle Central Library. **KAB**

"[Koolhaas has a] restless mind, conceptual brilliance, and [the] ability to make a building sing."

J. Carter Brown, Pritzker Prize Jury chairman

Minnaert Building (1997)

Architects Neutelings Riedijk Architects   **Location** Utrecht, Netherlands   **Style** Contemporary   **Material** Concrete

The Minnaert Building at the Uithof campus of Utrecht University is named for Marcel Minnaert (1893–1970), a Belgian astronomist with left-wing sensibilities, who became a pioneer of solar research at the university. The faculty building, which holds a key corner plot in the northwestern cluster of the Uithof, has several innovative design characteristics. Its striking, red exterior is typical of architects Neutelings Riedijk's interest in unusual formal solutions. The earth-colored, sprayed-on concrete facade features rippled elements that resemble the scaly surface of a lizard. This uneven, scar tissue–like effect was the result of a construction constraint because only a certain amount of concrete could be applied daily. The one-story, giant block lettering spelling "Minnaert" is a clever alternative to the traditional weight-bearing column. The most unusual feature, however, is a roof that is intended to leak. When it rains, openings in the ceiling allow water to fall into an interior pond, located in a large public space that serves as a gathering point for students. From here, it is pumped through a series of ceiling grilles into the lower floor, providing air conditioning for the computer labs. The warmed rainwater then flows back to the pond, where it cools during the night, ready for a new cycle the next day. The intentional ugliness of the building and its designers' refusal to project any artistic ideal, pays homage to the godfather of Dutch architecture, Rem Koolhaas. **KAB**

"You can only think of new things by questioning the old ones."

Neutelings Riedijk, architects

Villa VPRO (1997)

Architects MVRDV **Location** Hilversum, Netherlands **Style** Contemporary **Material** Concrete

The Netherlands has one of the highest population densities in Europe resulting in limited resources. It was therefore not surprising that some of the most groundbreaking work in architecture in the 1990s was unleashed by a group of young Dutch architects. MVRDV, with its unique blend of experimental formalism, is one of the practices to have had the greatest influence on contemporary Dutch design. Villa VPRO, the headquarters of the broadcasting company in Hilversum, is one of the most successful examples of this influence. The structure has a deep, almost square footprint due to site constraints, and this combines compactness with an unseen spatial differentiation. The concrete slab is a unifying element and spatial device that folds, ramps, and bends through the several floors of the building creating a continuous open space. Cuts, folds, and a courtyard form spaces that allow light to penetrate deep into the building. The result is an open-plan office where the distinction between inside and outside becomes blurred. The height differences in the interior, combined with the compartments created by the voids, allow for a wide range of working spaces. As a concept, the design challenges the idea of corridors and cellular offices. MVRDV's use of the folded slab as a structurally integral element, thus making columns redundant, could be one of the first truly revolutionary designs of twenty-first-century architecture. **LT**

"MVRDV pursues a fascination for radical methodical research: on density and on public realms."

MVRDV Architects design statement

WoZoCo (1997)

Architects MVRDV   **Location** Amsterdam, Netherlands   **Style** Contemporary   **Materials** Concrete, steel, wood

WoZoCo rather shakes up the usual stereotype of the cozy retirement cottage or bungalow. Thirteen of the hundred apartments in this block, reserved for people over fifty-five, are cantilevered out from its north facade into thin air—looking from afar like giant oversized balconies. At first sight this daring aesthetic seems purely an example of architectural gymnastics. However, it is a design solution that juggles the competing demands of the brief to increase density—getting one hundred apartments from a footprint for a block of eighty-seven—while maximizing the light inside and maintaining the green space outside. Extra costs for the structural bracing required to stabilize the cantilevered flats were offset against gains in the increased number of living units on the site. This is an ingenious solution to the pressure on this postwar garden suburb of Amsterdam to increase residential density. This pressure is typical for the country as a whole: the Netherlands is already one of the most densely populated countries on the planet and new design solutions are constantly being sought to balance the growth of the built environment against the maintenance of open public space—in a country where the land is often manmade. Over recent years, these pressing issues have resulted in the nurture of a very robust and experimental architectural culture in the Netherlands. MVRDV is one of the most celebrated Dutch practices to emerge from this milieu, with the questions of density and public space being central to their work, both built and published—they have written a series of books on the subject, beginning with the polemical *Farmax* in 1998. The WoZoCo building scheme has to be seen, both for its edgily unbalanced look, and to walk around and experience the unnerving feeling of standing underneath one of the massive cantilevered units. **RGW**

Wall-less House (1997)

Architect Shigeru Ban **Location** Karuizawa, Nagano, Japan
Style Minimalist **Materials** Concrete frame, steel

The Wall-less House is built on a steep, wooded hill. To provide a level site, its floor plate is cut back into the slope. However, rather than ending with a massive retaining wall at right angles, the floor plate slopes up and back on itself to become the roof slab. This continuous curving form makes a very rigid structure, that allows for only minimal support of the roof slab, just three slender columns, enabling almost complete openness of the interior to the outside world.

Internally, the elements of a traditional dwelling—kitchen, bathroom, and toilet—are all placed on a

> *"In the Wall-less House, the wall is an extension of the floor. I wanted to clarify the meaning of the wall."*
>
> Shigeru Ban, architect

"universal floor" without enclosure. With no walls or windows, a series of sliding panels and banks of cupboards, 7 feet (2 m) high, are used to divide the internal space and provide privacy when required.

This house is the eighth in a series of what Tokyo-born architect Shigeru Ban (b. 1957) calls "case study houses," referencing the Case Study program of John Entenza's *Arts and Architecture* magazine, which were designed as a new prototype for living in postwar California. Most explicitly, however, the design is inspired by Mies van de Rohe's Farnsworth House (1951), the first "glass" dwelling. Here, Ban takes this concept one step further, by replacing the glass walls with nothing, making it literally open to nature. With this radical, simple move, Ban directly questions the relationship between building and landscape. **RGW**

Kowloon Ventilation Building (1997)

Architect Terry Farrell **Location** Kowloon, Hong Kong, China
Style Industrial **Materials** Concrete, metal

In the not too distant past, a flight into Hong Kong was akin to a fairground ride. Kai Tak International Airport sat on land reclaimed from the harbor surrounded by skyscrapers. Approach demanded a stoic attitude or a stiff gin and tonic. When the new Chek Lap Airport was developed on an island just off Lantau, miles from downtown Hong Kong, it linked airport to city with the MTR subway line.

Pumped marine sand created the West Kowloon reclamation site. The land is public park and service system for the MTR. The Kowloon Ventilation Building,

> *"I am a great believer in cities as the most creative work of art that we have ever come up with."*
>
> Terry Farrell, architect

designed by Terry Farrell (b. 1939), sits on the southern tip of this site. Floodgates, power transformers, and ventilation units dictate the function, but not the form, of Farrell's building. Farrell says the shape was meant to reference the undulating landscape and the harbor waves, but it looks more like a crouched organism with four haunches raised above the main bulk of its body, ready to reverse evolution and slide back into an aquatic life. Mechanical fans ventilate the airport railway tunnels, and preventive floodgates control water. The building includes stairway entry/exit points for service workers and emergency evacuation points for civilians. Farrell's building is the only one of the series to be protected from eventual integration into new development. It will continue to be the West Kowloon sentry at water's edge. **DJ**

National Bank of Dubai (1997)

Architect Carlos Ott   **Location** Dubai, United Arab Emirates
Style Postmodernist   **Materials** Concrete, granite, glass

The National Bank of Dubai is a modern masterpiece of iconic imagery that punctuates the skyline of the United Arab Emirates's main city. The building is based on the form of the traditional *dhow*—the flat-bottomed sailboats that plied their trade along the banks of the Dubai Creek. Today, the *dhows* are without sails, but this visionary building perpetuates their former elegance, which is compounded by the smoothly curving sheet of glass that reflects the water and its boats.

Designed by Carlos Ott (*b.* 1946), the building is strikingly simple being formulated around two main geometric components, the "sail" and the "boat." Two granite columns support a shimmering glass curtain wall that curves toward the waterside and echoes the billowing of a sail. During daylight the glass reflects the sky and the water, whereas at sunset it is bathed in brilliant gold and silver light that lends the building an unearthly and surreal effect.

Beneath the tower and projecting to the front and back is the broadly horizontal banking hall, clad in deep green glass that is representative of the sea. Above the hall, is the curved aluminum roof that takes the shape of the "sail" tower as its form, but is used horizontally to symbolize the hull of the boat, and between the base of the tower and the aluminum roof lies an open space that further adheres to the image of the sail hovering over the boat.

Since studying design in his native Uruguay, Hawaii, and the United States, Ott has designed notable buildings throughout the world, and has contributed particularly to the architecture of the United Arab Emirates. With his inspiring realization of architectural modernity, he has created an iconic and mesmerizing building on Dubai's skyline. **TP**

Petronas Towers (1997)

Architect César Pelli   **Location** Kuala Lumpur, Malaysia   **Style** Postmodernist   **Materials** Reinforced concrete, steel, glass

Modern architectural history is littered with nations, companies, and architects battling to win the title of the world's tallest building, for reasons that vary from patriotic pride through corporate swagger, to personal ego. Petronas Towers in Kuala Lumpur, Malaysia, held that title for a short while and possibly for a mixture of all these reasons.

The building's chief wonder is, of course, its mighty scale. The twin towers, consisting of eighty-eight floors, were built for Malaysia's national oil company Petronas, which occupies one of the towers. These tapering towers are linked by a 190-foot long (58 m), vertiginous "skybridge" between the forty-first and forty-second floors, 558 feet (170 m) up.

Designed by Argentine-born, U.S. architect César Pelli (b. 1926), the building's towers were constructed largely of reinforced concrete. They are clad in a steel and glass facade designed to resemble the motifs found in Islamic art, reflecting Malaysia's Muslim religion. The floor plate design of the towers is also based on simple Islamic geometric forms—two interlocking squares that create a shape of eight-pointed stars. Superimposed on these are eight semicircles that soften the inner angles.

Owing to a shortage of steel and the huge cost of importing it at the time, the building was constructed from superstrength reinforced concrete—good for sway reduction, but twice as heavy as steel. Twenty-nine double-decker elevators whisk people around these high tech towers, which are also equipped with an array of intelligent systems that monitor fire protection, security, and environmental controls. **DT**

⬉ The brief was for a distinctive corporate statement, which the towers achieve through colossal height.

⬅ The towers are based on traditional Islamic design, combining circles with an eight-pointed plan shape.

Tree House (1998)

Architect Van der Merwe Miszewski Architects   **Location** Cape Town, South Africa   **Style** Contemporary   **Materials** Steel, timber, glass, stone

Nestling on the forested slopes of Table Mountain, this small but influential house leapfrogged its way to iconic status at the close of the millennium when it won a series of awards and was published all over the world. Critics were captivated by its jaunty humor, structural invention, and its eclectic fusion of forms.

Overlooking the city, the house manages to do what nearby houses—most of them stodgily anchored to the steep terrain by sprawling plans and flabby terraces—fail to do: it teeters. Aping the gawkily elegant umbrella pines all around, its trunklike columns soar upward before spreading out in an asymmetrical parasol of strut-branches, supporting a roof deck. The impression is of a lightweight pavilion built of trees, its head swaying in the wind while its base is rooted to the bedrock far below.

Despite playful features inside and out, the house—designed for art- and furniture-collecting clients—is restrained in its material palette and refined elevations. An almost stripped vertical order—heavy, opaque stone at the bottom and light, transparent glass at the top—is modulated by the shifting patterns of sliding doors and blinds. As well as changing from bottom to top, the elevation appears to transform through its depth. Internal walls peel away in a play of solid and void, surface and depth. Most dramatic is the curvilinear, maple-ply screen behind which a three-story drop offers views from street-level to the garden room below. The design mimics the exposed but enclosed childhood experience of a treehouse, drawing out the spirit of the site in a way that brings the architecture into dialogue with nature. **MJB**

↗ The open, asymmetrical frame and raised, off-center roof create an impression of awkward fragility.

→ The effect of the roof apparently lifted above its supporting walls is repeated in the lower structure.

Jean-Marie Tjibaou Cultural Center (1998)

Architects Renzo Piano Building Workshop   **Location** Noumea, New Caledonia   **Style** High Tech   **Materials** Iroko timber, stainless steel

> *"[With Kanak architecture] 'building the house' is every bit as important as 'the finished house.'"*

Renzo Piano, architect

⬆ Modeled on Kanak huts, the buildings' outer facades protect the inner structures from wind and heat.

➡ Built on the windward side of Grande Terre, the "huts" trace a single axis, as is common in Kanak villages.

Who said that great architecture is the exclusive privilege of Western civilization and the urban metropolis? The Jean-Marie Tjibaou Cultural Center, on Grande Terre, the main island of New Caledonia, confounds any such assumption. Dedicated to the celebration of the indigenous Kanak culture, it was named after local hero Jean-Marie Tjibaou, who gave his life fighting for independence from the French government in 1989. The center—a complex of ten units of different sizes and functions also known in the local pije language as *Ngan Jila*, which means quite literally "cultural center"—is the work of avant-garde, Italian architect Renzo Piano (*b.* 1937).

The separate units that make up the complex are amazing shell or masklike structures of three differing sizes and heights. This series of buildings expresses Piano's High-Tech architectural idiom infiltrated through traditional Kanak forms. However, these are not simple organic shapes. The ten vertical structures may resemble traditional Kanak huts, but in reality the whole complex is earthquake and cyclone resistant, and features a natural cross-ventilation system for perfect cooling and air circulation, as well as state-of-the-art technological support. The main construction material is stainless steel and Iroko, an amazing African rot-resistant type of timber, which in time takes on a silvery patina. The "huts" are linked together by a central path, a clear reminder of the Kanak village's traditional main ceremonial walkway.

Inspired by the cultural origins and vibrant identity of the Kanak people, the center encapsulates the intimate relationship of the Kanak with their natural environment. Piano emphasizes this by incorporating an "unfinished" feel into the center's design. This humanistic approach highlights the ever-evolving nature of the Kanak civilization and the harmonious symbiosis of the traditional and the modern. **ES**

No. 1
Poultry (1998)

Architect Stirling Wilford Associates **Location** London, England
Style Postmodernist **Materials** Stone, tiles

At one of London's most important junctions—flanked by the Bank of England and Mansion House and facing the Royal Exchange, with a major building by Sir Edwin Lutyens across the road—the latest arrival, No. 1 Poultry, is a confident, swaggering presence in banded colored stone, with a series of sculptural curves on a site suggesting a ship's prow. Unseen from the streets, the interior of the block is hollowed out into a triangular space looking up to the sky, where a startling facade of glazed tiles contains a regular grid of windows, each framed in an alternating pattern of bright pink, turquoise, and yellow colors. The "prow" of the building contains a restaurant, with its own separate, dramatic entrance, and a roof garden leading to the observation area above the clocktower.

As with all buildings by James Stirling (1926–1992), there is never a dull moment. Opinion is divided on whether this posthumously completed work ranks with his best, or whether Mies van der Rohe's earlier proposal for the site would have been better. One of the arguments against the Mies design was that its concept of a slab and plaza had become a cliche by the 1990s, and Stirling's alternative represents a typical solution of the late twentieth century, filling the site while making pedestrian routes through the urban block to replace a medieval street pattern, and opening a new route to the subway station at the same time. Although essentially a speculative office block, No. 1 Poultry gives more in return to the public than most other buildings in its class. **AP**

↖ Stirling's powerful, cylindrical No. 1 Poultry recalls the indomitable bulk of the Castel Sant'Angelo in Rome.

← In the triangular inner well, sections of blue, glazed tiles are bordered by more muted banded stone.

Villa Floriac (1998)

Architects Office for Metropolitan Architecture **Location** Bordeaux, France **Style** Contemporary **Material** Concrete

Mobius House (1998)

Architects UN Studio **Location** Het Gooi, Netherlands **Style** Contemporary **Materials** Glass, concrete

In 1994 Rem Koolhaas (*b.* 1944) and his Office for Metropolitan Architecture (OMA) were commissioned by a family to build them a new home (see page 548) on a hill with a panoramic view over the city of Bordeaux. One member, confined to a wheelchair and intending his life to center around the house, asked OMA to incorporate his special needs in the design.

Instead of designing a house on one floor, which would easily accommodate the wheelchair, the architect surprised his clients with a house on three levels, one on top of the other, with distinctively different ambiences. The ground floor, half carved into the hill, accommodates the kitchen and television room, and leads to a courtyard. The bedrooms of the family are on the top floor, built as a dark concrete box. Between these two levels is the glazed living room, from where the valley below and the city of Bordeaux may be contemplated.

An elevator platform, measuring 10 by 11.5 feet (3 x 3.5 m), comparable to the size of a room and well-equipped as an office, allows access to all three levels. Because of its vertical movement, the platform becomes part of the kitchen when it is on the ground floor, links with the living quarters on the middle level, and serves as a relaxed working space within the master bedroom on the top floor.

OMA has designed a complex case study house, and has surpassed the conventional in every detail. The concrete top floor, for example, rests on three legs. One of these legs, a cylinder that contains the circular staircase of the house, is located off-center. Although this displacement brings instability to the house, equilibrium is restored by a steel beam on top of the house, which is pulled by a cable in tension in a symbolic interpretation of life's uncertainties. **LT**

Situated in a quiet rustic suburb, the Mobius House (see page 549) is a radical departure from modern domesticity. Here the traditional family house is reconfigured as a Mobius strip: the familiar mathematical diagram shaped like a figure eight is used as the organizing principle. A three-dimensional computer model was used by UN Studio to chart the infinitely circular patterns of sleeping, working, eating, and living. The intertwining trajectory of the loop results in a design in which individual working spaces and bedrooms are aligned with collective areas

---

"The building that is unfinished, like the ruin that is in decay, has no functional purpose or use."

Ben van Berkel and Caroline Bos, architects

---

situated at the crossover points. Although the Mobius strip was the inspiration for the building, the formal structure is not a literal translation into architecture.

The house was built for husband-and-wife clients who both work from home. Unlike a traditional home with explicit divisions between functional and social areas, the spaces in the Mobius House have no beginning or end, and thus boundaries are blurred. This represents a brave response to the domestic program, by the architects as well as the clients.

Ben van Berkel (*b.* 1957) works under the wider auspices of UN Studio, whose work has been highly influential for a younger generation of architects and designers, including the United Nude fashion practice. West 8, which often collaborates with UN Studio, designed the landscape surrounding the house. **KAB**

Schoolhaus (1998)

Architect Valerio Olgiati **Location** Paspels, Switzerland **Style** Minimalist **Material** Concrete

Swiss architect Valerio Olgiati (*b*. 1958) does not build quickly. His small school in rural Switzerland took him four years to build but has drawn attention from all around the world for its gentle masterful approach in form and phenomenological approach to material and building—it is a school that will last long beyond the lifetime of its students. The village of Paspels is a scattered settlement with solitary buildings strewn across the landscape, rarely positioned by the roadside The setting is a fantastic mountain panorama, and the new schoolhouse sits easily within its environment. The key to understanding the building is that the rooms are oriented according to a series of distorted angles. In phenomenological terms, there are two main effects: the static system of rooms is set almost imperceptibly in motion and appears more "spatial," whereas from outside the core of the building seems more "bodily." With a square ground plan, the building consists of two concrete parts: an internal structure and an outer shell that, for climatic reasons, only touch where they are joined by shear connectors. The classrooms, clad in larch wood, are situated in the corners of the square, each opening in a different direction. Olgiati came to prominence with his Yellow House, an all-white cube painted roughly with chalklike texture that had no treatment. Similarly, the school has no decoration apart from the expressions of the concrete on the exterior and subtle visual tricks such as a method of extrusion with the classroom windows. The zones within the building have different frames, which subtly communicate a hierarchy of spaces within to the exterior. The window frames for the classrooms were mounted on the internal part of the wall, casting a pronounced shadow. Hallways have their window frames mounted on the exterior—flush with the wall with a bronzelike alloy frame. **BG**

Dominus Winery (1998)

Architect Herzog & de Meuron **Location** Yountville, California, USA **Style** Contemporary **Materials** Reinforced concrete, basalt, steel

The Napa Valley is the setting for this building that, though traditional in technique, seems somehow to break all the rules. The Dominus Winery was the first of a new generation of wineries in which architecture is asked to add another layer of prestige and glamour to the vintages produced. The massive size of the Dominus building—330 feet (100 m) long, 82 feet (25 m) wide, and 30 feet (9 m) high—is tempered by the use of local basalt, ranging in color from black to dark green. This basalt is packed with differing degrees of density into gabions—wire containers most often used to shore up river banks and sea walls. Here, the Swiss firm treats the functional gabions as aesthetic objects. The differing densities of stone allow light to pass through, creating delicate patterns within during the hot California daytime, and allowing the internal artificial lighting to leak out during the night so that the stones seem to emit starlight. The gabions

also work as a thermostat, keeping the temperatures in the storage areas at an even level. The firm is probably best known for their re-imagination of a disused power station in London, Tate Modern (2000). The same understanding of linear geometries can be seen in both Tate Modern and the Dominus Winery, where a simple harmony is achieved through the interplay of horizontal shapes and spaces, rather than by means of extravagant curves, or other aggressive architectural gestures. **GT**

> *"Herzog and de Meuron's work has infused architecture with an aesthetic energy."*
>
> Jorge Silvetti, Pritzker Prize judge (2001)

Jin Mao (1998)

Architects Skidmore, Owings & Merrill **Location** Shanghai, China **Style** Postmodern **Materials** Concrete, steel, glass, aluminum, granite

During 1990, Deng Xiaoping visited Shanghai and urged the municipal government to forge ahead with the development of Pudong, Shanghai's once neglected backyard. Within months, Pudong was leveled and the massive superstructures of nascent skyscrapers began to appear. Pre-eminent among all these structures was Jin Mao. At 1,380 feet (421 m), the tower, housing offices and a five-star hotel, was the tallest building in China, dwarfing its neighbors in Pudong. The elegant tapered structure shrouded in a sleek aluminum lattice frame and glass curtain raised the benchmark of architectural design.

Jin Mao's design relies on a unique structure that comprised an octagonal concrete core and a total of just sixteen exterior columns, which allowed each floor to be extremely open. One of the most notable characteristics of Jin Mao's exterior is the progressively stepped profile, which gives the tower a majestic posture and suggests a sense of elevation above the growing crowd of skyscrapers in Pudong. A fortuitous consequence of this sequential design is the hinted semblance to China's original skyscraper—the pagoda. Chinese characteristics abound in the design, most notably with the recurring association with the lucky number eight. The building is eighty-eight stories high; each segment is an eighth smaller than the previous; the inner core is octagonal; and the design competition that it won was held when Deng Xiaoping was eighty-eight years old.

A visit to this building is a must for the views of Shanghai and the vertiginous thirty-three-story hotel atrium that bores a hole out of the building's core. **ED**

⬉ Jin Mao's stepped profile gives it an organic look, as though it has just grown out of the ground.

⬅ Viewed from below, the jutting summits of each tier of stories recall the multiple eaves of a pagoda.

Thermal Baths (1998)

Architect Peter Zumthor **Location** Vals, Graubünden, Switzerland **Style** Minimalist **Material** Concrete

There are very few examples in the world where a building is able to manifest a single architect's philosophies, experiences, and feelings on materials, light, and logic in one space. Peter Zumthor (*b.* 1943) seems to achieve this unspoken harmony in almost every work he produces and this is felt most strongly in his masterpiece, the Thermal Baths at Vals.

Buried into the side of a spectacularly beautiful mountain range, the baths were built to supplement the industry of a small village. Using local stone, gneiss, quarried from the mountain and a concrete structure, Zumthor pushed his building into the earth, using stacks of finely cut and polished stone to create a labyrinth of small, almost sacred, cavelike pools spot-lit by carefully placed lamps. An open-air pool looks out at the surrounding panorama.

The experience is visceral, but in no way does this compromise on luxury as everywhere each space is choreographed perfectly. The main pool, although feeling dark and subterranean, sparkles with linear shafts of daylight cut from the roof above. Indeed, there is no sign from the outside that the building exists; it barely infringes on the mountain, but simply becomes part of the landscape.

The project took more than six years to complete and Zumthor continually visits and works there. The experience of Vals is one of both rich indulgence and a very fundamental feeling of architecture at its best: not background nor foreground but somewhere in between, shaping spaces and quietly orchestrating a very intentional, primal experience. It is something not to be missed. **BG**

↗ Clad with locally quarried gneiss, the thermal baths at Vals easily blend into their alpine surroundings.

→ At Vals, the bather encounters a world of stone and water, mainly lit by daylight penetrating from above.

Portugal Pavilion (1998)

Architect Álvaro Siza **Location** Lisbon, Portugal **Style** Modernist **Materials** Concrete, glass, steel, wood

Álvaro Siza (*b.* 1933) is arguably the greatest living Portuguese architect. His Portugal Pavilion was the centerpiece of the 1998 Lisbon EXPO, which had "oceans" as its theme. The pavilion features two large, concrete, partly tiled buildings connected by a large plaza that is covered by a vast, curved concrete roof like a huge sail or flag. The massive columns on the building seem to hint at the political architectural style that was popular during the Portuguese fascist dictatorship prior to the 1974 revolution.

This monumental pavilion was intended for use as a government building when EXPO ended, but it has remained empty apart from occasional exhibitions and launch events. There are now plans to establish Portugal's first international Architecture Museum on the site, although leading Portuguese contemporary art collector Joe Berardo has suggested that his vast collection, currently based at the Centro Cultural de Belém in Lisbon, could also one day be housed here.

The structure is poetic and breathtaking in its simplicity. Unlike many architects of international repute, the modus operandi of Siza's approach is to be creatively sensitive while focusing on the surroundings or physical context of the project. Hence, the inclusion of a small grove of olive trees in one of the building's courtyards in reference to Olivais, the name of the city district that is home to EXPO. As a result, the Portugal Pavilion complements the rest of the area, while also keeping in touch with the EXPO theme. The view of the river through the pavilion frames the river vista into a gargantuan photograph, a giant entrance to the river and the city at one and the same time. **MDC**

◥ Vacationers experience the odd sensation of standing beneath Siza's sagging concrete canopy.

◿ Simple but massive geometric supports help to define the unique space under the sheetlike roof.

B018 Nightclub (1998)

Architect Bernard Khoury   **Location** Beirut, Lebanon   **Style** Contemporary   **Materials** Steel, glass, wood

B018 is a nightclub that at first glance resembles a piece of military machinery. Designed by Bernard Khoury (b. 1968), the aerial view of this complex indicates a brutish, industrial facade. This central structure is surrounded by a parking carousel for sixty-four cars, and a floor spotlight system marks out each parking space, creating a dazzling halo effect at night.

The nightclub is located on the site of a former refugee camp that was heavily populated during the Lebanese civil war. Khoury intended this project to explore the contradictions inherent in building an entertainment complex on such a site. The project is built below the ground, its facade pressed into the earth's surface to avoid the exposure of a mass that could act as a rhetorical monument. The subterranean nightclub is accessed by dark, narrow steps that give the visitor a sense of entering a nuclear bunker. Having progressed through two consecutive "airlock" spaces, the visitor finally comes to a cavernous hall, with walls paneled in stained mahogany and layered with theatrical red curtains, as in a David Lynch movie.

Via a carefully angled mosaic of mirrors, the hydraulic opening of the roof reveals the surrounding Beirut cityscape as an urban backdrop to the patrons below. The eventual closing of the roof represents a voluntary disappearance—a gesture of quiet, meditative recess. If clubbing is about escape, then it is no wonder that many of the world's hotspots for hedonism are located deep underground. Yet a large number are also open-air wonderlands, offering people the chance to dance under the stars. B018 is a design masterpiece that offers both experiences. **AT**

↗ The nightclub, below ground level, is opened to the skies when the steel roof is hydraulically retracted.

→ At ground level, there is little to betray the presence of the cavernous and bunkerlike subterranean nightclub.

Kiasma Museum of Contemporary Art (1998)

Architect Steven Holl **Location** Helsinki, Finland
Style Minimalist **Materials** Zinc, aluminum, brass, concrete

Kiasma, designed by Steven Holl (*b.* 1947), sits in its surroundings like a peculiar, shy alien—situated at a busy road junction at the heart of Helsinki, close to a statue of the former president Mannerheim, the 1930s functionalist Post Office, and the Finnish Parliament building across the road. *Kiasma* means the crossing of two lines, like an "X." From the museum's foyer, the visitor can make choices about where to go, either toward the permanent exhibitions or into a temporary show. The building is also situated at an important street crossing. And then there is the mixture of soft and angular forms, light and heavy materials—in many ways the building represents a crossing.

The metal-clad exterior does not hint at the simple beauty within. The entrance hall opens up to the ceiling, with natural light pouring in from various directions. Moving through it, the building looks different from every angle, with a straight line here and a curve there, surprising views and pieces of sky visible through unexpected windows. The serenity of natural light contrasts with the rough interior surfaces, reminiscent of materials used in industrial spaces.

The Kiasma building serves its purpose perfectly. As the museum of contemporary art, it moves, fascinates, and challenges the visitor. Apart from its art and events program, the building serves as an impromptu meeting point; young skaters populate the building's surroundings, and in the summer the grass knolls at the back are a popular spot. Kiasma is nothing if not surprising. **RK**

↖ Clad in different metals, the building shimmers in the summer sunlight and is sleet-beaten in winter.

← From one side, a curving, metal-clad wall extends directly upward from the ground to form the roof.

Casa Nanon (1998)

Architect Ettore Sottsass   **Location** Lanaken, Belgium
Style Modernist   **Materials** Concrete, stone, glass

Ettore Sottsass (b. 1917) was born in Innsbruck, Austria, and studied architecture in Turin. He traveled widely in Europe, America, and Asia, finding inspiration for his signature style. Sottsass also found fame as a furniture and industrial designer and is noted for his innovative, experimental use of new materials, especially fiberglass.

Sottsass's passion for furniture design works in holistic harmony with his building designs. He created Casa Nanon for a fellow designer and art collector, Edmund Mourmans, who was also a close friend. This friendship allowed Sottsass to create a house truly

> ## "You don't save your soul painting everything in white."
>
> **Ettore Sottsass, architect**

designed around its owner and family—as well as their collection of birds, for which Sottsass incorporated aviaries into the shell of the house.

The house was specially designed for the family, with "secret staircases" for Mourmans's children to play and hide in, and creatively laid-out gardens. The whole project places an emphasis on togetherness, without intruding on individual privacy: at the core of the Mourmans's home is a courtyard, from which the other areas of the house emanate. The bedrooms, studies, and living area are on the ground floor, with the kitchen and library on the floor above. There is a strong emphasis on color, harmony, and accessibility, Rooms are seen and accessed from the courtyard through sliding glass doors that make the courtyard and the house essential parts of one another. **LH**

Karmøy Fishery Museum (1998)

Architects Snøhetta   **Location** Sletten, Vedavågen, Norway
Style Modernist   **Materials** Concrete, glass, juniper

Karmøy is an island located off the west coast of Norway. Its name comes from the Old Norse expression, *Kormt,* meaning shelter. Here, fishing has always been the mainstay of life. The rich history of the industry led to the construction of the Fishery Museum. Architects Snøhetta conceived a strong and intense building for the museum, which absorbs and becomes part of its immediate surroundings.

The limited budget for the Fishery Museum resulted in a simple, yet highly relevant and contextual building. It lies by a narrow inlet surrounded by hillocks and scattered housing. One elongated rectangular frame of in-situ concrete makes up the entire design. Only a few windows are positioned along the two long walls, but one large window at the end of the wall facing the water, lets in vast amounts of light to the gray concrete interior where a simple wooden ramp combines the second and third floors. Visitors enter the museum building from the landside; once inside, they are immediately drawn to the view of the fjord beyond the long exhibition room. Here the focus is clear: the collections housed indoors correspond to the natural world outside.

In a dramatic statement, the museum's end curtain wall cantilevers over the edge of the landscape, which drops down steeply to the waterside. This simple feature makes the building especially interesting. In an honest and open way, it brings instant contact with the lives of the fishermen and the fjord. The architects have applied a local craft technique to one of the museum's exterior walls; by using Einer—a coastal bush of the juniper family—they have woven wooden screens incorporating the contemporary architecture with the surrounding roughness of nature. **SML**

Oriente Station (1998)

Architect Santiago Calatrava **Location** Lisbon, Portugal **Style** Expressionist **Materials** Concrete, steel, glass

*"... typical of [Calatrava's] exciting
... railway stations, utilizing
beautiful and organic forms ..."*

Derek Avery, *Modern Architecture* (2003)

⬆ The vaulting supports of the fourth-story train station have been likened to the skeleton of a marine animal.

➡ Soaring high above the exiting trains, the station's roof canopy is clearly inspired by plant forms.

The Gare do Oriente transport terminus by the Spanish architect Santiago Calatrava (*b.* 1951) was commissioned by the city of Lisbon in 1993, after an international closed competition. It was intended to serve the great number of visitors expected for the Lisbon EXPO in 1998 and then act as a new city center hub. This project was part of Portugal's endeavor to rebrand itself as a vibrant modern nation.

In fact Oriente acts as a form of gateway between Lisbon and EXPO. The initial lofty aims for the project, as a catalyst for a new civic center, have never quite materialized. However, the place is always full of people because, in addition to being a transport terminus, it hosts fairs in its main foyer and is adjacent to a major shopping center, concert halls, and exhibition spaces. It will become even busier when the metro link with Lisbon Airport eventually opens.

The huge structure has three self-contained parts and is divided into four levels. The uppermost level carries the platforms, the middle levels have retail outlets and links to the shopping center, and the lower level has more connections to metro and bus terminii; it then emerges at the surface to serve as an entrance to EXPO city. Oriente displays the trademark Calatrava organic theme: seen from above, the main vaulted body of the train station resembles the huge concrete skeletal form of a marine animal, while the roof canopy is like a field of gigantic steel palms. Calatrava may have wanted to make an architectural reference to the oceanic theme of the 1998 EXPO.

Anyone passing through the station is struck by its immense scale and intricate nature. Despite its small number of ticket booths, lack of waiting rooms, and terrible bathrooms, it possesses an elegant, cathedral-like atmosphere. Due to the theatrical lighting scheme of the building it has an especially spectacular impact on the Lisbon skyline when darkness falls. **MDC**

Embassy Complex for the Nordic Countries (1999)

Architects Berger + Parkkinen Architekten **Location** Berlin, Germany **Style** High Tech **Materials** Concrete, timber, glass, copper

Since reunification, Berlin has been repopulated with embassies, and arguably the most original of these is the Embassy Complex for the Nordic Countries. Denmark, Iceland, Norway, Sweden, and Finland decided to house their embassies in one complex, with a shared building, the Felleshuset, for functions, dining, and a communal sauna. Berger + Parkkinen won the competition to design the complex, while the individual embassy buildings were designed by firms from the countries concerned. In these security-conscious times, the complex is daring both for housing five different nations in one compound and for the refreshing transparency of its architecture. The positions of each embassy reflects the geographical relationships of the countries, the whole being bound together by a copper panel wall that follows the site boundary. Within this palisade, the architects used timber, glass, perforated steel, and copper louvers to create a sense of lightness and elegance. Each embassy building includes a notable material from its home country, the most dramatic being a 50-foot-high (15 m) granite slab to create the narrow facade of the wedge-shaped Norwegian embassy. By contrast, a walkway canopy that connects the Felleshuset to the Danish embassy is made of translucent glass fiber. This is stretched over a frame and illuminated from within to make a glowing strand across the open end of the compound, an ethereal presence at night. **CB**

"A tension of emptiness is suspended between the buildings like an enduring memory of the whole."

Berger + Parkkinen, architects

Millennium Dome (1999)

Architect Richard Rogers Partnership **Location** London, England **Style** High Tech **Materials** PTFE fabric, steel

It is impossible to detach the Millennium Dome from the political controversy surrounding its conception, construction, and its eventual undignified decline. This is unfortunate because the building itself is inspirational. Its architect Richard, now Lord, Rogers (b. 1933) began his career with that other heavyweight of British architecture, Norman (now Lord) Foster. Their Team 4 practice pioneered the High-Tech style of design wherein many of the elements of a building's construction were not only exposed, but celebrated, becoming features of the building's design. Rogers continued in this tradition after Team 4 dissolved, most notably at the Pompidou Center in Paris. The Millennium Dome is not strictly speaking a dome because it is not self-supporting, but is held up by the twelve 328-foot-high (100 m) support towers. It is the world's largest single-roofed structure being 1,197 feet (365 m) in diameter, covering more than 1 million square feet (100,000 sq m). The number of towers and the diameter measurements make clever references to Greenwich Mean Time and to its location on the Greenwich meridian. The main body of the dome is a tensile fabric, PTFE, also known as Teflon, which is suspended by cables attached to the towers. So light is this construction that it is claimed that the air inside the dome weighs more than the building itself. The Millennium Dome remains an awesome space to enter and a beautiful structure to view from afar. **ER**

> *"[Richard Rogers] enthusiastically [embraces] a technological future with its accompanying aesthetic."*
>
> Dennis Sharp, architect and author

NatWest Media Centre (1999)

Architect Future Systems   **Location** London, England   **Style** Postmodernist   **Materials** Aluminum, glass

London's Marylebone Cricket Club (MCC) is something of a paradox. The club is renowned for its overbearing sense of tradition, yet—as its base at Lord's testifies—it has always taken risks with its architecture—none more so than when it commissioned Future Systems to design an ambitious new Media Centre. The white, aluminum monocoque (single shell) pod, which stands imperiously on two legs directly opposite the main pavilion, was prefabricated at Pendennis boatbuilder's yard in Cornwall. When it opened, this outlandish, Jetsons-style creation had the effect of reinvigorating the cricket ground and, even perhaps, played a small part in revitalizing the British game. The inside is painted a duck-egg blue—apparently inspired by the interior of a 1957 Ford Thunderbird—and is dominated by a tier of lecture worktables that can accommodate around 120 journalists. At the back of the building is a bar with curved walls, and on either side of the main room staircases, there are a string of surprisingly small studio spaces on a mezzanine level, which are used by broadcasters such as BBC Radio, Channel Five, and Sky Sports. That it provides a wonderful view across the MCC's playing field is beyond question, but there have been criticisms from some journalists who use the building. Experienced journalists tend to take the seats at the back of the seating area because toward the end of the day the front two rows can be dazzled by sunlight. The building is, therefore, far from perfect, although it remains a technically daring and provocative piece of architecture that usefully filled a dead space at the historic cricket ground. Perhaps most importantly, however, it proved that the United Kingdom's traditionally conservative establishment—even the stuffed shirts of the MCC—was willing to take risks and put its weight behind contemporary design. **GG**

Peckham Library (1999)

Architects Alsop and Stormer   **Location** London, England   **Style** Contemporary   **Materials** Concrete, glass, steel, weathered copper

If ever an area needed an architectural lift, it was Peckham, a dilapidated part of south London. It is almost impossible not to smile when you look at Peckham Library. Shaped like an inverted "L," wearing a bright orange beret, and tottering on the architects' now trademark stilts, the concrete-framed building has steel and glass curtain walling and is clad in weathered green copper, with pink, yellow, orange, blue, and green colored panels covering the north facade. Inside, it is dominated by the double-height library space, which also contains three stained and polished plywood pods suspended in the air. These were intended as more private reading areas, but are actually used as community spaces and offices. The floor below, meanwhile, houses a city council advice bureau. In fact, this is less a traditional library and more of a local hub. The building itself is ecologically sound, incorporating natural cross-ventilation (the budget

did not allow for air conditioning). Even touches that appear unnecessary serve a purpose. The idea behind the building's jaunty orange cap, for example, is to provide shade for the ventilation shafts and reduce the heat caused by the bright light in the main space. The building won the UK's prestigious architectural award, the Stirling Prize, in 2000, and has helped put Peckham on the map. This optimistic building may have its flaws, but it has been warmly embraced by the thousands of locals who use it every year. **GG**

> *"[Peckham Library] is classy architecture, it opens up new possibilities, and it works."*
>
> Hugh Pearman, architecture writer

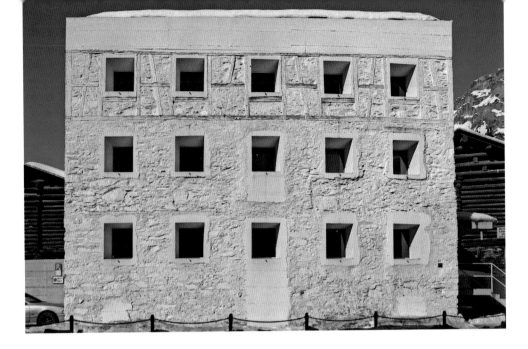

Yellow House (1999)

Architect Valerio Olgiati **Location** Flims, Graubünden, Switzerland **Style** Contemporary **Materials** Stone, *in situ* concrete, wood

Valerio Olgiati's (*b.* 1958) redesign of a nineteenth-century building in Flims constitutes a radical transformation of its character. Placed directly by the curving roadside, the Yellow House enjoys maximum impact on the cultural landscape of a town otherwise hidden from immediate view. This potential is fulfilled by the striking presence of the restored building: a timeless, deeply textured surface bearing the marks of construction, painted overall in white to emerge as a gloriously abstract volume. Its name—the Yellow House—is the last vestige of its past embodiment as a bourgeois town house with Neo-Classical stylistic pretensions. Olgiati's father, himself an architect, donated the old building to Flims on condition that it was renovated to become an exhibition space, painted white, and its covering replaced with a vernacular stone slab roof. Olgiati's design radicalizes these stipulations. Externally the building was stripped

of ornaments, the entrance rotated sideways, and all unnecessary openings filled in to create a seemingly neutral grid of windows. Internally the building was gutted and rebuilt in whitewashed timber, with the eccentric internal structure organizing the open plan into four unequal areas according to the ceiling beams' orientation. On the top floor, the dramatic encounter between this structure and the central roof geometry results in a "broken" pillar, symbolizing the power of challenging academic assumptions. **ID**

> *"The white lime-wash ... for its part gives the house itself the appearance of a 'vision.'"*
>
> Valerio Olgiati, architect

Ricola Marketing Building (1999)

Architects Herzog & de Meuron **Location** Laufen, Switzerland **Style** Contemporary **Materials** Steel, etched glass

For more than a decade Jacques Herzog (*b.* 1950) and Pierre de Meuron (*b.* 1950) have been dominating architectural headlines with high-profile projects, including museums, stadiums, and opera houses. The Ricola Marketing Building in Laufen is one of their smaller but equally important projects because it marks a turning point in the architects' work. It indicates a departure from the "decorated box" with its fluent internal spaces and a "de-materialized" facade. The skin of the building seems to be provided by ivy and vines growing from the roof. Built on a funnel-shaped site, this graceful structure intentionally lacks a defined shape and a perceivable volume. Herzog emphasized that his interest lay with "the external space, the interstitial space, as well as how the space penetrates the building." A wide perron that doubles up as a theaterlike gathering space leads from the representational entrance areas up to the office

floors. Here, spaces are not clearly defined, and glass walls set out territories within the open plan. Again the perception between inside and outside is blurred by the use of glass, providing a flow of space throughout the office. Only bespoke curtains seem to slow this flux, together with the living, planted skin of the outer facade. In this the Ricola Marketing Building combines architecture, nature, and art into one unified inhabitable concept that also reflects the value and the trade of the client in an ideal way. **LT**

"Herzog and de Meuron refine the traditions of Modernism to elemental simplicity..."

Ada Louise Huxtable, architecture critic

House in
Lège-Cap Ferret (1999)

Architects Anne Lacaton, Jean-Philippe Vassal **Location** Lège-Cap
Ferret, France **Style** Contemporary **Materials** Steel, concrete, glass

The Cap Ferret peninsula, with its sand dunes and pinewoods stretching between the Arcachon Bay and the Atlantic Ocean, is one of the favorite retreats for the inhabitants of nearby Bordeaux. The brother-and-sister clients for this house had fond memories of family picnics in the area. Their brief was simple: as large a living space as possible; total respect for the existing vegetation; and down-to-earth architecture.

Architects Anne Lacaton (*b.* 1955) and Jean-Philippe Vassal (*b.* 1954) were first known for their pioneering schemes for single-family houses, based

> ## "[Lacaton and Vassal's] use of new materials . . . enables them to offer optimal and ingenious solutions."

Andreas Ruby, architecture critic

on a highly creative use of technique and materials, ensuring the largest space possible for a given budget. The result here was a corrugated aluminum-coated basic volume raised on thin stilts anchored deep into the sand dune, wide open onto the breathtaking vista of the bay through the forest canopy. Inside, an open space for a simple, easygoing life; outside, the undulating sheeting beneath the house becomes an illuminated sky as it reflects the sun on the water. As requested, no disturbed landscape or topography, no massive foundations, no windbreak walls. No cut trees either: six of these, 98 foot (30 m) high and nearly 100 years old, grow through the house thanks to flexible, rainproof skylights that follow the movement of the trunks in the wind. This "tree house" stands halfway between a dream come true and common sense. **YN**

Poddar
Farmhouse (1999)

Architect Indrajeet Chatterjee **Location** Delhi, India
Style Postmodernist **Materials** Concrete, wood, granite, copper

The luxury of a countryside retreat in an urban context comes in the form of expansive farmhouses for the privileged residents of Delhi. These farmhouses have gained the reputation of being a surreal world of fiction. One can find houses modeled on Swiss chalets or Victorian mansions, all forming what is known as the Punjabi Baroque style. Within this environment, the Poddar Farmhouse is a refreshing change.

Owners of the Sirpur paper mills and a number of hotels, Poddar family members are leading patrons of contemporary Indian art, and their house sits as a

> ## "[Art] makes me look at the same thing—it could be an object or an idea—in a fresh way."

Anupam Poddar, owner

showcase for that collection. Situated in more than 2 acres (0.9 ha) of sprawling landscape, the house visually integrates with the outside space. The living areas are split over two levels, allowing the family to enjoy the stunning views of the landscape and lakes through the large expanses of uninterrupted glass. Primarily executed in exposed concrete bands and infill masonry blocks, externally the building has a quiet and stoic presence.

The highlight of the structure, however, is the elegant copper roof. Made to resemble a horizontal cascade, it spans the length of the residence. The underside of it is paneled in Myanmar teak giving the interior spaces, finished in granite and wood, a warm glow. The Poddar Farmhouse is ultimately a flight of fancy, elegantly grounded in its context. **LT**

Trinational
Environmental Center (1999)

Architect Zaha Hadid   **Location** Weil-am-Rhein, Germany
Style Deconstructivist   **Materials** Concrete, glass

Formerly called the Landesgartenschau pavilion, this boomerang-shaped building was commissioned from the Iraqi-born British architect Zaha Hadid (*b.* 1950) for the German national garden show "Green 99." At the time of its completion it was only the second building to have been realized by this now internationally famous architect. The starting point for the 460-foot-long (140 m) building, which contains an exhibition space and café, was to create a structure that both grew out of and complemented the landscape.

The most striking feature of the design is the way in which the long, snaking ramp gently rises from ground level at the rear of the building to double as a roof and viewing terrace. Hadid's ambition to create nonorthogonal, sculptural space is achieved here in a building made entirely from poured concrete. This material is clearly expressed inside, where a series of ramps bisects the section and walls are angled to give a sense of restless animation. Ribbons of windows are arranged to create geometric patterns on the facade, a detail that is particularly effective when the building is illuminated at night.

The green credentials of the project are subtly incorporated into its design, with features such as a cooling system buried under the "tail" of the structure and shady louvers provided on the windows. Although modest in scale, this building, now an environmental center, can be seen as a precursor to Hadid's later larger scale projects, such as her much-admired contemporary art center in Cincinnati. **MF**

↗ The long, concrete form of the Environmental Center rises above the ground and serves as a roof terrace.

→ Below the overarching concrete roof are two stories, the lower one set partially below ground level.

School of Architecture (1999)

Architects Lang Wilson Practice in Architecture Culture (LWPAC)   **Location** Valparaiso, Chile   **Style** Postmodernist   **Materials** Steel, glass

LWPAC's School of Architecture at the Universidad Técnica Federico Santa María is an award-winning project that represents one of the first architectural structures designed by a generation educated using both computers and traditional forms of representation, such as drawings and models. If common digitally designed architecture often indulges in complex shapes for no deep reason, the School of Architecture demonstrates how computers can influence design beyond its mere appearance. The tight schedule and the limited budget were incorporated into the project, turning them from constraining elements into design possibilities. Rather than housing the program in a series of separate and independent rooms, LWPAC tried to build into the design an idea of incompleteness by proposing a large undefined open space where several activities can take place. Students and teachers are invited to interact with the building, to take ownership of it, and determine where and when activities will happen. Ramps, double volumes, and mezzanines are the architectural elements that make interaction between the architecture and its users possible. The 8,500 square feet (790 sq m) of new space floats on top of the existing school, and is defined by a continuous metal roof that compresses and dilates the internal spaces. The skin of the building is partly covered by louvers that control the environmental conditions. In fact, this building does not have an air-conditioning system but relies on natural ventilation alone. For this reason, it is virtually a zero energy project that was built for just $35 per square foot. Beyond the deep conceptual reasons of the project, a visit to the school, with its sharp shape and uncompromising relation to the existing school, is to experience a modern, daring piece of contemporary architecture. **RB**

Blue Lagoon (1999)

Architects Vinnustofa Architects   **Location** Illahraun Lava Field, Grindavik, Iceland   **Style** Eco-Architecture   **Materials** Lava, concrete, steel, glass

The Blue Lagoon lies in the southwest of Iceland. The lagoon is a geothermal spa with an average temperature of approximately 104 degrees Fahrenheit (40° C). It is surrounded by lava stones and black sandy beaches, rich in silica and salt. This current design is part of a major building scheme to develop the lagoon to meet new public needs and health services. The hot underground is the artery of the complex, which includes a main outdoor pool, smaller interior pools, a restaurant, conference rooms, and health clinics. Due to its rich content of minerals, silica, and blue-green algae, the lagoon has an incredible blue color, and together with the hazy white steam the complex seemingly emerges as something out of this world. The architects let the natural resources of the site govern the design. Lava, rock-clad walls, and timber are important building materials, blending in with the natural surroundings. The concrete sections rest toward the lava landscape whereas the glazed facades open up toward the lagoon. Visitors enter the site by a 656-foot-long (200 m) timber pathway. The walkway transforms into a gully that continues as a wall of lava stones into the entry hall. The architects were particularly inspired by the seasonal change of the Northern light. During dark hours, lights come on around the lagoon; the inside and the outdoor melt together, creating a superb atmosphere in a subtle and elegant Icelandic way. **SML**

> *"[The design is] befriended by nature and inspired by its force and mystique."*
>
> Blanca E. Minervini, geothermal researcher

Nordea Headquarters (1999)

Architects Henning Larsen Architects **Location** Copenhagen, Denmark **Style** Modernist **Materials** Glass, copper, steel, granite

Building near historic sites requires a great deal of intuition and respect from the architect and the planners. It necessitates working with, not against, the existing structures, recognizing the past in order to build the new and modern. Such respectfulness is exemplified in the Nordea Headquarters. The architects have worked through every detail in a meticulous manner, with every element slick and polished. The building complex consists of six glass wings, each six stories high. They are positioned at a ninety degree angle to the inner harbor front. On the south side of the city, away from the harbor, is the main entrance to the bank—a U-shaped building clad with sandstone. It makes quite a contrast to the other buildings, which are light and almost weightless, not only because of the glass facades but also because all the glass sections have been enclosed and raised off the ground by frameworks of copper, which in

time will turn into a pale verdigris color. Similarly, at night, when lights wrap around and underneath the structure, the buildings appear to float off the ground, becoming a part of the canal rather than something solid and concrete. The anchor here, however, is the U-shaped building, which brings us back on land and within proximity of the late Baroque church. Such a meeting between the sumptuous Baroque style and the High Tech, polished bank stimulates a vibrant, architectural dialogue across the centuries. **SML**

> *"While most banks are closed off, Henning Larsen Architects have given this one a transparency…"*
>
> Henrik Steen Møller, author and architecture critic

Norwegian Petroleum Museum (1999)

Architects Lunde & Løvseth Arkitekter   **Location** Kjeringholmen, Stavanger, Norway   **Style** Postmodernist   **Materials** Steel, concrete, granite

The extraction of oil is an important industry in the city of Stavanger. Some twenty years after the oil boom, the geology and, in particular, the history of crude oil production in this region were celebrated in a museum that describes all aspects of this valuable resource. Significantly, the architects have carefully incorporated the features of a drilling platform in the design. The museum consists of five main sections. Facing the city lies a monumental block of gneiss rock that alludes to the Norwegian bedrock carrying the oil, whereas near the waterfront stands the single-story exhibition hall that is made of a glazed facade, gneiss, and black-slate flooring. Fronting the harbor and standing on platforms are three steel-and-glass cylinders, making the theme of this museum obvious. One cylinder acts as an exhibition room, another as a sample of a drilling platform, whereas the third incorporates a 46-foot-high (14 m) space, both above and below the water, where film projections of the sea are shown. It is from these platforms that visitors take in the beautiful view over the Stavanger Fjord. Entering the museum via the massive gray stone building, visitors are introduced to the origins of oil, and as they move through the exhibition the initial closed and solid structure opens up to incorporate the sea. Landing on the platform after learning of drilling and extraction, the journey ends where the story of oil begins: in the sea. **SML**

> *"[The design] is primarily a scenographic interpretation of the North Sea's oil installations . . ."*
>
> Lunde & Løvseth, architects

Burj al Arab (1999)

Architect Tom Wills Wright **Location** Dubai, United Arab Emirates **Style** High Tech, Postmodernist **Materials** Steel curtain with PTFE membrane

The Burj al Arab is recognized around the world as the beacon of the wondrous city of Dubai, similar in status to the Eiffel Tower in Paris and the Opera House in Sydney. It is a symbol of the economic boom and the decampment into the future of Dubai. At 1,053 feet (321 m) high, it is often referred to as the tallest hotel in the world and the first to virtually achieve the service equivalent of seven stars. Designed by Tom Wills Wright to be outstanding in every aspect, it was built to resemble the billowing sail of a *dhow*, a type of Arabian boat on an artificial island of the beach. Two "wings" arranged in a V-shape form a vast "mast," whereas the space between them houses a massive atrium, 590 feet (180 m) tall. Surprisingly, this allows for a small, albeit tall, lobby space around an impressive cascading water feature flanked by omnipresent, high-end boutiques and restaurants.

The hotel also boasts an impressive bar and dining area cantilevered 650 feet (200 m) above sea level, as well as rooftop tennis courts and a helicopter pad. There are 202 suites, each one arranged over two floors, ranging from 1,830 square feet (170 sq m) to an astonishing 8,400 square feet (780 sq m) in size. Whereas the exterior of this tower is expressed in terms of modern, High-Tech design, the interior is a slightly disappointing mix of luxurious styles with influences from both the East and the West. It poses a challenge to the senses and it is not only architects who eagerly await the time when the interiors will need to be refurbished. However, the Burj al Arab's truly iconic status may turn out to be short lived given Dubai's ongoing quest for the superlative. **LT**

↖ Burj al Arab's similarity to a *dhow* in full sail is reinforced by its unusual island site.

← The extravagant interior, while speaking of wealth and luxury, is not as admired as the elegant exterior.

Stalls and Abattoir (1999)

Architect Gion A. Caminada **Location** Vrin, Graubünden, Switzerland **Style** Minimalist **Materials** Wood, stone

Three agricultural buildings gently fan out out on the outskirts of the tiny settlement of Vrin. They form part of a wider strategy—called "Pro Vrin"—for this village of only 280 inhabitants. It concerns the extension and modernization of existing buildings and also new construction, all devised to ensure that Vrin remains a viable working community despite its small size. Caminada (b. 1957) acted as the planner and architect and is himself a local; his family comes from the same valley and his office is also situated there.

This particular scheme, commissioned by a local co-operative, was for an economically vital set of buildings for this farming community: winter stalls for cattle and an abattoir. The former are adjacent to the fields, while the latter, a smaller structure, is situated nearest to the village. The abattoir, used once a week on a Thursday, has a rubble-stone exterior base, traditional to the area, and an attic for curing meat.

Construction is of solid timber, using the traditional local "Strickbau" or "knit-building" technique. Caminada's background is apparent in the attention to the details of the timber construction— he trained as a carpenter before studying architecture.

This modest group of farm buildings is a pragmatic response to a community's needs and simultaneously great architecture. It shows how a respect for local building traditions does not have to result in a hackneyed pastiche vernacular. The sophisticated response to the brief underlines how a contemporary local vernacular is still possible—and desirable—even today when so many standardized industrial building techniques are in use. **RGW**

↗ Caminada's cattle stalls exemplify how Modernism can raise the standard of utilitarian constructions.

→ The buildings' sloping roofs and wooden construction owe much to traditional Swiss chalet design.

New Art Gallery (2000)

Architects Caruso St. John **Location** Walsall, England **Style** Minimalist **Materials** Concrete, wood, terra cotta

The opening of the New Art Gallery in Walsall marked a real change in fortunes for the small, industrial town in the West Midlands, near England's second largest city, Birmingham. The construction of the gallery was part of a new wave of arts buildings funded by public money in the United Kingdom.

Situated alongside a pool of water, landscaped by artist Richard Wentworth, its form is peculiar, square, minimalist. Clad in an unusual gray-tinged terra cotta, the skin often shines and sparkles in this perpetually rainy region. Behind this muted facade, the spaces are vast, light-filled, and generous. Rather than a conventional hierarchy of rooms in which one section of the museum takes priority over another, even weight has been given to the various parts of the collection. In this sense, the building inside has a domestic rather than a monumental scale. This idea has been emphasized throughout to make viewing the art a natural process. Each room is imbued with its own calm, still light; Douglas fir timber has been used generously in the ceilings, walls, and doors; and large windows frame views of Walsall.

The gallery is London-based architects Caruso St. John's first major project and propelled the practice, renowned for its precision architecture, into the spotlight. Their approach to design is meticulous, as demonstrated here with the handrails wrapped in deep brown leather and the walnut furniture. But it is the Douglas fir wood, used close-boarded as a lining to many parts of the building and as a softer foil to the concrete elements, that brings a rare warmth to this civic institution. **BG**

↖ The large windows are intended to mimic picture frames, giving visitors framed views of the city.

← The warm color of the wood interiors contrasts richly with the stark, sharp color of the exterior.

AutoTürme (2000)

Architects Henn Architekten   **Location** Wolfsburg, Germany   **Style** High Tech   **Material** Steel

A combination of technological efficiency and maverick design, Gemany's Volkswagen Autostadt—or Car City—is a monstrous monument to the twenty-first-century consumer. The 60-acre (24 ha), $417 million complex houses a hotel, restaurants, and a theme park of corporate automotive extravagance. The blueprint is simple: turn the manufacturing and purchase of a car into a theatrical event, replete with factory tours and festivals. And it has worked—more than 6,000 people visit the facility daily.

Central to the Autostadt's infrastructure are the AutoTürme—two twenty-story, glass-and-steel towers designed to store vehicles hot off the production-line conveyor belts. A twin-track rail system transfers up to 1,000 vehicles a day from the nearby VW plant. Once inside the glass tower, cars are hydraulically lifted at a speed of 5 feet (1.5 m) per second to their appointed pod. Each tower can accommodate 400 vehicles. The process is reversed when customers arrive to pick up their newly purchased Beetle or Jetta. The only flaw is that, while picking up the new family car, the consumer cannot see the car being brought down from its glassy outlook. The journey is only transmitted via screens as the consumer is briefed in the customer lounge, with the handover taking place in a rather ordinary showroom space. It is an efficient but rather unexciting birth experience.

Designed by the German architecture firm HENN Architekten, these towers are highrise buildings in their own right. It is not surprising that four new towers are planned to be built in the near future, provided that the car remains man's transport of choice. **LT**

↗ Crammed with cars awaiting new owners, the towers are a symbol of humankind's fetish for automobility.

→ Hydraulic elevators transfer factory-fresh products to temporary niches inside one of the towers.

Lohbach Residences (2000)

Architects Baumschlager & Eberle   **Location** Innsbruck, Austria   **Style** Modernist   **Materials** Concrete, copper

Social housing all over the world is one of the most neglected aspects of modern architecture. This often has disastrous results because these buildings stand as proof of how the urban environment influences social behavior. Social housing may even be considered to be an indicator of the health of a society or nation. It is therefore not surprising that one of the most successful housing projects of recent years is to be found in Austria's third largest city, Innsbruck, in a country that has so far largely resisted the concept of high-density, monofunctional public housing.

Masterminded by prominent local architects Guido Baumschlager and Dietmar Eberle, Lohbach Residences widens the perception of what housing can be. The complex is made up of an inspiring blend of well-laid-out apartments organized in six carefully placed building blocks, finished off with a high-quality facade that combines practicality with aesthetics. Mixed ownership ensures a balanced occupancy of different income brackets.

The facade is fitted with copper shutters that allow users to adapt their apartments to the different light conditions and take in views of the surrounding alpine landscape. All windows open up to the access balconies and terraces that continue around each house. Together with the partially open-plan layouts of the apartments, these simple interventions allow inhabitants easy access to contemporary living, with all rooms having access to the large exterior spaces. In addition, the housing blocks are designed for low energy consumption, setting the example of a more sustainable way of building in the future. **LT**

◥ Standing proud of the facades, the folding copper shutters are backed by balconies and access terraces.

◩ With apartment blocks facing each other, the shutters may be deployed for privacy as well as light control.

Al Faisaliyah Tower (2000)

Architects Norman Foster, Buro Happold   **Location** Riyadh, Saudi Arabia   **Style** High Tech   **Materials** Glass, reinforced concrete

The Al Faisaliyah Tower was part of the building boom for highrises in the Middle East, when at around the turn of the millenium skyscrapers were discovered by Arabian sheiks to be perfect status symbols. While many of the sprouting towers showed rather unremarkable facades of steel and glass, Norman Foster gave the Al Faisaliyah a more enduring appearance, using mainly reinforced concrete.

The tower is the central piece of the Al Faisaliyah Center comprising a hotel, apartments, shops, and offices. The four corner beams soar to to the spire at an altitude of 875 feet (267 m) in one smooth giant arc. Open decks are inserted at four levels as viewing galleries for visitors; framed by exposed K-braces, they allowed the corner pillars to be built more slenderly. The bracings divide the facade into three sections of nine, ten, and eleven stories. At the top, construction becomes more airy with large openings. The uppermost floors act as an outdoor observation platform, just above the "Globe"—a golden glass sphere, 79 feet (24 m) in diameter, that contains a three-level restaurant.

The building is a paradigm of ecological building techniques. In response to the extremely hot summers extensive passive energy control methods were developed, including external shading systems, special glass in the facade, and an air conditioning system that makes up to 50 tons of ice at night and uses it during the day to cool the building.

Upon completion in 2000 the Al Faisaliyah Tower was celebrated as the tallest building in Saudi Arabia, but only one year later it was superseded by the Kingdom Tower with which it now stands aligned in a direct axis. The Al Faisaliyah Tower still houses the country's highest restaurant, however, and it also boasts the world's largest stained-glass window in the five-story tower lobby. **FH**

Mason's Bend Community Center (2000)

Architects Rural Studio   **Location** Mason's Bend, Alabama, USA   **Style** Vernacular   **Materials** Steel, aluminum, metal, glass, clay

Mason's Bend sits in a crook on the Black Warrior River in Hale County. The residents are African-Americans and represent one of the poorest groups in an economically deprived region. Despite its isolation, the hamlet is known internationally as the heart of the Rural Studio architectural practice of Samuel Mockbee (1944–2001), based at Auburn University, Alabama. The Rural Studio collaborates with clients to design buildings that reflect the rural location, history, and materials, using funds that hover around $30,000, augmented by scavenged and donated materials. The Community Center is all spectacular roof. A hundred or so salvaged Chevrolet Caprice windshields, each layered over the next and interspersed with aluminum sheets, create an armadillo-like skin that cascades over a lightweight metal frame to meet low walls made of fine local clay mixed with cement and rammed between vertical molds. The depth of the walls—12 inches (30 cm)—is sufficient for stability and temperature control, but light enough to complement the roof. The earthen red color visually beds down the liquidity of the windshields. The walls are capped with a rusted metal gutter. In his work, Mockbee has been called a "missionary." But is it social welfare or a redistribution of commonly held assets? Mockbee found an exhilarating freedom from professional norms in Hale County, an area that, not incidentally, lacks inspectors to enforce building codes. **DJ**

" . . . [sustainability demonstrated] in a way most people don't have the gumption to demonstrate."

Norman Koonce, American Institute of Architects

Rose Center for Earth and Space (2000)

Architects Polshek Partnership   **Location** New York, New York, USA   **Style** High Tech   **Materials** Concrete, steel, glass

What looks like a cross between a giant space hopper and a balloon hijacked from the Macy's Thanksgiving Day parade is tethered within a 333,500-square-foot (30,982 sq m) glass cube on the edge of Central Park. This showstopper is the Hayden sphere within the American Museum of Natural History's Rose Center—a reinvented planetarium that reverses the traditional "me-centered" view of the universe by introducing us to a galactic economy of scale in which humanity assumes the role of mere speck of cosmic dust. The sphere is a globe of "water white" purified glass, 87 feet (26 m) in diameter, held together with gaskets that prevent buckling and distortion. The thin trusswork structure is revealed by the glass. The approach to the center amazes the viewer and promises an even bigger experience once inside, but the tight fit within means that the scale is best appreciated from the outside looking in. The circle shape is repeated at the center's entrance, but it is submerged so only a quarter of its curve appears in anticipation of the full globe inside. The Hayden sphere houses an internal planetarium and "Big Bang" theater. Supported by a tripod base, the sphere is wrapped by a serpentine "Scales of the Universe" walkway. The sphere guides understanding of the relative sizes of galaxies, planets, and stars, many of which appear inside as suspended models. The architecture of the Rose Center mixes steel-and-glass industrial elements with less sober, flamboyant touches such as black flooring, which appears to be laced with shimmering galaxy dust, and a lighting scheme that throws volumes of blue into the cube to create a night club atmosphere. Allied to a sweeping, look-at-me staircase that descends from the balcony, and a penthouse reached by glass elevators, this museum demands your attention. Obey. **DJ**

University of Toronto Graduate House (2000)

Architects Morphosis, Teeple Architects **Location** Toronto, Canada **Style** Contemporary **Materials** Perforated metal, steel, stucco

This compact residential ensemble is a rare North American example of perimeter housing. Rooms for 434 students are distributed in four interconnected blocks whose sizes respond to disparate elements in the complex's jumbled urban neighborhood. Municipal requirements dictated an accessible public space, rendered here as an interior courtyard, ringed by narrow pools of water, set one floor below street level. Graduate House sports some of architect Thom Mayne's (b. 1944) most rambunctious facades: layered, variegated surfaces of ribbed precast concrete, corrugated aluminum screens, perforated metal scrims, and mustard-colored stucco. The residence's showstopping feature, visible from afar, is a two-story corridor, glazed in ceramic fritted glass that spells out "University of Toronto." Built as a truss, the corridor brashly cantilevers over a side street like a Pop Art billboard, marking the entrance to the campus. The

designers overcame the project's notoriously low budget through dense and skillful planning. The skip-stop elevator scheme in the ten-story block, for instance, requires public corridors only every third floor, efficiently maximizing living space. A provocative landmark, Graduate House has had an important legacy in Toronto, opening the gates for other international architects to work in the city, and kick-starting a twenty-first-century debate about the role of contemporary architecture in civic life. **DMT**

"I like the way that university housing . . . has been conceptually stretched . . ."

Howard Davies, architect

Great Glasshouse (2000)

Architects Foster and Partners **Location** Lanarthne, Carmarthenshire, Wales **Style** High Tech **Materials** Glass, steel, concrete

One of the more esoteric reasons for visiting the Great Glasshouse is because it is the largest single-span glasshouse in the world. One of the more enjoyable reasons is to see a highly contemporary building blending with its immediate landscape context perfectly, and with some style. Situated in the Towy valley, the structure sits in an eighteenth-century Paxton landscape—the 568-acre (230 ha) Middleton estate that was described in a nineteenth-century sale catalogue as "richly ornamented by nature, and greatly improved by art." This description could equally apply today to the Glasshouse. Spanning some 324 feet (99 m), the building's spectacular dome consists of twenty-four tubular steel arches, which spring from a concrete ring beam. The Glasshouse is 311 feet (95 m) long by 180 feet (55 m) wide, and the roof boasts 785 panels of glass. As the distant cousin of the Eden Project in Cornwall, England—albeit by an entirely different High-Tech architect—the building seeks to reinvent the glasshouse for the twenty-first century and offer a model of sustainable development. This understandably green approach extends to biomass recycling, which is used to provide heating for some of the facilities. Elliptical in plan, the building swells from the ground like a glassy hillock, echoing the undulations of and blending seamlessly into the surrounding landscape. The Glasshouse rests its curved glass roof onto a retaining public wall that contains public and educational facilities. The building houses more than one thousand varieties of plants from several Mediterranean regions and research conducted here helps to conserve some of the rarest plants in the world. In 2006, the Glasshouse was voted Wales's top modern wonder ahead of Mount Snowdon (Wales's highest mountain), Welsh lamb, and the pop singer Tom Jones. **DT**

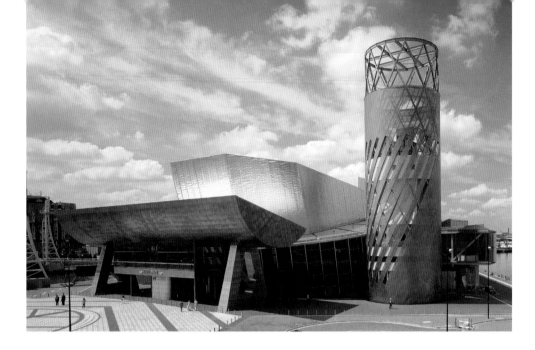

Lowry Centre (2000)

Architect Michael Wilford **Location** Salford, England **Style** Postmodernist **Materials** Glass, steel

The Manchester Ship Canal was built to bring international trade into the heart of Manchester. For eighty years it served this purpose, but the canal's inability to accommodate the new container ships brought about its decline; by 1982 the docks had closed. Salford City Council embarked on regenerating the area and was keen to anchor the redevelopment with a cultural project: a suitably impressive home for the city's enviable collection of work by artist L. S. Lowry. Michael Wilford (*b.* 1938) rose to the challenge and, only a month after the sudden death of his partner James Stirling, he presented a design for the Lowry Centre. The Lowry's waterside location leads to some inevitable nautical references, but Wilford avoids cliché and overt symbolism. The most obvious nautical reference is the circular "smoke stack" element but there are more subtle cues, such as thin metal lines in the blue terrazzo floor recalling longitude and latitude lines on nautical maps. The mix of textures and colors throughout the building combined with the sloping floors and obtuse connections between different areas can appear confusing, but prevents tedium. Wilford's use of color works to great effect in the interior, with brash oranges and reds in the entrance area merging to blues and purples. The Lowry engages the visitor visually, and more importantly satisfies the brief by creating a landmark cultural center in a harsh urban environment. **ER**

"The Lowry is the most complete example of the mature Wilford style in Britain."

Hugh Pearman, architecture critic

Liechtenstein Art Museum (2000)

Architects Morger-Degelo, Christian Kerez   **Location** Vaduz, Liechtenstein   **Style** Contemporary   **Materials** Concrete, basalt, glass

The principality of Liechtenstein nestles between Switzerland and Austria, and is home to only eleven villages, of which Vaduz is the capital. Famously the world's largest exporter of false teeth, Liechtenstein is also home to a phenomenal collection of art, and picturesque Vaduz now boasts the new Liechtenstein Art Museum. It is a building impossible to miss—a towering monolith of shiny gray-black concrete that sits as a resplendent statement of modernity under the cool gaze of a medieval castle. Quite apart from the museum's stunning simplicity, its geometric shape and striking facade represents a Herculean effort of planning—from start to finish the building was completed in just twenty-one months. The museum was designed by the architectural team of Morger-Degelo with Christian Kerez. The simplicity of their design is brilliant in its functionality, with a rectangular floorplan and four floors of carefully planned public and office areas. The realization of the building is visually dynamic, an impervious black box that encloses pure white interior spaces. The material used on the facade was a unique mix of green-and-black basalt mixed with river gravel, black pigment, Portland cement, and flue ash. The facade reflects the nearby shops, cafes, and snow-capped Alpine peaks and, quite unexpectedly, this structure becomes part of the landscape, absorbing the surroundings and mirroring the mood of the town. **BG**

> *"A new place of contemplation in a town where there is little architectural harmony."*
>
> Meinrand Morger, architect

British Embassy Berlin (2000)

Architects Michael Wilford & Partners   **Location** Berlin, Germany   **Style** Postmodernist   **Materials** Sandstone, glass, metal

The British Embassy was originally housed in a building constructed in 1868. It was badly damaged in World War II, and demolished in 1950. However, the land still belonged to the British state, and when the capital of Germany relocated to Berlin in 1991, it was decided to build a new embassy there. The British Embassy, located in the Pariser Platz area, is undoubtedly one of architect Michael Wilford's landmark works, a not to be missed Postmodern illusion. Very strict building guidelines apply in that area of Berlin, affecting the shape and volume of the structures as well as their materials; this is the main reason that led Wilford to come up with a unique solution to the restrictions. What you see from the road is a rather discreet box-shaped structure, with a rectangular-windowed sandstone facade and a traditional slanted roof, but do not be fooled; this is just scenery. Behind this conventional, almost classicist front, lies the most unconventional interior. An opening in the entrance reveals a two-story void with a centrally placed mature English oak tree, leading the visitor through to a surprisingly theatrical interior: a ceremonial staircase, two brightly colored volumes, the round purple conference room, and the light blue trapezoid information center. The embassy's facilities include a 200-seat conference room, the ambassador's dining room, a library, offices for 120 staff members, and a glass-covered winter garden that hosts the embassy's functions, trade fairs, and exhibitions. The building is a Postmodernist hymn, with an unexpectedly diverse glass-and-metal-clad interior, brightened by repeated lively colors. Berlin's British Embassy was Wilford's first commission after the pink-and-blue striped Wissenschaftszentrum on Landwehr Canal and was deservedly shortlisted for the Stirling Prize in 2001. **ES**

Palais de Justice (2000)

Architect Jean Nouvel   **Location** Nantes, France   **Style** Contemporary   **Materials** Steel, glass

The Palais de Justice represents a detailed polemic on the six fundamental values of authority and justice—rigor, clarity, greatness, sobriety, strength of purpose, and rationality. The building is a severe and symbolic black box of glass and steel and the interior spaces are vast, muted, and featureless, suggesting the assured presence of power. The stark structure itself brings to mind the idea of a cage and imprisonment. Even the landscape planting of ash trees conveys a symbol of repentance. Jean Nouvel believed that "Justice should express its power" and describes the building as being very "silent and balanced" and "clear and precise." The building is an uncompromising exercise in abstraction designed on a repetitive 26-by-26 feet (8 x 8 m) grid. The infinitely regular squares symbolize equality, and the glass structure symbolizes transparency. The grand entrance hall is a monumental symmetrical space of 37,680 square feet (3,500 sq m). Metallic screens, glazed walls, and polished black floors create a multitude of mirrors to encourage self-examination. The outer walls of the courtrooms are constructed from projecting and indented black wooden blocks. Inside the courtrooms a blood-red color of wood is used. Admirable for its extreme architectural and conceptual purity as an embodiment of the French justice system, one cannot fail to be indifferent to the Palais de Justice's aura, which seems to warn citizens of the unforgiving power of the law. **JEH**

> "What matters most is the intensity of the result as compared to what was pictured."
>
> Jean Nouvel, architect

Ecole Normale Supérieure (2000)

Architects Henri and Bruno Gaudin   **Location** Lyon, France
Style Expressionist   **Materials** Concrete, steel, glass

Henri Gaudin's work is informed by his interest in poetry, philosophy, and painting. It is essentially a reinterpretation, using contemporary materials and technology, of organic architecture and a repudiation of Corbusian rationalism.

Gaudin was joined by his son Bruno in 1995, and work on the Lyon campus of 20 acres (8 ha) was shared between father and son. Henri designed the main school (see page 548); Bruno was the architect of the Denis Diderot Library. The buildings enjoy seemingly random window shapes: many curves, mysterious

"Architecture ... must be symmetrical, but not completely, for pure symmetry is death itself."

Henri Gaudin, architect

angles, and odd-shaped openings. The library's external walls have large, differently shaped windows overlooking the gardens. The entrance hall has split-level galleries along the south and west walls. These are light, glazed with Pilkington Insulight glass, and decorated with colorful artworks by Albert Ràfols-Casamada and Alexandre Hollan. On the avenue the facade has a curving rhythm of six hemispherical windows beneath projecting bays. The campus is nicely landscaped by Atelier Acanthe; the college is proud of its herd of rare breed sheep! Henri Gaudin sought to relate the campus to the city, reflecting his belief that "each external area [should be] a place to be lived in." In logical, Cartesian France, Gaudin's organic architecture may appear radical but it is perhaps still nurtured by the classical tradition. **ATB**

Naked House (2000)

Architect Shigeru Ban   **Location** Kawagoe, Japan
Style Minimalist   **Materials** Plastic, polyethylene, fabric

Shigeru Ban's (b. 1957) buildings are innovative and aesthetically beautiful, openly embracing the world while remaining functionally true to the original brief. He is renowned for his use of "cheap" materials, such as plastic, cardboard, and bamboo. His revolutionary Naked House was built for a family of five: grandmother, parents, and two children. It allows all five inhabitants to live their lives without infringing on one another's space, yet it remains a cohesive home where no one is isolated.

The project, which encompassed both traditional

" ... populated by movable tatami rooms, Naked House is a lesson in material and spatial invention."

Architectural Review (2001)

Japanese architecture and Western ideas, takes its name from the translucent shell, which allows natural light in, imparting a feeling of living in a home without external walls. The internal walls can be moved around to create different living areas for differing purposes. The only non-moveable areas of the house are the kitchen, the bathroom, and some storage areas. These can be screened off, to make them "disappear."

Often compared externally to a warehouse, inside the home is airy, with an easily controlled climate. The house is also immensely practical—even the inner layers of the outside walls can be removed for cleaning. One of the chief inspirations for Naked House was the number of greenhouses near the site; it consciously echoes them and, as a result, blends harmoniously into its surrounding landscape. **LH**

Experience
Music Project (2000)

Architect Frank Gehry   **Location** Seattle, Washington, USA
Style Contemporary   **Materials** Steel, shotcrete, stainless steel

Paul G. Allen, owner of the world's largest collection of Jimi Hendrix memorabilia, first conceived the idea for the Experience Music Project (EMP) as a museum for his collection. Later the project evolved to become an interactive museum, a showcase for U.S. music, and a place to celebrate music and be inspired by it.

The building reflects the spirit of Hendrix and takes as its form a collision of guitar parts. Frank Gehry (*b.* 1929), who is a classical music fan, immersed himself in the music and culture of Hendrix to understand the driving force behind the rock star. He took several electric guitars to pieces, using the parts to form the basis for the museum's shape. The curvaceous flowing structure attempts to evoke the movement of music.

Technically the building was highly complex to devise. Gehry used a three-dimensional computer program called CATIA to assist with the engineering and structural elements. CATIA was initially developed for the design of Mirage fighter jets and Gehry is one of the few architects to have used it. The outer shell of the EMP is composed of more than 3,000 panels, with around seven painted-steel or aluminum shingles attached to each one. Each shingle was individually cut and shaped to create a multifaceted exterior surface that throws off distorted reflections and colors, and shimmers with constantly shifting patterns of light that add to the sense of movement in the building. Typically of Gehry's designs, the EMP is both functional space and art form, and is a Postmodern sculptural tribute to music. **TP**

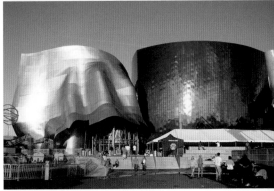

↗ The juxtaposition of unusual shapes and curves used in the exterior is repeated inside the museum.

→ Gehry's building displays a riot of colors—one of them is an allusion to Hendrix's rock classic "Purple Haze."

Cathedral of
Christ the Savior (2000)

Architect Based on design by Konstantin Thon **Location** Moscow, Russia
Style Renaissance Revival **Material** Concrete

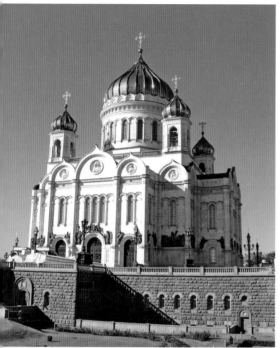

In Moscow, a rather fundamental quality of the city's architectural heritage is under attack: namely its authenticity. The reconstruction of the Cathedral of Christ the Savior forms part of the "romantic" stage of reconstruction that has taken place since the late 1980s and 1990s. The cathedral was the largest and one of the quickest of these reconstruction projects.

The original cathedral, with its visual dominance and proximity to the River Moscva and the Kremlin, was always an emotive site. Capable of holding 15,000 worshippers, it was massive in scale. However, when Stalin stated his goal of "wiping clean the slate of the past . . . and rebuilding the world from top to bottom," the cathedral was one of his many victims. He had it blown up on December 5, 1931. Stalin intended to replace it with a palace that at the time would be the tallest building in the world. The plan for the Palace of Soviets faltered, however, with the approach of World War II and the demise of Stalin. When the site flooded, it was turned into a huge public swimming pool.

The present cathedral is the legacy of Mayor Yury Luzhkov and a wave of popularity for Russian Orthodoxy after the fall of communism. The project was given to practicing architects and sparked a dangerous precedent. Today's bling incarnation is topped with a dome of fake gold. Its original stone details are reproduced in bronze and plastic, and the exterior is clad in a veneer of marble. Yet its mere presence, in its restored form, is a heartening symbol of a more romantic period of Russian history. **WB**

↖ The cathedral reincarnates in modern-day materials the original building, which was consecrated in 1883.

← The interior decoration reproduces works by Russian painters such as Vereshagin, Surikov, and Kramskoi.

Jamie Residence (2000)

Architect Escher GuneWardena   **Location** Pasadena, California, USA
Style Modernist   **Materials** Wood, glass, concrete

Perching on a precipitous slope above Pasadena, the Jamie Residence could easily be mistaken for a cantilevered Case Study House from the golden era of Californian Modernism. Completed in 2000, it was the first joint commission undertaken by Swiss-born Frank Escher and Sri Lankan Ravi GuneWardena.

Presented with the challenge of designing a 2,000-square-foot (186 sq m) family home on such a difficult site, the duo responded with a building that rekindles the west coast Modernist aesthetic and demonstrates a millennial sensitivity to the

---

"We are primarily interested in coming up with ... the simplest solution to a complex problem."

Frank Escher, architect

---

environment. To preserve the integrity of the site's topography and flora, the entire structure rests upon just two concrete pillars driven into the hillside. Upon these pillars sit steel beams that support the lightweight wooden balloon frame of the long, low building. Within the house, all the communal rooms are open plan, linking up with the balcony to form a continuous space offering panoramic views of Pasadena below, the San Rafael mountains to the west, and the San Gabriel mountains to the east. The bedrooms are located on the more private, hill-facing side of the house.

Recognizing its potential, artist Olafur Eliasson temporarily used the building as "an auratic pavilion of light and color" for his exhibition, *Meant To Be Lived In (Today I am Feeling Prismatic)*. **RDB**

Diamond Ranch High School (2000)

Architect Morphosis   **Location** Diamond Bar, California, USA
Style Contemporary   **Materials** Steel, metal

Sitting high on its Californian hillside location the Diamond Ranch High School (see page 548) fractures the sky with its dramatic silhouette. The 72-acre (29 ha) site that affords such impressive views was fraught with technical difficulties, and entailed two years of grading before construction could begin. Because Diamond Bar is a high-risk area for earthquakes, the school called for a flexible design—one that would adhere to the unstable geology of the location and to the constantly changing life of a busy school. The limited budget further influenced Morphosis architect Thom Mayne's (*b.* 1944) final structure.

The basic plan for the school is startlingly simple: at the top of the hill are the football fields, and at the bottom are the soccer pitches and tennis courts. In between are the buildings themselves, laid out in two horizontal rows with a "street" dividing them. This is where the simplicity of the plan dissolves into a highly sophisticated manipulation of space and expression of conceptual ideas associated with schools and learning. The two rows of buildings are divided into small pockets of space given over to classrooms divided by subject matter, and to administration and communal areas. Both rows interact, as children do, and there is a passage of movement between the two. The sense of small, separate areas of space coming together as a whole is effective, and lends the building an organic, encompassing feel.

The simple steel frame and metal cladding of the buildings was cost effective and allowed Mayne to develop the striking form of the school's components. Viewed as a whole, the buildings take on a sculptural quality with the folded and turned outline of the different roofs, in particular, reflecting the peaks and dips of the surrounding landscape. **TP**

Tate Modern (2000)

Architects Herzog & de Meuron   **Location** London, England   **Style** Minimalist   **Materials** Concrete, timber, steel, glass

General surprise greeted the announcement in 1994 that the Tate Gallery had acquired the defunct Bankside Power Station, and planned to convert it into a new museum of contemporary art. Could a building designed by Sir Giles Gilbert Scott (1880–1960) to generate electricity really be turned into an art gallery? An elite group of architects devised different schemes, including knocking down the building. In 1995 Herzog & de Meuron won the commission with a design that proposed only subtle interventions. Outside, the building retains much of its original appearance, with its monumental facade of brick and vertical strips of windows as well as the landmark chimney surmounted by a light-box. Yet inside the power station has been transformed. The vast turbine hall is seven stories high, with 35,500 square feet (3,400 sq m) of floor space. It forms the entrance lobby and doubles as a giant space for annual installations, whereas the main suites

of galleries are arranged over three floors across the front of the building. These galleries are a hodgepodge of spaces of different size and scale—some double-height, some with views over the River Thames—in which it is possible to get lost in an awe-inspiring maze of modern art. With their lightness of touch, handsome finishes, and exquisite details, the architects created a museum that works both for displaying art and for the millions of visitors who now know it as one of the world's best-loved buildings. **MF**

> *"London is ingrained into the fabric of the building like soot in bricks."*
>
> Rowan Moore, architecture critic

Hôtel Habita (2000)

Architects TEN Arquitectos **Location** Mexico City, Mexico **Style** Minimalist **Materials** Concrete-reinforced brick, frosted glass

The architects at Taller Enrique Norten Arquitectos (TEN) are internationally renowned for their artful renovations that concentrate on the manipulation of the skin of a structure to breathe new life into unremarkable constructions. Nowhere is this more evident than in the Hôtel Habita, the first boutique hotel in Mexico City but formerly an ugly brick and concrete five-storied 1950s apartment block. TEN wrapped the original facade in a glowing green carapace of frosted and translucent glass. The outer glazed wall is composed of a series of rectangular panels, attached by stainless-steel fittings, screening the old balconies and new circulation. The double skin acts as an aesthetic, acoustic, and climatic buffer, concealing ugly elements of the Mexico City skyline with bands of opaque glass while revealing better views in narrow strips of clear glass. Traffic noise, pollution, and the need for heating and cooling systems have been eliminated by the use of the envelope. What appears from a distance to be an expressionless mask comes to life on approach in an artful shadow-play. The subtle, ephemeral shapes of the guests moving behind the sandblasted glass exterior become a seductive open-air theater for passersby. At night the hotel metamorphoses as it is transformed into a constantly changing jewelry box of exotic color—a building of artistic elegance that protects its guests behind a magical glass bubble. **JH**

"I use light as a construction material that can be used as if it were reinforced concrete or iron."

Bernardo Gomez-Pimiento, TEN Arquitectos

With climate change a central issue, architects and planners now seek to integrate environmental efficiencies into their designs. The rise of the High-Tech style spotlights the importance of the operating systems that enable a building to function. Architecture becomes the art of the possible, with eco-architecture moving into the mainstream, highlighting the economic, political, and moral benefits of understanding the environmental impact of buildings. Most building activity across the world, however, repeats outdated values of the past, with developers prevailing and favoring Postmodernist pastiche as the style of the moment.

FAST *into* *the* FUTURE

2001–PRESENT

Vienna Twin Tower (2001)

Architect Massimiliano Fuksas   **Location** Vienna, Austria   **Style** High Tech   **Materials** Concrete, glass, steel

Towering over a low-level business district, the Vienna Twin Tower is a triumph of the slender high rise in a city that prohibited the construction of skyscrapers until as recently as the early 1990s. It is located in a new urban development known as Wienerberg City.

Wienerberg, a brick-making firm, ran a competition to encourage development in the area. The winner was the well-known and prolific architect Massimiliano Fuksas (*b.* 1944), who took on the awesome responsibility of designing a new city skyline. As well as office space, Fuksas's design included a ten-screen cinema, numerous shops, cafés, and restaurants.

Transparency underpins Fuksas's design; the skin of the building is made from nonreflecting glass, allowing the public visual access to the inner workings of the building. To gain unrestricted views, the heating and air-conditioning units have been hidden in the ceilings and floors wherever possible. Fuksas wanted this openness to create a connection between Vienna's inner urban areas and outer green areas.

The towers differ in height; one is thirty-seven floors high and the other thirty-five. Although they are connected by several glass multistory bridges, the two towers intersect at an odd angle, with the result that to a moving viewer below the shape and appearance of the towers appears to change and shift.

Fuksas also provided a master plan for additional infrastructure and social housing around the twin towers. These elegant glass forms symbolize Wienerberg City's growth as an area of regeneration, and are a lasting and artistic testament to Fuksas's philosophy of "less aesthetics, more ethics." **JM**

↖ The towers can be viewed through large skylights in the roof of the two-story pedestal on which they stand.

← The fifty-nine-degree angle between the two towers produces stimulating perspectives from ground level.

National Space Centre (2001)

Architect Nicholas Grimshaw **Location** Leicester, England **Style** High Tech **Materials** Concrete, ETFE, steel

Like a glistening chrysalis cloned with a rocket, the National Space Centre was a recipient of the British government's decision to aid a series of worthy Millennium projects with National Lottery money.

Situated on the banks of the River Soar in Abbey Meadows on a former stormwater tank site, and costing £52 million ($103 m)—half funded by the lottery—the building is the United Kingdom's largest tourist attraction devoted entirely to space exploration. It is also, however, a serious educational facility and research establishment affiliated with Leicester University.

Visitors enter through a low, square, research and planetarium block of perforated steel, built partially below ground. This double-height space is built on a lightweight 46-foot-grid (14 m) steel frame. A spiraling, landscaped, roof plane culminates in the geodesic dome of the planetarium. The real showstopper, however, is the tower itself, made up of a concrete core wrapped in a series of 9.8-feet-high (3 m) space-age ribs made from ETFE cushions. Inside the tower are two real rockets whose dimensions determined their home's 140 feet (42 m) height. These are the American Thor Able and the British Blue Streak rockets; each can be accessed via deck links.

The ETFE cushions that surround the building are highly efficient in terms of daylight and need only minimal support mechanisms. The Space Centre should be visited for its drama, organic form, and futuristic aesthetics, but also to glimpse a playful but at the same time serious building that perfectly expresses what it contains. **DT**

↗ The building's strange, chrysalis-like skin and form provoke curiosity as to what is half visible inside.

→ The ETFE (Ethylene TetrafluoroEthylene) skin has high corrosion resistance and strength in all weathers.

Eden Project (2001)

Architect Nicholas Grimshaw **Location** St. Austell, England **Style** High Tech **Materials** Steel, ETFE

"Grimshaw has always built for people. . . . [His works] show an engagement with people."

John Tusa, journalist and broadcaster

⬆ Banana plants flourish in the Humid Tropics Biome, which reaches 85-percent relative humidity.

➡ The Humid Tropics Biome and the Temperate Biome between them contain more than 100,000 plants.

In 1993, the UK government set up the National Lottery. Part of its function is to fund building projects through its "good causes" arm. This has proved a boon to a host of arts and other institutions looking to receive capital for their adventurous schemes. The Eden Project was one of the key recipients of this funding, having been awarded £43 million ($85 m) of the money targeted at the southwest, with the aim of transforming a disused china clay pit in Cornwall into a biosphere. It was money well spent.

The 57 acre (23 ha) environmental complex comprises a series of geodesic domes—biomes—each carefully designed and engineered to provide the right conditions to mimic those in various climates. The Eden Project was the brainchild of naturalist Tim Smit, who had already restored the Victorian gardens of Heligan, also in Cornwall, and local architect Jonathan Ball. It was designed by Sir Nicholas Grimshaw, the High-Tech architect famed for London Waterloo station's Eurostar terminal.

The biomes are made up of hexagons of various sizes, the largest of which are approximately 29 feet (9 m) across. The frame is galvanized tubular steel, glazed with a triple layer of ETFE foil. This foil is transparent to UV light, self-cleaning, recyclable, and should last for at least thirty years. Eden's scale is vast. The Humid Tropics Biome covers 51,148 square feet (15,590 sq m), it is 180 feet (55 m) tall, 328 feet (100 m) wide, and 656 feet (200 m) long. It is the biggest greenhouse in the world and tall enough to enclose the Tower of London or eleven double-decker buses piled on top of one another.

The Eden Project is a must-visit because of its scale, technological achievement, and because of the opportunity to marvel at how the lunar landscape of a former quarry can be transformed into a sanctuary for our planet's plant species. **DT**

International J. C. Decaux Headquarters (2001)

Architect Carlos Ferrater **Location** Madrid, Spain **Style** Contemporary **Materials** Steel, glass, wood

In 2001, J. C. Decaux, global manufacturers of street furniture—benches, bus shelters, billboards, and the like—moved their office headquarters for Southern Europe and Latin America to Spain. They had already identified a site for their new office, in the suburbs of Madrid, and held an architectural competition to find a design that would suit both the company and the location. Their new headquarters came about by "recycling" the old Martini & Rossi factory, a listed building that had been identified as one of Madrid's "landmark" structures. The 1959 factory had been designed by Jaime de Ferrater Ramoneda. Its protected building status represented a twenty-first century challenge: to create a state-of-the-art office, while keeping the majority of the building's original features in place. Internationally acclaimed, Barcelona-based architect Carlos Ferrater (b. 1944) is known for combining urban modernism with features of local, Mediterranean architecture. In 2001, the International J. C. Decaux Headquarters won the City of Madrid's prize for "restoration and rehabilitation." Inside, the Martini & Rossi factory featured a large, high-ceilinged space, comprising offices, warehouses, and working areas. The high, flat roof was supported by sweeping arches. Structurally, little was changed in the factory's interior, other than cosmetic and technological updating; the one major change was the introduction of skylights, installed above the new public areas to make maximum use of natural light. The spacious open-plan working areas were remodeled to provide office space. Externally, the old aluminum window frames were replaced as they had proved unsuccessful in the original factory and were considered a security risk. The entrance way was also remodeled, now taking full advantage of the high ceilings with an impressively spacious and welcoming lobby area. **LH**

Undercover Lab (2001)

Architect Klein Dytham Architecture **Location** Tokyo, Japan **Style** Minimalist **Materials** Brick, metal

Omotesando, Tokyo's most elegant avenue, is famous for being studded with the architectural jewels of the global luxury brands, but the tiny back streets threading off it are where the hidden treasures are to be found. Here you will find coruscating parades of Japanese street fashion; and, if observant, discover the enigmatic Undercover Lab. Klein Dytham Architecture created it for a local hero of these streets—famed fashion designer Jun Takahashi. The building is both quiet and powerfully striking. A massive tube clad in black metal, looking like a levitating shipping container, hovers beside the road, invisibly tied at its rear to a heavy cubic volume faced in recycled bricks imported from London. In contrast to the structural drama, the sobriety of the forms and materials seem at first difficult to square with Klein Dytham Architecture's usual palette of witty shapes and vivid color. Is this sober treatment maybe due to Mark

Dytham's whispered speculation that they are "Modernists at heart"? "No," Astrid Klein corrects, "we try not to have a style, because it would get boring to do the same thing every time." Each project is a new journey, with finding the destination part of the adventure. In this case the client is a dark magus of post-punk baroque with a love for London and rough-edged brick surfaces, who eschews the flashy strut of the main drag. Undercover Lab is both brand identity and modus operandi. **CMK**

> *"[The Undercover Lab] project is not about advertising ... it is about being understated."*
>
> **Klein Dytham Architecture**

Interbank Building (2001)

Architect Hans Hollein   **Location** Lima, Peru
Style Postmodernist   **Materials** Glass, titanium

As a strong critic of the formal rigidity of Functionalism, multi-award winning architect Hans Hollein (b. 1934) favors a rather relaxed attitude toward architecture, expressed by the inclusion of past stylistic references in his architectural vocabulary.

The Interbank Building in Lima (see page 786), strategically located near busy motorways, is open to virtually unobstructed view from all angles. The complex, accommodating bank offices, a 300-seat auditorium, trading room, café, bank branch, and parking lot, consists of four major elements: a twenty-

> "*[He] uses modern techniques to entice painterly effects from an aggressive mixture of styles.*"
>
> Jürgen Habermas, philosopher, on Hans Hollein

story-high curving glass tower block, a six-story Functionalist office slab, an Inca-inspired heavy stone plinth, and a sleek 24-hour operated cantilevered cube. Each has been expressed in its own materials from smooth glazing to rough-textured stone. This seemingly accidental juxtaposition of assorted architectural styles reveals its character when viewed from varying angles by alternating between bulky and slender, imposing and inconspicuous.

The most prominent part of the 289-foot (88 m) office block, was based on a crescent-shaped plan and adorned with a diagonal grid of satin-finish, titanium pipes covering the whole of the elevation and housing the external lighting system. After dusk the tower seems to transform itself into a colossal neon sign visible from miles away. **BK**

Casa pR34 (2001)

Architect Rojkind Arquitectos   **Location** Mexico City, Mexico
Style Modernist   **Materials** Rolled steel, steel plate, lava rock

The Casa pR34 (see page 787) is a very personal project. The client wanted to create an extension to his 1960s house as a present for his daughter, a promising dance student. He commissioned his friend Michel Rojkind, who had given up a career as a drummer in a Mexican rock band to study architecture.

Attached by a recessed, black-steel frame, Casa pR34 appears to "float" on top of the original structure, which had to be strengthened to support its weight. The little rooftop apartment, which measures 1,464 square feet (130 sq m), was inspired by the youthful, exuberant teenage ballerina. Two rounded and sensuous bright-red volumes interlock; caught in mid-dance, angles appear to come out of every curve. The steel plates, which wrap around the steel beam construction, were shaped in a panel-beating shop to resemble the contours of a human body in motion and, to add to the high-spirited aesthetic, spray-painted with cherry red car enamel.

Internally the living accommodation is organized on two levels: the first volume contains the kitchen, dining, and living area; the second, one flight down, the TV room and bedroom. The walls are covered in chipboard coated with an off-white resin to make the most of light in a limited space.

Like the relationship between parent and growing child, the house and the extension are at once linked yet independent. Although there are two separate entrances, with access to the addition reached by way of a spiraling staircase from the garage, the design incorporates the roof of the original structure. The terrace is paved with lava rocks that were used for the walls of the main house, and its acrylic skylights have become stools and benches at night illuminated by a spectacular LED system. **JH**

Apartment Building, Gasometer B (2001)

Architect Coop Himmelb(l)au **Location** Vienna, Austria
Style Deconstructivist **Materials** Reinforced concrete, cladding

In the the Viennese district of Simmering, four ornate, brick cylinders survive from the 1890s gasworks. After ceasing operation in 1984, they were abandoned and used for rave parties and movie locations. A first attempt to generate interest in turning them into apartments was unsuccessful due of a lack of transport links. A more complete urban regeneration project was needed, so a new metro extension was built. Different architects were commissioned for each of the four gas holders. These included Jean Nouvel and the Vienna-based practice Coop Himmel(l)au.

Gasometer B by Coop Himmelb(l)au is the only one to include a substantial structure outside the cylinder, as well as building within the drum. The tall tower, bent in the middle and standing on slanted legs, was first described as a "back pack," although later this was changed to a "shield." There is a connection between the two about halfway up the building via a "sky lobby," used as a social space by the residents. The outer face is smooth, with continuous bands of horizontal windows. In the base of the gasometer is a multifunctional events hall; the structure also houses offices. A shopping mall connects the new metro station with all four gasometers and the integration of mixed uses has successfully generated a village feeling in the development.

The shape-shifting work of the late Modernist avant-garde rarely interacts with protected historic buildings, but in Gasometer B, the result is mutually beneficial and worth a journey. **FH**

↗ Together, Gasometer B and the new building provide 360 apartments as well as office accommodation.

→ To the rear of the "shield" is a large conical court that allows light to the gasometer and the new building.

Musée de Prehistoire des Gorges de Verdon (2001)

Architects Foster and Partners   **Location** Quinson, France   **Style** Minimalist   **Materials** Dry stone, concrete, steel, glass

The Quinson region in Hautes Provence is rich in artifacts unique in Europe, spanning 500,000 years of human occupation. The construction of Europe's largest prehistory museum was justified by this wonderful collection and the sustained research work carried out here since the first excavations were undertaken in 1945. Bridging the gap between contemporary and vernacular architecture, the 43,056-square-foot (4,000 sq m) building creates a link with the existing village via a long dry-stone wall. Inside, a curved ramp leads to the vast foyer, and a series of subsequent display rooms nestle around a secluded heart: a replica of the Baume Bonne cave. The cave, which was the epicenter of the site, is now partly submerged by the Verdon river. Built in local stone and concrete of the same color, the museum displays a formal continuity with its environment while merging into the topography. The building is also highly energy efficient, an important consideration in an area of such natural beauty. Inside, attention is focused on the artifacts (through carefully designed lighting), the work of the researchers, and their dedicated facilities. The auditorium can also be used independently from the museum, an attribute that is popular with locals. Ten years after Massimiliano Fuksas's founding work for the Niaux cave in the Ardèche, Foster and Partners brought contemporary architecture into the oldest field of human knowledge. **YN**

"Such a pure building . . . a perfect integration into a subtle and harmonious site."

Michel Duffour, French politician

Imperial War Museum North (2001)

Architect Daniel Libeskind **Location** Manchester, England **Style** Deconstructivist **Materials** Steel, concrete, aluminum

Imperial War Museum North by Daniel Libeskind (b. 1946) is dedicated to the conflicts that shaped the twentieth century. Libeskind, who also designed the adjoining Lowry Footbridge, introduces a creatively expressive museum and a valuable force of regeneration. The museum's dramatic form is shaped by the composition of three oddly shaped aluminum-clad interlocking fragments from a broken globe—Earth, Air, and Water. These represent the three battlegrounds of war and provide the museum with its main functional spaces. The exhibition galleries are in Earth. Air has a generous and impressive shardlike entrance providing a viewing platform, along with education areas and an observatory on top. Water hosts the restaurant, café, and performance spaces, all with a beautiful canal view. The building looks sculptural and serene, but it is also challenging. Libeskind's "defragmentation" style—sloping floors,

ceilings, and complex asymmetric geometry—can prove disturbing. Our world today is represented by order and disorder: an explosion into fragments followed by their reassembling. Here, Libeskind has maturely perfected his techniques, producing a navigable building and rejuvenating a derelict site. The simple construction, low-maintenance, low-cost building, aims at articulating a new life for a run-down area through the integration of architecture, exhibition design, and past and future history. **ES**

"As Paul Valéry pointed out, the world is . . . threatened by two dangers: order and disorder."

Daniel Libeskind, architect

Walpen Residence (2001)

Architect Gion A. Caminada **Location** Blatten, Switzerland
Style Minimalist **Materials** Timber, stone

This house was commissioned by the director of a Swiss radio and television company, Armin Walpen, and his wife Ruth. They chose Gion A. Caminada (b. 1957) to be the architect of their second home, for his mastery of vernacular Swiss building techniques, in particular the use of traditional timber construction. Thus, in contrast to the rash of pastiche "jumbo chalets" that litter the outskirts of many Swiss mountain villages, the main bulk of the house is constructed of solid logs of larch, cut square but laid using the traditional technique of *Strickbau* or "knit-building"—so that they slot into each other and overlap at the corners.

The timber structure sits on a stone base—also traditional to Swiss architecture—which counteracts any unevenness in the site. The stones were gathered from the bed of a local stream—which used to be the common source for this building material in Switzerland: now it is usually imported from Italian quarries. At the northern end is the main entrance to the house, off which are enclosed storerooms including a wine cellar.

The upper floors of the house are divided by the stairwell: to the north are an office and guest room, one above each other, which run the full width of the house. To the south there is a large kitchen on the first floor and living room above, with bedrooms off it. This house is notable for being both uncompromisingly contemporary while exuding an unsentimental, traditional sense of "home" rooted in its site. **RGW**

↖ Swiss chalets were built over barns for cattle and their feed, and the Walpen Residence echoes this tradition.

← The rooms at ground level serve mainly for storage; residential accommodation is on the upper floors.

Children's Room (2001)

Architect Fernando Romero   **Location** Mexico City, Mexico
Style Contemporary   **Materials** Steel, foam, plaster

After graduating in Mexico, Fernando Romero moved to Europe, where he worked for Jean Nouvel first and later Rem Koolhaas, at the same time developing a personal architectural language to his work. In 1999 he returned to Mexico and started working on the concept of translation: transforming global ideas to meet local realities and gain their own unique style.

The project for a house extension to be used by children presented an ideal opportunity to clarify his ideas, although the site and the program presented a number of conflicts. First, the new building had to sit

---

"What we do [is create] structures that contain usable spaces with unique identities."

Fernando Romero, architect

---

next to a preexisting house built in a typical mid-century Mexican Modernist style. In addition, the very specific needs of the primary users—children—demanded a reconsideration of the traditional concerns about space and proportion.

Romero's design is a continuous snail-like space that provides a necessary sense of intimacy for the children. Walls fold onto themselves to become the floor, the ceiling, and even the long, curved stair that connects interior and exterior spaces. Without bearing any direct resemblance to the existing house, the design's clean lines and sensual geometries hint at the formal vocabulary of Central and South American Modernism. Romero was able to use his transformation ideals, turning the space into a uniquely apposite site for the children and the local area. **RB**

Aoki I House (2001)

Architect Jun Aoki   **Location** Tokyo, Japan
Style Modernist   **Materials** Concrete, steel, wood, leather

When Tokyo residents think of the Yoyogi Uehara neighborhood, the first image that comes to their mind is that of the park created on the site of a former U.S. barracks prior to the 1964 Olympics. The park is surrounded by a popular mix of 1920s and 1930s Japanese homes, dating from the early days of this garden suburb, augmented by modern masterpieces of residential architecture. The I House by Jun Aoki (b. 1956) certainly adds to the neighborhood's trendy veneer. Its impact comes not from from its size—the basement floor measures 400 square feet (37 sq m)—but from its uncommon, eye-catching design.

Between compliance with the Tokyo earthquake regulations, which enforce a minimum gap between properties, and recognition that adjacent building heights demanded a desperate quest for light and views, Aoki found a way to force his Abstract Modernism (some say Postmodernism) onto the challenging site. He added the personal touch that he had polished ever since leaving Arata Isozaki's office in 1991 to establish his own practice. A concrete shell made up of distorted intersecting planes encloses a domestic space balanced between two opposing masses linked by flow lines: the line of the upper floor and mezzanine floating above the stabilizing line of the basement dug into the ground. With the passage of natural light being skillfully orchestrated deep into the interior, Aoki confirms his taste for peculiar collisions in space design and ornamentation.

Aoki's I House came after his T, H, S, O, U, Z, B, L, and C ones, and before the K, Y, R, G, and F ones, not to mention the NMNL offices or the BF building (whether these were built or just remained paper architecture). Aoki will soon run out of vowels and consonants, but certainly not of ideas and determination. **YN**

National Museum of Australia (2001)

Architect Ashton Raggatt McDougall (ARM)   **Location** Canberra, Australia   **Style** Postmodernist   **Materials** Anodized aluminum, concrete

The National Museum of Australia has courted controversy since it opened in 2001, in particular for the building itself. To most visitors it probably looks like a cluster of unrelated, colorful blocks, at whose core stands a painted concrete park, The Garden of Australian Dreams. The idea behind the scheme was to extend the axes originally used by American architect Walter Burley Griffin for the design of Canberra, and then tangle them to form a huge three-dimensional knot. This notional knot weaves its way across the site, occasionally clashing with the museum. When it does it tears a section of the building away, leaving a red-colored trench in its wake. The most dramatic example of this can be seen in the entrance hall; the knot's only physical manifestation is the whirl that greets visitors as they enter the tiny car park. The wildly colored buildings represent the giant puzzle that is Australia's history, while their walls contain secret messages in giant braille. Some architectural references are obviously jokey—the windows in the main hall are shaped like the Sydney Opera House, for example—but one was extremely controversial. For the Gallery of First Australians, which discusses the history of the Aborigines, Raggatt imitated Daniel Libeskind's design for the Jewish Museum in Berlin. Libeskind was not impressed. Ultimately, it is a building that is loved and loathed; yet whatever you feel about it, it is a hugely daring piece of architecture. **GG**

"ARM ... takes pluralism to the limit at the National Museum of Australia."

Charles Jencks, *The Fatal Shore*

Aluminum Forest (2001)

Architect Micha de Haas   **Location** Houten, Netherlands   **Style** Contemporary   **Material** Aluminum

The Aluminum Forest is located in Houten, on the fringes of Utrecht in the Netherlands. The structure is the result of an architectural competition to create a working showcase for aluminum. Situated on a sloping bank and partially on top of water, the inhabitable part of the building floats atop a base of aluminum poles that serve as columns. The original proposal envisaged 1,200 columns, but the final plan includes 368 tubular, closely spaced columns about 19 feet (6 m) high. Like trees in a forest, some of the columns are slightly bent, providing drainage as well as service conduits to the spaces above. The flexible structure has been described as "lively," especially when there are strong winds. As its name suggests, it is built almost entirely from aluminum elements, which provides a strong symbolic function as the top section of the building is used for conferences and meetings for the aluminum industry. An elevator and

two aluminum staircases transport users to these rooms. Some components were made especially for the building, using among other things, aerospace technology. For example, the pink "pebbles" at the edge of the lake are, in fact, chunks of bauxite from which aluminum is smelted. Even the facade is clad in aluminum. Architect Micha de Haas (*b.* 1964) was inspired by the traditional lowlands landscape, in particular the regularly spaced trees whose tops merge into one mass of green foliage. An early model for the structure consisted of a matchbox on top of a pincushion. De Haas is fast becoming an important name in architecture. He studied in the Netherlands, and he has won several awards including the European Award for Technology and the Dedalo Minosse Under 40 Prize for the Aluminum Forest. The building is well worth seeing for its innovation, technique, and innate sense of theatricality. **KAB**

Århus University (2001)

Architects C. F. Møller Architects **Location** Århus, Denmark
Style Modernist, Functionalist **Materials** Brick, tiles

Skaparbyn Art Center (2001)

Architect Ralph Erskine **Location** Övägen, Sweden
Style Eco-Architecture, Functionalist **Material** Wood

Århus University was founded in 1928. After three years with study facilities in various buildings all over the city, it was decided to set up one campus and centralize the faculties. The entire site was originally designed by C. F. Møller in collaboration with Kay Fisker, Poul Stegmann, and landscape gardener Carl Theodor Sørensen between 1931 and 1942; from then on C. F. Møller, later C. F. Møller Architects, took over solely, working on university developments until 2001.

The university is located in the north part of Århus and is surrounded by lush park areas characterized by a deep moraine cleft. The landscape, together with the yellow-brick buildings, is harmonious and well placed for study. The many buildings are set closely together, and their uniform appearance is due to the consistent use of yellow bricks and tiles. These materials are repeated in the interior design—both the walls and the floors are covered with yellow tiles. Such consistency speaks of a respect for the construction materials and equally for the indoors and outdoors. A large open-air auditorium reinforces the message, seeming to merge with the grounds.

C. F. Møller was a pioneer of Danish Modernist and Functionalist architecture. In Århus University he mastered the synthesis of form, function, building materials, and the immediate surroundings. This ideal was carried through in the university's expansion between 1998 and 2001, when another five auditoriums were built, again in a uniform, rectangular style in yellow brick designed to conform to the original concept. In one auditorium, Danish artist Per Kirkeby has covered an area of 5,380 square feet (500 sq m) with a beautiful wall and ceiling painting, adding a sea of color to the clean, Functionalist, and unpretentious architecture. **SML**

The Skaparbyn Art Center (see page 786) is located on the Dalälven River close to Gävle on the east coast of Sweden. The center teaches creative courses such as ceramics, painting, weaving, and music. In the 1960s, Swedish artist Birger Forsberg became inspired by Egyptian architect Ramses Wissa Wassef's theories on children's innate artistic capabilities. Forsberg's ideas materialized in a unique and imaginative center, realized by architect Ralph Erskine (1914–2005).

The complex consists of seven main buildings that form a semicircle facing east and toward the river. The

> *"Functionalism is not a style but a method of thought ... that can increase our understanding."*
>
> Ralph Erskine, architect

houses contain workshops, offices, kitchens, sleeping areas, exhibition spaces, and a tower with views over the site and the river. Erskine has created a wonderful site, in complete symbiosis with its surroundings, for artistic inspiration and education. Here is no traffic, noise, nor pollution, but instead nature, fresh air, and serenity. Using wood throughout, the architect has built with the bordering forest as if all the buildings were lairs in the woods. Balconies and verandas appear on all the angular and sharp-edged buildings.

The communal spaces inside this creative village, such as the dining/meeting place, also promote instant contact and collaboration. Here people assemble in an open room, around a fireplace, and with an open view to the upper floors. There seem to be no limits to this free-flowing mindset. **SML**

Sendai Mediatheque (2001)

Architect Toyo Ito   **Location** Sendai, Japan
Style High Tech   **Materials** Steel, glass

Japan-based Toyo Ito (*b.* 1941) is considered one of the most innovative contemporary architects, combining High Tech and new media, passionately merging, from the early days of his career, the physical with the virtual world in his architectural experimentations. The Mediatheque of Sendai accommodates a library, art gallery, audiovisual archives, movie studio, and café, but is also the greatest representative of Ito's design attitude and dreamy High Tech info-architecture.

Ito's design came first in a competition of more than 200 entries. It used three basic elements—plates, tubes, and skin. The building has a characteristically transparent glass facade that leaves everything visible from the outside, from the activities on each level to the actual floor slabs and the structure's frame. The whole building is pulled together by thirteen vertical columns consisting of lattices of steel tubes. These rise from the ground floor and pass through every story to the roof, like giant tree trunks poking through the slabs. The tube-columns are differently sized and serve as the load-bearing elements, as well as carrying the utilities and assisting in the building's natural lighting.

The interiors of the floors are each the work of a different designer, including Kazuyo Sejima, K. T. Architecture, Ross Lovegrove, and Karim Rashid. In the transparency of the facade, the organic columns, the double heights used, and rich sun diffusion, the Mediatheque appears an "easy" building. The simple form and state-of-the-art technology produce an ideal cultural space to explore art and media. **ES**

↗ The transparent facade and use of tube-columns have resulted in a building that seems to float in its place.

→ Technological complexity coexists with elemental spatial simplicity at Sendai Mediatheque.

Kvarterhuset (2001)

Architect Dorte Mandrup Architects **Location** Copenhagen, Denmark **Style** Modernist **Materials** Glass, plywood, concrete

Since the late 1990s the National Secretariat for Urban Regeneration has worked on a total of twelve projects throughout Denmark. The overall purpose of these projects is to transform unsuccessful developments in urban areas where perhaps physical dilapidation, social problems, and crime dominate. One such project is Kvarterhuset (the Quarter House), which is located in southwest Copenhagen.

The building is a four-story extension of industrial premises dating from 1880, and today includes a public library, a café, a school, and meeting rooms. A large, open foyer connects to the library, and a white spiral staircase and white footbridges lead the public to the other floors as well as to the neighboring buildings. The glass box extension is lifted off the ground by leaning pillars of concrete, giving a sense of the magical. The bearing construction of the foyer is made of plywood with thermo glass panels set in a framework of pinewood, creating the impression of a light and airy environment.

The Quarter House is a fine-quality addition to its immediate surroundings, rejuvenating an area where rather heavy and dark brick buildings create a somber atmosphere. It is an open and inviting building, throwing light into the street and onto the buildings that tower two or three stories above it. Its presence imbues a sense of optimism and raises the expectations of the public who attend it for schooling, leisure time, and sports activities. The Quarter House functions as a much-needed community center in a built-up urban area where there are few outside public spaces for local inhabitants to meet. **SML**

↖ Standing on an array of oblique concrete pillars, the building looks like an urban "tree house."

← The raised glass box extension makes a lively contrast to the architectural landscape of the area.

Ekonologia House (2001)

Architect SWECO FFNS Architects **Location** Malmö, Sweden **Style** Eco-Architecture **Materials** Steel, fiber-cement, glass

Sweden's first international housing exhibition was held at Malmö in 2001. The purpose of the exposition was to display "the city of tomorrow in the ecologically sustainable information and welfare society." As part of the exhibition, architects from the European Union were invited to put forward a residential scheme displaying current trends as well as future ideas on sustainable architecture. The winning designs were erected in the urban district known as the European Village in Malmö, where the Swedish winning contribution, Ekonologia House, was constructed.

Ekonologia is a three-story, one-family house of approximately 1,798 square feet (167 sq m). It is built around a light steel frame with large glass facades and terraces. Protruding balconies offer views of the nearby canal. One half of the building appears open and airy; natural sunlight fills the space through the large windows, keeping an efficient level of energy within the house. With its slanted roof, this open section is extended a little further than the other half, which is finished with a flat top, emerging more rigid and closed. Keeping maintenance and waste of energy to a minimum, the architects have created a house for the future that is both financially and environmentally affordable. This combination of the economic and the ecological led to the name of the house. The designers have also included an up-to-date information technology system in Ekonologia House to control energy efficiency. All these features speak of "green architecture," a contemporary term used to describe new building tendencies that seek to protect the environment. **SML**

↗ Ekonologia House conforms to all the basic principles of sustainable architecture.

⇥ The building materials used are inorganic, low-maintenance, and energy efficient.

Alexandria Library (2001)

Architect Snøhetta Architects, Hamza Associates   **Location** Alexandria, Egypt
Style Contemporary   **Materials** Concrete, granite, aluminum

The idea of rebuilding the Bibliotheca Alexandrina was first launched in 1974 after visiting U.S. president Richard Nixon naively asked to see the ancient Library of Alexandria, which had disappeared some two millennia earlier. His gaffe prompted one of the truly grand public projects of the twentieth century.

Won in competition by the young Norwegian-based office of Snøhetta, the funding came from patrons as diverse as UNESCO, France, and Saddam Hussein. From afar it looks like an obliquely tilted solar disk. A grill of aluminum panels functions like the *mashrabyyra* screens over the windows of traditional Egyptian houses, with deftly incised northfacing clerestories that allow in daylight without glare.

While the overall form of the library appears to be a partially sunken cylindrical volume, it is actually a more complex geometry: the section of a doughnut-shaped torus. The magnificent reading room beneath the disk is structured like a hypostyle hall, with more than ninety slender concrete columns that rise to a maximum height of 138 feet (42 m). This is the largest research institution in the Middle East, and it was built to hold eight million volumes. There are constantly changing perspectives as one moves through the seven levels of the vast room. The enchanting play of natural light filtering into the interior, highlighted by rays from green-and-blue glass bricks embedded in the ceiling's structural grid, are conducive to metaphysical reflection. Chances are that those who come here to study probably feel like praying. **RI**

◹ The hot southern side is revetted with thick granite panels, producing a passive solar-heating system.

◁ The northern side of the disklike building plunges 40 feet (12 m) below the partial moat.

Blue Moon Aparthotel (2001)

Architect Foreign Office Architects **Location** Groningen, Netherlands **Style** Contemporary **Material** Corrugated steel

Resembling a giant upturned sea-container, the Aparthotel in Groningen (see page 787) is part of the Blue Moon scheme—masterminded by architect Toyo Ito (b. 1941) —to link architecturally two distinct parts of the city of Groningen. Foreign Office Architects (FOA) were one of four architectural practices who worked with Ito to present two designs; one for the Europapark area of the city, and one for the inner city.

The Aparthotel can be found in the inner city area, and is squeezed into a small square which is surrounded by docks, warehouses, and guesthouses.

> *"Each building is like a [unique] species … an antidote to homogenizing globalization."*
>
> Alejandro Zaera-Polo, architect

The site measures only 16 square feet (1.4 sq m), and the building is just four stories high. Despite these modest dimensions, FOA have managed to create a delightful building. When closed by day, it looks like a large steel container, but when the various guest rooms, bar, or restaurant are in use, the shutters open outward, giving the effect of a giant advent calendar. The building appears even more spectacular at night; the corrugated steel skin is finely perforated, so what appears as a solid mass by day becomes a spectacle of luminosity by night as the lights are turned on inside.

Husband-and-wife team Alejandro Zaera-Polo and Farshid Moussavi, who make up FOA, have won awards throughout the world for their singular vision of architecture, which insists that each building they design is rooted in its location and purpose. **BK**

Borusan (BMW) Expedition Center (2001)

Architect GAD Architects **Location** Istanbul, Turkey **Style** Postmodernist **Materials** Wood, glass, steel, rusted metal

The Fatih Forest in the Istanbul suburb of Maslak has always been a place where the metropolis's citizens could gain respite from the extreme temperatures in the summer months. The master plan for this area, conceived by GAD Architects, proposed to establish a differentiated set of venues at "Parkorman," to be used for sports activities and recreation in the daytime, and offering events or concerts at night. The motor firm BMW, one of the first to be attracted by this development scheme, commissioned GAD to design a "BMW Expedition Center" to serve as a training and educational space for company staff, but also as a showroom, public café, and event space.

The design of the building interacts with the existing landscape. The sloping site is dominated by century-old pine trees, which by law cannot be cut down. Thus, GAD designed the building as a "landscraper," being half dug into the undulating topology. During the building process, a part of the building had to be buried deep into the ground in order not to harm the roots of the pines. The impression of a building growing out of the slope is emphasized by a huge metal ramp that makes both levels accessible by car or bike.

The architects used durable and cost-efficient materials for the modular structure of the building. The huge window panels help to camouflage the 3,000-square-foot (284 sq m) volume during the day, but turn the illuminated café and showroom into one of the main attractions of Parkorman by night. The closed walls of the Expedition Center are of steel with a metal cladding that will rust over time, making the ageing of the material and the building visible. Gradually, the BMW Expedition Center will become a part of the landscape. **FH**

Jewish Museum (2001)

Architect Daniel Libeskind **Location** Berlin, Germany **Style** Deconstructivist **Materials** Reinforced concrete, zinc

> "I felt … I was implicated from the beginning, having lost most of my family in the Holocaust."

Daniel Libeskind, architect

⬆ Libeskind unofficially named this project "Between the Lines," referring to both fragmentation and continuity.

➡ These apparently random windows refer to a map of Berlin linking locations important in Jewish history.

There are few examples of contemporary architecture more talked about than the Jewish Museum in Berlin by Daniel Libeskind (*b*. 1946). Neither is it easy to find a building that leaves a stronger impression, both in appearance and content. The museum, an extension to the Baroque Kollegienhaus, a former Prussian courthouse, presents the history of Jews in Germany from the fourth century to the aftermath of the Holocaust and the present, through a heavily representational building program.

The design foundation revolves around three basic ideas: the Jewish multileveled contribution to Berlin's development, the spiritual and physical search to comprehend the meaning of the Holocaust, and the pan-European need to acknowledge this tragedy. The history and experience of Jewish suffering is told through a carefully studied multitude of symbolisms and references, leading to the creation of angular, unconventional spaces—with names such as Stair of Continuity, Garden of Exile and Emigration, and the Holocaust Void—boosted by the rich Jewish heritage. From above, the building looks like a single zigzagging line. This line incorporates three axes but also hides one more—the discontinuous Line of the Void, which visitors can see only through windows, represents the "embodiment of absence."

The Jewish Museum, built in the recognizable and particular Libeskind style, is the structure on which the renowned architect established his worldwide fame. It was also the one that held greatest emotional resonance for him, because so much of his family died in the Holocaust. The Jewish Museum is intended as a dialogue between the past and the future. It is an unprecedented project in postwar Germany; it urges us to rethink in more ways than one, not only historically and socially, but also in spatial terms, one of the greatest tragedies of modern history. **ES**

Magna Science Adventure Centre (2001)

Architect Wilkinson Eyre   **Location** Rotherham, England   **Style** High Tech   **Materials** Steel, glass

The Magna Science Adventure Centre, located in the once thriving steel town of Rotherham, was one of the visitor attractions that seemed to spring up like dandelions on the back of millennium-inspired lottery funding in the United Kingdom. However, unlike Sheffield's National Centre for Popular Music, Doncaster's Earth Centre, or, most famously, the Millennium Dome, this former steel mill avoided instant closure and remains open today. Bizarrely it even beat off stiff competition from the Eden Project to win the United Kingdom's most prestigious architecture award, the Stirling Prize, in 2001.

Surrounded by huge items of industrial detritus, this vast shed, clad in red steel, is a monument to the nation's industrial age. It has a brooding presence and is a genuine "dark satanic mill." Inside, huge hooks dangle imperiously from the ceiling, disused cranes have been left where they once stood, and old furnaces and railways remain, charred but intact.

While the original architecture is breathtaking, the new insertions scattered across the length of the building are more problematic. In four separate pods, suspended on steel ramps above the old floor of the mill, the exhibits investigate none-too-convincingly the elements required to make steel: water, fire, air, and earth. That said, it is not hard to understand why the Stirling judges were so captivated by the scheme. It is a reminder of an England that has almost vanished; a part of the nation's heritage lost to its new obsession with the "creative" industries. Yet, it has to be said that its success is largely down to the Edwardian engineers rather than the contemporary architects. **GG**

↖ The buildings of the Magna Science Adventure Centre rest on the grim remains of a once-thriving steel mill.

← One of the four pods housing the center's exhibits is suspended by steel ramps above the factory floor.

Parco della Musica Auditorium (2002)

Architect Renzo Piano **Location** Rome, Italy **Style** Contemporary **Materials** Roman brick, wood, lead, steel, travertine marble, concrete

This project was part of an urban regeneration development for the area lying between the lower parts of the Parioli Hill and Rome's former Olympic Village, which needed to be reincorporated into the neighboring districts and rendered functional for public use. Renzo Piano (b. 1937) designed an auditorium complex with all of his trademarks: a sensitivity for materials, site, and context coupled with a mastery of form, shape, and space. The complex consists of three state-of-the-art music halls—Sala Santa Cecilia (2,800 seats), Sala Sinopoli (1,200 seats), and Sala Petrassi (750 seats)—built around an open-air amphitheater, plus a foyer, a wooded park, and an archaeological museum. The glass-covered arcade at the front contains a restaurant and shops.

Each concert hall has a different dimension and function but the lead-covered roofs and cherry-wood panelled interiors guarantee superb acoustics all around, especially in the Sala Santa Cecilia, where symphonic concerts with choirs and large orchestras are held, as well as rock concerts. The stage and seating area of Sala Sinopoli can be adjusted to suit the requirements of a given type of performance, while the floor and ceiling of Sala Petrassi can be shifted to create a proscenium with drop curtains for operas or an open-scene stage for theatrical pieces, modern genres, and screen projections. A blue-and-red neon-light installation adds a dreamy touch to the continuous foyer that wraps around the base of the complex. Rome's cultural calendar is now buzzing with the eclectic program on offer at Europe's largest multifunctional complex. **AA**

⬈ The three harmonic chambers, wooden girders covered by steel, seem insectlike to some observers.

➡ The Sala Santa Cecilia, the largest auditorium, combines high technology with user comfort.

Dirty House (2002)

Architect David Adjaye **Location** London, England **Style** Minimalist **Materials** Concrete, brick, timber

Coated in deep brown, roughly textured anti-graffiti paint, the Dirty House stands defiantly among its Victorian neighbors looking more like a Minimalist sculpture than a home. Designed by architect David Adjaye (b. 1966), the house was originally a furniture factory but is now transformed into a purpose-built studio for artists Sue Webster and Tim Noble. A slight patina of the original bricks can be seen beneath the surface of the paint—most of the original openings were retained, giving the structure a sense of coherence to its surroundings—but its skin is startlingly different. Adjaye relishes differences and distinctions, and often refers to the oblique and playful—here, a slick, luminescent roof hovers above the dark, caustic exterior. The studios are concrete with bare white walls, but the residential suites have horizontal timber decking inside and out, along with grand, indulgent, sliding windows. Adjaye attended

London's Royal College of Art in the early 1990s, rubbing shoulders with the Young British Artists, including long-term collaborator Chris Ofili. Adjaye Associates was established in 1993 and the young Tanzanian-born architect quickly established a reputation for his immaculately finished East London houses. Adjaye's Dirty House is important, not only for its daring yet thoughtful and practical exterior cover, but also for that hint of deliberate and stylish indulgence that has had others follow in his wake. **BG**

"Spaces should seduce. I want to demystify this shroud that architecture has."

David Adjaye, architect

Vista (2002)

Architect Simon Conder **Location** Dungeness, England **Style** Contemporary **Materials** Wood, rubber

On the far southeast coast of England, a very small but special building clad entirely in black rubber sits quietly on a shingle beach. Its guest house, a silver caravan straight from the United States of the 1950s stands casually next door. In striking contrast with the land, sea, and sky behind it, the project has such clarity and simplicity that it is impossible not to warm to it. Architect Simon Conder was known for his careful refurbishments of barns and structures and his client's request was to refurbish a 1930s fishing hut to allow views of the sea. The architects stripped the hut back to its timbers and, picking up on the aesthetic of the old tarred cottages that still stand here, used waterproof black rubber to clad the building. The rubber skin obviates the need for gutters and drains because water simply runs off roof and walls into the surrounding shingle. Tough, watertight, breathable, the rubber absorbs the sun's heat, which is swept out

of the house in summer by the sea breeze. The entrance is through a fisherman's shed and a frameless glass passage; bathroom and chimney are separate structures. Floors, walls, and ceilings are all of the same light-colored plywood. Glass walls open out to the beach in summer, and a long folding window and side windows offer vistas up and down the coast. The gentle genius of this humble scheme is epitomized by a window in the bathroom specially designed to give views of the sea to anyone lying in the tub. **BG**

> "In its own small way, Vista is every bit as powerful as Foster's mighty, and special, 30 St. Mary Axe."
>
> Jonathan Glancey, architecture critic

Yokohama International Port Terminal (2002)

Architect Foreign Office Architects   **Location** Yokohama, Japan   **Style** Contemporary   **Materials** Steel, glass, wood

In 1994 the city of Yokohama held an international design competition for the reconstruction of the Osanbashi Pier in Tokyo Bay. The young London practice Foreign Office Architects (FOA) was selected, but due to a Japanese economic slump the project faced cancellation. But, a major change in fortune came when the decision was made to hold the 2002 soccer World Cup in Japan and South Korea, with Yokohama being given the honor of hosting the final. Any remaining fears for the project were dissipated.

From the outset the architects wanted to depart from the norm of a linear pier. The intention was to provide a pier where users could walk in on one path and walk out on a different one. The fundamental approach was to transform the ground into an active surface, using different materials and textures for each permutation of path along the upper levels. Just as the Port Terminal was seen as an interface between the open sea and the Tokyo-Yokohama metropolis, it was equally viewed as a transition space between the local people and arriving strangers.

Lifting flaps of skin from the ground and mutating them into contorted twists and turns, FOA enabled the building to transform into the landscape, and the landscape to merge seamlessly with the building. The Port Terminal pulls and stretches the city into the sea. The main level, below the landscaped roof surface, houses arrival and departure facilities with waiting areas, restaurants, and shops. Vertical movement is facilitated with a harmony of sloping floors, elevators, and ramps that connect the disparate levels, creating spatial continuity and flow. **AT**

⬉ The surface of the pier is configured to take users through tunnels and into extensive covered areas.

⬅ An arranged wooden boardwalk extends the ground of Yokohama into a ramped surface of shallow slopes.

Ilhavo Maritime Museum (2002)

Architects ARX Portugal **Location** Ilhavo, Portugal **Style** Contemporary **Materials** Concrete, slate, zinc panels, wood, marble

Ilhavo is a small fishing town on the coast of central Portugal. For centuries it was home to the so-called White Fleet, the Portuguese fishing boats that used to cruise in the North Atlantic for six months of the year, fishing for cod off the Newfoundland coast.

In the early 1970s, a museum was erected to pay tribute to the local fishermen who had given their lives to this harsh industry. Nearly thirty years later, the town decided to expand and remodel the existing building to give a new impetus to its collection of boats and maritime paraphernalia. ARX Portugal won the competition for the project with an imaginative proposal that combined a boldness of space and materials with sensuality. Now doubled in size, the new museum literally engulfs the original construction under saw-toothed roofing that is reminiscent of the ship sails beyond the suburban landscape. New and old spaces are distributed around an inner courtyard, the central pool of which reflects sunlight throughout the interior, underlining water as the common theme of the scheme. Out of the pool rises a black slate–clad tower, which is used for temporary exhibitions. A palette of white (plaster), black (slate), and gray (zinc) tones creates a fluid connection between the inner and outer spaces. The scale of the overall design helps to integrate the museum into the surrounding neighborhood, making it part of a clear urban strategy. With its steel and glass display cases, the graphic lettering on the facade, and the imposing presence of the new black tower floating on water, ARX skillfully demonstrate that their name is well-deserved: ARX—ARchiteXture (architecture, text, texture). **YN**

↗ The dark seas and cold light of the North Atlantic are suggested by black slate, gray zinc, and white plaster.

→ A fin in the white roofing commemorates Portugal's White Fleet of North Atlantic cod-fishing boats.

Laban Dance Centre (2002)

Architects Herzog & de Meuron   **Location** London, England   **Style** Minimalist   **Materials** Concrete, polycarbonate, glass, steel

This purpose-built center for contemporary dance includes dance studios, health facilities, a 300-seat theater, and a public café. It garnered great public acclaim when it won the Stirling Prize for Architecture in 2003. The front elevation presents a bold statement to the surrounding postindustrial landscape with its gentle, concave, "Cinemascope" curve aesthetics. The building can be interpreted as a singular and simple container, enveloped by a double-skinned wall. When viewing the exterior facade of Laban, the visitor first experiences the delicate external membrane of softly colored polycarbonate cladding. This layer was designed in conjunction with the artist Martin Craig-Martin, and is carefully illuminated from within to shape a vast semitranslucent light-box. This illusionary skin conceals a utilitarian, energy-saving, inner layer of insulation and glass panels. The dance studios themselves are pressed tightly up against this external

envelope, and utilize the exquisite pigmented transparency of the outer skin by offering passersby an ever-changing performance of silhouetted shadow puppets, created by the choreography being rehearsed within. The labyrinthine nature of the internal circulation is accentuated by the dramatic polychromy of the wall paints, the darkly toned interiors, and, most dramatically, the bold, gloss black-painted, spiral stair. This feature positions itself at the entrance to the building and marks a sculptural anchor—a similar technique is employed in the turbine hall at Tate Modern, also designed by Herzog & de Meuron. Painted black as tar and resembling a thick, concrete, drill bit driving its way through the floor of the building, the spiral stair contrasts strikingly with the lightness of the exterior facade, enabling the duality of the delicacy and dexterity of dance to manifest itself in the fabric of the building. **AT**

Beddington Zero Energy Development (2002)

Architects Bill Dunster Architects **Location** Beddington, England **Style** Eco-Architecture **Materials** Timber, solar panels

A pioneering, energy-efficient urban village located just south of London is Britain's first carbon-neutral eco-community. Designed by architect Bill Dunster alongside environmental consultants BioRegional Reclaimed, the Beddington Zero Energy Development (BedZED) prides itself on taking simple ideas of energy-saving and land use and putting them into best practice. The development consists of a mix of eighty-two economically constructed apartments, duplexes, town houses, and workspaces including community care and nurseries. One aim is that the buildings produce at least as much renewable energy as they consume. Houses have steep twenty-degree, south-facing aspects, their roofs peppered with photovoltaic panels and ventilation towers. The dwellings look south over their own gardens, with high daylight levels maintained in a deep plan by triple-glazed roof lights over stair voids. The homes are built using reclaimed timber, where possible, and all materials were locally sourced or recycled—ninety percent of the steel used was reclaimed from Brighton railway station. Rows are never longer than six units, and are porous to pedestrians and cyclists. A green transport plan with a "pedestrian first" approach, means that cars are restricted to the perimeter of the site. The houses are all fitted with waste and water-recyling units and a combined heat and power plan burns off-cuts from trees to supply energy. **BG**

> *"It looks devilish . . . cocking a snook at the mean Tudorbethan-meets-Belmarsh . . . next door."*
>
> Tom Dyckoff, architecture critic

Bergisel Ski Jump (2002)

Architect Zaha Hadid **Location** Innsbruck, Austria **Style** Deconstructivist **Materials** Concrete, metal, glass

The work of Iraqi-born architect Zaha Hadid (*b.* 1950) is often viewed as a complex, Deconstructivist collision of sharp angles and linear forms. With her Bergisel Ski Jump in Austria, this has given way to a necessarily organic, flowing form whose chief role is to throw skiers as far into the ether as possible.

The building peers down from its lofty perch atop Bergisel Mountain over downtown Innsbruck, replacing the old, outdated ski jump built by Horst Passer, and forming part of a larger refurbishment project for the Olympic Arena. Hadid describes it in the following way: "The assemblage of elements was resolved in the manner of nature, developing a seamless hybrid, where parts are smoothly articulated and fused into an organic unity."

Unlike other, one-dimensional ski jumps, this one includes specialized sports facilities and public spaces along with a café and viewing terrace in its cobra-like form. The jump is around 259 feet (90 m) long and at a height of some 164 feet (50 m). It is divided into a vertical, concrete tower and a café, which is reached by two elevators, and the jump section, which has a U-shaped profile. Bergisel Mountain, overlooking the town, was the venue of the great ski-jumping competitions during the Winter Olympics of 1964 and 1976. The jump is a stunning location from which to observe not only skiers as they jump to the ground but also the impressive Alpine landscape.

Hadid won the competition for the project in 1999, with the jump opening in 2002. She had found winning projects in the United Kingdom difficult until recently, especially after famously winning the competition to design the Cardiff Bay Opera House before the project was scrapped. However, the firm won plaudits for its BMW plant in Germany. Zaha Hadid won the Pritzker Prize for architecture in 2004—the first female recipient of the award. **DT**

"Without ever building, Hadid would have radically expanded architecture's repertoire."

Rolf Fehlbaum, chairman of the board of Vitra

⬆ Transparent safety barriers protect competitors on both sides of the central, snow-covered inrun.

➡ Reached by two elevators within the tower, the ski-jump complex includes a café and viewing platform.

Kingdom Center (2002)

Architects Ellerbe Becket, Omrania & Associates **Location** Riyadh, Saudi Arabia **Style** Postmodernist **Materials** Glass, steel, reinforced concrete

It took three years to select a winning project from more than a hundred entries in the architectural competition organized by Prince Alwaleed Bin Talal Bin Abdulaziz Al Saud, grandson of King Abdulaziz, the founder of Saudi Arabia. The brief called for "a simple, strong, monolithic and symmetrical structure," with the symbolic meaning and scale of the Eiffel Tower. Architects Ellerbe Becket proposed a 992-foot-tall (302 m) tower laid on an elliptical plan and topped by an inverted parabolic arch.

The luxury building accommodates a mixed-use area of 3 million square feet (278,000 sq m) and includes fourteen floors of office space with a large entrance lobby, a 225-room hotel, five floors of residential units, and a bank's headquarters. A three-story block, located at the base of the tower houses a shopping mall, a sports center with tennis courts and a pool, and a conference and wedding center accompanied by 3,000 underground parking spaces.

The unique design of the Kingdom Center is in part due to Riyadh's planning regulations, which limit the number of floors to thirty, while allowing a building height of up to 984 feet (300 m). The lower, thirty-story, habitable section of the building is executed in reinforced concrete, whereas the upper, 328-foot (100 m) hollow crown is constructed from lightweight steel trusses and spanned by a 184-foot (56 m) observation deck.

A blue, reflective glass curtain wall encases all the elevations, strengthening the structure's monolithic effect, and aluminum is used to highlight the parabolic opening at the top of the tower. The high quality interior mimics the exterior arch motif by its use in ceiling panels, furniture, and light fittings. Illuminated in continuously changing colors and dominating the Riyadh skyline, the Kingdom Center is an iconic symbol of Saudi Arabia's economic success. **BK**

Botanical Institute of Barcelona (2002)

Architect Carlos Ferrater   **Location** Barcelona, Spain   **Style** Minimalist   **Materials** Concrete, corten steel, wood, glass

Founded in 1882, the Botanical Institute of Barcelona is closely associated with the city's botanical garden, which began as the Acclimatization Garden of the 1929 Barcelona International Exhibition. The garden is located on the mountainside of the 500-acre (203 ha) Montjuïc Park. In the early 1990s, the Higher Council of Scientific Research (CSIC) held a competition for a new building for the institute, to be located in the upper, northwest section of the botanical garden.

The winner was Carlos Ferrater (*b.* 1944), whose works combine Modernist design with architectural characteristics of the neighboring buildings, and take their inspiration from Mediterranean precedents. Ferrater, along with other designers, was also commissioned to modernize the hard landscaping of the botanical garden. Some of the materials they used were also to feature strongly in the new building, notably corten steel, an unpainted alloy that on weathering forms a stable, rustlike exterior.

Ferrater's building consists of a long, narrow strip built on three levels. The first level is underground and is used for growing plants in low light. At ground level, glass windows in a wooden frame front an auditorium, exhibition hall, and public services. The upper level, accessed from the rear, projects forward over the garden and contains the institute's historic library, laboratories, and administrative offices.

The Botanic Garden of Barcelona is devoted to plants that grow in Mediterranean climates worldwide. With its white concrete and clean lines, Ferrater's Botanical Institute evokes Mediterranean architecture in apposite reference to the garden's purpose. **FR**

↗ At each end of the building, the side of the projecting upper volume lies flush with the concrete to its rear.

→ The cantilevered volume, clad in corten steel, appears heavy in comparison to the lightweight glass base.

La Maison Icône (2002)

Architects Périphériques Architectes **Location** Montreuil, France **Style** Contemporary **Materials** Wood, plastic, metal

La Maison Icône (Icon House) is an experimental interpretation of the traditional house: a lighthearted and functional response to the need for economical housing in the working-class district of Montreuil, to the east of Paris. The clients, Véronique Decker and Emmanuele Derid, were engaged in the design through a collective process of negotiation around the demands of individual living needs. Their requirements for the 5,618-square-foot (522 sq m) site included a big living room, five bedrooms, a kitchen, a study, a bathroom, and a garage, all surrounded by as large a garden as possible. The choice of cladding materials and organization of space responded to the low budget of $140,000 (€105,000), which meant that the design process was a mixture of spontaneity and architectural constraints. The image of the traditional four-walled and twin-gabled single-family house was the starting point. The architects developed themes based on the concept of customization, the art of camouflage, and low-tech versus glam style. The restricted budget meant that the building had to be constructed using alternative products and methods with characteristic components of plastic sheeting and wooden panels. The aim was to turn the ordinary into the deluxe, by adopting standardized, mass-produced materials from the building supplies store, and transform them into a sensual and flamboyant baroque object. The first impression of the house is of a temporary industrial structure with multiple drainpipes, irregularly placed windows, and doors with unusually deep thresholds. The garden facade is clad with resin-treated wooden panels with apertures cut for the openings. The house incorporated a skin of wire mesh creating a vertical garden to hide gutters, drainpipes, and air vents, and which will gradually be taken over by vegetation. **JEH**

Eso Hotel (2002)

Architects Auer+Weber+Assoziierte **Location** Cerro Paranal, Chile **Style** Contemporary **Materials** Concrete, glass

The Eso Hotel crouches in the Atacama Desert, where the red-colored land, littered with shards of stone and mounds of gravel, resembles a Martian landscape. Sun-baked during the day, temperatures plummet at night and winds sweeping in from the Andes toward the Pacific blast the unforgiving landscape. Architects Auer+Weber and engineers Mayr and Ludescher had to consider these factors in their design, in addition to considering how to limit the visual impact of a building in such a remote location. The hotel is in fact a private relaxation facility for the astronomers who visit the European Southern Observatory. The scientific facility is located on a high peak and looks down on the Eso Hotel, which to minimize light pollution is snuggled in a desert hollow at the foot of the incline. The success of the structure lies in its simplicity; a series of concrete modules set low to the ground. Behind the concrete block retaining walls lies a geodesic dome of polycarbonate sheeting, housing a courtyard and the swimming pool. Judicious planting here minimizes the effect of low humidity and tempers the rays of the sun. The dome is the only part of the building that rises above the horizon. The concrete used for construction was mixed with iron oxide to match the russet earth in which the structure sits, allowing it to blend in with the terrain. The Eso Hotel is an eloquent example of symbiosis between the natural and the manmade environment. **JH**

"A hotel like no other and one of the world's finest and most remarkable new buildings."

Jonathan Glancey, architecture critic

Bruges Concert Hall (2002)

Architects Robbrecht & Daem **Location** Bruges, Belguim **Style** Contemporary **Materials** Concrete, terra cotta

Sitting on the Zand, Bruges's main square, the massive Bruges Concert Hall (Brugge Concertgebouw) is at the heart of the old city, dwarfing the surrounding streetscape. Despite its bulk and uncompromising, angular modernity, it feels as though it could have been here for centuries. Designed by Belgian architects Paul Robbrecht and Hilde Daem, the structure was completed in time for Bruges's year as Capital of European Culture in 2002. The concert hall is an elemental, inscrutable building. It is not immediately obvious what its purpose is—it feels somewhat like a modern cathedral, although it also has a rural quality, and could almost be a giant barn. Defined by its simple but powerful geometry, the building descends from the square fly tower in a sequence of angled planes. These slants—along with the fact that the entire surface is a deep terracotta color—mean that the building makes intuitive reference to the surrounding city's pitched roofs. However, it meets the Zand in a less monumental way with a slightly detached volume known as the Lantern Tower, which contains the chamber music hall. Here, there is a facade of glass syncopated with long vertical louvers. The main auditorium is a striking space with inclined walls faced with grooved plaster panels that both limit reverberation and, from a distance, look almost like pleated fabric. The auditorium is located at the center of the building, which is insulated from the outside by the circulation spaces—an architectural promenade of exposed concrete geometry and spare, but beautiful, detailing. What is amazing about this building is how architects Robbrecht & Daem managed to create such an imposing mass so sensitively. The Bruges Concert Hall avoids being spectacular, but it has intensity and precision as an object that makes it linger in the mind. **JMc**

Downland Gridshell (2002)

Architects Edward Cullinan Architects **Location** Chichester, England **Style** Contemporary **Materials** Timber, glass

The Weald and Downland Open Air Museum is a collection of nearly fifty different historic buildings, dating from the thirteenth to nineteenth centuries, many of which have been saved from destruction. Carefully dismantled and conserved, they have been lovingly reconstructed in the Sussex countryside. Built in the museum's grounds is the Downland Gridshell—a purpose-built structure, designed by Edward Cullinan Architects, to house the museum's artifact collections, building conservation workshop, and timber store. The dominant feature of this building is the gridshell roof, constructed from oak strips known as "laths," which form a double-curvature shell. A diagonal grid of laths was formed, lowered into place, and bent into shape to create the full shell; it is secured to the edges of the timber framework. Inside, sunk below ground, is an environmentally controlled storage basement to hold the museum's

tools and artifacts, as well as a conservation studio for curators and researchers. Above, is the Jerwood Gridshell Space, funded by the Jerwood Foundation, which is a workshop where large pieces of timber-framed buildings can be laid out for conservation. Gridshell structures are rarely built and this was the first of its kind to be constructed in Britain. Both practical in function and stunning in design, it works with the surrounding landscape while reflecting the traditional craft of timber-framed construction. **FO**

> *"This project [was] created using a collection of materials that were previously thought unusable."*
>
> Steve Johnson, architect

Silodam (2002)

Architects MVRDV   **Location** Amsterdam, Netherlands   **Style** Contemporary   **Materials** Concrete; timber and brick cladding

When you walk along the wharf of Amsterdam's IJ River you are presented with a truly unusual sight— what appears to be a large colorful container ship floating on the water is actually an immense housing complex. This is Silodam, a building of innovative design created by Dutch architects MVRDV to help solve the housing shortage in Amsterdam.

Contained within the ten-story-high, 65-foot-deep (20 m) building are 157 apartments and 6,458 square feet (600 sq m) of commercial space. What is remarkable, however, is that these different industrial and living components are interwoven throughout the structure, meaning that floors fold and intersect with one another in intriguing and flexible ways and a system of passageways crisscross the entire building.

The different colors and materials used on the facades and in the interior corridors define what the space inside is being used for. This means each "neighborhood" of four to eight "houses" has its own identity. Furthermore, each housing unit differs both in orientation and size. A tenant can own half a block, a whole block, or a diagonal unit spanning two floors. The internal walls can even be moved or removed to suit individual tenants. Some units come with terraces or balconies, others with patios.

A pleasing living environment was a high priority in MVRDV's design and there are many individual and communal spaces throughout, including a restaurant. To make up for the lack of views for some residents, the causeway pierces the building and projects into the water, to form an accessible public terrace offering views over the historic harbor. The concrete pillars that hold up the structure also act as a "marina" where residents can moor their boats. With Silodam, MVRDV has succeeded in creating a multifunctional and eye-catching architectural unit that sits harmoniously within its surrounding environment. **JM**

> *"An example of truly innovative architecture expressing a new concept of spatial development."*
>
> Floriana De Rosa, architecture critic

⬆ The view from Silodam intentionally replicates the view from a large ship, creating a sense of space.

➡ The complex was a truly innovative way to solve the problem of Amsterdam's housing shortage.

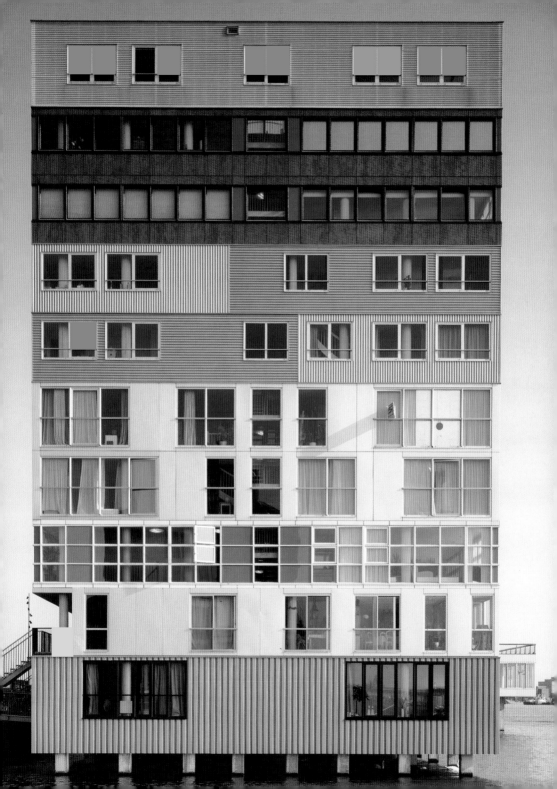

Philippi–Lansdowne Public Space (2002)

Architect Suzanne du Toit **Location** Cape Town, South Africa
Style Contemporary **Materials** Concrete, brick, gumpoles

South Africa's cities, like many in the Third World, are divided into haves and have-nots. During apartheid, urban geography expressed this division as racial separation. White wealth inhabited the town, in office blocks, gated communities, and suburban homes, while black poverty populated the township's prisonlike rows of low-cost houses, migrant workers' hostels, and shacks. Despite the advent of democracy in 1994, cities such as Cape Town are still divided. The challenge of transforming the township into a town remains high on the political agenda.

Philippi–Lansdowne Public Space is an innovative example of post-apartheid transformational urbanism. It attempts to chart a route from township to town, by creating an architectural framework that negotiates between the informal patterns of shack settlements and a formal spatial order. This design and others like it can help kick-start the slum's emergence into a modern and more dignified way of life. Yet it does not turn its back on the ingenuity of those who improvise: those who build informal homes from scraps of scavenged material, and build an informal economy as a way to cope with the everyday realities that overwhelm formal government.

A dialogue between formal and informal is expressed by the giant concrete and timber pergola. On its regimented public front it is rational and regular; on its back it is designed so that self-built shops and shacks can clip onto the parent structure. The beam at the junction between the formal and informal architecture is engineered to support a two-story building. It reminds us that the best urban design is always incomplete: while asserting a strong presence today, it does not prescribe a limit but rather opens up possibilities for tomorrow. **MJB**

Hydra Pier (2002)

Architects Asymptote **Location** Haarlemmermeer, Netherlands
Style Contemporary **Material** Glass

The Hydra Pier (see page 786) is a municipal pavilion located by Amsterdam's Schiphol Airport. Asymptote won an international competition to design this entrance pavilion for the 2002 Floriade, a gardening and flower festival held every ten years in the Netherlands. They describe the building as symbolic of the country's struggle between land and water, as well as the tension between nature and artifice.

Hydra Pier is situated in an artificially constructed pastoral landscape environment. The pavilion is conceived in two parts: an outdoor landscaped area, a

> *"We are . . . focused on building inspired worlds, be they domestic, institutional, urban, or digital."*
>
> Hani Rashid, Asymptote

potent reminder that most of this region was located underwater until it was reclaimed 150 years ago. The scheme consists of two parts: an outdoor landscaped area, which is sheltered by an overhanging roof, and a multimedia space for public events, which floats on the lake. This space is now used as a restaurant. A liquid sloping roof, which takes its inspiration from the wings of a Boeing 747, features a plane of cascading water that reflects the sky above, an acknowledgment that it is located under the flight path of one of Europe's busiest airports.

For Asymptote, architecture is not just about buildings, but the intersection of design, science, and technology. They have also "built" a virtual museum of digital art for the Guggenheim Museum in New York and designed a line of office furniture for Knoll. **KAB**

Simmons Hall
Dormitory (2002)

Architect Steven Holl   **Location** Cambridge, Massachusetts, USA
Style Postmodernist   **Material** Precast concrete panels

Architect Steven Holl (*b.* 1947) describes his concept for Simmons Hall at the Massachusetts Institute of Technology (MIT) as a "sponge." The sponge metaphor originates from Holl's idea of porosity—an openness that makes the building alive with both light and people. This "sponge" is, however, a ten-story-tall dormitory building that sleeps 350 students.

From the outside it resembles a cross between an enormous Rubik's cube—the openings are picked out with different colors—and a segment of a city, with windows and roof lines and those random shapes and spaces that make up the urban skyline. Holl's idea of an urban space is followed through in the provision of amenities to students; Simmons Hall is more than simply a place to study and to sleep. It possesses a theater, café, terraces, and street-level dining area.

Although the outline of the facade seems random, the structure is rigorously gridded. Each dorm room has nine windows, which can be individually opened or closed. The rigidity of this plan is offset by amorphous forms that sweep down through the building, bringing light into the internal spaces. It is as if, once the structure had been laid down, Holl found a place to play. A staircase curves upward, challenging the severity of the facade, while at the same time benefiting from the light filtered through the squared spaces. With this design, Holl allows light to enliven the interior throughout the fluctuations of the seasons, and points the way ahead for a new style of creating urban densities. **GT**

↗ With this building, Holl reinjects whimsy into the practicalities of mass housing.

→ The design is a pun on MIT's technology associations, resembling an old-fashioned computer board.

Hector Pieterson Museum (2002)

Architects Mashabane Rose Associates   **Location** Soweto, South Africa   **Style** Contemporary   **Materials** Red brick, glass, steel, concrete

On June 16, 1976, twelve-year-old Hector Pieterson was fatally wounded when the South African police opened fire on a Soweto crowd gathered to demonstrate against apartheid's education policy. That moment sparked off riots all over the country. A duty to mark and remember the wrongs of the past has underwritten national efforts to embrace a better future since the advent of democracy in 1994. Cultural projects, such as contemporary theater, express this objective, often in the form of testimony. Architecture also has a part to play in this reconfiguring of public culture, as witnessed by the Hector Pieterson Museum, erected to commemorate the uprising. Architects Mashabane Rose consulted local residents as to how they thought the new building should look. Most agreed that red brick—in keeping with the small, square, township houses built under the apartheid regime—should be used. As a result, the two-story

building appears to grow out of the urban texture of its surroundings. Inside, the space is cathedral-like, with a double-volume ceiling, concrete columns, and red-brick walls. The irregular shaped, but strategically placed, windows frame key views, making it clear to the visitor that the cultural history on display is rooted in real Soweto: these things happened and they happened here. A shale stone memorial to Hector and the other children who died in the uprising stands next to the museum. **MJB**

> *"[The museum] tells its story with a potent mix of historical fact and architectural expression."*
>
> Kerryn du Preez, journalist

Casa Vieja (2002)

Architect Mathias Klotz **Location** Santiago de Chile, Chile **Style** Contemporary **Materials** Concrete, glass, wood

In a profession where architects in their fifties are still considered to be "emergent," Mathias Klotz (b. 1965) represents an astonishing exception. Immediately after graduating in 1991, he was able to get direct commissions without the customary internship in some other architect's office. In a country that is 3,000 miles (4,828 km) long and has just 15 million people inhabiting it, space is in abundance. Consequently, the Chilean middle class has provided architects such as Klotz with plenty of opportunities to build their second homes. Casa Vieja injects new interest into schemes first adopted by the architects of the Modern movement. Although the exterior of the house follows the Modernist tradition by providing two long plates for the roof and floor of the villa, Klotz introduces subtle alterations to adapt it to local conditions. Here, the pure abstraction of European Modernism is contaminated by a rich, warm palette of local materials

ranging from rough concrete to wood. Klotz has morphed the geometric precision of avant-garde architecture to achieve specific spatial effects as seen in the sequence of spaces that lead to the entrance of the house. He creates a spatial compression by first lifting the path to the house through a ramp, which then slips under two cantilevering platforms clad in wood to finally lead to the narrow entrance door. The rear elevation has a long, generous opening that not only brings light into the four bedrooms, but also opens up onto a wooden deck facing the swimming pool. Casa Vieja represents an important step in Klotz's search for simple, clear solutions, and is unique in its specific use of materials and exploitation of the relationship between the architecture and the landscape. These efforts were acknowledged in 2001 when Klotz was awarded the Francesco Borromini Award for Young Architects. **RB**

Market Hall (2002)

Architects Miller & Maranta **Location** Aarau, Switzerland **Style** Minimalist **Material** Douglas fir timber

This building is basically a giant timber shed, its frame indistinguishable from its cladding. It was designed as a new market hall situated in the heart of the old Swiss town of Aarau. Its walls of regularly spaced wooden posts appear both open and closed depending on the angle from which you perceive the building, and allow plenty of light to penetrate. The construction is of Douglas fir, stained with natural oils. A single central column is all that is required to support the structure internally, strongly orientating and organizing the interior space, while allowing for maximum flexibility of use inside. Quintus Miller (*b.* 1961) and Paola Maranta (*b.* 1959) both studied architecture at the technical university ETH in Zurich and set up practice together in Basel. Their work is quietly dignified, designed to fit in and look as though it belongs naturally to its site, but not through slavish pastiche or historicism. Thus, this is a wooden building in the center of a mostly limestone old town. Yet it fits in perfectly, kinking at the middle to follow the old street pattern. The feeling inside is of a light, almost temporary market shed, while outside it has the presence of a reserved and significant public building, balancing its role as both a commercial and social hub for the small town. Miller was born in Aarau, which perhaps explains why this is such a perfectly judged intervention into the everyday life of the town, despite being an uncompromisingly modern structure. **RGW**

"[Market Hall] has mesmerizing patterns of slatted timbers, punctuated by shafts of light."

Jonathan Glancey, architecture critic

National Maritime Museum (2002)

Architects Long & Kentish   **Location** Falmouth, England   **Style** Vernacular   **Materials** English oak timber, steel

Beside the waters of Falmouth dock, one of the best natural harbors in Northern Europe, the angled, austere, English oak–clad walls of the National Maritime Museum heavily reference the form of the boat sheds that once made up the economy of this area on England's southwest coast. The main exhibition space is the Flotilla gallery, and indeed it recalls just that. A triple-height space is filled with small boats fully rigged and suspended at different heights, jostling for position and attention, set against the backdrop of a three-story-high, curving steel wall clad in thin birch ply. The design instantly relates to the prow of a ship making its way to dock. Throughout the building "porthole" lights reflect the building's theme. The collection is dominated by 140 boats donated by the National Maritime Museum in Greenwich, along with the collection of the Cornwall Maritime Museum. This museum project had a uniquely integrated approach to gallery and exhibition design, with its architects and exhibition designers working together from the outset. These bespoke elements add much to the museum experience—from the pool at the bottom to the remarkable Tidal Gallery, a room where two 16-foot-high (5 m) windows act as a living gauge to show the low and high water spring tides. There is also a library, a workshop, and a viewing tower. A reverence for thoughtful, quiet spaces has been serenely translated into this very British museum. **BG**

"[The museum demonstrates an] intelligent, beautifully made vernacular Modernism."

Tom Dyckhoff, architecture and design critic

Australian Centre for Contemporary Art (2002)

Architects Wood Marsh **Location** Melbourne, Australia **Style** Contemporary **Material** Corten steel

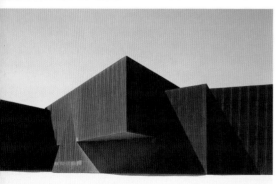

The hometown of this art center was dubbed "Marvelous Melbourne" in the 1880s as a tide of wealth flowed through the city from the adjacent gold fields; Melbourne then fell into conservative quietude for the next hundred years, interrupted briefly in the 1960s by the work of Modernist Robin Boyd. Architects Wood Marsh are part of the second wave of a generation that has earned the city consideration as an international design hotspot.

During its history, Melbourne has been torn between the Old and New Worlds. Encouraged by a relatively temperate climate, the Old World dream plays out in a myth of the Garden State that tries to clothe every space in green. Into this the architecture of Wood Marsh explodes with burnished and unapologetic form.

The Australian Centre for Contemporary Art (ACCA) consists of a foyer, offices, and five gallery spaces, and is situated at the center of Melbourne's Southbank arts complex, alongside the Malthouse Theatre. It forms a tight urban courtyard with the old brick theater complex to one side, and presents its steep, enigmatic rusted steel profile to the rest of the arts precinct across a wide plain of crushed gravel on the other. The structure evokes the poetry of the so-called "red center" of Australia—a miniature Uluru in a sand-colored setting relieved only by red brick lines.

ACCA has become one of Melbourne's most iconic buildings; its rust-red hulk is now a rallying symbol for accepting and celebrating the reality of the local climate and foregoing the dream of green that the settler city pursued for so long. **LVS**

↖ Deliberately made to look like rusting metal, the exterior contrasts with the modern, light interiors.

← The building celebrates Australia's cultural heritage by evoking the image of the sacred site of Uluru.

Esplanade–Theatres on the Bay (2002)

Architects Michael Wilford & Partners, DP Architects **Location** Singapore, Republic of Singapore **Style** High Tech **Materials** Glass, steel

With its pair of spiky domes looking rather like the eyes of an enormous fly, the Esplanade–Theatres on the Bay is an imposing sight on Singapore's Marina Bay. The arts center, the joint work of Michael Wilford & Partners and Singaporean firm, DP Architects, is not only a visual tour de force, but also a triumph of technological innovation.

The spikes, more than 2,000 of them in all, are a practical, state-of-the-art solution to a problem facing any architect in Singapore—the intensity of the tropical sun. Wilford's desire for a glazed, airy structure dictated that a complicated system of sunshades needed to be designed. Hence the spikes, each one of which is precisely angled to keep off the sun.

The Esplanade is open on three sides, taking full advantage of the views afforded by its spectacular location. The complex faces the sea to one side, with the Padang open park and Civic District on the others. The glazed structure of the building comes into its own in this respect, affording visitors unrestricted views of these local landmarks.

Inside, the center contains a 2,000-seat theater, a 1,800-seat concert hall, a 250-seat recital studio, and a 220-seat theater studio. These spaces provide an interesting counterpoint to the High-Tech exterior, making use of natural wood and, in the case of the main theater, using a gold-and-red color scheme that hints at a more vernacular style.

Ever since his early days working with James Stirling in the 1960s, Wilford has made a significant contribution to the world's public architecture and the Esplanade looks set to follow in that tradition. **GB**

↗ The sunshades were part inspired by the palm fronds and overlapping leaves found in indigenous designs.

→ Lit up at night, the domes create a dazzling spectacle that can be seen for miles around.

Telenor Headquarters (2002)

Architects NBBJ, HUS, PKA **Location** Oslo, Norway **Style** High Tech **Materials** Concrete, steel, glass

In 2002, one of the world's largest operators of mobile satellite services—Telenor—gathered together all its office units in Fornebu, just west of Oslo's city center. Today, the headquarters acts as a workplace for more than 7,000 people in a building that has been hailed as "the office of the future." There are no set, assigned desks because the employees are encouraged to access all information from "floating" worktops by plugging their laptops and mobiles into any data or power port. This is truly a mobile office concept. In a joint venture the U.S. architects NBBJ collaborated with the Norwegian practices, HUS and PKA. They envisioned building one large complex in order to realize the company's main wish to unite the resources of all the previous offices in one building, creating a communal space in which communication and work energy interact. The premises, which cover 34 acres (14 ha), is on the former site of Oslo International Airport, and makes extensive use of glass curtain walls, providing all the employees with stunning views over the Oslo Fjord and the surrounding mountains. Two curved glass boulevards, which have slanted walls, each link up to four glass and steel office blocks, which in turn are connected to public atriums. In between the boulevards there is a large common space, which acts as the spine of the building. This building is High Tech not simply because of the mobile and wireless concept that it communicates, but also through the practical elements of the structure. For example, shading devices that are automatically controlled by sensors regulate the heat created by the vast glazed facades, and there are also window blinds that are programmed to react to the position of the sun. The corporate desire for openness and transparency is echoed in the materials and construction of this state-of-the-art design. **SML**

Modern Art Museum of Fort Worth (2002)

Architect Tadao Ando **Location** Fort Worth, Texas, USA **Style** Modern **Materials** Steel, reinforced concrete, glass

Part of the brilliance of Tadao Ando (*b*. 1941) rests in the simple geometric form of his inspiring designs. By presenting the eye with clean, elegant, and satisfying lines he allows the mind the freedom to reflect, and his buildings, be they temples or museums, become sculptural, monumental, artistic endeavors that transcend their everyday functionality. The Modern Art Museum of Fort Worth, in Texas, is just such an example of Ando's manipulation and creation of space that caters both to the spirit and to humanity. One of the problems facing the architect in this project was the vast size of the site. It measures 473,600 square feet (44,000 sq m), and incorporates a garden and artificial lake, as well as a monumental gallery. The building is planned as a series of five interrelating rectangular blocks, or pavilions, which sit beside—or seemingly float on—the still, reflective waters of the artificial lake. Each block has a double structure, consisting of a concrete block encased by a 40-foot-high (12 m) glass wall, that blurs the definition of interior and exterior space. The lightness and uplifting quality of the expansive glass walls contrasts with the solidity of the concrete, thus creating a dynamic of conflicting energies. From the exterior the museum is immensely satisfying, the stillness and balance of its component parts combine in unrivaled harmony, while from the inside, the building becomes both a temple to art and to human inspiration. **TP**

"My hope is to help promote an architecture that welcomes humanity with a lasting effect."

Tadao Ando, architect

House in Corrubedo (2002)

Architect David Chipperfield **Location** Corrubedo, Spain **Style** Contemporary **Materials** Stone, concrete, white plaster cladding

Centrum Bank (2002)

Architect Hans Hollein **Location** Vaduz, Liechtenstein **Style** Postmodernist **Materials** Concrete, steel, glass

Seldom can an architect enjoy the chance to commission a building and thus dispense with the endless, unavoidable negotiations with clients. David Chipperfield (*b.* 1953) relished that chance when in 1996 he began looking for a site to build his own holiday house in Corrubedo, Galicia, on the Atlantic coast of Spain.

Mindful of both the beauty of this coastline and the needs of his family, Chipperfield rejected a passive attitude toward the surrounding context in favor of a more engaging relationship with it. From the main street the house has a faceted elevation punctured by few openings. The geometric irregularity of the street pattern is fully embraced and turned into the spatial logic of the plan of the house. At ground level, the choice of materials reinforces continuity with the local tradition: stone and concrete form the stable base of the house. From this level up, however, a much more open and weightless approach shapes the individual spaces. A long glass window provides an amazing view from the living room onto the ocean. Similarly on the top floor, a number of framed openings bring light into the two bedrooms and the spacious terrace.

The elevation facing the sea is paradigmatic of the spirit of this project. Whereas all the adjacent houses positioned most of the openings on the side facing the street, Chipperfield decided to invert that, not only to take advantage of the unique views, but to give each space a distinctive quality. At the same time, the fragmented profile of the house acknowledges the massing of the neighboring buildings.

With the house in Corrubedo, Chipperfield took the opportunity to stress the responsibility that architects have to weave together landscape and its users through manmade objects. **RB**

The tiny principality of Liechtenstein is reputedly the oldest tax haven in Europe. Today, most of the residents are engaged in providing financial services. Centrum Bank (see page 786) is a relatively small but distinguished private institution based in Vaduz, the capital. It was designed by Hans Hollein (*b.* 1934), the Pritzker Prize–winning architect who is also well known for his drawings, sculpture, and furniture designs.

Hollein conceived the building as a sculptural object—a "huge stone"—to be viewed from all sides, including from above. Although basically rectangular,

> *"To me architecture is not primarily the solution of a problem, but the making of a statement."*
>
> Hans Hollein, architect

the building is transformed by an asymmetrical, freely moving, upwardly swooping roof and gently curving walls into a structure that suggests the hull of a ship, Le Corbusier's chapel at Ronchamp, and even the exterior of the Colosseum in Rome, depending on the viewer's vantage point. From above, the three-dimensional, sculptural identity of the bank is clear because the roof's surface material is revealed as identical to the wall surfacing.

The sculptural shape integrates the bank with a built environment dating from an earlier period. The nearby mountains with their distant peaks are strongly suggested by the upward curve of the roof. Hollein creates architecture that echoes local topography, at the same time subtly transforming the local spirit of place into something wholly different. **FR**

Disney
Concert Hall (2003)

Architect Frank Gehry   **Location** Los Angeles, California, USA
Style Deconstructivist   **Materials** Stainless steel, stone

The billowing stainless steel forms of the Disney Concert Hall occupy an entire downtown block in Los Angeles; that they house an auditorium seems improbable. Yet these curved, flared, and collided volumes have a visual "rightness" amid the sober boxes of corporate L.A. The stainless steel is mostly satin finished; the original concave, polished finish caused a problematic glare of sunlight, and had to be altered.

The auditorium is essentially a rectangular box that sits within the block at an angle, disguised all around by the metallic volumes. Frank Gehry (*b*. 1929) has created billboard architecture on a spectacular scale, and at one place acknowledges this by exposing the steel armature that supports the panels. Despite a fifteen-year gestation and astonishing cost, the building is loved both by the city and by musicians.

During major events, the entrance doors can be fully retracted so the street seems to flow into the foyer. Inside, the spaces are generous and complex, the forms as extroverted as those on the outside. Timber "trees" disguise the steel frame and air-conditioning ducts. Roof lights are cleverly placed to bring daylight in and allow internal lighting to illuminate the external forms at night. The auditorium follows the "vineyard" layout, with the audience sitting in terraces around the stage, and has a tentlike ceiling of Douglas fir. The signage in the building is delightfully subtle: externally lettering is embossed in the stainless steel with a different grade of satin finish; inside, a wall honoring donors has stainless-steel lettering set into gray felt. **CB**

↗ The stainless-steel cladding of the concert hall gives off an intense glow in the Californian sunshine.

→ The hall, created as the new home of the Los Angeles Philharmonic Orchestra, has superb acoustics.

Selfridges (2003)

Architects Future Systems **Location** Birmingham, England **Style** Contemporary **Materials** Glass, steel, aluminum

New retail buildings in the United Kingdom are rarely exciting landmarks or icons. Selfridges in Birmingham can lay claim to be both. The scheme, designed by Future Systems, in the city's redeveloped Bull Ring, marked a key point in the revamp of England's second largest city after a long period from the 1960s onward of being regarded as a gloomy, grimy, overly concreted center that was in thrall to the automobile. That is no longer the case. Selfridges in Birmingham was the result of a commission from its illustrious former boss, Vittorio Radice. Driving past Lord's Cricket Ground in northwest London one day, Radice was struck by the form of its NatWest Media Centre and decided to opt for the same architect to design his new store. The 160,000-square-foot (14,864 sq m) Birmingham store is covered in a skin of 15,000 spun aluminum discs, said by architect Amanda Levete (*b.* 1959) to mimic the sequins on a famous Paco Rabanne dress. These discs allow the building to shimmer in the light, and the organic, amorphous form is a distinctive addition to the Birmingham skyline. Inside, the space is planned around a dramatic, roof-lit atrium, which is crisscrossed by a white "cat's cradle" of sculpted escalators and a smaller, but equally powerful, atrium. The store has won eight awards. Here, not only the customer, but the client, city dweller, and visitor, is always right, and the revitalization of a city center has been given a major push by progressive, characterful design. **DT**

> *"An ersatz urban cliff ... this is the department store as unalloyed architectural entertainment."*
>
> Jonathan Glancey, architecture critic

Kunsthaus (2003)

Architects Peter Cook, Colin Fournier **Location** Graz, Austria **Style** Contemporary **Materials** Reinforced concrete, acrylic, steel mesh

When Austria's second largest city, Graz, was awarded the honor of becoming European Capital of Culture for 2003, it needed something to celebrate the title, a gift to itself for the future. The Kunsthaus, a museum for contemporary art is the result. Dubbed the "friendly alien" by locals, the Kunsthaus is a bluish, shimmering blob of fun that eschews the normal white box favored by galleries, and bursts from its otherwise historic setting. It was designed by Colin Fournier (b. 1944) with Peter Cook (b. 1936), both professors of architecture at the Bartlett School in London, after they clinched the international competition held in 2000 as Spacelab Cook-Fournier. Cook in particular has inspired many architects with the experimental work he did with Archigram in the 1960s—the Kunsthaus's form owes something to that work. It is built primarily of reinforced concrete and clad in curvaceous, translucent, warm-blue acrylic paneling with white plaster and steel mesh on the interior. Its bulbous, biomorphic shape, which some people have likened to "mutant bagpipes," nestles on its site next to the River Mur. Inside, "travelators" connect the galleries while daylight streams in through nozzles in the roof. Outside at night—thanks to Berlin-based designers BIX—the facade becomes a shifting, pulsating surface animated by images and film. The Kunsthaus has style, exuberance, and panache, and its form sets a tension between the old and the new. **DT**

"Once you start actually building, then you occupy a different piece of history."

Peter Cook, professor and architect

Crooked House (2003)

Architect Szotynscy Zalewski Architekci   **Location** Sopot, Poland   **Style** Postmodernist   **Materials** Stone, glass, enameled tiles

The Krzywy Domek (Crooked House) is rapidly becoming one of the most recognizable landmarks of the small town of Sopot in northern Poland. It is located on the popular thoroughfare boasting the town's best selection of bars, restaurants, and shops, that is frequented by a bohemian crowd. The house won the Big Dreamers' Award, and was allegedly inspired by the work of the renowned Polish fairy-tale illustrator Jan Marcin Szancer and the Swedish artist and Sopot resident Per Dahlberg. A functionally designed, 43,000-square-foot (3,994 sq m) floorplan accommodates a variety of uses including commercial office space, retail units, food and drink facilities, a covered market, and a museum. Although the structure follows the building line and scale of the street, this is where any contextual constraints end. The external envelope appears to be its own reflection in a rippled water mirror. Curvaceously bent lines, bloated roof, luscious cornice and frieze, distorted door and window openings together create an illusion equal to that of stepping into a Surrealist painting. The turning-and-twisting nature of the building seems to be caught in a momentary stillness. The selection of materials for the facade interestingly highlights the building's quirkiness—the street-facing elevations are clad in limestone, while the use of glimmering, blue, enameled tiles convincingly animates the undulating curves of the roof. **BK**

> *"The city of Sopot was built on crazy ideas. This project is one of them."*
>
> Jacek Karnowski, Mayor of Sopot

Vacheron Constantin Watch Factory (2003)

Architect Bernard Tschumi **Location** Geneva, Switzerland **Style** High Tech **Materials** Aluminum, glass, steel, wood

The Vacheron Constantin Watch Factory sits as an autonomous object in the commercial zone of Plan-les-Ouates, once agricultural land on the periphery of Geneva. It unifies the management offices and production facilities of the Swiss manufacturer on a 110,300-square-foot (10,250 sq m) site. According to the wishes of the client, Bernard Tschumi (b. 1944) designed the watch factory to be a mixed image of novelty and tradition. It consists of two functional parts; a taller administrative and representative section, and a lower section housing all workshops. The core of the entire structure is almost completely transparent, with a concrete structure enveloped by generous vertical glass facades. Above this lies a thin, double-faced skin—shimmering metal on the outside and warm wooden veneer on the inside—like a blanket casually spread over the building. Except for the columns inside, all of the construction elements,

such as the girders for the roof are concealed between the wooden and metal skin, giving the surface of the facade, both inside and out, a perfect sleekness. The administrative section is organized vertically by a three-story atrium, cut by floating stairs, translucent walkways, and a vitreous lift. Natural light for the production facilities in the lower part of the building is provided by a generous prolate patio. This building certainly does not belong to Tschumi's experimental works of architecture, such as the Parc de la Villette or the Fresnoy Art Center. Nonetheless, it demonstrates the architect's intention to liberate architecture from stylistic expectations, and his devotion to new materials and technologies. The perfect functional partitioning, the representative design, and the relished commitment to high-tech materials and perfect details, make it a role model for industrial buildings in the twenty-first century. **FH**

Prada
Epicenter Store (2003)

Architects Herzog & de Meuron **Location** Tokyo, Japan
Style Contemporary **Materials** Glass, steel

International designer-clothing company Prada has an impressive recent history in commissioning unusual, not to say radical buildings. After the success of the company's flagship store in New York designed by Dutch architect Rem Koolhaas, and with others planned across the United States, Prada commissioned another leading practice, the thoughtful Swiss firm Herzog & de Meuron, to design its Tokyo outlet.

Built in the fashionable Aoyama district of Tokyo, the store is a six-story, five-sided glass "crystal" on a corner site made up of a series of diamond-shaped panes, and in a form that is reminiscent of a child's drawing of a pointed, roofed house. These panes—transparent shells at a human, display-window scale—are by turns flat, concave, and convex, with the effect that the building appears to breathe and move as one walks around it. Unusually for Tokyo, there is a plaza in front of the entrance, complete with trees and plants.

Inside the building, the effect is of a continuous space, achieved by the creation of structural cores and tubes that are extruded from the diamond shapes and morph into elevators, stairs, and fitting rooms. Hairy surfaces are mixed with viscous finishes, in materials such as pony skin and silicon, along with display tables of molded, transparent fiberglass. Below ground, the same oak has been used as at Tate Modern, England, with lacquered steel for the stairs and an ivory-colored carpet. This is a beautifully realized and stylish building, its honeycomb-like mesh acting as a perfect beacon for the expensive wares on offer inside. **DT**

↖ Despite the angles of the building, the mixture of concave and convex glazing softens its appearance.

← Because some of the glass is shaped, the building appears to breathe in and out as one walks around it.

Palais des Congrès (2003)

Architects Tétrault Dubuc Saia & Associates   **Location** Montreal, Canada   **Style** Contemporary   **Materials** Granite, concrete

Perhaps big box buildings like arenas, stadiums, and convention centers have no place downtown, but the Palais des Congrès turns size to its advantage. It engulfs three historic buildings, including the ten-story Art Deco Tramways Building, as well as a metro station, a fire station, and a new exhibition room touted as Canada's largest open-span space. By straddling the metro line and the trench housing the Ville-Marie expressway, the Palais des Congrès knits together Old Montreal with downtown's offices and shops, and has sparked urban renewal in the surrounding Quartier International. Inside, a 1,000-foot-long (300 m) promenade leads from the metro station on the east to a pair of giant glass canopies cantilevered over the sidewalk at the west entrance. The promenade links pedestrians to Montreal's celebrated underground city.

Mario Saia led the architectural consortium responsible for the design, which preserves the unloved 1983 convention center by Victor Prus—a linear, brutal concrete form. Their tour de force is an 80-foot-high (24 m) lobby on the west end, known as Hall Bleury, fronted by a quirky, multicolored glass curtain wall—a glittering counterpoint to Prus's iconic glass and steel tubular space frame. Capless glazing set in a grid of large panels makes sunlight dance over the interiors in green, yellow, orange, blue, and pink hues, brightening up drab convention proceedings.

This exuberant behemoth, stretching three city blocks, springs from the enduring Modernist ambition to create architecture out of infrastructure. The architects took daunting technical challenges, overwhelming functional requirements, and soul-destroying urban planning, and turned them into an urbane and vibrant showpiece. **DMT**

Social Housing (2003)

Architect Mario Garzaniti   **Location** Brussels, Belgium   **Style** Postmodernist   **Materials** Cor-ten steel, concrete

Rusty metal panels are normally seen as a sign of the structural damage of buildings. However, Belgian architect Mario Garzaniti (b. 1956) carefully constructed a stabilized, pre-rusted facade for an apartment building in the Schaerbeek area of Brussels.

The building occupies a narrow wedge-shaped site, housing a shop on the ground floor and two duplex apartments. Crammed against the firewall of the neighbors stands a slender slice of the building, which sets itself apart from the rusty hull; the internal stairs are situated here, along with the shop entrance

---

"There is a simplicity in the shape, which separates it from the hesitant attempts of other architects."

Rafael Magrou, architecture critic

---

and all facilities, stacked above each other, keeping a maximum of space for the rooms.

The eye-catching feature, however, is the facade. Cor-ten steel panels (which oxidize to give a brown finish) are riveted to stainless-steel profiles, which have then been attached to the concrete core. Flexible bands between the cor-ten panels and the stainless steel prevent any further corrosion. Window shutters are incorporated into the facade, filtering the light through their vertical slits. When closed, they lie flush with the outer shell, adding to the interesting patchwork of rusty nuances.

With its careful detailing and its ironic references to the adjacent tenements, Garzaniti's building forms a satisfactory architectural conclusion to the whole housing block. **FH**

Center
for Visual Arts (2003)

Architect João Mendes Ribeiro **Location** Coimbra, Portugal
Style Minimalist **Materials** Masonry, steel, wood

4 x 4
House (2003)

Architect Tadao Ando **Location** Kobe, Hyogo, Japan
Style Modernist **Material** Reinforced concrete

Coimbra is better known for the magnificent library of its university, by far the oldest in Portugal, than for architectural boldness. Yet there are exceptions, such as the subtle conversion of the west wing of the former Arts College into the Visual Arts Center, now at the center of student life. It was designed by local architect, and graduate from the Faculty of Architecture at the University of Oporto, João Mendes Ribeiro (b. 1960), who allows his architecture to be influenced by other disciplines. Mendes Ribeiro's approach to the Visual Arts Center was determined yet

"The ultimate aim is to create architecture that reveals the wish to condense itself."

João Mendes Ribeiro, architect

subtle, as he aimed to evoke archaeological memory while still retaining the city's modern image. Externally, the Visual Arts Center is diplomatic, and the plainness of Mendes Ribeiro's design aims for a peaceful coexistence between past and present. Inside, existing archaeological structures remained untouched, and are preserved underneath the floor, but the new areas are as modern as possible. At ground level is a flexible exhibition space with moving partitions; new gossamer metal stairs lead to the upper floor that has an imposing dividing wall. On one side of the wall lie laboratories, archives, and assembly rooms, while exhibition rooms, a library, and office spaces occupy the other. Mendes Ribeiro's clear, straightforward contemporary language creates a continuum between the old and the new. **YN**

Facing Awaji Island, the epicenter of the Hanshin earthquake that devastated the city of Kobe in 1995, the 4 x 4 House stands like a monument; its top-floor, glazed facade, complete with cruciform mullion, staring out over the Seto Inland Sea.

In this minimalist four-floored project, with a footprint measuring a mere 43 square feet (4 sq m), Tadao Ando (b. 1941) reveals his mastery in the design of small buildings. The brief was to conceive a house that would offer a rich living experience on a tiny plot of land located between the main railway line into Kobe and the beachfront. The severe concrete tower, with its square ground plan, was conceived as the largest structure possible in an area that today covers a tiny 70 square feet (6.5 sq m) parcel of land.

The restricted space meant that every detail had to be carefully considered and the building kept simple to make the most of the spectacular views over the bay. The first floor contains the entrance and the bathroom, the second floor the bedroom, the third a study, but it is the top floor accommodating the main living space that is the key to this tiny but beautifully conceived house. A perfect cube, the uppermost level has been designed on the same grid as the rest of the structure but has been displaced by 3 feet (1 m) toward the sea.

In miniature, the 4 x 4 House is an ideal example of Ando's precise geometric style, as well as his preoccupation with nature, which permeates the building through the top block's open views to front and back. Concrete, sky, and water blend in an aesthetic that combines the best of traditional Japanese architecture with a unique Modernist style. In 2004 a second 4 x 4 House, dubbed "The Sequel" by Ando, was constructed next to the original. **JH**

Estádio
Municipal de Braga (2003)

Architect Eduardo Souto de Moura   **Location** Braga, Portugal
Style Brutalist   **Material** Concrete

Designed by Souto de Moura (*b.* 1952), the soccer stadium at Braga is the architect's largest built project to date and secured his international reputation as an architect capable of transforming the environment. Portugal was awarded the rights to Euro 2004 soccer championship in 1999 when a promise of seven new and three rebuilt stadiums fought off competition from Spain. Although the Braga stadium was host to only two qualifying matches, it is the architectural *pièce de resistance* of the whole scheme.

One of Souto de Moura's most celebrated projects is the house at Trevessa do Souto (1998) in which he reshaped the terraced landscape to allow the building to nestle into a granite outcrop. At Braga he revisited the concept, but on an enormous scale. A series of controlled explosions blasted into the Monte Castro quarry to form a 98-foot-high (30 m) fissure, which allows the structure to literally "grow" out from the rock face.

Dispensing with the amphitheater iconography of stadium design, Souto de Moura has eliminated seating behind the goals: the northwest end housing a giant screen and the southeast a desolate rock wall—a natural sound amplifier for the chanting crowds. Shafts bring light into the circulation areas and rise to a panoramic viewing platform at roof level.

Like the Baroque cathedral that overlooks Braga, the material and sensual permanence of the stadium looks down on the town; a shrine not to religion but to the holy game of soccer. **JH**

↗ The tiered grandstands have been lightened by massive holes cut through the concrete.

→ The field and stands are protected by a retractable tensile awning guided along steel cables.

Amazing Whale Jaw (2003)

Architect Nio Architects   **Location** Hoofddorp, Netherlands   **Style** Contemporary   **Materials** Polystyrene foam, polyester

The Amazing Whale Jaw is a bus station located in the forecourt of the Hoofddorps Sparne Hospital. It was designed in homage to Oscar Niemeyer, the great Brazilian architect known for his curvilinear and organic forms. The building's unusual zoomorphic shape renders it more a sculpture than a bus station, and its strange morphology is at odds with its quiet suburban context. The open structure of the Whale Jaw also results in a dramatic *chiaroscuro* of light and shadow, providing protection from the elements but engaging them in a theatrical manner. The odd green color of the bus station adds to its notoriety. The most extraordinary thing about the Amazing Whale Jaw, however, is not its shape or pigmentation. It is instead the fact that it is the world's largest structure made out of synthetic materials. Restricted by a small budget ($1.3 million), the architects were forced to think creatively. The solution was a building constructed entirely from polystyrene foam and polyester, not typical building materials. Nio Architects is a young firm established in 2000 by Maurice Nio (*b.* 1959), who graduated from the well-respected Delft University of Technology. He is an unconventional architect and has previously caught the eye of the international architecture world for his design of waste facilities and a house for Brad Pitt. While the Amazing Whale Jaw is only a bus station, it merits a visit for its groundbreaking design and unexpected materials. **KAB**

"Like the white face of a geisha, every opinion and image can be projected onto the building . . ."

Maurice Nio, architect

An Turas (2003)

Architect Sutherland Hussey Architects   **Location** Island of Tiree, Scotland   **Style** Minimalist   **Materials** Blockwork, reinforced concrete, wood

A large-scale sculpture as much as a building, An Turas stands on the foreshore of a remote and beautiful Scottish island, a startling contemporary intervention in the landscape. Built as a shelter for passengers waiting for the local ferry, An Turas, "the journey" in Gaelic, represents a close collaboration between Sutherland Hussey and four established Scottish artists—Jake Harvey, Glen Onwin, Donald Urquhart, and Sandra Kennedy. The project was commissioned by the local arts enterprise organization. Having visited the location together, the artists and architects considered the various qualities that made the island distinctive, then devised the structure and its textures to draw out related themes. An Turas is formed of three main parts laid out as a long rectangle on plan— a tunnel, a bridge, and a glass box. Each part provides a different involvement with the surroundings, with the glass box being the main point of focus and allowing protected but delightfully engaging views across the bay. The white-walled tunnel protects the viewer from the harsh and frequent winds but is open to the sky, whereas the slatted sides of the bridge permit the patterns in the rocks and sand to be read. It is a pure and beautifully streamlined design and although it ostensibly performs its intended function as a passenger shelter, it is effectively a platform from which to comfortably engage with the surrounding topography. What makes it truly engaging though is the contrast its rectilinearity provides with the natural forms that surround it while simultaneously providing interaction with them. Here, Functionalism is secondary to inspiration, and at essence its closest architectural siblings are the viewing pavilions, belvederes, and follies that punctuate the more elaborately designed landscapes of Georgian Britain. **NC**

Schaulager (2003)

Architects Herzog & de Meuron   **Location** Basel, Switzerland   **Style** Contemporary   **Materials** Concrete, stone

The Emanuel Hoffmann-Stiftung foundation, based in Basel, began collecting art in 1933 and has works by nearly 150 artists. Originally these were displayed in the Basel Museum of Fine Arts or Contemporary Art Museum. Yet a major question remained: what to do with the invisible 99 percent of the collection? Local architects Jacques Herzog and Pierre de Meuron responded with a new kind of space for art, neither a museum nor a warehouse but something in between. Globally celebrated for their art galleries (Walker Art Center extension, Minneapolis; Goetz Collection, Munich; de Young Museum, San Francisco; Tate Modern, London), the Swiss pair have become renowned for their tendency to experiment with new forms. The interior of their Schaulager (or "exhibition warehouse") offers ideal space for storage, flexible enough to make any work available by appointment, while clearly expressing this functional requirement visually. They also created exhibition areas, offices, workshops, and an auditorium. The inner space gives a logical shape to the exterior, seemingly extruded from geometrical canons. Carefully designed, the indented entrance facade creates a courtyard that turns a dull lot in the outskirts of the city into a genuine urban space. German actor Karl Valentin once said "Kunst ist schön, macht aber viel Arbeit" (Art is nice, but that's a lot of work)—designing Schaulager was indeed a lot of work, but it was worth it. **YN**

"The strength of our buildings lies in their ability to produce an instant, visceral impact on the visitor."

Jacques Herzog and Pierre de Meuron, architects

Ferrari Research Center (2003)

Architect Massimiliano Fuksas   **Location** Modena, Italy   **Style** High Tech   **Materials** Glass, steel, concrete, aluminum

Located in the heart of the company's complex at Modena, the building houses the offices of the Ferrari Technical Management and the workshops developing new cars. The project by Massimiliano Fuksas (*b*. 1944) demonstrates a new poetic lightness in architecture, the constitutive element being the upper story, which is lifted up from the building itself as if it is floating. The square volumes are designed with black steel frames and dark-green-colored windows. This calls more attention to the elements of nature that are an integrated part of the building. The structure is arranged around a rectangular, precisely ordered bamboo garden creating a microclimate to improve working conditions. The roof of the lower volume is a large water basin, whereas the underside of the upper volume is clad in polished aluminum, creating a spectacular mirroring effect for the meeting rooms, the water, the pebbles, and the plants of the

basin. To enhance the floating effect, the load-bearing structures carrying the upper volume have been reduced as far as possible. The glass boxes of the meeting rooms are two of the few connecting points between the volumes. The rooms are accessible via the water basin on wooden walkways, and are colored in bright red and yellow, echoing Ferrari's brand colors. Rather than a building, Fuksas created an architectural landscape: an architecture devoted to innovation, ecology, and the human senses. **FH**

" … immaculately detailed, it is a passionate challenge to the banality of office work."

Richard Ingersoll, architect

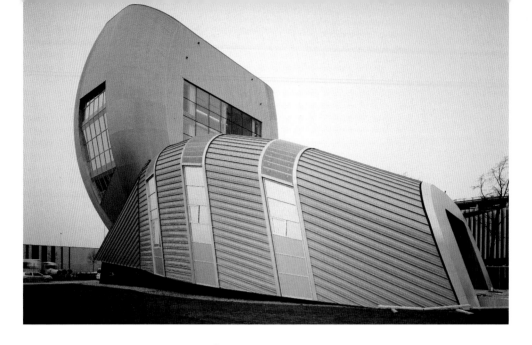

Living Tomorrow Pavilion (2003)

Architects UN Studio **Location** Amsterdam, Netherlands **Style** Expressionist **Materials** Concrete, metal

The unusual shape of the Living Tomorrow Pavilion houses a vision of how our home and work life will change as we embrace new technologies. The pavilion, a temporary structure, is a combination of a laboratory, a gallery, and an auditorium where companies can exhibit and test their technologies. Only recyclable materials or those with a low environmental impact were used in the construction of the 104-foot-high (32 m) building. Its metal-clad flowing curves and slopes demonstrate UN Studio's concept that the vertical and horizontal parts of the building should form one continuous, inside-out shape. Inside the building is a wealth of advanced technological features: you can use your phone to open locked doors and send your mail, or use the built-in computers to check your fridge inventory and order automatically cooked convenience foods. There are cocoon beds and bathroom mirrors that give you information on the weather and the news, and even washing machines that can detect a colored item among your whites. Living Tomorrow, the company behind the project, recognized the folly of trying continually to predict the future, so it put a time limit on it. Completed in 2004, the building was scheduled for demolition at the end of 2008 because the backers believed that by then everything exhibited within either would be out of date or already in daily use. These days, you need to rush to see the future. **JM**

> *"[I am] trying to make my projects endless, to create a bigger kind of capacity of continuity in them."*

Ben van Berkel, architect

Gormley Studio (2003)

Architects David Chipperfield Architects   **Location** London, England   **Style** Contemporary   **Materials** Steel, reinforced concrete, metal

The Gormley Studio fits in well with the industrial architecture of King's Cross. It is a converted warehouse, consisting of pitched roofs alongside a 10,763-square-foot (1,000 sq m), enclosed courtyard. The architect's brief was to accommodate Antony Gormley's working practices—drawing, sculpting, painting, welding, casting, and photography—within the space. The building was a collaboration between architect and client. David Chipperfield is passionate about historically generated architecture, basing his design on what exists rather than what could exist, and gently pushing the vernacular back into the picture, letting materials speak for themselves. Chipperfield explained that Gormley and he began with the concept of "a deluxe shed." To them it perhaps feels more like a gallery with its stark white walls, but as Gormley's practice gently dominates the space, this may change. Gormley wanted bright spaces, divided according to his working practices. The studio is made of seven bays, of which the large open studio is three. There is also a photographic studio and two smaller private workspaces, with the yard outside available for working on large-scale sculpture. Two angular, galvanized staircases connect the yard to the studios, punctuating the white roofs and giving the building a futuristic twist. The architecture provides seclusion and intimacy, space, calmness, and sharpness. It is inducive to creativity. **SL**

> *"The studio is a place of tremendous concentration, [a place] to be ... self-absorbed."*
>
> Antony Gormley, artist

Rosenthal Center for Contemporary Art (2003)

Architect Zaha Hadid **Location** Cincinnati, Ohio, USA **Style** Deconstructivist **Materials** Steel, concrete, glass, anodized aluminum

Cincinnati, a 200-year-old city straddling the Ohio River, presents the opiate blandness of many a second-tier U.S. city, but the university campus reveals another side: look-at-me faculty buildings by Frank Gehry, Michael Graves, Peter Eisenman, and Harry Cobb. Downtown, Zaha Hadid's Lois & Richard Rosenthal Center for Contemporary Arts, a facility of the city's Contemporary Arts Center (CAC), trumps them all.

With a tight, two-year construction schedule, the project was an exercise in discipline. Here stood the headquarters of Larry Flynt's *Hustler* empire. The architect's challenge was to compress the volumes into a vertical space that only offered two street-facing facades on a crossroads promising little opportunity for dramatic views of the building. Balancing the bulk of the building on an elegant glass-walled lobby, the ground floor is conceived as a continuation of the pavement section outside, itself stained a dark gray and inset with thin light boxes that direct the eye into the building. The floor runs through the lobby and, in the building's most dramatic gesture, makes a giant curve, running up to the roof. This creates an enormous fissure between the building and its neighbor that produces an immensely tall atrium.

Below, the architects have threaded a zigzag sequence of anodized aluminum-clad stairs that run back and forth, each flight 50–60 feet (15–18 m) long. Articulated flow—Hadid's signature gesture—is thus ingeniously folded into the very heart of the building. This urban carpet literally drags the street into the building and reflects the efforts of the CAC to reach out to a broad audience. **MI**

◹ The Rosenthal Center occupies a modest corner site of a mere 11,000 square feet (1,022 sq m).

◿ The complementary front and side elevations are enlivened by undulating, sculptural reliefs.

Casa Ponce (2003)

Architect Mathias Klotz   **Location** Buenos Aires, Argentina   **Style** Modernist   **Materials** Steel, concrete, glass

Located on the slope of the historic section of San Isidro Labrador to the north of Buenos Aires, this renowned work by Mathias Klotz (*b.* 1966) challenges the tolerance of the home in relation to the skills of modern architecture. Although a small supporting section is semi-underground, three-quarters of Casa Ponce is cantilevered and floats above the ground.

The house is not only a disturbing and spectacular architectural structure but also an overt metaphor for the fetish of contemporary architecture: the cantilevered box. On a 21,528-square-foot (2,000 sq m) lot in a dramatic rectangular shape, Klotz resolves the notoriously unchallenging single-family housing program with a provocative twist: he provides, on the narrow lot, open views of the Río de la Plata, located behind the property. The layout of the parallel bars along the length of the lot struggles with the problematic decision not to divide the lot in two.

A compact concrete bar rests on the edge that it shares with the lower-level glass box in the middle, and all the elements seem to float on a small semi-underground volume where the service rooms, the machine rooms, and the laundry room are housed. The bedrooms are on the upper level, with its fabulous garden deck, while the glass volume is the living room.

The functionality of such vertiginous cantilevers could be debated, as could the simple structural provocation of making weekend bathers seem to levitate; clearly, the work of this still young architect aims not only to provide heavenly views of the landscape, but also to add a bit of drama to life in these riverside suburbs. **PAB**

↗ The glazed communal area is raised high above the ground and enjoys views of the Río de la Plata.

➥ The long, cantilevered arm of the bedroom section is supported by the seemingly tiny block beneath.

International Center for Possibility Thinking (2003)

Architect Richard Meier   **Location** Los Angeles, California, USA   **Style** Postmodernist   **Materials** Glass, stainless steel, concrete

The Crystal Cathedral campus at Garden Grove in Los Angeles is home to three monuments of Modernist and Postmodernist architectural design, built by three of the world's most celebrated architects. The inspiring International Center for Possibility Thinking by Richard Meier (b. 1934) sits between the Crystal Cathedral, the first all-glass house of worship, designed by Philip Johnson (1906–2005) in 1980, and the soaring Tower of Hope, 1968, of Richard Neutra (1892–1970). The three buildings are located in such close proximity that the area between them functions almost as an outdoor room. Together they interrelate, aesthetically, spiritually, and functionally, while retaining the individual characters and expressions of their architects. In his career, Meier has based his designs on just a few specific concepts, and therefore his works seem a cohesive whole. His projects transcend their geography and location, and his ideals and inspiration are clearly defined in each building he creates. His approach is based loosely on Corbusian precepts—the interrelation of clean lines and geometric form—with an abiding admiration for the color white. The purity of his designs, combined with their essential whiteness, lends them a spiritual element that is present in both his public and domestic works, and is particularly prevalent in this building. The international center is an imposing four-story building sheathed in a skin of stainless steel and glass, with eight sliding, glass entrance doors that lead into a 40-foot-high (12 m) atrium. The extensive use of clear glass bathes the shining white interior in light, which is characteristically manipulated by Meier. The symbolic significance of Meier's building as the third part of the "trinity" of buildings on the campus is not lost, and it capacitates the roles of functionality and spirituality with an effortless sublimity. **TP**

Church of the Jubilee (2003)

Architect Richard Meier   **Location** Rome, Italy   **Style** Postmodernist   **Materials** Post-tensioned concrete, steel, glass, travertine, stucco

To celebrate the two-thousandth anniversary of the birth of Christ, the Vicariate of Rome opened a competition to six invited architects to design a new Catholic church for a housing estate in the Tor Tre Teste district of Rome. Richard Meier (*b.* 1934) won the commission with his inspiring design incorporating a church and community center. Glistening white and constructed around strong circular and angular forms, the church sits as an icon of Postmodernist architecture on a triangular site, surrounded by somewhat grimy 1970s apartment blocks. Three curved structures of the same radius but different heights are the most arresting aspect of the building. Symbolically they allude to the Holy Trinity, while functionally they divide the interior space, with the outer two curved walls enveloping the side chapel and baptistery and the largest one defining the main area of worship. The glazed skylights between the walls allow light to pour into the interior. The circular form of the three shell-like walls is in striking contrast to the tall and narrow wall against which they butt, and the angular lines of the community center. The three curved walls were a feat of engineering. The precast, white, post-tensioned concrete panels that make up the walls were positioned using a custom-built machine moving on rails. The smooth white concrete is photocatalytic, that is, it is self-cleaning, ensuring the longevity of its pristine appeal. **TP**

> *"Light is the means by which we are able to experience what we call sacred."*
>
> Richard Meier, architect

Slice House (2003)

Architects Procter-Rihl Architects   **Location** Porto Alegre, Brazil
Style Contemporary   **Materials** Concrete, glass

When the architecture firm Procter-Rihl was approached to design a new house for a retired history lecturer in Porto Alegre, the architects saw it as an opportunity to translate the practice's vision for cities and urban culture into its first built project.

First, the choice of a marginal, geometrically complex site, 12 feet (3.7 m) wide and 126 feet (38.5 m) long, implicitly demonstrates that no site is too small or too unimportant to be left aside. By treating the residual spaces with the same respect as the more monumental ones, Procter-Rihl was able to inject a

> *"Good architecture should have a role in questioning values . . . and engaging architectural debate."*
>
> Procter-Rihl Architects

sense of urbanity even in a small-scale intervention. An intention to invert traditional preconceptions about urban living is also demonstrated by the internal layout. A number of spatial effects and illusions are played out to enlarge the perception of the spaces. A non-orthogonal grid of partitions morphs the internal rooms, creating spatial variety. In turn this impacts on the prismatic shape of the outer volume and creates a dynamic composition enhanced by cuts to let in light.

The final product is not only a remarkable example of design for residual spaces but also an architectural and cultural hybrid. In fact, it mixes elements of the local culture such as the cult of the body through extroverted spaces, and the European interest in asymmetrical complexity is manifested in the overall composition of the project. **RB**

Minami Yamashiro Primary School (2003)

Architects Richard Rogers Partnership   **Location** Kyoto, Japan
Style High Tech   **Materials** Reinforced concrete, aluminum

The Minami Yamashiro Primary School is located in a small, remote village in the Kyoto prefecture, an area subject to rural depopulation. The brief was to design a low-budget facility to help restore civic pride, for use not only by the pupils but also as a community center for the adult inhabitants of the surrounding area: a mixed-use concept unusual for Japan.

The preparation of the site, in an elevated position overlooking the village, involved cutting away the top of a hill. The school itself occupies a quarter of the site; the rest is devoted to playing fields, an adjacent gym/village hall, and an outdoor swimming pool. Richard Rogers Partnership took the bold decision to use color, a striking element of the school's design that is rarely adopted in native Japanese architecture. The exterior of the auxiliary structures is enlivened with bright panels of primary colors; internally, color-coding is employed to differentiate usage: primaries for the youngest students to neutral tones for the adults.

To keep costs as low as possible, the obvious choice for the structure was a simple modular grid system. Flexible units, inspired by the traditional Japanese *tatami* mat, allow the school to adapt to its various requirements. The center of the building is dominated by the common hall, which is articulated by staircases and communication bridges and is surrounded by a series of adjustable classrooms. The multilevel upper space contains break areas while the lower levels are dedicated to specific lessons.

Sir Richard Rogers (*b.* 1933) is best known for his massive and bombastic architectural gestures: the Minami Yamashiro Primary School proves that size doesn't matter. The Royal Institute of British Architects, who gave an award to the building in 2004, described it as an "elegant East-meets-West building." **JH**

Casa
D'Água (2003)

Architect Isay Weinfeld   **Location** São Paulo, Brazil

Style Modernist   **Materials** Poured concrete, wood, rope

The design of the Casa d'Água has a subtle relevance in illustrating what has become to be known as Tropical Modernism. Reductive in essence, it has a sensuality and warmth missing in European houses of the same genre and serves as an antidote to the cold, monastic Minimalism so admired in recent years. Casa d'Água combines a contemporary aesthetic with vernacular building materials, and demonstrates a sound understanding of local climatic considerations. An unassuming, small domestic project, it gives visual expression to many of the characteristics found in the work of Isay Weinfeld (b. 1952): the texture of the stone walls, the delicacy of the woodwork, clean and well-defined volumes, and the judicious use of openings designed to catch natural light.

Although he does not welcome the comparison, Weinfeld is often compared to Oscar Niemeyer, who created a unique brand of modern architecture in Brasilia. Like Niemeyer, Weinfeld's striking mix of Modernist details linked with native Brazilian accents gives rise to an international style leavened by a relaxed geometry and Brazilian colors and textures.

Weinfeld has a hatred for the superfluous and decorative: his bold and elegant architecture reads as narrative imbued with the personal associations of his patrons. The plot at the Casa d'Água is long and narrow, which led Weinfeld to create a central patio dividing the building into two blocks. A narrow pool with large granite stones anchored to the bottom runs alongside the house and leads to this patio. **JH**

↗ The patio has a richly colored hardwood floor and is partly shaded by a screen of thick twine ropes.

→ The large granite stones in the pool next to the house bring a rugged sense of nature to the garden.

Usera Library (2003)

Architects Abalos & Herreros   **Location** Madrid, Spain   **Style** Contemporary   **Materials** Concrete, glass

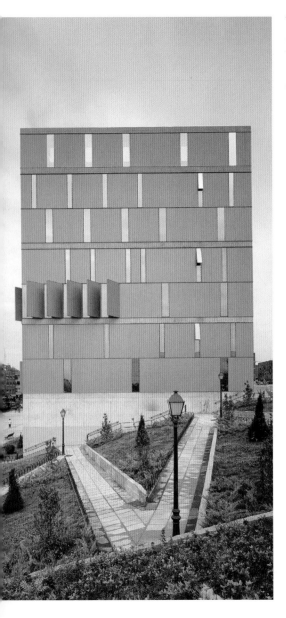

This public library in Usera, a southern suburb of Madrid, suggests a building in mythology: a golden tower, it has the appearance of the object of a quest. Its seductive power stems partly from its simple elegance and partly from the fact that it is intuitively understood as a sanctuary. That a cheap municipal building can be one of such symbolic potential is a real testament to its architects, the Madrid-based practice of Abalos & Herreros.

The tower—a form picked for its associations with learning—is a work of striking economy, as well as deception. It is actually only four stories high, not counting mezzanine floors, but the way the slender windows are ranked disguises this. Further, the facade continues upward one story beyond the roof to make the building seem taller than it is.

The facade itself is made of prefabricated panels with a platinum-colored, slightly reflective skin, with the result that the color of the building is constantly changing throughout the day. One of the wonderful details is the way in which certain windows have sunshades that appear to open and close like the covers of a book. These fixed shutters angle views toward particular parts of the city.

Inside, the library has a basic open layout with high ceilings and an extremely spare use of materials. The only decorative element is the wallpaper, made by U.S. artist Peter Halley, which has an abstract pattern derived from the text of Jorge Luis Borges's short story *The Library of Babel*. This wallpaper, together with the limited daylight coming in through the slit windows, creates a studious atmosphere.

The real richness of the building, though, is to be appreciated from outside, in the way that it communicates the idea of a library to the surrounding community with a language that is somehow both age-old and absolutely contemporary. **JMc**

30 St. Mary Axe (2004)

Architects Foster and Partners   **Location** London, England   **Style** High Tech   **Materials** Steel, glass

No. 30 St. Mary Axe, colloquially known as "The Gherkin" or "The Swiss Re Tower," is a distinctive addition to the London skyline and one that became an instant hit with capital dwellers and tourists alike. It was built during a key period in the modern-day development of the City of London, in the middle of an ongoing debate about tall buildings in the city center, and at a time of rising standards in architecture.

The tower, commissioned by the reinsurance group Swiss Re, is fashioned in the form of a sculptural, tapering cigar. The design allows for shops and an elegant public plaza space at its base, and a stunning, double-height rooftop viewing gallery and restaurant for tenants and their guests at its peak, just beneath a conical glass dome. The forty-story skyscraper also has a circular floorplate, and architects Foster and Partners, with ex-partner Ken Shuttleworth, created a sustainable energy system with maximum natural lighting whereby the aerodynamic form allows fresh air to be drawn up through its spiraling lightwells. This gives the exterior form a swirling, striped pattern of diamond shapes, while two skins create a natural chimney effect, reducing the need for air conditioning.

The building is significant as being one of a phase of tall building proposals for central London, which is otherwise relatively low-rise compared to other world cities. The site was formerly home to the 1903 Baltic Exchange building before it was damaged by an Irish Republican Army bomb in 1992.

Swiss Re sold the building, but continues to occupy thirteen levels. The Gherkin has won many major awards including the Stirling Prize in 2004. The landscaped plaza in which the building sits makes this even more of a public building, although it is not open to the public. The tower is a potent new symbol of prosperity, commerce, the future, and of the capital city of London itself. **DT**

Scottish Parliament Building (2004)

Architects Enric Miralles, RMJM **Location** Edinburgh, Scotland **Style** Contemporary **Materials** Concrete, timber, glass, steel, granite

With the passing of the Scotland Act 1998, the Scottish Parliament came into existence. Donald Dewar, the late Scottish Secretary, led the mission to create a new building that would house Scotland's first independent parliament for almost 300 years. In 1997, Dewar held an architectural competition, which was won jointly by Catalan architect Enric Miralles (1955–2000), and Scottish architecture practice RMJM. It was not, however, a match made in heaven. The complex is sited at the end of the Royal Mile in Edinburgh's Old Town opposite the Royal Palace at Holyrood. The location was controversial, there was a huge overspend on the initial budget of £40 million ($80 m), the building opened three years late, and the whole project was dogged by criticism and adverse publicity. The building, however, is a delight, and has won many plaudits for its design. With its central motifs of "upturned boats," interlocking, leaf-shaped

buildings topped with elegant skylights, and grass-roofed branchlike buildings merging into adjacent parkland, it achieves a poetic union between the Scottish landscape, its people, its culture, and the city of Edinburgh. Miralles, who like Dewar died in 2000, designed the building's Debating Chamber to emphasize the impression of parliament "sitting in the land" with garden paths and ponds linking the site to the landscape. Other elements include four tower buildings with committee rooms, briefing rooms, and staff offices, a media building, and a large, sky-lit foyer. The oft-photographed windows are of stainless steel, framed in oak with lattice oak sunscreens. Inside, the offices feature concrete, barrel-vaulted ceilings, oak furnishings, and window seats. The building is a tribute to its late architect and encapsulates a "Scottishness," individuality, and confidence in a new, independent future. **DT**

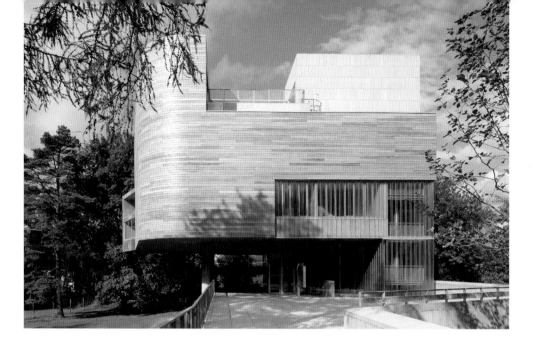

Lewis Glucksman Gallery (2004)

Architects Sheila O'Donnell, John Tuomey   **Location** Cork, Ireland   **Style** Modernist   **Materials** Concrete, limestone, Angela de Campigna wood

Ireland's most intriguing art space, the Lewis Glucksman Gallery, named for the Wall Street philanthropist who funded it, stands on a meadow beside the River Lee on the campus of University College, Cork. From a plinth of limestone and concrete, the building, shortlisted for the Stirling Prize in 2005, winds into the treetops in a series of dramatically cantilevered twists and turns, with limestone yielding to timber. Four interlocking galleries, stacked vertically, face variously toward the river, the city, and the university's original Neo-Gothic quadrangle, which was designed by Sir Thomas Deane in 1854. The architectural focus is on the individual galleries rather than on an imposing entrance hall. The architects, Sheila O'Donnell (b. 1953) and John Tuomey (b. 1954), both of whom worked with James Stirling in the late 1970s, were influenced by a museum exhibit of a Viking ship raised on stilts, and by an image from a poem by Seamus Heaney, Ireland's Nobel Prize–winning poet, of a celestial ship floating above the monastery of Clonmacnoise, "big hull rocked to a standstill." For Tuomey the building resembles a "celestial vessel straining over a stone terrain." The Glucksman Gallery is highly sympathetic to its surroundings. It is clad in limestone at various levels and the hardwood wrapped around the building mirrors its woodland setting. Existing trees were kept, and the building itself was held at tree-height. **BMC**

> *"What is really remarkable about this ... art gallery is that the more one looks, the better it gets."*
>
> Royal Institute of British Architects award (2005)

Sharp Centre for Design (2004)

Architects Alsop Architects **Location** Toronto, Canada **Style** Contemporary **Materials** Steel, metal

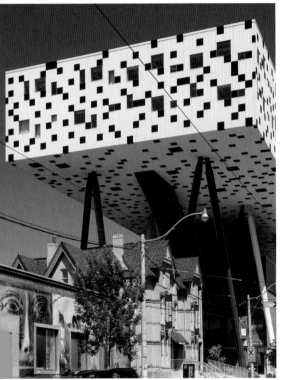

A structural marvel and a bold urban provocation, described as "Canada's version of the Pompidou Center" by Lisa Rochon, journalist for the *Globe and Mail*, the Sharp Centre for Design at the Ontario College of Art and Design in Toronto was a jolt for the staid reputations of its school and city. The first Canadian project by British architect Will Alsop (*b.* 1947), the Sharp Centre is an addition to the 130-year old Ontario College in downtown Toronto. It primarily houses classrooms and studio spaces.

Impossible to miss, the center is a two-story box, measuring 100 by 28 feet (30 x 8.5 m), lofted 85 feet (25 m) into the air by twelve slender steel caissons. The box is linked to the preexisting school below and to one side by umbilical circulation towers. The caissons, built of steel tubes used by the petroleum industry, are tied to concrete foundations that run 65 feet (20 m) deep. On its sides and underside the box is clad with metal siding painted black and white, and it has a randomized pattern of fenestration.

The center is a dramatically horizontal expression, in contrast to Toronto's best-known landmark, the CN Tower, which is one of the world's tallest buildings. Critics have been disappointed with the interiors, however. Budgetary limitations resulted in spaces that are largely conventional and simply appointed. Visitors are whisked up to the center in an elevator, and once there the windows present views that do not differ from those found in the surrounding buildings. There is a missed opportunity to highlight the procession from the ground to the rectangular volume, and to create a sense of floating above the city below. **AC**

↗ Architect Will Alsop has described his creation as being like a "tabletop."

← The boldly colored steel column "legs" hold aloft the massive horizontal slab of the building.

Stock Orchard Street (2004)

Architects Sarah Wigglesworth Architects **Location** London, England **Style** Eco-Architecture **Materials** Wood, steel and plastic sheeting

While taking the train from north London toward King's Cross station, there is one building that is certain to catch your eye: Stock Orchard Street by Sarah Wigglesworth (b. 1958). The bizarre structure, located just by the railway tracks, is the architect's house and studio, and owes its weird looks to the eco-consciousness of its creator, which won her the RIBA Sustainability Award. Sitting at the end of a Victorian row of houses, this complex represents a rare London example of eco-friendly urban living.

The unusual array of materials used are very low cost in both price and eco-footprint: gabions of concrete rubble, home-grown straw bales, corrugated clear plastic or steel sheeting, and sandbags. The large residential wing and the architectural studio are connected through a sequence of interior spaces, and a five-story library tower, all this surrounded by a food-growing garden. It may be said that the design lacks conventional elegance and perfection; it does not, however, ignore functionality, provided as it is with abundant natural light and ventilation, a carbon dioxide–controlling grass roof, and a naturally cooled food pantry.

Wigglesworth's experiment combines room both to live and work on the same location as well as providing space-covering basic food needs. This is a building one would expect to find in an eco-conscious suburb, a rural retreat of a city intellectual-turned-naturalist; yet it is in the middle of London. It has been described as an "urban oasis" for elegantly and durably demonstrating architecture sustainability where it is most needed. **ES**

↗ Stock Orchard Street has been described as "London's most environment-conscious building."

⇥ All the materials used are reclaimed or eco-friendly—functionality rather than aesthetics governs the design.

Perimeter Institute for Theoretical Physics (2004)

Architects Saucier & Perrotte **Location** Waterloo, Canada **Style** Minimalist **Materials** Steel, glass

On the shore of Ontario's Silver Lake, the Perimeter Institute for Theoretical Physics, a philanthropic private research institute, is built on land donated by the city of Waterloo. The impressive four-story building is an important example of contemporary Canadian architecture and was awarded a Governor General's Medal for Architecture in 2006. Geometric equations were used to formulate the "random" locations of the windows that punctuate its severe slate-black metal facade. Facing east toward the city, this attractive but anonymous wrapping belies a richly designed plan. Open and glazed to the north and south, the west facade frames a wide garden courtyard. Three bridges cross this public space and enter the main building at informal meeting spaces. Many of these elements were put forward by the client, who wanted to move away from the stereotypical notion of laboratories and create a feeling of warmth and informality. He specified open desk spaces, lounges, wood-burning fireplaces, and espresso machines, which infuse the offices with welcoming aromas, and creative rooms lined with blackboards to offer an opportunity for discussion. The design was inspired in part by theoretical physics itself; a subject rich in knowledge and information but somehow of uncertain form and substance. The Institute is a dynamic contribution to the cityscape, intended to raise the bar of both architecture and intellect for the city. **BG**

"[We wanted the facade to] express the complexity of scientific discourse within."

Saucier & Perrotte, architects

Chanel Tower (2004)

Architect Peter Marino **Location** Tokyo, Japan **Style** Minimalist **Materials** Glass, steel, aluminum

On first sight of this building, what is most striking is its sheer elegance—it is a perfect vessel for the clothes within. The structure, located in the stylish "Ginza" district of Tokyo, is the largest retail space for Chanel in the world and oozes Madame Chanel's love of the simple, graceful form. The sleek lines and minimal exterior allow the products inside to come to the fore. The brand's identity is inescapable: the distinctive "double C" logo adorns every lift button, and in the parking lot, a wall exhibits a giant Pop Art Chanel No. 5. New York–based architect Peter Marino refers to his unique style as "cross fertilization." Technology, interior design, and use of material come together to produce a structure that is ultramodern yet understated, structured yet sensual. His Chanel Tokyo is a ten-floor, 184-feet-high (56 m) temple to high fashion, crafted from stainless steel, aluminum, and glass, entwined to give the distinctive Chanel "tweed" effect, and houses a giant LED display on one of its walls, which comes alive every night. Designed by Israeli artist Michael Rovner, who worked with Marino on the Chanel buildings in Hong Kong and Osaka, the giant screen gives workers a breathtaking view by day and provides a blackened backdrop for the display by night. The tower's beauty comes from its stunningly simple shape and figure. The Chanel Tower in Tokyo is perfectly fitted to the surrounding area over which it gracefully resides. **DE**

"Glass is the new material of our age . . . and this is architecture born of new technology."

Peter Marino, architect

Flower Tower (2004)

Architect Edouard François **Location** Paris, France **Style** Eco-Architecture **Materials** Concrete, glass

"It looks like a giant display of potted plants … and it's one of the best places to live in Paris."

Jonathan Glancey, architecture critic

↑ The marbled effect of white and gray aggregates is visible on the only bamboo-free wall of the building.

→ Concrete pots and burgeoning bamboo signal the arrival of ecologically aware architecture in France.

The Maison Vegetale, or Flower Tower, is a social housing block disguised as a vertical urban garden wrapped in an outer screen of green bamboo plants. It promotes green design to make low-cost housing more attractive and environmentally sound, and differentiates the building from its fellows in a complex of twenty similar public housing blocks.

The monolithic 107,640-square-foot (10,000 sq m) structure relates to an adjacent park through the permanent presence of quick-growing bamboo in 380 concrete pots lining the balconies of thirty apartments on three sides of the ten-story building. The flowerpots have an irrigation system where fertilizer is added to the water in a basement storage tank and the solution is pumped up to the balconies. The result is a self-sustaining bamboo garden that remains constant throughout the year. Variety is added by the seasonal flowering of blue-violet morning glories. The bamboo grows to about 13 feet (4 m) and provides cool shade and privacy for the residents. One Flower Tower tenant decribed the effects of living in the building: "In the summer, with the windows open and the breeze flowing through the bamboo's grassy stalks, the effect is soporific, like sleeping in a tree." The greenery partly conceals the building's unique variegated two-tone concrete appearance, resulting from the deliberate specification of two aggregates for the walls, a white cement sourced from France and a gray color from Belgium.

Edouard François (b. 1957) is a protagonist of green architecture and sustainable development, with a cross-disciplinary approach between architecture, urbanism, and landscape design. His other projects include "Sprouting Building," in Montpellier (2000), with exterior walls featuring rocks held in place by a plant-covered, stainless-steel net, and the "Alliance Française" in New Delhi (2001). **JEH**

British Council Nairobi (2004)

Architects Squire and Partners **Location** Nairobi, Kenya
Style Modernist **Materials** Concrete, stone

The British Council offices in Nairobi were designed by the British architectural firm of Squire and Partners in collaboration with Kenyan architects and contractors.

Located on a ridge, the site nestles within a cluster of trees with primary access off a road running parallel to the ridge. The building sits perpendicular to this road—a linear block on a slope falling away from the road, which exploits the site and provides views across to the north of the city. From the street the bulk of the structure is concealed as the building is embedded in the slope and set back from the street edge. The wall of the compound retains a cut in the slope and is integrated into a landscaped water garden at its base.

The entrance to the office is down a pedestrian ramped approach and through a gatehouse; the main space is a double-height volume with large glazed ends that run the length of the building. This space contains the library and computers. A full-height screen runs the length of the building to minimize solar glare and keep the interiors cool. Here, there are eight "classrooms" for study, distance learning, and conferences. Below, a dramatic feature staircase connects to a café that opens out onto a stepped, landscaped terrace. Projecting over the main library on the second floor are offices, meeting rooms, and facilities for the fity-six British Council staff.

Materially, the architects utilized Nairobi blue stone and local terrazzo, along with stucco and concrete renders to the walls. Artist David Tremlett was commissioned to make pastel drawings on the walls and corridors of the Visual Arts Department; the rich colors chosen are typical of the African continent, blending in with the tones of the Kenyan soil, vegetation, and sky, and contributing to a building that sits easily in its surroundings. **GO**

Heyri Museum of Architecture (2004)

Architect Kyung-Kook Woo **Location** P'aju, Heyri, South Korea
Style Modernist **Materials** Concrete, steel, glass, wood

Following the thawing of relations between North and South Korea in the 1990s, pockets of redevelopment were initiated within the former Demilitarized Zone (DMZ) north of Seoul. Among these is the Heyri Art Valley, a community of writers, artists, architects, musicians, and cineastes located in lush terrain near P'aju and less than an hour by train from the capital. Conceived as an interactive marketplace for Korean artists and the international art-buying community, Heyri Art Valley is also a showcase of progressive architecture. More than

> *"Architecture is not the creation of something separate from nature and humanity."*
>
> Kyung-Kook Woo, architect

eighty buildings are already completed, including more than thirty museums, six galleries, and a movie production studio, with residences, shops, and schools for the artists and their families. Lots are available for a further 300-odd constructions.

The buildings of Heyri Art Valley are designed to serve the community and are mostly for mixed use. The Heyri Museum of Architecture (MOA), designed by South Korean architect and city planner Kyung-Kook Woo (b. 1946), has a café and is also the architect's private residence. The long, solid-looking, cantilevered, rectangular upper building rests on a partly glass-walled ground-floor space, creating Woo's avowed effect of "a mini eco-box floating in a forest." In winter, the brown of the building's copper cladding harmonizes with the leafless surrounding trees. **FR**

Cistercian Monastery
of Novy Dvur (2004)

Architect John Pawson **Location** Pilsen, Czech Republic
Style Minimalist **Materials** Plaster, concrete, timber, glass

Set in the beautiful Bohemian countryside of the Czech Republic, the Novy Dvur monastery is a must-see building yet one that only the privileged few will ever be able to enter. Cistercian monks depend on their monastery building to provide for all needs—as church, workplace, home, hospital, and farm. The order adheres to a specific architectural blueprint drawn up in the twelfth century by St. Bernard of Clairvaux, placing an emphasis on light and proportion rather than decoration.

The 250-acre (100 ha) site already included a Baroque manor house and three wings of agricultural buildings that framed a courtyard. Pawson elected to keep the buildings' basic silhouette, renovating the manor house and creating series of new spaces in the wings, which were completed with glazed, cantilevered cloisters. Upstairs the monks share a dormitory; each is allowed a cubicle with a curtain and there is a special section devoted to the order's snorers. The order prays every four hours so sound sleep is obviously an essential requirement. The material palette is predictably restrained with concrete, plaster, timber, and glass predominating.

While this sounds rather austere for the casual visitor at least, the space, which is completely whitewashed, is an uplifting experience. The church is a particular delight—rigorous and disciplined but beautifully lit. After a career spent creating upmarket shops, art galleries, and houses for the affluent, this is undoubtedly Pawson's defining moment. **GG**

↗ In drawing up his design, Pawson adhered to the principles laid down by St. Bernard in the 1100s.

→ The cautious melding of ancient baroque with new architecture has proved a harmonious blend.

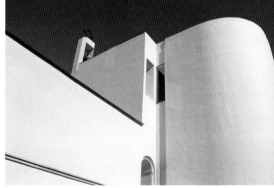

Langen Foundation (2004)

Architect Tadao Ando **Location** Neuss, Germany **Style** Contemporary **Materials** Concrete, steel, glass

In the early 1990s, NATO decided to give up its Pershing missile station on Hombroich Island, leaving behind a transformed military landscape with bunker systems and anti-shrapnel ramparts. In 1994 private art collector Karl-Heinrich Müller bought the island to transform it into a landscape of the arts; he also founded a museum for the Japanese art collection of the private Langen Foundation. Visitors enter the complex through a large cut-out in a widespread semicircular wall of concrete. A narrow path bordered by cherry trees leads around an artificial pond to the entrance of the main building. The building itself consists of three sections with an exhibition hall in each. The main building has a core of concrete blocks—the size of Japanese *tatami* mats—placed in a glass-and-steel envelope. This creates an area for contemplation that brings the surroundings to the permanent exhibition of Japanese art, breaking up the distinction of outside and inside. Because of its prominent position, the glass-sheathed concrete core of the main building represents the Langen Foundation. Two concrete buildings for special exhibitions are attached. With its lower part underground, the complex contains a slowly winding circuit of ramps. Long cuts in the gallery's ceilings allow natural light into the spaces inside. The building is known for the quality of Ando's "silklike" concrete, which suits this artificial, silent world perfectly. **FH**

"My main goal was to create ... [a] building with a simple form, to rapport with its environment."

Tadao Ando, architect

Stata Center (2004)

Architects Gehry Partners   **Location** Cambridge, Massachusetts, USA   **Style** Postmodernist   **Materials** Steel, concrete, brick, glass

The striking twists and tilts of the Stata Center, part of the Massachusetts Institute of Technology (MIT), was intended to reflect the freedom of ideas required for the research conducted there. It is built on the former site of Building 20, a timber-framed structure dating from World War II that was a famous breeding ground for the academic theories emanating from MIT. The 720,000-square-foot (66,890 sq m) complex, named after Ray and Maria Stata who helped finance it, contains three academic departments, and includes an auditorium, lecture rooms, and laboratories. Designed by Frank Gehry (b. 1929), this chaotic collage of shapes was made to be as informal as possible. Everything here is at odds with normal building design; different curves come together in unexpected ways, creating bulging, distorted, and crumpled forms, all built from materials ranging from glass and painted brickwork to brushed stainless steel. Gehry avoided "assigned space" to allow the the structure to continue evolving according to the inhabitants' needs. He also wanted to facilitate collisions of people by accident, to try to increase the likelihood of serendipitous and productive meetings of minds. Consequently, between the study areas are connecting spaces, where students can meet, relax, and share information. Daring, whimsical, and original, the Stata Center represents everything an academic institution should be—an inviting, flexible, fun place to work that encourages inventive thought. **JM**

"We think MIT buildings should be as intellectually interesting as the work that goes on inside them."

William Mitchell, dean of architecture, MIT

Seattle Public Library (2004)

Architects Office for Metropolitan Architecture, LMN Architects **Location** Seattle, Washington, USA **Style** Contemporary **Materials** Steel, glass

In 1998, a new public library initiative in Seattle called "Libraries for All" won overwhelming public support. The project included this makeover of the Central Library as an irregular-shaped, towering behemoth. Twenty-nine firms submitted designs for the new structure and the surprise winner was Rem Koolhaas (b. 1944) and his Office for Metropolitan Architecture in Rotterdam. Working with the local LMN Architects, he proposed an innovative, eleven-story, dazzling, avant-garde symphony of glass and steel, with an unorthodox, multifaceted exterior of eight unequal horizontal layers, each varying its size to suit its function. The Seattle Public Library building contains five main platforms. From Fifth Avenue you enter the Living Room—a vast empty space, 50 feet (15 m) high, surrounded by sloping glass walls. It contains the fiction section, and a large seating area where visitors can relax, read, and connect wirelessly to the Internet.

Another reading room is situated on the tenth level, providing impressive views over downtown and Elliott Bay. On levels six to nine, the entire non-fiction collection is housed on a continuous set of shelves, its Dewey decimal system classification uninterrupted, in a four-story Books Spiral. The fifth-floor Mixing Center is a reference section with wirelessly connected roving librarians on hand to answer questions and handle research needs. The library also includes a 275-seat auditorium and underground parking. **JM**

> *"The stacks . . . reinforce a sense of a world organized with machinelike precision."*
>
> Nicolai Ouroussoff, journalist

Wales Millennium Centre (2004)

Architects Capita Percy Thomas **Location** Cardiff, Wales **Style** Modernist **Materials** Slate, sandstone, glass, steel

The Wales Millennium Centre (Canolfan Mileniwm Cymru) was proposed as an artistic vision for Wales, a "stage for all" with a strong national identity. Envisioned by architect Jonathan Adams of Capita Percy Thomas, its distinctive shape was modeled on the great, solid, stratified land forms seen throughout Wales. This inspirational arts and cultural center includes a 1,852-seat theater, a 250-seat studio theater, as well as dance studios and rehearsal halls. Welsh symbolism abounds; the walls are made of slate collected from numerous Welsh quarries and laid in colored "strata" in a design inspired by the coastal cliffs at Southerdown. As the steel industry was so important to Wales in the past, the massive roof was built using a special type of champagne-colored, textured stainless steel that is resistant to the salt-laden air of Cardiff Bay. On the leaning roof, in 6.5-foot-high (2 m) glass-letter windows, stand two inscriptions,

one in English, "In these stones, horizons sing," and one in Welsh, "Creu gwir gwydr o ffwrnais awen," which translates as "Creating truth like glass from the furnace of inspiration." These words were written by Gwyneth Lewis, a popular Welsh poet, and are lit from within at night. With the acoustics being such an important consideration, the building was built from the inside out. The use of steel-framed structures enabled the performance spaces to be worked on as long as possible, to allow for fine-tuning before the outside was constructed. The acoustics needed to be flexible, and this was achieved by including a variety of sound-scattering or sound-absorbing surfaces that could be moved to achieve the desired balance. Opened only thirty-three months after construction began, Wales had its new cultural center. Few would argue it has fulfilled its brief to be "unmistakably Welsh and internationally outstanding." **JM**

Shanghai Oriental Arts Center (2004)

Architect Paul Andreu   **Location** Shanghai, China   **Style** High Tech   **Materials** Steel, glass

In the midst of Pudong New Area's extensive landscaping stands the organic form of the Shanghai Oriental Arts Center, designed by Paul Andreu (b. 1938). A bird's eye perspective reveals that the building resembles a five-petal flower, with five glazed lobes of varying size unfurling from a central core. Each of the five sections fulfills a particular function. Visitors gain access to the center via the first of these subdivisions, which serves as the entrance hall. From here admittance can be gained to the Philharmonic Performance Hall, Concert Hall, Exhibition Hall, or Opera Hall, located in the other four subdivisions. The organic references do not stop with the center's plan, however, as the entire interior of the building is intended to evoke nature. To this end all of the walls are covered in large, rounded, and glazed porcelain tiles resembling oversized pebbles. These hang from wires attached to the ceiling and bring great warmth to the interior. They also provide the building with coherence and make it appear more human in scale. The ceramic tiles continue through the wide passage that winds uninterrupted around each petal in turn. A peaceful oasis in the surrounding urban sprawl, the Shanghai Oriental Arts Center hosts a variety of dance and music performances and can be best appreciated at night. It is then that the interior drop lights, designed to resemble stars from a distance, richly illuminate the center and truly animate the building. **JF**

> *"What I am seeking in any project is at once its inner coherence … and its relationship to the outside."*
>
> Paul Andreu, architect

Netherlands Embassy (2004)

Architect Office for Metropolitan Architecture   **Location** Berlin, Germany   **Style** Contemporary   **Materials** Aluminum, steel, nonreflective glass

Berlin is a city with a history that architect Rem Koolhaas of the Office for Metropolitan Architecture (OMA) says, "causes great emotion for me, both good and bad." Located in the former East German sector of the city and backing onto one of its numerous canals, this building is surrounded by a contrasting array of structures dating from the Fascist and subsequent Communist eras. Consequently, perhaps, the embassy is an exercise in communication, something diplomats prize above everything else. From the sweeping drive that ramps up from Klosterstrasse into the heart of the embassy complex, to the aluminum-lined circulation route that weaves its clattering way through the ten or more stories of the building, the prevailing message is one of permissiveness, a social condition the Dutch have contrived to create for centuries. Doors slide open as you approach them—the mobile steel plate of the massive front door is a metaphor for the state's

legislative fluidity—and everywhere there are generous views outside, through occasional passages of glass flooring, via windows, and through apertures in the building's structure itself. Even the roof on the tenth floor peels back. The shape of the building has been dictated by its spaces, rather than the other way around. This sums up the OMA approach: first conceive a response to a situation and then form a structure to articulate it. The embassy's easy engagement with its context nullifies any grim historical echoes. Humor also helps in the mission. The glass-walled gym, with its lime-green, poured-resin floor, whispers that most Calvinist of desires—the wish to be seen to be working hard—although the effect here is more high camp than army camp. The ambassador's dining room, which juts out into the air with fake suicidal intent high up on the side of the building, is also droll. **MI**

Caltrans District 7 Headquarters (2004)

Architects Morphosis **Location** Los Angeles, California, USA **Style** Contemporary **Materials** Steel, aluminum, glass

The Caltrans District 7 Headquarters is what you might call billboard architecture. Designed for California's transportation authority by Thom Mayne of the Los Angeles–based firm Morphosis, it greets South Main Street with a barrier-like aluminum facade and a 40-foot-high (12 m) street number proclaiming "100." This is an uncompromising automotive language for what the writer Reyner Banham described in his book on Los Angeles as "a highly mobile population that measures distance in time at the wheel." Caltrans is a metallic monolith that looms over downtown in what can only be described as an intimidating way. The L-shaped, thirteen-story building contains over a million square feet (92,900 sq m) of office space, but for the observer the inside is inconsequential. This is a building of surfaces, a series of intersecting screens laid over a glass box. The east and west facades are made up of programmed aluminum panels that open

or close depending on the level of sunlight. Closed, they form an impenetrable wall—this building protects itself against sunlight the way an armored vehicle does against bullets. At night, however, the building opens up. Some of the louvers have colored lights on them so that at night the facade is made up of neon strips, giving the courtyard in front of the building a disco effect. This is not a beautiful building. It is dystopian, presenting a futuristic architecture of faceless power—but it is certainly impressive. **JMc**

> *"I do not build in an intentionally confrontational way, it is just who I am."*
>
> Thom Mayne, architect

Constitutional Court (2004)

Architects OMM Design Workshop **Location** Johannesburg, South Africa **Style** Modernist **Materials** Concrete, brick, slate

With the election of Nelson Mandela as president in 1994, a new constitution was drafted from scratch. A constitutional court was established and eleven judges appointed, but there was nowhere for them to exercise their powers. Three years later an architectural competition took a step closer to giving the supreme law of the land concrete expression in a new Constitutional Court building. The winning design, by OMM Design Workshop and Urban Solutions, was completed in 2004. Many aspects of the project symbolize victory over the past, not least the choice of site—that of Johannesburg's notorious "Old Fort" jail (1893), where Mahatma Ghandi and Nelson Mandela were former inmates. Today, justice dispensed here is cultural as well as legal, and design elements such as the "Great African Steps," commemorating heroes of South Africa's freedom struggle, signal a corrective realignment of history. Traditional African wisdom is associated with the gathering of elders under a tree. This motif is taken up as the court's emblem and reinterpreted metaphorically in the main public space of the building: the foyer. Tilted, mosaic-adorned columns, irregular skylights, and garlandlike chandeliers create a dappled, internal landscape, lending informality to the court's proceedings. In this project, also including a library, judges' chambers, administrative offices, and a garden, decorative crafts and modern construction methods are fused. **MJB**

> *"We wanted the new building to be a place where justice would be friendly, accessible, and warm."*
>
> Justice Albie Sachs, constitutional court judge

Museum of World Culture (2004)

Architects Brisac Gonzalez Architects   **Location** Göteborg, Sweden   **Style** Contemporary   **Materials** Concrete, steel, glass

In the Museum of World Culture, in Göteborg, the diversity of world cultures is brought to life through the medium of ever-changing exhibitions, and by an avoidance of any permanent displays. Together, the building and the exhibition programs create a versatile and exciting space.

London-based architects Cecile Brisac and Edgar Gonzalez wanted to emphasize the building's role as a place where all cultures are welcome and where understanding can be fostered. The six-story museum includes five exhibition halls, a research library, a café, a restaurant, a shop, and offices. Central to the building is a wide timber staircase that serves as the meeting point for all visitors to the museum.

Situated below a hill, the glass-and-concrete structure seems hidden and exposed at the same time; the west-facing facade, where the galleries are situated, appears rather solid and dense, whereas by contrast the facade toward the hill is glazed. A 141-foot-long (43 m) window draws passers-by inside the building, giving them clear views into the largest exhibition hall.

In one part of the building a large concrete wall beam, supporting four stories, protrudes 16 feet (5 m) over the footpath below, creating a dramatic and dizzying effect. Working in harmony, these features convey a building that communicates multiplicity and openness, the perfect setting for the museum's displays of world culture. With a mixture of solid concrete and floating and transparent glass, this building is alive with contrasts, symbolic of a world of similar diversity. **SML**

↖ The prevalent use of large panes of glass provides a feeling of space and an affinity with the landscape.

← Brisac's and Gonzalez's building was awarded Sweden's coveted Kaspar Salin Prize for Architecture.

Mirador (2004)

Architects MVRDV   **Location** Madrid, Spain   **Style** Contemporary   **Material** Concrete

This block of apartments presents an unusual variation on the traditional arrangement of having an open communal space at the center of a building to bring in light and air. Here, instead of the horizontal ground-level courtyard, there is a vertical one, five stories high, cutting a hole through the middle of the block on the thirteenth floor, 164 feet (50 m) above ground level.

The site is on the northeastern edge of Madrid, in the suburb of Sanchinarro, and the building was commissioned by the Madrid housing association EMVS, which has been an enthusiastic proponent of innovative housing over the last twenty-five years. MVRDV is a Dutch architectural practice known for its innovative solutions to issues of density and the provision of public space in new urban developments, particularly housing. In Amsterdam, the firm built an iconic apartment block, Silodam, that showcases surprising solutions to residential density.

MVRDV uses the term "superblock" to describe the Mirador: the variegated finishes of the facade—stone, concrete, tiles—disguise nine smaller blocks within the whole. These are all seemingly "glued" together to create the building. Each block offers a different type of accommodation, which therefore encourages a mixed community. This spectacular whole provides an instantly identifiable reference point for the surrounding area—important in a new area of the city that has been planned and built from scratch. However, while it undoubtedly draws attention to itself, the Mirador building also acts as a giant frame, drawing the gaze to views of the sky and the Guadarrama Mountains in the distance. **RGW**

↗ The varied facade delineates the different types of accommodation housed within.

→ An eye-catching swath of color dominates this striking high-rise residence.

Twenty-First Century Art Museum (2004)

Architects SANAA **Location** Kanazawa, Japan
Style Contemporary **Materials** Concrete, glass

This huge circular contemporary art museum, 370 feet (113 m) in diameter, makes a great impact on its setting in the historic city of Kanazawa. The glazed facades and entrances that face different directions provide a sense of openness, while the grass around the building allows visitors to stroll away from any roads confining the site. The art library, design gallery, and children's studio are placed along the periphery so that they can be visited separately, reflecting the community-focused approach of the museum. Surrounded by commercial, civic, and historic

> *"A place that children, the elderly, the disabled—anyone—can approach cheerfully and relax as desired."*
>
> *El Croquis*, architecture magazine

conservation areas, this museum "without a front or back" achieves an extreme accessibility.

This spatial strategy extends inside the museum. The fourteen boxlike gallery rooms can be accessed only through common corridors. Unlike a conventional museum with a dictated circulation, this arrangement allows visitors to move from one room to the other according to their choice. The inside of the building also offers a 360-degree panoramic view of the city.

Japanese architects Kazuyo Sejima and Ryue Nishizawa—who began collaborating under the name of their SANAA practice in 1995—have consistently questioned conventional ideas about architecture and space. Here, they radically reinterpret the idea of an art museum by closely examining the relationship of people to their environment. **TS**

Freedom Park (2004)

Architects Mphethi Morojele Architects, GAPP **Location** Pretoria, South Africa **Style** Eclectic **Materials** Stone, landscape materials

Billed as "the biggest monument to democracy in the world," Freedom Park's cultural aim was to bring about a deeper understanding of South Africa's heritage and, in so doing, celebrate freedom. A 128-acre (52 ha) site was developed to form a landscaped memorial, center of knowledge, interactive museum, commercial precinct, and library. Located in Pretoria, the heartland of the apartheid administration, the project was intended to realign the meaning of history, and thereby change relations between nation and citizen. Its aim is to repair the injuries inflicted by apartheid and, at the same time, ensure that lessons learned from the past are never forgotten.

The final aspects of the project are due for completion in 2009, but already in place are a garden of remembrance and the Sikhumbuto memorial, on which has been inscribed a poignant Wall of Names. The memorial also encompasses an eternal flame, an amphitheater, a place known as the Sanctuary, and a Gallery of Leaders, all of which honor those who fell in the fight to rescue South Africa from apartheid. The garden of remembrance was conceived as a setting for healing in which the trauma of dealing with past injustices can be released. Symbolizing the final resting place (*Isivivane*) of heroes whose sacrifice shaped South Africa, the garden's construction has involved both spiritual and physical coordination. A series of ceremonies around the country acknowledged seven historical conflicts and the role each locality played in them. Indigenous plants and soil from each of the provinces have been combined to bring together the different places and times in which lives have been lost for the sake of freedom. The site aims to bind all humanity in a common narrative, encompassing 3.6 billion years of history. **MB**

Santa Caterina Market (2004)

Architects Enric Miralles, EMBT **Location** Barcelona, Spain
Style Contemporary **Materials** Steel, wood, ceramic tiles

Santa Caterina Market is a vivid, exuberant masterpiece in the heart of Barcelona's gothic quarter. Reached via a knot of narrow streets between the cathedral and the medieval church of Santa Maria del Mar, it suddenly presents itself like a piece of urban theater.

It was designed by local architects EMBT, otherwise known as Enric Miralles and Benedetta Tagliabue. Like EMBT's more famous project, the Scottish Parliament, it took a long time to build—partly because of the archaeological remains discovered beneath it—and Miralles died before he could see it completed.

The most dramatic aspect of the market can only really be appreciated from the upper floors of the surrounding apartment buildings. Its billowing roof is a sea of vibrant colors laid out hexagonally in ceramic tiles. The tiles—a feast of oranges, lemon yellows, eggplant purples, florid greens—were made to order in Seville, and designed to evoke the fresh produce of the stalls beneath. The undulating roof structure hangs from three steel arches supported by a complex steel-and-wood framework, but for all its computer-generated sophistication, the roof is highly hand-crafted with the panels built out of laminated wood that had to be cut by hand to fit the awkward curves.

Three of the original nineteenth-century market's facades have been preserved, but the new one is in the inimitable, unpredictable language for which Miralles was famous. The building as a whole is very much in the tradition of Catalonia's history of flamboyantly individualistic craftsmen-architects. **JMG**

↗ EMBT's design has breathed vibrant new life into what had become a run-down market.

→ The roof's tiles were commissioned to emulate the fresh fruit and vegetables in the market underneath.

ARoS Århus Kunstmuseum (2004)

Architects Schmidt, Hammer & Lassen   **Location** Århus, Denmark   **Style** Modernist   **Materials** Red brick, glass, concrete

Founded in 1859, ARoS Århus Kunstmuseum was originally based in the attic of what was at one time a town hall, a courthouse, and a jail. To accommodate the growing art collections, a new, state-of-the-art, museum was required. This monumental new building covers more than 190,000 square feet (17,651 sq m). The voluminous, nine-story, 141-foot-high (43 m) building, consists of one large cube of red brick with a ground plan measuring 170 by 170 feet (52 x 52 m). Its compact solidity is raised by a glass curtain wall that wraps around most of the building at ground level. The museum appears heavy at the top and light at the base, as if the laws of gravity have been defied. Visitors enter the museum via two long ramps. Inside, a spectacular and dynamic room opens up and the weightiness experienced outside vanishes in favor of a brightly lit, open space where white concrete dominates. A large spiral staircase takes visitors to exhibition rooms for video installations and the museum's landmark sculpture—*Boy* by Australian artist Ron Mueck. Upstairs, more galleries are entered along white concrete crossings, which bridge over the museum's main "boulevard" below. ARoS was the first museum designed by architects Schmidt, Hammer & Lassen. Their intention was to not allow the design of the building to take precedence over the art within. They have successfully produced an exhibition space that creates flexibility. **SML**

"The project is genius by its way of symbolizing the rich coloring and power [of] the art collection."

Jens Erik Sørensen, director of ARoS

IT University of Copenhagen (2004)

Architects Henning Larsen Architects **Location** Ørestad, Denmark **Style** Contemporary **Materials** Metal-clad frame, concrete, glass

Situated to the south of Copenhagen's center, in the newly built town of Ørestad, the IT University is one of several buildings in an area of exciting architecture that includes Jean Nouvel's Danish Broadcasting Corporation television studios and concert hall, and the residential houses designed by Steven Holl. This architectural star-studded promenade lies within easy reach of the sea, the main airport, the newly built metro system, and the protected green site of Amager Common. The university building, which sits next to a 2,625-foot-long (800 m) canal, is arranged around a large central atrium, a space filled with light from the large five-story-high windows and the open glass and steel beam roof above. Different-sized glass boxes, which act as social meeting areas for students, are cantilevered out from the two parallel buildings linking this central space. The architects have added a lively dynamic to the space by allowing students, staff,

and passersby to glimpse what goes on inside the building. The result of such openness is a building that oozes activity and gives a sense of transparency and freedom for ideas, research, and inspiration. The building is elevated with a metal-clad frame that wraps around the entire structure. The glass facades are banded in different colors. Inside, color is also present; digital artwork displays designed by professor John Maeda project red and green on the surfaces of the atrium. When designing it, the architects paid great attention to the purpose of this new university. The ever-expanding nature of information technology seems naturally "at home" within these modern, clear-cut surroundings. Contemporary building technology and architectural transparency sit well with theories concerning the promotion of public information technology, an entrenched characteristic of the early part of the twenty-first century. **SML**

Utrecht
University Library (2004)

Architect Wiel Arets   **Location** Utrecht, Netherlands
Style Contemporary   **Materials** Concrete, cement, glass

In recent years, libraries have been assuming greater public importance and several prominent new libraries have been designed by the world's top architects. In designing his University Library for Utrecht, Wiel Arets (*b.* 1955) had to couple the pervasive use of digital technology with the need for silence and concentration.

Arets constrained his formal repertoire to a bare minimum: a box. Seen from the outside during the day, Utrecht University Library is a large, black block bearing little sign of what users will experience inside. The facades are subdivided by a modular grid of panels either constructed in black concrete or glass, which run uninterrupted from the top of the building to the basement to minimize the visual impact of the large parking area located at the bottom of the library. Inside a wide range of experiences are created by articulating the external black monolith within the reading rooms, lounge areas, auditorium, and exhibition spaces. Such richness is achieved despite Arets's limiting his color palette to black and white.

The central void where the checking desks are located is crucial in making the user aware of the spatial complexity of the library. A decorative pattern using CAD/CAM systems was applied to both glass and cement panels, and the glazed facade is utilized to control the amount of natural light in the building.

Arets seeks a careful balance between innovation and tradition, allowing the library readers a delicate mix between encounter and isolation. **RBZ**

↖ The amount of natural light allowed into the building can be regulated throughout the day.

← The austere exterior lends an air of sobriety to the library users' acquisition of knowledge.

Too-High Teahouse (2004)

Architect Terunobu Fujimori **Location** Nagano, Japan
Style Vernacular **Material** Wood

Today's Japanese architecture is not all about hypertechnology, sleek glass shapes, or twisted carbon-fiber trusses—and Terunobi Fujimori has always been an atypical figure. Both an architect and an architectural historian, he carried out surveys into working-class housing as well as historic buildings throughout Japan. Together with a writer and an illustrator, he set out to experiment with new territories in the urban environment. Quite late in his career he started designing houses (first of all for himself), then museums or other public-oriented buildings. His motto, somewhat against the mainstream, led him to explore, for the first time since the Japanese modernists, new ways of using natural and traditional building materials. For Fujimori, self-construction is also a way to efficiency.

His skills, which were duly recognized when he was chosen in 2006 to be the curator of the Japanese pavilion at the Venice architecture biennale, are apparent in most of his works. Yet the Too-High Teahouse, or Takasugi-an, is definitely a quintessential representation of Fujimori's credo.

After building several teahouses for friends (the teahouse is a typically Japanese archetype with no equivalent in Western culture), and finding it hard to "let them go," Fujimori decided to have another one built—this time for himself. Perched 20 feet (6 m) above ground on top of two improbable tree trunks, the hut is hard to define in relation to any typical school, typology, or tradition. This seemingly primitive cabin offers indeed a simple, sleek, white interior space with just a mat floor to sit or lie on. Most important of all was its opening onto a vast and beautiful scenery. Fujimori likened this to a person's own vision: without limits. **YN**

British Council Lagos (2005)

Architects Allies and Morrison **Location** Lagos, Nigeria
Style Modernist **Materials** Concrete, timber

In 2002, the British Council, an organization promoting educational and cultural relations, decided to relocate their activities in Lagos to a site in the residential area of Ikoyi. This was an exclusive European area during the British colonial period, featuring leafy trees and lush lawns set around large detached buildings. But, the city's rapid growth after independence saw a rise in violent crime, leading to the erection of high walls.

The British Council wanted a sense of openness to be conveyed by their new headquarters. Architects Allies and Morrison responded by replacing the wall

> *"A simple yet elegant building that intelligently mines and reinterprets the local vernacular…"*
>
> Catherine Slessor, *Architectural Review* (2006)

with a series of closely located vertical posts that delineate the extent of the site, but allow visual dialogue with the city. A simple, lawned front garden and gatehouse precede the building. The dominant entrance facade is a solar screen composed of large, vertical timber pieces closely arranged to reduce solar gain to the main glazed skin of the building.

Inside, the material palette becomes more robust, with a public foyer revealing board-shuttered concrete juxtaposed with timber. Openness is achieved as the functional volumes within are seamlessly fused with circulation ensuring a visual continuity from the street right through to the rear of the building.

The British Council challenges the urban context that it resides in, daring to open itself to a public who revel in being able to see so far into a building. **GO**

Yad Vashem Holocaust Museum (2005)

Architects Moshe Safdie and Associates   **Location** Jerusalem, Israel   **Style** Postmodernist   **Materials** Reinforced concrete, glass

> *"[The museum] is an element of an almost geological character interacting with fauna and flora."*
>
> Moshe Safdie, architect

⬆ Safdie commented that the Holocaust was so unusual, its story could not be housed in a conventional space.

➡ The rich landscape that surrounds the museum's buildings is a part of the contemplative experience.

Architect Moshe Safdie (*b*. 1938) was involved with the Yad Vashem redevelopment for many years, having completed the Children's Memorial in 1987 and the Memorial to the Deportées in 1995. The original complex, which opened in 1957, had few significant architectural features. The new campus, however, incorporating an art museum, exhibition pavilion, and synagogue, is characterized by strong architectural elements and firmly establishes Yad Vashem as a spiritual and cultural center that is visited annually by more than two million people. The Holocaust Museum is the culmination and core of the complex.

The brief for the design stipulated that it should combine the Holocaust's narrative with an experiential journey, and that the pastoral character of the natural landscape should be preserved. Safdie faced these challenges by conceiving a largely subterranean building. The 500-foot-long (152 m), raw concrete structure, designed to withstand the pressure of earth bearing down on it, cuts through the Mount of Remembrance like an angular spine. The triangular-shaped structure is exposed at the end nearest the entrance to the south, which cantilevers dramatically over the Ein Kerem valley floor. At the north exit, it explodes into a pair of symbolic wings that hover over the vibrant city of Jerusalem below.

Inside, the galleries are initially hidden on either side of the walkway. Separated by trenches signifying different stages of the Shoah—the mass murder of Jews by the Nazis—they gradually reveal themselves. The exposition ends in the Hall of Names. The ceiling of the hall is a 33-foot-high (10 m) cone displaying photos and testimony relating to many of the victims. Looking down through an opening in the floor, these are reflected in water at the base of an opposing cone sunk into the mountain bedrock below. The result is a perfect balance between building and message. **JH**

de Young Museum (2005)

Architects Herzog & de Meuron   **Location** San Francisco, California, USA   **Style** Contemporary   **Materials** Steel, copper panel facade

After the Loma Prieta earthquake of 1989, the de Young Museum was badly damaged and faced an uncertain future. Having first attempted to finance the repair with public funds, the museum's directors undertook a record-breaking, private, fundraising effort to build a new home for the collection. Jacques Herzog (b. 1950) and Pierre de Meuron (b. 1950) are well known for their work with innovative cladding systems, and the de Young Museum is a stunning example. Both inside and out, the visitor is aware of the building's "rain-screen" skin of perforated and stamped copper panels. The subtle pattern of the 7,200 panels is intended to evoke the dappled light falling through the surrounding foliage. As the copper oxidizes in the sea air, a varied patina of greens and browns will develop over time. The museum is made up of three parallel rectangles, skewed and parted to allow the landscape to slide in alongside galleries and

circulation spaces. At the north end, a nine-story tower twists as it rises to align with the city grid beyond. In many ways, the de Young rejects classical hierarchy and formal tradition. Instead of symmetry and historical sequence, the visitor can enter the museum from a number of entrances and flow from one area of the collection to another as they wish. The galleries intersect one another at angles that enhance a sense of exploration and create new opportunities for interpretation and comparison of the collection. **AC**

"The relationship of the de Young to nature is subtle and remarkably deft ..."

John King, journalist, *San Francisco Chronicle*

Parliament Palace (2005)

Architect Anca Petrescu **Location** Bucharest, Romania **Style** Neo-Classical **Materials** Marble, stone, wood

Only the U.S. Pentagon has a larger footprint than the Parliament Palace, a colossal edifice commissioned by Romanian dictator Nicolae Ceauşescu in Bucharest. The building of this behemoth led to the demolition of 20 percent of Bucharest's historic core and between 1984 and 1989 it consumed around 30 percent of Romania's gross national product. The genesis of the palace (formerly known as the House of the People) was an earthquake in 1977 that caused serious damage, although not in the Arsenal Hill area, the city's highest point. Ceauşescu initiated a design competition for a new building on Arsenal Hill. Five years later, Anca Petrescu, a young unknown architect, was chosen. Work began in 1984; for the next five years workers toiled in shifts twenty-four hours a day; there were never fewer than 20,000 on site. No expense was spared and Romanian-made materials were used exclusively. Meanwhile, the Romanian

people virtually starved. The fourteen-story building contains 3,200 rooms, 3,500 tons of crystal, and 900,000 tons of wood. By the time of Ceauşescu's execution in 1989, the building was 80 percent complete. The decade after his death was dominated by debate about what to do with it. Today, it is used as a conference center and tourist destination. In 2005, Petrescu completed the Senate Rooms in the heart of the building, finally ending a highly troubled and controversial twenty-one-year building process. **AM**

"Ceauşescu's legacy is a monstrous, though strangely impressive edifice ..."

Daniel McGrory, *The Times* (May 31, 2000)

Tod's (2005)

Architect Toyo Ito **Location** Tokyo, Japan **Style** Contemporary **Materials** Concrete, glass, steel

This abstract and dramatic L-shaped concrete-and-glass structure is a welcome addition to Omotesando, Tokyo's famously fashionable, tree-lined boulevard, an avenue which acts as an aspirational showcase for both Japan's flagship fashion stores and its cutting-edge architecture. Designed by Gold Medal award-winning Japanese architect Toyo Ito for Milan-based luxury leather goods outlet Tod's, the building needed to provide offices for the staff and be a customer boutique. As space on Omotesando is at a premium, the site was squeezed between two other buildings which only gave Ito a 109-foot (33 m) front facade to catch the customer's eye; his design successfully used the entire building to attract attention.

Ito built on his previous work at the Serpentine Gallery in London where he married the structural support with an outlandish concrete geometric surface pattern. Here, the structure's visible concrete exoskeleton, interlaced with hundreds of fragments of opaque and transparent glass, is based on silhouettes of the Zelkova trees that line the street outside.

Ito's striking concrete tree motif starts off as thick trunks at the base of the building which then split to form tapering branches at the higher levels. The pattern, visible from inside and outside the building, provides different daylight effects on the different floors. No supporting columns inside means the company can display their luxury goods to maximum effect. In a central district composed of signature shops by designer architects, Tod's still provides a profoundly beautiful visual statement which distinguishes Ito's design from the crowd. **JM**

↖ Toyo Ito has called for "a new abstract expressionism" to take architecture into the future.

← These "tree branches" are structural, meaning the inside needs no supporting columns.

Brick House (2005)

Architect Caruso St. John **Location** London, England **Style** Contemporary **Materials** Brick, concrete

A discreet black door beneath a Victorian archway marks the entrance to an ingenious and masterfully designed, family home in West London. Architects Caruso St. John, proponents of a particularly thoughtful and stylish brand of contemporary British Modernism, have defeated innumerable planning objections and negotiated what was a peculiarly shaped scrap of land into a vast and spacious home.

The commission for Brick House came from a wealthy family who had enjoyed the never-ending floor space and freedom of loft-living in New York, but who wanted a base in West London for their family. Due to the area's stringent residential laws, the house was not permitted to rise more than one story from ground level but despite being heavily overlooked on three sides, each bedroom was orientated and shaped to have its own courtyard.

The internal walls are constructed from pale, dusty, gently mottled yellow bricks—chosen to create a sense of home, security, and for that elemental feeling of brick-on-brick as well as their ability to absorb sound. The architects sourced the bricks from a company that specializes in railway station restoration. They ordered them in the thousands and, naturally, their construction is similarly immaculate. Brick House is also striking for the humble and subtle manner it carves its overtly domestic spaces. The vast concrete roof which yawns over the main living and kitchen area is as dramatic as it is photogenic, but it serves its function, designed to give the gentlest, calmest light over the kitchen and dining area—which is simply crying out to host fabulous parties. **BG**

↗ The color and depth of the mortar was chosen with as much care as the bricks themselves.

→ The problem of the site's potential lack of natural lighting was combated by strategic skylights.

Phæno Science Center (2005)

Architect Zaha Hadid   **Location** Wolfsburg, Germany   **Style** Deconstructivist   **Material** Reinforced concrete

This extraordinary building stands amid car factories in a German industrial town. By selecting Zaha Hadid (*b.* 1950) in an architectural competition, the judges guaranteed themselves an exciting, high-profile building, presumably aiming in part to boost the local tourist industry. They also took a risk, and sure enough the curators are paying the price for the appointment of such a star architect: nothing they can ever do with their displays can live up to the show-stoppingly theatrical building that houses them. The Phæno Science Center lifts its main floors off the ground on legs that are clear descendants of Le Corbusier's beloved *pilotis*. Hadid, however, thickens them to substantial cones in which she places the stairs and elevators up to the museum. Some of the cones stop at the floor level of the main volume, others go through it and up to support the roof. This building would not have been possible without sophisticated computer-assisted concrete engineering techniques. The building has echoes of science-fiction film sets, echoes of boats, and, in its strip windows set at crazy angles, distorted quotations from 1920s Modernist villas. The result is closer to the Modernist fantasy of a Bond villain's headquarters than to anything else. If the aim was to grab attention and draw people in, it is a huge success. Some in the architectural world mistrust the strong gestures of the center, but it is surely impossible not to be impressed by it. **BWC**

"Visitors to Phæno are not invited to find a place of repose, but of inspiration and scientific awe."

Kieran Long, architectural journalist

Reina Sofía Museum (2005)

Architect Jean Nouvel **Location** Madrid, Spain **Style** Contemporary **Materials** Glass, steel

Madrid's Museo Nacional Centro de Arte Reina Sofía is Spain's national museum of modern art. It is built on the site of the San Carlos Hospital commissioned by King Carlos III in the eighteenth century. The building has undergone several stages of conversion over the years to make it into a museum space. In 1980, Antonio Fernández Alba began work to restore and convert the building, and at the end of 1988, José Luis Iñiguez de Onzoño and Antonio Vázquez de Castro put the final touches to the modifications, whose most striking feature is three glass and steel lift towers. The most recent addition to the building has been a 86,100-square-foot (8,000 sq m) expansion to include two temporary exhibition spaces, an auditorium, a library, cafeteria, restaurant, and administration offices. The latest addition was designed by French architect Jean Nouvel (b. 1945), who is noted for creating structures that are sympathetic to their surroundings,

and for his use of steel and glass to play with shadow, light, and form. Nouvel has replaced three buildings that lay adjacent to the museum, so opening up a view of the museum's west facade. The museum's entrance is enclosed by a steel-and-glass tower containing lighting and projection screens. The tower completes a family of towers that surround the museum. The original building's stone pedestal has been extended into the new museum structure to become the floor of the temporary exhibition spaces, the restaurants, the library, and the offices. The three new buildings sit around a courtyard: the library lies to the south; the auditorium, protocol room, bar, and restaurant to the west; and the temporary exhibition spaces are to the north. The library captures light and shade from above using suspended, dome-shaped skylights. Steel louvers perforated in calligraphic patterns protect the large panels of etched glass. **CMK**

Central Building, BMW Plant (2005)

Architect Zaha Hadid **Location** Leipzig, Germany **Style** Deconstructivist **Materials** Concrete, steel, glass

BMW's tradition as a vehicle manufacturer with the highest principles and standards has carried through into the buildings this adventurous German car giant commissions. Hadid's dynamic scheme consists of a 430,500-square-foot (40,000 sq m) central building that forms the communications center of the whole factory complex. Animating and organizing the spaces like a giant, silent, child's toy, the building is linked by a production line conveyor belt to the body shop, paint shop, and assembly line, which can all be seen from the central hub. With cars in various states of undress passing overhead, accommodation in the form of offices and restaurants is arranged off this zigzagging central feature, so administrators can watch cars processing past to their engineer colleagues. Thus the building aims to break down traditional silos, mixing blue-collar and white-collar workers, industrial zones with exhibition space, work and play. The organization

of the building is transparent and flexible—in plan this lightning-bolt shape holds a generous lobby that allows for deep views into the building, while the courtyards admit daylight to the building's heart. The overall feeling is of measured, controlled, but stylish movement. Designed by an architect more famed for her arts than her industrial projects, to see this building is to witness efficiency and élan mixed in a sleek but powerful form as effortlessly as the cars that emerge at the factory's back door every day. **DT**

" . . . it took tremendous chutzpah for BMW to allow us to do this project."

Zaha Hadid, architect

Mercedes-Benz Museum (2005)

Architects UN Studio **Location** Stuttgart, Germany **Style** Deconstructivist **Material** Steel

UN Studio has long been refining its work to create an architectural language that speaks equally of its reverence for history, Baroque, and Modernism and of its passion for new forms and structures—of continuous surfaces, movement, twists, and Mobius strips. The Mercedes-Benz Museum is arguably the first example of the firm's work that achieves this. Their tour de force is appropriately a museum dedicated to the art of movement and engineering, and somehow the painstaking research and passion imbued by those glossy expensive cars merges seamlessly with UN Studio's genuinely new vocabulary of architecture that offers no boundaries—where spaces are not what they seem to be and materials offer opportunities not limits. The building is divided notionally into three but actually serves to be one continuously fluid space from top to bottom. The underlying geometry of the building is a series of interlocked circles and arcs, responding to the typology of the car. Two ramps descend from the top floor; two spiraling trajectories cross each other continuously like a double-helix so visitors can change paths and, because of the volume of space in the atrium, can navigate and orientate themselves very easily through the spaces and levels. The structure is concrete and required a great deal of testing for the twists to determine quality. An atrium core forms half of the structure; the supports on columns that are visible through the windows provide the other half. The UN Studio started out with the husband-and-wife team of architect Ben van Berkel and his wife, architecture and art writer Caroline Bos. Their architectural strategies and intrigues are rooted in an education at London's Architectural Association and also in the irreverent innovation of their native Netherlands, where they practice. **BG**

Casa da Música (2005)

Architects Office for Metropolitan Architecture   **Location** Porto, Portugal   **Style** Contemporary   **Materials** Concrete, corrugated glass, travertine

When the Portuguese city of Porto was named joint European Capital of Culture with Rotterdam in the Netherlands in 2001, it realized that it needed a landmark cultural building at the center of its activities. The Casa da Música, although it only appeared four years later, is the result. Ironically, the Portuguese chose a Dutch architect to mastermind their new icon. Rem Koolhaas (*b.* 1944) created a homage to music in a rich, sculptural, highly efficient but unusual structure. The 180-foot-tall (55 m) project was built on a travertine plaza just across from the Rotunda da Boavista, one of the city's main traffic centers. The white concrete load-carrying shell houses a main 1,300-seat concert hall enclosed at both ends by corrugated glass to aid acoustics and light, as well as a 350-seat concert hall, rehearsal rooms, and recording studios for the Porto National Orchestra. Koolhaas was initially determined to break with the tradition of a "shoe-box"–shaped concert hall, but admitted defeat when faced with the acoustics evidence from other international concert venues. Assisting the acoustics, the main concert hall's walls are of plywood, the wooden markings of which are enhanced by embossed gold leaf. The boxy, asymmetric building also features a terrace carved out of the sloping roofline, while a huge cut-out in the concrete skin connects the building to the rest of the urban landscape. It is a building for—and in touch with—its city. **DT**

> *"It is a building whose intellectual ardor is matched by its sensual beauty."*
>
> Nicolai Ouroussoff, *New York Times* critic

Allianz Arena (2005)

Architects Herzog & de Meuron **Location** Munich, Germany **Style** Contemporary **Materials** Reinforced concrete, ETFE

When Germany was awarded the honor of hosting the soccer World Cup in 2004, it needed a whole new series of stadiums to take the strain, and show itself off as a sport-loving, capable nation. The Allianz Arena was one of the most successful of this new breed. Designed by the architecture firm Herzog & de Meuron, Allianz Arena is most famous for its color scheme and futuristic appearance. Unusually, the stadium is home to two teams—Bayern Munich and TSV 1860. Bayern play in red, TSV in blue, so the architects devised a way in which the stadium could be transformed, glowing like a beacon in different colors from one week to the next. They chose to clad the 66,000 seater stadium in ETFE cushions which light up in red or blue—or white when the German national team plays. Inside modern stadiums, growing grass is often a difficult task because of the need to cram in as many fans as possible under large, overreaching roofs,

thereby restricting airflow. At Allianz Arena, the roof is constructed from 2,874 pneumatic panels made of transparent and translucent ETFE laminate, an exceptionally good conductor of light—allowing the grass to grow normally. The three-tiered stadium is a modern, adaptable, and popular classic—within a few months of opening day in 2005, the distinctive shape of the arena had inspired the nickname *Schlauchboot* —"inflatable boat." The name has stuck, but this innovative stadium is much more than that. **DT**

"[Herzog & de Meuron] reinvent everything with each new project and do it with such vigor."

Jack Pringle, Royal Institute of British Architects

National Assembly for Wales (2005)

Architect Richard Rogers Partnership **Location** Cardiff, Wales **Style** High Tech **Materials** Steel, glass, aluminum, wood

> " ... a building whose democratic function is clearly expressed under one dramatic roof."

Judges of the 2006 RIBA Stirling Prize

⬆ This dazzling glass ecological landmark is already proving to be an inspirational icon for Wales.

➡ The impressive curves of the natural wood roof structure take on a mushroomlike form.

Known as the Senedd—the Welsh word for senate—this innovative transparent building with views over Cardiff Bay houses the National Assembly for Wales.

Early in 1998 a competition was held challenging architects to design a twentieth-century building that would symbolize the ideas behind the new Welsh democracy. The winner was Richard Rogers (b. 1933), with an ecologically friendly building, which used openness as its underlying motif. Above a plinth of dark Welsh slate, see-through glass walls would attract people into the building and the installation of a circular viewing gallery over the funnel-shaped debating chamber would show that the fledgling Welsh government was to be publicly engaging. Like Norman Foster's Reichstag (1999) before it, this building would place the voting populace above the parliamentarians, meaning they could feel part of the democratic process.

Supported by six pairs of slender, steel columns, yet seeming to float above the glass pavilion and the courtyard outside, is a huge, undulating timber-clad roof. As part of its ecological remit, this vast 34,450 square feet (3,200 sq m) canopy collects enough rainwater annually to provide sufficient water for the building's lavatories, plant irrigation, and general cleaning.

At the roof's center is a 10.5-foot-high (6 m) rotating wind cowl, the largest of its type in Europe, which passively ventilates the building. Light enters through a glass lantern below this and is reflected by a conical mirror to provide natural illumination. The energy demands reduced by the roof, lantern, and funnel, along with the fact that the building is heated by passive heat exchangers and a biomass boiler which burns waste timber, helped it to win the Building Research Establishment's highest award for sustainable construction. **JM**

Big Dig House (2005)

Architect Single Speed Design, Paul Pedini   **Location** Lexington, Massachusetts, USA   **Style** Contemporary   **Materials** Steel, concrete

The Big Dig (not the house, but its namesake) is better known as the Boston boondoggle—the project to replace the 1950s elevated expressway through Boston with an underground road system. It represents the worst of American infrastructure development. Death, arrests, and threats of prosecution followed spiraling costs, massive underestimation of construction time, substandard materials, and demands by the attorney general for contractors to refund millions to taxpayers for "shoddy" work. There is, however, a small silver lining; it is the Big Dig House, created from the remains of the redundant solid engineering. It used 300 tons of rubble—mainly steel and concrete—from the Big Dig demolition. You could park an eighteen-wheel truck on the roof, such is the structural integrity of the house, demonstrated by the reduction of interior walls to one floor. It was conceptualized by Paul Pedini (b.

1954), who also acted as contractor for the architects, Single Speed Design. Construction time was decreased by using larger rescued parts—ramps, piers, and inversets—as found, which allowed the frame to go up in three days. The inversets—reinforced prefabricated concrete 10 feet (3 m) wide and variable lengths—are not part of the demolition, nor elements of the new build, but interim build features used for temporary site ramps and roads. Rather than send them to landfill, Pedini used them as one of the house components. At 4,300 square feet (399 m sq) for two people, and a build cost of $645,000 exclusive of land, the carbon footprint cost and financial outlay have yet to be amortized. Witness to a time when infrastructure was an investment in a collective future, the house also represents a future in which the reuse of deconstructed infrastructure shows recycling is not a chore but a challenge. **DJ**

Hotel Puerta América (2005)

Architects SGA Studio **Location** Madrid, Spain **Style** Eclectic **Materials** Concrete, glass

The facade of the Hotel Puerta América, designed by Jean Nouvel in a kaleidoscope of vibrantly colored PVC blinds, is adorned with words from Paul Eluard's poem "Liberté." Inside, twelve of the world's leading architects created twelve distinctive floors: go on an exploratory journey via the minimalist John Pawson, the fluid and sinuous curves of Zaha Hadid, the high-tech, yet sensuous serenity of Sir Norman Foster, and the erotic playgrounds of Jean Nouvel. Add to these the reception, restaurant, bar, roof-top spa, and subterranean garage, each again conceived by a different hand. Unusually, the client, Hoteles Silken, imposed few creative or budget restrictions. The individuals and practices selected were chosen for their expertise in various fields and they worked in total isolation from one another. This has led to criticism, such as the exterior bearing no relevance to the interior, the floors being internalized and unrelated, and the hotel itself being divorced from a wider urban context. Granted, circulation around the hotel is ill-conceived with little time or energy having been devoted to the lifts and staircases, but surely such negativity misses the point. The Puerta América is no normal hotel. It is more exhibition than architecture. Nouvel describes the building as a clutch of little songs rather than a symphony. The hotel is a destination in itself, and the sheer scale of this unique concept can only be celebrated. **JH**

> "[Hotel Puerta América] is a utopian hotel, a Statue of Liberty, an open book."
>
> Felipe Saez de Gordoa, architect

Walker Art Center (2005)

Architects Herzog & de Meuron **Location** Minneapolis, Minnesota, USA **Style** Contemporary **Materials** Reinforced concrete, aluminum, glass

In 1879 Thomas Barlow Walker put twenty of his favorite paintings on public view at his home in Minneapolis, Minnesota. Since that date, the museum has seen various incarnations, with the opening of its first purpose-built structure in 1925, followed by the present main building, by Edward Larrabee Barnes, in 1971. But what really put the Walker Art Center on the architectural map was the 2005 extension by Jacques Herzog (b. 1950) and Pierre de Meuron (b. 1950) who are renowned for building controversial structures.

The building, which doubled the size of the existing museum, is a fine example of the kind of postmillennium architecture that challenges or references Modernist masters such as Mies van der Rohe and Le Corbusier, but uses new technology and form to make something completely fresh. Herzog and de Meuron's building houses galleries, restaurants, a shop, and a theater. Its asymmetrical bulk is clad in 2,878 perforated aluminum panels stamped with crease patterns to resemble paper that has been scrunched up and flattened out again. Windows run in irregular-shaped strips across the facades.

The galleries—which contain fine works by Jasper Johns, Ellsworth Kelly, and Matthew Barney, among others—are arranged like discrete little buildings off streets lined with plum-colored bricks. There are canted, polished plaster walls, and ramped floors and touches of decoration, such as glass chandeliers and Baroque patterns on air vents. As Herzog has said of the firm's use of decoration: "It's something we like to freshen up and use, to challenge the taboos of Modernism." **MF**

◥ The Walker Art Center appears like a giant glistening iceberg on the street.

◁ Modest origins lie behind what is now regarded as one of the greatest collections of contemporary art.

Whitechapel Idea Store (2005)

Architects Adjaye Associates **Location** London, England **Style** Modernist **Materials** Concrete, glass cladding

What defines a public building? How can public institutions continue to function in a progressively privatized city? Adjaye Associates often address these questions through their public projects. For example, the two Idea Stores in East London are exemplary buildings as places for exchange and participation, in other words, as public spaces.

Perhaps, the secret ingredient of the Idea Store in Whitechapel lies in its name. Naming a public library an "Idea Store" radically alters the perception of how such an institution should relate to the community. The architects carefully read the different conditions of the site to come up with a design solution. The main library is housed in a four-story glass tower, whereas a two-story block containing services stretches toward the rear of the site. Thus, the design responds to the environs while maintaining a cohesive sense of unity.

At the entrance on busy Whitechapel Road, the glass tower announces the presence of the library. To enhance the sense of exchange between the building and the public street, the facade of the Idea Store is detached from the bulk of the structure so that it appears to include the sidewalk itself in the design. The rear elevation presents a different scenario: the library opens onto a supermarket and a parking lot. Here a low, dark block is shaped to mediate between the building and the supermarket. The context in which the Idea Store sits is best appreciated in the view from the fourth-floor café: subway stations, hospitals, markets, shops, and houses constitute the raw and chaotic material that public architecture must measure itself against to still participate in the life of cities. **RB**

↗ The blue and green colored glass panels on the facade reflect the colors of the adjacent market stalls.

→ At night the activities within the library become illuminated, drawing the viewer inside the building.

Green Building (2005)

Architects Terry Farrell & Partners   **Location** Manchester, England   **Style** Postmodernist   **Materials** Blue brick, concrete, wood

The relationship between built architecture and urban design has always been central to the work of Sir Terry Farrell (b. 1939). Creating at first an environment for which he then develops an architectural language means that his structures never live in a contextual vacuum. Nowhere is this more evident than the Green Building, which dominates Farrell's master plan for Mackintosh Village, the southern gateway into the radical regeneration of Manchester city center. Taking as his starting point the history and physical character of the place, Farrell's plan combines a series of new-builds with a refurbishment of the warehouses, which give the site—the birthplace of the world-famous Mackintosh raincoat—its nineteenth-century identity.

The building's sculptural form is based on the gasometer that once stood on the site. The concrete cylindrical drum, articulated by red cedar and pine timber balconies, is rendered in green, hence its name, which also alludes to the fact that the mixed-use building sets new standards in ecological design. Unusual for developments of this type, Farrell's iconic tower has several environmentally friendly features. The developer's brief stipulated that the building should reduce carbon dioxide emissions by 75 percent in its manufacture, construction, and operation. The silhouette of the drum culminates in a wind turbine, which generates power all year round. The latticework of steel girders at the top of the tower contains solar panels, which provide domestic hot water, and internally the top sky-lit atrium is the heart of both the ventilation and lighting systems for the building.

The Green Building successfully demonstrates that sustainability can be commercially applied to a building that contains not only thirty-two apartment units in the ten-story cylinder, but also a 120-child nursery and a doctor's office housed in the two-story plinth on which it sits. **JH**

Turning Torso (2005)

Architect Santiago Calatrava   **Location** Malmö, Sweden   **Style** Expressionist   **Materials** Reinforced concrete, steel, glass

After the opening of the Øresund Bridge in 2000, the European continent opened its doors to Sweden. Since then there has been a rapid growth in housing construction in and around the city of Malmö, situated in southwest Sweden, and in the neighboring city of Copenhagen. In an area otherwise characterized by low topography, Malmö has today been given a new and highly contrasting landmark, one that towers above the entire site with endless panoramic views stretching across the Øresund strait. To date, Turning Torso is the tallest building in Scandinavia and the second tallest in Europe.

This remarkable residential and office building is 623 feet (190 m) high. From base to top the structure rotates a total of 90 degrees. The shape of the building was based on one of Calatrava's sculptures called the *Twisting Torso*, which was made of nine cubes of white marble and fastened by a spinal column twisting 90 degrees. Today this sculptural project is realized through 54 floors, 147 apartments, and 5 elevators. The Torso is built around a reinforced concrete core, which is designed to give wind resistance—in stormy weather the top of the building moves up to a maximum of 1 foot (0.3 m). The core is further strengthened by an exoskeleton steel truss, which in turn is tied to large foundation slabs.

Owing to its height and the flat landscape of the area, the tower undoubtedly makes a huge impact on passersby, and because of the twisting shell, it also stands as a dynamic and moving monument, just as Calatrava envisioned with his sculpture. Moreover, and as the name implies, the tower also resembles the upper human body in movement. Turning Torso has received international acclaim, and in 2005 it won the Emporis Skyscraper Award. Members of the jury described the design as highly innovative, calling it "the epitome of structural expressionism." **SML**

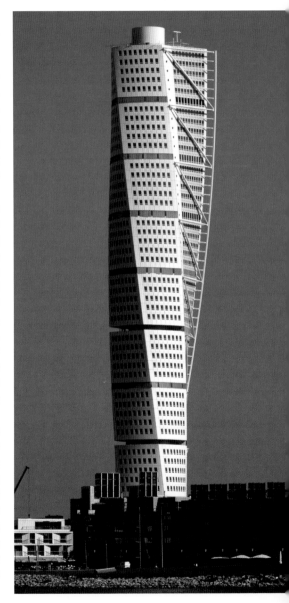

New Law Court (2005)

Architects Richard Rogers Partnership (RRP); VK Studios   **Location** Antwerp, Belgium   **Style** Contemporary   **Material** Concrete, steel

Richard Rogers (*b.* 1933) is often associated with schemes that create successful public space or enliven inner-city areas. Antwerp's New Law Court reflects a vision of the city as a humane and democratic place with a commitment to the regeneration of urban life. Built on a site on the southern fringe of the city area, originally cut off by a highway junction, the building acts as a gateway to the city by covering the highway and providing pedestrian access to the green spaces that surround the court building. The building—which features Rogers's trademark colored steel—fingers out into the landscaped parkland that extends right into the heart of the building. This central space is designed as a great public hall, traditionally known as the Salle des Pas Perdus, or Hall of Lost Footsteps. The courts, hearing rooms, and public space have spectacular views across the city and each of the thirty-six courtrooms is capped by a series of striking roof structures, creating a landmark in their own right. In an attempt to make the building more sustainable, all the main spaces and court rooms are flooded with natural light while natural ventilation is supplemented by low-velocity ventilation in the hearing rooms, using the thermal mass of the concrete structure to keep energy consumption to a minimum. Despite the building's mass, RRP created a structure that is sympathetic to the city and makes the workings of justice more transparent in every sense. **LT**

"[It] looks grand, yet subtle, and offers monumentality on a human scale."

Ivan Harbour, architect

Music Building (2005)

Architects 3 x Nielsen   **Location** Amsterdam, Netherlands   **Style** Modernist   **Materials** Glass, wood, concrete

In the former harbor area of Amsterdam resides the Music Building (Het Muziekgebouw). Its location—standing exposed by the waterfront—adds a significant architectural statement to the pier. This building caters for all the imaginable needs of conductors, musicians, and singers. The ceiling can be raised and lowered, and hydraulically operated platforms allow the floor to be slanted in order to create the optimal environment for musicians and performances. Designed by the Danish architects 3 x Nielsen, the Music Building houses two musical establishments: the Ijsbreker, which specializes in classical, modern, and improvised music, and the BIMhuis, which is a jazz club. The two institutions have their own concert halls, each of which has been fitted with flexible acoustic systems. In the classical music hall, for example, wonderful lighting effects of all imaginable colors are available and pulsate in rhythm with the music. Angular, hard-edged shapes are dominant characteristics throughout the building, giving the overall impression of an extremely sharp and powerful appearance. Together with the enormous glass facades, the cantilevered roof opens up to the river creating a link between the lively city in front and the musical life at the back. The public can enter the building during the day, independent of concerts and other events. Visitors walk from the pier onto staircases leading into the main foyer, where the café, a playground, and exhibition and audio areas are open to everyone. With a strong emphasis on glass and lighting, this building seems to be inducing music to flow freely in and out of the concert halls, and to drift out into the canals of beautiful Amsterdam. Such transparency is clearly experienced through the water, the sky, and the light, all of which are perennial subjects of the Dutch artistic tradition. **SML**

Tietgen Hall of Residence (2005)

Architects Boje Lundgaard, Lene Tranberg **Location** Copenhagen, Denmark **Style** Modernist **Materials** Concrete, oak, pine wood

In the Øresund area, in the south of Copenhagen, modern buildings have rapidly sprung up since the turn of the twenty-first century. Many of these buildings have similar architectural traits—angular and hard-edged outlines. By contrast, the Tietgen Hall of Residence brings organic curves and dimensions to the neighborhood's architecture. The building provides accommodation for up to 360 students. Five detached units, each of six residential stories, form a circle around a communal courtyard. The sections are joined by towers of stairs and lifts, making it possible to walk from one unit to another. The residential parts of the building are placed in the outer sections of the circular unit whereas the communal rooms, such as the study spaces and kitchen facilities, face the courtyard. All the rooms are organized in structural modules that vary in depth and size, creating a dynamic and vibrant environment. This results in the overall facade of the building appearing asymmetrical, which makes a fine contrast to the balanced, rotund shape of the structure. The designers were apparently inspired in this respect by the architecture of the Hakka people of southern China. The Hakka's style of building was for protective purposes, with thick walls and no windows at ground level, unlike the Tietgen Hall. In following a circular shape, however, the architects have designed a coherent and lively building. In 2006, Lundgaard and Tranberg received a prize known in Denmark as "Træprisen" (the Wood Award) because of their innovative use of timber in the Tietgen Hall. Wood breaks up the hard concrete framework, blending the manmade with the natural in a pleasant and harmonious way. Situated within close proximity to the university campus, this building strengthens the bond between knowledge and the students' everyday life. **SML**

Nobel Peace Center (2005)

Architect David Adjaye **Location** Oslo, Norway **Style** Contemporary **Materials** Sandblasted aluminum, polished brass, colored glass, wood

A hundred years after the first Nobel Peace Prize was awarded in 1905, the Nobel Peace Center was inaugurated in an old train station, dating from 1872, in central Oslo. The highly original interior utilizes a huge variety of colors and materials. It was principally designed by David Adjaye (b. 1966) with artistic contributions from designer David Small and artist Chris Ofili. The interplay between the old Classical exterior and the modern, high-tech elements inside creates a fascinating encounter. Adjaye also added a striking, theatrical element outside; visitors approach the center through an aluminum canopy with a curved floor and ceiling perforated with tiny holes, which represents a map of the world. Looking through this canopy, which frames the ground floor of the old station, the architecture from two different centuries is linked. Once inside, visitors are greeted by a wealth of colors and light effects. Open boxes, screens, and frames within frames dominate. Some areas have red resin coats on the walls and floors; in the entrance green and red lights go on and off, and in the Passage of Honor—a space dedicated to the current laureate—visitors are surrounded by polished brass. Traveling up the escalator, visitors enter a cedar-clad exhibition space and a felt-lined room for film screening. Such colorful, tactile qualities contribute to an exceptional building. Adjaye's captivating design demonstrates how architecture can convincingly use the past. **SML**

"My architecture is a series of 'host and skin' scenarios … they become skins that completely take over."

David Adjaye, architect

Juicy
House (2005)

Architects Atelier Bow-Wow   **Location** Tokyo, Japan
Style Contemporary   **Materials** Concrete, steel

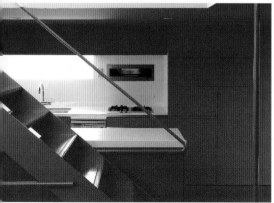

Yoshiharu Tsukamoto (*b.* 1965), who, together with Momoyo Kaijima (*b.* 1969), established the so-called "Atelier Bow-Wow" practice in Tokyo in 1992, is said to be the first to have talked about "post-bubble architecture," referring to buildings that arose in Japanese cities newly in recession. Unable to remake the city in their own image as Tadao Ando's generation had done, they accepted it as it was, making a name for themselves as one of the smartest, most peculiar practices in Japan today. Atelier Bow-Wow's work, deeply rooted in Tokyo's informal buildings, combines the inventive spontaneity of "Pet Architecture" (miniature buildings squeezed into tiny urban spaces), and the soundness of a certain "good" architecture. Tsukamoto and Kaijima believe that a building should reflect its owner's life and they favor generosity, however impertinent their houses may seem as they sidestep nearly every rule of urban or aesthetic etiquette in their bid to champion "right" architecture.

Somewhat odd, like most of their houses, the Juicy House is quirky but it also displays the neat perfection associated with Japanese architecture. Erected on a tiny, 800-square-foot (75 sq m) corner lot, with a building area of only 430 square feet (40 sq m), the fluid inner space is multiplied to infinity through carefully placed windows overlooking a sea of tile roofs. As brightly colored as freshly squeezed fruit juices, the partitions and stairs create a feeling of space and quietness that is challenged only by the playfulness that they display. Bow-Wow! **YN**

↖ A rich black-currant blue causes the Juicy House to stand out from its relatively drab neighbors.

↩ Brightly colored internal spaces and staircases account for much of the charm of the Juicy House.

Dulnyouk Publishing House (2005)

Architects Foreign Office Architects **Location** Paju Book City, South Korea **Style** Contemporary **Materials** Stone, wood

Paju Book City is situated just outside Seoul and forms part of South Korea's forward-looking infrastructure regeneration. The new development strategically centralizes the region's editorial business and includes buildings by Steven Holl, SANAA, and Foreign Office Architects (FOA). The master plan is by London-based Florian Beigel and the Architecture Research Unit.

The program for the Dulnyouk Publishing House, sited on the western edge of a hill above the "city," stipulated archive or storage, working areas, event spaces, and an apartment for guests, all within a 17,600-square-foot (1,635 sq m) floor area. FOA's concept was site specific in that the headquarters structure was oriented so as to avoid blockage of airflow between the hill and the river to the west. The building is set between a south-facing park and a north-facing mineral garden. The ingenuity of the design is the dialogue that the architects have developed between landscape and structure and between the back and front elevations. The building is designed as a folded screen, with the facades articulated in contrasting materials: the north elevation, which gives onto the parkland, is timber-framed; the south-facing parking garage facade is in stone. Internally the spaces are informed by the geometry of the building. The floors are alternately oriented toward one or other of the two gardens, so within the building the visitor sees an alternation of landscapes and facade styles. In effect, FOA have achieved two buildings for the price of one.

For the project FOA collaborated with the Korean architect Kim Young-Joon, who took over the executive design and supervision. Dulnyouk Publishing House presents a sympathetic symbiosis between architectural experimentation and indigenous sensibility. **JH**

Palace of Peace and Reconciliation (2006)

Architects Foster and Partners **Location** Astana, Kazakhstan **Style** High Tech **Materials** Stainless steel, glass, granite

The Palace of Peace and Reconciliation was built as the venue for the 2006 Congress of Leaders of World and Traditional Religions, a triennial event initiated and hosted by President Nursultan Nazarbayev of Kazakhstan. As well as being a highly unusual and striking work of contemporary architecture, the 203-foot-high (62 m) pyramid is a great feat of engineering and logistics. Astana is one of the world's most isolated capitals, yet the Palace was designed and built in less than two years. The envelope of the building—whose pyramidal form was chosen to

> *"Say what you like about Foster, there's no denying he's the man for the big architectural set piece."*
>
> Hugh Pearman, architectural critic

represent equality—is a lattice of stainless steel with pale gray, granite, triangular inserts. The steel frame, which was prefabricated in Turkey and shipped 2,485 miles (4,000 km) overland, "floats" on bearings above the concrete base, allowing it to expand and contract in the city's extreme temperature range.

The building is entered via a ground-level tunnel, which leads visitors into the heart of the pyramid. The lobby is clad in black granite tiles, giving it a heavy, brooding atmosphere. It holds a 1,500-seat opera house, and offers access to the upper levels via a 160-ton steel staircase. At the top of the stairs is Level Zero, a cavernous, white-walled void with views to the top of the pyramid. As well as the opera house, the palace includes a three-story museum, and the Hanging Gardens of Astana—two floors of lush foliage. **AM**

Red Location Museum of the People's Struggle (2006)

Architects Noero Wolff Architects   **Location** New Brighton, South Africa   **Style** Contemporary   **Materials** Prerusted iron, concrete, wood, steel

The Red Location Museum of the People's Struggle is a catalyst for regenerating a "township" reserved for black workers under South Africa's apartheid regime. The museum is the centerpiece of architect Noero Wolff's scheme, which incorporates a range of cultural buildings, civic spaces, educational institutions, and service facilities. The building's brief—to represent both a town of the future as well as a township that history should not forget—is more challenging than that suggested by its humdrum list of rooms, including exhibition spaces, offices, a restaurant, and a shop. As well as providing a springboard for local growth, the museum focuses attention outward, educating visitors about local heritage. Red Location was established in 1902, its name derived from a series of rust-red, corrugated iron barracks. These sheds, originally part of a Boer concentration camp, temporarily housed returning British soldiers before being used by black laborers. Prominent freedom fighters and significant struggle events are linked with sites in the township. The museum houses its exhibits in prerusted corrugated iron display rooms known as "memory boxes." These and other museum elements lie beneath an extended saw-tooth roof, reminiscent of a factory, which refers to the solidarity of workers caught up in resistance to apartheid. During the struggle the workplace represented a site of collective power at a time when black people's rights were denied. **MJB**

> *"Deliberately unglamorous, this is an architectural tour de force."*
>
> RIBA Lubetkin Prize panel (2006)

Coffee House, Jinhua Architecture Park (2006)

Architect Wang Shu **Location** Zhejiang Province, China **Style** Contemporary **Materials** Concrete, tiles

Not many people outside China have heard of Zhejiang Province, or its capital Hangzhou, once described by Marco Polo as "without doubt the finest and most splendid city in the world." In 2002, the municipal government of Jinhua, 80 miles (130 km) south of Hangzhou, established a new urban zone—the Jindong New District—in what used to be an agricultural area. The distinguished Beijing-born artist Ai Wei Wei (b. 1957) , son of the famous Jinhua poet, Ai Qin, was selected to contribute conceptual designs for the new development and, later, to develop a park on a long narrow site measuring 262 by 7,218 feet (80 x 2,200 m). Ai Wei Wei decided to develop a collective project, inviting five Chinese and eleven international architects and designers to contribute to the park. The construction of seventeen public pavilions in this park represents a minor museum of international architecture in China at the beginning of the twenty-first century and should be visited for its role in providing a physical snapshot of China's architectural landscape at this important juncture. Most notable among this collection of low-budget follies is Wang Shu's Coffee House. Based on the concept of a Chinese ink stone (used to grind ink sticks to make liquid ink), the purity of this building's form—a simple cube scarred only by a series of small square holes that puncture one side of the building—contrasts with its intensely detailed surface of tiny glazed tiles in different hues. The juxtaposition of simplicity of form and complexity of surface is a deliberate attempt by the architect to draw attention to the nature of architecture being about surface as much as it is about space. Wang Shu is head the architecture department at Hangzhou's College of Fine Art and also designed their new campus on the edge of Hangzhou's West Lake. **ED**

Kaurna Building (2006)

Architects John Wardle Architects, Hassell **Location** Adelaide, Australia **Style** Neo-Modernist **Materials** Concrete, glass

Named after a local indigenous people and home to architecture, design, and art schools, the Kaurna Building in Adelaide displays John Wardle's ability to turn problems into opportunities. A dense urban campus with an established pattern of linear buildings and repetitive finishes and details, not to mention a tight budget, were the constraints accompanying this commission. Wardle's association with Hassell brought local knowledge to the team. A raw concrete frame clad in exquisite precast panels, juxtaposed with areas of glazing, encloses a complex interplay of plan and section. A wide central staircase allows glimpses through the building and into teaching spaces, while exposed services and finishes provide teaching reference for the architecture students. Spaces are rarely completely separate and even academic staff have abandoned convention and moved into open-plan offices. Integration is established by lanes that connect the inner campus to the surrounding streets. New building facades contrast with the established built fabric through the use of arcades, awnings, balconies, bridges, and a cafe that sprawls between new and old buildings. The jagged building edges continue to the roofline, where they create a distinct silhouette. The building's large, almost unbroken glass front invites uninterrupted visual contact between interior and exterior, not least by night when the entire facade becomes a beacon of light. **MG**

"[Kaurna Building] exudes a unique Australian strength of character and idea."

Jury citation, RAIA Sir Zelman Cowan Award (2006)

The Public (2006)

Architect Alsop Architects **Location** West Bromwich, England **Style** Contemporary **Materials** Steel, glass

West Bromwich, in the Black Country region west of Birmingham, is famous for its soccer team, and not much else. However, it now has The Public (formerly called c/Plex), an arts center by one of Britain's leading architects, Will Alsop (*b.* 1947). The rectangular structure, clad in dark gray and silver metal, is enlivened by window openings in the form of magenta-rimmed fish shapes. Indeed, the building has been likened to an enormous fish tank. Because of financial problems the building is unfinished and is not open to the public, so the interior—normally an important feature of Alsop's buildings—is difficult to characterize. Alsop was strongly influenced by Cedric Price, whose ideas for the early 1960s project the Fun Palace are reflected in the form of The Public. It belongs with Alsop's Peckham Library (2000) in a late twentieth-century genre of reinvented public libraries, which provide social and recreational spaces in addition to their more traditional functions. The Public was originally intended to house galleries and studios, as well as a restaurant and cafe. Where social deprivation existed, it was relatively easy to win National Lottery funding at the turn of the twenty-first century. The Public was largely funded by Arts Council England, to give a permanent home to a local arts organization founded in 1974 by Sylvia King. Toward completion, it was revealed that considerable extra funding was needed, and in 2006, when Arts Council England refused a further grant, the organization was placed in receivership, leaving a question mark at the time of writing about its future. The Public has had a stormy infancy; if it can survive into adolescence or adulthood, it will become the architectural landmark of West Bromwich, and part of the strange story of Britain's alliance between lottery funding and the arts under Tony Blair's government. **AP**

Davies Alpine House (2006)

Architects Wilkinson Eyre **Location** London, England **Style** High Tech **Materials** Glass, metal

The first Alpine House at Kew Gardens was built in 1887 and there has been one here ever since. The original structure was made of timber and brick—vastly different from this splendid design by Wilkinson Eyre. The second Alpine House was in existence from 1981 until 2004, at which time a new structure was commissioned that would make the most of twenty-first-century technology and mimic the plants' natural conditions. The commission was won by London-based firm Wilkinson Eyre. When designing this structure, the architects took into account what effect their building would have not only on the plants but also on the ecological footprint of Kew Gardens. The Alpine House was made to be sustainable and energy efficient, while also recreating an Alpine habitat: artificial "rainfall," temperature, light, shade, and wind patterns were all taken into account. While seeking inspiration for the design, Wilkinson Eyre looked to both the natural and technological worlds—including marine and yacht building projects—adapting some of the methods to their own needs. The twin-arched structure contains 211 glass panels, stands 38 feet (11.5 m) tall, and includes a concrete base—an integral part of controlling the internal environment. It looks like an icy glacier, its smooth glass panes glinting in the sun, emulating a snow-capped mountain. Its glass is also a direct reference to the enormous glass palmhouse, for which Kew is so famous. **LH**

"This building seems to be all glass and hardly any steel. From certain angles, it is practically invisible."

Steve Rose, architectural critic

Sails and Winds Building (2006)

Architects David Chipperfield, b720 Arquitectos **Location** Valencia, Spain **Style** Modernist **Materials** Concrete, glass

The inducement for the Edificio Veles e Vents (Sails and Winds Building) was the America's Cup sailing competition, to be held out of Valencia for the first time in 2007. The building forms the centerpiece of the wholesale reorganization of Valencia's long-time neglected industrial port, providing a base for all America's Cup teams as well as a venue for visitors to watch the races. The elevated spectator decks, which extend from one side and include bars, restaurants, and shops, overlook a newly excavated canal that links the inner port to the offshore racing courses. The four-story building is conceived as a series of stacked and shifting horizontal planes. The deep, cantilevered floor slabs create unobstructed and shaded viewing decks around every floor. David Chipperfield (b. 1953) designed the entire building with a reduced palette of materials and plain, linear forms with perfectly clean details: white-painted steel trims at the edges of the concrete structure, ceilings covered by white metal panels, the internal floors coated with white resin. The predominantly white appearance of the interior is accentuated by brightly colored furniture. All outdoor floors have a solid timber decking, underscoring the shiplike appearance of the building. Chipperfield's entire architectural portfolio is characterized by a precise vocabulary of elegant forms and materials in a functional setting, but this building is no less than a masterpiece of timeless modern architecture. **FH**

"We want . . . to give a strong impression but the impression is . . . about the event and the boats."

David Chipperfield, architect

Casa Guerrero (2006)

Architect Alberto Campo Baeza   **Location** Cadiz, Spain
Style Modernist   **Materials** Concrete, plaster

In a small village on the outskirts of Zahora in southern Spain an anonymous white box with one solitary door seems more likely to be a contemporary art gallery or piece of minimalist sculpture than a weekend retreat. But this thoughtful Modernist cube is a striking contribution to an otherwise arid landscape.

The stark exterior reflects an obvious desire for privacy on the part of the client as well as an aesthetic idea of simplicity that is present in Alberto Campo Baeza's work. The Madrid-based architect has consistently built according to the stringent Modernist

> ## *"I like to think of this house as a secret garden, a closed paradise; it is a house to discover."*
> Alberto Campo Baeza, architect

principles of space, light, and simplicity. His buildings are a canvas for the sun to cast shadows and create forms, colors, and textures.

The four 26-foot-high (8 m) concrete walls of the house contain two vast open courtyards, flanking the central living space. Inside the courtyard, four carefully placed orange trees mark the entrance to the house and a low porch offers shade before entering the main space. On either side are bedrooms and bathrooms.

Baeza also built Casa Gaspo, belonging to the brother of the owner of Casa Guerrero, on this site. This kind of architecture—striving for simplicity and elegance—is the living dream of Mies van der Rohe, and there are few places in the world where it can work better than in Spain, and few better architects to execute it than Alberto Campo Baeza. **BG**

Municipal Theater and Auditorium (2006)

Architects Foreign Office Architects   **Location** Torrevieja, Spain
Style Contemporary   **Materials** Limestone, glass

Torrevieja is one of southeast Spain's major tourist destinations, and it has realized, perhaps a little belatedly, that one way to attract a new breed of visitors to the area is to commission contemporary architecture. However, when it came to the new Municipal Theater and Auditorium, instead of choosing one of the bigger names in contemporary architecture, the local council selected the relatively young practice, Foreign Office Architects (FOA).

The result is a building without any discernible signature; unlike many of their colleagues, FOA

> ## *"FOA has already been hugely influential in its computer-generated, landscaped architecture."*
> Architects Today

steadfastly refuse to produce more of the same. They are best known for their first major project, the Yokohama International Port Terminal (2002) in Japan, which thrust them into the architectural spotlight.

The 650-seat theater in Torrevieja continues in this highly original vein. Given a small plot of 49,190 square feet (4,570 sq m) in a corner site of one of the town's plazas, the architects cantilevered the auditorium off the ground, allowing "the plaza to penetrate the plot" through the glazed entrance. The foyer, box office, and café fill the ground floor and an excavated space below it, which has a pleasingly curvaceous ceiling, while the auditorium itself takes up almost the entire plan. Clearly this is an imposing building, but the fact that it is clad in a local limestone gives it a lovely lightness of touch. **GG**

Eureka Tower (2006)

Architect Fender Katsalidis   **Location** Melbourne, Australia
Style Postmodernist   **Materials** Concrete, steel, glass

The tag of "tallest building" is a hotly contested one. In Australia the race between Fender Katsalidis's Eureka Tower in Melbourne and the Q1 (by Atelier SDG) in Queensland finished neck and neck. According to the Council on Tall Buildings and Urban Habitat, there are four categories to determine height: pinnacle height; architectural top; roof height; and highest occupied floor. Q1 wins on the basis of the first two, and the ninety-two-floor Eureka Tower on the latter. The rivalry is similar to that between New York's Empire State and Chrysler Buildings, where the winner was ultimately decided by the height of the spire rising above the roof of the Empire State Building.

If the decider in Australia, however, was on the basis of sheer opulence and luxury, Eureka Tower would take the prize, for while Q1 may have a ten-story mini-rainforest sky garden sixty floors up, the entire top ten floors of the Eureka Tower are faced with gold. Built on reclaimed swampland, special foundations were needed to secure the 975-foot-high (297 m) tower, while at the top, construction was concluded when the crane at the summit of the tower was taken down by a smaller crane, which in its turn was dismantled by a crane smaller yet again (small enough to fit in the service elevator).

With its gold-plated windows, gym, cinema, bars, restaurants, and concierge services, the Eureka is aimed at the luxury end of the residential market, but it also incorporates environmental features. Glass-skin double glazing reduces heating and cooling costs and the elevator systems use magnet-hoist machinery, requiring less power than conventional ones. It is worth visiting the Eureka Tower simply to take an elevator up 935 feet (285 m) to the observation deck, and experience the stupendous views. **GT**

British High Commission (2006)

Architects Cullum and Nightingale   **Location** Kampala, Uganda   **Style** Contemporary   **Materials** Concrete, brick, terra cotta

The red-brick buildings of the British High Commission in Kampala rise up as if fused with Uganda's red earth. With a backdrop of lush trees and vegetation, the High Commission clearly stakes claims of permanence and belonging. The inspiration of the local brick palette is obvious in the cluster of buildings. By applying this palette liberally to roof, ground, and walls, Cullum and Nightingale could have created a monolith, but the articulation of the surfaces averts the potential for monotony. The complex is split into two realms, the main administrative building and a consular visa section, the different operational requirements forcing separate entrances from different roads. Interestingly, this hierarchy of public front and back entrances is a feature of some African dwellings. The intense tropical sun is shaded from the windows by terra-cotta louvers mounted on galvanized mild steel rod supports. There is an almost polite referencing of the modern African

market, the African village school, and the austere materiality of the broader context. The sophistication emerges in the banana-leaf concrete shuttering on tapered concrete columns, the careful and practical exposed metalwork, and the reflected light admitted via a clerestory above. Overall, the High Commission marks an interesting point in global cultural consumption, with Cullum and Nightingale confident in referencing critically the Ugandan and African context for what is essentially a patch of Britain. **GO**

" … neither a monument to the British empire nor to the architect but … a simple place to work …"

Tom Sanya, *Architects' Journal*, 2006

Museum of Modern Literature (2006)

Architects David Chipperfield Architects **Location** Marbach am Neckar, Germany **Style** Modernist **Materials** Concrete, stone

A brave move in a country where Fascism was given an aesthetic identity in the Neo-Classical excesses of Hitler's architect Albert Speer, the Literaturmuseum der Moderne—dubbed LiMo—stands like a Neo-Palladian temple on a rock plateau in Marbach Park. Birthplace of the dramatist Friedrich Schiller (1759–1805), the site is already the home of the National Schiller Museum (1903) and the Archive for German Literature, built in the 1970s. The terraced museum by Chipperfield (b. 1953) forms the third side of a large courtyard that acts as a gateway between the lower park and preexisting national monuments to German literature. The commission was awarded to Chipperfield's Berlin office in 2002, who chose to adopt this controversial style as a reaction to the site, along with Chipperfield's belief that no other approach is as appropriate for a structure dedicated to books and to learning. Chipperfield is known for his

Modernist approach, and the museum is no exception. This modern-day Parthenon is formed by a series of terraces embedded in the topography of the hillside. The most obvious structure is the glass entrance pavilion, the columns on its four symmetrical sides pared down to the bare minimum. Materials are simple to emphasize the bold aesthetic and rational architectural language of the building: local limestone for the floors, and concrete with the same limestone aggregate for the walls. The internal galleries situated in the lower building are lined with a rich and sensuous ipé wood, which has also been used in the mullions of the glazed facade behind the colonnade above. The warmth of the wood in these artificially lit exhibition spaces gives them a diurnal atmosphere which contrasts with the bright glazed galleries along the halls, balancing views inward to the internalized world of texts and outward to the valley below. **JH**

State Prison East Jutland (2006)

Architect Friis + Moltke Architects   **Location** Horsens, Denmark   **Style** Contemporary   **Materials** Concrete, steel, brick

Most prisons in Denmark were built at the beginning of the twentieth century. However, due to increasing security needs and a new focus on inmates' living conditions, the existing prisons do not live up to contemporary standards. The State Prison of East Jutland is a closed prison, the second of its kind in Denmark. The complex lies on a large open field close to the town of Horsens. Although there are no bars in front of the windows, the windows are made of armored glass and the frames are welded into the walls. The prison is ultramodern and holds up to 230 prisoners who each have a 129-square-foot (12 sq m) cell with their own toilet and shower. A distinctive feature of this two-story building is the way in which the architects have emphasized several units instead of one large structure. The prison's ring wall is 4,593 feet long (1,400 m) and the total length of the prison's fence measures 2.55 miles (4 km). The ceilings are

made of steel and the walls of reinforced concrete. The building is not a typical fortresslike prison; it is low built and the architects have taken into consideration that every prisoner must have his or her own view. The cluster of individual units makes it appear more like a group of homes than a large, grim institution. Inside, inmates encounter a thought-provoking sculpture by Danish artist Christian Lemmerz of a golden angel with breasts, wings, and tattoos. On one of the angel's arms it reads "God," and on the other, "Dog." **SML**

> *"There are those who consider that a prison might as well be situated below ground."*
>
> Martin Wienberg Mortensen, architect

Pull House (2006)

Architects Procter-Rihl **Location** Brattleboro, Vermont, USA **Style** Contemporary **Materials** Recycled wood, new wood, metal

One of the most interesting contemporary design firms is Procter-Rihl—the London-based partnership of Christopher Procter and Fernando Rihl. Their innovative designs revolve around key elements such as maintaining the cultural integrity of the location and devising sustainable, ecologically sound, and energy efficient buildings. They have a reputation for cutting-edge buildings such as the Slice House (2003) in Brazil, which made the most of a very narrow site. The partners demonstrate an acute cultural and climatic awareness when developing their commissions and Pull House is an outstanding example of this. The town of Brattleboro, Vermont, nestles in the Connecticut River valley, overlooked by a series of rolling hills and mountains. It is a place of outstanding natural beauty with a strong rural feel harking back to the dairy farming history of the area. Procter and Rihl have maintained this agricultural thread; the finished house combines traditional barn features—particularly apparent in the roof—with a surprising and playful manipulation of space and rational form. It is a building that relates to and respectfully acknowledges its location, while the extraordinary design creates a thoroughly twenty-first-century dwelling. One of the most pertinent considerations was Vermont's harsh winter climate. The entire house was designed with this in mind, from the steeply pitched roof to the positioning of the entry on the uphill side of the building where no snow collects. Furthermore, the house is hyper-insulated with structural insulated panels and triple-glazed windows that contribute to its energy efficiency. In addition to its strong focus on sustainability, Pull House is also one of the most imaginative of modern houses with its exciting manipulation of interior space and use of unusual geometric form. **TP**

Quai Branly Museum (2006)

Architect Jean Nouvel   **Location** Paris, France   **Style** Contemporary   **Materials** Concrete, glass, wood, vegetation

Described by Nouvel (*b.* 1945) as space organized around "the symbols of the forest, the river, and the obsessions of death and oblivion," this museum is an ensemble of four connected buildings comprising plate glass, natural woods, and concrete integrated through nature and vegetation. The dominant feature of the Musée du Quai Branly is an aerial, pierlike, rectangular box containing a 656-foot-long (200 m) exhibition hall perched on 33-foot-high (10 m) curved supporting pillars, "hovering" over an undulating landscaped garden. The external structure on the riverside facade presents a horizontal row of twenty-six protruding cubes in multicolored earth tones.

Inside, a five-story atrium and a spiraling 656-foot-long (200 m) ramp connect to the exhibition area and roof terrace. This space is one large gallery, divided by leather-covered partitions and devoted to the arts and civilizations of Africa, Asia, Oceania, and the Americas. The boxes protruding from the building reveal themselves to be thematic rooms, and freestanding display cabinets and ramped floors enable discovery of 3,500 exhibits on display. The reserve collection of 300,000 objects in storage is visible in a glass-fronted, central, circular vault. The facade and ceilings of a building containing the museum shop have been decorated by eight Australian aboriginal artists.

The garden is separated from the Quai Branly and River Seine by an 8,600-square-foot (800 sq m) vertical wall of vegetation, 40 feet (12 m) high, in which 15,000 plants were carefully arranged. The overwhelming metaphor is of the visitor as explorer discovering the building like a Mayan ruin in an overgrown jungle. Further, the museum addresses the question of *décontextualisation*—whether artifacts, exoticized and isolated from their ethnographic context, should be presented as aesthetic objects within the ethnocentric Western museum culture. **JEH**

> *"There is no hierarchy among the arts … it is upon this conviction … that this museum is founded."*
>
> Jacques Chirac, former president of France

⬆ An array of earth-colored cubes of different sizes cantilever out from the riverside exterior.

➡ Lush vegetation from the "living wall" contrasts with the inorganic materials of the structure.

Madrid Barajas
International Airport Terminal 4 (2006)

Architect Richard Rogers Partnership **Location** Madrid, Spain
Style High Tech **Materials** Glass, concrete, bamboo, steel

Madrid Barajas International Airport's Terminal 4 lies northwest of the existing terminals, and measures eleven million square feet (one million sq m). It is connected to a satellite building by a tunnel that runs under the runways. The terminal, its satellite, and two runways opened in 2006, and have doubled the airport's capacity to handle up to thirty-five million passengers a year, making Barajas the second largest airport in Europe, and tenth largest in the world. The terminal was designed by Richard Rogers (b. 1933) and Antonio Lamela and, and won them the Royal Institute of British Architects' Stirling Prize.

The spacious building's modular design has glass walls, and an undulating winglike roof of prefabricated steel supported by a concrete frame. Roof lights allow the upper level of the terminal to bask in natural light, reducing the need for artificial lighting and providing views of the aircraft and the mountains in the distance. Internally, the roof is clad in slatted, bamboo strips, and supported by Y-shaped steel beams painted to create a half-mile-long (1 km) view of graduated color. The gates are color coded for easy reference, with deep blue for north, and deep red for south.

Large courtyards divide the parallel floors that house the point of arrival, check-in, passport, security control, and departure lounges. These areas allow natural light down into the lower levels, and are spanned by glass and steel bridges. Air-conditioning outlets playfully resemble giant barcode readers and animate the baggage-collection stands. **CMK**

↖ The undulating waves of bamboo strips and boldly painted steel beams make the roof highly distinctive.

← The airport has the world's largest single terminal area, handling up to seventy million passengers annually.

South Essex Rape and Incest Crisis Centre (2006)

Architect Featherstone Associates **Location** Grays, England
Style Vernacular **Materials** Brick, wood

Olympic Tennis Center (2007)

Architects Dominique Perrault Architecture **Location** Madrid, Spain
Style High Tech **Materials** Glass, steel, wood

Featherstone Associates, led by Sarah Featherstone and considered to be one of the most promising young British architectural practices, was appointed by the South Essex Rape and Incest Crisis Centre (SERICC) to refurbish and extend their Grays center, based in a 1970s church hall. Spatial quality, sustainability, and technological innovation were to be primary in the design; fortunately, the practice were experienced in building such features into project development.

Perhaps the most characteristic feature of the building is its windows. Formed to resemble "listening

---

"It was very important that we understood the issues ... how the environment affects our emotions."

Sarah Featherstone, architect

---

ears," the two windows, podlike and clad with timber shingles, are the building's signature exterior marks. They also provide interior privacy for the counseling rooms. A central curved wall separates the counseling areas and the SERICC administrative offices, ensuring acoustic and visual discretion.

A high degree of understanding of the nature of SERICC's work was crucial to the design process. The designers studied "emotional diagrams" that represented both clients of the service and counseling workers' experiences of the center, and also analyzed the social, historical, and geographical patterns of the surrounding area. Featherstone Associates combined irregular, organic forms with distinctive materials, producing a sensitive yet spirited building with a strong contemporary identity. **ES**

The Olympic Tennis Center in Madrid, dubbed the "Magic Box" by its designer Dominique Perrault (b. 1953), is located next to an ecological lake, set in a large park. The tranquil landscape provides the perfect backdrop for Perrault's dramatic, large-scale luminous box—reflective by day, it is lit up by night to reveal the rigid geometry and bold colors of its interiors.

However, the crowning glory of the Magic Box—so called for both the external effects of light and color and for the events that can be viewed in its interior—is its series of adjustable metallic roofs. The three structures can be opened and closed either fully or partially depending on the weather, and on how the venue is being used, whether for a tennis match or a rock concert. The effect is like opening the flaps of an enormous cardboard box, with each flap angled to afford the best conditions for those within. As befits the headquarters of Spanish tennis, the center contains state-of-the-art facilities for both players and spectators, with three major courts accommodating crowds of 12,000, 5,000, and 3,000 spectators. In addition, there are a further sixteen outdoor courts, five indoor courts, and six covered training courts, as well as a swimming pool and restaurants.

Perrault is no stranger to designing sports stadia. Since establishing his practice in 1981, he has designed and built the Velodrome and the Olympic Swimming Pool in Berlin. He also competed to build London's 2012 Olympic swimming pool, and is currently working on a sports complex in Rouen, France, which is due for completion in 2009. These are in addition to numerous built projects, ranging from museums to educational buildings to factories, all of which are imbued with Perrault's desire to connect to a particular geography, site, and sense of history. **GB**

National Grand Theater of China (2007)

Architect Paul Andreu **Location** Beijing, China **Style** High Tech **Materials** Concrete, titanium, glass

A project of this type, scale, and audacity would not have been permitted in the historic core of any city other than in China. The National Grand Theater by Andreu (*b.* 1938) is a superlative example of iconic architecture of its time and place. A short distance from the Forbidden City and the adjacent Tiananmen Square—the heart and soul of Beijing—this structure courts controversy. Beloved by some for its bold design and radical approach to serving the arts, and despised by many for its huge budget ($324 million) and arguably inapt location, China's new National Theater is already a divisive building. While many Western architects in China enjoy a relatively free rein at the behest of their clients, China's ancient urban centers are being transformed irrevocably, sparking cultural debates that will doubtless last for decades.

The globular glass and titanium shell, 696 feet (212 m) across its longest axis and 471 feet (144 m) across its shortest, houses three separate venues in what the architect describes as a "city of theaters": a 2,461-seat opera house, a 2,017-seat concert hall, a 1,040-seat theater, plus numerous exhibition spaces, restaurants, and shopping areas. In the evening, these inner structures and spaces are revealed to the outside world through the glass exterior wall. From outside, the curved form, which is peeled back in the center to evoke an opening stage curtain, appears to float in a 381,980-square-foot (35,500 sq m) manmade lake that completely surrounds the structure. The apex of the curve reaches a height of 152 feet (46 m) above the lake. Access to the building is achieved via underground walkways. **ED**

↖ The panels of laminated, insulated glass allow the busy life of the theater to be viewed from outside.

← Sitting in a lake, the half ellipsoid structure has been likened by locals to an egg floating in water.

Prado Museum (2007)

Architect Rafael Moneo **Location** Madrid, Spain **Style** Modernist **Materials** Concrete, brick, granite, marble, oak, cedar, steel, bronze

When the Museo del Prado first opened its doors to the public in 1819, its exhibits totaled 311 Spanish paintings. By the millennium the Prado's collection had grown to more than 7,000 paintings, but lack of space in the museum building—the Palacio de Villanueva—meant that only half were displayed. The year 2007, however, saw the opening of a new wing, the first stage of an extension program; five years in the making and at a cost of $200 million, it added 183,000 square feet (17,000 sq m) to the museum and freed forty rooms of the Palacio for artwork display.

Spanish architect Rafael Moneo (*b.* 1937) designed the extension to house the museum's administration, conservation teams, a new library, a print and drawings gallery, a café and restaurant, an auditorium, and exhibition space. Most striking, and controversial, was his proposal to relocate, stone by stone, the fifteenth-century cloister of the nearby Church of San Jeronimo el Real to an upper floor of the new wing, where it would surround a new sculpture gallery.

From inside the new wing's spacious Modernist foyer the visitor can view the Baroque Palacio through floor-to-ceiling windows. The new spaces are impressive—the two exhibition spaces are perfect cubes—and the upper-floor sculpture gallery with its impeccably restored cloister is a thrill. Linking the museum buildings is a large underground area, roofed at ground level by a garden of clipped box hedges.

In his Prado extension, Moneo has turned his back on showy architecture and created a cool, restrained, Modernist structure that perfectly complements the opulence of its historic neighbor. **FR**

↗ The relocated cloister of the Church of San Geronimo lines the walls of the extension's sculpture gallery.

→ Sited next to the church, the extension overlooks the formal garden and, beyond that, the original Prado.

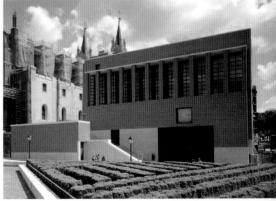

Matrimandir Meditation Center (2007)

Architect Roger Anger   **Location** Auroville, India   **Style** Expressionist   **Materials** Concrete, stainless steel, marble, gold leaf

> *When I spent a few minutes in the concentration chamber, I felt time is infinite; something echoed in me."*

A. P. J. Abdul Kalam, president of India

⬆ The golden globe of the building sits serenely in a landscaped area of red sandstone and lush plants.

➡ The gold-leaf coated, stainless-steel cladding gives the meditation center its shimmering golden hue.

Auroville, in the former French colony of Pondicherry, is an independent settlement inspired by the spiritual teachings of Sri Aurobindo. Intended to be an ideal city for spiritual seekers, it is steadily evolving according to the masterplan drawn up by Mirra Alfassa, known to Aurovilians as The Mother, the Paris-born spiritual partner of Sri Aurobindo. The project is being built under the supervision of French architect Roger Anger. The hub of this settlement is the Matrimandir Meditation Center, from which radiates the rest of the community in four sweeping zones—industrial, residential, cultural, and international.

A stunning modern-day architectural conception, situated in a expansive landscaped area referred to as Peace, the meditation center takes the form of a golden globe appearing to rise out of the earth as a symbol of spiritual consciousness. The center takes its golden hue from cladding formed of stainless-steel discs coated with gold leaf. Inside the globe, visitors slowly ascend to the core of the meditation center through spaces enclosed by pure white marble. The path they walk is covered in white carpet and the atmosphere is hushed and peaceful.

The ascending visitor is led into the core meditation chamber, a truly inspiring sight. Placed in the center is a manmade crystal 27.5 inches (70 cm) in diameter, reputed to be the largest optically perfect glass in the world. The sun's rays hit the crystal via a programmed heliostat mounted on the roof of the Matrimandir and provide the only source of light in the chamber. There are no organized rites or symbols within this space to distract visitors from their thoughts or direct them toward a specific religion.

The Matrimandir Meditation Center was conceived simply as an embodiment of peace. In its remarkable meditation chamber, one can rethink one's self—an experience truly worth having. **BS**

Museum for Ibere Camargo Foundation (2007)

Architect Álvaro Siza   **Location** Porto Alegre, Brazil
Style Contemporary   **Material** Concrete

As part of the celebrations for Porto Alegre's 500th anniversary, several Brazilian artists organized exhibitions in collaboration with foreign art institutions. The Ibere Camargo Foundation took that opportunity to provide the local community with its first museum of contemporary art.

Portuguese architect Álvaro Siza (b. 1933) won the competition to design the new museum with a bold structure coupling local culture with European sensibility. The relatively simple program—exhibition spaces, auditorium, bookstore, library and video library, café, offices, and artists' workshop—is basically split into two separate parts. A long raised platform accommodates all the technical spaces as well as dividing the public area of the building from the adjacent avenue.

The actual museum is a four-story structure positioned at the southwest end of the site and flanked by a tall cliff covered with vegetation. The two walls facing the cliff are straight and almost orthogonal to each other, whereas an irregular complex concrete element closes the figure on the side facing the water. The circulation system of the museum is beautifully exposed in the form of three hanging ramps that seem to embrace visitors entering the building through the plaza on the ground level.

Once inside the museum, the drastic separation of galleries and circulation spaces provides a clear hierarchy between the areas of rest and observation of the works on display. Meanwhile strategic openings are carefully positioned along the ramps to open up views toward the city.

Finally, Siza's use of white concrete—frequently utilized in Brazil's Modernist architecture—augments this elegant building's sculptural qualities. **RDB**

New Acropolis Museum (2007)

Architects Bernard Tschumi Architects, ARSY   **Location** Athens, Greece   **Style** Deconstructivist   **Materials** Glass, marble, concrete

Already a landmark in its own right, the New Acropolis Museum in Athens was designed by New York–based architect Bernard Tschumi (b. 1944), in collaboration with local architect Michael Photiadis of ARSY. The museum hosts the city's classical treasures from the Archaic to the Roman period, and is located on the southern base of the city's ancient sacred rock only 800 feet (244 m) away from the Parthenon.

The characteristic element of the design is light. Light-sensitive gallery spaces and transparent sections with big openings protect the valuable exhibits, and

"It's a museum inside the city … [combining] the most up-to-date technology and ancient materials."

Bernard Tschumi, architect

connect the new and the old worlds within Tschumi's Minimalist, trapezoidal creation. The architects kept to a simplicity of design and geometrical abstraction that allows the structure to blend naturally with the imposing historical setting, as well as with the contemporary fabric of Athens. The design placed a large, glass-enclosed gallery space, raised on slender pillars, over the seventh-century archaeological site.

The top-most level of the musuem building is a glass hall intended to house the Parthenon marbles, which are controversially kept by the British Museum in London. The entire hall is tilted to mirror the Parthenon, so that if the marbles are returned they will hang on the same axis as they once did on the Parthenon and visitors will also be able to look out on that historic structure. **ES**

Bahrain World Trade Center (2007)

Architects Atkins **Location** Manama, Bahrain
Style High Tech **Materials** Concrete, steel, glass

A shrine to commerce, with an environmental agenda? A futuristic building, borrowing from the designs of the past? Resolving such contradictions, the World Trade Center in Bahrain sets the standard for environmental construction. Ever since New York's Flatiron Building went up in 1902, creating a wind tunnel at its base (so much so that policemen had to be posted below to stop men loitering in the hope of seeing women's skirts being lifted up by the gusts), skyscrapers have created a latent, and generally untapped, energy resource.

Here, this energy is harnessed by means of three 164-foot (50 m) wind turbines set at intervals between the two tower blocks. Each of the blocks is shaped like a sail, and together they work like aerofoils, drawing and accelerating the wind to drive the propellers. The architects technologically perfected the design of traditional Arabian wind towers; the tapering design and curving shape of the 787-foot-high (240 m) towers mean that the wind rises perpendicularly between them, generating maximum power.

Atkins design iconic, landmark buildings and have been at the forefront of developments in the architectural playground of the newly emerging Middle East. Like windmills on a flat Dutch landscape or the billowing sails of a ship unfurled to meet the breeze, this edifice brings a new meaning to Louis Sullivan's adage that "whether it be the sweeping eagle in his flight or the open apple-blossom . . . form ever follows function, and this is the law." **GT**

↗ The sail-shaped towers of the center are a striking monument to commerce on the Manama skyline.

→ Supported by bridges, the turbines generate up to 15 percent of the center's electricity requirements.

Beijing National Stadium (2008)

Architects Herzog & de Meuron **Location** Beijing, China **Style** Contemporary **Materials** Steel, concrete, resin

> *"[We wanted to] create a new kind of urban site that will generate public life in this part of Beijing."*

Jacques Herzog, architect

⬆ The meshed "facade" of the stadium promises to be a memorable feature of Beijing's urban landscape.

➡ The stadium's interwoven, irregularly configured steel structure provides strength and visual interest.

Rising from the flat plain of north Beijing, the extraordinary shape of the National Stadium has already transformed the appearance of the city, giving a landmark to the far reaches of the famous north-south axis that runs through the center of the Forbidden City. The stadium is set on a gently sloped plinth, giving the impression that the building is a natural event emerging from the soil. With its mass of huge steel columns and struts, conceived as continuous limbs that rise from the ground and curve over the shoulder of the stadium before intermeshing into the enormous roof, the building displays an architectural intelligence never seen before in China and rarely rivaled elsewhere in the world.

Known as the "Bird's Nest" by the Chinese, a term that underscores their admiration for organic forms, the stadium achieves the considerable distinction of retaining its essentially sculptural quality despite its vast scale and its adroit fulfillment of a host of complex technical requirements. The stadium's most noticeable feature is the absence of a strict outer facade or curtain wall. Instead, a forest of columns produces a set of transitory spaces, neither exterior nor interior, that break down the monolithic mass of the building while emphasizing its tectonic qualities. The steel elements, while massive, hint at menacing movement. The area around the stadium has been designed to flow from it, with underground levels for access, media, and retail set beneath an urban park patterned to articulate the intermeshed design of the building.

Inside, the concrete bowl of the stadium provides seating for 91,000 spectators. Color is used sparingly—the steel is painted silver, the outer side of the concrete bowl and the stadium seating a dazzling red, and interior elements a matt black. This is not only a remarkable stadium but also a sourcebook of ideas for the new power of the twenty-first century. **MI**

Glossary

Abbasid, Aghlabid, Almohad
See **Islamic**

Ancient Egyptian
The culture and architecture of Ancient Egypt, ranging from 3150–31 BCE, when Egypt was absorbed into the Roman empire. The Egyptian style was imitated in Europe from the eighteenth century to the emergence of Art Deco in the twentieth century.

Ancient Greek
The culture and architecture of Ancient Greece, ranging from 1150 BCE to either the death of Alexander the Great in 323 BCE or the absorption of Greece into the Roman empire in 146 BCE. The high moment of Ancient Greek culture is considered to have been from 490–323 BCE, after which the term Hellenistic is used to describe the period until the Roman conquest. Some historians argue that Ancient Greek culture extended through to the third century CE, followed by the rise of Byzantine Constantinople (present-day Istanbul).

Ancient Shinto
Shinto is Japan's native religion, and is an animistic system of belief, involving the worship of *kami* or spirits that represent the genius of a place, object, or animal. Ancient Shinto architecture refers to shrines and other religious structures designed in a traditional style, featuring a gate or *torii*, made of two uprights and two crossbars signifying the line between the worlds of the living and the *kami*.

Art Deco
The design style popularized between 1920 and 1939, embracing a wide range of the arts, such as architecture, photography, fashion, graphic design, and film. The first global style to express the aspirations and technical capabilities of the Modern era, it originated in France and spread across the world, with variants in regions as diverse as North and South America, China, India, and South Africa. Speed, flight, and mass production were its watchwords, although a reuse of archaic architectural styles also featured, with its heyday evident in late-1920s New York City. It was replaced by Modernism and the International Style at the onset of World War II.

Art Nouveau
The idiosyncratic design style that flourished in Europe and elsewhere from the end of the nineteenth century to the outbreak of World War I. It is chiefly known for its very stylized curvilinear designs, often drawing on floral and organic forms. Highly expressive and eccentric, it was represented in architecture, furniture, glassware, textiles, street fittings, posters, and wallpapers. Among its proponents are some of the most original design names in European history. Regional variants include, among others, Jugendstil in Germany, Secession style in Vienna, and the work of masters such as Charles Rennie Mackintosh in Glasgow, Scotland, and Antonio Gaudí in Barcelona, Spain, where it was known as Catalan Modernisme.

Arts and Crafts
The design style and reform movement that arose in Britain, Scandinavia, and Germany and spread to the United States of America from 1880 to the onset of World War I. Developed in reaction to the then deadening fashion for historicist revival styles, the movement sought to return to a more immediate notion of creative expression in the fine and decorative arts, emphasizing the use of traditional materials and handmade techniques instead of mechanized production.

Bantu
A term describing a vast swath of peoples and their related languages and cultures, occupying central and southern Africa.

Baroque (Revival)
A period style in the visual arts, architecture, theater, and music starting from around 1600 in Italy and influencing much of Europe up to the eighteenth century. The Baroque overtly engages the senses, using dramatic composition, lighting, epic structural gestures, and, above all, a highly emotional palette. A key weapon used by the Catholic Church to convey in immediate terms the strictures of the Council of Trent (1545–63), which rallied the Church's forces against the Protestant Reformation. Neo-Baroque: imitative of the Baroque style.

Bauhaus
The style developed by the Bauhaus, the leading design school in Germany from 1919 to 1933, promulgated through architecture, textile and furniture design, graphics, ceramics, and photography. Led by Walter Gropius, Hannes Meyer, and Mies van der Rohe respectively on three sequential sites in Weimar, Dessau, and Berlin, the Bauhaus sought to unify art, craft, and technology, emphasizing the "new" objective truth of design in reaction to the overt emotionalism of Expressionism. The Bauhaus style is characterized by an attention to reductive form, simplicity of materials (albeit produced by machine), and a simple color palette.

Beaux Arts
An academic architectural style evolving from the Ecole des Beaux Arts, Paris, which reigned throughout the latter half of the nineteenth century,

spreading to all corners of the globe. Amalgamating historicist styles, it emphasized conventionally hierarchical arrangements of space, a close attention to historical detail, and a florid use of color and gilding.

Brutalist
The architectural style deriving from Modernism that became prominent in many European and U.S. cities between 1950 and 1975. Seen as a reaction to the neat purism of early Modernist architecture, its impetus came from the later work of the arch-Modernist architect Le Corbusier, especially his Unité d'Habitation, Marseilles (1952) and his Secretariat Building in Chandigarh, India (1953). Brutalist buildings employ highly boxy shapes and rough materials, such as concrete, on which the markings of wooden planks used to cast elements are visible.

Byzantine
The architecture and broader culture of the Byzantine empire, established along with its capital at Constantinople by the Roman Emperor Constantine in 306 and continuing until its eventual conquest by the Turks in 1453. Its architecture is characterized by the use of triangular squinches (inverted, concave pieces of masonry) linking square plan to dome, and luxurious interior use of colored and gilded mosaics and other decorations.

Cape Dutch
The architecture, culture, and peoples, mostly descended from German, Dutch, French, and other European stock, who between the seventeenth and nineteenth centuries occupied the western Cape of South Africa. Features of the style include rounded gabled facades, H-shaped floorplans, whitewashed walls, and thatched roofs.

Catalan Modernisme
See **Art Nouveau**

Celtic
A term used to describe the various ethnic peoples living in the western fringes of Europe, as well as their visual culture in which curling, animated, and highly complex designs are evident in buildings, tombs, memorials, jewelry, and other artifacts.

Classical, Neo-Classical
Buildings incorporating the three traditional orders of Classical Greek and Roman architecture: the Doric, Ionian, and the Corinthian. In use in Greece during the fifth century BCE, the orders have been reused and variously interpreted ever since. Neo-Classical is a term used to describe the revival of Classical Greek and Roman architecture and related decorative arts, notably in Europe and the United States of America throughout the latter half of the eighteenth century through to the end of the nineteenth century.

Eco-Architecture
An architectural design strategy, increasingly evident from the latter half of the twentieth century onward, that manifestly engages with or co-opts the local terrain, using regionally specific materials and placing sustainable building and maintenance systems at the heart of its practice.

Edwardian
The culture and architecture of the post-Victorian world between 1901 and 1918, especially those areas within the former British empire. Stylistically eclectic, but frequently reinterpreting the forms of the Baroque and Queen Anne periods in its projection of an Imperial style.

Expressionist
The highly emotive, individualistic style adopted by architects, artists, and composers in the first two decades of the twentieth century. Featuring swooping, curvilinear, and massy forms, its language owes much to imaginative formulations of theoretical physics, psychiatry, and social reform.

Fascist
The architectural style favored by twentieth-century totalitarian regimes, notably the Nazis and Italian Fascists, but also the later repressive regimes of Eastern Europe. Derived from a selective reading of Classical architecture, its use of repetitive sequencing, oversized scale, and emphasis on collective identity seeks to subordinate individual identity.

Franconian
An early medieval style, common to buildings located along the Rhine and its eventual tributaries that blends German and French styles.

Functionalist
The architectural style and theory debated in avant-garde circles in early twentieth-century Soviet Russia, and Western Europe and elsewhere, in which architecture must be seen to respond primarily to functional rather than aesthetic or emotional needs.

Georgian
Named after the Hanoverian monarchs, the architecture and design style produced in Britain throughout the eighteenth century and the early decades of the nineteenth century. Very loosely employing a Classical vocabulary based on Palladian precedents, Georgian buildings tend to have plain exteriors and complex interiors, generous in proportion and symmetrical in configuration.

Ghurid
See **Islamic**

Gothic (Perpendicular, Revival)

The architecture and design style developed across Europe from the early thirteenth century onward, favoring a use of soaring architectural elements, thin-ribbed ceilings, delicate tracery, and pointed spires and arches. Said to derive from a Germanic interest in the forests of their original homelands, the true impetus of the style is unknown. Evolving through a complex set of regional and periodic variants, this international and highly decorative style influenced artists, composers, producers of manuscripts, and others. Its greatest glories are arguably seen in the medieval churches of Europe. The Gothic was revived in the eighteenth and nineteenth centuries following and in reaction to the Classicist lessons of the Renaissance, reaching new heights in the early-mid-Victorian era when Gothic was considered a suitably nationalistic style for those cultures of Germanic origin.

Hellenistic

The architecture and culture of the Greek-speaking world following the death of Alexander the Great in 323 BCE; also, the term used to describe the eighteenth- and nineteenth-century revival of Greek as opposed to Roman Classical architecture.

High Tech

The style developed in the latter half of the twentieth century by leading architects such as Renzo Piano, Norman Foster, and Richard Rogers. Features an emphasis on the external display of conventionally hidden internal systems.

Ikkong

A building type common to traditional Korean architecture, which features hipped roofs and gables with double eaves. Ikkong buildings date from the seventh century through to the late nineteenth century.

Imperial Chinese

The traditional building style used by Imperial Chinese architects before the advent of Western architectural styles in the East. Favoring large, sloping roofs placed on almost insignificant walls, buildings in this style were produced with only minor variations for several thousand years within the Chinese sphere of influence.

Indo-Islamic

The architecture and culture that arose first in Northern India and then across the subcontinent and neighboring Afghanistan following the incursions of the Mughals into the region from 1526 to the decline of the empire in the 1720s. Incorporating Turkic, Persian, and Mongol innovations (such as the pillared archway) into native Hindu architecture, it combined the geometrical deftness and complex patterning of Islamic architecture with something of the rich sculptural sensibility of Hindu buildings.

International Style

The architecture produced between the 1920s and late 1930s by Modernist architects such as Mies van der Rohe, Hannes Meyer, Philip Johnson, and others, and named after the eponymous 1932 exhibition at the Museum of Modern Art, New York. Rejecting ornament, emphasizing glass, steel, and concrete, white rendering, and regular bands of windows, the style became internationally ubiquitous following the geographical dispersal of its leading exponents in the years leading up to and following World War II. Transplanting rigid principles to very different contexts across the world, it remained highly influential for decades and was the house-style favored by corporate America until the late 1960s and the reactionary rise of Postmodernism.

Irish

The culture and buildings produced on the island of Ireland and the western reaches of Scotland, notably by early Christian communities that were hermetic in nature and well integrated with the often harsh local environment, employing a functionalist, resilient, but still very beautiful vernacular style.

Islamic (Revival)

The architecture and culture of the Islamic world manifest in the first 300 years or so following the death of the Prophet Muhammad in 632 CE. Influenced by Persian, Roman, and Byzantine styles, its innovations lie in its blending of mathematically precise geometries and repetitive patterning with building forms that were entirely new, such as the mosque, minaret, *iwan* (open vaulted portal), and others that reflect the ritual observances inherent to Islam. Later Islamic architecture expresses different regional characteristics while broadly serving these same functions. Abbasid, Aghlabid, Almohad, Ghaznavid, Ghurid, Saadian, Safavid, Saminid, Sassanid, Shaybanid, Timurid, Tulunid, Umayyad: terms used to describe the changing dynasties, regional fiefdoms of Islamic rule, and respective architectural styles that featured across the pre-Modern Islamic world from its western reach in Moorish Spain to Persia, Afghanistan, and beyond. Mudéjar: vernacular architectural style influenced by the Moors who remained after the Christian Reconquest of Spain in the twelfth century, but also reflecting contemporary European styles. Islamic Revival: the reuse of traditional Islamic designs and motifs in later nineteenth-, twentieth-, and twenty-first-century architecture, sometimes adopted as a form of homage to original Islamic culture, unsullied by the fast-changing fashions inherent in Western architecture.

Italian Rationalist

A regional variant of the International style, aligned closely to the ideals of the Italian Fascists, but producing nonetheless some very fine buildings in which the Modernists' slogan of "form and function" is often elegantly realized.

Italianate

A term loosely describing the style developed first in Britain in the early 1800s, then spreading across Northern Europe and the outposts of the British empire and North America, that incorporated Italian Renaissance principles with a Neo-Classical sense of proportion. The style was often employed for private houses and official residences, featuring overhanging cornices and roofs, affiliated towers or belvedere, and simplified Venetian windows. Many Italianate buildings display great elegance together with an informal exuberance.

Jacobean

The architecture and design style evident in late sixteenth- and early seventeenth-century England, characterized in buildings by gabled facades, large windows, and much wood and plaster decoration internally. Evidence of a fashionable interest in the Renaissance, often filtered through French models, is often seen, although sometimes this is crudely interpreted. The Jacobean style declined following the more rigorous Classicism of Inigo Jones and his peers from 1616 onward.

Joseon

The name given in 1392 to what is now modern Korea by the successful warlord Yi Seong-gye, later King Taejo. The country was ruled by his dynasty for 500 years and was known by this name until 1910 with the Japanese annexation.

Jugendstil

See **Art Nouveau**

Jusimpo

A decorative style used in traditional Korean architecture during the Joseon period, characterized by the use of column-heads, or *gongpos*, adorning the top of each pillar supporting the eaves.

Khmer

The culture and architecture of the peoples occupying the area of present-day Cambodia between the ninth and fifteenth centuries. Khmer architecture features a profusion of sculptures and mythical serpents or *nagas* that are integrated into building facades, the use of corbel arches, and tiered temple structures set in broad courtyards said to resemble holy mountain ranges.

Lombard

A Germanic tribe that dominated Northern Italy between the sixth and eighth centuries. Lombard buildings are essentially early versions of the Romanesque, notable for their thick walls, plain elevations, repeated use of ornamental arches, and their generally earthbound, solid character.

Lutyens "Wrenaissance"

An aspect of the work of the Edwardian architect Sir Edwin Lutyens in the early years of the twentieth century, notable for its adroit, if rather fulsome, blend of quasi-Palladian and quasi-Baroque styles.

Mannerism

The style employed by architects, artists, and designers in sixteenth-century Italy and, to a lesser extent, elsewhere in Europe, that deliberately subverts the rediscovered, and generally sober Classicism of the earlier Renaissance, playfully employing and exaggerating elements of the design and decorative motifs in opposition to their original context and meaning. Mannerist architecture, like art of the same style, can appear rather intellectual and self-serving due to its witty specialisms, but some of the greatest architects, such as Michelangelo and Palladio, successfully worked in the Mannerist style.

Manueline

An architectural style particular to Portugal and named after King Manuel (1495–1521). Marking the transition from Late Gothic to the Renaissance, it incorporates decorative designs and architectural strategies encountered during the voyages of contemporary Portuguese explorers to India and beyond.

Mayan

The Mesoamerican civilization occupying the Yucatán Peninsula of present-day Mexico and beyond, between at least 400 BCE to the Spanish Conquest in the mid-sixteenth century CE, noted for its monumental buildings, giant causeways, inscribed landmarks, and painted reliefs. Mayan architecture was produced without metal tools or pulleys and featured stepped temple mounds, corbel arches and—due to the emphasis given to grand external elements such as ceremonial platforms, ball-courts, and temples—rather small internal spaces.

Minimalism

Architecture from which all but the essential structural forms have been expunged and where an explicit attention to the simplicity of materials is evident. Minimalism in architecture can be said to have its origins in the work of early Modernist pioneers such as Mies van der Rohe. While his "less is more" dictum and the work of the Constructivists was influential, Minimalist architecture is less programmatically ideological and creates through the absence of extraneous matter a contemplative space in which the thoughts of the architect and the perceptions of the viewer can meet.

Mission style

The style employed by architects working in California from the late nineteenth century to around 1925, that reflects an interest in sixteenth- and seventeenth-century Spanish colonial architecture in the area, notably in religious mission buildings, in which planar, white walls, simple low rooflines, and uncomplicated massing is evident.

Modernism
The architecture and social theory developed and promulgated in the first few decades of the twentieth century by architects such as Walter Gropius, Mies van der Rohe, and Le Corbusier, in which the eradication of historicism, ornament, and other "superfluous" elements highlighted the practice of architecture as a means of changing society to meet the rigors and opportunities of the Modern era. Rejecting the past and stressing the freedom of the individual, Modernist architecture owed much to the bold innovations of early Industrial architecture, notably in the manufacturing Midlands of the United Kingdom. It emphasized efficiency of performance, functional logic, and visual hygiene in its designs and was linked to the ethos of the machine age. Modernist buildings commonly employ glass facades, steel frames, and concrete for the floors and interior supports. Their floorplans are open and usually unencumbered by the traditional hierarchies of social space common to earlier architecture. The Modernist style became ubiquitous in the design of skyscrapers worldwide, producing urban landscapes that by the 1960s were criticized as sterile and unresponsive to local context.
See **International Style**

Mudéjar
See **Islamic**

Mughal
The Mughal peoples who from 1526 onward conquered the Indian subcontinent creating an empire that by 1700 stretched from modern-day Pakistan in the west, to Afghanistan and Bangladesh in the east and almost all of India. The architectural style incorporates Central Asian and Persian architectural styles with the native Hindi tradition. Characteristic elements include dome-shaped pavilions or *chhatris*, projecting eaves or *chhajjas*, and perforated stone screens.

Muromachi
The period in Japanese history from 1336 to 1573, under the Muromachi shogunate, when Japan established productive relationships with China, with the King of Japan describing himself as the Chinese Emperor's subject. Buddhism, in its Shinto guise, asserted itself as a national culture during this period, drawing inspiration from Chinese models across the arts and architecture.

Neolithic
The culture of the last part of the Stone Age, embracing a wide swath of farming peoples from across the world, and marking the stage of human technological development before the advent of metal tools.

Nguyen
A surname commonly found in Vietnamese culture, representing both a medieval dynastic power network and, to a lesser extent, actual clan ties. It has come to be synonymous with the Nguyen Dynasty that ruled Vietnam between 1802 and 1945.

Ottoman
The Turkish-led civilization that ruled from its capital at Constantinople from 1299 to 1922. Its architectural style emerged from its base in Edirne in the fourteenth and fifteenth centuries, and was based on Byzantine models, although Persian influences were crucial. Mimar Sinan, the sixteenth-century architect, is regarded as the prime exponent of Ottoman architecture, producing public buildings consisting of soaring vaulted ceilings and thin walls.

Typical features of later Ottoman domestic architecture include beautifully carved wooden balconies, projecting oriel window casements, and pierced wooden screens.

Palladian
The style derived from the architecture of Andrea Palladio (1508–80) by architects such as Inigo Jones in England, Jacob van Campen in the Netherlands, and Elias Holl in Germany. Palladio's architecture reworked Classical architectural rules, attempting to fuse ancient Roman ideals with the innovations of the Renaissance and Mannerism. Palladio's work was revived in early eighteenth-century Britain by fashionable avant-garde patrons such as Lord Burlington and architect collaborators such as William Kent.

Plateresque
An ornate form of Spanish architecture, especially the external facades of fifteenth- and sixteenth-century buildings in Spain and its colonial possessions, on which stucco, terra cotta, and other materials are carved with complex, swirling designs that resemble the craftwork of contemporaneous silversmiths (or *plateros*). Often unrelated to the structure of the building on which it has been applied, it is essentially a regional variant of Mannerism.

Postmodernism
An often fiercely critical engagement with the theories, programs, and architecture of Modernism, in which the latter's distrust of ornament and regional reference is turned on its head. Growing from the mid-1960s onward, it questions the rigorous precepts of Modernism and its fundamentalist subgenre, Functionalism. Postmodernist architecture employs decoration, color, and a certain playful self-referencing, occasionally drawing on Classical precedent

in its use of basic geometrical forms. Irony and apparent contradiction sum up the character of many buildings in this style.

Plečnik

The various architectural styles produced by the hugely talented, but artistically opportunistic Slovenian architect Jože Plečnik (1872–1957).

Prairie School

A late nineteenth-century style common to domestic buildings found in the American Midwest, with Frank Lloyd Wright its pioneering talent. A subgenre of the U.S. Arts and Crafts movement, Prairie style houses display expressive horizontality, with large overhanging roof eaves and ground-hugging, geometrically precise forms around the chimneys. A joyous use of local materials is often evident.

Pre-Columbian

The culture and peoples of America before the landing of Christopher Columbus in 1492 on American soil. The term also describes the indigenous cultures that briefly remained free of European influence immediately after this date.

Rajput

A Hindu caste, referring to a large population occupying modern-day Rajasthan, India. Rajput kingdoms rose to power in the seventh century, and ruled until the twelfth century, when Mughal invasions resulted in the subjugation of Rajput fiefdoms to Muslim authority, with Rajput-Mughal intermarriages a common feature among the nobility as the Mughal empire expanded.

Renaissance

The important shift in Western thought and artistic practice that developed between the fourteenth and seventeenth centuries, starting in Italy, specifically Siena, Florence, and Rome, and spreading across the whole of Europe. Renaissance art and architecture demonstrates an archaeologically-driven interest in the Classical heritage of ancient Greece and Rome, exploring its forms, ideals, and literature, and leading to advances in a range of scientific, philosophical, and artistic disciplines. The development of visual perspective was one of its immediate fruits. Renaissance architecture varies greatly in the degree to which it accurately reflects Classical precedent, but it should be seen as an ongoing dialogue between the past and present. Its impact continues today, with the use of an abstracted Classical architectural vocabulary in much Postmodern and even Modernist architecture.

Rococo

The style in the decorative arts and interior design that arose initially in France in the early years of the eighteenth century, spreading to Germany, Italy, and much of the rest of Europe (although it was rarely adopted in Britain and only with considerable caution). Charmingly inventive and characterized by a lightness of form, expressive assymetry, with curling, frondlike forms, and an opulent use of gold, it spoke of a change in attitudes following the reign of the French king Louis XIV, and a move among courtly society toward greater sensuality and playfulness. Some buildings, such as garden pavilions and other structures designed for temporary use, were constructed in the Rococo style, but it was rarely used for civic architecture, being instead the preferred style of rich patrons seeking relaxed private settings for themselves and their collections.

Romanesque

The style of architecture produced in Europe between the eleventh and twelfth centuries, featuring clearly comprehensible floorplans and elevations, often including rounded arches, barrel vaults, piers of evident section, and a bold use of geometrically patterned or figurative carving, particularly on the capitals of pillars. So-named by later historians to reflect the efforts of European stonemasons to emulate the achievements of Roman architecture, the Romanesque may have its origins in the architecture produced under the Carolingian kings of France between the seventh to tenth centuries. It precedes the lighter, more delicate architectural instincts of Gothic architecture, but is viewed highly for its sobriety of tone, emotional clarity, and sheer mastery of form. In the United Kingdom, the style is known as Norman, after the conquest of England by the Normans in the eleventh century.

Saadian

See **Islamic**

Safavid

See **Islamic**

Sailendra with Gupta influence

The architecture of the Buddhist and Hindu kingdom of Saliendra that occupied the Kedu Plain in the South-Central region of the island of Java, now part of Indonesia, rising to prominence between the seventh and eighth centuries. Borobudur is the culture's most famous architectural masterpiece. The Gupta empire occupied Northern India until around 550 CE, and had widespread trading links with the civilizations of the Indian Ocean and South East Asia in general.

Saminid

See **Islamic**

Sassanid

See **Islamic**

Seljuk

A Turkic people who arrived on the Anatolian plateau from Central Asia in the mid-eleventh century onward, carving out a massive empire in the Middle East that ranged from present-day Turkey, the Levant, and Persia to Afghanistan, Turkmenistan and beyond. Their architecture blended innovations drawn from Persian, Greek, and Arab sources and reached its peak in the twelfth century, with fine examples still existing in modern-day Iran. Their empire was depleted by Mongol invasions, with Turkic power in the region only reviving under their successors, the Ottomans.

Shaybanid
See **Islamic**

Shingle
An architectural style generally produced in the Eastern and North Western regions of the United States of America during the late nineteenth century, displaying a patriotic affection for the early buildings of the nation's seventeenth-century settlers. Shingle features deliberately aged roofs, often of low-profile, combined with turrets and gables to produce an eclectic silhouette, although inside the buildings are often roomy and well-appointed.

Sikh
The culture and architecture of the Sikh-dominated region of the Punjab in northern India. Sikh buildings, notably the *gurdwaras* or temples, have four basic types of floorplans—square, rectangular, octagonal, and cruciform—and they usually have domed roofs and elevations pierced by doorways on all sides, representing the openness of the faith to all. The interior and exterior facades tend to be highly decorated, with copper-gilt sheathing, inlay work (or *jaratkari*), plaster-of-Paris molding, or lattice serving as common features.

Spanish Colonial
The broadly Baroque vernacular style of architecture produced by the colonial settlers of the Spanish empire, who from the mid-sixteenth century onward

founded missions and urban centers in the "New World" of the North and South American continents.

Sudano-Sahelian
An architectural style found in the Sahel—the zone cutting horizontally across Africa and dividing the coastal Mahgreb cultures from the black African states south of the Sahara. Notable Sudano-Sahelian buildings from the sixteenth and seventeenth centuries remain the products of the Mali and Songhay empires centered in West Africa.

Sumerian
The culture of the geographical region lying between the Tigris and Euphrates Rivers in present-day Iraq.

Taoism
A loosely defined set of religious or philosophical beliefs of unknown ancient origin, deriving from mainland China but manifest throughout East Asia, united only by some core principles. These center on the wisdom of working with and not against Nature and universal harmony. The fulfilment of personal ego is seen as less preferable than the passive yielding to the flow of universal forces in which Nature plays a major role.

Timurid
See **Islamic**

Tudor
The period of English history under the rule of the Tudor dynasty from 1485 to 1603, in which buildings often feature half-timbering, steep roofs, narrow windows with fields of small glass panes, and highly decorative, sculptural chimneys. Oriel, or bay windows, are a speciality of Tudor architecture.

Tulunid
See **Islamic**

Umayyad
See **Islamic**

Venetian
The architectural style fostered by the Venetians from the fourteenth century onward, both in Venice and along their imperial outposts on the Adriatic and Ionian coasts. Venetian arched windows combine Byzantine, Arab, and Gothic influences, although the Venetian triple section window—much used by Palladio in the sixteenth century in his villas on the Veneto—is entirely different. Venetian Gothic was revived across Europe following the 1851–3 publication of British critic John Ruskin's book *The Stones of Venice*.

Victorian
The culture and architecture produced from 1837 to 1901, chiefly in the United Kingdom under the rule of Queen Victoria, but more generally describing the diversity of European architecture produced during the period, in which swings of taste between Gothic Revival and Classical styles produced initially imaginative reinterpretations of either strand as well as highly original combinations of these and other styles. Later, these reinterpretations became fixated by historicist polemic and were rebutted by a series of reformist movements, including the Arts and Crafts style in the United Kingdom.

Victorian Stick
An architectural style produced broadly in the United States of America during the late nineteenth century, featuring chiefly wooden elevations, integrated towers and turrets, wrap-around verandahs, decorative trimming on the roofline, steeply pitched gables and porches, and much finely turned wooden decorative edging. Not unlike Shingle-style architecture, but less solid in feel.

Viennese Secession
See **Art Nouveau**

Location Index

Page numbers in *italic* refer to illustrations.

Contributors

Florencia Alvarez (FA) studied architecture at the University of Buenos Aires, where she has been teaching since 2000. She has worked on collective projects that bring together experts and nonexperts to discuss urban topics, such as *Flood!* (2002) and *Chatheater* (2006). She has contributed to *Summa+* and to *Purple Journal*. She currently edits the architecture magazine, *UR*.

Anna Amari-Parker (AA) has traveled through Europe, Asia, and Latin America as a writer and editor. She has written on Dante Alighieri's *Divine Comedy* and contributed to the Encyclopedia of Decorative Arts. She lives and works in London.

Matthew Barac (MJB) teaches, writes about, and practices architecture. His research investigates the tension between symbolic and practical interpretations of South African cities, and his project "From Township to Town" won the 3rd International Bauhaus Award. He lives in London.

Charles Barclay (CB) is an architect, triathlete, and writer based in London. His practice recently won an international competition to design an all-timber observatory at Kielder, in Northumberland, England.

Juliet Barclay (JB) is a designer and writer working in London and Havana. She is the author of *Havana: Portrait of a City* (1996). She was formerly manager of the Oficina of the Restoration of Old Havana.

Kathy Batista (KAB) is Director of the MA Contemporary Art program at Sotheby's Institute of Art, New York. She has written extensively on art and architecture, and is the author of a forthcoming book about feminist art in Britain from the 1970s to 1990s.

Mary Beard (MB) is Professor of Classics at the University of Cambridge and Fellow of Newnham College; she is also Classics Editor of the *Times Literary Supplement*. Her books include *The Parthenon*, *The Invention of Jane Harrison*, and *The Roman Triumph*.

Jonathan Bell (JBL) is contributing architecture editor at *Wallpaper* magazine, where he also writes about automotive design. He has contributed to numerous art and design publications, and is the author of the books *Penthouse Living* and *21st Century House*.

Richard Bell (RDB) studied Visual Cultures at the University of Derby and completed a postgraduate Diploma in Publishing at the London College of Printing. He currently works for an educational publisher in London and as a freelance writer.

Pablo Bernard (PAB) studied architecture and fashion at the University of Buenos Aires, where he has been teaching since 2003. Currently he is editor of *Morgue*, a men's fashion magazine.

Will Black (WB) is Public Relations Manager for the UK office of the World Monuments Fund. He has written a book on Catherine the Great and, when not listening to the Pet Shop Boys, produces occasional features for the BBC's Russian Service.

Gavin Blyth (GB) studied for a Masters in architectural history before working for the Royal Institute of British Architects and going on to edit a photography magazine. He is now a freelance writer and editor specializing in architecture, design, and photography.

Roberto Bottazzi (RB) studied at the University of Florence and the University of British Columbia in Vancouver before moving to London in 2004. He teaches at the Royal College of Art and has exhibited his work and lectured in Italy, the United States, Canada, Austria, and Sweden.

Katherine Boyle (KGB) graduated from Bristol University with a first-class degree in History of Art, and has since been working as a Projects Assistant at the World Monuments Fund in Britain.

Alex Bremner (GAB) is an architectural historian at the University of Edinburgh. He studied architecture in Australia before moving to Britain to study at Cambridge University. He specializes in the history of nineteenth- and twentieth-century architecture.

Alex Brew (ADB) is a freelance writer with a focus on the arts and architecture. Her interest in temple and mosque architecture has been built on her extensive travel in the Indian subcontinent. She also promotes the arts and architecture at University College London (UCL), including at the UCL Bartlett.

Timothy Brittain-Catlin (TBC) has practiced as an architect and urban designer and now teaches the history and theory of architecture at the Architectural Association School of Architecture, London. He is a regular contributor to *The World of Interiors*.

Victor Buchli (VB) is Reader in Material Culture in the Department of Anthropology, University College London. He has written extensively on the Narkomfin (*An Archaeology of Socialism*) and is editor of *Home Cultures*, an interdisciplinary journal about the domestic sphere.

Barnabas Calder (BWC) is an architectural historian specializing in Modern architecture since World

War II. His particular interest is in the work of Sir Denys Lasdun and his fellow British Modernists, but he has also worked on Medieval and Baroque architecture.

Abe Cambier (AC) is an architect in Portland, Oregon, USA. He holds a graduate degree in architecture from the University of Oregon and an undergraduate degree from Michigan State University.

Jennie Cambier (JC) is an architect who lives, works, and plays in Portland, Oregon, USA. She holds a graduate degree in architecture from the University of Oregon and an undergraduate degree from Middlebury College in Vermont.

Neil Manson Cameron (NC) is an art historian and critic with a specialism in Scottish art and architecture. He works for the Royal Commission on the Ancient and Historical Monuments of Scotland and has published in various journals, newspapers, and magazines.

Mary Cooch (MC) is a freelance magazine and book journalist with a BA (Hons.) degree in History from London University. One of her special interests is pre-Renaissance art and architecture.

Louise Cooke (LC) is an archaeologist with a special interest in the archaeology, conservation, and contemporary use of earthen architecture. Her research has focused on Central Asia and in particular the World Heritage Site of Merv, Turkmenistan.

Michael DaCosta (MDC) has worked in the creative industries for more than seventeen years. He was cochair of the 2003 World Creative Forum, at Bloomberg London HQ, during the first London Design Festival. He also lectures, and is a contributing editor to *Art and Architecture Journal*.

Irina Davidovici (ID) is an architect based in London, where she has worked for Herzog & de Meuron on Tate Modern and the Laban Centre. She is currently writing her doctoral thesis at Cambridge University on contemporary Swiss architecture.

Edward Denison (ED) is a heritage consultant, writer, and photographer based in London and Shanghai. He has worked and published books on architectural heritage in Europe, Africa, and China, and is currently undertaking research on the influence of Modernism in China.

Antony Eastmond (AE) is Reader in the History of Byzantine Art at the Courtauld Institute of Art, University of London. He has a special interest in the arts of the Caucasus and artistic interchange with Islam.

Daniel Edon (DE) studied English Literature at the Roehampton Institute. He has written for the *North Eastern Evening Gazette* and for several style and fashion fanzines. He is an avid fan of the work of Peter Marino. Daniel lives in London and works for the publishing wing of the Chartered Insurance Institute.

Marie-Hélène Fabre (MHF) is an architect and researcher in urban planning and design. She is writing about the urban evolution of the Seoul metropolitan region in South Korea for her Ph.D. at Ecole Nationale des Ponts et Chaussées in France. She currently works as Education coordinator at the Ecole Speciale d'Architecture in Paris, France.

Marcus Field (MF) studied English and art history before working as a journalist at *The Architects' Journal*. He became editor of the art and design magazine *Blueprint* before moving to the *Independent on Sunday*, where he worked as the arts editor. He is the coauthor of *Lofts* and author of a monograph on the British architectural practice, Future Systems.

Henry Fletcher (HF) is a London-based architect with particular interests in urban development and earth construction. He has worked on projects in West Africa, Central and South Asia.

Jade Franklin (JF) studied History of Art at the University of Bristol. She lives in Shanghai, where she divides her time between working as a freelance writer and at the gallery, Shine Art Space.

Mads Gaardboe (MG) is Professor of Architecture and Head of the Louis Laybourne Smith School of Architecture and Design, University of South Australia. He studied architecture at the Royal Danish Academy of Art and Columbia University and has practiced in East Africa, the UK, and Australia.

Beatrice Galilee (BG) is a freelance architectural writer. She trained in architecture at Bath University and began writing for magazines and newspapers while studying. She is news editor for *Icon* magazine and a regular contributor to *Building Design*, *Frame* and *RIBA Journal*.

Eleanor Gawne (EG) is Assistant Director (Drawings and Archives Collections) at the British Architectural Library, RIBA. She cocurated the V&A + RIBA Architecture Gallery, and coauthored *Exploring Architecture: Buildings, Meaning and Making* (2004). Her specialism is twentieth-century British architecture.

Grant Gibson (GG) is an architecture and design journalist. A former editor of *Blueprint*, Grant has contributed to the *Observer*, *New Statesman*, *RIBA Journal*, *Frame*, and *Grafik*. He is also a contributing editor to the Dutch architecture title, *Mark*.

Maximilian Gwiazda (MJG) is from Munich. He is finishing his Ph.D. in the History and Philosophy of Architecture at Cambridge University, while working in Paris and Rome on postdoctoral fellowships.

Lucinda Hawksley (LH) is an art historian, biographer, and freelance writer, with a specialism in the nineteenth and early twentieth centuries. She is also a patron of the Charles Dickens Museum in London. She has written articles for magazines including *tate etc*, *English Heritage*, and *Time Out*. Her books include *Essential Pre-Raphaelites* and *Katey: The Life and Loves of Dickens's Artist Daughter*.

Florian Heilmeyer (FH) works and lives in Berlin. He studied architecture there and since 1996 has worked as a journalist writing about architecture, art, design, and town planning. He is a regular contributor to magazines in Germany, Austria, and Switzerland, including *Bauwelt*, *Deutsches Architektenblatt*, and *Graz Architecture Magazine*, and the architecture website *Werk.Bauen+Wohnen*.

Christian Hiller (CH) lives and works as a curatorial assistant in Berlin. He has an M.Phil. in media studies and has undertaken research at the Anthology Film Archives in New York. He is currently working on his postgraduate doctoral thesis "Landscape, Place and Space in the American Avant-garde."

Charles Hind (CWH) is Assistant Director (Special Collections) and H. J. Heinz Curator of Drawings at RIBA's British Architectural Library, which is housed at the Victoria & Albert Museum.

Jennifer Hudson (JH) is head of research at Laurence King Publishing and a freelance writer.

Jeremy Hunt (JEH) studied History of Art at Essex University and Goldsmiths College, London. He is editor of *The Art & Architecture Journal* and a freelance writer on art and architecture. He lives in Paris and London.

Richard Ingersoll (RI) is an architectural author whose books include *Sprawltown* and Volume One of *World Architecture: A Critical Mosaic*. He teaches at Syracuse University in Florence and writes as a critic for several international architecture magazines and newspapers.

Mark Irving (MI) is a writer, editor, and broadcaster, as well as a lecturer at Central Saint Martins, University of the Arts, London. He works with museums and arts organizations devising new content and enlivening their displays and publications. He is the General Editor of *1001 Buildings You Must See Before You Die*.

Denna Jones (DJ) is a U.S.-born, London-based writer, designer, and consultant who grew up in houses ranging from a Shoji-screen suburban in Hawaii to a mid-twentieth-century Modern in California. She works on urban design schemes across England.

Frank Kelsall (FK) has over forty years' experience in the preservation of historic buildings. After retiring from the conservation organization English Heritage in 1998, he founded the Architectural History Practice. He is currently President of the Society of Architectural Historians of Great Britain.

Carol King (CMK) is a freelance journalist. She has a degree in English Literature from the University of Sussex, and studied Fine Art at Central Saint Martins, London. She was delighted to write about some of the buildings she has seen during her world travels.

Riikka Kuittinen (RK) graduated in 2001 with a Masters degree from Goldsmiths College, London. Since then she has written about art and design, curated the Victoria & Albert Museum Print Collections, and worked on major exhibitions.

Bartek Kumor (BK) graduated from the department of architecture at the Silesian Technical University in Gliwice, Poland. He now lives and works in England, as an architect.

Phyllis Lambert (PL) is an architect and the Founding Director and Chair of the Board of Trustees of the Canadian Centre for Architecture. She is known internationally for her contribution to advancing contemporary architecture and for her concern for the social issues of urban conservation, and the role of architecture in the public realm.

Lucinda Lambton (LL) is a writer, photographer, and broadcaster who has worked both behind and in front of the lens nosing out architectural and historic flights of fancy. She has researched, written, and presented many films, including the BBC television series *Lucinda Lambton's Alphabet of Britain*. Her many books include *Temples of Convenience*, the best-selling history of the lavatory.

Signe Mellergaard Larsen (SML) has a Masters degree in Art History, from the Courtauld Institute of Art, London and a BA (Hons.) in Art History, from Plymouth University. She is a freelance writer, based in Copenhagen, and her research focuses on Nordic art and architecture from the nineteenth to twenty-first centuries.

Sophie Leighton (SL) is an assistant curator at the Victoria & Albert Museum, London, and previously edited and wrote guidebooks for National Trust properties, including mills, gardens, and country houses.

Bart Lootsma (BL) is Professor for Architectural Theory at Leopold-Franzens University, Innsbruck, Austria. He is a historian, critic, and curator in the fields of architecture, design, and the visual arts. He was an editor of *Forum de Architect* and *ARCHIS*, and his books include *Media and Architecture* and *The Naked City*.

Sally Mackay (SJM) studied architecture at Cambridge University and now works as an architect in London for Penoyre & Prasad. In 2005, she traveled to Ethiopia to visit the buildings of Lalibela, Aksum, Gonder, and Bahar Dar.

Brendan McCarthy (BMC) is arts editor of the weekly Catholic journal, *The Tablet*. He previously worked as a producer with BBC radio and television, and with the Irish broadcasting service, RTE.

Justin McGuirk (JMc) is editor of *Icon* magazine. He has written about architecture and design for numerous magazines and newspapers, as well as contributing to books and television programs. He has traveled extensively in the Middle East and Central Asia.

Alexandra McIntosh (ASM) writes on architecture, art, and urban issues in Canada. A member of the Centre de recherche urbaine de Montréal, she curates artistic projects that seek to engage the city. She is a writer and editor at the Canadian Centre for Architecture (CCA).

Jamie Middleton (JM) is a freelance writer and editor for various lifestyle magazines and books. Based in Bath, he has worked on a range of diverse subjects, from the Milau Bridge and Jaguar cars to laptops and fine wines.

Adam Mornement (AM) is a writer whose books include, *Corrugated Iron—Building on the Frontier, Extensions, Treehouses,* and *No Longer Notorious*.

Alison Morris (AMR) is a writer specializing in the fields of architecture and design. She

has worked in the studio of architect John Pawson for the past six years, and in 2002 she also edited the catalogues of the 8th Venice Architecture Biennale.

Stephen Anthony Murphy (SAM) has worked as an archaeologist in Ireland, England, France, Thailand, Singapore, and Japan. He is currently working on a Ph.D. in Southeast Asian archaeology at the School of Oriental and African Studies in London.

Yves Nacher (YN) is an architect, architecture critic, and a curator. He is head of the architecture department of the cultural agency of the French ministry of Foreign Affairs.

Fabrizio Nevola (FN) is Senior Lecturer in the History of Architecture at Oxford Brookes University. He received his Ph.D. from the Courtauld Institute of Art, London. He held fellowships at the Canadian Centre for Architecture (Montreal) and Harvard University's Villa I Tatti (Florence). He is the author of *Siena: Constructing the Renaissance City*.

John Julius Norwich (JJN) is the author of histories of Byzantium, Venice, and the Mediterranean. He has written and lectured on various aspects of world architecture and made a six-part television series for the BBC on the Antiquities of Turkey.

Giles Omezi (GO) is of mixed Nigerian and Jamaican parentage and studied architecture at the University of East London. He has worked for a number of UK-based architectural practices. He is currently Executive Director of Bukka, an urban research trust in London.

Fiona Orsini (FO) is Assistant Curator of the Drawings and Archives Collections at RIBA in London. She previously worked at the Museum of London on the Exploring Twentieth-Century London website.

Tamsin Pickeral (TP) is a freelance writer and researcher specializing in art, architecture, and horses. Her recent books include *30,000 Years of the Horse in Art, The Horse Owner's Bible, Van Gogh,* and *Charles Rennie Mackintosh*.

Alan Powers (AP) is an architectural historian and the author of numerous books, including *Britain: Modern Architectures in History, Modern: The Modern Movement in Britain, Living with Books,* and *The Twentieth Century House in Britain*. He teaches at the University of Greenwich in London.

Mark Powers (MP) works as an architect in London. He occasionally lectures at Cambridge University, where he studied, and at the Welsh School of Architecture in Cardiff. He has published articles in several journals, including *ARCHIS, Architecture Today,* and *Blueprint*. He is particularly interested in the relationships between architecture, people, and the city.

Joona Repo (JR) is currently engaged in Ph.D. research on Tibetan Buddhist refugee architecture in South Asia at the School of Oriental and African Studies in London. He specializes in Tibetan Buddhism and Tibetan art and culture in general.

Eddy Rhead (ER) is a freelance writer and photographer based in Manchester, England. He has a special interest in twentieth-century architecture and is Secretary of the North West Group of the Twentieth Century Society.

Frank Ritter (FR) is a freelance writer and editor specializing in architecture, gardens, and the visual arts. Most recently he edited *1001 Gardens You Must See Before You Die*.

Tsuto Sakamoto (TS) graduated from Waseda University in Tokyo and Columbia University in New York. He worked for Bernard Tschumi

Architects and Stan Allen Architects as a designer and currently teaches architectural design and theory at the National University of Singapore.

Justine Sambrook (JS) is an Assistant Curator at the Royal Institute of British Architects' Drawings and Archives Collections. She was cocurator of *On the Threshold: The Changing Face of Housing*, an exhibition in the V&A + RIBA Architecture Gallery at the Victoria & Albert Museum in London.

Emile G. L. Schrijver (EGS) is curator of the Bibliotheca Rosenthaliana, the Hebraica and Judaica special collection at Amsterdam University Library in the Netherlands. He is editor-in-chief of the yearbook, *Studia Rosenthaliana*. He has published on the history of Hebrew books and manuscripts, catalogued for auctioneers, bookdealers, and collectors, and contributed to numerous international exhibitions.

Bidisha Sinha (BS) works with Zaha Hadid Architects. She studied architecture at the School of Habitat Studies in New Delhi, India, where she graduated in 2000. She completed her Masters degree in Architecture and Urbanism at the Architectural Association in London. She is a licensed member of the Council of Architecture, India.

Ellie Stathaki (ES) was born in Greece and trained as an architect and architectural historian there, before moving to live in London's East End. She works at *Wallpaper* magazine, writes about architecture, and contributes regularly to the architectural press.

Sofia Sundstrom (IS) has a Masters degree in History of Art and is now undertaking a second Masters in Art and Archaeology at the School of Oriental and African Studies in London. She has written about the Swedish textile artist, Karin Larsson.

David Taylor (DT) is a freelance journalist specializing in architecture, property, and design. He is editor of the *London Property Review* and *Retail Property Review* and is also a member of the Commission for Architecture and the Built Environment's panel of writers in London.

Lars Teichmann (LT) is an Associate at Zaha Hadid Architects. Before joining the office in 2000, he studied architecture and urbanism at the Architectural Association in London, and in Germany. His work focuses in particular on investigating the interaction of spatial complexity and its functionality.

David Theodore (DMT) is a Research Associate at the School of Architecture, McGill University, Canada, where he teaches architectural design and studies the history of health-care architecture. He is also contributing editor at the design and architecture magazine, *Azure*, and is regional correspondent for *Canadian Architect*.

Abraham Thomas (AT) is Curator of Designs at the Victoria & Albert Museum in London. He curated the exhibition *Full Tilt*, which explored graphic design and photography at *Harpers Bazaar* and *Vogue* magazines in the 1940s and 1950s. He also cocurated *On The Threshold: The Changing Face of Housing*.

Gemma Tipton (GT) is a writer and critic of contemporary art and architecture based in Dublin. She writes for the *Irish Times* and is the author of *Space: Architecture for Art*.

Aidan Turner-Bishop (ATB) is a retired academic librarian. He is Chair of the North West England group of the Twentieth Century Society.

Juan Pablo Vacas (JPV) studied at the Contemporary Architecture Studies Center of Torcuato Di Tella University and the University of

Buenos Aires where he has been teaching since 2005. He contributes to several architectural publications.

Leon van Schaik (LVS) is Professor of Architecture (Innovation Chair) at RMIT University in Melbourne, Australia. His latest books are *Mastering Architecture* and *Design City Melbourne*.

Chakradhar Vittala (CV) studied architecture in Canada. She now works in London for the architectural practice Penoyre & Prasad.

Roger White (RW) is an architectural historian. He is a Fellow of the Society of Antiquaries, a contributing editor of *House & Garden* magazine, and the author of many books, catalogues, and articles.

Philip Wilkinson (PW) is the author of many books on architecture and history, including *The English Buildings Book* and *English Abbeys*. He also wrote the three volumes accompanying the BBC TV series *Restoration* and *Restoration Village*.

Katti Williams (KW) is a doctoral student at the University of Melbourne, Australia. Her thesis examines selected themes in the architecture, symbolism, and experience of large-scale World War I memorials across the world.

Rob Wilson (RGW) is an architect, curator, and writer, who works at the Royal Institute of British Architects as the Curator of Exhibitions. Recent exhibitions include *On the Threshold: the Changing Face of Housing* at the Victoria & Albert Museum and *Fantasy Architecture: 1500-2036* at the Hayward Gallery in London.

Yasushi Zenno (YZ) studied architectural history at Columbia University and is now working on his doctoral dissertation in Tokyo. He writes on architecture and contributed a chapter to the book *Charlotte Perriand: An Art of Living*.

Picture Credits

Karlsson - BKWinecom/Alamy **371 B:** Tony Morrison/South American Pictures **372** Per Karlsson - BKWinecom/Alamy **373 T:** Richard Bryant/Arcaid **373 B:** Richard Bryant/Arcaid **374 T:** Free Agents Limited/Corbis **374 B:** Svenja-Foto/zefa/Corbis **375 T:** Bernie Epstein/Alamy **375 B:** Bernie Epstein/Alamy **376** Joe Cornish/Arcaid **377** Arcaid/Alamy **378** Roland Halbe/Artur/View **379** Jochen Helle/Artur **380** Michael Freeman/Corbis **381** en:user:Fg2/© ARS, NY and DACS, London 2007 **382** Schuetze/Rodemann/akg-images **383** Murat Taner/zefa/Corbis **384 T:** Kevin Foy/Alamy **384 B:** Asia Photopress/Alamy **385 T:** Michael Jenner/Alamy **385 B:** Francesco Venturi/Corbis **386 T:** Arcaid/Alamy/©DACS, London 2007 **386 B:** Nathan Willock/View/©DACS, London 2007 **387 T:** ImageState/Alamy **387 B:** Bildagentur Hamburg/Alamy **388 T:** Pitu Cau/Alamy **388 B:** Paul Thompson; Eye Ubiquitous/Corbis **391 T:** Peter Horree/Alamy/©DACS, London 2007 **391 B:** Erich Lessing/akg-images/©DACS, London 2007 **392** Paul Raftery/View **393** Bildarchiv Monheim/akg-images **394 T:** Roland Halbe/Artur/View/©DACS, London 2007 **394 B:** Hilbich/akg-images/©DACS, London 2007 **395 T:** Index Stock Imagery/Photolibrary Group **395 B:** CSappa/Photolibrary Group **397 T:** Bildarchiv Monheim GmbH/Alamy/©DACS, London 2007 **397 B:** Bildarchiv Monheim GmbH/Alamy/©DACS, London 2007 **398** Dennis MacDonald/Alamy **399** Luc Boegly/Artedia/View/©DACS, London 2007 **400 T:** Patrik Engquist/Etsa/Corbis **400 B:** Sara Fhölenhag & Erik Holmqvist **402** David Clapp/Arcaid/©DACS, London 2007 **403** Tim Street-Porter/Esto/View **405 T:** Alexander Artamonov/fotoLibra/©DACS, London 2007 **405 B:** Tomas Riehle/Artur/View/©DACS, London 2007 **406** Luc Boegly/Artedia/View **407** Paul Raftery/View/©FLC/ADAGP, Paris and DACS, London 2007 **408 T:** Bildarchiv Monheim/Arcaid **408 B:** Bildarchiv Monheim GmbH/Alamy **410** Peter Mauss/ESTO/Arcaid **411** George Hammerstein/Solus-Veer/Corbis **412** Arcaid/Alamy **413** Richard Bryant/Arcaid **415 T:** Bildarchiv Monheim/Arcaid **415 B:** Bildarchiv Monheim/Arcaid **416** Collection Artedia/View **417** Jan Butchofsky-Houser/Corbis **419 T:** Bildarchiv Monheim/Arcaid **419 B:** Profimedia International sro/Alamy **420** Martyn Vickery/Alamy **421** Alain Nogues/Corbis Sygma **423 T:** Natalie Tepper/Arcaid **423 B:** Worldwide Picture Library/Alamy **424** Jeremy Horner/Corbis **425** Bildarchiv Monheim GmbH/Alamy **426** Bruce Coleman Inc/Alamy **427** Peter Mauss/ESTO/Arcaid **429 T:** Lightworks Media/Alamy **429 B:** Lightworks Media/Alamy **430 T:** Directphotoorg/Alamy **430 B:** Olivier Nord/Artedia/View **431 T:** Michael Halberstadt/Arcaid **431 B:** Collection Artedia/View **432 T:** Paul Thompson Images/Alamy **432 B:** Michael St Maur Sheil/Corbis **434** Yogi, Inc/Corbis **435** Nicholas Kane/Arcaid/Corbis **437** Kevin Foy/Alamy **438** Wolfgang Kaehler/Corbis **439** Andrea Jemolo/Corbis **440** Graeme and Pamela Shell/Photographers Direct **441** Courtesy Glaspaleis Heerlen **442 T:** Edifice **442 B:** Angelo Hornak/Corbis **444 T L:** Lee Snider/Photo Images/Corbis **444 T R:** imagebroker/Alamy **444 B L:** blickwinkel/Alamy **444 B R:** Aga Khan Trust for Culture **445 T:** Photo: Martti Kapanen, Alvar Aalto Museum **445 B:** National Trust Photolibrary/Alamy **446** Bernie Epstein/Alamy **447** Collection Artedia/View **448** Peter Cook/View **449** Klaus Frahm/Artur/View **450** Frank Nowikowski/South American Pictures **452** Andrew Garn **453** Andrew Garn **454** Daniel Kerek/Photographers Direct **455** f1 online/Alamy **457 T:** ©Edward Denison **457 B:** Jack Barker/Alamy **458 T:** Ian Middleton/Photographers Direct **458 B:** Jurij Skrlj/Photographers Direct **459 T:** Collection Artedia/View **459 B:** Eric Preau/Sygma/Corbis **460** Peter Cook/View **461** Richard A Cooke/Corbis/©ARS, NY and DACS, London 2007 **462** Andrew Hasson/Alamy **463** Photo: Martti Kapanen, Alvar Aalto Museum **465 T:** Bettmann/Corbis **465 B:** Lynn Goldsmith/Corbis **466** Courtesy Kyrkogårdsförvaltningen **467** Joel W Rogers/Corbis **468** Bildarchiv Monheim GmbH/Alamy **469** Will Pryce/Thames & Hudson/Arcaid **471 T:** wwwadamspicturelibrarycom_**471 B:** World Illustrated/Photoshot **472 T:** Jason P Howe/South American Pictures **472 B:** Jason P Howe/South American Pictures **473 T:** Roberto Schezen/Esto/View **473 B:** Andrea Jemolo/Corbis **475** Andrea Pistolesi/Tips Images **476** orkneypics/Alamy **477 T:** Alan Weintraub/Arcaid **477 B:** Alan Weintraub/Arcaid **478** Aga Khan Trust for Culture **479** David Sundberg/Esto/View **480 T:** Stijn Rolies/©DACS, London 2007 **480 B:** John Mitchell/Photographers Direct/©DACS, London 2007 **481 T:** Collection Artedia/View **481 B:** Collection Artedia/View **482** **483** David Lees/Corbis **484** Richard Bryant/Arcaid **485** Alan Weintraub/Arcaid/©DACS, London 2007 **486** Guenter Lachmuth/akg-images/©DACS, London 2007 **487** Paul Raftery/View/©FLC/ADAGP, Paris and DACS, London 2007 **489** Edifice **490** George Carter/Alamy **491** David LaSpina/Esto/View **492** Bildarchiv Monheim/Arcaid/©FLC/ADAGP, Paris and DACS, London 2007 **493** Dennis Gilbert/View **494** Alan Weintraub/Arcaid **495** Olivier Martin Gambier - FLC/Artedia/View/©FLC/ADAGP, Paris and DACS, London 2007 **496** Bildarchiv Monheim/Arcaid/©FLC/ADAGP, Paris and DACS, London 2007 **497** Ron Formby/Scottie Press **498 T:** Thomas A Heinz/Corbis **498 B:** DarleneBordwellcom/Photographers Direct **499 T:** ©2007 Barragan Foundation, Birsfelden, Switzerland/ProLitteris/©DACS, London 2007 **499 B:** ©2007 Barragan Foundation, Birsfelden, Switzerland/ProLitteris/©DACS, London 2007 **501 T:** Chris Hellier/Corbis/©FLC/ADAGP, Paris and DACS, London 2007 **501 B:** Stephane Couturier - FLC/Artedia/View/©FLC/ADAGP, Paris and DACS, London 2007 **502** Sherab/Alamy **503** ©DACS, London 2007 **504** Stijn Rolies **505** Kenneth Hamm/Photo Japan **506** AA World Travel Library/Alamy **507** World Pictures/Alamy **508 T:** Sylvie Bersout/Artedia/View **508 B:** Levilly/Andie/fotofinder/IPN **509 T:** David Rubinger/Corbis **509 B:** Israel images/Alamy **510** Luc Boegly/Artedia/View **511** Angelo Hornak/Corbis/©DACS, London 2007 **512** Architekturphoto/Arcaid **513** David Lees/Corbis **515 T:** Andrew Wong/Reuters/Corbis **515 B:** Carl & Ann Purcell/Corbis **516** Hervé Champollion/akg-images **517** Bildagentur/Tips Images **518 T:** David Sundberg/Esto/View**518 B:** David Sundberg/Esto/View **520** Architekturphoto/Arcaid **521** Alan Weintraub/Arcaid **523 T:** John Edward Linden/Arcaid **523 B:** John Edward Linden/Arcaid **524** Bildarchiv Monheim/Arcaid **525** Edifice **526 T:** John Perrin/View **526 B:** John Perrin/View **529 T:** Ted Streshinsky/ **529 B:** Ezra Stoller/ESTO **530** World Illustrated/Photoshot **531** Horst Ossinger/dpa/Corbis **32 T:** Chris George/Alamy **532 B:** Robert Harding Picture Library Ltd/Alamy **534** John Edward Linden/Arcaid **535** Kokyat Choong/Alamy **536 T:** Richard Bryant/Arcaid **536 B:** Bildarchiv Monheim GmbH/Alamy **537 T:** Jeremy Cockayne/Arcaid **537 B:** Richard Einzig/Arcaid **539 T:** Sara Fhölenhag & Erik Holmqvist **539 B:** Sara Fhölenhag & Erik Holmqvist **540** Angelo Hornak/Corb **541** lookGaleria/Alamy **542** Richard Waite/Arcaid **543** Mark Fiennes/Arcaid **544 T:** Bill Tingey/Arcaid **544 B:** Bill Tingey/Arcaid **545** Ezra Stoller/ESTO **547 T:** AM Corporation/Alamy **547 B:** Sandra Baker/Alamy **548 T L:** Paul Raftery/View **548 T R:** Atelier Kim Zwartz **548 B L:** OMA Photo: Hans Werlemann/©DACS, London 2007 **548 B R:** Collection Artedia/View **549 T:** Douglas Cardinal Architect Inc **549 B:** Moebius House, 1998, UNStudio/photo Christian Richter **550** Will Pryce/Thames & Hudson/Arcaid **551** Purcell Team/Alamy **552 T:** SkyScan/Corbis **552 B:** Bettmann/CORBIS **553 T:** Roland Halbe/Artur/View **553 B:** Roland Halbe/Artur/View **554 T:** Robert van der Hilst/CORBIS **554 B:** Scanpix Denmark **555 T:** Richard Bryant/Arcaid **555 B:** Gail Mooney/CORBIS **557** Hartmut Pohling/japan-photode **558** Michel Denance/Artedia/VIEW[**559** Richard Bryant/Arcaid **560** Michel Denance/Artedia/View **561** Bettmann/CORBIS **562** Sörens Foto & Ateljé/©DACS, London 2007 **563** Patrick Ashby/Alamy **564** Collection Artedia/VIEW **565** Alan Weintraub/Arcaid **566 T:** ©2007 Barragan Foundation, Birsfelden, Switzerland/ProLitteris/©DACS, London 2007 **566 B:** ©2007 Barragan Foundation, Birsfelden, Switzerland/ProLitteris/©DACS, London 2007 **568 T:** David Poole/Alamy **568 B:** Ashley Cooper/Alamy **569 T:** Richard Einzig/Arcaid **569 B:** Richard Einzig/Arcaid **571 T:** Michel Moch/Artedia/View **571 B:** Juergen Sorges/alg-images **573 T:** Denver Art Museum **573 B:** Denver Art Museum/Esto/View **574** Jonathan Littlejohn/Alamy **575** Bill Tingey/Arcaid **577 T:** Kevin Roche John Dinkeloo and Associates **577 B:** Kevin Roche John Dinkeloo and Associates **578 T:** Edifice **578 B:** Jiri Rezac/Alamy **580** ap-travel/Alamy/©DACS, London 2007 **581** Arcaid/Alamy **583** Robert Holmes/Corbis **584** Carl & Ann Purcell/CORBIS **585** L Clarke/CORBIS **587 T:** Alo Zanetta **587 B:** Marco D'Anna **588 T:** Roberto Schezen/Esto/View **588 B:** Roberto Schezen/Esto/View **590 T:** Charles & Josette Lenars/Corbis **590 B:** Charles & Josette Lenars/Corbis **592 T:** Angelo Hornak/Corbis **592 B:** Elmtree Images/Alamy **593 T:** Hemis/Alamy **593 B:** eStock Photo/Alamy **594 T:** Luc Boegly/Artedia/View **594 B:** Vanni Archive/Corbis **595 T:** Aga Khan Trust for Culture **595 B:** Aga Khan Trust for Culture **597 T:** Peter Cook/View **597 B:** Roberto Schezen/Esto/View **598** Macduff Everton/Corbis **599** Kevin R Morris/Corbis **601 T:** Edifice **601 B:** Pawel Libera/Corbis **602** Scanpix Denmark **603** Ezra Stoller/Esto **604** Herbert Spichtinger/zefa/Corbis **605** Michel Denance/Artedia/VIEW **607 T:** Photo: Tom Bernard; Courtesy Venturi, Scott Brown and Associates, Inc **607 B:** Photo: Tom Bernard; Courtesy Venturi, Scott Brown and Associates, Inc **608 T:** Richard Bryant/Arcaid **608 B:** Richard Bryant/Arcaid **609 T:** Colin Dixon/Arcaid **609 B:** Edifice **610** Jeremy Cockayne/Arcaid **611** Tim Street-Porter/Esto/VIEW **612 T:** Uyen Le/Alamy **612 B:** James P Blair/Corbis **613 T:** Ian Trower/Alamy **613 B:** Wendy Connett/Alamy **614 T:** JP Laffont/Sygma/Corbis **614 B:** Bettmann/CORBIS **617 T:** Alberto Flammer **617 B:** Alo Zanetta **618 T:** Harry Melchert/dpa/Corbis **618 B:** philosophygeek **619 T:** Richard Bryant/Arcaid **619 B:** Richard Bryant/Arcaid **621 T:** World Illustrated/Photoshot **621 B:** Bildarchiv Monheim GmbH/Alamy **622** Blom Piet/Artedia/View **623** Blom Piet/Artedia/View **624** Andanson James/Corbis Sygma **625** Robert H Carter **626** Edifice **627** Klaus Frahm/Artur/View **629** Ian Lambot/Arcaid **631 T:** Juergen Raible/akg-images **631 B:** Scott Frances/Esto/VIEW **632** Roberto Herrett/Alamy **633** Douglas Lander/Alamy **635 T:** Bildarchiv Monheim GmbH/Alamy **635 B:** Bildarchiv Monheim GmbH/Alamy **636** Grant Smith/Corbis **637** Robert O'Dea/akg-images **638 T:** Andres/babch **638 B:** Andres/babch **640** Jon Hicks/Corbis **641** Bob Krist/CORBIS **642** Harald A Jahn; Harald Jahn/CORBIS **643** Harald A Jahn; Harald Jahn/CORBIS **644** Viennaslide/babch **645** Stephane Couturier/Artedia/View **646** simo-images/Alamy **647** Luc Boegly/Artedia/View/©ADAGP, Paris and DACS, London 2007 **648** Ben Johnson/Arcaid/©ADAGP, Paris and DACS, London 2007 **649** Dieter Leistner/Artur/View **650 T:** Simon Woodcock/fotoLibra **650 B:** Jon Arnold Images/Alamy **652 T:** CZWG Architects **652 B:** CZWG Architects **653 T:** Timothy Hursley/Murphy Jahn Architects **653 B:** Donald Corner & Jenny Young/Artifice Images **655 T:** Kevin George/fotoLibra **655 B:** Richard List/Corbis **656** Thierry Prat/Sygma/Corbis **657** Hoberman Collection UK/Alamy **659 T:** Richard Bryant/Arcaid **659 B:** Richard Bryant/Arcaid **660 T:** Jeff Goldberg/Esto/View **660 B:** Jeff Goldberg/Esto/View **661 T:** Architectural Association/Amos Goldreich **661 B:** Architectural Association/Amos Goldreich **662** Roland Halbe/Artur/View **663** Jason Lindsey/Alamy **664** Bildarchiv Monheim/Arcaid **665** Architectural Association/Dennis Wheatley **667 T:** Sebastien Camboulive/Artedia/View **667 B:** Sebastien Camboulive/Artedia/View **668 T:** Michel Setboun/Corbis **668 B:** Ian Lambot/Arcaid **670** David Butow/CORBIS SABA **671** BL Images Ltd/Alamy **673 T:** Architectural Association/Alexander Franz/©ADAGP, Paris and DACS, London 2007 **673 B:** Architectural Association/Alexander Franz/©ADAGP, Paris and DACS, London 2007 **674** Dennis Gilbert/View **675** Norbert Miguletz **676** Nik Wheeler/Corbis **677** Jeremy Cockayne/Arcaid **678** Thomas Dix/archenova/Esto/View **679** Architectural Assocation/Thomas Hildebrand **680 T:** Daryl Mulvihill/fotoLibra **680 B:** Arcaid/Alamy **682** Abdul Hamid Abdullah/fotoLibra **683** artedia/view **684** /©DACS, London 2007 **685** Neil Harris/fotoLibra **686** Josep Lluís Mateo - MAP Arquitectos Photo Jordi Bernado **687** Natalie Tepper/Arcaid **688** Israel images/Alamy **689** Architectural Association/William Hailiang Chen **690** Bildarchiv Monheim/Arcaid **691** Paul Warchol/Vitra **692** Patrick Robert/Sygma/Corbis/©ADAGP, Paris and DACS, London 2007 **693** Richard Bryant/Arcaid **695 T:** Collection Artedia/VIEW **695 B:** VIEW Pictures Ltd/Alamy **696** Alan Weintraub/Arcaid **697** Peter Barber Architects **699 T:** Paul Warchol/Steven Holl Architects **699 B:** Paul Warchol/Steven Holl Architects **701 T:** Luc Boegly/Artedia/VIEW **701 B:** Luc Boegly/Artedia/VIEW **702** Architekturphoto/Arcaid **703** Niall MacLeod/Corbis **704 T:** lookGaleria/Alamy **704 B:** lookGaleria/Alamy **705 T:** Clive Collie/Fotolibra **705 B:** World Illustrated/Photoshot **707 T:** Collection Artedia/View **707 B:** Collection Artedia/View **708 T:** John Edward Linden/Arcaid **708 B:** John Edward Linden/Arcaid **709 T:** Morley von Sternberg/Arcaid **709 B:** Richard Glover/CORBIS **710** Bildarchiv Monheim GmbH/Alamy **711** ©Hiroyuki Hirai **712** Collection Artedia/View/©ADAGP, Paris and DACS, London 2007 **713** Aga Khan Trust for Culture **715 T:** Mark Harris/fotoLibra **715 B:** Sylvie Bersout/Artedia/VIEW **716 T:** Edifice/CORBIS **716 B:** Tigran Asatrjan/fotoLibra **717 T:** World Illustrated/Photoshot/©DACS, London 2007 **717 B:** World Illustrated/Photoshot/©DACS, London 2007 **719 T:** Carl Pedersen/Alamy **719 B:** Dirk Robbers/Artur/View **720** Edifice **721** Michael Moch/Artedia/View **722 T:** f1 online/Alamy **722 B:** Joern Sackermann/Alamy **724** Richard Bryant/Arcaid **725** Richard Bryant/Arcaid **726** John Gollings/Arcaid **727** World Illustrated/Photoshot **728** Luc Boegly/Artedia/View **729** Bill Tingey/Arcaid **730 T:** John Edward Linden/Arcaid **730 B:** John Edward Linden/Arcaid **731 T:** Robert Cesar/Artedia/View **731 B:** Robert Cesar/Artedia/

View 732 Nicholas Kane/Arcaid/©DACS, London 2007 733 World Illustrated/Photoshot 734 World Illustrated/Photoshot 735 Bildarchiv Monheim GmbH/Alamy 737 G P Bowater/Alamy 738 T: Ed Wheeler/CORBIS 738 B: Richard Bryant/Arcaid 739 T: Van der Merwe Miszewski Architects 739 B: Van der Merwe Miszewski Architects 740 Jacques Langevin/Corbis Sygma 741 John Gollings/Arcaid 742 T: Richard Bryant/Arcaid/Corbis 742 B: Richard Bryant/Arcaid 744 Lorenzo Nencioni/Alamy 745 Cephas Picture Library/Alamy 746 T: Olivier Martin Gambier/Artedia/VIEW 746 B: Tim Griffith/Esto/View 747 T: Nicholas Kane/Arcaid 747 B: Nicholas Kane 748 T: Luc Boegly/Artedia/VIEW 748 B: Luc Boegly/Artedia/VIEW 749 T: Bernard Khoury/DW5 749 B: Bernard Khoury/DW5 750 T: Jon Hicks/Corbis 751 B: World Illustrated/Photoshot 752 Luc Boegly/Artedia/VIEW 753 Luc Boegly/Artedia/VIEW 754 McCanner/Alamy 755 Sergio Pitamitz/CORBIS 756 Richard Davies 757 Richard Glover/View 758 World Illustrated/Photoshot 759 Architekturphoto/Arcaid 761 T: Architekturphoto/Arcaid 761 B: Architekturphoto/Arcaid 762 LWC Lang Wilson Practice in Architecture Culture 763 Chris Baker/fotoLibra 764 Scanpix Denmark 765 Jon Arnold Images/Alamy 766 T: George Hammerstein/Veer/Corbis 766 B: George Hammerstein/Veer/Corbis 767 T: Lucia Degonda/babch 767 B: Lucia Degonda/babch 768 T: Peter MacKinven/View 768 B: Peter MacKinven/View 769 T: Finbarr O'Reilly/Reuters/Corbis 769 B: Rainer Jensen/dpa/Corbis 770 T: Baumschlager & Eberle Photo Eduard Hueber, Arch Photo Inc 770 B: Baumschlager & Eberle Photo Eduard Hueber, Arch Photo Inc 771 AGRfoto/Alex Rowbotham/Alamy 772 Michael David Murphy 773 Bob Krist/Corbis 774 Tom Arban/Morphosis 775 Tim Graham/Corbis Sygma 776 Richard Bryant/Arcaid 777 Paul Raftery/View 778 Arcaid/Alamy 779 Michel Denance/Artedia/View/©ADAGP, Paris and DACS, London 2007 781 T: John Edward Linden/Arcaid 781 B: Douglas Peebles/CORBIS 782 T: Gillian Penney/fotoLibra 782 B: Abraham Nowitz/Corbis 784 Collection Artedia/VIEW 785 Latin Focus 786 T L: Studio Hollein 786 T R: Tovatt/photo Shigeo Ogawa 786 B L: World Illustrated/Photoshot 786 B R: Richard Bryant/Arcaid 787 T: Christian Richters/Artur/Esto/View 787 B: Rojkind Arquitectos (Michel Rojkind)/photo Jaime Navarro 788 T: Marco Cristofori/Corbis 788 B: Marco Cristofori/Corbis 789 T: Martine Hamilton Knight/Arcaid 789 B: Martine Hamilton Knight/Arcaid 790 Richard Bryant/Arcaid 791 Jason Hawkes/Corbis 792 Alejo Bagué 793 KleinDytham Architecture Photo: Kozo Takayama 795 T: Klaus Frahm/Artur/IPN 795 B: Hervé Champollion/akg-images 796 Richard Bryant/Arcaid 797 Richard Bryant/Arcaid 798 T: Lucinda Degonda/babch 798 B: Lucinda Degonda/babch 800 david sanger photography/Alamy 801 Chris Gascoigne/View 803 T: Natalie Tepper/Arcaid 803 B: Natalie Tepper/Arcaid 804 T: Josefin Widell Hultgren 804 B: Josefin Widell Hultgren 805 T: Josefin Widell Hultgren 805 B: Josefin Widell Hultgren 806 T: Sandro Vannini/CORBIS 806 B: Bibliotheca Alexandrina/epa/Corbis 808 John Edward Linden/Arcaid 809 Juergen Henkelmann Photography/Alamy 810 T: Chris Gascoigne/View 810 B: Chris Gascoigne/View 811 T: Richard Bryant/Arcaid 811 B: Richard Bryant/Arcaid 812 Stijn Rolies 813 Chris Gascoigne/View 814 T: Sue Barr/View 814 B: Sue Barr/View 815 T: Paul Raftery/View 815 B: Paul Raftery/View 816 Edifice 817 Benedict Luxmoore/Arcaid 818 Architekturphoto/Arcaid 819 Architekturphoto/Arcaid 820 James Sparshatt/CORBIS 821 T: Alejo Bagué 821 B: Alejo Bagué 822 Luc Boegly/Artedia/View 823 Roland Halbe/Artur/View 824 Jo Collins/Alamy 825 Benedict Luxmoore/Arcaid 826 Architekturphoto/Arcaid 827 Architekturphoto/Arcaid 829 T: Peter Aaron/Esto/View 829 B: Peter Aaron/Esto/View 830 Julius Lando/Alamy 831 Roland Halbe/Artur/View 832 Ruedi Walti/babch 833 Philip Linford/fotoLibra 834 T: Wolfram Janzer/Artur/VIEW 834 B: Wolfram Janzer/Artur/VIEW 835 T: Jon Hicks/Corbis 835 B: Tibor Bognar/Corbis 836 Robert Harding Picture Library Ltd/Alamy 837 Daniel Woo 839 T: Ted Soqui/Corbis 839 B: Juan Manuel Silva/Tips Images 840 Nicholas Kane/Arcaid 841 Monika Nikolic/Artur/VIEW 842 Sherab/Alamy 843 Peter Mauss/Esto/View 844 T: Sue Barr/View 844 B: Sue Barr/View 847 T: VIEW Pictures Ltd/Alamy 847 B: VIEW Pictures Ltd/Alamy 848 Arcaid/Alamy 849 VIEW Pictures Ltd/Alamy 850 Monika Nikolic/Artur/VIEW 851 Paolo Rosselli/Artur/VIEW 852 Nicholas Kane/Arcaid/©DACS, London 2007 853 Peter Cook/View 854 T: John Edward Linden/Arcaid 854 B: John Edward Linden/Arcaid 855 T: Roland Halbe/Artur/View 855 B: Roland Halbe/Artur/View 856 John Edward Linden/Arcaid 857 Arcaid/Alamy 857 B: Arcaid/Alamy 859 T: Arcaid/Alamy 859 B: Arcaid/Alamy 860 Roland Halbe/Artur/View 861 Richard Bryant/Arcaid 862 Nicholas Kane/Arcaid 863 Dennis Gilbert/View 864 T: Tim Griffith/Esto/View 864 B: Patrick Tweddle/fotoLibra 865 T: Edifice 865 B: Edifice 866 Marc Cramer 867 Collection Artedia/VIEW 868 Paul Raftery/View 869 Paul Raftery/View 871 T: Richard Glover/Arcaid 871 B: Richard Glover/Arcaid 872 Bildarchiv Monheim/Arcaid 873 Richard Mandelkorn/Esto/View 874 Art on File/Corbis/©DACS, London 2007 875 James Hughes/Alamy 876 Olivier Martin Gambier/Artedia/View/©ADAGP, Paris and DACS, London 2007 877 Living Tomorrow Pavilion, 2003, UNStudio/photo Christian Richters 878 Arcaid/Alamy 879 Huw Jones/Alamy 880 T: World Illustrated/Photoshot 880 B: Pixonnetcom/Alamy 881 T: Roland Halbe/Artur/View 881 B: Roland Halbe/Artur/View 883 T: Roland Halbe/Artur/View 883 B: Roland Halbe/Artur/View 884 Architekturphoto/Arcaid 885 Henning Larsen Architects Photo: Adam Mørk 886 T: Archenova/Arcaid 886 B: Archenova/Arcaid 888 Timothy Hursley 889 Timothy Hursley 890 Art on File/Corbis 891 Bernard Bisson/CORBIS SYGMA 892 T: Edmund Sumner/View 892 B: Edmund Sumner/View 893 T: Iona Marinescu/VIEW 893 B: Iona Marinescu/VIEW 894 Richard Bryant/Arcaid 895 Inigo Bujedo Aguirre/Arcaid/©ADAGP, Paris and DACS, London 2007 896 Dennis Gilbert/View 897 Harry Melchert/dpa/Corbis 898 Inigo Bujedo Aguirre/Arcaid/©DACS, London 2007 899 Franz-Marc Frei/Corbis 900 Grant Smith/View 901 James Brittain/View 902 SINGLE speed IMAGE 903 Archenova/Arcaid 904 T: Art on File/Corbis 904 B: Art on File/Corbis 905 T: Edmund Sumner/View 905 B: Edmund Sumner/View 906 Peter Cook/View 907 Jochen Helle/Artur/View 908 Grant Smith/View 909 Arnold De Bruin/FotoLibra 910 Josefin Widell Hultgren 911 Jon Hicks/Corbis 912 T: Edmund Sumner/View 912 B: Edmund Sumner/View 914 Noero Wolff Architects 915 Iwan Baan 916 Bronek Kaminski/FotoLibra 917 Andy Purcell/FotoLibra 918 Edmund Sumner/View 919 kolvenbach/Alamy 921 John Gollings/Arcaid 922 Cullum and Nightingale Architects Limited Photo Adrian Hobbs 923 Nathan Willock/View 924 Friis & Molltke 925 Procter-Rihl Architects Photo: Procter 926 Paul Raftery/View/©ADAGP, Paris and DACS, London 2007 927 Paul Raftery/View/©ADAGP, Paris and DACS, London 2007 928 T: Inigo Bujedo Aguirre/Arcaid 928 B: Richard Bryant/Arcaid 930 T: Ben McMillan/Arcaid/©ADAGP, Paris and DACS, London 2007 930 B: Yu Guiyou/Alamy/©ADAGP, Paris and DACS, London 2007 931 T: Inigo Bujedo Aguirre/View 931 B: Inigo Bujedo Aguirre/View 932 Christophe Boisvieux/Corbis 933 Floris Leeuwenberg/Cover Story/Corbis 935 T: World Illustrated/Photoshot 935 B: Gareth Dewar/FotoLibra 936 Getty Images 937 Archenova/Arcaid

Our sincere gratitude to the following people:

Jacket Design and Art Direction: Aki Nakayama

Editorial and Fact Checking: Becky Gee, Tobias Selin

Indexing: Ann Barrett

Image Research: Rod Teasdale

Translation: Georgina Turner, Marie-Hélène Fabre

Consultation: Alan Powers, Sarah Gaventa, Claire Catterall

Picture libraries:
Alamy– Tracey Day

Arcaid– Lynne Bryant and Gavin Jackson

Bildagentaur Baumann– Ursula Baumann

Corbis– John Moelwyn-Hughes

Getty– Hayley Newman

Fotolibra– Gwyn Headley and Yvonne Seeley

Photolibrary– Tim Kantoch

Photoshot– Colin Finlay

Photographers Direct, and all the photographers who contacted us through that site

William O'Reilly and the Aga Khan Trust for Culture

Christian Sarramon

Mats Nyström, Will Black, Louise Cooke, Edward Denison

And all the architects who generously supplied pictures from their archives for this project.

This book is dedicated to the memory of Hix.